Dynamic HTML
The Definitive Reference

Other resources from O'Reilly

oreilly.com

oreilly.com is more than a complete catalog of O'Reilly books. You'll also find links to news, events, articles, weblogs, sample chapters, and code examples.

oreillynet.com is the essential portal for developers interested in open and emerging technologies, including new platforms, programming languages, and operating systems.

Conferences

O'Reilly brings diverse innovators together to nurture the ideas that spark revolutionary industries. We specialize in documenting the latest tools and systems, translating the innovator's knowledge into useful skills for those in the trenches. Visit *conferences.oreilly.com* for our upcoming events.

Safari Bookshelf (*safari.oreilly.com*) is the premier online reference library for programmers and IT professionals. Conduct searches across more than 1,000 books. Subscribers can zero in on answers to time-critical questions in a matter of seconds. Read the books on your Bookshelf from cover to cover or simply flip to the page you need. Try it today for free.

THIRD EDITION

Dynamic HTML
The Definitive Reference

Danny Goodman

Beijing · Cambridge · Farnham · Köln · Paris · Sebastopol · Taipei · Tokyo

Dynamic HTML: The Definitive Reference, Third Edition
by Danny Goodman

Copyright © 1998, 2002, 2007 Danny Goodman. All rights reserved.
Printed in the United States of America.

Published by O'Reilly Media, Inc., 1005 Gravenstein Highway North, Sebastopol, CA 95472.

O'Reilly books may be purchased for educational, business, or sales promotional use. Online editions are also available for most titles (*safari.oreilly.com*). For more information, contact our corporate/institutional sales department: (800) 998-9938 or *corporate@oreilly.com*.

Editor: Tatiana Apandi
Production Editor: Adam Witwer
Proofreader: Audrey Doyle
Indexer: Johnna VanHoose Dinse

Cover Designer: Karen Montgomery
Interior Designer: David Futato
Illustrators: Robert Romano and Jessamyn Read

Printing History:

July 1998:	First Edition.
September 2002:	Second Edition.
December 2006:	Third Edition.

ISBN-10: 0-596-52740-3
ISBN-13: 978-0-596-52740-2
[C]

Table of Contents

Preface

I am going to admit a selfish motive for writing this book and, more recently, updating it to the third edition: I needed the finished product for my own consulting and development work. After struggling in the early Version 4 browser days with tangled online references and monstrous printed versions of Netscape, Microsoft, and World Wide Web Consortium (W3C) documentation for Dynamic HTML (DHTML) features, I had had enough. My human brain could no longer store the parallels and discrepancies of the hundreds of terms for HTML attributes, style sheets, and scriptable object models. And no browser maker was about to tell me how compatible a particular feature might be in another browser. It was clearly time to roll my own reference.

At first, I thought the project would be a relatively straightforward blending of content from available sources, with a pinch of my development experience thrown in for flavoring. But the more I examined the existing documents, the worse the situation became. Developer documentation from the browser makers, and even the W3C, contained inconsistencies and incomplete (if at times erroneous) information. From the very beginning, it was clear that I could not trust everything I read, but instead had to try as much as I could on as many browsers and browser versions as I could. Multiply all that code testing by the hundreds of HTML attributes, CSS properties, object properties, object methods, and events for the first edition...before I knew it, many extra months of day-and-night coding and writing were history.

Creating the second edition was no less harrowing. The W3C DOM had come on the scene, bringing entirely new concepts about object models. Reconciling the ideals of the W3C specifications against the development work on the Mozilla browser meant many hours combing through the browser's source code and bug reports for clues about what was broken, about-to-be-fixed, or put on hold for the future. Combining those developments with an ever-growing vocabulary in the proprietary Internet Explorer world, the amount of information had grown to unimaginable proportions: more than 15,000 unique instances of properties, methods, and event handlers supported by numerous document objects.

The need for this third edition grew from several stimuli. Although the Internet Explorer browser had been static for a number of years, the browser world was not standing still. Mozilla blossomed as an attractive alternative for many everyday users. On the Macintosh side of the aisle, the bundled Safari browser had established itself as the primary web access tool for a growing cadre of Mac OS X users. Undaunted by such competition, the Opera folks also kept up the development pace, adding in Opera 9 many bleeding-edge features, such as Web Forms 2.0. In the meantime, several W3C working groups finalized (or neared completion of) key Level 3 DOM and CSS modules, some of whose features were finding their way into non-IE browsers. Keeping track of which browser does what is no less difficult today than it has ever been.

That's all the more reason that I'm thrilled to produce this third edition, so that I have a DHTML reference that is always within arm's reach at my workstation. I even have the duct tape ready for the day when the cover surrenders to too many twists and turns.

I would be the last person on the planet to promise that this book is perfect in every way. While the predictability and reliability of DHTML scripting have increased significantly since the days of the first edition, I still find discrepancies between vendor or standards documentation and observable reality in mainstream browsers. In such cases, I document the reality. In doing so, I recall my high school physics teacher who would shout to the class, "Seeing is believing!" and then promptly demonstrate an optical illusion. I hope that my long experience in this field has helped me see through the illusions, so that I may relate the *true* reality.

What You Should Already Know

Because this is a reference book, it has been written with the assumption that you have at least dabbled in Dynamic HTML. You should already be HTML-literate and know the basics of client-side scripting in JavaScript. You need not be a DHTML expert, but even the supplementary online instructional sections are very much crash courses, intended for readers who are already comfortable with hand-coding web pages (or at least modifying the HTML generated by WYSIWYG authoring tools).

Contents of This Book

This book is divided into three parts:

Part I, *Dynamic HTML Reference*
> The chapters of Part I provide at-a-glance references for the tags, attributes, objects, properties, methods, and events of HTML, XHTML, CSS, DOM, and core JavaScript. These are the chapters I use all the time to look up the attributes of an HTML element or to see whether a particular object property is available

in the desired browser brands and versions. Every effort has been expended to present this information in a condensed yet meaningful format. At the same time, I have expanded compatibility coverage to include Safari and Opera browsers.

Part II, *Cross References*

The chapters in Part II slice through the information of Part I along different angles. Perhaps you recall the name of an attribute you found useful some time ago, but don't recall which elements provide that attribute. Here you can look up that attribute (or object property, method, or event type) to find all the items that recognize it.

Part III, *Appendixes*

Several appendixes provide quick lookup for a variety of values useful in HTML authoring and scripting. Appendix D has been expanded to include coverage of commands used across three browsers for user-editable content. A glossary also gives you quick explanations of some of the new and potentially confusing terminology of DHTML.

Conventions Used in This Book

Italic is used for:

- Pathnames, filenames, program names, email addresses, and web sites
- New terms where they are defined

Bold is used for:

- Keys
- GUI menu items and buttons

`Constant Width` is used for:

- Any HTML, CSS, or scripting term, including HTML tags, attribute names, object names, properties, methods, and event handlers
- All HTML and script code listings

`Constant Width Italic` is used for:

- Method and function parameters or assigned value placeholders that indicate an item is to be replaced by a real value in actual use

Additional Online Content

Readers of earlier editions will notice in this edition the absence of the chapters that expound on DHTML standards and application issues. Fear not! To make room for ever-expanding reference material in this third edition, I have updated those chapters (substantially in many cases) and made them available for immediate download at *http://www.oreilly.com/catalog/dhtmlref3*. The seven online sections are as follows:

> Online Section I, *The State of the Art: Standards*
> Online Section II, *Cross-Platform Compromises*
> Online Section III, *Adding Cascading Style Sheets to Documents*
> Online Section IV, *Changing Page Content and Styles*
> Online Section V, *Adding Dynamic Positioning to Documents*
> Online Section VI, *Scripting Events*
> Online Section VII, *XMLHttpRequest and Ajax*

Using Code Examples

This book is here to help you get your job done. In general, you may use the shell scripts in this book in your own scripts and documentation. You do not need to contact us for permission unless you're reproducing a significant portion of a script. For example, selling or distributing a CD-ROM of examples from O'Reilly books requires permission. Answering a question by citing this book and quoting a script does not require permission. Incorporating a significant amount of a script from this book into your product's code or documentation does require permission.

We appreciate, but do not require, attribution. An attribution usually includes the title, author, publisher, and ISBN. For example: "*Dynamic HTML: The Definitive Reference*, Third Edition, by Danny Goodman. Copyright 2007 O'Reilly Media, Inc., 978-0-596-52740-2."

If you feel your use of code examples falls outside fair use or them permission given above, feel free to contact us at *permissions@oreilly.com*.

Safari® Enabled

 When you see a Safari® enabled icon on the cover of your favorite technology book, that means the book is available online through the O'Reilly Network Safari Bookshelf.

Safari offers a solution that's better than e-books. It's a virtual library that lets you easily search thousands of top tech books, cut and paste code samples, download chapters, and find quick answers when you need the most accurate, current information. Try it free at *http://safari.oreilly.com*.

How to Contact Us

Please address comments and questions concerning this book to the publisher:

O'Reilly Media, Inc.
1005 Gravenstein Highway North
Sebastopol, CA 95472
(800) 998-9938 (in the United States or Canada)
(707) 829-0515 (international/local)
(707) 829-0104 (fax)

Your feedback on the quality of this book is important to us. If you discover any errors, bugs, typos, explanations that you cannot grok, or platform-specific issues not covered here, please let us know. You can email your bug reports and comments to us at:

bookquestions@oreilly.com

Also be sure to check the web page for this book, which lists errata, examples, or any additional information. You can access this page at:

http://www.oreilly.com/catalog/9780596527402

Previously reported errors and corrections are available for public view and further comment.

For more information about books, conferences, Resource Centers, and the O'Reilly Network, see the O'Reilly web site at:

http://www.oreilly.com

Acknowledgments

Despite the ever-increasing heft of the books I have written in the past several years, you'll have to take my word for it: I do not delight in making forests tremble with each added word. It's just that the subject matter has grown to outsized proportions. No matter how succinct one tries to be, the pages add up quickly.

A book of this scale and design complexity places enormous burdens on a great many people who turn my mere bytes into gorgeous pages and chapters. Thanks to Tim O'Reilly for continuing to be true to his author-friendly roots, while building a technology powerhouse whose reputation for quality is awe-inspiring. His editorial and production staffs consistently work miracles under extreme deadline pressures.

My true reward comes from having helped you unlock your own talent to create great solutions. Your encouragement has inspired me to do what I hope is an even better job this third time around to guide you through the newest advances in client-side scripting and web development. To new readers, I bid you welcome. Let's all have some fun exploring the power and promise of Dynamic HTML.

PART I

Dynamic HTML Reference

This part of the book, Chapters 1 through 5, is a complete reference to all the tags, attributes, objects, properties, methods, and event handlers for HTML, CSS, DOM, and core JavaScript.

CHAPTER 1

HTML and XHTML Reference

This chapter provides a complete list of HTML tags and attributes specified in the W3C recommendations for HTML 4.01 and XHTML 1.1 plus those implemented in yesterday's and today's mainstream browsers. This includes many items from the Web Hypertext Application Technology Working Group (WHATWG), such as Web Forms 2.0. Version information accompanies each tag and attribute so that you can see whether a particular entry applies to the browser(s) you must support. At a glance, you can see the version number of Internet Explorer (IE), pre-Mozilla Netscape Navigator (NN), Mozilla-based browsers (Moz), Safari (Saf), Opera (Op), and the W3C HTML specification (HTML) in which the item was first introduced. Because this book deals with Dynamic HTML, the history timeline goes back only to HTML 3.2, Netscape Navigator 2, and Internet Explorer 3. For derivatives of the Mozilla Foundation's browser (e.g., Firefox, Netscape 6 or later, Camino, etc.), see Appendix F. Although some DHTML facilities were available in early versions of Opera, this book starts its Opera history with version 7 from 2003, which coincides with the advent of the rendering engine that Opera uses today. Therefore, an item marked "Op 7" may have been supported by earlier versions.

Other than for Opera, if an item existed prior to one of these versions—or was available at the first release of newer browsers, such as Mozilla and Safari—and is still in use, it is simply marked "all." Where no implementation exists, I've used "n/a" to indicate that. Items valid for a single version show the number encased in pipe symbols (e.g., |4| for Version 4 only). Deprecated items are listed here because modern browsers support them for backward compatibility, and legacy code may rely on them. When an item has been not only deprecated, but removed from a standard, it is indicated with a "less than" symbol, as in <4. In a change from the last edition of this book, the NN indicators are only for Versions 2 through 4 of Netscape Navigator. Items that first appeared in Netscape 6 are covered by the Mozilla entries.

Following a section that lists attributes shared by all elements, this chapter is organized alphabetically by HTML element (or tag, if you prefer); within each element's description, attributes are listed alphabetically. The reference entries are designed so that it is easy to see which elements require end tags (in HTML), and whether attributes are optional or required. Scripted object references are displayed in the W3C DOM standard syntax style unless the item requires a different DOM style (e.g., the Navigator 4 layer element). Although the W3C DOM document.getElementById( ) syntax prevails in the listings, if IE supports the item through its DOM scripting, you can assume that the document.all reference style also applies in that environment. The description for an item details any significant differences between the various browser implementations of the item, but this reference is not intended to be a universal bug database.

All example code is formatted according to W3C HTML standards because the widest number of DHTML browsers support that format and all readers will be familiar with it. At the same time, however, the code demonstrates most practices encouraged for XHTML formatting, such as lowercase tag and attribute names and quoted attribute values of all types. The only XHTML formatting characteristics lacking from the example code are end tags for empty elements (such as the XHTML backward-compatible <br /> technique) and explicit value assignments to attributes that do not require them in HTML (such as the selected attribute of checkbox type input elements). These coding style variations are easy to modify on your own if your code must conform to XHTML validation (see Online Section I).

For in-depth coverage of event types related to event attributes mentioned in this chapter, see Chapter 3. To find out which, if any, HTML and XHTML DTDs support a particular element or attribute, consult Appendix E.

Attribute Value Types

Many HTML element attributes share similar data requirements. For the sake of brevity in the reference listings, this section describes a few common attribute value types in more detail than is possible within each listing. Whenever you see one of these attribute value types associated with an attribute, consult this section for a description of the type.

Length

A length value defines a linear measure of document real estate, such as the width of a table element. The unit of measurement can be any applicable unit that helps identify a position or space on the screen. HTML attribute length units are uniformly pixels, but in other content, such as that specified in Cascading Style Sheets (see Chapter 4), measurements can be in inches, picas, ems, or other relevant units. A single numeric value may represent a length when it defines the offset from an edge of an element. For example, a coordinate point (10,20) consists of two length values, denoting pixel measurements from the left and top edges of an element, respectively.

A length value applying to a horizontal or vertical space may also be represented as a percentage value, such as width="50%". Attributes associated with length values are deprecated in favor of corresponding CSS attributes for strict HTML 4 and XHTML conformance.

Identifier

An identifier (usually assigned to name or id attributes) is a name that adheres to strict syntactical rules. Most importantly, an identifier is one word with no whitespace allowed. If you need to use multiple words to describe an item, you can use the camelCase format (in which internal letters are capitalized) or an underscore character between the words. Most punctuation symbols are not permitted, but all numerals and alphabetical characters are. To avoid potential conflicts with scripting languages that refer to items by their identifiers, it is good practice to avoid using a numeral for the first character of an identifier.

URI and URL

The term Universal Resource Identifier (URI) is a broad term for an address of content on the Web. A Universal Resource Locator (URL) is a type of URI. For most web authoring, you can think of them as one and the same because most web browsers restrict their focus to URLs. A URL, commonly applied to href and src attributes, may be complete (including the protocol, host, domain, and the rest) or may be relative to the URL of the current document. In scriptable browsers, attributes that expect URI values can also accept the javascript: pseudo-protocol, which makes a script statement or function the destination of the link. This pseudo-protocol, while implemented widely, is not a formal standard and does not work in browsers with JavaScript disabled.

Language Code

There is an extensive list of standard codes that identify the spoken and written languages of the world. A language code always contains a primary language code, such as "en" for English or "zh" for Chinese. Common two-letter primary codes are cataloged in ISO-639 (an excerpted list of codes is available at *http://www.ietf.org/rfc/rfc1766.txt*). An optional subcode (separated from the primary code by a hyphen) may be used to identify a specific implementation of the primary language, usually according to usage within a specific country. Therefore, although "en" means English, "en-US" means a U.S.-specific version of English. The browser must support a particular language code for its meaning to be of any value to an element attribute.

Alignment Constants

The frequent presence of the `align` attribute among various elements (and the related but less pervasive `valign` attribute) is misleading when describing attribute values, because the attribute conveys different meanings for several element groups. Add to the mix several proprietary values that are implemented in some browsers, and it's easy to confuse which values to use when. That all such attributes are deprecated in favor of the CSS `text-align` (horizontal) and `vertical-align` properties is welcome relief to authors who code their layout exclusively with CSS (and for whom this section is largely irrelevant).

Element alignment is divisible into five categories, each with its own set of applicable elements and permissible values. Browsers accept case-insensitive values, but if you intend to continue working with these attributes, you should get in the habit of using all lowercase values to conform with the transitional DTDs.

Alignment outside the box

The first category governs the alignment of text that surrounds the rectangular space of the element bearing the `align` attribute. W3C HTML elements in this category include `applet`, `iframe`, `img`, `input`, and `object`. IE adds `embed`, `fieldset`, and `select` elements to the list, while deleting `iframe`. Here is a synopsis of various widely-supported `align` attribute settings for these elements and how they affect the display of the element and surrounding text content:

absbottom
> Text is aligned such that the bottom of any possible text rendering (including character descenders) is on the same horizontal line as the very bottom of the element.

absmiddle
> The middle of the text height (from descender to ascender) is aligned with the middle of the element height.

baseline
> The baseline of the text is on the same horizontal line as the very bottom of the element (note that character descenders extend below the baseline).

bottom
> The W3C sanctioned value that is the equivalent of `baseline`.

left
> If there is text starting on the same line as the element, the element is lowered to the next line and displayed flush left within the next outermost container context. Text that follows the element cinches up to the end of the text preceding the element, causing the text to wrap around the object or image (called *floating*). This is a W3C-sanctioned value.

middle
> The baseline of the text is aligned with the middle of the element height. This is a W3C-sanctioned value.

right
> If there is text starting on the same line as the element, the element is lowered to the next line and displayed flush right within the next outermost container context. Text that follows the element starts on the line immediately below the starting text, causing the text to wrap around the object or image (called floating). This is a W3C-sanctioned value.

texttop
> The very top of the element is on the same horizontal line as the ascenders of the preceding text.

top
> The top of the element is on the same horizontal line as the top of the tallest element (text or other kind of element) rendered in the line. This is a W3C-sanctioned value.

Text alignment inside the containing box

The legend element acts like a label for a form's fieldset element. The caption does the same for a table. Alignment of these elements applies to the location of the element's text relative to the rectangular space occupied by the form's fieldset border or table. Support for this element-attribute pair varies widely among modern browsers. The align attribute settings for this category are:

bottom
> Text is aligned at the bottom or below the related element's box. Browsers obey attribute value only for caption element. This attribute is a W3C-sanctioned value.

center
> Text is at the top or above the related element's box and centered horizontally. Although not a W3C-sanctioned value, this value is supported in modern browsers for the caption element, but not the legend element in Safari or Opera.

left
> Although this is a W3C-sanctioned value (where indications are that text should be to the left of the containing element), browsers align text at top left of box for legend; for caption, only Mozilla places caption text to the left of the element.

right
> Although this is a W3C-sanctioned value (where indications are that text should be to the right of the containing element), browsers align text at top right of box for legend; for caption, only Mozilla places caption text to the right of the element.

top

Text for legend aligned at top left of containing box; at top center for caption. This is a W3C-sanctioned value.

Horizontal alignment of a block element

This category is potentially confusing because of the perception of what a browser does when you set the align attribute for the p, div, h1 through h6, and hr elements. These block elements normally occupy a transparent box that is the full width of the next outermost container. For most elements, that container is the body element, which extends to nearly the full width of the browser window. Therefore, when you specify one of the three primary W3C-sanctioned attribute values to an element containing short strings—center, left, and right—it appears as though the element, itself, is being aligned. In truth, the element is in the exact same spot, taking up the same width as other body content, but the text inside is aligned per the attribute setting. If you specify a fixed-width style for the element, the align attribute continues to control the text inside the element, while the element hugs the left margin. To center the width-constrained element, you must nest it inside another full-width container, and set its align attribute to center.

To add to the confusion, the W3C HTML 4 transitional specification allows for a value of justify, while the strict HTML 4 and all XHTML specifications remove that value from text alignment types of align attributes (except for table element components). Browsers support the justify value when aligning these elements.

Horizontal text alignment in a table cell

In the W3C specification, text inside descendant nodes of the table element (tbody, tr, td, and the rest) can be aligned according to the values center, justify, left, and right. IE through Version 7, however, does not recognize the justify value for table components. If you wish to justify text in an IE table cell, wrap the text in a p or div container, and set that container's align attribute to justify.

Vertical text alignment inside an element

Vertical alignment within a table component requires the valign attribute, which has permissible values that resemble some of those of the align attribute. Those values are baseline, bottom, middle, and top.

Colors

A color value can be assigned either via a hexadecimal triplet or with a plain-language equivalent. A hexadecimal triplet consists of three pairs of hexadecimal (base 16) numbers that range between the values 00 and FF, corresponding to the red, green, and blue components of the color. The three pairs of numbers are bunched together and preceded by a pound sign (#) in the form #rrggbb. Therefore, the reddest of reds has all red (FF) and none (00) of the other two colors: #FF0000; pure blue is #0000FF. The letters A through F can also be lowercase.

This numbering scheme creates a huge number of potential combinations (over 16 million), but not all video monitors are set to distinguish among millions of colors. Therefore, you may wish to limit yourself to the more modest palette of colors known as the *web palette*. A fine reference of colors that work well on all browsers at popular bit-depth settings can be found at *http://www.lynda.com/hexh.html*.

The HTML recommendation also specifies a basic library of 16 colors that can be assigned by plain-language names. Note that the color names are case-insensitive. The names and their equivalent hexadecimal triplets are as follows:

Black	#000000	Maroon	#800000	Green	#008000	Navy	#000080
Silver	#C0C0C0	Red	#FF0000	Lime	#00FF00	Blue	#0000FF
Gray	#808080	Purple	#800080	Olive	#808000	Teal	#008080
White	#FFFFFF	Fuchsia	#FF00FF	Yellow	#FFFF00	Aqua	#00FFFF

In other words, the attribute settings bgcolor="Aqua" and bgcolor="#00FFFF" yield the same results.

Many years ago, Netscape deployed a much longer list of plain-language color equivalents, originally adopted from the X Window System palette known as X11 color names. These are detailed in Appendix A and are recognized by recent versions of mainstream browsers.

Shared HTML Element Attributes

A vast majority of elements found in HTML 4.x, XHTML 1.x, and today's browsers have numerous attributes in common. Rather than repeat the descriptions of these attributes ad nauseam in the reference listings, their details are listed here only once. These shared attributes do not appear in the attribute lists for each element in the rest of this chapter, but they are available in practically every element (within the browser or standard version range indicated in each listing). Obviously, the few shared attributes that are meaningless except for rendered elements may not be available to nonrendered elements. For example, it wouldn't make any sense to apply the tabindex attribute to a style element because the style element presents no content of its own on the page to which a user could tab. In a few cases, the W3C specifications do not implement common attributes in nonrendered elements, but the browsers support them because the W3C DOM establishes scriptable properties for those attributes. Consult Appendix E to verify HTML 4 and XHTML DTD support for a particular shared attribute. Here is a list of the shared attributes.

Attributes

accesskey	class	contenteditable	dir	disabled
hidefocus	id	lang	language	repeat
repeat-max	repeat-min	repeat-start	repeat-template	style
tabindex	title	unselectable	xml:lang	

accesskey
IE 4/5 NN n/a Moz 0.9 Saf 1 Op 7 HTML 4 (see text)

accesskey="*character*"   *Optional*

A single character key that either gives focus to an element (in some browsers) or activates a form control or link action. The browser and operating system determine the keyboard combination that the user must press with the access key to activate the link. For example, most Windows browsers require a press of the **Alt** key along with the designated access key, while Mac browsers use the **Ctrl** key as the modifier. Opera, on the other hand, has an entirely different sequence: **Shift+Esc** and then the access key.

Although accesskey is listed here as a widely shared attribute, that isn't strictly the case across all implementations. HTML 4 and most current browsers recognize this attribute for the following elements: a, area, button, input, label, legend, and textarea. To this list, IE 4 adds applet, body, div, embed, isindex, marquee, object, select, span, table, and td (but removes label and legend). IE 5 adds every other renderable element, but with a caution: except for input and other form-related elements, you must also assign a tabindex attribute to the IE 5 and later element (even if simply a value of zero for all) to let the accelerator key combination bring focus to the element. All other current mainstream browsers recognize this attribute for the select element.

Example
```
<a href="http://www.megacorp.com/toc.html" accesskey="t">Table of Contents</a>
<h2 class="subsection" accesskey="2" tabindex="0">Part Two</h2>
```

Value   Single character of the document set.

Default   None.

Object Model Reference
```
[window.]document.links[i].accessKey
[window.]document.anchors[i].accessKey
[window.]document.formName.elementName.accessKey
[window.]document.forms[i].elements[j].accessKey
[window.]document.getElementById(elementID).accessKey
```

class
IE 3 NN 4 Moz 0.9 Saf 1 Op 7 HTML 4

class="*className1[...classNameN]*"   *Optional*

An identifier generally used to associate an element with a style sheet rule defined for a class selector. See Online Section III. Use the class attribute only with visible (renderable) elements.

Example   `<a class="chapTitle" name="chapter3" id="chapter3">Chapter 3</a>`

Value   Case-sensitive identifier. Multiple classes can be assigned by separating the class names with spaces within the quoted attribute value.

Default   None.

Object Model Reference

`[window.]document.getElementById(`*`elementID`*`).className`

contenteditable   IE *5.5* NN *n/a* Moz *n/a* Saf *1.3/2* Op *9* HTML *n/a*

`contenteditable="`*`featureSwitch`*`"`   *Optional*

Boolean switch that enables or disables the user's ability to edit the element's content directly on the web page. For more information about scriptable editing in IE for Windows (also implemented in recent versions of Safari and Opera), visit *http://msdn.microsoft.com/ workshop/author/editing/editing_entry.asp.* For Mozilla, see the `document.designMode` property description in Chapter 2.

Example   `<p id="userArea" contenteditable="true">Enter your text here.</p>`

Value   `true | false | inherit`

Default   `inherit`

Object Model Reference

`[window.]document.getElementById(`*`elementID`*`).contentEditable`

dir   IE *5* NN *n/a* Moz *0.9* Saf *1* Op *7* HTML *4*

`dir="`*`direction`*`"`   *Optional*

Character rendering is either left-to-right or right-to-left. This attribute is usually set in concert with the `lang` attribute; it must be used to specify a character-rendering direction that overrides the current direction.

Example   `<a lang="ar" dir="rtl">`*`Some Unicode Arabic text characters here`*`</a>`

Value   `ltr | rtl`

Default   `ltr`

disabled   IE *4/5.5* NN *n/a* Moz *0.9* Saf *1* Op *7* HTML *4*

`disabled="`*`featureSwitch`*`"`   *Optional*

Boolean switch that enables or disables the user's ability to activate or otherwise access an element. This attribute is limited to interactive form control elements in HTML 4. IE 5.5 and later (Win32 only) also applies this attribute to most other renderable elements. Disabled elements are usually "greyed out" to distinguish themselves from other elements.

Example   `<input type="submit" name="sender" disabled="true">`

Value   `true | false`

Default   `false`

Object Model Reference
`[window.]document.getElementById(elementID).disabled`

hidefocus
IE *5.5* NN *n/a* Moz *n/a* Saf *n/a* Op *n/a* HTML *n/a*

`hidefocus="`*featureSwitch*`"`   *Optional*

Boolean switch that enables or disables the browser's ability to display a dotted focus rectangle around an element that has focus. The element continues to be able to receive focus if it is focusable by default or has the `tabindex` attribute set. Focus is necessary for some keyboard-only accessibility situations, but when this attribute is switched on, there is no visual clue about the focus state. Requires IE 5.5 or later (Win32 only).

Example   `<input type="image" src="sendme.jpg" hidefocus="true">`

Value   `true | false`

Default   `false`

Object Model Reference
`[window.]document.getElementById(elementID).hideFocus`

id
IE *4* NN *4* Moz *0.9* Saf *1* Op *7* HTML *4*

`id="`*elementIdertifier*`"`   *Optional*

A unique identifier that distinguishes this element from all the rest in the document. Can be used to associate a single element with a style rule naming this attribute value as an ID selector. An element can have an ID assigned for uniqueness as well as a class for inclusion within a group. See Online Section III.

Most browsers allow `id` attributes for nonrenderable elements, but if your code requires validation, be aware that the W3C HTML 4 and XHTML DTDs do not. Because all W3C DOM element objects have an `id` property, it is natural to assign an `id` attribute to nonrenderable elements if scripts must reference those elements. Or, your scripts may use other ways (e.g., the array returned by `document.getElementsByTagName( )`) to reference such elements.

Assign identifiers to `id` attributes in order to duplicate values previously only assigned to `name` attributes in elements that feature the `name` attribute. Current browser form controls still require `name` attributes for name/value pairs to be submitted with the form, and a elements acting as anchors still need `name` attributes. Be sure to assign an identifier to the `id` attribute of any element you intend to reference by script.

Example   `<h2 id="sect3Head">Section Three</h2>`

Value   Case-sensitive identifier.

Default   None.

Object Model Reference

[window.]document.getElementById(*elementID*).id

lang

IE *4* NN *3* Moz *0.9* Saf *1* Op *9* HTML *4*

lang="*languageCode*" *Optional*

The language being used for the element's attribute values and content. A browser can use this information to assist in proper rendering of content with respect to details such as treatment of ligatures (when supported by a particular font or required by a written language), quotation marks, and hyphenation. Other applications and search engines might use this information to aid the selection of spell-checking dictionaries and the creation of indices.

Example   <span lang="de">Deutsche Bundesbahn</span>

Value   Case-insensitive language code.

Default   Browser default.

Object Model Reference

[window.]document.getElementById(*elementID*).lang

repeat, repeat-max, repeat-min, repeat-start, repeat-template

IE *n/a* NN *n/a* Moz *n/a* Saf *n/a* Op *9* HTML *n/a*

(See text) *Optional*

Web Forms 2.0 (*http://www.whatwg.org*) lets you turn any HTML element into a *repetition block*, that is, one or more elements, which, as a group, require an unpredictable number of instances in a document. For example, an order form set up as a table element with a row containing fields for quantity and product number could begin with a two text entry controls (one would be an input of type number, while the other of type text with a pattern that matches the product numbering system for the company; as entries are made, an AJAX call in the background fetches the cost for display in another cell in the table row). If the user wishes to add to the order, the form needs a second row containing the same controls, but named differently so that the browser submits distinct data for each row. While DHTML scripts are capable of such actions with tables, the Web Forms 2.0 repetition block mechanism handles addition, deletion, and movement of repeated elements without scripting.

To make a table row (or other HTML container) a repetition block, assign the repeat attribute, as follows:

```
<tr id="item" repeat="template">
    <td><input type="number" name="row[item].quantity" value="1"></td>
    <td><input type="text" name="row[item].product" value=""></td>
    ...
</tr>
```

Notice that the names for each control have what looks like JavaScript array notation, with the ID of the repetition block (item in this case) inserted as the array index. When the form is submitted, the array notation is replaced in the control's name with an integer beginning with 0 for the first item (e.g., row0.quantity and row0.product for the first row).

Repetition blocks are controlled by input or button elements of type add, move-down, move-up, and remove. The template attribute of these controls point to the ID of the repetition block's outer container (the one with the repeat="template" attribute).

If you wish to begin layout of the form with a starting number of rows, you only need to compose the HTML for one row, and set the repeat-start attribute to the number of rows to appear initially. Similarly, you may provide upper and lower limits to the number of repetitions to be added or removed by setting the repeat-max and repeat-min attributes, respectively.

Example

```
<form action="..." method="POST">
<p>
<table>
<tr><th>Quantity</th><th>Item Number</th></tr>
<tbody>
    <tr id="item" repeat="template" repeat-start="2" repeat-min="1">
        <td><input type="number" name="row[item].quantity" value="1"></td>
        <td><input type="text" name="row[item].product" value=""></td>
        <td><input type="remove" /></td>
    </tr>
</tbody>
</table>
<button type="add" template="item">Add Item</button>
<p>
<input type="submit" />
</p>
</form>
```

Value   For repeat, the constant template or an integer for hard-coded items; for repeat-max, repeat-min, and repeat-start, an integer; for repeat-template, the ID of the element elsewhere in the document acting as the template.

Default   Maximum integer value (repeat-max); 0 (repeat-min); 0 (repeat-start in Opera, although the standard suggests 1).

style   IE 4 NN 4 Moz 0.9 Saf 1 Op 7 HTML 4

style="*styleSheetProperties*"   *Optional*

This attribute lets you set one or more style sheet rule property assignments for the current element. You may use the CSS or (for Navigator 4 only) JavaScript syntax for assigning style attributes. Use the style attribute only with visible (renderable) elements.

Example

```
<span style="color: green; font-size: 18px">Big, green, and bold</span>
```

Value   An entire CSS-syntax style sheet rule is enclosed in quotes. Multiple style attribute settings are separated by semicolons. Style sheet attributes are detailed in Chapter 4.

Default   None.

Object Model Reference

`[window.]document.getElementById(elementID).style`

tabindex
`IE 4  NN n/a  Moz 0.9  Saf 1  Op 7  HTML 4`

`tabindex="integer"`   *Optional*

A number that indicates the sequence of this element within the tabbing order of all focusable elements in the document. Tabbing order follows a strict set of rules. Elements that have values other than zero assigned to their `tabindex` attributes are first in line when a user starts tabbing in a page. Focus starts with the element with the lowest `tabindex` value and proceeds in order to the highest value, regardless of physical location on the page or in the document. If two elements have the same `tabindex` values, the element that comes earlier in the document receives focus first. Next come all elements that either don't support the `tabindex` attribute or have the value set to zero. These elements receive focus in the order in which they appear in the document. Note that reloading the current page does not necessarily restart the tabbing sequence from the "top." Therefore, controlling tabbing sequence is most helpful when the logic of your focusable elements is something other than the source code order of those elements (e.g., directing tabbing to fields down table columns rather than across rows).

HTML 4 and many browsers limit the `tabindex` attribute to the following elements: `a`, `area`, `button`, `input`, `object`, `select`, `textarea`. To this list, IE 4 adds `applet`, `body`, `div`, `embed`, `isindex`, `marquee`, `span`, `table`, and `td`. IE 5 adds every other renderable element. A negative value in IE and Mozilla 1.8 or later removes an element from tabbing order entirely.

Example   `<a href="chapter3.html" tabindex="3">Chapter 3</a>`

Value   Any integer from 0 through 32,767. In IE and Mozilla 1.8 or later, setting `tabindex` to a negative value causes the element to be skipped in tabbing order altogether.

Default   None.

Object Model Reference

`[window.]document.getElementById(elementID).tabIndex`

title
`IE 3  NN n/a  Moz 0.9  Saf 1  Op 7  HTML 4`

`title="advisoryText"`   *Optional*

An advisory description of the element. For HTML elements that produce visible content on the page, modern browsers render the content of the `title` attribute as a tooltip when the cursor rests on the element for a moment. For example, the table-related `col` element does not display content, so its `title` attribute is merely advisory. To generate tooltips in tables, assign `title` attributes to elements such as `table`, `tr`, `th`, or `td`.

The font and color properties of the tooltip are governed by the browser, and are not modifiable under script control. In IE/Windows, the tooltip is the standard small, light-yellow rectangle; in IE/Mac, the tooltip displays as a cartoon bubble in the manner of the Mac OS bubble help system. Mozilla tooltips are the same small rectangle on all OS versions. If no attribute is specified, the tooltip does not display.

You can assign any descriptive text you like to this attribute. Not everyone will see it, however, so do not put mission-critical information here. Browsers designed to meet web accessibility criteria might use this attribute's information to read information about a link or nontext elements to vision-impaired web surfers. Therefore, don't ignore this potentially helpful aid to describing an element's purpose on the page.

Although the compatibility listing for this attribute dates the attribute back to Internet Explorer 3 and HTML 3.2, it is newly ascribed to many elements starting with IE 4 and HTML 4.0.

Example	`<span title="United States of America">U.S.A.</span>`
Value	Any string of characters. The string must be inside a matching pair of (single or double) quotation marks.
Default	None.

Object Model Reference
`[window.]document.getElementById(elementID).title`

unselectable
IE *5.5*   NN *n/a*   Moz *n/a*   Saf *n/a*   Op *9*   HTML *n/a*

`unselectable="featureSwitch"`   *Optional*

Boolean switch that enables or disables the user's ability to select any portion of the element.

Example	`<p unselectable="on">...</p>`
Value	`on	off`
Default	`off`

xml:lang
IE *n/a*   NN *n/a*   Moz *n/a*   Saf *n/a*   Op *9*   HTML *X1.0*

`xml:lang="languageCode"`   *Optional*

This is the XML version of the HTML-only `lang` attribute, as specified in the W3C XML recommendation. Use this only in an XHTML-conforming document and in browsers that understand XML namespaces. XML processors other than current browsers can make content and display decisions based on values assigned to this attribute (e.g., display the element only if the browser and operating system support the language script style). Browser documents should continue to use the `lang` attribute, even when it duplicates the `xml:lang` attribute setting.

Example   `<span lang="de" xml:lang="de">Deutsche Bundesbahn</span>`

Value   Case-insensitive language code.

Shared Event Handler Attributes

Handler	IE/Windows	NN	Mozilla	IE/Mac	Safari	Opera	HTML
onactivate	5.5	n/a	n/a	n/a	n/a	n/a	n/a
onbeforeactivate	5.5	n/a	n/a	n/a	n/a	n/a	n/a
onbeforecopy	5	n/a	n/a	n/a	1.3/2	n/a	n/a
onbeforecut	5	n/a	n/a	n/a	1.3/2	n/a	n/a
onbeforedeactivate	5.5	n/a	n/a	n/a	n/a	n/a	n/a
onbeforeeditfocus	5	n/a	n/a	n/a	n/a	n/a	n/a
onbeforepaste	5	n/a	n/a	n/a	1.3/2	n/a	n/a
onblur	3/4	2	0.9	3/4	1	4	4
onclick	3/4	2	0.9	3/4	1	4	4
oncontextmenu	5	n/a	n/a	n/a	1.2	n/a	n/a
oncontrolselect	5.5	n/a	n/a	n/a	n/a	n/a	n/a
oncopy	5	n/a	n/a	n/a	n/a	n/a	n/a
oncut	5	n/a	n/a	n/a	n/a	n/a	n/a
ondblclick	4	4	0.9	4	1	7	4
ondeactivate	5.5	n/a	n/a	n/a	n/a	n/a	n/a
ondrag	5	n/a	n/a	n/a	1.3/2	n/a	n/a
ondragend	5	n/a	n/a	n/a	1.3/2	n/a	n/a
ondragenter	5	n/a	n/a	n/a	1.3/2	n/a	n/a
ondragleave	5	n/a	n/a	n/a	1.3/2	n/a	n/a
ondragover	5	n/a	n/a	n/a	1.3/2	n/a	n/a
ondragstart	5	n/a	n/a	n/a	1.3/2	n/a	n/a
ondrop	5	n/a	n/a	n/a	1.3/2	n/a	n/a
onfilterchange	4	n/a	n/a	n/a	n/a	n/a	n/a
onfocus	3/4	2	0.9	3/4	1	4	4
onfocusin	6	n/a	n/a	n/a	n/a	n/a	n/a
onfocusout	6	n/a	n/a	n/a	n/a	n/a	n/a
onhelp	4	n/a	n/a	5	n/a	n/a	n/a
onkeydown	4	4	0.9	4	1	5	4
onkeypress	4	4	0.9	4	1	5	4
onkeyup	4	4	0.9	4	1	5	4
onlosecapture	5	n/a	n/a	n/a	n/a	n/a	n/a
onmousedown	4	4	0.9	4	1	5	4

Handler	IE/Windows	NN	Mozilla	IE/Mac	Safari	Opera	HTML
onmouseenter	5.5	n/a	n/a	n/a	n/a	n/a	n/a
onmouseleave	5.5	n/a	n/a	n/a	n/a	n/a	n/a
onmousemove	4	4	0.9	4	1	5	4
onmouseout	3/4	2	0.9	3/4	1	4	4
onmouseover	3/4	2	0.9	3/4	1	4	4
onmouseup	4	4	0.9	4	1	5	4
onmousewheel	6	n/a	n/a	n/a	1.3/2	n/a	n/a
onmove	5.5	n/a	n/a	n/a	1	n/a	n/a
onmoveend	5.5	n/a	n/a	n/a	n/a	n/a	n/a
onmovestart	5.5	n/a	n/a	n/a	n/a	n/a	n/a
onpaste	5	n/a	n/a	n/a	n/a	n/a	n/a
onpropertychange	5	n/a	n/a	n/a	n/a	n/a	n/a
onreadystatechange	4	n/a	n/a	4	n/a	n/a	n/a
onresize	4	n/a	n/a	4	1.2	n/a	n/a
onresizeend	5.5	n/a	n/a	n/a	n/a	n/a	n/a
onresizestart	5.5	n/a	n/a	n/a	n/a	n/a	n/a
onselectstart	4	n/a	n/a	4	1.3/2	n/a	n/a

The evolution of shared event handler attributes over the course of scriptable browser history is not straightforward. While all renderable elements have the common mouse and keyboard event handler attributes starting with IE 4, Mozilla 0.9, and HTML 4, the earlier browsers implemented only some of these event attributes and only for interactive elements. Elements that have always responded to mouse clicks (e.g., form button controls, links, and image maps) supported onclick events. Links and image maps also generally support mouseover and mouseout events going way back. Microsoft brings a large repertoire of event handler attributes to Windows-only versions of Internet Explorer, and Apple has adopted many of them in Safari 1.3/2 to be used primarily in Dashboard widgets. For more details on each event type and other types not listed here, see Chapter 3.

Alphabetical Tag Reference

<a> IE *all* NN *all* Moz *all* Saf *all* Op *7* HTML *all*

<a>...</a> *HTML End Tag: Required*

The a element is the rare element that can be an anchor and/or a link, depending on the presence of the name and/or href attributes. As an anchor, the element defines a named location in a document to which any URL can reference by appending a hashmark and the anchor name to the document's URI (for example, *http://www.example.com/contents#a-c*). Names are identifiers assigned to the name attribute (or in newer browsers, the id attribute).

<a>

Content defined solely as an anchor is not (by default) visually differentiated from surrounding body content.

By assigning a URI to the href attribute, the element becomes the source of a hypertext link. Activating the link generally navigates to the URI assigned to the href attribute (or it may load other media into a helper application or plugin without changing the page). Unless modified by style sheets, links typically have a distinctive appearance in the browser, such as an underline beneath text (or border around an object) and a color other than the current content color. Attributes can define separate colors for three states: an unvisited link, a link being activated by the user, and a previously visited link (the linked document is currently in the browser cache). Such color control is deprecated in favor of CSS pseudo-classes (:link, :active, :visited, and a new state, :hover). An a element can be both an anchor and a link if, in the least, both the name (or id) and href attributes have values assigned to them.

Example

```
<a name="anchor3" id="anchor3">Just an anchor named "anchor3."</a>
<a href="#anchor3">A link to navigate to "anchor3" in the same document.</a>
<a name="anchor3" id="anchor3" href="http://www.example.com/index.html">
Go from here (anchor 3) to home page.</a>
```

Object Model Reference

```
[window.]document.links[i]
[window.]document.anchors[i]
[window.]document.getElementById(elementID)
```

Element-Specific Attributes

charset	coords	datafld	datasrc	href
hreflang	methods	name	rel	rev
shape	target	type	urn	

Element-Specific Event Handler Attributes

None. Anchor-only a elements have no event handlers in Navigator through Version 4.

charset

IE *n/a* NN *n/a* Moz *0.9* Saf *all* Op *7* HTML *4*

charset="*characterSet*"   *Optional*

Character encoding of the content at the other end of the link.

Example   `<a charset="csISO5427Cyrillic" href="moscow.html">Visit Moscow</a>`

Value   Case-insensitive alias from the character set registry (*ftp://ftp.isi.edu/in-notes/iana/assignments/character-sets*).

Default   Determined by browser.

coords
IE 6   NN n/a   Moz all   Saf all   Op 7   HTML 4

coords="coord1, ... coordN"   *Optional*

Although defined for the a element, the coords attribute applies to the area element for
client-side image maps. The area element "inherits" many attributes and behaviors of the a
element. See the area element.

datafld
IE 4   NN n/a   Moz n/a   Saf n/a   Op n/a   HTML n/a

datafld="columnName"   *Optional*

Used with IE data binding to associate a remote data source column name in lieu of an href
attribute for a link. The data source column must contain a valid URI (relative or absolute). A datasrc attribute must also be set for the element. Works only with text file data
sources in IE 5/Mac.

Example   `<a datasrc="DBSRC3" datafld="newsURL">Late-Breaking News</a>`

Value   Case-sensitive identifier.

Default   None.

Object Model Reference
```
[window.]document.links[i].dataFld
[window.]document.getElementById(elementID).dataFld
```

datasrc
IE 4   NN n/a   Moz n/a   Saf n/a   Op n/a   HTML n/a

datasrc="dataSourceName"   *Optional*

Used with IE data binding to specify the ID of the page's object element that loads the data
source object for remote data access. Content from the data source to be inserted into the a
element text is specified via the datafld attribute. Works only with text file data sources in
IE 5/Mac.

Example   `<a datasrc="DBSRC3" datafld="newsURL">Late-Breaking News</a>`

Value   Case-sensitive identifier.

Default   None.

Object Model Reference
```
[window.]document.links[i].dataSrc
[window.]document.getElementById(elementID).dataSrc
```

href
IE all   NN all   Moz all   Saf all   Op 7   HTML all

href="URI"   *Required for links*

The URI of the destination of a link. In browsers, when the URI is an HTML document,
the document is loaded into the current (default) or other window target (as defined by the
target attribute). For some other file types, the browser may load the destination content
into a plugin or save the destination file on the client machine. In the absence of the href

<a>

attribute, the element does not distinguish itself in a browser as a clickable link and may instead be only an anchor (if the name or id attribute is set).

Example   `<a href="part1/chap3.html">Chapter 3</a>`

Value

Any valid URI, including complete and relative URLs, anchors on the same page (anchor names prefaced with the # symbol), and the nonstandards-based javascript: pseudo-URL in scriptable browsers to trigger a script statement rather than navigate to a destination. Note that a link to a javascript: pseudo-URL will be inactive if scripting is disabled in a visitor's browser. Moreover, search engine spiders won't follow such links.

Default   None.

Object Model Reference

```
[window.]document.links[i].href
[window.]document.getElementById(elementID).href
```

Other link object properties allow for the extraction of components of the URL, such as protocol and hostname. See the a element in Chapter 2.

hreflang   IE 6   NN n/a   Moz 09   Saf all   Op n/a   HTML 4

hreflang="*languageCode*"   *Optional*

The language code of the content at the destination of a link. Requires that the href attribute also be set. This attribute is primarily an advisory attribute to help a browser prepare itself for a new language set if the browser is so enabled.

Example   `<a hreflang="HI" href="hindi/Chap3.html>Chapter 3 (in Hindi)</a>`

Value   Case-insensitive language code.

Default   Browser default.

methods   IE 4   NN n/a   Moz n/a   Saf n/a   Op n/a   HTML n/a

methods="*http-method*"   *Optional*

An advisory attribute about the functionality of the destination of a link. A browser could use this information to display special colors or images for the element content based on what the destination will do for the user.

Example
```
<a href="http://www.example.com/cgi-bin/search?chap3" methods="get">
Chapter 3</a>
```

Value   Comma-delimited list of one or more HTTP methods.

Default   None.

Object Model Reference

```
[window.]document.links[i].Methods
[window.]document.getElementById(elementID).Methods
```

<a>

name

name="*elementIdentifier*"   *Required for anchors*

The traditional way to signify an anchor position within a document. Other link elements can refer to the anchor by setting their href attributes to a URL ending in a pound sign (#) followed by the identifier. Omitting the name (and id) attribute for the a element prevents the element from being used as an anchor position. This attribute is interchangeable with the id attribute in recent browsers. The attribute is deprecated in XHTML 1.0, so you are encouraged to use both attributes (with the same identifier) to keep all browser generations happy. If the name and href attribute are set in the element, the element is considered both an anchor and a link.

Example   <a id="sect3" name="sect3">Section III</a>

Value   Case-sensitive identifier.

Default   None.

Object Model Reference
[window.]document.links[i].name
[window.]document.anchors[i].name
[window.]document.getElementById(*elementID*).name

rel

rel="*linkTypes*"   *Optional*

Defines the relationship between the current element and the destination of the link. Also known as a *forward link*, not to be confused in any way with the destination document whose address is defined by the href attribute. The HTML 4 recommendation defines several link types; it is up to the browser to determine how to employ the value. This attribute has meaning primarily for the link element, although there is significant room for future application for tasks such as assigning an a element (acting as a link) to a button in a static navigation bar pointing to the next or previous document in a series. The element must include an href attribute for the rel attribute to be applied.

Example   <a rel="next chapter" href="chapter3.html">Chapter 3</a>

Value
Case-insensitive, space-delimited list of HTML 4 standard link types applicable to the element. Sanctioned link types are:

alternate	appendix	bookmark	chapter
contents	copyright	glossary	help
index	next	prev	section
start	stylesheet	subsection	

In addition, IE 3 defined a fixed set of four values: same | next | parent | previous, but only next and previous continue to be supported in IE.

Default   None.

Object Model Reference
```
[window.]document.links[i].rel
[window.]document.getElementById(elementID).rel
```

rev   IE *3* NN *n/a* Moz *0.9* Saf *all* Op *n/a* HTML *4*
rev="*linkTypes*"   *Optional*

A reverse link relationship. Like the rel attribute, the rev attribute's capabilities are defined by the browser, particularly with regard to how the browser interprets and renders the various link types available in the HTML 4 specification. Given two documents (A and B) containing links that point to each other, the rev value of B is designed to express the same relationship between the two documents as denoted by the rel attribute in A. There is not yet much application of either the rel or rev attributes of the a element in mainstream browsers.

Example   `<a rev="previous" href="chapter2.html">Chapter 2</a>`

Value   Case-insensitive, space-delimited list of standard link types applicable to the element. See the rel attribute for sanctioned and supported link types.

Default   None.

Object Model Reference
```
[window.]document.links[i].rev
[window.]document.getElementById(elementID).rev
```

shape   IE *n/a* NN *n/a* Moz *all* Saf *all* Op *7* HTML *4*
shape="*shape*"   *Optional*

Defines the shape of a server-side image map area whose coordinates are specified with the coords attribute. See the area element.

target   IE *all* NN *all* Moz *all* Saf *all* Op *7* HTML *all*
target="*windowOrFrameName*"   *Optional*

If the destination document is to be loaded into a window or frame other than the current window or frame, you can specify where the destination document should load by assigning a window or frame name to the target attribute. Target frame names must be assigned to frames and windows as identifiers. Assign names to frames via the name and id attributes of the frame element; assign names to new windows via the second parameter of the window.open( ) scripting method. If you omit this attribute, the destination document replaces the document containing the link. An identifier other than one belonging to an existing frame or window opens a new window for the destination document. This attribute is applicable only when a value is assigned to the href attribute of the element.

A link element can have only one destination document and one target. If you want a link to change the content of multiple frames, you can use an a element's onclick event handler to fire a script that loads multiple documents. Set the location.href property of each frame to a desired URL.

Strict DTDs for HTML 4 and XHTML do not support the target attribute of any element because frames and windows are outside the scope of pure document markup. In fact, framesetting documents will not validate in the strict environment—thus the purpose of the separate frameset DTDs for HTML 4 and XHTML. If your documents must validate with these strict DTDs, and you wish to support targets, use scripts to set target properties of links, image maps, and forms after the page has loaded.

Example

```
<a target="display" href="chap3.html#sec2">Section 3.2</a>
<a target="_top" href="index.html">Start Over</a>
```

Value

Case-sensitive identifier when the frame or window name has been assigned via the target element's name and id attributes. Several reserved target names act as constants:

_blank
> Browser creates a new window for the destination document.

_content
> For Mozilla-based browsers only, when links appear in a browser sidebar and the destination is to be displayed in the primary content frame, regardless of its actual name.

_parent
> Destination document replaces the current frame's framesetting document (if one exists; otherwise, it is treated as _self).

_self
> Destination document replaces the current document in its window or frame.

_top
> Destination document is to occupy the entire browser window, replacing any and all framesets that may be loaded (also treated as _self if there are no framesets defined in the window).

Default   _self

Object Model Reference

```
[window.]document.links[i].target
[window.]document.getElementById(elementID).target
```

type   IE 6 NN n/a Moz n/a Saf n/a Op n/a HTML n/a

type="MIMEType"   Optional

An advisory about the content type of the destination document or resource. A browser might use this information to assist in preparing support for a resource requiring a multimedia player or plugin.

Example   `<a type="video/mpeg" href="ski4.mpeg">View Devil's Ghost slope</a>`

| Value | Case-insensitive MIME type. A catalog of registered MIME types is available from *ftp://ftp.isi.edu/in-notes/iana/assignments/media-types/*. |
| Default | None. |

urn

urn="*urn*"   *Optional*

A Uniform Resource Name version of the destination document specified in the href attribute. This attribute is intended to offer support in the future for the URN format of URI, an evolving recommendation under discussion at the IETF (see RFC 2141). Although supported in IE 4 and later, this attribute does not take the place of the href attribute.

Example   `<a urn="urn:foo:bar3" href="chapter3.html">Chapter 3</a>`

Value   A valid URN in the form of "urn:*NamespaceID*:*NamespaceSpecificString*".

Default   None.

Object Model Reference

```
[window.]document.links[i].urn
[window.]document.getElementById(elementID).urn
```

<abbr>

`<abbr>...</abbr>`   *HTML End Tag: Required*

The abbr element provides an encapsulation and enumeration mechanism for abbreviations that appear in the body text. For example, consider a web page that includes your company's address. At one point in the document, the abbreviation IA is used for Iowa. A spelling checker, language translation program, or speech synthesizer might choke on this abbreviation; a search engine would not include the word "Iowa" in its relevancy rating calculation. But by turning the IA text into an abbr element (and assigning a title attribute to it), you can provide a full-text equivalent that a search engine (if so equipped) can count; a text-to-speech program would read aloud the full state name instead of some guttural gibberish. Like many elements introduced in HTML 4.0, this one is intended to assist browser technologies that may not yet be implemented but could find their way into products of the future.

Mozilla and Opera render the abbr element with a dotted underline. The context menu in Mozilla for such an element contains a **Properties** choice, which leads to a displayed list of attributes and their values for the visitor.

A related element, acronym, offers the same services for words that are acronyms. Both elements are part of a larger group of what the HTML 4.0 recommendation calls *phrase elements*.

Example

```
Ottumwa, <abbr title="Iowa">IA</abbr> 55334<br>
<abbr lang="de" title="und so weiter">usw.</abbr>
```

Object Model Reference

[window.]document.getElementById(*elementID*)

Element-Specific Attributes

None.

Element-Specific Event Handler Attributes

None.

<acronym>

IE 4 NN *n/a* Moz 0.9 Saf *all* Op 7 HTML 4

<acronym>...</acronym>

HTML End Tag: Required

The acronym element provides an encapsulation and enumeration mechanism for acronyms that appear in the body text. For example, consider a web page that includes a discussion of international trade issues. At one point in the document, the acronym GATT is used for General Agreement on Tariffs and Trade. A spelling checker, language translation program, or speech synthesizer might choke on this acronym; a search engine would not include the word "tariffs" in its relevancy rating calculation. But by turning the GATT text into an acronym element (and assigning a title attribute to it), you can provide a full-text equivalent that a search engine (if so equipped) can count; a text-to-speech program would read aloud the full meaning of the acronym. Like many elements introduced in HTML 4.0, this one is intended to assist browser technologies that may not yet be implemented but could find their way into products of the future.

Mozilla and Opera render the acronym element with a dotted underline. The context menu in Mozilla for such an element contains a **Properties** choice, which leads to a displayed list of attributes and their values for the visitor.

A related element, abbr, offers the same services for words that are abbreviations. Both elements are part of a larger group of what the HTML 4 recommendation calls *phrase elements*.

Example

```
<acronym title="General Agreement on Tariffs and Trade">GATT</acronym>
<acronym lang="it" title="Stati Uniti">s.u.</acronym>
```

Object Model Reference

[window.]document.getElementById(*elementID*)

Element-Specific Attributes

None.

Element-Specific Event Handler Attributes

None.

<address>

IE *all* **NN** *all* **Moz** *all* **Saf** *all* **Op** *7* **HTML** *all*

`<address>...</address>`

HTML End Tag: Required

Prior to HTML 4, the address element was often regarded as a display formatting tag appropriate for displaying a page author's contact information on the page. Mainstream browsers display address elements in an italic font. But the increased focus on separating content from presentation in HTML 4 adds some extra meaning to this element. Search engines and future HTML (or XML) parsers may apply special significance to the content of this element, perhaps in cataloging author information separate from the hidden information located in meta elements. If you want to use this structural meaning of the element while keeping the rendering in line with the rest of your body text, you need to assign style sheet rules to override the browser's default formatting tendencies for this element. Any standard body elements, such as links, can be contained inside an address element.

Example

```
<address>
<p>Send comments to:<a href="mailto:jb@example.com">jb@example.com</a>
</p>
</address>
```

Object Model Reference

`[window.]document.getElementById(elementID)`

Element-Specific Attributes

None.

Element-Specific Event Handler Attributes

None.

<applet>

IE *3* **NN** *2* **Moz** *all* **Saf** *all* **Op** *7* **HTML** *3.2*

`<applet>...</applet>`

HTML End Tag: Required

You can embed an executable chunk of Java code in an HTML document in the form of an applet. An applet occupies a rectangular area of the page, even if it is only one-pixel square. An applet may require that some initial values be set from the HTML document. One or more param elements can be used to pass parameters to the applet before the applet starts running (provided the applet is written to accept these parameters). param elements go between the start and end tags of an applet element.

Applets are compiled by their authors into class files (filename suffix *.class*). An applet class file must be in the same directory as, or a subdirectory of, the HTML document that loads the applet. Key attributes of the applet element direct the browser to load a particular class file from the necessary subdirectory.

All user interface design for the applet is programmed into the applet in the Java language. One of the roles of attributes in the applet element is to define the size and other geographical properties of the applet for its rendering on the page. Recent browsers allow JavaScript scripts to communicate with the applet, as well as allowing applets to access document elements.

Note that HTML 4 deprecates the applet element in favor of the more generic object element. Support for embedding applets via the object element is improving, but is not universal. Browser support for the applet element will continue for some time to come, however.

Example

```
<applet code="simpleClock.class" name="myClock" width="400" height="50">
<param name="bgColor" value="black">
<param name="fgColor" value="yellow">
</applet>
```

Object Model Reference

```
[window.]document.applets[i]
[window.]document.appletName
[window.]document.getElementById(elementID)
```

Element-Specific Attributes

align	alt	archive	code	codebase
datafld	datasrc	height	hspace	mayscript
name	object	src	vspace	width

Element-Specific Event Handler Attributes

Handler	IE	Others	HTML
onafterupdate	4	n/a	n/a
onbeforeupdate	4	n/a	n/a
ondataavailable	4	n/a	n/a
ondatasetchanged	4	n/a	n/a
ondatasetcomplete	4	n/a	n/a
onerrorupdate	4	n/a	n/a
onrowenter	4	n/a	n/a
onrowexit	4	n/a	n/a

align
IE 3 NN 2 Moz *all* Saf *all* Op 7 HTML 3.2

align="*alignmentConstant*"   *Optional*

The align attribute determines how the rectangle of the applet aligns within the context of surrounding content. See the "Alignment Constants" earlier in this chapter for description of the possibilities defined in various browsers for this attribute.

Example

```
<applet code="simpleClock.class" name="myClock" align="absmiddle"
width="400" height="50"></applet>
```

Value   Case-insensitive constant value.

Default   bottom

Object Model Reference
```
[window.]document.applets[i].align
[window.]document.appletName.align
[window.]document.getElementById(elementID).align
```

alt   IE *3* NN *3* Moz *all* Saf *all* Op *7* HTML *3.2*
`alt="textMessage"`   *Optional*

If a browser does not have the facilities to load and run Java applets or if the browser has
Java support turned off in its preferences, the text assigned to the alt attribute is supposed
to display in the document where the applet element's tag appears. Typically, this text
provides advice on what the page visitor is missing by not being able to load the Java
applet. Unlike the noscript or noframes elements, there is no corresponding element for an
absent Java applet capability. In practice, browsers don't necessarily display this message
for applets that fail to load for a variety of reasons.

Example
```
<applet code="simpleClock.class" name="myClock" align="absmiddle"
alt="A Java clock applet." width="400" height="50"></applet>
```

Value   Any quoted string of characters.

Default   None.

archive   IE *7* NN *3* Moz *all* Saf *all* Op *7* HTML *4*
`archive="archiveFileURL"`   *Optional*

An author can package multiple Java class files into a single uncompressed *.zip* archive file
and let the browser load the entire set of classes at one time. This can offer a performance
improvement over loading just the main class file (specified by the code attribute) and then
letting the class loader fetch each additional class file as needed. The archive attribute
value points to the *.zip* archive file.

In addition to specifying the archive attribute, be sure to include a code attribute that
names the main class to load. The URL must also be relative to the codebase location.

The HTML specification allows multiple URLs to be specified (in a space-delimited list) for
additional class or other resource files. This design anticipates the use of the same attribute
with the object element, which the W3C has deemed the successor to the applet element.

Example
```
<applet code="ScriptableClock.class" archive="myClock.zip" width="400" height="50">
</applet>
```

Value   Case-sensitive URI.

Default   None.

Object Model Reference

```
[window.]document.applets[i].archive
[window.]document.appletName.archive
[window.]document.getElementById(elementID).archive
```

code
IE 3 NN 2 Moz *all* Saf *all* Op 7 HTML *3.2*

```
code="fileName.class"
```
Required

The name of the main class file that starts and runs the applet. If the codebase attribute is not specified, the code attribute must include a path from the directory that stores the HTML document loading the applet. You might get away with omitting the *.class* filename extension, but don't take any chances: be complete with the class name. Most servers are case-sensitive, so also match case of the actual class filename.

Example

```
<applet code="applets/ScriptableClock.class" width="400" height="50">
</applet>
```

Value   Case-sensitive *.class* filename or complete path relative to the HTML document.

Default   None.

Object Model Reference

```
[window.]document.applets[i].code
[window.]document.appletName.code
[window.]document.getElementById(elementID).code
```

codebase
IE 3 NN 2 Moz *all* Saf *all* Op 7 HTML *3.2*

```
codebase="path"
```
Optional

Path to the directory holding the class file designated in either the code or archive attribute. The codebase attribute does not name the class file, just the path. You can make this attribute a complete URL to the directory, but don't try to access a codebase outside of the domain of the current document: security restrictions may prevent the class from loading. A full path and filename can be set together in the code or object attribute, eliminating the need for the codebase attribute setting.

Example

```
<applet code="ScriptableClock.class" codebase="applets/" width="400" height="50">
</applet>
```

Value   Case-sensitive pathname, usually relative to the directory storing the current HTML document.

Default   None.

Object Model Reference

```
[window.]document.applets[i].codeBase
[window.]document.appletName.codeBase
[window.]document.getElementById(elementID).codeBase
```

datafld, datasrc

See the param element for IE data binding to Java applets.

height, width   IE *3* NN *2* Moz *all* Saf *all* Op *7* HTML *3.2*

width="*pixels*" height="*pixels*"   *Required*

The size that a Java applet occupies in a document is governed by the height and width attribute settings. Some browser versions might allow you to get away without assigning these attributes, letting the applet's own user interface design determine the height and width of its visible rectangle. As with images, however, it is more efficient for the browser's rendering engine when you explicitly specify the object's dimensions. Make a habit of supplying these values for all applets, as you should for all images or other visible external objects.

Example
<applet code="ScriptableClock.class" width="400" height="50"></applet>

Value   Positive integer pixel values. You cannot entirely hide an applet by setting values to zero, but you can reduce its height and width to one pixel in each dimension. If you want to hide an applet, do so with DHTML by setting its positioning display attribute to none.

Default   None.

Object Model Reference
```
[window.]document.applets[i].height
[window.]document.appletName.height
[window.]document.getElementById(elementID).height
[window.]document.applets[i].width
[window.]document.appletName.width
[window.]document.getElementById(elementID).width
```

hspace, vspace   IE *3* NN *2* Moz *all* Saf *all* Op *7* HTML *3.2*

hspace="*pixels*" vspace="*pixels*"   *Optional*

You can put some empty space ("air") between an applet and any surrounding content by assigning pixel values to the hspace and vspace attributes. The vspace attribute governs space above and below the applet; the hspace attribute governs space to the left and right of the applet. For browsers that are style sheet savvy, you are perhaps better served by using the padding and/or margin CSS properties to gain control down to individual sides, if you so desire.

Example
<applet code="ScriptableClock.class" width="400" height="50" hspace="3" vspace="4">
</applet>

Value   Positive integer pixel values (optionally quoted).

Default   0

Object Model Reference
```
[window.]document.applets[i].hspace
[window.]document.appletName.hspace
[window.]document.getElementById(elementID).hspace
[window.]document.applets[i].vspace
[window.]document.appletName.vspace
[window.]document.getElementById(elementID).vspace
```

id
IE 4   NN n/a   Moz all   Saf all   Op 7   HTML 4

`id="elementIdentifier"`   *Optional*

A unique identifier that distinguishes this element from others in the document. Can be used to associate a single element with a style rule naming this attribute value as an ID selector. An element can have an ID assigned for uniqueness as well as a class for inclusion within a group. See Online Section III.

If you assign an id attribute and not a name attribute, the value of the id attribute can be used as the applet's name in script reference forms that use the element name (document.appletName).

Example
```
<applet id="clocker" code="ScriptableClock.class" width="400" height="50">
</applet>
```

Value   Case-sensitive identifier.

Default   None.

Object Model Reference
```
[window.]document.applets[i].id
[window.]document.appletName.id
[window.]document.getElementById(elementID).id
```

mayscript
IE 4   NN 3   Moz 1.7.5   Saf all   Op n/a   HTML n/a

`mayscript`   *Optional*

Navigator 3 introduced a technology called LiveConnect, which allowed scripts to communicate with Java applets and vice versa (not yet implemented in Mozilla-based browsers). For security reasons, an applet's communications facilities with scripts must be explicitly switched on by the page author. By adding the mayscript attribute to the applet's tag, an applet that is written to take advantage of the document objects and scripts can address those items. In other words, the HTML is granting the applet the ability to reach scripts in the document. This attribute is a simple switch: when the attribute name is present, it is turned on.

One more step is required for an applet to communicate with JavaScript. The applet code must import a special Netscape class called *JSObject.class*. This class file and its companion exception class are built into the Java support in the Windows version of Internet Explorer 4 and later. Although the execution is not perfect in IE, applets can perform basic communication with scripts. Some Mozilla-based browser user installations require the installation of a Java runtime module/plugin to operate correctly.

Example

```
<applet code="ScriptableClock.class" width="400" height="50" mayscript>
</applet>
```

Value   No value assigned to the attribute. The presence of the attribute name sets turns on applet-to-script communication.

Default   Off.

name
IE 3 NN 2 Moz all Saf all Op 7 HTML 3.2

name="*elementIdentifier*"   *Optional*

If you are scripting an applet, it is usually more convenient to create a reference to the applet by using a unique name you assign to the applet. Then, if you edit the page and move or delete multiple applets on the page, you do not have to worry about adjusting index values to array-style references. In IE 4 and later or W3C DOM-compatible browsers, you have the option of omitting the name attribute and using the id attribute value in script references to the applet object.

Example

```
<applet name="clock2" code="ScriptableClock.class" width="400" height="50">
</applet>
```

Value   Case-sensitive identifier.

Default   None.

Object Model Reference

```
[window.]document.applets[i].name
[window.]document.appletName.name
[window.]document.getElementById(elementID).name
```

object
IE n/a NN n/a Moz n/a Saf n/a Op n/a HTML 4

object="*filename*"   *Optional*

Reference to the name of the file (relative to the codebase URI) that preserves the applet's state between sessions. When supported properly, this attribute replaces the code attribute, and the data file points to the applet's startup class file.

Example

```
<applet name="clock2" object="clockData.dat" width="400" height="50">
</applet>
```

Value   Case-sensitive filename.

Default   None.

Alphabetical Tag Reference | 33

Alphabetical
HTML Reference

<area>

Object Model Reference

```
[window.]document.applets[i].object
[window.]document.appletName.object
[window.]document.getElementById(elementID).object
```

src   IE 4   NN n/a   Moz n/a   Saf n/a   Op n/a   HTML n/a

src="URL"   *Optional*

Internet Explorer defines this attribute as the URL for an "associated file." This may be the same as the archive attribute defined in HTML and Navigator specifications. The src attribute is not a substitute for the code and/or codebase attributes.

Value   A complete or relative URL.

Default   None.

Object Model Reference

```
[window.]document.applets[i].src
[window.]document.appletName.src
[window.]document.getElementById(elementID).aex
```

vspace

See hspace.

width

See height.

<area>   IE *all*   NN *all*   Moz *all*   Saf *all*   Op 7   HTML *3.2*

<area>   *HTML End Tag: Forbidden*

A map element defines a client-side image map that is ultimately associated with an image or other object that occupies space on the page. The only job of the map element is to assign a name and a tag context for one or more area element definitions. Each area element defines how the page should respond to user interaction with a specific geographical region of the image or other object.

A client-side image map area can act like an a element link in that an area can link to a URL and assign another frame or window as the target for loading a new document. In fact, in the original scripting document object model, an area element is referenced as a link. It is not uncommon to use client-side area maps in a navigation bar occupying a slender frame of a frameset. This allows an artist to be creative with a menu design, while giving the page author the power to turn any segment of a larger image into a special-purpose link.

Example

```
<map name="nav">
<area coords="20,30,120,70" href="contents.html" target="display">
```

```
<area coords="20,80,145,190" href="contact.html" target="display">
</map>
```

Object Model Reference

```
[window.]document.links[i]
[window.]document.getElementById(elementID)
```

Element-Specific Attributes

alt	coords	href	nohref	shape
target				

Element-Specific Event Handler Attributes

None.

alt

IE 3 NN *n/a* Moz *all* Saf *all* Op 7 HTML *3.2*

```
alt="textMessage"
```
                                                                    Required

Nongraphical browsers can use the alt attribute setting to display a brief description of the meaning of the (invisible) image's hotspots. Keep in mind that recent handheld computers usually have nongraphical browsers (or allow graphics to be turned off for improved performance). Don't ignore the graphically impaired.

Example

```
<area coords="20,30,120,70" href="contents.html" target="display"
alt="Table of Contents">
```

Value   Any quoted string of characters.

Default   None.

Object Model Reference

```
[window.]document.getElementById(elementID).alt
```

coords

IE *all* NN *all* Moz *all* Saf *all* Op 7 HTML *3.2*

```
coords="coord1, ... coordN"
```
                                                                    Optional

Although the formal W3C definition for the coords attribute of an area element states that the attribute is optional, that doesn't mean that you can omit this attribute and expect an area to behave as it should. The coords attribute lets you define the outline of the area to be associated with a particular link or scripted action. Some third-party authoring tools can assist in determining the coordinate points for a hot area. You can also load the image into a graphics program that displays the cursor position in real time and then transfer those values to the coords attribute values.

Coordinate values are entered as a comma-delimited list. If two areas overlap, the area that is defined earlier in the HTML code takes precedence.

Example   `<area coords="20,30,120,70" href="contents.html" target="display">`

<area>

Value

Each coordinate is a length value, but the number of coordinates and their order depend on the shape specified by the shape attribute, which may optionally be associated with the element. For shape="rect", there are four coordinates (left, top, right, bottom); for shape="circle", there are three coordinates (center-x, center-y, radius); for shape="poly", there are two coordinate values for each point that defines the shape of the polygon (x1, y1, x2, y2, x3, y3,...xN, yN).

Default   None.

Object Model Reference

[window.]document.getElementById(*elementID*).coords

href
IE *all* NN *all* Moz *all* Saf *all* Op 7 HTML 3.2

href="*URI*"   *Required*

The URI of the destination of a link associated with the area. In a browser, when the URI is an HTML document, the document is loaded into the current (default) or other window target (as defined by the target attribute). For some other file types, the browser may load the destination content into a plugin or save the destination file on the client machine. Because some older browsers treat area elements as a elements, the href attribute must be defined in the area element for scripts in the old DOM to access various properties about the URL and for event handlers (such as onmouseover) to work.

Example   <area coords="20,30,120,70" href="contents.html" target="display">

Value   Any valid URI, including complete and relative URLs, anchors on the
                     same page (anchor names prefaced with the # symbol), and the
                     javascript: pseudo-URL in scriptable browsers to trigger a script state-
                     ment rather than navigate to a destination.

Default   None.

Object Model Reference

[window.]document.links[i].href
[window.]document.getElementById(*elementID*).href

Other link object properties allow for the extraction of components of the URL, such as protocol and hostname. See the link object in Chapter 2.

nohref
IE *all* NN *all* Moz *all* Saf *all* Op 7 HTML 3.2

nohref   *Optional*

Tells the browser that the area defined by the coordinates has no link associated with it (as not including any href attribute does). When you include this attribute, scriptable browsers no longer treat the element as a link. When an area element lacks an href attribute, the element no longer responds to user events. In IE 4 or later and W3C DOM browsers, you can turn this attribute on and off from a script by setting the corresponding noHref property to true or false.

Example   `<area coords="20,30,120,70" nohref>`

Value   The presence of this attribute sets its value to `true`. Extend for XHTML compliance by using `nohref="nohref"`.

Default   Off.

Object Model Reference
`[window.]document.getElementById(elementID).noHref`

shape   IE *all*   NN *all*   Moz *all*   Saf *all*   Op *7*   HTML *3.2*

`shape="shapeName"`   *Optional*

Defines the shape of the client-side area map whose coordinates are specified with the coords attribute. The shape attribute tells the browser how many coordinates to expect.

Example
```
<area shape="poly" coords="20,20,20,70,65,45" href="contents.html"
target="display">
```

Value
Case-insensitive shape constant. Each implementation defines its own set of shape names and equivalents, but there are common denominators across browsers (circle, rect, poly, and polygon).

Shape name	IE	Others	HTML
circ	•	—	•
circle	•	•	•
poly	•	•	•
polygon	•	•	—
rect	•	•	•
rectangle	•	—	—

Default   rect

Object Model Reference
`[window.]document.getElementById(elementID).shape`

target   IE *all*   NN *all*   Moz *all*   Saf *all*   Op *7*   HTML *3.2*

`target="windowOrFrameName"`   *Optional*

If the destination document is to be loaded into a window or frame other than the current window or frame, you can specify where the destination document should load by assigning a window or frame name to the target attribute. Target frame names must be assigned to frames and windows as identifiers. Assign names to frames via the name and id attributes of the frame element; assign names to new windows via the second parameter of the window.open( ) scripting method. If you omit this attribute, the destination document

Alphabetical
HTML Reference

<area>

replaces the document containing the link. This attribute is applicable only when a value is assigned to the href attribute of the element.

An area element can have only one destination document and one target. If you want a link to change the content of multiple frames, you can use an area element's onclick event handler (check Chapter 2 for supported browser versions) to fire a script that loads multiple documents. Set the location.href property of each frame to the desired URL.

Strict DTDs for HTML 4 and XHTML do not support the target attribute of any element because frames and windows are outside the scope of pure document markup. In fact, framesetting documents will not validate in the strict environment—thus the purpose of the separate frameset DTDs for HTML 4 and XHTML. If your documents must validate with these strict DTDs, and you wish to support targets, use scripts to set target properties of links, image maps, and forms after the page has loaded.

Example

```
<area coords="20,30,120,70" href="contents.html" target="display">
<area coords="140,30,180,70" href="index.html" target="_top">
```

Value

Case-sensitive identifier when the frame or window name has been assigned via the target element's name and id attributes. Several reserved target names act as constants:

_blank
    Browser creates a new window for the destination document.

_content
    For Mozilla-based browsers only, when links appear in a browser sidebar and the destination is to be deisplayed in the primary content frame, regardless of its actual name.

_parent
    Destination document replaces the current frame's framesetting document (if one exists; otherwise, it is treated as _self).

_self
    Destination document replaces the current document in its window or frame.

_top
    Destination document is to occupy the entire browser window, replacing any and all framesets that may be loaded (also treated as _self if there are no framesets defined in the window).

Default   _self

Object Model Reference

```
[window.]document.links[i].target
[window.]document.getElementById(elementID).target
```

<base>

<b>

IE *all* **NN** *all* **Moz** *all* **Saf** *all* **Op** *7* **HTML** *all*

`<b>...</b>`   *HTML End Tag: Required*

The b element—one of several font style elements in HTML 4—renders its content in a boldface version of the font face governing the next outermost HTML container. You can nest multiple font style elements to create combined styles, such as bold italic (`<b><i>bold-italic text</i></b>`).

It is up to the browser to fatten boldface display by calculating the character weight or by perhaps loading a bold version of the currently specified font. If you are striving for font perfection, it is best to use style sheets (and perhaps downloadable fonts if supported by your target browsers) to specify a true bold font family, rather than risk the browser's extrapolation of a boldface from a system font. The `font-weight` CSS style property provides quite granular control over the degree of bold applied to text if the font face supports such fine-tuning.

You can take advantage of the containerness of this element by assigning style sheet rules to some or all b elements in a page. For example, you may wish all b elements to be in a red color. By assigning the style rule b {`color:red`}, you can do it to all elements with only a tiny bit of code.

Although this element is not deprecated in HTML 4 or XHTML 1.0, it is losing favor to style sheets.

Example   `<p>This product is <b>new</b> and <b>improved</b>!</p>`

Object Model Reference
`[window.]document.getElementById(`*elementID*`)`

Element-Specific Attributes
None.

Element-Specific Event Handler Attributes
None.

<base>

IE *all* **NN** *all* **Moz** *all* **Saf** *all* **Op** *7* **HTML** *all*

`<base>`   *HTML End Tag: Forbidden*

A base element is defined inside a document's head element to instruct the browser about the URL path to the current document. This path is used as the basis for all relative URLs used to specify various src and href attributes in the document. The base element's URL should be a complete URL, including the document name (though browsers tend to support URLs to directories, too). The browser calculates the base URL path to the directory holding the document. If you specify `<base href="http://www.example.com/products/index.html">`, the href attribute of a link on that page to *widgets/framitz801.html* resolves to the full URL of *http://www.example.com/products/widgets/framitz801.html*. Similarly, a relative URL can walk up the hierarchy with the dot syntax. For example, from the base element defined earlier, an img element in the *index.html* page might be set for src=`"../images/logo.jpg"`. That reference resolves to *http://www.example.com/images/logo.jpg*.

<base>

By and large, today's browsers automatically calculate the base URL of the currently loaded document, thus allowing use of relative URLs without specifying a base element. This is especially helpful when you are developing pages locally and don't want to change the base element settings when you deploy the pages. The HTML 4 specification states that a document lacking a base element should by default use the current document's URL as the base URL.

You can also use the base element to define a default target for any link-type element in the document. Therefore, if all links are supposed to load documents into another frame, you can specify this target frame once in the base tag and not worry about target attributes elsewhere in the document. If you wish to override the default for a single link, you may do so by specifying the target attribute for that element (but see the note in the target attribute).

The only attribute this element has in common with other elements is the id attribute.

Example
```
<head>
<base href="http://www.example.com/index.html" target="_top">
</head>
```

Object Model Reference
```
[window.]document.getElementById(elementID)
```

Element-Specific Attributes

href   target

Element-Specific Event Handler Attributes
None.

href

IE *all*   NN *all*   Moz *all*   Saf *all*   Op 7   HTML *all*

href="*URL*"   *Optional*

The href attribute is a URL of a document whose server path is to be used as the base URL for all relative references in the document. This is typically the URL of the current document, but it can be set to another path if it makes sense to your document organization and directory structure.

Example   `<base href="http://www.example.com/products/index.html">`

Value   This should be a full and absolute URL to a document.

Default   Current document pathname.

Object Model Reference
```
[window.]document.getElementsByTagName("base")[0].href
[window.]document.getElementById(elementID).href
```

target

target="*windowOrFrameName*"   *Optional*

If all or most links and area maps on a page load documents into a separate window or frame, you can set the target attribute of the base element to take care of targeting for all of those elements. You can set the target attribute without setting the href attribute if you want to set only the base target reference.

Strict DTDs for HTML 4 and XHTML do not support the target attribute of any element because frames and windows are outside the scope of pure document markup. In fact, framesetting documents will not validate in the strict environment—thus the purpose of the separate frameset DTDs for HTML 4 and XHTML. If your documents must validate with these strict DTDs, and you wish to support targets, use scripts to set target properties of links, image maps, and forms after the page has loaded.

Example   <base target="rightFrame">

Value

Case-sensitive identifier when the frame or window name has been assigned via the target element's name attribute. Several reserved target names act as constants:

_blank

> Browser creates a new window for the destination document.

_content

> For Mozilla-based browsers only, when links appear in a browser sidebar and the destination is to be deisplayed in the primary content frame, regardless of its actual name.

_parent

> Destination document replaces the current frame's framesetting document (if one exists; otherwise, it is treated as _self).

_self

> Destination document replaces the current document in its window or frame.

_top

> Destination document is to occupy the entire browser window, replacing any and all framesets that may be loaded (also treated as _self if there are no framesets defined in the window).

Default   _self

Object Model Reference

[window.]document.getElementsByTagName("base")[0].target
[window.]document.getElementById(*elementID*).target

<basefont>

<basefont>   *HTML End Tag: Forbidden*

A basefont element advises the browser of some font information to be used as the basis for text rendering of the current page below the basefont element. You can apply this element in either the head or body portion of the document (although Microsoft recommends in the body only for IE 4 and later), and you can insert basefont elements as often as is needed to set the base font for a portion of the document. Be aware that basefont element settings do not necessarily apply to content in tables. If you want table content to resemble a custom basefont setting, you likely have to set the font styles to table elements separately.

The basefont element overrides the default font settings in the browser's user preferences settings. Like most font-related elements, the basefont element is deprecated in HTML 4 in favor of style sheets, and is removed from the HTML 4 and XHTML strict DTDs.

Example   `<basefont face="Times, serif" size="4">`

Element-Specific Attributes

color	face	name	size

Element-Specific Event Handler Attributes
None.

color
IE 3 NN n/a Moz all Saf all Op 7 HTML 4

`color="colorTripletOrName"`   *Optional*

Sets the font color of all text below the basefont element. Deprecated in HTML 4 in favor of the color CSS property.

Example   `<basefont color="Olive">`

Value   A hexadecimal triplet or plain-language color name. See Appendix A for acceptable plain-language color names.

Default   Browser default.

Object Model Reference
`[window.]document.getElementsByTagName("basefont")[0].color`

face
IE 4 NN n/a Moz all Saf all Op 7 HTML 4

`face="fontFaceName1[, ... fontFaceNameN]"`   *Optional*

You can assign a hierarchy of font faces to use for the default font of a section headed by a basefont element. The browser looks for the first font face in the comma-delimited list of font face names until it either finds a match in the client system or runs out of choices, at which point the browser default font face is used. Font face names must match the system font face names exactly. If you use this attribute (instead of the preferred style sheet property), you can always suggest a generic font face (serif, sans-serif) as the final choice. Deprecated in HTML 4 in favor of the font-family CSS property.

In IE 3, this attribute was called the name attribute.

Example   `<basefont face="Bookman, Times Roman, serif">`

Value	One or more font face names, including the recognized generic faces: `serif` | `sans-serif` | `cursive` | `fantasy` | `monospace`.
Default	Browser default.

Object Model Reference

`[window.]document.getElementsByTagName("basefont")[0].face`

name
IE |3| **NN** *n/a* **Moz** *n/a* **Saf** *n/a* **Op** *n/a* **HTML** *n/a*

`name="fontFaceName"` *Optional*

This was IE 3's version of what is today the `face` attribute. It accepts a single font face as a value. The `name` attribute is no longer used.

Value	A single font face name.
Default	Browser default.

size
IE *all* **NN** *n/a* **Moz** *all* **Saf** *all* **Op** *7* **HTML** *3.2*

`size="integerOrRelativeSize"` *Optional*

Font sizes referenced by the `size` attribute are on a relative size scale that is not tied to any one point size across operating system platforms. The default browser font size is 3. The range of acceptable values for the `size` attribute are integers from 1 to 7 inclusive. The exact point size varies with the operating system and browser design.

Users can often adjust the default font size in preferences settings. The `size` attribute overrides that setting. Moreover, `size` values can be relative to whatever font size is set in the preferences. By preceding an attribute value with a + or - sign, the browser's default size can be adjusted upward or downward, but always within the range of 1 through 7.

Example

```
<basefont size="4">
<basefont size="+3">
```

Value	Either an integer or relative value, consisting of a + or - symbol and an integer value.
Default	3

Object Model Reference

`[window.]document.getElementsByTagName("basefont")[0].size`

`<bdo>`
IE *5* **NN** *n/a* **Moz** *all* **Saf** *all* **Op** *7* **HTML** *4*

`<bdo>...</bdo>` *HTML End Tag: Required*

The name of the bdo element stands for *bidirectional override*. The `lang` and `dir` attributes of most elements are designed to take care of most situations involving the mixture of writing systems that compose text in opposite directions. The bdo element is designed to assist in instances when the normal bidirectional algorithms must be explicitly overridden, due to various conversions during text processing.

Example   <bdo dir="ltr">*someMixedScriptTextHere*</bdo>

Element-Specific Attributes
None.

Element-Specific Event Handler Attributes
None.

<bgsound>    IE *3* NN *n/a* Moz *n/a* Saf *n/a* Op *n/a* HTML *n/a*
<bgsound>   *HTML End Tag: Optional*

This Internet Explorer-only attribute lets you define a sound file that is to play in the background while the user visits the page. The element is allowed only inside the head element. With scripting, you can control the volume and how many times the sound track plays even after the sound file loads. Although an end tag is optional, there is no need for it because all specifications for the sound are maintained by attributes in the start tag. Only the id attribute is shared with other elements.

If you are going to use this tag, I strongly recommend making the background sound a user-selectable choice that is turned off by default. In office environments, it can be startling (if not embarrassing) to have background music or sounds unexpectedly emanate from a computer. Also be aware that there is likely to be some delay in the start of the music due to download time.

Example   <bgsound src="tunes/mazeppa.mid">

Object Model Reference
[window.]document.getElementById(*elementID*)

Element-Specific Attributes

balance   loop   src   volume

Element-Specific Event Handler Attributes
None.

# balance   IE *4* NN *n/a* Moz *n/a* Saf *n/a* Op *n/a* HTML *n/a*
balance="*signedInteger*"   *Optional*

A value that directs how the audio is divided between the left and right speakers. Once this attribute value is set in the element, its value cannot be changed by script control.

Example   <bgsound src="tunes/mazeppa.mid" balance="+2500">

Value   A signed integer between −10,000 and +10,000. A value of 0 is equally balanced on both sides. A negative value gives a relative boost to the left side; a positive value boosts the right side.

Default   0

Object Model Reference

[window.]document.getElementsByTagName("bgsound")[0].balance

loop   IE *3*   NN *n/a*   Moz *n/a*   Saf *n/a*   Op *n/a*   HTML *n/a*

loop="*integer*"   *Optional*

Defines the number of times the sound plays. If the attribute is absent or is present with any value other than -1, the sound plays at least once. Assigning a value of -1 means that the sound plays until the page is unloaded. Contrary to Microsoft's Internet Explorer SDK information, there does not appear to be a way to precache the sound without having it start playing.

Example   <bgsound src="tunes/mazeppa.mid" loop="3">

Value   No value assignment necessary for a single play. A value of 0 still causes a single play. Values above zero play the sound the specified number of times. Assign -1 to have the sound play indefinitely.

Default   -1

Object Model Reference

[window.] document.getElementsByTagName("bgsound")[0].loop

src   IE *3*   NN *n/a*   Moz *n/a*   Saf *n/a*   Op *n/a*   HTML *n/a*

src="*URL*"   *Optional*

A URL that points to the sound file to be played. The type of sound file that can be played is limited only by the audio facilities of the browser. Common audio formats, including MIDI, are supported in Internet Explorer without further plugin installation.

Example   <bgsound src="tunes/beethoven.mid">

Value   Any valid URL, including complete and relative URLs. The file must be in a MIME type supported by Internet Explorer or a plugin.

Default   None.

Object Model Reference

[window.] document.getElementsByTagName("bgsound")[0].src

<big>

volume
IE *4* NN *n/a* Moz *n/a* Saf *n/a* Op *n/a* HTML *n/a*

volume="*signedInteger*" *Optional*

An integer that defines how loud the background sound plays relative to the maximum sound output level as adjusted by user preferences in the client computer. Maximum volume—a setting of zero—is only as loud as the user has set in the **Sound** control panel. Attribute adjustments are negative values as low as –10,000 (although most users lose the sound at a value much higher than –10,000).

Example   `<bgsound src="tunes/beethoven.mid" volume="-500">`

Value   A signed integer value between –10,000 and 0.

Default   0

Object Model Reference
[window.] document.getElementsByTagName("bgsound")[0].volume

<big>
IE *all* NN *all* Moz *all* Saf *all* Op *7* HTML *3.2*

`<big>...</big>` *HTML End Tag: Required*

The big element—one of several font style elements in HTML 4—renders its content in the next font size (in HTML's 1 through 7 scale) larger than the previous body font size. If you nest big elements, the effects on the more nested elements are cumulative, with each nested level rendered one size larger than the next outer element. Default font size is dependent upon the browser, operating system, and user preferences settings. For more precise font size rendering, use style sheet rules.

Example   `<p>This product is <big>new</big> and <big>improved</big>!</p>`

Object Model Reference
[window.]document.getElementById(*elementID*)

Element-Specific Attributes
None.

Element-Specific Event Handler Attributes
None.

<blink>
IE *n/a* NN *all* Moz *1.01* Saf *n/a* Op *7* HTML *n/a*

`<blink>...</blink>` *HTML End Tag: Required*

The blink element is Marc Andreessen's contribution to horrifying web pages. All content of the element flashes on and off uncontrollably in a distracting manner. The more content you place inside the element, the more difficult it is to read between the flashes. Please don't use this tag. I beg you.

Example   `<blink>I dare you to read this...and not look at it.</blink>`

<body>

<blockquote>

<blockquote>...</blockquote>

IE *all* NN *all* Moz *all* Saf *all* Op *7* HTML *all*

HTML End Tag: Required

The blockquote element is intended to set off a long quote inside a document. Traditionally, the blockquote element has been rendered as an indented block, with wider left and right margins (about 40 pixels each), plus some extra whitespace above and below the block. Browsers will likely continue this type of rendering, although you are encouraged to use style sheets to create such displays (with or without the blockquote element). For inline quotations, see the q element.

Example

```
<blockquote>Four score and seven years ago...
shall not perish from the earth</blockquote>
```

Object Model Reference

[window.]document.getElementById(*elementID*)

Element-Specific Attributes

cite

Element-Specific Event Handler Attributes

None.

cite

IE *6* NN *n/a* Moz *all* Saf *all* Op *7* HTML *4*

cite="*URL*"

Optional

A URL pointing to an online source document from which the quotation is taken. This is not in any way a mechanism for copying or extracting content from another document. Presumably, this HTML 4 recommendation is to encourage future browsers and search engines to utilize a reference to online source material for the benefit of readers and surfers. The **Properties** choice for Mozilla's context menu for this element displays a small window that includes an active link to the URL assigned to the attribute. Current mainstream browsers provide no other functionality for this attribute.

Value   Any valid URL to a document on the World Wide Web, including absolute or relative URLs.

Default   None.

Element-Specific Event Handler Attributes

None.

<body>

<body>...</body>

IE *all* NN *all* Moz *all* Saf *all* Op *7* HTML *all*

HTML End Tag: Optional

After all of the prefatory material in the head portion of an HTML file, the body element contains the genuine content of the page that the user sees in the browser window (or may

<body>

hear from browsers that know how to speak to users). Before style sheets, the body element was the place where page authors could specify document-wide color and background schemes. A great many favorite attributes covering these properties are deprecated in HTML 4, in favor of style sheet rules that may be applied to the body element. Support for all these attributes, however, will remain in mainstream browsers for years to come.

The body element is also where window object event handler attributes are placed. For example, a window object as defined in most document object models has an onload event handler that fires when a document has finished loading into the current window or frame. Assigning that event handler as an element attribute is done in the body element.

Although it may appear from a variety of implications that the body element is the document object, this is not true. The document object has additional properties (such as the document. title) that are defined outside of the body element in an HTML document. In a W3C-DOM-aware browser, the document node tree puts more distance between the root document node and the body element: the document node is the parent of the html element; the html element is the parent of both the head and body elements.

Example

```
<body background="watermark.jpg" onload="init( );">
...
</body>
```

Object Model Reference

[window.]document.body

Element-Specific Attributes

alink	background	bgcolor	bgproperties	bottommargin
leftmargin	link	marginheight	marginwidth	nowrap
rightmargin	scroll	text	topmargin	vlink

Element-Specific Event Handler Attributes

Handler	IE	NN	Mozilla	Safari	Opera	HTML
onafterprint	5	n/a	n/a	n/a	n/a	n/a
onbeforeprint	5	n/a	n/a	n/a	n/a	n/a
onload	3	2	m18	1	7	4
onresize	4	4	m18	1	7	n/a
onscroll	4	n/a	1.0.1	1	n/a	n/a
onselect	4	n/a	n/a	n/a	n/a	n/a
onunload	3	2	m18	1	7	4

alink

alink="*colorTripletOrName*"   *Optional*

Establishes the color of a hypertext link when it is activated (being clicked on) by the user. This is one of three states for a link: unvisited, active, and visited. The color is applied to the link text or border around an image or object embedded within an a element. This attribute is deprecated in favor of the CSS :active pseudo-class style rule for an a element, as described in Chapter 4.

Example   <body alink="#FF0000">...</body>

Value   A hexadecimal triplet or plain-language color name. See Appendix A for acceptable plain-language color names.

Default   #FF0000 (typically).

Object Model Reference
[window.]document.alinkColor
[window.]document.body.aLink

background

background="*URL*"   *Optional*

Specifies an image file that is used as a backdrop to the text and other content of the page. Unlike normal images that get loaded into browser content, a background image loads in its original size (without scaling) and tiles to fill the available document space in the browser window or frame. Smaller images usually download faster but are obviously repeated more often in the background. Animated GIFs are also allowable but very distracting to the reader. When selecting a background image, be sure it is very muted in comparison to the main content so that the content stands out clearly. Background images, if used at all, should be extremely subtle or occupy space free of other content.

This attribute is deprecated in HTML 4 in favor of the background CSS property.

Example   <body background="watermark.jpg">...</body>

Value   Any valid URL to an image file, including complete and relative URLs.

Default   None.

Object Model Reference
[window.]document.body.background

bgcolor

bgcolor="*colorTripletOrName*"   *Optional*

Establishes a fill color (behind the text and other content) for the entire document. If you combine a bgcolor and background, any transparent areas of the background image let the background color show through. This attribute is deprecated in HTML 4 in favor of the background-color CSS property.

<body>

Example	`<body bgcolor="tan">...</body>`
Value	A hexadecimal triplet or plain-language color name. A setting of empty is interpreted as "#000000" (black). See Appendix A for acceptable plain-language color names.
Default	Varies with browser, browser version, and operating system.

Object Model Reference
`[window.]document.bgColor`
`[window.]document.body.bgColor`

bgproperties
IE 3   NN *n/a*   Moz *n/a*   Saf *all*   Op *n/a*   HTML *n/a*

`bgproperties="property"`   *Optional*

An Internet Explorer attribute that lets you define whether the background image (set with the background attribute or style sheet) remains in a fixed position or scrolls as a user scrolls the page. This can provide both intriguing and odd effects for the user. When the background image is set to remain in a fixed position, scrolled content flows past the background image very much like film credits roll past a background image on the screen.

Example
`<body background="watermark.jpg" bgproperties="fixed">...</body>`

| **Value** | If set to "fixed", the image does not scroll. Omit the attribute or set it to an empty string ("") to let the image scroll with the content. |
| **Default** | None. |

Object Model Reference
`[window.]document.body.bgProperties`

bottommargin
IE 4   NN *n/a*   Moz *n/a*   Saf *n/a*   Op *n/a*   HTML *n/a*

`bottommargin="integer"`   *Optional*

Establishes the amount of blank space between the very end of the content and the bottom of a scrollable page. The setting has no visual effect if the length of the content or size of the window does not cause the window to scroll. The default value is for the end of the content to be flush with the end of the document, but in the Macintosh version of Internet Explorer, there is about a 10-pixel margin visible even when the attribute is set to zero. Larger sizes are reflected properly. This attribute offers somewhat of a shortcut to setting the margin-bottom style sheet property for the body element.

Example	`<body bottommargin="20">...</body>`
Value	A string value of the number of pixels of clear space at the bottom of the document. A value of an empty string is the same as zero.
Default	0

Object Model Reference

[window.]document.body.bottomMargin

leftmargin
IE 3   NN *n/a*   Moz *n/a*   Saf *all*   Op 7   HTML *n/a*

leftmargin="*integer*"   *Optional*

Establishes the amount of blank space between the left edge of the content area of a window and the left edge of the content. This attribute offers somewhat of a shortcut to setting the margin-left style sheet property for the body element. As the outermost parent container in the renderable element hierarchy, this attribute setting fixes the left margin context for all nested elements in the document.

Example   <body leftmargin="25">...</body>

Value   A string value of the number of pixels of clear space at the left margin of the document. A value of an empty string is the same as zero.

Default   10 (IE/Windows); 8 (Others).

Object Model Reference

[window.]document.body.leftMargin

link
IE *all*   NN *all*   Moz *all*   Saf *all*   Op 7   HTML *3.2*

link="*colorTripletOrName*"   *Optional*

Establishes the color of a hypertext link that has not been visited (i.e., the URL of the link is not in the browser's cache). This is one of three states for a link: unvisited, active, and visited. The color is applied to the link text or border around an image or object embedded within an a element. This attribute is deprecated in favor of the :link pseudo-class style rule for an a element, as described in Chapter 4).

Example   <body link="#00FF00">...</body>

Value   A hexadecimal triplet or plain-language color name. See Appendix A for acceptable plain-language color names.

Default   #0000FF

Object Model Reference

[window.]document.linkColor
[window.]document.body.link

marginheight, marginwidth
IE *n/a*   NN *4*   Moz *all*   Saf *all*   Op 7   HTML *n/a*

marginheight="*integer*"marginwidth="*integer*"   *Optional*

Shortcut attributes to set the body's margins in lieu of CSS style sheets. Setting marginheight to a pixel value establishes a margin setting above and below the body content; marginwidth sets margins to the left and right of the body.

Example   <body marginheight="20" marginwidth="10">...</body>

Value	A string value of the number of pixels of clear space at each of the two sides affected by each attribute. A value of an empty string is the same as zero.
Default	0

nowrap

IE 4   NN *n/a*   Moz *n/a*   Saf *n/a*   Op *n/a*   HTML *n/a*

nowrap   *Optional*

Controls whether wide content should wrap within the body width.

Example	`<body nowrap>...</body>`
Value	The presence of the attribute sets its value to true.
Default	false

Object Model Reference

[window.]document.body.noWrap

rightmargin

IE 4   NN *n/a*   Moz *n/a*   Saf *all*   Op 7   HTML *n/a*

rightmargin="*integer*"   *Optional*

Establishes the amount of blank space between the right edge of the content area of a window and the right edge of the content. This attribute offers somewhat of a shortcut to setting the margin-right style sheet property for the body element. As the outermost parent container in the renderable element hierarchy, this attribute setting fixes the right margin context for all nested elements in the document. Be aware that IE on the Mac does not let content come as close to the right edge of the window as the Windows version.

Example	`<body rightmargin="25">... </body>`
Value	A string value of the number of pixels of clear space at the right margin of the document. A value of an empty string is the same as zero.
Default	10 (Windows); 0 (Macintosh).

Object Model Reference

[window.]document.body.rightMargin

scroll

IE 4   NN *n/a*   Moz *n/a*   Saf *n/a*   Op *n/a*   HTML *n/a*

scroll="*featureSwitch*"   *Optional*

Controls the presence of scrollbars when the content space exceeds the size of the current window. Without scrollbars, if you want your users to move around the page, you have to provide some scripted method of adjusting the scroll of the window. Be aware that Internet Explorer for the Mac always shows scrollbars when the document is too large for the window, even when the scroll attribute is set to no. For more modern control over scrollbars, use the overflow CSS property (plus IE-specific overflowX and overflowY properties).

Example	`<body scroll="no">...</body>`
Value	Constant values yes or no (case-insensitive).
Default	yes

Object Model Reference

`[window.]document.body.scroll`

text IE *all* NN *all* Moz *all* Saf *all* Op *7* HTML *3.2*

text="*colorTripletOrName*"   *Optional*

Establishes the color of body content in the document. Colors of individual elements within the document can override the document-wide setting. Because the default background color of browsers varies widely with browser brand, version, and operating system, it is advisable to set the bgcolor attribute (or equivalent style sheet rule) in concert with the document's text color. This attribute is deprecated in favor of the color style sheet property.

Example	`<body bgcolor="#FFFFFF" text="#c0c0c0">...</body>`
Value	A hexadecimal triplet or plain-language color name. See Appendix A for acceptable plain-language color names.
Default	#000000 (black).

Object Model Reference

`[window.]document.fgColor`
`[window.]document.body.text`

topmargin IE *3* NN *n/a* Moz *n/a* Saf *all* Op *7* HTML *n/a*

topmargin="*integer*"   *Optional*

Establishes the amount of blank space between the top edge of the content area of a window and the top edge of the content. This attribute offers somewhat of a shortcut to setting the margin-top style sheet property for the body element. As the outermost parent container in the renderable element hierarchy, this attribute setting fixes the top margin context for all nested elements in the document. Setting the topmargin attribute to zero or an empty string ("") pushes the content to the very top of the document content region.

Example	`<body topmargin="0">... </body>`
Value	A string value of the number of pixels of clear space at the top of the document. A value of an empty string is the same as zero.
Default	15 (IE/Windows); 8 (others).

Object Model Reference

`[window.]document.body.topMargin`

vlink

IE *all* NN *all* Moz *all* Saf *all* Op 7 HTML 3.2

vlink="*colorTripletOrName*"   *Optional*

Establishes the color of a hypertext link after it has been visited by a user (and the destination page is still in the browser's cache). This is one of three states for a link: unvisited, active, and visited. The color is applied to the link text or border around an image or object embedded within an a element. This attribute is deprecated in favor of the :visited pseudo-class style rule for an a element, as described in Chapter 4).

Example   <body vlink="teal">...</body>

Value   A hexadecimal triplet or plain-language color name. See Appendix A for acceptable plain-language color names.

Default   Varies with browser and operating system.

Object Model Reference
[window.]document.vlinkColor
[window.]document.body.vLink

IE *all* NN *all* Moz *all* Saf *all* Op 7 HTML *all*

                                              HTML End Tag: Forbidden

The br element forces a visible line break (carriage return and line feed) wherever its tag appears in the document. Browsers tend to honor the br element as a genuine line break, whereas paragraphs defined by the p element are given more vertical space between elements on the page. If the text containing the br element is wrapped around a floating image or other object, you can direct the next line (via the clear attribute or style sheet equivalent) to start below the object, rather than on the next line of the wrapped text.

Example
<p>I think that I shall never see
A poem lovely as a tree.</p>

Object Model Reference
[window.]document.getElementById(*elementID*)

Element-Specific Attributes

  clear

Element-Specific Event Handler Attributes
None.

clear

IE *all* NN *all* Moz *all* Saf *all* Op 7 HTML 3.2

clear="*constant*"   *Optional*

The clear attribute tells the browser how to treat the next line of text following a br element if the current text is wrapping around a floating image or other object. The value

<button>

you use depends on the side of the page to which one or more inline images are pegged and how you want the next line of text to be placed in relation to those images.

This attribute is deprecated in HTML 4 in favor of the clear style sheet property in CSS2.

Example
`<br clear="left">`

Value
Four string constants: all | left | none | right. HTML 4.0 includes what should be the default value: none. This value is listed in IE 3 documentation, but not for IE 4. You can set the property to none, and the browser either responds to the value or ignores it (yielding the same results).

Default
none

Object Model Reference
`[window.]document.getElementById(elementID).clear`

<button>

IE 4 NN n/a Moz all Saf all Op 7 HTML 4

`<button>...</button>`   *HTML End Tag: Required*

The button element is patterned after the input element (of types button, submit, and reset) but carries some extra powers, particularly when used as a submit-type button. Content for the button's label goes between the element's start and end tags, rather than being assigned as an attribute. Other elements can be used to generate the label content, including an img element if so desired (although client-side image maps of such images are strongly discouraged by the W3C). Although you can assign a style sheet to a button element, you can also wrap the label content inside an element (such as a span) and assign or override style rules just for that content.

When a button element is assigned a type of submit, the browser submits the button's name and value attributes to the server as a name/value pair, like other form elements. No special form handling is conveyed by a button when other types are specified.

In theory, a button element should be embedded within a form element. In practice, browsers have no problem rendering a free-standing button element. This might be acceptable when no related form elements (such as text boxes) need to be referenced by scripts associated with the button. Some scripting shortcuts (reading the form property of the event object's srcElement or target properties) simplify the scripted interactivity between form elements.

The W3C implemented this input element variant to offer browser makers a chance to create a different, richer-looking button. In practice, browser makers keep them the same (Mozilla), distinguish them slightly (IE 7), or display radically different elements (Safari). For Web Forms 2.0 (first implemented in Opera 9), the button element gains a number of attributes that accrue to all form control elements in that environment capable of submitting a form, but a button element's name/value pair is not submitted with the form.

Example

```
<button type="button" oneClick="doSomething( );">Click Here</button>
<button type="submit" id="sender" value="infoOnly">Request Info</button>
<button type="reset"><img src="clearIt.gif" height="20" width="18"></button>
```

Object Model Reference

[window.]document.getElementById(*elementID*)

Element-Specific Attributes

action	autofocus	datasrc	disabled	enctype
form	method	name	replace	target
template	type	value		

Element-Specific Event Handler Attributes

Handler	IE	Others	HTML
onafterupdate	4	n/a	n/a
onbeforeupdate	4	n/a	n/a
onrowenter	4	n/a	n/a
onrowexit	4	n/a	n/a

action, enctype, method, replace, target

For these Web Forms 2.0 extensions to a button element whose type attribute is set to submit, see the descriptions under the input element.

autofocus
IE *n/a* NN *n/a* Moz *n/a* Saf *n/a* Op *n/a* HTML *n/a*

autofocus="autofocus"   *Optional*

Web Forms 2.0 extension that brings focus to the element after the page loads. Should be assigned to only one form control element per page.

datafld
IE *4* NN *n/a* Moz *n/a* Saf *n/a* Op *n/a* HTML |4|

datafld="*columnName*"   *Optional*

Used with IE data binding to associate a remote data source column name with the label of a button. The data source column must be either plain text or HTML (see dataformatas). A datasrc attribute must also be set for the button element. Works only with text file data sources in IE 5/Mac.

This attribute was reserved in HTML 4, but was dropped in XHTML 1.0.

Example

```
<button type="button" datasrc="DBSRC3" datafld="label" onClick="getTopStory( );">
Latest News</button>
```

Value   Case-sensitive identifier.

Default   None.

<button>

Object Model Reference

[window.]document.getElementById(*elementID*).dataFld

dataformatas
IE 4 NN n/a Moz n/a Saf n/a Op n/a HTML |4|

dataformatas="*dataType*"   *Optional*

Used with IE data binding, this attribute advises the browser whether the source material arriving from the data source is to be treated as plain text or as tagged HTML. This attribute setting depends entirely on how the data source is constructed.

This attribute was reserved in HTML 4, but was dropped in XHTML 1.0.

Example

```
<button type="button" datasrc="DBSRC3"dataformatas="HTML" datafld="label"
onClick="getTopStory( );"> Latest News</button>
```

Value   IE recognizes two possible settings: text | html.

Default   text

Object Model Reference

[window.]document.getElementById(*elementID*).dataFormatAs

datasrc
IE 4 NN n/a Moz n/a Saf n/a Op n/a HTML |4|

datasrc="*dataSourceName*"   *Optional*

Used with IE data binding to specify the ID of the page's object element that loads the data source object for remote data access. Content from the data source is specified via the datafld attribute. Works only with text file data sources in IE 5/Mac.

This attribute was reserved in HTML 4, but was dropped in XHTML 1.0.

Example

```
<button type="button" datasrc="DBSRC3" datafld="label"
onClick="getTopStory( );"> Latest News</button>
```

Value   Case-sensitive identifier.

Default   None.

Object Model Reference

[window.]document.getElementById(*elementID*).dataSrc

form
IE n/a NN n/a Moz n/a Saf n/a Op 9 HTML n/a

form="*formID [formID]* ..."   *Optional*

Web Forms 2.0 extension that lets you associate a single form control element with one or more forms that do not enclose the controls. Because button elements are not confined to be descendants of form elements, the button elements may be located away from the form element. The form attribute connects the button element with one or more form elements on the page.

Example　　　　<button type="submit" form="orderForm">Submit Order</button>

Value　　　　ID of one or more form elements on the page. Multiple references are space-delimited.

Default　　　　None.

name　　　　　　　　　　　　　　IE 4　NN n/a　Moz all　Saf all　Op 7　HTML 4

name="*elementIdentifier*"　　　　　　　　　　　　　　　　　　　　　　*Optional*

For a button element, the name attribute can play two roles, depending on the type attribute setting. For all type attribute settings, the name attribute lets you assign an identifier that can be used in scripted references to the element (the id attribute is the preferred way to reference the element). For a button type of submit, the name attribute is sent as part of the name/value pair to the server at submit time.

Example
<button type="submit" name="sender" value="infoOnly">Request Info</button>

Value　　　　Case-sensitive identifier.

Default　　　　None.

Object Model Reference
[window.]document.getElementById(*elementID*).name

template　　　　　　　　　IE n/a　NN n/a　Moz n/a　Saf n/a　Op 9　HTML n/a

template="*elementID*"　　　　　　　　　　　　　　　　　　　　　　*Optional*

Web Forms 2.0 extension that lets you associate a button element with a repetition block—an HTML container that is repeated on the page. Such a repetition block allows the add-type button to add a copy of the block to the page, such as a new row in a table. This attribute ties together the button and block to be added, removed, or moved, depending on the setting of the type attribute.

Example　　　　<button type="remove" template="orderFormRow">Delete</button>

Value　　　　ID of an element on the page that has been set up as a repetition block.

Default　　　　None.

type　　　　　　　　　　　　　　IE 4　NN n/a　Moz all　Saf all　Op 7　HTML 4

type="*buttonType*"　　　　　　　　　　　　　　　　　　　　　　*Optional*

Defines the internal style of button for the browser. A button style is intended to be used to initiate scripted action via an event handler. A "reset" style behaves the same way as an input element whose type attribute is set to reset, returning all elements to their default

<canvas>

values. A "submit" style behaves the same way as an input element whose type attribute is set to submit. A button element whose type attribute is set to either reset or submit must be associated with a form for its implied action to be of any value to the page.

Example
```
<button type="reset"><img src="clearIt.gif" height="20" width="18"></button>
```

Value	Case-insensitive constant value from the following list of three standard HTML types: button | reset | submit. Web Forms 2.0 adds four additional choices for use with repetition blocks: add | move-down | move-up | remove.
Default	button

Object Model Reference
```
[window.]document.getElementById(elementID).type
```

value
IE *4* NN *n/a* Moz *all* Saf *all* Op *7* HTML *4*
```
value="text"
```
Optional

Preassigns a value to a button element that is submitted to the server as part of the name/value pair when the element is a member of a form.

Example
```
<button name="connections" id="connections" value="ISDN">ISDN</button>
```

Value	Any text string.
Default	None.

Object Model Reference
```
[window.]document.getElementById(elementID).value
```

<canvas>
IE *n/a* NN *n/a* Moz *1.8* Saf *2* Op *9* HTML *n/a*
```
<canvas></canvas>
```
HTML End Tag: Required

A canvas element defines a rectangular space in a document in which scripts may draw a variety of straight and curved lines for the display of items such as graphs and charts without resorting to fixed images. Regions may be filled with colors or gradients. The HTML element is essentially a placeholder for space in the document and therefore has few attributes associated with it. For more details on the drawing facilities available to the canvas element, see the canvas object in Chapter 2.

Safari does not require an end tag, but others encourage an end tag so that "fallback content" (i.e., text or an image that appears if the browser does not support the element) can be included with the document. Unfortunately, however, Safari 2 renders such fallback content along with the canvas space.

The canvas element derived from Apple's work on Safari, but is also being formalized in a document created by the Web Hypertext Application Technology Working Group

<caption>

(WHATWG) known as the Web Applications 1.0 specification. More details are available at *http://www.whatwg.org*.

Example   `<canvas id="myCanvas" height="300" width="300"></canvas>`

Object Model Reference
`[window.]document.getElementById(elementID)`

Element-Specific Attributes

height   width

Element-Specific Event Handler Attributes
None.

height, width   IE *n/a* NN *n/a* Moz *1.8* Saf *2* Op *9* HTML *all*

Optiona

`height="length"`
`width="length"`
Specify the dimensions, in pixels, of the rectangular space reserved for drawing by scripts.

Example   `<canvas id="pieChart" height="400" width="400"></canvas>`

Value   Positive integer values.

Default   Height: 150; width: 300

Object Model Reference
`[window.]document.getElementById(elementID).height`
`[window.]document.getElementById(elementID).width`

<caption>   IE *all* NN *all* Moz *all* Saf *all* Op *7* HTML *3.2*
`<caption>...</caption>`   *HTML End Tag: Required*

A caption element may be placed only inside a table element (and immediately after the `<table>` start tag) to denote the text to be used as a caption for the table. A caption applies to the entire table, whereas a table heading (th element) applies to a single column or row of the table. Only one caption element is recognized within a table element.

A table caption is usually a brief description of the table. A longer description may be written for the summary attribute of a table element for browsers that use text-to-speech technology. The primary distinguishing attribute of the caption element is align. Although deprecated in HTML 4, it lets you define where the caption appears in relation to the actual table.

Example
```
<table ...>
<caption class="tableCaptions">
   Table 3-2. Sample Inverse Framistan Values
```

<caption>

```
</caption>
...
</table>
```

Object Model Reference

[window.]document.getElementById(*elementID*)

Element-Specific Attributes

align   valign

Element-Specific Event Handler Attributes

None.

align
IE *all*   NN *all*   Moz *all*   Saf *all*   Op *7*   HTML *3.2*

align="*where*"   *Optional*

Determines how the caption is rendered in physical relation to the table. Not all versions of all browsers support the full range of possibilities for this attribute. Only top and bottom are universal among supporting browsers. IE and Opera place captions designated left and right above the table, rather than immediately to the left and right of it.

Browsers typically render a caption above or below a table in the running body font (unless modified by tag or style sheet) and centered horizontally on the table. If the caption is wider than the table, text is wrapped to the next line, maintaining center justification.

The align attribute is deprecated in HTML 4.0 in favor of the text-align and vertical-align style sheet properties.

Example   <caption align="top">Table II. Stock List</caption>

Value

Acceptable string values for this attribute vary with browser version. Select the one(s) from the following table that work for your deployment.

Value	IE 4+	NN 4	Mozilla	Safari	Opera	HTML 4
bottom	•	•	•	•	•	•
center	•	—	•	•	•	—
left	•	—	•	—	•	•
right	•	—	•	—	•	•
top	•	•	•	•	•	•

For implementation details, see the discussion of text alignment within a containing box in the "Alignment Constants" at the beginning of this chapter.

Default   top (in IE, center if valign attribute is also set).

Object Model Reference

[window.]document.getElementById(*elementID*).align

<center>

valign

valign="*where*"

The valign attribute was Internet Explorer's early attribute for placing a table caption above or below the table. Although this attribute is now a part of the align attribute, IE's special way of handling left, center, and right values of the align attribute give valign something to do. For example, you can use valign to set the caption below the table, and use align="right" to right-align the caption at the bottom. This combination is not possible with the HTML 4 attribute.

Example

```
<caption align="right" valign="bottom">Table 3-2. Fiber Content.</caption>
```

Value   Two possible case-insensitive values: bottom | top.

Default   top

Object Model Reference

[window.]document.getElementById(*elementID*).valign

<center>

<center>...</center>

The center element was introduced by Netscape and became widely used before the W3C-sanctioned div element came into being. It is clear, even from the HTML 3.2 documentation, that the HTML working group was never fond of this element. Momentum, however, carried the day, and this element found its way into the HTML 3.2 specification. The element is deprecated in HTML 4 in favor of the div element with a style sheet rule of text-align:center. In lieu of style sheets (but still deprecated in HTML 4), you can substitute a div element with align="center".

Content of a center element is aligned along an axis that runs down the middle of the next outermost containing element—usually the body or html element.

Example   <center>Don't do this.</center>

Object Model Reference

[window.]document.getElementById(*elementID*)

Element-Specific Attributes

None.

Element-Specific Event Handler Attributes

None.

<cite>

`<cite>...</cite>` *HTML End Tag: Required*

The cite element is one of a large group of elements that the HTML 4 recommendation calls *phrase elements*. Such elements assign structural meaning to a designated portion of the document. A cite element is one that contains a citation or reference to some other source material. This is not an active link but simply notation indicating what the element content is. Search engines and other HTML document parsers may use this information for other purposes (assembling a bibliography of a document, for example).

Browsers have free rein to determine how (or whether) to distinguish cite element content from the rest of the body element. Mainstream browsers elect to italicize the text. Override the default with a style sheet as you see fit.

Example

```
<p>Trouthe is the hyest thing that many may kepe.<br>
(Chaucer, <cite>The Franklin's Tale</cite>)</p>
```

Object Model Reference

`[window.]document.getElementById(elementID)`

Element-Specific Attributes

None.

Element-Specific Event Handler Attributes

None.

<code>

`<code>...</code>` *HTML End Tag: Required*

The code element is one of a large group of elements that the HTML 4 recommendation calls *phrase elements*. Such elements assign structural meaning to a designated portion of the document. A code element is one that is used predominantly to display one or more inline characters representing computer code (program statements, variable names, keywords, and the like).

Browsers have free rein to determine how (or whether) to distinguish code element content from the rest of the body element. Mainstream browsers elect to render code element content in a monospace font, usually in a slightly smaller font size than the default body font (although it is not reduced in IE 4 for the Macintosh). Override the default with a style sheet as you see fit.

Whitespace (including carriage returns) is treated the same way in code element content as it is in the browser's body element content. Line breaks must be manually inserted with br elements. See also the pre element for displaying preformatted text that observes all whitespace entered in the source code.

Example

```
<p>Initialize a variable in JavaScript with the <code>var</code> keyword.</p>
```

Object Model Reference

[window.]document.getElementById(*elementID*)

Element-Specific Attributes

None.

Element-Specific Event Handler Attributes

None.

<col>

IE *3* NN *n/a* Moz *all* Saf *all* Op *7* HTML *4*

<col>

HTML End Tag: Forbidden

The col element provides shortcuts to assigning widths and other characteristics (styles) to one or more subsets of columns within a table or within a table's column group. With this information appearing early in the table element, a browser equipped to do so starts rendering the table before all source code for the table has loaded (the time at which it would otherwise perform all of its geographical calculations).

You can use the col element in combination with the colgroup element or by itself. The structure depends on how you need to assign widths and styles to individual columns or contiguous columns. A col element can apply to multiple contiguous columns. By assigning an integer value to the span attribute, you direct the browser to apply the col element's width or style settings to said number of contiguous columns. The span attribute is similar to the colgroup element's colspan attribute. In concert with the colgroup element, the col element allows you to create a kind of subset of related columns within a colgroup set.

No matter how you address the column structure of your table, the total number of columns defined in all col and colgroup elements should equal the physical number of columns you intend for the table. The following three skeletal examples specify HTML 4 tables with six columns:

```
<table>
<col span="6">
...
</table>

<table>
<col>
<col span="4">
<col>
...
</table>

<table>
<colgroup>
<col span="2"></colgroup>
<colgroup span="4">
...
</table>
```

HTML 4 specifications for the col element exceed the implementation in most current browsers. For example, HTML 4 provides for alignment within a column to be around any character, such as the decimal point of a money amount. This kind of feature adds to the rationale behind the col element. For example, you can have a table whose first three columns are formatted one way, and fourth column is assigned a special style with its own alignment characteristics:

```html
<html>
<head>
<style type="text/css">
  .colHdrs {color:black}
  .normColumn {color:green}
  .priceColumn {color:red}
</style>
</head>
<body>
<table>
<colgroup class="normColumn" span="3"></colgroup>
<col class="priceColumn" align="char" char=".">
<thead class="colHdrs">
<tr><th>Stock No.<th>In Stock<th>Description<th>Price</tr>
<tbody>
<tr><td>8832<td>Yes<td>Brass Frobnitz<td>$255.98</tr>
<tr><td>8835<td>No<td>Frobnitz (black)<td>$98</tr>
...
</table>
</body>
</html>
```

Because attributes of the col and colgroup elements apply to the entire column, in the preceding example the style sheet rule for the thead overrides the color settings for the two column styles for the rows enclosed by the thead element. The preceding example works in IE 4 and later for Windows, except for the alignment of the final column, which is ignored.

Support indicated here for non-IE browsers is based on the browsers' DOM implementations. The DOMs report to scripts that the col element and its attributes exist (reflected as properties). But as of Mozilla 1.8, Safari 2, and Opera 9, the element does not perform its intended tasks.

Example　　　`<col class="dateCols" width="15" align="right">`

Object Model Reference
`[window.]document.getElementById(elementID)`

Element-Specific Attributes

align	ch	char	charoff	choff
span	valign	width		

Element-Specific Event Handler Attributes
None.

<col>

align

IE *3* NN *n/a* Moz *n/a* Saf *n/a* Op *8* HTML *4*

align="*alignConstant*"   *Optional*

Establishes the horizontal alignment characteristics of content within column(s) covered by the col element. The HTML 4 specification defines some values for the align attribute that are not yet reflected in the CSS specification. For example, there is no CSS equivalent for the alignment by character.

Example   <col class="dateCols" width="15" align="right">

Value

HTML 4 and IE/Opera have two sets of supported attribute values:

Value	IE & Opera	HTML 4
center	•	•
char	—	•
justify	—	•
left	•	•
right	•	•

The values center, left, and right are self-explanatory (and may be replicated through the CSS text-align property). The value justify is intended to space content so that text is justified down both left and right edges. For the value char, the char attribute must also be set to specify the character on which alignment revolves.

It is important to bear in mind that the align attribute applies to every row of every column spanned by a col element, including any th element you specify for the table. If you want a different alignment for the column header, override the setting with a separate align attribute or text-align style sheet property for the thead or individual th elements.

Default   left

Object Model Reference

[window.]document.getElementById(*elementID*).align

char

IE *n/a* NN *n/a* Moz *n/a* Saf *n/a* Op *n/a* HTML *4*

char="*character*"   *Optional*

The char attribute defines the text character used as an alignment point for text within a column. This attribute is of value only for the align attribute set to "char". Microsoft documents a ch attribute, which corresponds to the standards-based char attribute. In any case, the browser does not respond to either attribute.

Example   <col class="priceColumn" align="char" char=".">

Value   Any single text character.

Default   None.

charoff
IE *n/a* NN *n/a* Moz *n/a* Saf *n/a* Op *n/a* HTML *4*

charoff="*length*"   *Optional*

The charoff attribute lets you set a specific offset point at which the character specified by the char attribute is to appear within a cell. This attribute is provided in case the browser default positioning does not meet with the design goals of the table. Microsoft documents a choff attribute, which corresponds to the standards-based charoff attribute. In any case, the browser does not respond to either attribute.

Example   `<col class="priceColumn" align="char" char="." charoff="80%">`

Value   Any length value in pixels or percentage of cell space.

Default   None.

choff

See charoff.

span
IE *3* NN *n/a* Moz *n/a* Saf *n/a* Op *n/a* HTML *4*

span="*columnCount*"   *Optional*

Defines the number of adjacent columns for which the col element's attribute and style settings apply. If this attribute is missing, the col element governs a single column. You can combine multiple col elements of different span sizes as needed for your column subgrouping.

Example   `<col span="3">`

Value   Integer value greater than zero.

Default   1

Object Model Reference
`[window.]document.getElementById(elementID).span`

valign
IE *4* NN *n/a* Moz *n/a* Saf *n/a* Op *n/a* HTML *4*

valign="*alignmentConstant*"   *Optional*

Determines the vertical alignment of content within cells of the column(s) covered by the col element. You can override the vertical alignment for a particular cell anywhere in the column.

Example   `<col valign="middle">`

Value
Four constant values are recognized by both IE 4 and later for Windows and HTML 4: top | middle | bottom | baseline. With top and bottom, the content is rendered flush (or very close to it) to the top and bottom of the table cell. Set to middle (the default), the content floats perfectly centered vertically in the cell. When one cell's contents might wrap to

<colgroup>

multiple lines at common window widths (assuming a variable table width), it is advisable to set the valign attributes of all cells in the same row (or all col elements) to baseline. This assures that the character baseline of the first (or only) line of a cell's text aligns with the other cells in the row—usually the most aesthetically pleasing arrangement.

Default   middle

Object Model Reference

[window.]document.getElementById(*elementID*).vAlign

width
IE 4 NN *n/a* Moz *all* Saf *all* Op 7 HTML 4

width="*multiLength*"   *Optional*

Defines the maximum width for the column(s) covered by the col element. In practice, the browser won't render a column narrower than the widest contiguous stretch of characters not containing whitespace (e.g., the longest word). The precise measure of such a column width, of course, depends on the font characteristics of the content, as well.

Example   <col width="100">

Value

Internet Explorer accepts length values for the width in the form of pixel measures (without the "px" unit) or percentage of available horizontal space allocated to the entire table (width="25%").

The HTML 4 specification introduces an additional length measurement scheme to supplement the regular length measure. Called a proportional length (also MultiLength), this format features a special notation and geometry. It is best suited for situations in which a col element is to be sized based on the available width of the table space after all fixed length and percentage lengths are calculated. Using the proportional length notation (a number followed by an asterisk), you can direct the browser to divide any remaining space according to proportion. For example, if there is enough horizontal space on the page for 100 pixels after all other column width calculations are performed, three col elements might specify width attributes of 1*, 3*, and 1*. This adds up to a total of five proportional segments. The 100 available pixels are handed out to the proportional columns based on their proportion to the whole of the remaining space: 20, 60, and 20 pixels, respectively.

Default   Determined by browser calculation.

<colgroup>
IE 3 NN *n/a* Moz *all* Saf *n/a* Op 7 HTML 4

<colgroup>...</colgroup>   *HTML End Tag: Optional*

The colgroup element provides shortcuts to assigning widths and other characteristics (styles) to one or more subsets of columns within a table. With this information appearing early in the table element source code, a browser equipped to do so starts rendering the table before all source code for the table has loaded (at which time it would otherwise perform all of its geographical calculations).

You can use the colgroup element in combination with the col element or by itself. You may also define a colgroup that has col elements nested within to assist in defining subsets of columns that share some attribute or style settings. The need for the element's end tag is determined by the presence of standalone col elements following the colgroup element. For example, if you specify column groupings entirely with colgroup elements, end tags are not necessary under HTML:

```
<table>
<colgroup span="2" width="30">
<colgroup span="3" width="40">
<thead>
```

If you have a freestanding col element following the colgroup element, you must clearly end the colgroup element before the standalone col element:

```
<table>
<colgroup class="leftCols">
<col width="30">
<col width="20">
</colgroup>
<col class="priceCol" width="25">
<thead>
...
```

The structure depends on how you need to assign widths and styles to individual columns or contiguous columns. To create a column grouping that consists of multiple adjacent columns, use the span attribute. This is entirely different from the colspan attribute of a td element, which has the visual impact of joining adjacent cells together as one. The span attribute helps define the number of columns to be treated structurally as a group (for assigning attribute and style sheet settings across multiple columns, regardless of the column content).

No matter how you address the column structure of your table, the total number of columns defined in all col and colgroup elements should equal the physical number of columns you intend for the table. The following three skeletal examples specify HTML 4 tables with six columns:

```
<table>
<colgroup span="6">
...
</table>

<table>
<col>
<colgroup span="4">
<col>
...
</table>

<table>
<colgroup>
    <col span="2">
</colgroup>
<colgroup span="4">
...
</table>
```

<colgroup>

HTML 4 specifications for the colgroup element exceed the implementation in most current browsers. For example, HTML 4 provides for alignment within a column to be around any character, such as the decimal point of a money amount. This kind of feature adds to the rationale behind the col element (see the col element for an example).

Syntactically, there is little difference between a colgroup and col element. A colgroup element, however, lends a structural integrity to a group of columns that is rendered differently when the containing table element specifies rules="groups"; the browser draws rule lines (standard table borders in IE) only between colgroup elements, and not col elements.

Support indicated here for non-IE browsers is based on the browser's DOM implementation. The DOM reports to scripts that the colgroup element and its attributes exist (reflected as properties). But as of Mozilla 1.8 and Opera 9, the element does not perform its intended tasks.

Example   `<colgroup class="dateCols" width="15" align="right">`

Object Model Reference
`[window.]document.getElementById(elementID)`

Element-Specific Attributes

align	char	charoff	span	valign
width				

Element-Specific Event Handler Attributes
None.

align   IE 3 NN *n/a* Moz *n/a* Saf *n/a* Op 8 HTML 4
`align="alignConstant"`   *Optional*

Establishes the horizontal alignment characteristics of content within column(s) covered by the colgroup element. The HTML 4 specification defines settings for the align attribute that are not yet reflected in the CSS specification. For example, there is no CSS equivalent for the alignment by character.

Example
`<colgroup class="dateCols" width="15" align="right" span="3">`

Value
HTML 4 and IE have two sets of attribute values.

Value	IE and Opera	HTML 4
center	•	•
char	—	•
justify	—	•
left	•	•
right	•	•

The values center, left, and right are self-explanatory. The value justify is intended to space content so that text is justified down both left and right edges. For the value char, the char attribute must also be set to specify the character on which alignment revolves. In the HTML 4 specification example, content that does not contain the character appears to be right-aligned to the location of the character in other rows of the same column.

It is important to bear in mind that the align attribute applies to every row of a column, including any th element you specify for the table. If you want a different alignment for the column header, override the setting with a separate align attribute or text-align style sheet property for the thead or individual th elements.

Default   left

Object Model Reference
[window.]document.getElementById(*elementID*).align

char   IE *n/a* NN *n/a* Moz *n/a* Saf *n/a* Op *n/a* **HTML 4**
char="*character*"   *Optional*

The char attribute defines the text character used as an alignment point for text within a column. This attribute is of value only for the align attribute set to "char". Microsoft documents a ch attribute, which corresponds to the standards-based char attribute. In any case, the browser does not respond to either attribute.

Example   <colgroup class="priceCols" align="char" char="." span="2">

Value   Any single text character.

Default   None.

charoff   IE *n/a* NN *n/a* Moz *n/a* Saf *n/a* Op *n/a* **HTML 4**
charoff="*length*"   *Optional*

The charoff attribute lets you set a specific offset point at which the character specified by the char attribute is to appear within a cell. This attribute is provided in case the browser default positioning does not meet with the design goals of the table. Microsoft documents a choff attribute, which corresponds to the standards-based charoff attribute. In any case, the browser does not respond to either attribute.

Example
<colgroup class="priceColumn" align="char" char="." charoff="80%" span="2">

Value   Any length value in pixels or percentage of cell space.

Default   None.

span

IE 3 NN *n/a* Moz *n/a* Saf *n/a* Op *n/a* HTML 4

span="*columnCount*" *Optional*

Defines the number of adjacent columns for which the colgroup element's attribute and style settings apply. If this attribute is missing, the colgroup element governs a single column. You can combine multiple colgroup elements of different span sizes as needed for your column subgrouping.

Example   <colgroup span="3">

Value   Integer value greater than zero.

Default   1

Object Model Reference

[window.]document.getElementById(*elementID*).span

valign

IE 3 NN *n/a* Moz *n/a* Saf *n/a* Op *n/a* HTML 4

valign="*alignmentConstant*" *Optional*

Determines the vertical alignment of content within cells of the column(s) covered by the colgroup element. You can override the vertical alignment for a particular cell anywhere in the column.

Example   <colgroup valign="middle">

Value

Four constant values are recognized by both IE 4 and HTML 4: top | middle | bottom | baseline. With top and bottom, the content is rendered flush (or very close to it) to the top and bottom of the table cell. Set to middle (the default), the content floats perfectly centered vertically in the cell. When one cell's contents might wrap to multiple lines at common window widths (assuming a variable table width), it is advisable to set the valign attributes of all cells in the same row (or all colgroup elements) to baseline. This assures that the character baseline of the first (or only) line of a cell's text aligns with the other cells in the row—usually the most aesthetically pleasing arrangement.

Default   middle

Object Model Reference

[window.]document.getElementById(*elementID*).vAlign

width

IE 3 NN *n/a* Moz *all* Saf *n/a* Op 7 HTML 4

width="*multiLength*" *Optional*

Defines the maximum width for the column(s) covered by the colgroup element. In practice, the browser won't render a column narrower than the widest contiguous stretch of characters not containing whitespace (e.g., the longest word). The precise measure of such a column width, of course, depends on the font characteristics of the content, as well.

Example   <colgroup width="100">

Value

Length values for the width are in the form of pixel measures (without the "px" unit) or percentage of available horizontal space allocated to the entire table (width="25%").

An alternate variation of the proportional length value is described in the HTML 4.0 specification. For a colgroup element, you can specify width="0*" to instruct the browser to render all columns according to the minimum width necessary to display the content of the cells in the column. For a browser to make this calculation, it must load all table contents, thus eliminating the possibility of incremental rendering of a long table. For more information about proportional lengths, see the width attribute of the col element.

Default   Determined by browser calculation.

<comment>   IE *all* NN *n/a* Moz *all* Saf *all* Op *7* HTML *n/a*
`<comment>...</comment>`   *HTML End Tag: Required*

The comment element is an artifact of early Internet Explorer browsers. It was intended as a plain-language tag alternate to the `<!--comment-->` comment element. IE does not render content inside the comment element, but all other browsers do. Do not use this element. Further details are omitted here to reduce the incentive to use the element.

<datalist>   IE *all* NN *all* Moz *all* Saf *all* Op *9* HTML *all*
`<option>...</option>`   *End Tag: Required*

The datalist element is a Web Forms 2.0 element that provides semantic context for predefined items associated with all input elements having text entry fields. Individual items are specified by option elements nested within the datalist element.

The datalist element must have an identifier assigned to its id attribute. A form control element that is associated with the list must then have a list attribute, whose value is the ID of the datalist element. Users are not required to make a choice from the data list options (the text entry field is fully editable by default), but the listed options can speed data entry for familiar or (if the browser is so equipped) recent entries.

Example
```
<label>Enter your operating system:<input type="text" name="os" list="oses" />
</label>
<datalist id="oses">
   <option value="">
   <option value="Windows Vista">
   <option value="Windows XP">
   <option value="Windows 98">
   <option value="Mac OS X">
   <option value="Linux">
</datalist>
```

Object Model Reference
`[window.]document.getElementById(elementID)`

Element-Specific Attributes

None

Element-Specific Event Handler Attributes

None.

`<dd>`

IE *all* NN *all* Moz *all* Saf *all* Op 7 HTML *all*

`<dd>...</dd>`

HTML End Tag: Optional

The dd element is a part of the dl, dt, dd triumvirate of elements used to create a definition list in a document. The entire list is bracketed by the dl element's tags. Each definition term is denoted by a leading dt element tag, and the definition for the term is denoted by a leading dd element tag. A schematic of a definition list sequence for three items looks as follows:

```
<dl>
    <dt>Term 1</dt>
    <dd>Definition 1</dd>
    <dt>Term 2</dt>
    <dd>Definition 2</dd>
    <dt>Term 3</dt>
    <dd>Definition 3</dd>
</dl>
```

A dt element is an inline element, whereas a dd element can contain block-level content, including bordered text, images, and other objects. End tags are optional for both dt and dd elements because the next start tag automatically signals the end of the preceding element. The entire list, however, must close with an end tag for the encapsulating dl element.

Although the HTML specification forces no particular way of rendering a definition list, mainstream browsers are in agreement in left-aligning a dt element and indenting any dd element that follows it. No special font formatting or visual elements are added by the browser, but you are free (if not encouraged) to assign styles as you like. If you want to stack multiple terms and/or definitions, you can place multiple dt and/or dd elements right after each other in the source code.

Because HTML is being geared toward context-sensitive tagging, avoid using definition lists strictly as a formatting trick (to get some indented text). Use style sheets and adjustable margin settings to accomplish formatting tasks.

In Navigator 4, any styles assigned to dt and dd elements by way of the class, id, or style attribute do not work. If you wish to assign the same style attributes to both the dt and dd elements, assign the style to the dl element; otherwise, wrap each dt and dd element with a span element whose styles the nested dt and dd elements inherit. This workaround is observed by other browsers, although it is not necessary for IE-only documents that will never render in NN 4.

Example

```
<dl>
    <dt>Z-scale</dt>
    <dd>A railroad modeling scale of 1:220. The smallest mass-produced
```

```
      commercial model scale.</dd>
</dl>
```

Object Model Reference

[window.]document.getElementById(*elementID*)

Element-Specific Attributes

None.

Element-Specific Event Handler Attributes

None.

<del>

IE *4* NN *n/a* Moz *all* Saf *all* Op *7* HTML *4*

<del>...</del>

HTML End Tag: Required

The del element and its companion, ins, define a format that shows which segments of a document's content have been marked up for deletion (or insertion) during the authoring process. This is far from a workflow management scheme, but in the hands of a supporting WYSIWYG HTML authoring tool, these elements can assist in controlling generational changes of a document in process.

Text contained by this element is rendered as a strikethrough style (whereas ins elements are underlined). The HTML 4 specification includes two potentially useful attributes for preserving hidden information about the date and time of the alteration and some descriptive text about the change.

Example

```
<p>Four score and
<del cite="Fixed the math">eight</del><ins>seven</ins> years ago...</p>
```

Object Model Reference

[window.]document.getElementById(*elementID*)

Element-Specific Attributes

cite   datetime

Element-Specific Event Handler Attributes

None.

cite

IE *6* NN *n/a* Moz *all* Saf *all* Op *7* HTML *4*

cite="*text*"

Optional

A description of the reason for the change or other notation to be associated with the element, but normally hidden from view. In Mozilla, the context menu for such an element contains a **Properties** choice, which leads to a displayed list of attributes and their values for the visitor. Or, your DHTML scripts can access the information through the element object's cite property, and add value to the presentation.

<del>

Example   `<del cite="Fixed the math --A.L.">eight</del>`

Value   Any string of characters. The string must be inside a matching pair of (single or double) quotation marks.

Default   None.

Object Model Reference
`[window.]document.getElementById(elementID).cite`

datetime

IE 6 NN *n/a* Moz *all* Saf *all* Op 7 HTML 4

`datetime="datetimeString"`   *Optional*

The date and time the deletion was made. This information is most likely to be inserted into a document with an HTML authoring tool designed to track content insertions and deletions. Data from this attribute can be recalled later as an audit trail to changes of the document. There can be only one `datetime` attribute value associated with a given `del` element. In Mozilla, the context menu for such an element contains a **Properties** choice, which leads to a displayed list of attributes and their values for the visitor. Or, your DHTML scripts can access the information through the element object's `dateTime` property, and add value to the presentation.

Example   `<del datetime="2001-09-11T08:56:00-04:00">SomeDeleteTextHere</del>`

Value

The `datetime` attribute requires a value in a special date-time format that conveys information about the date and time in such a way that the exact moment can be deduced from any time zone around the world. Syntax for the format is as follows: *yyyy-MM-ddThh:mm:ssTZD*.

yyyy
    Four-digit year

MM
    Two-digit month (01 through 12)

dd
    Two-digit date (01 through 31)

T
    Uppercase "T" to separate date from time

hh
    Two-digit hour in 24-hour time (00 through 23)

mm
    Two-digit minute (00 through 59)

ss
    Two-digit second (00 through 59)

TZD
    Time Zone Designator

<dfn>

There are two formats for the Time Zone Designator. The first is simply the uppercase letter "Z", which stands for UTC (Coordinated Universal Time—also called "Zulu"). The other format indicates the offset from UTC that the time shown in *hh:mm:ss* represents. This time offset consists of a plus or minus symbol and another pair of *hh:mm* values. For time zones west of Greenwich Mean Time (which, for all practical purposes is the same as UTC), the operator is a negative sign because the main *hh:mm:ss* time is earlier than UTC; for time zones east of GMT, the offset is a positive value. For example, Pacific Standard Time is eight hours earlier than UTC: when it is 6:00 P.M. in the PST zone, it is 2:00 A.M. the next morning at UTC. Thus, the following examples all represent the exact same moment in time (Time Zone Designator shown in boldface for clarification only):

2003-01-30T02:00:00**Z**	UTC
2003-01-29T21:00:00-**05:00**	Eastern Standard Time
2003-01-29T18:00:00-**08:00**	Pacific Standard Time
2003-01-30T13:00:00+**11:00**	Sydney, Australia

For more details about this way of representing time, see the ISO-8601 standard.

Default   None.

<dfn>

IE *3* NN *n/a* Moz *all* Saf *all* Op *7* HTML *3.2*

`<dfn>...</dfn>`   *HTML End Tag: Required*

The dfn element is one of a large group of elements that the HTML 4 recommendation calls *phrase elements*. Such elements assign structural meaning to a designated portion of the document. A dfn element signifies the first usage of a term in a document (its defining instance). A common technique in documents is to italicize an important vocabulary term the first time it is used in a document. This is generally the place in the document where the term is defined so that it may be used in subsequent sentences with its meaning understood. By default, mainstream browsers italicize all text within a dfn element. You can, of course, easily define your own style for dfn elements with a style sheet rule.

Example
```
<p>Concerto composers usually provide a space for soloists to show off
technical skills while reminding the audience of various themes used
throughout the movement. This part of the concerto is called the <dfn>
cadenza</dfn>.</p>
```

Object Model Reference
[window.]document.getElementById(*elementID*)

Element-Specific Attributes
None.

Element-Specific Event Handler Attributes
None.

<dir>

<dir>

IE *all* NN *all* Moz *all* Saf *all* Op 7 HTML *all*

<dir>...</dir>

HTML End Tag: Required

The original idea of the dir element was to allow browsers to generate multicolumn lists of items. Virtually every browser, however, treats the dir element the same as a ul element, to present an unordered single column list of items (usually preceded by a bullet). The dir element is deprecated in HTML 4 and does not validate against strict HTML 4 or XHTML DTDs. You should be using the ul element, in any case, because you are assured backward compatibility and forward compatibility should this element ever disappear from the browser landscape entirely. Everything said here also applies to the deprecated menu element.

Example

```
Common DB Connector Types:
<dir>
    <li>DB-9</li>
    <li>DB-12</li>
    <li>DB-25</li>
</dir>
```

Object Model Reference

[window.]document.getElementById(*elementID*)

Element-Specific Attributes

compact

Element-Specific Event Handler Attributes

None.

compact

IE 3 NN *n/a* Moz *n/a* Saf *n/a* Op *n/a* HTML 3.2

compact

Optional

A Boolean attribute originally designed to let browsers render the list in a more compact style than normal (smaller line spacing between items). In practice, mainstream browsers do not adjust their rendering in response to this attribute.

Example   <dir compact>...</dir>

Value   The presence of this attribute makes its value true.

Default   false

<div>

IE *all* NN *all* Moz *all* Saf *all* Op 7 HTML 3.2

<div>...</div>

HTML End Tag: Required

The div element gives structure and context to any block-level content in a document. Unlike some other structural elements that have very specific connotations attached to

<div>

them (the p element, for instance), the author is free to give meaning to each particular div element by virtue of the element's attribute settings and nested content. Each div element becomes a generic block-level container for all content within the required start and end tags.

It is most convenient to use the div element as a wrapper for multielement content that is to be governed by a single style sheet rule. For example, if a block of content includes three paragraphs, rather than assign a special font style to each of the p elements, you can wrap all three p elements with a single div element whose style sheet defines the requested font style. Such a style sheet could be defined as an inline style attribute of the div element or assigned via the class or id attribute, depending on the structure of the rest of the document.

div elements are block-level elements. If you need an arbitrary container for inline content, use the span element, instead.

Example   `<div class="sections" id="section3">...</div>`

Object Model Reference
`[window.]document.getElementById(elementID)`

Element-Specific Attributes

align	datafld	dataformatas	datasrc	nowrap

Element-Specific Event Handler Attributes
None.

align   IE 3   NN 2   Moz all   Saf all   Op 7   HTML 3.2
`align="alignmentConstant"`   *Optional*

See details for horizontal alignment within a block element in the "Alignment Constants" at the beginning of this chapter.

Example   `<div align="center">Part IV</div>`

Value
Constant value. Navigator 4, Internet Explorer 4 or later (Windows), and current browsers recognize all four constants specified in loose HTML 4: center | left | right | justify. IE 4 for the Macintosh does not recognize the justify setting.

Default   left or right, depending on direction of current language.

Object Model Reference
`[window.]document.getElementById(elementID).align`

datafld
IE 4 NN *n/a* Moz *n/a* Saf *n/a* Op *n/a* HTML |4|

datafld="*columnName*"   *Optional*

Used with IE data binding to associate a remote data source column name with the HTML content of a div element. The data source column must be HTML (see dataformatas). datasrc and dataformatas attributes must also be set for the div element. Works only with text file data sources in IE 5/Mac.

This attribute was reserved in HTML 4, but was dropped in XHTML 1.0.

Example   \<div datasrc="DBSRC3" datafld="sec3" dataformatas="HTML"\>\</div\>

Value   Case-sensitive identifier.

Default   None.

Object Model Reference

[window.]document.getElementById(*elementID*).dataFld

dataformatas
IE 4 NN *n/a* Moz *n/a* Saf *n/a* Op *n/a* HTML |4|

dataformatas="*dataType*"   *Optional*

Used with IE data binding, this attribute advises the browser whether the source material arriving from the data source is to be treated as plain text or as tagged HTML. A div element should receive data only in HTML format. Works only with text file data sources in IE 5/Mac.

This attribute was reserved in HTML 4, but was dropped in XHTML 1.0.

Example   \<div datasrc="DBSRC3" datafld="sec3" dataformatas="HTML"\>\</div\>

Value   IE recognizes two possible settings: text | html

Default   text

Object Model Reference

[window.]document.getElementById(*elementID*).dataFormatAs

datasrc
IE 4 NN *n/a* Moz *n/a* Saf *n/a* Op *n/a* HTML |4|

datasrc="*dataSourceName*"   *Optional*

Used with IE data binding to specify the ID of the page's object element that loads the data source object for remote data access. Content from the data source is specified via the datafld attribute. Works only with text file data sources in IE 5/Mac.

This attribute was reserved in HTML 4, but was dropped in XHTML 1.0.

Example   \<div datasrc="DBSRC3" datafld="sec3" dataformatas="HTML"\>\</div\>

Value   Case-sensitive identifier.

Default   None.

Object Model Reference

[window.]document.getElementById(*elementID*).dataSrc

nowrap

nowrap   *Optional*

The nowrap attribute overrides the normal block model for a div element. When the attribute is turned on, text streams to the right unless broken by other interlaced elements. Indiscriminate use may lead to excessively wide pages that force users to scroll horizontally over long distances.

Example   <div id="bigBlock" nowrap>...</div>

Value   The presence of the attribute sets its value to true.

Default   false

<dl>

<dl>...</dl>   *HTML End Tag: Required*

The dl element is a part of the dl, dt, dd triumvirate of elements used to create a definition list in a document. The entire list is bracketed by the dl element's tags. Each definition term is denoted by a leading dt element tag, and the definition for the term is denoted by a leading dd element tag. A schematic of a definition list sequence for three items looks like the following:

```
<dl>
    <dt>Term 1</dt>
    <dd>Definition 1</dd>
    <dt>Term 2</dt>
    <dd>Definition 2</dd>
    <dt>Term 3</dt>
    <dd>Definition 3</dd>
</dl>
```

The entire list must close with an end tag for the encapsulating dl element. Note that the dl element is the container of the entire list, which means that inheritable style sheet rules assigned to the dl element apply to the nested dt and dd elements. Unwanted inheritances can be overridden in the dt and dd elements.

Although the HTML specification forces no particular way of rendering a definition list, mainstream browsers are in agreement in left-aligning a dt element and indenting any dd element that follows it. No special font formatting or visual elements are added by the browser, but you are free (if not encouraged) to assign styles as you like. If you want to stack multiple terms and/or definitions, you can place multiple dt and/or dd elements right after each other in the source code.

Because HTML is being geared toward context-sensitive tagging, avoid using definition lists strictly as a formatting trick (to get some indented text). Use style sheets and adjustable margin settings to accomplish formatting.

Example

```
<dl>
    <dt>Z-scale</dt>
    <dd>A railroad modeling scale of 1:220. The smallest mass-produced
    commercial model scale.</dd>
</dl>
```

Object Model Reference

[window.]document.getElementById(*elementID*)

Element-Specific Attributes

compact

Element-Specific Event Handler Attributes
None.

compact

compact   IE *3*   NN *3*   Moz *n/a*   Saf *n/a*   Op *n/a*   HTML *3.2*

compact   *Optional*

When set to true (by virtue of its presence in the dl element tag), the compact Boolean attribute instructs the browser to render a related dt and dd pair on the same line if space allows. The criterion for determining this space (as worked out in both Navigator and Internet Explorer) is related to the amount of indentation normally assigned to a dd element (indentation size differs slightly with operating system). With compact turned on, if the dt element is narrower than the indentation space, the dd element is raised from the line below and displayed on the same line as its dt element. Because the width of characters in proportional fonts varies so widely, there is no hard-and-fast rule about the number of characters of a dt element that lets the dd element come on the same line. But this compact styling is intended for dt elements consisting of only a few characters. This attribute is deprecated in HTML 4, and does not validate in strict HTML 4 or XHTML.

Example   `<dl compact>`*ListItems*`</dl>`

Value   Presence of the attribute name enables the feature.

Default   Off.

Object Model Reference

[window.]document.getElementById(*elementID*).compact

 `<!DOCTYPE>`

                                  IE *all*   NN *all*   Moz *all*   Saf *all*   Op *7*   HTML *3.2*

`<!DOCTYPE...>`   *HTML End Tag: Forbidden*

The DOCTYPE element is not an HTML element, but rather a comment in the Standard Generalized Markup Language (SGML) format (as are so-called HTML comments in the `<!-- ... -->` style). This element must be the first element in a document, except as noted below for XHTML documents, and must always precede the `<html>` tag element. It advises the browser as to the document type definition (DTD) that the HTML source code is designed to follow. All browsers have a default document type that defines which elements and element attributes the browser supports (and that the browser has the internal programming to support—buggy or otherwise). Specifying a document type for a more modern DTD does not empower an older browser to support elements and attributes for which it is not coded. Conversely, specifying a constricted DTD does not prevent a browser from recognizing and supporting backward-compatible or proprietary elements and attributes.

A DOCTYPE element contains several unlabeled attribute values that specify such details as the name for the outermost document tag (html for our purposes), the organization responsible for the DTD, the address of the actual DTD file (called a *system identifier*), a plain-language name for the definition (including version number, if necessary), and the like. For example, the following DOCTYPE refers to an HTML 4.01 DTD that includes all deprecated elements and attributes:

```
<!DOCTYPE HTML PUBLIC "-//W3C//DTD HTML 4.01 Transitional//EN"
        "http://www.w3.org/TR/html401/loose.dtd">
```

The next example points to the XHTML 1.1 DTD, which does not include deprecated items nor frames:

```
<!DOCTYPE html PUBLIC "-//W3C//DTD XHTML 1.1//EN"
        "http://www.w3.org/TR/xhtml11/DTD/xhtml11.dtd">
```

Additionally, if you specify an XHTML DTD, you should include one of the following SGML-processing instruction tags prior to the DOCTYPE declaration:

```
<?xml version="1.0"?>
<?xml version="1.0" encoding="UTF-8"?>
```

The latter version includes a setting for character set encoding, which may alternatively be set in a <meta> tag. The W3C HTML and XHTML validators encourage documents to declare their character-encoding type in one way or the other.

For the most part, web authors include a DOCTYPE element to facilitate validation of the HTML source code prior to publication on the Web. But some modern browsers behave slightly differently based on the details of the DOCTYPE comment at the start of the document. Both IE 6 or later, Mozilla, and some other browsers operate in one of two "modes," depending on the details of the DOCTYPE attribute values. One mode points to backward compatibility with implementations that came before, and diverge from, the W3C standards; the other mode causes the browser to behave more in keeping with W3C recommendations. The differences between the two modes lay primarily in fine layout details that are more carefully defined in modern-day CSS and DOM specifications. For simple layouts, you probably won't notice the difference in modes. But if your pages rely upon style sheets or backgrounds for tables, form control alignment (especially in tables), precise font sizing or spacing, and pixel-perfect CSS positioning with respect to the document edges and positioned element sizes, you need to pay attention to the DOCTYPE details in your documents.

It is difficult to guide you through every compatibility detail, but a couple of broad recommendations should keep you on track. First, if you are pleased with the layouts of your current pages or templates, you will probably be best served by continuing to use DOCTYPE settings that keep you in backward-compatible mode (the Mozilla engineers call it "quirks"

<!DOCTYPE>

mode; Microsoft has no particular name for the mode). But if you are generating new content, especially for the newer browsers, you should gravitate toward the "strict" (Mozilla) or "standards-compatible" (IE) mode settings.

The number of DOCTYPE attribute values in common use today is mind boggling, and the rules that govern which attributes force each browser into a particular mode are not 100% in sync across browsers. But here are a few of the more common DOCTYPE tags that force modern browsers into backward-compatible mode, regardless of browser:

```
<!DOCTYPE HTML PUBLIC "-//W3C//DTD HTML 3.2 Final//EN">
<!DOCTYPE HTML PUBLIC "-//IETF//DTD HTML 3.0//EN">
<!DOCTYPE HTML PUBLIC "-//W3C//DTD HTML 4.01 Transitional//EN">
```

A couple of points worth noting. First, all of the above examples declare HTML DTDs no later than HTML 4.01, and none are XHTML. Second, none of the above examples includes a system identifier URI to a reference *.dtd* file. Also, if you omit the DOCTYPE element entirely, the browser applies the equivalent of the old internal DTDs.

Note: IE 6 has a flaw that causes it to revert to quirks mode if you specify an XHTML DOCTYPE and precede the document with the <? xml ... ?> declaration. The problem is fixed in IE 7.

Now here are common DOCTYPE tags that force modern browsers into the modern, standards-based mode:

```
<!DOCTYPE HTML PUBLIC "-//W3C//DTD HTML 4.0 Transitional//EN"
        "http://www.w3.org/TR/REC-html40/loose.dtd">
<!DOCTYPE HTML PUBLIC "-//W3C//DTD HTML 4.0 Frameset//EN"
        "http://www.w3.org/TR/REC-html40/frameset.dtd">
<!DOCTYPE HTML PUBLIC "-//W3C//DTD HTML 4.0//EN"
        "http://www.w3.org/TR/REC-html40/strict.dtd">
<!DOCTYPE html PUBLIC "-//W3C//DTD XHTML 1.0 Transitional//EN"
        "http://www.w3.org/TR/xhtml1/DTD/xhtml1-transitional.dtd">
<!DOCTYPE html PUBLIC "-//W3C//DTD XHTML 1.0 Frameset//EN"
        "http://www.w3.org/TR/xhtml1/DTD/xhtml1-frameset.dtd">
<!DOCTYPE html PUBLIC "-//W3C//DTD XHTML 1.0 Strict//EN"
        "http://www.w3.org/TR/xhtml1/DTD/xhtml1-strict.dtd">
<!DOCTYPE html PUBLIC "-//W3C//DTD XHTML 1.1//EN"
        "http://www.w3.org/TR/xhtml11/DTD/xhtml11.dtd">
```

All HTML 4.x/strict and XHTML DTDs switch on standards-compatible mode, with or without the URLs. Including the URL with HTML 4.x transitional and frameset DTDs invokes the standards-compatible mode.

To learn more about the impact of the DTD choice on DOM and CSS features in the latest browsers, see Chapter 2 (client- and offset- properties, the body object, the document.compatMode property) and Chapter 3 (height and width attributes). Appendix E shows which HTML 4 elements and attributes are supported by each of the most popular HTML 4.01 and XHTML 1.0 DTDs for validation purposes.

Object Model Reference

[window.]document.firstChild

Element-Specific Attributes

Attributes are unlabeled.

Element-Specific Event Handler Attributes

None.

<dt>

IE *all*   NN *all*   Moz *all*   Saf *all*   Op 7   HTML *all*

`<dt>...</dt>`

HTML End Tag: Optional

The dt element is a part of the dl, dt, dd triumvirate of elements used to create a definition list in a document. The entire list is bracketed by the dl element's tags. Each definition term is denoted by a leading dt element tag, and the definition for the term is denoted by a leading dd element tag. A schematic of a definition list sequence for three items looks like the following:

```
<dl>
    <dt>Term 1</dt>
    <dd>Definition 1</dd>
    <dt>Term 2</dt>
    <dd>Definition 2</dd>
    <dt>Term 3</dt>
    <dd>Definition 3</dd>
</dl>
```

A dt element is an inline element, whereas a dd element can contain block-level content, including bordered text, images, and other objects. End tags are optional in HTML for both dt and dd elements because the next start tag automatically signals the end of the preceding element. The entire list, however, must close with an end tag for the encapsulating dl element.

Although the HTML specification forces no particular way of rendering a definition list, mainstream browsers are in agreement in left-aligning a dt element and indenting any dd element that follows it. No special font formatting or visual elements are added by the browser, but you are free (if not encouraged) to assign styles as you like. If you want to stack multiple terms and/or definitions, you can place multiple dt and/or dd elements right after each other in the source code.

Because HTML is being geared toward context-sensitive tagging, avoid using definition lists strictly as a formatting trick (to get some indented text). Use style sheets and adjustable margin settings to accomplish formatting.

In Navigator 4, any styles assigned to dt and dd elements by way of the class, id, or style attribute do not work. If you wish to assign the same style attributes to both the dt and dd elements, assign the style to the dl element; otherwise, wrap each dt and dd element with a span element whose styles the nested dt and dd elements inherit. This workaround is observed by other browsers, although it is not necessary for documents that will never render in NN 4.

Example

```
<dl>
    <dt>Z-scale</dt>
    <dd>A railroad modeling scale of 1:220. The smallest mass-produced
    commercial model scale.</dd>
</dl>
```

<em>

Object Model Reference
[window.]document.getElementById(*elementID*)

Element-Specific Attributes
None.

Element-Specific Event Handler Attributes
None.

<em>

IE *all* NN *all* Moz *all* Saf *all* Op 7 HTML *all*

<em>...</em>

HTML End Tag: Required

The em element is one of a large group of elements that the HTML 4 recommendation calls *phrase elements*. Such elements assign structural meaning to a designated portion of the document. An em element is one that is to be rendered differently from running body text to designate emphasis.

Browsers have free rein to determine how (or whether) to distinguish em element content from the rest of the body element. Both Navigator and Internet Explorer elect to italicize the text. Override the default with a style sheet as you see fit.

Example
```
<p>The night was dark, and the river's churning waters were <em>very</em>
cold.</p>
```

Object Model Reference
[window.]document.getElementById(*elementID*)

Element-Specific Attributes
None.

Element-Specific Event Handler Attributes
None.

<embed>

IE 3 NN 2 Moz *all* Saf *all* Op 7 HTML *n/a*

<embed>...</embed>

HTML End Tag: Optional/Required

An embed element allows you to load media and file types other than those natively rendered by the browser. Typically, such external data requires a plugin or helper application to properly load the data and display its file. Notice that this element has been supported by both Navigator and Internet Explorer since Versions 2 and 3, respectively, but the element never became a part of the HTML standard vocabulary. The HTML 4 specification recommends the object element as the one to load the kind of external data covered by the embed element in the browsers. Navigator 4 and later and Internet Explorer 4 and later also support the object element, and you should gravitate toward that element for embedded elements if your visitor browser base can support it.

<embed>

Despite the goal of standardizing on the object element, not all browsers support it on all operating systems. Mozilla, for instance, prefers the embed element, while IE prefers the object element. To accommodate these disparities, you can specify both elements such that the current browser uses the element it understands. For example, the following code loads a Flash animation into all browsers that have the Flash plugin installed:

```
<object width="425" height="350">
    <param name="movie" value="http://www.example.com/vid/2bq"></param>
    <embed src="http://www.example.com/vid/2bq" type="application/x-shockwave-flash"
    width="425" height="350"></embed>
</object>
```

Bear in mind that for data types that launch plugins, the control panel displayed for the data varies widely among browsers, operating systems, and the plugins the user has installed for that particular data type. It is risky business trying to carefully design a layout combining a plugin's control panel and surrounding text or other elements.

The list of attributes for the embed element is a long one, but pay special attention to the browser compatibility rating for each attribute. Because the plugin technologies for IE/Windows, IE/Mac, and Navigator are not identical, neither are the attribute sets. Even so, it is possible to assign an embed element in one document that works on both browser brands when the embedded element does not rely on an attribute setting not supported in one of the browsers. Some plugins, however, may require or accept attribute name/value pairs that are not listed for this element. At least in the case of Navigator and Mozilla, all attributes (including those normally ignored by the browser) and their values are passed to the plugin. Therefore, you must also check with the documentation for a plugin to determine what, if any, extra attributes may be supported or required. The object element gets around this object-specific attribute problem by letting you add any number of param elements tailored to the object, as was shown.

Example

```
<embed name="jukebox" src="jazz.aif" height="100" width="200"></embed>
```

Object Model Reference

```
[window.]document.embeds[elementName]
[window.]document.getElementById(elementID)
```

Element-Specific Attributes

align	alt	height	hidden	name
pluginspage	pluginurl	src	type	units
width				

Element-Specific Event Handler Attributes

None.

<embed>

align
IE *4* NN *n/a* Moz *all* Saf *all* Op *7* HTML *n/a*

align="*where*'   *Optional*

If the embedded object (or player control panel) occupies space on the page, the align attribute determines how the object is rendered in physical relation to the element's next outermost container. If some additional text is specified between the start and end tags of the embed element, the align attribute also affects how that text is rendered relative to the object's rectangular space.

Most of the rules for alignment-constant values cited at the beginning of this chapter apply to the embed element. Precise layout becomes difficult because the HTML page author usually isn't in control of the plugin control panel that is displayed on the page. Dimensions for the element that work fine for one control panel are totally inappropriate for another.

Typically, align attributes are deprecated in HTML 4 in favor of the align style sheet property. But if you are using the embed element for backward compatibility, stick with the align attribute.

Example
```
<embed src="jazz.aif" align="left" height="100" width="200"></embed>
```

Value
Each browser defines a different set of values for this attribute. Select the one(s) from the following table that work for your deployment:

Value	IE	Others
absbottom	•	—
absmiddle	•	—
baseline	•	—
bottom	•	•
left	•	•
middle	•	•
right	•	•
texttop	•	—
top	•	•

Default   bottom

Object Model Reference
```
[window.]document.embeds[elementName].align
[window.]document.getElementById(elementID).align
```

alt

alt="*textMessage*"   *Optional*

If Internet Explorer does not have the facilities to load and run the external media, the text assigned to the alt attribute is supposed to display in the document where the embed element's tag appears. Typically, this text provides advice on what the page visitor is missing by not being able to load the data (although IE also presents a dialog about how to get plugin information from an online source).

Use the alt attribute with care. If the external data is not a critical part of your page's content, you may just want the rest of the page to load without calling attention to the missing media controller in lesscapable browsers. The alternate message may be more disturbing to the user than a missing media player.

The equivalent powers are available in Navigator with the noembed element.

Example

<embed src="jazz.aif" alt="Sound media player" height="10" width="20"></embed>

Value   Any quoted string of characters.

Default   None.

height, width

height="*length*" width="*length*"   *Required*

The size that an embedded object (or its plugin control panel) occupies in a document is governed by the height and width attribute settings. Some browser versions might allow you to get away without assigning these attributes, letting the plugin's own user interface design determine the height and width of its visible rectangle. It is best to specify the exact dimensions of a plugin's control panel whenever possible. (Control panels vary with each browser and even between different plugins for the same browser.) In some cases, the control panel does not display if you fail to supply enough height on the page for the control panel. If you assign values that are larger than the actual control panel, the browser reserves that empty space on the page, which could interfere with your intended page design.

Example   <embed src="jazz.aif" height="150" width="250"></embed>

Value

Positive integer values (optionally quoted) or percentage values (quoted). You cannot entirely hide an embedded object's control panel by setting values to zero (one pixel always shows and occupies space), but you can reduce its height and width to one pixel in each dimension. If you want to hide a plugin, do so with DHTML by setting its positioning display attribute to none.

Default   None.

Object Model Reference

[window.]document.embeds[i].height
[window.]document.getElementById(*elementID*).height

<embed>

```
[window.]document.embeds[i].width
[window.]document.getElementById(elementID).width
```

hidden

IE 4   NN n/a   Moz 0.9   Saf n/a   Op 7   HTML n/a

hidden="true" | "false"   *Optional*

The hidden attribute is a switch that lets you set whether the embedded data's plugin control panel appears on the screen. When you set the hidden attribute, the height and width attributes are overridden.

Example   <embed src="soothing.aif" hidden="true"></embed>

Value   true | false

Default   false

Object Model Reference

```
[window.]document.embeds[i].hidden
[window.]document.getElementById(elementID).hidden
```

name

IE 3   NN 2   Moz all   Saf all   Op 7   HTML n/a

name="elementIdentifier"   *Optional*

If you are scripting a plugin (especially in Navigator via LiveConnect), it is usually more convenient to create a reference to the embedded element by using a unique name you assign to the item. Thus, if you edit the page and move or delete multiple embed elements on the page, you do not have to worry about adjusting index values to array-style references (document.embeds[embedName]). For W3C DOM browsers, however, use the id attribute and document.getElementById( ).

Example

<embed name="jukebox" id="jukebox" src="jazz.aif" height="15" width="25"></embed>

Value   Case-sensitive identifier.

Default   None.

Object Model Reference

```
[window.]document.embeds[i].name
[window.]document.getElementById(elementID).name
```

pluginspage

IE 4   NN 4   Moz all   Saf all   Op 7   HTML n/a

pluginspage="URL"   *Optional*

If the MIME type of the data file assigned to the embed element's src attribute is not supported by an existing plugin or helper application in the browser, the pluginspage attribute is intended to provide a URL for downloading and installing the necessary plugin. Mozilla, however, tries to use its own plugin registry as a resource.

Example

```
<embed name="jukebox" src="jazz.aif" height="150" width="250"
pluginspage="http://www.example.com/plugin/install/index.html">
</embed>
```

Value	Any valid URL.
Default	None.

pluginurl

IE *n/a* NN |4| Moz *n/a* Saf *n/a* Op *n/a* HTML *n/a*

pluginurl="*URL*"   *Optional*

Navigator 4 (only) introduced the power (a feature called Smart Update) to allow somewhat automatic installation of browser components. If a user does not have the necessary plugin installed for your embed element's data type, the pluginurl can point to a Java Archive (JAR) file that contains the plugin and digitally signed objects to satisfy security issues surrounding automatic installation (via Netscape's Java Installation Manager). A JAR file is both digitally signed and compressed (very much along the lines of a *.zip* file), and is created with the help of Netscape's JAR Packager tool.

You can include both the pluginspage and pluginurl attributes in an embed element's tag to handle the appropriate browser version. Navigator 2 and 3 respond to the pluginspage attribute, whereas Navigator 4 gives precedence to the pluginurl attribute when it is present.

Example

```
<embed name="jukebox" src="jazz.aif" height="150" width="250"
pluginurl="http://www.example.com/plugin/install.jar">
</embed>
```

Value	Any valid URL to a JAR file.
Default	None.

src

IE *3* NN *2* Moz *all* Saf *all* Op *7* HTML *n/a*

src="*URL*"   *Optional*

The src attribute is a URL to a file containing data that is played through the plugin. For most uses of the embed element, this attribute is required, but there are some circumstances in which it may not be necessary (see the type attribute). Browsers used to rely on the filename extension to determine which plugin to load (based on browser preferences settings for plugins and helper applications), but now commonly make decisions based on the content type.

Example

```
<embed name="babyClip" src="Ugachaka.avi" height="150" width="250"></embed>
```

Value	A complete or relative URL.
Default	None.

Object Model Reference
```
[window.]document.embeds[i].src
[window.]document.getElementById(elementID).src
```

type   IE *n/a*   NN *2*   Moz *all*   Saf *all*   Op *7*   HTML *n/a*

type="*MIMEtype*"   *Optional*

Early Navigator versions anticipated the potential of a plugin not requiring any outside data file. Instead, such a plugin would more closely resemble an applet. If such a plugin is to be put into your document, you still use the embed element but specify just the MIME type instead of the data file URL (in the src attribute). This assumes, of course, that the MIME type is of such a special nature that only one possible plugin would be mapped to that MIME type in the browser settings. Today, however, browsers rely on the type attribute to dtermine which plugins to be used with the external media. Specify both the src and type attribute in an embed element tag.

Example
```
<embed src="hooha.fbz" type="application/x-frobnitz" height="150" width="250">
</embed>
```

Value
Any valid MIME type name as a quoted string, including the type and subtype portions delimited by a forward slash. A catalog of registered MIME types is available from *ftp://ftp. isi.edu/in-notes/iana/assignments/media-types/*.

Default   None.

units   IE *3*   NN *n/a*   Moz *n/a*   Saf *n/a*   Op *n/a*   HTML *n/a*

units="*measurementUnitType*"   *Optional*

The units attribute is supposed to dictate the kind of measurement units used for the element's height and width attribute values. Internet Explorer appears to treat the measurements in pixels, regardless of this attribute's setting.

Example   `<embed src="jazz.aif" height="150" width="250" units="en"></embed>`

Value   Internet Explorer values are px or em.

Default   px

Object Model Reference
```
[window.]document.embeds[i].units
[window.]document.getElementById(elementID).units
```

width

See height.

<fieldset>

<fieldset>

IE *4* **NN** *n/a* **Moz** *all* **Saf** *all* **Op** *7* **HTML** *4*

`<fieldset>...</fieldset>`   *HTML End Tag: Required*

A fieldset element is a structural container for form elements (as distinguished from the functional containment of the form element). In fact, you can define multiple fieldset elements within a single form element to supply context to logical groupings of form elements. For example, one fieldset element might contain text input fields for name and address info; another fieldset might be dedicated to credit card information.

Supporting browsers boost the attractiveness of this element by automatically drawing a rule around the form elements within each fieldset container. You can also attach a label that gets embedded within the rule by defining a legend element immediately after the start tag of a fieldset element. By default, the box extends the full width of the next outermost container geography—usually the document body or html element. If you'd rather have the box cinch up around the visible form elements, you have to set the width style sheet property for the element.

Example

```
<form method="POST" action="...">
<fieldset>
<legend>Credit Card Information</legend>
...inputElementsHere...
</fieldset>
</form>
```

Object Model Reference

`[window.]document.getElementById(elementID)`

Element-Specific Attributes

align   form

Element-Specific Event Handler Attributes
None.

align

IE *4* **NN** *n/a* **Moz** *n/a* **Saf** *n/a* **Op** *n/a* **HTML** *n/a*

`align="where"`   *Optional*

The align attribute appears only in Internet Explorer, and its implementation is far from consistent across operating systems. In theory, the attribute should control the alignment of input elements it contains. This is true in the Macintosh version of IE, but in the Windows version (especially in IE 6), the settings have minor effect on the fieldset element rule. It is best to let the default setting take precedence, and override with style sheets.

Example   `<fieldset align="right">...</fieldset>`

Value   Allowed values are left | center | right.

Default   left

Object Model Reference

[window.]document.getElementById(*elementID*).align

form
IE *n/a* NN *n/a* Moz *n/a* Saf *n/a* Op 9 HTML *n/a*

form="*formID [formID]* ..."   *Optional*

Web Forms 2.0 extension that lets you associate a fieldset element with one or more forms that do not enclose the fieldset element.

Value   ID of one or more form elements on the page. Multiple references are space-delimited.

Default   None.

##
IE *all* NN *all* Moz *all* Saf *all* Op 7 HTML *3.2*

<font>...</font>   *HTML End Tag: Required*

A font element is a container whose contents are rendered with the font characteristics defined by the element's attributes. This element is deprecated in HTML 4 in favor of font attributes available in style sheets that are applied directly to other elements or the arbitrary span container for inline font changes. This element will be supported for a long time to come to allow backward compatibility with web pages designed for older browsers, however.

For nested tables in Navigator 4, style sheet inheritance frequently breaks down. Inserting font wrappers around content inside a td element can fortify your control over the design. Going forward, use font elements only as a last resort if a browser version balks at obeying CSS font rules.

The font element evolved over its lifetime, adding new attributes along the way to work in the more mature browsers. Navigator included some proprietary attributes for Version 4 (only) that are better served by style sheets for cross-browser compatibility.

Example   <font face="Times, serif" size="4">

Object Model Reference

[window.]document.getElementById(*elementID*)

Element-Specific Attributes

color	face	point-size	size	weight

Element-Specific Event Handler Attributes

None.

<font>

color

color="*colorTripletOrName*" *Optional*

Sets the font color of all text contained by the font element. This attribute is deprecated in HTML 4 in favor of style sheets.

Example `<font color="Olive">...</font>`

Value A hexadecimal triplet or plain-language color name. See Appendix A for acceptable plain-language color names.

Default Browser default.

Object Model Reference

[window.]document.getElementById(*elementID*).color

face

face="*fontFamilyName1[, ... fontFamilyNameN]*" *Optional*

You can assign a hierarchy of font families to use for a segment of text contained by a font element. The browser looks for the first font family in the comma-delimited list of font family names until it either finds a match on the client system or runs out of choices, at which point the browser default font family is used. Font family names must match the system font family names exactly. If you use this attribute (instead of the preferred font-family style sheet property), you can always suggest a generic font face (serif, sans-serif) as the final choice.

Example `<font face="Bookman, Times Roman, serif">...</font>`

Value One or more font family names, including the recognized generic faces: serif | sans-serif | cursive | fantasy | monospace.

Default Browser default.

Object Model Reference

[window.]document.getElementById(*elementID*).face

point-size

point-size="*pointSize*" *Optional*

The point-size attribute is Navigator 4's nonCSS equivalent of setting the font size by specific point size (rather than by relative font size directed by the size attribute). If you assign a value to the point-size attribute and set the font-size style attribute, the style attribute takes precedence. If you are aiming for cross-browser deployment, I suggest using style sheets exclusively for precise point or pixel sizes.

Example `<font point-size="14">...</font>`

Value A positive integer, representing the desired point size.

Default Browser default.

<form>

size

size="*integerOrRelativeSize*"

Font sizes referenced by the size attribute are the relative size scale that is not tied to any one point size across operating system platforms. The default browser font size is 3. The range of acceptable values for the size attribute are integers from 1 to 7 inclusive. The exact point size varies with the operating system and browser design.

Users can often adjust the default font size in preferences settings. The size attribute over-rides that setting. Moreover, size values can be relative to whatever font size is set in the preferences. By preceding an attribute value with a + or - sign, the browser's default size can be adjusted upward or downward, but always within the range of 1 through 7.

Example

```
<font size="4">...</font>
<font size="+3">...</font>
```

Value   Either an integer (quoted or not quoted) or a quoted relative value consisting of a + or - symbol and an integer value.

Default   3

Object Model Reference

[window.]document.getElementById(*elementID*).size

weight

weight="*boldnessValue*"

The weight attribute is Navigator 4's nonCSS equivalent of setting the font weight with a regular attribute rather than by style sheet rule. The attribute is unreliable, so the font-weight CSS style property is a better choice.

Value   Integer value between 100 and 900 in increments of 100. A value of 900 is the maximum boldness setting.

Default   Unknown.

<form>

<form>...</form>

Despite the importance of HTML forms in communication between web page visitors and the server, a form element at its heart is nothing more than a container of controls. Most, but not all, form controls are created in the document as input elements. Even if user inter-action with input elements is not intended for submission to a server (perhaps some client-side scripting requires interaction with the user), such input elements are contained by a form element—and must be nested inside a form element to render at all in Navigator 4 or earlier.

A document may contain any number of form elements, but a client may submit the settings of controls from only one form at a time. Therefore, the only time it makes sense to divide a series of form controls into multiple form elements is when the control groups can be submitted independently of each other. If you need to logically or structurally group controls while maintaining a single form, use the fieldset element to create the necessary subgroupings of controls.

When a form is submitted to the server, all controls that have name attributes assigned to them pass both their names and values—in name/value pairs—to the server for further processing (or possibly as an email attachment or message with the help of a browser's e-mail module). A Common Gateway Interface (CGI) program running on the server can accept and dissect the name/value pairs for further processing (adding a record to a server database or initiating a keyword search, for example). The server program is invoked via URL to the program assigned to the action attribute.

Inside browsers, the submission process consists of a few well-defined steps. The process begins with the browser assembling a form data set out of the name/value pairs of form controls. The name comes from the value assigned to the name attribute. A control's value depends on the type of control. For example, a text input element's value is the content appearing in the text box at submission time; for a radio button within a radio group (all of whose name attributes are assigned the same value), the value assigned to the value attribute of the selected radio button is inserted into the name/value pair for the radio group.

The W3C recommendations prefer that form controls use their id attributes in name/value pairs. As of the newest browsers now available, however, only the name attribute is recognized as an identifier for the submitted name/value pair.

The second step of submission encodes the text of each name/value pair. A + symbol is substituted for each space character. Reserved characters (as defined by RFC 1738) are escaped, and all other nonalphanumeric characters are converted to hexadecimal representations (in the form %HH, where HH is the hex code for the ASCII value of the character). Name and value components of each name/value pair are separated by an = symbol, and each name/value pair is delimited with an ampersand (&).

In the final step, the method attribute setting determines how the escaped form data set is transmitted to the server. With a method of get, the form data set is appended to the URL stated in the action attribute, separated by a ? symbol. With a method of post and a default enctype, the data set is transmitted as a kind of (non-email) message to the server. Data submitted via the GET method is limited in character length, while the POST method offers unlimited data length and no echoed display in the browser's Address box.

Form submission can be canceled in modern browsers with the help of scripts that perform validation checking or other functions triggered by the onsubmit event. This event fires prior to the form being submitted. If the event handler evaluates to return false or the default event is canceled (e.g., evt.preventDefault( )), the form is not submitted, and the user may continue to edit the form elements.

The Web Forms 2.0 standard (first implemented in Opera 9) offers internal validation mechanisms that put more "intelligence" into the form controls (e.g., a text entry field can have a regular expression pattern assigned to it as an attribute). See the input element in this chapter and the ValidityState object in Chapter 2 for additional details.

<form>

Example

```
<form name="orders" method="POST" action="http://www.example.com/cgi-bin/order">
...
</form>
```

Object Model Reference

```
[window.]document.forms[i]
[window.]document.forms[formName]
[window.]document.formName
[window.]document.getElementById(elementID)
```

Element-Specific Attributes

accept	accept-charset	acceptcharset	action	autocomplete
data	enctype	method	name	replace
target				

Element-Specific Event Handler Attributes

Handler	IE	NN	Others	HTML
onreset	4	3	all	4
onsubmit	3	2	all	4

accept   IE *n/a* NN *n/a* Moz *n/a* Saf *n/a* Op *9* HTML *4*

accept="*MIMETypeList*"   *Optional*

Intended for use with input elements of type file, the accept attribute lets you specify one or more MIME types for allowable files to be uploaded to the server when the form is submitted. The predicted implementation of this attribute would filter the file types listed in file dialogs used to select files for uploading. In a way, this attribute provides client-side validation of a file type so that files not conforming to the permitted MIME type are not even sent to the server.

Example   `<form accept="text/html, image/gif" ...>...</form>`

Value   Case-insensitive MIME type (content type) value. For multiple items, a comma-delimited list is allowed. A catalog of registered MIME types is available from *ftp://ftp.isi.edu/in-notes/iana/assignments/media-types/*.

Default   None.

accept-charset, acceptcharset   IE *5* NN *n/a* Moz *all* Saf *all* Op *7* HTML *4*

accept-charset="*MIMETypeList*"   *Optional*

A server advisory (for servers that are equipped to interpret the information) about which character sets it must receive from a client form. The hyphenated version is from the HTML 4 specification, but IE 5 and later also implement an alternate attribute whose name has no hyphen.

<form>

Example   `<form accept-charset="it, es" ...>...</form>`

Value

Case-insensitive alias from the character set registry (*ftp://ftp.isi.edu/in-notes/iana/ assignments/character-sets*). Multiple character sets may be delimited by commas. The reserved value, unknown, is supposed to represent the character set that the server used to generate the form for the client.

Default   unknown

action   IE *all* NN *all* Moz *all* Saf *all* Op *7* HTML *all*

`action="URL"`   *Optional*

Specifies the URL to be accessed when the form is being submitted. When the form is submitted to a server for further processing, the URL may be to a CGI program or to an HTML page that includes server-side scripts. (Those scripts execute on the server before the HTML page is downloaded to the client.) As a result of the submission, the server returns an HTML page for display in the client. If the returned display is to be delivered to a different frame or window, the target attribute must be specified accordingly.

Implementations of submitting a form by email (specifying a mailto: URL for the action attribute) across all browsers are very uneven—you may be missing form submissions from many users. If CGI processing of forms is beyond your expertise, search for third-party FormMail services that forward forms to you via email.

If you omit the action attribute and the form is submitted, the current page reloads itself, returning all form elements to their default values.

Example

`<form method="POST" action="http://www.example.com/orders/order.html">`

Value   A complete or relative URL.

Default   None.

Object Model Reference

```
[window.]document.forms[i].action
[window.]document.forms[formName].action
[window.]document.formName.action
[window.]document.getElementById(elementID).action
```

autocomplete   IE *5* NN *n/a* Moz *n/a* Saf *n/a* Op *n/a* HTML *n/a*

`autocomplete="featureSwitch"`   *Optional*

If an IE user has automatic form completion preference enabled, the autocomplete attribute governs the feature for the entire form. IE preserves (in an encrypted fashion) previous text and password entries, and presents a repeat visitor with one or more choices to complete the field entry. If the field is for data commonly stored in a user's vCard, you can specify vcard-name attributes for text and password type input elements to let the browser pre-fill or assist the entry of a particular named field that matches one of the preferences entries.

For more details on how AutoComplete works in HTML forms, visit *http://msdn.microsoft. com/workshop/author/forms/autocomplete_ovr.asp*.

Example   `<form method="POST" action="register.pl" autocomplete="on">`

Value   Constants: on | off.

Default   off

Object Model Reference

```
[window.]document.forms[i].autoComplete
[window.]document.forms[formName].autoComplete
[window.]document.formName.autoComplete
[window.]document.getElementById(elementID).autoComplete
```

data   IE *n/a* NN *n/a* Moz *n/a* Saf *n/a* Op *n/a* HTML *n/a*

`data="URI"`   *Optional*

Web Forms 2.0 extension that allows a form to retrieve initial values for controls from an external XML file. The specification provides some details of the structure and namespaces to be used for the file. Visit *http://www.whatwg.org* for further information.

Example

```
<form name="registration" method="POST" action="register.pl" data="form/reg_default.
xml">
```

Value   Uniform Resource Identifier.

Default   None.

enctype   IE *all* NN *all* Moz *all* Saf *all* Op *7* HTML *all*

`enctype="MIMEType"`   *Optional*

Sets a MIME type for the data being submitted to the server with the form. For typical form submissions (where the method attribute is set to POST), the default value is the proper content type. If you include a file input element, specify "multipart/form-data" as the enctype attribute.

Example

```
<form method="POST" enctype="text/plain" action="mailto:orders@example.com">
...
</form>
```

Value   MIME type (content type) value. For multiple items, a comma-delimited list is allowed.

Default   application/x-www-form-urlencoded

Object Model Reference

```
[window.]document.forms[i].encoding
[window.]document.forms[formName].encoding
```

```
[window.]document.formName.encoding
[window.]document.getElementById(elementID).encoding
```

method
IE *all* NN *all* Moz *all* Saf *all* Op *7* HTML *all*

method="GET" | "POST"   *Optional*

Forms may be submitted via two possible HTTP methods: GET and POST. These methods determine whether the form element data is sent to the server appended to the action attribute URL (GET) or as a transaction message body (POST). In practice, when the action and method attributes are not assigned in a form element, the form performs an unconditional reload of the same document, restoring form controls to their default values.

Example

```
<form method="POST" action="http://www.example.com/orders/order.html">
...
</form>
```

Value   Constant values of GET or POST. Browsers respond to upper- or lowercase values. Web Forms 2.0 adds the following values: put | delete.

Default   GET

Object Model Reference

```
[window.]document.forms[i].method
[window.]document.forms[formName].method
[window.]document.formName.method
[window.]document.getElementById(elementID).method
```

name
IE *3* NN *2* Moz *all* Saf *all* Op *7* HTML *4.01*

name="elementIdentifier"   *Optional*

Assigns an identifier to the entire form element. This value is particularly useful in writing scripts for older browsers that reference the form or its nested controls. Newer browsers support the preferred id attribute for this purpose, but the name attribute is still needed for form submission.

Example

```
<form name="orders" id="orders" method="POST"
action="http://www.example.com/cgi-bin/order">
...
</form>
```

Value   Case-sensitive identifier.

Default   None.

Object Model Reference

```
[window.]document.forms[i].name
[window.]document.forms[formName].name
[window.]document.formName.name
[window.]document.getElementById(elementID).name
```

replace

replace="*type*"

Optional

Web Forms 2.0 extension that associates instructions to a form with how to process the data returned from the server after the form is submitted. The choice is whether the response replaces the original document in the browser (the default) or the browser should apply returned values to the form, rather than retrieve initial form data (if a URL is assigned to the data attribute of the form element).

Example

```
<form name="registration" method="POST" action="register.pl"
data="form/reg_default.xml" replace="values">
```

Value   One of two constant values: document | values.

Default   document

target

target="*windowOrFrameName*"

Optional

If the HTML document returned from the server after it processes the form submission is to be loaded into a window or frame other than the current window or frame, you can specify where the returned document should load by assigning a window or frame name to the target attribute. Target frame names must be assigned to frames and windows as identifiers. Assign names to frames via the name attribute of the frame element; assign names to new windows via the second parameter of the window.open( ) scripting method. If you omit this attribute, the returned document replaces the document containing the form element. An identifier other than one belonging to an existing frame or window opens a new window for the returned document.

If the form is located in a subwindow, and you want the target to be the main window, you must first use a script to assign an identifier to the name property of the main window. Use that name as the value of the form's target attribute.

Strict DTDs for HTML 4 and XHTML do not support the target attribute of any element because frames and windows are outside the scope of pure document markup. In fact, framesetting documents will not validate in the strict environment—thus the purpose of the separate frameset DTDs for HTML 4 and XHTML. If your documents must validate with these strict DTDs, and you wish to support targets, use scripts to set target properties of links, image maps, and forms after the page has loaded.

A form element can have only one returned document and one target. If you want a form submission to change the content of multiple frames, you can include a script in the returned document whose onload event handler loads or dynamically writes a document into a different frame. (Set the location.href property of each frame to a desired URL.)

Example

```
<form method="POST" action="http://www.example.com/cgi-bin/order" target="new">
...
</form>
```

Value

Case-sensitive identifier when the frame or window name has been assigned via the target element's name attribute. Four reserved target names act as constants:

_blank
> Browser creates a new window for the destination document

_parent
> Destination document replaces the current frame's framesetting document (if one exists; otherwise, it is treated as _self)

_self
> Destination document replaces the current document in its window or frame

_top
> Destination document is to occupy the entire browser window, replacing any and all framesets that may be loaded (also treated as _self if there are no framesets defined in the window)

Default   _self

Object Model Reference

```
[window.]document.forms[i].target
[window.]document.forms[formName].target
[window.]document.formName.target
[window.]document.getElementById(elementID).target
```

<frame>   IE 3   NN 2   Moz all   Saf all   Op 7   HTML 4

<frame>   *HTML End Tag: Forbidden*

The frame element defines properties of an individual window space that is some fractional portion of the entire browser window. A frame element must be defined within the context of a frameset element. It is the frameset that defines the row and column arrangement of a related group of frames.

A browser treats a frame as a separate browser window within the browser application's window. As such, each frame window can load its own content, independent of other frames. Although no attributes of the frame element are required, assigning a value to the name attribute is highly recommended if you have forms or links whose returned or destination document is to be displayed in a different frame. Scripting among multiple frames also benefits greatly from names assigned to frames because it makes references to those frames (and their contents) more easily understandable to someone reading the script code. Note that among recent W3C DTDs, the frame element validates only in the HTML 4.01 Transitional DTD and the Frameset DTDs for both HTML 4.01 and XHTML 1.0. See Appendix E.

Example

```
<frameset cols="150,*">
    <frame name="navbar" src="nav.html">
    <frame name="main" src="page1.html">
</frameset>
```

Object Model Reference

[window.]*frameName*
[window.]frames[i]
[window.]document.getElementById(*elementID*)

Element-Specific Attributes

allowtransparency	bordercolor	datafld	datasrc
frameborder	height	longdesc	marginheight
marginwidth	name	noresize	scrolling
security	src	width	

Element-Specific Event Handler Attributes

None.

allowtransparency

IE 5.5   NN *n/a*   Moz *n/a*   Saf *n/a*   Op *n/a*   HTML *n/a*

allowtransparency="*featureSwitch*"

Optional

More applicable to the iframe element, the allowtransparency attribute, when engaged, turns the frame's background transparent. See the iframe element.

bordercolor

IE 4   NN 3   Moz *all*   Saf *n/a*   Op *n/a*   HTML *n/a*

bordercolor="*colorTripletOrName*"

Optional

If your frameset displays borders (as set with the border attribute of the frameset element), but you want a subset of the frames in the frameset to be rendered with a border color different from the rest, you can assign a color to the bordercolor attribute of an individual frame element. Mixing border colors in a frameset exposes your HTML to the risk of different rendering techniques of each browser and operating system. Not only do the precise pixel composition of borders vary, but each browser and operating system may resolve conflicts between colored borders differently. If you assign a color to only some frames of a frameset, be sure to test the look on as many browser versions and operating systems as possible to evaluate the visual effect of your color choices. IE 6 and IE 7 can render unpredictably if you try to color the border of a single frame.

Example   <frame name="navbar" src="nav.html" bordercolor="salmon">

Value   A hexadecimal triplet or plain-language color name. See Appendix A for acceptable plain-language color names.

Default   None.

Object Model Reference

[window.]document.getElementById(*elementID*).borderColor

<frame>

datafld
IE *4*   NN *n/a*   Moz *n/a*   Saf *n/a*   Op *n/a*   HTML *n/a*

datafld="*columnName*"   *Optional*

Used with IE data binding to associate a remote data source column name in lieu of an src attribute for a frame element. The data source column must contain a valid URI (relative or absolute). A datasrc attribute must also be set for the element. Works only with text file data sources in IE 5/Mac.

Example	<frame datasrc="DBSRC3" datafld="newsURL">
Value	Case-sensitive identifier.
Default	None.

Object Model Reference
[window.]document.getElementById(*elementID*).dataFld

datasrc
IE *4*   NN *n/a*   Moz *n/a*   Saf *n/a*   Op *n/a*   HTML *n/a*

datasrc="*dataSourceName*"   *Optional*

Used with IE data binding to specify the ID of the page's object element that loads the data source object for remote data access. Content from the data source is specified via the datafld attribute. Works only with text file data sources in IE 5/Mac.

Example	<frame datasrc="DBSRC3" datafld="newsURL">
Value	Case-sensitive identifier.
Default	None.

Object Model Reference
[window.]document.getElementById(*elementID*).dataSrc

frameborder
IE *3*   NN *3*   Moz *all*   Saf *all*   Op *8*   HTML *4*

frameborder="*borderSwitch*"   *Optional*

Controls whether an individual frame within a frameset displays a border. The setting is supposed to override the frameborder attribute setting of the containing frameset element. Controlling individual frame borders appears to be a problem for most browsers in most operating system versions. Turning off the border of one frame may have no effect if all adjacent frames have their borders on. Feel free to experiment with the effects of turning some borders on and some borders off, but be sure to test the final effect on all browsers and operating systems used by your audience. You can rely more comfortably on the frameborder attribute of the entire frameset.

Example	<frame name="navbar" src="nav.html" frameborder="0">
Value	On-off values for this attribute vary with the source. HTML 4 specifies the values of 1 (on) and 0 (off). Navigator 3 and 4 use yes and no. Internet Explorer 4 and later and other supporting browsers accept both sets of values.

Default   1

Object Model Reference

[window.]document.getElementById(*elementID*).frameBorder

height, width

IE *4* NN *n/a* Moz *n/a* Saf *n/a* Op *n/a* HTML *n/a*

height="*length*" width="*length*"   *Optional*

Microsoft HTML documentation for IE says that the height and width attributes control the size of a frame. In practice in IE, these attributes have no direct control over the appearance of the frames within a frameset. Instead, the cols and rows attributes of the containing frameset govern the initial geometry of a frame. Do not use these attributes.

longdesc

IE *6* NN *n/a* Moz *all* Saf *all* Op *n/a* HTML *4*

longdesc="*URL*"   *Optional*

Specifies a URL of a document that contains a longer description of the element than what the content of the title attribute reveals. One application of this attribute in future browsers is to retrieve an annotated description of the element for users who cannot read the browser screen. The **Properties** choice for Mozilla's context menu for this element displays a small window that includes an active link to the URL assigned to the attribute. Current mainstream browsers provide no other functionality for this attribute.

Example

<frame longdesc="navDesc.html" title="Navigation Bar" src="navbar.html">

Value   Any valid URI, including complete and relative URLs.

Default   None.

Object Model Reference

[window.]document.getElementById(*elementID*).longDesc

marginheight, marginwidth

IE *3* NN *n/a* Moz *all* Saf *all* Op *7* HTML *4*

marginheight="*pixelCount*" marginwidth="*pixelCount*"   *Optional*

The number of pixels between the inner edge of a frame and the content rendered inside the frame. The marginheight attribute controls space along the top and (when scrolled) the bottom edges of a frame; the marginwidth attribute controls space on the left and right edges of a frame. The HTML 4 specification leaves default behavior up to browsers.

Without any prompting, browsers automatically insert a margin of 14 (IE/Windows) or 8 (others) pixels inside a frame. But if you attempt to override the default behavior, be aware that setting any one of these two attributes causes the value of the other to go to zero. Therefore, unless you want the content to be absolutely flush with various frame edges, you need to assign values to both attributes.

Example   <frame src="navbar.html" marginheight="20" marginwidth="14">

Value   Any positive integer value or zero.

Default   14 (IE/Windows) or 8 (others).

Object Model Reference

```
[window.]document.getElementById(elementID).marginHeight
[window.]document.getElementById(elementID).marginWidth
```

name   IE 3   NN 2   Moz *all*   Saf *all*   Op 7   HTML 4

```
name="elementIdentifier"
```
Optional

When links and forms must load their destination or returned documents into frames other than the one holding the link or form, those elements have `target` attributes indicating which frame receives the new content. To direct such content to a frame, the frame must have a value assigned to its `name` attribute. That same value is assigned to the `target` attribute of the `a` or `form` element. Client-side scripting also uses the frame's name in building references to other frames or content in other frames. It is good practice to assign a unique identifying name to all frames.

The `name` attribute is deprecated in XHTML. To validate under the Frameset XHTML DTD, assign the same identifier to the element's `name` and `id` attributes.

Example   `<frame name="navbar" id="navbar" src="nav.html">`

Value   Case-sensitive identifier.

Default   None.

Object Model Reference

```
[window.]frameName.name
[window.]frames[i].name
[window.]document.getElementById(elementID).name
```

noresize   IE 3   NN 2   Moz *all*   Saf *all*   Op 7   HTML 4

```
noresize
```
Optional

Frame borders can be resized by the user dragging the border perpendicular to the axis of the border edge. When present, the `noresize` attribute instructs the browser to prevent the frame's edges from being manually resized by the user. All border edges of the affected `frame` element become locked, meaning that all edges that extend to other frames in the frameset remain locked as well.

Example   `<frame src="navbar.html" noresize>`

Value   The presence of the attribute in HTML makes the frame nonresizable.

Default   Frames are resizable by default.

Object Model Reference

```
[window.]document.getElementById(elementID).noResize
```

scrolling
IE 3 NN 2 Moz all Saf all Op 7 HTML 4

`scrolling="auto" | "no" | "yes"`
Optional

By default, browsers add vertical and/or horizontal scrollbars when the content loaded into a frame exceeds the visible content region of the frame. Scrollbars can affect the layout of some content because they occupy space normally devoted to content (that is, the frame does not expand to accommodate scrollbars). Also, due to differences in default font sizes in browsers and operating system versions, a given collection of text content may display differently in different clients. If you want to prevent scrollbars from appearing in the frame, set the scrolling attribute to no; if you want scrollbars to be in the frame at all times, set the attribute to yes. In the latter case, if the content does not require scrolling, the scrollbars are disabled. In some older versions of Navigator, the automatic scrollbars remain visible, even if content not requiring them is subsequently loaded into a frame. In Navigator 4 and other mainstream browsers, the automatic scrollbars appear only when needed.

Setting the scrolling attribute to no should be used only after you have tested on all browsers and platforms that mission-critical content is always visible in the frame. If the frame is set to not scroll and has the noresize attribute set, some users might not be able to see all the content of the frame.

Example	`<frame src="navbar.html" scrolling="no">`
Value	Constant values: auto | no | yes.
Default	auto

Object Model Reference
`[window.]document.getElementById(elementID).scrolling`

security
IE 6 NN n/a Moz n/a Saf n/a Op n/a HTML n/a

`security="restricted"`
Optional

When activated, this attribute raises the security level of the frame to the Restricted level of the Windows Security preferences settings. Such a frame's content may not execute scripts.

Example	`<frame src="navbar.html" security="restricted">`
Value	Constant value: restricted.
Default	None.

src
IE 3 NN 2 Moz all Saf all Op 7 HTML 4

`src="URL"`
Optional

Defines the URL of the content to be loaded into the frame element. The URL can be an absolute URL or one relative to the URL of the document containing the frameset specifications. You may also use the javascript: pseudo-URL to have the returned value of a script appear in the frame. For example, if you want a frame to be blank when the frameset loads, you can define a function in the frameset document that returns a blank HTML page. The

<frameset>

src attribute for each soon-to-be-blank frame invokes the function from the vantage point of the child frame:

```
<html>
<script language="JavaScript">
function blank( ) {
    return "<html></html>"
}
</script>
<frameset cols="50%,50%">
    <frame name="leftFrame" src="javascript:parent.blank( )">
    <frame name="rightFrame" src="javascript:parent.blank( )">
</frameset>
</html>
```

Another type of blank page is available from some browsers and versions via the about: blank URL, which draws from an internal blank page.

Example   `<frame src="navbar.html">`

Value   A complete or relative URL or a javascript: pseudo-URL.

Default   None.

Object Model Reference
`[window.]document.getElementById(elementID).src`

width

See height.

<frameset>

IE 3 NN 2 Moz *all* Saf *all* Op 7 HTML 4

`<frameset>...</frameset>`   *HTML End Tag: Required*

Defines the layout of a multiple-frame presentation in a browser's application window. The primary duty of the frameset element is to specify the geographical layout—in a row and column array—of rectangular frames. Attributes defined in a frameset element apply to all frame elements nested within (unless overridden by a similar attribute for a specific frame). A frameset element's tag takes the place in an HTML document that is normally devoted to the body element.

You may nest a frameset element within a frameset element. This tactic allows you to subdivide a frame from the outer frameset element into two or more frames. For example, if you define one frameset element with three rows and two columns, you get a total of six frames:

```
<frameset rows="33%, 33%, 34%" cols="50%, 50%">
    <frame name="r1c1" id="r1c1"...>
    <frame name="r1c2" id="r1c2"...>
    <frame name="r2c1" id="r2c1"...>
    <frame name="r2c2" id="r2c2"...>
    <frame name="r3c1" id="r3c1"...>
    <frame name="r3c2" id="r3c2"...>
</frameset>
```

Figure 1-1 shows the resulting frame organization.

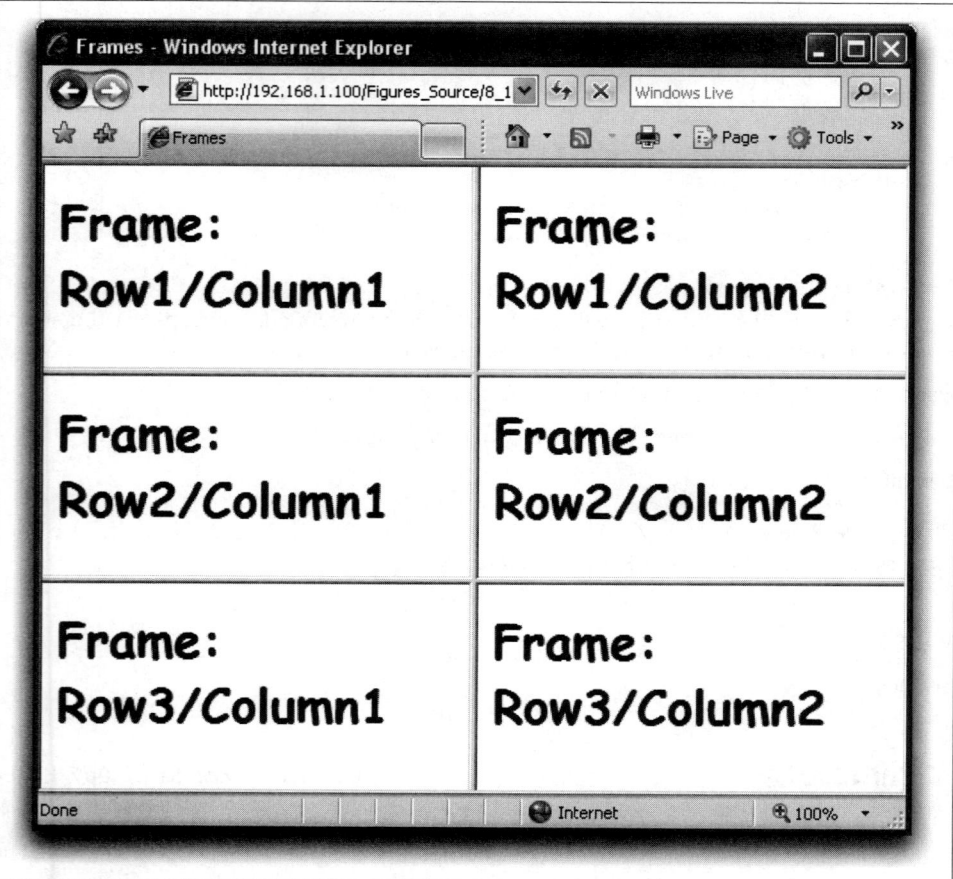

Figure 1-1. A three-row, two-column frameset

On the other hand, if you nest a frameset where a frame definition goes, that frame is divided into whatever frame organization is defined by that nested frameset. Consider the following nested frameset:

```
<frameset rows="33%, 33%, 34%">
    <frame name="r1" id="r1"...>
    <frameset cols="50%, 50%">
        <frame name="r2c1" id="r2c1"...>
        <frame name="r2c2" id="r2c2"...>
    </frameset>
    <frame name="r3" id="r3"...>
</frameset>
```

This produces the frame organization shown in Figure 1-2.

<frameset>

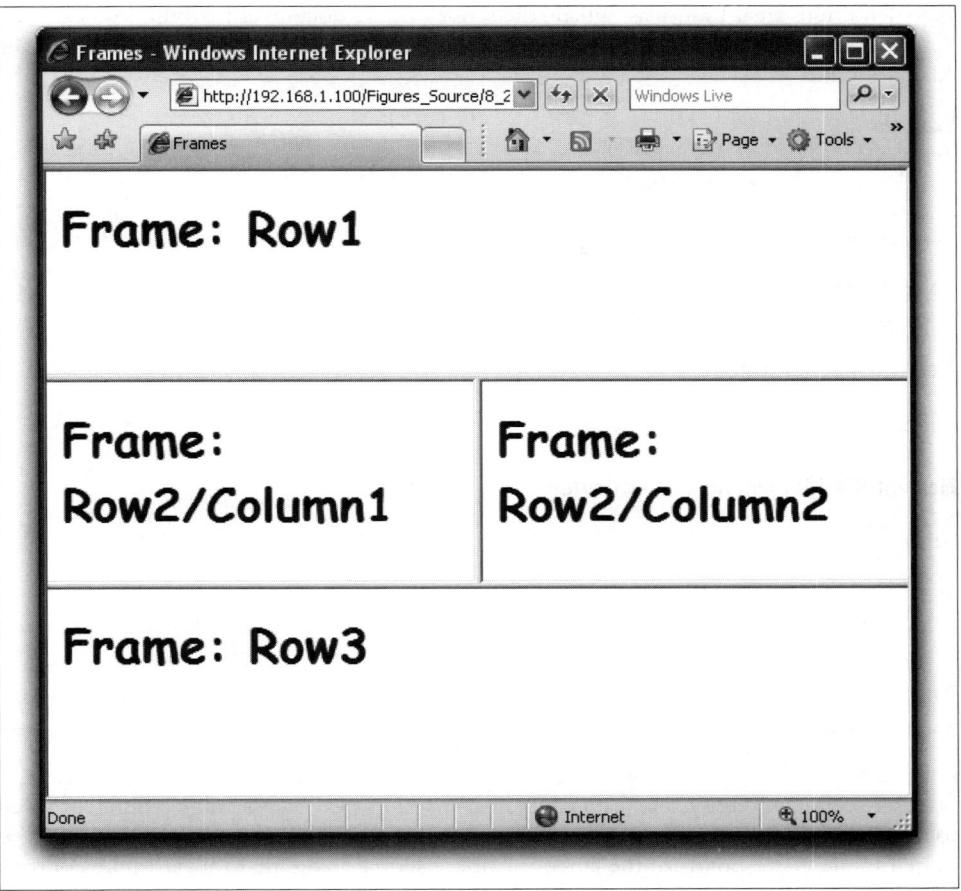

Figure 1-2. A nested frameset

You may nest frameset elements as deeply as your page design requires. Be aware that frames can devour memory resources of browsers on some operating systems. Not all users appreciate frames that display borders, even when such a structure may make logical sense for your page design.

The outermost frameset document is the one whose title attribute governs the display in the browser window title bar. Documents loaded into individual frames have no control over title bar display, although for reasons of scripting and potential application in future browsers, the title attribute of framed documents should be set anyway.

If you wish to offer an option for a user to remove a frameset, you can supply a link or button that invokes a script. The script should set the top.location.href property to the URL of the single most important document of the pages loaded into frames (the primary content).

Strict DTDs for HTML 4 and XHTML explicitly exclude support for frameset and frame elements (and target attributes of other elements that point to frames). These document type definitions treat frames as outside the scope of pure document markup. You can validate a framesetting document with the HTML 4 transitional and frameset DTDs or the XHTML frameset DTD.

Example

```
<frameset cols="150,*">
    <frame name="navbar" id="navbar" src="nav.html">
    <frame name="main" id="main" src="page1.html">
</frameset>
```

Object Model Reference

[window.]document.getElementById(*elementID*)

Element-Specific Attributes

border	bordercolor	cols	frameborder	framespacing	rows

Element-Specific Event Handler Attributes

Handler	IE	NN	Others	HTML
onload	3	2	all	4
onunload	3	2	all	4

border

IE *4* NN *3* Moz *all* Saf *all* Op *7* HTML *n/a*

border="*pixelCount*"   *Optional*

Frames display 3-D borders by default. The default thickness of that border varies with browser and operating system. You can adjust this thickness by assigning a different value to the border attribute of the frameset. Only the outermost frameset element of a system of nested framesets responds to the border attribute setting. Note that this attribute controls inter-frame borders, and not a border around the frameset.

Navigator and Mozilla are consistent across Windows and Macintosh platforms by displaying a default border that is the same thickness as when the border attribute is set to 5. For IE, the default value is 6 in Windows and 1 on the Mac (although the actual rendering is far more than one pixel wide). Any single setting you make for the border attribute therefore does not look the same on all browsers. Moreover, at smaller settings, some browsers react strangely. IE 6 won't display a border in Windows when the value is 4 or less; Mozilla loses its 3-D effect when the value is 2 or less.

This hodge-podge deployment of frame borders may make you shy away from using them altogether (set the border attribute to 0). In some cases, however, borders provide reassuring visual contexts for frame content that requires a scrollbar. Having a scrollbar appear floating in a browser window might be disconcerting to some viewers.

That the HTML 4 specification does not include a border attribute might lead one to believe it prefers the use of style sheet borders instead of borders tied only to frames. At most, however, a border-related CSS style property affects only a border around the entire frameset, and has no impact on borders between frames.

Example   `<frameset cols="150,*" border="0">...</frameset>`

Value   An integer value. A setting of zero eliminates the border entirely. Although the value is supposed to represent the precise pixel thickness of borders in the frameset, this is not entirely true for all operating systems or browsers.

Default   See description.

Object Model Reference

`[window.]document.getElementById(elementID).border`

bordercolor
            IE *4* NN *3* Moz *all* Saf *n/a* Op *n/a* HTML *n/a*

`bordercolor="colorTripletOrName"`   *Optional*

Establishes the rendering color for all visible borders in a frameset. A `bordercolor` setting in an outermost `frameset` element may be overridden by a `bordercolor` attribute of a nested `frameset` element (for the nested frameset's frames only) or an individual `frame` element. Browsers resolve conflicts of colors assigned to adjacent frames differently. Test your color combinations carefully if you mix border colors.

Example   `<frameset cols="150,*" bordercolor="salmon">...</frameset>`

Value   A hexadecimal triplet or plain-language color name. See Appendix A for acceptable plain-language color names.

Default   Browser default, usually a shade of gray with black or blue highlighting for the 3-D effect.

Object Model Reference

`[window.]document.getElementById(elementID).borderColor`

cols
            IE *3* NN *2* Moz *all* Saf *all* Op *7* HTML *4*

`cols="columnLengthsList"`   *Optional*

Defines the sizes or proportions of the column arrangement of frames in a frameset. If you intend to use the `frameset` element to create frames in multiple columns, you must assign a list of values to the `cols` attribute, with one value per column.

Column size is defined in one of three ways:

- An absolute pixel size
- A percentage of the width available for the entire frameset
- A wildcard (*) to represent all available remaining space after other pixels and percentages have been accounted for

Use an absolute pixel size when you want the width of a frame to be the same no matter how the user has sized the overall browser window. This is especially useful when the frame is to display an object of fixed width, such as an image. Use a percentage when you want the frame width to be a certain proportion of the frameset's width, no matter how the user has adjusted the size of the overall browser window. If you use all percentage values

<frameset>

for the cols attribute, they should add up to 100%. If the values don't add up to 100%, the browser makes the columns fit anyway. Finally, use the asterisk wildcard value to let the browser calculate the width of one frame when all other frames in the frameset have fixed or percentage values assigned to them. Separate the values within the attribute value string with commas.

You can mix and match all three types of values in the attribute string. For example, consider a three-column frameset. If you want the leftmost column to be exactly 150 pixels wide, but the middle column must be 50% of the total frameset width, set the value as follows:

```
<frameset cols="150,50%,*">
```

The precise width of the two rightmost frames is different with each browser window's width adjustment. The rightmost frame width in this example is roughly equal to one half the width of the frameset minus the 150 pixels reserved for the leftmost frame.

You may define an invisible column to the right. Use percentage values for visible columns, and make sure they total 100%. Then assign the asterisk value for the final column.

To create a regular grid of frames, assign values to both the cols and rows attributes in the frameset element's tag. For an irregular array, you must nest frameset elements, as shown in the description of the frameset element, earlier in this section.

Example   `<frameset cols="25%,50%,25%">...</frameset>`

Value   Comma-separated list of pixel, percentage, or wildcard (*) values. Internet Explorer 4 for the Macintosh exhibits incorrect behavior with some combinations that include a wildcard value.

Default   100%

Object Model Reference

`[window.]document.getElementById(elementID).cols`

frameborder   IE 3 NN 3 Moz all Saf all Op n/a HTML n/a

`frameborder="borderSwitch"`   *Optional*

Controls whether all frames within the frameset display a border (acting as dividers between frame edges). The frameborder attribute of frame elements can override the frameset element's setting for this attribute, but some frame organizations don't lend themselves well to eliminating frames from subgroups of frames. Override the frameset element's attribute with caution, and test on all browsers and operating system platforms.

Example   `<frameset cols="25%,50%,25%" frameborder="no">...</frameset>`

Value   On-off values for this attribute vary with the browser. Navigator uses yes and no. Internet Explorer 4 and later accepts both yes | no and 1 | 0. For cross-browser compatibility, use the yes/no pairing.

Default   yes

Object Model Reference

`[window.]document.getElementById(elementID).frameBorder`

framespacing

framespacing="*pixelLength*"   *Optional*

The Internet Explorer framespacing attribute is an older version of the border attribute. The older attribute is supported in current IE versions for backward compatibility. The behavior of the framespacing attribute is more uniform across operating system versions of IE: a setting of 10 pixels generates a border between frames that is essentially identical in both Windows and Mac versions. For an IE-only deployment, the framespacing attribute is a more accurate way to create borders that look the same across operating system versions.

Example   `<frameset cols="25%,50%,25%" framespacing="7">...</frameset>`

Value   A positive integer. Unlike the border attribute, however, a setting of zero does not remove the border. Use the frameborder attribute to hide borders entirely.

Default   2

Object Model Reference

[window.]document.getElementById(*elementID*).frameSpacing

rows

rows="*rowLengthsList*"   *Optional*

Defines the sizes or proportions of the row arrangement of frames in a frameset. If it is the intent to use the frameset element to create frames with multiple rows, you must assign a list of values to the rows attribute, with one value per row.

Row size is defined in one of three ways:

- An absolute pixel size
- A percentage of the height available for the entire frameset in the browser window
- A wildcard (*) to represent all available remaining space in the browser window after other pixels and percentages have been accounted for

Use an absolute pixel size when you want the height of a frame row to be the same no matter how the user has sized the overall browser window. This is especially useful when the frame is to display an object of fixed height, such as an image. Use a percentage when you want the frame height to be a certain proportion of the frameset's height, no matter how the user has adjusted the size of the overall browser window. If you use all percentage values for the rows attribute, they should add up to 100%. If the values don't add up to 100%, the browser makes the rows fit anyway. Finally, use the asterisk wildcard value to let the browser calculate the height of one row when all other rows in the frameset have fixed or percentage values assigned to them. Separate the values within the attribute value string with commas.

You can mix and match all three types of values in the attribute string. For example, consider a three-row frameset. If you want the bottom row to be exactly 80 pixels high to accommodate a navigation bar, but the middle row must be 50% of the total frameset height, set the value as follows:

```
<frameset rows="*,50%,80">
```

The precise height of the two topmost frames is different with each browser window's height adjustment. The topmost frame height in this example is roughly equal to one half the height of the frameset minus the 80 pixels reserved for the bottom row.

You may define an invisible row at the bottom. Use percentage values for visible rows, and make sure they total 100%. Then assign the asterisk value for the final row.

To create a regular grid of frames, assign values to both the cols and rows attributes in the frameset element's tag. For an irregular array, you must nest frameset elements, as shown in the description of the frameset element, earlier in this section.

Example	`<frameset rows="25%,50%,25%">...</frameset>`
Value	Comma-separated list of pixel, percentage, or wildcard (*) values. Internet Explorer 4 for the Macintosh exhibits incorrect behavior with some combinations that include a wildcard value.
Default	100%

Object Model Reference

`[window.]document.getElementById(elementID).rows`

<h1>, <h2>, <h3>, <h4>, <h5>, <h6>

IE *all* NN *all* Moz *all* Saf *all* Op 7 HTML *all*

HTML End Tag: Required

```
<h1>...</h1>, <h2>...</h2>, <h3>...</h3>
<h4>...</h4>, <h5>...</h5>, <h6>...</h6>
```

HTML defines a series of six heading levels with associated numbers that are intended to signify the relative importance of the section below the heading. The h1 element represents the most important, whereas h6 represents the least important. HTML document parsers can examine a page's tags to create a table of contents based on the headings. This means that for proper document structure, these heading levels should be used in sequence, without skipping levels for aesthetic purposes.

It is up to the browsers to determine the default font, weight, and other characteristics of each level. Each heading element is rendered on its own line, with no line break or paragraph elements necessary to begin the content of the section titled with the heading. Figure 1-3 shows examples of how Internet Explorer 7 and Firefox 1.5 render all six heading levels in Windows. By and large, this pattern applies to other browser versions and operating systems.

You can always override the browser's rendering style for any heading level or individual heading with style sheet rules.

Example

```
<h1>The Solar System</h1>
<p>Floating gracefully within the Milky Way galaxy is our Solar System.  ...</p>
<h2>The Sun</h2>
<p>At a distance of 93,000,000 miles from Earth, the Sun...</p>
<h3>The Planets</h3>
<p>Nine recognized planets revolve around the Sun. ...</p>
```

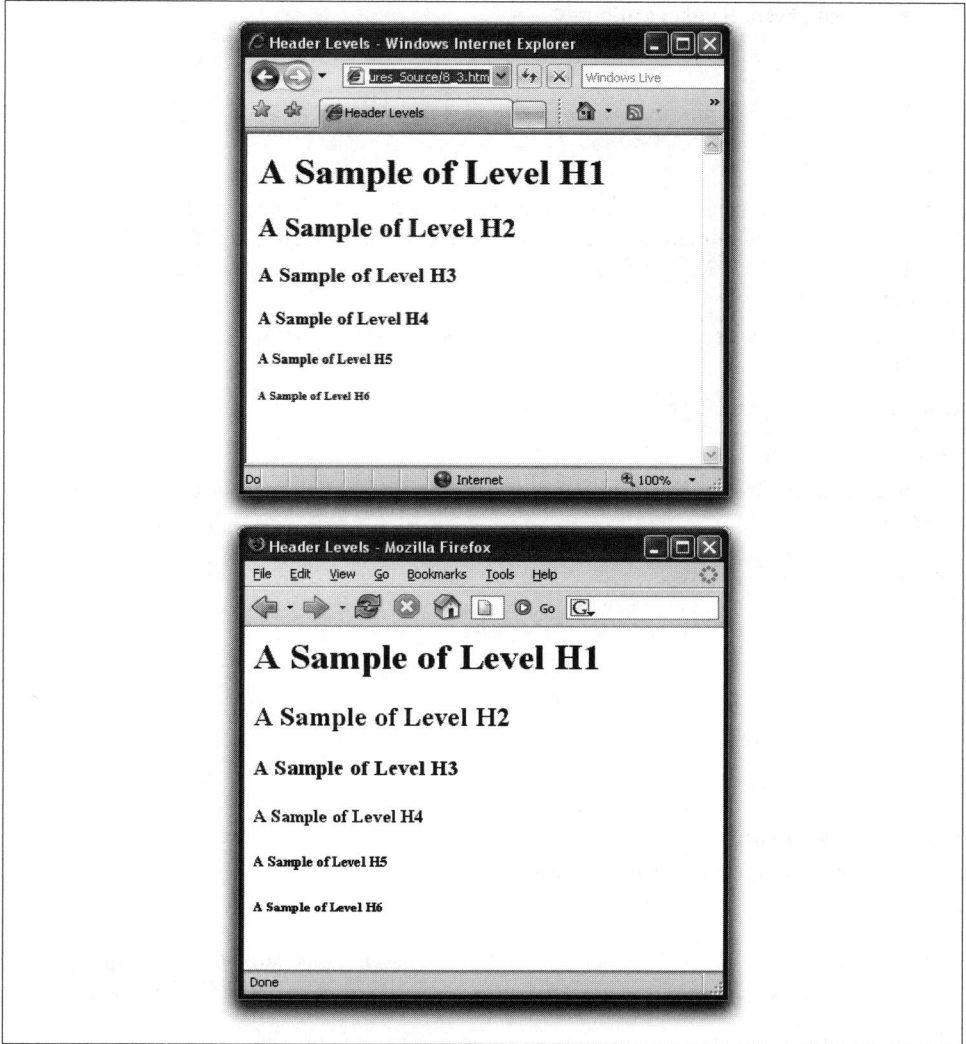

Figure 1-3. Heading levels in Internet Explorer 7 and Firefox 1.5

```
<h4>Mercury</h4>
...
```

Object Model Reference

[window.]document.getElementById(*elementID*)

Element-Specific Attributes

align

<head>

Element-Specific Event Handler Attributes
None.

align

IE *all* NN *all* Moz *all* Saf *all* Op 7 HTML *3.2*

align="*where*" *Optional*

Determines how the element's text is aligned inside the element's block. Mainstream browsers support alignment values for center, left, and right alignment. Transitional HTML 4 (but not XHTML) adds the possibility of a fully justified alignment for multilined content, as well.

The align attribute is deprecated in HTML 4 in favor of the text-align style sheet property.

Example   <h1 align="center">Article I</h1>

Value

The following table shows values for the align attribute. Values may be treated as case-insensitive values.

Value	IE 4+	Others	HTML4
center	•	•	•
justify	—	—	•
left	•	•	•
right	•	•	•

Default   left

Object Model Reference
[window.]document.getElementById(*elementID*).align

<head>

IE *all* NN *all* Moz *all* Saf *all* Op 7 HTML *all*

<head>...</head> *HTML End Tag: Optional*

The head element contains document information that is generally not rendered as part of the document in the browser window. At most, a browser displays the title element's content in the browser window's titlebar.

The content of the head element consists entirely of other elements that are intended to assist the browser in working with document data. Another classification of data, handled in one or more meta elements, can also assist search engines and document parsers to learn more about the document based on abstract information supplied by the author. The table below shows the elements that may be nested inside a head element according to three different specifications.

Although the HTML 4 or XHTML standards do not explicitly support the id attribute, browsers permit the attribute as part of their support for W3C DOM common properties of all elements.

Element	IE 4+	NN 4 and Mozilla	HTML 4 and XHTML
base	•	•	•
basefont	•	•	—
bgsound	•	—	—
isindex	—	•	•
link	•	•	•
meta	•	•	•
nextid	•	—	—
object	—	—	•
script	•	•	•
style	•	•	•
title	•	•	•

Example

```
<head>
<meta name="Author" content="Danny Goodman">
<style type="text/css">
    h1 {color:cornflowerblue}
</style>
</head>
```

Object Model Reference

```
[window.]document.getElementsByTagName("head")[0]
[window.]document.getElementById(elementID)
```

Element-Specific Attributes

profile

Element-Specific Event Handler Attributes

None.

profile

IE 6 NN n/a Moz all Saf all Op n/a HTML 4

profile="URLList"   Optional

A meta data profile is a separate file that defines one or more metadata property behaviors. The W3C leaves the precise application of this attribute to the whims of the browsers makers. Current browsers do nothing special as a result of assigning this attribute.

Example

```
<head profile="http://www.example.com/profiles/common">
    <meta name="Author" content="Jane Smith">
    <meta name="keywords" content="benefits,insurance,">
    ...
</head>
```

Value Any valid URL or browser profile constant.

Default Browser default.

Object Model Reference
```
[window.]document.firstChild.firstChild.profile
[window.]document.getElementsByTagName("head")[0].profile
[window.]document.getElementById(elementID).profile
```

\<hr\>

IE *all* NN *all* Moz *all* Saf *all* Op *7* HTML *all*

\<hr\>

HTML End Tag: Forbidden

The hr element draws a horizontal rule according to visual rules built into the browser with a variety of attribute controls. As a block element, the hr element starts and ends its rule on its own line, as if the element were surrounded by br elements. This element is not a content container, and many of the attributes that have been in use for a long time are deprecated in HTML 4 in favor of style sheet rules. The HTML recommendation leaves default appearance specifications up to the browser maker.

Example `<hr align="center" width="80%" />`

Object Model Reference
```
[window.]document.getElementById(elementID)
```

Element-Specific Attributes

align	color	noshade	size	width

Element-Specific Event Handler Attributes
None.

align

IE *all* NN *all* Moz *all* Saf *all* Op *7* HTML *3.2*

align="*where*"

Optional

Determines how the hr element is rendered in physical relation to the next outermost container (usually the body or html element). The align attribute is deprecated in HTML 4 in favor of the align style sheet property.

Example `<hr align="right" />`

Value One of three case-insensitive values: center | left | right.

Default center

Object Model Reference
```
[window.]document.getElementById(elementID).align
```

<hr>

color

color="*colorTripletOrName*"   *Optional*

Sets the color of the hr element. Setting the color attribute also turns on the noshade attribute.

Example   <hr color="salmon">

Value   A hexadecimal triplet or plain-language color name. See Appendix A for acceptable plain-language color names.

Default   None.

Object Model Reference
[window.]document.getElementById(*elementID*).color

noshade

noshade   *Optional*

The presence of the noshade attribute tells the browser to render the rule as a flat (not 3-D) line. In Internet Explorer only, if you set the color attribute, the browser changes the default line style to a no-shade style.

Example   <hr noshade>

Value   The presence of the attribute turns on no-shade rendering.

Default   Off.

Object Model Reference
[window.]document.getElementById(*elementID*).noShade

size

size="*pixelCount*"   *Optional*

You can override the default thickness of the hr element by assigning a value to the size attribute. The size attribute is deprecated in HTML 4 in favor of the height style sheet property.

Example   <hr size="4">

Value   Any positive integer. A setting of zero still draws a one-pixel thick rule.

Default   2

Object Model Reference
[window.]document.getElementById(*elementID*).size

<html>

width

width="*length*"   *Optional*

Defines the precise pixel width or percentage of available width (relative to the containing element) to draw the hr element rule. This attribute is deprecated in HTML 4 in favor of the width style sheet property.

Example   <hr width="75%">

Value   Any length value in pixels or percentage of available space.

Default   100%

Object Model Reference

[window.]document.getElementById(*elementID*).width

<html>

<html>...</html>   *HTML End Tag: Optional*

The html element is the container of the entire document content, including the head element. Typically, the html element start tag is the second line of an HTML file, following the Document Type Definition (DTD) statement (see the DOCTYPE element earlier in this chapter). If no DTD is provided in the file (it assumes the browser's default DTD), the html start tag becomes the first line of the file. The end tag should be in the last line of the file (but it does not have to stand on its own line).

Although the html element doesn't render per se, it is the root positioning context of a document in a purely W3C-compliant environment. This applies to W3C DOM browsers (Mozilla, Safari, Opera) and IE 6, the latter only when certain DOCTYPE definitions start the document. Otherwise, IE for Windows (this goes for IE 4 through IE 5.5) treats the body element as the root positioning context. If you don't specify margins, borders, or padding for the body element, you probably won't notice the difference.

The HTML 4 and XHTML standards do not include explicit support for id, class, or style attributes, but modern DHTML browsers support them.

Example

```
<html>
<head>
    ...
</head>
<body>
    ...
</body>
</html>
```

Element-Specific Attributes

version	xmlns

Element-Specific Event Handler Attributes
None.

version

version="*string*"   *Optional*

The version attribute is deprecated in HTML 4 and was never adopted by the major browsers until the desire to claim standards compliance led the maker to introduce the dead-end attribute. Originally intended to specify the HTML DTD version supported by the document, this information is universally supplied in the separate DTD statement (in the DOCTYPE element) above the html element in the document. Do not use this attribute.

Value   Any string of characters. The string must be inside a matching pair of (single or double) quotation marks.

Default   None.

xmlns

xmlns="*namespaceSpec*"   *Optional*

The W3C attribute and its fixed URI value should be in the html element of every XHTML document. Microsoft uses this attribute to allow IE 5 and later for Windows to reference elements that belong to non-HTML sources, such as the Microsoft implementation of behaviors (generic external script modules that can be applied to any element).

The xmlns attribute has two possible assignment operators, depending upon its usage. The equals sign (=) is used to assign a namespace specification (typically a URI) to a default namespace to be used by the current element and any of its child elements. The colon (:) is used to assign a namespace specification (URI) to a namespace prefix (so that the prefix acts like a shortcut namespace reference when used to denote attributes belonging to a particular namespace).

A common example is the you can use in an XHTML document to signify that the document is to use (by default) the W3C XHTML DTD as the source of meaning for elements and attributes in the rest of the document:

```
<html xmlns="http://www.w3.org/1999/xhtml" xml:lang="en" lang="en">
```

Namespace prefixes are used (primarily in XML documents) when you have a mixture of DTDs from multiple sources governing the element and attribute rules of the document. For example:

```
<html xmlns:au="http://www.writers.org/2002/author-guidelines">
```

Once the au prefix is assigned, it can be used in other elements within the scope of the <html> element to signify an attribute defined by the DTD associated with the namespace URI (theoretically allowing the "custom" attribute to validate correctly):

```
<p au:license="Creative Commons">...</p>
```

Example (IE 5+/Windows)
```
<html xmlns:MSIE>...</html>
```

Value

For XHTML, a fixed URI string: http://www.w3.org/1999/xhtml. For IE 5 and later namespace references, just a prefix name (MSIE for built-in behaviors), or a prefix and URI that acts as an additional identifier for the prefix. Note the colon delimiter.

Default   None.

‹i›

IE *all*   NN *all*   Moz *all*   Saf *all*   Op *7*   HTML *all*

‹i›...‹/i›   *HTML End Tag: Required*

The i element—one of several font style elements in HTML 4—renders its content in an italic version of the font face governing the next outermost HTML container. You can nest multiple font style elements to create combined styles, such as bold italic (‹b›‹i›bold-italic text‹/i›‹/b›).

It is up to the browser to italicize a system font or perhaps load an italic version of the currently specified font. If you are striving for font perfection, it is best to use style sheets (and perhaps downloadable fonts if supported by your target browsers) to specify a true italic font family, rather than risk the browser's extrapolation of an italic face from a system font.

You can take advantage of the containerness of this element by assigning style sheet rules to some or all i elements in a page. For example, you may wish all i elements to be in a red color. By assigning the style rule i{color:red}, you can apply the color to all elements with only a tiny bit of code.

Although this element is not deprecated in HTML 4, it would not be surprising to see it lose favor to the font-style style sheet property in the future.

Example   ‹p›This product is ‹i›new‹/i› and ‹i›improved‹/i›!‹/p›

Object Model Reference

[window.]document.getElementById(*elementID*)

Element-Specific Attributes

None.

Element-Specific Event Handler Attributes

None.

‹iframe›

IE *3*   NN *n/a*   Moz *all*   Saf *all*   Op *7*   HTML *4*

‹iframe›...‹/iframe›   *HTML End Tag: Required*

An iframe element creates an inline frame within the natural flow of a document's content. The frame is a rectangular space into which you may load any other HTML document (or use scripts to dynamically write content to the space). If you assign a value to the name attribute of an iframe element, you may supply that name as the value of a target attribute of a, form, or other element that lets you define a target for a destination or returned document.

<iframe>

Although an iframe element's rectangular space begins immediately following the content that comes before it (including in a line of text), all content following the end tag starts on the next line following the frame rectangle. Text leading up to the iframe element can be aligned in the same ways that text can be aligned around an img or object element.

Content between the start and end tags is ignored by browsers that support the iframe element. All others display such content as inline HTML content (as a way to let users know what they're missing and perhaps provide a link to related information). The Navigator 4 element that comes closest to the functionality and behavior of the iframe element is the ilayer element.

In most respects, an iframe behaves like a frame element, but without the need for a frameset. In fact, the element acts so much like a frame that if you reference it through frame referencing syntax (window.*frameName*), the returned object is the same type as a window object, rather than a frame element object.

While the iframe element validates in the transitional HTML 4 DTD along with the frame and frameset elements, only the iframe validates in the transitional XHTML DTD. The iframe validates in the frameset DTDs for HTML 4 and XHTML.

Example

```
<iframe src="quotes.html" width="150" height="90">
<a href="quotes.html" target="new" style="color:darkred">
 Click here to see the latest quotes </a>
</iframe>
```

Object Model Reference

[window.]document.getElementById(*elementID*)

Element-Specific Attributes

align	allowtransparency	datafld	datasrc	frameborder
height	hspace	longdesc	marginheight	marginwidth
name	scrolling	security	src	vspace
width				

Element-Specific Event Handler Attributes

None.

align

IE 3 NN *n/a* Moz *all* Saf *all* Op 7 HTML 4

align="*alignmentConstant*"   *Optional*

Determines how the rectangle of the iframe element aligns within the context of surrounding content. See "Alignment Constants" earlier in this chapter for a description of the possibilities defined for this element's attribute.

Example

```
<iframe src="quotes.html" width="150" height="90" align="center"></iframe>
```

Value   Case-insensitive constant value.

<iframe>

Default   left

Object Model Reference
[window.]document.getElementById(*elementID*).align

allowtransparency   IE *5.5* NN *n/a* Moz *n/a* Saf *n/* Op *n/a* HTML *n/a*
allowtransparency="*true*"   *Optional*

Specifies whether the background plane of the iframe element is transparent or opaque. To allow the main document to show through the iframe, set the allowtransparency attribute to true and either leave the iframe's background-color style property at its default setting (transparent) or set it explicitly to transparent. Note that this transparency affects the iframe element, independent of any document loaded into the iframe. Therefore, if you want a background style to affect only the iframe, you must set the allowtransparency attribute of the iframe to true and set the background of the element that appears behind any document loaded into the iframe (provided the document's background is transparent). An allowtransparency attribute setting of false (the default) does not allow background styles associated with the iframe element to be visible (but background styles in the iframe's nested document will be visible).

Example
<iframe src="album.html" height="400" width="400" allowtransparency="true"></iframe>

Value   Constant values: true | false

Default   false

Object Model Reference
[window.]document.getElementById(*elementID*).allowTransparency

datafld   IE *4* NN *n/a* Moz *n/a* Saf *n/a* Op *n/a* HTML *n/a*
datafld="*columnName*"   *Optional*

Used with IE data binding to associate a remote data source column name in lieu of a src attribute for an iframe element. The data source column must contain a valid URI (relative or absolute). A datasrc attribute must also be set for the element. Works only with text file data sources in IE 5/Mac.

Example   <iframe datasrc="DBSRC3" datafld="newsURL"></iframe>

Value   Case-sensitive identifier.

Default   None.

Object Model Reference
[window.]document.getElementById(*elementID*).dataFld

<iframe>

datasrc
IE *4*   NN *n/a*   Moz *n/a*   Saf *n/a*   Op *n/a*   HTML *n/a*

datasrc="*dataSourceName*"   *Optional*

Used with IE data binding to specify the ID of the page's object element that loads the data source object for remote data access. Content from the data source is specified via the datafld attribute. Works only with text file data sources in IE 5/Mac.

Example   <iframe datasrc="DBSRC3" datafld="newsURL"></iframe>

Value   Case-sensitive identifier.

Default   None.

Object Model Reference
[window.]document.getElementById(*elementID*).dataSrc

frameborder
IE *3*   NN *n/a*   Moz *all*   Saf *all*   Op *n/a*   HTML *4*

frameborder="*borderSwitch*"   *Optional*

Controls whether the iframe element displays a border. If you want linked-in documents to look as if they are embedded as part of the main document, turn off the frameborder attribute.

Example
<iframe src="quotes.html" width="150" height="90" frameborder="no"></iframe>

Value   On-off values for this attribute vary with the source. HTML 4 specifies the values of 1 (on) and 0 (off). Internet Explorer 4 and other supporting browsers accept the HTML value and yes or no.

Default   1

Object Model Reference
[window.]document.getElementById(*elementID*).frameBorder

height, width
IE *4*   NN *n/a*   Moz *all*   Saf *all*   Op *7*   HTML *4*

height="*length*" width="*length*"   *Optional*

These attributes establish the dimensions of the iframe element. Both attributes are deprecated in HTML 4 in favor of CSS height and width style properties.

Example   <iframe src="news.html" height="200" width="200">

Value   Any length value in pixels or percentage of available space.

Default   A width of 300 pixels; a height of 150 pixels.

Object Model Reference
[window.]document.getElementById(*elementID*).height
[window.]document.getElementById(*elementID*).width

hspace, vspace

IE *4* NN *n/a* Moz *n/a* Saf *n/a* Op *7* HTML *n/a*

hspace="*pixelCount*" vspace="*pixelCount*"   *Optional*

These attributes set padding around an iframe element within the content flow. The hspace attribute controls padding along the left and right edges (horizontal padding), and the vspace attribute controls padding along the top and bottom edges (vertical padding). Adding such padding provides an empty cushion around the frame. As an alternate (and to achieve cross-browser compatibility), you can specify the various margin style sheet settings, especially if you want to open space along only one edge.

Example   <iframe src="news.html" hspace="20" vspace="10">

Value   Any positive integer.

Default   0

Object Model Reference

[window.]document.getElementById(*elementID*).hspace
[window.]document.getElementById(*elementID*).vspace

longdesc

IE *6* NN *n/a* Moz *all* Saf *all* Op *n/a* HTML *4*

longdesc="*URL*"   *Optional*

Specifies a URL of a document that contains a longer description of the element than what the content of the title attribute reveals. One application of this attribute in future browsers is to retrieve an annotated description of the element for users who cannot read the browser screen. The **Properties** choice for Mozilla's context menu for this element displays a small window that includes an active link to the URL assigned to the attribute. Current mainstream browsers provide no other functionality for this attribute.

Example

<iframe longdesc="newsDesc.html" title="Navigation Bar" src="news.html">
</iframe>

Value   Any valid URI, including complete and relative URLs.

Default   None.

marginheight, marginwidth

IE *3* NN *n/a* Moz *all* Saf *all* Op *7* HTML *4*

marginheight="*pixelCount*" marginwidth="*pixelCount*"   *Optional*

Determine the number of pixels between the inner edge of a frame and the content rendered inside the frame. The marginheight attribute controls space along the top and (when scrolled) the bottom edges of a frame; the marginwidth attribute controls space on the left and right edges of a frame. The HTML 4 specification leaves default behavior up to browsers.

Browsers insert their default margins (in the range between 8 and 14 pixels) inside a frame. But if you attempt to override the default behavior, be aware that setting any one of these two attributes causes the value of the other to go to zero. Therefore, unless you want the content to be absolutely flush with various frame edges, you need to assign values to both attributes.

Example

<iframe src="news.html" marginheight="20" marginwidth="14"></iframe>

Value   Any positive integer value or zero.

Default   Varies with browser and operating system.

Object Model Reference

[window.]document.getElementById(*elementID*).marginHeight
[window.]document.getElementById(*elementID*).marginWidth

name

name="*elementIdentifier*"   *Optional*

When links and forms must load their destination or returned documents into frames other than the one holding the link or form, those elements have target attributes indicating which frame receives the new content. To direct such content to a frame, the frame must have a value assigned to its name attribute. That same value is assigned to the target attribute of the a or form element.

Example   <iframe name="news" id="news" src="news.html"></iframe>

Value   Case-sensitive identifier.

Default   None.

Object Model Reference

[window.]document.getElementById(*elementID*).name

scrolling

scrolling="*featureSwitch*"   *Optional*

By default, browsers add vertical and/or horizontal scrollbars when the content loaded into an inline frame exceeds the visible content region of the element. Scrollbars can affect the layout of some content because they occupy space normally devoted to content (that is, the frame does not expand to accommodate scrollbars). Also, due to differences in default font sizes in browsers and operating system versions, a given collection of text content may display differently in different clients. If you want to prevent scrollbars from appearing in the frame, set the scrolling attribute to no; if you want scrollbars to be in the frame at all times, set the attribute to yes. In the latter case, if the content does not require scrolling, the scrollbars are visible, but disabled.

Setting the scrolling attribute to no should be used only after you have tested that mission-critical content is always visible in the frame on all browsers and platforms. If the frame is set to not scroll, some users might not be able to see all content of the frame.

<iframe>

In lieu of this attribute, you may also use the CSS overflow style property. Microsoft provides extra axis-specific control over scrollbars via their overflow-x and overflow-y style properties.

Example	<iframe src="news.html" scrolling="no"></iframe>
Value	Constant values: auto | no | yes.
Default	auto

Object Model Reference
[window.]document.getElementById(*elementID*).scrolling

security   IE 6   NN *n/a*   Moz *n/a*   Saf *n/a*   Op *n/a*   HTML *n/a*
security="restricted"   *Optional*

When activated, this attribute raises the security level of the inline frame to the Restricted level of the Windows Security preferences settings. Such a frame's content may not execute scripts.

Example	<iframe src="news.html" security="restricted"></iframe>
Value	Constant value: restricted.
Default	None.

src   IE 3   NN *n/a*   Moz *all*   Saf *all*   Op 7   HTML 4
src="*URL*"   *Optional*

Defines the URL of the content to be loaded into the iframe element. The URL can be an absolute URL or one relative to the URL of the document containing the frameset specifications. You may also use the javascript: pseudo-URL to have the returned value of a script appear in the frame. If you omit the src attribute, the frame opens empty.

Example	<iframe src="news.html"></iframe>
Value	A complete or relative URL or a javascript: pseudo-URL.
Default	None.

Object Model Reference
[window.]document.getElementById(*elementID*).src

vspace

See hspace.

width

See height.

<ilayer>

IE *n/a*   NN |4| Moz *n/a*   Saf *n/a*   Op *n/a*   HTML *n/a*

<ilayer>...</ilayer>   *HTML End Tag: Required*

An ilayer element is an inline version of the Navigator 4-specific layer element. In some respects, the ilayer element works like the iframe element in Internet Explorer, but an ilayer is automatically regarded as a positionable element in Navigator 4's object model (e.g., like a block-level element with a CSS position: attribute set to relative). As a result, many of the attributes are the same as the layer element and are named according to the Navigator 4 way of positioning, sizing, and stacking positionable elements.

Content for an ilayer element can be read in from a separate file (with the src attribute) or wired into the current document by placing the HTML between the start and end tags. You can include both types of content in the same ilayer element. Content from the src document is rendered first (as its own block-level element), with additional content starting on its own line below the external content's rectangle.

Example

<ilayer id="thingy1" src="quotes.html" width="150" height="90"></ilayer>

Object Model Reference

[window.]document.*layerName*

Element-Specific Attributes

above	background	below	bgcolor	clip
height	id	left	name	src
top	visibility	width	z-index	

Element-Specific Event Handler Attributes

Handler	NN	Others	HTML
onblur	4	n/a	n/a
onfocus	4	n/a	n/a
onload	4	n/a	n/a
onmousedown	4[a]	n/a	n/a
onmouseout	4[a]	n/a	n/a
onmouseover	4[a]	n/a	n/a
onmouseup	4[a]	n/a	n/a

[a] Event capture mode only.

above

IE *n/a*   NN |4| Moz *n/a*   Saf *n/a*   Op *n/a*   HTML *n/a*

above="*layerID*"   *Optional*

Names the positionable element that is to be above (in front of) the current ilayer in the stacking order. This is a different way to set the z-index attribute that does not rely on an arbitrary numbering system. If you use the above attribute, do not use the below or z-index attribute for the same ilayer element.

Example   <ilayer id="thingy4" src="quotes.html" above="thingy3"></ilayer>

Value   Case-sensitive identifier.

Default   None.

Object Model Reference
[window.]document.*layerName*.above

background   IE *n/a* NN |4| Moz *n/a* Saf *n/a* Op *n/a* HTML *n/a*
background="*URL*"   *Optional*

Specifies an image file that is used as a backdrop to the text and other content of the ilayer element. Unlike normal images that get loaded into browser content, a background image loads in its original size (without scaling) and tiles to fill the available layer space. Smaller images download faster but are obviously repeated more often in the background. Animated GIFs are also allowable but very distracting to the reader. When selecting a background image, be sure it is very muted in comparison to the main content so that the content stands out clearly. Background images, if used at all, should be extremely subtle.

Example
<ilayer id="thingy4" src="quotes.html" background="blueCrinkle.jpg"></ilayer>

Value   Any valid URL to an image file, including complete and relative URLs.

Default   None.

Object Model Reference
[window.]document.*layerName*.background

below   IE *n/a* NN |4| Moz *n/a* Saf *n/a* Op *n/a* HTML *n/a*
below="*layerID*"   *Optional*

Names the positionable element that is to be below (behind) the current ilayer in the stacking order. This is a different way to set the z-index attribute that does not rely on an arbitrary numbering system. If you use the below attribute, do not use the above or z-index attribute for the same ilayer element.

Example   <ilayer id="thingy4" src="quotes.html" below="thingy5"></ilayer>

Value   Case-sensitive identifier.

Default   None.

Object Model Reference
[window.]document.*layerName*.below

bgcolor

bgcolor="*colorTripletOrName*"   *Optional*

Establishes a fill color (behind the text and other content) for the entire layer rectangle. If you combine a bgcolor and background, any transparent areas of the background image let the background color show through.

Example	<ilayer src="quotes.html" bgcolor="tan"></ilayer>
Value	A hexadecimal triplet or plain-language color name. A setting of empty is interpreted as "#000000" (black). See Appendix A for acceptable plain-language color names.
Default	Varies with operating system.

Object Model Reference
[window.]document.*layerName*.bgColor

clip

clip="[*leftPixel, topPixel,*] *rightPixel, bottomPixel*"   *Optional*

A clipping region is a rectangular view to the full ilayer content. Only content that is within the clipping rectangle can be seen on the page. The default value of the clip attribute is determined by the space required to display the content as it naturally flows into the element. Setting the clip attribute lets you rein in long content that might flow beyond a fixed rectangle desired for the page design.

Example	<ilayer src="quotes.html" clip="50,50"></ilayer>

Value

clip attribute values are pixel measures from the top and left edges of the element as it flows in the document. The order of values is clockwise from the left edge, around the rectangle sides: left, top, right, bottom. If you supply only two values, Navigator assumes the left and top values are zero, meaning that you wish to adjust only the right and bottom edges. Thus, a setting of "50,50" means that the clipping region is 50-pixels square, starting at the top-left corner of the layer's rectangle. If you want the same size view, but starting 10 pixels in from the left, the clip attribute setting becomes "10,0,60,50".

Default   Naturally flowing viewing area of ilayer content.

Object Model Reference
[window.]document.*layerName*.clip.left
[window.]document.*layerName*.clip.top
[window.]document.*layerName*.clip.right
[window.]document.*layerName*.clip.bottom

height, width

IE *n/a* NN |4| Moz *n/a* Saf *n/a* Op *n/a* HTML *n/a*

height="*length*" width="*length*"   *Optional*

Define the minimum size of the layer as it flows in the document. When you add content to the layer, however, the attribute settings do not restrict the amount of the content that is visible along either axis. For example, if you display an image in an ilayer that is 120 pixels wide by 90 pixels high, the actual visible size of an ilayer element whose height and width attributes are set to a smaller size expands to allow the full image to appear. The same happens to text or other content: the viewable region expands to allow all content to appear. To restrict the visible portion of the content, set the clip attribute.

Setting the height and width attributes to specific sizes is helpful when you are creating a colored or patterned rectangle (via the bgcolor or background attributes) to act as an underlying layer beneath some other positioned content. Without content pushing on the edges of the ilayer, the height and width attributes set the clipping region to their sizes.

Example   `<ilayer bgcolor="yellow" height="100" width="100"></ilayer>`

Value   Positive integer values (optionally quoted) or percentage values (quoted). You can reduce both values to zero to not only hide the element (which you can also do with the visibility attribute), but prevent the element from occupying any page space.

Default   Naturally flowing viewing area of ilayer content.

Object Model Reference

```
[window.]document.layerName.height
[window.]document.layerName.width
```

id

IE *n/a* NN |4| Moz *n/a* Saf *n/a* Op *n/a* HTML *n/a*

id="*elementIdentifier*"   *Optional*

A unique identifier that distinguishes this element from all the rest in the document. This is the identifier used as values for the above and below attributes. Scripts also use the id attribute value as the ilayer element's name for object references.

Example
`<ilayer id="oldYeller" bgcolor="yellow" height="100" width="100"></ilayer>`

Value   Case-sensitive identifier.

Default   None.

Object Model Reference

```
[window.]document.layerName.name
```

left, top

IE *n/a* NN |4| Moz *n/a* Saf *n/a* Op *n/a* HTML *n/a*

left="*pixelCount*" top="*pixelCount*" *Optional*

Define the positioned offset of the left and top edges of the layer relative to the spot in the document where the ilayer element would normally appear. The precise location relative to the page varies because an ilayer element is an inline layer, which means it can start anywhere within normally flowing HTML content. When you set either of these attributes, Navigator 4 preserves the space in the document where the ilayer element appears, rather than cinch up surrounding content to fill space vacated by the element that has shifted its location. You are therefore likely to set these attributes for an ilayer only when attempting to accomplish a look tailored to very customized content (perhaps an ilayer amid inflow images).

Example   <ilayer bgcolor="yellow" left="10" top="50"></ilayer>

Value   Positive integer values (optionally quoted).

Default   0

Object Model Reference

[window.]document.*layerName*.left
[window.]document.*layerName*.top

name

IE *n/a* NN |4| Moz *n/a* Saf *n/a* Op *n/a* HTML *n/a*

name="*elementIdentifier*" *Optional*

A unique identifier that distinguishes this element from all the rest in the document. This is the identifier used as values for the above and below attributes. The name attribute is interchangeable with the id attribute for object references.

Example

<ilayer name="oldYeller" bgcolor="yellow" height="100" width="100"></ilayer>

Value   Case-sensitive identifier.

Default   None.

Object Model Reference

[window.]document.*layerName*.name

src

IE *n/a* NN |4| Moz *n/a* Saf *n/a* Op *n/a* HTML *n/a*

src="*URL*" *Optional*

To load the content of an external HTML file into an ilayer element, assign the URL of that file to the src attribute. Any HTML content between the ilayer start and end tags is rendered on the page after the content loaded from the src URL. If you omit the src attribute, only content between the tags is rendered. Scripts can change the corresponding object property (src) after the document has loaded to dynamically change content within the ilayer element (without reloading the main document).

Example	<ilayer src="quotes.html"></ilayer>
Value	A complete or relative URL.
Default	None.

Object Model Reference

[window.]document.*layerName*.src

top

See left.

visibility

IE *n/a*   NN |4| Moz *n/a*   Saf *n/a*   Op *n/a*   HTML *n/a*

visibility="*visibilityConstant*"   *Optional*

Determines whether Navigator 4 displays the ilayer element. The default behavior is for a layer to inherit the visibility attribute of its next outermost (parent) layer. For an ilayer element that is part of the basic document body, this means that the layer is seen by default (the base layer is always visible). To hide a layer when the page loads, set the visibility attribute to "hidden". You need to set the attribute to "show" only if the ilayer element is nested within another layer with a visibility value that is set to (or is inherited as) "hidden".

Regardless of the visibility attribute setting, an ilayer element always occupies its normal inflow space in the document. This allows Navigator 4 to change the visibility on the fly (via scripting) without reloading the document. (Navigator 4 does not automatically reflow changed content.)

Example	<ilayer src="quotes.html" visibility="hidden"></ilayer>
Value	One of the accepted constants: hidden | inherit | visible.
Default	inherit

Object Model Reference

[window.]document.*layerName*.visibility

width

See height.

z-index

IE *n/a*   NN |4| Moz *n/a*   Saf *n/a*   Op *n/a*   HTML *n/a*

z-index="*layerNumber*"   *Optional*

Controls the positioning of layers along the Z-axis (front-to-back) of the document relative to the next outermost layer container. When the z-index values of two or more positionable elements within the same container (such as the base document layer) are identical numbers, the loading order of the elements in the HTML source code controls the stacking

<img>

order, with the later elements stacked in front of earlier ones. The default z-index value for all positionable elements is zero. Therefore, if you want only one positionable element to appear in front of all the others that stack in their default order, you simply assign any positive value (even 1) to that stand-out element. Stacking order of positionable elements can be changed on-the-fly via scripting. See also the above and below attributes.

Example   `<ilayer src="quotes.html" z-index="1"></ilayer>`

Value   Any integer.

Default   0

Object Model Reference
`[window.]document.layerName.zIndex`

<img>

IE *all*   NN *all*   Moz *all*   Saf *all*   Op *7*   HTML *all*

`<img>`

HTML End Tag: Forbidden

The img element displays a graphical image in whatever MIME types the browser is equipped to handle. Common image types are GIF and JPEG, but modern browsers are frequently capable of decoding bitmapped images in PNG and BMP formats (unless helper application settings reroute those file types to external applications). img elements are inline elements, appearing anywhere in the document you specify, including in the middle of a line of text. A large number of attributes affecting visual presentation of the element are deprecated in HTML 4 in favor of style sheet rules. You will be able to use the attributes safely for many browser generations to come, however, because of the need to be backward compatible with the large collection of image-laden documents already on the Web. Note, too, that if you intend to use style sheets for img element borders and margins in Navigator 4, you must wrap the img element inside div or span elements and assign the style sheets to the surrounding element. This workaround works with all other CSS-aware browsers, so you can use style sheets in cross-browser deployment.

If you want to make an entire image a clickable link, wrap the img element inside an a element. To eliminate the typical link border around the image, set the border attribute to 0. And for image maps (where different segments of an image link to different destinations), the HTML recommendation encourages the use of client-side image maps (via the usemap attribute) over the server-side image map (ismap). For nonlinking action, you can assign an onclick event handler to an image in IE 4 or later and W3C DOM browsers. The downside is that you'll have to control the cursor style with the :hover CSS pseudo-class (Mozilla, Safari, IE 7, Opera 9) or other events.

To be backward compatible with earlier scriptable browsers, it is advisable to include height and width attribute assignments in all img element tags. When values are assigned to these attributes, the browser renders pages more quickly because it doesn't have to wait for the image to load in order to determine its size and organize other content on the page.

Example
`<img src="mtRushmore.jpg" height="90" width="120" alt="Mount Rushmore" />`

Object Model Reference

```
[window.]document.imageName
[window.]document.images[i]
[window.]document.getElementById(elementID)
```

Element-Specific Attributes

align	alt	border	datafld	datasrc
dynsrc	galleryimage	height	hspace	ismap
longdesc	loop	lowsrc	name	src
start	suppress	usemap	vspace	width

Element-Specific Event Handler Attributes

Handler	IE	NN	Others	HTML
onabort	4	3	all	n/a
onerror	4	3	all	n/a
onload	4	3	all	n/a

align

IE *all* NN *all* Moz *all* Saf *all* Op 7 HTML *all*

align="*where*"   *Optional*

Determines how the img element is rendered in physical relation to the element's next outermost container and surrounding content. Some settings also let you "float" the image to the left or right margin and let surrounding text wrap around the image (but no wrapping with a centered image).

Most of the rules for alignment-constant values cited at the beginning of this chapter apply to the img element. Typically, align attributes are deprecated in HTML 4 in favor of the style sheet properties.

Example

```
<img src="surferDude.gif" align="right" alt="Surfer" height="100" width="200">
```

Value

Each browser defines a different set of values for this attribute. Although the align attribute has a long heritage, not all values do. The more esoteric values, such as absmiddle and baseline, were added to browser offerings in Navigator 3 and Internet Explorer 4, but not added to the W3C repertoire. Assigning different values to multiple images in the same vicinity on the page can result in unpredictable rendering and positioning of the images and surrounding content. Select value(s) from the following table that work for your deployment:

Value	IE 4+	NN 3+/Mozilla/Safari	Opera	HTML 4
absbottom	•	•	•	—
absmiddle	•	•	•a	—

Value	IE 4+	NN 3+/Mozilla/Safari	Opera	HTML 4	
baseline	•	•	•	—	
bottom	•	•	•	•	
left	•	•	•	•	
middle	•	•	•	•	
right	•	•	•	•	
texttop	•	•	—	—	
top	•	•	•	•	

a Unlike other supporting browsers, Opera does not differentiate absmiddle from middle. Both are treated the same way that other browsers treat middle.

Default   bottom

Object Model Reference

```
[window.]document.imageName.align
[window.]document.images[i].align
[window.]document.getElementById(elementID).align
```

alt   IE *all* NN *all* Moz *all* Saf *all* Op *7* HTML *all*

alt="*textMessage*"   *Required*

In a world littered with graphical browsers, it is often hard to remember that not every browser downloads images or that not every web surfer can see the images. Aside from those using VT100 terminals with browsers such as Lynx, pocket computers often offer better performance when images don't have to be downloaded and rendered. Vision impaired users may not be able to see an image, but could benefit by knowing what an image is about. Text-only browsers display the text assigned to an img element's alt attribute where the img element appears on the page. Browsers that speak the page's text also speak the alt text. The alt attribute should contain a brief description of what the image is (or an empty string for images used as space fillers). The HTML recommendation considers this capability so important that it calls the alt attribute a requirement for the img element.

Example

```
<img src="navbar.gif" usemap="#nav" alt="Navigation Bar" width="400" height="50">
```

Value   Any quoted string of characters.

Default   None.

Object Model Reference

```
[window.]document.imageName.alt
[window.]document.images[i].alt
[window.]document.getElementById(elementID).alt
```

border

border="*pixels*"   *Optional*

Controls the thickness of a border around an img element. Default rendering of the border is in black, but if the img element is wrapped inside an a element, the border takes on the document's various link colors (depending on link state). If you want a different color for a plain border, use style sheets (with the appropriate div or span wrapper for Navigator 4). When a link surrounds the image, you can eliminate the colored border altogether by setting the border attribute value to zero.

Example

```
<img src="surferDude.gif" alt="Surfer" border="3" height="100" width="200">
```

Value   Any integer pixel value.

Default   0

Object Model Reference

```
[window.]document.imageName.border
[window.]document.images[i].border
[window.]document.getElementById(elementID).border
```

datafld

datafld="*columnName*"   *Optional*

Used with IE data binding to associate a remote data source column name with the src attribute URL of an img element. A datasrc attribute must also be set for the img element. Works only with text file data sources in IE 5/Mac.

Example

```
<img datasrc="DBSRC3" alt="Current Radar" datafld="img3URL" height="100"
width="150">
```

Value   Case-sensitive identifier.

Default   None.

Object Model Reference

```
[window.]document.imageName.dataFld
[window.]document.images[i].dataFld
[window.]document.getElementById(elementID).dataFld
```

datasrc

datasrc="*dataSourceName*"   *Optional*

Used with IE data binding to specify the ID of the page's object element that loads the data source object for remote data access. Content from the data source is specified via the datafld attribute. Works only with text file data sources in IE 5/Mac.

<img>

Example

```
<img datasrc="DBSRC3" alt="Current Radar" datafld="img3URL" height="100"
width="150">
```

Value   Case-sensitive identifier.

Default   None.

Object Model Reference

```
[window.]document.imageName.dataSrc
[window.]document.images[i].dataSrc
[window.]document.getElementById(elementID).dataSrc
```

dynsrc   IE *4* NN *n/a* Moz *n/a* Saf *n/a* Op *n/a* HTML *n/a*

dynsrc="*URL*"   *Optional*

Internet Explorer 4 and later allows video clips (and VRML) to be displayed via the img
element (as an alternate to the embed or object element). To help the browser differentiate
between a dynamic and static image source, you use the dynsrc attribute in place of the src
attribute to load the video clip. All other visual aspects of the img element are therefore
immediately applicable to the rectangular region devoted to playing the video clip. See also
the loop attribute for controlling the frequency of clip play and the start attribute.

Example   `<img dynsrc="snowman.avi" loop="3" height="100" width="150">`

Value   Any valid URL, including complete and relative URLs.

Default   None.

Object Model Reference

```
[window.]document.images[i].dynsrc
[window.]document.imageName.dynsrc
[window.]document.getElementById(elementID).dynsrc
```

galleryimg   IE |*6*| NN *n/a* Moz *n/a* Saf *n/a* Op *n/a* HTML *n/a*

dynsrc="*featureSwitch*"   *Optional*

Sets whether images that are at least 130 pixels high and wide display the Windows OS
"My Pictures" toolbar during mouse rollovers in IE 6. This tool bar provides quick-click
shortcuts to save, print, or email the image. You cannot control which buttons appear in
the toolbar.

Example

```
<img src="rushmore.jpg" alt="Mount Rushmore" height="240" width="550"
galleryimg="no">
```

Value   Constant value: yes | true | no | false.

Default   yes

Object Model Reference

[window.]document.images[i].galleryImg
[window.]document.*imageName*.galleryImg
[window.]document.getElementById(*elementID*).galleryImg

height, width

IE *all* NN *all* Moz *all* Saf *all* Op *7* HTML *3.2*

height="*length*" width="*length*"   *Optional*

Define the dimensions for the space on the page reserved for the image, regardless of the actual size of the image. For best performance (and backward script compatibility), you should set these attributes to the actual pixel height and width of the source image. If you supply a different measure, the browser scales the image (not very well) to fit the space defined by these attributes.

Example   <img src="surferDude.gif" alt="Surfer" height="100" width="200">

Value   Positive integer values or percentage values.

Default   Actual size of source image.

Object Model Reference

[window.]document.*imageName*.height
[window.]document.images[i].height
[window.]document.getElementById(*elementID*).height
[window.]document.*imageName*.width
[window.]document.images[i].width
[window.]document.getElementById(*elementID*).width

hspace, vspace

IE *all* NN *all* Moz *all* Saf *all* Op *7* HTML *3.2*

hspace="*pixelCount*" vspace="*pixelCount*"   *Optional*

Define a margin that acts as whitespace padding around the visual content of the img element. The hspace establishes a margin on the left and right sides of the image rectangle; the vspace establishes a margin on the top and bottom sides of the image rectangle. Both attributes are deprecated in HTML 4 in favor of the margin- or padding-related CSS properties.

Example   <img src="desk3.gif" alt="My Desktop" vspace="10" hspace="10">

Value   Integer representing the number of pixels for the width of the margin on the relevant sides of the img element's rectangle.

Default   0

Object Model Reference

[window.]document.*imageName*.hspace
[window.]document.images[i].hspace
[window.]document.getElementById(*elementID*).hspace
[window.]document.*imageName*.vspace
[window.]document.images[i].vspace
[window.]document.getElementById(*elementID*).vspace

ismap

ismap   *Optional*

The Boolean `ismap` attribute tells the browser that the `img` element is acting as a server-side image map. To turn an image into a server-side image map, wrap the `img` element with an a element whose `href` attribute points to the URL of the CGI program that knows how to interpret the click coordinate information. The browser appends coordinate information about the click to the URL like a GET form method appends form element data to the `action` attribute URL. In the following example, if a user clicks at the coordinate point 50, 25, the browser sends "http://www.example.com/cgi-bin/nav.pl?50,25" to the server. A server CGI program named `nav.pl` might examine the region in which the coordinate point appears and send the relevant HTML back to the client.

Browsers also allow client-side image maps (see the `usemap` attribute), which operate more quickly for the user because there is no communication with the server to carry out the examination of the click coordinate point.

Example
```
<a href="http://www.example.com/cgi-bin/nav" target="main">
<img src="navbar.gif" alt="Navigation Bar" ismap height="90" width="120">
</a>
```

Value   The presence of the attribute turns the feature on.

Default   Off.

Object Model Reference
```
[window.]document.imageName.isMap
[window.]document.images[i].isMap
[window.]document.getElementById(elementID).isMap
```

longdesc

longdesc="*URL*"   *Optional*

Specifies a URL of a document that contains a longer description of the element than what the content of the `alt` or `title` attributes reveal. One application of this attribute in future browsers is to retrieve an annotated description of the element for users who cannot read the browser screen. The **Properties** choice for Mozilla's context menu for this element displays a small window that includes an active link to the URL assigned to the attribute. Current mainstream browsers provide no other functionality for this attribute.

Example
```
<img longdesc="navDesc.html" alt="Navigation Bar" src="navbar.jpg">
```

Value   Any valid URL, including complete and relative URLs.

Default   None.

Object Model Reference
```
[window.]document.imageName.longDesc
[window.]document.images[i].longDesc
[window.]document.getElementById(elementID).longDesc
```

loop
IE 3   NN *n/a*   Moz *n/a*   Saf *n/a*   Op *n/a*   HTML *n/a*

loop="*loopCount*"   *Optional*

If you specify a video clip with the dynsrc attribute, the loop attribute controls how many times the clip should play ("loop") after it loads. If you set the value to zero, the clip loads but does not play initially. Video clips that are not currently running play when the user double-clicks on the image, but you may need to provide instructions for that on the page because there are no other obvious controls. This attribute does not control animated *.gif* playback.

Example

```
<img dynsrc="snowman.avi" alt="Snowman Movie"loop="3" height="100" width="150">
```

Value   Any positive integer or zero.

Default   1

Object Model Reference
```
[window.]document.imageName.loop
[window.]document.images[i].loop
[window.]document.getElementById(elementID).loop
```

lowsrc
IE 4   NN 3   Moz *all*   Saf *n/a*   Op *n/a*   HTML *n/a*

lowsrc="*URL*"   *Optional*

Not everyone has a fast Internet connection and that high-resolution images can take a long time to download to the client. To fill the void, the lowsrc attribute lets the author specify a URL of a lower-resolution (or alternate) image to download into the document space first. The lowsrc image should be the same pixel size as the primary src image.

Example

```
<img src="navbar.jpg" alt="Navigation Bar" lowsrc="navbarBW.jpg" height="60"
width="300">
```

Value   Any valid URL, including complete and relative URLs.

Default   None.

Object Model Reference
```
[window.]document.imageName.lowsrc
[window.]document.images[i].lowsrc
[window.]document.getElementById(elementID).lowsrc
```

name
IE 4   NN 3   Moz *all*   Saf *all*   Op 7   HTML 4

name="*elementIdentifier*"   *Optional*

If you are scripting an image (especially swapping precached images), backward-compatible scripting utilizes the name attribute value to reference the img object because the id attribute did not exist. References by name are more reliable than by numeric index within the document.images array because you can rearrange or delete images at any time and still maintain references to the remaining named images. For modern browsers only, you can use the id attribute value in place of the name attribute.

Example

```
<img name="mugshot" id="mugshot" alt="My face" src="janem.jpg" height="90"
width="80">
```

Value   Case-sensitive identifier.

Default   None.

Object Model Reference
```
[window.]document.images[i].name
[window.]document.imageName.name
[window.]document.getElementById(elementID).name
```

src   IE *all*   NN *all*   Moz *all*   Saf *all*   Op *7*   HTML *all*
```
src="URL"
```                                                                                      *Required*

URL to a file containing image data that is displayed through the img element. With the exception of specifying a dynsrc attribute in Internet Explorer for video clips or datasrc for IE data binding, the src attribute is required if you want to see any image in the img element space. The browser must be equipped to handle the image MIME type. On the World Wide Web, the most common image formats are GIF and JPEG. HTML or XHTML validation, of course, requires the src attribute and doesn't accept the IE attribute alternatives.

Example   `<img src="surferDude.gif" alt="Surfer" height="100" width="200">`

Value   A complete or relative URL.

Default   None.

Object Model Reference
```
[window.]document.images[i].src
[window.]document.imageName.src
[window.]document.getElementById(elementID).src
```

start   IE *4*   NN *n/a*   Moz *n/a*   Saf *n/a*   Op *n/a*   HTML *n/a*
```
start="videoStartType"
```                                                                                      *Optional*

Whenever you set the dynsrc attribute of an img to display a video clip in Internet Explorer, you can direct the element to start playing the video immediately after the video file loads or when the user rolls the cursor over the image. The start attribute lets you decide the best user interface for your page.

Example

```
<img dynsrc="snowman.avi" loop="1" start="mouseover" height="100" width="150">
```

Value   One of the two case-insensitive constant values: fileopen | mouseover.

Default   fileopen

Object Model Reference
```
[window.]document.images[i].start
[window.]document.imageName.start
[window.]document.getElementById(elementID).start
```

suppress   IE *n/a* NN |4| Moz *n/a* Saf *n/a* Op *n/a* HTML *n/a*

suppress="*featureSwitch*"   *Optional*

When engaged, this attribute prevents Navigator 4 from displaying the generic image icon, alt text, and raised image area while the image is downloading. If the image fails to load, the artifacts appear in the image space as if the attribute were not turned on.

Example
```
<img src="surferDude.gif" alt="Surfer" height="150" width="250" suppress="true">
```

Value   Boolean string value: true | false.

Default   false

usemap   IE *all* NN *all* Moz *all* Saf *all* Op *7* HTML *3.2*

usemap="*mapURL*"   *Optional*

You can define a client-side image map with the help of the map and area elements. The map element is a named container for one or more area elements. Each area element sets a "hot" area on an image and assigns a link destination (and other settings) for a response to the user clicking in that region. The purpose of the usemap attribute is to establish a connection between the img element and a named map element in the same document. In some respects, the map element's name is treated like an anchor in that the "address" of the map element is the element's name preceded by a # symbol.

Example
```
<img src="navbar.gif" alt="Navigation Bar" usemap="#navigation"
height="90" width="120">
```

Value   A URL to the map element in the same document (a hash symbol plus the map name).

Default   None.

Object Model Reference
```
[window.]document.imageName.useMap
[window.]document.images[i].useMap
[window.]document.getElementById(elementID).useMap
```

vspace

See hspace.

width

See height.

<input>

<input>

IE *all* **NN** *all* **Moz** *all* **Saf** *all* **Op** *7* **HTML** *all*

HTML End Tag: Forbidden

An input element is sometimes known as a form control, although not all input elements are visible on the page. For the most part, an input element provides a place for users to enter text, click buttons, and make selections from lists. The data gathered from this interaction can be submitted to a server-side program (when the surrounding form element is submitted), or it may be used strictly on the client as a way for users to interact with client-side scripts. Server applications also commonly embed session data in a page's hidden input elements so that the data gets submitted with the next form submission—one way to cascade data gathering across multiple form pages without maintaining the data temporarily on the server between page deliveries.

Prior to HTML 4, input elements were supposed to be wrapped by a form element in all instances. This restriction is loosening up, but Navigator 4 still requires the form wrapper in order to render input elements.

The primary attribute that determines the kind of control displayed on the page is the type attribute. This attribute can have one of the following values in standard HTML: button, checkbox, file, hidden, image, password, radio, reset, submit, or text.* The Web Forms 2.0 standard (first natively supported in Opera 9 and detailed at *http://www.whatwg.org/specs/*) offers several other input types: add, date, datetime, datetime-local, email, month, move-up, move-down, number, range, time, url, and week. Not all input element types utilize the full range of attributes defined for the input element; sometimes a single attribute has different powers with different element types. For each attribute of the input element, the listing specifies the types to which it applies. Although the textarea element has its own tag, it is often treated like another form control.

Example

```
<form method="POST" action="http://www.example.com/cgi-bin/query.pl">
First Name: <input type="text" name="first" id="first" maxlength="15"><br>
Last Name: <input type="text" name="last" id="last" maxlength="25"><br>
ZIP Code: <input type="text" name="zip" id="zip" maxlength="10"><br>
<input type="reset">
<input type="submit">
</form>
```

---

* Apple has implemented two additional input element types (search and range) which are intended for use in Dashboard widgets. The search type displays a Mac OS X search field, while the range type displays a slider control. Although these elements render in Safari 2, their details are not documented here. Instead, consult the Safari HTML Reference at *http://developer.apple.com/documentation/AppleApplications/Reference/SafariHTMLRef/SafariHTMLRef.pdf*.

Object Model Reference

[window.]document.*formName.inputName*   // but not img type
[window.]document.forms[i].elements[j] // but not img type
[window.]document.getElementById(*elementID*)

Element-Specific Attributes

accept	accesskey	action	align	alt
autocomplete	autofocus	border	checked	datafld
datasrc	disabled	dynsrc	enctype	form
height	hspace	inputmode	ismap	list
loop	lowsrc	max	maxlength	method
min	name	pattern	readonly	replace
required	size	src	start	step
template	type	usemap	value	vcard_name
vspace	width			

Element-Specific Event Handler Attributes

Handler	IE	NN	Opera	Others	HTML
onafterupdate	4	n/a	n/a	n/a	n/a
onbeforeupdate	4	n/a	n/a	n/a	n/a
onchange	3	2	all	all	4
onformchange	n/a	n/a	9	n/a	n/a
onforminput	n/a	n/a	9	n/a	n/a
oninvalid	n/a	n/a	9	n/a	n/a
onselect	3	2	all	all	4

Not all events are active in all input types.

accept

IE 6 NN *n/a* Moz *all* Saf *all* Op 7 HTML 4

accept="*MIMETypeList*"   *Optional*

Specifies one or more MIME types for allowable files to be uploaded to the server when the form is submitted. The HTML 4 provides this attribute in case a browser wishes to incorporate some file type filtering prior to submitting a form with a file input element. In current mainstream browsers, this attribute has no practical impact on file selection or submission.

Input Types   file

Example   <input type="file" accept="text/html, image/gif" ...>

Value   MIME type (content type) value. For multiple items, a comma-delimited list is allowed. Web Forms 2.0 allows wildcards for MIME type ranges.

Default   None.

accesskey
IE 4 NN n/a Moz all Saf all Op 7 HTML 4

accesskey="*character*"   *Optional*

See the description of this shared attribute at the beginning of this chapter for general characteristics. For file input types, pressing the accesskey combination places the text pointer in the associated text box, but does not "click" the Browser button.

Input Types   All rendered types.

action
IE n/a NN n/a Moz n/a Saf n/a Op 9 HTML n/a

action="*URI*"   *Optional*

Web Forms 2.0 extension that allows a submission of the enclosing form to a URI different from the regular form when the input element is clicked.

Input Types   image, submit

align
IE all NN all Moz all Saf all Op 7 HTML 3.2

align="*alignmentConstant*"   *Optional*

Determines how the rectangle of the input image aligns within the context of the surrounding content. See "Alignment Constants" earlier in this chapter for a description of the possibilities for this attribute with img elements.

Input Types   image

Example   <input type="image" name="icon" src="icon.gif" align="absmiddle">

Value   Alignment-constant value applied to elements outside the image rectangle.

Default   left

Object Model Reference

```
[window.]document.formName.inputName.align
[window.]document.forms[i].elements[j].align
[window.]document.getElementById(elementID).align
```

alt
IE 4 NN n/a Moz all Saf all Op 7 HTML 4

alt="*textMessage*"   *Optional*

Provides text description of the input element image while the image downloads, in lieu of rendered images, or for text-to-speech browsers. Behaves just like the alt attribute of the img element.

Input Types   image

Example   <input type="image" name="icon" src="sndIcon.gif" alt="Sound Icon">

Value   Any quoted string of characters.

Default   None.

Object Model Reference

[window.]document.*formName*.*inputName*.alt
[window.]document.forms[i].elements[j].alt
[window.]document.getElementById(*elementID*).alt

autocomplete
IE *5* NN *n/a* Moz *n/a* Saf *n/a* Op *n/a* HTML *n/a*

autocomplete="*featureSwitch*"
Optional

If an IE user has automatic form completion preference enabled, the autocomplete attribute governs the feature for the entire form. IE preserves (in an encrypted fashion) previous text and password entries, and presents a repeat visitor with one or more choices to complete the field entry. If the field is for data commonly stored in a user's vCard, you can specify vcard_name attributes for text and password type input elements to let the browser pre-fill or assist the entry of a particular named field that matches one of the preferences entries. For more details on how AutoComplete works in HTML forms, visit *http://msdn.microsoft.com/workshop/author/forms/autocomplete_ovr.asp*.

Web Forms 2.0 specifies similar usage of this attribute, but does not rely on the proprietary Microsoft vCard system. Instead, it lets any supporting browser use whatever internal mechanism it wishes for preserving values that can be offered for automatic completion in subsequent entries.

Input Types   password, text; all text-oriented input types for Web Forms 2.0.

Example

<input type="text" name="homephone" vcard_name="vCard.Home.Phone" autocomplete="on">

Value   Constants: on | off.

Default   off

Object Model Reference

[window.]document.*formName*.*inputName*.autoComplete
[window.]document.forms[i].elements[j].autoComplete
[window.]document.getElementById(*elementID*).autoComplete

autofocus
IE *n/a* NN *n/a* Moz *n/a* Saf *n/a* Op *n/a* HTML *n/a*

autofocus="autofocus"
Optional

Web Forms 2.0 extension that brings focus to the element after the page loads. Should be assigned to only one form control element per page.

Input Types   All rendered types.

border

IE *4(Mac)*   NN *4*   Moz *all*   Saf *n/a*   Op *n/a*   HTML *n/a*

border="*pixels*" *Optional*

Specifies the thickness of a border around the input element image. Navigator 4 (only) places a border around the image by default. Set the border attribute to zero to remove the border.

Input Types   image

Example   <input type="image" name="icon" src="sndIcon.gif" border="0">

Value   Any integer pixel value.

Default   2 (Navigator 4) or 0 (All others).

Object Model Reference

[window.]document.*formName*.*inputName*.border
[window.]document.forms[i].elements[j].border
[window.]document.getElementById(*elementID*).border

checked

IE *all*   NN *all*   Moz *all*   Saf *all*   Op *7*   HTML *4*

checked *Optional*

A Boolean attribute that designates whether the current checkbox or radio input element is turned on when the page loads. In the case of a radio button grouping, only one input element should have the checked attribute. Scripts can modify the internal value of this attribute after the page has loaded. When the form is submitted, an input element that has its checked attribute turned on sends its name/value pair as part of the form data. The name/value pair consists of values assigned to the name and value attributes for the element. If no value is assigned to the value attribute, the string value "active" or "on" is automatically assigned when the checkbox or radio button is highlighted. This is fine for checkboxes because each one should be uniquely named. However, all radio buttons in a related group must have the same name for browsers to handle the automatic highlighting and unhighlighting within the group. See the name attribute below.

Input Types   checkbox, radio

Example

<input type="checkbox" name="addToList" checked>Send email updates to this web site.

Value   The presence of this attribute turns on its property.

Default   Off.

Object Model Reference

[window.]document.*formName*.*inputName*.checked
[window.]document.forms[i].elements[j].checked
[window.]document.getElementById(*elementID*).checked

<input>

datafld
IE 4 NN n/a Moz n/a Saf n/a Op n/a HTML |4|

datafld="*columnName*"   *Optional*

Used with IE 4 data binding to associate a remote data source column name with parts of various input elements. A datasrc attribute must also be set for the element. Works only with text file data sources in IE 5/Mac.

This attribute was reserved in HTML 4, but was dropped in XHTML 1.0.

Input Types   button, checkbox, hidden, password, radio, text

Example

```
<input type="text" name="first" datasrc="DBSRC3" datafld="firstName">
```

Value   Case-sensitive identifier.

Default   None.

Object Model Reference

```
[window.]document.formName.inputName.dataFld
[window.]document.forms[i].elements[j].dataFld
[window.]document.getElementById(elementID).dataFld
```

datasrc
IE 4 NN n/a Moz n/a Saf n/a Op n/a HTML |4|

datasrc="*dataSourceName*"   *Optional*

Used with IE data binding to specify the ID of the page's object element that loads the data source object for remote data access. Content from the data source is specified via the datafld attribute. Works only with text file data sources in IE 5/Mac.

This attribute was reserved in HTML 4, but was dropped in XHTML 1.0.

Input Types   button, checkbox, hidden, password, radio, text

Example

```
<input type="text" name="first" datasrc="DBSRC3" datafld="firstName">
```

Value   Case-sensitive identifier.

Default   None.

Object Model Reference

```
[window.]document.formName.inputName.dataSrc
[window.]document.forms[i].elements[j].dataSrc
[window.]document.getElementById(elementID).dataSrc
```

disabled
IE 4 NN n/a Moz all Saf all Op 7 HTML 4

disabled   *Optional*

A disabled input element appears grayed out on the screen and cannot be activated by the user. A disabled form control cannot receive focus and does not become active within the tabbing order rotation. IE/Windows extends this to mean that if one radio button in a group is disabled, the entire group is disabled. Not so in IE/Mac or other browsers, which let unhighlighted buttons uncheck a disabled checked member of the group via scripting.

The name/value pair of a disabled input element is not sent to the server when the form is submitted. input elements that normally perform submissions do not submit their form when disabled.

The disabled attribute is a Boolean type, which means that in HTML format, its presence in the attribute sets its value to true. Its value can also be adjusted after the fact by scripting (see the input object in Chapter 2).

Input Types	All.
Example	`<input type="submit" disabled value="Ready to Submit">`
Value	The presence of the attribute disables the element.
Default	`false`

Object Model Reference
```
[window.]document.formName.inputName.disabled
[window.]document.forms[i].elements[j].disabled
[window.]document.getElementById(elementID).disabled
```

dynsrc
IE 4   NN *n/a*   Moz *n/a*   Saf *n/a*   Op *n/a*   HTML *n/a*

`dynsrc="URL"`   *Optional*

Internet Explorer 4 and later allows video clips (and VRML) to be displayed via an image type input element. To help the browser differentiate between a dynamic and static image source, you use the dynsrc attribute in place of the src attribute to load the video clip. All other visual aspects of the input type input element are therefore immediately applicable to the rectangular region devoted to playing the video clip. See also the loop attribute for controlling the frequency of clip play and the start attribute.

Input Types   image

Example
```
<input type="image" dynsrc="submit.avi" alt="Submit Button" loop="3" height="100"
width="150">
```

Value	Any valid URL, including complete and relative URLs.
Default	None.

Object Model Reference
```
[window.]document.formName.inputName.dynsrc
[window.]document.forms[i].elements[j].dynsrc
[window.]document.getElementById(elementID).dynsrc
```

<input>

enctype

IE *n/a* NN *n/a* Moz *n/a* Saf *n/a* Op 9 HTML *n/a*

`enctype="`*`MIMEType`*`"` *Optional*

Web Forms 2.0 extension that allows (in concert with other attributes, such as `action`) a submission of the enclosing form to a URI and enclosure MIME type different from the regular form when the `input` element is clicked.

Input Types   image, submit

form

IE *n/a* NN *n/a* Moz *n/a* Saf *n/a* Op 9 HTML *n/a*

`form="`*`formID [formID] ...`*`"` *Optional*

Web Forms 2.0 extension that lets you associate a single form control element with one or more forms that do not enclose the controls. Because `input` elements in Web Forms 2.0 are not confined to be descendants of `form` elements, the `input` elements may be located away from the `form` element. The `form` attribute connects the `input` element with one or more `form` elements on the page.

Input Types   All rendered types.

Example   `<input type="text" id="searchText" form="GoogleSearch" />`

Value   ID of one or more `form` elements on the page. Multiple references are space-delimited.

Default   None.

height, width

IE 4 NN 4 Moz *all* Saf *all* Op 7 HTML *n/a*

`height="`*`pixels`*`" width="`*`pixels`*`"` *Optional*

Defines the dimensions of the image used for the `input` element. If you omit these attributes, the browser waits for the image to load before allocating space on the page for the element.

Input Types   image

Example   `<input type="image" src="submit.jpg" height="20" width="60">`

Value   Positive integers.

Default   Default image size.

hspace, vspace

IE 4 NN *n/a* Moz *all* Saf *all* Op 7 HTML *n/a*

`height="`*`pixels`*`" width="`*`pixels`*`"` *Optional*

Establishes extra padding around the image (and, thus, the `input` element) to keep other content at a minimum distance. The `hspace` controls the padding thickness of both the left and right edges; `vspace` does the same for top and bottom. Safari adds support for other input element types.

Input Types   image

<input>

Example
```
<input type="image" src="submit.jpg" alt="Submit Button"
height="20" width="60" hspace="10" vspace="20">
```

Value   Positive integers.

Default   0

inputmode

inputmode="*ScriptToken [ModifierToken]*"   *Optional*

Web Forms 2.0 extension (adopted whole from the W3C XForms 1.0 specification at *http://www.w3.org/TR/xforms/sliceE.html*) that directs the browser to display the appropriate text input user interface for a written language. Consult the W3C XForms 1.0 documents for details.

Input Types   email, password, text, url

Example   `<input type="text" id="searchText" inputmode="hiragana" />`

Value   Written language script token with an optional modifier token (space-delimited). Tokens generally correspond to Unicode scripts (*http://www.unicode.org/unicode/reports/tr24/*).

Default   None.

ismap

ismap   *Optional*

The Boolean ismap attribute tells the browser that the image representing the input element is acting as a server-side image map. Unlike the img element, the image type input element has an action (submitting the form) associated with it, so no surrounding a element is required. The browser appends coordinate information about the click to the URL of the form's action. See the usemap attribute for client-side image map details.

Input Types   image

Example
```
<input type="image src="navbar.gif" alt="Navigation Bar" ismap height="90"
width="120">
```

Value   The presence of the attribute turns the feature on.

Default   Off.

Object Model Reference
```
[window.]document.formName.inputName.isMap
[window.]document.forms[i].elements[j].isMap
[window.]document.getElementById(elementID).isMap
```

<input>

list
IE *n/a* NN *n/a* Moz *n/a* Saf *n/a* Op 9 HTML *n/a*

list="*datalistElementID*"   *Optional*

Web Forms 2.0 extension that lets you associate a set of predefined entries tailored for the input type, yet the input element also allows for text entry of a value not in the list. Predefined entries are coded as option elements inside a Web Forms 2.0 datalist element. The list attribute's value is the ID of the datalist element containing the predefined entries. In Opera's implementation, predefined entries appear as a pick list below the input element when the element has focus.

Input Types   date, datetime, datetime-local, email, month, number, range, text, time, url, week

Example
```
<label>Enter your operating system:<input type="text" name="os" list="oses" />
</label>
<datalist id="oses">
   <option value="">
   <option value="Windows Vista">
   <option value="Windows XP">
   <option value="Windows 98">
   <option value="Mac OS X">
   <option value="Linux">
</datalist>
```

Value   ID of the associated datalist element.

Default   None.

loop
IE 3 NN *n/a* Moz *n/a* Saf *n/a* Op *n/a* HTML *n/a*

loop="*loopCount*"   *Optional*

If you specify a video clip with the dynsrc attribute, the loop attribute controls how many times the clip should play ("loop") after it loads. If you set the value to zero, the clip loads but does not play initially. Video clips that are not currently running play when the user double-clicks on the image, but you may need to provide instructions for that on the page because there are no other obvious controls.

Input Types   image

Example
```
<input type="image" dynsrc="snowman.avi" alt="Snowman Movie" loop="3"
height="100" width="150">
```

Value   Any positive integer or zero.

Default   1

Object Model Reference
```
[window.]document.formName.inputName.loop
[window.]document.forms[i].elements[j].loop
[window.]document.getElementById(elementID).loop
```

lowsrc

lowsrc="*URL*"   *Optional*

Provides a URL to an alternate low-resolution image to be loaded initially if the src image is taking a long time to load.

Input Types   image

Example
```
<input type="image" src="navbar.jpg" alt="Navigation Bar" lowsrc="navbarBW.jpg"
height="60" width="300">
```

Value   Any valid URL, including complete and relative URLs.

Default   None.

Object Model Reference
```
[window.]document.formName.inputName.lowsrc
[window.]document.forms[i].elements[j].lowsrc
[window.]document.getElementById(elementID).lowsrc
```

max, min

                                                                                Optional

max="*rangeMaximum*"
min="*rangeMinimum*"

Web Forms 2.0 extension that lets you specify the minimum and maximum values for an input element designed for numeric, date, time, and file upload data. If a user enters values outside of these boundaries, the browser sets the rangeUnderflow or rangeOverflow properties of the ValidityState object, which scripts may inspect for further error indications to the user.

Input Types   date, datetime, datetime-local, file, month, number, range, time, week

Example
```
<input type="time" name="apptTime" min="09:00" max="17:00" />
```

Value
For number and range types, a positive or negative integer or floating-point number; for date type, an ISO 8601 format value (e.g., 2007-03-15); for combinations of date and time, an ISO 8601 format value (e.g., 2007-03-15T08:00:00, with a trailing Z if not the local variant); for month type, an ISO format value (e.g., 2007-03); for week type, an ISO 8601 format value (e.g., 2007W3); for file type, a positive integer indicating the number of allowed files to be uploaded with the form.

Default   None.

<input>

maxlength

IE *all* NN *all* Moz *all* Saf *all* Op 7 HTML *all*

maxlength="*characterCount*" *Optional*

Defines the maximum number of characters that may be typed into a text field input element. In practice, browsers beep or otherwise alert users when a typed character would exceed the maxlength value. There is no innate correlation between the maxlength and size attributes. If the maxlength allows for more characters than fit within the specified width of the element, the browser provides horizontal scrolling (albeit awkward for many users) to allow entry and editing of the field.

Input Types   password, text

Example   <input type="text" name="ZIP" maxlength="10">

Value   Positive integer.

Default   Unlimited.

Object Model Reference

[window.]document.*formName*.*inputName*.maxLength
[window.]document.forms[i].elements[j].maxLength
[window.]document.getElementById(*elementID*).maxLength

method

IE *n/a* NN *n/a* Moz *n/a* Saf *n/a* Op 9 HTML *n/a*

method="GET" | "POST" *Optional*

Web Forms 2.0 extension (when used with other extensions, such as the action attribute) that allows a submission for the enclosing form to a URI different and even method from the regular form when the input element is clicked.

Input Types   image, submit

name

IE *all* NN *all* Moz *all* Saf *all* Op 7 HTML *all*

name="*elementIdentifier*" *Optional/Required*

If the input element is part of a form being submitted to a server, the name attribute is required if the value of the element is to be submitted with the form. For forms that are in documents for the convenience of scripted form elements, input element names are not required.

The identifier you assign to the name attribute becomes part of the name/value pair submitted to the server. Radio button elements that are to act as a mutually exclusive group must all have the same name attribute value. In some browsers, failure to include a name attribute assignment disallows user access to checkbox or radio input elements.

The HTML 4 and XHTML specifications encourage using the id attribute in place of the name attribute throughout your pages. Mainstream browsers do not submit data from input elements bearing an id assignment but no name assignment. For consistency with DHTML-scripted DOM access of all elements, it's good practice to assign both attributes, even using the same identifier for both (except for radio buttons, whose IDs need to be unique, while their names are shared). Let the name attribute carry the element's value to the server, while scripts reach the elements via their IDs—especially in browsers that provide the IE `document.all.elementID` or W3C DOM `document.getElementById(elementID)` referencing syntax. Perhaps reluctantly, the strict XHTML DTD validates the `name` attribute for input elements so that validated pages will function within the reality of former and current browser implementations.

Input Types	All.
Example	`<input type="text" name="ZIP" id="ZIP" maxlength="10">`
Value	Case-sensitive identifier.
Default	None.

Object Model Reference

```
[window.]document.formName.inputName.name
[window.]document.forms[i].elements[j].name
[window.]document.getElementById(elementID).name
```

pattern
IE *n/a* NN *n/a* Moz *n/a* Saf *n/a* Op *9* HTML *n/a*

`pattern="regularExpression"`   *Optional*

Web Forms 2.0 extension that lets you specify a regular expression pattern that the user's input must match to pass validation.

Input Types   email, password, text, url

Example
```
<input pattern="[A-Z][0-9]{7}" name="partNum"
    title="A part number is an uppercase letter followed by seven numbers." />
```

Value	A regular expression (but not surrounded by the slash symbols, as used in JavaScript regular expressions).
Default	None.

readonly
IE *4* NN *n/a* Moz *all* Saf *all* Op *7* HTML *4*

`readonly`   *Optional*

When the `readonly` attribute is present, the text field input element cannot be edited on the page by the user (although scripts can modify the content). A field marked as `readonly` should not receive focus within the tabbing order (although IE 4 and later for the Macintosh allows the field to receive focus and beeps if a user tries to type).

Input Types	password, text
Example	`<input type="text" name="ZIP" readonly>`
Value	The presence of the attribute sets its value to true.
Default	`false`

<input>

Object Model Reference

[window.]document.*formName*.*inputName*.readOnly
[window.]document.forms[i].elements[j].readOnly
[window.]document.getElementById(*elementID*).readOnly

replace
IE n/a NN n/a Moz n/a Saf n/a Op 9 HTML n/a

replace="*type*"   *Optional*

Web Forms 2.0 extension that associates instructions to a submission form control with how to process the data returned from the server after the form is submitted. The choice is whether the response replaces the original document in the browser (the default) or the browser should apply returned values to the form, rather than retrieve initial form data (if a URL is assigned to the data attribute of the form element).

Input Types   image, submit

Example

```
<input type="submit" replace="values" action="http://example.com/custRecord.jsp"
    method="POST" />
```

Value   One of two constant values: document | values.

Default   document

required
IE n/a NN n/a Moz n/a Saf n/a Op 9 HTML n/a

required="required"   *Optional*

Web Forms 2.0 extension that signifies whether the input element's value is required for submission. Sets the missingValue property of the ValidityState object to true if the element receives no value.

Input Types   checkbox, date, datetime, datetime-local, email, file, month, number, password, radio, range, text, time, url, week

size
IE all NN all Moz all Saf all Op 7 HTML all

size="*elementWidth*"   *Optional*

In practice, the size attribute is limited to describing the width of text field input elements based on the number of characters that display. The actual rendered width is calculated based on the font setting (or default font) for the element, but the results are not always perfect. Variations in font rendering (and the ability to specify alternate font faces and sizes in newer browsers) sometimes lead to unexpectedly narrower fields. Therefore, it is not wise to automatically set the size and maxlength attributes to the same value without testing the results on a wide variety of browsers and operating systems with worst-case data (for example, all "m" or "W" characters in proportional fonts). The HTML 4 specification indicates that the size attribute might be applied to other input element types (as pixels, rather than characters), but as of recent browsers, this is not the case. In the meantime, you can use CSS properties to make buttons wider than the default size that tracks the width of the value attribute string.

<input>

Input Types	password, text
Example	<input type="text" name="ZIP" maxlength="10" size="12">
Value	Any positive integer.
Default	20

Object Model Reference
```
[window.]document.formName.inputName.size
[window.]document.forms[i].elements[j].size
[window.]document.getElementById(elementID).size
```

src   IE *all* NN *all* Moz *all* Saf *all* Op *7* HTML *all*

src="*URL*"   *Required*

URL to a file containing image data that is displayed through the input element of type image. The browser must be equipped to handle the image MIME type. On the World Wide Web, the most common image formats are GIF and JPEG.

Input Types	image
Example	<input type="image" name="icon" src="sndIcon.gif" border="0">
Value	A complete or relative URL.
Default	None.

Object Model Reference
```
[window.]document.formName.inputName.src
[window.]document.forms[i].elements[j].src
[window.]document.getElementById(elementID).src
```

start   IE *4* NN *n/a* Moz *n/a* Saf *n/a* Op *n/a* HTML *n/a*

start="*videoStartType*"   *Optional*

Whenever you set the dynsrc attribute of an image type input element to display a video clip in Internet Explorer, you can direct the element to start playing the video immediately after the video file loads or when the user rolls the cursor over the image. The start attribute lets you decide the best user interface for your page.

Input Types	image

Example
```
<input type="image" dynsrc="submit.avi" alt="Submit Button" loop="1"
start="mouseover" height="100" width="150">
```

Value	One of the two case-insensitive constant values: fileopen	mouseover.
Default	fileopen

<input>

Object Model Reference

[window.]document.*formName*.*inputName*.start
[window.]document.forms[i].elements[j].start
[window.]document.getElementById(*elementID*).start

step
IE *n/a*   NN *n/a*   Moz *n/a*   Saf *n/a*   Op 9   HTML *n/a*

step="*precision*"   *Optional*

Web Forms 2.0 extension that lets you specify the incremental values permitted in the
input element. If a min and/or max attribute is set, those values set boundaries for data
entered by the user; otherwise a zero boundary is used (with 1970-01-01T00:00:00.0Z
being the zero point for date-related elements).

Input Types   date, datetime, datetime-local, file, month, number, range, time, week

Example

```
<input type="time" name="apptTime" min="09:00" max="17:00" value="09:00"
step="900" />
```

Value   For number and range types, a positive or negative integer or floating-
point number; for date, week, and month types, an integer representing a
number of days, weeks, or months, respectively; for combinations of
date and time, a number of seconds.

Default   60 (datetime, datetime-local, time); 1 (others).

target
IE *n/a*   NN *n/a*   Moz *n/a*   Saf *n/a*   Op 9   HTML *n/a*

target="*windowOrFrameName*"   *Optional*

Web Forms 2.0 extension that allows (in concert with other attributes, such as action) the
page returned from a submission of the enclosing form to appear in a window or frame
different from the destination of the page returned from regular form when the input
element is clicked.

Input Types   image, submit

template
IE *n/a*   NN *n/a*   Moz *n/a*   Saf *n/a*   Op 9   HTML *n/a*

template="*repeatedBlockId*"   *Optional*

Web Forms 2.0 extension that lets you associate an add type input element to an element
(typically a tr element) that has been coded to act as a template for the possibility of having
repeated blocks of content added to the form. The repeatable element has its repeat
attribute set to template, and the add element's template attribute points to the ID of the
repeated element. For example, when clicked, the add element adds a new row to the table
with the same cell arrangement as the template.

Input Types   add

<input>

Example

```
<form>
    <table>
        <tr>
            <th>Product</th>
            <th>Quantity</th>
        </tr>
        <tr id="order" repeat="template">
            <td><input type="text" name="row[order].product" value=""></td>
            <td><input type="text" name="row[order].quantity" value="1"></td>
        </tr>
    </table>
    <p><button type="add" template="order">Add Row</button></p>
    <p><button type="submit">Submit</button></p>
</form>
```

Value   A repeated element's id attribute value.

Default   None.

type

type="*elementType*"   *Required*

Advises the browser how to render the input element (or even whether the element should be rendered at all). Possible choices for all browsers are as follows.

Type	Description
button	A clickable button whose action must be scripted. Its label is assigned by the value attribute. If you want to use HTML to format the label of a button, use the button element instead.
checkbox	A free-standing checkbox that provides two states (active/on and inactive/off). Its label is created by HTML text before or after the input element tag (also see the label element). The value attribute value is submitted with a form.
file	A button and field that lets the user select a local file for eventual uploading to the server. A click of the button generates a File dialog, and the name (or pathname) of the selected file appears in the field. The server must have a CGI script (invoked by the form's action attribute URI) to accept the incoming file at submission time.
hidden	An invisible field often used to carry over database or state data from submission to submission without bothering the user with its content (or having to store the temporary data on the server). The name/value pair is submitted with the form.
image	A graphical button whose sole default action is to submit the form. The coordinate points x,y of the click on the image are submitted as two name/value pairs linked by an ampersand character: inputName.x=n&inputName.y=m.
password	A text field that presents bullets or asterisks for each typed character to ensure over-the-shoulder privacy for the user. The plain-language text is submitted as the value for this element.
radio	One of a related group of on-off buttons. Assigning the same value to the name attribute of multiple radio buttons assembles them in a related group. Clicking on one button in the group activates it while unhighlighting all others. The value attribute value of the activated member is submitted with a form.

<input>

Type	Description
reset	A button whose sole job is to revert the form's elements to the values they had when the form initially loaded into the client. A custom label can be assigned via the `value` attribute.
submit	A button whose sole job is to submit the form. A custom label can be assigned by the `value` attribute. If `name` and `value` attributes are assigned for the element, their values are submitted with the form.
text	A one-line field for typing text that gets submitted as the value of the element (in a URL-encoded format). For a multiple-line field, see the `textarea` element.

Apple includes support in Safari 2 for two additional types (search and range), but these types are intended for use in Dashboard widgets rather than web pages.

The Web Forms 2.0 standard (first implemented in Opera 9) adds a number of intelligent input types, most of which have user interface features to facilitate entry of accurate form data (original HTML types are also enhanced with data entry validation powers). Those new types are as follows.

Type	Description
add	A clickable button that adds a repeated block of HTML content that has been coded as a repetition block.
date	A text entry field for date data in the ISO 8601 format (e.g., 2007-03-15).
datetime	A text entry field for date and UTC time data in the ISO 8601 format (e.g., 2007-03-15T21:45:00Z).
datetime-local	A text entry field for date and local time data in the ISO 8601 format (e.g., 2007-03-15T15:45:00).
email	A text entry field for an email address formatted according to RFC 2882 (section 3.4.1).
month	A text entry field for numeric entry of a combination of year and month (e.g., 2007-03).
move-down	A clickable button that moves the nearest ancestor repetition block down by one increment (e.g., moving a table row down one row).
move-up	A clickable button that moves the nearest ancestor repetition block up by one increment (e.g., moving a table row up one row).
number	A text entry field for numeric entry only.
range	An element that facilitates user choice of a value within a predefined range. The design is up to the browser maker, but a typical design is a slider control.
remove	A clickable button that removes a repeated block of HTML content.
time	A text entry field for time data in the ISO 8601 format (e.g., 23:45:00).
url	A text entry field for an Internet address in the Internationalized Resource Identifier format of RFC3987 (*http://www.ietf.org/rfc/rfc3987.txt*).
week	A text entry field for numeric entry of a combination of year and week (e.g., 2007W22).

Input Types   All.

Example

```
<input type="button" value="Toggle Sound" onclick="toggleSnd( )">
<input type="checkbox" name="connections" value="ISDN">ISDN
<input type="file" name="uploadFile">
<input type="hidden" name="prevState" id="prevState" value="modify">
<input type="image" name="graphicSubmit" src="submit.jpg" height="40" width="40">
```

```
<input type="password" name="password" maxlength="12" size="20">
<input type="radio" name="creditCard" value="Visa">Visa
<input type="reset">
<input type="submit" value="Send Encrypted">
Social Security Number:<input type="text" name="ssn" value="###-##-####"
onclick="validateSSN(this)">
```

Value   Any one of the known input element types: button | checkbox | file | hidden | image | password | radio | reset | submit | text.

Default   text

Object Model Reference

```
[window.]document.formName.inputName.type
[window.]document.forms[i].elements[j].type
[window.]document.getElementById(elementID).type
```

usemap

IE 6 NN n/a Moz all Saf all Op 7 HTML 4

usemap="*mapURL*"   *Optional*

You can define a client-side image map for an image type input element with the help of the map and area elements. The map element is a named container for one or more area element. Each area element sets a "hot" area on an image and assigns a link destination (and other settings) for a response to the user clicking in that region. The purpose of the usemap attribute is to establish a connection between the image type input element and a named map element in the same document. In some respects, the map element's name is treated like an anchor in that the "address" of the map element is the element's name preceded by a # symbol.

Input Types   image

Example

```
<input type="image" src="submit.gif" alt="Submit Button" usemap="#submitter"
height="90" width="120">
```

Value   A URL to the map element in the same document (a hash symbol plus the map name).

Default   None.

Object Model Reference

```
[window.]document.formName.inputName.useMap
[window.]document.forms[i].elements[j].useMap
[window.]document.getElementById(elementID).useMap
```

value

IE all NN all Moz all Saf all Op 7 HTML all

value="*text*"   *Optional/Required*

Preassigns a value to an input element that is submitted to the server as part of the name/value pair for the element. Some input element types are not submitted (an unchecked

<input>

radio button, for example), but any value you associate with all but the button or reset type input element reaches the server when the element is submitted.

In the case of text and password input elements, the value attribute contains a default entry. As the user makes a change to the content of the text field, the value changes, although the source code does not. When a form is reset (via a reset input element), the default values are put back into the text fields.

The value attribute is required only for checkbox and radio input elements. For input elements that are rendered as standard clickable buttons, the value attribute defines the label that appears on the button.

Input Types   All.

Example   `<input type="checkbox" name="connections" value="ISDN">ISDN`

Value   Any text string.

Default   None.

Object Model Reference

```
[window.]document.formName.inputName.defaultValue
[window.]document.forms[i].elements[j].defaultValue
[window.]document.getElementById(elementID).defaultValue
[window.]document.formName.inputName.value
[window.]document.forms[i].elements[j].value
[window.]document.getElementById(elementID).value
```

vcard_name   IE 5   NN *n/a*   Moz *n/a*   Saf *n/a*   Op *n/a*   HTML *n/a*

`vcard_name="vcardField"`   *Optional*

If an IE user has automatic form completion preference enabled, the autocomplete attribute governs the feature for the entire form. If the field is for data commonly stored in a user's vCard, you can specify vcard_name attributes for text and password type input elements to let the browser pre-fill or assist the entry of a particular named field that matches one of the preferences entries. For more details on how AutoComplete works in HTML forms, visit *http://msdn.microsoft.com/workshop/author/forms/autocomplete_ovr.asp*.

Input Types   password, text

Example

`<input type="text" name="homephone" vcard_name="vCard.Home.Phone" autocomplete="on">`

Value

Constants: vCard.Business.City | vCard.Business.Country | vCard.Business.Fax | vCard. Business.Phone | vCard.Business.State | vCard.Business.StreetAddress | vCard.Business. URL | vCard.Business.Zipcode | vCard.Cellular | vCard.Company | vCard.Department | vCard. DisplayName | vCard.Email | vCard.FirstName | vCard.Gender | vCard.Home.City | vCard.Home. Country | vCard.Home.Fax | vCard.Home.Phone | vCard.Home.State | vCard.Home. StreetAddress | vCard.Home.Zipcode | vCard.Homepage | vCard.JobTitle | vCard.LastName | vCard.MiddleName | vCard.Notes | vCard.Office | vCard.Pager.

<ins>

Default   None.

Object Model Reference

```
[window.]document.formName.inputName.vcard_name
[window.]document.forms[i].elements[j].vcard_name
[window.]document.getElementById(elementID).vcard_name
```

vspace

See hspace.

width

See height.

<ins>   IE 4 NN n/a Moz all Saf all Op 7 HTML 4

`<ins>...</ins>`   *HTML End Tag: Required*

The ins element and its companion, del, define a format that shows which segments of a document's content have been marked up for insertion (or deletion) during the authoring process. This is far from a workflow management scheme, but in the hands of a supporting WYSIWYG HTML authoring tool, these elements can assist in controlling generational changes of a document in process.

Browsers that support this element render text contained by the element as underlined (whereas del elements are in a strikethrough style). The HTML 4 specification includes two potentially useful attributes for preserving hidden information about the date and time of the alteration and some descriptive text about the change.

Example

```
<p>Four score and
<del cite="Fixed the math">eight</del><ins>seven</ins> years ago...</p>
```

Object Model Reference

```
[window.]document.getElementById(elementID)
```

Element-Specific Attributes

cite   datetime

Element-Specific Event Handler Attributes
None.

cite

IE 6 NN *n/a* Moz *all* Saf *all* Op 7 HTML 4

cite="*text*" *Optional*

A description of the reason for the change or other notation to be associated with the element, but normally hidden from view. In Mozilla, the context menu for such an element contains a **Properties** choice, which leads to a displayed list of attributes and their values for the visitor. Or, your DHTML scripts can access the information through the element object's cite property, and add value to the presentation.

Example   `<ins cite="Fixed the math --A.L.">seven</ins>`

Value   Any string of characters. The string must be inside a matching pair of (single or double) quotation marks.

Default   None.

Object Model Reference

`[window.]document.getElementById(elementID).cite`

datetime

IE 6 NN *n/a* Moz *all* Saf *all* Op 7 HTML 4

datetime="*datetimeString*" *Optional*

The date and time the insertion was made. This information is most likely to be added into a document with an HTML authoring tool designed to track content insertions and deletions. Data from this attribute can be recalled later as an audit trail to changes of the document. There can be only one datetime attribute value associated with a given ins element. In Mozilla, the context menu for such an element contains a **Properties** choice, which leads to a displayed list of attributes and their values for the visitor. Or, your DHTML scripts can access the information through the element object's dateTime property, and add value to the presentation.

Example

`<ins datetime="2001-09-11T08:56:00-04:00">SomeInsertedTextHere</ins>`

Value

The datetime attribute requires a value in a special date-time format that conveys information about the date and time in such a way that the exact moment can be deduced from any time zone around the world. Syntax for the format is as follows: *yyyy-MM-ddThh:mm:ssTZD*.

yyyy
    Four-digit year

MM
    Two-digit month (01 through 12)

dd
    Two-digit date (01 through 31)

T
    Uppercase "T" to separate date from time

hh
    Two-digit hour in 24-hour time (00 through 23)

mm

Two-digit minute (00 through 59)

ss

Two-digit second (00 through 59)

TZD

Time Zone Designator

There are two formats for the Time Zone Designator. The first is simply the uppercase letter "Z", which stands for UTC (Coordinated Universal Time—also called "Zulu"). The other format indicates the offset from UTC that the time shown in *hh:mm:ss* represents. This time offset consists of a plus or minus symbol and another pair of *hh:mm* values. For time zones west of Greenwich Mean Time (which, for all practical purposes is the same as UTC), the operator is a negative sign because the main *hh:mm:ss* time is earlier than UTC; for time zones east of GMT, the offset is a positive value. For example, Pacific Standard Time is eight hours earlier than UTC: when it is 6:00 P.M. in the PST zone, it is 2:00 A.M. the next morning at UTC. Thus, the following examples all represent the exact same moment in time (Time Zone Designator shown in boldface for clarification only):

2003-01-30T02:00:00**Z**	UTC
2003-01-29T21:00:00**-05:00**	Eastern Standard Time
2003-01-29T18:00:00**-08:00**	Pacific Standard Time
2003-01-30T13:00:00**+11:00**	Sydney, Australia

For more details about this way of representing time, see the ISO-8601 standard.

Default   None.

<isindex>

IE *all* **NN** *all* **Moz** *all* **Saf** *all* **Op** *n/a* **HTML** *all*

<isindex>   *HTML End Tag: Forbidden*

The isindex element is a longtime holdover from the earliest days of HTML and is deprecated in HTML 4 in favor of the text input element. The isindex element tag belongs in the head element. In modern browsers, it is rendered as a simple text field between two hr elements. When a user types text into the field and presses the **Enter/Return** key, the content of the field is URL-encoded (with + symbols substituted for spaces) and sent to the server with the URL of the current document. A CGI program on the server must know how to process this URL and return HTML for display in the current window or frame.

Example

```
<head>
<isindex prompt="Enter a search string:">
</head>
```

Object Model Reference

```
[window.]document.getElementById(elementID)
```

Element-Specific Attributes

`prompt`

Element-Specific Event Handler Attributes
None.

prompt
IE *all* NN *all* Moz *all* Saf *all* Op *n/a* HTML 4

`prompt="message"`   *Optional*

This attribute lets you assign the prompt message that appears with the element.

Example	`<isindex prompt="Enter a search string:">`
Value	Any quoted string.
Default	None.

<kbd>
IE *all* NN *all* Moz *all* Saf *all* Op 7 HTML *all*

`<kbd>...</kbd>`   *HTML End Tag: Required*

The kbd element is one of a large group of elements that the HTML 4 recommendation calls *phrase elements*. Such elements assign structural meaning to a designated portion of the document. A kbd element is one that displays text that a user is supposed to type on the keyboard, presumably to fill a text field or issue some command.

Browsers have free rein to determine how (or whether) to distinguish kbd element content from the rest of the body element. Most browsers elect to use a monospace font for the text. Override the default with a style sheet as you see fit.

Example
`<p>If you don't know the answer, type <kbd>NONE</kbd> into the text box.</p>`

Object Model Reference
`[window.]document.getElementById(elementID)`

Element-Specific Attributes
None.

Element-Specific Event Handler Attributes
None.

<keygen>
IE *n/a* NN 3 Moz *all* Saf *all* Op 7 HTML *n/a*

`<keygen>`   *HTML End Tag: Forbidden*

A keygen element allows a form to be submitted with key encryption, where the server expects a form to be packaged with an encrypted key. The client browser must have a digital certificate installed. The user sees two results of including the keygen element inside a form element. First, a select list of available encryption key sizes is rendered in the form where the keygen element appears. When the user submits the form, the user may see one or more security-related dialogs for confirmation. This element builds on the public-key encryption systems in Navigator and Netscape's Certificate Management System (CMS). Documentation is available at *http://www.redhat.com/docs/manuals/cert-system/admin/ overview.htm*.

Example

```
<form ...>
...
<keygen name="encryptedOrder" challenge="39457582201">
</form>
```

Element-Specific Attributes

| challenge | keytype | name | pqg |

Element-Specific Event Handler Attributes

None.

challenge

IE *n/a* NN *3* Moz *all* Saf *all* Op *7* HTML *n/a*

challenge="*challengeString*"   *Required*

If the server is equipped to interpret a challenge string for verification of an encrypted package, the challenge attribute is the challenge string. If you assign an empty string to the attribute, the key is encoded as an IA5STRING.

Example   `<keygen name="encryptedOrder" challenge="39457582201">`

Value   Any string.

Default   Empty string.

keytype

IE *n/a* NN *3* Moz *all* Saf *n/a* Op *n/a* HTML *n/a*

keytype="*keyType*"   *Optional/Required*

Sets the type of key to be created by the CMS prior to submitting the form data. This attribute is required only for the secondary type, DSA.

Example

`<keygen name="encryptedOrder" challenge="39457582201" keytype="DSA">`

Value   One of two constant values: RSA | DSA.

Default   RSA

name

IE *n/a* NN *3* Moz *all* Saf *all* Op *7* HTML *n/a*

name="*identifier*"   *Required*

Encrypting a form turns the entire form into a value that is part of a name/value pair. The name attribute assigns the "name" part of the name/value pair. If the server successfully decrypts the package, the individual form element name/value pairs are available to the server for further processing.

Example   <keygen name="encryptedOrder" challenge="39457582201">

Value   Case-insensitive identifier.

Default   None.

pqg

IE *n/a* NN *3* Moz *all* Saf *n/a* Op *n/a* HTML *n/a*

pqg="*dssParams*"   *Optional/Required*

If you specify the DSA key type for the keytype attribute, you must also assign associated parameter values to the pqg attribute. An explanation of the algorithms used to derive these values may be found at *ftp://ftp.ietf.org/internet-drafts/draft-ietf-pkix-ipki-pkalgs-05.txt*.

<label>

IE *4* NN *n/a* Moz *all* Saf *all* Op *7* HTML *4*

<label>...</label>   *HTML End Tag: Required*

The label element defines a structure and container for the label associated with an input element. Because the rendered labels for most form controls are not part of the control element's tag, the label element provides a way for an author to associate the context of the label with its control. A label element also simplifies assigning uniform styles to all form labels.

You have two ways to provide the association. One is to assign the id attribute value of the control to the for attribute of the label element. The other is to wrap the input element inside a label element. The latter is possible only if the label and control are part of running body content; if you must physically separate the label from the control because they exist inside separate td elements of a table, you must use the for attribute linkage. Whether the label is rendered in front of or after the control depends entirely on the relative locations of the tags in the source code.

Example

```
<form>
<label>Company:<input type="text" name="company"></label><br>
<label for="stateEntry">State:</label>
<input type="text" name="state" id="stateEntry">
...
</form>
```

Object Model Reference

[window.]document.getElementById(*elementID*)

Element-Specific Attributes

accesskey   datafld   dataformatas   datasrc   for

Element-Specific Event Handler Attributes
None.

accesskey
IE *4* NN *n/a* Moz *all* Saf *all* Op *7* HTML *4*

accesskey="*character*"   *Optional*

A character key (in combination with one or more modifier keys) that brings focus to, or activates, the associated input element. See the description of this shared attribute at the beginning of this chapter for general characteristics.

Example   `<label for="stateEntry" accesskey="s">State:</label>`

Value   Single character of the document set.

Default   None.

Object Model Reference
`[window.]document.getElementById(elementID).accessKey`

datafld
IE *4* NN *n/a* Moz *n/a* Saf *n/a* Op *n/a* HTML *n/a*

datafld="*columnName*"   *Optional*

Used with IE data binding to associate a remote data source column name with the label of an input element. The data source column must be either plain text or HTML (see dataformatas). A datasrc attribute must also be set for the label element. Works only with text file data sources in IE 5/Mac.

Example
```
<label for="stateEntry" datasrc="DBSRC3" datafld="label" dataformatas="HTML">
</label>
```

Value   Case-sensitive identifier.

Default   None.

Object Model Reference
`[window.]document.getElementById(elementID).dataFld`

dataformatas
IE *4* NN *n/a* Moz *n/a* Saf *n/a* Op *n/a* HTML *n/a*

dataformatas="*dataType*"   *Optional*

Used with IE data binding, this attribute advises the browser whether the source material arriving from the data source is to be treated as plain text or as tagged HTML. This attribute setting depends entirely on how the data source is constructed. Works only with text file data sources in IE 5/Mac.

<label>

Example

```
<label for="stateEntry" datasrc="DBSRC3" datafld="label" dataformatas="HTML">
</label>
```

Value   IE recognizes two possible settings: text | html.

Default   text

Object Model Reference

[window.]document.getElementById(*elementID*).dataFormatAs

datasrc   IE 4 NN *n/a* Moz *n/a* Saf *n/a* Op *n/a* HTML *n/a*

datasrc="*dataSourceName*"   *Optional*

Used with IE data binding to specify the ID of the page's object element that loads the data source object for remote data access. Content from the data source is specified via the datafld attribute. Works only with text file data sources in IE 5/Mac.

Example

```
<label for="stateEntry" datasrc="DBSRC3" datafld="label" dataformatas="HTML">
</label>
```

Value   Case-sensitive identifier.

Default   None.

Object Model Reference

[window.]document.getElementById(*elementID*).dataSrc

for   IE 4 NN *n/a* Moz *all* Saf *all* Op 7 HTML 4

for="*inputElementIdentifier*"   *Optional*

A unique identifier that is also assigned to the id attribute of the input element to which the label is to be associated. The for attribute is necessary only when you elect not to wrap the input element inside the label element, in which case the for attribute performs the binding between the two elements.

Example   `<label for="stateEntry">State:</label>`

Value   Case-sensitive identifier.

Default   None.

Object Model Reference

[window.]document.getElementById(*elementID*).htmlFor

<layer>

<layer>

IE *n/a* NN |4| Moz *n/a* Saf *n/a* Op *n/a* HTML *n/a*

<layer>...</layer>   *HTML End Tag: Required*

A layer element is a positionable element in Navigator 4's object model (e.g., like a block-level element whose CSS position attribute is set to absolute). As a result, many of the attributes are named according to the Navigator 4 way of positioning, sizing, and stacking positionable elements. The element was removed for the subsequent move to Mozilla, and will not be implemented in new browsers or W3C standards.

Content for a layer element can be read from a separate file (with the src attribute) or wired into the current document by placing the HTML between the start and end tags. You can include both types of content in the same layer element. Content from the src document is rendered first (as its own block-level element), with additional content starting on its own line below the external content's rectangle.

A layer element can be positioned anywhere within a document and can overlap content belonging to other layers (including the base document layer). Under link or script control, content for an individual layer can be changed without having to reload the other content on the page. Moreover, layer elements may be nested inside one another.

Example

```
<layer bgcolor="yellow" src="instrux.html" width="200" height="300"></layer>
```

Object Model Reference

[window.]document.*layerName*

Element-Specific Attributes

above	background	below	bgcolor	clip
height	id	left	pagex	pagey
src	top	visibility	width	z-index

Element-Specific Event Handler Attributes

Handler	NN	IE/Others	HTML
onblur	4	n/a	n/a
onfocus	4	n/a	n/a
onload	4	n/a	n/a
onmousedown	4[a]	n/a	n/a
onmouseout	4[a]	n/a	n/a
onmouseover	4[a]	n/a	n/a
onmouseup	4[a]	n/a	n/a

[a] Event capture mode only.

Alphabetical
HTML Reference

above

above="*layerID*"   *Optional*

Names the positionable element that is to be above (in front of) the current layer in the stacking order. This is a different way to set the z-index attribute that does not rely on an arbitrary numbering system. If you use the above attribute, do not use the below or z-index attribute for the same layer element.

Example

```
<layer id="instrux" bgcolor="yellow" src="instrux.html" above="help1"
width="200" height="300">
</layer>
```

Value   Case-sensitive identifier.

Default   None.

Object Model Reference

[window.]document.*layerName*.above

background

background="*URL*"   *Optional*

Specifies an image file that is used as a backdrop to the text and other content of the layer element. Unlike normal images that get loaded into browser content, a background image loads in its original size (without scaling) and tiles to fill the available layer space. Smaller images download faster but are obviously repeated more often in the background. Animated GIFs are also allowable but very distracting to the reader. When selecting a background image, be sure it is very muted in comparison to the main content so that the content stands out clearly. Background images, if used at all, should be extremely subtle.

Example

```
<layer background="blueCrinkle.jpg" src="instrux.html" width="200" height="300">
</layer>
```

Value   Any valid URL to an image file, including complete and relative URLs.

Default   None.

Object Model Reference

[window.]document.*layerName*.background

below

below="*layerID*"   *Optional*

Names the positionable element that is to be below (behind) the current layer in the stacking order. This is a different way to set the z-index attribute that does not rely on an arbitrary numbering system. If you use the below attribute, do not use the above or z-index attribute for the same layer element.

Example

```
<layer bgcolor="yellow" src="instrux.html" width="200" height="300"
below="thankyou">
</layer>
```

Value   Case-sensitive identifier.

Default   None.

Object Model Reference

[window.]document.*layerName*.below

bgcolor   IE *n/a*   NN |4| Moz *n/a*   Saf *n/a*   Op *n/a*   HTML *n/a*

bgcolor="*colorTripletOrName*"   *Optional*

Establishes a fill color (behind the text and other content) for the entire layer rectangle. If you combine a bgcolor and background, any transparent areas of the background image let the background color show through.

Example

```
<layer bgcolor="yellow" src="instrux.html" width="200" height="300"></layer>
```

Value   A hexadecimal triplet or plain-language color name. A setting of empty is interpreted as "#000000" (black). See Appendix A for acceptable plain-language color names.

Default   Varies with operating system.

Object Model Reference

[window.]document.*layerName*.bgColor

clip   IE *n/a*   NN |4| Moz *n/a*   Saf *n/a*   Op *n/a*   HTML *n/a*

clip="[*leftPixel, topPixel,*]*rightPixel,bottomPixel*"   *Optional*

A clipping region is a rectangular view to the full layer content. Only content that is within the clipping rectangle can be seen on the page. The default value of the clip attribute is either the default size of the content or the layer element's width by the automatically flowing content length. Setting the clip attribute lets you rein in long content that might flow beyond a fixed rectangle desired for the page design.

Example

```
<layer bgcolor="yellow" src="instrux.html" clip="50,50" width="200" height="300">
</layer>
```

Value

clip attribute values are pixel measures from the top and left edges of the element as it flows in the document. The order of values is clockwise from the left edge, around the rectangle sides: left, top, right, bottom. If you supply only two values, Navigator 4 assumes the left and top values are zero, meaning that you wish to adjust only the right and bottom edges. Thus, a setting of "50,50" means that the clipping region is 50 pixels square, starting at the top-left corner of the layer's rectangle. If you want the same size view starting 10 pixels in from the left, the clip attribute setting becomes "10,0,60,50".

Default Naturally flowing viewing area of layer content.

Object Model Reference

```
[window.]document.layerName.clip.left
[window.]document.layerName.clip.top
[window.]document.layerName.clip.right
[window.]document.layerName.clip.bottom
```

height, width
IE *n/a* NN |4| Moz *n/a* Saf *n/a* Op *n/a* HTML *n/a*

height="*length*" width="*length*"   *Optional*

Define the minimum size of the layer element. When you add content to the layer during initial loading, however, the attribute settings do not restrict the amount of the content that is visible along either axis. For example, if you display an image in a layer that is 120 pixels wide by 90 pixels high, the actual visible size of a layer element whose height and width attributes are set to a smaller size expands to allow the full image to appear. The same happens to text or other content: the viewable region expands to allow all content to appear. To restrict the visible portion of the content, set the clip attribute.

Setting the height and width attributes to specific sizes is helpful when you are creating a colored or patterned rectangle (via the bgcolor or background attributes) to act as an underlying layer beneath some other positioned content. Without content pushing on the edges of the layer, the height and width attributes set the clipping region to their sizes.

Example
```
<layer bgcolor="yellow" src="instrux.html" width="200" height="300"></layer>
```

Value Positive integer values or percentage values. You can reduce both values to zero to not only hide the element (which you can also do with the visibility attribute), but also prevent the element from occupying any page space.

Default Naturally flowing viewing area of layer content.

Object Model Reference

```
[window.]document.layerName.height
[window.]document.layerName.width
```

id
IE *n/a* NN |4| Moz *n/a* Saf *n/a* Op *n/a* HTML *n/a*

id="*elementIdentifier*"   *Optional*

A unique identifier that distinguishes this element from all the rest in the document. This is the identifier used as values for the above and below attributes. Scripts also use the id attribute value as the layer element's name for object references.

Example

```
<layer id="oldYeller" bgcolor="yellow" src="instrux.html" width="200" height="300">
</layer>
```

Value   Case-sensitive identifier.

Default   None.

Object Model Reference

```
[window.]document.layerName.name
```

left, top
IE *n/a* NN |4| Moz *n/a* Saf *n/a* Op *n/a* HTML *n/a*

`left="pixelCount" top="pixelCount"`   *Optional*

Define the positioned offset of the left and top edges of the layer relative to the spot in the document where the layer element would normally appear in source code order. This precise location relative to the page varies unless you also set the pagex and pagey attributes, which absolutely position the element in the document space. Unlike what it does for the ilayer element, Navigator does not preserve the space in the document where a layer element appears. The element is placed in its own plane, and the surrounding source code content is cinched up—usually overlapping the layer content unless the layer is positioned elsewhere.

Example

```
<layer bgcolor="yellow" src="instrux.html" width="200" height="300" left="10"
top="50">
</layer>
```

Value   Positive integer values (optionally quoted).

Default   0

Object Model Reference

```
[window.]document.layerName.left
[window.]document.layerName.top
```

pagex, pagey
IE *n/a* NN |4| Moz *n/a* Saf *n/a* Op *n/a* HTML *n/a*

`pagex="pixelCount" pagey="pixelCount"`   *Optional*

To truly position a layer element with repeatable accuracy, you can use the top-left corner of the document (page) as the point of reference. When you set the pagex and/or pagey attributes, you establish an offset for the left and top edges of the layer element relative to the corresponding edges of the entire document. Therefore, the zero point for a vertically scrolled page may be above the visible area of the browser window.

Example

```
<layer bgcolor="yellow" src="instrux.html" width="200" height="300" pagex="50"
pagey="350">
</layer>
```

Value   Positive integer values (optionally quoted).

Default   0

Object Model Reference
[window.]document.*layerName*.pageX
[window.]document.*layerName*.pageY

---

src   IE *n/a* NN |4| Moz *n/a* Saf *n/a* Op *n/a* HTML *n/a*

src="*URL*"   *Optional*

To load the content of an external HTML file into a layer element, assign the URL of that file to the src attribute. Any HTML content between the layer start and end tags is rendered on the page after the content is loaded from the src URL. If you omit the src attribute, only content between the tags is rendered. Scripts can change the corresponding object property (src) after the document has loaded to dynamically change content within the layer element (without reloading the main document).

Example
\<layer bgcolor="yellow" src="instrux.html" width="200" height="300">\</layer>

Value   A complete or relative URL.

Default   None.

Object Model Reference
[window.]document.*layerName*.src

---

top

See left.

---

visibility   IE *n/a* NN |4| Moz *n/a* Saf *n/a* Op *n/a* HTML *n/a*

visibility="*visibilityConstant*"   *Optional*

Determines whether Navigator 4 displays the layer element. The default behavior is for a layer to inherit the visibility attribute of its next outermost (parent) layer. For a layer element that is part of the basic document body, this means that the layer is seen by default (the base layer is always visible). To hide a layer when the page loads, set the visibility attribute to "hidden". You need to set the attribute to "show" only if the layer element is nested within another layer (or ilayer) whose visibility value is set to (or is inherited as) "hidden".

Example
\<layer bgcolor="yellow" src="instrux.html" width="200" height="300"
pagex="50" pagey="350" visibility="hidden">
\</layer>

Value   One of the accepted constants: hidden | inherit | visible.

Default   inherit

Object Model Reference
[window.]document.*layerName*.visibility

width

See height.

z-index   IE *n/a* NN |4| Moz *n/a* Saf *n/a* Op *n/a* HTML *n/a*
z-index="*layerNumber*"   *Optional*

Controls the positioning of layers along the Z-axis (front-to-back) of the document relative to the next outermost layer container. When the z-index values of two or more positionable elements within the same container (such as the base document layer) are identical numbers, the loading order of the elements in the HTML source code controls the stacking order, with the later elements stacked in front of earlier ones. The default z-index value for all positionable elements is zero. Therefore, if you want only one positionable element to appear in front of all the others that stack in their default order, you simply assign any positive value (even 1) to that standout element. Stacking order of positionable elements can be changed on-the-fly via scripting. See also the above and below attributes.

Example
```
<layer bgcolor="yellow" src="instrux.html" width="200" height="300" z-index="1">
</layer>
```

Value   Any integer.

Default   0

Object Model Reference
[window.]document.*layerName*.zIndex

<legend>   IE *4* NN *n/a* Moz *all* Saf *all* Op *7* HTML *4*
<legend>...</legend>   *HTML End Tag: Required*

The legend element acts as a label for a fieldset element. In visual browsers, this usually means that the label is visually associated with the group border rendered for the fieldset element. A text-to-speech browser might read the label aloud as a user navigates through a form. Place the legend element immediately after the start tag of the fieldset element for the association to stick. Because the content of the legend element is HTML content, you can assign styles to make the label stand out, if you like.

Example
```
<form method="POST" action="...">
<fieldset>
<legend>Credit Card Information</legend>
...inputElementsHere...
```

```
<legend>

</fieldset>
</form>
```

Object Model Reference

[window.]document.getElementById(*elementID*)

Element-Specific Attributes

accesskey   align

Element-Specific Event Handler Attributes

None.

accesskey   IE 5 NN *n/a* Moz *all* Saf *n/a* Op *n/a* HTML 4

accesskey="*character*"   *Optional*

A single character key that brings focus to, or activates, the first focusable control of the form associated with the legend element. See the description of this shared attribute at the beginning of this chapter for general characteristics.

Example   `<legend accesskey="c">Credit Card Information</legend>`

Value   Single character of the document set.

Default   None.

Object Model Reference

[window.]document.getElementById(*elementID*).accessKey

align   IE 4 NN *n/a* Moz *all* Saf *n/a* Op *n/a* HTML 4

align="*where*"   *Optional*

Controls the alignment of the legend element with respect to the containing fieldset element. See the discussion about text alignment inside a containing box in "Alignment Constants," earlier in this chapter.

Example   `<legend align="right">Credit Card Information</legend>`

Value   Allowed values in HTML 4 are bottom | left | right | top. IE 4 and later and Mozilla add center.

Default   left

Object Model Reference

[window.]document.getElementById(*elementID*).align

<li>

<li>

IE *all* **NN** *all* **Moz** *all* **Saf** *all* **Op** *7* **HTML** *all*

`<li>...</li>`   *HTML End Tag: Optional*

The li element is a single list item that is nested inside an ol or ul list container. The outer container determines whether the li item is preceded with a number or letter (indicating sequence within an order) or a symbol that doesn't connote any particular order. A special category of style sheet properties are devoted to list formatting.

If you apply a style sheet rule to an li element to adjust the color in Navigator 4, only the leading symbol is colored. To color the text as well, wrap the li element inside a span element and apply the style to the span element. This workaround operates fine in other CSS-capable browsers.

Example

```
<ul>
    <li>Larry</li>
    <li>Moe</li>
    <li>Curly</li>
</ul>
```

Object Model Reference

`[window.]document.getElementById(elementID)`

Element-Specific Attributes

type	value

Element-Specific Event Handler Attributes

None.

type

IE *all* **NN** *all* **Moz** *all* **Saf** *all* **Op** *7* **HTML** *3.2*

`type="labelType"`   *Optional*

The type attribute provides some flexibility in how the browser displays the item's leading symbol or sequence number. Values are divided into two groups, with one group each dedicated to ol and ul items. For an unordered list (ul), you can specify whether the leading symbol should be a disc, circle, or square; for an ordered list (ol), the choices are among letters (uppercase or lowercase), Roman numerals (uppercase or lowercase), or Arabic numerals. The type attribute is deprecated in HTML 4 in favor of the list-style-type style sheet property.

Be aware that in Version 4 browsers, the type attribute for a li element sets the type for subsequent li elements in the list unless overridden by a type attribute setting in another li element. More recent versions restrict the effect to the current li element. In general, though, it is best to set the type attribute of the ol or ul element and let that setting govern all nested elements.

Example   `<li type="square">Chicken Curry</li>`

Value

When contained by a ul element, possible values are disc | circle | square. When contained by an ol element, possible values are A | a | I | i | 1. Sequencing is performed automatically as shown in the following table.

Type	Example
A	A, B, C, …
a	a, b, c, …
I	I, II, III, …
i	i, ii, iii, …
1	1, 2, 3, …

Default   1 and disc.

Object Model Reference
[window.]document.getElementById(*elementID*).type

value   IE *all* NN *all* Moz *all* Saf *all* Op 7 HTML 3.2

value="*number*"   *Optional*

The value attribute applies only when the li element is nested inside an ol element. You can manually set the number used as a starting point for the sequencing of ordered list items. This can come in handy when you need to break up an ol element with some running text that is not part of the list.

Even though the value assigned to this attribute is a number, it does not affect the type setting. For example, setting value to 3 when type is A means that the sequence starts from that li element with the letter C.

Example
<li value="3">Insert Tab C into Slot M. Tighten with a wingnut.</li>

Value   Any positive integer.

Default   1

Object Model Reference
[window.]document.getElementById(*elementID*).value

   IE *3* NN *4* Moz *all* Saf *all* Op 7 HTML *all*

<link>   *HTML End Tag: Forbidden*

Unlike the a element (informally called a link when it contains an href attribute), the link element belongs inside the head element and is a place for the document to establish links with external documents, such as style sheet definition files or font definition files. By and large, browsers have yet to exploit the intended powers of this element. A variety of attributes let the author establish relationships between the current document and potentially related documents. In theory, some of these relationships could be rendered as part of the document or browser controls. Implementations of this element as of current browsers are rather weak compared to the HTML 4 specification. At the same time, several attributes (and all event handlers) defined in the HTML 4 specification and listed among shared items at the beginning of this chapter aren't very helpful because they more typically apply to elements that actually display content on the page. No explicit document content is rendered as a result of the link element. Some of those attributes may be associated with the link element by mistake or merely for consistency within the rendering engines.

When used to import stylesheets, this element's title attribute can play a non-intuitive role. By adding a title attribute when the rel attribute is set to stylesheet, you instruct modern browsers to treat the imported stylesheet as being author-preferred. If the browser allows users to choose from multiple author-supplied style sheets (e.g., see the View->Page Style menu choice in Firefox), the preferred one is listed first.

Example

```
<head>
<title>Section 3</title>
<link rev="Prev" href="sect2.html">
<link rel="Next" href="sect4.html">
<link rel="stylesheet" type="text/css" href="myStyles.css">
</head>
```

Object Model Reference

[window.]document.getElementById(*elementID*)

Element-Specific Attributes

charset	href	hreflang	media	rel
rev	src	target	type	

Element-Specific Event Handler Attributes

None.

charset

IE *n/a* NN *n/a* Moz *all* Saf *all* Op *7* HTML *4*

charset="*characterSet*"   *Optional*

Character encoding of the content at the other end of the link.

Example   \<link charset="csISO5427Cyrillic" href="moscow.html"\>

Value   Case-insensitive alias from the character set registry (*ftp://ftp.isi.edu/in-notes/iana/assignments/character-sets*).

Default   Determined by browser.

Alphabetical
HTML Reference

<link>

href

`href="URI"`   *Required*

The URI of the document associated with the link (also known in W3C jargon as the *destination*, even though there is no page navigation involved). Navigator 4 also uses the `src` attribute for this purpose.

Example   `<link rel="Prev" href="sect2.html" src="sect2.html">`

Value   Any valid URI, including complete and relative URLs.

Default   None.

Object Model Reference
`[window.]document.getElementById(elementID).href`

hreflang

`hreflang="languageCode"`   *Optional*

The language code of the content at the destination of a link. Requires that the `href` attribute also be set. This attribute is primarily an advisory attribute to help a browser prepare itself for a new language set if the browser is so enabled.

Example   `<link hreflang="HI" href="hindi/Chap3.html">`

Value   Case-insensitive language code.

Default   Browser default.

Object Model Reference
`[window.]document.getElementById(elementID).hrefLang`

media

`media="descriptorList"`   *Optional*

Sets the intended output device for the content of the destination document pointed to by the `href` attribute. The `media` attribute looks forward to the day when browsers are able to tailor content to specific kinds of devices such as pocket computers, text-to-speech digitizers, or fuzzy television sets. In the meantime, you can use it to specify separate external style sheets that are to be applied when the browser page is sent to a printer. The HTML 4 specification defines a number of constant values for anticipated devices, but the list is open-ended, allowing future browsers to tailor output to yet other kinds of media and devices.

Example
`<link rel="Glossary" href="gloss.html" media="screen, tv, handheld">`

Value
Constant values. Multiple values can be grouped together in a comma-delimited list within a quoted string. Values defined in HTML 4 are `all` | `aura` | `braille` | `handheld` | `print` |

projection | screen | tty | tv . Current browsers support the following values: all | print | screen.

Default   screen

Object Model Reference

[window.]document.getElementById(*elementID*).media

rel
IE *3* NN *4* Moz *all* Saf *all* Op *7* HTML *3.2*

rel="*linkTypes*"   *Optional*

Defines the relationship between the current element and the destination of the link. The HTML 4 recommendation defines several link types; it is up to the browser to determine how to employ the value. The element must include an href attribute for the rel attribute to be applied.

Example   <link rel="Next" href="sect6.html">

Value

Case-insensitive, space-delimited list of standard link types applicable to the document and browser. HTML 4-sanctioned link types are:

alternate	appendix	bookmark	chapter
contents	copyright	glossary	help
index	next	prev	section
start	stylesheet	subsection	

Current browsers use stylesheet to link in an external CSS file. Navigator 4 recognizes stylesheet and fontdef. In IE 5 and later for Windows, you can also use the value shortcut icon (with the space) and assign a URL to a custom icon file (*.ico*) on your server so that your icon appears in the Favorites list if the user chooses to add the page to his list.

Default   None.

Object Model Reference

[window.]document.getElementById(*elementID*).rel

rev
IE *4* NN *n/a* Moz *all* Saf *all* Op *n/a* HTML *4*

rev="*linkTypes*"   *Optional*

A reverse link relationship. Like the rel attribute, the rev attribute's capabilities are defined by the browser, particularly with regard to how the browser interprets and renders the various link types available in the HTML 4 specification. Given two documents (A and b) containing links that point to each other, the rev value of b is designed to express the same relationship between the two documents as denoted by the rel attribute in A. Current browsers provide no practical functionality for this attribute.

Example   <link rev="Prev" href="sect4.html">

Value　　　　　　Case-insensitive, space-delimited list of HTML 4 standard link types applicable to the element. See the rel attribute for sanctioned link types.

Default　　　　　　None.

Object Model Reference

[window.]document.getElementById(*elementID*).rev

---

src
IE *n/a*　NN *4*　Moz *n/a*　Saf *all*　Op *7*　HTML *n/a*

src="*URL*"　　　　　　　　　　　　　　　　　　　　　　　　　*Optional*

The URL of the destination of a link. In the case of content to be brought into the browser, the location of the resource.

Example

<link rel="fontdef" src="fonts/garamond.pfr" href="fonts/garamond.pfr">

Value　　　　　　Any valid URL, including complete and relative URLs.

Default　　　　　　None.

---

target
IE *4*　NN *n/a*　Moz *all*　Saf *all*　Op *7*　HTML *4*

target="*windowOrFrameName*"　　　　　　　　　　　　　　　*Optional*

Presumably, the target attribute is provided in HTML 4 as a way to specify the destination for the display of a document at the other end of the href attribute of the link element, such as a link to the next page in a series.

Value

Identifier when the frame or window name has been assigned via the target element's name attribute. Four reserved target names act as constants:

_blank
> Browser creates a new window for the destination document

_parent
> Destination document replaces the current frame's framesetting document (if one exists; otherwise, it is treated as _self)

_self
> Destination document replaces the current document in its window or frame

_top
> Destination document is to occupy the entire browser window, replacing any and all framesets that may be loaded (also treated as _self if there are no framesets defined in the window)

IE for Windows implements two other values: _search (IE 5 and later) and _media (IE 6). These supposedly direct the browser to load linked content into the browser's Search pane and Media Bars, respectively. Because browsers don't yet support relationships for which this attribute would be useful, precise implementation details are not clear.

Default　　　　　　　_self

Object Model Reference

[window.]document.getElementById(*elementID*).target

type   IE *4* NN *4* Moz *all* Saf *all* Op *7* HTML *4*

type="*MIMEType*"   *Optional*

An advisory about the content type of the destination document or resource. In practice, this attribute has been used so far to prepare the browser for the style sheet type being linked to.

Example

<link rel="stylesheet" type="text/css" href="styles/mainStyle.html">

Value   Case-insensitive MIME type. A catalog of registered MIME types is available from *ftp://ftp.isi.edu/in-notes/iana/assignments/media-types*.

Default   None.

Object Model Reference

[window.]document.getElementById(*elementID*).type

<listing>   IE *all* NN *all* Moz *all* Saf *all* Op *7* HTML *<4*

<listing>...</listing>   *HTML End Tag: Required*

The listing element displays its content in a monospace font as a block element, as in computer code listings rendered 132 columns wide. In most browsers, the font size is also reduced from the default size. Browsers observe carriage returns and other whitespace in element content. This element has been long deprecated in HTML and has even been removed from the HTML 4.0 specification. You are encouraged to use the pre element instead.

Example

```
<listing>
&lt;script language="JavaScript"&gt;
   document.write("Hello, world.")
&lt;/script&gt;
</listing>
```

Object Model Reference

[window.]document.getElementById(*elementID*)

Element-Specific Attributes

None.

Element-Specific Event Handler Attributes

None.

<map>

IE *all* NN *all* Moz *all* Saf *all* Op *7* HTML *3.2*

<map>...</map>

HTML End Tag: Required

A map element is a container for area elements that define the location and links of hotspots of client-side image maps. The primary purpose of the map element is to associate an identifier (the name attribute) that the usemap attribute points to when turning an img element into a client-side image map. Most other attributes are style-related and may be applied to the map element so that they are inherited by elements nested within.

Example

```
<img src="images/logo.gif" alt="Scroll to the bottom for navigation links."
height="300" width="250" usemap="#navigation">
<map name="navigation">
<area shape="rect" coords="0,0,100,100" href="products.html">
<area shape="rect" coords="0,100,300,100" href="support.html">
</map>
```

Object Model Reference

[window.]document.getElementById(*elementID*)

Element-Specific Attributes

  name

Element-Specific Event Handler Attributes

None.

name

IE *all* NN *all* Moz *all* Saf *all* Op *7* HTML *3.2*

name="*identifier*"

Required

The identifier to which the usemap attribute of an img element points. Because the usemap attribute is actually a URL type, its value resembles that of a link to an anchor: the name is preceded by a hash symbol (only in the usemap attribute). Despite XHTML's preference for id attributes over name attributes, browsers continue to rely on the name attribute as the connection between an image and an area map. Strict HTML 4 and XHTML DTDs continue to validate the name attribute.

Example	<map name="navigation"> ...</map>
Value	Case-sensitive unique identifier.
Default	None.

Object Model Reference

[window.]document.getElementById(*elementID*).name

<marquee>

<marquee>

IE 3 NN n/a Moz 1.0.1 Saf all Op 8 HTML n/a

`<marquee>...</marquee>`   *HTML End Tag: Optional*

The marquee element was first implemented in Internet Explorer. It displays HTML content in a scrolling region on the page. Scrolled content goes between the start and end tags. It is now supported by mainstream browsers, although not with the depth of its inventor.

Example

```
<marquee behavior="slide" direction="left" width="250" bgcolor="white">
Check out our monthly specials.
</marquee>
```

Object Model Reference

`[window.]document.getElementById(elementID)`

Element-Specific Attributes

behavior	bgcolor	datafld	dataformatas	datasrc
direction	height	hspace	loop	scrollamount
scrolldelay	truespeed	vspace	width	

Element-Specific Event Handler Attributes

Handler	IE	Others	HTML
onafterupdate	4	n/a	n/a
onbounce	4	n/a	n/a
onfinish	4	n/a	n/a
onstart	4	n/a	n/a

behavior

IE 3 NN n/a Moz 1.0.1 Saf all Op 8 HTML n/a

`behavior="motionType"`   *Optional*

Sets the motion of the content within the rectangular space reserved for the marquee element. You have a choice of three motion types.

Example

```
<marquee behavior="slide" direction="left" width="250" bgcolor="white">
...</marquee>
```

Value

One of the case-insensitive marquee element motion types:

alternate
> Content alternates between marching left and right. The only value supported in Mozilla until version 1.7.

scroll

Content scrolls (according to the direction attribute) into view and out of view before starting again.

slide

Content scrolls (according to the direction attribute) into view, stops at the end of its run, blanks, and then starts again.

Default   scroll

Object Model Reference

[window.]document.getElementById(*elementID*).behavior

bgcolor   IE *3* NN *n/a* Moz *1.0.1* Saf *all* Op *8* HTML *n/a*

bgcolor="*colorTripletOrName*"   *Optional*

Establishes a fill color (behind the text and other content) for the rectangular space reserved for the marquee element.

Example

```
<marquee behavior="slide" direction="left" width="250" bgcolor="white">
...</marquee>
```

Value   A hexadecimal triplet or plain-language color name. A setting of empty is interpreted as "#000000" (black). See Appendix A for acceptable plain-language color names.

Default   Varies with browser, browser version, and operating system.

Object Model Reference

[window.]document.getElementById(*elementID*).bgColor

datafld   IE *4* NN *n/a* Moz *n/a* Saf *n/a* Op *n/a* HTML *n/a*

datafld="*columnName*"   *Optional*

Used with IE data binding to associate a remote data source column name with the content scrolled by the marquee element. The data source column must be either plain text or HTML (see dataformatas). A datasrc attribute must also be set for the marquee element. Works only with text file data sources in IE 5/Mac.

Example

```
<marquee behavior="slide" direction="left" width="200"
datasrc="DBSRC3" datafld="news" dataformatas="HTML"></marquee>
```

Value   Case-sensitive identifier.

Default   None.

Object Model Reference

[window.]document.getElementById(*elementID*).dataFld

dataformatas

dataformatas="*dataType*" *Optional*

Used with IE data binding, this attribute advises the browser whether the source material arriving from the data source is to be treated as plain text or as tagged HTML. This attribute setting depends entirely on how the data source is constructed. Works only with text file data sources in IE 5/Mac.

Example

```
<marquee behavior="slide" direction="left" width=200
datasrc="DBSRC3" datafld="news" dataformatas="HTML"></marquee>
```

Value   Constant values: text | html.

Default   text

Object Model Reference

[window.]document.getElementById(*elementID*).dataFormatAs

datasrc

datasrc="*dataSourceName*" *Optional*

Used with IE data binding, this attribute advises the browser whether the source material arriving from the data source is to be treated as plain text or as tagged HTML. Works only with text file data sources in IE 5/Mac.

Example

```
<marquee behavior="slide" direction="left" width="200"
datasrc="DBSRC3" datafld="news" dataformatas="HTML"></marquee>
```

Value   Case-sensitive identifier.

Default   None.

Object Model Reference

[window.]document.getElementById(*elementID*).dataSrc

direction

direction="*scrollDirection*" *Optional*

A marquee element's content may scroll in one of four directions (only left and right in Safari). For optimum readability in languages written left to right, it is easier to grasp the content when it scrolls either to the left or downward.

Example

```
<marquee behavior="slide" direction="left" width="200">...</marquee>
```

Value   Four possible directions: down | left | right | up.

Default   left

Object Model Reference

[window.]document.getElementById(*elementID*).direction

height, width   IE 3   NN *n/a*   Moz *1.0.1*   Saf *all*   Op 8   HTML *n/a*

height="*length*" width="*length*"   *Optional*

A marquee element renders itself as a rectangular space on the page. You can override the default size of this rectangle by assigning values to the height and width attributes. The default value for height is determined by the font size of the largest font assigned to content in the marquee. Default width is set to 100% of the width of the next outermost container (usually the document body). The width defines how much space is used at one time or another by horizontally scrolling content. When the marquee is embedded within a td element that lets the browser determine the table cell's calculated width, you must set the width of the marquee element or risk having the browser set it to 1, making the content unreadable.

If you want extra padding around the space, see the hspace and vspace attributes.

Note that in Mozilla, the element's width can be specified only as a percentage or via the CSS width property. In Safari, you can make the element tall, but the text does not scroll vertically.

Example

```
<marquee behavior="slide" direction="left" height="20" width="200">
...
</marquee>
```

Value   Any length value in pixels or percentage of available space.

Default   A width of 100%; a height of 12 pixels.

Object Model Reference

[window.]document.getElementById(*elementID*).height
[window.]document.getElementById(*elementID*).width

hspace, vspace   IE 3   NN *n/a*   Moz *n/a*   Saf *all*   Op *n/a*   HTML *n/a*

hspace="*pixelCount*" vspace="*pixelCount*"   *Optional*

Internet Explorer provides attributes for setting padding around a marquee element. The hspace attribute controls padding along the left and right edges (horizontal padding), whereas the vspace attribute controls padding along the top and bottom edges (vertical padding). Adding such padding provides an empty cushion around the marquee's rectangle. As an alternative, you can specify the various margin style sheet settings, especially if you want to open space along only one edge.

Example

```
<marquee behavior="slide" direction="left" height="20" width="200"
hspace="10" vspace="15">...</marquee>
```

Value   Any positive integer.

Default   0

Object Model Reference
[window.]document.getElementById(*elementID*).hspace
[window.]document.getElementById(*elementID*).vspace

loop   IE *3* NN *n/a* Moz *n/a* Saf *all* Op *8* HTML *n/a*
loop="*count*"   *Optional*

Sets the number of times the marquee element scrolls its content. After the final scroll, the content remains in a fixed position. Constant animation can sometimes be distracting to page visitors, so if you have the marquee turn itself off after a few scrolls, you may be doing your visitors a favor.

Example
```
<marquee behavior="slide" direction="left" height="20" width="200" loop="3">
...</marquee>
```

Value   Any positive integer if you want the scrolling to stop. Otherwise, set the value to -1 or infinite.

Default   -1

Object Model Reference
[window.]document.getElementById(*elementID*).loop

scrollamount   IE *3* NN *n/a* Moz *1.0.1* Saf *all* Op *8* HTML *n/a*
scrollamount="*pixelCount*"   *Optional*

marquee content looks animated by virtue of the browser clearing and redrawing its content at a location offset from the previous location (in a direction set by the direction attribute). You can make the scrolling appear faster by increasing the amount of space between positions of each drawing of the content; conversely, you can slow down the scrolling by decreasing the space. See also scrolldelay.

Example
```
<marquee behavior="slide" direction="left" height="20" width="200" scrollamount="2">
...</marquee>
```

Value   Any positive integer.

Default   6

Object Model Reference
[window.]document.getElementById(*elementID*).scrollAmount

scrolldelay

IE 3 NN *n/a* Moz *1.0.1* Saf *all* Op *8* HTML *n/a*

scrolldelay="*milliseconds*" *Optional*

Apparent scrolling speed can be influenced by the frequency of the redrawing of the content as its position shifts with each redraw (see scrollamount). Increasing the scrolldelay value slows down the scroll speed, whereas decreasing the value makes the scrolling go faster. Be aware that on slower computers, you can reach a value at which no increase of speed is discernible no matter how small you make the scrolldelay value (see truespeed).

Example

```
<marquee behavior="slide" direction="left" height="20" width="200"
scrolldelay="100">
...</marquee>
```

Value   Any positive integer representing the number of milliseconds between content redraws.

Default   85 (Windows 95); 90 (Macintosh).

Object Model Reference

[window.]document.getElementById(*elementID*).scrollDelay

truespeed

IE 4 NN *n/a* Moz *n/a* Saf *all* Op *n/a* HTML *n/a*

truespeed *Optional*

The marquee element includes a built-in speed bump to prevent scrolling from being accidentally specified as too fast for visitors to read. If you genuinely intend the content to scroll very fast, you can include the truespeed attribute to tell the browser to honor scrolldelay settings below 60 milliseconds.

Example

```
<marquee behavior="slide" direction="left" height="20" width="200"
scrolldelay="45" truespeed>...</marquee>
```

Value   The presence of this attribute sets the value to true.

Default   false

Object Model Reference

[window.]document.getElementById(*elementID*).trueSpeed

vspace

See hspace.

width

See height.

<menu>

<menu>...</menu>   *HTML End Tag: Required*

The original idea of the menu element was to allow browsers to generate single-column lists of items. Virtually every browser, however, treats the menu element the same as a ul element to present an unordered single column list of items (usually preceded by bullets). The menu element is deprecated in HTML 4. You should be using the ul element for it in any case, because you are assured backward compatibility and forward compatibility should this element ever disappear from the browser landscape. Everything said here also applies to the deprecated dir element.

Example
```
Common DB Connector Types:
<menu>
    <li>DB-9</li>
    <li>DB-12</li>
    <li>DB-25</li>
</menu>
```

Object Model Reference
[window.]document.getElementById(*elementID*)

Element-Specific Attributes

compact

Element-Specific Event Handler Attributes
None.

compact

compact   *Optional*

A Boolean attribute originally designed to let browsers render the list in a more compact style than normal (smaller line spacing between items).

Example   <menu compact>...</menu>

Value   The presence of this attribute makes its value true.

Default   false

Object Model Reference
[window.]document.getElementById(*elementID*).compact

<meta>

<meta>   *HTML End Tag: Forbidden*

A meta element conveys hidden information about the document. Some browsers respond to this element to derive header information that may be important to the document but is

Alphabetical
HTML Reference

not sent by the server in response to the request for the document. The element is also used to embed document information that some search engines use for indexing and categorizing documents on the World Wide Web.

More than one meta element may be included in a document, and all meta elements belong nested inside the head element. The specific purpose of each meta element is defined by its attributes. Typically, a meta element reduces to a name/value pair that is of use to either the server or the client. For example, most browsers recognize attribute settings that force the page to reload (or redirect to another page) after a timed delay. This would be useful in a page whose content is updated minute-by-minute, because the browser keeps reloading the latest page as often as indicated in the meta element.

Several other elements and attributes in HTML 4 contain the same kind of metadata that might otherwise be located in meta elements. Use the avenue that is best suited to your intended server and browser environments. See also the address, del, ins, link, and title elements, as well as the profile attribute of the head element.

Much mythology surrounds meta element usage. Some attribute values affect only some browsers (controlling the browser cache, for example), and not all search engine bots respond to meta tag attribute values the same way (if at all). At the same time, commonly-used powers, such as refresh, are frowned upon by the standards. There are no mandated standards for acceptable values, but the W3C validators for HTML 4 and XHTML point toward acceptance of the character set value shown in the example below.

Example

```
<head profile="http://www.example.com/profiles/common">
    <meta name="Author" content="Jane Smith">
    <meta name="keywords" content="benefits,insurance,plan">
    <meta http-equiv="refresh"
    content="1;URL=http://www.example.com/truindex.html">
    <meta http-equiv="Content-Type" content="text/html;
    charset=ISO-8859-5">
</head>
```

Element-Specific Attributes

content	http-equiv	name	scheme

Element-Specific Event Handler Attributes
None.

content
IE *all* NN *all* Moz *all* Saf *all* Op *7* HTML *all*

content="*valueString*"
Required

The equivalent of the value of a name/value pair. The attribute is usually accompanied by either a name or http-equiv attribute, either of which act as the name portion of the name/ value pair. Specific values of the content attribute vary with the value of the name or http-equiv attribute. Sometimes, the content attribute value contains multiple values. In such cases, the values are delimited by commas, semicolons, or whatever delimiter the browser expects for that content. Some of these values may be name/value pairs in their own right, such as the content for a refresh meta element. The first value is a number representing the number of seconds delay before loading another document; the second value indicates a URL of the document to load after the delay expires.

Example

```
<meta http-equiv="refresh"
content="2;URL=http://www.example.com/basicindex.html">
```

Value   Any string of characters. The string must be inside a matching pair of (single or double) quotation marks.

Default   None.

Object Model Reference

```
[window.]document.getElementById(elementID).content
```

http-equiv

IE *all* NN *all* Moz *all* Saf *all* Op *7* HTML *all*

```
http-equiv="identifier"
```
Optional

When a server sends a document to the client with the HTTP protocol, a number of HTTP header fields are sent along, primarily as directives to the client about the content on its way. meta elements can add to those HTTP headers when the http-equiv attribute is assigned to a document. Browsers convert the http-equiv and content attribute values into the HTTP response header format of "name: value" and treat them as if they came directly from the server.

Web standards define a long list of HTTP headers (see *Webmaster in a Nutshell* by Stephen Spainhour and Valerie Quercia, published by O'Reilly), but some of the more common values are shown in the following examples. Not all browsers respond to all header types, and some browsers respond to browser-specific headers (e.g., the IE 6 MSTHEMECOMPATIBLE header). You can have either the http-equiv or name attribute in a meta element, but not both.

Example

```
<meta http-equiv="refresh"
content="1,http://www.example.com/truindex.html">
<meta http-equiv="Content-Type" content="text/html; charset=ISO-8859-5">
<meta http-equiv="expires" content="Sun, 15 Jan 1998 17:38:00 GMT">
```

Value   Any string identifier.

Default   None.

Object Model Reference

```
[window.]document.getElementById(elementID).httpEquiv
```

name

IE *all* NN *all* Moz *all* Saf *all* Op *7* HTML *all*

name="*identifier*" *Optional*

An identifier for the name/value pair that constitutes the meta element. Typically, the attribute value is a plain-language term that denotes the purpose of the meta element, such as "author" or 'keywords". You can assign a value to either the name or http-equiv attribute, but not both, in the same meta element.

Example

```
<meta name="Author" content="Jane Smith">
<meta name="keywords" content="benefits,insurance,plan">
```

Value   Any string identifier.

Default   None.

Object Model Reference

[window.]document.getElementById(*elementID*).name

scheme

IE *6* NN *n/a* Moz *all* Saf *n/a* Op *n/a* HTML *4*

scheme="*identifier*" *Optional*

Provides one more organizational layer to metadata supplied with a document. For example, a university campus with several libraries might generate documents associated with each of the libraries. Assuming that a browser is equipped to interpret metadata about this, one approach at assembling the tags is to create a separate name attribute value for each library: name="law", name="main", name="engineering", and so on. But it may also be necessary to associate these name values with a specific university. The scheme attribute could be called into service to align the metadata with a particular university: scheme="Harvard". Now, other university library systems could use the same organization of name attributes, but the scheme attribute clearly associates a given meta element with a specific university and library. Again, this assumes that the browser is empowered to do something special with this metaknowledge.

Example   `<meta scheme="Chicago" name="classicalFM" content="98.7">`

Value   Any string identifier.

Default   None.

Object Model Reference

[window.]document.getElementById(*elementID*).scheme

<multicol>

IE *n/a* NN *3* Moz *n/a* Saf *n/a* Op *n/a* HTML *n/a*

<multicol>...</multicol> *HTML End Tag: Required*

A Navigator-specific (Versions 3 and 4) element that renders its content in any number of evenly spaced flowing columns on the page. The way this element flows content might remind you of a desktop publishing program that automatically flows long content into column space that has been defined for the page. There is no equivalent for this element in HTML or Internet Explorer, but a CSS-related proposal for a multicolumn layout property may find its way into CSS3 (*http://www.w3.org/1999/06/WD-css3-multicol-100-623*).

Example

```
<multicol cols="2" gutter="20" width="500">LongFlowingHTMLContent
</multicol>
```

Element-Specific Attributes

cols	gutter	width

Element-Specific Event Handler Attributes
None.

cols
IE *n/a* NN *3* Moz *n/a* Saf *n/a* Op *n/a* HTML *n/a*

```
cols="columnCount"
```
Required

Defines the number of columns across which the browser distributes and renders the content of the element. For a given width of the content, the browser does its best to make each column the same length. The proposed CSS equivalent attribute is `column-number`.

Example

```
<multicol cols="2" gutter="20" width="500">LongFlowingHTMLContent
</multicol>
```

Value	Any positive integer.
Default	1

gutter
IE *n/a* NN *3* Moz *n/a* Saf *n/a* Op *n/a* HTML *n/a*

```
gutter="pixelCount"
```
Optional

Specifies the number of pixels to be placed between columns. The browser then calculates the width of the content columns by subtracting all the gutters from the total available width. The proposed CSS equivalent attribute is `column-gap`.

Example

```
<multicol cols="2" gutter="20" width="500">LongFlowingHTMLContent
</multicol>
```

Value	Any positive integer.
Default	10

width

width="*elementWidth*"   *Optional*

Defines the total width of the columns plus gutters. You can specify the width in pixels or as a percentage of the width of the next outer container (usually the document body). The proposed CSS equivalent attribute is the existing width attribute.

Example

```
<multicol cols="2" gutter="20" width="500">LongFlowingHTMLContent
</multicol>
```

Value   Any length value in pixels or percentage of available space.

Default   100%

<nextid>

<nextid>   *HTML End Tag: Prohibited*

The nextid element was at one time intended to assist document-editing application. It went inside a document's head element. Deprecated in HTML 2.0, it is no longer used.

<nobr>

<nobr>...</nobr>   *HTML End Tag: Required*

The nobr element instructs the browser to render its content without wrapping the text to the next line at the right edge of the window or container. Even if there are carriage returns in the source code for the element's content, the browser flows the text as one line. Although this might seem convenient in circumstances involving careful layout of pages, it may mean the user has to scroll horizontally to view the text—not something most users like to do. Despite the longevity of the nobr element in commercial browsers, it has never been mentioned in formal HTML recommendations.

Example

```
<nobr>
Now is the time for all good men to
come to the aid of their country, even if
the text forces them to scroll horizontally.
</nobr>
```

Object Model Reference

[window.]document.getElementById(*elementID*)

Element-Specific Attributes

None.

Element-Specific Event Handler Attributes

None.

<noembed>

<noembed>...</noembed>

The noembed element isolates advisory content that displays in browsers incapable of working with plugins. All content between the start and end tags of the noembed element is not rendered in plugin-enabled browsers, but is rendered in other browsers (which ignore the tag but not the content). There are no attributes for this element.

Example

```
<embed name="jukebox" src="jazz.aif" height="100" width="200"></embed>
<noembed>
To play the music associated with this page, you need a modern graphical browser.
</noembed>
```

Element-Specific Attributes

None.

Element-Specific Event Handler Attributes

None.

<noframes>

<noframes>...</noframes>

The noframes element contains HTML that is rendered by browsers incapable of displaying frames. Browsers that are capable of displaying frames ignore the noframes element and all content it contains. Content for this element should instruct the user about using frames or perhaps offer a link to a frameless version of the page. The most common location for the noframes element is inside a frameset element. The HTML 4 specification, however, sees nothing wrong with embedding the element in a rendered document, if it makes sense for your application. It could be useful if your page employs an iframe element, and you want browsers not equipped for that element to alert users about what they're missing.

All standard attributes of the noframes element were added to support Cascading Style Sheets. This seems odd, because it would seem very unlikely that a browser would support CSS but not frames (with the exception of Navigator 4's lack of iframe support).

Example

```
<frameset cols="150,*">
    <frame name="navbar" src="nav.html">
    <frame name="main" src="page1.html">
    <noframes>Your browser does not support frames.
    Click <a href="noFramesIndex.html">here</a> for a frameless version.
    </noframes>
</frameset>
```

Element-Specific Attributes

None.

Element-Specific Event Handler Attributes

None.

<nolayer>

IE *n/a* NN |4| Moz *n/a* Saf *n/a* Op *n/a* HTML *n/a*

`<nolayer>...</nolayer>`

HTML End Tag: Required

Navigator 4 provides a tag for isolating advisory content that displays in browsers that don't recognize the layer element. All content between the start and end tags of the nolayer element is not rendered in Navigator 4 but is rendered in other browsers (which ignore the tag but not the content). You can place the nolayer element anywhere you want, but be aware that it won't be positioned like the layer element is intended to be. Nonlayer browsers render the nolayer element's content.

There are no attributes for this element. If you attempt to set style sheet rules for the nolayer element, they are ignored by browsers such as Internet Explorer. You can, however, wrap the nolayer element inside a div or span element to associate a style sheet rule with the advisory text.

Example

```
<layer bgcolor="yellow" src="instrux.html" width=200 height=300></layer>
<nolayer>
You are not seeing some content that requires Netscape Navigator 4 to view.
</nolayer>
```

Element-Specific Attributes

None.

Element-Specific Event Handler Attributes

None.

<noscript>

IE *4* NN *3* Moz *all* Saf *all* Op *7* HTML *4*

`<noscript>...</noscript>`

HTML End Tag: Required

The noscript element is intended to display content when a browser is not set to run the scripts embedded in the current document. When a user disables scripting in a browser, the noscript element's content is rendered wherever it falls in the source code. For older browsers, and those that don't support scripting, the noscript element is ignored, which means that its content is rendered within the next outermost container's context. Going forward, the HTML 4.0 specification recommends that browsers also render the noscript element's content when scripts earlier in the document are of a language type not supported or enabled in the browser. Also, if an HTML 4-compatible browser should be developed that lacks scripting altogether, it, too, should render the noscript element's contents. But in practice, scriptable browsers render the content of this element only if scripting is turned off in the browser preferences.

All standard attributes of the noscript element were added to support Cascading Style Sheets, internationalization, and events for HTML 4.

Example

```
<noscript>
This document contains programming that requires a scriptable browser, such
as Microsoft Internet Explorer or Netscape Navigator. You may not have full
access to this page's powers at this time.
</noscript>
```

Element-Specific Attributes

None.

Element-Specific Event Handler Attributes

None.

<object>

IE *3* NN *4* Moz *all* Saf *all* Op *7* HTML *4*

`<object>...</object>`

HTML End Tag: Required

The object element supplies the browser with information to load and render data types that are not natively supported by the browser. If the browser must load some external program (a Java applet, a plugin, ActiveX object, or some other helper), the information about the content that is to be rendered is contained by the object element, its attributes, and optionally, associated param elements nested inside of it. Although today's browsers recognize elements such as applet and embed, the HTML specification indicates that the trend is to combine all of this into the object element. Internet Explorer has long favored the object element.

The HTML 4 specification allows nesting of object elements to give the browser a chance to load alternate content if no plugin or other necessary content aids are available in the browser. Essentially, the browser should be able to walk through nested object elements until it finds one it can handle. For example, the outer object element may try to load an MPEG2 video; if no player is available, the browser looks for the next nested object, which is a JPEG still image from the video; if the browser is not a graphical browser, it would render some straight HTML that is the most nested item (although not as an object element) within the hierarchy of nested objects:

```
<div>
<object data="proddemo.mpeg" type="application/mpeg">
    <object data="prodStill.jpg" type="image/jpeg">
        The all-new Widget 3000!
    </object>
</object>
</div>
```

See also the embed element for an example that blends the object and embed elements to accommodate a wide range of browsers.

To determine which attributes apply to a particular content type or object and what their values look like, you have to rely on documentation from the supplier of the object or plugin. That same documentation should let you know whether the functionality is available across browser brands and operating systems.

<object>

Example

```
<object id="earth" classid="clsid:83A38BF0-B33A-A4FF-C619A82E891D">
<param name="srcStart" value="images/earth0.gif">
<param name="frameCount" value="12">
<param name="loop" value="-1">
<param name="fps" value="10">
</object>
```

Element-Specific Attributes

align	alt	archive	border	classid
code	codebase	codetype	data	declare
height	hspace	name	standby	type
usemap	vspace	width		

Element-Specific Event Handler Attributes

None.

align

IE 3   NN 4   Moz all   Saf all   Op 7   HTML 4

`align="alignmentConstant"` *Optional*

Determines how the rectangle of the object element aligns within the context of surrounding content. See the discussion about alignment of elements with respect to content outside an element's box in "Alignment Constants," earlier in this chapter.

Example	`<object ... align="baseline"></object>`
Value	Constant value. See "Alignment Constants."
Default	bottom

Object Model Reference

`[window.]document.getElementById(elementID).align`

archive

IE 6   NN n/a   Moz all   Saf all   Op n/a   HTML 4

`archive="URIList"` *Optional*

A space-delimited list of URIs of files that support the loading and running of the object element. By explicitly specifying the files in the archive attribute, the browser doesn't have to wait for the supporting files to be called by the content running in the object element. Instead, the supporting files can be downloaded simultaneously with the primary content. The archive attribute may also include URIs assigned to the classid or data attributes, but one of these two attributes still needs to point to the primary content URI. Current browsers provide no particular functionality for this attribute.

Example

```
<object ... archive="/images/anim3.gif/images/anim4.gif"></object>
```

<object>

Value   A complete or relative URL.

Default   None.

Object Model Reference

[window.]document.getElementById(*elementID*).archive

border   IE 6 NN *n/a* Moz *all* Saf *n/a* Op *n/a* HTML *4*

border="*pixels*"   *Optional*

The thickness of a border around the object element. The attribute is deprecated in HTML 4 in favor of style sheet borders. If you use the object element to load an image for a client-side image map, you can set the border attribute to zero to eliminate the typical link border in IE 5/Mac (see usemap later in this section).

Example   <object ... border="4"></object>

Value   Any integer pixel value.

Default   None.

Object Model Reference

[window.]document.getElementById(*elementID*).border

classid   IE 3 NN 4 Moz *all* Saf *all* Op 7 HTML *4*

classid="*URL*"   *Optional*

The URL of the object's implementation. This attribute typically directs the browser to load a program, an applet, or a plugin class file. In Internet Explorer, the URL can point to the *CLSID* directory that stores all of the IDs for registered ActiveX controls, such as DirectAnimation. You must obtain the classid value from the supplier of an ActiveX control (or root around the Registry with **Regedit** if you know what you're looking for). In Navigator 4 and Mozilla, the Java Archive (JAR) Installation Manager attempts to install a plugin from the classid URL if the plugin is not installed for data specified in the data attribute. Eventually, this attribute may be used to load Java applets (IE 4 includes a code attribute to handle this now), but through Version 6 of both browsers, Java applets are not yet supported in this fashion in current browsers.

Example

<object id="earth" classid="clsid:83A38BF0-B33A-A4FF-C619A82E891D"></object>

Value   A complete or relative URL.

Default   None.

Object Model Reference

[window.]document.*elementID*.classid

code

IE 4   NN *n/a*   Moz *n/a*   Saf *n/a*   Op *n/a*   HTML *n/a*

code="*fileName.class*"   *Optional*

Internet Explorer uses the code attribute to allow the object element to perform the same job as an applet element, using the same kind of attributes. The code attribute value is the name of the Java applet class file. If the class file is in a directory other than the document, the path to the directory must be assigned to the codebase attribute, just like in the applet element. Parameters are passed to applets via param elements, just like the ones nested inside applet elements. IE appears to preserve the classid attribute for referencing ActiveX controls only.

Example   <object code="fileReader.class" codebase="classes"></object>

Value   Applet class filename.

Default   None.

Object Model Reference
[window.]document.*elementID*.code

codebase

IE 3   NN 4   Moz *all*   Saf *all*   Op 7   HTML 4

codebase="*path*"   *Optional*

Path to the directory holding the class file designated in either the code or classid attribute. The codebase attribute does not name the class file, just the path. You can make this attribute a complete URL to the directory, but don't try to access a codebase outside of the domain of the current document.

Example   <object code="fileReader.class" codebase="classes"></object>

Value   Case-sensitive pathname, usually relative to the directory storing the current HTML document.

Default   None.

Object Model Reference
[window.]document.getElementById(*elementID*).codeBase

codetype

IE 3   NN *n/a*   Moz *all*   Saf *all*   Op *n/a*   HTML 4

codetype="*MIMEType*"   *Optional*

An advisory about the content type of the object referred to by the classid attribute. A browser might use this information to assist in preparing support for a resource requiring a multimedia player or plugin. If the codetype attribute is missing, the browser looks next for the type attribute setting (although it is normally associated with content linked by the data attribute URL). If both attributes are missing, the browser gets the content type information from the resource as it downloads.

Example
```
<object classid="clsid:83A38BF0-B33A-A4FF-C619A82E891D"
codetype="application/x-crossword"></object>
```

Value	Case-insensitive MIME type. A catalog of registered MIME types is available from *ftp://ftp.isi.edu/in-notes/iana/assignments/media-types/*.
Default	None.

Object Model Reference

[window.]document.getElementById(*elementID*).codeType

data
IE 3 NN 4 Moz all Saf all Op 7 HTML 4

data="*URL*"   *Optional*

URL of a file containing data for the object element (as distinguished from the object itself). For data with a content type that can be opened (and viewed or played) with any compatible object or plugin, the data and type attributes are generally sufficient to launch the plugin and get the content loaded. But if the content requires a very specific plugin or ActiveX control, you should include a classid attribute that points to the object's implementation as well. In that case, you can specify the content type with either the codetype or type attributes. Relative URLs are calculated relative to the codebase attribute, if one is assigned; otherwise the URL is relative to the document's URL.

Example	`<object data="proddemo.mpeg" type="application/mpeg"></object>`
Value	A complete or relative URL.
Default	None.

Object Model Reference

[window.]document.getElementById(*elementID*).data

declare
IE 6 NN n/a Moz all Saf all Op n/a HTML 4

declare   *Optional*

The presence of the declare attribute instructs the browser to regard the current object element as a declaration only, without instantiating the object. A browser may use this opportunity to precache data that does not require the object being loaded or run. Another object element pointing to the same classid and/or data attribute values, but without the declare attribute, gets the object running. Current mainstream browsers provide no particular functionality for this attribute.

Example

`<object classid="clsid:83A38BF0-B33A-A4FF-C619A82E891D" declare></object>`

Value	The presence of the attribute sets it to true.
Default	false

Object Model Reference

[window.]document.getElementById(*elementID*).declare

<object>

height, width

IE 3   NN 4   Moz all   Saf all   Op 7   HTML 4

height="*length*" width="*length*"   *Optional*

The size that an embedded object (or its plugin control panel) occupies in a document is governed by the height and width attribute settings. Some browser versions might allow you to get away without assigning these attributes and letting the plugin's own user interface design determine the height and width of its visible rectangle. It is best to specify the exact dimensions of a plugin's control panel or the data (in the case of images) whenever possible (control panels vary with each browser and even between different plugins for the same browser). In some cases, the object may not display if you fail to supply enough height on the page. In other instances, if the player fails to load, the space may not be reserved. If you assign values that are larger than the actual object or its control panel and the object loads successfully, the browser reserves that empty space on the page, which could interfere with your intended page design.

When an object is scriptable, and you don't want its controller to appear, you can set its dimensions to zero or one. Place the tag at the end of the document.

Example   <object data="blues.aif" height="150" width="250"></object>

Value   Positive integer values (optionally quoted) or percentage values (quoted).

Default   None.

Object Model Reference
[window.]document.getElementById(*elementID*).height
[window.]document.getElementById(*elementID*).width

hspace, vspace

IE 3   NN n/a   Moz all   Saf n/a   Op 7   HTML 4

hspace="*pixelCount*" vspace="*pixelCount*"   *Optional*

A margin that acts as whitespace padding around the visual content of the object element's rectangular space. hspace establishes a margin on the left and right sides of the rectangle; vspace establishes a margin on the top and bottom sides of the rectangle.

Example
<object data="blues.aif" height="150" width="250" vspace="10" hspace="10"></object>

Value   Integer representing the number of pixels for the width of the margin on the relevant sides of the object element's rectangle.

Default   0

Object Model Reference
[window.]document.getElementById(*elementID*).hspace
[window.]document.getElementById(*elementID*).vspace

<object>

name

name="*elementIdentifier*"   *Optional*

The HTML 4 specification provides for a name attribute of the object element for instances in which the object is part of a form that is submitted to the server. The name attribute in this case performs the same function as the name attribute of an input element; it acts as a label for some data being submitted. The code that is loaded into the object element must be programmed to return a value if it is to be submitted via an HTML form. Current mainstream browsers list support for this attribute for compatibility claims, but do not respond to its value. Use the id attribute to assign an identifier that scripts use to reference the object.

Example
```
<object name="embedded" classid="clsid:83A38BF0-B33A-A4FF-C619A82E891D"
height="150" width="250"></object>
```

Value   Case-sensitive identifier.

Default   None.

Object Model Reference
[window.]document.getElementById(*elementID*).name

standby

standby="*HTMLText*"   *Optional*

HTML content to be displayed while the object is loading. This attribute has not been implemented in most current browsers (although it works in IE 5/Mac); presumably the message is to be displayed in the rectangular region intended for the object element, just as the alt message appears in an img element space while the image loads.

Example
```
<object classid="clsid:83A38BF0-B33A-A4FF-C619A82E891D"
height="150" width="250" standby="Loading movie..."></object>
```

Value   Any HTML content.

Default   None.

type

type="*MIMEType*"   *Required*

An advisory about the content type of the data referred to by the data attribute. A browser might use this information to assist in preparing support for a resource requiring a multimedia player or plugin. The data element first looks to the codetype attribute for this information. But if the codetype attribute is missing, the browser looks next for the type attribute setting. If both attributes are missing, the browser tries to get the content type information from the resource as it downloads. To be on the safe side, always specifiy a MIME type for image data (e.g., image/jpeg or image/gif).

<ol>

Example

```
<object data="movies/prodDemo.mpeg" type="application/mpeg"></object>
```

Value   Case-insensitive MIME type. A catalog of registered MIME types is available from *ftp://ftp.isi.edu/in-notes/iana/assignments/media-types/*.

Default   None.

Object Model Reference

```
[window.]document.getElementById(elementID).type
```

usemap   IE 6   NN *n/a*   Moz *all*   Saf *all*   Op 7   HTML 4
usemap="*mapURL*"   *Optional*

The HTML 4 specification lists the usemap attribute for an object element, thus offering the possibility of using the object element to load an image that gets used as an image map. Current browsers provide this capability.

Assign the URI of the image to the data attribute, and assign a MIME type for the image to the type property. Create a separate map element with one or more nested area elements, and assign the map element's name identifier to the object element's usemap attribute. IE/Windows pads the image and adds scrollbars, so you may not achieve successful cross-browser deployment.

Example

```
<object data='navbar.jpg" type="image/jpeg" alt="Navigation Bar" usemap="#navbarMap"
border="0"></object>
```

Value   See the usemap attribute of the img element.

Default   None.

Object Model Reference

```
[window.]document.getElementById(elementID).useMap
```

vspace

See hspace.

width

See height.

<ol>   IE *all*   NN *all*   Moz *all*   Saf *all*   Op 7   HTML *all*
<ol>...</ol>   *HTML End Tag: Required*

The ol element is a container for an ordered list of items. An "ordered list" means that the items are rendered with a leading sequence number or letter (depending on the type attribute setting or list-style-type style sheet property setting). Content for each list item is defined by a nested li element. If you apply a style sheet rule to an ol element, the style is inherited by the nested li elements.

Example
```
<ol>
    <li>Choose Open from the File menu.</li>
    <li>Locate the file you wish to edit, and click on the filename.</li>
    <li>Click the Open button.</li>
</ol>
```

Object Model Reference
[window.]document.getElementById(*elementID*)

Element-Specific Attributes

compact	start	type

Element-Specific Event Handler Attributes
None.

compact

IE *4* NN *n/a* Moz *all* Saf *all* Op *n/a* HTML *3.2*

compact   *Optional*

A Boolean attribute originally designed to let browsers render the list in a more compact style than normal (smaller line spacing between items). Although listed as a supported attribute for HTML compatibility, the compact attribute has no effect on mainstream browsers. Use style sheets to control element sizes and line spacing.

Example	`<ol compact>...</ol>`
Value	The presence of this attribute makes its value true.
Default	false

start

IE *all* NN *all* Moz *all* Saf *all* Op *7* HTML *all*

start="*number*"   *Optional*

Assigns a custom starting number for the sequence of items in the ol element. This is convenient when a sequence of items must be disturbed by running body text. Although the value is a number, the corresponding Arabic numeral, Roman numeral, or alphabet letter (controlled by the type attribute) is used to render the value.

Example	`<ol start="5"> ...</ol>`
Value	Any positive integer.
Default	None.

Object Model Reference
[window.]document.getElementById(*elementID*).start

<optgroup>

type

type="*labelType*"   *Optional*

The type attribute provides some flexibility in how the sequence number is displayed in the browser. For an ordered list, the choices are among letters (uppercase or lowercase), Roman numerals (uppercase or lowercase), or Arabic numerals. The type attribute is deprecated in HTML 4 in favor of the list-style-type style sheet property.

Example

<ol type="a">...</ol>

Value

Possible values are A | a | I | i | 1. Sequencing is performed automatically as follows.

Type	Example
A	A, B, C, ...
a	a, b, c, ...
I	I, II, III, ...
i	i, ii, iii, ...
1	1, 2, 3, ...

Default   1

Object Model Reference

[window.]document.getElementById(*elementID*).type

<optgroup>

<optgroup>...</optgroup>   *HTML End Tag: Required*

The optgroup element is a container for option elements within a select element. Each optgroup can represent a subgroup of options within the total list of select elements. Each browser and operating system has its own default styles to differentiate an optgroup label from selectable and indented options. In IE 5/Mac, the presence of optgroup elements turns a popup menu into a two-level hierarchical menu.

Example

```
<select name="carCos">
    <optgroup label="American">
        <option value="General Motors">General Motors</option>
        <option value="Ford">Ford Motor Company</option>
        <option value="Chrysler">DaimlerChrysler</option>
    </optgroup>
    <optgroup label="Japanese">
        <option value="Toyota">Toyota</option>
        <option value="Honda">Honda</option>
        <option value="Nissan">Nissan</option>
    </optgroup>
</select>
```

Object Model Reference

[window.]document.getElementById(*elementID*)

Element-Specific Attributes

disabled   label

Element-Specific Event Handler Attributes

None.

disabled   IE *5/6* NN *n/a* Moz *all* Saf *n/a* Op *7* HTML *4*

disabled   *Optional*

The presence of this attribute disables the optgroup element and its nested option elements. Other optgroup elements remain enabled.

Example	<optgroup label="Engineering" disabled>
Value	The presence of this attribute sets its value to true.
Default	false

Object Model Reference

[window.]document.getElementById(*elementID*).disabled

label   IE *5/6* NN *n/a* Moz *all* Saf *all* Op *7* HTML *4*

label="*labelText*"   *Required*

The text of the select element entry for the optgroup is defined by the label attribute. This is plain text, not HTML, and the user cannot select this text from the list.

Example	<optgroup label="Engineering" disabled>
Value	Any string of characters. The string must be inside a matching pair of (single or double) quotation marks.
Default	None.

Object Model Reference

[window.]document.getElementById(*elementID*).label

<option>   IE *all* NN *all* Moz *all* Saf *all* Op *7* HTML *all*

<option>...</option>   *HTML End Tag: Optional*

The option element defines an item that appears in a select element listing, whether the listing is in a pop-up menu or scrolling list. option elements associated with a select element must be nested within the start and end tags of the select element.

select elements supply name/value pairs when the element is submitted as part of a form element. Typically, the name attribute of the select element and the value attribute of the selected option are submitted as the name/value pair. Therefore, it is important to assign a meaningful value to the value attribute of each option element in a select list. You can use the value attribute to disguise user-unfriendly (but server- or script-friendly) values from the user, while presenting a user-friendly entry that appears in the select list. Content for the human-readable entry of a select list is entered after the option element's start tag. The end tag is optional because the entry is delimited either by the next option element start tag or the select element's end tag. See also the optgroup attribute for possible future grouping of option elements into hierarchical menu groupings.

Example

```
<select name="chapters">
    <option value="1">Chapter 1</option>
    <option value="2">Chapter 2</option>
    <option value="3">Chapter 3</option>
    <option value="4">Chapter 4</option>
</select>
```

Object Model Reference

```
[window.]document.formName.selectName.optionName
[window.]document.forms[i].elements[j].options[k].optionName
[window.]document.getElementById(elementID)
```

Element-Specific Attributes

disabled	label	selected	value

Element-Specific Event Handler Attributes

None.

disabled

IE *5(Mac)* NN *n/a* Moz *all* Saf *n/a* Op *7* HTML *4*

disabled   *Optional*

The presence of this attribute disables the option element in the list. Note that although the attribute disables the list choice in IE 5/Mac, as of Version 7, IE/Windows provides no other functionality for this attribute.

Example   `<option value="Met101" disabled>Meteorology 101</option>`

Value   The presence of this attribute sets its value to true.

Default   `false`

Object Model Reference

```
[window.]document.formName.selectName.optionName.disabled
[window.]document.forms[i].elements[j].options[k].optionName.disabled
[window.]document.getElementById(elementID).disabled
```

label

label="*labelText*"   *Required*

The label attribute is included in HTML 4.0 in anticipation of possible hierarchical select lists. The label is intended to be a shorter alternate entry for an option element when it is rendered hierarchically. It overrides the normal text associated with the option element. Note that IE 5/Mac and Safari incorrectly display the label attribute value in lieu of the element's text. Other current browsers provide no practical functionality for this attribute except for Opera 9, which uses this attribute in the Web Forms 2.0 context to provide a friendly label for an item in a datalist element (e.g., a web site title, while the option's value attribute is a URL).

Example
```
<option label="Meteo 101" value="met101">Meteorology 101</option>
```

Value   Any string of characters. The string must be inside a matching pair of (single or double) quotation marks.

Default   None.

selected

selected   *Optional*

The presence of the selected attribute preselects the item within the select element. When the select element is set to multiple, more than one option element may have the selected attribute set.

Example   `<option value="met101" selected>Meteorology 101</option>`

Value   The presence of this attribute sets its value to true.

Default   false

Object Model Reference
```
[window.]document.formName.selectName.optionName.selected
[window.]document.forms[i].elements[j].options[k].selected
[window.]document.getElementById(elementID).selected
```

value

value="*text*"   *Optional*

Associates a value with an option that may or may not be the same as the text displayed in the select element. When the select element is in a form submitted to the server, the value of the value attribute is assigned to the name/value pair for the select element if the option has been selected by the user (or is designated as selected with that attribute and the user has made no other selection). For scripting purposes, the value attribute might contain values such as URLs or string representations of objects that may subsequently be processed by scripts.

Example   `<option value="met101">Meteorology 101</option>`

Value   Any string of characters. The string must be inside a matching pair of (single or double) quotation marks.

Default   None.

Object Model Reference

```
[window.]document.formName.selectName.optionName.value
[window.]document.forms[i].elements[j].options[k].optionName.value
[window.]document.getElementById(elementID).value
```

IE *n/a* NN *n/a* Moz *n/a* Saf *n/a* Op *9* HTML *n/a*

`<output>...</output>`   *HTML End Tag: Required*

A Web Forms 2.0 output element can be associated with a form control to display HTML content under script control, usually as a result of a form-related event occurring. The element is an inline element, like a span element, but unlike other form controls, the output element's value is not submitted with the form. The element does, however, become a member of the form's elements array.

One use is to display advisory or transient information while a user interacts with the form. For example, an initially empty output element might be adjacent to one of the text entry fields in a form. An event handler monitoring user input of the field (via the forminput event) could check various ValidityState object properties and display a relevant error message if the data being entered is invalid.

Example

```
<script type="text/javascript"> // <![CDATA[
function validateField(evt) {
   var form = evt.target.form;
   var errField = form.elements[evt.target.name + "Error"];
   if (evt.target.validity.typeMismatch) {
      errField.value = 'You must enter a time (hh:mm).';
   } else if (evt.target.validity.stepMismatch) {
      errField.value = 'Appointments must begin at 0, 15, 30, or 45 past the hour.';
   } else if (evt.target.validity.rangeUnderflow) {
      errField.value = 'The earliest appointment is 9:00 am.';
   } else if (evt.target.validity.rangeOverflow) {
      errField.value = 'The last appointment is 5:00 pm.';
   } else if (evt.target.validity.valueMissing) {
      errField.value = 'You must enter a time.';
   } else {
      errField.value = '';
   }
   evt.preventDefault();
// ]]>
}
</script>
...
<form action="..." method="get" >
<p><label>Desired appointment time:
```

```
<input type="time" name="apptTime" min="09:00" max="17:00" value="09:00"
   step="900" required="required" onforminput="validateField(event)" />
</label>
<output name="apptTimeError" />
</p>
<p>
<input type="submit" />
</p>
</form>
```

Object Model Reference

[window.]document.getElementById(*elementID*)

Element-Specific Attributes

for	form	name

Element-Specific Event Handler Attributes

None.

for

for="*elementID [elementID]* ..."   *Optional*

Specifies the IDs of one or more other elements that are related to the option element. The specific usage is dependent upon the browser.

Value	One or more space-delimited element ID attributes.
Default	None.

Object Model Reference

None.

form

form="*formID [formID]* ..."   *Optional*

Lets you associate the output element with one or more forms that do not enclose the control. Because output elements in Web Forms 2.0 are not confined to be descendants of form elements, the output elements may be located away from the form element. The form attribute connects the output element with one or more form elements on the page.

Input Types	All rendered types.
Example	<output form="appointmentForm" name="apptTimeError" />
Value	ID of one or more form elements on the page. Multiple references are space-delimited.
Default	None.

<p>

name

name="*elementIdentifier*"   *Optional*

An identifier that can be used for script access via the form's elements array. You can also assign an identifier to the id attribute and use document.getElementById( ) if you prefer.

Example   `<output form="appointmentForm" name="apptTimeError" />`

Value   Case-sensitive identifier.

Default   None.

Object Model Reference

```
[window.]document.formName.elementName.name
[window.]document.forms[i].elements[j].name
[window.]document.getElementById(elementID).name
```

<p>

`<p>...</p>`   *HTML End Tag: Optional*

A p element defines a paragraph structural element in a document. With HTML 4, the p element is formally a block-level element, which means that content for a p element begins on its own line, and content following the p element starts on its own line. No other block-level elements may be nested inside a p element. If you omit the end tag (not permissible in XHTML), the element ends at the next block-level element start tag.

The nature of the p element has changed over time. In early implementations of HTML, the element represented only a paragraph break (a new line with some extra line spacing). Version 4 and later browsers render p elements in a hybrid way such that the start tag of a p element inserts a line space before the block. This means that a p element cannot start at the very top of a page unless it is positioned via CSS. Use the p element for structural purposes, rather than formatting purposes.

The content of a p element does not recognize extra whitespace that appears in the source code. Other elements, such as pre, render content just as it is formatted in the source code.

Example

```
<p>This is a simple, one-sentence paragraph.</p>
<p>This second paragraph starts on its own line, with a little extra
line spacing.</p>
```

Object Model Reference

```
[window.]document.getElementById(elementID)
```

Element-Specific Attributes

```
align
```

Element-Specific Event Handler Attributes

None.

<param>

align
IE *all* NN *all* Moz *all* Saf *all* Op *7* HTML *3.2*

align="*where*" *Optional*

Determines how the paragraph text is justified within the box that the p element occupies. See the discussion about horizontal alignment for a block element's content in "Alignment Constants," earlier in this chapter.

The align attribute is deprecated in HTML 4 in favor of the text-align style sheet property.

Example   ...

Value   Text alignment values are center | justify | left| right, although the justify value does not validate in strict HTML or XHTML DTDs.

Default   left

Object Model Reference
[window.]document.getElementById(*elementID*).align

<param>
IE *3* NN *2* Moz *all* Saf *all* Op *7* HTML *3.2*

<param> *HTML End Tag: Forbidden*

The param element may be nested within an applet or object element to pass parameters to the Java applet or object (typically, an ActiveX control in IE or a plugin) as it is being loaded. Parameters provide ways for HTML authors to adjust settings of an applet or object without having to recode the applet or object. A parameter typically passes a name/ value pair, which is assigned to the name and value attributes. You can have more than one param element per applet or object. The documentation for the applet or object should provide you with the information necessary to pass those parameter values.

Example
```
<applet code="simpleClock.class" name="myClock" width="400" height="50">
<param name="bgColor" value="black">
<param name="fgColor" value="yellow">
</applet>
```

Object Model Reference
[window.]document.getElementById(*elementID*)

Element-Specific Attributes

datafld	dataformatas	datasrc	name	type
value	valuetype			

Element-Specific Event Handler Attributes
None.

datafld

IE 4   NN *n/a*   Moz *n/a*   Saf *n/a*   Op *n/a*   HTML *n/a*

datafld="*columnName*"   *Optional*

Used with IE data binding to associate a remote data source column name with the parameter passed to a Java applet or object. In the following example, data from a data source's column named backColor is assigned to the value attribute, even though the attribute is not explicitly shown in the tag. More complex relationships are also possible with both object and applet elements. datafld works only with text file data sources in IE 5/Mac.

Example

```
<param name="bgColor" datasrc="DBSRC2" dataformatas="text" datafld="backColor">
```

Value	Case-sensitive identifier.
Default	None.

dataformatas

IE 4   NN *n/a*   Moz *n/a*   Saf *n/a*   Op *n/a*   HTML *n/a*

dataformatas="*dataType*"   *Optional*

Used with IE data binding, this attribute advises the browser whether the source material arriving from the data source is to be treated as plain text or as tagged HTML. This attribute setting depends entirely on how the data source is constructed and what kind of data the param element is expecting. dataformatas works only with text file data sources in IE 5/Mac.

Example

```
<param name='bgColor" datasrc="DBSRC2" dataformatas="text" datafld="backColor">
```

Value	IE recognizes two possible settings: text | html.
Default	text

datasrc

IE 4   NN *n/a*   Moz *n/a*   Saf *n/a*   Op *n/a*   HTML *n/a*

datasrc="*dataSourceName*"   *Optional*

Used with IE data binding to specify the ID of the page's object element that loads the data source object for remote data access. Content from the data source is specified via the datafld attribute. datasrc works only with text file data sources in IE 5/Mac.

Example

```
<param name="bgColor" datasrc="DBSRC2" dataformatas="text" datafld="backColor">
```

Value	Case-sensitive identifier.
Default	None.

<param>

name

name="*elementIdentifier*"   *Required*

Assigns an identifier for the parameter that the applet or object is expecting. Parameters generally supply a name/value pair. An applet, for example, includes a routine that fetches each parameter by name and assigns the passed value to a variable within the applet. Documentation for the applet or object should provide a list of names and value types corresponding to the param elements.

Example   `<param name="loop" value="4">`

Value   Case-sensitive identifier.

Default   None.

type

type="*MIMEType*"   *Optional*

When the valuetype attribute is set to "ref", the type attribute value advises the browser about the content type of the file referenced by the URL assigned to the value attribute. Omit the type attribute for other settings of the valuetype attribute.

Example
```
<param name="help" value="http://www.example.com/help.html" valuetype="ref"
type="text/html">
```

Value   Case-insensitive MIME type. A catalog of registered MIME types is available from *ftp://ftp.isi.edu/in-notes/iana/assignments/media-types/*.

Default   None.

Object Model Reference
`[window.]document.getElementById(`*elementID*`).type`

value

value="*runTimeParameterValue*"   *Optional*

The parameter value to be passed to an applet or object as the executable program or data loads. Parameter values are passed as string values, and it is up to the applet or object to perform the necessary internal coercion of the data to the desired data type. The value attribute is listed as optional because there may be instances in which the presence of the param element name attribute may be sufficient for the object. Once the applet or object loads its associated parameter values, scripts cannot dynamically modify those values unless the applet or object is scriptable and exposes methods designed to modify the values.

Example   `<param name="loop" value="4">`

Value   Any string value.

Default   None.

Object Model Reference

[window.]document.getElementById(*elementID*).value

valuetype

IE 6 NN *n/a* Moz *all* Saf *all* Op 7 HTML 4

valuetype="*paramValueType*"

Optional

object element parameters can come in three flavors: data, object, and ref. The valuetype attribute uses these constants to tell the browser how to treat the value assigned to the value attribute for passing to the object. When the valuetype is data, the value attribute is passed as a plain text string. A valuetype of object means that the value attribute consists of an identifier (id attribute value) of some other object element defined earlier in the same document. The other object may be one whose declare attribute is set, and now the parameter values are being passed to instantiate the object. When valuetype is ref, the value attribute is a URL that points to a file or other resource where runtime values are stored (perhaps a set of parameter values).

Example

```
<param name='anime" value="http://www.example.com/params/animation.txt"
valuetype="ref" type="text/html">
```

Value	Three possible constant values: data | object | ref.
Default	data

Object Model Reference

[window.]document.getElementById(*elementID*).valueType

<plaintext>

IE *all* NN *all* Moz *all* Saf *all* Op 7 HTML <4

<plaintext>...</plaintext>

HTML End Tag: Optional

The plaintext element displays its content in a monospace font as a block element, but with a twist. All document source code coming after the start tag is rendered as-is in the browser window. You cannot turn off the plaintext element. Even the end tag is rendered as-is. This element has been long deprecated in HTML and has even been removed from the HTML 4.0 specification. You are encouraged to use the pre element instead.

Example

```
<p>The rest of the HTML code follows:</p>
<plaintext>
...
</plaintext>
```

Object Model Reference

[window.]document.getElementById(*elementID*)

Element-Specific Attributes

None.

Element-Specific Event Handler Attributes

None.

<pre>

IE *all*   NN *all*   Moz *all*   Saf *all*   Op *7*   HTML *all*

`<pre>...</pre>`   *HTML End Tag: Required*

The pre element defines a block of preformatted text. Preformatted text is usually rendered by default in a monospace font and, more importantly, it preserves the whitespace (multiple spaces between words and new lines) entered into the source code for the content. Unlike the deprecated plaintext element, the pre element doesn't ignore HTML tags. Instead, it passes such tags onto the browser for normal rendering. If you want to display HTML tags in a block of preformatted text, use entities for the less-than (<) and greater-than (>) symbols. This prevents the HTML tags from being interpreted as genuine tags but renders the symbols within the preformatted text block.

Browsers ignore a whitespace line break immediately following a pre element start tag in case you wish to start the content on a new line in the source code, as shown in the example below.

The HTML 4 specification is adamant about the pre element maintaining its monospaced font size and line spacing. It lists the following elements that should not be included inside a pre element: applet, basefont, big, font, img, object, small, sub, and sup. Any one of these destroys the fixed-size pitch of the pre element. The recommendation also encourages authors to avoid overriding the monospaced font settings with style sheets.

One last admonition concerns using tab characters to indent or align text within a pre element. Not all browsers render tab characters the same way. Avoid potential problems by using space characters and let the pre element's preservation of whitespace do the job. No nonbreaking space entities ( ) are necessary in a pre element.

Example

```
<p>Here is the script example:</p>
<pre>
&lt;script language="JavaScript"&gt;
   document.write("Hello, world.")
&lt;/script&gt;
</pre>
```

Object Model Reference

`[window.]document.getElementById(elementID)`

Element-Specific Attributes

cols   width   wrap

Element-Specific Event Handler Attributes

None.

cols
IE *n/a* NN *all* Moz *all* Saf *n/a* Op *n/a* HTML *n/a*

`cols="columnCount"` *Optional*

The maximum number of characters per line of preformatted code. This proprietary attribute automatically sets the `wrap` attribute to `true`. Without this attribute, the source code formatting (or `width` attribute, where supported) governs the line width.

Example   `<pre cols="80">...</pre>`

Value   Any positive integer.

Default   None.

width
IE *n/a* NN *n/a* Moz *all* Saf *n/a* Op *n/a* HTML *4*

`width="columnCount"` *Optional*

The HTML 4 specification introduces the `width` attribute to allow you to set a maximum number of characters to be rendered on a preformatted line of text. Presumably, browsers that support this attribute in the future will wrap lines so that words do not break in the middle. Without this attribute, the source code formatting governs the line width. Navigator and Mozilla provide this functionality with the `cols` attribute, while Mozilla also supports the `width` attribute. Note that the CSS `width` property does not affect this element.

Example   `<pre width="80">...</pre>`

Value   Any positive integer.

Default   None.

wrap
IE *n/a* NN *all* Moz *all* Saf *n/a* Op *n/a* HTML *n/a*

`wrap` *Optional*

The presence of the `wrap` attribute instructs Navigator and Mozilla to wrap preformatted text so that text does not run beyond the right edge of the browser window or frame. `wrap` is set to `true` automatically when the `cols` attribute is set.

Example   `<pre wrap>...</pre>`

Value   The presence of the attribute sets its value to `true`.

Default   `false`

`<q>`
IE *4* NN *n/a* Moz *all* Saf *all* Op *7* HTML *4*

`<q>...</q>` *HTML End Tag: Required*

The q element is intended to set off an inline quote inside a document. The HTML 4 specification indicates that browsers should automatically surround the content of a q element with language-sensitive quotation marks, and that authors should not include quotes. All mainstream browsers supports this requirement, except for IE in Windows (through version 7). IE 5/Mac inserts quotes, but if the element's parent container is not left-aligned, the quotes float out of place. If you need quotes around quoted text in a cross-browser environment, you have no choice at this point but to include them yourself and not use the q element. For a block-level quotation, see the blockquote element.

Example

```
<p>The preamble to the u.s. Constitution begins,
<q>We the People of the United States</q></p>
```

Object Model Reference

[window.]document.getElementById(*elementID*)

Element-Specific Attributes

cite

Element-Specific Event Handler Attributes

None.

cite

IE *6* NN *n/a* Moz *all* Saf *all* Op *7* HTML *4*

cite="*URL*"   *Optional*

A URL pointing to an online source document from which the quotation is taken. This is not in any way a mechanism for copying or extracting content from another document. Presumably, the purpose of this HTML 4 recommendation is to encourage future browsers and search engines to utilize a reference to online source material for the benefit of readers and surfers. Version 6 browsers provide no practical functionality for this attribute.

Value   Any valid URL to a document on the World Wide Web, including absolute or relative URLs.

Default   None.

<rb>

IE *n/a* NN *n/a* Moz *n/a* Saf *n/a* Op *n/a* HTML *X1.1*

<rb>...</rb>   *End Tag: Required*

The rb element denotes the base text within a ruby-enhanced section of content. This is the regular text to which ruby annotation is added. IE 5 and later supports ruby text, but the rb element is not explicitly supported, and is assumed to automatically apply to text other than what is encased inside rt elements.

Example

```
<ruby>
  <rb>03</rb><rt>Month</rt>
  <rb>04</rb><rt>Day</rt>
  <rb>2003</rb><rt>Year</rt>
</ruby>
```

Object Model Reference

[window.]document.getElementById(*elementID*)

Element-Specific Attributes

None.

Element-Specific Event Handler Attributes

None.

<rbc>, <rtc>

IE *n/a* NN *n/a* Moz *n/a* Saf *n/a* Op *n/a* HTML *X1.1*

<rbc>...</rbc> <rtc>...</rtc>   *End Tag: Required*

If you want to string together a contiguous sequence of ruby base items and their associated ruby text items, you can group all base items and all text items together inside rbc and rtc containers, respectively. The number of items inside the rbc and rtc elements should be the same so that the browser can keep the base and ruby text items together. Using this approach does not degrade well in browsers that do not support ruby text.

Example

```
<ruby>
  <rbc>
    <rb>03</rb><rb>04</rb><rb>2003</rb>
  </rbc>
  <rtc>
    <rt>Month</rt><rt>Day</rt><rt>Year</rt>
  </rtc>
</ruby>
```

Object Model Reference

[window.]document.getElementById(*elementID*)

Element-Specific Attributes

None.

Element-Specific Event Handler Attributes

None.

<rp>

IE *5* NN *n/a* Moz *n/a* Saf *n/a* Op *n/a* HTML *X1.1*

<rp>...</rp>   *End Tag: Required*

The ruby markup module features the rp element to ease compatibility with browsers that don't support ruby markup directly. Non-ruby browsers render both the rp and rt element content as inline text. The rp element gives you a chance to include parentheses (or other character) around the ruby text so that the ruby text acts as an inline label. Content of each rp element is traditionally either a left or right parenthesis symbol. A complete rp element goes before and after each rt element. Browsers that support ruby text ignore the rp element content, and, thus, don't display the parentheses.

Example

```
<ruby>
  <rb>03</rb><rp>(</rp><rt>Month</rt><rp>)</rp>
  <rb>04</rb><rp>(</rp><rt>Day</rt><rp>)</rp>
  <rb>2003</rb><rp>(</rp><rt>Year</rt><rp>)</rp>
</ruby>
```

Object Model Reference

[window.]document.getElementById(*elementID*)

Element-Specific Attributes

None.

Element-Specific Event Handler Attributes

None.

<rt>

IE *5* **NN** *n/a* **Moz** *n/a* **Saf** *n/a* **Op** *n/a* **HTML** *X1.1*

`<rt>...</rt>`   *End Tag: Required*

The rt element contains the text that is the annotation for a corresponding rb element. Browsers that support ruby text usually render rt elements in a smaller font size than the base text. Through style sheet assignment, you can also use alternate font families. You can also assign a different language set for the ruby text via the xml:lang attribute of the rt element.

Example

```
<ruby>
  <rb>03</rb><rt>Month</rt>
  <rb>04</rb><rt>Day</rt>
  <rb>2003</rb><rt>Year</rt>
</ruby>
```

Object Model Reference

[window.]document.getElementById(*elementID*)

Element-Specific Attributes

name   rbspan

Element-Specific Event Handler Attributes

None.

---

name

IE *5* **NN** *n/a* **Moz** *n/a* **Saf** *n/a* **Op** *n/a* **HTML** *n/a*

`name="elementIdentifier"`   *Optional*

Sets an identifier for the element.

Value   Case-sensitive string.

Default   None.

rbspan

IE *n/a* NN *n/a* Moz *n/a* Saf *n/a* Op *n/a* HTML *X1.1*

rbspan="*integer*"   *Optional*

In some cases, you may want one rt element to span two or more contiguous rb elements. Assign the number of rb elements to the rt element's rbspan attribute. The mechanism is similar to the td element colspan attribute.

Value   Integer number of rb elements.

Default   1

<ruby>

IE *5* NN *n/a* Moz *n/a* Saf *n/a* Op *n/a* HTML *X1.1*

<ruby>...</ruby>   *End Tag: Required*

Ruby text is small-font annotation that usually appears above or below the main body text (or to one side in vertically oriented writing systems). The name comes from a small font that was used in typography to create the small annotation text. Ruby text is more commonly employed in pictographic languages, where the ruby text supplies a pronunciation guide to the main text pictographic symbols. But ruby text can be used with Latin alphabet languages, too.

The ruby element is a master container for all content to be affected by ruby markup, including the main text. The main text is known as the *ruby base*, while the annotation is called *ruby text*. Each of these types has its own tag (rb and rt, respectively), and any such tags must be encased within a ruby element. IE implemented the basics of ruby markup starting with Version 5 (Windows and Mac).

The W3C ruby markup specification was developed independently of the HTML recommendation, and was added to XHTML 1.1 as one of the first modules to take advantage of the extensible nature of XHTML.

Example

```
<ruby>
   <rb>03</rb><rt>Month</rt>
   <rb>04</rb><rt>Day</rt>
   <rb>2003</rb><rt>Year</rt>
</ruby>
```

Object Model Reference

[window.]document.getElementById(*elementID*)

Element-Specific Attributes

name

Element-Specific Event Handler Attributes

None.

name

name="*elementIdentifier*"   *Optional*

Sets an identifier for the element.

Value   Case-sensitive string.

Default   None.

<s>

<s>...</s>   *HTML End Tag: Required*

The s element renders its content as strikethrough text. This element is identical to the strike element; it was adopted because it more closely resembled the one-character element names for other type formatting (such as b, i, and u elements). In any case, both s and strike elements are deprecated in HTML 4 in favor of the text-decoration:line-through style sheet property.

Example
```
<p>If at first you don't succeed, <s>do it over</s> try, try again.</p>
```

Object Model Reference
```
[window.]document.getElementById(elementID)
```

Element-Specific Attributes
None.

Element-Specific Event Handler Attributes
None.

<samp>

<samp>...</samp>   *HTML End Tag: Required*

The samp element is one of a large group of elements that the HTML 4 recommendation calls *phrase elements*. Such elements assign structural meaning to a designated portion of the document. A samp element is one that contains text that is sample output from a computer program or script. This is different from a code example, which is covered by the code element.

Browsers have free rein to determine how (or whether) to distinguish samp element content from the rest of the body element. Current mainstream browsers elect to render the text in monospace font. Override the default with a style sheet as you see fit.

Example
```
<p>When you press the Enter key, you will see <samp>Hello, world!</samp>
on the screen.</p>
```

Object Model Reference
```
[window.]document.getElementById(elementID)
```

<script>

Element-Specific Attributes
None.

Element-Specific Event Handler Attributes
None.

<script>

IE *3* NN *2* Moz *all* Saf *all* Op *7* HTML *4*

<script>...</script>

HTML End Tag: Required

The script element provides a container for lines of script code written in any scripting language that the browser is capable of interpreting. Script statements that are not written inside a function definition are executed as the page loads; function definitions are loaded but their execution is deferred until explicitly invoked by user or system action (events). You can have more than one script element in a document, and you may include script elements written in different script languages within the same document.

An important shift in attribute syntax is introduced with HTML 4. To specify the scripting language of the statements within a script element, the language attribute has been used since the first scriptable browsers. HTML 4 deprecates that attribute in favor of the type attribute, whose value is a MIME type. Until you know for certain that your page visitors use only newer browsers that support the type attribute, you should include both attributes in documents for long-term backward compatibility with older browsers. The language attribute validates with transitional DTDs.

All but the earliest scriptable browsers also allow script statements to be imported into the document from a document whose URL is specified for the src attribute.

Very old, nonscriptable browsers don't recognize the script element and may attempt to render the script statements as regular HTML content. To prevent this, the long-held practice was to wrap the script statements inside HTML block comment markers. The end-of-comment marker (-->) must be preceded by a JavaScript comment marker (//) to prevent JavaScript from generating a script error.

If you are deploying your content in XHTML, you must enclose your script statements in an XML CDATA section to let XHTML validators accept script symbols (< and &) that are illegal content characters under XML. At the same time, a sufficient number of browsers in use today do not understand CDATA markup. As a compromise that appeases all browser types and validators, combine CDATA markup with script comment symbols, as shown in the example below. Or you can avoid the entire issue by importing scripts from external *.js* files.

Example

```
<script type="text/javascript" language="JavaScript">
// <![CDATA[
function howdy( ) {
    alert("Hello, HTML world!");
}
// ]]>
</script>

<script type="text/javascript" src="scripts/myscript.js"></script>
```

<script>

Element-Specific Attributes

charset	defer	event	for	language
src	type	version	xml:space	

Element-Specific Event Handler Attributes
None.

charset

IE *n/a* NN *n/a* Moz *all* Saf *all* Op *7* HTML *4*

charset="*characterSet*"   *Optional*

Character encoding of the content in the file referred to by the src attribute.

Example
<script charset="csISO5427Cyrillic" src="moscow.js"> . . . </script>

Value   Case-insensitive alias from the character set registry (*ftp://ftp.isi.edu/in-notes/iana/assignments/character-sets*).

Default   Determined by browser.

defer

IE *4* NN *n/a* Moz *n/a* Saf *n/a* Op *n/a* HTML *4*

defer   *Optional*

The presence of the defer attribute instructs the browser to render regular HTML content without looking for the script to generate content as the page loads. This is an advisory attribute only. The browser doesn't have to hold up rendering further HTML content as it parses the content of the script element in search of document.write( ) statements. Of the current browsers, only IE responds to the defer attribute.

Example
<script type="text/javascript" language="JavaScript" defer>...</script>

Value   The presence of this attribute sets its value to true.

Default   false

Object Model Reference
[window.]document.getElementById(*elementID*).defer

event

IE *4* NN *n/a* Moz *n/a* Saf *all* Op *7* HTML |*4*|

event="*eventName*"   *Optional*

Internet Explorer's event model allows the binding of object events to script elements with the help of the event and for attributes. As the page loads, the browser registers each script element with its event and object binding so that when the object generates the event, the script statements inside the script element execute—without having to write event handlers for the objects or wrap the script statements inside function definitions.

Event values are written either as unquoted event names or as quoted event names formatted as functions (with trailing parentheses and optional parameter names). Use this type of script-event binding only in Internet Explorer, if at all. Other browsers attempt to execute the script statements while the page loads. The transitional HTML 4 DTD reserves this attribute for possible future use, but the reservation doesn't hold for XHTML 1.0.

Example
```
<script for="window" event="onresize( )">...</script>
```

Value	Case-sensitive event name or the event name as a function inside a quote pair. The object described in the for attribute must support the event named in the event attribute.
Default	None.

Object Model Reference
```
[window.]document.getElementById(elementID).event
```

for
IE 4 NN *n/a* Moz *n/a* Saf *all* Op 7 HTML |4|

for="*elementID*"   *Optional*

Internet Explorer's event model allows the binding of object events to script elements with the help of the event and for attributes. As the page loads, the browser registers each script element with its event and object binding so that when the object generates the event, the script statements inside the script element execute—without having to write event handlers for the objects or wrap the script statements inside function definitions. Use the unique id attribute value of the element whose event you wish to handle. Use this type of script-event binding only in Internet Explorer. Nonsupporting browsers attempt to execute the script statements while the page loads. The transitional HTML 4 DTD reserves this attribute for possible future use, but the reservation doesn't hold for XHTML 1.0.

Example
```
<script for="firstNameEntry" event="onchange( )">...</script>
```

Value	Case-sensitive ID value of the event-generating element. The object described in the for attribute must support the event named in the event attribute.
Default	None.

Object Model Reference
```
[window.]document.getElementById(elementID).htmlFor
```

language
IE 3 NN 2 Moz *all* Saf *all* Op 7 HTML 4

language="*scriptingLanguage*"   *Optional*

Sets the scripting language for script statements defined in the element. This attribute is deprecated in HTML 4 (in favor of the type attribute), but it has been so widely used since the first days of scriptable browsers that its use and support will continue for a long time to

---

<script>

come. Moreover, it is so far the only accepted way to convey the JavaScript version for the script block (e.g., see the Array object in Chapter 5).

Example   `<script language="JavaScript">...</script>`

Value

Internet Explorer 4 and later recognize five case-insensitive language names: JavaScript | JScript | vbs | vbscript | ECMAScript. Navigator and Mozilla recognize only JavaScript. Safari, and Opera recognize JavaScript | JScript | ECMAScript.

Versions of JavaScript are also supported in appropriate browsers. To keep the attribute values one-word identifiers, the version numbers are tacked onto the end of the "JavaScript" language name. The following table summarizes the browsers in which each JavaScript version was introduced.

Version	First Introduction
JavaScript	NN 2, IE 3
JavaScript 1.1	NN 3
JavaScript 1.2	NN 4, IE 4
JavaScript 1.5	Mozilla 1.8
JavaScript 1.6	Mozilla 1.8
JavaScript 1.7	Firefox 2.0

As for current browsers, IE 7 is still on JavaScript 1.3, while Safari and Opera are up to JavaScript 1.5.

When script elements are assigned a version later than what a browser has implemented, older browsers that don't support the named version ignore the script elements.

Default   JScript (IE); JavaScript (others)

Object Model Reference

`[window.]document.getElementById(elementID).language`

---

src   IE 4 NN 3 Moz *all* Saf *all* Op 7 HTML 4
`src="URL"`   *Optional*

Imports a file of script statements from an external file. Once the external statements are loaded, the browser treats them as if they were embedded in the main HTML document.

In theory, you should be able to add script statements inside a script element that loads an external script library file. In practice, it is more reliable to provide a separate script element for each external library file and for in-document scripts.

Current implementations limit the src attribute to point to JavaScript external files. Such files must have a *.js* filename extension, and the server must have the extension and `application/x-javascript` MIME type set to serve up such files.

<script>

When assigning the src attribute in an XHTML document, browsers may not like the shortcut end tag format. Don't think of the tag as an empty element, but rather as one with content that arrives from an external source. Use an explicit </script> end tag.

Example

```
<script language="JavaScript" type="text/javascript" src="stringParseLib.js">
</script>
```

Value   Any valid URL. Current browsers require files with names that end in the *.js* extension. A complete URL may help overcome difficulties in earlier browsers that implement this feature.

Default   None.

Object Model Reference

```
[window.]document.getElementById(elementID).src
```

type
IE 4 NN *n/a* Moz *all* Saf *all* Op 7 HTML 4

```
type="MIMEType"
```
Required

An advisory about the content type of the script statements. The content type should tell the browser which scripting engine to use to interpret the script statements. The type attribute will eventually replace the language attribute as the one defining the scripting language in which the element's statements are written. To be compatible with future and past browsers, you may include both the language and type attributes in a script element.

Example

```
<script type="text/javascript" language="JavaScript">...</script>
```

Value

Case-insensitive MIME type. Values are limited to one(s) for which a particular browser is equipped. IE 4 and later and all other scriptable browsers accept text/javascript and application/x-javascript for scripts in an ECMAScript-compatible language. IE also accepts the following types: text/ecmascript, text/jscript, text/vbs (IE/Windows), text/vbscript (IE/Windows), and text/xml (IE 5 and later).

Default   None.

Object Model Reference

```
[window.]document.getElementById(elementID).type
```

version
IE *n/a* NN *n/a* Moz *all* Saf *n/a* Op *n/a* HTML *n/a*

```
version="x.y"
```
Optional

This attribute is listed here as a possible future implementation for Mozilla-based browsers. Most of the pieces that support this attribute (to complement the type attribute) are in place in the Mozilla browser engine but are not yet connected.

Example   `<script type="text/javascript" version="1.5">...</script>`

Value　　　　Language version expressed as major and minor version integers, separated by a period.

xml:space　　　　　　　IE *n/a*　NN *n/a*　Moz *n/a*　Saf *n/a*　Op *n/a*　HTML *X1.0*
xml:space="*preserve*"　　　　　　　　　　　　　　　　　　　　　　　　　　*Optional*

An XHTML parser is supposed to expunge all source code whitespace as it processes the document. This removal may harm scripts. By including the XML namespace space attribute, you instruct the parser to keep source code whitespace of script element content intact.

Example　　　　`<script type="text/javascript" xml:space="preserve">...</script>`

Value　　　　Constant value: preserve.

Default　　　　None.

\<select\>　　　　　　IE *all*　NN *all*　Moz *all*　Saf *all*　Op *7*　HTML *all*
\<select\>...\</select\>　　　　　　　　　　　　　　　　　　　　　*HTML End Tag: Required*

The select element displays information from nested option elements as either a scrolling list or pop-up menu in a document. Users typically make a selection from the list of items (or multiple selections from a scrolling list if the size attribute is set greater than 1 and the multiple attribute is set). The value attribute of the selected option item is submitted as the value part of a name/value pair to the server with a form. When the element is set to allow multiple selections, multiple ampersand-delimited name/value pairs (repeating the name of the element) are submitted with the form. Navigator 4 requires that a select element be placed inside a form element.

Example
```
<select name="chapters">
    <option value="chap1.html">Chapter 1</option>
    <option value="chap2.html">Chapter 2</option>
    <option value="chap3.html">Chapter 3</option>
    <option value="chap4.html">Chapter 4</option>
</select>
```

Object Model Reference
```
[window.]document.formName.selectName
[window.]document.forms[i].elements[j]
[window.]document.getElementById(elementID)
```

Element-Specific Attributes

accesskey	align	autofocus	data	datafld
datasrc	disabled	form	multiple	name
size	tabindex			

<select>

Element-Specific Event Handler Attributes

Handler	IE	NN	Opera	Others	HTML
onafterupdate	4	n/a	n/a	n/a	n/a
onbeforeupdate	4	n/a	n/a	n/a	n/a
onchange	3	2	all	all	4
onformchange	n/a	n/a	9	n/a	n/a
onforminput	n/a	n/a	9	n/a	n/a
oninvalid	n/a	n/a	9	n/a	n/a

accesskey
IE 4 NN *n/a* Moz *n/a* Saf *n/a* Op *n/a* HTML *n/a*

accesskey="*character*"   *Optional*

See the description of this shared attribute at the beginning of this chapter for general characteristics.

align
IE 4 NN *n/a* Moz *n/a* Saf *n/a* Op *n/a* HTML *n/a*

align="*alignmentConstant*"   *Optional*

Determines how the rectangle of the select element (particularly when the size attribute is set greater than 1) aligns within the context of surrounding content. See "Alignment Constants," earlier in this chapter. Note that only Internet Explorer supports the align attribute for the select element.

Example   <select name="chapters" multiple align="baseline">...</select>

Value   Case-insensitive constant value.

Default   bottom (IE/Windows); absmiddle (IE/Macintosh).

Object Model Reference
[window.]document.*formName.selectName*.align
[window.]document.forms[i].elements[j].align
[window.]document.getElementById(*elementID*).align

autofocus
IE *n/a* NN *n/a* Moz *n/a* Saf *n/a* Op *n/a* HTML *n/a*

autofocus="autofocus"   *Optional*

Web Forms 2.0 extension that brings focus to the element after the page loads. Should be assigned to only one form control element per page.

<select>

data
IE *n/a* NN *n/a* Moz *n/a* Saf *n/a* Op *n/a* HTML *n/a*

data="*URI*"   *Optional*

Web Forms 2.0 extension that allows a form to retrieve initial values for controls from an external XML file. The specification provides some details of the structure and namespaces to be used for the file. Visit *http://www.whatwg.org/* for further information.

Example
<select name="departments" data="form/departments.xml">...</select>

Value   Uniform Resource Identifier.

Default   None.

datafld
IE *4* NN *n/a* Moz *n/a* Saf *n/a* Op *n/a* HTML |4|

datafld="*columnName*"   *Optional*

Used with IE data binding to associate a remote data source column name to the selectedIndex property of a select element (i.e., a zero-based index value of the item currently selected in the list, as described in the select object of Chapter 2). As such, you can use data binding only with select elements that do not specify the multiple attribute. A datasrc attribute must also be set for the element. Works only with text file data sources in IE 5/Mac.

This attribute was reserved in HTML 4 but was dropped in XHTML 1.0.

Example
```
<select name="chapters" datasrc="DBSRC3" datafld="chapterRequest">
    <option value="chap1.html">Chapter 1</option>
    <option value="chap2.html">Chapter 2</option>
    <option value="chap3.html">Chapter 3</option>
    <option value="chap4.html">Chapter 4</option>
</select>
```

Value   Case-sensitive identifier.

Default   None.

Object Model Reference
```
[window.]document.formName.selectName.dataFld
[window.]document.forms[i].elements[j].dataFld
[window.]document.getElementById(elementID).dataFld
```

datasrc
IE *4* NN *n/a* Moz *n/a* Saf *n/a* Op *n/a* HTML |4|

datasrc="*dataSourceName*"   *Optional*

Used with IE data binding to specify the ID of the page's object element that loads the data source object for remote data access. Content from the data source is specified via the datafld attribute. Works only with text file data sources in IE 5/Mac.

This attribute was reserved in HTML 4, but was dropped in XHTML 1.0.

Alphabetical
HTML Reference

<select>

Example

```
<select name="chapters" datasrc="#DBSRC3" datafld="chapterRequest">
    <option value="chap1.html">Chapter 1</option>
    <option value="chap2.html">Chapter 2</option>
    <option value="chap3.html">Chapter 3</option>
    <option value="chap4.html">Chapter 4</option>
</select>
```

Value   Case-sensitive identifier.

Default   None.

Object Model Reference

```
[window.]document.formName.selectName.dataSrc
[window.]document.forms[i].elements[j].dataSrc
[window.]document.getElementById(elementID).dataSrc
```

disabled   IE *4* NN *n/a* Moz *all* Saf *all* Op *7* HTML *4*

disabled   *Optional*

The presence of this attribute disables the entire select element and its nested option elements. The element receives no events when it is disabled. You can also disable individual options through those elements' disabled properties.

Example

```
<select name="chapters" disabled>
    <option value="chap1.html">Chapter 1</option>
    <option value="chap2.html">Chapter 2</option>
    <option value="chap3.html">Chapter 3</option>
    <option value="chap4.html">Chapter 4</option>
</select>
```

Value   The presence of this attribute sets its value to true.

Default   false

Object Model Reference

```
[window.]document.formName.selectName.disabled
[window.]document.forms[i].elements[j].disabled
[window.]document.getElementById(elementID).disabled
```

form   IE *n/a* NN *n/a* Moz *n/a* Saf *n/a* Op *9* HTML *n/a*

form="*formID [formID]* ..."   *Optional*

Web Forms 2.0 extension that lets you associate a single form control element with one or more forms that do not enclose the controls. Because select elements in Web Forms 2.0 are not confined to be descendants of form elements, the select elements may be located away from the form element. The form attribute connects the select element with one or more form elements on the page.

<select>

Input Types	All rendered types.
Example	`<select id="chapters" form="bookSearch" />`
Value	ID of one or more form elements on the page. Multiple references are space-delimited.
Default	None.

multiple

IE *all*   NN *all*   Moz *all*   Saf *all*   Op *7*   HTML *all*

`multiple`   *Optional*

The presence of the `multiple` attribute instructs the browser to render the `select` element as a list box and to allow users to make multiple selections from the list of options. By default, the `size` attribute is set to the number of nested `option` elements, but the value may be overridden with the `size` attribute setting. Users can select contiguous items by **Shift**-clicking on the first and last items of the group. To make discontiguous selections, Windows users must **Ctrl**-click on each item; Mac users must **Command**-click on each item. The `multiple` attribute has no effect when `size` is set to 1 to display a pop-up menu.

Example

```
<select name="equipment" multiple>
    <option value="monitor">Video monitor</option>
    <option value="modem">Modem</option>
    <option value="printer">Printer</option>
    ...
</select>
```

Value	The presence of this attribute sets its value to `true`.
Default	`false`

Object Model Reference

```
[window.]document.formName.selectName.multiple
[window.]document.forms[i].elements[j].multiple
[window.]document.getElementById(elementID).multiple
[window.]document.formName.selectName.type
[window.]document.forms[i].elements[j].type
[window.]document.getElementById(elementID).type
```

name

IE *all*   NN *all*   Moz *all*   Saf *all*   Op *7*   HTML *all*

`name="elementIdentifier"`   *Optional*

The name submitted as part of the element's name/value pair with the form. It is similar to the name attribute of input elements.

Example

```
<select name="cpu" id="cpu">
    <option value="486">486</option>
    <option value="pentium">Pentium</option>
```

<select>

```
    <option value="pentium2">Pentium II</option>
    ...
</select>
```

Value   Case-sensitive identifier.

Default   None.

Object Model Reference
[window.]document.*formName.selectName*.name
[window.]document.forms[i].elements[j].name
[window.]document.getElementById(*elementID*).name

size   IE *all* NN *all* Moz *all* Saf *all* Op *7* HTML *all*

size="*rowCount*"   *Optional*

Controls the number of rows of option elements that appear in the select element. With a value of 1, the select element displays its content as a pop-up menu; with a value greater than 1, option items are rendered in a list box. Browsers control the width of the element, based on the widest text associated with nested option elements.

Example
```
<select name="equipment" size="3">
    <option value="monitor">Video monitor</option>
    <option value="modem">Modem</option>
    <option value="printer">Printer</option>
    ...
</select>
```

Value   Any positive integer.

Default   1

Object Model Reference
[window.]document.*formName.selectName*.size
[window.]document.forms[i].elements[j].size
[window.]document.getElementById(*elementID*).size

tabindex   IE *4* NN *n/a* Moz *all* Saf *all* Op *7* HTML *4*

tabindex="*integer*"   *Optional*

Facilitates accessibility to a complex form control. Once the select element has focus, the user can continue using the keyboard to make item choices. See the discussion about this attribute earlier in this chapter.

<small>

IE *3* NN *2* Moz *all* Saf *all* Op *7* HTML *3.2*

<small>...</small>

HTML End Tag: Required

The small element renders its content in a relative size one level smaller than the text preceding the element. Given the font element's way of specifying sizes in a range of 1 through 7, the small element displays its content one size smaller than the text that comes before it. This attribute is the same as specifying <font size=-1>.

Example   <p>Let's get really <small>small</small>.</p>

Object Model Reference

[window.]document.getElementById(*elementID*)

Element-Specific Attributes

None.

Element-Specific Event Handler Attributes

None.

<spacer>

IE *n/a* NN *3* Moz *n/a* Saf *n/a* Op *n/a* HTML *n/a*

<spacer>

HTML End Tag: Forbidden

As a solution to the need for creating blank space without forcing   entities, incessant <p> tags, or transparent images, Navigator 3 introduced the spacer element. This element creates empty space within a line of text, between lines, or as a rectangular space. Some of this functionality can be re-created in a cross-browser implementation with style sheets. The element is supported only in Navigator 3 and Navigator 4.

Example

<p>This is one line of a paragraph.
<spacer type="vertical" size="36">
And this completes the paragraph with a three-line gap from the first line.</p>

Element-Specific Attributes

align	height	size	type	width

Element-Specific Event Handler Attributes

None.

align

IE *n/a* NN *3* Moz *n/a* Saf *n/a* Op *n/a* HTML *n/a*

align="*alignmentConstant*"

Optional

Determines how a block type of spacer element aligns within the context of surrounding content. See "Alignment Constants" earlier in this chapter for a description of the possibilities.

<spacer>

Example
<spacer type="block" height="90" width="40" align="absmiddle">

Value   Case-insensitive constant value.

Default   bottom

height, width
IE n/a NN 3 Moz n/a Saf n/a Op n/a HTML n/a

height="*length*" width="*length*"   *Required*

The size that a block type spacer element occupies in a document is governed by the height and width attribute settings. These attributes apply only when the type attribute is block.

Example   <spacer type="block" height="150" width="250">

Value   Positive integer or percentage values.

Default   0

size
IE n/a NN 3 Moz n/a Saf n/a Op n/a HTML n/a

size="*pixelCount*"   *Optional*

The number of pixels of whitespace to insert either horizontally or vertically, depending on whether the type attribute is set to line or vertical. If the type attribute is set to block, the size attribute is ignored.

Example   <spacer type="line" size="40">

Value   Any positive integer.

Default   0

type
IE n/a NN 3 Moz n/a Saf n/a Op n/a HTML n/a

type="*spacerType*"   *Required*

Defines which of the three spacer geometries is being specified for the spacer element. A type of line adds empty space in the same line of text as the preceding content; a type of vertical (or vert) adds empty space between lines of text; and a type of block defines a rectangular space that extends in two dimensions. For the line and vertical types, the size attribute must be assigned; for the block type, the height and width attributes must be assigned.

Example   <spacer type="line" size="40">

Value   Any of four case-insensitive constant values: block | line | vertical | vert.

Default   line

<span>

width

See height.

<span>

<div align="right">IE 3 NN 4 Moz all Saf all Op 7 HTML 4</div>

`<span>...</span>`

<div align="right">*HTML End Tag: Required*</div>

The span element gives structure and context to any inline content in a document. Unlike some other structural elements that have very specific connotations attached to them (the p element, for instance), the author is free to give meaning to each particular span element by virtue of the element's attribute settings and nested content. Each span element becomes a generic container for all content within the required start and end tags.

It is convenient to use the span element as a wrapper for a small inline chunk of content that is to be governed by a style sheet rule. For example, if you want to differentiate a few words in a paragraph with the equivalent of a small caps look, you would wrap the affected words with a span element whose style sheet defines the requested font and text styles. Such a style sheet could be defined as an inline style attribute of the span element or assigned via the class or id attribute depending on the structure of the rest of the document.

If you need an arbitrary container for block-level content, use the div element.

Example

```
<span style="font-size:10pt; text-transform:uppercase">
30-day special offer</span>
```

Object Model Reference

`[window.]document.getElementById(elementID)`

Element-Specific Attributes

datafld	dataformatas	datasrc

Element-Specific Event Handler Attributes

None.

datafld

<div align="right">IE 4 NN n/a Moz n/a Saf n/a Op n/a HTML |4|</div>

`datafld="columnName"`

<div align="right">*Optional*</div>

Used with IE data binding to associate a remote data source column name with the HTML content of a span element. The data source column must be HTML (see dataformatas). datasrc and dataformatas attributes must also be set for the span element. Works only with text file data sources in IE 5/Mac.

This attribute was reserved in HTML 4, but was dropped in XHTML 1.0.

Example

`<span datasrc="DBSRC3" datafld="quote" dataformatas="HTML">...</span>`

<strike>

Value   Case-sensitive identifier.

Default   None.

Object Model Reference

[window.]document.getElementById(*elementID*).dataFld

dataformatas   IE *4*   NN *n/a*   Moz *n/a*   Saf *n/a*   Op *n/a*   HTML |4|

dataformatas="*dataType*"   *Optional*

Used with IE data binding, this attribute advises the browser whether the source material arriving from the data source is to be treated as plain text or as tagged HTML. A span element should receive data only in HTML format.

This attribute was reserved in HTML 4, but was dropped in XHTML 1.0.

Example

```
<span datasrc="DBSRC3" datafld="quote" dataformatas="HTML">...</span>
```

Value   Case-insensitive constants: html | text.

Default   text

Object Model Reference

[window.]document.getElementById(*elementID*).dataFormatAs

datasrc   IE *4*   NN *n/a*   Moz *n/a*   Saf *n/a*   Op *n/a*   HTML |4|

datasrc="*dataSourceName*"   *Optional*

Used with IE data binding to specify the ID of the page's object element that loads the data source object for remote data access. Content from the data source is specified via the datafld attribute. Works only with text file data sources in IE 5/Mac.

This attribute was reserved in HTML 4, but was dropped in XHTML 1.0.

Example

```
<span datasrc="DBSRC3" datafld="quote" dataformatas="HTML">...</span>
```

Value   Case-sensitive identifier.

Default   None.

Object Model Reference

[window.]document.getElementById(*elementID*).dataSrc

\<strike\>   IE *3*   NN *3*   Moz *all*   Saf *all*   Op *7*   HTML *3.2*

\<strike\>...\</strike\>   *HTML End Tag: Required*

The strike element renders its content as strikethrough text. This element is identical to the s element, which was adopted because it more closely resembled the one-character

<style>

element names for other type formatting (such as b, i, and u elements). In any case, both strike and s elements are deprecated in HTML 4 in favor of the text-decoration:line-through style sheet property. Neither strike nor s elements validate with strict HTML 4 or XHTML DTDs.

Example

```
<p>If at first you don't succeed, <strike>do it over</strike> try, try again.</p>
```

Object Model Reference

```
[window.]document.getElementById(elementID)
```

Element-Specific Attributes

None.

Element-Specific Event Handler Attributes

None.

<strong>

IE *all* NN *all* Moz *all* Saf *all* Op *7* HTML *all*

```
<strong>...</strong>
```
HTML End Tag: Required

The strong element is one of a large group of elements that the HTML 4 recommendation calls *phrase elements*. Such elements assign structural meaning to a designated portion of the document. A strong element is one that contains text that indicates a stronger emphasis than the em element. Whereas an em element is typically rendered as italic text, a strong element is generally rendered as boldface text. Override the default with a style sheet as you see fit.

Example

```
<p>Don't delay. <strong>Order today</strong> to get the maximum discount.
</p>
```

Object Model Reference

```
[window.]document.getElementById(elementID)
```

Element-Specific Attributes

None.

Element-Specific Event Handler Attributes

None.

<style>

IE *3* NN *4* Moz *all* Saf *all* Op *7* HTML *4*

```
<style>...</style>
```
HTML End Tag: Required

The style element is a container for style sheet rules. Use the style element only inside the head element. You may include more than one style element in a head element (see the media attribute).

<style>

Very old browsers may attempt to render the content of a style element. To prevent that, you can wrap the style sheet rules inside HTML comment tags. See Online Section III for details on the makeup of style sheet rules.

Example
```
<style type="text/css">
h1 {font-size: 18pt; text-transform: capitalize}
p  {font-size: 12pt}
</style>
```

Object Model Reference
```
[window.]document.getElementsByTagName("style")[i]
[window.]document.getElementById(elementID)
```

Element-Specific Attributes

disabled	media	type

Element-Specific Event Handler Attributes
None.

disabled

IE 4 NN *n/a* Moz *n/a* Saf *n/a* Op *n/a* HTML *n/a*

disabled   *Optional*

Disables the entire style element, as if it didn't exist in the document. IE/Mac responds to this attribute starting in Version 5.

The disabled attribute is a Boolean type, which means that its presence in the attribute sets its value to true. Its value can also be adjusted after the fact by scripting (see the style object in Chapter 2).

Example   `<style type="text/css" disabled>...</style>`

Value   The presence of the attribute disables the element.

Default   `false`

Object Model Reference
```
[window.]document.getElementsByTagName("style")[i].disabled
[window.]document.getElementById(elementID).disabled
```

media

IE 4 NN *n/a* Moz *all* Saf *all* Op 7 HTML 4

media="*descriptorList*"   *Optional*

Sets the intended output device for the content of the element. The media attribute looks forward to the day when browsers are able to tailor content to specific kinds of devices such as pocket computers, text-to-speech digitizers, or fuzzy television sets. These days, it is used mostly to provide an alternate style sheet for printed output. The HTML 4 specification defines a number of constant values for anticipated devices, but the list is open-ended, allowing future browsers to tailor output to yet other kinds of media and devices.

Example   <style type="text/css" media="print">...</style>

Value

Case-sensitive constant values. Multiple values can be grouped together in a comma-delimited list within a quoted string. Values defined in HTML 4 are all | aura | braille | handheld | print | projection | screen | tty | tv. Current browsers support the following values: all | print |screen.

Default   all

Object Model Reference

[window.]document.getElementsByTagName("style")[i].media
[window.]document.getElementById(*elementID*).media

type   IE *4* NN *4* Moz *all* Saf *all* Op *7* HTML *4*

type="*MIMEType*"   *Required*

The type attribute tells the browser which style sheet syntax to use to interpret the style rules defined in the current element.

Example   <style type="text/css">...</style>

Value   Case-insensitive MIME type. A type accepted by all mainstream browsers is "text/css". Navigator 4 (only) also recognizes "text/javascript" when using JavaScript syntax style sheets.

Default   text/css

Object Model Reference

[window.]document.getElementsByTagName("style")[i].type
[window.]document.getElementById(*elementID*).type

<sub>   IE *3* NN *2* Moz *all* Saf *all* Op *7* HTML *3.2*

<sub>...</sub>   *HTML End Tag: Required*

The sub element is a typographical element that instructs the browser to render its content as a subscript in a font size consistent with the surrounding content. Browsers tend to render this content in a smaller size than surrounding content.

Example

<p>A hydronium ion (H<sub>3</sub>O) has one more hydrogen atom than regular water.
</p>

Object Model Reference

[window.]document.getElementById(*elementID*)

Element-Specific Attributes

None.

Element-Specific Event Handler Attributes

None.

<sup>

IE *3* NN *2* Moz *all* Saf *all* Op *7* HTML *3.2*

`<sup>...</sup>`

HTML End Tag: Required

The sup element is a typographical element that instructs the browser to render its content as a superscript in a font size consistent with the surrounding content. Browsers tend to render this content in a smaller size than surrounding content.

Example   `<p>This book is published by O'Reilly<sup>&#153;</sup>.</p>`

Object Model Reference

`[window.]document.getElementById(elementID)`

Element-Specific Attributes

None.

Element-Specific Event Handler Attributes

None.

<table>

IE *all* NN *all* Moz *all* Saf *all* Op *7* HTML *3.2*

`<table>...</table>`

HTML End Tag: Required

The table element is a container for additional elements that specify the content for a table. A table consists of rows and columns of content. Other elements related to the table element are caption, col, colgroup, tbody, td, tfoot, th, thead, and tr. The purpose of the table element is to define a number of visible attributes that apply to the entire table, regardless of the number of rows or columns within it. Many of these attributes can be overridden for a given row, column, or cell. The number of rows and columns is strictly a factor of the structure of tr and td elements within the table. It is advisable to include a tbody section in every table if your scripts will modify the table's content.

Tables have been used for a relatively long time not only to organize rows and columns of content but also to position content. With no visible borders, table rows and columns can be set to empty space. With the wide browser adoption of CSS 2, web designers now rarely use tables for layout purposes. Tables are, instead, reserved for presentations of truly tabular data—data whose context within a document dictates that it be organized and presented in tabular format.

Deeply nested tables (tables within tables) can cause problems in some browsers. Navigator 4 has severe difficulty with style sheet inheritance and overall performance in complex tables (nesting beyond three levels is asking for trouble). IE 5/Mac can inexplicably explode cell dimensions when scripts create or modify table-related elements. The simpler you keep your table structure, the more reliable your pages will be across browsers. Heavy editing of table structures in visual HTML authoring tools can leave hidden complexities (e.g., lots of empty cells) in your source code. Temporarily turn on a thin table border to see the exact row and column structure (some web development browser extensions also let you see where tables are on the page).

Example

```
<table cols="3">
<thead>
<tr>
<th>Time</th><th>Event</th><th>Location</th>
</tr>
</thead>
<tbody>
<tr>
<td>7:30am-5:00pm</td><td>Registration Open</td><td>Main Lobby</td>
</tr>
<tr>
<td>9:00am-12:00pm</td><td>Keynote Speakers</td><td>Cypress Room</td>
</tr>
</tbody>
</table>
```

Object Model Reference

[window.]document.getElementById(*elementID*)

Element-Specific Attributes

align	background	bgcolor	border	bordercolor
bordercolordark	bordercolorlight	cellpadding	cellspacing	cols
datapagesize	datasrc	frame	height	hspace
layout	rules	summary	vspace	width

Element-Specific Event Handler Attributes

Handler	NN	IE	HTML
onafterupdate	n/a	4	n/a
onbeforeupdate	n/a	4	n/a
onrowenter	n/a	4	n/a
onrowexit	n/a	4	n/a

align

IE *all* NN *all* Moz *all* Saf *all* Op *7* HTML *3.2*

align="*where*"   *Optional*

Determines how the table is aligned relative to the next outermost container (usually the document body or html element). The align attribute is deprecated in HTML 4 in favor of style sheet properties.

Example	<table align="center">...</table>
Value	Alignment constant: center | left | right.

Default   left

Object Model Reference

[window.]document.getElementById(*elementID*).align

background   IE *3* NN *4* Moz *all* Saf *all* Op *7* HTML *n/a*
background="*URL*"   *Optional*

Specifies an image file that is used as a backdrop to the table. Unlike normal images that get loaded into browser content, a background image loads in its original size (without scaling) and tiles to fill the available table space. Smaller images download faster but are obviously repeated more often in the background. Animated GIFs are also allowable, but very distracting to the reader. When selecting a background image, be sure it is very muted in comparison to the main content so that the content stands out clearly. Background images, if used at all, should be extremely subtle.

Navigator 4 can be quirky with this attribute. Be prepared to wrap your main table (without a background) inside another `table` element, whose `background` property has a graphic file assigned to it.

Example   `<table background="watermark.jpg">...</table>`

Value   Any valid URL to an image file, including complete and relative URLs.

Default   None (table is transparent).

Object Model Reference

[window.]document.getElementById(*elementID*).background

bgcolor   IE *3* NN *3* Moz *all* Saf *all* Op *7* HTML *3.2*
bgcolor="*colorTripletOrName*"   *Optional*

Establishes a fill color (behind the text and other content) for the entire table. If you combine a `bgcolor` and `background`, any transparent areas of the background image let the background color show through. This attribute is deprecated in HTML 4 in favor of the background-color style property.

Example   `<table bgcolor="tan">...</table>`

Value   A hexadecimal triplet or plain-language color name. A setting of empty is interpreted as "#000000" (black). See Appendix A for acceptable plain-language color names.

Default   Varies with browser, browser version, and operating system.

Object Model Reference

[window.]document.getElementById(*elementID*).bgColor

border

border="*pixelCount*"   *Optional*

The thickness (in pixels) of the border drawn around a table element. If you set the border attribute to any value, browsers by default render narrow borders around each of the cells inside the table. With a table element's border showing, the thickness of internal borders between cells is defined by the cellspacing attribute of the table element.

If you include only the border attribute without assigning any value to it, the browser renders default-sized borders around the entire table and between cells, unless overridden by other attributes.

Browsers render the border in a 3-D style, with the border appearing to be raised around the flat content in the cells. Numerous other attributes affect the look of the border, including: bordercolor, bordercolordark, bordercolorlight, frame, and rules. The type of border rendered for tables is different from the borders defined by style sheet rules. You get better control of the border look by using the dedicated attributes of the table element.

Example   <table border="1">...</table>

Value   A positive integer value.

Default   0

Object Model Reference

[window.]document.getElementById(*elementID*).border

bordercolor

bordercolor="*colorTripletOrName*"   *Optional*

The colors used to render some of the pixels that create the illusion of borders around cells and the entire table. The border attribute must have a nonzero value assigned for the color to appear. The 3-D effect of borders in is created by careful positioning of light (or white) and dark lines around the page's background or default color (see Figure 1-4). Standard colors are usually shades of gray and white, depending on the browser.

Applying color to a table border has a different effect in Internet Explorer and all other supporting browsers. Internet Explorer and Safari apply the color to all lines that make up the border. The net effect is to flatten the 3-D effect (refer to the bordercolordark and bordercolorlight attributes to color borders and maintain the 3-D effect in IE). In Navigator and Mozilla, the color is applied to what is normally the darker of the two shades used to create the border. Moreover, the browsers automatically adjust the darkness of some of the lines to enhance the 3-D effect of the border.

Example   <table bordercolor="green" border="2">...</table>

Value   A hexadecimal triplet or plain-language color name. A setting of empty is interpreted as "#000000" (black). See Appendix A for acceptable plain-language color names.

Default   Varies with browser and operating system.

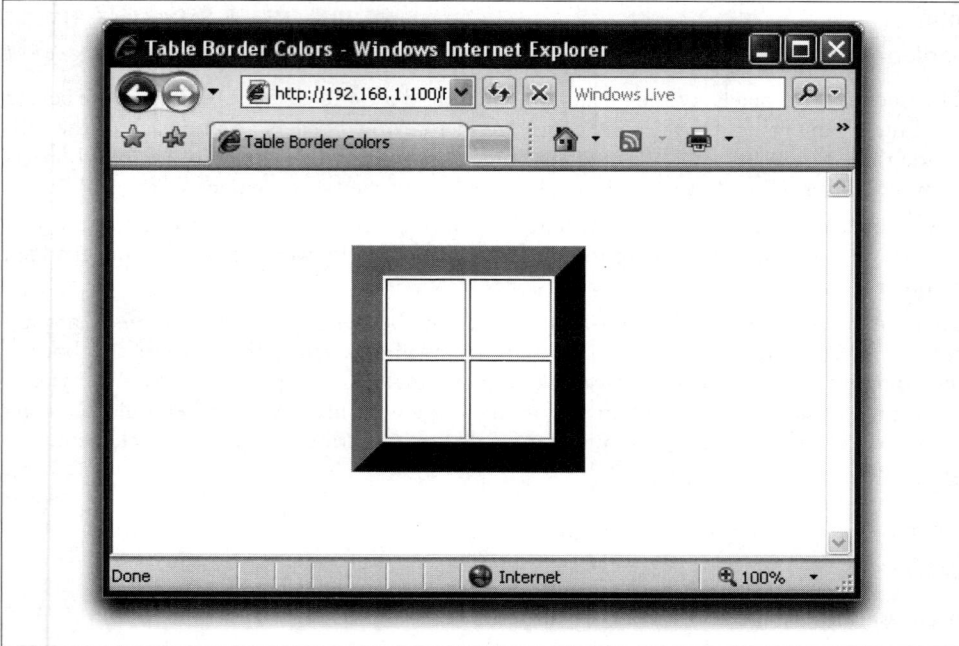

Figure 1-4. Components of table border color

Object Model Reference
[window.]document.getElementById(*elementID*).borderColor

bordercolordark, bordercolorlight
IE *3* NN *n/a* Moz *n/a* Saf *n/a* Op *n/a* HTML *n/a*

bordercolordark="*colorTripletOrName*" bordercolorlight="*colorTripletOrName*"   *Optional*

The 3-D effect of table borders in Internet Explorer is created by careful positioning of light and dark lines around the page's background or default color (see Figure 1-4Figure 1-4). You can independently control the colors used for the dark and light lines by assigning values to the bordercolordark and bordercolorlight attributes. The border attribute must have a nonzero value assigned for the colors to appear.

Typically, you should assign complementary colors to the pair of attributes. There is also no rule that says you must assign a dark color to bordercolordark. The attributes merely control a well-defined set of lines so you can predict which lines of the border change with each attribute.

To achieve the identical look in IE and browsers that support table border colors, you must determine the complementary colors that other browsers use for the 3-D effect from the bordercolor attribute. Then assign those values to the bordercolordark and bordercolorlight attributes. You may place all three attributes in the same <table> tag.

Example
```
<table bordercolordark="darkred" bordercolorlight="salmon" border="3">...</table>
```

Value	A hexadecimal triplet or plain-language color name. A setting of empty is interpreted as "#000000" (black). See Appendix A for acceptable plain-language color names.
Default	Varies with operating system.

Object Model Reference

```
[window.]document.getElementById(elementID).borderColorDark
[window.]document.getElementById(elementID).borderColorLight
```

cellpadding

IE 3 NN all Moz all Saf all Op 7 HTML 3.2

`cellpadding="length"` *Optional*

The amount of empty space between the border of a table cell and the content of the cell. Note that this attribute applies to space *inside* a cell. Without setting this attribute, most browsers render text content so that its leftmost pixels abut the left edge of the cell. If the table displays borders, adding a few pixels of breathing space between the border edge and the content makes the content more readable. Large padding may also be desirable in some design instances. This attribute is not as noticeable when the table does not display borders (in which case the cellspacing attribute can assist in adjusting the space between cells).

Example `<table border="2" cellpadding="3">...</table>`

Value

Any length value in pixels or percentage of available space. Percentage values are based on the total available space in the horizontal and vertical dimensions of the cell. For example, a value of 10% means that the left and right padding will each be 5% of the total width of the cell; the top and bottom padding will each be 5% of the total height of the cell.

Default 0

Object Model Reference

```
[window.]document.getElementById(elementID).cellPadding
```

cellspacing

IE 3 NN all Moz all Saf all Op 7 HTML 3.2

`cellspacing="length"` *Optional*

The amount of empty space between the outer edges of each table cell. If you set the border attribute of the table element to any positive integer value, the effect of setting cellspacing is to define the thickness of borders rendered between cells. Even without a visible border, the readability of a table often benefits from cell spacing.

Example `<table border="2" cellspacing="10">...</table>`

Value Any positive integer.

Default 0 (no table border); 2 (with table border).

Object Model Reference

```
[window.]document.getElementById(elementID).cellSpacing
```

cols

cols="*columnCount*"   *Optional*

The number of columns of the table. The HTML specification never adopted this attribute. In HTML 4, the functionality of this attribute is covered by the colgroup and col elements. In the meantime, the cols attribute is recognized by older and current browsers. The attribute assists the browser in preparation for rendering the table. Without this attribute, the browser relies on its interpretation of all downloaded tr and td elements to determine how the table is to be divided.

Example   <table cols="4">...</table>

Value   Any positive integer.

Default   None.

Object Model Reference

[window.]document.getElementById(*elementID*).cols

datapagesize

datapagesize="*recordCount*"   *Optional*

Used with IE data binding, this attribute advises the browser how many instances of a table row must be rendered to accommodate the number of data source records set by this attribute. A common application is setting a table cell to display a text input element whose datafld attribute is bound to a particular column of the data source (the datasrc is set in the table element). If the datapagesize attribute is set to 5, the browser must display five rows of the table (but the row is specified in the HTML only once).

Example

```
<table datasrc="DBSRC3" datapagesize="5">
<tr>
  <td><input type="text" datafld="stockNum"></td>
  <td><input type="text" datafld="qtyOnHand"></td>
</tr>
</table>
```

Value   Any positive integer.

Default   None.

Object Model Reference

[window.]document.getElementById(*elementID*).dataPageSize

datasrc

datasrc="*dataSourceName*"   *Optional*

Used with IE data binding to specify the ID of the page's object element that loads the data source object for remote data access. Content from the data source is specified via the datafld attribute.

A block of contiguous records can be rendered in the table when you also set the datapagesize attribute of the table. Works only with text file data sources in IE 5/Mac.

Example   `<table datasrc="DBSRC3" datapagesize="5">...</table>`

Value   Case-sensitive identifier.

Default   None.

Object Model Reference
`[window.]document.getElementById(elementID).dataSrc`

frame   IE 3 NN n/a Moz all Saf n/a Op 7 HTML 4
`frame="frameConstant"`   *Optional*

Defines which (if any) sides of a table's outer border (set with the border attribute) are rendered. This attribute does not affect the interior borders between cells. Including the border attribute without assigning any value to it is the same as setting the frame attribute to border. All settings can be replicated with CSS border-related properties if you prefer.

Example   `<table border="3" frame="void">...</table>`

Value

Any one case-insensitive frame constant:

above
    Renders border along top edge of table only
below
    Renders border along bottom edge of table only
border
    Renders all four sides of the border (default in IE and NN)
box
    Renders all four sides of the border (same as border)
hsides
    Renders borders on top and bottom edges of table only (a nice look)
lhs
    Renders border on left edge of table only
rhs
    Renders border on right edge of table only
void
    Hides all borders (default in HTML 4)
vsides
    Renders borders on left and right edges of table only

Default   Mozilla: void (when border=0); border (when border is any other value).
Internet Explorer: border.

Object Model Reference
`[window.]document.getElementById(elementID).frame`

height, width

IE 3 NN *all* Moz *all* Saf *all* Op *7 (width)* HTML *3.2 (width)*

height="*length*" width="*length*" *Optional*

The rectangular dimensions of a table that may be different from the default size as calculated by the browser. When the values for these attributes are less than the minimum space required to render the table cell content, the browser overrides the attribute settings to make sure that all content appears, even if it means that text lines word-wrap. You can also stretch the dimensions of a table beyond the browser-calculated dimensions. Extra whitespace appears inside table cells to make up the difference. If you specify just one attribute, the browser performs the necessary calculations to automatically adjust the dimension along the other axis.

Note that the height attribute is not in the HTML specification. The assumption there is that the table height is calculated by the browser to best show all cell content given either the default or attribute-established width. Because different browsers on different operating systems can render text content in varying relative font sizes, it is not unusual to let the height of a table be calculated by the browser.

Example <table width="80%">...</table>

Value Any length value in pixels or percentage of available space.

Default Governed by content, but width not to exceed 100% of the next outermost container. All browsers but Mozilla accept percentage values beyond 100%, which may cause the table's container to display scroll bars and perhaps disturb the graphical integrity of the layout design.

Object Model Reference

[window.]document.getElementById(*elementID*).height
[window.]document.getElementById(*elementID*).width

hspace, vspace

IE *n/a* NN *n/a* Moz *all* Saf *all* Op *n/a* HTML *n/a*

hspace="*pixels*" vspace="*pixels*" *Optional*

Inserts transparent padding outside the edges of the entire table on the page. Use CSS-padding-related attributes instead. Note that Mozilla responds to these table element attributes only in "quirks" mode (see DOCTYPE element).

Example <table hspace="20" vspace="40">...</table>

Value Integer pixel count.

Default 0

layout

IE *n/a* NN *n/a* Moz *all* Saf *n/a* Op *n/a* HTML *n/a*

layout="*layoutType*" *Optional*

Controls the table-layout-rendering algorithm. A value of fixed directs the browser to size the table and cells according to explicit height and width settings, rather than respecting content size minimums. This attribute mimics the table-layout CSS property.

<table>

Example	`<table layout="fixed" width="500">...</table>`
Value	Constant values: auto | `fixed`.
Default	auto

rules

`rules="rulesConstant"`   *Optional*

Defines where (if at all) interior borders between cells are rendered by the browser. In addition to setting the table to draw borders to turn the cells into a matrix, you can also set borders to be drawn only to separate rows, columns, or any sanctioned cell grouping (thead, tbody, tfoot, colgroup, or col). The border attribute must be present—either as a Boolean or set to a specific border size—for any cell borders to be drawn. IE 5/Mac leaves gaps in inter-cell borders where rules are removed. In browsers that support table border colors, the same color is applied to rules.

| Example | `<table border="3" rules="groups">...</table>` |

Value

Any one case-insensitive rules constant:

all
: Renders borders around each cell

cols
: Renders borders between columns only

groups
: Renders borders between cell groups as defined by the thead, tfoot, tbody, colgroup, or col elements

none
: Hides all interior borders

rows
: Renders borders between rows only

Default   none (when border=0); all (when border is any other value).

Object Model Reference

`[window.]document.getElementById(elementID).rules`

summary

`summary="text"`   *Optional*

A textual description of the table, including, but not limited to, instructions that nonvisual browsers might follow to describe the purpose and organization of the table data. The **Properties** choice for Mozilla's context menu for this element displays a small window that includes an active link to the URL assigned to the attribute. Current mainstream provide no other functionality for this attribute.

<tbody>

Example

```
<table summary="Order form for entry of up to five products.">...</table>
```

Value   Any quoted string of characters.

Default   None.

vspace

See hspace.

width

See height.

<tbody>

```
<tbody>...</tbody>
```

HTML End Tag: Optional

A tbody element is an arbitrary container of one or more rows of table cells. More than one tbody element may be defined within a single table element. Use the tbody element to define structural segments of a table that may require their own styles or border treatments (see the rules attribute). A tbody element is the row-oriented equivalent of the colgroup element for columns. Other types of row groupings available are the tfoot and thead elements, neither of which overlaps with a tbody element.

Example

```
<table cols="3">
<thead>
<tr>
<th>Time</th><th>Event</th><th>Location</th>
</tr>
</thead>
<tbody>
<tr>
<td>7:30am-5:00pm</td><td>Registration Open</td><td>Main Lobby</td>
</tr>
<tr>
<td>9:00am-12:00pm</td><td>Keynote Speakers</td><td>Cypress Room</td>
</tr>
</tbody>
</table>
```

Object Model Reference

```
[window.]document.getElementById(elementID)
```

Element-Specific Attributes

align	bgcolor	ch	char	charoff
choff	valign			

Element-Specific Event Handler Attributes

None.

align

align="*alignConstant*"   *Optional*

Establishes the horizontal alignment characteristics of content within the row(s) covered by the tbody element.

Example   <tbody align="center">

Value

HTML 4 and various browsers implement different sets of attribute values.

Value	IE/Windows	Others	HTML 4
center	•	•	•
char	—	—	•
justify	—	•	•
left	•	•	•
right	•	•	•

The values center, left, and right are self-explanatory. The value justify spaces multiline content so that text is justified down both left and right edges. For the value char, the char attribute must also be set to specify the character on which alignment revolves. In the HTML 4 specification example, content that does not contain the character appears to be right-aligned to the location of the character in other rows of the same column.

It's important to bear in mind that the align attribute applies to every cell of every row within the tbody. If you want a different alignment for the row header, override the setting with a separate align attribute or text-align style sheet property for the thead or individual th elements.

Default   left

Object Model Reference

[window.]document.getElementById(*elementID*).align

bgcolor

bgcolor="*colorTripletOrName*"   *Optional*

Establishes a fill color (behind the text and other content) for the cells contained by the tbody element.

Example   <tbody bgcolor="tan">

Value   A hexadecimal triplet or plain-language color name. A setting of empty is interpreted as "#000000" (black). See Appendix A for acceptable plain-language color names.

Default   Varies with browser, browser version, and operating system.

Object Model Reference

[window.]document.getElementById(*elementID*).bgColor

char   IE *n/a* NN *n/a* Moz *n/a* Saf *n/a* Op *n/a* HTML 4

char="*character*"   *Optional*

The char attribute defines the text character used as an alignment point for text within a
cell contained by the tbody element. This attribute is of value only for the align attribute
set to "char". Microsoft documents a ch attribute, which corresponds to the standards-
based char attribute. In any case, the browser does not respond to either attribute.

Example   <tbody align="char" char=".">

Value   Any single text character.

Default   None.

charoff   IE *n/a* NN *n/a* Moz *n/a* Saf *n/a* Op *n/a* HTML 4

charoff="*length*"   *Optional*

The charoff attribute lets you set a specific offset point at which the character specified by
the char attribute is to appear within a cell contained by the tbody element. This attribute is
provided in case the browser default positioning does not meet with the design goals of the
table. Microsoft documents a choff attribute, which corresponds to the standards-based
charoff attribute. In any case, the browser does not respond to either attribute.

Example   <tbody align="char" char="." charoff="80%">

Value   Any length value in pixels or percentage of cell space.

Default   None.

choff

See charoff.

valign   IE *4* NN *n/a* Moz *all* Saf *all* Op *7* HTML 4

valign="*alignmentConstant*"   *Optional*

Determines the vertical alignment of content within cells of the column(s) covered by the
tbody element. You can override the vertical alignment for a particular cell anywhere in the
column.

Example   <tbody valign="bottom">

<td>

Value

Four constant values: top | middle | bottom | baseline. With top and bottom, the content is rendered flush (or very close to it) to the top and bottom of the table cell. Set to middle (the default), the content floats perfectly centered vertically in the cell. When one cell's contents might wrap to multiple lines at common window widths (assuming a variable table width), it is advisable to set the valign attribute to baseline. This assures that the character baseline of the first (or only) line of a cell's text aligns with the other cells in the row—usually the most aesthetically pleasing arrangement.

Default   middle

Object Model Reference

[window.]document.getElementById(*elementID*).vAlign

<td>

IE *all* NN *all* Moz *all* Saf *all* Op *7* HTML *3.2*

<td>...</td>   *HTML End Tag: Optional*

The td element is a container for content that is rendered inside one cell of a table element. One cell is the intersection of a column and row. Other elements related to the td element are caption, col, colgroup, table, tbody, tfoot, th, thead, and tr. In addition to providing a wrapper for a cell's content, the td element defines a number of visible attributes that apply to a single cell, often overriding similar attributes set in lesser-nested elements in the table.

Four attributes—abbr, axis, headers, and scope—are included in the HTML 4 specification in anticipation of nonvisual browsers that will use text-to-speech technology to describe content of an HTML page—a kind of "verbal rendering." Although these attributes are briefly described here for the sake of completeness, there is much more to their application in nonvisual browsers than is relevant in this book on Dynamic HTML. Consult the HTML 4 recommendation for more details.

Example

```
<table cols="3">
<thead>
<tr>
<th>Time</th><th>Event</th><th>Location</th>
</tr>
</thead>
<tbody>
<tr>
<td>7:30am-5:00pm</td><td>Registration Open</td><td>Main Lobby</td>
</tr>
<tr>
<td>9:00am-12:00pm</td><td>Keynote Speakers</td><td>Cypress Room</td>
</tr>
</tbody>
</table>
```

Object Model Reference

[window.]document.getElementById(*elementID*)

<td>

Element-Specific Attributes

abbr	align	axis	background	bgcolor
bordercolor	bordercolordark	bordercolorlight	ch	char
charoff	choff	colspan	datafld	dir
headers	height	nowrap	rowspan	scope
valign	width			

Element-Specific Event Handler Attributes

Handler	IE	Others	HTML
onafterupdate	4	n/a	n/a
onbeforeupdate	4	n/a	n/a
onrowenter	4	n/a	n/a
onrowexit	4	n/a	n/a

abbr
IE 6   NN n/a   Moz all   Saf all   Op n/a   HTML 4

abbr="*text*"   *Optional*

Provides an abbreviated string that describes the cell's content. This is usually a brief label that a nonvisual browser would speak to describe what the value of the cell represents. The **Properties** choice for Mozilla's context menu for this element displays a small window that includes an active link to the URL assigned to the attribute. Current mainstream browsers provide no other functionality for this attribute.

Example   <td abbr="Main Event">Keynote Speakers</td>

Value   Any quoted string.

Default   None.

Object Model Reference
[window.]document.getElementById(*elementID*).abbr

align
IE all   NN all   Moz all   Saf all   Op 7   HTML 3.2

align="*alignConstant*"   *Optional*

Establishes the horizontal alignment characteristics of content within the cell covered by the td element.

Example   <td align="center">

Value

HTML 4 and various browsers implement different sets of attribute values.

Value	IE/Windows and NN 4	Others	HTML 4
center	•	•	•
char	—	—	•
justify	—	•	•
left	•	•	•
right	•	•	•

The values center, left, and right are self-explanatory. The value justify spaces multiline content so that text is justified down both left and right edges. For the value char, the char attribute must also be set to specify the character on which alignment revolves. In the HTML 4 specification example, content that does not contain the character appears to be right-aligned to the location of the character in other rows of the same column.

Default   left

Object Model Reference
[window.]document.getElementById(*elementID*).align

axis   IE 6   NN *n/a*   Moz *all*   Saf *all*   Op *n/a*   HTML 4
axis="*text*"   *Optional*

Provides an abbreviated string that describes the cell's category. This is usually a brief label that a nonvisual browser would speak to describe what the value of the cell represents. The **Properties** choice for Mozilla's context menu for this element displays a small window that includes an active link to the URL assigned to the attribute. Current mainstream browsers provide no other functionality for this attribute.

Example   <td axis="event">Keynote Speakers</td>

Value   Any quoted string.

Default   None.

Object Model Reference
[window.]document.getElementById(*elementID*).axis

background   IE 3   NN 4   Moz *all*   Saf *all*   Op 7   HTML *n/a*
background="*URL*"   *Optional*

Specifies an image file that is used as a backdrop to the cell. Unlike normal images that get loaded into browser content, a background image loads in its original size (without scaling) and tiles to fill the available cell space. Smaller images download faster but are obviously repeated more often in the background. Navigator 4, however, requires a minimum image size of 16 by 16 pixels. Animated GIFs are also allowable, but very distracting to the reader. When selecting a background image, be sure it is very muted in comparison to the main content so that the content stands out clearly. Background images, if used at all, should be extremely subtle.

Example	`<td background="watermark.jpg">`
Value	Any valid URL to an image file, including complete and relative URLs.
Default	None.

Object Model Reference

`[window.]document.getElementById(elementID).background`

bgcolor
IE 3   NN 3   Moz all   Saf all   Op 7   HTML 3.2

`bgcolor="colorTripletOrName"` *Optional*

Establishes a fill color (behind the text and other content) for the cell defined by the td element.

Example	`<td bgcolor="yellow">`
Value	A hexadecimal triplet or plain-language color name. A setting of empty is interpreted as "#000000" (black). See Appendix A for acceptable plain-language color names.
Default	Varies with browser, browser version, and operating system.

Object Model Reference

`[window.]document.getElementById(elementID).bgColor`

bordercolor
IE 3   NN n/a   Moz n/a   Saf n/a   Op n/a   HTML n/a

`bordercolor="colorTripletOrName"` *Optional*

The colors used to render some of the pixels that create the illusion of borders around cells and the entire table. Internet Explorer applies the color to all four lines that make up the interior border of a cell. Therefore, colors of adjacent cells do not collide. A cell's border color can be different from the table's border color.

Example	`<td bordercolor="green">`
Value	A hexadecimal triplet or plain-language color name. A setting of empty is interpreted as "#000000" (black). See Appendix A for acceptable plain-language color names.
Default	Varies with browser and operating system.

Object Model Reference

`[window.]document.getElementById(elementID).borderColor`

bordercolordark, bordercolorlight
IE 3   NN n/a   Moz n/a   Saf n/a   Op n/a   HTML n/a

Optional

`bordercolordark="colorTripletOrName"`
`bordercolorlight="colorTripletOrName"`

The 3-D effect of table borders in Internet Explorer is created by careful positioning of light and dark lines around the page's background or default color (see Figure 1-4 in the table

<td>

element discussion). You can independently control the colors used for the dark and light lines by assigning values to the bordercolordark (left and top edges of the cell) and bordercolorlight (right and bottom edges) attributes.

Typically, you should assign complementary colors to the pair of attributes. There is also no rule that says you must assign a dark color to bordercolordark. The attributes merely control a well-defined set of lines so you can predict which lines of the border change with each attribute.

Example `<td bordercolordark="darkred" bordercolorlight="salmon">`

Value A hexadecimal triplet or plain-language color name. A setting of empty is interpreted as "#000000" (black). See Appendix A for acceptable plain-language color names.

Default Varies with operating system.

Object Model Reference

`[window.]document.getElementById(elementID).borderColorDark`
`[window.]document.getElementById(elementID).borderColorLight`

---

char   IE *n/a* NN *n/a* Moz *n/a* Saf *n/a* Op *n/a* HTML *n/a*

`char="character"`   *Optional*

The char attribute defines the text character used as an alignment point for text within a cell. This attribute is of value only for the align attribute set to "char". Microsoft documents a ch attribute, which corresponds to the standards-based char attribute. In any case, the browser does not respond to either attribute.

Example `<td align="char" char=".">203.00</td>`

Value Any single text character.

Default None.

---

charoff   IE *n/a* NN *n/a* Moz *n/a* Saf *n/a* Op *n/a* HTML *4*

`charoff="length"`   *Optional*

The charoff attribute lets you set a specific offset point at which the character specified by the char attribute is to appear within a cell. This attribute is provided in case the browser default positioning does not meet with the design goals of the table. Microsoft documents a choff attribute, which corresponds to the standards-based charoff attribute. In any case, the browser does not respond to either attribute.

Example `<td align="char" char="." charoff="80%">`

Value Any length value in pixels or percentage of cell space.

Default None.

choff

See charoff.

colspan

IE *all* NN *all* Moz *all* Saf *all* Op 7 HTML 3.2

colspan="*columnCount*"   *Optional*

The number of columns across which the current table cell should extend itself. For each additional column included in the colspan count, one less td element is required for the table row. If you set the align attribute to center or right, the alignment is calculated on the full width of the td element across the specified number of columns. Unless the current cell also specifies a rowspan attribute, the next table row returns to the original column count.

Example   `<td colspan="2" align="center">`

Value   Any positive integer, usually 2 or larger.

Default   1

Object Model Reference

[window.]document.getElementById(*elementID*).colSpan

datafld

IE 4 NN *n/a* Moz *n/a* Saf *n/a* Op *n/a* HTML *n/a*

datafld="*columnName*"   *Optional*

Used with IE data binding to associate a remote data source column name with the content of a table cell. A datasrc (and optionally a datapagesize) attribute must also be set for the enclosing table element. Works only with text file data sources in IE 5/Mac.

Example

```
<table datasrc="DBSRC3" datapagesize="5">
<tr>
  <td datafld='stockNum'></td>
  <td datafld='qtyOnHand'></td>
</tr>
</table>
```

Value   Case-sensitive identifier.

Default   None.

headers

IE 6 NN *n/a* Moz *all* Saf *all* Op *n/a* HTML 4

headers="*cellIDList*"   *Optional*

Points to one or more th or td elements that act as column or row headers for the current table cell. The assigned value is a space-delimited list of id attribute values that are assigned to the relevant th elements. A nonvisual browser could speak the cell's header before the content of the cell to help listeners identify the nature of the cell content. Although some maintstream browsers claim support for this attribute, none have yet connected support for it.

Example
```
<tr>
<th id="hdr1">Product Number</th>
<th id="hdr2">Description</th>
</tr>
<tr>
<td headers="hdr1">0392</td>
<td headers="hdr2">Round widget</td>
</tr>
```

Value   A space-delimited list of case-sensitive IDs assigned to cells that act as headers to the current cell.

Default   None.

height, width   IE *all*   NN *all*   Moz *all*   Saf *all*   Op 7   HTML *3.2*

height="*length*" width="*length*"   *Optional*

The rectangular dimensions of a cell that may be different from the default size as calculated by the browser. When the values for these attributes are less than the minimum space required to render the table cell content, the browser overrides the attribute settings to make sure that all content appears, even if it means that text lines word-wrap. You can also stretch the dimensions of a table beyond the browser-calculated dimensions. Extra whitespace appears inside table cells to make up the difference. If you specify just one of these attributes, the browser performs all necessary calculations to automatically adjust the dimension along the other axis. The cell must have some content assigned to it, or it may close up to minimum size.

Due to the regular nature of tables, if you set a custom height for one cell in a row taller than the others, the entire row is set to that height; similarly, setting the width of a cell to wider than others in the same column causes the width of all cells in the column to be the same size.

Both the height and width attributes are deprecated in HTML 4 in favor of height and width style sheet properties (which are not available for table cells in Navigator 4).

Example   `<td width="80%" height="30">`

Value   Any length value in pixels or percentage of available space.

Default   Based on content size.

Object Model Reference
```
[window.]document.getElementById(elementID).height
[window.]document.getElementById(elementID).width
```

nowrap

IE *all* NN *all* Moz *all* Saf *all* Op 7 HTML *3.2*

nowrap

Optional

The presence of the nowrap attribute instructs the browser to render the cell as wide as is necessary to display a line of nonbreaking text on one line. Abuse of this attribute can force the user into a great deal of inconvenient horizontal scrolling of the page to view all of the content. The nowrap attribute is deprecated in HTML 4 in favor of the white-space:nowrap CSS property.

Example   <td nowrap>

Value   The presence of this attribute sets its value to true.

Default   false

Object Model Reference
[window.]document.getElementById(*elementID*).noWrap

rowspan

IE *all* NN *all* Moz *all* Saf *all* Op 7 HTML *3.2*

rowspan="*rowCount*"

Optional

The number of rows through which the current table cell should extend itself downward. For each additional row included in the rowspan count, one less td element is required for the next table row in that cell's position along the row.

Example   <td rowspan="2">

Value   Any positive integer, usually 2 or larger.

Default   1

Object Model Reference
[window.]document.getElementById(*elementID*).rowSpan

scope

IE 6 NN *n/a* Moz *all* Saf *all* Op *n/a* HTML 4

scope="*scopeConstant*"

Optional

Used more with a th element than with a td element, the scope attribute sets the range of cells (relative to the current cell) that behave as though the current cell is the header for those cells. For tables whose structure is quite regular, the scope attribute is a simpler way of achieving what the headers attribute does, without having to define id attributes for the header cells. Although some mainstream browsers claim support for this attribute, none have yet connected support for it.

Example
```
<tr>
<th scope="col">Product Number</th>
<th scope="col">Description</th>
</tr>
<tr>
```

<td>

```
<td>0392</td>
<td>Round widget</td>
</tr>
```

Value

One of four recognized scope constants:

col
> Current cell text becomes header text for every cell in the rest of the column.

colgroup
> Current cell text becomes header text for every cell in the rest of the colgroup element.

row
> Current cell text becomes header text for every cell in the rest of the tr element.

rowgroup
> Current cell text becomes header text for every cell in the rest of the tbody element.

Default None.

valign

IE *all* NN *all* Moz *all* Saf *all* Op *7* HTML *3.2*

valign="*alignmentConstant*" *Optional*

Determines the vertical alignment of content within the td element. A value you set for an individual cell overrides the same attribute setting for outer containers, such as tr and tbody.

Example `<td valign="bottom">`

Value

Four constant values: top | middle | bottom | baseline. With top and bottom, the content is rendered flush (or very close to it) to the top and bottom of the table cell. Set to middle (the default), the content floats perfectly centered vertically in the cell. When one cell's contents might wrap to multiple lines at common window widths (assuming a variable table width), it is advisable to set the valign attribute to baseline. This assures that the character baseline of the first (or only) line of a cell's text aligns with the other cells in the row—usually the most aesthetically pleasing arrangement.

Default middle

Object Model Reference
[window.]document.getElementById(*elementID*).vAlign

width

See height.

<textarea>

<textarea>

<textarea>...</textarea>   *HTML End Tag: Required*

The textarea element is a multiline text input control primarily used inside form elements (required in Navigator 4 or earlier). Unlike the text type input element, a textarea element can be sized to accept more than one line of text. Word-wrapping is available on current browsers, and users may enter carriage return characters (a combination of characters ASCII decimal 13 and 10) inside the text box. When a textarea element is inside a submitted form, the name/value pair is submitted, with the value being the content of the text box (and the name attribute must be assigned). The CGI program on the server must be able to handle the possibility of carriage returns in the text data.

If you wish to display text in the textarea element when it loads, that text goes between the start and end tags; otherwise, there are no intervening characters in the source code between start and end tags. A label for the textarea element must be placed before or after the element, and may be encased in a label element for structural purposes (optionally in newer browsers).

Example

```
<textarea rows="5" cols="60" name="notes">Use this area for extra notes.
</textarea>
```

Object Model Reference

```
[window.]document.formName.elementName
[window.]document.forms[i].elements[j]
[window.]document.getElementById(elementID)
```

Element-Specific Attributes

accept	autofocus	cols	datafld	datasrc
disabled	form	inputmode	maxlength	name
readonly	required	rows	wrap	

Element-Specific Event Handler Attributes

Handler	IE	NN	Opera	Others	HTML
onafterupdate	4	n/a	n/a	n/a	n/a
onbeforeupdate	4	n/a	n/a	n/a	n/a
onchange	3	2	all	all	4
onformchange	n/a	n/a	9	n/a	n/a
onforminput	n/a	n/a	9	n/a	n/a
oninvalid	n/a	n/a	9	n/a	n/a
onscroll	3	n/a	n/a	n/a	4
onselect	3	2	all	all	4

<textarea>

accept

IE *n/a* NN *n/a* Moz *all* Saf *n/a* Op *n/a* HTML *n/a*

accept="*MIMETypeList*"   *Optional*

A Web Forms 2.0 extension, the accept attribute specifies one or more MIME types for allowable content to be entered into the element. If the browser provides alternate input editors for content other than straight text, this attribute prepares the element for the content and encodes it correctly for submission with the form.

Example   <textarea name="newsItem" accept="message/news"></textarea>

Value   MIME type (content type) value. For multiple items, a comma-delimited list is allowed. Web Forms 2.0 allows wildcards for MIME type ranges.

Default   None.

autofocus

IE *n/a* NN *n/a* Moz *n/a* Saf *n/a* Op *n/a* HTML *n/a*

autofocus="autofocus"   *Optional*

Web Forms 2.0 extension that brings focus to the element after the page loads. Should be assigned to only one form control element per page.

cols

IE *all* NN *all* Moz *all* Saf *all* Op *7* HTML *all*

cols="*columnCount*"   *Optional*

The width of the editable space of the textarea element. The value represents the number of monofont characters that are to be displayed within the width. For a browser that supports style sheet font sizes, the actual width changes accordingly.

Example   <textarea cols="40">...</textarea>

Value   Any positive integer.

Default   Varies with browser and operating system.

Object Model Reference

[window.]document.*formName.elementName*.cols
[window.]document.forms[i].elements[j].cols
[window.]document.getElementById(*elementID*).cols

datafld

IE *4* NN *n/a* Moz *n/a* Saf *n/a* Op *n/a* HTML *n/a*

datafld="*columnName*"   *Optional*

Used with IE data binding to associate a remote data source column name with the content of the textarea element. A datasrc attribute must also be set for the element. Works only with text file data sources in IE 5/Mac.

Example

<textarea name="summary" datasrc="DBSRC3" datafld="summary"></textarea>

Value   Case-sensitive identifier.

<textarea>

Default   None.

Object Model Reference
[window.]document.*formName*.*elementName*.dataFld
[window.]document.forms[i].elements[j].dataFld
[window.]document.getElementById(*elementID*).dataFld

datasrc   IE 4 NN *n/a* Moz *n/a* Saf *n/a* Op *n/a* HTML *n/a*
datasrc="*dataSourceName*"   *Optional*

Used with IE data binding to specify the ID of the page's object element that loads the data source object for remote data access. Content from the data source is specified via the datafld attribute. Works only with text file data sources in IE 5/Mac.

Example
<textarea name="summary" datasrc="DBSRC3" datafld="summary"></textarea>

Value   Case-sensitive identifier.

Default   None.

Object Model Reference
[window.]document.*formName*.*elementName*.dataSrc
[window.]document.forms[i].elements[j].dataSrc
[window.]document.getElementById(*elementID*).dataSrc

disabled   IE 4 NN *n/a* Moz *all* Saf *all* Op 7 HTML 4
disabled   *Optional*

A disabled textarea element can't be activated by the user. A disabled textarea cannot receive focus and doesn't become active within the tabbing order rotation. The name/value pair of a disabled element is not sent when the form is submitted.

The disabled attribute is a Boolean type, which means that its presence in the attribute sets its value to true. Its value can also be adjusted after the fact by scripting (see the textarea object in Chapter 2).

Example   <textarea disabled></textarea>

Value   The presence of the attribute disables the element.

Default   false

Object Model Reference
[window.]document.*formName*.*elementName*.disabled
[window.]document.forms[i].elements[j].disabled
[window.]document.getElementById(*elementID*).disabled

form

form="*formID [formID] ...*"   *Optional*

Web Forms 2.0 extension that lets you associate a single form control element with one or more forms that do not enclose the controls. Because textarea elements in Web Forms 2.0 are not confined to be descendants of form elements, the textarea elements may be located away from the form element. The form attribute connects the textarea element with one or more form elements on the page.

Example   `<textarea name="notes" form="orderForm"></textarea>`

Value   ID of one or more form elements on the page. Multiple references are space-delimited.

Default   None.

inputmode

inputmode="*ScriptToken [ModifierToken]*"   *Optional*

Web Forms 2.0 extension (adopted whole from the W3C XForms 1.0 specification at *www.w3.org/TR/xforms/sliceE.html*) that directs the browser to display the appropriate text input user interface for a written language. Consult the W3C XForms 1.0 documents for details.

Example   `<textarea name="notes_jp" inputmode="hiragana"></textarea>`

Value   Written language script token with an optional modifier token (space-delimited). Tokens generally correspond to Unicode scripts (*http://www.unicode.org/unicode/reports/tr24/*).

Default   None.

name

name="*elementIdentifier*"   *Optional*

If the textarea element is part of a form being submitted to a server, the name attribute is required if the value of the element is to be submitted with the form. Newer DOMs encourage assigning the same identifier to the id attribute for uniform script references to the element object.

Example   `<textarea name="comments" id="comments"></textarea>`

Value   Case-sensitive identifier.

Default   None.

Object Model Reference
```
[window.]document.formName.elementName.name
[window.]document.forms[i].elements[j].name
[window.]document.getElementById(elementID).name
```

readonly

IE 4 NN n/a Moz all Saf all Op 7 HTML 4

readonly   <i>Optional</i>

When the readonly attribute is present, the textarea element cannot be edited on the page by the user (although scripts can modify the content). A textarea marked as readonly receives focus within the tabbing order. Users can still select and copy text from a read-only textarea.

Example   <textarea name="instructions" readonly></textarea>

Value   The presence of the attribute sets its value to true.

Default   false

Object Model Reference

[window.]document.*formName.elementName*.readOnly
[window.]document.forms[i].elements[j].readOnly
[window.]document.getElementById(*elementID*).readOnly

required

IE n/a NN n/a Moz n/a Saf n/a Op 9 HTML n/a

required="required"   <i>Optional</i>

Web Forms 2.0 extension that signifies whether the textarea element's value is required for submission. Sets the missingValue property of the ValidityState object to true if the element receives no value.

rows

IE all NN all Moz all Saf all Op 7 HTML all

rows="*rowCount*"   <i>Optional</i>

The height of the textarea element based on the number of lines of text that are to be displayed without scrolling. The value represents the number of monospace-font character lines that are to be displayed within the height before the scrollbar becomes active. For a browser that supports style sheet font sizes, the actual width changes accordingly.

Example   <textarea rows="5" cols="40"></textarea>

Value   Any positive integer.

Default   Varies with browser and operating system.

Object Model Reference

[window.]document.*formName.elementName*.rows
[window.]document.forms[i].elements[j].rows
[window.]document.getElementById(*elementID*).rows

wrap

IE 4 NN 2 Moz all Saf all Op 7 HTML n/a

wrap="*wrapType*"   <i>Optional</i>

The wrap attribute tells the browser whether it should wrap text in a textarea element and whether wrapped text should be submitted to the server with soft returns converted to

<tfoot>

hard carriage returns. The HTML specification is silent on the subject, while major browsers have, over the years, clouded the attribute values. But more recently, the mainstream browsers are coming together on a set of three attribute values: off, soft, and hard.

When set to soft, the text automatically wraps as the user types, but the carriage returns and line feeds (CRLFs) do not go with the text when the form is submitted. With a setting of hard, wrapping occurs, and the CRLFs introduced by wrapping become part of the textarea's value submitted to the server (but not for Safari). Old synonyms for the soft value include virtual and physical. A setting of off means that typing beyond the right edge of the rectangle forces the textarea to scroll horizontally. Only a press of the Return key causes the text insertion pointer to advance to the next line.

Example	`<textarea name="comments" wrap="hard"></textarea>`
Value	Constant values: hard | off | soft.
Default	soft

Object Model Reference

```
[window.]document.formName.elementName.wrap
[window.]document.forms[i].elements[j].wrap
[window.]document.getElementById(elementID).wrap
```

<tfoot>

IE 3 NN *n/a* Moz *all* Saf *all* Op 7 HTML 4

`<tfoot>...</tfoot>`   *HTML End Tag: Optional*

A tfoot element is a special-purpose container of one or more rows of table cells rendered at the bottom of the table. Typically, the tfoot element mirrors the thead element content for users who have scrolled down the page (or for future browsers that scroll inner table content). No more than one tfoot element may be defined within a single table element, and the tfoot element should be located in the source code *before* any tbody elements defined for the table. A tfoot element is a row grouping, like the tbody and thead elements. Navigator 4 ignores the tfoot tag and therefore renders the nested tr element(s) as regular tr elements in source code order.

Example

```
<table cols="3">
<thead>
<tr>
<th>Time</th><th>Event</th><th>Location</th>
</tr>
</thead>
<tfoot>
<tr>
<th>Time</th><th>Event</th><th>Location</th>
</tr>
</tfoot>
<tbody>
<tr>
<td>7:30am-5:00pm</td><td>Registration Open</td><td>Main Lobby</td>
```

```
<tfoot>

</tr>
<tr>
<td>9:00am-12:00pm</td><td>Keynote Speakers</td><td>Cypress Room</td>
</tr>
</tbody>
</table>
```

Object Model Reference

[window.]document.getElementById(*elementID*)

Element-Specific Attributes

align	bgcolor	ch	char	charoff
choff	valign			

Element-Specific Event Handler Attributes

None.

align

align="*alignConstant*"   *Optional*

Establishes the horizontal alignment characteristics of content within the row(s) covered by the tfoot element.

Example   <tfoot align="center">

Value

HTML 4 and various browsers implement different sets of attribute values.

Value	IE/Windows	Others	HTML 4
center	•	•	•
char	—	—	•
justify	—	•	•
left	•	•	•
right	•	•	•

The values center, left, and right are self-explanatory. The value justify spaces multiline content so that text is justified down both left and right edges. For the value char, the char attribute must also be set to specify the character on which alignment revolves. In the HTML 4 specification example, content that does not contain the character appears to be right-aligned to the location of the character in other rows of the same column.

It's important to bear in mind that the align attribute applies to every cell of every row within the tfoot, including any th element you specify for the table. If you want a different alignment for the row header, override the setting with a separate align attribute or text-align style sheet property for the individual th elements.

Default   left

<tfoot>

Object Model Reference

[window.]document.getElementById(*elementID*).align

bgcolor   IE *4* NN *n/a* Moz *all* Saf *all* Op *7* HTML *n/a*

bgcolor="*colorTripletOrName*"   *Optional*

Establishes a fill color (behind the text and other content) for the cells contained by the tfoot element.

Example	<tfoot bgcolor="tan">
Value	A hexadecimal triplet or plain-language color name. A setting of empty is interpreted as "#000000" (black). See Appendix A for acceptable plain-language color names.
Default	Varies with browser, browser version, and operating system.

Object Model Reference

[window.]document.getElementById(*elementID*).bgColor

char   IE *n/a* NN *n/a* Moz *n/a* Saf *n/a* Op *n/a* HTML *4*

char="*character*"   *Optional*

The char attribute defines the text character used as an alignment point for text within a cell contained by the tfoot element. This attribute is of value only for the align attribute set to "char". Microsoft documents a ch attribute, which corresponds to the standards-based char attribute. In any case, the browser does not respond to either attribute.

Example	<tfoot align="char" char=".">
Value	Any single text character.
Default	None.

charoff   IE *n/a* NN *n/a* Moz *n/a* Saf *n/a* Op *n/a* HTML *4*

charoff="*length*"   *Optional*

The charoff attribute lets you set a specific offset point at which the character specified by the char attribute is to appear within a cell contained by the tfoot element. This attribute is provided in case the browser default positioning does not meet with the design goals of the table. Microsoft documents a choff attribute, which corresponds to the standards-based charoff attribute. In any case, the browser does not respond to either attribute.

Example	<tfoot align="char" char="." charoff="80%">
Value	Any length value in pixels or percentage of cell space.
Default	None.

choff

See charoff.

valign

IE *4*   NN *n/a*   Moz *all*   Saf *all*   Op *7*   HTML *4*

valign="*alignmentConstant*"   *Optional*

Determines the vertical alignment of content within cells of the column(s) covered by the tfoot element. You can override the vertical alignment for a particular cell anywhere in the column.

Example   <tfoot valign="bottom">

Value

Four constant values: top | middle | bottom | baseline. With top and bottom, the content is rendered flush (or very close to it) to the top and bottom of the table cell. Set to middle (the default), the content floats perfectly centered vertically in the cell. When one cell's contents might wrap to multiple lines at common window widths (assuming a variable table width), it is advisable to set the valign attribute to baseline. This assures that the character baseline of the first (or only) line of a cell's text aligns with the other cells in the row—usually the most aesthetically pleasing arrangement.

Default   middle

Object Model Reference

[window.]document.getElementById(*elementID*).vAlign

<th>

IE *all*   NN *all*   Moz *all*   Saf *all*   Op *7*   HTML *3.2*

<th>...</th>   *HTML End Tag: Optional*

The th element is a container for content that is rendered inside one cell of a table element in a format that distinguishes it as a header. Most browsers render the content as boldface. A cell is the intersection of a column and row. Other elements related to the th element are caption, col, colgroup, table, tbody, td, tfoot, thead, and tr. In addition to providing a wrapper for a cell's content, the th element defines a number of visible attributes that apply to a single cell, often overriding similar attributes set in lesser-nested elements in the table.

Four attributes—abbr, axis, headers, and scope—are included in the HTML 4 specification in anticipation of nonvisual browsers that will use text-to-speech technology to describe content of an HTML page—a kind of "verbal rendering." Although these attributes are briefly described here for the sake of completeness, there is much more to their application in nonvisual browsers than is relevant in this book on Dynamic HTML. Consult the HTML 4 recommendation for more details.

Example

```
<table cols="3">
<thead>
<tr>
<th>Time</th><th>Event</th><th>Location</th>
```

<th>

```
</tr>
</thead>
<tbody>
<tr>
<td>7:30am-5:00pm</td><td>Registration Open</td><td>Main Lobby</td>
</tr>
<tr>
<td>9:00am-12:00pm</td><td>Keynote Speakers</td><td>Cypress Room</td>
</tr>
</tbody>
</table>
```

Object Model Reference

`[window.]document.getElementById(elementID)`

Element-Specific Attributes

abbr	align	axis	background	bgcolor
bordercolor	bordercolordark	bordercolorlight	ch	char
charoff	choff	colspan	datafld	headers
height	nowrap	rowspan	scope	valign
width				

Element-Specific Event Handler Attributes

Handler	IE	Others	HTML	
onafterupdate	4	n/a	n/a	
onbeforeupdate	4	n/a	n/a	
onrowenter	4	n/a	n/a	
onrowexit	4	n/a	n/a	

abbr

IE 6 NN *n/a* Moz *all* Saf *all* Op *n/a* HTML 4

`abbr="text"`   *Optional*

Provides an abbreviated string that describes the cell's content. This is usually a brief label that a nonvisual browser would speak to describe what the value of the cell represents. The **Properties** choice for Mozilla's context menu for this element displays a small window that includes an active link to the URL assigned to the attribute. Current mainstream browsers provide no other functionality for this attribute.

Example	`<th abbr="What">Event</th>`
Value	Any quoted string.
Default	None.

align
IE *all* NN *all* Moz *all* Saf *all* Op *7* HTML *3.2*

`align="`*`alignConstant`*`"` *Optional*

Establishes the horizontal alignment characteristics of content within the cell covered by the th element.

Example   `<th align="center">`

Value

HTML 4 and various browsers implement different sets of attribute values.

Value	IE/Windows and NN 4	Others	HTML 4
center	•	•	•
char	—	—	•
justify	—	•	•
left	•	•	•
right	•	•	•

The values center, left, and right are self-explanatory. The value justify spaces multi-line content so that text is justified down both left and right edges. For the value char, the char attribute must also be set to specify the character on which alignment revolves. In the HTML 4 specification example, content that does not contain the character appears to be right-aligned to the location of the character in other rows of the same column.

Default   left

Object Model Reference

`[window.]document.getElementById(`*`elementID`*`).align`

axis
IE *6* NN *n/a* Moz *all* Saf *all* Op *n/a* HTML *4*

`axis="`*`text`*`"` *Optional*

Provides an abbreviated string that describes the cell's category. This is usually a brief label that a nonvisual browser would speak to describe what the value of the cell represents. The **Properties** choice for Mozilla's context menu for this element displays a small window that includes an active link to the URL assigned to the attribute. Current mainstream browsers provide no other functionality for this attribute.

Example   `<th axis="event">Events</th>`

Value   Any quoted string.

Default   None.

Object Model Reference

`[window.]document.getElementById(`*`elementID`*`).axis`

<th>

background

background="*URL*"   *Optional*

Specifies an image file that is used as a backdrop to the cell. Unlike normal images that get loaded into browser content, a background image loads in its original size (without scaling) and tiles to fill the available cell space. Smaller images download faster but are obviously repeated more often in the background. Navigator 4, however, requires a minimum image size of 16 by 16 pixels. Animated GIFs are also allowable, but very distracting to the reader. When selecting a background image, be sure it is very muted in comparison to the main content so that the content stands out clearly. Background images, if used at all, should be extremely subtle.

Example   `<th background="watermark.jpg">`

Value   Any valid URL to an image file, including complete and relative URLs.

Default   None.

Object Model Reference
`[window.]document.getElementById(elementID).background`

bgcolor

bgcolor="*colorTripletOrName*"   *Optional*

Establishes a fill color (behind the text and other content) for the cell defined by the th element.

Example   `<th bgcolor="yellow">`

Value   A hexadecimal triplet or plain-language color name. A setting of empty is interpreted as "#000000" (black). See Appendix A for acceptable plain-language color names.

Default   Varies with browser, browser version, and operating system.

Object Model Reference
`[window.]document.getElementById(elementID).bgColor`

bordercolor

bordercolor="*colorTripletOrName*"   *Optional*

The colors used to render some of the pixels that create the illusion of borders around cells and the entire table. Internet Explorer applies the color to all four lines that make up the interior border of a cell. Therefore, colors of adjacent cells do not collide.

Example   `<th bordercolor="green">`

Value   A hexadecimal triplet or plain-language color name. A setting of empty is interpreted as "#000000" (black). See Appendix A for acceptable plain-language color names.

Default   Varies with browser and operating system.

Object Model Reference

`[window.]document.getElementById(elementID).borderColor`

bordercolordark, bordercolorlight   IE 3   NN *n/a*   Moz *n/a*   Saf *n/a*   Op *n/a*   HTML *n/a*

Optional

```
bordercolordark="colorTripletOrName"
bordercolorlight="colorTripletOrName"
```

The 3-D effect of table borders in Internet Explorer is created by careful positioning of light and dark lines around the page's background or default color (see Figure 1-4Figure 1-4 in the table element discussion). You can independently control the colors used for the dark and light lines by assigning values to the bordercolordark (left and top edges of the cell) and bordercolorlight (right and bottom edges) attributes.

Typically, you should assign complementary colors to the pair of attributes. There is also no rule that says you must assign a dark color to bordercolordark. The attributes merely control a well-defined set of lines so you can predict which lines of the border change with each attribute.

Example   `<th bordercolordark="darkred" bordercolorlight="salmon">`

Value   A hexadecimal triplet or plain-language color name. A setting of empty is interpreted as "#000000" (black). See Appendix A for acceptable plain-language color names.

Default   Varies with operating system.

Object Model Reference

`[window.]document.getElementById(elementID).borderColorDark`
`[window.]document.getElementById(elementID).borderColorLight`

char   IE *n/a*   NN *n/a*   Moz *n/a*   Saf *n/a*   Op *n/a*   HTML 4

`char="character"`   *Optional*

The char attribute defines the text character used as an alignment point for text within a cell. This attribute is of value only for the align attribute set to "char". Microsoft documents a ch attribute, which corresponds to the standards-based char attribute. In any case, the browser does not respond to either attribute.

Example   `<th align="char" char=".">$325.10</th>`

Value   Any single text character.

Default   None.

<th>

charoff

charoff="*length*" *Optional*

The charoff attribute lets you set a specific offset point at which the character specified by the char attribute is to appear within a cell. This attribute is provided in case the browser default positioning does not meet with the design goals of the table. Microsoft documents a choff attribute, which corresponds to the standards-based charoff attribute. In any case, the browser does not respond to either attribute.

Example `<th align="char" char="." charoff="80%">`

Value Any length value in pixels or percentage of cell space.

Default None.

choff

See charoff.

colspan

colspan="*columnCount*" *Optional*

The colspan attribute specifies the number of columns across which the current table cell should extend itself. For each additional column included in the colspan count, one less th or td element is required for the table row. If you set the align attribute to center or right, the alignment is calculated on the full width of the th element across the specified number of columns. Unless the current cell is also specifies a rowspan attribute, the next table row returns to the original column count.

Example `<th colspan="2" align="right">`

Value Any positive integer, usually 2 or larger.

Default 1

Object Model Reference

[window.]document.getElementById(*elementID*).colSpan

datafld

datafld="*columnName*" *Optional*

Used with IE data binding to associate a remote data source column name with the content of a table header cell. A datasrc (and optionally, a datapagesize) attribute must also be set for the enclosing table element. Works only with text file data sources in IE 5/Mac.

Example
```
<table datasrc="DBSRC3" datapagesize="5">
<tr>
  <th datafld="stockNum"></th>
  <th datafld="qtyOnHand"></th>
```

```
<th>

</tr>
</table>
```

Value   Case-sensitive identifier.

Default   None.

headers

IE 6   NN n/a   Moz all   Saf all   Op n/a   HTML 4

```
headers="cellIDList"
```
Optional

Points to one or more th or td elements that act as column or row headers for the current table cell. The assigned value is a space-delimited list of id attribute values that are assigned to the relevant th elements. A nonvisual browser could speak the cell's header before the content of the cell to help listeners identify the nature of the cell content. Although aome mainstream browsers claim support for this attribute, none have yet connected support for it.

Example

```
<tr>
<th id="hdr1">Product Number</th>
<th id="hdr2">Description</th>
</tr>
<tr>
<th headers="hdr1">0392</th>
<th headers="hdr2">Round widget</th>
</tr>
```

Value   A space-delimited list of case-sensitive IDs assigned to cells that act as headers to the current cell.

Default   None.

height, width

IE all   NN all   Moz all   Saf all   Op 7   HTML 3.2

```
height="length" width="length"
```
Optional

The rectangular dimensions of a cell that may be different from the default size as calculated by the browser. When the values for these attributes are less than the minimum space required to render the table cell content, the browser overrides the attribute settings to make sure that all content appears, even if it means that text lines word-wrap. You can also stretch the dimensions of a table beyond the browser-calculated dimensions. Extra whitespace appears inside table cells to make up the difference. If you specify just one of these attributes, the browser performs all necessary calculations to automatically adjust the dimension along the other axis.

Due to the regular nature of tables, if you set a custom height for one cell in a row taller than the others, the entire row is set to that height; similarly, setting the width of a cell to wider than others in the same column causes the width of all cells in the column to be the same size.

<th>

Both the height and width attributes are deprecated in HTML 4 in favor of height and width style sheet properties (which are not available for table cells in Navigator 4).

Example   `<th width="80%" height="30">`

Value   Any length value in pixels or percentage of available space.

Default   Based on content size.

Object Model Reference
```
[window.]document.getElementById(elementID).height
[window.]document.getElementById(elementID).width
```

nowrap   IE *all* NN *all* Moz *all* Saf *all* Op 7 HTML *3.2*
nowrap   *Optional*

The presence of the nowrap attribute instructs the browser to render the cell as wide as is necessary to display a line of nonbreaking text on one line. Abuse of this attribute can force the user into a great deal of inconvenient horizontal scrolling of the page to view all of the content. The nowrap attribute is deprecated in HTML 4. The nowrap attribute is deprecated in HTML 4 in favor of the white-space:nowrap CSS property and value.

Example   `<th nowrap>`

Value   The presence of this attribute sets its value to true.

Default   false

Object Model Reference
```
[window.]document.getElementById(elementID).noWrap
```

rowspan   IE *all* NN *all* Moz *all* Saf *all* Op 7 HTML *3.2*
rowspan="*rowCount*"   *Optional*

The number of rows through which the current table cell should extend itself downward. For each additional row included in the rowspan count, one less th or td element is required for the next table row in that cell's position along the row.

Example   `<th rowspan="2">`

Value   Any positive integer, usually 2 or larger.

Default   1

Object Model Reference
```
[window.]document.getElementById(elementID).rowSpan
```

<th>

scope

scope="*scopeConstant*"   *Optional*

The range of cells (relative to the current cell) that behave as though the current cell is the header for those cells. For tables whose structure is quite regular, the scope attribute is a simpler way of achieving what the headers attribute does, without having to define id attributes for the header cells. Although some mainstream browsers claim support for this attribute, none have yet connected support for it.

Example

```
<tr>
<th scope="col">Product Number</th>
<th scope="col">Description</th>
</tr>
<tr>
<td>0392</td>
<td>Round widget</td>
</tr>
```

Value

One of four recognized scope constants:

col
> Current cell text becomes header text for every cell in the rest of the column.

colgroup
> Current cell text becomes header text for every cell in the rest of the colgroup element.

row
> Current cell text becomes header text for every cell in the rest of the tr element.

rowgroup
> Current cell text becomes header text for every cell in the rest of the tbody element.

Default   None.

valign

valign="*alignmentConstant*"   *Optional*

Determines the vertical alignment of content within the td element. A value you set for an individual cell overrides the same attribute setting for outer containers, such as tr and tbody.

Example   <th valign="bottom">

Value

Four constant values: top | middle | bottom | baseline. With top and bottom, the content is rendered flush (or very close to it) to the top and bottom of the table cell. Set to middle (the default), the content floats perfectly centered vertically in the cell. When one cell's contents might wrap to multiple lines at common window widths (assuming a variable table width), it is advisable to set the valign attribute to baseline. This assures that the character base-

<thead>

line of the first (or only) line of a cell's text aligns with the other cells in the row—usually the most aesthetically pleasing arrangement.

Default   middle

Object Model Reference
[window.]document.getElementById(*elementID*).vAlign

width

See height.

<thead>

<thead>...</thead>   *HTML End Tag: Optional*

A thead element is a special-purpose container of one or more rows of table cells rendered at the top of the table. No more than one thead element may be defined within a single table element, and the thead element should be located in the source code immediately after the table element's start tag. You are free to use any combination of td and th elements you like within the thead element. A thead element is a row grouping, like the tbody and tfoot elements. Navigator 4 ignores the thead tag and therefore renders the nested tr element(s) as regular tr elements in source code order.

Example

```
<table cols="3">
<thead>
<tr>
<th>Time</th><th>Event</th><th>Location</th>
</tr>
</thead>
<tfoot>
<tr>
<th>Time</th><th>Event</th><th>Location</th>
</tr>
</tfoot>
<tbody>
<tr>
<td>7:30am-5:00pm</td><td>Registration Open</td><td>Main Lobby</td>
</tr>
<tr>
<td>9:00am-12:00pm</td><td>Keynote Speakers</td><td>Cypress Room</td>
</tr>
</tbody>
</table>
```

Object Model Reference
[window.]document.getElementById(*elementID*)

<thead>

Element-Specific Attributes

align	bgcolor	ch	char	charoff
choff	valign			

Element-Specific Event Handler Attributes
None.

align

IE 4   NN *n/a*   Moz *all*   Saf *all*   Op 7   HTML 4

align="*alignConstant*" *Optional*

Establishes the horizontal alignment characteristics of content within the row(s) covered by the thead element.

Example
<thead align="center">

Value
HTML 4 and various browsers implement different sets of attribute values.

Value	IE/Windows	Others	HTML 4
center	•	•	•
char	—	—	•
justify	—	•	•
left	•	•	•
right	•	•	•

The values center, left, and right are self-explanatory. The value justify spaces multiline content so that text is justified down both left and right edges. For the value char, the char attribute must also be set to specify the character on which alignment revolves. In the HTML 4 specification example, content that does not contain the character appears to be right-aligned to the location of the character in other rows of the same column.

It is important to bear in mind that the align attribute applies to every cell of every row within the thead, including any th element you specify for the table. If you want a different alignment for the row header, override the setting with a separate align attribute or text-align style sheet property for the individual th elements.

Default   left

Object Model Reference
[window.]document.getElementById(*elementID*).align

<thead>

bgcolor

bgcolor="*colorTripletOrName*"   *Optional*

Establishes a fill color (behind the text and other content) for the cells contained by the thead element.

Example	<thead bgcolor="tan">
Value	A hexadecimal triplet or plain-language color name. A setting of empty is interpreted as "#000000" (black). See Appendix A for acceptable plain-language color names.
Default	Varies with browser, browser version, and operating system.

Object Model Reference

[window.]document.getElementById(*elementID*).bgColor

char

char="*character*"   *Optional*

The char attribute defines the text character used as an alignment point for text within a cell contained by the thead element. This attribute is of value only for the align attribute set to "char". Microsoft documents a ch attribute, which corresponds to the standards-based char attribute. In any case, the browser does not respond to either attribute.

Example	<thead align="char" char=".">
Value	Any single text character.
Default	None.

charoff

charoff="*length*"   *Optional*

The charoff attribute lets you set a specific offset point at which the character specified by the char attribute is to appear within a cell contained by the thead element. This attribute is provided in case the browser default positioning does not meet with the design goals of the table. Microsoft documents a choff attribute, which corresponds to the standards-based charoff attribute. In any case, the browser does not respond to either attribute.

Example	<thead align="char" char="." charoff="80%">
Value	Any length value in pixels or percentage of cell space.
Default	None.

choff

See charoff.

<title>

valign

IE 4 NN *n/a* Moz *all* Saf *all* Op 7 HTML 4

valign="*alignmentConstant*"   *Optional*

Determines the vertical alignment of content within cells of the column(s) covered by the thead element. You can override the vertical alignment for a particular cell anywhere in the column.

Example   <thead valign="bottom">

Value

Four constant values: top | middle | bottom | baseline. With top and bottom, the content is rendered flush (or very close to it) to the top and bottom of the table cell. Set to middle (the default), the content floats perfectly centered vertically in the cell. When one cell's contents might wrap to multiple lines at common window widths (assuming a variable table width), it is advisable to set the valign attribute to baseline. This assures that the character baseline of the first (or only) line of a cell's text aligns with the other cells in the row—usually the most aesthetically pleasing arrangement.

Default   middle

Object Model Reference

[window.]document.getElementById(*elementID*).vAlign

<title>

IE *all* NN *all* Moz *all* Saf *all* Op 7 HTML *all*

<title>...</title>   *HTML End Tag: Required*

The title element identifies the overall content of a document. The element content is not displayed as part of the document, but browsers display the title in the browser application's window titlebar. Only one title element is permitted per document and it must be located inside the head element. It is all right to be somewhat verbose in assigning a document title because not everyone will access the document in sequence through your web site. Give the document some context as well.

Example   <title>Declaration of Independence</title>

Object Model Reference

[window.]document.getElementById(*elementID*)

Element-Specific Attributes

None.

Element-Specific Event Handler Attributes

None.

<tr>

<tr>...</tr>

A tr element is a container for one row of cells. Each cell within a row may be a th or td element. Every row requires at least a start tag to instruct the browser to begin rendering succeeding cell elements on the next line of the table. Other special-purpose row groupings available are the tfoot and thead, as well as the more generic tbody grouping element.

Example
```
<table cols="3">
<thead>
<tr>
<th>Time</th><th>Event</th><th>Location</th>
</tr>
</thead>
<tbody>
<tr>
<td>7:30am-5:00pm</td><td>Registration Open</td><td>Main Lobby</td>
</tr>
<tr>
<td>9:00am-12:00pm</td><td>Keynote Speakers</td><td>Cypress Room</td>
</tr>
</tbody>
</table>
```

Object Model Reference
[window.]document.getElementById(*elementID*)

Element-Specific Attributes

align	background	bgcolor	bordercolor	bordercolordark
bordercolorlight	ch	char	charoff	choff
height	valign	width		

Element-Specific Event Handler Attributes
None.

align

align="*alignConstant*"

Establishes the horizontal alignment characteristics of content within the row.

Example   <tr align="center">

Value   HTML 4 and various browsers implement different sets of attribute values.

<tr>

Value	IE/Windows	Others	HTML 4
center	•	•	•
char	—	—	•
justify	—	•	•
left	•	•	•
right	•	•	•

The values center, left, and right are self-explanatory. The value justify spaces multiline content so that text is justified down both left and right edges. For the value char, the char attribute must also be set to specify the character on which alignment revolves. In the HTML 4 specification example, content that does not contain the character appears to be right-aligned to the location of the character in other rows of the same column.

It is important to bear in mind that the align attribute applies to every cell within the tr element, including any th element you specify for the table. If you want a different alignment for the row header, override the setting with a separate align attribute or text-align style sheet property for the tr or individual th elements.

Default   center

Object Model Reference
[window.]document.getElementById(*elementID*).align

background   IE *n/a* NN *4* Moz *all* Saf *all* Op *7* HTML *n/a*
background="*URL*"   *Optional*

Specifies an image file that is used as a backdrop to the entire row of cells. Unlike normal images that get loaded into browser content, a background image loads in its original size (without scaling) and tiles to fill the available cell space. Smaller images download faster but are obviously repeated more often in the background. Navigator 4, however, requires a minimum image size of 16 by 16 pixels. Animated GIFs are also allowable, but very distracting to the reader. When selecting a background image, be sure it is very muted in comparison to the main content so that the content stands out clearly. Background images, if used at all, should be extremely subtle.

Example   <tr background="watermark.jpg">

Value   Any valid URL to an image file, including complete and relative URLs.

Default   None.

Object Model Reference
[window.]document.getElementById(*elementID*).background

<tr>

bgcolor

bgcolor="*colorTripletOrName*"   *Optional*

Establishes a fill color (behind the text and other content) for the cells contained by the `tr` element.

Example   `<tr bgcolor="lavender">`

Value   A hexadecimal triplet or plain-language color name. A setting of empty is interpreted as "#000000" (black). See Appendix A for acceptable plain-language color names.

Default   Varies with browser, browser version, and operating system.

Object Model Reference
`[window.]document.getElementById(elementID).bgColor`

bordercolor

bordercolor="*colorTripletOrName*"   *Optional*

The color used to render some of the pixels that create the illusion of borders around cells and the entire table. Internet Explorer applies the color to all four lines that make up the interior border of a cell. Therefore, colors of adjacent cells do not collide.

Example   `<tr bordercolor="green">`

Value   A hexadecimal triplet or plain-language color name. A setting of empty is interpreted as "#000000" (black). See Appendix A for acceptable plain-language color names.

Default   Varies with browser and operating system.

Object Model Reference
`[window.]document.getElementById(elementID).borderColor`

bordercolordark, bordercolorlight

Optional

bordercolordark="*colorTripletOrName*"
bordercolorlight="*colorTripletOrName*"

The 3-D effect of table borders in Internet Explorer is created by careful positioning of light and dark lines around the page's background or default color (see Figure 1-4 in the `table` element discussion). You can independently control the colors used for the dark and light lines by assigning values to the `bordercolordark` (left and top edges of the cell) and `bordercolorlight` (right and bottom edges) attributes.

Typically, you should assign complementary colors to the pair of attributes. There is also no rule that says you must assign a dark color to `bordercolordark`. The attributes merely control a well-defined set of lines so you can predict which lines of the border change with each attribute.

Example	`<tr bordercolordark="darkred" bordercolorlight="salmon">`
Value	A hexadecimal triplet or plain-language color name. A setting of empty is interpreted as "#000000" (black). See Appendix A for acceptable plain-language color names.
Default	Varies with operating system.

Object Model Reference

```
[window.]document.getElementById(elementID).borderColorDark
[window.]document.getElementById(elementID).borderColorLight
```

char
IE *n/a* NN *n/a* Moz *n/a* Saf *n/a* Op *n/a* HTML *4*

`char="character"`   *Optional*

The char attribute defines the text character used as an alignment point for text within a cell contained by the tr element. This attribute is of value only for the align attribute set to "char". Microsoft documents a ch attribute, which corresponds to the standards-based char attribute. In any case, the browser does not respond to either attribute.

Example	`<tr align="char" char=".">`
Value	Any single text character.
Default	None.

charoff
IE *n/a* NN *n/a* Moz *n/a* Saf *n/a* Op *n/a* HTML *n/a*

`charoff="length"`   *Optional*

The charoff attribute lets you set a specific offset point at which the character specified by the char attribute is to appear within a cell contained by the tr element. This attribute is provided in case the browser default positioning does not meet with the design goals of the table. Microsoft documents a choff attribute, which corresponds to the standards-based charoff attribute. In any case, the browser does not respond to either attribute.

Example	`<tr align="char" char="." charoff="80%">`
Value	Any length value in pixels or percentage of cell space.
Default	None.

choff

See charoff.

valign

`valign="alignmentConstant"`   *Optional*

Determines the vertical alignment of content within cells of the column(s) covered by the tr element. You can override the vertical alignment for a particular cell anywhere in the row.

Example   `<tr valign="bottom">`

Value

Four constant values: `top | middle | bottom | baseline`. With `top` and `bottom`, the content is rendered flush (or very close to it) to the top and bottom of the table cell. Set to `middle` (the default), the content floats perfectly centered vertically in the cell. When one cell's contents might wrap to multiple lines at common window widths (assuming a variable table width), it is advisable to set the `valign` attribute to `baseline`. This assures that the character baseline of the first (or only) line of a cell's text aligns with the other cells in the row—usually the most aesthetically pleasing arrangement.

Default   `middle`

Object Model Reference

`[window.]document.getElementById(elementID).vAlign`

<tt>

`<tt>...</tt>`   *HTML End Tag: Required*

The tt element renders its content as monospaced text (indicating a teletype output). The element is intended to be strictly a formatting—as opposed to a contextual—element. If you are looking for a contextual setting for computer program code or input, see the code, kbd, and samp elements. As with most font-related elements, the use of style sheets is preferred.

Example   `<p>The computer said, <tt>"That does not compute."</tt></p>`

Object Model Reference

`[window.]document.getElementById(elementID)`

Element-Specific Attributes

None.

Element-Specific Event Handler Attributes

None.

<u>

`<u>...</u>`   *HTML End Tag: Required*

The u element renders its content as underlined text. This element is deprecated in HTML 4 in favor of the `text-decoration:underline` style sheet property. The element does not validate in strict HTML 4 or XHTML DTDs, and may confuse users who regard any under-lined text as a clickable link, regardless of color.

Example   `<p>You may already be a <u>winner</u>!</p>`

Object Model Reference
`[window.]document.getElementById(elementID)`

Element-Specific Attributes
None.

Element-Specific Event Handler Attributes
None.

<ul>

IE *all* NN *all* Moz *all* Saf *all* Op 7 HTML *all*

`<ul>...</ul>`   *HTML End Tag: Required*

The ul element is a container for an unordered list of items. An "unordered list" means that the items are rendered with a leading symbol (depending on the type attribute setting or list-style-type style sheet property setting) that implies no specific order of items other than by virtue of location within the list. Content for each list item is defined by a nested li element. If you apply a style sheet rule to a ul element, the style is inherited by the nested li elements (except for occasional odd behavior in Navigator 4 only).

Example

```
<ul>
    <li>Africa</li>
    <li>Antarctica</li>
    <li>Asia</li>
    <li>Australia</li>
    <li>Europe</li>
    <li>North America</li>
    <li>South America</li>
</ul>
```

Object Model Reference
`[window.]document.getElementById(elementID)`

Element-Specific Attributes

compact   type

Element-Specific Event Handler Attributes
None.

<var>

compact

IE 4 NN n/a Moz all Saf all Op n/a HTML 3.2

compact   *Optional*

A Boolean attribute originally designed to let browsers render the list in a more compact style than normal (smaller line spacing between items). Although listed as a supported attribute for HTML compatibility, the compact attribute has no effect on mainstream browsers. Use style sheets to control element sizes and line spacing.

Example   `<ul compact>...</ul>`

Value   The presence of this attribute makes its value true.

Default   `false`

type

IE all NN all Moz all Saf all Op 7 HTML 3.2

type="*labelType*"   *Optional*

The type attribute provides some flexibility in how the leading symbol or sequence number is displayed in the browser. You can specify whether the leading symbol should be a disc, circle, or square. A disc is a filled circle (also known as a bullet). The square type is rendered as an outline in early Macintosh browsers, and as a filled square in Windows and modern browsers of all OS types. The type attribute is deprecated in HTML 4 in favor of the list-style-type style sheet property.

Example   `<ul type="disc">...</ul>`

Value   Possible values are circle | disc | square.

Default   `disc`

Object Model Reference
[window.]document.getElementById(*elementID*).type

<var>

IE all NN all Moz all Saf all Op 7 HTML all

<var>...</var>   *HTML End Tag: Required*

The var element is one of a large group of elements that the HTML 4 recommendation calls *phrase elements*. Such elements assign structural meaning to a designated portion of the document. A var element is one that is used predominantly to display one or more inline characters representing a computer program variable name.

Browsers have free rein to determine how (or whether) to distinguish var element content from the rest of the body element. Current mainstream browsers elect to render var element content in an italic font. Override the default with a style sheet as you see fit.

Example   `<p>The value of <var>offsetWidth</var> becomes 20.</p>`

Object Model Reference
[window.]document.getElementById(*elementID*)

<wbr>

Element-Specific Attributes

None.

Element-Specific Event Handler Attributes

None.

<wbr>

IE *all* NN *all* Moz *n/a* Saf *n/a* Op *n/a* HTML *n/a*

<wbr>   *HTML End Tag: Forbidden*

If you use the nobr element to define content that should have no word-wrapping or line breaks, you can use the wbr element to advise the browser that it can break up the content if the width of the browser window requires it. The locations of these provisional breaks are marked in the source code with the wbr element. In a sense, the nobr and wbr elements give the author control over word-wrapping of running content. Neither element is included in the HTML specification, and the wbr element continues forward only in Internet Explorer.

Example

```
<nobr>This is a long line of text that could run on and on, <wbr>forcing
the browser to display the horizontal scrollbar after awhile.</nobr>
```

Object Model Reference

[window.]document.getElementById(*elementID*)

Element-Specific Attributes

None.

Element-Specific Event Handler Attributes

None.

<xml>

IE *5* NN *n/a* Moz *n/a* Saf *n/a* Op *n/a* HTML *n/a*

<xml>...</xml>   *HTML End Tag: Required*

IE 5 and later for Windows supports XML data islands, which are self-contained, unrendered blocks of XML data within an HTML page. The XML data may be delivered as part of the HTML document (embedded between the start and end tags) or loaded from an external source. Once the XML data is loaded, Microsoft's XML DOM (which in many ways resembles the Core portion of the W3C DOM) allows script access to the data for custom rendering. It is more common these days to use the XMLHttpRequest object and JavaScript to blend XML data into an HTML page. See Online Section VII.

Example

```
<xml id="xmlData">
  <xmlresults>
    <!-- xml data here -->
  </xmlresults>
</xml>
```

Object Model Reference
[window.]document.getElementById(*elementID*)

Attributes

src

Event Handler Attributes
None.

---

src   IE *5* NN *n/a* Moz *n/a* Saf *n/a* Op *n/a* HTML *n/a*

src="*URI*"   *Optional*

Points to an external source of XML data to be loaded into the element.

Example
<xml id="xmldata" src="http://www.magacorp.com/data/2003Forecast.xml></xml>

Value   Any valid URI whose return value contains XML data.

Default   None.

Object Model Reference
[window.]document.getElementById(*elementID*).src

<xmp>   IE *all* NN *all* Moz *all* Saf *all* Op *7* HTML *<4*

<xmp>...</xmp>   *HTML End Tag: Required*

The xmp element displays its content in a monospace font as a block element, as in computer code listings rendered 80 columns wide. In most browsers, the font size is also reduced from the default size. Browsers observe carriage returns and other whitespace in element content. This element has long been deprecated in HTML and has even been removed from the HTML 4 specification. You are encouraged to use the pre element instead. Note that in the example below, only Opera converts the entities into characters.

Example
```
<xmp>
&lt;script language="JavaScript"&gt;
   document.write("Hello, world.");
&lt;/script&gt;
</xmp>
```

Object Model Reference
[window.]document.getElementById(*elementID*)

Element-Specific Attributes
None.

<!--comment-->

Element-Specific Event Handler Attributes

None.

<!--comment-->

IE *all* NN *all* Moz *all* Saf *all* Op 7 HTML *all*

`<!--comment-->`   *HTML End Tag: Forbidden*

A comment element allows the author to insert content that the browser does not render, but is visible to anyone viewing the source code. Although the HTML standard states that a space between the -- characters and right angle bracket is permissible, most browsers require that there be no space within the sequence.

Microsoft uses the non-rendering behavior of HTML comments in other browsers to implement a system of directives called *conditional comments*. First introduced with IE 5 for Windows, conditional comments offer an additional way of specifying HTML content that is to render only in specific IE versions from 5 onward or render only in browsers other than IE 5 or specific later versions. Controlling the rendering are expressions inside the comment tag, such as whether the current browser is IE 6 or later.

There are two types of conditional comments: *downlevel-hidden* and *downlevel-revealed*. The former allows you to supply HTML code that is rendered only in designated versions of IE 5 or later; the latter lets you supply HTML that is render *only* in browsers other than designated IE 5 or later versions. Each type has a slightly different syntax.

A downlevel-hidden conditional comment has the following syntax:

```
<!--[if expression]> HTMLContent <![endif]-->
```

IE 5 and later for Windows understand that the square brackets with if and endif directives are explicitly for conditional comments, and will render the *HTMLContent* portion if the *expression* evaluates to true. Other browsers treat the entire comment as a plain HTML comment, and won't render anything.

A downlevel-revealed conditional comment has the following syntax:

```
<![if expression]> HTMLContent <![endif]>
```

Note that there are no hyphens in this form. Browsers other than IE 5 or later will always render the *HTMLContent* portion. If you also want, say, IE 5 and 5.5 to render the content, but not IE 6 or later, you create an *expression* that tells IE to render the *HTMLContent* portion also for those IE browsers whose versions are less than 6, as in the following:

```
<![if lt IE 6]
<script type="text/javascript" language="JavaScript">
    // statements for non-IE and pre-IE6 here
</script>
<![endif]>
```

An expression consists of a feature (IE is the only one supported to date), a comparison operator (omitting the operator means "equals"), and a version number (5 or later). Accepted comparison operators are lt (less than), gt (greater than), lte (less than or equal to), and gte (greater than or equal to). You can also negate the expression with a ! symbol in front of the feature (e.g., `<![if !IE 7]>`, meaning if IE is not version 7).

For more details on precise version vectors and other tips, visit *http://msdn.microsoft.com/workshop/author/dhtml/overview/ccomment_ovw.asp*.

<!--comment-->

Example   `<!-- layout inspired by www.example.com/catalog.html -->`

Object Model Reference

Via adjacent node references or walking the document tree by node type.

Element-Specific Attributes

None.

Element-Specific Event Handler Attributes

None.

CHAPTER 2

Document Object Model Reference

This chapter focuses on objects in documents—the scriptable entities that a browser maintains in its memory whenever a document is loaded. Most of these objects are created for you when the browser interprets the tags embedded within the content of the document. But many more objects exist solely for the purposes of scripting activities, such as event processing, window manipulation, creating and populating documents with new objects, reading the client's system environment, and even XML data that is part of an AJAX exchange with a server.

An object is described by its properties, methods, collections (or arrays) of nested items, and events. The Dynamic HTML features that you associate with a document rely entirely upon the objects and the properties, methods, and events that are supported by the browsers used by the page's visitors. The scriptable object model of early browsers was a simple one, with relatively few objects, and those objects had short lists of implemented properties, methods, and events. Today's model, however, is huge, due to a greatly expanded object model for Microsoft Internet Explorer 4 and, more recently, the addition of a completely new (and still growing) abstract object model designed by the W3C. That newest object model, the W3C DOM, is the model for which any new DHTML scripting should be targeted, as it is supported to various extents by all modern mainstream scriptable browsers.

To help you choose the right objects, properties, methods, and event handlers for the type of page development you're doing, this chapter lists every client-side Dynamic HTML-related object defined by Microsoft (IE), pre-Mozilla Netscape (NN), Mozilla (Moz), Safari (Saf), Opera 7 or later (Op), and the W3C (DOM), including some DOM Level 3 modules nearing completion. From these listings, you should be able to judge whether a particular object or its properties, methods, or events will work for your application.

If cross-browser support is essential for your application, pay close attention to the browser support and version information for each entry. The version number represents the first version of a particular browser to support the term (Opera compatibility ratings begin with version 7). Where no implementation exists, I use "n/a" to indicate that. Items valid for only a single version show the number encased in pipe symbols (e.g., |4|: for Version 4 only). For derivatives of the Mozilla Foundation's browser (e.g., Firefox, Netscape 6 or later, Camino, etc.), see Appendix F. Be aware that some items may not be available on all operating system platforms for a particular browser brand and version (particularly true for Internet Explorer 5). These distinctions are noted wherever the anomalous behavior could be substantiated by actual testing on the Win32 and Macintosh platforms. For example, IE 5 means both Windows and Mac versions, while IE 5(Win) is Windows only; IE 5.5 or later are Windows only.

Following a section that lists properties, methods, and events shared by all HTML element objects in the latest browsers, this chapter is organized alphabetically by object type. HTML element object types appear as their corresponding HTML element's tag name (in XHTML lowercase form). Scripts do not reference elements by these names, except when they use tag name strings as method parameters (e.g., `document.getElementsByTagName("h1")`). Instead, scripts reference such element objects by the various ways that scripts produce valid references to element objects. The most common is to assign an identifier to the `id` attribute of the element, and use that identifier to create a reference with syntax such as the following W3C DOM method:

    document.getElementById("elementID")

where the parameter is a string of the element's identifier. Numerous other properties throughout the object models evaluate to valid element object references, without requiring an explicit reference to the identifer. For example, an event object contains a property that evaluates to a valid reference to the element that was the target of the event. A script statement can then use that reference to access the element object's properties or methods, as needed.

The very large W3C DOM vocabulary contains many terms that do not come into common use even in today's browsers. For example, the element object listed in this chapter as the `div` object is formally known in the W3C DOM as the `HTMLDivElement` object. For the sake of compactness, this chapter does not list the W3C DOM HTML element objects as separate entries, but see "Static W3C HTML DOM Objects" below for further details.

Property Value Types

Many properties share similar data requirements. For the sake of brevity in the reference listings, this section describes a few common property value types in more detail than is possible within the listings. Whenever you see one of these property value types associated with a property, consult this section for a description of the type.

Length

A length value defines a linear measure of document real estate. The unit of measurement can be any applicable unit that helps identify a position or space on the screen. For properties that reflect HTML attributes, length units are uniformly pixels, but in other content, such as that specified in Cascading Style Sheets (see Chapter 4), measurements can be in inches, picas, ems, or other relevant units. A single numeric value may represent a length when it defines the offset from an edge of an element. For example, a coordinate point (10,20) consists of two length values, denoting pixel measurements from the left and top edges of an element, respectively.

Identifier

An identifier is a name that adheres to some strict syntactical rules. Most important is that an identifier is one word with no whitespace allowed. If you need to use multiple words to describe an item, you can use the intercapitalized format (in which internal letters are capitalized, also known as lowerCamelCase) or an underscore character between the words. Most punctuation symbols are not permitted, but all numerals and alphabetical characters are. Scripting languages do not allow the use of a numeral for the first character of an identifier.

URI and URL

The term *Universal Resource Identifier* (URI) is a broad term for an address of content on the Web (while an Internationalized Resource Identifier—IRI—is an address that can include Unicode characters to accommodate non-ASCII characters). A Universal Resource Locator (URL) is a type of URI. For most web authoring, you can think of them as one and the same, since most web browsers restrict their focus to URLs. A URL may be complete (including the protocol, host, domain, and the rest) or may be relative to the URL of the current document. In the latter case, this means the URL may consist of an anchor, file, or pathname. An object property that refers to a URL requires that the text of the URL be represented as a quoted string.

Language Code

There is an extensive list of standard codes that identify the spoken and written languages of the world. A language code always contains a primary language code, such as "en" for English or "zh" for Chinese. Common two-letter primary codes are cataloged in ISO 639. An optional subcode (separated from the primary code by a hyphen) may be used to identify a specific implementation of the primary language, usually according to usage within a specific country. Therefore, while "en" means all of English, "en-US" means a U.S.-specific version of English. The browser must support a particular language code for its meaning to be of any value to an element attribute.

Colors

A color value can be assigned either via a hexadecimal triplet or with a plain-language equivalent. A hexadecimal triplet consists of three pairs of hexadecimal (base 16) numbers that range between the values 00 and FF, corresponding to the red, green, and blue components of the color. The three pairs of numbers are bunched together and preceded by a pound sign (#) in the form #rrggbb. Therefore, the reddest of reds has all red (FF) and none (00) of the other two colors: #FF0000; pure blue is #0000FF. The letters A through F can also be lowercase. For values that apply to style sheet properties, a color may also be represented in the RGB (red-green-blue) format consistent with CSS conventions (see Chapter 4).

These numbering schemes obviously lead to a potentially huge number of combinations (over 16 million). In the early days of the Web, typical PC display settings (throttled by limitations in processing power and memory) limited output to 256 colors, meaning that subtle differences among the 16 million potential colors were lost on visitors who had those settings. As a result, web content authors commonly used what became known as a *web-safe palette* consisting of 216 distinguishable colors. Although today's computers have sufficient processing power and memory to accommodate millions of colors with ease, some page designers continue to adhere to the more limited palette to ensure backward compatibility. A fine online reference of colors that work well on all browsers and PC color display settings can be found at *http://www.lynda.com/hex.asp*.

The HTML recommendation also specifies a basic library of 16 colors that can be assigned by plain-language names. Note that the color names are case-insensitive. The names and their equivalent hexadecimal triplets are as follows:

Black	#000000	Maroon	#800000	Green	#008000	Navy	#000080
Silver	#C0C0C0	Red	#FF0000	Lime	#00FF00	Blue	#0000FF
Gray	#808080	Purple	#800080	Olive	#808000	Teal	#008080
White	#FFFFFF	Fuchsia	#FF00FF	Yellow	#FFFF00	Aqua	#00FFFF

In other words, the attribute settings bgcolor="Aqua" and bgcolor="#00FFFF" yield the same results.

Many years ago, Netscape deployed a much longer list of plain-language color equivalents, originally adopted from the X Window System palette known as X11 color names. These are detailed in Appendix A, and are recognized by recent versions of mainstream browsers.

About client- and offset- Properties

In Internet Explorer 4, Microsoft introduced a set of size and position properties for elements that render as part of the regular body content (i.e., not positioned via

CSS). These properties had the potential to assist scripts in their tasks of determining locations and dimensions of body content so that positioned elements could be moved in relation to these fixed elements. The properties are:

clientHeight	clientLeft	clientTop	clientWidth
offsetHeight	offsetLeft	offsetTop	offsetWidth

The sad news is that between buggy behavior under fairly common circumstances in IE/Windows, and a different philosophy behind their implementation in IE/Mac, these properties can be difficult to work with. Add to this mix the fact that Microsoft tried to mend the errors for IE 6 by altering the playing field when the DOCTYPE element puts the browser into "standards-compliant" mode (and fixing the genuine measurement bugs while in that mode). If that weren't enough, early Mozilla versions implemented some of these non-W3C properties for the convenience of DHTML authors, but in a way that comes closer to the old IE/Windows mode (minus the measurement bugs) than to the IE 6 standards-compliant mode. Confusing? You bet!

The primary measurement discrepancies among browsers and compatibility modes have to do with element padding (if any is applied) and the positioning context for the element (even for nonpositioned elements). The number of permutations of oddities introduced by element and style sheet combinations boggles the mind, so I'll take one example of a common task—using a script to place the content of a CSS-positioned element directly atop the content of an inline element—to demonstrate the range of possible problem areas with a variety of browsers and compatibility modes. Because the properties described in this section are not part of the W3C DOM (as of Level 2), it is difficult to say which approach is "correct." It's more a question of how to use these properties to accomplish your desired tasks on your target browsers.

For this scenario, the following tag was inserted into an arbitrary place within a document so that its precise location would vary with browser, window size, and other environmental conditions:

```
<img id="fixedImg" src="bkgnd.jpg" alt="Locator box" height="90"
    width="120" style="padding:2px; border:3px solid green; margin:5px">
```

I use an image here because its content is the same size regardless of browser, and will let us see how the various size properties report the element's overall or content size (i.e., we're not at the mercy of font rendering vaguaries). Including padding, border, and margin settings for this fixed element will illustrate that some of these style attributes can impact topographical information about the element in the document. Table 2-1 shows the values for relevant size and position properties for several browsers and compatibility modes.

Table 2-1. Comparative property values (pixels) for a 120-by-90 pixel inline element

Property name	IE 7 (Quirks mode)	IE 7 (CSS mode)	FF 1.5 (CSS mode)	Saf 2	Op 9 (CSS mode)
clientLeft	3	3	n/a	n/a	3
clientTop	3	3	n/a	n/a	3
offsetLeft	15	5	13	5	13
offsetTop	243	228	251	215	229
clientWidth	120	124	124	124	124
clientHeight	90	94	94	94	94
offsetWidth	126	130	130	130	130
offsetHeight	96	100	100	100	100
naturalWidth	n/a	n/a	120	n/a	n/a
naturalHeight	n/a	n/a	90	n/a	n/a
width	120	124	120	120	120
height	90	94	90	90	90
offsetParent.clientLeft	2	0	n/a	n/a	0
offsetParent.clientTop	2	0	n/a	n/a	0
offsetParent.offsetLeft	0	10	0	8	0
offsetParent.offsetTop	0	15	0	8	0

Table 2-1 reveals a great deal about how various browsers report the location and size of an inline element. Some of the precise numbers, such as the location coordinates, are not critical measures because each browser renders surrounding content slightly differently, and any scripts that rely on the position will read the live values in each case. But several very important details are worth noting for this particular element insertion:

- IE 6 and 7 in backward-compatible ("quirks") mode calculates the heights and widths the same as IE for Windows all the way back to Version 4. This is good for backward compatibility.

- In IE 6 and 7 in quirks mode, the offset sizes include the border thicknesses on both sides of the content.

- In standards mode, IE 6 and 7 calculate the offsetLeft and offsetTop properties in relation to the offsetParent element; the offsetParent element has its own offset values. The actual position must take into account the offsetParent's offset values.

- In standards mode, IE 6 and 7 report width and height properties influenced by the padding thickness. This is wrong, because these properties should reflect the height and width attribute values of the element (even `getAttribute( )` returns the incorrect values).

- IE 6 and 7 in standards mode, Mozilla, Safari, and Opera report identical `offsetWidth` and `offsetHeight` values, all of which include the padding and border thicknesses, but not the margins.

The main point to understand here is that when you attempt to mix absolute-positioned elements with elements rendered as part of the main document, the client and offset properties of the fixed items can be both helpful and tricky, depending on the level of standards compatibility dictated by your DOCTYPE, and whether the elements have borders, margins, and padding associated with them. In standards-compatible mode, you will likely have to take offsetParent coordinates of fixed elements into account. Almost any task is possible, but it may require much trial, error, and cross-browser testing to achieve the desired results with your combination of elements. Don't be surprised if a complex element design and precision positioning task across the domains of fixed elements, positioned elements, and event coordinates takes hard work to accomplish.

Default Property Values

Many property listings provide what appear to be explicit default values, but this can be deceiving. The trend in recent browsers is for an element object property to return an empty string when the property reflects an HTML attribute not explicitly assigned in the source code. But an empty string is equally misleading, because the element may behave according to a default specification, even when no attribute is assigned. The `align` property of a block-level element is a good example. Unless instructed otherwise, the element usually behaves as if its `align` property were set to `left`, yet the default property returns as an empty string because no `align` attribute is explicitly set in the markup.

In these cases, the listings in this chapter display the default values under which the element object behaves. This choice simply provides a shortcut so that when you see a list or range of possible property values, you don't have to look up the corresponding attribute in Chapter 1 to find the HTML default value. Where the default value is listed as "None," this means that there is no default HTML behavior and the default value is, indeed, an empty string.

Events

Objects that can receive events have events listed in their main entries. In a change from previous editions of this book, events are listed by their event type—the version without the leading "on" prefix. When you choose to bind an event handler function to an object via its event property, use the "on" prefix format, as described in "Binding Event Handlers to Elements" in Online Section VI.

The selection of events listed for each object is based on a couple of factors. First, just as most HTML 4.0 elements have intrinsic events associated with them, those same events are listed in this chapter with the objects that reflect the HTML element. As such, it may seem odd that an element that has almost no visual presence on a page has keyboard and mouse events. Those events are listed just the same, even though the likelihood of your scripting them is next to nil.

Second, the Internet Explorer and W3C DOM event bubbling models (see Online Section VI) dictate that it is possible for an event from one element to bubble up through the element containment hierarchy all the way to a root node or element. This means that essentially every event that can appear in the most nested element is also available in all elements higher up the containment chain. In other words, virtually every element that acts as a container can have virtually every bubbling event type associated with it. You can read more about the characteristics of each event type in Chapter 3.

Static W3C HTML DOM Objects

Shared DOM Reference

One category of DOM object not explicitly detailed in this chapter is the one containing the static DOM objects from which each HTML element object instance is derived. By and large you won't ever have need to script these static objects directly, although you will see their names crop up in your debugging in browsers such as Mozilla and recent versions of Safari and Opera. For example, if you ask the alert( ) method to display the reference to a p element object in Mozilla, the reference is converted to a string form as follows:

```
[object HTMLParagraphElement]
```

This is not the object's JavaScript type (which is just object). But it means that the p element in question is an instance of the W3C DOM HTMLParagraphElement object. In browsers that support direct access to the static object (Mozilla, Safari after version 2.0.4, and Opera 8 or later), you have the luxury of adding properties and methods to the prototype property of any such object. Thus, any new instance that your scripts create has those new properties and methods built into them (see the Array. prototype description in Chapter 5 for an example of this JavaScript mechanism).

The W3C DOM Level 2 module for HTML elements defines the static objects in the following list. All of these objects inherit the properties and methods of the HTMLElement object, also listed below. Descriptions for these items can be found later in this chapter under the HTML element object names (e.g., HTMLParagraphElement is covered under the p object).

HTMLAnchorElement	HTMLAppletElement	HTMLAreaElement
HTMLBaseElement	HTMLBaseFontElement	HTMLBodyElement
HTMLBRElement	HTMLButtonElement	HTMLDirectoryElement
HTMLDivElement	HTMLDListElement	HTMLElement
HTMLFieldSetElement	HTMLFontElement	HTMLFormElement
HTMLFrameElement	HTMLFrameSetElement	HTMLHeadElement
HTMLHeadingElement	HTMLHRElement	HTMLHtmlElement
HTMLIFrameElement	HTMLImageElement	HTMLInputElement
HTMLIsIndexElement	HTMLLabelElement	HTMLLegendElement
HTMLLIElement	HTMLLinkElement	HTMLMapElement
HTMLMenuElement	HTMLMetaElement	HTMLModElement
HTMLObjectElement	HTMLOListElement	HTMLOptGroupElement
HTMLOptionElement	HTMLParagraphElement	HTMLParamElement
HTMLPreElement	HTMLQuoteElement	HTMLScriptElement
HTMLSelectElement	HTMLStyleElement	HTMLTableCaptionElement
HTMLTableCellElement	HTMLTableColElement	HTMLTableElement
HTMLTableRowElement	HTMLTableSectionElement	HTMLTextAreaElement
HTMLTitleElement	HTMLUListElement	

When a browser implements an element that is not part of the HTML 4 and W3C DOM specification, it typically extends the HTMLDivElement or HTMLSpanElement object with behaviors and/or styles to give that elements it's special characteristics. Thus, Mozilla reports that a marquee element is derived from the HTMLSpanElement object.

Shared Object Properties, Methods, and Events

Both the proprietary Internet Explorer DOM and W3C DOM expose a wide range of properties (including event handler properties) and methods almost universally across objects that reflect HTML elements. Rather than repeat the descriptions of these items ad nauseam in the reference listing, I am listing these shared details only once. Due to the large number of shared items (95 properties, 74 methods, and 72 event types), these shared items do not appear in the lists of properties, methods, and events for each object in the rest of this chapter, but they are available for practically every HTML element object (within the browser or standard version range indicated in each listing).

Obviously, the shared properties or methods that are meaningless except for rendered element objects may not be available to nonrendered elements. For example, invoking the IE scrollIntoView( ) method of a style element object is meaningless because the style element presents no content of its own on the page to which a window could scroll. Such items are typically part of the DOMs simply because the browsers' internal architectures utilize an inheritance mechanism that empowers all element objects with the same basic items, even if they have no particular application. You should get to know the shared items well, and refer to the object-specific items later in this chapter when you need their special powers.

In the following item descriptions, the example code uses the term *elementID* to refer to the identifier assigned to the id attribute of the element. In your scripts, substitute the object's true ID for the placeholder used here.

Shared Element Object Properties

ATTRIBUTE_NODE	CDATA_SECTION_NODE	COMMENT_NODE
DOCUMENT_FRAGMENT_NODE	DOCUMENT_NODE	DOCUMENT_POSITION_CONTAINED_BY
DOCUMENT_POSITION_CONTAINS	DOCUMENT_POSITION_DISCONNECTED	DOCUMENT_POSITION_FOLLOWING
DOCUMENT_POSITION_IMPLEMENTATION_SPECIFIC	DOCUMENT_POSITION_PRECEDING	DOCUMENT_TYPE_NODE
ELEMENT_NODE	ENTITY_NODE	ENTITY_REFERENCE_NODE
NOTATION_NODE	PROCESSING_INSTRUCTION_NODE	TEXT_NODE
accessKey	all[]	attributes[]
baseURI	behaviorUrns[]	canHaveChildren
canHaveHTML	childNodes[]	children
cite	className	clientHeight
clientLeft	clientTop	clientWidth
contentEditable	currentStyle	dateTime
dir	disabled	document
filters[]	firstChild	hideFocus
id	innerHTML	innerText
isContentEditable	isDisabled	isMultiLine
isTextEdit	lang	language
lastChild	localName	namespaceURI
nextSibling	nodeName	nodeType
nodeValue	offsetHeight	offsetLeft
offsetParent	offsetTop	offsetWidth
outerHTML	outerText	ownerDocument
parentElement	parentNode	parentTextEdit
prefix	previousSibling	readyState
recordNumber	repeatMax	repeatMin
repeatStart	repetitionBlocks[]	repetitionIndex
repetitionTemplate	repetitionType	runtimeStyle
scopeName	scrollHeight	scrollLeft
scrollTop	scrollWidth	sourceIndex
style	tabIndex	tagName
tagUrn	textContent	title
uniqueID	unselectable	

Shared Element Object Methods

addBehavior( )	addEventListener( )	addRepetitionBlock( )
addRepetitionBlockByIndex( )	appendChild( )	applyElement( )
attachEvent( )	blur( )	clearAttributes( )
click( )	cloneNode( )	compareDocumentPosition( )
componentFromPoint( )	contains( )	createControlRange( )
detachEvent( )	dispatchEvent( )	doScroll( )
dragDrop( )	fireEvent( )	focus( )
getAdjacentText( )	getAttribute( )	getAttributeNode( )
getAttributeNodeNS( )	getAttributeNS( )	getBoundingClientRect( )
getClientRects( )	getElementsByTagName( )	getElementsByTagNameNS( )
getExpression( )	getFeature( )	getUserData( )
hasAttribute( )	hasAttributeNS( )	hasAttributes( )
hasChildNodes( )	insertAdjacentElement( )	insertAdjacentHTML( )
insertAdjacentText( )	insertBefore( )	isDefaultNamespace( )
isEqualNode( )	isSameNode( )	isSupported( )
lookupNamespaceURI( )	lookupPrefix( )	mergeAttributes( )
moveRepetitionBlock( )	normalize( )	releaseCapture( )
removeAttribute( )	removeAttributeNode( )	removeAttributeNS( )
removeBehavior( )	removeChild( )	removeEventListener( )
removeExpression( )	removeNode( )	removeRepetitionBlock( )
replaceAdjacentText( )	replaceChild( )	replaceNode( )
scrollIntoView( )	setActive( )	setAttribute( )
setAttributeNode( )	setAttributeNodeNS( )	setAttributeNS( )
setCapture( )	setExpression( )	setUserData( )
swapNode( )	toString( )	

Shared Element Object Events

Events	IE (Win)	IE (Mac)	Mozilla	Safari	Opera	W3C DOM
DOMActivate[a]	n/a	n/a	n/a	1.3/2	n/a	2
DOMAttrModified[a]	n/a	n/a	n/a	n/a	9	2
DOMCharacterDataModified[a]	n/a	n/a	n/a	n/a	n/a	2
DOMFocusIn[a]	n/a	n/a	n/a	1.3/2	9	2
DOMFocusOut[a]	n/a	n/a	n/a	1.3/2	9	2
DOMNodeInserted[a]	n/a	n/a	n/a	n/a	9	2
DOMNodeInsertedIntoDocument[a]	n/a	n/a	n/a	n/a	n/a	2
DOMNodeRemoved[a]	n/a	n/a	n/a	n/a	n/a	2
DOMNodeRemovedFromDocument[a]	n/a	n/a	n/a	n/a	n/a	2

Events	IE (Win)	IE (Mac)	Mozilla	Safari	Opera	W3C DOM
DOMSubtreeModified[a]	n/a	n/a	n/a	1.3/2	n/a	2
activate	5.5	n/a	n/a	n/a	n/a	n/a
afterupdate[b]	4	5	n/a	n/a	n/a	n/a
beforeactivate	6	n/a	n/a	n/a	n/a	n/a
beforecopy	5	n/a	n/a	1.3/2	n/a	n/a
beforecut	5	n/a	n/a	1.3/2	n/a	n/a
beforedeactivate	5.5	n/a	n/a	n/a	n/a	n/a
beforeeditfocus	5	n/a	n/a	n/a	n/a	n/a
beforepaste	5	n/a	n/a	1.3/2	n/a	n/a
beforeupdate[b]	4	5	n/a	n/a	n/a	n/a
blur[c]	3	3.01	all	all	7	2
cellchange[d]	5	n/a	n/a	n/a	n/a	n/a
click[c]	3	3.01	all	all	all	2
contextmenu	5	n/a	all	all	n/a	n/a
controlselect	5.5	n/a	n/a	n/a	n/a	n/a
copy	5	n/a	n/a	1.3/2	n/a	n/a
cut	5	n/a	n/a	1.3/2	n/a	n/a
dataavailable[d]	4	n/a	n/a	n/a	n/a	n/a
datasetchanged[d]	4	n/a	n/a	n/a	n/a	n/a
datasetcompleted	4	n/a	n/a	n/a	n/a	n/a
dblclick[c]	4	4	all	n/a	all	n/a
deactivate	5.5	n/a	n/a	n/a	n/a	n/a
drag	5	n/a	n/a	1.3/2	n/a	n/a
dragend	5	n/a	n/a	1.3/2	n/a	n/a
dragenter	5	n/a	n/a	1.3/2	n/a	n/a
dragleave	5	n/a	n/a	1.3/2	n/a	n/a
dragover	5	n/a	n/a	1.3/2	n/a	n/a
dragstart	5	n/a	n/a	1.3/2	n/a	n/a
drop	5	n/a	n/a	1.3/2	n/a	n/a
errorupdate[b]	4	5	n/a	n/a	n/a	n/a
filterchange	4	n/a	n/a	n/a	n/a	n/a
focus[c]	3	3.01	all	all	all	2
focusin	6	n/a	n/a	n/a	n/a	n/a
focusout	6	n/a	n/a	n/a	n/a	n/a
help[c]	4	5	n/a	n/a	n/a	n/a
keydown[c]	4	4	all	all	all	3
keypress[c]	4	4	all	all	all	3

Events	IE (Win)	IE (Mac)	Mozilla	Safari	Opera	W3C DOM
keyup[c]	4	4	all	all	all	3
layoutcomplete	5.5	n/a	n/a	n/a	n/a	n/a
losecapture	5	n/a	n/a	n/a	n/a	n/a
mousedown[c]	4	4	all	all	all	2
mouseenter	5.5	n/a	n/a	n/a	n/a	n/a
mouseleave	5.5	n/a	n/a	n/a	n/a	n/a
mousemove[c]	4	4	all	all	all	2
mouseout[c]	3	3.01	all	all	all	2
mouseover[c]	3	3.01	all	all	all	2
mouseup[c]	4	4	all	all	all	2
mousewheel	6	n/a	n/a	n/a	n/a	n/a
move	5.5	n/a	n/a	n/a	n/a	n/a
moveend	5.5	n/a	n/a	n/a	n/a	n/a
movestart	5.5	n/a	n/a	n/a	n/a	n/a
paste	5	n/a	n/a	1.3/2	n/a	n/a
propertychange	5	n/a	n/a	n/a	n/a	n/a
readystatechange[e]	4	n/a	1.0.1	1.2	8	n/a
resize[c]	4	4	all	all	all	2
resizeend	5.5	n/a	n/a	n/a	n/a	n/a
resizestart	5.5	n/a	n/a	n/a	n/a	n/a
rowenter[d]	4	n/a	n/a	n/a	n/a	n/a
rowexit[d]	4	n/a	n/a	n/a	n/a	n/a
rowsdeleted[d]	5	n/a	n/a	n/a	n/a	n/a
rowsinserted[d]	5	n/a	n/a	n/a	n/a	n/a
scroll[f]	4	4	n/a	n/a	n/a	2
selectstart	4	4	n/a	1.3/2	n/a	n/a

[a] Event type assignable only via the addEventListener( ) method for any node.

[b] Exposed as property for all elements in IE 6+, but applies only to elements that support data binding: a, bdo, button, custom, div, frame, iframe, img, input (checkbox, hidden, password, radio, text), label, legend, marquee, rt, ruby, select, span, and textarea.

[c] Shared among all element objects only in recent browsers. Earlier implementations and compatibilities are listed with applicable objects throughout this chapter.

[d] Exposed as property for all elements in IE 6+, but applies only to applet, object, and xml elements set for data binding.

[e] Exposed as property for all elements in IE 6+, but applies only to applet, document, frame, frameSet, iframe, img, link, object, script, and xml elements unless an HTML behavior is attached to the element.

[f] Exposed as property for all elements in IE 6+, but applies only to applet, bdo, body, custom, div, embed, map, marquee, object, table, and textarea elements and the window object.

ATTRIBUTE_NODE, CDATA_SECTION_NODE, COMMENT_NODE, DOCUMENT_FRAGMENT_NODE, DOCUMENT_NODE, DOCUMENT_TYPE_NODE, ELEMENT_NODE, ENTITY_NODE, ENTITY_REFERENCE_NODE, NOTATION_NODE, PROCESSING_INSTRUCTION_NODE, TEXT_NODE

NN *n/a*   Moz *all*   Saf *all*   Op *7*   DOM *1*

Read-only

This set of constants belongs to the root Node object of the W3C DOM, and is therefore inherited by all document-level nodes and elements (except in Safari and Opera, where they are properties of the Node object only). Each property corresponds to an integer value associated with the nodeType property of every DOM node. You can use these properties as a more plain-language way to indicate the node type your script is looking for in comparisons or similar operations.

Example

```
if (myObject.nodeType == Node.ELEMENT_NODE) {
    // process as an element here
}
```

Value

Integer corresponding to DOM node type as follows:

Property	nodeType value
ELEMENT_NODE	1
ATTRIBUTE_NODE	2
TEXT_NODE	3
CDATA_SECTION_NODE	4
ENTITY_REFERENCE_NODE	5
ENTITY_NODE	6
PROCESSING_INSTRUCTION_NODE	7
COMMENT_NODE	8
DOCUMENT_NODE	9
DOCUMENT_TYPE_NODE	10
DOCUMENT_FRAGMENT_NODE	11
NOTATION_NODE	12

Default   Constant values (above).

DOCUMENT_POSITION_CONTAINED_BY, DOCUMENT_POSITION_CONTAINS, DOCUMENT_POSITION_DISCONNECTED, DOCUMENT_POSITION_FOLLOWING, DOCUMENT_POSITION_IMPLEMENTATION_SPECIFIC, DOCUMENT_POSITION_PRECEDING

IE *n/a*   NN *n/a*   Moz *1.7*   Saf *n/a*   Op *n/a*   DOM *3*

Read-only

This set of constants belongs to the root Node object of the W3C DOM, and is therefore inherited by all document-level nodes and elements (including attribute nodes). Each property corresponds to a bitmask value used in calculations of node position comparisons. See the shared compareDocumentPosition( ) method for details on usage. Some of these constants were implemented in Mozilla as early as version 1.4, but the name of one constant changed in 1.7 and later.

Example

```
if (document.body.compareDocumentPosition(document.body.parentNode) ==
   (Node.DOCUMENT_POSITION_PRECEDING | Node.DOCUMENT_POSITION_CONTAINS)) {
   // statements
}
```

Value

Integer corresponding to values as follows:

Property	Mask value	Integer value
DOCUMENT_POSITION_CONTAINED_BY	0x10	16
DOCUMENT_POSITION_CONTAINS	0x08	8
DOCUMENT_POSITION_DISCONNECTED	0x01	1
DOCUMENT_POSITION_FOLLOWING	0x04	4
DOCUMENT_POSITION_IMPLEMENTATION_SPECIFIC	0x20	32
DOCUMENT_POSITION_PRECEDING	0x02	2

Default   Constant values (above).

accessKey

IE *4*   NN *n/a*   Moz *all*   Saf *all*   Op *7*   DOM *1*

Read/Write

This is the character key that either gives focus to an element (in some browsers) or activates a form control or link action. The browser and operating system determine if the user must press a modifier key (e.g., **Ctrl**, **Alt**, or **Command**) with the access key to activate the link. Most Windows browsers require a press of the **Alt** key along with the designated access key, while Mac browsers use the **Ctrl** key as the modifier. Opera, on the other hand, has an entirely different sequence: **Shift+Esc** and then the access key

Although listed here as a widely shared property, that isn't strictly the case across all implementations. Per the W3C DOM, Mozilla, Safari, and Opera recognizes this property only for the following elements: a, area, button, input, label, legend, and textarea. To this list, IE 4 adds applet, body, div, embed, isindex, marquee, object, select, span, table, and td (but removes label and legend). IE 5 adds every other renderable element, but with a caution. Except for input and other form-related elements, you must also assign a tabindex attribute or tabIndex property value to the IE 5 and later element (even if it's simply a value of zero for all) to let the accelerator key combination bring focus to the element. All other current mainstream browsers recognize this property for the select element.

Example   document.links[3].accessKey = "n";

Value   Single alphanumeric (and punctuation) keyboard character.

Default   Empty string.

all[ ]   IE 4　NN *n/a*　Moz *1.7*　Saf *n/a*　Op *7*　DOM *n/a*

Read-only

Returns an array of all HTML element objects contained by the current element (only for the document object in Mozilla—see document.all for details). Items in this array are indexed (zero-based) in source code order. The collection transcends generations of nested elements such that document.all[ ] exposes every element in the entire document. See the all object for a list of this property value's own set of properties and methods.

As with all collections, you may use the traditional JavaScript array syntax (with square brackets around the index value) or IE's JScript alternative (with parentheses around the index value). If you are aiming for cross-browser deployment for collections that are available on both platforms, use the square brackets.

Unless you develop strictly for IE browsers, you should use W3C DOM references via document.getElementById( ), implemented in IE 5 and later and all other mainstream browsers.

Syntax
```
object.all(index).objectPropertyOrMethod
object.all[index].objectPropertyOrMethod
object.all("elementID").objectPropertyOrMethod
object.all["elementID"].objectPropertyOrMethod
object.all.elementID.objectPropertyOrMethod
```

Example   var inpVal = document.all.first_name.value;

Value   Array (collection) of element object references in HTML source code order.

Default   Current document's model.

attributes[ ]   IE 5　NN *n/a*　Moz *all*　Saf *all*　Op *7*　DOM *1*

Read-only

Returns a named node map object (W3C DOM type NamedNodeMap), which resembles an array (collection) of attribute objects (W3C DOM type Attr), but also has some methods of its own to facilitate accessing a member of this array. This property is inherited from the Node object, but its value is null for all node types other than elements (because elements are the only node types that contain attributes). IE's attributes array contains entries for all attributes of the element's internal DTD, plus any custom (expando) attributes explicitly set in the HTML source code in IE 6 or later. Scripted changes to the element's attributes or their values are not reflected in this array.

For non-IE browsers, the attributes array contains entries only for those attributes explicitly defined in the HTML source code for the element, including custom attributes. Scripted changes to attributes (additions or deletions) or their values are reflected in the attribute objects referenced by the attributes array.

In lieu of the named node map object methods, you may access individual attribute objects via standard JavaScript array syntax. By and large, however, it is far more convenient to access HTML element attribute values for scripting purposes either via their reflection as element object properties or via the element's getAttribute() and setAttribute() methods. For W3C DOM details (which are useful for XML document parsing), see the Attr and NamedNodeMap objects for properties and methods of these objects.

Example

```
var ldAttr = document.getElementById("myImg").attributes.getNamedItem("longdesc");
```

Value   Collection (IE) or named node map (others) of attribute object references in source code (Mozilla), alphabetical-by-name (IE/Mac), or haphazard (IE/Windows) order.

Default   Current element's model.

baseURI
IE n/a   NN n/a   Moz all   Saf n/a   Op n/a   DOM 3
Read-only

This is a property of the Node object (proposed for DOM Level 3 Core) that reveals the base URI (full path to the source) from which the node was served. For example, each node copied from an XML document loaded into a document.implementation object reveals its baseURI, which is different from that of the HTML page performing the rendering.

Example   `var nodeSrc = myXMLDoc.firstChild.childNodes[14].baseURI;`

Value   Full URI string.

Default   Current node's internal value.

behaviorUrns[ ]
IE 5(Win)   NN n/a   Moz n/a   Saf n/a   Op n/a   DOM n/a
Read-only

Provides an array of Uniform Resource Names for all external behaviors (.htc files) associated with the element through style sheet syntax. Perhaps for security reasons, the strings entries of this array are always empty.

Example

```
var htcCount = document.getElementById(elementID).behaviorUrns.length;
```

Value   Array of (empty) strings.

Default   Array of length 0.

canHaveChildren

IE 5(Win) NN n/a Moz n/a Saf n/a Op n/a DOM n/a

Read-only

Specifies whether the current element may act as a container of other elements. The property value is based on IE for Windows built-in HTML DTDs, which define several elements (such as br) that may not have child nodes inserted into them.

Example

```
if (elementRef.canHaveChildren) {
    // statements to insert or append child elements
}
```

Value   Boolean value: true | false.

Default   Element-specific.

canHaveHTML

IE 5.5 NN n/a Moz n/a Saf n/a Op n/a DOM n/a

Read-only and Read/Write

Specifies whether the current element may act as a container of other content with HTML markup. The property reports identical information as canHaveChildren for regular HTML elements. For IE HTML Components (defined in an XML-based *.htc* file), the property is read/write, and directs the browser how to treat the custom element defined by the component.

Example

```
if (elementRef.canHaveHTML) {
    // statements to insert content with HTML markup
}
```

Value   Boolean value: true | false.

Default   Element-specific.

childNodes[ ]

IE 5 NN n/a Moz all Saf all Op 7 DOM 1

Read-only

This is a property of the W3C DOM Node object that consists of an array of references to all child nodes (a node list) in the next deeper level of the node hierarchy (whether part of the document node tree or free-standing document fragments not yet inserted into the document tree). To reach more deeply nested nodes, you must access the childNodes array of each child node of the current node. A vital property for walking through a node tree. See the NodeList object for the properties and methods of this kind of array.

Example

```
for (var i = 0; i < nodeRef.childNodes.length; i++) {
    if (nodeRef.childNodes[i].nodeType == document.ELEMENT_NODE) {
        // operate on an element
    }
}
```

Value   Array of node object references.

Default   Array of length zero.

children[ ]

IE 4 NN n/a Moz n/a Saf 1.2 Op 7 DOM n/a

Read-only

Returns an array of all first-level HTML element objects contained by the current element. This collection differs from the all[] collection in that it contains references only to the immediate children of the current element (whereas the all[] collection transcends generations). For example, document.body.children[] might contain a form, but no reference to form elements nested inside the form. Items in this array are indexed (zero-based) in source code order. In contrast to the childNodes[] array, the scope of this property is the element, not the node. See the children object. The W3C DOM equivalent is the childNodes property.

Example

```
for (var i = 0; i < elementRef.children.length; i++) {
    if (elementRef.children[i].tagName == "FORM") {
        // operate on a form element
    }
}
```

Value   Array of element object references.

Default   Array of length zero.

cite

IE 6 NN n/a Moz all Saf all Op 7 DOM 1

Read/Write

This property (along with dateTime) is shared among all phrase element objects in IE 6 or later, but in truth, it officially belongs only to the blockquote, q, del, and ins element objects (see those element descriptions in Chapter 1 for details on the corresponding attribute in the context of the element). Because the property is shared by four objects, Microsoft may have found it more convenient to implement the property internally for a larger related set of HTML element objects. Or it may be a mistake. Whatever the reason, do not expect this property in as many element objects as exposed in recent IE versions. Compatibility ratings for other browsers and the DOM apply to the property only in its intended element objects.

Value   Any valid URL to a document on the World Wide Web, including absolute or relative URLs.

Default   Empty string.

className

IE 4   NN n/a   Moz all   Saf all   Op 7   DOM 1

Read/Write

This is an identifier generally used to associate an element with a style sheet rule defined for a class selector. You can alter the class association for an element by script. If the document includes an alternate class selector and style rule, adjusting the element's className property can provide a shortcut for adjusting many style properties at once.

Example
```
document.getElementById("elementID").className = "altHighlighted";
```

Value   Case-sensitive string. Multiple class names are space-delimited within the string.

Default   Empty string.

clientHeight, clientWidth

IE 4   NN n/a   Moz 1.0.1   Saf all   Op 7   DOM n/a

Read-only

Broadly speaking, these provide the height and width of the element's content, but with minor variations with respect to element padding among various operating system versions of IE and compatibility modes controlled by the DOCTYPE declaration. Not available for all element types in IE for Macintosh. For Mozilla, values are zero except when an element's content overflows the viewable area, in which case the values reveal the dimensions of the viewable area (e.g., the browser window's content region for the document.body element). See the "About client- and offset- Properties" at the beginning of this chapter for details.

Example   `var midHeight = document.body.clientHeight/2;`

Value   Integer pixel value.

Default   0

clientLeft, clientTop

IE 4   NN n/a   Moz n/a   Saf n/a   Op n/a   DOM n/a

Read-only

Broadly speaking, these provide the left and top coordinates of the element's content within the box that includes the element's padding, but with minor variations among various operating system versions of IE. Not available for all element types in IE for Macintosh. See the "About client- and offset- Properties" at the beginning of this chapter for details. More useful information for inline element positioning generally comes from the offsetLeft and offsetTop properties. For CSS-positioned elements (including changing an element's position), use style object properties, such as left and top, and (in IE only) pixelLeft and pixelTop.

| **Value** | Integer pixel value. |
| **Default** | 0 |

contentEditable

IE 5.5 NN *n/a* Moz *n/a* Saf 1.2 Op 9 DOM *n/a*

Read/Write

Controls whether the element is editable by the user via live content-editing facilities built into the browser. User changes are not preserved on the server without intervention by the server, usually via client-side script capture of modified content and submission via form or XMLHttpRequest. Scripts should alter the appearance of an element (border, background color, etc.) when in edit mode to highlight the mode for the user (Safari does this automatically by giving the element a glowing blue border). By default, all child elements inherit the edit mode setting of an element. See the move event in Chapter 3 for an extended example.

Example	document.getElementById("*elementID*").contentEditable = "true";
Value	String constant: false | inherit | true.
Default	inherit

currentStyle

IE 5 NN *n/a* Moz *n/a* Saf *n/a* Op 9 DOM *n/a*

Read-only

Returns a style object with properties that reflect the effective values being applied to the element. This property takes into account style sheet rules defined in a style element, imported from external style sheet files, and inline style attributes. Because the style property reflects only inline style attributes, the currentStyle property is more valuable for reading initial values after a document loads. To modify style attributes, you can use the element's style object properties. For similar capabilities with W3C DOM syntax, see the window.getComputedStyle( ) method.

Example

var currSize = document.getElementById("*elementID*").currentStyle.fontSize;

| **Value** | style object reference. |
| **Default** | The effective style object. |

dateTime

IE 6 NN *n/a* Moz *all* Saf *all* Op 7 DOM 1

Read/Write

This property (along with cite) is shared among all phrase element objects in IE 6 or later, but in truth, it officially belongs only to the del and ins element objects (see those element descriptions in Chapter 1 for details on the corresponding attribute in the context of the element). Because the property is shared by four objects, Microsoft may have found it more convenient to implement the property internally for a larger related set of HTML element objects. Or it may be a mistake. Whatever the reason, do not expect this property in as many element objects as IE 6 exposes. Compatibility ratings for other browsers and the DOM apply to the property only in its intended element objects.

| **Value** | Date string. |
| **Default** | Empty string. |

dir

IE 5 NN *n/a* Moz *all* Saf *all* Op 7 DOM 1
Read/Write

Indicates the direction of character rendering for the element's text whose characters are not governed by inherent directionality according to the Unicode standard and default browser language system. Character rendering is either left-to-right or right-to-left.

| **Value** | ltr | rtl (case insensitive string). |
| **Default** | ltr |

disabled

IE 4 NN *n/a* Moz *all* Saf *all* Op 7 DOM 2
Read/Write

Specifies whether the element is available for user interaction. When set to true, the element cannot receive focus or be modified by the user, and it typically appears grayed out on the page. This property is available for all HTML element objects in IE 5.5 and later. For IE 4 and IE 5, it applies only to form controls, while Mozilla, Safari, and Opera recognize the property for form controls and the style element object. A disabled form control's name/value pair is not submitted with its form.

Example	document.getElementById("myButton").disabled = true;
Value	Boolean value: true	false.
Default	false

document

IE 4 NN *n/a* Moz *n/a* Saf *1.2* Op 7 DOM *n/a*
Read-only

Returns a reference to the document object that contains the current element. Potentially helpful for functions that act on object references retrieved from event properties or passed as ID strings. The corresponding W3C DOM property is ownerDocument.

Example	var currDoc = document.getElementById("elementID").document;
Value	document object reference.
Default	The current document object.

filters[ ]

IE 4(Win)   NN n/a   Moz n/a   Saf n/a   Op n/a   DOM n/a

Read-only

Returns an array of all filter objects contained by the current element. Applies only to the following element objects: bdo, body, button, div, fieldset, img, input, marquee, rt, ruby, span, table, td, textarea, and th. See the filter object for referencing syntax.

Value   Array of filter object references.

Default   Array of length zero.

firstChild, lastChild

IE 5   NN n/a   Moz all   Saf all   Op 7   DOM 1

Read-only

Returns a reference to the first or last child node (respectively) of the current element node. Most commonly, these child nodes are text nodes nested inside an element. For a simple element containing only one text node, both properties return a reference to the same text node. More complex constructions, such as tr elements, can have other element nodes (td elements) as their child nodes, but some browsers may turn source code carriage returns between elements into text nodes. Therefore, it's a good idea to validate the type of node returned by either property before acting on it.

Example
```
if (document.getElementById("elementID").firstChild.nodeType == 3) {
    // process as a text node
}
```

Value   Node object (including text node, HTML element node, etc.) reference.

Default   null

hideFocus

IE 5.5   NN n/a   Moz n/a   Saf n/a   Op n/a   DOM n/a

Read/Write

Specifies whether the browser should display a dotted focus rectangle around the element if it has focus. The element continues to be able to receive focus if it is focusable by default or has the tabindex attribute set. When this property is set to true, there is no visual clue about the focus state.

Example   document.getElementById("elementID").hideFocus = true;

Value   Boolean value: true | false.

Default   false

id

IE 4   NN n/a   Moz all   Saf all   Op 7   DOM 1

Read/Write

Specifies a unique identifier that distinguishes this element from all the rest in the document. The value of this property is most often used to assemble references to elements, but

---

you can loop through all elements to see if there is a match of an id value. It is generally not a good idea to change this property's value for an element already in the document tree. But if a script creates a new element object (via the document.createElement( ) method, for instance), it can assign a unique identifier to this object's id property, and then add the element to the document tree.

Example   `var headID = document.getElementsByTagName("head")[0].id;`

Value   String.

Default   Empty string.

innerHTML

IE 4   NN n/a   Moz all   Saf all   Op 7   DOM n/a
Read-only and Read/Write

Indicates the rendered text and HTML tags (i.e., all source code) between the start and end tags of the current element. A change to this property that includes HTML tags is rendered through the HTML parser, as if the new value were part of the original source code. You may change this property only after the document tree has fully loaded and rendered. Changes to the innerHTML property are not reflected in the source code when you view the source in the browser. This property is read-only in Internet Explorer for the col, colgroup, frameset, html, style, table, tbody, tfoot, thead, title, and tr element objects.

Although the W3C DOM does not support this element, all modern mainstream browsers do for convenience. Assigning a string lacking HTML tags to the innerHTML property has the same effect as assigning the string to the IE-only innerText property. In IE, you can read or write the source code that includes the element's tags via the outerHTML property.

Example

`document.getElementById("elementID").innerHTML = "How <i>now</i> brown cow?";`

Value   String that may or may not include HTML tags.

Default   Empty string.

innerText

IE 4   NN n/a   Moz n/a   Saf all   Op 7   DOM n/a
Read/Write

Indicates the rendered text (but not any tags) of the current element. If you want the rendered text as well as any nested HTML tags, see innerHTML. Any changes to this property are not rendered through the HTML parser, meaning that any HTML tags you include are treated as displayable text content only. You may change this property only after the document tree has fully loaded and rendered. Changes to the innerText property are not reflected in the source code when you view the source in the browser. An equivalent W3C DOM Level 3 property supported by recent versions of Mozilla and Opera is textContent.

Example

`document.getElementById("elementID").innerText = "How now brown cow?";`

Value   String.

Default   Empty string.

isContentEditable

IE 5.5 NN n/a Moz n/a Saf 1.2 Op 9 DOM n/a

Read-only

Specifies whether the current element has user editing engaged. Reveals the actual editing state as either explicitly set for the element (by element attribute or scripted property) or inherited from its ancestor tree.

Example

```
if (document.getElementById("elementID").isContentEditable) {
    // process the editable element
}
```

Value   Boolean value: true | false.

Default   false

isDisabled

IE 5.5 NN n/a Moz n/a Saf n/a Op n/a DOM n/a

Read-only

Specifies whether the current element is disabled. Reveals the actual disabled state as either explicitly set for the element (by element attribute or scripted property) or inherited from its ancestor tree.

Example

```
if (document.getElementById("elementID").isDisabled) {
    // process the disabled element
}
```

Value   Boolean value: true | false.

Default   false

isMultiLine

IE 5.5 NN n/a Moz n/a Saf n/a Op n/a DOM n/a

Read-only

Specifies whether the current element allows content to extend across multiple lines. Most text containers allow multiple lines, but other kinds of elements, such as a text input element are restricted to single line rendering.

Example

```
if (document.getElementById("elementID").isMultiLine) {
    // process the element as a potential multiple-line element
}
```

Value   Boolean value: true | false.

Default   Element default.

isTextEdit

Specifies whether the element can be used to create an IE/Windows TextRange object (via the createTextRange( ) method). Only body, button, text type input, and textarea elements are permitted to have text ranges created for their content.

Example
```
if (document.getElementById("elementID").isTextEdit) {
    var rng = document.getElementById("elementID").createTextRange( );
}
```

Value	Boolean value: true | false.
Default	Element default.

lang

Indicates the written language being used for the element's attribute and property values. Other applications and search engines might use this information to aid selection of spellchecking dictionaries and creating indices.

Example	document.getElementById("elementID").lang = "de";
Value	Case-insensitive language code.
Default	Browser default.

language

Indicates the scripting language for script statements defined in the element.

Example	document.getElementById("elementID").language = "vbscript";
Value	Case-insensitive scripting language name as string: javascript | jscript | vbs | vbscript.
Default	jscript

lastChild

See firstChild.

Shared DOM Reference

These three properties apply primarily to XML document elements with tags that are defined with the help of XML namespaces. A simplified example of such a document follows:

```
<?xml version="1.0" encoding="ISO-8859-1"?>
<results xmlns:libBook="http://catalog.umv.edu/schema">
<libBook:title libBook:rareBooks="true">De Principia</libBook:title>
</results>
```

The properties reveal details about the element's naming characteristics. A localName is the equivalent of the nodeName property of the element, that is, the tag name within the scope of the entire document, even if the tag name is reused by another element originating from another namespace. The prefix, however, links the element with a prefix name that is normally defined with an xmlns attribute of a container in the XML document. This helps your script identify the namespace to which the element is associated. A further binding is revealed through the namespaceURI property, which returns the URI string assigned to the xmlns attribute of a container element. Although all three properties belong to the Node object, their values are null (or, rather, should be null, but in Mozilla are empty strings) for node types other than element and attribute nodes.

Example

```
var allTitles = document.getElementsByTagName("title");
for (var i = 0; i < allTitles.length; i++) {
    if (allTitles[i].prefix == "libBook" &&
        allTitles[i].namespaceURI.indexOf("catalog.umv.edu") != -1) {
        // process title elements from the desired namespace here
    }
}
```

Value   Strings.

Default   For localName, the element's tag name. For others, an empty string.

namespaceURI

See localName.

nextSibling, previousSibling   IE *5*   NN *n/a*   Moz *all*   Saf *all*   Op *7*   DOM *1*

Returns a reference to the next or previous node (respectively) in the document tree at the same nested level as the current node. If there is no node in the position indicated by the property name, the property returns null. For a lone text node inside an element node, both properties return null. Node sequence is determined intially by source code order, but script changes to the document tree are reflected in the nodes returned by these properties.

Example	`var nextNode = document.getElementById("`*`elementID`*`").nextSibling;`
Value	Node object (including text node, HTML element node, etc.) reference.
Default	`null`

nodeName

IE 5 NN *n/a* Moz *all* Saf *all* Op 7 DOM 1

Read-only

Returns a string that identifies the name of the node as influenced by the node type. For element and attribute node types, the property returns the tag name and attribute name, respectively. For many other kinds of nodes, which have no inherent label associated with them, the nodeName property returns a fixed string indicating the node type, such as #text for a text node and #document for the root document node. For elements, the property returns the same string value as the element object's tagName property. Note that supporting browsers return element tag strings in all uppercase, regardless of source code style or DOCTYPE specification.

Example

```
if (document.getElementById("elementID").nextSibling.nodeName == "#text") {
    // process as a text node
}
```

| **Value** | Fixed string for #cdata-section, #document, #document-fragment, and #text nodes; variable string for attribute, element, and other node types. |
| **Default** | Node-specific. |

nodeType

IE 5 NN *n/a* Moz *all* Saf *all* Op 7 DOM 1

Read-only

Returns an integer that corresponds to a node type as specified in the W3C DOM. This is the preferred property to use to test a node object for its type (rather than the nodeName property values). Every node type has a value, but not all browsers that support the nodeType property support all node types as objects. The integer values have corresponding constants associated with them, which you can use to make more verbose, but easier-to-read script comparisons for node type processing (see the ATTRIBUTE_NODE property earlier in this chapter). Note that there is no way to distinguish element types (e.g., root Element node versus an HTMLElement node) via the nodeType property. Also note that IE 6 and IE 7 erroneously report a DOCTYPE element as a comment node type.

Example

```
if (document.getElementById("elementID").firstChild.nodeType == 1) {
    // process as an element
}
```

Value

Integer values according to the following table.

Value	Node type
1	ELEMENT_NODE
2	ATTRIBUTE_NODE
3	TEXT_NODE
4	CDATA_SECTION_NODE
5	ENTITY_REFERENCE_NODE
6	ENTITY_NODE
7	PROCESSING_INSTRUCTION_NODE
8	COMMENT_NODE
9	DOCUMENT_NODE
10	DOCUMENT_TYPE_NODE
11	DOCUMENT_FRAGMENT_NODE
12	NOTATION_NODE

Default   Node-specific.

nodeValue

IE *5* NN *n/a* Moz *all* Saf *all* Op *7* DOM *1*

Read/Write

Although the nodeValue property belongs to every node type, it is particularly helpful for text nodes because the property provides read/write access to the actual rendered text content of a text node. This property provides the W3C DOM canonical access to reading and modifying the text node nested inside an element, assuming your script addresses the nodeValue property of, say, an element's firstChild node. The property returns null for element nodes, so do not think of it as a pure replacement for the innerText or innerHTML convenience properties. The property returns the value assigned to an attribute when used with an attribute node. See also the more recent textContent property.

Example

```
document.getElementById("elementID").firstChild.nodeValue = "New Text!";
```

Value   String, although IE for Windows may return an attribute node's value as a Number data type if the value consists of a numeric value. You should always assign a string to this property.

Default   Empty string.

offsetHeight, offsetWidth

IE *4* NN *n/a* Moz *all* Saf *all* Op *7* DOM *n/a*

Read-only

Broadly speaking, provide the height and width of the element's content, but with minor variations with respect to element borders and padding among various operating system versions of IE and compatibility modes controlled by the DOCTYPE declaration. The trend is to include the measure of borders and padding, but not margins in these values. Although not part of the W3C DOM, these properties are implemented in all modern mainstream browsers as a convenience. See the "About client- and offset- Properties" at the beginning of this chapter for details.

Example   `var midpoint = document.getElementById("elementID").offsetWidth/2;`

Value   Integer pixel count.

Default   Element-specific.

offsetLeft, offsetTop

IE 4 NN *n/a* Moz *all* Saf *all* Op 7 DOM *n/a*

Read-only

Broadly speaking, provide the left and top coordinates of the element's box, but with minor variations with respect to the coordinate system context (vis-à-vis the offsetParent element) influenced by various operating system versions of IE and compatibility modes controlled by the DOCTYPE declaration. Although not part of the W3C DOM, these properties are implemented in all modern mainstream browsers as a convenience. See the "About client- and offset- Properties at the beginning of this chapter for details. For positioned elements, you should rely more on the element's style properties that control location in the document or browser viewing space.

Example

```
if (document.getElementById("elementID").offsetLeft <= 20 &&
document.getElementById("elementID").offsetTop <=40) {
    ...
}
```

Value   Integer pixel count.

Default   Element-specific.

offsetParent

IE 4 NN *n/a* Moz *all* Saf *all* Op 7 DOM *n/a*

Read-only

Returns a reference to the object that is the current element's offset positioning context. For most elements on an IE page and all elements in a Mozilla, Safari, and Opera page, this is the body object. But elements in IE that are wrapped in div elements or are cells of a table have other parents. Moreover, for complex nested elements, you will find occasional variations in the object returned by this property, depending on browser version. For example, the offsetParent property of a td element is the next outermost tr element in IE 4, while later versions and now modern mainstream browsers regard the enclosing table element as the offset parent. See the "About client- and offset- Properties" at the beginning of this chapter for an example of using this property to calculate the precise position of an inline element.

Example

`var containerLeft = document.getElementById("elementID").offsetParent.offsetLeft;`

Value   Object reference.

Default   body object.

outerHTML

Indicates the rendered text and HTML tags (i.e., all source code), including the start and end tags, of the current element. If you want only the rendered text, see outerText. For the source code that excludes the current element's tags, see innerHTML. A change to this property that includes HTML tags is rendered through the HTML parser, as if the new value were part of the original source code. You may change this property only after the document tree has fully loaded and rendered, and, in the process, you can even change the type of element it is or replace the element with straight text content. Changes to the outerHTML property are not reflected in the source code when you view the source in the browser. To add to existing HTML, see the insertAdjacentHTML( ) method. The W3C DOM equivalent requires extensive manipulation of node-level objects, as shown in Online Section IV.

Example
```
document.getElementById("elementID").outerHTML =
    "<acronym id="quotes">NI<i>M</i>BY</acronym>";
```

Value   String that may or may not include HTML tags.

Default   Empty string.

outerText

Indicates the rendered text (but not any tags) of the current element. If you want the rendered text as well as the element's HTML tags, see outerHTML. Any changes to this property are not rendered through the HTML parser, meaning that any HTML tags you include are treated as displayable text content only. You may change this property only after the document has fully loaded. Changes to the outerText property are not reflected in the source code when you view the source in the browser.

Example   `document.getElementById("elementID").outerText = "UNESCO";`

Value   String.

Default   Empty string.

ownerDocument

Returns a reference to the document object that contains the current node. Potentially helpful for functions that act on object references retrieved from event properties or passed as ID strings. Also equivalent to the document property in IE.

Example   `var currDoc = document.getElementById("elementID").ownerDocument;`

Value   document object reference.

Default   The current document object.

parentElement

Returns a reference to the next outermost element in the HTML containment hierarchy. An element's HTML parent is not necessarily the same as the object returned by the offsetParent property. The parentElement concerns itself strictly with source code containment, while the offsetParent property looks to the next outermost element that is used as the coordinate system for measuring the location of the current element. For example, if the main document contains a p element with an em element nested inside, the em element has two parents. The p element is the returned parentElement value (due to the HTML source code containment), while the body element is the returned offsetParent value (due to coordinate space containment).

You can jump multiple parent levels by cascading parentElement properties, as in:

```
document.getElementById("elementID").parentElement.parentElement;
```

You can then use references to access a parent element's properties or methods.

The corresponding property for the W3C DOM is parentNode.

Example
```
document.getElementById("elementID").parentElement.style.fontSize = "14pt";
```

Value   Element object reference.

Default   Element-specific.

parentNode

Returns a reference to the next outermost node (usually an element) that acts as a container to the current node in the document tree. The relationship between the current node and its parent is purely structural, and is not concerned with positioning context. A parent node is one that completely encases the current node—not to be confused with sibling nodes, which, at best, reside on just one side of the current node. You can use the same cascading tricks as shown for the IE parentElement property, but it is hazardous to completely equate results from the element-centric IE-only properties with results from the W3C DOM node-centric properties (even though recent IE versions support both views of the world).

Example
```
if (document.getElementById("elementID").parentNode.nodeType == 1) {
    document.getElementById("elementID").parentNode.style.fontSize = "14pt";
}
```

Value   Element object reference.

Default   Node-specific.

parentTextEdit

Returns a reference to the next highest element up the HTML containment hierarchy that is of a type that allows a TextRange object to be created with it. This property may have to reach through many levels to find a suitable object. This property always returns null in IE for the Macintosh because of lack of support for text ranges.

Example

```
var rangeElement = document.getElementById("elementID").parentTextEdit;
var rng = rangeElement.createTextRange( );
```

Value   Element object reference.

Default   body object.

prefix

See localName.

previousSibling

See nextSibling.

readyState

Returns the current download status of the object's content. If a script (especially one initiated by a user event) can perform some actions while the document is still loading, but must avoid other actions until the entire page has loaded, this property provides intermediate information about the loading process. You should use its value in condition tests. The value of this property changes during loading as the loading state changes. Each change of the property value fires a readyStateChange event (the event does not bubble).

When introduced with IE 4, the property was available for only the document, embed, img, link, object, script, and style objects. IE 5 expanded coverage to all HTML element objects.

Example

```
if (document.readyState == "loading") {
    //statements for alternate handling while loading
}
```

Value

For all but the object element, one of the following values (as strings): uninitialized | loading | loaded | interactive | complete. Some elements may allow the user to interact with partial content, in which case the property may return interactive until all loading has completed. Not all element types return all values in sequence during the loading process. The object element returns numeric values for these five states. They range from 0 (uninitialized) to 4 (complete).

Default   None.

recordNumber

IE *4* NN *n/a* Moz *n/a* Saf *n/a* Op *n/a* DOM *n/a*

Read-only

Used with IE data binding, returns an integer representing the record within the data set that generated the element (i.e., an element whose content is filled via data binding). Values of this property can be used to extract a specific record from an Active Data Objects (ADO) record set (see recordset property). Although this property is defined for all IE element objects, the other properties related to data binding belong to a subset of elements.

Example
```
<script for="tableTemplate" event="onclick">
    myDataCollection.recordset.absoluteposition = this.recordNumber;
    ...
</script>
```

Value   Integer.

Default   null

repeatMax, repeatMin

IE *n/a* NN *n/a* Moz *n/a* Saf *n/a* Op *9* DOM *n/a*

Read/Write

Used with Web Forms 2.0, an integer representing the maximum and minimum (respectively) number of instances of the element allowed within a repetition block (scripted representations of the repeat-max and repeat-min attributes). If you assign a new value that is beyond the current state (e.g., setting a new maximum lower than the current number of repeated items), the browser tries to recover the best it can (e.g., disabling the Add button), but does not eliminate out-of-bounds items. See the shared repeat attribute in Chapter 1.

Example   document.getElementById("order").repeatMax = 10;

Value   Integer.

Default   Highest possible JavaScript integer (repeatMax); 0 (repeatMin).

repeatStart

IE *n/a* NN *n/a* Moz *n/a* Saf *n/a* Op *9* DOM *n/a*

Read/Write

Used with Web Forms 2.0, an integer representing the starting index number to be appended to form control element names when the browser assembles instances of repeated items in the document (a scripted representation of the repeat-start attribute).

Example   document.getElementById("order").repeatStart = 1;

Value   Integer.

Default   Opera 9 uses 0 as the default, but the Web Forms 2.0 standard suggests 1.

Shared DOM Reference

repetitionBlocks

Used with Web Forms 2.0, returns an array of repetition blocks (HTML element objects) currently associated with the repeat template. For example, if there are three table rows generated from a repeat template, the element acting as the template has a repetitionBlocks property consisting of three items. Each item (a tr element object in this example) is a repetition block, with a repeat attribute (repetitionIndex property) value. Reading the length property of this array lets your script see how many rows have been added by the user or script.

Example

```
if (document.getElementById("order").repetitionBlocks > 10) {
    // process items from form with more than 10 items
}
```

Value   Array.

Default   Array of zero length.

repetitionIndex

Used with Web Forms 2.0, returns an integer reflecting the repeat attribute of a repeated element. Left to its own devices, a browser assigns the same value to this attribute/property as the index value plugged into the index value's placeholder in form control names. Changing this property of one repeated item does not alter the form control names or the attribute/property of other items associated with the same template.

Example

```
if (document.getElementById("order").repetitionBlocks > 10) {
    // process items from form with more than 10 items
}
```

Value   Array.

Default   Array of zero length.

repetitionTemplate

Used with Web Forms 2.0, returns a reference to the HTML element object that is acting as the template for the current repetition element. For example, the repetitionTemplate property of one of the repeated table rows points to the tr element in the source code containing specifications (attributes) about its repetition behavior. This is particularly helpful if you have a reference to a reptition block read from the repetitionBlocks property, and wish to obtain a reference to the element governing repetition behavior.

Example
```
var templateRow =
document.forms["orderform"].elements["row0.quantity"].parentNode.parentNode.
repetitionTemplate;
```
Value   HTML element object reference.

Default   None.

repetitionType

Used with Web Forms 2.0, returns an integer signifying whether the element is a repetition block, repetition template, or exhibiting no repetition behavior. The integer corresponds to one of the defined RepetitionElement object types, as shown in the following table.

Code	Constant
0	REPETITION_NONE
1	REPETITION_TEMPLATE
2	REPETITION_BLOCK

Example
```
if (document.getElementById("orders").repetitionType == 1) {
    // process repetition template here
}
```
Value   Integer values: 0 (none), 1 (repetition template), or 2 (repetition block).

Default   0

runtimeStyle

Returns a style object whose individual style properties convey values only if they are explicitly set via the regular style sheet processes. Unlike the currentStyle object, system default style sheet properties are not reflected. You can set individual style properties of this runtimeStyle object, but doing so transcends (some might say violates) normal cascading precedence. Any property you assign by script overrides all other settings for that style property governing that element, including values assigned to the element tag's style attribute and style property. For example, if you assign the value red to an element's style.color property, and assign the value green to the same element's runtimeStyle.color property, the element's text appears in green, even though the more specific style.color property still preserves the red value. At that point the element's currentStyle.color property also returns green, because that is the effective style governing the element at that instant.

You can use the runtimeStyle object to assign multiple style properties by reassigning a CSS syntax rule to the runtimeStyle.cssText property. Assign an empty string to the cssText property to remove all in-line attribute values, allowing the regular style sheet cascade to control the element's effective style.

Example

```
document.getElementById("elementID").runtimeStyle.cssText =
  "border: 5px blue solid";
```

Value	style object reference.
Default	The effective style object and its explicitly defined style attribute values.

scopeName, tagUrn   IE *5(Win)*   NN *n/a*   Moz *n/a*   Saf *n/a*   Op *n/a*   DOM *n/a*

Read-only

For custom elements employing XML namespaces, the scopeName property returns the identifier that associates the tag name with a namespace that is defined elsewhere in the document via the xmlns attribute. All plain HTML elements return a value of HTML for this property. The tagUrn property returns the URI specified for the namespace. The corresponding properties in the W3C DOM are prefix and namespaceURI.

Example

```
var allTitles = document.getElementsByTagName("title");
for (var i = 0; i < allTitles.length; i++) {
    if (allTitles[i].scopeName == "libBook" &&
        allTitles[i].tagUrn.indexOf("catalog.umv.edu") != -1) {
        // process title elements from the desired namespace here
    }
}
```

Value	Strings.
Default	HTML for scopeName; empty string for tagUrn.

scrollHeight, scrollWidth   IE *4*   NN *n/a*   Moz *1.0.1*   Saf *all*   Op *7*   DOM *n/a*

Read-only

Originally implemented in IE 4 for elements that either scrolled or influenced an element's scroll (body, button, caption, div, fieldset, legend, marquee, and textarea), these properties return the pixel dimensions of an element, including elements that are larger than the viewable area in the browser window. This is in contrast to the clientHeight and clientWidth properties for scrollable elements, which return dimensions of only visible portions of the element. IE for the Macintosh, however, interprets the intent of the scroll-properties differently, returning the dimensions of the visible portion.

Starting in IE 5 for Windows, all HTML elements have these properties, and the values for nonscrolling elements are the same as the offsetHeight and offsetWidth properties. Mozilla, Safari, and Opera implement these properties for all elements, returning the height and width of the element, whether or not it's in view. The important point is that for key elements, such as the body, the properties mean different things and can disrupt cross-platform operation.

Example	var midPoint = document.body.scrollHeight/2;
Value	Positive integer or zero.
Default	None.

scrollLeft, scrollTop

IE 4   NN *n/a*   Moz *1.0.1*   Saf *all*   Op *7*   DOM *n/a*

Read/Write

Provide the distance in pixels between the actual left or top edge of the element's physical content and the left or top edge of the visible portion of the content. Setting these properties allows you to use a script to adjust the scrolling of content within a scrollable container, such as text in a textarea element or an entire document in the browser window or frame. When the content is not scrolled, both values are zero. Setting the scrollTop property to 15 scrolls the document upward by 15 pixels in the window; the scrollLeft property is unaffected unless explicitly changed. The property values change as the user adjusts the scrollbars. This is important for some event-driven positioning tasks in IE for Windows because the coordinate system for event offset measurements are with respect to the visible area of a page in the browser window. You must add document.body scrolling factors to align event coordinates with body content positions (see the element dragging example in Online Section VI). Starting with IE 5 for Windows, the scrollLeft and scrollTop properties are available for all HTML element objects, but values for unscrollable elements are zero.

Example	document.body.scrollTop = 40;
Value	Positive integer or zero.
Default	0

sourceIndex

IE 4   NN *n/a*   Moz *n/a*   Saf *n/a*   Op *7*   DOM *n/a*

Read-only

Returns the zero-based index of the element among all elements in the document. Elements are numbered according to their source code order, with the first element given a sourceIndex of zero.

Example

var whichElement = document.getElementById("*elementID*").sourceIndex;

Value	Positive integer or zero.
Default	Element-specific.

style

IE 4   NN *n/a*   Moz *all*   Saf *all*   Op *7*   DOM *1*

Read/Write

Indicates the style object associated with the element, as set by values explicitly assigned to the element's style attribute in the tag. In W3C DOM object terminology, this object more specifically is called a CSSStyleDeclaration object. This property is the gateway to

Shared DOM Reference

reading and writing individual style sheet property settings for an element. To read the effective style sheet properties governing an element (including imported style sheet attributes), see the currentStyle property earlier in this chapter (for IE) and the AbstractView.getComputedStyle( ) method (for W3C DOM browsers).

Example   document.getElementById("*elementID*").style.fontSize = "14pt";

Value   style object.

Default   None.

tabIndex

IE 4 NN *n/a* Moz *all* Saf *all* Op 7 DOM 1

Read/Write

This is a number that indicates the sequence of this element within the tabbing order of all focusable elements in the document. Tabbing order follows a strict set of rules. Elements that have values other than zero assigned to their tabIndex properties are first in line when a user starts tabbing in a page. Focus starts with the element with the lowest tabIndex value and proceeds in order to the highest value, regardless of physical location on the page or in the document. If two elements have the same tabIndex values, the element that comes earlier in the document receives focus first. Next come all elements that either don't support the tabIndex property or have the value set to zero. These elements receive focus in the order in which they appear in the document.

The W3C DOM and most modern browsers limit the tabIndex property to the following element objects: a, area, button, input, object, select, textarea. To this list, IE 4 adds applet, body, div, embed, isindex, marquee, span, table, and td. IE 5 adds every other renderable element. A negative value in IE and Mozilla 1.8 or later removes an element from tabbing order entirely.

Example   document.getElementById("link3").tabIndex = 6;

Value   Integer.

Default   0

tagName

IE 4 NN *n/a* Moz *all* Saf *all* Op 7 DOM 1

Read-only

Returns the name of the tag of the current element. Tag names are always returned in all uppercase letters for purposes of string comparisons, regardless of source code style or DOCTYPE declaration.

Example   var theTag = document.getElementById("*elementID*").tagName;

Value   String.

Default   Element-specific.

tagUrn

See scopeName.

textContent

Reflects the text string of a node, including the combined text nodes within an element. For example, if a p element has a nested em element, the textContent property of the p element consists of the complete text of both elements, as if the em element were not present. If you assign a string to the property, all nested content of that element is replaced by the new text as a single text node. In this regard, the textContent property is the W3C DOM equivalent of the IE innerText property.

Example

```
document.getElementById("elementID").textContent = "This is some new text.";
```

Value   String.

Default   Empty string.

title

Provides an advisory description of the element. When the element is one that has a physical presence on the page, the browser renders the value of this property as a floating text label when the cursor rests atop the element for a moment. The size, font characteristics, and color of this label are not within control of scripting.

Example   `document.getElementById("elementID").title = "Hot stuff!";`

Value   String.

Default   Empty string.

uniqueID

Returns an identifier string that is unique among all object identifiers on the page. Used primarily to assign an ID to newly created elements when you don't mind the browser using its own naming scheme to invent the name. Most commonly used as a property of the document object, but it is accessible through any existing element object reference. The identifier is perfectly valid for use as string a parameter to methods that require an element ID.

Example

```
var newElem = document.createElement("p");
newElem.id = document.uniqueID;
```

Value   String.

Default   Browser-generated.

unselectable

IE 5.5   NN n/a   Moz n/a   Saf n/a   Op 9   DOM n/a
Read/Write

Controls whether the current element's content can be selected by the user. The setting is not necessarily inherited by child elements.

Example   document.getElementById("*elementID*").unselectable = "on";

Value   String constant: on | off.

Default   Empty string.

addBehavior( )

IE 5(Win)   NN n/a   Moz n/a   Saf n/a   Op n/a   DOM n/a

addBehavior('*URL*')

Attaches an internal or external IE behavior to the current element. After a script attaches the behavior, the element responds to events defined for the behavior (if any), and provides access to properties and methods associated with the behavior. An external behavior file must be served from the same domain (and protocol) as the current page. For more information on applying IE/Windows behaviors, visit *http://msdn.microsoft.com/workshop/ author/behaviors/overview.asp*.

Returned Value   Integer serial number usable as a parameter for the removeBehavior( ) method.

Parameters

URL

For external behaviors, a relative or absolute URL to the *.htc* file on the server. For internal behaviors, a special format as described in the next item.

#default#behaviorName

where *behaviorName* is one of the following built-in behaviors: anchorClick | anim | clientCaps | download | homePage | httpFolder | mediaBar | saveFavorite | saveHistory | saveSnapshot | userData.

addEventListener( )

IE n/a   NN n/a   Moz all   Saf all   Op 7   DOM 2

addEventListener("*eventType*", *listenerFunction*, *useCapture*)

Binds an event handler function to the current node so that the function executes when an event of a particular type arrives at the node either as event target or during event propagation. Note that W3C DOM events propagate through text nodes, as well as element nodes. The node listens for the event type either during event capture or event bubbling propagation, depending upon the setting of the Boolean third parameter. You may invoke this method multiple times for the same node but with different parameter values to assign as many event handling behaviors as you like, but only one listener function may be invoked for the same event and propagation type. If the event listener is added on a temporary basis, it should be removed via the removeEventListener( ) method.

Returned Value   None.

Parameters

eventType

A string of one event type (without the "on" prefix) known to the browser's object model. The W3C DOM knows the following event types (all but the DOM-prefixed ones implemented in modern browsers):

abort	blur	change
click	DOMActivate	DOMAttrModified
DOMCharacterDataModified	DOMFocusIn	DOMFocusOut
DOMNodeInserted	DOMNodeInsertedIntoDocument	DOMNodeRemoved
DOMNodeRemovedFromDocument	DOMSubtreeModified	error
focus	load	mousedown
mousemove	mouseout	mouseover
mouseup	reset	resize
scroll	select	submit
unload		

listenerFunction

A reference to the function to execute when the node hears the event type in the specified propagation mode. As this is a reference to a function object, do not surround the name in quotes, nor include the parentheses of the function. An anonymous function is also permitted for this reference. At execution time, the browser automatically passes the current event object as a parameter to the listener function.

useCapture

A Boolean value. If true, the node listens for the event type only while the event propagates toward the target node (in event capture node). If false, the node listens only when the event bubbles outward from the event target. If the current node is the target of the event, either Boolean value may be used.

addRepetitionBlock( )   IE *n/a* NN *n/a* Moz *n/a* Saf *n/a* Op *9* DOM *n/a*

addRepetitionBlock(*blockReferenceOrNull*)

Inserts a new repetition block among a group of blocks associated with the current element (assuming the current element is a repetition template). Invoking this method is the scripted equivalent of a user clicking an add-type input element.

Returned Value   Reference to the inserted element.

Parameters

blockReferenceOrNull

If you pass null as the parameter (not an empty parameter), the new element is appended as the last repetition block. Or you can pass a reference to the specific repetition block within the group (e.g., a value obtained from the repetitionBlocks array), after which the new block is to be inserted.

addRepetitionBlockByIndex( ) IE n/a NN n/a Moz n/a Saf n/a Op 9 DOM n/a

addRepetitionBlockByIndex(*blockReferenceOrNull, newRepeatIndex*)

Inserts a new repetition block among a group of blocks associated with the current element (assuming the current element is a repetition template). Invoking this method is the scripted equivalent of a user clicking an add-type input element. The second parameter lets you assign a custom index to the newly inserted repetition block.

Returned Value   Reference to the inserted element.

Parameters

blockReferenceOrNull
> If you pass null as the parameter (not an empty parameter), the new element is appended as the last repetition block. Or you can pass a reference to the specific repetition block within the group (e.g., a value obtained from the repetitionBlocks array), after which the new block is to be inserted.

newRepeatIndex
> Integer value.

appendChild( ) IE 5 NN n/a Moz all Saf all Op 7 DOM 1

appendChild(*nodeObject*)

Inserts a new node after the end of the last child node of the current node object. The current node object must be capable of containing child nodes, otherwise the method throws an exception. This method is the most common way to append a dynamically created element, text node, or document fragment to an existing element or node, such as a script might do when assembling a chunk of new content for a document. But if the node reference passed as a parameter with the appendChild( ) method points to an existing node in the document tree, that node is first removed from the tree, and then appended to the end of the list of child nodes in the current object. This provides a shortcut way to move a node from one location to the end of a container.

Appending one text node as a sibling to an existing text node does not join the two text nodes together. To combine all sibling text nodes into one large text node, invoke the parent's normalize( ) method.

Returned Value   Reference to the appended node.

Parameters

nodeObject
> Reference to any node object of a type that makes sense to become a child of the current object. It may be from dynamically generated content (e.g., text node, element, or document fragment) or a node from the existing document tree.

applyElement( ) IE 5(Win) NN n/a Moz n/a Saf n/a Op n/a DOM n/a

applyElement(*elementObject*[, *type*])

Inserts a new element as either a child element of the current object or as the new parent of the current object, depending on the value of the second parameter. The default behavior is to wrap the current object with the new element. But you may also choose to insert the new element as a child element. In this case, if the current object is in the document tree (as opposed to simply floating in memory after being created with document.createElement( )) and already has child elements nested inside it, the newly applied element is inserted in such a way that the previous children become children of the inserted element (i.e., grand-children of the current object). This wrapping behavior is unique among IE element insertion methods and can have significant impact on the document tree. Use with caution.

Returned Value   Reference to the newly added element object.

Parameters

elementObject
> Reference to any dynamically generated or existing element object from the document tree.

type
> Optional string value: inside (the new element becomes the sole, first child of the current object); outside (the new element becomes the parent of the current object). The default is outside.

attachEvent( )   IE 5(Win) NN n/a Moz n/a Saf n/a Op 7 DOM n/a
attachEvent("*eventName*", *functionReference*)

Binds an event handler function to an element object for a particular event type. Similar in operation to the W3C DOM addEventListener( ) method. If you bind an event handler through the attachEvent( ) method, you should disengage the binding via the detachEvent( ) method.

Returned Value   Boolean value true if the binding is successful.

Parameters

eventName
> String version of the event name, including the "on" prefix. Although not case-sensi-tive, all-lowercase values are recommended.

functionReference
> A reference to the function to execute when the element receives the event either as the event target or through event propagation. As this is a reference to a function object, do not surround the name in quotes, nor include the parentheses of the function. No parameters may be passed to the function.

blur( )   IE 3 NN 2 Moz all Saf all Op 7 DOM 1

Removes focus from the current object, at which time the object's blur event fires. Note that the range of elements capable of focus and blur (both the event and method) is limited in all browsers except for more recent versions of IE (see the shared tabindex attribute in Chapter 1). Most reliably for backward compatibility, apply the blur( ) method to blatantly focusable elements, such as text input and textarea elements. Assigning the attribute onfocus="this.blur( );" to a text input element, for instance, is a crude but effective backward-compatible way to largely disable a field for browsers that do not provide genuine element disabling.

Use blur( ) and focus( ) methods in moderation on the same page. You can inadvertently trigger endless loops of blurring and focusing if alert dialog boxes are involved along the way. Moreover, be aware that when you invoke the blur( ) method on one object, some other object (perhaps the window object) receives a focus event.

Returned Value None.

Parameters None.

clearAttributes( ) IE 5(Win) NN n/a Moz n/a Saf n/a Op n/a DOM n/a

Removes all attributes from the current element except for the id and name attributes (if specified). Any rendering characteristics influenced by the element's attributes that are removed also no longer apply to the element.

Returned Value None.

Parameters None.

click( ) IE 4 NN 2 Moz all Saf all Op 7 DOM 1

Simulates the click action of a user on the element, and fires a click event. Don't expect all elements that normally change their graphical state when clicked by the user to simulate the same state change during the scripted click. For example, some Macintosh browser versions fail to change the checked state of a checkbox when a script invokes a click( ) method on the checkbox. In this case, invoke the click( ) method only if a click event handler executes some code; but also set the checked property of the checkbox as desired.

Returned Value None.

Parameters None.

cloneNode( ) IE 5 NN n/a Moz all Saf all Op 7 DOM 1
cloneNode(*deepBoolean*)

Copies the current node to memory, and returns a reference to the node copy (which is not part of the document tree). Because the clone is a full-fledged node, you can perform additional node-related operations on the clone before inserting the node elsewhere in the document tree. Beware, however, that id attributes of cloned elements are the same as the original. Change the id properties of those elements in the fragment before reintroducing the clone into the document tree.

The Boolean parameter determines whether the clone is of only the current node or the current node and all nested nodes. Note that if you clone a simple element container and set the parameter to false, the text node inside the element does not become part of the cloned copy.

Returned Value Reference to document fragment in memory.

Parameters

deepBoolean

Boolean value that controls whether the copy includes all nested nodes (true) or only the current node (false). Parameter is optional in IE, with a default value of false.

compareDocumentPosition( ) IE *n/a* NN *n/a* Moz *1.4* Saf *n/a* Op *n/a* DOM *3*

compareDocumentPosition(*nodeReference*)

Returns an integer signifying the relative node tree position of the *nodeReference* parameter compared to the element on which the method is invoked. As this method belongs to the Node object, it is inherited by all types of nodes, including HTML element nodes and attribute nodes.

The returned value is determined by calculations of hexadecimal bitmask values corresponding to six different comparision states. Given the hypothetical expression NodeA.compareDocumentPosition(NodeB), the six values, their constant names, and meanings are as follows:

Value	Constant	Description
0x01	DOCUMENT_POSITION_DISCONNECTED	The two nodes are disconnected (and are thus implementation specific).
0x02	DOCUMENT_POSITION_PRECEDING	NodeB comes before NodeA.
0x04	DOCUMENT_POSITION_FOLLOWING	NodeB comes after NodeA.
0x08	DOCUMENT_POSITION_CONTAINS	NodeB contains NodeA (and thus NodeB comes before NodeA).
0x10	DOCUMENT_POSITION_CONTAINED_BY	NodeB is contained by NodeA (and thus NodeB comes after NodeA).
0x20	DOCUMENT_POSITION_IMPLEMENTATION_SPECIFIC	The browser determines the comparative order.

Bitmasks are used because it is possible for one comparison to meet more than one state. For example, consider the following expression:

```
document.body.compareDocumentPosition(document.body.parentNode)
```

In a typical HTML document, the body's parent node is the html element. Therefore, the expression returns a value of 10 because the html element comes before the body (mask of 0x02) and the html element contains the body element (mask of 0x08). To use the constant values in a comparison when two states may be present, use the bitwise OR operator (|), as follows:

```
if (document.body.compareDocumentPosition(document.body.parentNode) ==
    (Node.DOCUMENT_POSITION_PRECEDING | Node.DOCUMENT_POSITION_CONTAINS)) {
    // statements
}
```

If the two node references point to the same node, the method returns zero.

Returned Value Integer.

Parameters

nodeReference
    Reference to any node either within the current document or outside of it (e.g., a document fragment node).

componentFromPoint( )   IE *5(Win)*   NN *n/a*   Moz *n/a*   Saf *n/a*   Op *n/a*   DOM *n/a*

`componentFromPoint(x, y)`

Returns a string that denotes where the coordinate points are in the element. For elements that display scroll bars, the returned value reveals precisely which piece of the scroll bar is at the coordinate location. If you engage Microsoft's document editing mode, additional pieces, such as draggable size handlers, are also indicated in the returned value. For areas of elements not displaying scroll bars or edit handles, you can also determine whether the coordinate is inside or outside the element, which is handy for collision detection between event coordinates and the element.

The most common source for coordinate parameter values is the event object, especially the `event.clientX` and `event.clientY` properties. You can apply these values directly, as in:

```
var where = event.srcElement.componentFromPoint(event.clientX, event.clientY);
```

Returned Value

One of the string values in the following table:

Returned string values	Description
empty string	Inside the element content area
`outside`	Outside the element content area
`handleBottom`	Edit mode resize handle at bottom
`handleBottomLeft`	Edit mode resize handle at bottom left
`handleBottomRight`	Edit mode resize handle at bottom right
`handleLeft`	Edit mode resize handle at left
`handleRight`	Edit mode resize handle at right
`handleTop`	Edit mode resize handle at top
`handleTopLeft`	Edit mode resize handle at top left
`handleTopRight`	Edit mode resize handle at top right
`scrollbarDown`	Scroll bar down arrow
`scrollbarHThumb`	Scroll bar horizontal thumb control
`scrollbarLeft`	Scroll bar left arrow
`scrollbarPageDown`	Scroll bar page-down region
`scrollbarPageLeft`	Scroll bar page-left region
`scrollbarPageRight`	Scroll bar page-right region
`scrollbarPageUp`	Scroll bar page-up region
`scrollbarRight`	Scroll bar right arrow
`scrollbarUp`	Scroll bar up arrow
`scrollbarVThumb`	Scroll bar vertical thumb control

Parameters

x

> Positive or negative pixel count relative to the top of the screen.

y

> Positive or negative pixel count relative to the left edge of the screen

contains( )

IE 4 NN *n/a* Moz *n/a* Saf *n/a* Op 7 DOM *n/a*

`contains(`*elementReference*`)`

Returns whether the current element contains the specified element.

Returned Value   Boolean value: `true` | `false`.

Parameters

elementReference

> A fully formed element object reference (e.g., `document.getElementById("myDIV")`).

createControlRange( )

IE 5(Win) NN *n/a* Moz *n/a* Saf *n/a* Op *n/a* DOM *n/a*

Though implemented for many HTML element objects, this method should be used only with the `selection` object. See the `createControlRange( )` method of the `selection` object for details.

detachEvent( )

IE 5(Win) NN *n/a* Moz *n/a* Saf *n/a* Op *n/a* DOM *n/a*

`detachEvent("`*eventName*`",` *functionReference*`)`

Removes a previously attached event handler function binding from an element object for a particular event type. Similar in operation to the W3C DOM `removeEventListener( )` method. The event property equivalent of the `detachEvent( )` method is to assign `null` to the event property.

Returned Value   None.

Parameters

eventName

> String version of the event name, including the "on" prefix. Applicable event types include any event from IE/Windows extensive list of shared event types. Although not case-sensitive, all-lowercase values are recommended.

functionReference

> A reference to the function to execute when the element receives the event either as the event target or through event propagation. As this is a reference to a function object, do not surround the name in quotes, nor include the parentheses of the function.

dispatchEvent( )

dispatchEvent(*eventObjectReference*)

Directs an event to fire on the current node. Used primarily when artificially creating an event by script, and then sending that event to a node for its event listener function to execute. The event object passed as a parameter must have an event type specified, but other properties of the event object (such as mouse event location or character key) may also be set when initializing the newly created event object. The following script fragment creates a generic mouse event, initializes the event as a mousedown type that bubbles and is cancelable, and sends the event to an element with the ID myNode:

```
var newEvt = document.createEvent("MouseEvents");
newEvt.initEvent("mousedown", true, true);
document.getElementById("myNode").dispatchEvent(newEvt);
```

See the W3C DOM Event, MouseEvent, and UIEvent objects for more details. The corresponding method for IE/Windows-only is fireEvent( ).

Returned Value   The W3C DOM specification indicates a Boolean value of false is returned if any event listener function that executes in response to the dispatchEvent( ) method also invokes the event.preventDefault( ) method. Otherwise the method returns true.

Parameters

eventObjectReference
A reference to an event object. Most commonly this object is created and initialized by associated script statements.

doScroll( )

doScroll(["*scrollAction*"])

Controls the scrolling of any element that displays scroll bars. Because most HTML elements can use style sheets to hardwire a height and width, while having the overflow style attribute to scroll, the doScroll( ) method is applicable to any element.

Rather than scrolling to a coordinate position, the doScroll( ) method simulates the click on a scroll bar control or region as directed by the parameter. Each invocation of the method triggers the onscroll event for the element. Invoke this method through a separate function that gets called from setTimeout( ) if the script sequence leading up to the scroll involves reflowing of the page (to let IE catch up with rendering).

Returned Value   None.

Parameters

scrollAction
The string name of one scroll bar region. If omitted, the default value applied is scrollbarDown. Most regions have interchangable long and short names, as shown in the following list:

```
scrollbarDown (or down)
scrollbarHThumb
scrollbarLeft (or left)
```

```
scrollbarPageDown (or pageDown)
scrollbarPageLeft (or pageLeft)
scrollbarPageRight (or pageRight)
scrollbarPageUp (or up)
scrollbarVThumb
```

dragDrop( ) IE *5.5* NN *n/a* Moz *n/a* Saf *n/a* Op *n/a* DOM *n/a*

Triggers an ondragstart event for the current element, allowing a mouse event handler function to initiate script execution related to the start of dragging even before the user has actually begun to drag the element. Returns a Boolean true when the user releases the mouse button after the physical drag operation.

Returned Value   Boolean value: true | false.

Parameters   None.

fireEvent( ) IE *5.5* NN *n/a* Moz *n/a* Saf *n/a* Op *n/a* DOM *n/a*

fireEvent("*eventType*"[, *eventObjectReference*])

Directs an event to fire on the current element. Used primarily when artificially creating an event by script, and then sending that event to an element for its event handler function to execute. You can send a simple event of any type you wish. Such a generic event object has four properties automatically assigned to it:

```
cancelBubble = false;
returnValue = true;
srcElement = reference-to-current-element;
type = event-type-specified-as-the-parameter;
```

Or you may pass along an event object that has more details associated with it, such as the event location or character key. The following script fragment creates a generic event object, assigns some properties to it, and then sends the event (as an onclick event) to an element with the ID myElem:

```
var newEvt = document.createEventObject( );
newEvt.clientX = 50;
newEvt.clientY = 300;
newEvt.cancelBubble = true;
document.getElementById("myElem").fireEvent("onclick", newEvt);
```

See the IE event object for more details. The corresponding W3C DOM method is dispatchEvent( ).

Returned Value   Boolean value (true | false) signifying whether the event fired successfully.

Parameters

eventType
> String value of the "on" version of the event name (e.g., "onmousedown").

eventObjectReference
> An optional reference to an event object, usually one that is created anew.

focus( )

Gives focus from the current object, at which time the object's focus event fires. Most reliably for backward compatibility, apply the focus( ) method to blatantly focusable elements, such as text input and textarea elements.

To give a text box focus and pre-select all the text in the box, use the sequence of focus( ) and select( ) methods on the element. If this sequence is to occur after windows change (such as after an alert dialog box closes), place the methods in a separate function, and invoke this function through the setTimeout( ) method following the alert( ) method for the dialog. This allows IE/Windows to sequence statement execution correctly.

Returned Value   None.

Parameters   None.

getAdjacentText( )

getAdjacentText("*where*")

Returns the text (excluding HTML tags and attributes) in and around the current element in the direction indicated by one of four parameter values. The text segment extends only until the next element start or end tag. For example, consider the following HTML:

```
<p>This is a very <span id="mySpan">short</span> paragraph.</p>
```

Invoking the getAdjacentText( ) method on the span element with each of the four parameter values yields the values as shown here:

```
document.getElementById("mySpan").getAdjacentText("beforeBegin")
    // returns: "This is a very "
document.getElementById("mySpan").getAdjacentText("afterBegin")
    // returns: "short"
document.getElementById("mySpan").getAdjacentText("beforeEnd")
    // returns: "short"
document.getElementById("mySpan").getAdjacentText("afterEnd")
    // returns: " paragraph."
```

In this case the afterBegin and beforeEnd parameters return the same value because no elements are inside the span element. Invoking the method on the outer p element and the afterBegin parameter yields the text up to the start of the span element. In some document tree structures, this method returns the equivalent of W3C DOM's child node nodeValue properties.

Returned Value   String, which may contain leading or trailing spaces, depending on the structure of the text fragment inside the element.

Parameters

where

One of four constant string values (case-insensitive).

Constant	Description
beforeBegin	Text in front of current element's start tag back to preceding tag
afterBegin	Text after current element's start tag until next (start or end) tag

Constant	Description
beforeEnd	Text in front of current element's end tag back to the preceding (start or end) tag
afterEnd	Text after current element's end tag until next (start or end) tag

getAttribute( )

IE 4 NN n/a Moz all Saf all Op 7 DOM 1

getAttribute(*attributeName*)
getAttribute(*attributeName*[,*caseSensitivity*])

Returns the value of the named attribute within the current element. If the attribute is reflected in the object model as a property, this method returns the same value as when reading the object's property. This is the preferred method for reading an element object attribute (i.e., property) value under the W3C DOM.

The attribute name you pass as a parameter is not case-sensitive in current browsers. IE, however, provides an optional second parameter that lets you force case-sensitivity in the attribute naming. This might encourage the reuse of the same attribute name but with different case letters—an ill-advised practice.

See the setAttribute( ) method for assigning values to attributes and creating new attribute/value pairs.

Returned Value   The W3C DOM (as implemented in Mozilla, Safari, and Opera) specifies that attribute values are exclusively string data types. IE, however may return an attribute value as a string, number, or Boolean.

Parameters

attributeName
> The (case-insensitive by default) attribute name used in the HTML tag (not including the = symbol). While IE lets you switch between case-sensitivity settings, other browsers do not demand case-sensitivity, even when the DOCTYPE is set to an XHTML variant. But given the trend toward case-sensitive XHTML, it is best to get into the case-sensitive habit.

caseSensitivity
> An optional integer value for IE only. Default value is 0 (not case-sensitive). If 1, the attribute in the HTML tag must match the case of the *attributeName* parameter exactly for its value to be returned.

getAttributeNode( )

IE 6 NN n/a Moz all Saf all Op 7 DOM 1

getAttributeNode(*attributeName*)

Returns a reference to the attribute node (Attr object) associated with the name passed as a parameter. This type of node is the same kind that populates the array returned by an element's attributes property, but the getAttributeNode( ) method gives you direct access to the Attr node object by name. More helpful in XML documents, where an attribute can convey important data associated with the element. See the Attr object for details about that node type.

Returned Value   Reference to an Attr object.

Parameters

attributeName

The attribute name used in the tag (not including the = symbol). Browsers do not demand case-sensitivity. But given the trend toward case-sensitive XHTML, it is best to get into the case-sensitive habit.

getAttributeNodeNS( )   IE *n/a* NN *n/a* Moz *all* Saf *all* Op *7* DOM *2*

getAttributeNodeNS("*namespaceURI*", "*localName*")

Returns a reference to the local-named Attr object with a matching namespace URI within the current element. This method works like getAttributeNS( ) but accommodates attributes for XML documents that are labeled according to a namespace specification.

Returned Value   Reference to an Attr object.

Parameters

namespaceURI

URI string matching a URI assigned to a label earlier in the document.

localName

The local name portion of the attribute.

getAttributeNS( )   IE *n/a* NN *n/a* Moz *all* Saf *all* Op *7* DOM *2*

getAttributeNS("*namespaceURI*", "*localName*")

Returns the value of the local-named attribute with a matching namespace URI within the current element. This method works like getAttribute( ) but accommodates attributes for XML documents that are labeled according to a namespace specification. The following simple XML document uses a namespace for an attribute of the libBook:title element:

```
<?xml version="1.0" encoding="ISO-8859-1"?>
<results xmlns:libBook="http://catalog.umv.edu/schema">
<libBook:title libBook:rareBooks="true">De Principia</libBook:title>
</results>
```

To retrieve the value of the libBook:rareBooks attribute, the method for the element would include the getAttributeNS( ) method call with the following parameters:

```
getAttributeNS("http://catalog.umv.edu/schema", "rareBooks")
```

Returned Value   The W3C DOM, Netscape, Safari, and Opera return attribute values exclusively as string data types.

Parameters

namespaceURI

URI string matching a URI assigned to a label earlier in the document.

localName

The local name portion of the attribute.

getBoundingClientRect( )

Returns an IE TextRectangle object that describes the rectangular space occupied by the current element (including nontext elements, such as images). The rectangle (which has properties for top, right, bottom, and left coordinates) is as wide as the widest point of the content (e.g, the longest line of a word-wrapped paragraph) and as tall as the sum of all content. To obtain measures of rectangles for individual lines of a text element, see the getClientRects( ) method.

Returned Value   TextRectangle object.

Parameters   None.

getClientRects( )

Returns an array of IE TextRectangle objects. Each entry of the array is a TextRectangle object for a single line of a multiline text element. Lines that have different font sizes or line heights will be encased by rectangles that are of different heights. See the TextRectangle object for its properties. To obtain one TextRectangle object for an entire element, use the getBoundingClientRect( ) method.

Returned Value   Array of TextRectangle objects.

Parameters   None.

getElementsByTagName( )

getElementsByTagName("*tagName*")

Returns an array of all descendant elements of the current element whose tag name matches the parameter of the method. Elements in the array include children, grandchildren, and so on, and are in the source code order. The current element is not included in the array. If there are no matches, the array has a length of zero.

IE 5/Macintosh, IE 6/Windows, and all other supporting browsers let you specify the quoted asterisk wildcard character as a parameter to return an array of all descendant elements, regardless of tag name. Be aware, however, that different browsers may exhibit slight differences in their document tree structures that result in wildcard parameter array lengths that don't match each other.

Returned Value   Array of zero or more element references.

Parameters

tagName
> The (case-insensitive by default) tag name for desired elements. Or an asterisk that acts as a wildcard character to signify all tag names.

getElementsByTagNameNS( )

IE *n/a* NN *n/a* Moz *all* Saf *all* Op *7* DOM *2*

getElementsByTagNameNS("*namespaceURI*", "*localName*")

Returns an array of all descendant elements of the current element which have a local name that matches the second parameter of the method, and a namespace URI (assigned elsewhere in the document as a namespace declaration) that matches the first method parameter. Elements in the array include children, grandchildren, and so on, and are in the source code order. The current element is not included in the array. If there are no matches, the array has a length of zero. Applies primarily to XML documents.

Returned Value   Array of zero or more element references.

Parameters

namespaceURI
 URI string matching a URI assigned to a label earlier in the document.

localName
 The local name portion of the tag name.

getExpression( )

IE *5(Win)* NN *n/a* Moz *n/a* Saf *n/a* Op *n/a* DOM *n/a*

getExpression("*attributeName*")

Returns a string version of the script expression used in a corresponding setExpression( ) method call on an attribute of the current element. The setExpression( ) method assigns a script expression used to calculate the value assigned to the attribute. The expression is calculated automatically in response to some event types and to the document.recalc( ) method. To read the current value of the attribute, you must use the eval( ) function on the string returned by the getExpression( ) method. See the setExpression( ) method later in this section.

Returned Value   String.

Parameters

attributeName
 Name of the current element's attribute to which an expression is assigned by the setExpression( ) method.

getFeature( )

IE *n/a* NN *n/a* Moz *1.7.2* Saf *n/a* Op *n/a* DOM *3*

getFeature("*feature*", "*version*")

The W3C DOM spec states that this method returns an object implementing the APIs of the feature/version combination passed as parameters. As of Mozilla 1.8.1, the method returns an object that does not expose itself to scripts. There also appears as yet to be no validation checking on the parameter values, other than their quantity. See the implementation.hasFeature( ) method.

Returned Value   Object.

Parameters

feature

    Name of a DOM feature, such as Core, HTML, or Events corresponding to DOM modules.

version

    String consisting of the DOM level, such as 1.0 or 3.0.

getUserData( )   IE *n/a* NN *n/a* Moz *(1.7.2)* Saf *n/a* Op *n/a* DOM *3*

getUserData("*key*")

The W3C DOM spec states that this method returns an object of any type that had been associated with the current node via the setUserData( ) method. Multiple objects may be associated with a node, and they are distinguished by their keys (labels). Although recent versions of Mozilla have implemented this method to some extent (e.g., the browser checks for the presence of a parameter), invoking the method from a web page throws a NS_DOM_NOT_IMPLEMENTED error as of Mozilla 1.8.1.

Returned Value   Object of any JavaScript type.

Parameters

key

    String identifying a label with which the data was preserved via setUserData( ).

hasAttribute( )   IE *n/a* NN *n/a* Moz *all* Saf *all* Op *7* DOM *1*

hasAttribute("*attributeName*")

Returns a Boolean value true if the current element has an attribute whose name matches the method parameter.

Returned Value   Boolean value: true | false.

Parameters

attributeName

    The case-sensitive attribute name to search for.

hasAttributeNS( )   IE *n/a* NN *n/a* Moz *all* Saf *all* Op *7* DOM *2*

hasAttributeNS("*namespaceURI*", "*localName*")

Returns a Boolean value true if the current element has an attribute with a local name that matches the method's second parameter, and a namespace URI (assigned elsewhere in the document as a namespace declaration) that matches the first method parameter.

Returned Value   Boolean value: true | false.

Parameters

namespaceURI

    URI string matching a URI assigned to a label earlier in the document.

localName

    The local name portion of the attribute name.

hasAttributes( )

Returns a Boolean value true if the current element has any attributes explicitly assigned within the tag.

Returned Value   Boolean value: true | false.

Parameters   None.

hasChildNodes( )

Returns a Boolean value true if the current node contains one or more child nodes.

Returned Value   Boolean value: true | false.

Parameters   None.

insertAdjacentElement( )

`insertAdjacentElement("`*where*`", ` *elementObjectReference*`)`

Inserts an element object into the designated position relative to the current element. Typically, the element object about to be inserted is created separately (for example, via `document.createElement( )`) or it may be a reference to an object already in the document tree, and the method essentially moves the object to its new location with the help of the `insertAdjacentElement( )` method.

The destination is governed by the first attribute, which consists of one of four values that determine where the insertion occurs, as follows.

Position	Insert new element
BeforeBegin	Before start tag of current element, as a previous sibling
AfterBegin	Immediately after current element's start tag, as a first child element
BeforeEnd	Immediately before current element's end tag, as a last child element
AfterEnd	After end tag of current element, as a next sibling

Although the effects on the document element tree are well-defined, the rendered result varies with the combination of inline and block elements you use as the current and inserted element objects. Inserting a block-level element (such as a div or p element) causes that element to render on the next line and at the left edge of the block-level positioning context (such as the body or td element). Applying the W3C DOM appendChild( ) method on elements is the equivalent of the insertAdjacentElement( ) method with the beforeEnd position parameter.

Returned Value   Reference to the inserted element object.

Parameters

where

String value of one of the following case-insensitive constants: BeforeBegin | AfterBegin | BeforeEnd | AfterEnd. The first and last locations are outside the HTML tags of the current element; the middle two locations are between the tags and element content.

elementObjectReference
Reference to any valid element object either existing in the document tree or created dynamically.

insertAdjacentHTML( )   IE *4* NN *n/a* Moz *n/a* Saf *n/a* Op *7* DOM *n/a*

`insertAdjacentHTML("where", HTMLText)`

Inserts a text string into the designated position relative to the element's existing HTML. If HTML tags are part of the text to be inserted, the browser interprets the tags and performs the desired rendering.

Returned Value   None.

Parameters

where
String value of one of the following constants: BeforeBegin | AfterBegin | BeforeEnd | AfterEnd. The first and last locations are outside the HTML tags of the current element; the middle two locations are between the tags and element content.

HTMLText
String value of the text and/or HTML to be inserted in the desired location.

insertAdjacentText( )   IE *4* NN *n/a* Moz *n/a* Saf *n/a* Op *7* DOM *n/a*

`insertAdjacentText("where", text)`

Inserts text into the designated position relative to the element's existing HTML. If HTML tags are part of the text to be inserted, the tags are shown literally on the page.

Returned Value   None.

Parameters

where
String value of one of the following constants: BeforeBegin | AfterBegin | BeforeEnd | AfterEnd. The first and last locations are outside the HTML tags of the current element; the middle two locations are between the tags and element content.

HTMLText
String value of the text to be inserted in the desired location.

insertBefore( )   IE *5* NN *n/a* Moz *all* Saf *all* Op *7* DOM *1*

`insertBefore(newChildNode, referenceChildNodeOrNull)`

Inserts a node as a child of the current node (usually the current node is an element) before one of the other child nodes of the current node. The new child can be a reference to an existing node in the document tree (in which case it is removed from its original position when this method is invoked). The child node may also be created anew as any valid DOM node type, including a document fragment (which may hold HTML tags) or `Attr` (the latter implemented for IE 6 or later and all other supporting browsers).

The second parameter allows you to specify a reference point among existing child nodes, in front of which the new child node is inserted. Alternatively, if you specify `null` as the second parameter (or omit the parameter in IE), the new node is inserted as the last child of the current node—the same result as the `appendChild()` method.

Returned Value   Reference to the inserted node object.

Parameters

newChildNode
    Any valid node object that can be a child of a parent node.

referenceChildNodeOrNull
    Any child node of the current node, or `null`.

isDefaultNamespace( )   IE *n/a* NN *n/a* Moz *1.7.2* Saf *n/a* Op *9* DOM *3*

`isDefaultNamespace("`*namespaceURI*`")`

Returns a Boolean `true` if the current node's default namespace matches that of the parameter.

Returned Value   Boolean value: `true` | `false`.

Parameters

namespaceURI
    A string of the URI for the namespace to test.

isEqualNode( )   IE *n/a* NN *n/a* Moz *1.7.2* Saf *n/a* Op *n/a* DOM *3*

`isEqualNode(`*nodeReference*`)`

Returns a Boolean `true` if the current node is equal to the node passed as a parameter according to a specific set of equality rules. The two nodes must have identical values for the properties `localName`, `namespaceURI`, `nodeName`, `nodeType`, `nodeValue`, and `prefix`; both nodes must also have equal values for their `attributes` and `childNodes` properties. The relative positions of the two nodes within the document tree are not taken into account for equality. Two nodes shown to be the same (`isSameNode()`) would also be equal.

Returned Value   Boolean value: `true` | `false`.

Parameters

nodeReference
    A reference to a different node to test for equality against the current node.

isSameNode( )   IE *n/a* NN *n/a* Moz *1.7.2* Saf *n/a* Op *n/a* DOM *3*

`isSameNode(`*nodeReference*`)`

Returns a Boolean `true` if the current node is the very same node as the one passed as a parameter.

Returned Value   Boolean value: true | false.

Parameters

nodeReference
> A reference to a different node to test for sameness against the current node.

isSupported( )   IE *n/a*   NN *n/a*   Moz *all*   Saf *all*   Op *7*   DOM *2*

isSupported("*feature*", "*version*")

Returns a Boolean true if the current node supports (i.e., conforms to the required specifications of) a stated W3C DOM module and version. While the document.implementation object's hasFeature( ) method performs the same test, it does so on the entire browser application. The isSupported( ) method performs the test on an individual node, allowing you to verify feature support for the current node type. Parameter values for isSupported( ) are the same as for document.implementation.hasFeature( ).

It is up to the browser maker to validate that the DOM implemented in the browser conforms with each module before allowing the browser to return true for the module. That doesn't necessarily mean that the implementation is bug-free or consistent with other implementations. Caveat scriptor.

In theory, you could use this method to verify module support prior to accessing a property or invoking a method, as in the following fragment that assumes myElem is a reference to an element node:

```
if (myElem.isSupported("CSS", "2.0")) {
    myElem.style.color = "green";
}
```

In practice, object detection is a better solution because W3C DOM support reporting facilities are not implemented across all mainstream browsers yet and are certainly not backward compatible.

Returned Value   Boolean value: true | false.

Parameters

feature
> As of W3C DOM Level 2, permissible case-sensitive module name strings are: Core, XML, HTML, Views, StyleSheets, CSS, CSS2, Events, UIEvents, MouseEvents, MutationEvents, HTMLEvents, Range, Traversal.

version
> String representation of the major and minor version of the DOM module cited in the first parameter. For the W3C DOM Level 2, the version is 2.0, even when the DOM module supports another W3C standard that has its own numbering system. Thus, the test for HTML DOM module support is for Version 2.0, even though HTML is at 4.x.

Shared DOM Reference

lookupNamespaceURI( )

lookupNamespaceURI("*prefix*")

Returns the URI (string) for a node if the prefix passed as a parameter matches that of a previously defined namespace. Used primarily with XML documents.

Returned Value   String URI.

Parameters

prefix

A string consisting of a namespace prefix.

lookupPrefix( )

lookupPrefix("*namespaceURI*")

Returns the prefix (string) for a node if the namespace URI passed as a parameter matches that of a previously defined namespace. Used primarily with XML documents. Some earlier versions of Mozilla had implemented this method under the name lookupNamespacePrefix( ).

Returned Value   String prefix name.

Parameters

namespaceURI

A string of the URI for a namespace.

mergeAttributes( )

mergeAttributes(*modelElementReference*[, *preserveIDs*])

Copies attribute name/value pairs from the element specified as a parameter to the current element. This is helpful for copying a large set of attributes from an existing element to a newly created element. By default, the copy does not include the id or name attributes so that the two elements maintain separate identifiers for scripting and form purposes. Starting with IE 5.5, an optional Boolean second parameter, when set to false, duplicates id and name attributes as well.

Returned Value   None.

Parameters

modelElementReference

Reference to an existing element that serves as a model for attribute name/value pairs to be copied to the current element.

preserveIDs

An optional Boolean value. If false, the id and name attributes from the model element are not copied to the current element. The default for this parameter is true.

moveRepetitionBlock( )

moveRepetitionBlock(*distance*)

Moves a repetition block up or down as the scripted equivalent of the move-up and move-down input element types. The parameter integer determines both the direction and how far the current block is to be moved. A negative value moves the element up by the passed number; a positive value moves the element down by the passed number.

Returned Value   None.

Parameters

distance
> A positive or negative integer specifying how far to move the current element among its siblings. Negative values move upward; positive values move downward.

normalize( )

Collapses all sibling text nodes of the current (element) node into a single text node. Invoking this method may be needed after inserting or removing child nodes of an element, especially if your node walking (traversal) scripts expect contiguous text to be contained by a single text node. The W3C DOM considers a document tree to be normal only if a text node has no other text nodes as siblings. Note that the method is crash-prone in IE 6.

Returned Value   None.

Parameters   None.

releaseCapture( )

Turns off mouse event capture mode that had been engaged earlier by the setCapture( ) method. In the IE event model, mouse event capture is designed for temporary use, such as processing mouse events while a custom context menu (implemented as a positioned div element) is activated. IE event capture is also released automatically by several user actions: giving focus to another window, frame, or the browser's Address box; scrolling a window; displaying a system dialog box; or displaying the true context menu.

Returned Value   None.

Parameters   None.

removeAttribute( )

removeAttribute("*attributeName*")
removeAttribute("*attributeName*"[, *caseSensitivity*])

Removes the named attribute from the current element. An IE 4 requirement that limited attribute removal to attributes that had been added with the setAttribute( ) method is not applicable in IE 5 and later or elsewhere. Removing an attribute does not change the source code when viewed through the browser, but does affect how the browser renders the element. The attribute value or node is also no longer available after removal.

Returned Value   In IE, Boolean `true` if successful; `false` if the attribute doesn't exist. No returned value in other supporting browsers (or W3C DOM specification).

Parameters

attributeName

The (case-insensitive by default) attribute name used in the HTML tag (not including the = symbol). While IE lets you switch between case-sensitivity settings, Netscape 6 does not demand case-sensitivity. But given the trend toward case-sensitive XHTML, it is best to get into the case-sensitive habit.

caseSensitivity

An optional integer value for IE only. Default value is 0 (not case-sensitive). If 1, the attribute in the HTML tag must match the case of the *attributeName* parameter exactly for its value to be returned.

removeAttributeNode( )   IE *6* NN *n/a* Moz *all* Saf *all* Op *7* DOM *1*

`removeAttributeNode(`*attrObjectReference*`)`

Removes the attribute from the current element indicated by the parameter reference to an existing `Attr` node object. This provides an alternate way to remove an attribute from an element if the script has only a reference to the `Attr` node object, rather than its name. Removing an attribute node does not change the source code when viewed through the browser, but does affect how the browser renders the element. The attribute value or node is no longer available after removal.

Returned Value   Reference to the removed `Attr` object, which is no longer part of the document tree, but may now be inserted elsewhere in the document tree.

Parameters

attrObjectReference

A reference to an `Attr` node object associated with the current element.

removeAttributeNS( )   IE *n/a* NN *n/a* Moz *all* Saf *all* Op *7* DOM *2*

`removeAttributeNS("`*namespaceURI*`", "`*localName*`")`

Removes the local-named attribute with a matching namespace URI from the current element. This method works like `removeAttribute( )` but accommodates attributes for XML documents that are labeled according to a namespace specification. The following simple XML document uses a namespace for an attribute of the `libBook:title` element:

```
<?xml version="1.0" encoding="ISO-8859-1"?>
<results xmlns:libBook="http://catalog.umv.edu/schema">
<libBook:title libBook:rareBooks="true">De Principia</libBook:title>
</results>
```

To remove the value of the `libBook:rareBooks` attribute, the method for the element would include the `removeAttributeNS( )` method call with the following parameters:

```
removeAttributeNS("http://catalog.umv.edu/schema", "rareBooks")
```

Returned Value None.

Parameters

namespaceURI
> URI string matching a URI assigned to a label earlier in the document.

localName
> The local name portion of the attribute.

removeBehavior( ) IE 5(Win) NN n/a Moz n/a Saf n/a Op n/a DOM n/a

`removeBehavior(behaviorID)`

Disconnects the association between the current element and a behavior that had been made earlier via the addBehavior( ) method. The parameter is the value that had been returned by the addBehavior( ) method, which you must preserve as a variable between invocation of the two methods.

Returned Value Boolean value true if the removal is successful; otherwise false.

Parameters

behaviorID
> Integer serial number initially generated by the addBehavior( ) method for the current element and behavior type.

removeChild( ) IE 5 NN n/a Moz all Saf all Op 7 DOM 1

`removeChild(childNodeReference)`

Removes a child node from the current element. The parameter must be a reference to an existing child node nested inside the current element. Once removed, the child node is no longer part of the document tree, but is still preserved in memory. The method returns a reference to the removed node so that you may modify it and place it elsewhere in the document tree. Note that you can command one node to remove one of its children, but you cannot command a node to remove itself (but see removeNode( ) for IE).

Returned Value A reference to the removed node.

Parameters

childNodeReference
> Reference to an existing child node.

removeEventListener( ) IE n/a NN n/a Moz all Saf all Op 7 DOM 2

`removeEventListener("eventType", listenerFunction, useCapture)`

Cuts a previously established event binding between an event handler function and the current node. This method assumes that an event listener was added to the node at some prior time. To ensure removal of the desired event listener, use the identical three parameters for removeEventListener( ) that you used for addEventListener( ). You may invoke this method multiple times for the same node but with different parameter values so as not to disturb other event listeners assigned to the same node. Invoke this method only if user interaction with the node improves with the particular event handling turned off.

Returned Value   None.

Parameters

eventType

A string of one event type (without the "on" prefix) known to the browser's object model. The W3C DOM knows the following event types (all but the DOM-prefixed ones implemented in modern browsers):

abort	blur	change
click	DOMActivate	DOMAttrModified
DOMCharacterDataModified	DOMFocusIn	DOMFocusOut
DOMNodeInserted	DOMNodeInsertedIntoDocument	DOMNodeRemoved
DOMNodeRemovedFromDocument	DOMSubtreeModified	error
focus	load	mousedown
mousemove	mouseout	mouseover
mouseup	reset	resize
scroll	select	submit
unload		

listenerFunction

A reference to the function to execute when the node hears the event type in the specified propagation mode. As this is a reference to a function object, do not surround the name in quotes, nor include the parentheses of the function. At execution time, the browser automatically passes the current event object as a parameter to the listener function.

useCapture

A Boolean value. If true, the node listens for the event type only while the event propagates toward the target node (in event capture node). If false, the node listens only when the event bubbles outward from the event target. If the current node is the target of the event, either Boolean value may be used.

removeExpression( )   IE 5(Win) NN n/a Moz n/a Saf n/a Op n/a DOM n/a

removeExpression("*attributeName*")

Disengages an expression that had been assigned previously to an element's attribute (assigned via the setExpression( ) method). Invoking the removeExpression( ) method turns off the automatic expression re-evaluation that might alter the attribute value in response to user activity (or explicit recalculation via the document.recalc( ) method). But the value assigned to the attribute as a result of the most recent calculation remains in effect, even after the expression is removed.

Returned Value   Boolean true if the removal is successful; otherwise false.

Parameters

attributeName
Name of the current element's attribute to which an expression had been assigned by the setExpression( ) method.

removeNode( )   IE 5(Win)   NN n/a   Moz n/a   Saf n/a   Op 7   DOM n/a

removeNode([*childrenFlag*])

Removes the current node from the document tree. The method returns a reference to the removed node so that you may modify it and place it elsewhere in the document tree. By default, the method removes only the current node and none of its child nodes. Removing a container node without its children can wreak havoc with the document tree, especially for complex elements, such as tables.

Returned Value   A reference to the removed node.

Parameters

childrenFlag
Optional Boolean value: false (default) removes only the current node; true removes current node and all nested child nodes.

removeRepetitionBlock( )   IE n/a   NN n/a   Moz n/a   Saf n/a   Op 9   DOM n/a

Removes the current repetition block from its parent. This is the scripted equivalent of the remove-type input element.

Returned Value   None.

Parameters   None.

replaceAdjacentText( )   IE 5(Win)   NN n/a   Moz n/a   Saf n/a   Op n/a   DOM n/a

replaceAdjacentText("*where*", "*newText*")

Replaces a contiguous block of text that is adjacent to the current element with new text. This method operates only on rendered text characters, and not HTML tags.

The text to be removed (and the spot where new text goes) is governed by the first attribute, which consists of one of four values that determine where the insertion occurs, as follows.

Position	Replace...
BeforeBegin	Text in front of current element's start tag back to preceding tag
AfterBegin	Text after current element's start tag until next (start or end) tag
BeforeEnd	Text in front of current element's end tag back to the preceding (start or end) tag
AfterEnd	Text after current element's end tag until next (start or end) tag

Replacement of text has no effect on the structure of the document tree because you are simply replacing the value of one text node with a different value.

Returned Value   String of the removed text.

Parameters

where

String value of one of the following case-insensitive constants: BeforeBegin | AfterBegin | BeforeEnd | AfterEnd. The first and last locations are outside the HTML tags of the current element; the middle two locations are between the tags and element content.

newText

String of text to be inserted where old text is removed. If the text contains HTML tags, the tag characters are displayed as-is.

replaceChild( )   IE 5 NN *n/a* Moz *all* Saf *all* Op 7 DOM 1

replaceChild(*newChildNodeReference, oldChildNodeReference*)

Replaces one child node of the current node with a new child node. Typically, this is used with element nodes, but can also be used with Attr node objects. Parameters point to the incoming and outgoing child nodes, respectively. The new child node may be created anew or may be a reference to a node that exists elsewhere in the document tree. In the latter case, invoking the replaceChild( ) method removes the node from its original location in the document tree, and puts it into the child node position of the node referenced by the second parameter. The method returns a reference to the removed node so that you may modify it and place it elsewhere in the document tree. Note that you can command one node to replace one of its children, but you cannot command a node to replace itself (but see replaceNode( ) and swapNode( ) for IE).

Returned Value   A reference to the removed node.

Parameters

newChildNodeReference

Reference to a node that will replace an existing node.

oldChildNodeReference

Reference to an existing child node that is to be replace.

replaceNode( )   IE 5(Win) NN *n/a* Moz *n/a* Saf *n/a* Op *n/a* DOM *n/a*

replaceNode(*newNodeObjectReference*)

Replaces the current node with a new node. The new node may be created anew (e.g., a text node or element) or may be a reference to a node that exists elsewhere in the document tree. In the latter case, invoking the replaceNode( ) method removes the node from its original location in the document tree, and puts it into the current node's.

Returned Value   Reference to the removed node.

Parameters

newNodeObjectReference

Reference to the node object that will replace the current node.

scrollIntoView( ) IE 4 NN n/a Moz n/a Saf 2.02 Op 7 DOM n/a

scrollIntoView([*showAtTop*])

Scrolls the content holding the current element so that the element is brought into view. The default behavior is to display the element so that its top is at the top of the scroll space. But you may also align the element at the bottom of the scroll space, if you prefer.

Returned Value   None.

Parameters

showAtTop

> An optional Boolean value. If true (the default), the top of the content is positioned at the top of the scroll space; if false, the bottom of the content is positioned at the bottom of the scroll space.

setActive( ) IE 5.5 NN n/a Moz n/a Saf n/a Op n/a DOM n/a

Makes the current element the active element without scrolling the page to bring the active element into view. Nor does the method change focus between windows or frames if the method is invoked across window object boundaries. The element, however, receives an onfocus event when the method is invoked.

Returned Value   None.

Parameters   None.

setAttribute( ) IE 4 NN n/a Moz all Saf all Op 7 DOM 1

setAttribute("*attributeName*", *value*)
setAttribute("*attributeName*", *value*[, *caseSensitivity*])

Sets the value of the named attribute within the current element. If the attribute is reflected in the object model as a property, this method acts the same as assigning a value to the object's property. Even so, the W3C DOM declares the setAttribute( ) method as the preferred way to adjust an attribute value (and the getAttribute( ) method for reading the value).

If the attribute does not yet exist in the element, the setAttribute( ) method adds the attribute as a name/value pair to the element (except in IE 4 through 5.5, the newly added attribute is not reported as part of the element's attributes collection).

IE treats the attribute names more as object property names. Therefore, when a discrepancy exists between the attribute and corresponding property names (e.g., class versus className), IE requires the property name version. To assign a new value to the class attribute of an element for both IE and other browsers, you should branch the code to invoke the method only once per browser type to avoid adding an unused className attribute to the Mozilla, Safari, and Opera element. For purposes of object detection, a browser that supports the W3C DOM approach returns a string value type for the element's getAttribute("class") method.

Values you assign to an attribute must be all strings for non-IE browsers (per the W3C spec). IE allows other data types (such as Number and Boolean), but if you assign, say, a numeric value in string form, the data type gets converted so that getAttribute( ) returns the value in IE's preferred data type.

Attribute names in W3C browsers are not case-sensitive, but you should get in the habit of using all lowercase attribute names (in the direction of XHTML). IE is case-sensitive about attribute names for this method by default. An optional third parameter for IE lets you control whether the attribute name should be treated in a case-sensitive manner. Avoid playing case-sensitivity tricks with attribute names (two different attributes with the same spelling but different case characteristics). If you use all lowercase attribute names for all your code, you can omit the third IE parameter while staying W3C DOM compliant.

Using setAttribute( ) in IE to assign a value to element attributes responsible for loading external content (e.g., a script element's src attribute) is prone to failure. Be prepared to revert to assigning the value to the corresponding property of the element object.

Returned Value   None.

Parameters

attributeName
> The attribute name used in the HTML tag (except as noted above for IE).

value
> For Mozilla, Safari, and Opera, the attribute value as a string data type. For IE, the attribute value as a string, number, or Boolean, as dictated by the attribute's data type. Strings are safe for all values, although IE internally converts the data types as necessary.

caseSensitivity
> An optional integer value for IE only. If 1 (the default), the attribute in the HTML tag must match the case of the *attributeName* parameter exactly for its value to be set (allowing for multiple attribute names with the same spelling but different cases to coexist). If 0, the *attributeName* parameter aligns itself with the first attribute with the same name, regardless of case.

setAttributeNode( )   IE 6 NN *n/a* Moz *all* Saf *all* Op 7 DOM 1

setAttributeNode(*attrObjectReference*)

Inserts or replaces an attribute in the current element. The parameter is a reference to an Attr node object that is either created anew or references from another element in the document tree. When the setAttributeNode( ) method is invoked, the browser first looks for a match between the new attribute's name and existing attribute names. If there is a match, the new attribute replaces the original one; otherwise, the new attribute is added to the attributes of the element. Adding an attribute node does not change the source code when viewed through the browser, but may affect how the browser renders the element if the attribute affects the visual representation of the element. The value of the new attribute may be retrieved via the getAttribute( ) method.

Returned Value   Reference to a replaced Attr object (which is no longer part of the document tree) or null for an insertion.

Parameters

attrObjectReference
> A reference to an `Attr` node object created through `document.createAttribute( )` or an `Attr` node from another element in the document tree.

setAttributeNodeNS( )

`setAttributeNodeNS(`*attrObjectReference*`)`

Inserts or replaces an attribute in the current element. The parameter is a reference to an `Attr` node object that is either created anew or references from another element in the document tree. When the `setAttributeNodeNS( )` method is invoked, the browser first looks for a match between the new attribute's pairing of local name and namespace URI and existing attribute local names and namespace URIs. If there is a match, the new attribute replaces the original one; otherwise, the new attribute is added to the attributes of the element. Adding an attribute node does not change the source code when viewed through the browser, but may affect how the browser renders the element if the attribute affects the visual representation of the element. The value of the new attribute may be retrieved via the `getAttributeNS( )` method.

Returned Value   Reference to a replaced `Attr` object (which is no longer part of the document tree) or `null` for an insertion.

Parameters

attrObjectReference
> A reference to an `Attr` node object created through `document.createAttributeNS( )` or an `Attr` node from another element in the document tree.

setAttributeNS( )

`setAttributeNS("`*namespaceURI*`", "`*qualifiedName*`", "`*value*`")`

Inserts or replaces an attribute in the current element. If a match exists among the element's attributes for both the namespace URI and the qualified name passed as parameters, the new value is assigned to the existing attribute. If there is no match, the attribute is added to the element.

Returned Value   None.

Parameters

namespaceURI
> URI string matching a URI assigned to a label earlier in the document.

qualifiedName
> The full name for the attribute, consisting of the local name prefix (if any), a colon, and the local name.

value
> The string value for the attribute.

setCapture( )

setCapture([`containerFlag`])

Initiates IE capture mode for all click-related mouse events (onclick, ondblclick, onmousedown, onmousemove, onmouseout, onmouseover, onmouseup), sending all event processing for those events to the current element, regardless of the actual event target. Useful for mouse modality required while handling custom context menus or dragging. While capture is engaged, the event.srcElement property for each event holds a reference to the element that would normally receive the event, but only the capture-mode element's event handlers actually process the events. When your modal effect is no longer needed, disengage capture mode with the releaseCapture( ) method. IE event capture is also released automatically by several user actions: giving focus to another window, frame, or the browser's Address box; scrolling a window; displaying a system dialog box; or displaying the true context menu.

Starting with IE 5.5, an optional parameter provides more control over event propagation when a user triggers a mouse event atop an element whose parent has the capture mode set. The default behavior (parameter omitted or set to true) causes the parent container to intercept events, as you would expect. But if you set the parameter to false, you direct events to proceed intially to their event targets (descendant elements of the capture-mode element). Such events can then bubble upward as normal; all other mouse events proceed directly to the capture-mode element. For example, if you invoke the setCapture( ) method on an element that contains a form with clickable form controls, you will probably want to use the false parameter so that mouse actions (such as clicking in text boxes) reach their intended targets even while capture mode is on. Otherwise, descendant elements won't respond to mouse activity, and the form controls will act as if they were disabled.

Returned Value   None.

Parameters

containerFlag
> Boolean true (default) to let current element (if a container) capture all mouse events, or false to let mouse events reach their intended targets before bubbling.

setExpression( )

setExpression("`propertyName`", "`expression`", ["`scriptLanguage`"])

Assigns a script expression to an element object's property as a way to calculate dynamically a value for the property. This method works with properties of element objects and their style objects if you like. The expression is re-evaluated automatically for most user-oriented events, or you may explicitly force re-evaluation at any time via the recalc( ) method.

Assigning an expression to an element attribute can take the place of some event handling, such as maintaining position relationships among elements when a user resizes the browser window. For example, to keep an element horizontally centered in the browser window, you could use one of the following techniques to apply an expression to the element's style.left property. The first example demonstrates the syntax (also for IE 5 for Windows or later) for assigning an expression as an inline attribute for the the element:

```
<div id='heading' style="position:absolute; left:expression(
  document.body.clientWidth/2-document.getElementById("heading").offsetWidth/2);
```

Alternatively, a function invoked at load time could include the following statement:

```
document.getElementById("heading").style.setExpression("left",
  "document.body.clientWidth/2-document.getElementById('heading').offsetWidth/2;",
  "JScript");
```

In both cases, the same expression calculates the coordinate position for the element's left edge relative to the current viewable width of the body element. Because this expression depends on a body element dimension property, the browser knows that it should re-evaluate any expression that might be impacted by a change in the body size caused by window resizing.

Be sure the resulting value of the expression you assign is the desired data type for the attribute you are setting. Isolate and run some initial tests on the expression before assigning it to the setExpression( ) method. Otherwise debugging will be more difficult.

If you want an expression to assign a value to an attribute and force that value to stick, use the removeExpression( ) method to prevent any further re-evaluation of the attribute value.

Returned Value   None.

Parameters

propertyName
> The name of the attribute being controlled by the expression, but in case-sensitive property name form (e.g., use the className property name instead of the corresponding class attribute name).

expression
> A string that contains the script expression to be evaluated. The expression must evaluate to a value suitable for the property named in the first parameter, so multiple, semicolon-delimited statements are not allowed. References to other elements should be complete references. Early implementations may balk at references that include arrays.

scriptLanguage
> One of three constant strings: JScript | JavaScript | VBScript. The default is JScript.

setUserData( )   IE *n/a* NN *n/a* Moz *(1.7.2)* Saf *n/a* Op *n/a* DOM *3*

getUserData("*key*", *object, userDataHandler*)

The W3C DOM spec states that this method associates an object of any type with the current node (and the data can be later retrieved via the getUserData( ) method). Multiple objects may be associated with a node, and they are distinguished by their keys (labels). The object can be any valid JavaScript object type. The third parameter is a reference to a handler function that gets invoked when the node is adopted (via document.adoptNode( )), cloned (via cloneNode( )), deleted, imported (via document.importNode( )), or renamed (via document.renameNode( )). Although recent versions of Mozilla have implemented this method to some extent (e.g., the browser checks for the presence of parameters), invoking the method from a Web page throws a NS_DOM_NOT_IMPLEMENTED error as of Mozilla 1.8.1.

Returned Value   Object of any JavaScript type that had been passed as the second parameter.

Parameters

key

> String identifying a label with which the data is to be preserved.

object

> JavaScript object of any type or null to delete previously set data.

userDataHandler

> Reference to a function that is to be invoked when the node is adopted, cloned, deleted, imported, or renamed. The function is invoked with five parameters, as follows: an integer representing the type of operation (cloned = 1, imported = 2, deleted = 3, renamed = 4, adopted = 5); a string with the key; the preserved data object; reference to node being operated on; reference to newly created node after the operation (or null, if none).

swapNode( )   IE 5(Win) NN n/a Moz n/a Saf n/a Op n/a DOM n/a

swapNode(*otherNodeObject*)

Exchanges the current node (in the document tree) with a different node passed as a parameter. The other node object can be created anew, or it can be a reference to a node elsewhere in the document tree. In the latter case, the result is the same as a bi-directional exchange, where the two nodes essentially change places. If the two nodes are of different node types or element display types (e.g., an inline versus a block-level element), the rendering of the document may be affected significantly.

Returned Value   Reference to the node from which the method is invoked (i.e., the current node).

Parameters

otherNodeObject

> Reference to any node object, usually another node in the document tree.

toString( )   IE 4 NN 4 Moz *al* Saf *all* Op 7 DOM *n/a*

Returns a string representation of the element object. You'll encounter similarities for some elements among Mozilla, Safari, and Opera in the content of the string, but there are no guarantees. For example all three browsers return [HTMLParagraphElement] for a p element, but an em element reports [HTMLSpanElement] in Mozilla and just [HTMLElement] in Safari and Opera. Internet Explorer simply returns [object] for all types.

Returned Value   Browser-dependent string

Parameters   None.

Alphabetical Object Reference

a

The a object reflects the a element, regardless of whether the element is set up to be an anchor, link, or both. Early versions of Netscape Navigator and Internet Explorer treat this object only as a member of the links[] and/or anchors[] arrays of a document. Starting with IE 4 and all browsers supporting the W3C DOM, you can access the object through supported element object reference syntax (e.g., the document.all[] collection for IE or document.getElementById() for IE 5 and later and W3C browsers).

HTML Equivalent   <a>

Object Model Reference
[window.]document.links[i]
[window.]document.anchors[i]
[window.]document.getElementById("*elementID*")

Object-Specific Properties

charset	coords	dataFld	dataFormatAs	dataSrc	hash
host	hostname	href	hreflang	Methods	mimeType
name	nameProp	pathname	port	protocol	protocolLong
rel	rev	search	shape	target	text
type	urn				

Object-Specific Methods
None.

Object-Specific Events

Event	IE	Mozilla	Safari	Opera	W3C DOM
blur	•	•	—	•	—
click	•	•	•	•	•
dblclick	•	•	—	•	—
focus	•	•	—	•	—
help	•	—	—	—	—
mousedown	•	•	•	•	•
mousemove	•	•	•	•	•
mouseout	•	•	•	•	•
mouseover	•	•	•	•	•
mouseup	•	•	•	•	•

Anchor-only a objects have no events in Navigator through Version 4.

charset

IE *6* NN *n/a* Moz *all* Saf *all* Op *7* DOM *1*

Read/Write

Character encoding of the document's content.

Example
```
if (document.getElementById("myAnchor").charset == "csISO5427Cyrillic") {
    // process for Cyrillic charset
}
```

Value Case-insensitive alias from the character set registry (*ftp://ftp.isi.edu/in-notes/iana/assignments/character-sets*).

Default Determined by browser.

coords

IE *6* NN *n/a* Moz *all* Saf *all* Op *7* DOM *1*

Read/Write

Defines the outline of an area to be associated with a particular link or scripted action. This property is a member of the a object, but really belongs to the area object, which inherits the properties of the a object. Coordinate values are entered as a comma-delimited list. If hotspots of two areas should overlap, the area that is defined earlier in the code takes precedence.

Example
```
document.getElementById("mapArea2").coords = "25, 5, 50, 70";
```

Value
Each coordinate is a length value, but the number of coordinates and their order depend on the shape specified by the shape attribute, which may optionally be associated with the element. For shape="rect", there are four coordinates (left, top, right, bottom); for shape="circle" there are three coordinates (center-x, center-y, radius); for shape="poly" there are two coordinate values for each point that defines the shape of the polygon.

Default None.

dataFld

IE *4* NN *n/a* Moz *n/a* Saf *n/a* Op *n/a* DOM *n/a*

Read/Write

Used with IE data binding to associate a remote data source column value in lieu of an href attribute for a link. The datasrc attribute must also be set for the element. Setting both the dataFld and dataSrc properties to empty strings breaks the binding between element and data source. Works only with text file data sources in IE 5/Mac.

Example `document.getElementById("hotlink").dataFld = "linkURL";`

Value Case-sensitive identifier of the data source column.

Default None.

dataFormatAs

IE 4 NN n/a Moz n/a Saf n/a Op n/a DOM n/a

Read/Write

Used with IE data binding, this property advises the browser whether the source material arriving from the data source is to be treated as plain text or as tagged HTML.

Example   `document.getElementById("hotlink").dataFormatAs = "HTML";`

Value   IE recognizes two possible settings: `text | html`.

Default   `text`

dataSrc

IE 4 NN n/a Moz n/a Saf n/a Op n/a DOM n/a

Read/Write

Used with IE data binding to specify the ID of the page's object element that loads the data source object for remote data access. Content from the data source to be inserted into the a element text is specified via the `datafld` property. Setting both the `dataFld` and `dataSrc` properties to empty strings breaks the binding between element and data source. Works only with text file data sources in IE 5/Mac.

Example   `document.all.hotlink.dataSrc = "#DBSRC3";`

Value   Case-sensitive identifier of the data source.

Default   None.

hash

IE 3 NN 2 Moz all Saf all Op 7 DOM 1

Read/Write

Provides that portion of the `href` attribute's URL following the # symbol, referring to an anchor location in a document. Do not include the # symbol when setting the property.

Example

```
document.getElementById("myLink").hash = "section3";
document.links[2].hash = "section3";
```

Value   String.

Default   None.

host

IE 3 NN 2 Moz all Saf all Op 7 DOM 1

Read/Write

This is the combination of the hostname and port (if any) of the server of the destination document for the link. If the port is explicitly part of the URL, the hostname and port are separated by a colon, just as they are in the URL. If the port number is not specified in an HTTP URL for IE, it automatically returns the default, port 80.

Example

```
document.getElementById("myLink").host = "www.megacorp.com:80";
document.links[2].host = "www.megacorp.com:80";
```

| **Value** | String of hostname optionally followed by a colon and port number. |
| **Default** | Depends on server. |

hostname

IE 3   NN 2   Moz *all*   Saf *all*   Op 7   DOM 1
Read/Write

This is the hostname of the server (i.e., a "two-dot" address consisting of server name and domain) of the destination document for the link. The hostname property does not include the port number.

Example

```
document.getElementById("myLink").hostname = "www.megacorp.com";
document.links[2].hostname = "www.megacorp.com";
```

| **Value** | String of hostname (server and domain). |
| **Default** | Depends on server. |

href

IE 3   NN 2   Moz *all*   Saf *all*   Op 7   DOM 1
Read/Write

Provides the URL specified by the element's href attribute.

Example

```
document.getElementById("myLink").href = "http://www.megacorp.com";
document.links[2].href = "http://www.megacorp.com";
```

| **Value** | String of complete or relative URL. |
| **Default** | None. |

hreflang

IE 6   NN *n/a*   Moz *all*   Saf *all*   Op 7   DOM 1
Read/Write

Provides the language code of the content at the destination of a link. Requires that the href attribute or property also be set.

Example	`document.getElementById("myLink").hreflang = "DE";`
Value	Case-insensitive language code.
Default	None.

Methods

IE 4   NN *n/a*   Moz *n/a*   Saf *n/a*   Op *n/a*   DOM *n/a*
Read/Write

Provides an advisory attribute about the functionality of the destination of a link. A browser could use this information to display special colors or images for the element content based on what the destination does for the user, but Internet Explorer does not appear to do anything with this information.

Example   document.links[1].Methods = "post";

Value   Any valid HTTP method as a string.

Default   None.

mimeType

Returns a plain-language version of the MIME type of the destination document at the other end of the link specified by the href attribute. You could use this information to set the cursor type during a mouse rollover. Don't confuse this property with the navigator. mimeTypes[] array and individual mimeType objects that Netscape Navigator refers to. This is not available in IE 4/Macintosh.

Example
```
if (document.getElementById("myLink").mimeType == "GIF Image") {
    ...
}
```

Value   A plain-language reference to the MIME type as a string.

Default   None.

name

This is the identifier associated with an element that turns it into an anchor. You can also use the name as part of the object reference.

Example
```
if (document.links[12].name == "section3") {
    ...
}
```

Value   Case-sensitive identifier that follows the rules of identifier naming: it may contain no whitespace, cannot begin with a numeral, and should avoid punctuation except for the underscore character.

Default   None.

nameProp

Returns just the filename, rather than the full URL, of the href attribute set for the element.

Example

```
if (document.getElementById("myLink").nameProp == "logo2.gif") {
    ...
}
```

Value   String.

Default   None.

pathname   IE 3 NN 2 Moz all Saf all Op 7 DOM 1
Read/Write

Provides the pathname component of the URL assigned to the element's href attribute. This consists of all URL information following the last character of the domain name, including the initial forward slash symbol.

Example

```
document.getElementById("myLink").pathname = "/images/logoHiRes.gif";
document.links[2].pathname = "/images/logoHiRes.gif";
```

Value   String.

Default   None.

port   IE 3 NN 2 Moz all Saf all Op 7 DOM 1
Read/Write

Provides the port component of the URL assigned to the element's href attribute. This consists of all URL information following the colon after the last character of the domain name. The colon is not part of the port property value.

Example

```
document.getElementById("myLink").port = "80";
document.links[2].port = "80";
```

Value   String (a numeric value as string).

Default   None.

protocol   IE 3 NN 2 Moz all Saf all Op 7 DOM 1
Read/Write

Indicates the protocol component of the URL assigned to the element's href attribute. This consists of all URL information up to and including the first colon of a URL. Typical values are: "http:", "file:", "ftp:", and "mailto:".

Example   `document.getElementById("secureLink").protocol = "https:";`

Value   String.

Default   None.

protocolLong

Read-only

Provides a verbose description of the protocol implied by the URL of the href attribute or href property. Appears to be deprecated.

Example
```
if (document.getElementById("myLink").protocolLong ==
    "HyperText Transfer Protocol") {
    // statements for treating document as server file
}
```

Value   String.

Default   None

rel

Read/Write

Defines the relationship between the current element and the destination of the link. Also known as a *forward link*, not to be confused in any way with the destination document whose address is defined by the href attribute. Mainstream browsers do not take advantage of this attribute for the a element, but you can treat the attribute as a kind of parameter to be checked and/or modified under script control. See the discussion of the a element's rel attribute in Chapter 1 for a glimpse of how this property may be used in the future.

Value
Case-insensitive, space-delimited list of HTML 4.0 standard link types (as a single string) applicable to the element. Sanctioned link types are:

alternate	appendix	bookmark	chapter	contents
copyright	glossary	help	index	next
prev	section	start	stylesheet	subsection

Default   None.

rev

Read/Write

Defines the relationship between the current element and the destination of the link. Also known as a *reverse link*. This property is not exploited yet in mainstream browsers, but you can treat the attribute as a kind of parameter to be checked and/or modified under script control. See the discussion of the a element's rev attribute in Chapter 1 for a glimpse of how this property may be used in the future.

Value   Case-insensitive, space-delimited list of HTML 4.0 standard link types (as a single string) applicable to the element. See the rel property for sanctioned link types.

Default   None.

search   IE *3* NN *2* Moz *all* Saf *all* Op *7* DOM *1*

Read/Write

Provides the URL-encoded portion of a URL assigned to the href attribute that begins with the ? symbol. A document that is served up as the result of the search also may have the search portion available as part of the window.location property. You can modify this property with a script. Doing so sends the URL and search criteria to the server. You must know the format of data (usually name/value pairs) expected by the server to perform this properly.

Example

```
document.getElementById("searchLink").search="?p=Tony+Blair&d=y&g=0&s=a&w=s&m=25";
document.links[1].search="?p=Tony+Blair&d=y&g=0&s=a&w=s&m=25";
```

Value   String starting with the ? symbol.

Default   None.

shape   IE *6* NN *n/a* Moz *all* Saf *all* Op *7* DOM *1*

Read/Write

Indicates the shape of a server-side image map area, with coordinates that are specified with the COORDS attribute. Intended for use by the area object, which inherits the properties of the a object.

Example   `document.getElementById("myLink").shape = "circle";`

Value   Case-insensitive shape constant as string: default | rect | rectangle | circle | poly | polygon.

Default   rect

target   IE *3* NN *2* Moz *all* Saf *all* Op *7* DOM *1*

Read/Write

Provides the name of the window or frame that is to receive content as the result of navigating to a link. Such names are assigned to frames by the frame element's name attribute; for subwindows, the name is assigned via the second parameter of the window.open( ) method. If you need the services of a target attribute to open a linked page in a blank browser window and you also need the markup to validate under strict HTML or XHTML DTDs (see Online Section VI), you can omit the target attribute in the code, but you must assign a value to the a element's target property by script after the page loads.

Example
```
document.getElementById("homeLink").target = "_top";
document.links[3].target = "_top";
```

Value   String value of the window or frame name, or any of the following
                constants (as a string): _parent | _self | _top | _blank. The _parent value
                targets the frameset to which the current document belongs; the _self
                value targets the current window; the _top value targets the main
                browser window, thereby eliminating all frames; and the _blank value
                creates a new window of default size.

Default   None.

text

Returns the text between the a element's start and end tags. This property pre-dates the
W3C DOM and should be used only if needed for Navigator 4 (even though Mozilla, Safar,
and Opera support it).

Value   String value.

Default   None.

type

This is the MIME type of the destination document at the other end of the link specified by
the href attribute. A browser might use this information to assist in preparing support for a
resource requiring a multimedia player or plugin.

Example
```
if (document.getElementById("myLink").type == "image/jpeg") {
    ...
}
```

Value   Case-insensitive MIME type. A catalog of registered MIME types is avail-
                able from *ftp://ftp.isi.edu/in-notes/iana/assignments/media-types/*.

Default   None.

urn

Indicates a Uniform Resource Name (URN) version of the destination document specified
in the href attribute. This attribute is intended to offer support in the future for the URN
format of URI, an evolving recommendation under discussion at the IETF (see RFC 2141).
Although supported in IE, this attribute does not take the place of the href attribute.

Example   `document.getElementById("link3").urn = "http://www.megacorp.com";`

Value   Complete or relative URN as a string.

Default   None.

abbr, acronym, cite, code, dfn, em, kbd, samp, strong, var
IE *4* NN *n/a* Moz *all* Saf *all* Op *7* DOM *1*

All these objects reflect the corresponding HTML phrase elements of the same name. Each of these phrase elements provides a context for an inline sequence of content. Some of these elements are rendered in ways to distinguish themselves from running text. See the HTML element descriptions in Chapter 1 for details. From a scripted standpoint, all phrase element objects share the same set of properties, methods, and events.

HTML Equivalent

```
<abbr>
<acronym>
<cite>
<code>
<dfn>
<em>
<kbd>
<samp>
<strong>
<var>
```

Object Model Reference

```
[window.]document.getElementById("elementID")
```

Object-Specific Properties

None.

Object-Specific Methods

None.

Object-Specific Events

None.

AbstractView

See the window object.

address
IE *4* NN *n/a* Moz *all* Saf *all* Op *7* DOM *1*

The address object reflects the address element.

HTML Equivalent   `<address>`

Object Model Reference

[window.]document.getElementById("*elementID*")

Object-Specific Properties

None.

Object-Specific Methods

None.

Object-Specific Events

None.

all

A collection of elements nested within the current element (only document.all is partially supported in Mozilla). A reference to document.all, for example, returns a collection (array) of all element objects contained by the document, including elements that may be deeply nested inside the document's first level of elements. The collection is sorted in source code order of the element tags. You can retrieve a reference to an element with its ID by any of the following syntaxes:

```
document.all.elementID
document.all["elementID"]
document.all("elementID")
document.all.item("elementID")
document.all.namedItem("elementID")
```

The W3C DOM equivalent (the document.getElementById( ) method) operates only from the document object, providing global reach to elements throughout the entire document. Note that Mozilla's support for document.all operates only in quirks mode, and displays a warning message in the JavaScript/Error Console with each usage. Additionally, if you test for the existence of document.all in an if condition, the browser returns a value as if document.all does not exist—thus preventing scripts that use document.all as an Internet Explorer browser detector from executing within Mozilla.

Object Model Reference

elementReference.all

Object-Specific Properties

length

Object-Specific Methods

item( )   namedItem( )   tags( )   urns( )

Object-Specific Events

None.

length

Read-only

Returns the number of elements in the collection.

Example   var howMany = document.all.length;

Value   Integer.

item( )

item(*index*[, *subindex*])

Returns a single object or collection of objects corresponding to the element matching the index value (or, optionally, the index and subindex values).

Returned Value   One object or collection (array) of objects. If there are no matches to the parameters, the returned value is null.

Parameters
index

When the parameter is a zero-based integer, the returned value is a single element corresponding to the specified item in source code order (nested within the current element); when the parameter is a string, the returned value is a collection of elements whose id or name properties match that string.

subindex

If you specify a string value for the first parameter, you can use the second parameter to specify a zero-based index that retrieves the specified element from the collection whose id or name properties match the first parameter's string value.

namedItem( )

namedItem(*IDOrName*)

Returns a single object or collection of objects corresponding to the element matching the parameter string value.

Returned Value   One object or collection (array) of objects. If there are no matches to the parameters, the returned value is null.

Parameters
IDOrName

The string that contains the same value and case as the desired element's id or name attribute.

tags( )

tags(*tagName*)

Returns a collection of objects (among all objects nested within the current element) whose tags match the *tagName* parameter.

Returned Value A collection (array) of objects. If there are no matches to the parameters, the returned value is an array of zero length.

Parameters

tagName
> A case-insensitive string that contains the element tag name only (no angle brackets), as in document.all.tags("p").

urns( ) IE *4* NN *n/a* Moz *n/a* Saf *n/a* Op *n/a* DOM *n/a*

urns(*URN*)

Returns a collection of nested element objects that have behaviors attached to them and whose URNs match the *URN* parameter.

Returned Value A collection (array) of objects. If there are no matches to the parameters, the returned value is an array of zero length.

Parameters

URN
> A string with a local or external behavior file URN.

anchors IE *3* NN *2* Moz *all* Saf *all* Op *7* DOM *1*

A collection of all a elements with assigned name attributes that make them behave as anchors (instead of links). Collection members are sorted in source code order. All browsers let you use array notation to access a single anchor in the collection (e.g., document.anchors[0], document.anchors["section3"]). Internet Explorer also allows the index value to be placed inside parentheses instead of brackets (e.g., document.anchors(0)). If you want to use the anchor's name as an index value (always as a string identifier), be sure to use the value of the name attribute, rather than the id attribute. To use the id attribute in a reference to an anchor, access the object via a document.all.*elementID* (in IE only) or document.getElementById("*elementID*") reference. Recent browsers include additional methods that provide named or indexed access.

Object Model Reference

document.anchors

Object-Specific Properties

length

Object-Specific Methods

item( )   namedItem( )   tags( )   urns( )

Object-Specific Events

None.

length

Returns the number of elements in the collection.

Example   `var howMany = document.anchors.length;`

Value   Integer.

item( )

```
item(index[, subindex])
item(index)
```

Returns a single anchor object or collection of anchor objects corresponding to the element matching the index value (or, optionally in IE, the index and subindex values).

Returned Value   One anchor object or collection (array) of anchor objects. If there are no matches to the parameters, the returned value is `null`.

Parameters

index

When the parameter is a zero-based integer (per the W3C spec), the returned value is a single element that corresponds to the specified item in source code order. When the parameter is a string (IE), the returned value is a collection of elements whose `id` or `name` properties match that string.

subindex

In IE only, if you specify a string value for the first parameter, you can use the second parameter to specify a zero-based index that retrieves the specified element from the collection with `id` or `name` properties that match the first parameter's string value.

namedItem( )

```
namedItem(IDOrName)
```

Returns a single anchor object or collection of anchor objects corresponding to the element matching the parameter string value.

Returned Value   One anchor object or collection (array) of anchor objects. If there are no matches to the parameters, the returned value is `null`.

Parameters

IDOrName

The string that contains the same value as the desired element's `id` or `name` attribute.

tags( )

```
tags(tagName)
```

Returns a collection of objects (among all objects nested within the current collection) with tags that match the *tagName* parameter. Implemented in all IE, Safari, and Opera collections (see the `all.tags( )` method), but redundant for collections of the same element type.

urns( )

urns(*URN*)

See the all.urns( ) method.

applet

The applet object reflects the applet element. Note that although no object-specific methods are listed here, applets expose public properties and methods to scripts through LiveConnect, where supported. In particular, if you iterate through the properties and methods of an applet in a Mozilla-based browser, you will find a long list of public methods that are specific to the applet currently loaded into the applet element.

HTML Equivalent   <applet>

Object Model Reference
[window.]document.*appletName*
[window.]document.getElementById("*elementID*")

Object-Specific Properties

align	alt	altHTML	archive	code
codeBase	dataFld	dataSrc	height	hspace
name	object	vspace	width	

Object-Specific Methods
None.

Object-Specific Event Properties
None.

align

Read/Write

Defines the alignment of the element within its surrounding container. See "Alignment Constants" at the beginning of Chapter 1 for the various meanings that different values bring to this property.

Example   document.getElementById("myApplet").align = "center";

Value   Any of the alignment constants: absbottom | absmiddle | baseline | bottom | left | middle | right | texttop | top.

Default   left

alt

IE 6   NN n/a   Moz all   Saf all   Op 7   DOM 1

Read/Write

This is the text message to be displayed if the object or applet fails to load. There is little indication that setting this property on an existing applet object has any visual effect.

Example   `document.myApplet.alt= "Image Editor Applet";`

Value   Any quoted string of characters, but HTML tags are not interpreted.

Default   None.

altHTML

IE 4   NN n/a   Moz n/a   Saf n/a   Op n/a   DOM n/a

Read/Write

Provides the HTML content to be displayed if the object or applet fails to load. This can be a message, static image, or any other HTML that best fits the scenario. There is little indication that setting this property on an existing applet object has any visual effect.

Example   `document.myApplet.altHTML = "<img src='appletAlt.gif'>";`

Value   Any quoted string of characters, including HTML tags.

Default   None.

archive

IE 6   NN n/a   Moz all   Saf all   Op 7   DOM 1

Read-only

Reflects the archive attribute of the applet element. Only partially implemented in the browsers. See the discussion of the archive attribute in Chapter 1.

Example

```
if (document.applets["clock"].archive == "myClock.zip") {
    // process for the found class file
}
```

Value   Case-sensitive URI as a string.

Default   None.

code

IE 4   NN n/a   Moz all   Saf all   Op 7   DOM 1

Read-only

Provides the name of the Java applet class file set to the code attribute.

Example

```
if (document.applets["clock"].code == "XMAScounter.class") {
    // process for the found class file
}
```

Value   Case-sensitive applet class filename as a string.

Default   None.

codeBase

IE 4 NN *n/a* Moz *all* Saf *all* Op 7 DOM 1

Read-only

Provides the path to the directory holding the class file designated in the code attribute. The codebase attribute does not name the class file, just the path.

Example

```
if (document.applets["clock"].codeBase == "classes") {
    // process for the found class file directory
}
```

Value   Case-sensitive pathname, usually relative to the directory storing the current HTML document.

Default   None.

dataFld

IE 4 NN *n/a* Moz *n/a* Saf *n/a* Op *n/a* DOM *n/a*

Read/Write

It is unclear how you would use this property with an applet object because the dataFld and dataSrc properties (as set in element attributes) are applied to individual param elements.

Value   Case-sensitive identifier of the data source column.

Default   None.

dataSrc

IE 4 NN *n/a* Moz *n/a* Saf *n/a* Op *n/a* DOM *n/a*

Read/Write

It's unclear how you would use this property with an applet object because the dataFld and dataSrc properties (as set in element attributes) are applied to individual param elements.

Value   Case-sensitive identifier of the data source.

Default   None.

height, width

IE 4 NN *n/a* Moz *all* Saf *all* Op 7 DOM 1

Read/Write

Indicate the height and width in pixels of the element as set by the tag attributes. Changing the values does not necessarily change the actual rectangle of the applet after it has loaded.

Example   `var appletHeight = document.myApplet.height;`

Value   Integer.

Default   None.

hspace, vspace

IE *4* NN *n/a* Moz *all* Saf *all* Op *7* DOM *1*

Read/Write

Indicate the pixel measure of horizontal and vertical margins surrounding an applet. The hspace property affects the left and right edges of the element equally; the vspace affects the top and bottom edges of the element equally. These margins are not the same as margins set by style sheets, but they have the same visual effect.

Example

```
document.getElementById("myApplet").hspace = 5;
document.getElementById("myApplet").vspace = 8;
```

Value   Integer of pixel count.

Default   0

name

IE *4* NN *n/a* Moz *all* Saf *all* Op *7* DOM *1*

Read-only

This is the identifier associated with the applet. Use the name when referring to the object in the form document.*appletName*.

Value   Case-sensitive identifier that follows the rules of identifier naming: it may contain no whitespace, cannot begin with a numeral, and should avoid punctuation except for the underscore character.

Default   None.

object

IE *4* NN *n/a* Moz *all* Saf *all* Op *7* DOM *n/a*

Read-only

Returns a reference to the applet object so that a script can access a property or method of the applet whose name is identical to a property or method of the applet element object. Although the functional version of this property is available only in IE, other supporting browsers simply return an empty string for its value.

Value   In IE, an applet object (not the applet element object) reference; in other supporting browsers, an empty string.

Default   None.

vspace

See hspace.

width

See height.

applets
IE *3* NN *2* Moz *all* Saf *all* Op *7* DOM *1*

A collection of all the Java applets in the current element, sorted in source code order. Navigator and Internet Explorer let you use array notation to access a single applet in the collection (e.g., document.applets[0], document.applets["clockApplet"]). Internet Explorer allows the index value to be placed inside parentheses instead of brackets (e.g., document.applets(0)). If you wish to use the applet's name as an index value (always as a string identifier), use the value of the name attribute rather than the id attribute. To use the id attribute in a reference to an applet, access the object via a document.all.*elementID* (in IE only) or document.getElementById("*elementID*") reference.

Object Model Reference
document.applets[i]

Object-Specific Properties

length

Object-Specific Methods

item( )   namedItem( )   tags( )

length
IE *3* NN *2* Moz *all* Saf *all* Op *7* DOM *1*

Read-only

Returns the number of elements in the collection.

Example   var howMany = document.applets.length;

Value   Integer.

item( )
IE *4* NN *n/a* Moz *all* Saf *all* Op *7* DOM *1*

item(*index*[, *subindex*]) item(*index*)

Returns a single applet object or collection of applet objects corresponding to the element matching the index value (or, optionally in IE, the index and subindex values).

Returned Value   One applet object or collection (array) of applet objects. If there are no matches to the parameters, the returned value is null.

Parameters
index
> When the parameter is a zero-based integer, the returned value is a single element corresponding to the specified item in source code order (nested within the current element); when the parameter is a string, the returned value is a collection of elements whose id or name properties match that string.

subindex
> In IE only, if you specify a string value for the first parameter, you can use the second parameter to specify a zero-based index that retrieves the specified element from the collection whose id or name properties match the first parameter's string value.

namedItem( )

IE 6 NN *n/a* Moz *all* Saf *all* Op 7 DOM 1

namedItem(*IDOrName*)

Returns a single applet object or collection of applet objects corresponding to the element matching the parameter string value.

Returned Value   One applet object or collection (array) of applet objects. If there are no matches to the parameters, the returned value is null.

Parameters

IDOrName
> The string that contains the same value as the desired element's id or name attribute.

tags( )

IE 4 NN *n/a* Moz *n/a* Saf *all* Op 7 DOM *n/a*

tags(*tagName*)

Returns a collection of objects (among all objects nested within the current collection) with tags that match the *tagName* parameter. Implemented in all IE, Safari, and Opera collections (see the all.tags( ) method), but redundant for collections of the same element type.

area

IE 4 NN *n/a* Moz *all* Saf *all* Op 7 DOM 1

The area object reflects the area element, which defines the shape, coordinates, and destination of a clickable region of a client-side image map. Navigator and Internet Explorer treat an area object as a member of the links collection, since an area object behaves much like a link, but for a segment of an image.

HTML Equivalent

<area>

Object Model Reference

```
[window.]document.links[i]
[window.]document.getElementById("elementID")
```

Object-Specific Properties

alt	coords	hash	host	hostname
href	noHref	pathname	port	protocol
search	shape	target		

Object-Specific Methods
None.

Object-Specific Events
None.

alt

Read/Write

Future nongraphical browsers may use the alt property setting to display a brief description of the meaning of the (invisible) image's hotspots.

Example   document.getElementById("*elementID*").alt = "To Next Page";

Value   Any quoted string of characters.

Default   None.

coords

Read/Write

Defines the outline of the area to be associated with a particular link or scripted action. Coordinate values are entered as a comma-delimited list. If hotspots of two areas should overlap, the area that is defined earlier in the code takes precedence.

Example   document.getElementById("mapArea2").coords = "25, 5, 50, 70";

Value

Each coordinate is a pixel length value, but the number of coordinates and their order depend on the shape specified by the shape attribute, which may optionally be associated with the element. For shape="rect", there are four coordinates (left, top, right, bottom); for shape="circle", there are three coordinates (center-x, center-y, radius); for shape="poly", there are two coordinate values for each point that defines the shape of the polygon.

Default   None.

hash

Read/Write

This is that portion of the href attribute's URL following the # symbol, referring to an anchor location in a document. Do not include the # symbol when setting the property.

Example   document.getElementById("mapArea2").hash = "section3";

Value   String.

Default   None.

host

Read/Write

Provides the combination of the hostname and port (if any) of the server of the destination document for the area link. If the port is explicitly part of the URL, the hostname and port are separated by a colon, just as they are in the URL. If the port number is not specified in an HTTP URL for IE, it automatically returns the default, port 80.

Alphabetical DOM
Reference

Example

document.getElementById("mapArea2").host = "www.megacorp.com:80";

Value　　　　　　　String of hostname optionally followed by a colon and port number.

Default　　　　　　Depends on server.

hostname

Read/Write

Provides the hostname of the server (i.e., a two-dot address consisting of server name and domain) of the destination document for the area link. The hostname property does not include the port number.

Example　　　　　　document.areas[2].hostname = "www.megacorp.com";

Value　　　　　　　String of hostname (server and domain).

Default　　　　　　Depends on server.

href

Read/Write

This is the URL specified by the element's href attribute.

Example　　　　　　document.areas[2].href = "http://www.megacorp.com";

Value　　　　　　　String of complete or relative URL.

Default　　　　　　None.

noHref

Read/Write

Specifies whether the area defined by the coordinates has a link associated with it. When you set this property to true, scriptable browsers no longer treat the element as a link.

Example　　　　　　document.areas[4].noHref = "true";

Value　　　　　　　Boolean value: true | false.

Default　　　　　　false

pathname

Read/Write

Provides the pathname component of the URL assigned to the element's href attribute. This consists of all URL information following the last character of the domain name, including the initial forward slash symbol.

Example

document.getElementById("myLink").pathname = "/images/logoHiRes.gif";

Value   String.

Default   None.

port   IE 3   NN 2   Moz all   Saf all   Op 7   DOM 1
Read/Write

Provides the port component of the URL assigned to the element's href attribute. This consists of all URL information following the colon after the last character of the domain name. The colon is not part of the port property value.

Example   document.getElementById("myLink").port = "80";

Value   String (a numeric value as string).

Default   None.

protocol   IE 3   NN 2   Moz all   Saf all   Op 7   DOM 1
Read/Write

Indicates the protocol component of the URL assigned to the element's href attribute. This consists of all URL information up to and including the first colon of a URL. Typical values are "http:", "file:", "ftp:", and "mailto:".

Example   document.getElementById("secureLink").protocol = "https:";

Value   String.

Default   None.

search   IE 3   NN 2   Moz all   Saf all   Op 7   DOM 1
Read/Write

This is the URL-encoded portion of a URL assigned to the href attribute that begins with the ? symbol. A document that is served up as the result of the search also may have the search portion available as part of the window.location property. You can modify this property with a script. Doing so sends the URL and search criteria to the server. You must know the format of data (usually name/value pairs) expected by the server to perform this properly.

Example

document.getElementById("searchLink").search="?p=Tony+Blair&d=y&g=O&s=a&w=s&m=25";

Value   String starting with the ? symbol.

Default   None.

shape

IE 4 NN n/a Moz all Saf all Op 7 DOM 1

Read/Write

Indicates the shape of a server-side image map area with coordinates that are specified with the coords attribute.

Example   `document.getElementById("area51").shape = "circle";`

Value   Case-insensitive shape constant as string: default | rect | rectangle | circle | poly | polygon.

Default   RECT (IE); empty string but rect implied (Mozilla).

target

IE 3 NN 2 Moz all Saf all Op 7 DOM 1

Read/Write

This is the name of the window or frame that is to receive content as the result of navigating to an area link. Such names are assigned to frames by the frame element's name attribute; for subwindows, the name is assigned via the second parameter of the window. open( ) method. If you need the services of a target attribute to open a linked page in a blank browser window and you also need the HTML to validate under strict HTML or XHTML DTDs, you can omit the target attribute in the code, but assign a value to the area element's target property by script after the page loads.

Example   `document.getElementById("homeArea").target = "_blank";`

Value

String value of the window or frame name, or any of the following constants (as a string): _parent | _self | _top | _blank. The _parent value targets the frameset to which the current document belongs; the _self value targets the current window; the _top value targets the main browser window, thereby eliminating all frames; and the _blank value creates a new window of default size.

Default   None.

areas

IE 4 NN n/a Moz all Saf all Op 7 DOM 1

A collection of all area elements associated with a map element. Notice that individual items of an areas collection are also members of the document-wide links collection (document. links[] array). But the members of an areas collection are local to a single map element.

Object Model Reference `document.getElementById("mapElementID").areas`

Object-Specific Properties

    length

Object-Specific Methods

    item( )   namedItem( )   tags( )   urns( )

length

IE 4 NN n/a Moz all Saf all Op 7 DOM 1

Read-only

Returns the number of elements in the collection.

Example   `var howMany = document.areas.length;`

Value   Integer.

item( )

IE 4 NN n/a Moz all Saf all Op 7 DOM 1

`item(`*index*`[, `*subindex*`])` `item(`*index*`)`

Returns a single `area` object or collection of `area` objects corresponding to the element matching the index value (or, optionally in IE, the index and subindex values).

Returned Value   One area object or collection (array) of area objects. If there are no matches to the parameters, the returned value is `null`.

Parameters

index
> When the parameter is a zero-based integer, the returned value is a single element corresponding to the specified item in source code order (nested within the current element); when the parameter is a string, the returned value is a collection of elements whose `id` or `name` properties match that string.

subindex
> In IE only, if you specify a string value for the first parameter, you can use the second parameter to specify a zero-based index that retrieves the specified element from the collection whose `id` or `name` properties match the first parameter's string value.

namedItem( )

IE 6 NN n/a Moz all Saf all Op 7 DOM 1

`namedItem(`*IDOrName*`)`

Returns a single `area` object or collection of `area` objects corresponding to the element matching the parameter string value.

Returned Value   One area object or collection (array) of area objects. If there are no matches to the parameters, the returned value is `null`.

Parameters

IDOrName
> The string that contains the same value as the desired element's `id` or `name` attribute.

tags( )

IE 4 NN n/a Moz n/a Saf all Op 7 DOM 1

`tags(`*tagName*`)`

Returns a collection of objects (among all objects nested within the current collection) with tags that match the *tagName* parameter. Implemented in all IE, Safari, and Opera collections (see the `all.tags( )` method), but redundant for collections of the same element type.

urns( )   IE 5(Win)   NN n/a   Moz n/a   Saf n/a   Op n/a   DOM n/a

urns(*URN*)

See the all.urns( ) method.

Attr, attribute   IE 4   NN n/a   Moz all   Saf all   Op 7   DOM 1

An abstract representation of an element's attribute name/value pair is an object known in the W3C DOM vernacular as the Attr object; in IE terminology, it is called an attribute object. They are different names for the same object. An attribute object is created in both environments via the document.createAttribute( ) method; the reference to the attribute object then becomes the parameter to an element's setAttributeNode( ) method to insert that attribute object into the element. For example:

```
var newAttr = document.createAttribute("author");
newAttr.value = "William Shakespeare";
document.getElementById("hamlet").setAttributeNode(newAttr);
```

Some W3C DOM element methods (most notably, the getAttributeNode( ) method) return attribute objects, which have properties that may be accessed like any scriptable object.

In the W3C DOM abstract model, the Attr object inherits all properties and methods of the Node object. Some Node object properties, however, are not inherited by the attribute object in IE/Windows until Version 6, even though they are implemented for element and text nodes in Version 5.

HTML Equivalent   Any name/value pair inside a start tag.

Object Model Reference

[window.]document.getElementById("*elementID*").attributes[*i*]
[window.]document.getElementById("*elementID*").attributes.item(*i*)
[window.]document.getElementById("*elementID*").attributes.getNamedItem[*attrName*]

Object-Specific Properties

expando	name	ownerElement	specified	value

Object-Specific Methods
None.

Object-Specific Events
None.

expando   IE 6   NN n/a   Moz n/a   Saf n/a   Op n/a   DOM n/a

Read-only

Returns Boolean true if the attribute, once it is inserted into an element, is not one of the native attributes for the element. This property is false for an attribute created by document.createAttribute( ) until the attribute is added to the element (via the setAttributeNode( ) method), at which time the property's value is reevaluated within the context of the element's native attributes.

Example
```
var isCustomAttr =
  document.getElementById("book3928").getAttributeNode("author").expando;
```

Value   Boolean value: true | false.

Default   false

name   IE 5 NN n/a Moz all Saf all Op 7 DOM 1

This is the name portion of the name/value pair of the attribute. It is identical to the nodeName property of the Attr node. You may not modify the name of an attribute by script because other dependencies may lead to document tree confusion. Instead, replace the old attribute with a newly created one, the name of which is a required parameter of the document.createAttribute( ) method.

Example
```
if (myAttr.name == "author") {
    // process author attribute
}
```

Value   String value.

Default   Empty string, although creating a new attribute requires a name.

ownerElement   IE n/a NN n/a Moz all Saf all Op 7 DOM 2

Refers to the element that contains the current attribute object. Until a newly created attribute is inserted into an element, this property is null.

Example
```
if (myAttr.ownerElement.tagName == "fred") {
    // process attribute of <fred> element
}
```

Value   Element node reference.

Default   null

specified   IE 5 NN n/a Moz all Saf all Op 7 DOM 1

Returns Boolean true if the value of the attribute is explicitly assigned in the source code or adjusted by script. If the browser reflects an attribute that is not explicitly set (IE does this), the specified property for that value is false, even though the attribute may have a default value determined by the document's DTD. The W3C DOM Level 2 recommends (and Safari and Opera support) that the specified property of a freshly created Attr object should be true, but both IE 6+ and Mozilla leave it false until the attribute is inserted into an element.

Example

```
if (myAttr.specified) {
    // process attribute whose value is something other than DTD default
}
```

Value   Boolean value: true | false.

Default   false

value   IE 6   NN *n/a*   Moz *all*   Saf *all*   Op 7   DOM 1

Read/Write

Provides the value portion of the name/value pair of the attribute. Identical to the nodeValue property of the Attr node, as well as data accessed more directly via an element's getAttribute( ) and setAttribute( ) methods. If you create a new attribute object, you can assign its value via the value property prior to inserting the attribute into the element. Attribute node values are always strings, including in IE, which otherwise allows Number or Boolean data types for the corresponding properties.

Example

```
document.getElementById("hamlet").getAttributeNode("author").value = "Shakespeare";
```

Value   String value.

Default   Empty string, except in IE/Windows, which returns the string undefined
                   (that is, not a value whose type evaluates to the undefined value).

attributes, NamedNodeMap   IE 5   NN *n/a*   Moz *all*   Saf *all*   Op 7   DOM 1

The object returned by the attributes property of every W3C DOM element object is a collection (array) of references to Attr (a.k.a. attribute) objects. An attribute type of node always has a name associated with it, which opens the way for methods of the collection of such nodes to access them directly by name, rather than iterating through the array in search of a matching node name. In the W3C DOM structure, the abstract representation of this array of named nodes is called the NamedNodeMap object, which shares some properties and methods of the IE attributes object. Since both objects refer to the same parts of a document tree, they are treated here together. A couple of other W3C DOM collections are also of the NamedNodeMap variety, but your primary contact with the NamedNodeMap in HTML documents is as a collection of Attr objects. Collection members are sorted in source code order.

There are more direct ways to access an attribute of an element (such as the getAttribute( ) or getAttributeNode( ) methods of all elements). The property and methods shown here, however, assume that your script has been handed a collection of attributes independent of their host element, and your processing starts from that point.

Object Model Reference

elementReference.attributes

Object-Specific Properties

length

Object-Specific Methods

| getNamedItem( ) | getNamedItemNS( ) | item( ) | removeNamedItem( ) |
| removeNamedItemNS( ) | setNamedItem( ) | setNamedItemNS( ) | |

Object-Specific Events

None.

length
IE 5   NN n/a   Moz all   Saf all   Op 7   DOM 1

Read-only

Returns the number of elements in the collection.

| **Example** | var howMany = document.getElementById("myTable").attributes.length; |
| **Value** | Integer. |

getNamedItem( )
IE 6   NN n/a   Moz all   Saf all   Op 7   DOM 1

getNamedItem("*attributeName*")

Returns a single Attr object corresponding to the attribute whose node name matches the parameter value.

| **Returned Value** | Reference to one Attr object. If there is no match to the parameter value, the returned value is null. |

Parameters

attributeName
   String corresponding to the name portion of an attribute's name/value pair.

getNamedItemNS( )
IE n/a   NN n/a   Moz all   Saf all   Op 7   DOM 2

getNamedItemNS("*namespaceURI*", "*localName*")

Returns a single Attr object with a local name and namespace URI that match the parameter values.

| **Returned Value** | Reference to one Attr object. If there is no match to the parameter values, the returned value is null. |

Alphabetical DOM
Reference

Parameters

namespaceURI
> URI string matching a URI assigned to a label earlier in the document.

localName
> The local name portion of the attribute.

item( )   IE 5   NN *n/a*   Moz *all*   Saf *all*   Op 7   DOM 1

item(*index*)

Returns a single Attr object corresponding to the element matching the index value.

Returned Value   Reference to one Attr object. If there is no match to the index value, the returned value is null. Unlike some other collections in IE, a string index value is not allowed for the attributes object.

Parameters

index
> A zero-based integer corresponding to the specified item in source code order.

removeNamedItem( )   IE 6   NN *n/a*   Moz *all*   Saf *all*   Op 7   DOM 1

removeNamedItem("*attributeName*")

Removes from the collection a single Attr object corresponding to the attribute whose node name matches the parameter value.

Returned Value   Reference to the removed Attr object. If there is no match to the parameter value, the returned value is null.

Parameters

attributeName
> String corresponding to the name portion of an attribute's name/value pair.

removeNamedItemNS( )   IE *n/a*   NN *n/a*   Moz *all*   Saf *all*   Op 7   DOM 2

removeNamedItemNS("*namespaceURI*", "*localName*")

Removes from the collection a single Attr object whose local name and namespace URI match the parameter values.

Returned Value   Reference to the removed Attr object. If there is no match to the parameter values, the method generates an error.

Parameters

namespaceURI
> URI string matching a URI assigned to a label earlier in the document.

localName
> The local name portion of the attribute.

setNamedItem( ) IE 6 NN n/a Moz all Saf all Op 7 DOM 1

setNamedItem(*attrObjectReference*)

Inserts a single `Attr` object into the current collection of attributes. If the destination of the attribute is an existing element, you may also use the `setAttributeNode( )` method on the element to insert the `Attr` object. When the `setNamedItem( )` method is invoked, the browser first looks for a match between the new attribute's name and existing attribute names within the collection. If there is a match, the new attribute replaces the original one; otherwise, the new attribute is added to the collection.

Returned Value Reference to an `Attr` object either created anew or referenced from elsewhere in the document tree.

Parameters

attrObjectReference
> A reference to an `Attr` node object created through `document.createAttribute( )` or an `Attr` node from another element in the document tree.

setNamedItemNS( ) IE n/a NN n/a Moz all Saf all Op 7 DOM 2

setNamedItemNS(*attrObjectReference*)

Inserts a single `Attr` object into the current collection of attributes. If the destination of the attribute is an existing element, you may also use the `setAttributeNodeNS( )` method on the element to insert the `Attr` object. When the `setNamedItemNS( )` method is invoked, the browser first looks for a match between the new attribute's pairing of local name and namespace URI and existing attribute local names and namespace URIs within the collection. If there is a match, the new attribute replaces the original one; otherwise, the new attribute is added to the collection.

Returned Value Reference to an `Attr` object either created anew or referenced from elsewhere in the document tree.

Parameters

attrObjectReference
> A reference to an `Attr` node object created through `document.createAttributeNS( )` or an `Attr` node from another element in the document tree.

Audio IE n/a NN n/a Moz n/a Saf n/a Op 9 DOM n/a

The Audio object is a script-only control, whose standard is under the guidance of the WHATWG. Opera 9 is the first mainstream browser to support the object, whose purpose is to give scripts a standardized way of loading, playing, and stopping background sound. There is no plugin control panel automatically displayed by the browser, so it is up to the page designer to offer controls, if needed.

To use the object, create an instance of it by invoking the constructor function, passing as the sole parameter, the URL of the sound file to load. Opera 9 currently supports .wav files:

```
var aud = new Audio("sample.wav");
```

You can use the `load` event to trigger the `play( )` method.

Object Model Reference

new Audio("*audioFile*")

Object-Specific Properties

None.

Object-Specific Methods

loop( )   play( )   stop( )

Object-Specific Events

Event	IE	Mozilla	Safari	Opera	W3C DOM
error	—	—	—	•	—
load	—	—	—	•	—

loop( )   IE *n/a* NN *n/a* Moz *n/a* Saf *n/a* Op *9* DOM *n/a*

loop([*count*])

Controls how many times the loaded sound should play when the play( ) method is invoked. If the parameter is empty, the sound plays continuously.

Returned Value   None

Parameters

count

An integer controlling how many times the sound is to play.

play( ), stop( )   IE *n/a* NN *n/a* Moz *n/a* Saf *n/a* Op *9* DOM *n/a*

Begins or halts the playback through the instance of the Audio object. The file must be completely loaded before playback can begin. When you stop the playback, the playback counter is reset to zero, and the playback pointer is set to the beginning of the file.

Returned Value   None.

Parameters   None.

b, big, i, s, small, strike, tt, u   IE *4* NN *n/a* Moz *all* Saf *all* Op *7* DOM *1*

All these objects reflect the HTML font-related style elements of the same name. Each of these elements specifies a rendering style for an inline sequence of content governed by each browser's default internal style sheet rules. All the elements are deprecated in HTML 4 in favor of style sheet attributes. See the HTML element descriptions in Chapter 1 for details. From a scripted standpoint, all font-related style element objects share the same set of properties, methods, event handlers, and collections.

HTML Equivalent

```
<b>
<big>
<i>
<s>
<small>
<strike>
<tt>
<u>
```

Object Model Reference

[window.]document.getElementById("*elementID*")

Object-Specific Properties

None.

Object-Specific Methods

None.

Object-Specific Events

None.

base

IE *4* NN *n/a* Moz *all* Saf *all* Op *7* DOM *1*

A base object instructs the browser about the URL path to the current document. This path is then used as the basis for all relative URLs that are used to specify various src and href attributes throughout the document.

HTML Equivalent   `<base>`

Object Model Reference

[window.]document.getElementById("*elementID*")

Object-Specific Properties

href   target

Object-Specific Methods

None.

Object-Specific Events

None.

href

IE *4* NN *n/a* Moz *all* Saf *all* Op *7* DOM *1*

Read/Write

Provides the URL of a document whose server path is to be used as the base URL for all relative references in the document. This is typically the URL of the current document, but it can be set to another path if it makes sense to your document organization and directory structure.

Example	`document.getElementById("myBase").href = "http://www.megacorp.com";`
Value	String of complete or relative URL.
Default	Current document pathname.

target

Provides the name of the window or frame that is to receive content as the result of navigating to a link or any other action on the page that loads a new document. Such names are assigned to frames by the `frame` element's `name` attribute; for subwindows, the name is assigned via the second parameter of the `window.open( )` method. If you need the services of a `target` attribute to open a linked page in a blank browser window and you also need the HTML to validate under strict HTML or XHTML DTDs, you can omit the `target` attribute in the code, but assign a value to the `base` element's `target` property by script after the page loads.

Example	`document.getElementById("myBase").target = "_blank";`

Value

String value of the window or frame name, or any of the following constants (as a string): `_parent` | `_self` | `_top` | `_blank`. The `_parent` value targets the frameset to which the current document belongs; the `_self` value targets the current window; the `_top` value targets the main browser window, thereby eliminating all frames; and the `_blank` value creates a new window of default size.

Default	`_self`

basefont

A basefont element advises the browser of some font information to be used as the basis for text rendering of the current page below the basefont element. The basefont element overrides the default font settings in the browser's user preferences settings.

If you intend to alter this element by script, do so only via the properties shown here or W3C DOM-compatible document tree manipulations. Other approaches either risk the display of the document or are not permitted by the browser.

HTML Equivalent   `<basefont>`

Object Model Reference
`[window.]document.getElementById("elementID")`

Object-Specific Properties

color	face	size

Object-Specific Methods
None.

Object-Specific Events
None.

color
IE 4   NN *n/a*   Moz *all*   Saf *all*   Op 7   DOM 1
Read/Write

Sets the font color of all text below the basefont element.

Example   `document.getElementsByTagName("basefont")[0].color = "#c0c0c0";`

Value   Case-insensitive hexadecimal triplet or plain-language color name as a string. See Appendix A for acceptable plain-language color names.

Default   Browser default.

face
IE 4   NN *n/a*   Moz *all*   Saf *all*   Op 7   DOM 1
Read/Write

Indicates a hierarchy of font faces to use for the default font of a section headed by a basefont element. The browser looks for the first font face in the comma-delimited list of font face names until it either finds a match in the client system or runs out of choices, at which point the browser default font face is used. Font face names must match the system font face names exactly.

Example
`document.getElementById("myBaseFont").face = "Bookman, Times Roman, serif";`

Value   One or more font face names in a comma-delimited list within a string. You may use real font names or the recognized generic faces: serif | sans-serif | cursive | fantasy | monospace.

Default   Browser default.

size
IE 4   NN *n/a*   Moz *all*   Saf *all*   Op 7   DOM 1
Read/Write

Provides the size of the font in the 1-7 browser relative scale.

Example   `document.getElementById("myBaseFont").size = "+1";`

Value   Either an integer (as a quoted string) or a quoted relative value consisting of a + or - symbol and an integer value.

Default   3

Alphabetical DOM Reference

bdo

The bdo element is designed to assist in instances when, due to various conversions during text processing, the normal bidirectional algorithms must be explicitly overridden. The primary property of this object is dir, which is shared among all other element objects.

HTML Equivalent   <bdo>

Object-Specific Properties
None.

Object-Specific Methods
None.

Object-Specific Events
None.

bgsound

A bgsound element defines a sound file that is to play in the background while the user visits the page. Set properties to control the volume and how many times the sound track plays even after the sound file has loaded. A few properties, such as innerHTML and innerText, are exposed in the Windows version, but they don't apply to an element that does not have an end tag.

HTML Equivalent   <bgsound>

Object Model Reference
[window.]document.getElementById("*elementID*")

Object-Specific Properties

balance	loop	src	volume

Object-Specific Methods
None.

Object-Specific Events
None.

balance

Read-only

Specifies how the audio is divided between the left and right speakers. Once this attribute value is set in the element, its value cannot be changed by script control.

Example
var currBal = document.getElementsByTagName("bgsound")[0].balance;

Value	A signed integer between –10,000 and +10,000. A value of 0 is equally balanced on both sides. A negative value means the left side is dominant; a positive value means the right side is dominant.
Default	0

loop

Specifies the number of times the sound plays. Assigning a value of –1 means the sound plays continuously until the page is unloaded.

Example	`document.getElementById("mySound").loop = 3;`
Value	Integer.
Default	1

src

Provides the URL of the sound file to be played. Change tunes by assigning a new URL to the property. The new tune plays according to the loop property setting.

Example	`document.getElementById("tunes").src = "sounds/blues.aif";`
Value	Complete or relative URL as a string.
Default	None.

volume

Specifies how loud the background sound plays relative to the maximum sound output level as adjusted by user preferences in the client computer. Maximum volume—a setting of zero—is only as loud as the user has set the **Sound** control panel. Attribute adjustments are negative values as low as –10,000 (although most users lose the sound at values much higher than that value).

Example	`var currVolume = document.getElementById("themeSong").volume;`
Value	Integer.
Default	Varies with operating system and sound settings.

big

See b.

blockquote

IE 4 NN n/a Moz all Saf all Op 7 DOM 1

The blockquote object reflects the blockquote element, which is intended to set off a long, block-level quote inside a document.

HTML Equivalent   <blockquote>

Object Model Reference

[window.]document.getElementById("*elementID*")

Object-Specific Properties

  cite

Object-Specific Methods

None.

Object-Specific Events

None.

cite

IE 5(Mac)/6(Win) NN n/a Moz all Saf all Op 7 DOM 1

Read/Write

Provides a URL pointing to an online source document from which the quotation is taken. This is not in any way a mechanism for copying or extracting content from another document. No mainstream browser does anything special with this information.

Value   Any valid URL to a document on the World Wide Web, including absolute or relative URLs.

Default   None.

body

IE 4 NN n/a Moz all Saf all Op 7 DOM 1

The body object reflects the body element, which is distinct from the document object. The body object refers to just the element and its nested content. There can be only one body element in an HTML page, so both the IE and W3C DOMs provide a shortcut reference to the object, document.body. Event handlers listed here appear as attributes in the <body> tag, but in truth are document-level events (best referenced in property form as document. *eventName*). While IE for the Mac doesn't share the sets of client and scroll properties with all element objects, those properties are defined for the body object.

In its effort to institute the standards-compatible mode in IE 6 for Windows (see the DOCTYPE element in Chapter 1), Microsoft has rendered useless the old trick of using the body element's clientHeight and clientWidth properties to obtain the equivalent of Netscape's window.innerHeight and window.innerWidth properties. In standards-compatibility mode (where document.compatMode == "CSS1Compat"), you must use the html element's clientHeight and clientWidth properties to find these values. Use these effective reference shortcuts:

```
document.body.parentNode.clientHeight
document.body.parentNode.clientWidth
```

Most properties unique to the body element affect presentation aspects, which are better controlled through CSS rules applied to the body selector.

HTML Equivalent   <body>

Object Model Reference

[window.]document.body

Object-Specific Properties

aLink	background	bgColor	bgProperties	bottomMargin
leftMargin	link	noWrap	rightMargin	scroll
text	topMargin	vLink		

Object-Specific Methods

createControlRange( )   createTextRange( )

Object-Specific Methods

Event	IE (Win)	Mozilla	Safari	Opera	W3C DOM
afterprint	•	—	—	—	—
beforeprint	•	—	—	—	—
beforeunload	•	—	—	—	—
load	•	•	•	•	•
select	—	•	•	—	—
unload	•	•	•	•	•

aLink   IE 4 NN n/a Moz all Saf all Op 7 DOM 1

Read/Write

Indicates a color of a hypertext link as it is being clicked. The color is applied to the link text or border around an image or object embedded within an a element. See also link and vLink properties for unvisited and visited link colors. The deprecated but backward-compatible version of this property is the alinkColor property of the document object. Largely superceded in modern practice by the :active pseudo-class.

Example   document.body.aLink = "green";

Value   A hexadecimal triplet or plain-language color name. See Appendix A for acceptable plain-language color names.

Default   #0000FF

background

Read/Write

Provides the URL of the background image for the entire document. If you set a bgColor to the element as well, the color appears if the image fails to load; otherwise, the image overlays the color.

Example

```
document.body.background = "images/watermark.jpg";
```

Value Complete or relative URL to the background image file.

Default None.

bgColor

Read/Write

Provides the background color of the element. Even if the bgcolor attribute or bgColor property is set with a plain-language color name, the returned value is always a hexadecimal triplet.

Example `document.body.bgColor = "yellow";`

Value A hexadecimal triplet or plain-language color name. See Appendix A for acceptable plain-language color names.

Default Varies with browser and operating system.

bgProperties

Read/Write

Specifies whether the background image remains in a fixed position or scrolls as a user scrolls the page. When the background image is set to remain in a fixed position, scrolled content flows past the background image very much like film credits roll past a background image on the screen.

Example `document.body.bgProperties = "fixed";`

Value An empty string (indicating the normal scrolling behavior) or the case-insensitive constant string fixed.

Default Empty string.

bottomMargin

Read/Write

Indicates the amount of blank space between the very end of content and the bottom of a scrollable page. The setting has no visual effect if the length of the content or size of the window does not cause the window to scroll. The default value is for the end of content to be flush with the end of the document, but in the Macintosh version of Internet Explorer, there is about a 10-pixel margin visible even when the property is set to zero. Larger sizes are reflected properly. This property offers somewhat of a shortcut or alternative to setting the `marginBottom` style sheet property for the body element object.

Example   `document.body.bottomMargin = 20;`

Value   An integer value (zero or greater) of the number of pixels of clear space at the bottom of the document.

Default   0

leftMargin

IE 4 NN n/a Moz n/a Saf n/a Op n/a DOM n/a

Read/Write

Provides the width in pixels of the left margin of the body element in the browser window or frame. By default, the browser inserts a small margin to keep content from abutting the left edge of the window. Setting the property to an empty string is the same as setting it to zero.

Example   `document.body.leftMargin = 16;`

Value   Integer of pixel count.

Default   10 (Windows); 8 (Macintosh).

link

IE 4 NN n/a Moz all Saf all Op 7 DOM 1

Read/Write

Indicates the color of a hypertext link that has not been visited (that is, the URL of the link is not in the browser's cache). This is one of three states for a link: unvisited, active, and visited. The color is applied to the link text or border around an image or object embedded within an element. This property has the same effect as setting the document object's `linkColor` property. Largely superceded in modern practice by the `:link` pseudo-class.

Example   `document.body.link = "#00FF00";`

Value   A hexadecimal triplet or plain-language color name. See Appendix A for acceptable plain-language color names.

Default   #0000FF

noWrap

IE 4 NN n/a Moz n/a Saf n/a Op n/a DOM n/a

Read/Write

Specifies whether the browser should render the body content as wide as necessary to display a line of nonbreaking text on one line. Abuse of this attribute can force the user into a great deal of inconvenient horizontal scrolling of the page to view all of the content.

Example   `document.body.noWrap = "true";`

Value   Boolean value: `true` | `false`.

Default   `false`

rightMargin

IE 4　NN *n/a*　Moz *n/a*　Saf *n/a*　Op *n/a*　DOM *n/a*

Read/Write

Provides the width in pixels of the right margin of the body element in the browser window or frame. By default, the browser inserts a small margin to keep content from abutting the right edge of the window (except on the Macintosh). Setting the property to an empty string is the same as setting it to zero.

Example　　　　document.body.leftMargin = 16;

Value　　　　Integer of pixel count.

Default　　　　10 (Windows); 0 (Macintosh).

scroll

IE 4　NN *n/a*　Moz *n/a*　Saf *n/a*　Op *n/a*　DOM *n/a*

Read/Write

Specifies whether the window (or frame) displays scrollbars when the content exceeds the window size. If your document specifies a standards-compatible DOCTYPE definition (see Chapter 1), the scroll property does not respond to changes for the body element. Nor does the html element object gain this property, as Microsoft's developer documentation purports.

Example　　　　document.body.scroll = "no";

Value　　　　Not exactly a Boolean value. Requires one of the following string values: yes | no | auto.

Default　　　　yes

text

IE 4　NN *n/a*　Moz *all*　Saf *all*　Op *7*　DOM *1*

Read/Write

Indicates the color of text for the entire document body. Equivalent to the foreground color, and generally superceded in practice by the CSS color property..

Example　　　　document.body.text = "darkred";

Value　　　　A hexadecimal triplet or plain-language color name. See Appendix A for acceptable plain-language color names.

Default　　　　Browser default (user customizable).

topMargin

IE 4　NN *n/a*　Moz *n/a*　Saf *n/a*　Op *n/a*　DOM *n/a*

Read/Write

Provides the width in pixels of the top margin of the body element in the browser window or frame. By default, the browser inserts a small margin to keep content from abutting the top edge of the window. Setting the property to an empty string is the same as setting it to zero.

Example	`document.body.topMargin = 16;`
Value	Integer of pixel count.
Default	15 (Windows); 8 (Macintosh).

vLink

Indicates the color of a hypertext link that has been visited recently. The color is applied to the link text or border around an image or object embedded within an a element. See also link and aLink properties for unvisited and clicked link colors. The deprecated but backward-compatible version of this property is the vlinkColor property of the document object. Largely superceded in modern practice by the :vlink pseudo-class.

Example	`document.body.vLink = "gold";`
Value	A hexadecimal triplet or plain-language color name. See Appendix A for acceptable plain-language color names.
Default	Varies with browser and operating system.

createControlRange( )

When content of an element is in user editing mode, this method creates a controlRange collection—a collection of all contiguous elements currently selected.

Returned Value	controlRange collection.
Parameters	None.

createTextRange( )

Creates a TextRange object from the rendered text content of the current element. See the TextRange object for details.

Returned Value	TextRange object.
Parameters	None.

br

The br object reflects the br element.

HTML Equivalent   `<br>`

Object Model Reference
`[window.]document.getElementById("elementID")`

Object-Specific Properties

```
clear
```

Object-Specific Methods
None.

Object-Specific Events
None.

clear

IE 4   NN n/a   Moz all   Saf all   Op 7   DOM 1

Read/Write

Tells the browser how to treat the next line of text following a br element if the current text is wrapping around a floating image or other object. The value you use depends on the side of the page to which one or more inline images are pegged and how you want the next line of text to be placed in relation to those images.

Example	document.getElementById("specialBreak").clear = "all";
Value	Case-insensitive string of any of the following constants: all | left | none | right.
Default	none

button

IE 4   NN n/a   Moz all   Saf all   Op 7   DOM 1

The button object reflects the button element. See the discussion of the button element in Chapter 1 to see how it differs from the input element of type button. Opera 9 implements numerous properties and methods for its Web Forms 2.0 support.

HTML Equivalent   <button>

Object Model Reference
[window.]document.getElementById("elementID")

Object-Specific Properties

action	autofocus	dataFld	dataFormatAs	dataSrc
enctype	form	forms	htmlTemplate	labels
method	name	replace	status	target
type	validationMessage	validity	value	willValidate

Object-Specific Methods

checkValidity( )	createTextRange( )	dispatchChange( )
dispatchFormChange( )	setCustomValidity( )	

Object-Specific Event Properties
None.

action

Web Forms 2.0 extension that allows a submission of the enclosing form to a URI different from the regular form when the button element is clicked (and its type is set to submit).

Example	document.getElementById("myButton").action = "redirect.php";
Value	URI string.
Default	None.

autofocus

Web Forms 2.0 extension that brings focus to the element after the page loads. Should be assigned to only one form control element per page. The button's type must be set to submit.

Example	document.getElementById("myButton").autofocus = true;
Value	Boolean: true | false.
Default	false

dataFld

Used with IE data binding to associate a remote data source column name to a button object's label. A datasrc attribute must also be set for the element. Setting both the dataFld and dataSrc properties to empty strings breaks the binding between element and data source.

Example	document.getElementById("myButton").dataFld = "linkURL";
Value	Case-sensitive identifier of the data source column.
Default	None.

dataFormatAs

Used with IE data binding, this property advises the browser whether the source material arriving from the data source is to be treated as plain text or as tagged HTML.

Example	document.getElementById("myButton").dataFormatAs = "html";
Value	String constant values: text | html.
Default	text

dataSrc

IE 4 NN n/a Moz n/a Saf n/a Op n/a DOM n/a

Read/Write

Used with IE data binding to specify the ID of the page's object element that loads the data source object for remote data access. Content from the data source is specified via the datafld attribute in the button element. Setting both the dataFld and dataSrc properties to empty strings breaks the binding between element and data source.

Example	document.getElementById("myButton").dataSrc = "DBSRC3";
Value	Case-sensitive identifier of the object element.
Default	None.

enctype

IE n/a NN n/a Moz n/a Saf n/a Op 9 DOM n/a

Read/Write

Web Forms 2.0 extension that allows (in concert with other properties, such as action) a submission of the enclosing form to a URI and enclosure MIME type different from the regular form when the button element is clicked (and its type is set to submit).

Example	document.getElementById("myButton").enctype = "text/plain";
Value	MIMEtype string.
Default	None.

form

IE 4 NN n/a Moz all Saf all Op 7 DOM 1

Read-only

Returns a reference to the form element that contains the current element (if any). In the Web Forms 2.0 environment, you can reassign a button to be associated with a different form via the setAttribute( ) method.

Example	var theForm = event.srcElement.form;
Value	Object reference.
Default	None.

forms

IE n/a NN n/a Moz n/a Saf n/a Op 9 DOM n/a

Read-only

Web Forms 2.0 extension that returns an array (NodeList) of references to form objects with which the current button element is associated.

Example	var formList = document.getElementById("myButton").forms;
Value	Array.
Default	One-item array with a reference to any enclosing form element.

htmlTemplate

Web Forms 2.0 extension that returns a reference to the element object (a RepetitionElement object) whose ID matches that of the current button element's template attribute (which must be set for this property to be anything other than null).

Example
var repeatTemplate = document.getElementById("myButton").htmlTemplate;

Value	Element object reference.
Default	null

labels

Web Forms 2.0 extension that returns an array (HTMLCollection) of references to label element objects associated with the current button element.

Example	var allLabels = document.getElementById("myButton").labels;
Value	Array of label element object references.
Default	Empty array.

method

Web Forms 2.0 extension (when used with other extensions, such as the action attribute) that allows a submission for the enclosing form to a URI different and even method from the regular form when the button element is clicked (and its type is set to submit).

Example	document.getElementById("myButton").method = "get";
Value	String of method type.
Default	get

name

This is the identifier associated with the element when used as a form control. The value of this property is submitted as one-half of the name/value pair when the form is submitted to the server. Names are hidden from user view, since control labels are assigned via other means, depending on the control type. Form control names may also be used by script references to the objects.

Example	document.forms[0].compName.name = "company";

Alphabetical DOM Reference

Value	Case-sensitive identifier that follows the rules of identifier naming: it may contain no whitespace, cannot begin with a numeral, and should avoid punctuation except for the underscore character.
Default	None.

replace

Web Forms 2.0 extension that associates instructions to a submission form control with how to process the data returned from the server after the form is submitted. The choice is whether the response replaces the original document in the browser (the default) or the browser should apply returned values to the form, rather than retrieve initial form data (if a URL is assigned to the data attribute of the form element).

Example	`document.getElementById("myButton").replace = "values";`
Value	One of two constant values: document | values.
Default	document

status

Unlike the status property of other types of form controls, the property has no visual or functional impact on the button.

Value	Boolean value: true | false; or null.
Default	null

target

Web Forms 2.0 extension that allows (in concert with other attributes, such as action) the page returned from a submission of the enclosing form to appear in a window or frame different from the destination of the page returned from regular form when the button element is clicked (and its type is set to submit).

Example	`document.getElementById("myButton").target = "_blank";`
Value	Frame or window name as a string.
Default	None (signifying the current window or frame).

type

Specifies whether the button element is specified as a button, reset, or submit style button. Web Forms 2.0 also adds types that facilitate control of repetition blocks.

Example
```
if (evt.target.type == "button") {
    // process button element
}
```

Value For all supporting browsers, one of the three constants (as a string): button | reset | submit. For browsers supporting Web Forms 2.0, additional string constants: add | move-down | move-up | remove.

Default button

validationMessage

IE *n/a* NN *n/a* Moz *n/a* Saf *n/a* Op 9 DOM *n/a*

Read-only

Web Forms 2.0 extension that returns a browser-generated message if the form control fails to validate according to its specifications. This property is meant more for text-oriented form controls, where an empty string means that the entry validates properly. For a button element, this property is always an empty string.

Value Empty string.

Default Empty string.

validity

IE *n/a* NN *n/a* Moz *n/a* Saf *n/a* Op 9 DOM *n/a*

Read-only

Web Forms 2.0 extension that returns a ValidityState object. For a button element, all members of the returned object are false, except for the valid property, which is true. See the ValidityState object.

Value ValidityState object.

Default ValidityState object.

value

IE 4 NN *n/a* Moz *all* Saf *all* Op 7 DOM 1

Read-only

Provides the current value associated with the form control that is submitted with the name/value pair for the element. Unlike the button-type input element object, this value property's value is unseen by the user; the label is set by the element's content (innerHTML property or nested node).

Example `var val = document.getElementById("myButton").value;`

Value String.

Default None.

Alphabetical DOM
Reference

willValidate

Web Forms 2.0 extension that returns a Boolean value indicating whether the form control element meets criteria for validating under the Web Forms 2.0 mechanism. A button element is not one of the correct types, and therefore always returns false.

Value	Boolean value: true	false.
Default	false

checkValidity( )

Web Forms 2.0 method that returns a Boolean value representing whether the form control element meets its validity criteria—ultimately, whether the validity.valid property is true. Because that value is always true for a button element, the checkValidity( ) method always returns true.

Returned Value	Boolean value: true	false.
Parameters	None.

createTextRange( )

Creates a TextRange object containing the button's label text. See the TextRange object.

Returned Value	TextRange object.
Parameters	None.

dispatchChange( ), dispatchFormChange( )

Web Forms 2.0 methods that fire the change and formchange events on the current element. You could, for example "convert" a click event to a change or formchange event by having the onclick event handler invoke either method.

Returned Value	None.
Parameters	None.

setCustomValidity( )
setCustomValidity([*errorString*])

Web Forms 2.0 method that sets the customError Boolean value of the validity property (itself a ValidityState object). This method has no effect on button elements and throws a NOT_SUPPORTED_ERR error.

Returned Value	None.

Parameters

errorString

If null or an empty string, the parameter resets the validity object's customError property, signifying the form control is not valid. An error string is to be remembered by the browser (during the current session) so that it displays the string upon subsequent validation failures.

canvas

The canvas object reflects the canvas element (as defined in the Web Applications 1.0 specification of the WebHypertext Application Technology Working Group (WHATWG). This object is simply the DOM element within the document tree. To perform graphic operations inside the canvas element space, first obtain the canvas rendering context object (via getContext( )), and then invoke methods of that object (see the CanvasRenderingContext2D object).

HTML Equivalent   <canvas>

Object Model Reference

[window.]document.getElementById("*elementID*")

Object-Specific Properties

height	width

Object-Specific Methods

getContext( )	toDataURL( )

Object-Specific Events

None.

height, width
Read/Write

Determine pixel dimensions of the graphical drawing space of the element. You can change the size of the element by script even if the dimensions are set by element attributes.

Example   document.getElementById("myCanvas").width = 450;

Value   Integer pixel values.

Default   0

getContext( )   IE *n/a* NN *n/a* Moz *1.8* Saf *2* Op *n/a* DOM *n/a*

getContext("*contextID*")

Returns a reference to the drawing space (called a context) in the element. See the CanvasRenderingContext2D object for the methods you can invoke to specify and draw lines and shapes in to appear in the canvas element.

Returned Value   Canvas context object (CanvasRenderingContext2D).

Parameters

contextID

> A string that identifies which drawing context to reference from the canvas element. Early generation implementations have only a two-dimensional context, named 2D.

toDataURL( )   IE *n/a* NN *n/a* Moz *1.8.1* Saf *n/a* Op *n/a* DOM *n/a*

toDataURL(["*MIMEType*"])

Returns a string in the form of a URI (starting with a data: protocol) containing the binary representation of the image rendered in the element. The default MIME type is image/png, but you can specify others, as supported by the browser (e.g., Mozilla also supports image/jpeg).

Returned Value   URI String.

Parameters

MIMEType

> A string denoting the MIME type for the data to be returned by the method.

CanvasRenderingContext2D   IE *n/a* NN *n/a* Moz *1.8* Saf *2* Op *n/a* DOM *n/a*

This object is returned by the canvas element object's getContext( ) method, and provides the drawing mechanism for the space within the rendered element. Properties and methods of this object control the drawing operations that only scripts can perform inside a canvas element. Eventually there will likely be other types of contexts that allow drawing in, say, three-dimensional space. This particular context is limited to two-dimensional drawing along x and y axes. Safari 2 internally calls this object Context2D.

As a simple example of a typical coding sequence, the following function draws a smiley face using arcs of two different line thicknesses:

```
function draw( ) {
    var canvas = document.getElementById("mycanvas");
    var ctxt = canvas.getContext("2d");
    ctxt.fillStyle = "rgb(255,225,0)";
    ctxt.beginPath( );
    ctxt.lineWidth = 2;
    ctxt.arc(75,75,50,0,Math.PI*2,true);
    ctxt.fill( );
    ctxt.moveTo(65,65);
    ctxt.arc(60,65,5,0,Math.PI*2,true);
    ctxt.moveTo(95,65);
```

```
        ctxt.arc(90,65,5,0,Math.PI*2,true);
        ctxt.stroke( ); // render arcs thus far
        ctxt.beginPath( );
        ctxt.moveTo(110,75);
        ctxt.lineWidth = 4;
        ctxt.arc(75,75,35,0,Math.PI,false);
        ctxt.stroke( ); // render thicker arc
    }
```

The range of properties and methods for drawing images and animations in a canvas context is large. Effective usage of some of the methods benefit from knowledge of color gradients, geometry, and even illustration techniques—all subjects beyond the scope of this reference. You can get a good introduction to how to apply the properties and methods discussed here at *http://developer.mozilla.org/en/docs/Canvas_tutorial*.

Object Model Reference

[window.]document.getElementById("*canvasElementID*").getContext("2D")

Object-Specific Properties

canvas	fillStyle	globalAlpha
globalCompositeOperation	lineCap	lineJoin
lineWidth	miterLimit	shadowBlur
shadowColor	shadowOffsetX	shadowOffsetY
strokeStyle		

Object-Specific Methods

arc( )	arcTo( )	beginPath( )
bezierCurveTo( )	clearRect( )	clip( )
closePath( )	createLinearGradient( )	createPattern( )
createRadialGradient( )	drawImage( )	fill( )
fillRect( )	lineTo( )	moveTo( )
quadraticCurveTo( )	rect( )	restore( )
rotate( )	save( )	scale( )
stroke( )	strokeRect( )	translate( )

Object-Specific Event Properties

None.

---

canvas

IE *n/a*   NN *n/a*   Moz *1.8*   Saf *2*   Op *n/a*   DOM *n/a*

Read-only

A reference to the canvas element from which the current context was derived. This is a convenience property that lets a reusable script refer back to the original element, perhaps to adjust the element's height or width properties.

Example   myContext.canvas.width = 450;

Alphabetical DOM
Reference

| **Value** | HTML element reference. |
| **Default** | Containing canvas element reference. |

fillStyle

IE n/a NN n/a Moz 1.8 Saf 2 Op n/a DOM n/a

Read/Write

Specifies the color, gradient, or pattern to be used to fill a shape.

Example	myContext.fillStyle = "rgb(255, 0, 0)";
Value	For a color, any valid CSS3 color value as a string, including color names, numeric RGB, and numeric RGBA (alpha for transparency) values. For gradient or pattern, any object created by the gradient or pattern generation methods of the canvas context object.
Default	rgb(0, 0, 0) (black).

globalAlpha

IE n/a NN n/a Moz 1.8 Saf 2 Op n/a DOM n/a

Read/Write

Specifies the transparency level for all shapes or images prior to their rendering.

Example	myContext.globalAlpha = 0.5;
Value	Floating point number from 0 to 1.0, with 0 being completely transparent and 1.0 being completely opaque.
Default	1.0 (opaque).

globalCompositeOperation

IE n/a NN n/a Moz 1.8 Saf 2 Op n/a DOM n/a

Read/Write

Specifies the type of masking (if any) between a new shape (to be rendered after setting the property) and existing content within the canvas context.

Example	myContext.globalCompositeOperation = "destination-in";
Value	One of 12 string constants: copy | darker | destination-atop | destination-in | destination-out | destination-over | lighter | source-atop | source-in | source-out | source-over
Default	source-over (new shapes are drawn atop existing content with no clipping).

lineCap

IE n/a NN n/a Moz 1.8 Saf 2 Op n/a DOM n/a

Read/Write

Specifies the way endpoints of lines are to be rendered. By default, a line ends with a square edge at the endpoint coordinates specified by a method such as lineTo( ). But lines can also be drawn so that the ends are rendered with filled semicircles (whose radius is one-half the line width) or a rectangle (whose height is one-half the line width). These latter two styles cause the line cap to render slightly beyond the endpoint coordinates for the extra caps.

Example myContext.lineCap = "round";

Value One of three string constants: butt | round | square.

Default butt

lineJoin
IE *n/a* NN *n/a* Moz *1.8* Saf *2* Op *n/a* DOM *n/a*
Read/Write

Specifies the way to render the meeting points of two lines. By default, two lines meet in a miter joint such that the outer edges of the lines meet at one point. But line can also meet with a rounded or beveled joint.

Example myContext.lineJoin = "bevel";

Value One of three string constants: bevel | miter | round.

Default miter

lineWidth
IE *n/a* NN *n/a* Moz *1.8* Saf *2* Op *n/a* DOM *n/a*
Read/Write

Specifies the thickness of a line to be drawn for a shape. The unit of measure is canvas coordinate space units (typically pixels). Note that when a method draws a line according to coordinates, the coordinates are applied to the centerline of the line, which may cause a wide line to position, say, a rectangle drawn with the fillRect( ) method to be positioned slightly differently than you expect.

Example myContext.lineWidth = 5;

Value Positive floating-point number.

Default 1.0

miterLimit
IE *n/a* NN *n/a* Moz *1.8* Saf *2* Op *n/a* DOM *n/a*
Read/Write

Specifies the ratio of the miter length (the distance from the inside joint to the outside joint).

Example myContext.miterLimit = 17.5;

Value Positive floating point number.

Default 10.0

shadowBlur

IE *n/a* NN *n/a* Moz *n/a* Saf *2* Op *n/a* DOM *n/a*
Read/Write

Specifies the number of coordinate space units adjacent to a shape that is to be covered by a shadow.

Example	myContext.shadowBlur = 3;
Value	Positive floating point number.
Default	1.0

shadowColor

IE *n/a* NN *n/a* Moz *n/a* Saf *2* Op *n/a* DOM *n/a*
Read/Write

Specifies the color to be used for a shape's shadow.

Example	myContext.shadowColor = "rgb(90, 90, 90)";
Value	CSS3-compatible color specification as a string.
Default	black

shadowOffsetX, shadowOffsetY

IE *n/a* NN *n/a* Moz *n/a* Saf *2* Op *n/a* DOM *n/a*
Read/Write

Specify the horizontal (x) and vertical (y) distances in coordinate space units of the shadow in relation to the shapes about to be drawn. Positive values are up and to the right; negative values are down and to the left.

Example	myContext.shadowOffsetX = 5;
Value	Positive or negative floating point number.
Default	0

strokeStyle

IE *n/a* NN *n/a* Moz *1.8* Saf *2* Op *n/a* DOM *n/a*
Read/Write

Specifies the color, gradient, or pattern to be used to draw lines or the outlines of shapes.

Example	myContext.strokeStyle = "rgb(255, 0, 0)";
Value	For a color, any valid CSS3 color value as a string, including color names, numeric rgb, and numeric rgba (alpha for transparency) values. For gradient or pattern, any object created by the gradient or pattern generation methods of the canvas context object.
Default	rgb(0, 0, 0) (black).

arc( )

arc(*x, y, radius, startAngle, endAngle, counterClockwiseFlag*)

Specifies an arc to be drawn in the canvas context from the current point in the path. The arc is drawn along a path defined by two endpoints measured as angles (in radians) around the x,y origin. As with all path-related methods, this method belongs between a beginPath( ) and a stroke( ) method call.

Returned Value   None.

Parameters

x, y
> Horizontal (x) and vertical (y) coordinates (in canvas coordinate units as number values) of the center point of the circle defined by the arc.

radius
> Length, in canvas coordinate units as a number value, of the radius of the circle of which the arc is a part.

startAngle, endAngle
> Points along the circle where the arc begins and ends, specified in radians as number values.

counterClockwiseFlag
> Boolean value indicating the direction of the arc from start to end: true for counter-clockwise; false for clockwise.

arcTo( )

arc(*x1, y1, x2, y2, radius*)

Specifies an arc to be drawn in the canvas context from the current point in the path. The arc is drawn along a path that has one point tangent to the line from the current position to point (*x1, y1*), one point tangent to the line from from the point (*x1, y1*) to the point (*x2, y2*), and that has radius *radius*.

Returned Value   None.

Parameters

x1, y1
> Horizontal (x) and vertical (y) coordinates (in canvas coordinate units as number values) of the start point of the arc.

x2, y2
> Horizontal (x) and vertical (y) coordinates (in canvas coordinate units as number values) of the endpoint of the arc.

radius
> Length, in canvas coordinate units as a number value, of the radius of the circle of which the arc is a part.

beginPath( )   IE *n/a* NN *n/a* Moz *1.8* Saf *2* Op *n/a* DOM *n/a*

Resets the context's path list to empty and moves the pointer to 0, 0 to get ready to accept new path specifications for another shape. This method is automatically invoked when the context is first created.

Returned Value   None.

Parameters   None.

bezierCurveTo( )   IE *n/a* NN *n/a* Moz *1.8.1* Saf *2* Op *n/a* DOM *n/a*

bezierCurveTo(cp1x, cp1y, cp2x, cp2y, x, y)

Specifies a cubic Bézier curve to be drawn in the canvas context from the current point in the path to an endpoint specified by *x* and *y*. The precise shape of the curve is guided by two control point coordinates, one for the start point (*cp1x*, *cp1y*), the other for the endpoint (*cp2x*, *cp2y*).

Returned Value   None.

Parameters

cp1x, cp1y

> Horizontal (x) and vertical (y) coordinates (in canvas coordinate units as number values) of the control point that influences the shape of the curve at the start point.

cp2x, cp2y

> Horizontal (x) and vertical (y) coordinates (in canvas coordinate units as number values) of the control point that influences the shape of the curve at the endpoint.

x, y

> Horizontal (x) and vertical (y) coordinates (in canvas coordinate units as number values) of the endpoint of the curve.

clearRect( )   IE *n/a* NN *n/a* Moz *1.8.1* Saf *2* Op *n/a* DOM *n/a*

clearRect(x, y, width, height)

Erases the canvas context for the region specified by parameters. You can selectively erase multiple rectangular regions, or clear the entire canvas. A generic script can obtain the size of the canvas via the canvas.height and canvas.width properties.

Returned Value   None.

Parameters

x, y

> Horizontal (x) and vertical (y) coordinates (in canvas coordinate units as number values) of the top-left corner of the rectangle to clear.

width, height

> Width and height (in canvas coordinate units as number values) of the rectangle to be cleared. Neither value can be zero.

clip( )   IE *n/a* NN *n/a* Moz *1.8.1* Saf *2* Op *n/a* DOM *n/a*

After establishing a path through other methods, invoke clip( ) to create a clipping region for the canvas context. Thereafter, new shapes will appear only within the clipping region. Clipping regions can be any shape you create using the various path methods.

Returned Value   None.

Parameters   None.

closePath( )   IE *n/a* NN *n/a* Moz *1.8.1* Saf *2* Op *n/a* DOM *n/a*

Draws a straight line between the current path point and the first point of the path.

Returned Value   None.

Parameters   None.

createLinearGradient( )   IE *n/a* NN *n/a* Moz *1.8.1* Saf *2* Op *n/a* DOM *n/a*
createLinearGradient(*x0, y0, x1, y1*)

Creates and returns a CanvasGradient object (assignable to a context's fillStyle and strokeStyle properties) for a straight line gradient. A linear gradient has a start and endpoint within the context space, specified as parameters to the method. Once you have the gradient object, you can then assign colors to various points along the length of the gradient via the addColorStop( ) method of a gradient object. For example, the following code sequence creates a linear gradient that transitions from white to red along a diagonal starting at the top-left corner of the context, extending to 200 pixels down and across:

```
var ctxt = document.getElementById("mycanvas").getContext("2d");
var gradient = ctxt.createLinearGradient(0, 0, 200, 200);
gradient.addColorStop(0, "white");
gradient.addColorStop(1, "red");
ctxt.fillStyle = gradient;
ctxt.fillRect(0, 0, 200, 200);
```

The first parameter of addColorStop( ) is a floating-point number between 0 (the start point of the gradient) and 1 (the endpoint of the gradient). You can specify multiple color stops along the way.

Returned Value   CanvasGradient object.

Parameters

x0, y0
   Horizontal (x) and vertical (y) coordinates (in canvas coordinate units as number values) of the start point of the gradient.

x1, y1
   Horizontal (x) and vertical (y) coordinates (in canvas coordinate units as number values) of the endpoint of the gradient.

createPattern( )   IE *n/a*   NN *n/a*   Moz *1.8.1*   Saf *2*   Op *n/a*   DOM *n/a*

createPattern(*imageObjectRef*, "*repeatStyle*")

Creates and returns a CanvasPattern object (assignable to a context's fillStyle and strokeStyle properties) whose original image becomes either a shape fill pattern or stroke pattern. The image object to be passed as a first parameter can be created through familiar DOM techniques, as follows:

```
var img = new Image( );
img.src = "myImage.png";
var pattern = ctxt.createPattern(img, "repeat");
```

Then assign the resulting object to the context's fillStyle or strokeStyle properties.

Returned Value   CanvasPattern object.

Parameters

imageObjectRef

> Reference to an image object whose src property points to an image URL. Some browsers may also support assigning an image object that has been returned by the canvas element's dataToURL( ) method.

repeatStyle

> One of four constant strings: no-repeat | repeat | repeat-x | repeat-y.

createRadialGradient( )   IE *n/a*   NN *n/a*   Moz *1.8.1*   Saf *2*   Op *n/a*   DOM *n/a*

createRadialGradient(*x0, y0, r0, x1, y1, r1*)

Creates and returns a CanvasGradient object (assignable to a context's fillStyle and strokeStyle properties) for a gradient that extends outward from a center circle or point to a distance specified by radius values measured from the center point. A radial gradient has a start and endpoint within the context space, specified as parameters to the method. Once you have the gradient object, you can then assign colors to various points along the length of the gradient via the addColorStop( ) method of a gradient object.

Returned Value   CanvasGradient object.

Parameters

x0, y0

> Horizontal (x) and vertical (y) coordinates (in canvas coordinate units as number values) of the start point of the gradient.

x1, y1

> Horizontal (x) and vertical (y) coordinates (in canvas coordinate units as number values) of the endpoint of the gradient.

r0, r1

> Radius distances (in canvas coordinate units as number values) from the center point to the location of the start point (r0) and the endpoint (r1).

drawImage( )

```
drawImage(imageOrCanvas, dx, dy)
drawImage(imageOrCanvas, dx, dy, dw, dh)
drawImage(imageOrCanvas, sx, sy, sw, sh, dx, dy, dw, dh)
```

Copies an imported (or generated) image into the canvas context at a designated location within the context. The method has three different versions, depending on the number of parameters you specify.

Returned Value   None.

Parameters

dx, dy

> Horizontal (x) and vertical (y) coordinates (in canvas coordinate units as number values) of the top-left corner of the image within the canvas context (referred to as the destination).

dw, dh

> Width and height (in canvas coordinate units as number values) of the image.

sx, sy

> Horizontal (x) and vertical (y) coordinates (in canvas coordinate units as number values) of the top-left corner of the image scaled within the original image space.

dw, dh

> Width and height (in canvas coordinate units as number values) of the scaled image.

fill( )

Fills spaces defined by the current path, using the color, gradient, or pattern assigned to the `fillStyle` property.

Returned Value   None.

Parameters   None.

fillRect( )

```
fillRect(x, y, width, height)
```

Paints the region specified by parameters with the color, gradient, or pattern assigned to the `fillStyle` property.

Returned Value   None.

Parameters

x, y

> Horizontal (x) and vertical (y) coordinates (in canvas coordinate units as number values) of the top-left corner of the rectangle to paint.

width, height

> Width and height (in canvas coordinate units as number values) of the rectangle to be painted. Neither value can be zero.

lineTo( )
IE *n/a* NN *n/a* Moz *1.8.1* Saf *2* Op *n/a* DOM *n/a*

lineTo(*x*, *y*)

Adds a line to the path from the current path point to the coordinates specified as parameters, after which the current point is the passed coordinates.

Returned Value   None.

Parameters

x, y

> Horizontal (x) and vertical (y) coordinates (in canvas coordinate units as number values) of the endpoint of the line.

moveTo( )
IE *n/a* NN *n/a* Moz *1.8.1* Saf *2* Op *n/a* DOM *n/a*

moveTo(*x*, *y*)

Moves the current point to the specified coordinate position, and also begins a subpath using the point as the starting position.

Returned Value   None.

Parameters

x, y

> Horizontal (x) and vertical (y) coordinates (in canvas coordinate units as number values) of the new position.

quadraticCurveTo( )
IE *n/a* NN *n/a* Moz *1.8.1* Saf *2.02* Op *n/a* DOM *n/a*

quadraticCurveTo(*cp1x*, *cp1y*, *x*, *y*)

Specifies a quadratic Bézier curve to be drawn in the canvas context from the current point in the path to an endpoint specified by *x* and *y*. The precise shape of the curve is guided by control point coordinates *cp1x* and *cp1y*.

Returned Value   None.

Parameters

cp1x, cp1y

> Horizontal (x) and vertical (y) coordinates (in canvas coordinate units as number values) of the control point that influences the shape of the curve relative to both the start and endpoints of the curve.

x, y

> Horizontal (x) and vertical (y) coordinates (in canvas coordinate units as number values) of the endpoint of the curve.

rect( )
IE *n/a* NN *n/a* Moz *1.8.1* Saf *2* Op *n/a* DOM *n/a*

rect(*x*, *y*, *width*, *height*)

Creates a separate subpath that defines a rectangle at the specified position and dimensions. The method then sets the current point to 0,0.

Returned Value   None.

Parameters

x, y

> Horizontal (x) and vertical (y) coordinates (in canvas coordinate units as number values) of the top-left corner of the rectangle path.

width, height

> Width and height (in canvas coordinate units as number values) of the rectangle path.

restore( )   IE *n/a* NN *n/a* Moz *1.8.1* Saf *2* Op *n/a* DOM *n/a*

Pops the topmost drawing from the internal drawing state stack. Use save( ) to push onto the stack.

Returned Value   None.

Parameters   None.

rotate( )   IE *n/a* NN *n/a* Moz *1.8.1* Saf *2* Op *n/a* DOM *n/a*

rotate(*angle*)

Has the effect of rotating the canvas context (called a transformation matrix), and should be invoked before drawing in the transformed state.

Returned Value   None.

Parameters

angle

> The clockwise rotation angle in radians.

save( )   IE *n/a* NN *n/a* Moz *1.8.1* Saf *2* Op *n/a* DOM *n/a*

Pushes the current state of the drawing onto an internal drawing state stack. Use restore( ) to pop from the stack.

Returned Value   None.

Parameters   None.

scale( )   IE *n/a* NN *n/a* Moz *1.8.1* Saf *2* Op *n/a* DOM *n/a*

scale(*x, y*)

Adjusts the scale of the canvas context by multiples specified for the horizontal and vertical axes.

Returned Value   None.

Alphabetical DOM
Reference

Parameters

x, y

Floating-point numbers representing the multiplication factor for scaling the context in the horizontal (x) and vertical (y) axes.

stroke( )   IE *n/a*   NN *n/a*   Moz *1.8.1*   Saf *2*   Op *n/a*   DOM *n/a*

Draws the current path in the canvas context, using the settings of the `lineJoin`, `lineWidth`, `miterLimit`, and `strokeStyle` properties.

Returned Value   None.

Parameters   None.

strokeRect( )   IE *n/a*   NN *n/a*   Moz *1.8.1*   Saf *2*   Op *n/a*   DOM *n/a*

`fillRect(x, y, width, height)`

Draws a rectangular outline in the parameter-driven location and dimensions using the values assigned to the `lineJoin`, `lineWidth`, `miterLimit`, and `strokeStyle` properties.

Returned Value   None.

Parameters

x, y

Horizontal (x) and vertical (y) coordinates (in canvas coordinate units as number values) of the top-left corner of the rectangle to paint.

width, height

Width and height (in canvas coordinate units as number values) of the rectangle to be painted.

translate( )   IE *n/a*   NN *n/a*   Moz *1.8.1*   Saf *2*   Op *n/a*   DOM *n/a*

`translate(x, y)`

Moves the origin point of the canvas context to the coordinates specified as parameters.

Returned Value   None.

Parameters

x, y

Floating-point numbers representing the offsets along the horizontal (x) and vertical (y) axes that define the new origin point of the canvas context.

caption   IE *4*   NN *n/a*   Moz *all*   Saf *all*   Op *7*   DOM *1*

The caption object reflects the caption element, which must always be nested inside a table element. IE/Mac implements the client and scroll property sets for this object.

HTML Equivalent   `<caption>`

Object Model Reference
[window.]document.getElementById("*elementID*")

Object-Specific Properties

align   vAlign

Object-Specific Methods
None.

Object-Specific Events
None.

align

Read/Write

Determines the position of the caption in the table. See the align attribute of the caption element in Chapter 1 for details on the interaction between the align and vAlign attributes and properties in IE for Windows. The W3C DOM uses the align property predominantly for placing the caption above or below the table.

Example   document.getElementById("myCaption").align = "bottom";

Value   Any of the following constants (as a string): bottom | left | right | top.

Default   top

vAlign

Read/Write

Specifies whether the table caption appears above or below the table.

Example   document.getElementById("tabCaption").vAlign = "bottom"

Value   Case-insensitive constant (as a string): bottom | top.

Default   top

cells

A collection of all td elements contained within a single tr element. Collection members are sorted in source code order.

Object Model Reference
document.getElementById("*rowID*").cells

Object-Specific Properties

length

cells

Object-Specific Methods

item( )   namedItem( )   tags( )   urns( )

Object-Specific Events
None.

length

Read-only

Returns the number of elements in the collection.

Example
var howMany = document.getElementById("myTable").rows[0].cells.length;

Value   Integer.

item( )

item(*index*[, *subindex*]) item(*index*)

Returns a single td object or collection of td objects corresponding to the element matching the index value (or, optionally in IE, the index and subindex values).

Returned Value   One td object or collection (array) of td objects. If there are no matches to the parameters, the returned value is null.

Parameters
index
When the parameter is a zero-based integer, the returned value is a single element corresponding to the specified item in source code order (nested within the current element); when the parameter is a string (IE only), the returned value is a collection of elements whose id properties match that string.

subindex
In IE only, if you specify a string value for the first parameter, you can use the second parameter to specify a zero-based index that retrieves the specified element from the collection whose id properties match the first parameter's string value.

namedItem( )

namedItem("*ID*")

Returns a single td object or collection of td objects corresponding to the element matching the parameter string value.

Returned Value   One td object or collection (array) of td objects. If there are no matches to the parameters, the returned value is null.

Parameters

ID

The string that contains the same value as the desired element's id attribute.

tags( )
IE *4*   NN *n/a*   Moz *n/a*   Saf *n/a*   Op *n/a*   DOM *n/a*

tags("*tagName*")

Returns a collection of objects (among all objects nested within the current collection) whose tags match the *tagName* parameter. Implemented in all IE collections (see the all. tags( ) method), but redundant for collections of the same element type.

urns( )
IE *5(Win)*   NN *n/a*   Moz *n/a*   Saf *n/a*   Op *n/a*   DOM *n/a*

urns(*URN*)

See the all.urns( ) method.

center
IE *4*   NN *n/a*   Moz *all*   Saf *all*   Op *7*   DOM *1*

The center object reflects the center element. The W3C DOM does not support the deprecated HTML 4 center element. For backward compatibility, Mozilla treats the element as earlier browsers do, but the scriptable element is treated as a span object, whose default text-align style is set to center.

HTML Equivalent   <center>

Object Model Reference

[window.]document.getElementById("*elementID*")

Object-Specific Properties

None.

Object-Specific Methods

None.

Object-Specific Events

None.

checkbox

See input.

CharacterData

See Text.

childNodes, NodeList　　　　　IE 4　NN n/a　Moz all　Saf all　Op 7　DOM 1

The object returned by the childNodes property of several W3C DOM objects is a collection (array) of references to Node objects that are immediate children of the current node object. In the W3C DOM structure, the abstract representation of this array is called the NodeList object, which shares some properties and methods of the IE childNodes object. Since both objects refer to the same parts of a document tree, they are treated here together. Collection members are sorted in source code order.

Object Model Reference
nodeReference.childNodes

Object-Specific Properties

length

Object-Specific Methods

item( )　　　　　　　　　　　　　　urns( )

Object-Specific Events
None.

length　　　　　　　　　　IE 4　NN n/a　Moz all　Saf all　Op 7　DOM 1
Read-only

Returns the number of nodes in the collection.

Example　　　　var howMany = document.getElementById("myTable").attributes.length;

Value　　　　　Integer.

item( )　　　　　　　　　　IE 5　NN n/a　Moz all　Saf all　Op 7　DOM 1
item(*index*)

Returns a single Node object corresponding to the element matching the index value.

Returned Value　　Reference to one Node object. If there is no match to the index value, the returned value is null. Unlike some other collections in IE, a string index value is not allowed for the childNodes object.

Parameters
index
　　A zero-based integer corresponding to the specified item in source code order (nested within the current node).

urns( )

urns(*URN*)

See the all.urns( ) method.

children

A collection of all elements contained in the current element. Note that unlike the childNodes collection, children counts only elements and not text nodes. Collection members are sorted in source code order. Internet Explorer lets you use array notation or parentheses to access a single element in the collection.

Object Model Reference

```
document.getElementById("elementID").children(i)
document.getElementById("elementID").children[i]
```

Object-Specific Properties

length

Object-Specific Methods

| item( ) | namedItem( ) | tags( ) | urns( ) |

Object-Specific Events

None.

length

Read-only

Returns the number of elements in the collection.

Example

```
var howMany = document.body.children.length;
```

Value   Integer.

item( )

item(*index*)

Returns an element object corresponding to the element matching the index value in source code order.

Returned Value   Reference to an element object. If there is no matches to the parameter, the returned value is null.

Parameters

index

A zero-based integer corresponding to the specified item in source code order (nested within the current element).

namedItem( )   IE 6 NN *n/a* Moz *n/a* Saf *all* Op 7 DOM *n/a*

namedItem(*IDOrName*)

Returns an element object or collection of objects corresponding to the element matching the parameter string value.

Returned Value   One element object or collection (array) of element objects. If there are no matches to the parameters, the returned value is null.

Parameters

IDOrName

The string that contains the same value as the desired element's id or name attribute.

tags( )   IE 4 NN *n/a* Moz *n/a* Saf *all* Op 7 DOM *n/a*

tags(*tagName*)

Returns a collection of objects (among all objects nested within the current collection) whose tags match the *tagName* parameter. Implemented in all IE collections (see the all. tags( ) method), but redundant for collections of the same element type.

urns( )   IE 5(Win) NN *n/a* Moz *n/a* Saf *n/a* Op *n/a* DOM *n/a*

urns(*URN*)

See the all.urns( ) method.

cite

See abbr.

clientInformation

See navigator.

clipboardData   IE 5(Win) NN *n/a* Moz *n/a* Saf *n/a* Op *n/a* DOM *n/a*

The clipboardData object (accessible as a property of a window or frame object) allows script access to the Windows system clipboard as a temporary container that scripts in IE 5 and later for Windows can use to transfer text data, particularly during script-controlled operations that simulate cutting, copying, and pasting, or that control dragging. Your script controls what data is stored in the clipboardData object, such as just the text of an element, an element's entire HTML, or the URL of an image. For example, a page for children could display simple icon images of several different kinds of animals. If the user starts dragging the dog icon, the script initiated by the img element's onDragStart event handler stores a custom attribute value of that element (perhaps the URL of a pretty dog photo) into the clipboardData object. When the user drops the icon into the designated area, the onDrop event handler's function reads the clipboardData object's data and loads the photo image into position on the page.

Data stored in this object survives navigation to other pages within the same domain and protocol. Therefore, you can use it to pass text data (including arrays that have been converted to strings by the Array.join( ) method) from one page to another without using cookies or location.search strings.

For more information on transferring data via this object and the event.dataTransfer object, visit *http://msdn.microsoft.com/workshop/author/datatransfer/overview.asp*.

HTML Equivalent   None.

Object Model Reference
[window.]clipboardData

Object-Specific Properties

dropEffect   effectAllowed

Object-Specific Methods

clearData( )   getData( )   setData( )

Object-Specific Events
None.

dropEffect, effectAllowed

IE *5(Win)* NN *n/a* Moz *n/a* Saf *n/a* Op *n/a* DOM *n/a*

Read/Write

These two properties belong to the clipboardData object by inheritance from the dataTransfer object, to which they genuinely apply. Ignore these properties for the clipboardData object.

clearData( )

IE *5(Win)* NN *n/a* Moz *n/a* Saf *n/a* Op *n/a* DOM *n/a*

clearData([*dataFormat*])

Removes data from the clipboardData object.

Returned Value   None.

Parameters

dataFormat

> An optional string specifying a single format for the data to be removed. Earlier plans to allow multiple data types appear to have fallen through. As of IE 6, the only reliable format is Text. Omitting the parameter removes all data of all types.

getData( )
IE *5(Win)* NN *n/a* Moz *n/a* Saf *n/a* Op *n/a* DOM *n/a*

getData(*dataFormat*)

Returns a copy of data from the clipboardData object. The clipboardData contents remain intact for subsequent reading in other script statements.

Returned Value   String.

Parameters

dataFormat

> A string specifying the format for the data to be read. Earlier plans to allow multiple data types appear to have fallen through. As of IE 6, the only reliable format is Text.

setData( )
IE *5(Win)* NN *n/a* Moz *n/a* Saf *n/a* Op *n/a* DOM *n/a*

setData(*dataFormat, stringData*)

Stores string data in the clipboardData object. Returns Boolean true if the assignment is successful

Returned Value   Boolean value: true | false.

Parameters

dataFormat

> A string specifying the format for the data to be read. Earlier plans to allow multiple data types appear to have fallen through. As of IE 6, the only reliable format is Text. While the method accepts URL as a format, reading a set value in that format is not successful.

stringData

> Any string value, including strings that contain HTML tags.

code

See abbr.

col
IE *4* NN *n/a* Moz *all* Saf *all* Op *7* DOM *1*

The col object reflects the col element. The element provides ways of assigning single or multiple adjacent columns to groups for convenience in assigning styles, widths, and other visual treatments to columns within a table.

HTML Equivalent   <col>

Object Model Reference
[window.]document.getElementById("*elementID*")

Object-Specific Properties

align	ch	chOff	span	vAlign
width				

Object-Specific Methods
None.

Object-Specific Events
None.

align

IE *4* NN *n/a* Moz *all* Saf *all* Op *7* DOM *1*

Read/Write

Defines the horizontal alignment of content within cells covered by the col element.

Example	document.getElementById("myCol").align = "center";
Value	Any of the three horizontal alignment constants: center | char | left | right.
Default	left

ch

IE *6* NN *n/a* Moz *all* Saf *all* Op *n/a* DOM *1*

Read/Write

Defines the text character used as an alignment point for text within a column or column group (reflecting the char attribute). This property is normally of value only for the align attribute set to "char". In practice, however, none of the supporting browsers respond to this property.

Example	document.getElementById("myCol").ch = ".";
Value	Single character string.
Default	None.

chOff

IE *6* NN *n/a* Moz *all* Saf *all* Op *n/a* DOM *1*

Read/Write

Defines the offset point at which the character specified by the char attribute is to appear within a cell. In practice, none of the supporting browsers respond to this property.

Example	document.getElementById("myCol").chOff = "80%";
Value	String value of the number of pixels or percentage (within the cell).
Default	None.

span

Read/Write

Provides the number of adjacent columns for which the element's attribute and style settings apply.

Example   document.getElementById("myCol").span = 2;

Value   Integer.

Default   1

vAlign

Read/Write

Provides the manner of vertical alignment of text within the column grouping's cells.

Example   document.getElementById("myCol").vAlign = "baseline";

Value   Case-insensitive constant (as a string): baseline | bottom | middle | top.

Default   middle

width

Read/Write

Provides the width in pixels of each column of the column grouping. Changes to these values are immediately reflected in reflowed content on the page.

Example   document.getElementById("myCol").width = 150;

Value   Integer.

Default   None.

colgroup

The colgroup object reflects the colgroup element, which provides ways of assigning multiple adjacent columns to groups for convenience in assigning styles, widths, and other visual treatments.

HTML Equivalent   <colgroup>

Object Model Reference

[window.]document.getElementById("*elementID*")

Object-Specific Properties

align	ch	chOff	span	vAlign
width				

Object-Specific Methods
None.

Object-Specific Events
None.

align

IE 4 NN *n/a* Moz *all* Saf *n/a* Op 7 DOM 1

Read/Write

Defines the horizontal alignment of content within cells covered by the colgroup element.

Example	document.getElementById("myColgroup").align = "center";
Value	Any of the three horizontal alignment constants: center | char | left | right.
Default	left

ch

IE 4 NN *n/a* Moz *all* Saf *n/a* Op *n/a* DOM 1

Read/Write

Defines the text character used as an alignment point for text within a column or column group (reflecting the char attribute). This property is normally of value only for the align attribute set to "char". In practice, none of the supporting browsers respond to this property.

Example	document.getElementById("myColgroup").ch = ".";
Value	Single character string.
Default	None.

chOff

IE 4 NN *n/a* Moz *all* Saf *n/a* Op *n/a* DOM 1

Read/Write

Defines the offset point at which the character specified by the char attribute is to appear within a cell. In practice, none of the supporting browsers respond to this property.

Example	document.getElementById("myColgroup").chOff = "80%";
Value	String value of the number of pixels or percentage (within the cell).
Default	None.

span

IE 4 NN *n/a* Moz *all* Saf *n/a* Op 7 DOM 1

Read/Write

Provides the number of adjacent columns for which the element's attribute and style settings apply.

Example	document.getElementById("myColgroup").span = 2;

Alphabetical DOM Reference

Value   Integer.

Default   1

vAlign   IE *4* NN *n/a* Moz *all* Saf *n/a* Op *7* DOM *1*

Read/Write

Provides the manner of vertical alignment of text within the column grouping's cells.

Example   `document.getElementById("myColgroup").vAlign = "baseline";`

Value   Case-insensitive constant (as a string): `baseline` | `bottom` | `middle` | `top`.

Default   `middle`

width   IE *4* NN *n/a* Moz *all* Saf *all* Op *7* DOM *1*

Read/Write

Provides the width in pixels of each column of the column grouping. Changes to these values are immediately reflected in reflowed content on the page.

Example   `document.getElementById("myColgroup").width = 150;`

Value   Integer.

Default   None.

comment, Comment   IE *4* NN *n/a* Moz *all* Saf *all* Op *7* DOM *1*

The comment object reflects the ! element in an HTML document. But in a W3C DOM environment, such as Mozilla, this object is not a genuine element in the context of the W3C DOM abstract model. Instead, the object is simply a special kind of node, whose nodeType value of 8 identifies it as a Comment node. A Comment node has the following inheritance chain in the DOM abstract model: Node->CharacterData->Comment. While a Comment node has special values automatically assigned to some of its properties (such as nodeValue), a Comment node has no properties or methods beyond the ones inherited from the Node and CharacterData objects. Node properties and methods are discussed earlier in this chapter among the shared items; CharacterData properties and methods are covered in detail with the Text object, which also inherits from CharacterData, and is more likely to be scripted.

To reference a comment element, use relative element or node properties. While IE provides an id property by virtue of its inheritance model, you cannot assign an identifier to the element via an id attribute. Such an element in IE does, however, have a tag name value of !. Therefore, you can reference an IE HTML comment element via the collection of elements returned by the document.all.tags("!") method. You can reference comment nodes in Mozilla only for comments delivered with the document within the body element, not the head. In Safari, you can reference only comment nodes added through scripting (e.g., via document.createComment( ) and any of the node insertion methods).

HTML Equivalent `<!--comment text-->`

Object Model Reference
nodeReference

Object-Specific Properties

data	length	text

Object-Specific Methods

appendData( )   deleteData( )   insertData( )   replaceData( )
substringData( )

Object-Specific Events
None.

---

data   IE 6   NN *n/a*   Moz *all*   Saf *all*   Op 7   DOM 1
Read/Write

Provides the text content of the comment. See Text.data.

---

length   IE 6   NN *n/a*   Moz *all*   Saf *all*   Op 7   DOM 1
Read-only

Provides the character count of the comment data. See Text.length.

---

text   IE 4   NN *n/a*   Moz *n/a*   Saf *n/a*   Op 7   DOM *n/a*
Read/Write

Provides the text content of the element. Due to the nature of this element in IE, the value of the text property is identical to the values of the innerHTML and outerHTML properties. Changes to this property do not affect the text of the comment as viewed in the browser's source code version of the document. This property is not available in IE 4/Macintosh. For modern cross-browser access, use the data property.

Example
```
document.all.tags("!")[4].text = "Replaced comment, but no one will know.";
```

Value   String.

Default   None.

---

appendData( ), deleteData( ), insertData( ), replaceData( ), substringData( )   IE 6   NN *n/a*   Moz *all*   Saf *all*   Op 7   DOM 1

Provide methods for manipulating comment text. See these methods in the Text object.

Context2D

See CanvasRenderingContext2D.

---

controlRange
IE 5(Win) NN n/a Moz n/a Saf n/a Op n/a DOM n/a

The controlRange object is a collection of element objects that had been selected from within an editable container (i.e., its contentEditable property is true), and created via the document.body.controlRange( ) or document.selection.createRange( ) methods. In a typical editing application, users can select whatever contiguous elements the editor allows within the container. A script can then iterate through the controlRange collection (perhaps filtering out elements such as img elements) and perform operations (including commands via the execCommand( ) method) on the elements within the collection. Microsoft has a demo of this feature at *http://msdn.microsoft.com/library/default.asp?url=/workshop/samples/author/dhtml/collections/controlrange.htm*.

Object Model Reference
controlRangeReference

Object-Specific Properties

length

Object-Specific Methods

add( )	addElement( )	execCommand( )
item( )	queryCommandEnabled( )	queryCommandIndeterm( )
queryCommandState( )	queryCommandSupported( )	queryCommandValue( )
remove( )	scrollIntoView( )	select( )

Object-Specific Events
None.

---

add( )
IE 5 NN n/a Moz n/a Saf all Op n/a DOM n/a

add(*elementRef*[, *index*])

Adds an element (from the createElement( ) method) to the current collection.

Returned Value   None.

Parameters
elementRef

> A fully formed element object reference, usually generated by the createElement( ) method.

index

> An optional integer indicating where in the collection the new element should be placed.

addElement( )   IE *5(Win)*   NN *n/a*   Moz *n/a*   Saf *all*   Op *n/a*   DOM *n/a*

add(*elementRef*)

Adds an element to the current collection. This method is specifically designed for the controlRange collection. The new element should be contiguous with existing elements in the collection if you intend to invoke execCommand( ) or select( ) methods.

Returned Value   None.

Parameters

elementRef
> A fully formed element object reference.

execCommand( )

See the TextRange.execCommand method for details.

item( )   IE *5(Win)*   NN *n/a*   Moz *n/a*   Saf *all*   Op *n/a*   DOM *n/a*

item(*index*)

Returns a single object from the collection.

Returned Value   One object reference. If there are no matches to the parameters, the returned value is null.

Parameters

index
> Zero-based integer.

queryCommandEnabled( ), queryCommandIndeterm( ), queryCommandState( ), queryCommandSupported( ), queryCommandValue( )

See the corresponding method description in the TextRange object for details.

remove( )   IE *5(Win)*   NN *n/a*   Moz *n/a*   Saf *all*   Op *n/a*   DOM *n/a*

remove(*index*)

Deletes an element from the current collection. Simply specify the zero-based index value of the element you wish to remove from the collection.

Returned Value   None.

Parameters

index
> A zero-based integer indicating which item in the collection should be deleted.

scrollIntoView( ) IE 5(Win) NN n/a Moz n/a Saf all Op n/a DOM n/a

See scrollIntoView( ) in the shared methods at the beginning of this chapter.

select( ) IE 5(Win) NN n/a Moz n/a Saf all Op n/a DOM n/a

Selects all the elements within the controlRange collection.

Returned Value   None.

Parameters   None.

CSSCharsetRule, CSSFontFaceRule, CSSImportRule, CSSMediaRule, CSSPageRule, CSSStyleRule, CSSUnknownRule

See CSSRule.

cssRule, CSSRule, rule IE 5 NN n/a Moz all Saf all Op 9 DOM 2

A style sheet rule object is a member of the collection of styleSheet objects in the document. The IE and W3C DOMs have different syntax for referencing each of these rule objects. For IE, the reference is via the rules collection (a single object being known as a rule object); for W3C, as implemented in IE 5 for the Macintosh, Mozilla, Safari, and Opera 9, the reference is via the cssRules collection (a single object being known as a cssRule object). Note that the cssRule object is not in the Windows version of IE through Version 7. Additionally, security restrictions built into IE 6 and 7 prevent scripts from accessing the rules collection of a styleSheet object. Therefore, even though properties and methods below show IE support, those properties and methods are not truly available, and cause "Access denied" security errors.

The W3C DOM abstract object of a cssRule is called the CSSRule object, but that form of the object name is important only to scripters who wish to modify the prototype properties and methods of the CSSRule object in Mozilla. The W3C DOM goes further to define special types of CSSRule objects for each of the @ rule types (CSSImportRule, CSSMediaRule, and so on—see the type property for a list of all types). A member of the cssRules collection can be any one of those types, and is identified as such by its type property. Each type has its own set of properties and/or methods that apply to that cssRule type. In the property and method listings below, observe the type(s) for which they apply. By and large, however, the rules you will script are of the CSSStyleRule type, which are the typical rules that have selectors pointing to various elements in a document.

Use scriptable access to a rule or cssRule object with caution. If you modify a rule's selector or style definition, the changes affect the entire document, and could, with a misplaced colon, ruin other rules in the document. To toggle among two or more styles for a single element, class, or element type, it is generally more reliable and efficient to use other techniques that work with multiple rules (swapping className assignments on elements) or multiple style sheets (enabling and disabling styleSheet objects). But for the sake of the completeness of the object model, the W3C DOM in particular provides full access to style sheet rule pieces if you absolutely need them.

Object Model Reference
```
document.styleSheets[i].rules[j]  // pre-IE 6
document.styleSheets[i].cssRules[j]
```

Object-Specific Properties

cssRules	cssText	encoding	href
media	parentRule	parentStyleSheet	readOnly
selectorText	style	styleSheet	type

Object-Specific Methods

deleteRule()	insertRule()

Object-Specific Events
None.

cssRules

IE *n/a* NN *n/a* Moz *all* Saf *all* Op 9 DOM 2

Read-only

Returns a collection of cssRule objects nested within an @media rule.

W3C DOM CSSRule Types
CSSMediaRule

Value	Reference to a cssRules collection object.
Default	Array of zero length.

cssText

IE *5(Mac)* NN *n/a* Moz *all* Saf *all* Op 9 DOM 2

Read/Write

Indicates the complete text of the style sheet rule, including selector and attribute name/value pairs inside curly braces. IE 6 for Windows provides no equivalent property. In supporting browsers, changes do not influence the object or rendering.

W3C DOM CSSRule Types
All.

Example
```
document.styleSheets[0].cssRules[2].cssText = "td {text-align:center}";
```

Value	String.
Default	None.

encoding

Read-only

Returns the character set code (e.g., ISO-8859-1 or UTF-8) associated with an @charset rule.

W3C DOM CSSRule Types
CSSCharsetRule

Value	String.
Default	None.

href

Read-only

Returns the URI of the external style sheet file imported via an @import rule.

W3C DOM CSSRule Types
CSSImportRule

Value	String.
Default	None.

media

Read-only

Returns the media type specified for an @import or @media rule.

W3C DOM CSSRule Types
CSSImportRule
CSSMediaRule

Value	String constant for media types supported by the browser (e.g., screen or print).
Default	all

parentRule

Read-only

Refers to the cssRule object that contains the current cssRule, such as a rule nested inside an @ rule.

W3C DOM CSSRule Types
All.

Example	var superRule = document.styleSheets[0].cssRules[1].parentRule;
Value	cssRule object reference.
Default	null

parentStyleSheet

Refers to the styleSheet object that contains the current cssRule. Allows a function that might be passed a reference to a cssRule object to obtain a reference to the containing styleSheet object, possibly to learn more about what else is in the style sheet.

W3C DOM CSSRule Types
All.

Example	`var ss = document.styleSheets[0].cssRules[3].parentStyleSheet;`
Value	styleSheet object reference.
Default	Current object.

readOnly

Returns Boolean true for rules that arrive to a document via an @import rule or a link element. Such rules may not be modified by script, although an element governed by such a rule can have individual style properties modified because the modifications are made to the element's own style property, and not the rule object.

Example
```
if (!document.styleSheets[2].cssRules[0].readOnly) {
    // not read-only, so OK to modify here
}
```

Value	Boolean value: true | false.
Default	Varies with rule type.

selectorText

Indicates the selector portion of the style sheet rule. Although this property is read/write (except in IE 5/Mac), changes do not influence the object or rendering.

W3C DOM CSSRule Types
CSSPageRule
CSSStyleRule

Example
```
document.styleSheets[0].cssRules[2].selectorText = "td.leftHeaders";
```

Value	String.
Default	None.

Alphabetical DOM Reference

style

Returns a style object with properties that reflect the attribute settings of the current rule. This is the same kind of style object associated with elements in the document (corresponding to the W3C DOM CSSStyleDeclaration object). If you must modify style sheet settings at the rule level, do so via the style property of the rule or cssRule. Changes register themselves immediately, and the elements affected by the rule render their changes accordingly.

W3C DOM CSSRule Types
CSSFontRule
CSSPageRule
CSSStyleRule

Example
```
var oneRule;
if (document.styleSheets) {
    if (document.styleSheets[0].cssRules) {
        oneRule = document.styleSheets[2].cssRules[1];
    } else if (document.styleSheets[0].rules) {
        oneRule = document.styleSheets[2].rules[1];
    }
}
if (oneRule) {
    oneRule.style.color = "red";
    oneRule.style.fontWeight = "bold";
}
```

Value	Reference to a style (W3C CSSStyleDeclaration) object.
Default	Current style object.

styleSheet

Returns a reference to the styleSheet object contained by the imported style sheet. From here you can inspect cssRule objects belonging to that styleSheet object—essentially drilling down one more level to the styleSheet object structure of the remote style sheet file.

W3C DOM CSSRule Types
CSSImportRule

Value	styleSheet object reference.
Default	None.

type

Returns an integer corresponding to one of seven `cssRule` types, as defined by the W3C DOM. Every `cssRule` object in Mozilla comes equipped with plain-language constant properties corresponding to the rule types, as follows.

Constant	Equivalent integer
cssRuleReference.UNKNOWN_RULE	0
cssRuleReference.STYLE_RULE	1
cssRuleReference.CHARSET_RULE	2
cssRuleReference.IMPORT_RULE	3
cssRuleReference.MEDIA_RULE	4
cssRuleReference.FONT_FACE_RULE	5
cssRuleReference.PAGE_RULE	6

W3C DOM CSSRule Types
All.

Example
```
var oneRule = document.styleSheets[2].cssRules[1];
if (oneRule.type == oneRule.IMPORT_RULE) {
    // process @import rule
}
```

Value   Integer.

Default   1

deleteRule( )

deleteRule(*index*)

Removes the zero-based index numbered rule from the current @media rule.

W3C DOM CSSRule Types
CSSMediaRule

Returned Value   None.

Parameters
index
> A zero-based integer corresponding to the specified item in source code order.

insertRule( )

IE *n/a* NN *n/a* Moz *all* Saf *all* Op *9* DOM *2*

insertRule("*rule*", *index*)

Inserts a new rule (selector text and style attributes) into the current @media rule at the position indicated by the second parameter.

W3C DOM CSSRule Types
CSSMediaRule

Returned Value   Integer of inserted position.

Parameters
rule
>   A string containing selector and curly braced style attributes comprising the rule to be inserted.

index
>   A zero-based integer corresponding to the specified item in source code order.

cssRules, CSSRuleList, rules

IE *4* NN *n/a* Moz *all* Saf *all* Op *9* DOM *2*

A collection of cssRule (W3C DOM browsers) or rule (IE 4 and later, but not accessible in IE 6 or 7 for security reasons) objects that are members of a styleSheet object. The W3C DOM abstract representation of this collection is called a CSSRuleList object. Members of this collection are accessed only via their integer index number, but you may iterate through the collection and examine properties of each rule object (such as the selectorText property) to distinguish one rule from another.

Object Model Reference
IE (Windows, pre-IE 6)
>   document.styleSheets[i].rules

Others
>   document.styleSheets[i].cssRules

Object-Specific Properties

length

Object-Specific Methods

item( )

Object-Specific Events
None.

length

Read-only

Returns the number of elements in the collection, including @ rules.

Example   `var howMany = document.styleSheets[1].cssRules.length;`

Value   Integer.

item( )

`item(index)`

Returns a style sheet rule object corresponding to the rule matching the index value in source code order.

Returned Value   Reference to a `cssRule` or `rule` object, depending on the object model. If there are no matches to the parameters, the returned value is `null`.

Parameters

index
> A zero-based integer corresponding to the specified item in source code order (nested within the current `styleSheet` object).

CSSStyleDeclaration

See style.

CSSStyleSheet

See styleSheet.

currentStyle

The `currentStyle` object (a property of all HTML element objects in IE 5 and later for Windows) provides read-only access to the effective (cascaded) style properties applied to the current element, including properties influenced by linked, imported, and explicit style sheet settings. This object is a property of all renderable HTML element objects and stands in contrast to an element's `style` object, which reports, and allows modification of, style sheet properties explicitly assigned to the inline `style` attribute.

Object Model Reference

`[window.]document.getElementById("elementID").currentStyle`

Object-Specific Properties

See the `style` object.

Object-Specific Methods

See the style object.

Object-Specific Events

None.

custom, HTMLUnknownElement   IE 5 NN *n/a* Moz *all* Saf *all* Op 7 DOM 1

Provides scriptable access to author-defined elements. Such elements share properties, methods, and event handlers of generic HTML element objects, and usually have custom attributes associated with them. Internet Explorer exposes custom attributes as properties of the element object.

HTML Equivalent   *<user-defined-tag>*

Object Model Reference

[window.]document.getElementById("*elementID*")

Object-Specific Properties

None.

Object-Specific Methods

None.

Object-Specific Events

None.

dataTransfer   IE 5(Win) NN *n/a* Moz *n/a* Saf 2 Op *n/a* DOM *n/a*

The dataTransfer object (accessible as a property of the event object) is a temporary container that scripts in IE 5 or later for Windows and Safari 2 can use to transfer text data, particularly during script-controlled operations that simulate cutting, copying, and pasting, or that control dragging. Your script controls what data is stored in the dataTransfer object, such as just the text of an element, an element's entire HTML, or the URL of an image. For example, a page for children could display simple icon images of several different kinds of animals. If the user starts dragging the dog icon, the script initiated by the img element's ondragstart event handler can store a custom attribute value of that element (perhaps the URL of a pretty dog photo) into the dataTransfer object. When the user drops the icon into the designated area, the ondrop event handler's function reads the dataTransfer object's data, and loads the photo image into position on the page.

Even though an event object changes its properties with each new event action, the dataTransfer object preserves its data from one event to the next, until a script removes the data from the object or other data is stored in it. Properties of the dataTransfer object distinguish its powers from those of the clipboardData object. By setting the dropEffect and effectAllowed properties, your scripts can control the type of cursor icon that appears during drag and drop operations. Example 2-1 demonstrates how the properties and methods of the dataTransfer object can be wired to dragging events such that the cursor changes to a "copy" style when rolled atop a desired drop target.

Example 2-1. Using the dataTransfer object

```html
<html>
<head>
<title>dataTransfer Demo</title>
<style type="text/css">
td {text-align:center}
th {text-decoration:underline}
.cyan {color:cyan}
.yellow {color:yellow}
.magenta {color:magenta}
#blank1 {text-decoration:underline}
</style>
<script type="text/javascript">
// set stage when dragging a desired source element
function setupDrag(evt) {
    evt = (evt) ? evt : window.event;
    var elem = (evt.target) ? evt.target : evt.srcElement;
    if (elem.nodeType == 3) {elem = elem.parentNode;}
    if (elem.tagName != "TD") {
        // don't allow dragging for any other elements
        evt.returnValue = false;
        if (evt.preventDefault) {evt.preventDefault();}
    } else {
        // set cursor to look like copy action
        evt.dataTransfer.effectAllowed = "copy";
        // store dragged cell text to transfer
        evt.dataTransfer.setData("Text", elem.innerHTML);
    }
}
// perform drop operations
function handleDrop( evt) {
    evt = (evt) ? evt : window.event;
    var elem = (evt.target) ? evt.target : evt.srcElement;
    var passedData = event.dataTransfer.getData("Text");
    if (passedData) {
        // show drop target cursor
        event.dataTransfer.dropEffect = "copy";
        // apply data to drop target
        elem.innerHTML = passedData;
        elem.className = passedData;
        if (document.selection) {
            document.selection.empty();
        }
    }
}
// we're dragging/copying, but not to here
function cancelDefault(evt) {
    evt = (evt) ? evt : window.event;
    // set cursor to "No" symbol
    evt.dataTransfer.dropEffect = "copy";
```

```
        evt.returnValue = false;
        if (evt.preventDefault) {evt.preventDefault();}
}
</script>
</head>
<body ondragstart="setupDrag(event);">
<table cellpadding="5">
<tr><th>Select and Drag Your Favorite Color</th></tr>
<tr><td>cyan</td></tr>
<tr><td>yellow</td></tr>
<tr><td>magenta</td></tr>
</table>

<p>My favorite color is <span id="blank1" ondragenter="cancelDefault(event);"
ondragover="cancelDefault(event);" ondrop="handleDrop(event);">
     </span> .</p>
</body>
</html>
```

For more information on transferring data via this object and the clipboardData object, visit *http://msdn.microsoft.com/workshop/author/datatransfer/overview.asp.*

HTML Equivalent   None.

Object Model Reference
[window.]event.dataTransfer

Object-Specific Properties

dropEffect	effectAllowed

Object-Specific Methods

clearData( )	getData( )	setData( )

Object-Specific Events
None.

---

dropEffect, effectAllowed

IE 5(Win)   NN n/a   Moz n/a   Saf 2   Op n/a   DOM n/a

Read/Write

These two properties work together but at different stages along a dragging operation that involves the dataTransfer object. They both control the appearance of the cursor during the drag and drop process. Assign a cursor style at the beginning of a drag operation via the ondragstart event and effectAllowed property. The drop target's ondragover and ondragenter event handlers should set the dropEffect property to the desired cursor style, and also set the event.returnValue property to false. This opens the way for the ondrop event handler not only to set the cursor via the dropEffect property, but to process the drop action. See Example 2-1 for a simple demonstration of the interaction of all these events and properties.

Example

`event.dataTransfer.dropEffect= "copy";`

Value   Case-insensitive constant (as a string): copy | link | move | none.

Default   none

clearData( )   IE 5(Win)   NN n/a   Moz n/a   Saf 2   Op n/a   DOM n/a

`clearData([dataFormat])`

Removes data from the dataTransfer object.

Returned Value   None.

Parameters

dataFormat
> An optional string specifying the format for the data to be removed. Earlier plans to allow multiple data types appear to have fallen through. The only reliable format is Text. Omitting the parameter deletes all data of all types.

getData( )   IE 5(Win)   NN n/a   Moz n/a   Saf 2   Op n/a   DOM n/a

`getData(dataFormat)`

Returns a copy of data from the dataTransfer object. The dataTransfer contents remain intact for subsequent reading in other script statements.

Returned Value   String.

Parameters

dataFormat
> A string specifying the format for the data to be read. Earlier plans to allow multiple data types appear to have fallen through. The only reliable format is Text.

setData( )   IE 5(Win)   NN n/a   Moz n/a   Saf 2   Op n/a   DOM n/a

`setData(dataFormat, stringData)`

Stores string data in the dataTransfer object. Returns Boolean true if the assignment is successful

Returned Value   Boolean value: true | false.

Parameters

dataFormat
> A string specifying the format for the data to be read. Earlier plans to allow multiple data types appear to have fallen through. The only reliable format is Text. While the method accepts URL as a format, reading a set value in that format is not successful.

stringData
> Any string value, including strings that contain HTML tags.

dd

IE *4* NN *n/a* Moz *all* Saf *all* Op *7* DOM *1*

The dd object reflects the dd element.

HTML Equivalent   <dd>

Object Model Reference
[window.]document.getElementById("*elementID*")

Object-Specific Properties
noWrap

Object-Specific Methods
None.

Object-Specific Events
None.

noWrap

IE *4* NN *n/a* Moz *n/a* Saf *n/a* Op *n/a* DOM *n/a*

Read/Write

Specifies whether the browser should render the element as wide as is necessary to display a line of nonbreaking text on one line. Abuse of this attribute can force the user into a great deal of inconvenient horizontal scrolling of the page to view all of the content.

Example	document.getElementById("wideBody").noWrap = "true";
Value	Boolean value: true | false.
Default	false

del

IE *4* NN *n/a* Moz *all* Saf *all* Op *7* DOM *1*

The del object reflects the del element.

HTML Equivalent   <del>

Object Model Reference
[window.]document.getElementById("*elementID*")

Object-Specific Properties

cite	dateTime

Object-Specific Methods
None.

Object-Specific Events
None.

cite, dateTime

Read/Write

These two properties are listed among the shared properties earlier in this chapter due to an implementation oddity in IE 6 and 7. IE 5/Macintosh, Mozilla, Safari, and Opera correctly implement these properties only for the del and ins objects, as specified in the W3C DOM, but in no mainstream browser do they convey any special powers. See the shared cite and dateTime properties.

dfn

See abbr.

Dialog Helper

The Dialog Helper object is an ActiveX control delivered with IE 6 and 7 that provides a short assortment of potentially useful system and document information; the method also displays a color selector dialog from which your scripts can obtain a user's color choice. Most typically, it would be used when scripting IE's edit mode, where users need to make color, font, and element choices. But you might find the object's properties and methods useful in traditional browser document settings.

Loading this object into the page requires the following <object> tag:

```
<object id="dlgHelper" classid="clsid:3050f819-98b5-11cf-bb82-00aa00bdce0b"
        width="0px" height="0px">
</object>
```

Because this object is not rendered, you may place its tag in the head portion of your document. You may also assign your choice of identifier to the id attribute. Once the object is loaded, reference it as a global object in the window.

HTML Equivalent   None.

Object Model Reference
[window.]document.getElementById("*elementID*")

Object-Specific Properties

blockFormats	fonts

Object-Specific Methods

ChooseColorDlg( )	getCharset( )

Object-Specific Events
None.

blockFormats

Read-only

Returns a collection of plain-language names of block-level elements supported by the browser. Unlike other IE collections, to read the number of items, you must access its Count property, rather than length property. The names of items returned are strings, such as "Heading 1" and "Numbered List" (corresponding to the h1 and ol elements, respectively). Access each item in the collection via the collection's item( ) method.

Example

```
var blockList = dlgHelper.blockFormats;
var blockNames = new Array( );
for (var i = 0; i < blockList.Count; i++) {
    blockNames[blockNames.length]= blockList.item(i);
}
```

Value   Array of strings

Default   Implementation-dependent.

fonts

Read-only

Returns a collection of plain-language names of system fonts. Unlike other IE collections, to read the number of items, you must access its Count property, rather than length property. The names of items returned are strings, such as "MS Sans Serif" and "Verdana". Access each item in the collection via the collection's item( ) method.

Example

```
var fontList = dlgHelper.fonts;
var fontNames = new Array( );
for (var i = 0; i < fontList.Count; i++) {
    fontNames [fontNames .length]= fontList .item(i);
}
```

Value   Array of strings

Default   Implementation-dependent.

ChooseColorDlg( )

```
ChooseColorDlg([initialHexColor])
```

Displays a color selector dialog box, and returns a decimal number corresponding to the color chosen by the user. To apply the color to style or other color property settings, you may have to convert the decimal value to a suitable hexadecimal triplet value of the *#RRGGBB* format. The following fragment demonstrates the sequence of obtaining the color, converting it to the desired base and digit count, and assigning the value to a style property:

```
var colorChoice = dlgHelper.ChooseColorDlg( );
var hexColor = colorChoice.toString(16);
```

```
    while (hexColor.length < 6) {hexColor = "0" + hexColor;}
    document.body.style.color = "#" + hexColor;
```

If the user selects a custom color in the dialog and adds it to a little shortcut box, the color does not reappear in the box the next time the dialog appears. But a custom color can still be pre-selected by passing its hex value as a parameter to the method.

Returned Value   Decimal integer of the selected color (0 through as many colors of the client settings).

Parameters

initialHexColor

Optional hexadecimal number that presets the initially selected color in the dialog box.

getCharset( )   IE 6 NN *n/a* Moz *n/a* Saf *n/a* Op *n/a* DOM *n/a*

getCharset("*fontName*")

Returns an integer corresponding to a constant associated with a character set known by the operating system. Among the common values returned for font families installed on Latin-based systems are 0 (for plain ANSI character set) and 2 (for a symbol set). The required parameter is the name of a font to inspect for its character set. Such names may be retrieved from the fonts property of the Dialog Helper object:

```
    var setID = dlgHelper.getCharset(dlgHelper.fonts.item(4));
```

Not all Windows versions have the same character set suite installed.

Returned Value   Integer.

Parameters

fontName

String name of installed system font.

dir   IE 4 NN *n/a* Moz *all* Saf *all* Op 7 DOM 1

The dir object reflects the dir element. This element, originally intended as a multicolumn list format, is treated the same as the ul element.

HTML Equivalent   <dir>

Object Model Reference

[window.]document.getElementById("*elementID*")

Object-Specific Properties

compact

Object-Specific Methods

None.

Object-Specific Events

None.

compact   IE *5(Mac)/6(Win)*   NN *n/a*   Moz *all*   Saf *all*   Op *7*   DOM *1*

Read/Write

Provided for this element for the sake of compatibility with the W3C DOM standard. However, mainstream browsers do not act upon this property or its corresponding attribute.

Value   Boolean value: `true` | `false`.

Default   `false`

directories, locationbar, menubar, personalbar, scrollbars, statusbar, toolbar   IE *n/a*   NN *4*   Moz *all*   Saf *n/a*   Op *n/a*   DOM *n/a*

These objects belong to the `window` object and represent portions of the "chrome" surrounding the content area of the browser window (the `directories` object was added to the list for Mozilla). With signed scripts in Navigator 4 or Mozilla (and the user's permission), you can dynamically hide and show these elements in a browser window. These features can also be turned off via the third parameter of the `window.open( )` method, but only when generating a new window. To change the visibility of these items in an existing window, signed scripts are required. Other browsers offer no equivalent functionality for a window that is already open.

Object Model Reference

```
[window.]directories
[window.]locationbar
[window.]menubar
[window.]personalbar
[window.]scrollbars
[window.]statusbar
[window.]toolbar
```

Object-Specific Properties

`visible`

Object-Specific Methods

None.

Object-Specific Events

None.

visible

Read/Write

Accessible only through signed scripts in Navigator 4 or Mozilla, determines whether the window chrome feature is displayed.

Example

```
netscape.security.PrivilegeManager.enablePrivilege("UniversalBrowserWrite");
window.statusbar.visible = "false";
netscape.security.PrivilegeManager.revertPrivilege("UniversalBrowserWrite");
```

Value   Boolean value: true | false.

Default   true

div

The div object reflects the div element. This element creates a block-level element often used for element positioning or containment grouping of several related elements. The client and scroll properties are active in IE for the Macintosh.

HTML Equivalent   `<div>`

Object Model Reference

`[window.]document.getElementById("elementID")`

Object-Specific Properties

align	dataFld	dataFormatAs	dataSrc	noWrap

Object-Specific Methods
None.

Object-Specific Events
None.

align

Read/Write

Defines the horizontal alignment of content within the element's box. Unless otherwise reined in, the box width is that of the next outermost positioning context—usually the body.

Example   `document.getElementById("myDIV").align = "center";`

Value   Any of the three horizontal alignment constants: center | left | right.

Default   left

dataFld

IE 4 NN *n/a* Moz *n/a* Saf *n/a* Op *n/a* DOM *n/a*

Read/Write

Used with IE data binding to associate a remote data source column name to a div element's content. A datasrc attribute must also be set for the element. Setting both the dataFld and dataSrc properties to empty strings breaks the binding between element and data source. Works only for text data sources in IE 5 for the Macintosh.

Example   document.getElementById("myDiv").dataFld = "comment";

Value   Case-sensitive identifier of the data source column.

Default   None.

dataFormatAs

IE 4 NN *n/a* Moz *n/a* Saf *n/a* Op *n/a* DOM *n/a*

Read/Write

Used with IE data binding, this property advises the browser whether the source material arriving from the data source is to be treated as plain text or as tagged HTML.

Example   document.getElementById("myDiv").dataFormatAs = "text";

Value   String constants: text | html.

Default   text

dataSrc

IE 4 NN *n/a* Moz *n/a* Saf *n/a* Op *n/a* DOM *n/a*

Read/Write

Used with IE data binding to specify the ID of the page's object element that loads the data source object for remote data access. Content from the data source is specified via the datafld attribute. Setting both the dataFld and dataSrc properties to empty strings breaks the binding between element and data source.

Example   document.getElementById("myDiv").dataSrc = "DBSRC3";

Value   Case-sensitive identifier of the data source.

Default   None.

noWrap

IE 4 NN *n/a* Moz *n/a* Saf *n/a* Op *n/a* DOM *n/a*

Read/Write

Specifies whether the browser should render the element as wide as is necessary to display a line of nonbreaking text on one line. Abuse of this attribute can force the user into a great deal of inconvenient horizontal scrolling of the page to view all of the content. The corresponding attribute is deprecated.

Example   document.getElementById("wideDiv").noWrap = "true";

Value   Boolean value: true | false.

Default   false

dl   IE *4* NN *n/a* Moz *all* Saf *all* Op *7* DOM *1*

The dl object reflects the dl element. This element is the wrapper for a definition list grouping.

HTML Equivalent   <dl>

Object Model Reference
[window.]document.getElementById("*elementID*")

Object-Specific Properties
compact

Object-Specific Methods
None.

Object-Specific Events
None.

compact   IE *4* NN *n/a* Moz *all* Saf *all* Op *7* DOM *1*
Read/Write

When set to true, the compact property instructs the browser to render a related dt and dd pair on the same line if space allows. This compact styling is intended for dt elements consisting of only a few characters.

Example   document.getElementById("maindl").compact = true;

Value   Boolean value: true | false.

Default   false

document   IE *3* NN *2* Moz *all* Saf *all* Op *7* DOM *1*

The document object represents both the content viewed in the browser window or frame and the other content of the HTML file loaded into the window or frame. Thus, all information from the head portion of the file is also part of the document object. The document object has no name other than its hard-wired object name: document.

For a browser with internal architecture based closely on the W3C DOM, this document object represents the HTMLDocument object—a special kind (internal subclass) of the core module's Document object, suited to holding HTML documents. In other words, the HTMLDocument object inherits the properties and methods of the core Document and Node objects (sharing facilities with XML documents) and gets additional properties and methods that apply only to HTML documents. Of course, there is the conceptual incongruity about whether an HTMLDocument is applicable to an XHTML document because such a document theoretically is an XML document. But, in practice, even an XHTML document becomes an HTML document for scripting purposes, and has all the HTMLDocument properties and methods available to it.

One more important practical side to a W3C DOM implementation (as evidenced by implementations in Mozilla, Safari, and Opera) is that the document object internally implements document-level properties and methods from other DOM modules, such as views, events, and styles. Each of these modules defines an object (DocumentEvent, DocumentRange, DocumentStyle, and DocumentView) that provides a vital connection between the HTMLDocument and these add-on module features. Thus, it is the styleSheets property of the DocumentStyle object in the W3C DOM that the scriptable document object described here uses to reach the styleSheet objects and their rules. And the DocumentEvent object links in its createEvent( ) method that allows the scriptable document object to generate an event outside the normal user- or system-created events. All of these features become subsumed by the document object you reference and script in Mozilla and other W3C DOM-centric browsers. The precise source module for a particular feature is not important to the scripter—all you need to know is that the properties and methods belong to the scriptable document object.

Object Model Reference

[window.]document

Object-Specific Properties

activeElement	alinkColor	all[]	anchors[]
applets[]	bgColor	body	charset
characterSet	compatMode	contentType	cookie
defaultCharset	defaultView	designMode	doctype
documentElement	documentURI	domain	domConfig
embeds[]	expando	fgColor	fileCreatedDate
fileModifiedDate	fileSize	fileUpdatedDate	forms[]
frames[]	height	ids[]	images[]
implementation	inputEncoding	lastModified	layers[]
linkColor	links[]	location	media
mimeType	nameProp	namespaces[]	parentWindow
plugins[]	preferredStylesheetSet	protocol	readyState
referrer	scripts[]	security	selectedStylesheetSet
selection	strictErrorChecking	styleSheets[]	tags[]
title	URL	URLUnencoded	vlinkColor
width	xmlEncoding	xmlStandalone	xmlVersion

Object-Specific Methods

addBinding( )	adoptNode( )
captureEvents( )	clear( )
close( )	createAttribute( )
createAttributeNS( )	createCDATASection( )

createComment( )

createDocumentFragment( )

createElement( )

createElementNS( )

createEntityReference( )

createEvent( )

createEventObject( )

createNodeIterator( )

createProcessingInstruction( )

createRange( )

createStyleSheet( )

createTextNode( )

createTreeWalker( )

elementFromPoint( )

execCommand( )

getAnonymousElementByAttribute( )

getAnonymousNodes( )

getBindingParent( )

getElementById( )

getElementsByName( )

getOverrideStyle( )

getSelection( )

handleEvent( )

hasFocus( )

importNode( )

loadBindingDocument( )

normalizeDocument( )

open( )

postMessage( )

queryCommandEnabled( )

queryCommandIndeterm( )

queryCommandState( )

queryCommandSupported( )

queryCommandText( )

queryCommandValue( )

recalc( )

releaseEvents( )

removeBinding( )

renameNode( )

routeEvent( )

write( )

writeln( )

Object-Specific Events

Event	IE	Others	DOM	
selectionchange	4	n/a	n/a	
stop	4	n/a	n/a	

activeElement

IE *4* NN *n/a* Moz *n/a* Saf *n/a* Op *7* DOM *n/a*

Read-only

Refers to the object that is currently designated as the active element in the document. To learn more about the returned object, you'll need to examine the object's tagName, id, or other properties. Because buttons and other elements may not receive focus on all platforms, the returned value of this property may vary with operating system. While an element (especially a form control) that receives focus also becomes active, an element might be active, but due to other settings in newer IE versions, does not have focus. See the shared setActive( ) method.

Example   var currObj = document.activeElement;

Value   Element object reference.

Default   None.

alinkColor

IE 3   NN 2   Moz *all*   Saf *all*   Op 7   DOM *n/a*

Read/Write

Specifies the color of a hypertext link as it is being clicked. The color is applied to the link text or border around an image or object embedded within all a elements in the document. See also linkColor and vlinkColor properties for unvisited and visited link colors. Replaced in the W3C DOM by the aLink property of the body object or in CSS by the :active pseudo-class. Dynamically changed values for alinkColor are not reflected on the page in pre-Mozilla Navigator.

Example	document.alinkColor = "green";
Value	A hexadecimal triplet or plain-language color name. See Appendix A for acceptable plain-language color names.
Default	#0000FF

all[ ]

IE 4   NN *n/a*   Moz 1.7   Saf *all*   Op 7   DOM *n/a*

Read-only

The all property is a member of all containers in IE 4 or later and Opera 7 or later, but a member of only the document object in Mozilla 1.7 or later. This property was added to Mozilla as a convenience for old scripts that used document.all references without conditional branches that tested for the existence of the property. As such, Mozilla recognizes document.all only in pages marked up in quirks mode (see the DOCTYPE element in Chapter 1), but even there does not expose the property as being valid in an if conditional expression. The normal IE practice of referencing elements by document.all.*elementID* and referencing an element solely by its ID work in Mozilla in quirks mode. See the all collection object earlier in this chapter.

Value	A collection of element objects in the document.
Default	The current collection.

anchors[ ]

IE 3   NN 2   Moz *all*   Saf *all*   Op 7   DOM 1

Returns an array of all anchor objects in the current document. This includes a elements that are designed as either anchors or combination anchors and links. Items in this array are indexed (zero-based) in source code order.

Example	var aCount = document.anchors.length;
Value	Array of anchor element objects.
Default	Array of length zero.

applets[ ]

Returns an array of all Java applet objects in the current document. An applet must be started and running before it is counted as an object. Items in this array are indexed (zero-based) in source code order.

Example	var appletCount = document.applets.length
Value	Array of applet element objects.
Default	Array of length zero.

bgColor

Read/Write

Provides the background color of the document. Even if the bgcolor attribute or bgColor property is set with a plain-language color name, the returned value is always a hexadecimal triplet.

The modern preference to managing a document's background color is via the CSS background property for the body element.

Example	document.bgColor = "yellow";
Value	A hexadecimal triplet or plain-language color name. See Appendix A for acceptable plain-language color names.
Default	Varies with browser and operating system.

body

Read-only

Returns a reference to the body object defined by the body element within the document. This property is used as a gateway to the body object's properties.

Example	document.body.style.marginLeft = "15px";
Value	Object reference.
Default	The current body object.

charset

Read/Write

Indicates the character encoding of the document's content. For other browsers, use the document.characterSet property.

Example
```
if (document.charset == "csISO5427Cyrillic") {
    // process for Cyrillic charset
}
```

Value   Case-insensitive alias from the character set registry (*ftp://ftp.isi.edu/in-notes/iana/assignments/character-sets*).

Default   Determined by browser.

characterSet

Indicates the character encoding of the document's content.

Example
```
if (document.characterSet == "ISO-8859-1") {
    // process for standard Latin character set
}
```

Value   Case-insensitive alias from the character set registry (*ftp://ftp.isi.edu/in-notes/iana/assignments/character-sets*).

Default   Determined by browser.

compatMode

Returns the compatibility mode for the document, as controlled by the DOCTYPE element's content. See the DOCTYPE element discussion in Chapter 1 for details on how to force the browser to treat a document in either backward compatibility or standards compatibility mode for element positioning and other implementation details. Because the choice of mode can impact some style property results, you can use this property to branch between two calculations in a shared library so that they treat the current document correctly, regardless of mode.

Example
```
if (document.compatMode == "BackCompat") {
    // process as "quirks" mode
}
```

Value   String constant: BackCompat | CSS1Compat.

Default   BackCompat

contentType

Returns the MIME type for the document, as conveyed by the server.

Example
```
if (document.contentType != "text/html") {
    // process for alternative MIME type
}
```

Value	String.
Default	text/html

cookie

Indicates the HTTP cookie associated with the domain of the document and stored on the client machine. The Mozilla browsers group all cookie data together into a single file, while IE creates a separate file for each domain's cookie data.

Reading and writing the cookie property are not parallel operations. Reading a cookie property returns a semicolon-delimited list of name/value pairs in the following format:

```
name=value
```

Up to 20 of these pairs can be stored in the cookie property for a given domain (regardless of the number of HTML documents used in that web site). A total of 4,000 characters can be stored in the cookie, but it is advisable to keep each name/value pair to less than 2,000 characters in length. It is up to your scripting code to parse the cookie property value for an individually named cookie's value.

Writing cookie property values allows more optional pairs of data associated with a single name/value pair. Cookie data must be a string, but you can deconstruct an array into a string via the Array.join( ) method for writing the cookie value, and then use String. split( ) to reconstruct the array after reading the cookie data. The format is as follows:

```
document.cookie = "name=value
    [; expires=timeInGMT]
    [; path=pathName]
    [; domain=domainName]
    [; secure]";
```

No matter how many optional subproperties you set per cookie, only the name/value pair may be retrieved. All cookie data written to the cookie property is maintained in the browser's memory until the browser quits. If an expiration date has been made part of the cookie data and that time has not yet expired, the cookie data is saved to the actual cookie file; otherwise, the cookie data is discarded. The browser automatically deletes cookie data that has expired when the browser next starts.

Example

```
var exp = new Date( );
var nowPlusOneWeek = exp.getTime( ) + (7 * 24 * 60 * 60 * 1000);
exp.setTime(nowPlusOneWeek);
document.cookie = "userName=visitor; expires=" + exp.toGMTString( );
```

Value	Cookie data as string. See description.
Default	None.

Alphabetical DOM Reference

defaultCharset

IE 4   NN *n/a*   Moz *n/a*   Saf *n/a*   Op *n/a*   DOM *n/a*

Read-only

Indicates the character encoding of the content of the document.

Example	var cset = document.defaultCharset;
Value	Case-insensitive alias from the character set registry (*ftp://ftp.isi.edu/in-notes/iana/assignments/character-sets*).
Default	Determined by browser.

defaultView

IE *n/a*   NN *n/a*   Moz *all*   Saf *all*   Op 7   DOM 2

Read-only

Returns a reference to the W3C DOM abstract representation of a "viewer" that renders the document (the formal name for the object is AbstractView). In Mozilla and Opera, this object equates to the window or frame object that contains the document. A script function that has access to a document object (such as via the element object's ownerDocument property) can obtain a valid reference to the document's window in these browsers via this defaultView property. Safari, on the other hand, returns a reference just to an instance of the AbstractView object. The document's view (in either object referencing scheme) includes knowledge about cascaded style rules applied to each element. See Online Section V for an example of obtaining the effective style of an element with the help of the document.defaultView property and the getComputedStyle( ) method.

Example

```
var elem = document.getElementById("myDiv");
var vw = document.defaultView;
var currStyle = vw.getComputedStyle(elem, "");
var elemLeft = currStyle.getPropertyValue("left");
```

Value	Reference to a window object in Mozilla and Opera; reference to an instance of the AbstractView object in Safari that implements the W3C DOM ViewCSS object (also supported by Mozilla and Opera).
Default	The document's window or view.

designMode

IE 5.5   NN *n/a*   Moz 1.3   Saf 1.3/2   Op 9   DOM *n/a*

Read/Write

Controls whether the document can be edited by the user. Because this property governs the entire document, it is prudent to create a separate, editable portion of the main page inside an iframe element, and engage the designMode property for the iframe's document.

When designMode is on, supporting browsers also make additional document methods available to the scripter, particularly those that execute commands (e.g., execCommand( )) to apply font and other text stylings to user-selected text in an editable document.

For an introduction to the use of designMode and related features in the Mozilla environment, visit: *http://developer.mozilla.org/en/docs/Rich-Text_Editing_in_Mozilla*.

Example	`document.getElementById("editMe").designMode = "on";`
Value	String constant: off | on. Internet Explorer also allows Inherit.
Default	off (W3C); Inherit (IE)

doctype

Returns a reference to the DOCTYPE element object (the same as the W3C DOM abstract DocumentType node object). The property returns a reference value only if the DOCTYPE is specified in the document; otherwise the property returns null. See the DocumentType object for properties available in various browsers. In a pure W3C DOM environment, the doctype property is inherited from the core document object, and is thus available to XML documents, as well.

Example	`var docsType = document.doctype;`
Value	Node reference.
Default	None.

documentElement

Returns a reference to the root element node of the document. For HTML documents, the reference is to the html element that encompasses the document's head and body elements. In a pure W3C DOM environment, the documentElement property is inherited from the core document object, and is thus available to XML documents, as well.

Example	`var rootElem = document.documentElement;`
Value	Element node reference.
Default	The current html element object.

documentURI

Denotes the Uniform Resource Identifier of the current document. The value is the same as location.href, and can be used in the same way to navigate to a different URI, if desired.

Example	`document.documentURI = "http://www.megacorp.com";`
Value	Complete or relative URI as a string.
Default	The current document's URI.

domain

IE 4 NN 3 Moz all Saf all Op 7 DOM 1

Read/Write

Provides the hostname of the server that served up the document. If documents from different servers on the same domain must exchange content with each other, the domain properties of both documents must be set to the same domain to avoid security restrictions. Normally, if the hosts don't match, browser security disallows access to the other document's form data. This property allows, for example, a page from the *www* server to communicate with a page served up by a secure server.

Example   document.domain = "megaCorp.com";

Value   String of the domain name that two documents have in common (exclusive of the server name).

Default   None.

domConfig

IE n/a NN n/a Moz n/a Saf n/a Op n/a DOM 3

Read-only

Returns a DOMConfiguration object, which reveals information about numerous configuration features of the current document. These features are typically of more use when working with XML documents.

Example   var paramList = document.domConfig.parameterNames;

Value   DOMConfiguration object.

Default   Current DOMConfiguration object.

embeds[]

IE 4 NN 3 Moz all Saf all Op 7 DOM n/a

Returns an array of all embedded objects (embed elements) in the current document. Items in this array are indexed (zero-based) in source code order.

Example   var embedCount = document.embeds.length;

Value   Array of embed object references.

Default   Array of zero length.

expando

IE 4 NN n/a Moz n/a Saf n/a Op n/a DOM n/a

Read/Write

Specifies whether scripts in the current document allow the creation and use of custom properties assigned to the document object. The extensible nature of JavaScript allows scripters to create a new object property by just assigning a value to it (as in document. stooge = "Curly"). This also means the document accepts incorrectly spelled property assignments, such as forgetting to set a middle letter of a long property name to uppercase (marginLeftColor). Such assignments are accepted without question, but the desired result is nowhere to be seen. If you don't intend to create custom properties, consider setting document.expando to `false` in an opening script statement as you author a page. This could help prevent spelling errors from causing bugs. The setting affects only scripts in the current document.

Example	document.expando = false;
Value	Boolean value: `true` | `false`.
Default	`true`

fgColor

IE *3* NN *2* Moz *all* Saf *all* Op *7* DOM *n/a*
Read/Write

Provides the foreground (text) color for the document. While you can change this property in all versions of Navigator, the text does not change dynamically in versions prior to 6. Still supported in current browsers, this property better handled via the `document.body.text` property or, better still, CSS color property settings.

Example	document.fgColor = "darkred";
Value	A hexadecimal triplet or plain-language color name. See Appendix A for acceptable plain-language color names.
Default	Browser default (usually `black`).

fileCreatedDate

IE *4(Win)* NN *n/a* Moz *n/a* Saf *n/a* Op *n/a* DOM *n/a*
Read-only

Returns a string of the date (but not the time) that the server (or local filesystem) reports the currently loaded file was created. Starting with IE 5, the date information is formatted as mm/dd/yyyy. The value may be corrupted if the server supplies the data in a format that IE does not expect.

Example	var dateObj = new Date(document.fileCreatedDate);
Value	Date string.
Default	None.

fileModifiedDate

IE *4(Win)* NN *n/a* Moz *n/a* Saf *n/a* Op *n/a* DOM *n/a*
Read-only

Returns a string of the date (but not the time) that the server (or local file system) reports the currently loaded file was most recently modified. Starting with IE 5, the date information is formatted as mm/dd/yyyy. The value may be corrupted or incorrect if the server supplies the data in a format that IE does not expect.

Example	var dateObj = new Date(document.fileModifiedDate);
Value	Date string.
Default	None.

Alphabetical DOM Reference

fileSize

IE *4* NN *n/a* Moz *n/a* Saf *n/a* Op *n/a* DOM *n/a*

Read-only

Returns the number of bytes for the size of the currently loaded document. IE for Windows returns this value as a string, while IE for Macintosh returns a number value (an important distinction if you need to perform math operations on the value).

Example   `var byteCount = parseInt(document.fileSize, 10);`

Value   Integer as string (Windows) or number (Mac).

Default   None.

fileUpdatedDate

IE *5.5* NN *n/a* Moz *n/a* Saf *n/a* Op *n/a* DOM *n/a*

Read-only

Returns an empty string. Apparently not officially supported for the document object.

forms[ ]

IE *3* NN *2* Moz *all* Saf *all* Op *7* DOM *1*

Read-only

Returns an array of all `form` objects (form elements) in the current document. Items in this array are indexed (zero-based) in source code order, but may also be accessed by using the form's name as a string index value.

Example   `var elemCount = document.forms[0].elements.length;`

Value   Array of `form` objects.

Default   Array of zero length.

frames[ ]

IE *4* NN *n/a* Moz *n/a* Saf *n/a* Op *n/a* DOM *n/a*

Read-only

Returns an array of all `iframe` objects (iframe element objects, not to be confused with window-like `frame` objects) in the current document. Items in this array are indexed (zero-based) in source code order. For cross-browser compatibility with modern browsers, use `document.getElementsByTagName("iframe")` instead.

Example   `var iframeCount = document.frames.length;`

Value   Array of `iframe` objects.

Default   Array of zero length.

height, width

IE *n/a* NN *4* Moz *all* Saf *all* Op *n/a* DOM *n/a*

Read-only

Return the pixel dimensions of the entire rendered document. These values coincide with the `offsetHeight` and `offsetWidth` property values for the `document.body.parentNode` (i.e., the html element) object. Since neither property pairing is yet sanctioned by the W3C DOM, you might prefer the offset pair, because they are at least cross-browser compatible.

Example	var howTall = document.height;
Value	Number of pixels.
Default	Current document size.

ids[ ]   IE *n/a* NN |4| Moz *n/a* Saf *n/a* Op *n/a* DOM *n/a*
Read-only

Used with the Navigator 4-only JavaScript syntax of style sheets, the ids[] collection is part of a reference to a single ID and the style property assigned to it in the syntax form [document.]ids.*idName.stylePropertyName*. For a list of related properties, see the tags object listing in this chapter.

images[ ]   IE *4* NN *3* Moz *all* Saf *all* Op *7* DOM *1*
Read-only

Returns an array of all img element objects in the current document node tree (exclusive of pre-cached images loaded via the new Image( ) constructor). Items in this array are indexed (zero-based) in source code order, and may be accessed by number or by string name. The presence of this property indicates support for live, swappable images.

Example	document.images["home"].src = "images/homeHilite.jpg";
Value	Array of img element objects.
Default	Array of zero length.

implementation   IE *5(Mac)/6(Win)* NN *n/a* Moz *all* Saf *all* Op *7* DOM *1*
Read-only

Returns a reference to the W3C DOMImplementation object, which represents, to a limited degree, the environment that makes up the document container—the browser, for our purposes. Methods of the object let you see which DOM modules the browser reports supporting. This object is also a gateway to creating virtual W3C Document and DocumentType objects outside of the current document tree. Thus, in Mozilla you can use the document.implementation property as a start to generating a nonrendered document for external XML documents. See the DOMImplementation object for details about the methods and their browser support.

Example
var xDoc = document.implementation.createDocument("", "theXdoc", null);

Value	Reference to a DOMImplementation object.
Default	Current DOMImplementation object.

inputEncoding

IE *n/a*   NN *n/a*   Moz *1.8*   Saf *n/a*   Op *n/a*   DOM *3*
Read-only

Returns the character encoding type specified for the document. The value is influenced by encoding specifications in the document, such as a meta element that specifies a charset.

Example
```
if (document.inputEncoding == "ISO-8859-5") {
    // process for ISO-8859-5 character encoding
}
```

Value   Character encoding type as a string, or null if the document is created outside of the current document node tree.

Default   UTF-8

lastModified

IE *3*   NN *2*   Moz *all*   Saf *all*   Op *7*   DOM *n/a*
Read-only

Provides the date and time (as a string) on which the server says the document file was last modified. Some servers don't supply this information at all or correctly. Only in recent browsers is the date string in a form suitable as a parameter for a Date object constructor.

Example   document.write(document.lastModified);

Value   String representation of a date and time.

Default   None.

layers[ ]

IE *n/a*   NN |4| Moz *n/a*   Saf *n/a*   Op *n/a*   DOM *n/a*
Read-only

Returns an array of all Navigator 4-only layer element objects in the current document. Also included in the array are references to other HTML elements with style sheets that set the element to be relative- or absolute-positioned (in which case, Navigator 4 treats those elements as layer objects). Items in this array are indexed (zero-based) in source code order, and may be accessed by number or by string name. As a dead-end feature implemented only in Navigator 4, the presence of this property indicates support for the unique referencing requirements for Netscape layers.

Example
```
if (document.layers) {
    // use document.layers[] syntax for references
}
```

Value   Array of layer objects or their equivalent.

Default   Array of zero length.

linkColor

Indicates the color of a hypertext link that has not been visited (that is, the URL of the link is not in the browser's cache). This is one of three states for a link: unvisited, active, and visited. The color is applied to the link text or border around an image or object embedded within an a element. Changes to this property do not dynamically change the link color in Navigator 4 or earlier. In modern browsers, you should be using the W3C DOM alternative, document.body.link, or, better still, the :link CSS pseudo-class.

Example	document.link Color= "#00FF00";
Value	A hexadecimal triplet or plain-language color name. See Appendix A for acceptable plain-language color names.
Default	#0000FF

links[ ]

Returns an array of all area element objects and a element objects that have href attributes assigned to them (i.e., they are clickable links). Items in the array are in source code order.

Example

```
for (var i = 0; i < document.links.length; i++) {
    // iterate through document.links[] array
}
```

Value	Array of area and a (set up as link) element objects.
Default	Array of zero length.

location

Indicates the URL of the current document. This property was deprecated because it may conflict with the window.location property, but browsers continue to support it. Use either the widely implemented document.URL property, or, better, the window.location.href property.

Example	document.location = "products/widget33.html";
Value	A full or relative URL as a string.
Default	Document URL.

media

IE 5.5   NN *n/a*   Moz *n/a*   Saf *n/a*   Op *n/a*   DOM *n/a*

Read/Write

Returns a string indicating the output medium for which the content is formatted. The property returns an empty string as of IE 6, and throws a security error if you assign accepted string values (all, print, or screen) to it. Avoid using this property with the document object.

mimeType

IE 5.5   NN *n/a*   Moz *n/a*   Saf *n/a*   Op *n/a*   DOM *n/a*

Read-only

Returns a string indicating the basic document type, but not in a MIME format. For an HTML document, the string returned changed starting with IE 5.5 to HTML Document. Do not confuse this document object property with the Netscape, Mozilla, and IE/Mac navigator.mimeTypes property, which is an entirely different animal.

Example	var what = document.mimeType;
Value	String.
Default	HTML Document

nameProp

IE 6   NN *n/a*   Moz *n/a*   Saf *n/a*   Op *n/a*   DOM *n/a*

Read-only

Returns a string containing the same data as document.title, including an empty string if no title element exists in the document. This property may not be officially supported for the document object in IE.

Value	String.
Default	Empty string.

namespaces[ ]

IE 5.5   NN *n/a*   Moz *n/a*   Saf *n/a*   Op *n/a*   DOM *n/a*

Read-only

Returns a collection of IE namespace objects implemented in the current document. A namespace object is a gateway to loading external behaviors. For more details, visit *http://msdn.microsoft.com/workshop/author/behaviors/overview/elementb_ovw.asp*.

Example	var IENSCount = document.namespaces.length;
Value	Array of namespace object references.
Default	Array of zero length.

parentWindow

Returns a reference to the window object (which may be a frame in a frameset) that contains the current document. Use this reference to access the window's properties and methods directly. The returned value is the same as the window reference from the document.

Example	var siblingCount = document.parentWindow.frames.length;
Value	window or frame object reference.
Default	window object.

plugins[ ]

Returns an array of all embedded objects (embed elements) in the current document. Items in this array are indexed (zero-based) in source code order. Do not confuse this collection with the navigator.plugins collection.

Example	var embedCount = document.plugins.length;
Value	Array of embed object references.
Default	Array of zero length.

preferredStylesheetSet

Returns the title property value of the imported style sheet marked up to be the document author's preferred one, according to HTML 4 specifications for the link element.

Example

```
if (document.preferredStylesheetSet == "main") {
    // statements to work on 'main' style sheet rules
}
```

Value	String.
Default	Empty string.

protocol

Returns a plain-language string describing the protocol used to load the current document. Unlike the location.protocol property's literal value (e.g., http: or file:), the document. protocol is human-readable (e.g., Hypertext Transfer Protocol or File Protocol).

Example

```
if (document.protocol == "File Protocol") {
    // process for file access in IE
}
```

Alphabetical DOM Reference

Value	Plain-language string.
Default	Current document's protocol type.

readyState

IE 4 NN *n/a* Moz *n/a* Saf *all* Op 7 DOM *n/a*

Read-only

Returns the current download status of the document content. If a script (especially one initiated by a user event) can perform some actions while the document is still loading, but must avoid other actions until the entire page has loaded, this property provides intermediate information about the loading process. You would use its value in condition tests. The value of this property changes during loading as the loading state changes. Each change of the property value fires a readystatechange event.

Example

```
if (document.readyState == "loading") {
    // statements for alternate handling
}
```

Value	One of the following values (as strings): complete	interactive	loading	uninitialized. Some elements may allow the user to interact with partial content, in which case the property may return interactive until all loading has completed.
Default	None.

referrer

IE 3 NN 2 Moz *all* Saf *all* Op 7 DOM 1

Read-only

Returns a string of the URL of the page from which the current page was accessed, provided the original page had a link to the current page. Many server logs capture this information as well. Scripts can see whether the visitor reached the current document from specific origins and perhaps present slightly different content on the page accordingly. If the visitor arrived by another method, such as typing the document URL into a browser dialog or by selecting a bookmark, the referrer property returns an empty string. Many versions of IE for Windows fail to report the correct referrer URL, often showing the URL of the current page instead.

Example

```
if (document.referrer) {
    document.write("<p>Thanks for following the link to our web site.</p>");
}
```

Value	String.
Default	None.

scripts[ ]

Read-only

Returns an array of all script objects (script elements) in the current document. Each script object may contain any number of functions. The scripts[] collection counts the number of actual <script> tags in the document. Items in this array are indexed (zero-based) in source code order.

Example	`var scriptCount = document.scripts.length;`
Value	Array of script element references.
Default	Array of zero length.

security

Read-only

Returns a string describing the security policy in force for the current document.

Example	`var secPolicy = document.security;`
Value	String.
Default	`This type of document does not have a security certificate.`

selectedStylesheetSet

Read/Write

Returns the title property value of the imported style sheet marked up to be the document author's preferred one and currently selected. This appears to be an experimental property (see *http://hixie.ch/specs/css/dom/altss/altss-1.0-pre7*).

Value	String.
Default	Empty string.

selection

Read-only

Returns a selection object. To work with text that has been selected by the user or script, you must convert the selection to a TextRange object. Access to the text of a Mozilla or Safari selection is via the window.getSelection( ) method.

Example	`var range = document.selection.createRange( );`
Value	Object reference.
Default	None.

strictErrorChecking

IE *n/a* NN *n/a* Moz *1.8* Saf *n/a* Op *n/a* DOM *3*

Read/Write

Boolean value that controls whether the browser throws exceptions for DOM operations.

Example   `document.strictErrorChecking = false;`

Value   Boolean value: `true` | `false`.

Default   `true`

styleSheets[ ]

IE *4* NN *n/a* Moz *all* Saf *all* Op *7* DOM *2*

Read-only

Returns an array of all `styleSheet` objects in the current document. Each style sheet object may contain any number of style sheet rules. The `styleSheets[]` collection counts the number of actual `<style>` tags in the document as well as `<link>` tags that load external style sheet files. Items in this array are indexed (zero-based) in source code order. An `@import` style sheet object is accessible via a `styleSheet` object's `cssRule.styleSheet` property. See the `styleSheet` object.

Example

```
for (var i = 0; i < document.styleSheets.length; i++) {
    // loop through each styleSheet object
}
```

Value   Array of `styleSheet` object references.

Default   Array of zero length.

tags[ ]

IE *n/a* NN |*4*| Moz *n/a* Saf *n/a* Op *n/a* DOM *n/a*

Read-only

Used with the Navigator 4-only JavaScript syntax of style sheets, the `tags[]` collection is part of a reference to a single tag type and the style property assigned to it. For a list of properties, see the `tags` object listing in this chapter. Do not confuse this Navigator use of the `tags[]` collection with Internet Explorer's use of the `tags[]` collection that belongs to the `all` collection.

Example   `document.tags.H1.color= "red";`

Value   Array of Navigator 4 JavaScript Style Sheet tag object references.

Default   Array of zero length.

title

IE *3* NN *2* Moz *all* Saf *all* Op *7* DOM *1*

Read/Write

Unlike the `title` property for objects that reflect HTML elements, the `document.title` property refers to the content of the `title` element defined in the head portion of a document. The title content appears in the browser's titlebar to help identify the document. This is also the content that goes into a bookmark listing for the page. Although the property is read/write, don't be surprised if a browser version does not alter the window titlebar in response for security reasons.

Example   `document.title = "Fred\'s Home Page";`

Value   String.

Default   None.

URL

IE 4 NN 3 Moz *all* Saf *all* Op 7 DOM 1

Read/Write

Provides the URL of the current document. The value is the same as `location.href`. The `document.URL` property evolved as a replacement for `document.location` to avoid potential confusion (by scripters and JavaScript interpreter engines) between the `location` object and `document.location` property.

Example   `document.URL = "http://www.megacorp.com";`

Value   Complete or relative URL as a string.

Default   The current document's URL.

URLUnencoded

IE 5.5 NN *n/a* Moz *n/a* Saf *n/a* Op *n/a* DOM *n/a*

Read-only

Returns the URL of the current document, but with any URL-encoded characters returned to their plain-language version (e.g., %20 is converted to a space character). The returned value is the same as if applying the JavaScript `decodeURI( )` function to `document.URL`.

Example   `var straightPath = document.URLUnencoded;`

Value   Complete or relative URL as a string.

Default   The current document's URL.

vlinkColor

IE 3 NN 2 Moz *all* Saf *all* Op 7 DOM *n/a*

Read/Write

Color of a hypertext link that has been visited recently. The color is applied to the link text or border around an image or object embedded within an a element. See also `alinkColor` and `linkColor` properties for clicked and unvisited link colors. Changes to this property do not dynamically change the link color in Navigator 4 or earlier. In modern browsers, you should use the W3C DOM alternative, `document.body.vLink`, or, better still, the CSS : visited pseudo-class.

Example   `document.vlinkColor = "gold";`

Value   A hexadecimal triplet or plain-language color name. See Appendix A for acceptable plain-language color names.

Default   Varies with browser and operating system.

width

See height.

xmlEncoding, xmlStandalone, xmlVersion

IE *n/a*   NN *n/a*   Moz *1.8*   Saf *n/a*   Op *n/a*   DOM *3*

See text

These three properties reflect information in an XML document's XML declaration. For example, in the following declaration

```
<?xml version="1.0" standalone="yes"?>
```

The xmlVersion property reports 1.0 and xmlStandalone returns true. Because there is no character encoding declared, the xmlEncoding property returns an empty string. The xmlVersion property is read-only, while the other two are read-write.

Although Mozilla 1.8 and 1.8.1 support these properties, they are not completely implemented, and may report incorrect values.

Value   Strings (xmlVersion and xmlEncoding); Boolean (xmlStandalone).

Default   Should be null, false, and null (respectively), but in Mozilla 1.8 and 1. 8.1 evaluate to an empty string, false, and an empty string (respectively).

addBinding( ), getAnonymousElementByAttribute( ), getAnonymousNodes( ), getBindingParent( ), loadBindingDocument( ), removeBinding( )

IE *n/a*   NN *n/a*   Moz *all*   Saf *n/a*   Op *n/a*   DOM *n/a*

This series of Mozilla document object methods are part of a browser programming feature called Extensible Binding Language (XBL), an adjunct to the XML-based mechanism that the browser uses for generating user interface skins. To learn more about XBL, visit *http://www.mozilla.org/docs/xul/xulnotes/xulnote_xbl.html*.

adoptNode( )

IE *n/a*   NN *n/a*   Moz *1.7.8*   Saf *n/a*   Op *7*   DOM *3*

adoptNode(nodeReference)

Removes a node from another document and brings it into the context of the current document. You can then use other methods of the current document to insert the node into the desired location in the document tree.

Returned Value   Reference to adopted node.

Parameters

nodeReference
> A reference to the node (usually in another document) you intend to adopt into the current document.

captureEvents( )   IE *n/a* NN *4* Moz *all* Saf *all* Op *8* DOM *n/a*

captureEvents(*eventTypeList*)

Instructs the browser to grab events of a specific type before they reach their intended target objects. The object invoking this method must then have event handlers defined for the given event types to process the event. Although this method is part of the Navigator 4 event model, it continues to be supported in Mozilla, as well as Safari and Opera 8 or later, creating the equivalent of a W3C DOM capture-mode event listener for the document object. While the method may be convenient, you should direct new code to the W3C DOM event listener syntax as described in Online Section VI.

Returned Value   None.

Parameters

eventTypeList
> A comma-separated list of case-sensitive event types as derived from the available static Event object constants, such as Event.CLICK or Event.MOUSEMOVE.

clear( )   IE *3* NN *2* Moz *all* Saf *all* Op *7* DOM *n/a*

Removes the current document from the window or frame, usually in preparation to open a new stream for writing new content. The document.write( ) and document.writeln( ) methods automatically invoke this method. Many bugs with the document.clear( ) method plagued earlier browser versions. Even today, it is best to let the document writing methods handle the job for you. The W3C DOM explicitly omits this method.

Returned Value   None.

Parameters   None.

close( )   IE *3* NN *2* Moz *all* Saf *all* Op *7* DOM *1*

Closes the document writing stream to a window or frame. If a script uses document.write( ) or document.writeln( ) to generate all-new content for a window or frame (which will replace the entire current document with the newly written content), you must append a document.close( ) method to make sure the entire content is written to the document. Omitting this method may cause some content not to be written. This method also prepares the window or frame for a brand new set of content with the next document writing method. Do not, however, use document.close( ) if you use the document writing methods to dynamically write content to a page while loading from the server.

Returned Value   None.

Parameters   None.

createAttribute( ) IE 5(Mac)/6(Win) NN n/a Moz all Saf all Op 7 DOM 1

createAttribute("*attributeName*")

Generates in memory an instance of an attribute node (Attr object). A typical sequence is to create the attribute, assign a value to it via its nodeValue property, and then insert the Attr node into an element's attribute list via the element's setAttributeNode( ) method.

Returned Value   Attr node object reference.

Parameters

attributeName
   A case-sensitive string of the attribute's name.

createAttributeNS( ) IE n/a NN n/a Moz all Saf all Op 8 DOM 2

createAttributeNS("*namespaceURI*", "*qualifiedName*")

Generates in memory an instance of an attribute node (Attr object) whose name is defined in an external namespace. A typical sequence is to create the attribute, assign a value to it via its nodeValue property, and then insert the Attr node into an element's attribute list via the element's setAttributeNodeNS( ) method.

Returned Value   Attr node object reference.

Parameters

namespaceURI
   URI string that will match a URI assigned to a label earlier in the document into which the attribute is eventually added.

qualifiedName
   The full name for the attribute, consisting of the local name prefix (if any), a colon, and the local name.

createCDATASection( ) IE 5(Mac) NN n/a Moz all Saf all Op 8 DOM 1

createCDATASection("*data*")

Generates in memory an instance of a character data section node (CDATASection object) in an XML (including XHTML) document.

Returned Value   CDATASection node object reference.

Parameters

data
   String data that comprises the content of the section.

createComment( ) IE 5(Mac)/6(Win) NN n/a Moz all Saf all Op 7 DOM 1

createComment("*commentText*")

Generates in memory an instance of a comment node (comment object with a nodeValue of 8). A typical sequence is to create the Comment node, then insert it into the desired location of the document tree via any node's appendChild( ) or insertBefore( ) method. Only partially implemented in IE 5/Mac.

Returned Value   Comment node object reference.

Parameters

commentText

    String containing the comment data.

createDocumentFragment( )   IE *5(Mac)/6(Win)*   NN *n/a*   Moz *all*   Saf *all*   Op *7*   DOM *1*

Generates in memory an instance of an empty document fragment node (DocumentFragment object). This node becomes an arbitrary holder for assembling a sequence of nodes that ultimately get appended or inserted into a document tree. See the DocumentFragment object for more details.

Returned Value   DocumentFragment node object reference.

Parameters   None.

createElement( )   IE *4*   NN *n/a*   Moz *all*   Saf *all*   Op *7*   DOM *1*

createElement("*tagName*")

Generates in memory an instance of an element object associated with the tag passed as a parameter to the method. The method is limited to area, img, and option elements in IE 4; all elements are permitted in other supporting browsers. A newly created element has no attribute values assigned (except any default values assigned according to the DTD), nor is the element yet part of the document tree. Assign attributes (such as the type for an input element or id for any element), and append or insert the element into the document tree. This sequence is the W3C DOM approach to generating new content (in place of the Microsoft proprietary innerHTML convenience property implemented in many modern browsers).

Returned Value   Element object reference.

Parameters

tagName

    A string of the tag name of the new element: document.createElement("option"). IE also allows a complete start tag string, complete with angle brackets and attribute name/value pairs. Only the straight tag name is supported by the W3C DOM specification.

createElementNS( )   IE *n/a*   NN *n/a*   Moz *all*   Saf *all*   Op *8*   DOM *2*

createElementNS("*namespaceURI*", "*qualifiedName*")

Generates in memory an instance of an element object associated with namespace, label, and tag passed as parts of the method's parameters. A newly created element has no attribute values assigned (except any default values assigned according to the DTD), nor is the element yet part of the document tree. Assign attributes (such as the type for an input element or id for any element), and append or insert the element into the document tree.

Returned Value   Element object reference.

Parameters

namespaceURI
> URI string that will match a URI assigned to a label earlier in the document into which the attribute is eventually added.

qualifiedName
> The full name for the attribute, consisting of the local name prefix (if any), a colon, and the local name.

createEntityReference( )   IE *5(Mac)* NN *n/a* Moz *all* Saf *all* Op *n/a* DOM *1*
createEntityReference("*entityName*")

Generates in memory an instance of an entity reference node object for an XML document. Only partial support provided in IE 5/Mac.

Returned Value   Entity reference node object reference.

Parameters

entityName
> String value.

createEvent( )   IE *n/a* NN *n/a* Moz *all* Saf *all* Op *7* DOM *2*
createEvent("*eventType*")

Generates in memory an instance of a W3C DOM Event object of a particular event category. After the generic event is created, it must be initialized (via one of several initialization methods) as a particular event type, along with other properties appropriate for the event category. The following sequence creates a mousedown event and sends it to an element:

```
var evt = document.createEvent("MouseEvents");
evt.initEvent("mousedown", true, true);
document.getElementById("myElement").dispatchEvent(evt);
```

Such an event might then be handed to an element (via the element's dispatchEvent( ) method) so that the element's event listener can process the event as if it had been generated by a user clicking the mouse button.

Returned Value   Event object object reference.

Parameters

eventType
> String constant for one of the event categories in all supporting browsers: HTMLEvents, KeyEvents (not specified in the W3C DOM Level 2), MouseEvents, MutationEvents, or UIEvents. DOM Level 3 restructures this list with all-new (singular) event categories

(supported starting with Mozilla 1.7.5 and Opera 8): Event (formerly HTMLEvents), KeyboardEvent, MouseEvent, MutationEvent, MutationNameEvent, TextEvent, or UIEvent.

createEventObject( )   IE *5.5* NN *n/a* Moz *n/a* Saf *n/a* Op *n/a* DOM *n/a*

createEventObject([*existingEventObject*])

Generates in memory an instance of an empty IE DOM event object. After the generic event is created, its properties can be stuffed with pertinent values to help the event be processed. Then the event acts as a parameter to an element's fireEvent( ) method, at which point the event type is associated with the event. The following sequence creates a mousedown event and sends it to an element:

```
var evt = document.createEventObject( );
document.getElementById("myElement").fireEvent("onmousedown", evt);
```

You can also use an existing event object as a model for a script-generated event. Pass the current event object as a parameter to the createEventObject( ) method, and modify the properties of the new object as you see fit.

Returned Value   event object reference.

Parameters
existingEventObject

Reference to an event object either generated by the user or script. The new event assumes all properties of the existing event object.

createNodeIterator( )   IE *n/a* NN *n/a* Moz *n/a* Saf *1.3/2* Op *8* DOM *2*

createNodeIterator(*rootNode, whatToShow, filterFunction, entityRefExpansion*)

Generates in memory an instance of a NodeIterator object. This method has the same set of parameters as the createTreeWalker( ) method.

Returned Value   NodeIterator object reference.

Parameters
rootNode

Reference to a node in the document tree that becomes the first node in the NodeIterator object's list of nodes.

whatToShow

Integer value corresponding to one of several built-in filters that allow nodes of a single type to be included in the NodeIterator object returned by the method. The NodeFilter object contains constants that should be used as plain-language substitutes for this value:

NodeFilter.SHOW_ALL	NodeFilter.SHOW_ATTRIBUTE
NodeFilter.SHOW_CDATA_SECTION	NodeFilter.SHOW_COMMENT
NodeFilter.SHOW_DOCUMENT	NodeFilter.SHOW_DOCUMENT_FRAGMENT
NodeFilter.SHOW_DOCUMENT_TYPE	NodeFilter.SHOW_ELEMENT
NodeFilter.SHOW_ENTITY	NodeFilter.SHOW_ENTITY_REFERENCE

```
        NodeFilter.SHOW_NOTATION              NodeFilter.SHOW_PROCESSING_INSTRUCTION
        NodeFilter.SHOW_TEXT
```

filterFunction

Reference to a user function that can further filter nodes that are included in the `NodeIterator` object. The function has a single parameter (a reference to a node to test, invoked automatically by the `NodeIterator` object). The value returned by the function determines whether the node being tested is to be included in the list of nodes. Returned values are integers, but the `NodeFilter` object provides three constants you should use as plain-language substitutes:

```
        NodeFilter.FILTER_ACCEPT              NodeFilter.FILTER_REJECT
        NodeFilter.FILTER_SKIP
```

Because a `NodeIterator` object does not maintain its list of nodes as a hierarchy, the values `NodeFilter.FILTER_REJECT` and `NodeFilter.FILTER_SKIP` pass over a node without any effect on child nodes. See the `TreeWalker` object for an example of this kind of function.

entityRefExpansion

Boolean value that controls whether the content of entity reference nodes (found predominantly in XML documents) should be treated as hierarchical nodes (`true`) or not (`false`).

createProcessingInstruction( )   IE *5(Mac)* NN *n/a* Moz *all* Saf *all* Op *8* DOM *1*

createProcessingInstruction("*target*", "*data*")

Generates in memory an instance of a processing instruction node object in an XML document. Only partial support provided in IE 5/Mac.

Returned Value   Processing instruction node object reference.

Parameters

target

String value.

data

String value.

createRange( )   IE *n/a* NN *n/a* Moz *all* Saf *1.2* Op *n/a* DOM *2*

Creates a blank `Range` object, whose boundary points are collapsed to the point before the first character of the rendered body text. The method returns a reference to that `Range` object, which you then use to adjust its boundary points, invoke its methods, and so on. See the `Range` object for details of its language features.

Returned Value   W3C DOM `Range` object reference.

Parameters   None.

createStyleSheet( )

createStyleSheet(["*url*"[, *index*]])

This method performs the same actions in IE for Windows and Macintosh, but their returned values differ. Moreover, the specific actions in the document tree depend upon the parameters passed with the method. When no parameters are included, the method inserts a blank `style` element into the document tree. This `style` element, however, is not reflected in the `document.styleSheets` collection until you add one or more style rules to the object. But if you specify a URL to an external .css file as the first parameter, the method creates and inserts a `link` element into the document's head section, bringing the external style rules to life immediately.

IE for Windows always returns a reference to a `styleSheet` object; IE for Macintosh returns a reference to the newly inserted element, which will be a `style` or `link` element, depending on the parameter makeup. The inserted `style` element reference is of little help for adding a rule because you can't reference the `styleSheet` object. For cross-operating-system compatibility, it's best to use this method only for external style sheets.

Returned Value   `styleSheet` object reference (Windows); `style` or `link` element object reference (IE 5 and later for Macintosh).

Parameters

url
>   A string of the URL of an external .css style sheet definition file.

index
>   Optional zero-based integer that indicates where among the `styleSheets[]` collection this new style sheet should be inserted. Default behavior is to append to the end of the collection, but this may affect cascading rules for your document. See Online Section III.

createTextNode( )

createTextNode("*text*")

Generates in memory an instance of a text node (W3C DOM Text object) whose `nodeValue` consists of the untagged text content passed as a parameter. A newly created text node is not yet part of the document tree. Append or insert the node into the document tree or document fragment being assembled for later document insertion. This sequence is the W3C DOM approach to generating new content (in place of the Microsoft proprietary `innerText` convenience property implemented in some browsers).

Returned Value   Text node object reference.

Parameters

text
>   A string of characters to be rendered as content when inserted into the document tree.

createTreeWalker( )   IE *n/a*   NN *n/a*   Moz *1.0.1*   Saf *1.3/2*   Op *8*   DOM *2*

createTreeWalker(*rootNode*, *whatToShow*, *filterFunction*, *entityRefExpansion*)

Generates in memory an instance of a TreeWalker object.

Returned Value   TreeWalker object reference.

Parameters

rootNode

> Reference to a node in the document tree that becomes the first node in the TreeWalker object's list of nodes.

whatToShow

> Integer value corresponding to one of several built-in filters that allow nodes of a single type to be included in the TreeWalker object returned by the method. The NodeFilter object contains constants that should be used as plain-language substitutes for this value:

NodeFilter.SHOW_ALL	NodeFilter.SHOW_ATTRIBUTE
NodeFilter.SHOW_CDATA_SECTION	NodeFilter.SHOW_COMMENT
NodeFilter.SHOW_DOCUMENT	NodeFilter.SHOW_DOCUMENT_FRAGMENT
NodeFilter.SHOW_DOCUMENT_TYPE	NodeFilter.SHOW_ELEMENT
NodeFilter.SHOW_ENTITY	NodeFilter.SHOW_ENTITY_REFERENCE
NodeFilter.SHOW_NOTATION	NodeFilter.SHOW_PROCESSING_INSTRUCTION
NodeFilter.SHOW_TEXT	

filterFunction

> Reference to a user function that can further filter nodes that are included in the TreeWalker object. The function has a single parameter (a reference to a node to test, invoked automatically by the TreeWalker object). The value returned by the function determines whether the node being tested is to be included in the list of nodes. Returned values are integers, but the NodeFilter object provides three constants you should use as plain-language substitutes:

NodeFilter.FILTER_ACCEPT	NodeFilter.FILTER_REJECT
NodeFilter.FILTER_SKIP	

With a return value of NodeFilter.FILTER_SKIP, descendant nodes of the skipped node may still qualify as members of the TreeWalker node list (provided they survive other filtering). A return value of NodeFilter.FILTER_REJECT removes both the node under test and its descendants from consideration as members of the TreeWalker object. See the TreeWalker object for an example of this kind of function.

entityRefExpansion

> Boolean value that controls whether the content of entity reference nodes (found predominantly in XML documents) should be treated as hierarchical nodes (true) or not (false).

elementFromPoint( )

elementFromPoint(x, y)

Returns a reference to the object directly underneath the pixel coordinates specified by the x (horizontal) and y (vertical) parameters. For an element to be recognized, it must be capable of responding to mouse events. Also, if more than one element is positioned in the same location, the element with the highest zIndex value or, given equal zIndex values, the element that comes last in the source code order is the one returned.

Returned Value   Element object reference.

Parameters

x

Horizontal pixel measure relative to the left edge of the window or frame.

y

Vertical pixel measure relative to the top edge of the window or frame.

execCommand( )

execCommand("commandName"[, UIFlag[, value]])

Executes the named command. In IE, most commands require that a TextRange object be created first for an insertion point, while in the rest, the command impacts either the current text insertion point or selection. See Appendix D for a list of commands.

Returned Value   Boolean value: true if command was successful; false if unsuccessful.

Parameters

commandName

A case-insensitive string value of the command name. See Appendix D.

UIFlag

Optional Boolean value: true to display any user interface triggered by the command (if any); false to prevent such display.

value

A parameter value for the command.

getAnonymousElementByAttribute( )

See addBinding( ).

getAnonymousNodes( )

See addBinding( ).

getBindingParent( )

See addBinding( ).

getElementById( )   IE 5   NN *n/a*   Moz *all*   Saf *all*   Op 7   DOM 1

getElementById("*elementID*")

Returns a reference to an element node from the document tree whose id attribute value matches the parameter value. If there is no match, the method returns null. This method, although a chore to type while observing its case-sensitive name, is the gateway for scripts in W3C DOM-capable browsers to communicate with element objects.

Returned Value   Reference to element node object.

Parameters

elementID
   String of the desired element's ID.

getElementsByName( )   IE 5   NN *n/a*   Moz *all*   Saf *all*   Op 7   DOM 1

getElementsByName("*elementName*")

Returns an array of references to all element nodes from the document tree whose name attribute value matches the parameter value. If there is no match, the method returns null. When an element supports both the name and id attribute, IE for Windows and Opera include an element in the returned array even if only the id attribute is set to the parameter value. Other supporting browsers match only elements that have name attributes explicitly set to the parameter value (as prescribed in the W3C DOM spec).

Returned Value   Array of references to element node object.

Parameters

elementName
   String of the desired element's name.

getOverrideStyle( )   IE *n/a*   NN *n/a*   Moz *n/a*   Saf *n/a*   Op *n/a*   DOM 2

getOverrideStyle(*elementReference, pseudoElement*)

Returns a style object (CSSStyleDeclaration type) for the element passed as a parameter. This method allows a script to get (and then set via setProperty( )) style sheet properties of XML documents, which don't have the style convenience facilities of HTML documents. While Safari 1.3/2 implements the method, the returned value is empty.

Returned Value   Style object of type CSSStyleDeclaration.

Parameters

elementReference
   Reference to a single element object in the document.

pseudoElement
   String denoting a pseudo-element, if necessary; otherwise null.

getSelection( )

In Navigator 4, this method captures the current text selection in the document. The method is deprecated in Mozilla in favor of the window.getSelection( ) method (which returns a sophisticated selection object, rather than just text). Invoking from the document object in Mozilla displays a warning in the JavaScript/Error Console window, but does not throw a full-fledged exception. The IE equivalent is reading the selection property.

Returned Value String.

Parameters None.

handleEvent( )

handleEvent(*event*)

Instructs the document object to accept and process the Navigator 4-only event whose specifications are passed as the parameter to the method. The object must have an event handler for the event type to process the event.

Returned Value None.

Parameters

event
    A Navigator 4 event object.

hasFocus( )

Returns Boolean true if the document or any element in the document has focus. A background process, such as a function invoked through setTimeout( ) can find out if the document's window is currently the front window on the Desktop.

Returned Value Boolean value: true | false.

Parameters None.

importNode( )

importNode(*nodeReference, deepBoolean*)

Imports a node object from another loaded document into the current document, but not yet place the node into the document tree. In many ways, importNode( ) works like cloneNode( ), but it assumes that the source node may exist in an entirely different document tree context (especially in an XML document). W3C DOM rules for this method govern what properties and attributes of the source node make the journey and what happens to them upon their arrival. For example, an Attr node loses its ownerElement (i.e., its value becomes null) when imported from an element in one document into a fragment-like state in the new document—until the attribute gets added to an element in the new document. Nodes of Document and DocumentType types are not importable.

The importNode( ) method does not assume the responsibility of persistence between documents. That's where, for instance, a JavaScript variable comes into play. As with cloneNode( ), the importNode( ) method does not disturb the source node (unlike adoptNode( ), which removes the source node from its original location).

Returned Value   Reference to the imported copy of the node object.

Parameters

nodeReference
Reference to a node in a different loaded document (including a nonrendered document loaded into the browser by way of the document.implementation.createDocument( ) method).

deepBoolean
Boolean value that controls whether the copy includes all nested nodes (true) or only the current node (false). Required, but applicable primarily to element nodes.

loadBindingDocument( )

See addBinding( ).

normalizeDocument( )   IE *n/a* NN *n/a* Moz *n/a* Saf *n/a* Op *n/a* DOM *3*

Among other actions, performs the equivalent of invoking the normalize( ) method on all elements in the document at once. Other actions may be influenced by specific settings of the DOMConfiguration object for the current document.

Returned Value   None.

Parameters   None.

open( )   IE *3* NN *2* Moz *all* Saf *all* Op *7* DOM *1*

open(["*MIMEType*"][, "replace"])

Opens the output stream for writing to the current window or frame. If document.clear( ) has not already been invoked, it is automatically invoked in response to the document.open( ) method. If you are writing HTML text, you can omit this method, and start right in with document.write( ) or document.writeln( ).

Returned Value   None.

Parameters

MIMEType
Advises the browser of the MIME type of the data to be written in subsequent statements. Navigator supports "text/html" | "text/plain" | "image/gif" | "image/jpeg" | "image/xbm" | "plugIn". Only "text/html" is supported in Internet Explorer.

replace
The presence of this parameter directs the browser to replace the entry in the history list for the current document with the document about to be written.

postMessage( )

```
postMessage("messageText")
```

Permits the transfer of text data from one document to another, even if the two documents are served from different domains. Both documents have to be loaded and the destination document must have a suitable reference available for the method to work. For example if the main document includes an iframe element containing a document from another domain, the main document can reference the other document and send it a text message:

```
var destDoc = document.getElementById("myIframe").contentDocument;
destDoc.postMessage("blue");
```

The following event handler binding in the destination document processes the event to change the background color of the document in the iframe element:

```
document.addEventListener("message", receiver, false);
function receiver(evt) {
    if (evt.domain == "example-friendly-place.com") {
        document.body.style.backgroundColor = evt.data;
    }
}
```

String data could obviously be assigned to other script variables in the destination document, including data that can be evaluated into arrays and objects (JavaScript Object Notation). This mechanism comes from the WHATWG Web Applications 1.0 specification (*http://whatwg.org/specs/web-apps/current-work*).

Returned Value   None.

Parameters

messageText
   String value to be passed to another document.

queryCommandEnabled( )

```
queryCommandEnabled("commandName")
```

Specifies whether the command can be invoked in light of the current state of the document or selection.

Returned Value   Boolean value: true if enabled; false if not.

Parameters

commandName
   A case-insensitive string value of the command name. See Appendix D.

queryCommandIndeterm( )

```
queryCommandIndeterm("commandName")
```

Specifies whether the command is in an indeterminate state.

Returned Value   Boolean value: true | false.

Parameters

commandName

    A case-insensitive string value of the command name. See Appendix D.

queryCommandState( )   IE *4(Win)* NN *n/a* Moz *n/a* Saf *1.3/2* Op *9* DOM *n/a*

queryCommandState("*commandName*")

Determines the current state of the named command.

Returned Value   true if the command has been completed; false if the command has not completed; null if the state cannot be accurately determined.

Parameters

commandName

    A case-insensitive string value of the command name. See Appendix D.

queryCommandSupported( )   IE *4(Win)* NN *n/a* Moz *n/a* Saf *1.3/2* Op *9* DOM *n/a*

queryCommandSupported("*commandName*")

Determines whether the named command is supported by the document object.

Returned Value   Boolean value: true | false.

Parameters

commandName

    A case-insensitive string value of the command name. See Appendix D.

queryCommandText( )   IE *4(Win)* NN *n/a* Moz *n/a* Saf *1.3/2* Op *9* DOM *n/a*

queryCommandText("*commandName*")

Returns text associated with the command.

Returned Value   String.

Parameters

commandName

    A case-insensitive string value of the command name. See Appendix D.

queryCommandValue( )   IE *4(Win)* NN *n/a* Moz *n/a* Saf *1.3/2* Op *9* DOM *n/a*

queryCommandValue("*commandName*")

Returns the value associated with the command, such as the name font of the selection.

Returned Value   Depends on the command.

Parameters

commandName

    A case-insensitive string value of the command name. See Appendix D.

recalc( )

recalc([allBoolean])

Forces the recalculation of expressions assigned to element attributes via the setExpression( ) method. Needed only when automatic recalculation isn't triggered by user action, but affected values might have changed.

Returned Value   None.

Parameters

allBoolean

When set to true, forces all dynamic attribute expressions in the document to recalculate. The default false lets browser decide which expressions are affected by changes since the last manual or automatic recalculation.

releaseEvents( )

releaseEvents(eventTypeList)

The opposite of document.captureEvents( ), this method turns off event capture at the document level for one or more specific events named in the parameter list. Although this method is part of the Navigator 4 event model, it continues to be supported in Mozilla, as well as Safari and Opera 8 or later, performing the equivalent of a W3C DOM event listener removal for the document object. While the method may be convenient, you should direct new code to the W3C DOM event listener syntax as described in Online Section VI.

Returned Value   None.

Parameters

eventTypeList

A comma-separated list of case-sensitive event types as derived from the available Event object constants, such as Event.CLICK or Event.MOUSEMOVE.

removeBinding( )

See addBinding( ).

renameNode( )

renameNode(nodeReference, "namespaceURI", "qualifiedName")

Renames an element or attribute node in the current document. An element's name in this context is its tag name.

Returned Value   Reference to the newly renamed node (if the renaming took effect).

Parameters

nodeReference

Reference to the node whose name is to be changed.

namespaceURI

String of the namespace URI, or an empty string of no namespace is involved.

qualifiedName
Full name of the element or attribute, including namespace prefix, if applicable.

routeEvent( )   IE *n/a* NN *4* Moz *all* Saf *n/a* Op *n/a* DOM *n/a*

routeEvent(*event*)

Used inside an event handler function, this method directs Navigator 4 to let the event pass to its intended target object. The method does not cause an error in Mozilla, but it does not perform any action.

Returned Value   None.

Parameters

event
A Navigator 4 event object

write( ), writeln( )   IE *3* NN *2* Moz *all* Saf *all* Op *7* DOM *n/a*

write("*string1*"[, ..."*stringN*"]) writeln("*string1*"[, ..."*stringN*"])

When invoked as the page loads, these methods can dynamically add content to the page. When invoked after the page has loaded, a single method invocation clears the current document, opens a new output stream, and writes the content to the window or frame. A document.close( ) method is required afterward. Because the first document.write( ) or document.writeln( ) method destroys the current document, do not use two or more writing statements to create a new document. Instead, load the content into one variable and pass that variable as the parameter to a single document.write( ) or document.writeln( ) method.

Using document.write( ) for <script> tags is tricky in many early browsers because it typically interprets the writing of the end script tag as meaning the end of the script doing the writing. You should have success, however, if you split the end script tag into string sections:

```
document.write("<" + "/script>");
```

If you include the "hide script" comment trick, write it this way:

```
document.write("//--" + ">");
```

The difference between the two methods is that document.writeln( ) adds a carriage return to the source code it writes to the document. This is not reflected in the rendered content, but can make reading the dynamic source code easier in browser versions that support dynamic content source viewing.

Returned Value   None.

Parameters

string
Any string value, including HTML tags.

Document

IE *n/a* **NN** *n/a* **Moz** *all* **Saf** *all* **Op** *8* **DOM** *1*

The document object described earlier is, in the W3C DOM structure, more specifically an HTMLDocument node, a member of the HTML module of the standard. The HTMLDocument node inherits the properties and methods of the Document node (with an uppercase "D" described here, and defined in the W3C DOM Core module). This is the pure, abstract Document node, and all that is needed to contain an unrendered XML document.

Mozilla and Opera 9 extend this node with a load( ) method that allows scripts to load XML documents into a plain (and unseen) Document node. Such a node is created via the document.implementation.createDocument( ) method. Scripts can then access the XML data in that document through regular W3C DOM document tree properties and methods. The XMLHttpRequest object, however, is now the preferred way to load external XML data into the browser.

To help reinforce in your mind the heritage of the document object you normally script (that is, the instance of the HTMLDocument node represented in each window's document), I show the lists of properties and methods for the core Document object. For descriptions of all these properties and methods—except for the uninherited load( ) method—see the document object, earlier in this chapter.

Object Model Reference

documentNodeReference

Object-Specific Properties

doctype	documentElement	documentURI
domConfig	implementation	inputEncoding
strictErrorChecking	XMLEncoding	XMLStandalone
XMLVersion		

Object-Specific Methods

adoptNode( )	createAttribute( )
createAttributeNS( )	createCDATASection( )
createComment( )	createDocumentFragment( )
createElement( )	createElementNS( )
createEntityReference( )	createProcessingInstruction( )
createTextNode( )	getElementById( )
getElementsByTagName( )	getElementsByTagNameNS( )
importNode( )	load( )
normalizeDocument( )	rename( )

Object-Specific Event Properties

None.

load( )   IE *n/a*   NN *n/a*   Moz *all*   Saf *n/a*   Op *9*   DOM *n/a*

load("*URI*")

Loads an XML file into the current Document object. Attempting to load other types of files (such as HTML) throws an exception. The server must be configured to send the file as the text/xml content type.

Returned Value   None.

Parameters

URI

     A string of the URI to an external XML file.

DocumentEvent

See document.

DocumentFragment   IE *6*   NN *n/a*   Moz *all*   Saf *all*   Op *7*   DOM *1*

The W3C DCM DocumentFragment object is essentially a context-free container of other DOM nodes. In other words, you can use all node properties and methods to assemble a sequence of element and text nodes outside of the document tree, but not influenced by the containment that the DocumentFragment provides. If you then append or insert the DocumentFragment node into the document tree, the DocumentFragment container disappears, and its node contents stand on their own within the context of their position in the document tree. The DocumentFragment isn't necessary to assemble content that is wrapped by an element node, because the element node can act as both the temporary container outside the document tree and the container after insertion into the document tree. But if one or both ends of a content segment end in a text node, the DocumentFragment node provides a transparent bucket to keep the string of nodes together until they are dropped into the document.

Create an empty DocumentFragment container via the document.createDocumentFragment( ) method. A DocumentFragment type of node inherits all properties and methods of the Node object (for inserting and appending other nodes you create), and adds nothing of its own other than its silent ability to hold other nodes. Do not confuse a DocumentFragment node with a string of tagged text that gets assigned to the innerHTML property of an element. The W3C DOM (as of Level 3) provides no such string-to-node-hierarchy conversion.

Object Model Reference

documentFragmentNodeReference

Object-Specific Properties

None.

Object-Specific Methods

None.

Object-Specific Events
None.

DocumentRange

See document.

DocumentStyle

See document.

DocumentTraversal　　　　IE *n/a*　NN *n/a*　Moz *1.0.1*　Saf *1.3/2*　Op *8*　DOM *2*

The DocumentTraversal object is defined in the Traversal module of the W3C DOM, where it defines the createNodeIterator( ) and createTreeWalker( ) methods. These methods (and the otherwise invisible DocumentTraversal interface) are blended into the document object so that scripts can access them as document.createTreeWalker( ) and createNodeIterator( ).

DocumentType　　　　IE *5(Mac)*　NN *n/a*　Moz *all*　Saf *n/a*　Op *7*　DOM *1*

Reflects the DOCTYPE element, if one arrives to the browser as part of the document flow. The DocumentType object is its own node type in the W3C DOM, and, just as indicated in its position in a document's source code, exists outside of the content portion of the document tree. Access to this object in supported browsers is via the document.doctype property. If no DOCTYPE element exists in the file, the property returns null.

Properties of the DocumentType object expose individual pieces of the data within the DOCTYPE tag, whose structure is determined by SGML standards. The W3C DOM Level 2 specification provides placeholder properties for these pieces, and both Mozilla and Opera implement most of them to one degree or other. But it is clear from the DOM specification that work on aligning the two worlds is not complete.

Object Model Reference
documentTypeNodeReference

Object-Specific Properties

entities	internalSubset	name	notations	publicId	systemId

Object-Specific Methods
None.

Object-Specific Events
None.

entities

Returns an array of nested Entity nodes within the DOCTYPE element. An Entity is formatted according to the following syntax (which would appear inside the DOCTYPE element's angle brackets):

```
[<!ENTITY publicID "systemID">]
```

Primarily applicable to XML documents.

Value	Array (technically, a NamedNodeMap data type) of Entity node object references.
Default	null

internalSubset

Returns a string value of the internal subset portion of the element.

Value	String.
Default	Empty string.

name

Returns a string value of the name portion of the element. The name is the first word that follows the DOCTYPE element's tag name. In the context of this book's subject, all HTML and XHTML documents show this value to be html. Note that although this object and property are implemented in IE 5/Macintosh, that browser returns the entire inner string value of the DOCTYPE element, starting with the html name.

Value	String.
Default	html

notations

Returns an array of references to Notation nodes within the DOCTYPE element.

Value	Array (technically, a NamedNodeMap data type) of Notation node object references.
Default	null

publicId

Returns a string value of the public identifier portion of the element. This data reveals the type of DTD, as in "-//W3C//DTD XHTML 1.0 Strict//EN".

Value	String.
Default	Empty string.

systemId

Returns a string value of the system identifier portion of the element. This data typically reveals the URI of DTD, as in "http://www.w3.org/TR/xhtml1/DTD/xhtml1-strict.dtd".

Value	String.
Default	Empty string.

DocumentView

See document.

DOMException

Some operations on W3C DOM objects can trigger errors, or, in the vernacular of Java-Script 1.5, throw exceptions, if something goes wrong. The W3C DOM defines an object that conveys a code number corresponding to a well-defined (if limited) list of exceptions. For example, if you attempt to append one text node as a child of another text node, the appendChild( ) method of such an operation throws an exception whose code number is 3. This number corresponds to the exception that signals an attempt to perform an illegal or logically impossible action on a DOM hierarchy (a text node can't have any child nodes).

The job of conveying the DOM exception information to a scripter falls to the hosting environment, rather than the DOM. Because JavaScript, starting with version 1.5, already has an exception handling mechanism, the task of blending the DOMException system with Java-Script exception handling fell first to Mozilla. The new mechanism permits different kinds of error objects to circulate through the exception handling operations, thus leaving the original system intact, while extending the mechanism to accommodate not only the W3C DOM DOMException object, but some browser-specific errors, as well. Processing of exceptions of all kinds continues to take place in the catch block of a try/catch construction, and all information about the exception is still passed as an object through a single parameter to the catch block.

Mozilla's DOM exception object (which embodies the W3C DOMException object) arrives at the catch block with a longer list of properties and methods associated with it than does an exception arising from other causes (e.g., trying to use a JavaScript variable that has not been initialized). The distinguishing property of a DOMException object, missing from the other types, is the code property. Moreover, any code value between 1 and 17 indicates an exception type known to the formal DOM specification through Level 3. Mozilla uses code numbers starting with 1000 for its list of browser-specific exceptions.

If you wish to process true W3C DOM exceptions along their own execution path, you can use a construction similar to the following (which allows for the DOMException list to grow to 999 in future iterations):

```
try {
    // your DOM-related statement goes here
}
catch(e) {
    if (typeof e.code == "number") {
        if (e.code < 1000) {
            // process DOMException object here
        } else {
            // process Netscape DOM exception object here
        }
    } else {
        // process language or other exceptions here
    }
}
```

Of course, it is highly unlikely that exception details will be of benefit to users, but they are invaluable to you during development. For more on exception handling, see the error object in Chapter 5.

Object Model Reference

errorObjectReference

Object-Specific Properties

code

Object-Specific Methods

None.

Object-Specific Events

None.

code

IE *n/a* NN *n/a* Moz *all* Saf *all* Op *7* DOM *1*

Read-only

Provides an integer corresponding to one of the defined DOM error types. The following table lists all code values, their constant equivalents, and examples of what kinds of problems throw the exception.

Code	Constant	Most likely cause
1	INDEX_SIZE_ERR	An integer offset parameter is out of the range of the target object.
2	DOMSTRING_SIZE_ERR	Property string value is too large for the hosting language.
3	HIERARCHY_REQUEST_ERR	Appending a child to a node not capable of children.

Code	Constant	Most likely cause
4	WRONG_DOCUMENT_ERR	Inserting a node created from a different document (without passing through the import process).
5	INVALID_CHARACTER_ERR	Assigning an identifier with an illegal character.
6	NO_DATA_ALLOWED_ERR	Assigning data to a node that doesn't allow data.
7	NO_MODIFICATION_ALLOWED_ERR	Assigning a value to a read-only property.
8	NOT_FOUND_ERR	Method parameter reference to a nonexistent node in the object's scope.
9	NOT_SUPPORTED_ERR	Invoking an XML-only method in an HTML document.
10	INUSE_ATTRIBUTE_ERR	Method parameter to an Attr node that already belongs to another element (without cloning the Attr first).
11	INVALID_STATE_ERR	Referencing a node that is not readable or writable.
12	SYNTAX_ERR	A slippery keyboard.
13	INVALID_MODIFICATION_ERR	Modifying the type of a node.
14	NAMESPACE_ERR	Namespace mismatch or malformed name.
15	INVALID_ACCESS_ERR	You can't go there.
16	VALIDATION_ERR	An attempted node operation would invalidate the Node.
17	TYPE_MISMATCH_ERR	The object is the wrong type.

Example

```
if (e.code == e.INVALID_CHARACTER_ERR) {
    // process for an illegal identifier character
}
```

Value   Integer

Default   Determined by error.

DOMImplementation

See implementation.

DOMParser   IE *n/a* NN *n/a* Moz *1.0.1* Saf *1.2* Op *8* DOM *n/a*

The DOMParser object transforms a string of XML markup into an XML document object (node type of 9). Browsers use this object internally, but the object is available to your scripts, if needed for other tasks. Mozilla exposes the parseFromBuffer() and parseFromStream() methods of the object, but some of the necessary parameters are data types not available to client-side scripts associated with web pages.

Object Model Reference

new DOMParser()

Object Properties   None.

Object Methods

parseFromString( )

Object-Specific Events
None.

parseFromString( )   IE *n/a* NN *n/a* Moz *1.0.1* Saf *1.2* Op *8* DOM *n/a*

parseFromString("*string*", "*MIMEType*")

If successful, returns a document object whose content consists of the node tree specified in the string passed as a parameter.

Returned Value   document object.

Parameters
string

XML markup as a string value to be converted into a complete XML document.

MIMEType

A content type (as a string), such as text/xml, application/xml, or application/xhtml+xml.

dt   IE *4* NN *n/a* Moz *all* Saf *all* Op *7* DOM *1*

The dt object reflects the dt element.

HTML Equivalent   <dt>

Object Model Reference
[window.]document.getElementById("*elementID*")

Object-Specific Properties
noWrap

Object-Specific Methods
None.

Object-Specific Events
None.

noWrap   IE *4* NN *n/a* Moz *n/a* Saf *n/a* Op *n/a* DOM *n/a*
Read/Write

Specifies whether the browser should render the element as wide as is necessary to display a line of nonbreaking text on one line. Abuse of this attribute can force the user into a great deal of inconvenient horizontal scrolling of the page to view all of the content.

Example   document.getElementById("wideItem").noWrap = "true";

Value	Boolean value: true | false.
Default	false

Element

The W3C DOM Element object is from the Core module and represents the kind of element object you find in true XML documents. This node type inherits properties and methods from the root Node object and adds capabilities that let it act as a container of other nodes. Elements in HTML documents are of the HTMLDocument type, which inherits form this Element object. All properties and methods of the Element object are shared among all HTML element objects, as described at the beginning of this chapter. DOM Level 3 may include some additional properties and methods, which are not yet implemented in any browser.

Object Model Reference

elementNodeReference

Object-Specific Properties

tagName

Object-Specific Methods

getAttribute( )	getAttributeNode( )	getAttributeNodeNS( )
getAttributeNS( )	hasAttribute( )	hasAttributeNS( )
removeAttribute( )	removeAttributeNode( )	removeAttributeNS( )
setAttribute( )	setAttributeNode( )	setAttributeNodeNS( )
setAttributeNS( )		

Object-Specific Event Properties

None.

ElementCSSInlineStyle

The W3C DOM ElementCSSInlineStyle object is from the StyleSheets module and represents style settings assigned to an element through an explicit style attribute. The HTMLElement object (and thus, all elements in HTML documents) gets its style property as a result of its connection with the ElementCSSInlineStyle object (the object's only property is style, which is what HTML elements pick up). Scripts don't ever touch this object, but dynamic styles in the W3C DOM couldn't exist without it in the abstract model.

Object Model Reference

None.

Object-Specific Properties
None.

Object-Specific Methods
None.

Object-Specific Events
None.

elements

A collection of all elements contained within a form. Collection members are sorted in source code order. Because each form element includes a type property, scripts can loop through all elements in search of elements of a specific type (e.g., all checkbox elements).

Object Model Reference
```
document.forms[i].elements
document.formName.elements
```

Object-Specific Properties
length

Object-Specific Methods

item( )   namedItem( )   tags( )

Object-Specific Events
None.

length

Read-only

Returns the number of form control elements in the collection.

Example   `var howMany = document.forms[0].elements.length;`

Value   Integer.

item( )

```
item(index[, subindex])
item(index)
```

Returns a single form control object or collection of form control objects corresponding to the element matching the index value (or, optionally in IE, the index and subindex values).

Returned Value   One form control object or collection (array) of form control objects. If there are no matches to the parameters, the returned value is null.

Parameters

index

When the parameter is a zero-based integer (per the W3C spec), the returned value is a single element that corresponds to the specified item in source code order. When the parameter is a string (IE), the returned value is a collection of elements whose id or name properties match that string.

subindex

In IE only, if you specify a string value for the first parameter, you can use the second parameter to specify a zero-based index that retrieves the specified element from the collection with id or name properties that match the first parameter's string value.

namedItem( )   IE 6 NN *n/a* Moz *all* Saf *all* Op 7 DOM 1

`namedItem(IDOrName)`

Returns a single form control object or collection of form control objects corresponding to the element matching the parameter string value.

Returned Value   One form control object or collection (array) of form control objects. If there are no matches to the parameters, the returned value is null.

Parameters

IDOrName

The string that contains the same value as the desired element's id or name attribute.

tags( )   IE 4 NN *n/a* Moz *n/a* Saf *all* Op 7 DOM *n/a*

`tags(tagName)`

Returns a collection of objects (among all objects nested within the current collection) with tags that match the *tagName* parameter. Implemented in all IE, Safari, and Opera collections (see the `all.tags( )` method), but redundant for collections of the same element type.

em

See abbr.

embed   IE 4 NN 3 Moz *all* Saf *all* Op 7 DOM *n/a*

The embed object reflects the embed element. Although the W3C standards point to the object element as being the one to load external content that trigger things like media players, the Mozilla browser still prefers the embed element for such tasks. Properties and methods exposed by the player pass through the embed object so that scripts treat the embed object as if its list of scriptable powers is extended. Properties listed here are the properties that the element object, rather than an external controller, exposes to scripts.

Note that IE 5 for the Macintosh treats the embed object more like the object object, and exposes properties more closely aligned with an object or applet than an embed object. It's of little consequence, however, because IE/Mac does not let scripts communicate with external players or controllers.

HTML Equivalent   `<embed>`

Object Model Reference
`[window.]document.getElementById("elementID")`
`[window.]document.embeds[i]`

Object-Specific Properties

align	height	hidden	name	palette
pluginspage	src	type	units	width

Object-Specific Methods

`getSVGDocument( )`

Object-Specific Events
None.

---

align
IE *5(Mac)* NN *n/a* Moz *all* Saf *n/a* Op *n/a* DOM *n/a*

Read/Write

Defines the alignment of the element within its surrounding container. See the "Alignment Constants" at the beginning of Chapter 1 for the various meanings that different values bring to this property.

Example   `document.getElementById("audioPlayer").align = "center";`

Value   Any of the alignment constants: `absbottom` | `absmiddle` | `baseline` | `bottom` | `left` | `middle` | `right` | `texttop` | `top`.

Default   `left`

---

height, width
IE *4* NN *n/a* Moz *all* Saf *all* Op *n/a* DOM *n/a*

Read/Write

Provide the height and width in pixels of the element as set by the tag attributes. Changing the values does not necessarily change the actual rectangle of the applet after it has loaded.

Example   `var controllerHeight = document.embeds["audioPlayer"].height;`

Value   Integer.

Default   0

hidden

Specifies whether the embedded data's plugin control panel appears on the screen. Changes to this property force the page to reflow its content to make room for the plugin control panel or close up space around a newly hidden panel.

Example   `document.embeds["jukebox"].hidden = true;`

Value   Boolean value: `true` | `false`.

Default   `false`

name

Reflects the `name` attribute value of the element's tag.

Example   `document.embeds["myEmbed"].name = "tunes";`

Value   Case-sensitive identifier that follows the rules of identifier naming: it may contain no whitespace, cannot begin with a numeral, and should avoid punctuation except for the underscore character.

Default   None.

palette

Returns the setting of the `palette` attribute of the embed element object.

Value   String.

Default   None.

pluginspage

Indicates the URL for downloading and installing the plugin necessary to run the current object's embedded data.

Value   A complete or relative URL as a string.

Default   None returned, but Internet Explorer has its own default URL for plugin information.

Alphabetical DOM Reference

src

IE 4   NN *n/a*   Moz *all*   Saf *all*   Op 7   DOM 1

Read/Write

Indicates URL of the external content file associated with the object. Although some controllers may respond to changes of this attribute, it is more reliable to load a different file into the controller via its own loading method or property.

Example	`document.embeds["myEmbed"].src = "tunes/dannyboy.wav";`
Value	Complete or relative URL as a string.
Default	None.

type

IE *n/a*   NN *n/a*   Moz *all*   Saf *n/a*   Op *n/a*   DOM *n/a*

Read-only

Indicates the MIME type of the external data assigned to the element's type attribute.

Example	`var dataMIME = document.embeds["myEmbed"].type;`
Value	Any valid MIME type name as a quoted string, including the type and subtype portions delimited by a forward slash.
Default	None.

units

IE *4(Win)*   NN *n/a*   Moz *n/a*   Saf *n/a*   Op *n/a*   DOM *n/a*

Read/Write

Specifies the unit of measure for the height and width dimensions of the element. Internet Explorer appears to treat all settings as pixels.

Example	`document.getElementById("myEmbed").units = "ems";`
Value	Any of the following case-insensitive constants (as a string): `pixels` | `px` | `em`.
Default	`pixels`

width

See height.

getSVGDocument( )

IE 6   NN *n/a*   Moz *1.8*   Saf *1.3/2*   Op 9   DOM *n/a*

Returns a reference to the document object containing the XML data within the *.svg* document. You can then invoke W3C DOM Core methods on the object.

Returned Value	Reference to the *.svg* document object loaded into the embed element.
Parameters	None.

embeds

IE *4* NN *n/a* Moz *all* Saf *all* Op *7* DOM *1*

A collection of all embed elements contained in the current element. Collection members are sorted in source code order. Internet Explorer lets you use array notation or parentheses to access a single element in the collection.

Object Model Reference
document.embeds

Object-Specific Properties
length

Object-Specific Methods

item( )   namedItem( )   tags( )

length

IE *4* NN *n/a* Moz *all* Saf *all* Op *7* DOM *1*

Read-only

Returns the number of elements in the collection.

Example   var howMany = document.embeds.length;

Value   Integer.

item( )

IE *4* NN *n/a* Moz *all* Saf *all* Op *7* DOM *1*

item(*index*[, *subindex*])
item(*index*)

Returns a single embed element object or collection of embed element objects corresponding to the element matching the index value (or, optionally in IE, the index and subindex values).

Returned Value   One embed element object or collection (array) of embed element objects. If there are no matches to the parameters, the returned value is null.

Parameters
index

When the parameter is a zero-based integer (per the W3C spec), the returned value is a single element that corresponds to the specified item in source code order. When the parameter is a string (IE), the returned value is a collection of elements whose id or name properties match that string.

subindex

In IE only, if you specify a string value for the first parameter, you can use the second parameter to specify a zero-based index that retrieves the specified element from the collection with id or name properties that match the first parameter's string value.

namedItem( )

IE 6   NN *n/a*   Moz *all*   Saf *all*   Op 7   DOM 1

namedItem(*IDOrName*)

Returns a single embed element object or collection of embed element objects corresponding to the element matching the parameter string value.

Returned Value   One form control object or collection (array) of form control objects. If there are no matches to the parameters, the returned value is null.

Parameters

IDOrName

> The string that contains the same value as the desired element's id or name attribute.

tags( )

IE 4   NN *n/a*   Moz *n/a*   Saf *all*   Op 7   DOM *n/a*

tags(*tagName*)

Returns a collection of objects (among all objects nested within the current collection) with tags that match the *tagName* parameter. Implemented in all IE, Safari, and Opera collections (see the all.tags( ) method), but redundant for collections of the same element type.

Entity, EntityReference

IE 4   NN *n/a*   Moz *all*   Saf *all*   Op 7   DOM 1

The Entity object (one of the node types) is an abstract representation in the W3C DOM of an element that is treated in an XML document as a storage unit. Some entities define a name that can be used by other elements (including other entities) as a shortcut reference to the information stored in the entity. This latter reference is represented in the W3C DOM as an EntityReference node type. You can see many examples of Entity elements in DTD documents. For more details on the application of Entity elements, see the XML specification at *http://www.w3.org/TR/REC-xml*.

event

IE 4   NN 4   Moz *all*   Saf *all*   Op 7   DOM 2

The event object contains information about a user- or system-generated event. But there are three different kinds of event objects, one for each of the event object models deployed in browsers: IE for Windows, Navigator 4, and the W3C DOM (as implemented in Mozilla, Safari, and Opera). IE 5 for Macintosh implements a hybrid of the IE for Windows and W3C DOM version. See Online Section VI for examples of processing events in a cross-browser environment. It is rare that an event object property applies to more than one of the event models, so pay special attention to the browser compatibility listings for each of the following properties.

The W3C DOM event object is more complex in some ways due to the object-oriented nature of the underlying W3C DOM Event object structure. Rather than being an all-encompassing object (as the IE event object is), the W3C DOM event object exposes different sets of properties and methods depending on the classification of event. All event classes share the properties and methods of the W3C DOM root Event object. But actual event object instances belong to one of the Event object's subclasses (and sometimes, sub-

subclasses). These subclasses are known as UIEvent (so-called user interface events such as DOMFocusIn), MouseEvent (including the well-known mouse events), MutationEvent (events that signal a scripted change to the node structure of the document), and, in DOM Level 3, TextEvent (typing-related events) and KeyboardEvent (pressing keyboard keys). Prior to the DOM Level 3 keyboard-related events being finalized, Mozilla and other W3C DOM browsers implemented a temporary keyboard events classification under the name KeyEvent, which is a subclass of UIEvent, although it borrows some MouseEvent properties for scripting convenience.

By and large, this functional division of objects won't impact your W3C DOM event processing because an event listener function for a particular kind of event will be looking for properties associated with that event. The event class is of little concern. Still, it is instructive to see the way event object properties and methods cascade through this object-oriented structure. The following table illustrates the distribution of properties (some of them unique to Mozilla) among W3C DOM event classes.

	Event	UI	Mouse	Keyboard	Text	Mutation
Event properties						
bubbles	•	•	•	•	•	•
cancelable	•	•	•	•	•	•
cancelBubble[a]		•	•	•	•	
currentTarget	•	•	•	•	•	•
eventPhase	•	•	•	•	•	•
originalTarget	•	•	•	•		•
target	•	•	•	•	•	•
timeStamp	•	•	•	•	•	•
type	•	•	•	•	•	•
UIEvent properties						
detail		•	•	•	•	
view		•	•	•	•	
MouseEvent properties						
altKey			•	•	•	
button			•			
clientX			•			
clientY			•			
ctrlKey			•	•	•	
metaKey			•	•	•	
relatedTarget			•			
screenX			•			
screenY			•			
shiftKey			•	•	•	

event

	Event	UI	Mouse	Keyboard	Text	Mutation
KeyboardEvent properties						
charCode[b]				•		
isChar[b]				•		
keyCode[b]				•		
rangeOffset[b]				•		
rangeParent[b]				•		
TextEvent property						
data					•	
MutationEvent properties						
attrChange						•
attrName						•
newValue						•
prevValue						•
relatedNode						•

[a] IE property implemented in Mozilla for cross-browser convenience.
[b] Implemented in Mozilla and Safari in lieu of final W3C DOM Level 3 keyboard events specification.

And the following table illustrates the distribution of methods among W3C DOM event classes.

	Event	UI	Mouse	Keyboard	Text	Mutation
Event methods						
initEvent( )	•	•	•	•	•	•
getPreventDefault( )	•	•	•	•		•
preventDefault( )	•	•	•	•	•	•
stopPropagation( )	•	•	•	•	•	•
UIEvent methods						
initUIEvent( )		•				
MouseEvent methods						
initMouseEvent( )			•			
KeyboardEvent methods						
initKeyEvent( )				•		
TextEvent methods						
initTextEvent( )					•	
MutationEvent methods						
initMutationEvent( )						•

The event object in Mozilla also implements the properties of the old Navigator 4 static Event object, and it inherits an enormous list of W3C DOM TextEvent object constants that represent nonalphanumeric keyboard key codes (which have constant names like *eventObject*.DOM_VK_PAGE_UP). In the meantime, however, these keyboard constants have been dropped from the proposed DOM Level 3 Events module. Therefore, if you explore the properties of an event object in Mozilla, you will continue to see these constants represented. A list of properties for the Navigator 4 static Event object appears in the Event object discussion following the current foray through an instance of an event.

As described in detail throughout Online Section VI, you must use different script techniques to obtain a reference to an event object in the IE and W3C DOM event models. Once you have that reference, you are well on your way to equalizing event processing across browsers. The example fragments that follow assume that previous script statements have obtained a reference to the browser-specific event object (usually shown in the example as stored in a variable called evt).

Object Model Reference

NN and W3C DOM
> eventObj

IE
> [window.]event

Object-Specific Properties

altKey	altLeft	attrChange	attrName
behaviorCookie	behaviorPart	bookmarks	boundElements
bubbles	button	cancelable	cancelBubble
charCode	clientX	clientY	contentOverflow
ctrlKey	ctrlLeft	currentTarget	data
dataFld	dataTransfer	detail	eventPhase
explicitOriginalTarget	fromElement	isChar	isTrusted
keyCode	layerX	layerY	metaKey
modifiers	newValue	nextPage	offsetX
offsetY	originalTarget	pageX	pageY
prevValue	propertyName	qualifier	rangeOffset
rangeParent	reason	recordset	relatedNode
relatedTarget	repeat	returnValue	screenX
screenY	shiftKey	shiftLeft	srcElement
srcFilter	srcUrn	target	timeStamp
toElement	type	view	wheelDelta
which	x	y	

Object-Specific Methods

getPreventDefault( )	initEvent( )	initKeyEvent( )	initMouseEvent( )
initMutationEvent( )	initUIEvent( )	preventDefault( )	stopPropagation( )

Object-Specific Event Properties

None.

altKey

Returns true if the left or right **Alt** key is down at the time the event fired.

Example

```
if (evt.altKey) {
    //handle case of Alt key down
}
```

Value	Boolean value: true | false.
Default	false

altLeft

Returns true if the left **Alt** key is down at the time the event fired.

Example

```
if (evt.altLeft) {
    //handle case of left Alt key down
}
```

Value	Boolean value: true | false.
Default	false

attrChange

Returns an integer code corresponding to the type of change made to an Attr node as the result of a DOMAttrModified event type of W3C DOM mutation event. Every mutation event object has three constants that also correspond to the integer values, which you can use to make more verbose, but easier-to-read script comparisons for DOMAttrModified event processing. The values and constants are shown in the following table. Although Safari implements the property, it does not support the event type that triggers events with this property. Manually created mutation events, however, have the property.

Value	Constant	Description
1	*evtObj*.MODIFICATION	Changed value of existing Attr node
2	*evtObj*.ADDITION	The Attr node was added to the document tree
3	*evtObj*.REMOVAL	The Attr node was removed from the document tree

Example

```
if (evt.attrChange == evt.MODIFICATION) {
    // do post-processing of attribute value change
}
```

Value   Integer value: 1 | 2 | 3.

Default   None.

attrName
IE *n/a* NN *n/a* Moz *all* Saf *all* Op *8* DOM *2*

Read-only

Returns a string version of the name of an `Attr` node affected by a `DOMAttrModified` event type of W3C DOM mutation event. Although Safari implements the property, it does not support the event type that triggers events with this property. Manually created mutation events, however, have the property.

Example   `var changedAttr = evt.attrName;`

Value   String value.

Default   Empty string.

behaviorCookie, behaviorPart, bookmarks, boundElements
IE *6* NN *n/a* Moz *n/a* Saf *n/a* Op *n/a* DOM *n/a*

Read-only

These properties are returned by the event object in IE 6 and 7 (with values 0, 0, null, and the empty array, respectively), but Microsoft does not document them. Perhaps they will be supported and implemented in a future version.

bubbles
IE *n/a* NN *n/a* Moz *all* Saf *all* Op *7* DOM *2*

Read-only

Returns Boolean `true` if the default behavior of the event is to allow the event to bubble through the element hierarchy.

Example

```
if (evt.bubbles) {
    // handle case of the event bubbling
}
```

Value   Boolean value: `true` | `false`.

Default   Event type-specific.

Alphabetical DOM
Reference

button

IE 4 NN *n/a* Moz *all* Saf *all* Op 7 DOM 2

Read-only

Inidicates which mouse button was pressed to trigger the mouse event. Be aware that the typical Macintosh has only a one-button mouse. Also, if you want to intercept the right-click context menu in IE/Windows, use the oncontextmenu event handler.

A significant discrepancy exists between the IE and W3C DOM implementations with respect to the numbers returned for this property. The W3C DOM, as implemented in Mozilla and others, specifies a value of zero to indicate the left (primary) button. IE for Windows supports additional values for mouse button combinations.

Example

```
if (evt.button == 2) {
    // handle event for right button
}
```

Value

Integer value according to the following table.

Button(s)	IE	W3C DOM
No button	0	null
Left (primary)	1	0
Middle	4	1
Right	2	2
Left + Right	3	n/a
Left + Middle	5	n/a
Right + Middle	6	n/a
Left + Middle + Right	7	n/a

Default   0

cancelable

IE *n/a* NN *n/a* Moz *all* Saf *all* Op 7 DOM 2

Read-only

Returns Boolean true if the event is of the type that can have its default behavior on the target element cancelled via the preventDefault( ) method.

Example

```
if (evt.cancelable ) {
    evt.preventDefault( );
}
```

Value   Boolean: true | false.

Default   Event type-specific.

cancelBubble

Specifies whether the event should propagate (bubble) up the element container hierarchy. You usually only need to set this property to true to override the default behavior and prevent the event from going any further. Other browsers implements this IE property for convenience. The W3C DOM equivalent is the stopPropagation( ) method of the event object.

Example   evt.cancelBubble = true;

Value   Boolean: true | false.

Default   false

charCode

Returns an integer corresponding to the Unicode value of the character generated by the key that fired the event. The character code is different from the key code, as the character code distinguishes between upper- and lowercase letters (for example, 97 for "a" and 65 for "A"), whereas the keyCode value is the same for that key, regardless of the character created from it. This property generally contains a value only for onkeypress events; the value is zero for keydown and keyup events. For the IE equivalent, see the keyCode property.

(The W3C DOM Level 3 Events module does not offer an exact substitute, but suggests the data property will convey the Unicode value for a character, such as the string U+0041 for the capital letter A.)

Example
```
if (evt.charCode > 96 && evt.charCode < 123) {
    evt.target.value += String.fromCharCode(evt.charCode - 32);
    evt.preventDefault( );
}
```

Value   Integer.

Default   Event-specific.

clientX, clientY

Indicate the horizontal (x) and vertical (y) coordinate of the mouse at the moment the current event fired. These coordinates are relative to the viewable document area of the browser window or frame. To convert these coordinates to the document's in IE, be sure to add the body element's scroll values (or html element's scroll values in IE 6 and 7 standards-compatible mode). For Mozilla, Safari, and Opera, the pageX and pageY properties provide coordinates in the document's space.

Example

```
if ((evt.clientX >= 10 && evt.clientX <= 20) &&
(evt.clientY >= 50 && evt.clientY <= 100)) {
    // process code for click in hot zone bounded by 10,50 and 20,100
}
```

| **Value** | Integer of pixel values. |
| **Default** | None. |

contentOverflow

IE 5.5 NN n/a Moz n/a Saf n/a Op n/a DOM n/a
Read-only

Returns Boolean true if as-yet unrendered content requires a new layout rectangle to handle the overflow content. The property applies only to the onlayoutcomplete event if you deploy custom print or print preview templates. For more on the C++ programming required for such templates, visit *http://msdn.microsoft.com/library/default.asp?url=/ workshop/browser/hosting/printpreview/reference/reference.asp.*

| **Value** | Boolean: true \| false. |
| **Default** | false |

ctrlKey

IE 4 NN n/a Moz all Saf all Op 7 DOM 2
Read-only

Returns true if the left or right **Control** key was pressed at the instant the event fired. See Online Section VI for testing for this key in cross-browser event handling code.

Example

```
if (evt.ctrlKey) {
    // process for Control key being down
}
```

| **Value** | Boolean value: true \| false. |
| **Default** | false |

ctrlLeft

IE 5.5 NN n/a Moz n/a Saf n/a Op n/a DOM n/a
Read-only

Returns true if the left **Control** key was pressed at the instant the event fired.

Example

```
if (evt.ctrlLeft) {
    // process for left Control key being down
}
```

| **Value** | Boolean value: true \| false. |
| **Default** | false |

currentTarget

IE *n/a* NN *n/a* Moz *all* Saf *all* Op *7* DOM *2*

Read-only

Returns a reference to the node whose event listener is currently processing the event. Allows a function to know whether it is invoked from the actual target node or a different node during event propagation.

Example
```
if (evt.currentTarget.nodeType == 1) {
    // process at element level for possible text node target
}
```

Value   Reference to a node in event propagation hierarchy.

Default   Reference to event target.

data

IE *|4|* NN *n/a* Moz *n/a* Saf *n/a* Op *n/a* DOM *n/a*

Read-only

Provides accessory data associated with the Navigator 4-only dragdrop event. The data property returns the URL of the item being dropped onto the window or frame. This property name may be adopted for the TextEvent in the W3C DOM Level 3 Events module.

Example   var srcDoc = evtObj.data;

Value   String.

Default   None.

dataFld

IE *5(Win)* NN *n/a* Moz *n/a* Saf *n/a* Op *n/a* DOM *n/a*

Read/Write

Used with IE data binding, the dataFld property holds the name of the data source object's field associated with the column of the HTML table. This property contains a value after an oncellchange event in a table generated via data binding.

Value   String.

Default   Empty string.

dataTransfer

IE *5(Win)* NN *n/a* Moz *n/a* Saf *1.3/2* Op *n/a* DOM *n/a*

Read-only

Returns a reference to the dataTransfer object to facilitate moving customized data between source and destination elements during a drag-and-drop operation. See the dataTransfer object for details of its usage.

Value   Reference to dataTransfer object.

Default   None.

detail

IE *n/a* NN *n/a* Moz *all* Saf *all* Op *7* DOM *2*

Read-only

Returns an integer conveying event type-specific additional information. For mouse button events, the number indicates how many times the user clicked the mouse on the same coordinate position as the previous click without moving the cursor away from the location. Moving the cursor resets the counter to zero in preparation for the next press and release of the mouse button. For a DOMActivate event type, the detail property returns 1 for activation by a simple user action (click or tab), and 2 for a more complex action (a double-click).

Example

```
if (evt.type == "click" && evt.detail > 5) {
    alert("Relax, dude!");
}
```

Value   Integer.

Default   Event-type specific.

eventPhase

IE *n/a* NN *n/a* Moz *all* Saf *all* Op *7* DOM *2*

Read-only

Returns an integer conveying whether the event listener is processing the event while in the capture phase, at the event target, or in the bubbling phase. W3C DOM event objects also implement plain-language constants corresponding to the three values.

Example

```
if (evt.eventPhase == evt.AT_TARGET) {
    // process event listener from the event target
}
```

Value

Integer value from the following table.

Value	Constant
1	*eventObjectReference*.CAPTURING_PHASE
2	*eventObjectReference*.AT_TARGET
3	*eventObjectReference*.BUBBLING_PHASE

Default   2

explicitOriginalTarget

IE *n/a* NN *n/a* Moz *1.4* Saf *n/a* Op *n/a* DOM *n/a*

Read-only

Returns a reference to the node that received the actual event. Because the target property changed in Mozilla 1.4 to point to an element object (rather than, say, a text node contained by an element), the explicitOriginalTarget property provides access to the precise node that received the event. There is a technical difference between explicitOriginalTarget and originalTarget that concerns what is known as anonymous content that is more of an issue in XUL development for Mozilla browsers. In an HTML document, the two properties reference the same node.

Example
```
if (evt.explicitOriginalTarget !== evt.target) {
    ...
}
```

Value	Element or node object reference.
Default	None.

fromElement

Returns a reference to the object where the cursor was located just prior to the mouseover or mouseout event.

Example
```
if (evt.fromElement.id == "lowerLevel") {
    ...
}
```

Value	Element object reference.
Default	None.

isChar

Returns true if the keyboard event is from a character key. In practice Mozilla returns false for all keys, including function keys. Use onkeydown or onkeyup event handlers to process noncharacter keys.

Value	Boolean value: true | false.
Default	true

isTrusted

Returns true if the event was generated as the result of a user action. Events artifically created by script (e.g., via the document.createEvent( ) mechanism) have this event object property set to false.

Value	Boolean value: true | false.
Default	true

keyCode

IE *4* NN *n/a* Moz *all* Saf *all* Op *7* DOM *n/a*

Read/Write

You'll find different handling of this property among mainstream browsers for the keypress event, but the all browsers treat the keyCode property the same way for onkeydown and onkeyup event handlers. For these events, the keyCode property returns the code associated with the keyboard key, irrespective of the character that might be generated by that key. On a typical Latin character set keyboard, the **A** key generates the code 65. Modifier keys generate their own events and codes as they are pressed and released.

For the onkeypress event, IE, Safari, and Opera return a significant value, corresponding to the ASCII integer value of the actual character displayed in a text box by typing the character (e.g., 65 for "A" and 97 for "a"). The equivalent property in Mozilla for the keypress event is charCode. See Online Section VI about processing keyboard events.

Example

```
if (evt.keyCode == 65) {
    ...
}
```

Value   Integer.

Default   None.

layerX, layerY

IE *n/a* NN *4* Moz *all* Saf *all* Op *n/a* DOM *n/a*

Read-only

Provide the horizontal (x) and vertical (y) coordinate of the mouse at the moment the current event fired. These coordinates are relative to the containing layer. If no layers or positionable elements have been defined, the default layer of the base document is used as a reference point, thus equivalent to the pageX and pageY properties. In Mozilla, these properties are measured relative to the element's own rectangular space for text and password input elements, textarea elements, and select elements.

Example

```
if ((evt.layerX >= 10 && evt.layerX <= 20) &&
(evt.layerY >= 50 && evt.layerY <= 100)) {
    // process code for click in hot zone bounded by 10,50 and 20,100
}
```

Value   Integer of pixel values.

Default   None

metaKey

IE *n/a* NN *n/a* Moz *all* Saf *all* Op *7* DOM *n/a*

Read-only

Returns true if the keyboard's **Meta** key (**Command** key on the Macintosh keyboard) was pressed at the instant the event fired.

Example
```
if (evt.metaKey) {
    // process for meta key being down
}
```

Value	Boolean value: true	false.

Default	false

modifiers

Provides an integer that represents the keyboard modifier key(s) being held down at the time the Navigator 4-only event fired. You can use the & operator with a series of static Event object constants to find out whether a particular modifier key was pressed. See Online Section VI.

Example	`var altKeyPressed = evt.modifiers & Event.ALT_MASK;`
Value	Integer.
Default	0

newValue, prevValue

Return a string with the new and previous values (respectively) of data associated with DOMAttrModified and DOMCharacterDataModified event types of the W3C DOM mutation events class. This information could be useful for creating an undo buffer for changes to an element's attribute or the content of a CharacterData node.

Example	`undoAttrBuffer = {attrNode:evt.relatedNode, oldVal:evt.prevValue};`
Value	String value.
Default	Empty string.

nextPage

Returns a string indicating whether the next page of a custom print template will appear on a left- or right-facing page. For more on the C++ programming required for templates, visit *http://msdn.microsoft.com/library/default.asp?url=/workshop/browser/hosting/printpreview/ reference/reference.asp.*

Value	String constant: left	right	(empty string).
Default	Empty string.

Alphabetical DOM Reference

offsetX, offsetY

IE *4* NN *n/a* Moz *n/a* Saf *n/a* Op *n/a* DOM *n/a*

Read-only

Provide the left and top coordinates of the mouse pointer relative to the containing element (exclusive of padding, borders, or margins) when the event fired. You can determine the containing element via the `offsetParent` property. See the "About client- and offset- Properties at the beginning of this chapter for information on offset measurement anomalies in Internet Explorer.

Example

```
if (evt.offsetX <= 20 && evt.offsetY <=40) {
    ...
}
```

Value	Integer pixel count.
Default	None.

originalTarget

IE *n/a* NN *n/a* Moz *all* Saf *n/a* Op *n/a* DOM *n/a*

Read-only

Returns a reference to a node that Mozilla internally treats as the genuine first target of the event. By and large, this information isn't helpful to DHTML scripting, because it dives into the internal construction of certain elements (e.g., in early versions of Mozilla, an `input` element of type text has a `div` element nested inside of it, but the DOM node tree does not see the `div` element as a child node of the `input` element). For many events and event targets, the `target` and `originalTarget` properties reference the identical node, but when an element contains a text node, the `target` property is internally set to the text node's parent—the containing element.

Value	Node object reference
Default	Element-specific.

pageX, pageY

IE *n/a* NN *n/a* Moz *all* Saf *all* Op *7* DOM *n/a*

Read-only

Provide the left and top coordinates of the element's content relative to the top-left corner of the page area when the event fired. The measurements ignore any scrolling of the page.

Example

```
if (evt.pageX <= 20 && evt.pageY <=40) {
    ...
}
```

Value	Integer pixel count.
Default	None.

prevValue

See newValue.

propertyName

Returns a string containing the name of the object property that changed during an onpropertychange event. For other event types, the value is an empty string. If the changed property is a property of a property (e.g., a property of an element's style property), the returned value shows the "dot" version, such as style.color.

Example

```
if (evt.propertyName.indexOf("style") == 0) {
    // perform further processing on a changed style
}
```

Value   String property name.

Default   Empty string.

qualifier

For use with IE data binding events (such as ondatasetcomplete). Returns a string value signifying a data source member, which may then be used as a parameter to access a data source's named recordset. Consult the Microsoft documentation for the Data Source Object you use to see if it provides qualifier data.

Value   String.

Default   Empty string.

rangeOffset

Returns an integer of the character offset within a node that the Mozilla DOM considers a potential Range endpoint. The reference to the node is found in the associated rangeParent property of the event object. These two values can be passed as parameters to W3C DOM Range object methods for setting a start or endpoint. Thus, a mousedown event listener could establish the start point of a range, while a mouseup event listener function could set the endpoint—both functions feeding rangeParent and rangeOffset values to the Range object methods.

Example

```
var rng;
function processMouseDown(evt) {
    rng = document.createRange( );
    rng.setStart(evt.rangeParent, evt.rangeOffset);
}
```

Value   Integer.

Default   0

rangeParent

IE *n/a* NN *n/a* Moz *all* Saf *n/a* Op *n/a* DOM *n/a*

Read-only

Returns a reference to a document tree node that would be a suitable start or endpoint for a W3C text range. Use in concert with the rangeOffset property.

Example
```
function processMouseUp(evt) {
    rng.setEnc(evt.rangeParent, evt.rangeOffset);
}
```

Value   Reference to a node.

Default   None.

reason

IE *4* NN *n/a* Moz *n/a* Saf *n/a* Op *n/a* DOM *n/a*

Read/Write

Returns a code associated with an ondatasetcomplete event signifying whether the IE data binding data transfer was successful or, if incomplete, whether the transfer stopped due to an error or a stoppage by the client or user. This property must be examined in an event handler for the ondatasetcomplete event. In IE 4, the property is read-only. Although IE 5/ Mac includes this property of the event object, it does not implement the associated event.

Example
```
if (evt.reason == 2) {
    alert("An error occurred during the most recent update.");
}
```

Value

One of three possible integer values:

0

    Transfer was successful

1

    Transfer aborted

2

    An error halted the transfer

Default   None.

recordset

IE *5(Win)* NN *n/a* Moz *n/a* Saf *n/a* Op *n/a* DOM *n/a*

Read/Write

Returns a reference to an IE data binding recordset object associated with a data-related event.

Value   Object reference.

Default   None.

relatedNode

IE *n/a* NN *n/a* Moz *all* Saf *all* Op *7* DOM *2*

Read-only

Returns a reference to a node that is affected by the action that triggers some W3C DOM mutation events. This provides a more direct route to a node that is impacted by the event, according to the following table.

Mutation event type	eventObj.relatedNode reference
DOMNodeInserted	Parent node of inserted node
DOMNodeRemoved	Original parent node of removed node
DOMAttrModified	Attr node

For other mutation event types, the property returns null; for other event classes, the property returns undefined.

Example   var newParent = evt.relatedNode;

Value   Reference to a node, null, or undefined.

Default   None.

relatedTarget

IE *n/a* NN *n/a* Moz *all* Saf *all* Op *7* DOM *2*

Read-only

Returns a reference to a rendered node in the document tree that was the previous or next target for events, depending on the event type. For a mouseover event type, the relatedTarget property refers to the node from which the cursor arrived; for a mouseout event, the relatedTarget property refers to the node to which the cursor departed. The corresponding IE functionality is in the fromElement and toElement properties of the IE event object.

Example   var beenThere = evt.relatedTarget;

Value   Reference to a node.

Default   None.

repeat

IE *5(Win)*   NN *n/a*   Moz *n/a*   Saf *n/a*   Op *n/a*   DOM *n/a*

Read/Write

For an onkeydown event only, returns Boolean true if the key has been down long enough to enter auto-repeat mode. You can prevent auto-repeated keys from being entered into a field with the following example.

Example
```
function handleKeyDown( ) {
    if (evt.repeat) {
        evt.returnValue = false;
    }
}
```

Value   Boolean value: true | false.

Default   false

returnValue

IE *4*   NN *n/a*   Moz *n/a*   Saf *1.2*   Op *7*   DOM *n/a*

Read/Write

Provides the value to be returned to the event's source element to allow or prohibit the element's default action connected with the event. If you set event.returnValue to false, the element does not carry out its normal operation, such as navigating to a link or submitting the form. This property does not influence an actual value you may wish to return from an event handler function.

Example   evt.returnValue = false;

Value   Boolean value: true | false, or undefined.

Default   undefined

screenX, screenY

IE *4*   NN *4*   Moz *all*   Saf *all*   Op *7*   DOM *2*

Read-only

Provide the horizontal and vertical pixel coordinate points where the cursor was located on the video screen when the event occurred. The top-left corner of the screen is point 0,0. There is no particular coordination with the browser window or document, unless you have positioned the window and know where the active window area is in relation to the screen.

Example
```
if (evt.screenX < 5 || evt.screenY < 5) {
    alert("You\'re too close to the edge!");
}
```

Value   Any positive integer or zero.

Default   0

shiftKey

Read-only

Returns true if the left or right **Shift** key was pressed at the instant the event fired.

Example

```
if (evt.shiftKey) {
    // process for Shift key being down
}
```

Value	Boolean value: true | false.
Default	false

shiftLeft

Read-only

Returns true if the left **Shift** key was pressed at the instant the event fired.

Example

```
if (evt.shiftLeft) {
    // process for left Shift key being down
}
```

Value	Boolean value: true | false.
Default	false

srcElement

Read-only

Refers to the element object that initially received the current event. This property is convenient in `switch` constructions for an event handler function that handles the same event type for a number of different elements. The corresponding property for the W3C DOM is target.

Example

```
switch (evt.srcElement.id) {
    case "myDIV":
        ...
    ...
}
```

Value	Element object reference.
Default	None.

srcFilter

IE 4(Win)   NN n/a   Moz n/a   Saf n/a   Op n/a   DOM n/a

Read-only

Refers to the filter object that fired an onfilterchange event.

Value   Filter object reference.

Default   None.

srcUrn

IE 5(Win)   NN n/a   Moz n/a   Saf n/a   Op n/a   DOM n/a

Read-only

String of the URN of an attached behavior that fired an event.

Value   String.

Default   null

target

IE n/a   NN n/a   Moz all   Saf all   Op 7   DOM 2

Read-only

Refers to the object that is the intended destination of the current event. In early versions of Mozilla and Safari prior to version 2.02, the target property can refer to a text node, even if the event handler is defined for the element that surrounds the text node. Your event processing for such a scenario must take the nodeType into account to equalize the reference to the surrounding element for both IE and Navigator. Beginning with version 1.4, Mozilla's event target is automatically redirected to a text node's containing element. If you need a reference to the receiving text node in Mozilla, use originalTarget or explicitOriginalTarget.

Example   var elem = (evt.target) ? evt.target : evt.srcElement;

Value   Node object reference.

Default   None.

timeStamp

IE n/a   NN n/a   Moz all   Saf all   Op 7   DOM 2

Read-only

Provides an integer signifying a milliseconds value you can use as a relative indicator of when an event occurred. Although the W3C DOM suggests the value should be the time since 1 January 1970 (the Java and JavaScript epoch), you cannot rely on that value. But you can compare the timeStamp property value for two events to derive the elapsed time between events.

Example   var clickTime = evt.timeStamp;

Value   Integer.

Default   Current timestamp.

toElement

Read-only

Returns a reference to the element object to which the cursor has moved that triggered the onmouseout event.

Example
```
if (evt.toElement.id == "upperLevel") {
    ...
}
```
Value   Element object reference.

Default   None.

type

Read-only

Indicates the type of the current event (without the "on" prefix). Values are all lowercase.

Example
```
if (evt.type == "change") {
    ...
}
```
Value   Any event name (without the "on" prefix) as a string.

Default   None.

view

Read-only

Returns a reference to the W3C DOM view (i.e., the window or frame object in Mozilla's implementation, and the document.defaultView in Safari and Opera) in which the event occurred.

Example   `var whichWin = evt.view;`

Value   Reference to a window type of object.

Default   Current window.

wheelDelta

Read-only

Returns an integer indicating which direction the user rolled the mouse wheel (for a mouse equipped with a wheel) during an onmousewheel event. A positive value means the user rolled the wheel toward the screen; a negative value means the opposite direction.

Alphabetical DOM Reference

Example
```
if (evt.wheelDelta > 0) {
    ...
}
```
Value   Integer, typically 120 or -120.

Default   None.

which   IE *n/a* NN *4* Moz *all* Saf *all* Op *7* DOM *n/a*
Read-only

Returns a value relevant to the type of event. For mouse events, the property value is an integer indicating which mouse button was used (1 is the left button; 3 is the right button). For keyboard events, the property value is an integer of the keyboard character ASCII code. This property survives in Mozilla and elsewhere as a carryover from the Navigator 4 event model. Use the button, charCode, and keyCode properties if you no longer need to support Navigator 4.

Example
```
if (evt.which == 65) {
    ...
}
```
Value   Integer.

Default   None.

x, y   IE *4* NN *n/a* Moz *n/a* Saf *all* Op *7* DOM *n/a*
Read-only

Return the horizontal and vertical pixel coordinates of the mouse pointer at the time the event occurred. For all but relative-positioned elements, the coordinate system is the body element (or html element in IE 6 and later standards-compatible mode). If the event occurs inside a relative-positioned element's rectangle, the coordinate system is limited to that element's space (the element's top left corner being 0,0). A value of -1 is returned if the pointer was outside of the document area of the browser window.

Example
```
if (evt.x < 20 && evt.y < 30) {
    ...
}
```
Value   Integer.

Default   None.

getPreventDefault( )   IE *n/a* NN *n/a* Moz *all* Saf *n/a* Op *n/a* DOM *n/a*

Returns Boolean `true` if the `preventDefault( )` method has been invoked for the current event object. Essentially lets a script inquire about the prevent-default state. This method is a Mozilla extension to the W3C DOM events module.

Returned Value   Boolean value: `true` | `false`.

Parameters   None.

initEvent( )   IE *n/a* NN *n/a* Moz *all* Saf *all* Op *7* DOM *2*

`initEvent("`*eventType*`", `*bubblesFlag*`, `*cancelableFlag*`)`

Performs the minimum initialization required on an event object that is generated by `document.createEvent( )`. After a script-generated event is initialized, it may be used as a parameter to a node's `dispatchEvent( )` method.

Returned Value   None.

Parameters

eventType
> String identifier for the event's type, such as `click`, `mousedown`, `keypress`, `DOMAttrModified`, and so on. You should limit the event type to those suitable to the classification of the event you created (e.g., a `click` event type for `document.createEvent("MouseEvent")`).

bubblesFlag
> Boolean value (`true` | `false`) determining whether the event's default propagation behavior is to bubble.

cancelableFlag
> Boolean value (`true` | `false`) determining whether the event's default action may be prevented via the `preventDefault( )` method.

initKeyEvent( )   IE *n/a* NN *n/a* Moz *all* Saf *all* Op *n/a* DOM *3*

`initKeyEvent("`*eventType*`", `*bubblesFlag*`, `*cancelableFlag*`, `*view*`, `*ctrlKeyFlag*`, `*altKeyFlag*`, `*shiftKeyFlag*`, `*metaKeyFlag*`, `*keyCode*`, `*charCode*`)`

Initializes a newly created event object with a complete set of property values associated with any keyboard event. Mozilla implemented its own version of the keyboard event initialization method because the W3C DOM had not yet addressed keyboard events. Safari has also adopted it for now. All parameters must be present, and must be set to default values (such as `false` for Boolean key flags or zero for integer code numbers) if the values are not significant for the event type.

Returned Value   None.

Parameters

eventType
> String identifier for the event's type: `keydown`, `keypress`, `keyup`.

Alphabetical DOM Reference

bubblesFlag

Boolean value (`true` | `false`) determining whether the event's default propagation behavior is to bubble.

cancelableFlag

Boolean value (`true` | `false`) determining whether the event's default action may be prevented via the `preventDefault( )` method.

view

Reference to the window or frame object (Mozilla) or `document.defaultView` (Safari) in which the dynamically generated event is supposed to have occurred.

ctrlKeyFlag

Boolean value (`true` | `false`) of the **Control** key state for this event.

altKeyFlag

Boolean value (`true` | `false`) of the **Alt** key state for this event.

shiftKeyFlag

Boolean value (`true` | `false`) of the **Shift** key state for this event.

metaKeyFlag

Boolean value (`true` | `false`) of the **Meta** key (e.g., Macintosh Command key) state for this event.

keyCode

Integer key code for this event.

charCode

Integer character code for this event.

initKeyboardEvent( )   IE *n/a* NN *n/a* Moz *n/a* Saf *n/a* Op *n/a* DOM *3*

initKeyEvent("*eventType*", *bubblesFlag*, *cancelableFlag*, *view*, *keyIdentifier*, *keyLocation*, *modifierList*)

Initializes a newly created event object with a complete set of property values associated with any keyboard event. Parameters for this method may change because as of this writing, the Level 3 Events module is not finalized. All parameters must be present, and must be set to default values (such as `false` for Boolean key flags or zero for integer code numbers) if the values are not significant for the event type.

Returned Value   None.

Parameters

eventType

String identifier for the event's type: keydown, keypress, keyup.

bubblesFlag

Boolean value (`true` | `false`) determining whether the event's default propagation behavior is to bubble.

cancelableFlag

Boolean value (`true` | `false`) determining whether the event's default action may be prevented via the `preventDefault( )` method.

view

    Reference to the window or frame object in which the dynamically generated event is supposed to have occurred.

keyIdentifier

    String value denoting which key the event is simulating. Values come from a long list of constant values (e.g., F1 and Home) and Unicode character references (e.g., U+0041). A complete list is available at *http://www.w3.org/TR/DOM-Level-3-Events/events.html#Events-KeyboardEvent-keyIdentifier*.

keyLocation

    Integer indicating which section of the keyboard is to be simulated for the event: 0 (standard); 1 (left); 2 (right); 3 (numeric keypad).

modifierList

    A space-delimited string of modifier keys to be signaled as being pressed during this simulated event. Common values include: Alt, AltGraph, CapsLock, Control, Meta, NumLock, Scroll, Shift.

initMouseEvent( )　　　　　IE *n/a*　NN *n/a*　Moz *all*　Saf *all*　Op 7　DOM 2

initMouseEvent("*eventType*", *bubblesFlag*, *cancelableFlag*, *view*, *detailVal*, *screenX*, *screenY*, *clientX*, *clientY*, *ctrlKeyFlag*, *altKeyFlag*, *shiftKeyFlag*, *metaKeyFlag*, *buttonCode*, *relatedTargetNodeRef*)

Initializes a newly created event object with a complete set of property values associated with any mouse event. All parameters must be present, and must be set to default values (such as false for Boolean key flags, zero for integer values, or null for a node reference) if the values are not significant for the event type.

Returned Value　None.

Parameters

eventType

    String identifier for the event's type, such as click, mousedown, mousemove, mouseout, mouseover, mouseup.

bubblesFlag

    Boolean value (true | false) that determines whether the event's default propagation behavior is to bubble.

cancelableFlag

    Boolean value (true | false) that determines whether the event's default action may be prevented via the preventDefault( ) method.

view

    Reference to the window or frame object in which the dynamically generated event is supposed to have occurred.

detailVal

    Integer code for detail data associated with the event.

screenX

    Integer for horizontal screen coordinate.

screenY
   Integer for vertical screen coordinate.
clientX
   Integer for horizontal browser window coordinate.
clientY
   Integer for vertical browser window coordinate.
ctrlKeyFlag
   Boolean value (true | false) of the **Control** key state for this event.
altKeyFlag
   Boolean value (true | false) of the **Alt** key state for this event.
shiftKeyFlag
   Boolean value (true | false) of the **Shift** key state for this event.
metaKeyFlag
   Boolean value (true | false) of the **Meta** key(e.g., Macintosh **Command** key) state for this event.
buttonCode
   Integer button code for this event.
relatedTargetNodeRef
   Reference to node receiving the previous or next mouse event.

initMutationEvent( )   IE *n/a* NN *n/a* Moz *all* Saf *all* Op *8* DOM *2*

initMutationEvent("*eventType*", *bubblesFlag*, *cancelableFlag*, *relatedNodeRef*, *prevValue*, *newValue*, *attrName*, *attrChangeCode*)

Initializes a newly created event object with a complete set of property values associated with any mutation event. All parameters must be present, and must be set to default values (such as false for Boolean key flags or zero for integer code numbers) if the values are not significant for the event type.

Returned Value   None.

Parameters
eventType
   String identifier for the event's type: DOMAttrModified, DOMCharacterDataModified, DOMNodeInserted, DOMNodeInsertedIntoDocument, DOMNodeRemoved, DOMNodeRemovedFrom-Document, DOMSubtreeModified.
bubblesFlag
   Boolean value (true | false) determining whether the event's default propagation behavior is to bubble.
cancelableFlag
   Boolean value (true | false) determining whether the event's default action may be prevented via the preventDefault( ) method.
relatedNode
   Reference to a node associated with the event. Applicable only to DOMNodeInserted, DOMNodeRemoved, DOMAttrModified event types.

prevValue

String of previous value for an `Attr` or `CharacterData` node. Applicable only to `DOMAttrModified` and `DOMCharacterDataModified` event types.

newValue

String of new value for an `Attr` or `CharacterData` node. Applicable only to `DOMAttrModified` and `DOMCharacterDataModified` event types.

attrName

String of the name of an `Attr` node. Applicable only to the `DOMAttrModified` event type.

attrChangeCode

Integer for the code corresponding to the type of change the event simulates. Applicable only to the `DOMAttrModified` event type.

initUIEvent( )   IE *n/a*   NN *n/a*   Moz *all*   Saf *all*   Op *7*   DOM *2*

`initUIEvent("`*eventType*`",` *bubblesFlag, cancelableFlag, view, detailVal*`)`

Initializes a newly created event object with a complete set of property values associated with any UI event. All parameters must be present, and must be set to default values (such as `false` for Boolean key flags or zero for integer values) if the values are not significant for the event type.

Returned Value   None.

Parameters

eventType

String identifier for the event's type, such as `DOMFocusIn`, `DOMFocusOut`, `DOMActivate`.

bubblesFlag

Boolean value (`true | false`) determining whether the event's default propagation behavior is to bubble.

cancelableFlag

Boolean value (`true | false`) determining whether the event's default action may be prevented via the `preventDefault( )` method.

view

Reference to the window or frame object in which the dynamically generated event is supposed to have occurred.

detailVal

Integer code for detail data associated with the event.

preventDefault( )   IE *n/a*   NN *n/a*   Moz *all*   Saf *all*   Op *7*   DOM *2*

Instructs the current event to bypass the normal operation it performs on the node. Once set, the mode cannot be undone for the current event. The following W3C DOM event listener function for an keypress event allows only numbers to be entered into a text field:

```
function numsOnly(evt) {
    if (evt.charCode < 48 || evt.charCode > 57) {
        evt.preventDefault( );
    }
}
```

This method is the equivalent of assigning false to the IE event.returnValue property, or having an event handler evaluate to return false.

Returned Value   None.

Parameters   None.

stopPropagation( )   IE n/a NN n/a Moz all Saf all Op 7 DOM 2

Prevents the current event from propagating through the capture or bubbling hierarchy beyond the node currently processing the event. This method performs the same action as assigning false to the event object's cancelBubble property (for bubbling propagation only).

Returned Value   None.

Parameters   None.

Event   IE 4 NN |4| Moz all Saf all Op n/a DOM n/a

The Event object is a static object (originating in Navigator 4) that contains a large set of case-sensitive constant values you can use to test user- or system-generated events for keyboard modifiers and event types (see the modifiers and type properties of the event object). These constant values evaluate to mathematically related integers. This same object continues to be supported in Mozilla and Safari, primarily for backward compatibility with the Navigator 4 event capture syntax.

Object Model Reference
Event

Object-Specific Properties

ABORT	ALT_MASK	BACK	BLUR	CHANGE
CLICK	CONTROL_MASK	DBLCLICK	DRAGDROP	ERROR
FOCUS	FORWARD	HELP	KEYDOWN	KEYPRESS
KEYUP	LOAD	LOCATE	META_MASK	MOUSEDOWN
MOUSEDRAG	MOUSEMOVE	MOUSEOUT	MOUSEOVER	MOUSEUP
MOVE	RESET	RESIZE	SCROLL	SELECT
SHIFT_MASK	SUBMIT	UNLOAD	XFER_DONE	

Event   IE n/a NN n/a Moz all Saf all Op 8 DOM 2

The W3C DOM Event object is an abstract object that contains the properties and methods shared by every instance of a W3C DOM event. This object type is also the generic event object created from the document.createEvent( ) method. See the discussion of the event object earlier in this chapter for property and method support for this object and how these items are inherited by more specific event types.

Object Model Reference
Event

Object-Specific Properties

AT_TARGET	bubbles	BUBBLING_PHASE	cancelable
CAPTURING_PHASE	currentTarget	eventPhase	target
timeStamp	type		

Object-Specific Methods

initEvent( )   preventDefault( )   stopPropagation( )

EventListener
IE *n/a* NN *n/a* Moz *all* Saf *all* Op *7* DOM *2*

The W3C DOM EventListener object is nothing more than a reference to a script function that is invoked by a node in response to an event. Its existence in the W3C DOM offers a convenient way for the specification to signify the data type of the second parameter to the *nodeObject*.addEventListener( ) and *nodeObject*.removeEventListener( ) methods, described earlier in this chapter.

EventTarget
IE *n/a* NN *n/a* Moz *all* Saf *all* Op *7* DOM *2*

The W3C DOM EventTarget object is the Events module connection with nodes that actually receive events. All node objects (especially text and element nodes in an HTML document tree) implement the EventTarget object, thus giving those nodes the three methods that belong to the EventTarget object: addEventListener( ), dispatchEvent( ), and removeEventListener( ). In other words, every node in a document is also a potential EventTarget object.

external
IE *4(Win)* NN *n/a* Moz *n/a* Saf *n/a* Op *n/a* DOM *n/a*

The external object is used primarily by developers who use Internet Explorer as a component for their applications and require access to custom extensions to the document object model. But you might add one or two of this object's methods into your work for an IE/Windows audience.

The following syntax example asks a user for permission to insert a script-controlled bookmark into the browser's Favorites list:

```
external.AddFavorite("URL", "Favorites List Label");
```

The following syntax example loads another URL into the a target window or frame (or the current window if the third parameter is an empty string), and then performs a text find for the third parameter string:

```
external.NavigateAndFind("URL", "searchString", "targetFrameName");
```

For more details, visit *http://msdn.microsoft.com/workshop/browser/overview/overview.asp*.

fieldset

The fieldset object reflects the fieldset element. IE 5 for Macintosh implements the client and scroll measurement properties for this object.

HTML Equivalent   <fieldset>

Object Model Reference
[window.]document.getElementById("elementID")

Object-Specific Properties

align   form

Object-Specific Methods
None.

Object-Specific Events
None.

align

Defines the horizontal alignment of the element within its surrounding container. In practice, this property has little effect on the fieldset object or its contents in IE 4. It behaves erratically in IE 6 for Windows, but responds as expected in IE 5 for Macintosh.

Example	document.getElementById("myFieldset").align = "center";
Value	Any of the three horizontal alignment constants: center | left | right.
Default	left

form

Returns a reference to the next outermost form element object in the document tree. Multiple fieldset element objects within the same form element reference the same form element object.

Example	var theForm = document.getElementById("myFieldset").form;
Value	Reference to a form element object.
Default	None.

fileUpload

See input.

filters[]

IE 4(Win) NN n/a Moz n/a Saf n/a Op n/a DOM n/a

Provides a collection of all filters associated with the current element. Internet Explorer lets you use array notation or parentheses to access a single element in the collection. Filters are not available in IE for the Macintosh.

Object Model Reference
```
document.getElementById("elementID").filters
```

Object-Specific Properties

length

Object-Specific Methods

item( )   namedItem( )

length

IE 4(Win) NN n/a Moz n/a Saf n/a Op n/a DOM n/a

Read-only

Returns the number of filters in the collection.

Example
```
var howMany = document.body.filters.length;
```

Value   Integer.

item( )

IE 4(Win) NN n/a Moz n/a Saf n/a Op n/a DOM n/a

```
item(index)
```

Returns a filter object corresponding to the filter that matches the index value in source code order.

Returned Value   Reference to a filter object. If there are no matches to the parameter, the returned value is null.

Parameters
index
   A zero-based integer corresponding to the specified item in source code order.

namedItem( )

IE 4(Win) NN n/a Moz n/a Saf n/a Op n/a DOM n/a

```
namedItem(IDOrName)
```

Returns a filter object or collection of objects corresponding to the filter matching the parameter string value.

Returned Value   One filter object or collection (array) of filter objects. If there are no matches to the parameters, the returned value is null.

Parameters

IDOrName
> The string that contains the same value as the desired filter's name.

font

IE 4 NN *n/a* Moz *all* Saf *all* Op 7 DOM 1

The font object reflects the font element.

HTML Equivalent   <font>

Object Model Reference
[window.]docunent.getElementById("*elementID*")

Object-Specific Properties

color	face	size

Object-Specific Methods
None.

Object-Specific Events
None.

color

IE 4 NN *n/a* Moz *all* Saf *all* Op 7 DOM 1

Read/Write

Sets the font color of all text contained by the font element.

Example   document.getElementById("myFont").color = "red";

Value   Case-insensitive hexadecimal triplet or plain-language color name as a string. See Appendix A for acceptable plain-language color names.

Default   Browser default.

face

IE 4 NN *n/a* Moz *all* Saf *all* Op 7 DOM 1

Read/Write

Provides a hierarchy of font faces to use for the content surrounded by the current font object. The browser looks for the first font face in the comma-delimited list of font face names until it either finds a match in the client system or runs out of choices, at which point the browser default font face is used. Font face names must match the system font face names exactly.

Example
document.getElementById("myFont").face = "Bookman, Times Roman, serif";

Value	One or more font face names in a comma-delimited list within a string. You may use real font names or the recognized generic faces: serif | sans-serif | monospace.
Default	Browser default.

size

The size of the font in the 1–7 browser relative scale. For more accurate font size settings, see the `style.fontSize` property later in this chapter.

Example	`document.getElementById("fontSpec2").size = "+1";`
Value	Either an integer (as a quoted string) or a quoted relative value consisting of a + or - symbol and an integer value.
Default	3

fonts

For details on this IE/Windows object, see the `fonts` property of the Dialog Helper object earlier in this chapter.

form

The `form` object reflects the `form` element. The `form` object can be referenced in all scriptable browsers via the value assigned to its tag `name` attribute or by the index of the forms array contained by every document. For browsers that support the `id` attribute (IE 4 and later and W3C DOM browsers), you may also use the element object reference formats that employ the element's ID. To assemble a reference to a nested form control object (such as input and textarea element objects), you have a choice again of using backward compatible references that include the `form` object as part of the reference (as in `document.formName.controlName`); or in more modern browsers, you can reference the control element directly via its unique ID.

HTML Equivalent   `<form>`

Object Model Reference
```
[window.]document.formName
[window.]document.forms[i]
[window.]document.form["formName"]
[window.]document.getElementById("elementID")
```

Object-Specific Properties

accept	acceptCharset	action	autocomplete	data
elements[]	encoding	enctype	length	method
name	replace	target	templateElements	

Object-Specific Methods

checkValidity( )   dispatchFormChange( )   dispatchFormInput( )
handleEvent( )   reset( )   resetFromData( )
submit( )

Object-Specific Events

Events	IE	Mozilla	Safari	Opera	W3C DOM
formchange[a]	—	—	—	•	—
forminput[a]	—	—	—	•	—
reset	•	•	•	•	•
submit	•	•	•	•	•

[a] Web Forms 2.0 event implemented in Opera 9.

accept

IE *n/a* NN *n/a* Moz *n/a* Saf *n/a* Op *9* DOM *n/a*

Read/Write

Controls the type(s) of files that all file-type input elements in the current form may upload.

Example   document.entryForm.accept= "image/gif, image/jpeg";

Value   String of MIME types. Multiple MIME types should be delimited by commas.

Default   Empty string.

acceptCharset

IE *5* NN *n/a* Moz *all* Saf *all* Op *7* DOM *1*

Read/Write

A server advisory (for servers that are equipped to interpret the information) about which character sets it must receive from a client form.

Example   document.entryForm.acceptCharset= "it, es";

Value   Case-insensitive string from the character set registry (*ftp://ftp.isi.edu/in-notes/iana/assignments/character-sets*). Multiple character sets may be delimited by commas.

Default   Empty string, except in IE/Windows, with a default of UNKNOWN.

action

IE *3* NN *2* Moz *all* Saf *all* Op *7* DOM *1*

Read/Write

Provides the URL to be accessed when a form is being submitted. Script control of this property lets one form be submitted to different server processes based on user interaction with the rest of the form.

Example

document.entryForm.action = "http://www.megacorp.com/cgi-bin/altEntry";

Value	Complete or relative URL.
Default	None.

autocomplete

Read/Write

When an IE user has automatic form completion preference enabled and the page author has set the autocomplete attribute of the form element, this property lets you control whether automatic completion is to be enabled. For more details on how AutoComplete works in HTML forms, visit *http://msdn.microsoft.com/workshop/author/forms/ autocomplete_ovr.asp*.

Example	document.entryForm.autocomplete = "off";
Value	String values: on | off.
Default	None.

data

Read/Write

Web Forms 2.0 extension that allows a form to retrieve initial values for controls from an external XML file. The specification provides some details of the structure and namespaces to be used for the file. Visit *http://www.whatwg.org/* for further information.

Example	document.entryForm.autocomplete = "off";
Value	URL string.
Default	Empty string.

elements[]

Read-only

Returns an array of all form control objects contained by the current form.

Example

```
for (var i = 0; i < document.entryForm.elements.length; i++) {
    if (document.entryForm.elements[i].type == "text") {
        document.entryForm.elements[i].value = "";
    }
}
```

Value	Array of element object references.
Default	Array of length zero.

encoding

IE 3 NN 2 Moz *all* Saf *n/a* Op 7 DOM *n/a*

Read/Write

Specifies the MIME type for the data being submitted to the server with the form. For typical form submissions (where the method attribute is set to post), the default value is the proper content type. But if you change the action property for a form by script, consider whether you require a custom encoding for the purpose. See also the encType property.

Example	document.orderForm.encoding = "text/plain";
Value	Case-insensitive MIME type (content type) value as a string. For multiple items, a comma-delimited list is allowed in a single string.
Default	"application/x-www-form-urlencoded" in IE and Opera; empty string in Mozilla.

enctype

IE 5(Mac)/6(Win) NN *n/a* Moz *all* Saf *all* Op 7 DOM 1

Read/Write

Provides the W3C DOM property name for what had been the encoding property of earlier DOM implementations. Current browsers support both property names. See the encoding property.

Example	document.orderForm.enctype = "text/plain";
Value	Case-insensitive MIME type (content type) value as a string. For multiple items, a comma-delimited list is allowed in a single string.
Default	"application/x-www-form-urlencoded" in IE and Opera. Empty string in Mozilla and Safari.

length

IE 3 NN 2 Moz *all* Saf *all* Op 7 DOM 1

Read-only

Specifies the number of form control elements in the form. You can use this property in lieu of the length of the form's elements array.

Example
```
for (var i = 0; i < document.forms[0].length; i++)
    ...
}
```

Value	Integer.
Default	0

method

IE 3 NN 2 Moz *all* Saf *all* Op 7 DOM 1

Read/Write

Forms may be submitted via two possible HTTP methods: get and post. These methods determine whether the form element data is sent to the server appended to the action attribute URL (get) or as a transaction message body (post). In practice, when the action and method attributes are not assigned in a form element, the form performs an unconditional reload of the same document, restoring form controls to their default values.

Example   `document.entryForm.method = "post";`

Value   Either of the following constant values as a string: get | post.

Default   get

name

IE *3*   NN *2*   Moz *all*   Saf *all*   Op *7*   DOM *1*

Read/Write

This is the identifier associated with the form. This information is not submitted with the form, but a form's name is used in references to the form and nested form elements. Despite the modern standards' preference for the id attribute, many browsers still require that a form be assigned a name attribute to allow the form to be submitted.

Example   `var firstFormName = document.forms[0].name;`

Value   Case-sensitive identifier that follows the rules of identifier naming: it may contain no whitespace, cannot begin with a numeral, and should avoid punctuation except for the underscore character.

Default   None.

replace

IE *n/a*   NN *n/a*   Moz *n/a*   Saf *n/a*   Op *9*   DOM *n/a*

Read/Write

Web Forms 2.0 extension that associates instructions to a form with how to process the data returned from the server after the form is submitted. The choice is whether the response replaces the original document in the browser (the default) or the browser should apply returned values to the form, rather than retrieve initial form data (if a URL is assigned to the data attribute of the form element).

Example   `document.getElementById("myform").replace = "values";`

Value   One of two string values: document | values.

Default   document

target

IE *3*   NN *2*   Moz *all*   Saf *all*   Op *7*   DOM *1*

Read/Write

The name of the window or frame that is to receive content returned by the server after the form is submitted. Such names are assigned to frames by the frame element's name attribute; for subwindows, the name is assigned via the second parameter of the window.open( ) method. Because the corresponding target attribute is not recognized by strict HTML or XHTML validators, you can omit the attribute to survive validation, yet still direct form results to another window by assigning a value to the form's target property in script after the page has loaded or at submit time.

Example document.getElementById("myForm").target = "_blank";

Value

String value of the window or frame name, or any of the following constants (as a string): _parent | _self | _top | _blank. The _parent value targets the frameset to which the current document belongs; the _self value targets the current window; the _top value targets the main browser window, thereby eliminating all frames; and the _blank value (or any unused identifier, for that matter) creates a new window of default size.

Default None (which implies the current window or frame).

templateElements IE *n/a* NN *n/a* Moz *n/a* Saf *n/a* Op 9 DOM *n/a*

Read-only

Web Forms 2.0 extension that returns an array of form control elements in the current form that make up repetition templates.

Value Array (collection) of HTML element object references.

Default Empty array.

checkValidity( ) IE *n/a* NN *n/a* Moz *n/a* Saf *n/a* Op 9 DOM *n/a*

Web Forms 2.0 extension that forces validity checking on all form controls set up for automatic validation. Returns a Boolean true if all controls validate per their individual specifications.

Returned Value Boolean: true | false.

Parameters None.

dispatchFormChange( ) IE *n/a* NN *n/a* Moz *n/a* Saf *n/a* Op 9 DOM *n/a*

Web Forms 2.0 extension that forces the formchange event to fire on all elements in the form, thereby causing any event handlers for formchange events on individual elements to fire.

Returned Value None.

Parameters None.

dispatchFormInput( ) IE *n/a* NN *n/a* Moz *n/a* Saf *n/a* Op 9 DOM *n/a*

Web Forms 2.0 extension that forces the forminput event to fire on all elements in the form, thereby causing any event handlers for forminput events on individual elements to fire.

Returned Value None.

Parameters   None.

handleEvent( )   IE *n/a*   NN |4| Moz *n/a*   Saf *n/a*   Op *n/a*   DOM *n/a*

handleEvent(*event*)

Instructs the object to accept and process the event whose specifications are passed as the parameter to the method. The object must have an event handler for the event type to process the event.

Returned Value   None.

Parameters

event
>   A Navigator 4 event object.

reset( )   IE *4*   NN *3*   Moz *all*   Saf *all*   Op *7*   DOM *1*

Performs the same action as a click of a reset-type input element. All form controls revert to their default values.

Returned Value   None.

Parameters   None.

resetFromData( )   IE *n/a*   NN *n/a*   Moz *n/a*   Saf *n/a*   Op *9*   DOM *n/a*

resetFromData(*XMLDocument*)

Web Forms 2.0 extension that sets initial values to control elements in the current form according to specifications in the XML document object passed as a parameter. The Web Forms 2.0 specification contains details on the specialized structure of this type of document. Visit *http://www.whatwg.org/* for further information.

Returned Value   None.

Parameters

XMLDocument
>   An XML document object in the same structure as the ones that load externally from a URL you can assign to the data property.

submit( )   IE *4*   NN *3*   Moz *all*   Saf *all*   Op *7*   DOM *1*

Performs the same action as a click of a submit-type input element. This method does not fire the onSubmit event handler.

Returned Value   None.

Parameters   None.

forms
IE 3 NN 2 Moz all Saf all Op 7 DOM 1

A collection of all form objects in the document.

Object Model Reference

document.forms

Object-Specific Properties

length

Object-Specific Methods

item( )　　　　namedItem( )　　　　tags( )　　　　urns( )

Object-Specific Events

None.

length
IE 3 NN 2 Moz all Saf all Op 7 DOM 1

Read-only

Returns the number of elements in the collection.

Example　　　var howMany = document.forms.length;

Value　　　Integer.

item( )
IE 4 NN n/a Moz all Saf all Op 7 DOM 1

item(*index*[, *subindex*]) item(*index*)

Returns a single object or collection of objects corresponding to the element matching the index value (or, optionally in IE/Windows, the index and subindex values).

Returned Value　　　One object or collection (array) of objects. If there are no matches to the parameters, the returned value is null.

Parameters

index

When the parameter is a zero-based integer (as required for the W3C DOM), the returned value is a single element corresponding to the said numbered item in source code order (nested within the current element). When the parameter is a string (allowed by IE/Windows), the returned value is a collection of elements with id or name properties that match that string.

subindex

If you specify a string value for the first parameter (in IE/Windows), you may use the second parameter to specify a zero-based integer to retrieve a specific element from the collection with id or name properties that match the first parameter's string value.

namedItem( )

namedItem(*IDOrName*)

Returns a single object (W3C DOM) or collection of objects corresponding to the element matching the parameter string value.

Returned Value   One object (W3C DOM) or collection (array) of objects. If there are no matches to the parameters, the returned value is null.

Parameters

IDOrName
   The string that contains the same value as the desired element's id or name attribute.

tags( )

tags(*tagName*)

Returns a collection of objects (among all objects within the current collection) with tags that match the *tagName* parameter. Redundant here, because all elements have the same form tag.

Returned Value   A collection (array) of objects. If there are no matches to the parameters, the returned value is an array of zero length.

Parameters

tagName
   A string that contains the element tag, as in document.forms.tags("form").

urns( )

urns(*URN*)

Returns a collection of nested element objects that have behaviors attached to them and URNs that match the *URN* parameter.

Returned Value   A collection (array) of objects. If there are no matches to the parameters, the returned value is an array of zero length.

Parameters

URN
   A string with a local or external behavior file URN.

frame

The frame object reflects the frame element, which can be generated only inside a frameset element. Be sure to distinguish the difference between the frame element object (described here) and the window object that a frame makes possible. Properties and methods of a frame element object tend to reflect the aspects associated with the HTML element and its attributes. The content of the frame is a window (a view in the W3C DOM terminology), which has been scriptable from the beginning, and contains a document. Reference a frame element object via its ID, even if you assign the same identifier to a frame element's id and name attributes. For example, from a script residing in one frame's document, reach the frame element object via:

```
parent.document.getElementById("TOCFrame")
```

But to reach the same frame in its capacity as a window (and thus access its scripts and document), the reference from the same script would be either of the following:

```
parent.TOCFrame
parent.frames["TOCFrame"]
```

If a script is processing a reference to the frame element object, you can jump the fence between the element object and its content via the contentDocument or contentWindow properties described below, provided the document containing the script and the target frame's document are served from the same server and domain. But there are numerous security pitfalls in attempting to access content in another frame. Internet Explorer, in particular, is quick to generate an "Access denied" error because the browser maker has had to tighten its security bolts further than is convenient for many scripters.

HTML Equivalent   <frame>

Object Model Reference

[*windowRef*.]document.getElementById("*frameID*")

Object-Specific Properties

allowTransparency	borderColor	contentDocument	contentWindow
dataFld	dataSrc	frameBorder	height
longDesc	marginHeight	marginWidth	name
noResize	scrolling	src	width

Object-Specific Methods
None.

Object-Specific Events
None.

allowTransparency   IE 6   NN *n/a*   Moz *n/a*   Saf *n/a*   Op *n/a*   DOM *n/a*

Read/Write

Specifies whether the frame background can be transparent. Because an underlying frameset does not have a background color or image, this property is not helpful for a frame. It does apply, however, to the related iframe element object.

Value   Boolean value: true | false.

Default   false

borderColor

IE 4   NN *n/a*   Moz *n/a*   Saf *n/a*   Op *n/a*   DOM *n/a*

Read/Write

Color of the frame's border. This property more accurately belongs to the frameset element, but is exposed as a frame object property in the IE DOM.

Example   `parent.document.getElementById("myFrame").borderColor = "salmon";`

Value   A hexadecimal triplet or plain-language color name. A setting of empty is interpreted as "#000000" (black). See Appendix A for acceptable plain-language color names.

Default   Varies with operating system.

contentDocument

IE *n/a*   NN *n/a*   Moz *all*   Saf *all*   Op 7   DOM 2

Read-only

Returns a reference to the document object loaded into the frame element object. Through that document object, you can access one of the document's elements via the getElementById( ) method, or access the containing window object via the document's defaultView property. For IE/Windows, use the contentWindow property to jump from frame element object to its content.

Example
```
var frameElem = parent.document.getElementById("myFrame");
var doc = frameElem.contentDocument;
```

Value   Reference to a document node.

Default   Current document node.

contentWindow

IE 5.5   NN *n/a*   Moz 1.0.1   Saf *all*   Op 7   DOM *n/a*

Read-only

Returns a reference to the window object generated by the frame element. Through that window object, you can access the document object and then any one of the document's elements. The W3C DOM provides the contentDocument property to jump from frame element object to its content. But if you are trying to reach script variables or functions in the frame, the contentWindow (or W3C DOM-friendly contentDocument.defaultView) provides access to the script context.

Example
```
var frameElem = parent.document.getElementById("myFrame");
var win = frameElem.contentWindow;
```

Value   Reference to a window object.

Default   Current window object.

dataFld

IE *4* NN *n/a* Moz *n/a* Saf *n/a* Op *n/a* DOM *n/a*

Read/Write

Used with IE data binding to associate a remote data source column name to the frame's src attribute. A datasrc attribute must also be set for the element. Setting both the dataFld and dataSrc properties to empty strings breaks the binding between element and data source. Works only with text file data sources in IE 5/Mac.

Example	parent.document.getElementById("myFrame").dataFld = "srcURL";
Value	Case-sensitive identifier of the data source column.
Default	None.

dataSrc

IE *4* NN *n/a* Moz *n/a* Saf *n/a* Op *n/a* DOM *n/a*

Read/Write

Used with IE data binding to specify the ID of the page's object element that loads the data source object for remote data access. Setting both the dataFld and dataSrc properties to empty strings breaks the binding between element and data source. Works only with text file data sources in IE 5/Mac.

Example	parent.document.getElementById("myFrame").dataSrc = "DBSRC3";
Value	Case-sensitive identifier of the data source.
Default	None.

frameBorder

IE *4* NN *n/a* Moz *all* Saf *all* Op *7* DOM *1*

Read/Write

Controls whether an individual frame within a frameset displays a border. Controlling individual frame borders appears to be a problem for most browsers in most operating system versions. Turning off the border of one frame may have no effect if all adjacent frames have their borders on. Feel free to experiment with the effects of turning some borders on and some borders off, but be sure to test the final effect on all browsers and operating systems used by your audience. Rely more comfortably on the frameborder attribute or frameBorder property of the entire frameset.

Example	parent.document.getElementById("frame2").frameBorder = "no";
Value	String values of 1 (on) and 0 (off) as well as yes and no.
Default	yes

height, width

IE *4* NN *n/a* Moz *n/a* Saf *n/a* Op *n/a* DOM *n/a*

Read-only

Return the height and width in pixels of the frame. Dimensions include frame chrome (scrollbars). Adjust a frame's size via the frameset object's rows or cols properties.

Example	var frHeight = parent.document.getElementById("myFrame").height;

| **Value** | Integer. |
| **Default** | Current height and width. |

longDesc

IE *5(Mac)/6(Win)* NN *n/a* Moz *all* Saf *all* Op *7* DOM *1*
Read/Write

Reflects the longDesc attribute of the frame element. Modern mainstream browsers provide no significant functionality for this attribute or property.

| **Value** | URL string. |
| **Default** | Empty string. |

marginHeight, marginWidth

IE *4* NN *n/a* Moz *all* Saf *all* Op *7* DOM *1*
Read/Write

Indicate the number of pixels between the inner edge of a frame and the content rendered inside the frame. The marginHeight property controls space along the top and (when scrolled) bottom edges of a frame; the marginWidth attribute controls space on the left and right edges of a frame.

Without any prompting, browsers automatically insert a small margin inside a frame (generally between 8 and 14 pixels depending on browser and operating system). But if you attempt to override the default behavior, be aware that setting any one of these two attributes causes the value of the other to go to zero. Therefore, unless you want the content to be absolutely flush with various frame edges, you need to assign values to both attributes.

Example

```
parent.document.getElementById("myFrame").marginHeight = 14;
parent.document.getElementById("myFrame").marginWidth = 5;
```

| **Value** | Positive integer value or zero. |
| **Default** | Varies with browser and operating system. |

name

IE *4* NN *n/a* Moz *all* Saf *all* Op *7* DOM *1*
Read/Write

This is the identifier associated with a frame for use as the value assigned to target attributes or as script references to the frame. The value is usually assigned via the name attribute, but it can be modified by script if necessary.

Example	`parent.document.getElementById("myFrame").name = "results";`
Value	Case-sensitive identifier that follows the rules of identifier naming: it may contain no whitespace, cannot begin with a numeral, and should avoid punctuation except for the underscore character.
Default	None.

noResize

IE 4 NN n/a Moz all Saf all Op 7 DOM 1

Read/Write

Indicates whether the frame can be resized by the user. All border edges of the affected frame element become locked, meaning all edges that extend to other frames in the frameset remain locked as well.

Example	`parent.document.getElementById("myFrame").noResize = "true";`
Value	Boolean value: true | false.
Default	`false`

scrolling

IE 4 NN n/a Moz all Saf all Op 7 DOM 1

Read/Write

Controls the treatment of scrollbars for a frame when the content exceeds the visible area of the frame. You can force a frame to display scrollbars at all times or never. Or you can let the browser determine the need for scrolling. In many supporting browsers, changing the value of this property has no effect.

Example	`parent.document.getElementById("mainFrame").scrolling = "yes";`
Value	String values of 1 (on) and 0 (off) as well as yes, no, and auto.
Default	`auto`

src

IE 4 NN n/a Moz all Saf all Op 7 DOM 1

Read/Write

Provides the URL of the external content file loaded into the frame. To change the content, assign a new URL to the property. For cross-platform applications, you can also set the `location.href` property of the frame to load a different document into the frame using window-related references (`parent.frameName.location.href = "newDoc.html"`).

Example

`parent.document.getElementById("myFrame").src = "images/altNavBar.jpg";`

Value	Complete or relative URL as a string.
Default	None.

width

See height.

frames

IE 3 NN 2 Moz all Saf all Op 7 DOM n/a

A collection of all frame objects defined in the window or frame. Only the first-level frames are exposed to the frameset object. To find further nested frames requires digging into the frames collections of nested `frameset` objects. The collection also includes `iframe` elements defined in the window's document.

Object Model Reference [*windowRef.*]`frames`

Object-Specific Properties

length

Object-Specific Methods

item( )   namedItem( )

length   IE 3 NN 2 Moz *all* Saf *all* Op 7 DOM *n/a*
Read-only

Returns the number of child frames defined in the frameset whose window starts the reference. Broken in some sub-versions of pre-1.0 versions of Mozilla.

Example   var howMany = parent.frames.length;

Value   Integer.

item( )   IE 4 NN *n/a* Moz *n/a* Saf *all* Op *n/a* DOM *n/a*
item(*index*)

Returns a single `window` object corresponding to the element matching the index value in source code order.

Returned Value   window object.

Parameters
index
   A zero-based integer.

namedItem( )   IE 4 NN *n/a* Moz *n/a* Saf *n/a* Op *n/a* DOM *n/a*
namedItem(*IDOrName*)

Returns a single object or collection of objects corresponding to the element matching the parameter string value.

Returned Value   One object or collection (array) of objects. If there are no matches to the parameters, the returned value is `null`.

Parameters
IDOrName
   The string that contains the same value as the desired element's `id` or `name` attribute.

Alphabetical DOM
Reference

frameset

IE 4   NN *n/a*   Moz *all*   Saf *all*   Op 7   DOM 1

The frameset object reflects the frameset element. Be sure to distinguish the difference between the frameset element object (described here) and the window object that a frameset makes possible. Properties and methods of a frameset element object tend to reflect the aspects associated with the HTML element and its attributes. The content of the frameset element is a window (a view in the W3C DOM terminology), which has been scriptable from the beginning, and contains a document (although with no renderable elements beyond the nested frame elements). Reference a frameset element object via its ID. For example, from a script residing in one frame's document, reach the frameset element object via:

    parent.document.getElementById("myFrameset")

But to reach the frameset's window (and thus access its scripts and document), the reference from the same script would be either of the following:

    parent
    top

If a script is processing a reference to the frameset element object, you can jump the fence between the element object and its content via the ownerDocument property of the element (described among the shared properties earlier in this chapter).

HTML Equivalent   <frameset>

Object Model Reference
[*windowRef.*]document.getElementById("*framesetID*")

Object-Specific Properties

border	borderColor	cols	frameBorder	frameSpacing	rows

Object-Specific Methods
None.

Object-Specific Events

Event	IE	Mozilla	Safari	Opera	W3C DOM
afterprint	•	—	—	—	—
beforeprint	•	—	—	—	—
beforeunload	•	—	—	—	—
load	•	•	•	•	•
resize	•	•	•	•	—
unload	•	•	•	•	•

border

IE 4   NN *n/a*   Moz *n/a*   Saf *n/a*   Op *n/a*   DOM *n/a*

Read/Write

Thickness of the spaces between frames in a frameset in pixels. Only the outermost frameset element of a system of nested framesets responds to the border property setting.

Internet Explorer treats the default thicknesses for Windows and Macintosh differently, so be aware that the same value may look different on each operating system platform.

Example   `top.document.getElementById("myFrameset").border = 4;`

Value   An integer value. A setting of zero eliminates the border entirely. While the value is supposed to represent the precise pixel thickness of borders in the frameset, this is not entirely true for all operating systems or browsers.

Default   6 (IE Windows); 1 (IE Mac).

borderColor

IE *4* NN *n/a* Moz *n/a* Saf *n/a* Op *n/a* DOM *n/a*

Read/Write

Color of borders between frames of the frameset. The `borderColor` property of an individual frame overrides the `frameset` object's setting.

Example

`parent.document.getElementById("myFrameset").borderColor = "salmon";`

Value   A hexadecimal triplet or plain-language color name. A setting of empty is interpreted as `"#000000"` (black). See Appendix A for acceptable plain-language color names.

Default   Varies with operating system.

cols

IE *4* NN *n/a* Moz *all* Saf *all* Op *7* DOM *1*

Read/Write

Defines the sizes or proportions of the column arrangement of frames in a frameset. Column size is defined in one of three ways:

- An absolute pixel size
- A percentage of the width available for the entire frameset
- A wildcard (*) to represent all available remaining space after other pixels and percentages have been accounted for

Exercise extreme care when scripting a change to this property. Altering the composition of a frameset on the fly might disrupt scripts that communicate across frames. Reducing the number of columns may destroy documents whose scripts or objects support scripts in other frames or the parent. It is safest to maintain the same number of columns, but use this property to adjust the widths of existing frame columns. If your scripts rely on the frameset's `onresize` event handler, be sure to test on as many platforms as possible that the event is firing in response to script changes of these properties.

Example   `parent.document.getElementById("framesetter").cols = "40%,60%";`

Value   Comma-separated list (as a string) of pixel, percentage, or wildcard (*) values.

Default   100%

frameBorder

IE 4 NN n/a Moz n/a Saf n/a Op n/a DOM n/a

Read/Write

Controls whether the frameset displays borders between frames. Adjusting this property does not dynamically change the border visibility in Internet Explorer for Windows.

Example `parent.document.getElementById("framesetter").frameBorder = "no";`

Value Internet Explorer 4 accepts the string values of 1 (on) and 0 (off) as well as yes and no.

Default yes

frameSpacing

IE 4 NN n/a Moz n/a Saf n/a Op n/a DOM n/a

Read/Write

The amount of spacing in pixels between frames within a frameset. Adjusting this property does not dynamically change the frame spacing in Internet Explorer for Windows.

Example `parent.document.getElementById("framesetter").frameSpacing = 5;`

Value Integer.

Default 2

rows

IE 4 NN n/a Moz all Saf all Op 7 DOM 1

Read/Write

The sizes or proportions of the row arrangement of frames in a frameset. See the cols property for additional details of selecting values for the rows property.

Example `document.getElementById("myFrameset").rows = "20%, 300, *";`

Value String of comma-delimited list of pixel or percentage values, or the * wildcard character.

Default None.

h1, h2, h3, h4, h5, h6

IE 4 NN n/a Moz all Saf all Op 7 DOM 1

These objects reflect the HTML header elements of the same names. See the description of the elements in Chapter 1 for examples of how various browsers render each of the header sizes.

HTML Equivalent

```
<h1>
<h2>
<h3>
<h4>
<h5>
<h6>
```

Object Model Reference
[window.]document.getElementById("*elementID*")

Object-Specific Properties
align

Object-Specific Methods
None.

Object-Specific Events
None.

align

IE *4* NN *n/a* Moz *all* Saf *all* Op *7* DOM *1*

Read/Write

Defines the horizontal alignment of the element within its surrounding container.

Example	document.getElementById("myHeader").align = "center";
Value	Any of the three horizontal alignment constants: center | left | right.
Default	left

head

IE *4* NN *n/a* Moz *all* Saf *all* Op *7* DOM *1*

The head object reflects the head element. Accessing this object via its ID reference may not work in the Windows version of IE 4. You should use the document.all.tags[] collection instead. For IE 5 and later and W3C DOM browsers, you can reference the element via its ID, the document.getElementsByTagName("head")[0] array reference, or document.body.previousSibling.

HTML Equivalent <head>

Object Model Reference
[window.]document.getElementById("*elementID*")
[window.]document.getElementsByTagName("head")[0]

Object-Specific Properties
profile

Object-Specific Methods
None.

Object-Specific Events
None.

profile

IE 4 NN n/a Moz all Saf all Op 7 DOM 1
Read/Write

Returns the URL string assigned to the optional profile attribute. In modern mainstream browsers, nothing special occurs as a result of assigning a value to this property.

Value   URL string.

Default   Empty string.

hidden

See input.

history

IE 3 NN 2 Moz all Saf all Op 7 DOM n/a

During a browser session, the browser uses the history object to maintain a list of URLs visited by the user. This list (stored as an array) is used by the browser to assist with navigation via the **Back** and **Forward** buttons. Due to the sensitive nature of the private information stored in the history object, not many of the details are exposed to scripts that could capture such information and surreptitiously submit it to a server. In more recent browser versions, each window maintains its own history object.

To answer a frequently asked question: no, you cannot block or disable the **Back** button's action. At most, you can prevent the current page from being entered into the browser's history when a user clicks on a link from the page. Accomplish this by scripting the links with the location.replace( ) navigation method. Navigator 4 and Mozilla (with signed scripts and the user's explicit approval) can remove the toolbar from the browser window (see the locationbar object discussion). Or, you can open a new window without the toolbar (see the window.open( ) method).

Object Model Reference
[window.]history

Object-Specific Properties

current	length	navigationMode	next
previous			

Object-Specific Methods

back( )	forward( )	go( )	item( )

Object-Specific Events
None.

current, next, previous

IE *n/a* NN *4* Moz *all* Saf *n/a* Op *(see text)* DOM *n/a*

Read-only

The URL of the current, next, and previous URLs in the history array. Opera supports only the current property. The next and previous property information is private and can be retrieved in Navigator 4 or Mozilla only with signed scripts and the user's approval.

Example

```
netscape.security.PrivilegeManager.enablePrivilege("UniversalBrowserRead");
var prevURL = parent.otherFrame.history.previous;
netscape.security.PrivilegeManager.revertPrivilege("UniversalBrowserRead");
```

Value   URL string.

Default   None.

length

IE *3* NN *2* Moz *all* Saf *all* Op *7* DOM *n/a*

Read-only

The number of items in the history list. Even with this information, you are not allowed to extract a specific history entry except with signed scripts and the user's permission in Navigator 4 or Mozilla.

Example

```
if (history.length > 4) {
    ...
}
```

Value   Integer.

Default   None.

navigationMode

IE *n/a* NN *n/a* Moz *n/a* Saf *n/a* Op *9* DOM *n/a*

Read/Write

Opera 9 lets users and page authors control whether the browser should always use "fast" history navigation (which does not trigger load and unload events and thus displays pages from history faster), the compatible way (which does trigger those events), or its best guess at which mode should be used on a page-by-page basis.

Example   `history.navigationMode = "fast";`

Value   String values: automatic | compatible | fast.

Default   automatic

back( )

IE *3* NN *2* Moz *all* Saf *all* Op *7* DOM *n/a*

The basic action is to navigate to the previously viewed document, similar to the click of the browser's **Back** button. You can direct the back( ) method to a specific window or frame, thus bypassing the default behavior of the **Back** button. For example, repeated calls to `parent.otherFrame.history.back( )` eventually run out of history for the frame and then cease to do anything further. On the other hand, repeated calls to `top.history.back( )` are the same as clicking the **Back** button, conceivably backing out of the frameset entirely if it wasn't the first document loaded in the current browser session.

Returned Value   None.

Parameters   None.

forward( )
IE 3   NN 2   Moz *all*   Saf *all*   Op 7   DOM *n/a*

The basic action is to navigate to the same URL that the browser's **Forward** button leads to (if it is active). Similar cautions about the window's history from the `history.back( )` method apply here, as well.

Returned Value   None.

Parameters   None.

go( )
IE 3   NN 2   Moz *all*   Saf *all*   Op 7   DOM *n/a*

`go(stepCount | "URL")`

Navigates to a specific position in the history listing.

Returned Value   None.

Parameters
`stepCount`

> An integer representing how many items away from the current listing the browser should use to navigate. A value of zero causes the current page to reload; a value of -1 is the same as `back( )`; a value of -2 is the URL two steps back from the current item in history.

`URL`

> A URL or (in Navigator) document title stored in the history listing.

item( )
IE *n/a*   NN 4   Moz *all*   Saf *n/a*   Op *n/a*   DOM *n/a*

`item(itemNumber)`

Returns the URL at a specific location in the history list. Requires Netscape/Mozilla signed scripts and the user's explicit permission to retrieve this private information.

Returned Value   URL string.

Parameters
`itemNumber`

> An integer representing the number of item within the history list. The range of acceptable values is 0 through the `history.length` minus 1.

hr

The hr object reflects the hr element.

HTML Equivalent   <hr>

Object Model Reference
[window.]document.getElementById("*elementID*")

Object-Specific Properties

align	color	noShade	size	width

Object-Specific Methods
None.

Object-Specific Events
None.

align

Read/Write

Defines the horizontal alignment of the element within its surrounding container.

Example   document.getElementById("myHR").align = "center";

Value   Any of the three horizontal alignment constant strings: center | left | right.

Default   center

color

Read/Write

Sets the color scheme of the horizontal rule. If the rule is rendered in 3D, complementary colors are automatically assigned to the shaded area.

Example   document.getElementById("myHR").color = "red";

Value   Case-insensitive hexadecimal triplet or plain-language color name as a string. See Appendix A for acceptable plain-language color names.

Default   Browser default.

noShade

Read/Write

Indicates whether the browser should render the rule as a flat (not 3D) line. In Internet Explorer only, if you set the color property, the browser changes the default line style to a no-shade style. In IE, once noShade is set to true, shading cannot later be restored.

Example	document.getElementById("bar2").noShade = "true";
Value	Boolean value: true | false.
Default	false

size

IE 4 NN *n/a* Moz *all* Saf *all* Op 7 DOM 1

Read/Write

Provides the thickness in pixels of the horizontal rule.

Example	document.getElementById("rule2").size = 3;
Value	Positive integer.
Default	2

width

IE 4 NN *n/a* Moz *all* Saf *all* Op 7 DOM 1

Read/Write

Provides the width of the rule either in pixels (as an integer) or a percentage (as a string) of the next outermost block-level container.

Example	document.getElementById("bar3").width = "70%";
Value	Integer (for pixels) or string (for pixels or percentage).
Default	100%

html

IE 4 NN *n/a* Moz *all* Saf *all* Op 7 DOM 1

The html object reflects the html element.

HTML Equivalent   <html>

Object Model Reference
[window.]document.getElementById("*elementID*")
[window.]document.body.parentNode
[window.]document.documentElement

Object-Specific Properties
version

Object-Specific Methods
None.

Object-Specific Events
None.

version
IE 5(Mac)/6(Win) NN n/a Moz all Saf all Op 7 DOM 1

Read/Write

Reflects the deprecated version attribute of the html element. Present in modern browsers, but not functional. See the DocumentType object.

Value   String.

Default   Empty string.

HTMLCollection
IE 5(Mac)/6(Win) NN n/a Moz all Saf all Op 7 DOM 1

The HTMLCollection object is an abstract representation in the W3C DOM of any collection of HTML element objects, all of which exist in the same document tree and have the same tag. For example, in the eyes of the W3C DOM, the document.images array is an HTMLCollection object. All entries are img element object references. JavaScript treats such collections as arrays for access to individual entries via array notation, along with the help of the HTMLCollection's sole property, length. Alternatively, you can use the two methods (item( ) and namedItem( )) to reference a single entry in the collection. All instances of the HTMLCollection object (such as document.images) inherit the property and methods listed below from the abstract HTMLCollection object. See descriptions of each instance in this chapter (anchors, applets, areas, cells, elements, forms, images, links, options, rows, tBodies, and non-W3C DOM element collections all, children, embeds, and frames).

Object-Specific Properties

length

Object-Specific Methods

item( )   namedItem( )

Object-Specific Events
None.

length
IE 5(Mac)/6(Win) NN n/a Moz all Saf all Op 7 DOM 1

Read-only

Returns the number of elements in the collection.

Example   var howMany = document.myForm.elements.length;

Value   Integer.

item( )

item(*index*)

Returns one object from the collection corresponding to the object matching the index value in source code order. IE implements another variation of this method for some (but not all) of its collections with an optional secondary parameter.

Returned Value   Reference to an element object. If there are no matches to the parameter, the returned value is null.

Parameters

index
> A zero-based integer corresponding to the specified item in source code order.

namedItem( )

namedItem(*IDOrName*)

Returns one object from the collection corresponding to the object matching the parameter string value.

Returned Value   Reference to an element object. If there are no matches to the parameters, the returned value is null.

Parameters

IDOrName
> The string that contains the same value as the desired filter's name.

HTMLDocument

The HTMLDocument object is an abstract representation in the W3C DOM of the document node for an HTML document tree. Scripts reference this object via the document object.

This object inherits properties and methods from a chain of node objects in the W3C DOM core module, namely the root Node object and the Document object. To this set of properties and methods, the HTMLDocument object adds properties and methods that apply specifically to HTML documents (in contrast to XML documents)—properties such as referrer and body, and methods such as write( ). Browser implementations add numerous additional proprietary properties and methods. See the full discussion of the scriptable implementations of the HTMLDocument object within the document object discussion earlier in this chapter.

Object-Specific Properties

anchors[ ]	applets[ ]	body	cookie
domain	forms[ ]	images[ ]	links[ ]
referrer	title	URL	

Object-Specific Methods

close( )	getElementsByName( )	open( )
write( )	writeln( )	

HTMLElement

IE *4* **NN** *n/a* **Moz** *all* **Saf** *all* **Op** *7* **DOM** *1*

Every scriptable element object in modern browsers is, at its core, a descendant of the basic HTMLElement abstract object in the W3C DOM. The HTMLElement, itself, inherits properties and methods from the Node and Element chain in the core DOM module. To this inherited set of features, the HTMLElement adds properties that apply to HTML elements (in contrast to XML elements), including the className, dir, id, lang, and title properties. All individual HTML element objects, such as HTMLBodyElement and HTMLFormElement, inherit their characteristics from the HTMLElement object. That's one reason why the list of shared properties and methods at the beginning of this chapter is so long: it includes items inherited from the long chain of Node to Element to HTMLElement.

Knowing the terminology of the DOM abstract object names (e.g., HTMLBodyElement) is not essential knowledge to scripting element objects. That is to say, the abstract object names almost never appear in scripts because scripts reference instances of such HTML objects by way of their identifiers or through properties of other objects (such as *eventObject*.target). The only time you are likely to see these abstract names is during debugging, when you use alert( ) methods or other tools to inspect the object referenced by a variable. Mozilla reports such object references as instances of a specific HTML element class (e.g., HTMLParagraphElement or HTMLInputElement). This information, in itself, is often far more helpful than IE's reporting of the reference being just [object].

Object-Specific Properties

className	dir	id	lang
title			

Object-Specific Methods
None.

i

See b.

iframe

IE *4* **NN** *n/a* **Moz** *all* **Saf** *all* **Op** *7* **DOM** *1*

The iframe object reflects the iframe element. Be aware that, in Internet Explorer, a number of properties defined for this object have no effect on the object nor any default value, but are implemented because the element shares its internal structure with other elements that use those properties.

HTML Equivalent   `<iframe>`

Object Model Reference
`[window.]document.getElementById("elementID")`

Object-Specific Properties

align	allowTransparency	border	contentDocument	contentWindow
dataFld	dataSrc	frameBorder	frameSpacing	height
hspace	location	longDesc	marginHeight	marginWidth
name	noResize	scrolling	src	vspace
width				

Object-Specific Methods
None.

Object-Specific Events
None.

align

IE 4   NN n/a   Moz all   Saf all   Op 7   DOM 1
Read/Write

Defines how the element is aligned relative to surrounding text content. Most values set the vertical relationship between the element and surrounding text. For example, to align the bottom of the element with the baseline of the surrounding text, the `align` property value would be `baseline`. An element can be "floated" along the left or right margin to let surrounding text wrap around the element.

Example   `document.getElementById("myIframe").align = "absmiddle";`

Value   Any of the following alignment constant values (as a string): `absbottom` | `absmiddle` | `baseline` | `bottom` | `right` | `left` | `none` | `texttop` | `top`.

Default   `bottom`

allowTransparency

IE 6   NN n/a   Moz n/a   Saf n/a   Op n/a   DOM n/a
Read/Write

Specifies whether the `iframe` background can be transparent. For the background of the main document to show through both the `iframe` and its document, the document's `background-color` style attribute must be set to `transparent`.

Example   `document.getElementById("myIframe").allowTransparency = true;`

Value   Boolean value: `true` | `false`.

Default   `false`

border

IE *4(Win)* NN *n/a* Moz *n/a* Saf *n/a* Op *n/a* DOM *n/a*

Read/Write

Although defined for the iframe element object in IE/Windows, the border property has no value nor does assigning a value affect the appearance of the element.

contentDocument

IE *n/a* NN *n/a* Moz *all* Saf *all* Op *7* DOM *2*

Read-only

Returns a reference to the document object loaded into the iframe element object. Through that document object, you can access one of the document's elements via the getElementById() method, or access the containing window object via the document's defaultView property. For IE/Windows, use the contentWindow property to jump from iframe element object to its content.

Example
```
var iframeElem = parent.document.getElementById("myIframe");
var doc = iframeElem.contentDocument;
```

Value   Reference to a document node.

Default   Current document node.

contentWindow

IE *5.5* NN *n/a* Moz *1.0.1* Saf *all* Op *7* DOM *n/a*

Read-only

Returns a reference to the window object generated by the iframe element. Through the window object, you can access the document object and then any one of the document's elements. The W3C DOM provides the contentDocument property to jump from iframe element object to its content. But if you are trying to reach script variables or functions in the frame, the contentWindow (or W3C DOM-friendly contentDocument.defaultView) provides access to the script context.

Example
```
var iframeElem = parent.document.getElementById("myIframe");
var win = iframeElem.contentWindow;
```

Value   Reference to a window node.

Default   Current window node.

dataFld

IE *4* NN *n/a* Moz *n/a* Saf *n/a* Op *n/a* DOM *n/a*

Read/Write

Used with IE data binding to associate a remote data source column name with the value of the src property. A datasrc attribute must also be set for the element. Setting both the dataFld and dataSrc properties to empty strings breaks the binding between element and data source. Works only with text file data sources in IE 5/Mac.

Example	document.getElementById("myIframe").dataFld = "frameURL";
Value	Case-sensitive identifier of the data source column.
Default	None.

dataSrc

Used with IE data binding to specify the ID of the page's object element that loads the data source object for remote data access. Setting both the dataFld and dataSrc properties to empty strings breaks the binding between element and data source. Works only with text file data sources in IE 5/Mac.

Example	document.getElementById("myIframe").dataSrc = "DBSRC3";
Value	Case-sensitive identifier of the data source.
Default	None.

frameBorder

Controls whether the iframe element displays a border.

Example	document.getElementById("myIframe").frameBorder = "0";
Value	String values: 1 (on) | 2 (off)
Default	Empty string or 1.

frameSpacing

The amount of spacing in pixels between frames within a frameset. This property has no effect on an inline frame in Internet Explorer.

height, width

Provide the pixel or percentage measure of the iframe element's height and width.

Example
```
document.getElementById("myIframe").height = "200";
document.getElementById("myIframe").width = "500";
```

| **Value** | Length string. |
| **Default** | 300 (width); 150 (height). |

hspace, vspace

Read/Write

Provide the pixel measure of horizontal and vertical margins surrounding an inline frame. The hspace property affects the left and right edges of the element equally; the vspace property affects the top and bottom edges of the element equally. These margins are not the same as margins set by style sheets, but they have the same visual effect.

Example

```
document.getElementById("myIframe").hspace = 5;
document.getElementById("myIframe").vspace = 8;
```

Value	Integer of pixel count.
Default	0

location

Read/Write

This property borrows the location property of the window object created by the iframe element. It is a full-fledged location object, but if you wish to load a new URL into an iframe, use the cross-browser src property.

longDesc

Read/Write

Reflects the longDesc attribute of the iframe element. Mainstream browsers provide no significant functionality for this attribute or property.

Value	URL string.
Default	Empty string.

marginHeight, marginWidth

Read/Write

Control the number of pixels between the inner edge of a frame and the content rendered inside the frame. An adjustment to either property sets the other property to zero, eliminating the default margin provided by the browser.

Value	Positive integer value or zero.
Default	Varies with browser and operating system.

name

Read/Write

This is the identifier associated with an `iframe` for use as the value assigned to target attributes or as script references to the frame. The value is usually assigned via the `name` attribute, but it can be modified by script if necessary.

Value	Case-sensitive string identifier that follows the rules of identifier naming: it may contain no whitespace, cannot begin with a numeral, and should avoid punctuation except for the underscore character.
Default	None.

noResize

Read/Write

Specifies whether the frame can be resized by the user. Not applicable to an `iframe` element.

scrolling

Read/Write

Specifies the treatment of scrollbars for an `iframe` when the content exceeds the visible area of the `iframe`. You can force an `iframe` to display scrollbars at all times or never. Or you can let the browser determine the need for scrolling. It is not uncommon for browsers to ignore scripted changes to this property. Make your choice in the element's `scrolling` attribute.

Example	`document.getElementById("myIframe").scrolling = "no";`
Value	One of three constants (as a string): auto | no | yes.
Default	auto

src

Read/Write

Indicates the URL of the external content file loaded into the current element. To change the content, assign a new URL to the property.

Example	`document.getElementById("myIframe").src = "section2.html";`
Value	Complete or relative URL as a string.
Default	None.

vspace

See hspace.

width

See height.

ilayer

See layer.

Image IE 4 NN 3 Moz *all* Saf *all* Op 7 DOM *n/a*

Use the constructor function the static Image object (new Image( )) to create a nondisplayed img object in the browser's memory. By assigning an image file's URL to the src property of such an instance, you instruct the browser to precache the image in the browser. You may then assign the src property of the undisplayed instance to the src property of an img object in the document tree to swap the existing image with the pre-cached one. An instance of the Image object is a DOM img element, whose properties, methods, and events are described with that object.

Object Model Reference

Image

Object-Specific Properties

prototype

Object-Specific Methods

None.

prototype IE 4 NN 3 Moz *all* Saf *all* Op 7 DOM *n/a*
Read/Write

This is a property of the static Image object. Use the prototype property to assign new properties and methods to future instances of images created in the current document. See the Array.prototype property in Chapter 5 for usage of this object property.

Example   Image.prototype.exif = "";

Value   Any data, including function references.

images IE 4 NN 3 Moz *all* Saf *all* Op 7 DOM 1

A collection (array) of all img objects contained by the document. This object is implemented only in browser versions that treat images as objects. Therefore, you can use the existence of this array object as a conditional switch surrounding statements that swap or preload images:

```
if (document.images) {
    // process img element objects here
}
```

Alphabetical DOM Reference

Object Model Reference
document.images

Object-Specific Properties

length

Object-Specific Methods

item( )   namedItem( )   tags( )   urns( )

length   IE 4   NN 3   Moz all   Saf all   Op 7   DOM 1

Read-only

Returns the number of elements in the collection.

Example   var howMany = document.images.length;

Value   Integer.

item( )   IE 4   NN n/a   Moz all   Saf all   Op 7   DOM 1

item(*index*[, *subindex*]) item(*index*)

Returns a single image object or collection of image objects corresponding to the element matching the index value (or, optionally in IE, the index and subindex values).

Returned Value   One object or collection (array) of objects. If there are no matches to the parameters, the returned value is null.

Parameters
index

> When the parameter is a zero-based integer (required in W3C DOM implementations), the returned value is a single element corresponding to the said numbered item in source code order (nested within the current element). When the parameter is a string, the returned value is a collection of elements with id or name properties that match that string.

subindex

> If you specify a string value for the first parameter (IE only), you may use the second parameter to specify a zero-based integer to retrieve a specific element from the collection with id or name properties that match the first parameter's string value.

namedItem( )   IE 6   NN n/a   Moz all   Saf all   Op 7   DOM 2

namedItem(*IDOrName*)

Returns a single object corresponding to the element matching the parameter string value.

Returned Value   One object reference. If there are no matches to the parameters, the returned value is null.

Parameters

IDOrName
>   The string that contains the same value as the desired element's id or name attribute.

tags( )

tags(*tagName*)

Returns a collection of objects (among all objects within the current collection) with tags that match the *tagName* parameter. Redundant here, because all elements have the same img tag.

Returned Value   A collection (array) of objects. If there are no matches to the parameters, the returned value is an array of zero length.

Parameters

tagName
>   A string that contains the element tag, as in document.images.tags("img").

urns( )

urns(*URN*)

Returns a collection of nested element objects that have behaviors attached to them and URNs that match the *URN* parameter.

Returned Value   A collection (array) of objects. If there are no matches to the parameters, the returned value is an array of zero length.

Parameters

URN
>   A string with a local or external behavior file URN.

img

The img object reflects the img element. This object shares the same properties as the static Image object, which you can use to pre-cache images without rendering them on the page.

HTML Equivalent   `<img>`

Object Model Reference
```
[window.]document.imageName
[window.]document.images[i]
[window.]document.images["imageName"]
[window.]document.getElementById("elementID")
```

Object-Specific Properties

align	alt	border	complete
dataFld	dataFormatAs	dataSrc	dynsrc

fileCreatedDate	fileModifiedDate	fileSize	fileUpdatedDate
height	href	hspace	isMap
longDesc	loop	lowsrc	lowSrc
mimeType	name	nameProp	naturalHeight
naturalWidth	protocol	src	start
useMap	vspace	width	x
y			

Object-Specific Methods
None.

Object-Specific Events

Events	IE	Mozilla	Safari	Opera	W3C DOM
abort	•	•	•	•	•
error	•	•	•	•	•
load	•	•	•	•	—

align
IE 4 NN n/a Moz all Saf all Op 7 DOM 1

Read/Write

Defines how the element is aligned relative to surrounding text content. Most values set the vertical relationship between the element and surrounding text. For example, to align the bottom of the element with the baseline of the surrounding text, the align property value would be baseline. An element can be "floated" along the left or right margin to let surrounding text wrap around the element.

Example   document.logoImg.align = "absmiddle";

Value   Any of the following alignment constant values (as a string): absbottom | absmiddle | baseline | bottom | right | left | none | texttop | top.

Default   bottom

alt
IE 4 NN n/a Moz all Saf all Op 7 DOM 1

Read/Write

Indicates the text to be displayed (or spoken) where the img element appears on the page when a browser does not download graphics (or is waiting for the image to download). The text is usually a brief description of what the image is. Be aware that the size of the image area on the page may limit the amount of assigned text visible on the page. Make sure the description is readable.

Example   document.corpLogo.alt = "MegaCorp Logo";

Value   String value.

Default   None.

border

IE 4　NN 3　Moz *all*　Saf *all*　Op 7　DOM 1
Read/Write

Provides the thickness of the border around an element (in pixels). This property is read-only in Navigator up to version 4.

Example　　　　　document.logoImage.border = 4;

Value　　　　　An integer value. A setting of zero removes the border entirely.

Default　　　　　0

complete

IE 4　NN 3　Moz *all*　Saf *n/a*　Op 7　DOM *n/a*
Read-only

Reveals whether the img element's src or lowsrc image file has fully loaded. Note that Navigator 4 provides an incorrect true reading before the image has completely loaded.

Example
```
if (document.logo.complete) {
    // safe to process the image object
}
```

Value　　　　　Boolean value: true | false.

Default　　　　　false

dataFld

IE 4　NN *n/a*　Moz *n/a*　Saf *n/a*　Op *n/a*　DOM *n/a*
Read/Write

Used with IE data binding to associate a remote data source column name with the src property of the img object. A datasrc attribute must also be set for the element. Setting both the dataFld and dataSrc properties to empty strings breaks the binding between element and data source. Works only with text file data sources in IE 5/Mac.

Example　　　　　document.myImage.dataFld = "logoURL";

Value　　　　　Case-sensitive identifier of the data source column.

Default　　　　　None.

dataFormatAs

IE 4　NN *n/a*　Moz *n/a*　Saf *n/a*　Op *n/a*　DOM *n/a*
Read/Write

This property is a member of the img element object in IE, but does not apply to img because data binding values are linked to the src attribute, rather than rendered content.

dataSrc

Read/Write

Used with IE data binding to specify the ID of the page's object element that loads the data source object for remote data access. Setting both the dataFld and dataSrc properties to empty strings breaks the binding between element and data source. Works only with text file data sources in IE 5/Mac.

Example	document.myImage.dataSrc = "DBSRC3";
Value	Case-sensitive identifier of the data source.
Default	None.

dynsrc

Read/Write

URL of a video clip to be displayed through the img element. Changing this property loads a new video clip into the image object. See also the loop property for controlling the frequency of video clip play.

Example	document.images[3].dynsrc = "snowman.avi";
Value	Complete or relative URL as a string.
Default	None.

fileCreatedDate

Read-only

Returns a string of the date (but not the time) that the server (or local filesystem) reports the currently loaded file was created. By loading an image into a nonrendered Image object, a script can determine the date of the image (but more accurately from the fileUpdatedDate property). IE 4's value is a long date format, but starting with IE 5, the date information is formatted as mm/dd/yyyy. The value may be corrupted if the server supplies the data in a format that IE does not expect. Implemented in IE 5/Mac, but the value is empty.

Example	var dateObj = new Date(document.logoImg.fileCreatedDate);
Value	Date string.
Default	None.

fileModifiedDate

Read-only

Returns a string of the date (but not the time) that the server (or local filesystem) reports the currently loaded file was most recently modified. IE 4's value is a long date format, but starting with IE 5, the date information is formatted as mm/dd/yyyy. The value may be corrupted or incorrect if the server supplies the data in a format that IE does not expect. Implemented in IE 5/Mac, but the value is empty.

Example	var dateObj = new Date(document.logoImg.fileModifiedDate);
Value	Date string.
Default	None.

fileSize

Returns the number of bytes for the size of the currently loaded image. IE for Windows returns this value as a string, while IE for Macintosh returns a number value (although its value is 0).

Example	var byteCount = parseInt(document.fileSize, 10);
Value	Integer as string (Windows) or number (Mac).
Default	None.

fileUpdatedDate

For an image file retrieved from a server, this property may more accurately reflect the date the file was last uploaded to the server than the other date-related properties. Local files commonly return an empty string. Implemented in IE 5/Mac, but the value is empty.

Example	var dateObj = new Date(document.logoImg.fileUpdatedDate);
Value	Date string.
Default	None.

height, width

Provide the height and width in pixels of the image rendered in the img element. Changes to these values are immediately reflected in reflowed content on the page in all supporting browsers except NN 4 and earlier. Be aware that images scale to fit the new dimension.

Example	document.prettyPicture.height = 250;
Value	Integer.
Default	None.

href

The URL specified by the element's src attribute. Identical to, and deprecated in favor of, the src property.

Example	document.logoImage.href = "images/fancyLogo.gif";

| **Value** | String of complete or relative URL. |
| **Default** | None. |

hspace, vspace

IE 3   NN 4   Moz all   Saf all   Op 7   DOM 1
Read/Write

Provide the pixel measure of horizontal and vertical margins surrounding an image object. The hspace property affects the left and right edges of the element equally; the vspace affects the top and bottom edges of the element equally. These margins are not the same as margins set by style sheets, but they have the same visual effect. Properties are read-only in NN 4 and earlier.

Example

```
document.logo.hspace = 5;
document.logo.vspace = 8;
```

| **Value** | Integer of pixel count. |
| **Default** | 0 (IE, Safari, Opera), -1 (Mozilla). |

isMap

IE 4   NN n/a   Moz all   Saf all   Op 7   DOM 1
Read/Write

Indicates whether the img element is acting as a server-side image map. For an image to be a server-side image map, it must be wrapped with an a element whose href attribute points to the URL of the CGI program that knows how to interpret the click coordinate information. The browser appends coordinate information about the click to the URL as a get form method appends form element data to the action attribute URL.

More recent browsers allow client-side image maps (see the useMap property), which operate more quickly for the user, because there is no communication with the server to carry out the examination of the click coordinate point.

Example	document.navMap.isMap = true;
Value	Boolean value: true | false.
Default	false

longDesc

IE 5(Mac)/6(Win)   NN n/a   Moz all   Saf all   Op 7   DOM 1
Read/Write

Reflects the longDesc attribute of the img element. Mainstream browsers provide no significant functionality for this attribute or property.

| **Value** | URL string. |
| **Default** | Empty string. |

loop

Read/Write

If you specify a video clip with the dynsrc attribute, the loop property controls how many times the clip should play (loop). Changing to a value of -1 is equal to a continuous loop.

Example   document.movieImg.loop = 3;

Value   Integer.

Default   1

lowsrc

Read/Write

Indicates the URL of a lower-resolution (or alternate) image to download into the document space if the image of the src attribute will take a long time to download. The lowsrc image should be the same pixel size as the primary src image. It makes sense to change the lowsrc property only if you are also going to change the src property. In this case, make sure you change the lowsrc property first so that the browser knows how to handle the long download for the src image.

Note that early Mozilla versions also implemented a second variation of this property with a different capitalization: lowSrc. Neither version is indicated in the W3C DOM.

Example   document.productImage.lowsrc = "images/widget43LoRes.jpg";

Value   Any complete or relative URL as a string.

Default   None.

mimeType

Read-only

Returns a plain-language description of the MIME type for the image. This property may not be officially supported by Microsoft, but it correctly reports values for typical image types served from both local disks and servers.

Example
```
if (document.productImage.mimeType.indexOf("JPEG") != -1) {
    // process condition for jpeg image
}
```

Value   String value such as JPEG Image or GIF Image.

Default   None.

name

IE *3* NN *2* Moz *all* Saf *all* Op *7* DOM *1*

Read/Write

This is the identifier associated with the image object for use in scripted references to the object, such as via the `document.images` array.

Example   `var imgName = document.images[3].name;`

Value   Case-sensitive string identifier that follows the rules of identifier naming: it may contain no whitespace, cannot begin with a numeral, and should avoid punctuation except for the underscore character.

Default   None.

nameProp

IE *5(Win)* NN *n/a* Moz *n/a* Saf *n/a* Op *n/a* DOM *n/a*

Read-only

Returns the filename (without the rest of the URL path) of the current image. Simplifies examination of current image content.

Example
```
if (document.images[3].nameProp == "menuOn.jpg") {
    document.image[3].src = "../images/menuOff.jpg";
}
```

Value   Case-sensitive string filename and extension.

Default   None.

naturalHeight, naturalWidth

IE *n/a* NN *n/a* Moz *all* Saf *n/a* Op *n/a* DOM *n/a*

Read-only

Return the unscaled height and width of the image, in pixels. Allows scripts to find the true dimensions of the original image in case scripts or incorrect element attributes have scaled the image.

Example
```
document.logoImg.height = document.logoImg.naturalHeight;
document.logoImg.width = document.logoImg.naturalWidth;
```

Value   Integer.

Default   None.

protocol

IE *4(Win)/5(Mac)* NN *n/a* Moz *n/a* Saf *n/a* Op *n/a* DOM *n/a*

Read-only

Returns the protocol component of the URL associated with the element. Windows and Macintosh versions return values in different formats. For the Windows version, the values are in expanded plain language (e.g., File Protocol or HyperText Transfer Protocol); for the Mac version, values resemble location.protocol values (e.g., file: or http:).

Value   String.

Default   None.

src   IE 4 NN 3 Moz *all* Saf *all* Op 7 DOM 1

Read/Write

Provides the relative or complete URL of the image file currently loaded or to be loaded into the img element. Loading an image of a different size into an existing img element forces the element to resize to the new image's dimensions except in the following browsers: Netscape 3, Netscape 4, and IE 3 for the Macintosh. Reading this property returns the complete URL, regardless of how the URL form assigned the value originally.

Example   document.image[3].src = "../images/menuOff.jpg";

Value   URL string.

Default   None.

start   IE 4 NN *n/a* Moz *n/a* Saf *n/a* Op *n/a* DOM *n/a*

Read/Write

If you specify a video clip with the dynsrc attribute, the start property controls the action that causes the clip to start running.

Example   document.movieImg.start = "mouseover";

Value   String constant: fileopen | mouseover.

Default   fileopen

useMap   IE 4 NN *n/a* Moz *all* Saf *all* Op 7 DOM 1

Read/Write

Provides the URL of the map element in the same document that contains client-side image map hot areas and links. The value includes the hashmark assigned with the map name in the usemap attribute of the img element.

Example   document.images[0].useMap = "#altMap";

Value   A string starting with a hashmark and the name of the map element.

Default   None.

vspace

See hspace.

width

See height.

x, y   IE *n/a* NN *4* Moz *all* Saf *all* Op *n/a* DOM *n/a*

Provide the horizontal and vertical pixel coordinates of the top-left corner of the image relative to the page. These are Navigator-only properties, corresponding to the offsetLeft and offsetTop properties of Internet Explorer.

Example   var imageFromTop = document.logoImg.y;

Value   Integer.

Default   None.

implementation   IE *5(Mac)/6(Win)* NN *n/a* Moz *all* Saf *all* Op *7* DOM *1*

The implementation object (the JavaScript reference for the W3C DOMImplementation object) represents, to a limited degree, the environment that makes up the document container— the browser for our purposes. You can reach this object via the document.implementation property.

Methods of the object let you see which DOM modules the browser reports supporting. In W3C DOM browsers, this object is also a gateway to creating virtual W3C Document and DocumentType objects outside of the current document tree. Thus, in supporting W3C DOM browsers you can use the document.implementation property as a start to generating a nonrendered document for external XML documents.

Opera implements several methods that are defined in the W3C DOM Level 3 Load and Save module: createLSInput( ), createLSOutput( ), createLSParser( ), and createLSSerializer( ). For details on these methods, consult the W3C recommendation at *http://www.w3.org/TR/DOM-Level-3-LS/load-save.html*.

Object Model Reference
document.implementation

Object-Specific Properties
None.

Object-Specific Methods

createCSSStyleSheet( )	createDocument( )	createDocumentType( )
createHTMLDocument( )	hasFeature( )	

Object-Specific Events
None.

createCSSStyleSheet( )
IE *n/a* NN *n/a* Moz *n/a* Saf *1.2* Op *n/a* DOM *2*

createCSSStyleSheet("*title*", "*mediaList*")

Returns a reference to a newly created virtual styleSheet object with no rules. You can add rules via the styleSheet.addRule( ) method. Unfortunately, as the W3C DOM recommendation admits, there is no mechanism for associating a styleSheet object created in this manner with a document to offer any practical application. For programmatic insertion of style sheet settings, use the addRule( ) method for an existing styleSheet object in the document tree.

Returned Value   Reference to a styleSheet object not yet associated with a Document object.

Parameters

title
 String containing an advisory title.

mediaList
 String of comma-delimited media (e.g., screen, print) for which the style sheet is intended.

createDocument( )
IE *n/a* NN *n/a* Moz *all* Saf *all* Op *7* DOM *2*

createDocument("*namespaceURI*", "*qualifiedName*", *docTypeReference*)

Returns a reference to a newly created virtual W3C DOM Document (not the document node of an HTML document) object. Mozilla extends this Document object with a load( ) method that permits the loading of XML documents into the browser's memory—now superceded by the XMLHttpRequest object.

Returned Value   Reference to an empty Document node object.

Parameters

namespaceURI
 String of the namespace URI for a new XML document element.

qualifiedName
 String identifier for the qualified name for the new document element.

docTypeReference
 Reference to a DocumentType node (which may be generated from the document. implementation.createDocumentType( ) method).

createDocumentType( )
IE *n/a* NN *n/a* Moz *all* Saf *all* Op *7* DOM *1*

createDocumentType("*qualifiedName*", "*publicID*", "*systemID*")

Returns a reference to a newly created virtual W3C DOM DocumentType object. You can feed the object returned from this method to the document.implementation.createDocument( ) method.

Returned Value   Reference to a DocumentType object not yet associated with a Document object.

Parameters

qualifiedName
> String identifier for the qualified name for the new document element.

publicID
> String of the public identifier for the DOCTYPE.

systemID
> String of the system identifier (typically, the URI of the DTD file) for the DOCTYPE.

createHTMLDocument( )　　　　　IE *n/a*　NN *n/a*　Moz *n/a*　Saf *1.2*　Op *7*　DOM *2*
```
createHTMLDocument("title")
```

Returns a reference to a newly created virtual W3C DOM HTMLDocument (not the document node of an HTML document) object. This document is a skeleton document (<HTML><HEAD> <TITLE>*titleParameterText*</TITLE></HEAD></HTML>), into which you may append elements of your own creation.

Returned Value　　Reference to an empty HTMLDocument object.

Parameters

title
> String of the document's title, which is inserted as the content of the title element.

hasFeature( )　　　　　IE *5(Mac)/6(Win)*　NN *n/a*　Moz *all*　Saf *all*　Op *7*　DOM *1*
```
hasFeature("feature", "version")
```

Returns a Boolean true if the browser application supports (i.e., conforms to the required specifications of) a stated W3C DOM module and version. The closely related isSupported( ) method performs the same test on an individual node, allowing you to verify feature support for the current node type. Parameter values for the two methods are identical.

It is up to the browser maker to validate that the DOM implemented in the browser conforms with each module before allowing the browser to return true for the module. That doesn't necessarily mean that the implementation is bug-free or consistent with other implementations. Caveat scriptor.

In theory, you could use this method to verify module support prior to accessing a property or invoking a method. The following script fragment from the head portion of a document dynamically links a different external style sheet file for "true" CSS2 support:
```
var cssFile;
if (document.implementation.hasFeature("CSS", "2.0")) {
    cssFile = "styles/corpStyle2.css";
} else {
    cssFile = "styles/corpStyle1.css";
}
document.write("<link rel='stylesheet' type='text/css' href='" + cssFile + "'>");
```

More browsers support this browser-wide method than the element-specific method, which may help more developers deploy it sooner.

Returned Value   Boolean value: true | false.

Parameters

feature

As of W3C DOM Level 2, permissible case-sensitive module name strings are: Core, XML, HTML, Views, StyleSheets, CSS, CSS2, Events, UIEvents, MouseEvents, MutationEvents, HTMLEvents, Range, Traversal, and Views. Level 3 adds more features, such as LS (the Load and Save module), BasicEvents, TextEvents, and KeyboardEvents.

version

String representation of the major and minor version of the DOM module cited in the first parameter. For the W3C DOM Level 2, the version is 2.0, even when the DOM module supports another W3C standard that has its own numbering system. Thus, the test for HTML DOM module support is for Version 2.0, even though HTML is at 4.x.

imports   IE 4 NN *n/a* Moz *n/a* Saf *n/a* Op *n/a* DOM *n/a*

A collection (array) of styleSheet objects imported into an explicit styleSheet object via the @import rule. In other words, a styleSheet object that employs an @import treats that imported style sheet as a nested object, but one that is, itself, a full-fledged styleSheet object. Thus, you can access the rule objects within each imported style sheet. The following example iterates through all of the document's styleSheet objects in search of imported style sheets:

```
for (var i = 0; i < document.styleSheets.length; i++) {
    for (var j = 0; j < document.styleSheets[i].imports.length; j++) {
        // process each imported style sheet, referenced
        // here as document.styleSheets[i].imports[j]
    }
}
```

Object Model Reference

document.styleSheets[*i*].imports

Object-Specific Properties

length

Object-Specific Methods

item( )

length   IE 4 NN *n/a* Moz *n/a* Saf *n/a* Op *n/a* DOM *n/a*

Read-only

Returns the number of objects in the collection.

Example   var howMany = document.styleSheets[i].imports.length;

Value   Integer.

item( )   IE 4   NN n/a   Moz n/a   Saf n/a   Op n/a   DOM n/a

item(*index*)

Returns a single imported styleSheet object corresponding to the index value in source code order of @import rules. IE 5 for Macintosh erroneously returns null.

Returned Value   Reference to an imported styleSheet object. If there are no matches to the parameters, the returned value is null.

Parameters

index

> Zero-based integer.

input   IE 4   NN n/a   Moz all   Saf all   Op 7   DOM 1

The input object reflects the input element. Most input element types were at least partially accessible to scripts dating all the way back to the first scriptable browsers. But Internet Explorer from version 4 onward, as well as Mozilla, Safari, and Opera from the past few years all provide script access to a wide range of properties.

In the W3C DOM specification, all input element objects share the same properties, even when the properties don't necessarily apply (the checked property of an input element of type text, for example). To reduce potential confusion, the discussions here for input types note the type or types for which each property and method truly applies (just like the corresponding entry for the input HTML element in Chapter 1).

A few properties and methods that don't appear here in the lists of object-specific items are worth highlighting. While the IE DOM (especially in the Windows versions) ascribes properties such as accessKey, disabled, and tabIndex to virtually every HTML element, the W3C DOM is typically more parsimonious in handing out these properties to elements. But input elements are the right places for these properties, and you'll find full implementations in all modern browsers. The same goes for the blur( ), click( ), and focus( ) methods, which are described among the shared items earlier in this chapter.

One input type that can cause initial headaches is the radio type. To allow a group of radio input elements to work their exclusive magic (checking one unchecks another) requires that all elements have the same identifier assigned to the name attribute (and thus name property). This means all like-named radio objects become a collection (array) of radio objects. It may be necessary, therefore, to reference an individual radio button as an item in an array. The entire array, of course, has a length property you can use to assist in looping through all radio objects within the group, if necessary, to find which one is checked, and retrieve that object's value:

```
var radioGrp = document.forms[0].myRadio;
for (var i = 0; i < radioGrp.length; i++) {
    if (radioGrp[i].checked) {
        alert("The value of the chosen button is " + radioGrp [i].value);
    }
}
```

Many properties and methods listed below are the exclusive realm of Web Forms 2.0, whose first implementation is in Opera 9. Item descriptions clearly indicate when they apply to Web Forms 2.0. Consult the input element in Chapter 1 for more details about setting up input elements to be Web Forms 2.0 friendly.

All event types listed here are available in all scriptable browsers. Mouse and keyboard events, of course, are shared among all rendered HTML elements, as described at the beginning of this chapter. Consult Chapter 9 to see which input types recognize each event type tailored for input elements.

Object Model Reference

```
[window.]document.formName.elementName
[window.]document.forms[i].elements[i]
[window.]document.getElementById("elementID")
```

Object-Specific Properties

accept	action	alt	autocomplete	autofocus
checked	complete	dataFld	dataSrc	defaultChecked
defaultValue	dynsrc	enctype	form	forms[]
height	hspace	htmlTemplate	indeterminate	inputmode
labels[]	list	loop	lowsrc	max
maxLength	method	min	name	pattern
readOnly	replace	required	selectedOption	selectionEnd
selectionStart	size	src	start	status
step	target	type	useMap	validationMessage
validity	value	valueAsDate	valueAsNumber	width
willValidate				

Object-Specific Methods

checkValidity()	createTextRange()	dispatchChange()
dispatchFormChange()	handleEvent()	select()
setCustomValidity()		

Object-Specific Events

Event
change
invalid (Web Forms 2.0)
select

accept

IE 4 NN n/a Moz all Saf all Op 7 DOM 1

Read/Write

Provides an optional advisory property consisting of a string of one or more comma-delimited MIME types of files that are being uploaded. Values have no impact on this element in current browsers.

Input Types	file
Example	document.entryForm.myFileUpload.accept = "image/gif";
Value	String.
Default	None.

action

IE *n/a* NN *n/a* Moz *n/a* Saf *n/a* Op *9* DOM *n/a*

Read/Write

Web Forms 2.0 extension that allows a submission of the enclosing form to a URI different from the regular form when the button element is clicked (and its type is set to submit).

Input Types	image, submit
Example	document.getElementById("redirSubmit").action = "redirect.php";
Value	URI string.
Default	None.

alt

IE *4* NN *n/a* Moz *all* Saf *all* Op *7* DOM *1*

Read/Write

Provides text to be displayed (or spoken) where the image-type input element appears on the page when a browser does not download graphics (or is waiting for the image to download). See the alt property of the img object for more details.

Input Types	image

autocomplete

IE *n/a* NN *n/a* Moz *n/a* Saf *n/a* Op *9* DOM *n/a*

Read/Write

Web Forms 2.0 extension that specifies whether the browser's automatic text field completion function is engaged. Although the property is a member of text-related input elements in Opera 9, changing the value does not affect operation.

Input Types	Text-oriented input types for Web Forms 2.0.
Value	String value: on | off.
Default	on

autofocus

IE *n/a* NN *n/a* Moz *n/a* Saf *n/a* Op *9* DOM *n/a*

Read/Write

Web Forms 2.0 extension that brings focus to the element after the page loads. Should be assigned to only one form control element per page.

Input Types	All rendered input types for Web Forms 2.0.

| **Value** | Boolean value: true | false. |
| **Default** | false |

checked

Determines whether the button is selected or turned on by the user or script. Checkboxes operate independently of each other. Only radio or checkbox objects with the checked property set to true have their name/value pair submitted with the form. To find out whether the form element is set to be checked when the page loads, see the defaultChecked property. Scripts can change this property even if the element is disabled.

Input Types   checkbox, radio

Example
```
if (document.choiceForm.myRadio[0].checked) {
    //process first radio button
}
```

| **Value** | Boolean: true | false. |
| **Default** | false |

complete

Reveals whether the image-type input element's src or lowsrc image file has fully loaded. See the complete property of the img object for more details.

Input Types   image

dataFld

Used with IE data binding to associate a remote data source column name to a button object's value property. A datasrc attribute must also be set for the element. Setting both the dataFld and dataSrc properties to empty strings breaks the binding between element and data source. Works only with text file data sources in IE 5/Mac.

Input Types   button, checkbox, hidden, password, radio, text

Example   document.myForm.myButton.dataFld = "linkURL";

Value   Case-sensitive identifier of the data source column.

Default   None.

dataSrc

Read/Write

Used with IE data binding to specify the ID of the page's object element that loads the data source object for remote data access. Content from the data source is specified via the dataFld attribute. Setting both the dataFld and dataSrc properties to empty strings breaks the binding between element and data source. Works only with text file data sources in IE 5/Mac.

Input Types	button, checkbox, hidden, password, radio, text
Example	document.myForm.myButton.dataSrc = "DBSRC3";
Value	Case-sensitive identifier of the data source.
Default	None.

defaultChecked

Read/Write

Specifies whether the element has the checked attribute set in the tag. You can compare the current checked property against defaultChecked to see whether the state of the control has changed since the document loaded. Changing this property does not affect the current checked status.

Input Types   checkbox, radio

Example
```
var cBox = document.forms[0].checkbox1
if (cBox.checked != cBox.defaultChecked) {
    // process for changed state
}
```

Value	Boolean value: true | false.
Default	Determined by HTML tag attribute.

defaultValue

Read/Write

Returns the string assigned to the value attribute of the element in the source code (except in IE for Windows, which returns an empty string). A user must manually select a file for uploading, so pre-setting or attempting to alter this value is a waste of time.

Input Types	file, hidden, password, text
Example	var initVal = document.entryForm.myFileUpload.defaultValue;
Value	String.
Default	None.

dynsrc

Provides the URL of a video clip to be displayed through the image-type input element's image. See the dynsrc property of the img object for more details.

Input Types   image

enctype

Web Forms 2.0 extension that allows (in concert with other properties, such as action) a submission of the enclosing form to a URI and enclosure MIME type different from the regular form when the submit button or image is clicked.

Input Types   image, submit

Example   `document.getElementById("mySubmit").enctype = "text/plain";`

Value   MIMEtype string.

Default   None.

form

Returns a reference to the form element that contains the current element. When processing an event from this element, the event handler function automatically has access to the input element (as the event object's target or srcElement property). By reading the form property, the script can easily access other controls within the same form.

In a Web Forms 2.0 environment, a form control (via the form attribute) may be associated with a form element that does not contain the control in the document tree. The property points to whichever form element is associated with the control.

Input Types   All types.

Example   `var theForm = evt.srcElement.form;`

Value   form element object reference.

Default   None.

forms

Web Forms 2.0 extension that returns an array (NodeList) of references to form objects with which the current input element is associated.

Example   `var formList = document.getElementById("myButton").forms;`

Value   Array.

Default   One-item array with a reference to any enclosing form element.

height, width

IE 4   NN *n/a*   Moz *all*   Saf *all*   Op 7   DOM 1

Read/Write

Indicate the height and width in pixels of the image rendered in the input element. See the height and width properties of the img object for more details.

Input Types   image

hspace, vspace

IE 4   NN *n/a*   Moz *all*   Saf *all*   Op 7   DOM 1

Read/Write

Indicate the pixel measure of horizontal and vertical margins surrounding an image-type input object. See the hspace and vspace properties of the img object for more details.

Input Types   image

htmlTemplate

IE *n/a*   NN *n/a*   Moz *n/a*   Saf *n/a*   Op 9   DOM *n/a*

Read-only

Web Forms 2.0 extension that returns a reference to the element object (a RepetitionElement object) whose ID matches that of the current form control's template attribute (which must be set for this property to be anything other than null).

Input Types   add

Example
```
var repeatTemplate = document.getElementById("myButton").htmlTemplate;
```
Value   Element object reference.

Default   null

indeterminate

IE 4   NN *n/a*   Moz *n/a*   Saf *n/a*   Op *n/a*   DOM *n/a*

Read/Write

Indicates whether a checkbox is visually represented as being neither checked nor unchecked, yet still active. This middle ground is rendered differently for different operating systems. In Windows, the checkbox is grayed out (with the checkmark still visible if it was there originally) but still active. On the Macintosh, the checkbox displays a hyphen inside the box. The indeterminate state usually means some change elsewhere on the page has likely affected the setting of the checkbox, requiring the user to verify the checkbox's setting for accuracy. An "indeterminate" checkbox is submitted with the form.

Input Types   checkbox

Example   document.orderForm.2DayAir.indeterminate = true;

Value   Boolean value: true | false.

Default   false

inputmode

Web Forms 2.0 extension (adopted whole from the W3C XForms 1.0 specification at *http://www.w3.org/TR/xforms/sliceE.html*) that directs the browser to display the appropriate text input user interface for a written language. Consult the W3C XForms 1.0 documents for details.

Input Types   `email`, `password`, `text`, `url`

Example   `document.orderForm.searchText.inputmode = "hiragana";`

Value   Written language script token with an optional modifier token (space-delimited). Tokens generally correspond to Unicode scripts (*http://www.unicode.org/unicode/reports/tr24/*).

Default   None.

labels

Web Forms 2.0 extension that returns an array (HTMLCollection) of references to `label` element objects associated with the current form control element.

Input Types   All rendered types.

Example   `var textboxLabels = document.getElementById("searchBox").labels;`

Value   Array of `label` element object references.

Default   Empty array.

list

Web Forms 2.0 extension associates a set of predefined entries tailored for the input type, yet the input element also allows for text entry of a value not in the list. Predefined entries are coded as `option` elements inside a Web Forms 2.0 `datalist` element. The `list` attribute's value is the ID of the `datalist` element containing the predefined entries. In Opera's implementation, predefined entries appear as a pick list below the input element when the element has focus.

Input Types   `date`, `datetime`, `datetime-local`, `email`, `month`, `number`, `range`, `text`, `time`, `url`, `week`

Example   `var whichList = document.getElementById("opsystems").list;`

Value   Reference to the associated `datalist` element object.

Default   None.

loop

IE 4 NN n/a Moz n/a Saf n/a Op n/a DOM n/a

Read/Write

If you specify a video clip with the dynsrc attribute, the loop property controls how many times the clip should play (loop). See the loop property of the img object for more details.

Input Types   image

lowsrc

IE 4 NN n/a Moz n/a Saf n/a Op n/a DOM n/a

Read/Write

Provides the URL of a lower-resolution (or alternate) image to download into the document space if the image of the src attribute will take a long time to download. See the lowsrc property of the img object for more details.

Input Types   image

max, min

IE n/a NN n/a Moz n/a Saf n/a Op 9 DOM n/a

Read/Write

Web Forms 2.0 extension that lets you specify the minimum and maximum values for an input element designed for numeric, date, time, and file upload data. If a user enters values outside of these boundaries, the browser sets the rangeUnderflow or rangeOverflow properties of the ValidityState object, which scripts may inspect for further error indications to the user.

Input Types   date, datetime, datetime-local, file, month, number, range, time, week

Example
```
document.getElementById("apptTime").min = "09:00";
document.getElementById("apptTime").max = "17:00";
```

Value
For number and range types, a positive or negative integer or floating-point number; for date type, an ISO 8601 format value (e.g., 2007-03-15); for combinations of date and time, an ISO 8601 format value (e.g., 2007-03-15T08:00:00, with a trailing Z if not the local variant); for month type, an ISO format value (e.g., 2007-03); for week type, an ISO 8601 format value (e.g., 2007W3); for file type, a positive integer indicating the number of allowed files to be uploaded with the form.

Default   None.

maxlength

IE 4 NN n/a Moz all Saf all Op 7 DOM 1

Read/Write

Defines the maximum number of characters that may be typed into a text field input element. In practice, browsers beep or otherwise alert users when a typed character would exceed the maxlength value. There is no innate correlation between the maxlength and size attributes. If the maxlength allows for more characters than fit within the specified width of the element, the browser provides horizontal scrolling (albeit awkward for many users) to allow entry and editing of the field.

Input Types	password, text
Example	document.getElementById("ZIP").maxlength=10;
Value	Positive integer.
Default	Unlimited.

method

Web Forms 2.0 extension (when used with other extensions, such as the action attribute) that allows a submission for the enclosing form to a URI different and even method from the regular form when the element is clicked (and its type is set to submit).

Input Types	image, submit
Example	document.getElementById("submitHere").method = "get";
Value	String of method type.
Default	get

name

This is the identifier associated with the form control. The value of this property is submitted as one-half of the name/value pair when the form is submitted to the server. Names are hidden from user view, since control labels are assigned via other means, depending on the control type. Form control names may also be used by script references to the objects. Despite the modern standards' preference for the id attribute, many browsers still require that a form control be assigned a name attribute to allow the control's value to be submitted.

Example	document.orderForm.myButton.name = "Win32";
Value	Case-sensitive string identifier that follows the rules of identifier naming: it may contain no whitespace, cannot begin with a numeral, and should avoid punctuation except for the underscore character.
Default	None.

pattern

Web Forms 2.0 extension that lets you specify a regular expression pattern that the user's input must match to pass validation.

Alphabetical DOM Reference

Input Types	email, password, text, url
Example	document.getElementById("partNum").pattern = "[A-Z][0-9]{7}"
Value	A regular expression (but not surrounded by the slash symbols, as used in JavaScript regular expressions).
Default	None.

readOnly

IE 4 NN *n/a* Moz *all* Saf *all* Op 7 DOM 1

Read-only

Specifies whether the form element can be edited on the page by the user. A form control that has a readOnly property set to true may still be modified by scripts, even though the user may not alter the content.

Input Types   password, text

Example
```
if (document.forms[0].myText.readOnly) {
    ...
}
```

Value	Boolean value: true	false.
Default	false

replace

IE *n/a* NN *n/a* Moz *n/a* Saf *n/a* Op 9 DOM *n/a*

Read/Write

Web Forms 2.0 extension that associates instructions to a submission form control with how to process the data returned from the server after the form is submitted. The choice is whether the response replaces the original document in the browser (the default) or the browser should apply returned values to the form, rather than retrieve initial form data (if a URL is assigned to the data attribute of the form element).

Input Types	image, submit
Example	document.getElementById("submitMe").replace = "values";
Value	One of two string values: document	values.
Default	document

required

IE *n/a* NN *n/a* Moz *n/a* Saf *n/a* Op 9 DOM *n/a*

Read/Write

Web Forms 2.0 extension that signifies whether the input element's value is required for submission. Sets the missingValue property of the ValidityState object to true if the element receives no value.

Input Types	checkbox, date, datetime, datetime-local, email, file, month, number, password, radio, range, text, time, url, week
Value	Boolean value: true | false.
Default	false

selectedOption

Web Forms 2.0 extension that returns a reference to the option element (within a datalist element) currently selected by the user. In Opera 9, the property is implemented, but always returns null.

| **Input Types** | date, datetime, datetime-local, email, month, number, range, text, time, url, week |

Example

```
var optionElem = document.getElementById("opsystems").selectedOption;
```

| **Value** | Reference to the selected option element object. |
| **Default** | None. |

selectionEnd, selectionStart

The selectionEnd and selectionStart properties are convenience properties that allow scripts to get and set the endpositions of a text selection within a text-oriented input element. Values are zero-based integer counters of positions between characters in the text entered into the field. When both properties have the same value, the visual result is the same as a text insertion pointer. For example, to place the cursor at the end of a text box, set the two values to the element's text length (see the textLength property). The equivalent IE functionality requires creating an IE text range in the element, adjusting the range's endpoints, and selecting the range (see the TextRange object).

| **Input Types** | password, text |

Example

```
var elem = document.forms[0].myPassword;
elem.selectionEnd = elem.textLength;
elem.selectionStart = elem.textLength;
```

| **Value** | Positive integer. |
| **Default** | None. |

size

IE 4 NN *n/a* Moz *all* Saf *all* Op 7 DOM 1

Read/Write

Roughly speaking, the width in characters that the input box should be sized to accommodate. In practice, the browser does not always accurately predict the proper width even when all characters are the same, as they are in the password object. See details in the size attribute discussion for the input element in Chapter 1. There is no interaction between the size and maxLength properties for this object.

Input Types	password, text
Example	document.forms[0].myPassword.size = 12;
Value	Integer.
Default	20

src

IE 4 NN *n/a* Moz *all* Saf *all* Op 7 DOM 1

Read/Write

Provides the relative or complete URL of the image file currently loaded or to be loaded into the image-type input element. See the src property of the img object for more details.

Input Types	image

start

IE 4 NN *n/a* Moz *n/a* Saf *n/a* Op *n/a* DOM *n/a*

Read/Write

If you specify a video clip with the dynsrc attribute, the start property controls the action that causes the clip to start running. See the start property of the img object for more details.

Input Types	image

status

IE 4 NN *n/a* Moz *n/a* Saf *n/a* Op *n/a* DOM *n/a*

Read/Write

Specifies whether the element is highlighted/checked. This property is identical to the checked property.

Input Types   checkbox, radio

Example
```
if (document.forms[0].56KbpsBox.status) {
    ...
}
```

Value	Boolean value: true | false.
Default	None.

step

Web Forms 2.0 extension that lets you specify the incremental values permitted in the input element. If a min and/or max attribute is set, those values set boundaries for data entered by the user; otherwise, a zero boundary is used (with 1970-01-01T00:00:00.0Z being the zero point for date-related elements).

Input Types	`date`, `datetime`, `datetime-local`, `file`, `month`, `number`, `range`, `time`, `week`
Example	`document.getElementById(""apptTime").step = "900";`
Value	For number and range types, a positive or negative integer or floating-point number as a string; for date, week, and month types, an integer (as a string) representing a number of days, weeks, or months, respectively; for combinations of date and time, a number of seconds as a string.
Default	60 (`datetime`, `datetime-local`, `time`); 1 (others).

target

Web Forms 2.0 extension that allows (in concert with other attributes, such as action) the page returned from a submission of the enclosing form to appear in a window or frame different from the destination of the page returned from a regular form when a submit-type element is clicked.

Input Types	`image`, `submit`
Example	`document.getElementById("submitMe").target = "_blank";`
Value	Frame or window name as a string.
Default	None (signifying the current window or frame).

type

Returns the type of form control element. The value is returned in all lowercase letters. It may be necessary to cycle through all form elements in search of specific types to do some processing on (e.g., emptying all form controls of type "text" while leaving other controls untouched). See the input element's type attribute description in Chapter 1 for more details about each type.

Input Types	All types.

Example

```
if (document.forms[0].elements[3].type == "button") {
    // process button input type here
}
```

Value

Any of the following constants (as a string): button | checkbox | file | hidden | image | password | radio | reset | select-multiple | select-one | submit | text | textarea (image type is not accessible to pre-Mozilla Netscape Navigator). Web Forms 2.0 browsers (like Opera 9) have the following additional type string values: add | date | datetime | datetime-local | email | month | move-down | move-up | number | range | remove | time | url | week.

Default   text

useMap   IE *4* NN *n/a* Moz *all* Saf *all* Op *7* DOM *1*
Read/Write

Provides the URL of the map element in the same document that contains client-side image map hot areas and links to be applied to the image. See the useMap property of the img object for more details.

Input Types   image

validationMessage   IE *n/a* NN *n/a* Moz *n/a* Saf *n/a* Op *9* DOM *n/a*
Read-only

Web Forms 2.0 extension that returns a browser-generated message if the form control fails to validate according to its specifications. This property is meant more for text-oriented form controls, where an empty string means that the entry validates properly. For a button element, this property is always an empty string.

Input Types   All types, including special Web Forms 2.0 types.

Value   Empty string.

Default   Empty string.

validity   IE *n/a* NN *n/a* Moz *n/a* Saf *n/a* Op *9* DOM *n/a*
Read-only

Web Forms 2.0 extension that returns a ValidityState object. For a button element, all members of the returned object are false, except for the valid property, which is true. See the ValidityState object.

Input Types   All types, including special Web Forms 2.0 types.

Value   ValidityState object.

Default   ValidityState object.

value

Indicates the current value associated with the form control that is submitted with the name/value pair for the element. All values are strings, and it is through this property that scripts insert text into text fields. Browsers return the actual characters typed by the user, including the password type so you can retrieve an entered password for further processing before submission (or perhaps for storage in the cookie). For a button type, the value property controls the label of a form control: the text that appears on the button. A button input element is not submitted with the form.

Input Types	All types except image.
Example	document.forms[0].myButton.value = "Undo";
Value	String.
Default	None.

valueAsDate

Web Forms 2.0 extension that returns the value of the form control in a standardized fashion, as noted below.

Input Types	datetime, date, time, week, month.

Value

String values as follows: for datetime type, the selected value in a form like that of the toString( ) method of a JavaScript date object (e.g., Sat, 26 Aug 2006 07:06:00 GMT-0700); for date type, the selected date at 00:00 UTC; for time type, the selected time on January 1, 1970; for week type, the date value of the Monday at 00:00 UTC for the selected week; for month type, the first day of the selected month at 00:00 UTC. For all other types, null.

Default	null

valueAsNumber

Web Forms 2.0 extension that returns a number (where possible) representing the entered data. Date and time types are converted to milliseconds since January 1, 1970 at 00:00 UTC.

Input Types	All text entry types.
Value	Number value or NaN.
Default	NaN

width

See height.

willValidate

Read-only

Web Forms 2.0 extension that returns a Boolean value indicating whether the form control element meets criteria for validating under the Web Forms 2.0 mechanism. A button element is not one of the correct types, and therefore always returns false.

Input Types	All types.
Value	Boolean value: true | false.
Default	false

checkValidity( )

Web Forms 2.0 method that returns a Boolean value representing whether the form control element meets its validity criteria—ultimately, whether the validity.valid property is true.

Input Types	All types.
Returned Value	Boolean value: true | false. Always true for button type elements.
Parameters	None.

createTextRange( )

Creates a TextRange object containing the button's label text. See the TextRange object for details.

Input Types	password, text
Returned Value	TextRange object.
Parameters	None.

dispatchChange( ), dispatchFormChange( )

Web Forms 2.0 methods that fire the change and formchange events on the current element. You could, for example "convert" a click event to a change or formchange event by having the onclick event handler invoke either method.

Input Types	All types.
Returned Value	None.
Parameters	None.

handleEvent( )

handleEvent(*event*)

Instructs the object to accept and process the event whose specifications are passed as the parameter to the method. The object must have an event handler for the event type to process the event. Navigator 4 only.

Input Types   button | checkbox | file | password | radio | reset | select-multiple | select-one | submit | text | textarea

Returned Value   None.

Parameters

event

A Navigator 4 event object.

select( )

Selects all the text displayed in the form element. Usually requires that the element have focus prior to invoking this method.

Input Types   password, text

Returned Value   None.

Parameters   None.

setCustomValidity( )

setCustomValidity([*errorString*])

Web Forms 2.0 method that sets the customError Boolean value of the validity property (itself a ValidityState object). If the method does not impact an element type, it throws a NOT_SUPPORTED_ERR error.

Input Types   All types.

Returned Value   None.

Parameters

errorString

If null or an empty string, the parameter resets the validity object's customError property, signifying the form control is not valid. An error string is to be remembered by the browser (during the current session) so that it displays the string upon subsequent validation failures.

ins

The ins object reflects the ins element.

HTML Equivalent   <ins>

Alphabetical DOM Reference

Object Model Reference
[window.]document.getElementById("*elementID*")

Object-Specific Properties

cite   dateTime

Object-Specific Methods
None.

Object-Specific Events
None.

cite, dateTime   IE *5(Mac)/6(Win)* NN *n/a* Moz *all* Saf *all* Op *7* DOM *1*
Read/Write

These two properties are listed among the shared properties earlier in this chapter due to an IE implementation oddity. IE 5/Macintosh and W3C DOM browsers correctly implement these properties only for the del and ins objects, as specified in the W3C DOM, but in no mainstream browser do they convey any special powers. See the shared cite and dateTime properties earlier in this chapter.

isindex   IE *5* NN *n/a* Moz *all* Saf *all* Op *7* DOM *1*

The isindex object reflects the ancient HTML isindex element. IE arbitrarily converts this element into a text-type input object in its DOM, and even creates a form element around it. Avoid using this element.

HTML Equivalent   <isindex>

Object-Specific Properties
prompt

prompt   IE *5(Mac)* NN *n/a* Moz *all* Saf *all* Op *7* DOM *1*
Read/Write

Provides the prompt message for the text entry field.

Value   String.

Default   None.

kbd

See abbr.

label

IE *4* **NN** *n/a* **Moz** *all* **Saf** *all* **Op** *7* **DOM** *1*

The label object reflects the label element.

HTML Equivalent `<label>`

Object Model Reference
`[window.]document.getElementById("elementID")`

Object-Specific Properties

control	dataFld	dataFormatAs	dataSrc	form
forms	htmlFor			

Object-Specific Methods
None.

Object-Specific Events
None.

control

IE *n/a* **NN** *n/a* **Moz** *n/a* **Saf** *n/a* **Op** *9* **DOM** *n/a*
Read-only

Web Forms 2.0 extension that returns a reference to the input element with which the current label element is associated.

Example   `var inpElem = document.getElementById("myLabel").control;`

Value   Reference to an input element

Default   None.

dataFld

IE *4* **NN** *n/a* **Moz** *n/a* **Saf** *n/a* **Op** *n/a* **DOM** *n/a*
Read/Write

Used with IE data binding to associate a remote data source column name with the displayed text of the input element label. A datasrc attribute must also be set for the element. Setting both the dataFld and dataSrc properties to empty strings breaks the binding between element and data source. Works only for text data sources in IE 5 for the Macintosh.

Example   `document.getElementById("myLabel").dataFld = "labelText";`

Value   Case-sensitive string identifier of the data source column.

Default   None.

Alphabetical DOM
Reference

dataFormatAs
IE *4* NN *n/a* Moz *n/a* Saf *n/a* Op *n/a* DOM *n/a*
Read/Write

Used with IE data binding, this property advises the browser whether the source material arriving from the data source is to be treated as plain text or as tagged HTML. Works only for text data sources in IE 5 for the Macintosh.

Example   `document.forms[0].myLabel.dataFormatAs = "html";`

Value   IE 4 recognizes two possible settings: text | html.

Default   text

dataSrc
IE *4* NN *n/a* Moz *n/a* Saf *n/a* Op *n/a* DOM *n/a*
Read/Write

Used with IE data binding to specify the ID of the page's object element that loads the data source object for remote data access. Setting both the dataFld and dataSrc properties to empty strings breaks the binding between element and data source. Works only for text data sources in IE 5 for the Macintosh.

Example   `document.getElementById("myLabel").dataSrc = "DBSRC3";`

Value   Case-sensitive identifier of the data source.

Default   None.

form
IE *5(Mac)/6(Win)* NN *n/a* Moz *all* Saf *all* Op *7* DOM *1*
Read-only

Returns a reference to the next outermost form element object in the document tree. Multiple label element objects within the same form element reference the same form element object.

Example   `var theForm = document.getElementById("myLabel").form;`

Value   Reference to a form element object.

Default   None.

forms
IE *n/a* NN *n/a* Moz *n/a* Saf *n/a* Op *9* DOM *n/a*
Read-only

Web Forms 2.0 extension that returns an array (NodeList type) containing references to the form elements with which the input element contained by the current label element is associated.

Example   `var inpForms = document.getElementById("myLabel").forms;`

Value   Reference to an input element

Default   None.

htmlFor

IE *4* NN *n/a* Moz *all* Saf *all* Op *7* DOM *1*

Read/Write

Provides the element id of the input element to which the label is associated (the value of the for attribute). Binds the label element to a particular input element.

Example	document.getElementById("label3").htmlFor = "chkbox3";
Value	String.
Default	None.

layer

IE *n/a* NN |4| Moz *n/a* Saf *n/a* Op *n/a* DOM *n/a*

The layer object reflects the layer and ilayer elements. Found in Navigator 4 only. Other elements (such as div and span) that have style sheet position attributes set to absolute or relative are arbitrarily converted to layer objects in Navigator 4.

HTML Equivalent

<ilayer>
<layer>

Object Model Reference[window.]document.*layerName*

Object-Specific Properties

above	background	below	bgColor	clip
hidden	left	name	pageX	pageY
parentLayer	siblingAbove	siblingBelow	src	top
visibility	zIndex			

Object-Specific Methods

captureEvents( )	handleEvent( )	load( )	moveAbove( )
moveBelow( )	moveBy( )	moveTo( )	moveToAbsolute( )
releaseEvents( )	resizeBy( )	resizeTo( )	routeEvent( )

Object-Specific Events

Handler	NN	Others	DOM
blur	4	n/a	n/a
focus	4	n/a	n/a
load	4	n/a	n/a
mouseout	4	n/a	n/a
mouseover	4	n/a	n/a
mouseup	4	n/a	n/a

Alphabetical DOM
Reference

above, below

IE *n/a* NN |4| Moz *n/a* Saf *n/a* Op *n/a* DOM *n/a*

Read-only

Return a reference to the positionable element whose stacking z-order is above or below the current element. These properties operate in the context of all positionable elements in a document. If the current element is the highest element, the above property returns null. To restrict the examination of next higher or lower elements within a single layer context, see siblingAbove and siblingBelow. To adjust the stacking order with respect to specific objects, see the moveAbove( ) and moveBelow( ) methods.

Example   var nextHigher = document.myILayer.above;

Value   Object reference or null.

Default   None.

background

IE *n/a* NN |4| Moz *n/a* Saf *n/a* Op *n/a* DOM *n/a*

Read/Write

This property holds an image object that has a src property that can be set to change the image used for the layer's background. In other words, you must set the src property of the layer's background object to change the image.

Example   document.myIlayer.background.src = "images/newlogo.gif";

Value   An image object property, such as src.

Default   None.

bgColor

IE *n/a* NN |4| Moz *n/a* Saf *n/a* Op *n/a* DOM *n/a*

Read/Write

Provides the background color of the element. While you may set the value with either a hexadecimal triplet or plain-language color value, values returned from the property are for some reason the decimal equivalent of the hexadecimal RGB version. The default behavior is a transparent background created with a bgColor property value of null.

Example   document.myIlayer.bgColor = "yellow";

Value   A hexadecimal triplet or plain-language color name. See Appendix A for acceptable plain-language color names. Returned values are the decimal equivalent of the hexadecimal value. A value of null sets the background to transparent.

Default   null (transparent).

clip

IE *n/a* NN |4| Moz *n/a* Saf *n/a* Op *n/a* DOM *n/a*

Read/Write

Defines a clipping region of a positionable element. This property is treated more like an object in itself, in that you adjust its values through six properties: clip.top, clip.left, `clip.bottom`, `clip.right`, `clip.width`, and `clip.height`. Adjust the side(s) or dimension(s) of your choice. All values represent pixel values.

Example	`document.myIlayer.clip.width = 150;`
Value	Integer.
Default	None.

hidden

Specifies whether the object is visible on the page. When the object is hidden, its surrounding content does not close the gap left by the element.

Example	`document.myIlayer.hidden = false;`
Value	Boolean value: `true`	`false`.
Default	`false`

left

For positionable elements, defines the position (in pixels) of the left edge of an element's box (content plus left padding, border, and/or margin) relative to the left edge of the next outermost block content container. For the relative-positioned layer, the offset is based on the left edge of the inline location of where the element would normally appear in the content.

Example	`document.myIlayer.left = 45;`
Value	Integer.
Default	0

name

This is the identifier associated with a layer for use as the value assigned to `target` attributes or as script references to the frame. If no value is explicitly assigned to the `id` attribute, Navigator automatically assigns the `name` attribute value to the `id` attribute.

Example
```
if (document.layers[2].name == "main") {
    ...
}
```

| **Value** | Case-sensitive identifier that follows the rules of identifier naming: it may contain no whitespace, cannot begin with a numeral, and should avoid punctuation except for the underscore character. |
| **Default** | None. |

pageX, pageY

IE *n/a* NN |4| Moz *n/a* Saf *n/a* Op *n/a* DOM *n/a*
Read/Write

Provide the horizontal (x) and vertical (y) position of the object relative to the top and left edges of the entire document.

Example   document.myIlayer.pageX = 400;

Value   Integer.

Default   None.

parentLayer

IE *n/a* NN |4| Moz *n/a* Saf *n/a* Op *n/a* DOM *n/a*
Read-only

Returns a reference to the next outermost layer in the containment hierarchy. For a single layer in a document, its parentLayer is the window object.

Example
```
if (parentLayer != window) {
    ...
}
```

Value   Object reference (a layer or window).

Default   window

siblingAbove, siblingBelow

IE *n/a* NN |4| Moz *n/a* Saf *n/a* Op *n/a* DOM *n/a*
Read-only

Return a reference to the positionable element whose stacking z-order is above or below the current element, but only within the context of the shared parentLayer. If the current element is the highest element, the siblingAbove property returns null. To widen the examination of next higher or lower elements to a document-wide context, see above and below. To adjust the stacking order with respect to specific objects, see the moveAbove( ) and moveBelow( ) methods.

Example   var nextHigher = document.myILayer.siblingAbove;

Value   Object reference or null.

Default   None.

src

IE *n/a* NN |4| Moz *n/a* Saf *n/a* Op *n/a* DOM *n/a*
Read/Write

Indicates the URL of the external content file loaded into the current element. To change the content, assign a new URL to the property.

Assigning a new URL to this property does not work with inline layers (ilayer elements) in Navigator 4. Instead the current source document is removed, and other page elements can be obscured. Avoid setting this property for inline layers. The same goes for the load( ) method.

Example	document.myIlayer.src = "swap2.html";
Value	Complete or relative URL as a string.
Default	None.

top

For positionable elements, defines the position of the top edge of an element's box (content plus top padding, border, and/or margin) relative to the top edge of the next outermost block content container. All measures are in pixels. When the element is a relative-positioned inline layer, the offset is based on the top edge of the inline location of where the element would normally appear in the content.

Example	document.myIlayer.top = 50;
Value	Integer.
Default	0

visibility

Indicates the state of the positioned element's visibility. Surrounding content does not close the space left by an element whose visibility property is set to hide (or the CSS version, hidden). If you set the property to the CSS syntax values (hidden | visible), they are converted internally to the JavaScript versions and returned from the property in that format.

Example	document.myIlayer.visibility = "hide";
Value	One of the constant values (as a string): hide	inherit	show.
Default	inherit

zIndex

For a positioned element, determines the stacking order relative to other elements within the same parent container. See Online Section IV for details on relationships of element layering amid multiple containers.

Example	document.myIlayer.zIndex = 3;
Value	Integer.
Default	0

captureEvents( )

IE *n/a*   NN |4| Moz *n/a*   Saf *n/a*   Op *n/a*   DOM *n/a*

captureEvents(*eventTypeList*)

Instructs the browser to grab events of a specific type before they reach their intended target objects. The object invoking this method must then have event handlers defined for the given event types to process the event.

Returned Value   None.

Parameters

eventTypeList
> A comma-separated list of case-sensitive event types as derived from the available Event object constants, such as Event.CLICK or Event.MOUSEMOVE.

handleEvent( )

IE *n/a*   NN |4| Moz *n/a*   Saf *n/a*   Op *n/a*   DOM *n/a*

handleEvent(*event*)

Instructs the object to accept and process the event whose specifications are passed as the parameter to the method. The object must have an event handler for the event type to process the event.

Returned Value   None.

Parameters

event
> A Navigator 4 event object.

load( )

IE *n/a*   NN |4| Moz *n/a*   Saf *n/a*   Op *n/a*   DOM *n/a*

load("*URL*", *newLayerWidth*)

This method lets you load a new document into a layer object. It does not work properly in Navigator 4 for ilayer elements. The existing document is unloaded from the layer, but the new one does not load as you'd expect. There is no satisfactory workaround except to transform the element into a layer.

Returned Value   Boolean value: true if the document loading was successful.

Parameters

URL
> String value of the complete or relative URL of the document to be loaded into the layer.

newLayerWidth
> Integer value in pixels of a resized width of the element to accommodate the new content.

moveAbove( ), moveBelow( )

IE *n/a*   NN |4| Moz *n/a*   Saf *n/a*   Op *n/a*   DOM *n/a*

moveAbove(*layerObject*) moveBelow(*layerObject*)

These methods shift the z-order of the current layer to a specific location relative to another, sibling layer. This is helpful if your script is not sure of the precise zIndex value of a layer you want to use as a reference point for the current layer's stacking order. Use moveAbove( ) to position the current layer immediately above the layer object referenced as a parameter.

Returned Value   None.

Parameters

layerObject

> Reference to another layer object that shares the same parent as the current layer.

moveBy( )

IE *n/a*   NN |4| Moz *n/a*   Saf *n/a*   Op *n/a*   DOM *n/a*

moveBy(*deltaX, deltaY*)

A convenience method that shifts the location of the current element by specified pixel amounts along both axes. To shift along only one axis, set the other value to zero. Positive values for *deltaX* shift the element to the right; negative values to the left. Positive values for *deltaY* shift the element downward; negative values upward. This method comes in handy for path animation under the control of a setInterval( ) or setTimeout( ) method that moves the element in a linear path over time.

Returned Value   None.

Parameters

deltaX

> Positive or negative pixel count of the change in horizontal direction of the element.

deltaY

> Positive or negative pixel count of the change in vertical direction of the element.

moveTo( ), moveToAbsolute( )

IE *n/a*   NN |4| Moz *n/a*   Saf *n/a*   Op *n/a*   DOM *n/a*

moveTo(*x, y*) moveToAbsolute(*x, y*)

Convenience methods that shift the location of the current element to a specific coordinate point. The differences between the two methods show when the element to be moved is nested inside another positioned container (e.g., a layer inside a layer). The moveTo( ) method uses the coordinate system of the parent container; the moveToAbsolute( ) method uses the coordinate system of the page. For a single layer on a page, the two methods yield the same result.

Returned Value   None.

Parameters

x

> Positive or negative pixel count relative to the top of the reference container, whether it is the next outermost layer (moveTo( )) or the page (moveToAbsolute( )).

y

Positive or negative pixel count relative to the left edge of the reference container, whether it is the next outermost layer (moveTo( )) or the page (moveToAbsolute( )).

releaseEvents( )   IE *n/a*   NN |4| Moz *n/a*   Saf *n/a*   Op *n/a*   DOM *n/a*

releaseEvents(*eventTypeList*)

The opposite of *layerObj*.captureEvents( ), this method turns off event capture at the layer level for one or more specific events named in the parameter list. See Online Section VI.

Returned Value   None.

Parameters

eventTypeList
A comma-separated list of case-sensitive event types as derived from the available Event object constants, such as Event.CLICK or Event.MOUSEMOVE.

resizeBy( )   IE *n/a*   NN |4| Moz *n/a*   Saf *n/a*   Op *n/a*   DOM *n/a*

resizeBy(*deltaX, deltaY*)

A convenience method that shifts the width and height of the current element by specified pixel amounts. To adjust along only one axis, set the other value to zero. Positive values for *deltaX* make the element wider; negative values make the element narrower. Positive values for *deltaY* make the element taller; negative values make the element shorter. The top and left edges remain fixed; only the right and bottom edges are moved.

Returned Value   None.

Parameters

deltaX
Positive or negative pixel count of the change in horizontal dimension of the element.
deltaY
Positive or negative pixel count of the change in vertical dimension of the element.

resizeTo( )   IE *n/a*   NN |4| Moz *n/a*   Saf *n/a*   Op *n/a*   DOM *n/a*

resizeTo(*x, y*)

Convenience method that adjusts the height and width of the current element to specific pixel sizes. The top and left edges of the element remain fixed, while the bottom and right edges move in response to this method.

Returned Value   None.

Parameters

x
Width in pixels of the element.
y
Height in pixels of the element.

---

routeEvent( )

routeEvent(*event*)

Used inside an event handler function, this method directs Navigator to let the event pass to its intended target object.

Returned Value   None.

Parameters

event

A Navigator 4 event object.

legend

The legend object reflects the legend element. A legend element must be nested inside and immediately after the fieldset element associated with a form or group of form controls.

HTML Equivalent   <legend>

Object Model Reference

[window.]document.getElementById("*elementID*")

Object-Specific Properties

align	form	forms

Object-Specific Methods

None.

Object-Specific Events

None.

align

Read/Write

Controls the alignment of the legend element with respect to the containing fieldset element. The permissible values do not always work as planned in Internet Explorer 4. Be sure to check your desired setting on all operating system platforms of your intended audience.

Example   document.getElementById("myLegend").align = "center";

Value   Any one of the following constant values (as a string): bottom | center | left | right | top.

Default   left

form
IE 5(Mac)/6(Win) NN n/a Moz all Saf all Op 7 DOM 1

Read-only

Returns a reference to the next outermost form element object in the document tree. Multiple legend element objects within the same form element reference the same form element object.

Example   var theForm = document.getElementById("myLegend").form;

Value   Reference to a form element object.

Default   None.

forms
IE n/a NN n/a Moz n/a Saf n/a Op 9 DOM n/a

Read-only

Web Forms 2.0 extension that returns an array (NodeList type) containing references to the form elements with which the input element contained by the current legend element is associated.

Example   var inpForms = document.getElementById("myLegend").forms;

Value   Reference to an input element

Default   None.

li
IE 4 NN n/a Moz all Saf all Op 7 DOM 1

The li object reflects the li element nested inside an ol or ul element.

HTML Equivalent   <li>

Object Model Reference
[window.]document.getElementById("*elementID*")

Object-Specific Properties

type	value

Object-Specific Methods
None.

Object-Specific Events
None.

type
IE 4 NN n/a Moz all Saf all Op 7 DOM 1

Read/Write

Indicates the manner in which the leading bullets, numbers, or letters of items in the list are displayed. Bullet styles are displayed when the li element is nested inside a ul element;

numbers and letters are displayed for an ol element. If your script changes the type for a single li object, be aware that the change affects all subsequent li elements in the same list.

Example

```
document.getElementById("instruxListItem3").type = "a";
document.getElementById("point4").type = "square";
```

Value

For an ol style list, possible values are: A | a | I | i | 1. Sequencing is performed automatically as shown in the following table.

Type	Example
A	A, B, C, ...
a	a, b, c, ...
I	I, II, III, ...
i	i, ii, iii, ...
1	1, 2, 3, ...

For a ul-style list, possible values are: circle | disc | square.

Default   1 and disc (although values are empty unless the corresponding attribute is explicitly assigned).

value

IE 4 NN n/a Moz all Saf all Op 7 DOM 1

Read/Write

Indicates the number of the item within an ordered list. This property applies to an li element only when it is nested inside an ol element, and only when the corresponding attribute is explicitly assigned in the HTML code. The default value for unadjusted numbering is always 0 in IE, Safari, and Opera and -1 in Mozilla. If you set the value property of one item in the list, the following items continue the sequence from the new value. Modifying the property value does not adjust the rendered numbering.

Example

```
if (document.getElementById("step5").value > 0) {
    ...
}
```

Value   Integer.

Default   0 or -1.

link

IE 4 NN n/a Moz all Saf all Op 7 DOM 1

The link object reflects the link element. Note that many of the properties listed here are not available for scripting in the object unless their corresponding attributes are set initially in the HTML tag. Moreover, because the element's attributes act as directives while the document loads, assigning new values to the corresponding properties generally has no effect (even though the properties are read/write). This includes: href, rel, rev, and type. As a reminder, the disabled property (described among the shared properties earlier in this chapter) lets all supporting browsers turn on and off a linked style sheet.

HTML Equivalent   `<link>`

Object Model Reference`[window.]document.getElementById("elementID")`

Object-Specific Properties

charset	href	hreflang	media	rel
rev	sheet	styleSheet	target	type

Object-Specific Methods
None.

Object-Specific Events

Event	IE	Opera 9	Others	DOM
error	•	•	—	—
load	•	•	—	—

charset

IE 4 NN n/a Moz all Saf all Op 7 DOM 1

Read/Write

Indicates the character encoding of the content at the other end of the link.

Example   `var charCoding = document.getElementById("myLink").charset;`

Value   Case-insensitive alias from the character set registry (*ftp://ftp.isi.edu/in-notes/iana/assignments/character-sets*).

Default   None.

href

IE 4 NN n/a Moz all Saf all Op 7 DOM 1

Read/Write

Provides the URL specified by the element's href attribute. In IE/Windows, you can assign a new URL to this property to load in an alternate style sheet after the fact.

Example   `document.getElementById("styleLink").href = "altStyles.css";`

Value   String of complete or relative URL.

Default   None.

hreflang

IE 6   NN n/a   Moz all   Saf all   Op 7   DOM 1

Read/Write

Specifies the language code of the content at the destination of a link. Requires that the href attribute or property also be set.

Example   document.getElementById("myLink").hreflang = "DE";

Value   Case-insensitive language code.

Default   None.

media

IE 4   NN n/a   Moz all   Saf all   Op 7   DOM 1

Read/Write

Specifies the intended output device for the content of the destination document pointed to by the href attribute. The media property looks forward to the day when browsers are able to tailor content to specific kinds of devices such as pocket computers, text-to-speech digitizers, or fuzzy television sets.

Example

```
if (document.getElementById("link3").media == "print") {
    // process for print output
}
```

Value   Any one of the following constant values as a string: all | print | screen.

Default   all

rel

IE 4   NN n/a   Moz all   Saf all   Op 7   DOM 1

Read/Write

Defines the relationship between the current element and the external item pointed to by the link. Also known as a *forward link*, not to be confused in any way with the destination document whose address is defined by the href attribute. This property is not fully exploited in mainstream browsers, but you can treat the attribute as a kind of parameter to be checked and/or modified under script control.

Example

```
if (document.getElementById("link3").rel == "alternate stylesheet") {
    // process for alternate style sheet
}
```

Value

Case-insensitive, space-delimited list of HTML 4 standard link types (as a single string) applicable to the element. Sanctioned link types are:

alternate	appendix	bookmark	chapter
contents	copyright	glossary	help

index	next	prev	section
start	stylesheet	subsection	

Default   None.

rev

Read/Write

Defines the relationship between the current element and the destination of the link. Also known as a *reverse link*. This property is not fully exploited in mainstream browsers, but you can treat the attribute as a kind of parameter to be checked and/or modified under script control.

Value   Case-insensitive, space-delimited list of HTML 4 standard link types (as a single string) applicable to the element. See the rel property for sanctioned link types.

Default   None.

sheet

Read-only

Returns a reference to the styleSheet object (CSSStyleSheet object in W3C DOM terminology) linked into the current document when a style sheet is specified as the target of the link element. IE for Windows provides a similar property: styleSheet.

Example   var extSS = document.getElementById("link3").sheet;

Value   styleSheet object reference.

Default   None.

styleSheet

Read-only

This nonstandard convenience property returns a reference to the styleSheet object linked into the current document when a style sheet is specified as the target of the link element. Mozilla and Safari provide a similar property: sheet.

Example   var extSS = document.getElementById("link3").styleSheet;

Value   styleSheet object reference.

Default   None.

target

Read/Write

Indicates the window or frame name to be the recipient of linked content. Default value (equivalent of _self) is the desired setting for linked style sheets.

Example	document.getElementById("link4").target = "frame2";
Value	String value of the window or frame name, or any of the following constants (as a string): _parent	_self	_top	_blank.
Default	None.

type

Read/Write

Indicates an advisory MIME type declaration about the data being loaded from an external source. For example, an external style sheet would be text/css. This information is usually set in the element tag's type attribute.

Example

```
if (document.getElementById("myStyle").type == "text/css") {
    ...
}
```

Value	MIME type string.
Default	None.

links

A collection of all a and area elements that have assigned href attributes that make them behave as links (instead of only anchors). Collection members are sorted in source code order. Navigator and Internet Explorer let you use array notation to access a single link in the collection (document.links[0] or document.links["section3"], for example). If you wish to use the link's name as an index value (always as a string identifier), be sure to use the value of the name attribute, rather than the id attribute. To use the id attribute in a reference to an anchor, access the object via a document.all.*elementID* (in IE only) or document.getElementById(*"elementID"*) reference.

Object Model Reference
document.links

Object-Specific Properties

length

Object-Specific Methods

item( )	namedItem( )	tags( )	urns( )

Object-Specific Events

None.

length

IE 2 NN 3 Moz *all* Saf *all* Op 7 DOM 1

Read-only

Returns the number of elements in the collection.

Example	`var howMany = document.links.length;`
Value	Integer.

item( )

IE 4 NN *n/a* Moz *all* Saf *all* Op 7 DOM 1

`item(index)` `item(index[, subindex])`

Returns a single object or collection of objects corresponding to the element matching the index value (or, optionally in IE/Windows, the index and subindex values).

Returned Value	One object or collection (array) of objects. If there are no matches to the parameters, the returned value is `null`.

Parameters

index

> When the parameter is a zero-based integer (as required for Mozilla), the returned value is a single element corresponding to the said numbered item in source code order (nested within the current element). When the parameter is a string (allowed by IE/Windows), the returned value is a collection of elements with id or name properties that match that string.

subindex

> If you specify a string value for the first parameter (in IE/Windows), you may use the second parameter to specify a zero-based integer to retrieve a specific element from the collection with id or name properties that match the first parameter's string value.

namedItem( )

IE 6 NN *n/a* Moz *all* Saf *all* Op 7 DOM 1

`namedItem(IDOrName)`

Returns a single object (in W3C DOM browsers) or collection of objects corresponding to the element matching the parameter string value.

Returned Value	One object (in W3C DOM browsers) or collection (array) of objects. If there are no matches to the parameters, the returned value is `null`.

Parameters

IDOrName

> The string that contains the same value as the desired element's id or name attribute.

tags( )   IE *4*   NN *n/a*   Moz *n/a*   Saf *n/a*   Op *7*   DOM *n/a*

tags(*tagName*)

Returns a collection of objects (among all objects within the current collection) with tags that match the *tagName* parameter. Lets you distinguish among collections of a and area elements.

Returned Value   A collection (array) of objects. If there are no matches to the parameters, the returned value is an array of zero length.

Parameters

tagName
     A string that contains the element tag, as in document.links.tags("a").

urns( )   IE *5(Win)*   NN *n/a*   Moz *n/a*   Saf *n/a*   Op *n/a*   DOM *n/a*

urns(*URN*)

Returns a collection of nested element objects that have behaviors attached to them and URNs that match the *URN* parameter.

Returned Value   A collection (array) of objects. If there are no matches to the parameters, the returned value is an array of zero length.

Parameters

URN
     A string with a local or external behavior file URN.

LinkStyle   IE *4*   NN *n/a*   Moz *all*   Saf *all*   Op *7*   DOM *2*

The LinkStyle object is a W3C DOM abstract object that gets blended into the link element object. Through this blending, the Mozilla and Safari link element object gains the sheet property, which provides a reference to the styleSheet object linked into the current document through a link element.

Object Model Reference

document.getElementById("*linkElementID*")

Object-Specific Properties

sheet

Object-Specific Methods

None.

Object-Specific Events

None.

sheet

IE *n/a*   NN *n/a*   Moz *all*   Saf *all*   Op *n/a*   DOM *2*

Read-only

Returns a reference to the styleSheet object (CSSStyleSheet object in W3C DOM terminology) linked into the current document when a style sheet is specified as the target of the link element. IE for Windows provides a similar property for a link element object: styleSheet.

Example	var extSS = document.getElementById("link3").sheet;
Value	styleSheet object reference.
Default	None.

listing

IE *4*   NN *n/a*   Moz *n/a*   Saf *n/a*   Op *n/a*   DOM *n/a*

The listing object reflects the listing element.

HTML Equivalent   <listing>

Object Model Reference
[window.]document.getElementById("*elementID*")

Object-Specific Properties
None.

Object-Specific Methods
None.

Object-Specific Events
None.

location

IE *3*   NN *2*   Moz *all*   Saf *all*   Op *7*   DOM *n/a*

There is one location object in each window or frame. The object stores all information about the URL of the document currently loaded into that window or frame. By assigning a new URL to the href property of the location object, you instruct the browser to load a new page into the window or frame. This is the primary way of scripting the loading of a new page:

```
location.href = "newPage.html";
```

A script in one frame can reference the location object in another frame to load a new document into that other frame:

```
parent.otherFrameName.location.href = "newPage.html";
```

Security restrictions prevent a script in one frame from accessing location object information in another frame if the document in the second frame does not come from the same domain (and the same server, unless the document.domain properties of the two documents are set to match) as the document with the nosy script. This prevents a rogue script from monitoring navigation in another frame to external web sites. In Navigator 4 and Mozilla, you can overcome the security restriction with the help of signed scripts, but the user still has to give explicit permission for a script to access location object information outside the script's domain.

As a window-related object, the location object is not part of the formal W3C DOM Level 1 or 2 specifications (which leave windows for future versions). But the location object and its properties are well-entrenched in scripting vernacular, and should continue to be supported for a long time coming.

Object Model Reference
[*windowRef*.]location

Object-Specific Properties

hash	host	hostname	href	pathname	port	protocol	search

Object-Specific Methods

assign()	reload()	replace()

Object-Specific Events
None.

hash

IE 3 NN 2 Moz *all* Saf *all* Op 7 DOM *n/a*

Read/Write

Indicates that portion of a URL following the # symbol, referring to an anchor location in a document. This property contains its data only if the user has explicitly navigated to an anchor, and is not just scrolling to it. Do not include the # symbol when setting the property.

Example	location.hash = "section3";
Value	String.
Default	None.

host

IE 3 NN 2 Moz *all* Saf *all* Op 7 DOM *n/a*

Read/Write

Provides the combination of the hostname and port (if any) of the server that serves up the current document. If the port is explicitly part of the URL, the hostname and port are separated by a colon, just as they are in the URL.

Example
```
if (location.host == "www.megacorp.com:80") {
    ...
}
```
Value   String of hostname, optionally followed by a colon and port number.

Default   Depends on server.

hostname

IE 3   NN 2   Moz *all*   Saf *all*   Op 7   DOM *n/a*
Read/Write

Provides the combination of the hostname of the server (i.e., a two-dot address consisting of server name and domain) that serves up the current document. The hostname property does not include the port number.

Example
```
if (location.hostname == "www.megacorp.com") {
    ...
}
```
Value   String of hostname (server and domain).

Default   Depends on server.

href

IE 3   NN 2   Moz *all*   Saf *all*   Op 7   DOM *n/a*
Read/Write

Provides the complete URL of the document loaded in the window or frame. Assigning a URL to this property is how you script navigation to load a new document into the window or frame (although Internet Explorer also offers the equivalent window.navigate( ) method).

Example   `location.href = "http://www.megacorp.com";`

Value   String of complete or relative URL.

Default   None.

pathname

IE 3   NN 2   Moz *all*   Saf *all*   Op 7   DOM *n/a*
Read/Write

Provides the pathname component of the URL. This consists of all URL information following the last character of the domain name, including the initial forward slash symbol.

Example   `location.pathname = "/images/logoHiRes.gif";`

Value   String.

Default   None.

port

IE 3   NN 2   Moz *all*   Saf *all*   Op 7   DOM *n/a*
Read/Write

Provides the port component of the URL, if one exists. This consists of all URL information following the colon after the last character of the domain name. The colon is not part of the port property value.

Example	`location.port = "80";`
Value	String (a numeric value as string).
Default	None.

protocol

Provides the protocol component of the URL. This consists of all URL information up to and including the first colon of a URL. Typical values are: "http:", "file:", "ftp:", and "mailto:".

Example
```
if (location.protocol == "file:") {
    // statements for treating document as local file
}
```

| **Value** | String. |
| **Default** | None. |

search

Provides the URL-encoded portion of a URL that begins with the ? symbol. A document that is served up as the result of the search also may have the search portion available as part of the window.location property. You can modify this property by script. Doing so sends the URL and search criteria to the server. You must know the format of data (usually name/value pairs) expected by the server to perform this properly. You can also pass string data between separate pages by appending a search string to the next page's URL. While the search string appendage does not affect retrieval of the page, the string arrives with the new page in the new page's location object. A script in the new page can read and dissect the location.search property to place the passed values in variables that scripts in the page may use for their processing.

Example	`location.search="?p=Tony+Blair&d=y&g=0&s=a&w=s&m=25";`
Value	String starting with the ? symbol.
Default	None.

assign( )

`assign("URL")`

This method was intended to be hidden from view of scripters, but remains available for now. It performs the same action as assigning a URL to the location.href property. The assign( ) method is listed here for completeness and should not be used.

| **Returned Value** | None. |

Parameters

URL

> A string version of a complete or relative URL of a document to be loaded into a window or frame.

reload( )   IE 4   NN 3   Moz *all*   Saf *all*   Op 7   DOM *n/a*

reload([*unconditional*])

Performs a hard reload of the document associated with the location object. This kind of reload resets form elements to their default values (for a soft reload, use history.go(0)). By default, the reload( ) method performs a conditional-get action, which retrieves the file from the browser cache if the file is still in the cache (and the cache is turned on). To force a reload from the server, force an unconditional-get by adding the true Boolean parameter.

Returned Value   None.

Parameters

unconditional

> An optional Boolean value. If true, the browser performs an unconditional-get to force a reload of the document from the server, rather than the browser cache.

replace( )   IE 4   NN 3   Moz *all*   Saf *all*   Op 7   DOM *n/a*

replace("*URL*")

Loads a new document into the reference window and replaces the browser's history listing entry of the current document with the entry of the new document. Thus, some interim page that you don't want appearing in history (to prevent the **Back** button from ever returning to the page) can be removed from the history and replaced with the entry of the newly loaded document.

Returned Value   None.

Parameters

URL

> A string version of a complete or relative URL of a document to be loaded into a window or frame.

locationbar

See directories.

map   IE 4   NN *n/a*   Moz *all*   Saf *all*   Op 7   DOM 1

The map object reflects the map element.

HTML Equivalent   <map>

Object Model Reference

[window.]document.getElementById("*elementID*")

Object-Specific Properties

areas[]   name

Object-Specific Methods
None.

Object-Specific Events
None.

areas[ ]

IE *4* NN *n/a* Moz *all* Saf *all* Op *7* DOM *1*

Read-only

Indicates a collection of all area element objects nested inside the map element.

Example
```
for (var i = 0; i < document.getElementById("myMap").areas.length; i++) {
    oneMap = document.getElementById("myMap").areas[i];
    ...
}
```

Value	Array of area element objects.
Default	Array of length zero.

name

IE *4* NN *n/a* Moz *all* Saf *all* Op *7* DOM *1*

Read/Write

This is the identifier associated with the client-side image map specification. A map element contains all the area elements that define the hotspots of an image and their link destinations. The name assigned to the map element is the one cited by the usemap attribute of the img element. This binds the map definitions to the image.

Example	document.getElementById("myMap").name = "altMap";
Value	Case-sensitive string identifier that follows the rules of identifier naming: it may contain no whitespace, cannot begin with a numeral, and should avoid punctuation except for the underscore character.
Default	None.

marquee

IE *4* NN *n/a* Moz *1.0.1* Saf *n/a* Op *n/a* DOM *n/a*

The marquee object reflects the marquee element. Mozilla's implementation is in the form of an XUL extension (built-in). A number of properties and methods used internally by the add-on are exposed to scripts, but there is little or no need to reference them. If you are interested in the inner workings, you can learn a lot by viewing the XML and JavaScript Mozilla source code for the module (*http://lxr.mozilla.org/seamonkey/source/layout/style/xbl-marquee/xbl-marquee.xml*).

HTML Equivalent   `<marquee>`

Object Model Reference
`[window.]document.getElementById("elementID")`

Object-Specific Properties

behavior	bgColor	dataFld	dataFormatAs	dataSrc
direction	height	hspace	loop	scrollAmount
scrollDelay	trueSpeed	vspace	width	

Object-Specific Methods

start( )   stop( )

Object-Specific Events

Event	IE	Others	DOM
bounce	•	—	—
finish	•	—	—
start	•	—	—

behavior

IE *4*   NN *n/a*   Moz *1.0.1*   Saf *n/a*   Op *n/a*   DOM *n/a*

Read/Write

Specifies the motion of the content within the rectangular space set aside for the marquee element. You have a choice of three motion types.

Example   `document.getElementById("newsBanner").behavior = "slide";`

Value
Case-insensitive marquee element motion types:

alternate
Content alternates between marching left and right.

scroll
Content scrolls (according to the direction attribute or property) into view and out of view before starting again.

slide
Content scrolls (according to the direction attribute or property) into view, stops at the end of its run, blanks, and then starts again.

Default   scroll

bgColor

Background color of the element. This color setting is not reflected in the style sheet backgroundColor property. Even if the bgcolor attribute or bgColor property is set with a plain-language color name, the returned value is always a hexadecimal triplet.

Example document.getElementById("myBanner").bgColor = "yellow";

Value A hexadecimal triplet or plain-language color name. See Appendix A for acceptable plain-language color names.

Default Inherits body background color.

dataFld

Used with IE data binding to associate a remote data source column name with the content of the marquee element. A datasrc attribute must also be set for the element. Setting both the dataFld and dataSrc properties to empty strings breaks the binding between element and data source. Works only with text file data sources in IE 5/Mac.

Example document.getElementById("myBanner").dataFld = "hotNews";

Value Case-sensitive string identifier of the data source column.

Default None.

dataFormatAs

Used with IE data binding, this property advises the browser whether the source material arriving from the data source is to be treated as plain text or as tagged HTML.

Example document.getElementById("myBanner").dataFormatAs = "text";

Value IE recognizes two possible settings: text | html.

Default text

dataSrc

Used with IE data binding to specify the ID of the page's object element that loads the data source object for remote data access. Setting both the dataFld and dataSrc properties to empty strings breaks the binding between element and data source. Works only with text file data sources in IE 5/Mac.

Example document.getElementById("myBanner").dataSrc = "DBSRC3";

Value Case-sensitive string identifier of the data source.

Alphabetical DOM
Reference

Default   None.

direction   IE 4   NN n/a   Moz 1.0.1   Saf n/a   Op n/a   DOM n/a

Read/Write

Specifies the direction of the scroll within the element space.

Example   `document.getElementById("myBanner").direction = "down";`

Value   Four possible case-insensitive directions: down | left | right | up.

Default   `left`

height, width   IE 4   NN n/a   Moz 1.0.1   Saf n/a   Op n/a   DOM n/a

Read/Write

Provide the height and width in pixels of the element. Changes to these values are immediately reflected in reflowed content on the page.

Example   `document.getElementById("myBanner").height = 250;`

Value   Integer.

Default   None.

hspace, vspace   IE 4   NN n/a   Moz n/a   Saf n/a   Op n/a   DOM n/a

Read/Write

Provide the pixel measure of horizontal and vertical margins surrounding the element. The hspace property affects the left and right edges of the element equally; the vspace affects the top and bottom edges of the element equally. These margins are not the same as margins set by style sheets, but they have the same visual effect.

Example
```
document.getElementById("myBanner").hspace = 5;
document.getElementById("myBanner").vspace = 8;
```

Value   Integer of pixel count.

Default   0

loop   IE 4   NN n/a   Moz n/a   Saf n/a   Op n/a   DOM n/a

Read/Write

Sets the number of times the element scrolls its content. After the final scroll, the content remains in a fixed position. Constant animation can sometimes be distracting to page visitors, so if you have the marquee turn itself off after a few scrolls, you may be doing your visitors a favor.

Example   `document.getElementById("myBanner").loop = 3;`

Value   Any positive integer if you want the scrolling to stop after that number of
                   times. Otherwise, set the value to -1.

Default   -1

scrollAmount
IE *4* NN *n/a* Moz *1.0.1* Saf *n/a* Op *n/a* DOM *n/a*

Read/Write

Specifies the amount of space between positions of each drawing of the content. The
greater the space, the faster the text appears to scroll. See also scrollDelay.

Example   document.getElementById("myBanner").scrollAmount = 4;

Value   Positive integer.

Default   6

scrollDelay
IE *4* NN *n/a* Moz *1.0.1* Saf *n/a* Op *n/a* DOM *n/a*

Read/Write

Specifies the amount of time in milliseconds between each drawing of the content. The
greater the delay, the slower the text appears to scroll. See also scrollAmount.

Example   document.getElementById("myBanner").scrollDelay = 100;

Value   Positive integer.

Default   85 (Windows 95); 90 (Macintosh).

trueSpeed
IE *4* NN *n/a* Moz *n/a* Saf *n/a* Op *n/a* DOM *n/a*

Read/Write

Specifies whether the browser should honor scrolldelay attribute settings below 60 milliseconds. The default setting (false) prevents accidental settings that scroll too fast for most
readers.

Example   document.getElementById("myBanner").trueSpeed = "true";

Value   Boolean value: true | false.

Default   false

vspace
See hspace.

width
See height.

start( )   IE 4   NN n/a   Moz 1.0.1   Saf 1.3/2   Op n/a   DOM n/a

Starts the marquee element scrolling if it has been stopped. If the method is invoked on a stopped element, the onstart event handler also fires in response.

Returned Value   None.

Parameters   None.

stop( )   IE 4   NN n/a   Moz 1.0.1   Saf 1.3/2   Op n/a   DOM n/a

Stops the scrolling of the marquee element. The content remains on the screen in the precise position it was in when the method was invoked. Restart via the start( ) method.

Returned Value   None.

Parameters   None.

MediaList   IE n/a   NN n/a   Moz all   Saf 1.2   Op 9   DOM 2

The MediaList object is an abstract representation in the W3C DOM of a collection of string names for media specified for a particular styleSheet object. The media property of a styleSheet object returns a value that is a MediaList object (IE 6 and 7 incorrectly return a string value). Media types (such as print, screen, aural, and so on) are specified for the style sheet either via the media attribute of a link element or an @media rule in a style element. Media support beyond print and screen types (and the default all type) is rather limited, so the details of this object are not yet important.

Object-Specific Properties

  length   mediaText

Object-Specific Methods

  appendMedium( )   deleteMedium( )   item( )

Object-Specific Events
None.

length   IE n/a   NN n/a   Moz all   Saf 1.2   Op 9   DOM 2

Read-only

Returns the number of items in the collection.

Example   var howMany = document.styleSheets[0].media.length;

Value   Integer.

mediaText

Returns the entire string of comma-delimited media names.

Example   var allMedia = document.styleSheets[0].media.mediaText;

Value   String.

appendMedium( ), deleteMedium( )

appendMedium("*mediumType*") deleteMedium("*mediumType*")

Adds or removes a medium type from the list. In early (pre-1.0) Mozilla, the methods are incorrectly named append( ) and delete( ).

Returned Value   None.

Parameters

mediumType
    String of recognized media type (e.g., print, screen).

item( )

item(*index*)

Returns one media name string from the collection corresponding to the item matching the index value in source code order.

Returned Value   String.

Parameters   *index*
    A zero-based integer corresponding to the specified item in source code order.

menu

The menu object reflects the menu element.

HTML Equivalent   <menu>

Object Model Reference
[window.]document.getElementById("*elementID*")

Object-Specific Properties

compact	type

Object-Specific Methods
None.

Object-Specific Events
None.

compact

IE 5(Mac)/6(Win) NN n/a Moz all Saf all Op 7 DOM 1

Read/Write

Provided for this element for the sake of compatibility with the W3C DOM standard. However, mainstream browsers do not act upon this property or its corresponding attribute.

Value   Boolean value: true | false.

Default   false

type

IE 6 NN n/a Moz n/a Saf n/a Op n/a DOM n/a

Read/Write

Implemented in IE 6 and 7 due to internal element relationships with the ol and ul element objects. Ignore for the menu element object.

menubar

See directories.

meta

IE 4 NN n/a Moz all Saf all Op 7 DOM 1

The meta object reflects the meta element.

HTML Equivalent   <meta>

Object Model Reference
[window.]document.getElementById("*elementID*")

Object-Specific Properties

charset	content	httpEquiv	name	scheme	url

Object-Specific Methods
None.

Object-Specific Events
None.

charset

IE 4 NN n/a Moz n/a Saf n/a Op n/a DOM n/a

Read/Write

Indicates the character encoding of the content in the file associated with the href attribute. This property does not change the setting of the charset attribute of a name/value pair contained by the content attribute or property. For now the charset property has little or no effect on a document.

Example
```
if (document.all.myMeta.charset == "csISO5427Cyrillic") {
    // process for Cyrillic charset
}
```

Value   Case-insensitive alias from the character set registry (*ftp://ftp.isi.edu/in-notes/iana/assignments/character-sets*).

Default   Determined by browser.

content   IE 4   NN *n/a*   Moz *all*   Saf *all*   Op 7   DOM 1
Read/Write

This is the equivalent of the value of a name/value pair. The property's corresponding content attribute is usually accompanied by either a name or http-equiv attribute, either of which acts as the name portion of the name/value pair. Specific values of the content attribute vary with the value of the name or http-equiv attribute. Sometimes the content attribute value contains multiple values. In such cases, the values are delimited by a semicolon. Some of these multiple values may be name/value pairs in their own right, such as the content for a refresh meta element. The first value is a number representing the number of seconds of delay before loading another document; the second value is a name/value pair indicating a URL of the document to load after the delay expires.

Despite the following example, changing the content property on a loaded document may not produce the desired effect if the browser relies on the incoming value as the document loads.

Example
```
document.getElementById("refreshMeta").content =
    "5,http://www.giantco.com/basicindex.html";
```

Value   String.

Default   None.

httpEquiv   IE 4   NN *n/a*   Moz *all*   Saf *all*   Op 7   DOM 1
Read/Write

This is the equivalent of the name of a name/value pair. The property's corresponding http-equiv attribute is usually accompanied by a content attribute, which acts as the "value" portion of the name/value pair. The author may elect to use the name attribute instead of the http-equiv attribute, but only one may be set. Adjust only the property corresponding to the attribute used in the meta element's tag. Then be sure to set the content property with a value that makes sense with the httpEquiv or name property.

Example   `document.getElementById("refreshMeta").httpEquiv = "expires";`

Value   String.

Default   None.

name
IE 4 NN n/a Moz all Saf all Op 7 DOM 1
Read/Write

This is an identifier for the name/value pair that constitutes the meta element. The value is typically a plain-language term that denotes the purpose of the meta element, such as "author" or "keywords". Either the name or httpEquiv properties can have a value, but not both, in the same meta element.

Example	document.getElementById("detailMeta").name = "keywords";
Value	String.
Default	None.

scheme
IE 4 NN n/a Moz all Saf all Op 7 DOM 1
Read/Write

Reflects the scheme attribute, but as yet has no particular functionality in current browsers. See the scheme attribute of the meta element in Chapter 1 for information about the intended purpose of this property.

Value	String.
Default	None.

url
IE 4 NN n/a Moz n/a Saf n/a Op n/a DOM n/a
Read/Write

Although implemented in IE browsers, this property no longer appears to be officially supported.

mimeType
IE 5(Mac) NN 3 Moz all Saf all Op 8 DOM n/a

The mimeType object belongs to the navigator object. The object represents a MIME type specification. Its properties let scripts find out if the browser is equipped to handle a specific MIME type of external content before it is loaded from the server. All these properties are mirrored in the internal document displayed when you choose Navigator's **About Plug-ins** menu option. Internet Explorer 5 for the Macintosh implements this scheme, but Explorer for Windows uses an entirely different system for determining support for external media via the object element.

Object Model Reference
navigator.mimeTypes[i]

Object-Specific Properties

description	enabledPlugin	suffixes	type

Object-Specific Methods
None.

Object-Specific Events
None.

description

Returns the brief description of the plugin. This information is embedded in the plugin by its developer. Be aware that the precise wording of this description may vary for the same plugin written for different operating systems.

Example   `var descr = navigator.mimeTypes["video/mpeg"].description;`

Value   String.

Default   None.

enabledPlugin

Returns a `plugin` object reference corresponding to the plugin currently set to play any incoming data formatted according to the current MIME type. You can then dig deeper into properties of the returned `plugin` object to retrieve, say, its name.

Example
`var plugName = navigator.mimeTypes["video/mpeg"].enabledPlugin.name;`

Value   plugin object reference.

Default   None.

suffixes

Returns a comma-delimited string list of file suffixes associated with the `mimeType` object, as supported by the plugin enabled for that MIME type. For example, the suffixes that the QuickTime plugin acknowledges for the type video/avi are:

    avi, vfw

If you loop through all `mimeType` objects registered in the browser to find a match for a specific suffix, you can then find out whether the matching `mimeType` object has a plugin installed for it (via the `enabledPlugin` property).

Example   `var suff = navigator.mimeTypes["audio/mpeg"].suffixes;`

Value   String.

Default   None.

type
IE *5(Mac)* NN *3* Moz *all* Saf *all* Op *8* DOM *n/a*

Read-only

Returns a string version of the MIME type associated with the mimeType object. You could, for example, loop through all the mimeType objects in search of the one that matches a specific MIME type (application/x-midi) and examine that mimeType object further to see whether it is currently supported and enabled.

Example   var MType = navigator.mimeTypes[3].type;

Value   String.

Default   None.

MouseEvent
IE *n/a* NN *n/a* Moz *all* Saf *all* Op *7* DOM *2*

The W3C DOM MouseEvent object is an abstract object that contains the properties and methods shared by every instance of a W3C DOM mouse-related event. This object inherits characteristics from the W3C DOM Event and UIEvent objects. The properties (information such as click coordinates) and methods of this object are blended into the directly scripted event object. See the discussion of the event object earlier in this chapter for specific property and method support for this object and how these items are inherited by more specific event types.

MutationEvent
IE *n/a* NN *n/a* Moz *all* Saf *all* Op *8* DOM *2*

The W3C DOM MutationEvent object is an abstract object that contains the properties and methods shared by every instance of a W3C DOM event that concerns itself with the modification of the document tree. This object inherits characteristics from the W3C DOM Event. The properties (information such as references to the node affected by the change) and methods of this object are blended into the directly scripted event object. See the discussion of the event object earlier in this chapter for specific property and method support for this object and how these items are inherited by more specific event types.

NamedNodeMap

See attributes.

navigator
IE *3* NN *2* Moz *all* Saf *all* Op *7* DOM *n/a*

The navigator object in many ways represents the browser application. As such, the browser is outside the scope of the document object model. Even so, the navigator object plays an important role in scripting, because it allows scripts to see what browser and browser version is running the script. In addition to several key properties that both Navigator and Internet Explorer have in common, each browser also extends the property listing of this object in ways that would generally benefit all browsers. IE duplicates this object under the clientInformation object name, but for cross-browser compatibility, you can use the navigator object reference in all browsers.

Object Model Reference

navigator
[window.]navigator

Object-Specific Properties

appCodeName	appMinorVersion	appName	appVersion
browserLanguage	cookieEnabled	cpuClass	language
mimeTypes[]	onLine	oscpu	platform
plugins[]	product	productSub	securityPolicy
systemLanguage	userAgent	userLanguage	userProfile
vendor	vendorSub		

Object-Specific Methods

javaEnabled( )	preference( )	taintEnabled( )

Object-Specific Events
None.

appCodeName

IE 3 NN 2 Moz *all* Saf *all* Op 7 DOM *n/a*

Read-only

Reveals the code name of the browser. Almost all scriptable browsers and versions return Mozilla, which was the code name for an early version of Navigator (a combination of the early freeware name of the Mosaic browser and Godzilla). The Mozilla character is Netscape's corporate mascot, but all browsers that license the original Mosaic technology (including IE) return Mozilla.

Example	var codeName = navigator.appCodeName;
Value	Mozilla
Default	Mozilla

appMinorVersion

IE 4 NN *n/a* Moz *n/a* Saf *n/a* Op 7 DOM *n/a*

Read-only

With succeeding generations of Internet Explorer, this property returns a dizzying range of values, most of which are not useful for typical version detection. IE 5.x for Windows returns an appVersion value of 4.0, with the appMinorVersion reporting the first digit to the right of the decimal. In IE 6 for Windows, the appMinorVersion returns a string signifying a build or patch code number, such as ;Q313675;. Use with extreme caution.

Example	var subVer = navigator.appMinorVersion;

Value   String.

Default   Depends on browser version.

appName

Reveals the model name of the browser.

Example   `var isIE = navigator.appName == "Microsoft Internet Explorer";`

Value   String values. Netscape Navigator, Mozilla, and Safari: `Netscape`; IE: `Microsoft Internet Explorer`; Opera 9: `Opera`. Some other browsers return these values to appear to be compatible with one of the mainstream browsers.

Default   Depends on browser.

appVersion

Reveals a version number of the browser engine, along with minimal operating system platform information (a subset of the information returned by `userAgent`). Sample returned values are as follows.

Internet Explorer:

```
4.0 (compatible; MSIE 6.0; Windows 98; Q312461)
4.0 (compatible; MSIE 7.0; Windows NT 5.1)
```

Mozilla:

```
5.0 (Macintosh; en-US)
```

Safari:

```
5.0 (Macintosh; U; PPC Mac OS X; en-us) AppleWebKit/418.8 (KHTML, like Gecko) Safari/
419.3
```

Opera:

```
9.01 (Windows NT 5.1; U; en)
```

Note that the version number at the start of the value (up to the first whitespace) is not necessarily indicative of the actual browser application version, but rather of the fundamental engine. Thus, IE application Versions 4 through 7 (and perhaps later) all report engine Version 4.0; Mozilla and Safari are based on what they term engine generation 5.0 (although they use entirely different engines). Browser application version information is found elsewhere either in the `appVersion`, `userAgent`, or other `navigator` object properties. Do not use the first word of the `appVersion` value for any kind of browser version detection that influences which DOM or JavaScript language features are supported by the browser. In browsers leading up to Version 4, this property correctly reflected the application version, but that is no longer the case.

While it may appear that the precise Internet Explorer version is embedded in this property's value (as `MSIE X.XX`), there are occasional mismatches in some versions. To inspect this portion of the version string, the `navigator.userAgent` property is more reliable.

Example	`var isVer4Min = parseInt(navigator.appVersion) >= 4;`
Value	String.
Default	Depends on browser.

browserLanguage

IE *4* NN *n/a* Moz *n/a* Saf *n/a* Op *7* DOM *n/a*

Read-only

Provides the default written language of the browser. Other browsers use the `navigator.language` property.

Example	`var browLangCode = navigator.browserLanguage;`
Value	Case-insensitive language code as a string, such as en.
Default	Browser default.

cookieEnabled

IE *4* NN *n/a* Moz *all* Saf *all* Op *7* DOM *n/a*

Read-only

Returns whether the browser allows reading and writing of cookie data.

Example
```
if (cookieEnabled) {
    setCookieData(data);
}
```

| **Value** | Boolean value: true \| false. |
| **Default** | Depends on browser preference setting. |

cpuClass

IE *4* NN *n/a* Moz *n/a* Saf *n/a* Op *n/a* DOM *n/a*

Read-only

Returns a string reference of the CPU of the client computer. Common Intel microprocessors (including Pentium-class CPUs and Macintoshes running Windows emulators) return x86, while PowerPC Macintoshes return PPC. This value tells you only about the basic hardware class, not the operating system or specific CPU speed or model number.

Example
```
if (navigator.cpuClass == "PPC") {
    // statements specific to PowerPC clients
}
```

| **Value** | String. |
| **Default** | Depends on client hardware. |

language

IE *n/a*   NN *4*   Moz *all*   Saf *all*   Op *7*   DOM *n/a*

Read-only

Indicates the written language for which the browser version was created. The language is specified in the ISO 639 language code scheme (such as en-us). Internet Explorer provides this information via the navigator.browserLanguage property.

Example	var mainLang = navigator.language;
Value	Case-insensitive language code as a string.
Default	Browser default.

mimeTypes

IE *5(Mac)*   NN *4*   Moz *all*   Saf *all*   Op *7*   DOM *n/a*

Read-only

Returns an array of mimeType objects supported by installed plugins in the browser. IE for Windows provides this property for syntactical compatibility, but it always returns an array of zero length. See the mimeType object.

Example	var videoPlugin = navigator.mimeTypes["video/mpeg"].enabledPlugin;
Value	Array of mimeType objects.
Default	Browser default.

onLine

IE *4*   NN *n/a*   Moz *1.7*   Saf *n/a*   Op *n/a*   DOM *n/a*

Read-only

Specifies whether the browser is set for online or offline browsing. Pages may wish to invoke live server actions when they load in online mode, but avoid these calls when in offline mode. Use this Boolean property to build such conditional statements.

Example
```
if (navigator.onLine) {
    document.write("<applet ...>");
    ...
}
```

Value	Boolean value: true | false.
Default	true

oscpu

IE *n/a*   NN *n/a*   Moz *all*   Saf *n/a*   Op *n/a*   DOM *n/a*

Read-only

Returns a string containing operating system or central processing unit information about the client machine. Values vary widely across systems. Windows clients are divided roughly into two categories: non-NT and NT. The former includes Windows 95, 98, and ME (oscpu values of Win95, Win98, and Win 9x 4.90, respectively). The NT category includes Windows NT 4 (WinNT4.0) and Windows XP (Windows NT x.x). Macintosh systems all report the CPU type and the absence or presence of Mac OS X (PPC or PPC Mac OS X). Unix systems report both the operating system and CPU type. The oscpu value is also a part of the userAgent value. Formatting for this information is not the same in Internet Explorer's corresponding cpuClass or userAgent properties.

Example

```
if (navigator.oscpu.indexOf("Win") != -1) {
    document.write("You are running a Windows computer.");
}
```

| **Value** | String. |
| **Default** | System dependent. |

platform

IE 4 NN 4 Moz all Saf all Op 7 DOM n/a

Read-only

Returns the name of the operating system or hardware platform of the browser. For Windows 95/NT, the value is Win32; for a Macintosh running a PowerPC CPU, the value is MacPPC. At least for the major platforms I've been able to test, mainstream browsers agree on the returned values. Using this property to determine the baseline facilities of the client in a conditional expression can help the page optimize its output for the device.

Example

```
if (navigator.platform == "Win32") {
    document.write("<link rel='stylesheet' type='text/css' href='css/stylePC.css'>");
}
```

| **Value** | String. |
| **Default** | System dependent. |

plugins[ ]

IE 5(Mac) NN 3 Moz all Saf all Op 7 DOM n/a

Read-only

Returns a collection of plugin objects recognized by the browser to facilitate script determination of the browser's support for a particular external media type. IE 4 and later for Windows implement this property, but only as a dummy placeholder that always returns an array of length zero. See the mimeType and plugin objects.

Example	var plugInCount = navigator.plugins.length;
Value	Array of plugin object references.
Default	None.

Alphabetical DOM Reference

product, productSub

IE *n/a* NN *n/a* Moz *all* Saf *all* Op *n/a* DOM *n/a*

Read-only

Return a string identifying the software engine behind the browser. In Mozilla and Safari, the product property returns Gecko, while the productSub property returns a development build number (in string form).

Example	var prod = navigator.product;
Value	String.
Default	Browser dependent.

securityPolicy

IE *n/a* NN *4* Moz *all* Saf *n/a* Op *n/a* DOM *n/a*

Read-only

Returns a string in Navigator 4 revealing the browser's encryption level (that is, the domestic or export encryption policy to which the browser adheres). With the loosening of U.S. encryption export laws, Mozilla implements one encryption type across all versions. In Mozilla, this property returns an empty string.

Value	String.
Default	None.

systemLanguage

IE *4* NN *n/a* Moz *n/a* Saf *n/a* Op *n/a* DOM *n/a*

Read-only

Specifies the code for the default written language used by the operating system. If you have multi-lingual content available, you can use this property to insert content in specific languages.

Example

```
if (navigator.systemLanguage == "nl") {// document.write( ) some Dutch content
}
```

Value	Case-insensitive language code.
Default	Usually the browser default (en for English-language Internet Explorer available in the United States).

userAgent

IE *3* NN *2* Moz *all* Saf *all* Op *7* DOM *n/a*

Read-only

Provides information about the browser software, including version, operating system platform, and brand. This is the most complete set of information about the browser, whereas appVersion and appName properties provide subset (and not always correct) data. Typical data for the userAgent property looks like the following examples from a selection of browsers:

```
Mozilla/4.0 (compatible; MSIE 7.0; Windows NT 5.1)
Mozilla/5.0 (Macintosh; U; PPC Mac OS X Mach-O; en-US; rv:1.8.0.6) Gecko/20060728
Firefox/1.5.0.6
Mozilla/5.0 (Macintosh; U; PPC Mac OS X; en-us) AppleWebKit/418.8 (KHTML, like Gecko)
Safari/419.3
Opera/9.01 (Windows NT 5.1; U; en)
```

Do not rely on the length or position of any part of this data, as it may vary with the browser, version, and proxy server used at the client end. Instead, use the indexOf( ) method to check for the presence of a desired string. To extract only the actual application version number for IE, use the following function:

```
function readIEVersion( ) {
    var ua = navigator.userAgent;
    var IEOffset = ua.indexOf("MSIE ");
    return parseFloat(ua.substring(IEOffset + 5, ua.indexOf(";", IEOffset)));
}
```

Example

```
if (navigator.userAgent.indexOf("MSIE") != -1) {
    var isIE = true;
}
```

Value   String.

Default   Browser dependent.

userLanguage   IE 4 NN *n/a* Moz *n/a* Saf *n/a* Op 7 DOM *n/a*
Read-only

The default written language of the browser, based on the operating system user profile setting (if one exists). The property defaults to the browserLanguage property.

Example   var userLangCode = navigator.userLanguage;

Value   Case-insensitive language code as a string.

Default   Browser default.

userProfile   IE 4 NN *n/a* Moz *n/a* Saf *n/a* Op *n/a* DOM *n/a*
Read-only

The userProfile property is, itself, an object that lets scripts request permission to access personal information stored in the visitor's user profile (for Win32 versions of Internet Explorer 4 through 6). See the userProfile object.

Example

```
navigator.userProfile.addReadRequest("vcard.displayname");
navigator.userProfile.doReadRequest("3", "MegaCorp Customer Service");
var custName = navigator.userProfile.getAttribute("vcard.displayname");
navigator.userProfile.clearRequest( );
if (custName) {
    ...
}
```

Value userProfile object reference; null in IE 7.

Default Browser default.

vendor, vendorSub IE *n/a* NN *n/a* Moz *all* Saf *all* Op *n/a* DOM *n/a*

Read-only

Return a string identifying the company that is using the browser engine. For example, Netscape 7 returns simply Netscape, while Safari returns Apple Computer, Inc. Mozilla's own product, Firefox, returns an empty string. The vendorSub property (not implemented in Safari) returns the version release in detail (in string form).

Example
```
if (parseFloat(navigator.vendorSub, 10) >= 6.2) {
    // OK, meets minimum Netscape requirement
}
```

Value String.

Default Browser dependent.

javaEnabled( ) IE *4* NN *3* Moz *all* Saf *all* Op *7* DOM *n/a*

Returns whether Java is turned on in the browser. This method obviously won't help you in a nonscriptable browser (or scriptable browser that doesn't support the property), but if scripting is enabled, it does tell you whether the user has Java turned off in the browser preferences.

Returned Value Boolean value: true | false.

Parameters None.

preference( ) IE *n/a* NN *4* Moz *all* Saf *n/a* Op *n/a* DOM *n/a*

preference(*name*[, *value*])

By way of signed scripts in Navigator 4 and Mozilla, you can access a wide variety of user preferences settings. These include even the most detailed items, such as whether the user has elected to download images or whether style sheets are enabled. Most of these settings are intended for scripts used by network administrators to install and control the user settings of enterprise-wide deployment of Navigator. Consult the Netscape developer web site for further information about these preferences settings (*http://developer.netscape.com/docs/manuals/communicator/preferences/*).

Returned Value Preference value in a variety of data types.

Parameters
name
> The preference name as a string, such as general.always_load_images.

value
> An optional value to set the named preference.

taintEnabled( )

Returns whether data tainting is turned on in the browser. This security mechanism was never fully implemented in Navigator, but the method that checks for it is still included in newer versions of Navigator and Mozilla for backward compatibility. Internet Explorer and Opera also include it for compatibility, even though it always returns false.

Returned Value   Boolean value: true | false.

Parameters   None.

nobr

The nobr object reflects the nobr element.

HTML Equivalent   `<nobr>`

Object Model Reference
`[window.]document.getElementById("elementID")`

Object-Specific Properties
None.

Object-Specific Methods
None.

Object-Specific Events
None.

Node

The Node object is an abstract representation in the W3C DOM of the fundamental content building block in a document. All pieces of content that you can address in the W3C DOM model are nodes: unnamed contiguous strings of text between tags, tagged elements, name/value attribute pairs, special-purpose elements such as comments, DOCTYPE declarations, and even the document, itself, to name several.

A Node object has a large set of properties and methods, most of which concern a node's relationships to surrounding nodes. Properties listed below in all uppercase letters are either constants or bit masks. The objects in a document that scripts read and control are defined as descendants of the basic Node object; this means that the most common content-bearing objects that DHTML scripts work with—HTML elements, text nodes, and element attributes—all share this set of properties and methods to start (and are described at the beginning of this chapter among the shared properties and methods). Then, as needed for their powers as HTML elements, they accrue additional properties and/or methods that give them their special powers.

While the nodeness of the W3C DOM codifies the inheritance relationships among different pieces of a document's content, the model presents a conceptual framework and granularity that at times seems tedious compared to the shortcut HTML-ness of both the first-generation DOM and the Microsoft DOM. But the ultimate goal is to provide a single model that works for both XML and HTML documents (in either their pure HTML or XML-ized versions).

Object Model Reference

Node

Object-Specific Properties

ATTRIBUTE_NODE	CDATA_SECTION_NODE
DOCUMENT_FRAGMENT_NODE	COMMENT_NODE
DOCUMENT_NODE	DOCUMENT_POSITION_CONTAINED_BY
DOCUMENT_POSITION_CONTAINS	DOCUMENT_POSITION_DISCONNECTED
DOCUMENT_POSITION_FOLLOWING	DOCUMENT_POSITION_IMPLEMENTATION_SPECIFIC
DOCUMENT_POSITION_PRECEDING	DOCUMENT_TYPE_NODE
ELEMENT_NODE	ENTITY_NODE
ENTITY_REFERENCE_NODE	NOTATION_NODE
PROCESSING_INSTRUCTION_NODE	TEXT_NODE
attributes	baseURI
childNodes	firstChild
lastChild	localName
namespaceURI	nextSibling
nodeName	nodeType
nodeValue	ownerDocument
parentNode	prefix
previousSibling	textContent

Object-Specific Methods

appendChild( )	cloneNode( )
compareDocumentPosition( )	getFeature( )
getUserData( )	hasAttributes( )
hasChildNodes( )	insertBefore( )
isDefaultNamespace( )	isEqualNode( )
isSameNode( )	isSupported( )
lookupNamespaceURI( )	lookupPrefix( )
normalize( )	removeChild( )
replaceChild( )	setUserData( )

NodeFilter
IE n/a   NN n/a   Moz 1.0.1   Saf 1.3/2   Op 8   DOM 2

The NodeFilter object provides a mechanism for the NodeIterator and TreeWalker objects to determine which nodes or classes of nodes are to be accepted or rejected for inclusion into one of the special node lists. The lone accept( ) method is invoked silently by the

NodeInterator and TreeWalker objects whenever the objects are asked to point to the next node in sequence. The NodeFilter object is also the holder of two sets of constants that are used in a variety of creation method calls and user-defined filter functions. See the TreeWalker object for an example, and the document.createTreeWalker( ) method for application of the constants.

Object Model Reference

NodeFilter

Object-Specific Properties

FILTER_ACCEPT	FILTER_REJECT	FILTER_SKIP
SHOW_ALL	SHOW_ATTRIBUTE	SHOW_CDATA_SECTION
SHOW_COMMENT	SHOW_DOCUMENT	SHOW_DOCUMENT_FRAGMENT
SHOW_DOCUMENT_TYPE	SHOW_ELEMENT	SHOW_ENTITY
SHOW_NOTATION	SHOW_PROCESSING_INSTRUCTION	SHOW_TEXT

Object-Specific Methods

accept( )

Object-Specific Events

None.

accept( )

IE *n/a* NN *n/a* Moz *1.0.1* Saf *1.3/2* Op *8* DOM *2*

accept(*nodeReference*)

Returns an integer signifying whether a node is to be included in the NodeIterator or TreeWalker object's list. This method is invoked automatically by the objects whenever one of their pointer-moving methods is invoked.

Returned Value   Integer value, each of which has a corresponding constant value associated with the NodeFilter object: 1 (NodeFilter.FILTER_ACCEPT); 2 (NodeFilter.FILTER_REJECT); 3 (NodeFilter.FILTER_SKIP).

Parameters

nodeReference
    Reference to the document tree node under test. Passed automatically to the method when invoked by the NodeInterator and TreeWalker objects.

NodeIterator

IE *n/a* NN *n/a* Moz *n/a* Saf *1.3/2* Op *8* DOM *2*

The NodeIterator object is a "live" list of nodes that meet the criteria defined by the document.createNodeIterator( ) method. The list is a simple list of node references in source code order, but the list items do not bear any parent or descendant relationships to each other. The createNodeIterator( ) method describes the node where the list begins and which nodes (or classes of nodes) are exempt from the list by way of filtering (see the TreeWalker object for an example of this kind of filtering).

The NodeIterator object maintains a kind of pointer inside the list (so that your scripts don't have to). Methods of this object let scripts access the next or previous node in the list, while moving the pointer one position in either direction. If scripts modify the document tree after the NodeIterator is created, changes to the document tree are automatically reflected in the sequence of nodes in the NodeIterator.

Object Model Reference
NodeIteratorReference

Object-Specific Properties

expandEntityReference	filter	root	whatToShow

Object-Specific Methods

detach( )	nextNode( )	previousNode( )

Object-Specific Events
None.

expandEntityReference, filter, root, whatToShow
IE *n/a* NN *n/a* Moz *n/a* Saf *1.3/2* Op *8* DOM *2*

Read-only

See these properties of the TreeWalker object.

detach( )
IE *n/a* NN *n/a* Moz *n/a* Saf *1.3/2* Op *8* DOM *2*

Disconnects the current NodeIterator object from the document tree. Items in the list are no longer accessible once the method is invoked.

Returned Value None.

Parameters None.

nextNode( ), previousNode( )
IE *n/a* NN *n/a* Moz *n/a* Saf *1.3/2* Op *8* DOM *2*

Moves the internal NodeIterator pointer one position forward (nextNode( )) or backward (previousNode( )), while returning a reference to the node through which the pointer passed en route.

Returned Value Reference to a node in the document tree.

Parameters None.

NodeList

The NodeList object is an abstract representation in the W3C DOM of a collection of nodes of any type. Any W3C DOM property or method that returns a collection of nodes returns an object of type NodeList. For example, the Node object's childNodes property and the Element object's getElementsByTagName( ) method both return NodeList objects. JavaScript exposes a NodeList collections as an array that has the familiar length property. Scripts can reference individual items in the array through integer array indexes (inside square brackets) or via the NodeList object's item( ) method.

Some node types have their own collections (e.g., NamedNodeMap for a collection of attribute nodes and the HTMLCollection for a collection of HTML element nodes). These other collection objects have extra properties and methods that are meaningful only to the types of nodes inside the collections. For instance, because text nodes (one of the simplest type of Node object) do not have a property that can contain an identifier, the NodeList object does not include a method to reference an item by its ID. But an HTMLCollection object (consisting entirely of the more complex HTMLElement types of nodes) includes another method (namedItem( )) that lets scripts reference an item by its ID as well as integer index. The distinctions among collection object types are readily apparent when you compare the properties and methods of the collection objects you actually script (see the descriptions in this chapter of the attributes and images objects, for example). The W3C DOM terminology, on the other hand, is not a factor in scripts.

Object-Specific Properties

length

Object-Specific Methods

item( )

noframes, noscript

The noframes object reflects the noframes element, and the noscript object reflects the noscript element.

HTML Equivalent

<noframes>
<noscript>

Object Model Reference

[window.]document.getElementById("*elementID*")

Object-Specific Properties

None.

Object-Specific Methods

None.

Object-Specific Events

None.

Notation
IE *n/a* NN *n/a* Moz *1.0.1* Saf *n/a* Op *8* DOM *1*

The Notation object (one of the node types) is an abstract representation in the W3C DOM of a portion of a DOCTYPE declaration. In particular, a Notation object contains properties for reading the public and system IDs cited by the DOCTYPE.

object
IE *4* NN *n/a* Moz *all* Saf *all* Op *7* DOM *1*

The object object reflects the object element. This is an updated way of embedding other media and external data into a document (through a plugin or, in IE for Windows, an ActiveX control). The depth and quality of implementation of this object (vis-à-vis the W3C specifications) is uneven across browser brands and versions. The most consistent implementation is in IE for Windows for loading ActiveX controls.

HTML Equivalent   <object>

Object Model Reference

[window.]document.getElementById("*elementID*")

Object-Specific Properties

align	alt	altHtml	archive	BaseHref
border	classid	code	codeBase	codeType
contentDocument	data	dataFld	dataSrc	declare
form	height	hspace	name	object
standby	type	useMap	vspace	width

Object-Specific Methods

None.

Object-Specific Events

Handler	IE	Mozilla	Safari	Opera	DOM
abort	—	—	•	—	•
error	•	—	•	—	•
load	—	—	•	—	•

align
IE *4* NN *n/a* Moz *all* Saf *all* Op *7* DOM *1*

Read/Write

Defines how the element is aligned relative to surrounding text content. Most values set the vertical relationship between the element and surrounding text. For example, to align the bottom of the element with the baseline of the surrounding text, the align property value would be baseline. An element can be "floated" along the left or right margin to let surrounding text wrap around the element.

Example   document.getElementById("myObject").align = "absmiddle";

Value   Any of the following alignment constant values (as a string): absbottom | absmiddle | baseline | bottom | right | left | none | texttop | top.

Default   bottom

alt   IE 6 NN *n/a* Moz *n/a* Saf *n/a* Op *n/a* DOM *n/a*
Read/Write

Indicates the text to be displayed (or spoken) where the object element appears on the page when a browser doesn't download graphics (or is waiting for the image to download). Presumably, Microsoft implemented this nonstandard property for occasions when the object element is used for the display of images, rather than the more common img element.

Example   document.getElementById("logoDisplay").alt = "MegaCorp Logo";

Value   String value.

Default   None.

altHtml   IE 4 NN *n/a* Moz *n/a* Saf *n/a* Op *n/a* DOM *n/a*
Read/Write

Provides HTML content to be displayed if the object or applet fails to load. This can be a message, static image, or any other HTML that best fits the scenario. There are inconsistencies in Internet Explorer with regard to this property name's case. The Win32 version requires altHtml; the Mac version requires altHTML.

Example
document.getElementById("myObject").altHtml = "<img src='objectAlt.gif'>";

Value   Any quoted string of characters, including HTML tags.

Default   None.

archive   IE 6 NN *n/a* Moz *all* Saf *all* Op 7 DOM 1
Read/Write

Reflects the archive attribute of the object element, but current mainstream browsers assign no functionality to either the attribute or property.

Value   String value.

Default   None.

BaseHref

IE 4(Win) NN n/a Moz n/a Saf n/a Op n/a DOM n/a

Read-only

Returns the URL of the document containing the object element. Most commonly, the value is the same as the location.href of the current window. Note the unusual letter case.

Example   `var where = document.getElementById("myObject").BaseHref;`

Value   URL string.

Default   Current document's URL.

border

IE 6 NN n/a Moz all Saf all Op 7 DOM 1

Read/Write

Controls the thickness of the border in pixels. For cross-browser compatibility use string values.

Example   `document.getElementById("myObject").border = "5";`

Value   Number as string.

Default   0

classid

IE 4 NN n/a Moz n/a Saf n/a Op n/a DOM n/a

Read-only

Provides the URL of the object's implementation. In Internet Explorer, the URL can point to the client computer's *CLSID* directory (with a clsid: URL) that stores all the IDs for registered ActiveX controls, such as DirectX or Media Player. IE 4 for Macintosh names this property classID, but the name was repaired to all lowercase in IE 4.5. The W3C DOM omits this property, even though HTML 4 includes the corresponding attribute.

Example

```
if (document.getElementById("soundObject").classid ==
    "clsid:83A38BF0-B33A-A4FF-C619A82E891D"){
    // process for the desired sound object
}
```

Value   String (including the clsid: protocol for local ActiveX controls).

Default   None.

code

IE 4 NN n/a Moz all Saf all Op 7 DOM 1

Read-only

Provides the name of the Java applet class file set to the code attribute of the object element (when using an object element in lieu of an applet element—if supported by your browsers).

Example
```
if (document.getElementById("clock").code == "Y2Kcounter.class") {
    // process for the found class file
}
```

Value	Case-sensitive applet class filename as a string.
Default	None.

codeBase

Read-only

This is the path to the directory holding the class file designated in either the code or classid attribute. The codebase attribute does not name the class file, just the path.

Example
```
if (document.getElementById("clock").codeBase == "classes") {
    // process for the found class file directory
}
```

Value	Case-sensitive pathname, usually relative to the directory storing the current HTML document.
Default	None.

codeType

Read/Write

Provides an advisory about the content type of the object referred to by the classid attribute. A browser might use this information to assist in preparing support for a resource requiring a multimedia player or plugin. If the codetype property is set to an empty string, the browser looks next for the type attribute setting (although it is normally associated with content linked by the data attribute URL). If both attributes have no (or empty) values set, the browser gets the content type information from the resource as it downloads.

Example
```
document.getElementById("gameTime").codeType = "application/x-crossword";
```

Value	Case-insensitive MIME type. A catalog of registered MIME types is available from *ftp://ftp.isi.edu/in-notes/iana/assignments/media-types/*.
Default	None.

contentDocument

Read-only

Refers to a document node created by the object element, if any.

Value	Document node reference or null.
Default	null

data

IE *4* NN *n/a* Moz *n/a* Saf *n/a* Op *n/a* DOM *n/a*

Read-only

URL of a file containing data for the object element (as distinguished from the object itself). Relative URLs are calculated relative to the codebase attribute if one is assigned; otherwise, the URL is relative to the document's URL.

Example   var objDataURL = document.getElementById("soundEffect").data;

Value   A complete or relative URL as a string.

Default   None.

dataFld

IE *4* NN *n/a* Moz *n/a* Saf *n/a* Op *n/a* DOM *n/a*

Read/Write

Used with IE data binding to associate a remote data source column name to an object element attribute determined by properties set in the object. A datasrc attribute must also be set for the element. Setting both the dataFld and dataSrc properties to empty strings breaks the binding between element and data source.

Example   document.getElementById("myObject").dataFld = "streamURL";

Value   Case-sensitive identifier of the data source column.

Default   None.

dataSrc

IE *4* NN *n/a* Moz *n/a* Saf *n/a* Op *n/a* DOM *n/a*

Read/Write

Used with IE data binding to specify the ID of the page's object element that loads the data source object for remote data access (an object element other than the current one). Setting both the dataFlc and dataSrc properties to empty strings breaks the binding between element and data source.

Example   document.getElementById("myObject").dataSrc = "DBSRC3";

Value   Case-sensitive identifier of the data source.

Default   None.

declare

IE *6* NN *n/a* Moz *all* Saf *all* Op *8* DOM *1*

Read/Write

Reflects the declare attribute. Has no effect on the content in current mainstream browsers.

Value   Boolean value: true | false.

Default   false

form

IE *4* NN *n/a* Moz *all* Saf *all* Op *7* DOM *1*

Read-only

Returns a reference to the form element that contains the current element (if any). This property is appropriate only if the object is acting as a form control.

Value   Object reference or null.

Default   None.

height, width

IE *4* NN *n/a* Moz *all* Saf *all* Op *7* DOM *1*

Read/Write

Provide the height and width of the element, in pixels. Changes to these values are immediately reflected in reflowed content on the page.

Example   document.getElementById("myObject").height = 250;

Value   Integer.

Default   None.

hspace, vspace

IE *4* NN *n/a* Moz *all* Saf *all* Op *7* DOM *1*

Read/Write

Provide the pixel measure of horizontal and vertical margins surrounding an object element. The hspace property affects the left and right edges of the element equally; the vspace affects the top and bottom edges of the element equally. These margins are not the same as margins set by style sheets, but they have the same visual effect.

Example
document.getElementById("myObject").hspace = 5;
document.getElementById("myObject").vspace = 8;

Value   Integer of pixel count as string.

Default   0

name

IE *4* NN *n/a* Moz *all* Saf *all* Op *7* DOM *1*

Read/Write

This is the identifier associated with the object element. If the object should be one that goes inside a form, the name property is submitted as one-half of the name/value pair when the form is submitted to the server.

Example   document.getElementById("myObject").name = "company";

Value   Case-sensitive string identifier that follows the rules of identifier naming: it may contain no whitespace, cannot begin with a numeral, and should avoid punctuation except for the underscore character.

Default   None.

object   IE 4 NN *n/a* Moz *n/a* Saf *n/a* Op *n/a* DOM *n/a*

Read-only

Provides a reference to a wrapper around an object to allow access to document object model properties of the object element when the names may be confused with internal property naming of the object. For example, if the code loaded into an object element had a property named hspace, the script reference document.getElementById("reader").object. hspace would retrieve that internal property, rather than the hspace property of the HTML element. The object property wrapper tells the JavaScript interpreter to access the property of the external object loaded into the element, and not the property of the HTML element itself.

Example   `var objCode = document.getElementById("reader").object.code;`

Value   Object reference.

Default   None.

standby   IE 5(Mac)/6(Win) NN *n/a* Moz *all* Saf *all* Op 8 DOM 1

Read-only

This will eventually assume the duty of the alt attribute for displaying a message during loading. Currently has no effect on the element.

Value   String.

Default   None.

type   IE 4 NN *n/a* Moz *all* Saf *all* Op 7 DOM 1

Read/Write

Provides an advisory about the MIME type of the external data to be loaded into the object. The browser looks to the type property value if the codeType property is null.

Example
```
if (document.getElementById("myObject").type == "image/jpeg") {
   ...
}
```

Value   Case-insensitive MIME type. A catalog of registered MIME types is available from *ftp://ftp.isi.edu/in-notes/iana/assignments/media-types/*.

Default   None.

useMap

Read/Write

Provides the URL of the map element in the same document that contains client-side image map hot areas and links. The value includes the hash mark assigned with the map name in the usemap attribute of the object element.

Example document.getElementById("logoViewer").useMap = "#altMap";

Value A string starting with a hash mark and the name of the map element.

Default None.

vspace

See hspace.

width

See height.

ol

The ol object reflects the ol element.

HTML Equivalent <ol>

Object Model Reference
[window.]document.getElementById("*elementID*")

Object-Specific Properties

compact	start	type

Object-Specific Methods
None.

Object-Specific Events
None.

compact

Read/Write

When set to true, the compact property should instruct the browser to render items in the list in a more compact format. This property has no effect in mainstream browsers.

Example document.getElementById("myOL").compact = true;

Value Boolean value: true | false.

Default   false

start   IE 4   NN *n/a*   Moz *all*   Saf *all*   Op 7   DOM 1
Read/Write

Indicates the starting number for the sequence of items in the ol element. This is convenient when a sequence of items must be disturbed by running body text. While the value is a number, the corresponding Arabic numeral, Roman numeral, or alphabet letter renders the value. When no value is set as an attribute, different browsers assign different default values (see below)

Example   `document.getElementById("sublist2").start = 6;`

Value   Integer.

Default   1 (IE, Opera); -1 (Mozilla); 0 (Safari).

type   IE 4   NN *n/a*   Moz *all*   Saf *all*   Op 7   DOM 1
Read/Write

Indicates the manner in which the leading numbers or letters of items in the list are displayed.

Example   `document.getElementById("instruxList").type = "a";`

Value

Possible values are: A | a | I | i | 1. Sequencing is performed automatically as shown in the following table.

Type	Example
A	A, B, C, ...
a	a, b, c, ...
I	I, II, II, ...
i	i, ii, iii, ...
1	1, 2, 3, ...

Default   None specified, although behavior is that of 1.

optgroup   IE 5(Mac)/6(Win)   NN *n/a*   Moz *all*   Saf *all*   Op 7   DOM 1

The optgroup object reflects the optgroup element, which must be nested inside a select element and surround option elements. See the optgroup element in Chapter 1 for browser support details of this element. The disabled property (described among the shared properties earlier in this chapter) is available for this object, and it influences the disabled status of nested option elements.

HTML Equivalent   `<optgroup>`

Object Model Reference
[window.]document.getElementById("*elementID*")

Object-Specific Properties
label

Object-Specific Methods
None.

Object-Specific Events
None.

---

label

IE *5(Mac)/6(Win)* NN *n/a* Moz *all* Saf *all* Op *9* DOM *1*

Read/Write

Reflects the label attribute of the optgroup element.

Value   String.

Default   None.

---

option

IE *3* NN *2* Moz *all* Saf *all* Op *7* DOM *1*

The option object reflects the option element, which must be nested inside a select element. References to option objects most often use its parent select object, with the option object treated as one member of an array of options belonging to that select object. With modern browsers, you can also reference an option object directly via its ID. The disabled property (described among the shared properties earlier in this chapter) is available for IE 4 and later and W3C DOM browsers.

You can modify the set of options in a select object in browsers starting with Netscape 3 and Explorer 4 with backward-compatible code that continues to work in the newest browsers. If the modification entails replacing existing options with a different list of the same length, you can simply assign new values to text, value, and selected properties of each option in the select object's options array. But if the list has a different number of options, you are better served by removing all existing option objects and inserting new ones. A constructor function for a new Option object lets you create objects one at a time, and then assign them to positions within the options array. Syntax for the constructor is as follows:

```
var newOpt = new Option("text", "value", isDefaultSelectedFlag, isSelectedFlag);
```

The following function demonstrates the typical steps involved in rewriting a select object's list of options:

```
function setSelect(selectElemObj) {
    // remove existing options
    selectElemObj.options.length = 0;
    // create and assign options, one by one
    selectElemObj.options[0] = new Option("Hercule Poirot", "poirot", false, false);
    selectElemObj.options[1] = new Option("Miss Marple", "marple", false, false);
```

```
        ...
    }
```

In a production environment, the values for the constructor parameters would most likely be delivered to the page as an array of objects, allowing the stuffing of new options to be carried out inside a for loop. For additional approaches to this task, see the options.add( ) method (for IE, Mozilla, and Opera) and the select.add( ) method (for IE 5 or later and W3C DOM browsers).

HTML Equivalent   `<option>`

Object Model Reference
```
[window.]document.formName.selectName.options[i]
[window.]document.forms[i].elements[i].options[i]
[window.]document.getElementById("elementID")
```

Object-Specific Properties

defaultSelected	form	index	label	selected	text	value

Object-Specific Methods
None.

Object-Specific Events
None.

---

defaultSelected

IE 3 NN 2 Moz all Saf all Op 7 DOM 1
Read/Write

Determines whether an element has the selected attribute set in the tag. You can compare the current selected property against defaultSelected to see whether the state of the select control has changed since the document loaded. Changing this property does not affect the current selected status.

Example
```
var listItem = document.forms[0].selector.options[2];
if (listItem.selected != listItem.defaultSelected) {
    // process for changed state
}
```

Value   Boolean value: true | false.

Default   Determined by HTML tag attribute.

---

form

IE 4 NN n/a Moz all Saf all Op 7 DOM 1
Read-only

Returns a reference to the form object that contains the select element and its options.

Example   `var theForm = document.getElementById("myOption3").form;`

Value	form object reference.
Default	None.

index

Read-only

Returns the zero-based index integer value of the current option object within the collection of options of the select element. The select object's selectedIndex property returns the index value of the option that is currently selected.

Example	var whichItem = document.getElementById("myOption3").index;
Value	Integer.
Default	None.

label

Read/Write

Reflects the label attribute of the option element. This property is intended for use with hierarchical menus, but it is not operational in browsers except for IE 5/Mac, where it returns the same value as the text property.

Value	String.
Default	None.

selected

Read/Write

Determines whether the list option has been selected by the user, meaning that its value is submitted with the form. Scripts can modify the value to select an item algorithmically. To find out which option is selected, it is more efficient to use the select object's selectedIndex property, rather than looping through all options in search of those whose selected properties are true. The exception to this is when the select element is set to allow multiple selections, in which case you need to cycle through them all to find the chosen items.

Example	document.forms[0].selectList.options[3].selected = true;
Value	Boolean value: true | false.
Default	false

text

Read/Write

Provides the text associated with the option element (this property pre-dates the ability to read or write the text node content of an option element). This text is located between the start and end tags; it is what appears in the select element on screen. A hidden value associated with the list item can be stored, retrieved, and changed via the value property.

Example
```
var list = document.forms[0].selectList;
var listItemText = list.options[list.selectedIndex].text;
```

Value   String.

Default   None.

value   IE 4   NN 4   Moz all   Saf all   Op 7   DOM 1
Read/Write

Provides the value associated with the option element. If the option element has a value attribute or value property set, this is the value returned for the value property; otherwise, the property returns an empty string.

Example   `var itemValue = document.forms[0].selectList.options[2]value;`

Value   String.

Default   None.

options   IE 3   NN 2   Moz all   Saf all   Op 7   DOM 1

An array of option elements nested within a select object. The W3C DOM Level 2 classifies this object as an HTMLOptionsCollection.

Object Model Reference
```
[window.]document.formName.selectName.options
[window.]document.forms[i].elements[i].options
[window.]document.getElementById("selectElementID").options
```

Object-Specific Properties

length   selectedIndex

Object-Specific Methods

add( )   item( )   namedItem( )   remove( )   tags( )   urns( )

length   IE 3   NN 2   Moz all   Saf all   Op 7   DOM 1
Read/Write

Returns the number of elements in the collection. You can assign a value of zero to this property to empty the options from the select element.

Example   `var howMany = document.forms[0].mySelect.options.length;`

Value   Integer.

selectedIndex

Returns a zero-based integer indicating which option within the collection is currently selected. This is a nonstandard alernate to the selectedIndex property of the containing select element object.

Example   `var whichOne = document.forms[0].mySelect.options.selectedIndex;`

Value   Zero-based integer.

add( )

`add(elementRef[, index])`

Adds an already-created element (from the createElement( ) method) to the current collection. The element must be of the option type. By default, the new element is added as the last item of the collection unless you specify an index value as a second parameter (in which case all existing items from that index position get pushed down by one). The following example sequence appends a new item to a select object:

```
var newElem = document.createElement("option");
newElem.text = "Freddie";
newElem.value = "Freddie Mercury";
document.forms[1].rockers.options.add(newElem);
```

Notice that a generic object is created first. Then its properties are stuffed with values, and the new element is added to the select element.

For an example of a cross-browser and backward-compatible approach to this task, see the option object discussion. Also see the select.add( ) method for a W3C DOM approach that works with all W3C DOM browsers.

Returned Value   None.

Parameters

elementRef

> A fully formed element object reference, usually generated by the createElement( ) method.

index

> An optional integer indicating where in the collection the new element should be placed.

item( )

`item(index[, subindex])`
`item(index)`

Returns a single object or collection of objects corresponding to the element matching the index value (or, optionally, the index and subindex values).

Returned Value   One object or collection (array) of objects. If there are no matches to the parameters, the returned value is null.

Parameters
index

When the parameter is a zero-based integer, the returned value is a single element corresponding to the specified item in source code order (nested within the current element); when the parameter is a string (IE only), the returned value is a collection of elements with id properties that match that string.

subindex

In IE only, if you specify a string value for the first parameter, you can use the second parameter to specify a zero-based index that retrieves the specified element from the collection with id properties that match the first parameter's string value.

namedItem( )   IE 6   NN *n/a*   Moz *all*   Saf *all*   Op 7   DOM *1*
```
namedItem("ID")
```

Returns a single option object corresponding to the element matching the parameter string value.

Returned Value   One option object. If there are no matches to the parameters, the returned value is null.

Parameters
ID

The string that contains the same value as the desired element's id attribute.

remove( )   IE 4   NN *n/a*   Moz *n/a*   Saf *all*   Op 7   DOM *n/a*
```
remove(index)
```

Deletes an element from the current collection. Simply specify the zero-based index value of the option element you wish to remove from the collection belonging to a select element. The following example deletes the first item from a select object:

```
document.forms[1].rockers.options.remove(0);
```

The process for removing an option element is entirely different in other browsers. To delete an item, assign null to the item in the collection. For example, the Mozilla version of the preceding IE example is as follows:

```
document.forms[1].rockers.options[0] = null;
```

Regardless of the browser-specific process of removing an option from the select object, the length of the options array collapses to fill the space.

Returned Value   None.

Parameters
index

A zero-based integer indicating which item in the collection should be deleted.

tags( )

tags("*tagName*")

Returns a collection of objects (among all objects nested within the current collection) with tags that match the *tagName* parameter. Implemented in all IE collections (see the all.tags( ) method), but redundant for collections of the same element type.

urns( )

urns(*URN*)

See the all.urns( ) method.

output

The output object reflects the Web Forms 2.0 output element. See the output element in Chapter 1 for implementation details and usage. Because the output object is another type of Web Forms 2.0 form control, it shares its properties and methods with the input object. Both methods are superfluous for this object because its data is never validated nor submitted with the form. See the input object for details on the properties and methods listed below.

HTML Equivalent   <output>

Object Model Reference

[window.]document.getElementById("*elementID*")

Object-Specific Properties

defaultValue	form	forms	name
value	validationMessage	validity	willValidate

Object-Specific Methods

checkValidity( )	setCustomValidity( )

p

The p object reflects the p element.

HTML Equivalent   <p>

Object Model Reference

[window.]document.getElementById("*elementID*")

Object-Specific Properties

align

Object-Specific Methods
None.

Object-Specific Events
None.

align

Determines how the paragraph text is justified within the p element's box.

Example   `document.getElementById("myP").align = "center";`

Value   Any of the three horizontal alignment string constants: `center` | `left` | `right`.

Default   `left`

page

The page object is a special type of style rule created via an @page CSS rule. In the W3C DOM, this object (known as the `CSSPageRule` object) inherits properties of the `CSSRule` object. But as of IE 6 for Windows, the page object does not adhere to this inheritance structure. This object lays the foundation for a more fully implemented notion of page boxes expected in future browser versions.

HTML Equivalent
```
<style type="text/css">
@page {specifications}
</style.
```

Object Model Reference
```
[window.]document.styleSheets[i].pages[j]
```

Object-Specific Properties

pseudoClass	selectorText	style

Object-Specific Methods
None.

Object-Specific Events
None.

pseudoClass

Returns the name of the pseudo-class associated with the @page rule (if any).

Example	var pClass = document.styleSheets[2].pages[0].pseudoClass;
Value	String pseudo-class names (including leading colon): :first | :left | :right.
Default	None.

selectorText

IE 5.5 NN n/a Moz n/a Saf n/a Op n/a DOM 2

Read/Write

Provides the selector of the @page rule (if any).

Example	document.styleSheets[2].pages[0].selectorText = ":right";
Value	String.
Default	None.

style

IE n/a NN n/a Moz n/a Saf n/a Op n/a DOM 2

Read-only

Returns the style object (of type CSSStyleDeclaration in the W3C DOM) reflecting the style attributes and properties of the @page rule.

Value	style object reference.
Default	None.

pages

IE 5.5 NN n/a Moz n/a Saf n/a Op n/a DOM n/a

Provides an array of page objects (@page rules) nested within a styleSheet object.

Object Model Reference
[window.]document.styleSheets[i].pages

Object-Specific Properties
length

Object-Specific Methods
item( )

Object-Specific Events
None.

length

IE 5.5 NN n/a Moz n/a Saf n/a Op n/a DOM n/a

Read-only

Returns the number of objects in the collection.

Example	var howMany = document.styleSheets[0].pages.length;

Value   Integer.

item( )   IE 5.5   NN *n/a*   Moz *n/a*   Saf *n/a*   Op *n/a*   DOM *n/a*

item(*index*)

Returns a single object corresponding to the element matching the index value.

Returned Value   Reference to a page object. If there are no matches to the parameters, the returned value is null.

Parameters

index

A zero-based integer corresponding to the specified item in source code order.

param   IE 5   NN *n/a*   Moz *all*   Saf *all*   Op 7   DOM 1

The param object reflects the param element, which passes variable values to ActiveX objects (IE/Windows only), Java applets, and some plugins. Such programs are written to read parameter name/value pairs during initialization so the values are ready to go when the program starts (e.g., the URL of a sound file). IE for Windows commonly assigns a full suite of parameters to some ActiveX controls, even though only a handful might be explicitly defined in the source code. Although properties are read/write, assigning new values after the page has loaded does not convey the new values to the external program.

HTML Equivalent   <param>

Object Model Reference

[window.]document.getElementById("*elementID*")

Object-Specific Properties

name	type	value	valueType

Object-Specific Methods
None.

Object-Specific Events
None.

name   IE 5   NN *n/a*   Moz *all*   Saf *all*   Op 7   DOM 1

Read/Write

This is the name of the external program's parameter to which a value in the param element applies.

Example   var pName = document.getElementById("audioParam2").name;

Value   String.

Default   None.

type

Provides the MIME type for a param element with a valuetype attribute set to "ref".

Example
```
if (document.getElementById("myParam").valueType == "ref") {
    var pType = document.getElementById("myParam").type;
}
```

Value Case-insensitive MIME type as string. A catalog of registered MIME types is available from *ftp://ftp.isi.edu/in-notes/iana/assignments/media-types/*.

Default None.

value

Indicates the string value assigned to a named parameter for the external program.

Example `var pVal = document.getElementById("volumeParam").value;`

Value String.

Default None.

valueType

Indicates the string classification of the parameter set by the element.

Example `var pValType = document.getElementById("volumeParam").valueType;`

Value String constant: data | object | ref.

Default data

password

See input.

personalbar

See directories.

plaintext

IE 4 NN n/a Moz all Saf all Op 7 DOM 1

The plaintext object reflects the plaintext element. Note that the Win32 version of Internet Explorer 4 incorrectly evaluates the innerHTML, innerText, outerHTML, and outerText property values to include all document content following the start tag for the element. This element is deprecated in favor of the pre element.

HTML Equivalent   <plaintext>

Object Model Reference
[window.]document.getElementById("*elementID*")

Object-Specific Properties
None.

Object-Specific Methods
None.

Object-Specific Events
None.

plugin

IE 5(Mac) NN 3 Moz all Saf all Op 7 DOM n/a

A plugin object represents a single plugin that is registered with the browser at launch time. Access to a single plugin is normally via the navigator.plugins array. It is also common to use the navigator.mimeTypes array and associated properties to uncover whether the browser has the desired plugin installed before loading external content. Most of the properties provide scripted access to information normally found in the **About Plug-ins** window available from Navigator's **Help** menu and IE/Macintosh **File Helper** preferences. IE for Windows uses a different technique (involving the object element loading ActiveX controls) to determine support for playing external media.

Object Model Reference
navigator.plugins[i]

Object-Specific Properties

description	filename	length	name

Object-Specific Methods
None.

description

IE 5(Mac) NN 3 Moz all Saf all Op 7 DOM n/a

Read-only

Provides a brief plain-language description of the plugin supplied by the plugin manufacturer.

Example	var descr = navigator.plugins[2].description;
Value	String.
Default	None.

filename

Read-only

Returns the filename of the plugin binary. Some early browser versions returned the complete pathname, but modern browsers return only the filename.

Example	var file = navigator.plugins[2].filename;
Value	String.
Default	None.

length

Read-only

Returns the number of MIME types supported by the plugin. Don't confuse this property with the length property of the entire navigator.plugins array, which measures how many plugin objects are known to the browser.

Example	var howManyMIMEs = navigator.plugins[2].length;
Value	Integer.
Default	None.

name

Read-only

Returns the name of the plugin assigned to it by its manufacturer. You cannot, however, be guaranteed that a plugin designed for multiple operating systems has the same name across all versions.

Example	var pName = navigator.plugins[2].name;
Value	Integer.
Default	None.

plugins

All mainstream browsers have a plugins array, but they are quite different collections of objects. For Netscape Navigator, Mozilla, Safar, and Opera, the plugins array is a property of the navigator object. Each item in the navigator.plugins array represents a plugin that is installed in the browser (actually just registered with the browser when the browser last loaded). See the plugin object.

On the Windows side, Internet Explorer's plugins collection belongs to the document object and essentially mirrors the embeds collection: a collection of all embed elements in the document. An embed element may well, indeed, launch a plugin, but not necessarily. Nor does Internet Explorer for Windows provide JavaScript access to the installed plugins in the same way that browsers such as Navigator and Mozilla do (IE for Macintosh provides no such access).

Object Model Reference

IE
    document.plugins

NN, Mozilla, Safari, Opera
    navigator.plugins

Object-Specific Properties

length

Object-Specific Methods

item( )   namedItem( )   refresh( )

length

IE *4*   NN *3*   Moz *all*   Saf *all*   Op *7*   DOM *n/a*

Read-only

Returns the number of elements in the collection.

Example

```
var IEhowMany = document.plugins.length;
var NNhowMany = navigator.plugins.length;
```

Value   Integer.

item( )

IE *4(Win)*   NN *n/a*   Moz *all*   Saf *all*   Op *7*   DOM *n/a*

item(*index*[, *subindex*]) item(*index*)

Returns a single object or collection of objects corresponding to the item matching the index value (or, optionally, the index and subindex values).

Returned Value   One object or collection (array) of objects. If there are no matches to the parameters, the returned value is null.

Parameters

index
    When the parameter is a zero-based integer, the returned value is a single element corresponding to the specified item in source code order (nested within the current element). When the parameter is a string (IE only), the returned value is a collection of elements with name properties that match that string.

subindex
> In IE only, if you specify a string value for the first parameter, you can use the second parameter to specify a zero-based index that retrieves the specified element from the collection with name properties that match the first parameter's string value.

namedItem( )

namedItem("*name*")

Returns a single plugin (NN) or embed (IE) object corresponding to the element matching the parameter string value.

Returned Value   One plugin (NN) or embed (IE) object. If there are no matches to the parameters, the returned value is null.

Parameters

name
> The string that contains the same value as the desired object's name attribute.

refresh( )

Instructs the browser to reregister plugins installed in the plugins directory. This allows a browser to summon a newly installed plugin without forcing the user to quit and relaunch the browser.

Returned Value   None.

Parameters   None.

popup

A popup object is a featureless rectangular space that has none of the typical browser window chrome (borders, scrollbars, title bar, etc.) nor any reference path back to the main document. Scripts must create the popup object to a specific size and location, and populate the window with content by assigning an HTML string to the popup's document.body. innerHTML property. Your scripts must also help this region stand out from the document by assigning background colors and borders to either the popup's document.body.style property or the styles of elements inside the popup.

While this popup object holds what is essentially a document object, it is not related to the window object in any way, and therefore may not load external documents. It does, however, have the helpful characteristic of transcending frame and even browser window borders, giving the appearance of an operating-system level HTML content holder. Thus, you could use it for a drop-down menu or an annotation that needs to flow across frame borders or extend beyond the browser window edge.

A popup is a transient visual element. A click anywhere outside of the popup causes the popup to disappear. But you can assign the full range of mouse events to the elements in the popup's document, for effects such as rollovers and menu item clicks. The HTML content may also contain images.

To create a popup object, use the `window.createPopup( )` method. Here is a simple example of the typical creation, population, and display sequence:

```
var popup = window.createPopup( );
var bod = popup.document.body;
bod.style.border = "3px solid #ff8800";
bod.style.padding = "2px";
bod.style.backgroundColor = "lightyellow";
bod.innerHTML =
  "<p style='font-family:Arial, sans-serif; font-size:10px'>Some popup text.</p>";
popup.show(100, 100, 100, 26, document.body);
```

Object Model Reference

popupObjectRef

Object-Specific Properties

document	isOpen

Object-Specific Methods

hide( )	show( )

Object-Specific Events
None.

document

IE 5.5 NN n/a Moz n/a Saf n/a Op n/a DOM n/a

Read-only

Returns a reference to the document object inside the popup object. Most (but not all) regular document object properties apply to the popup's document object. It is the primary gateway to assigning HTML content to the popup. This property is read-only, but the document object's properties are read/write to allow you to assign values to its content.

Example   `popupRef.document.body.innerHTML = "<p>Howdy, pardner!</p>";`

Value   document object reference.

Default   The current document object.

isOpen

IE 5.5 NN n/a Moz n/a Saf n/a Op n/a DOM n/a

Read-only

Returns a Boolean value revealing whether the popup object is visible. Even after the popup object is hidden, its content is still accessible to scripts.

Example

```
if (popupRef.isOpen) {
    popupRef.hide( );
}
```

| **Value** | Boolean value: true | false. |
| **Default** | false |

hide( )

Hides the popup object. Generally invoked from scripts triggered by user actions on the popup's content.

| **Returned Value** | None. |
| **Parameters** | None. |

show( )

show(*left, top, width, height*[, *positioningElemRef*])

Shows the popup object, usually after its content has been assigned. All dimensions and position are set via parameters. The position may optionally be established relative to an element in the main document. Position and positioning element parameters may come from event object properties (event.clientX, event.clientY, and event.srcElement).

Returned Value   None.

Parameters

left
> Horizontal pixel coordinate relative to the left edge of the screen or, if specified by the optional parameter, an HTML element.

top
> Vertical pixel coordinate relative to the top edge of the screen or, if specified by the optional parameter, an HTML element.

width
> Outer pixel width of the popup space.

height
> Outer pixel height of the popup space.

positioningElemRef
> An optional reference to any element accessible to the script invoking the method. Establishes a coordinate context for the *left* and *top* parameters.

pre

The pre object reflects the pre element for preformatted text.

HTML Equivalent   <pre>

Object Model Reference
[window.]document.getElementById("*elementID*")

Alphabetical DOM Reference

Object-Specific Properties
width

Object-Specific Methods
None.

Object-Specific Events
None.

width

IE 6 NN *n/a* Moz *all* Saf *all* Op 7 DOM 1

Read/Write

Provides the character column count for the monospaced content of the element.

Example	document.getElementById("codeExample2").width = 40;
Value	Integer.
Default	-1 (Mozilla); 0 (Safari, Opera); none (IE).

ProcessingInstruction

IE *n/a* NN *n/a* Moz *n/a* Saf *n/a* Op *n/a* DOM 1

The ProcessingInstruction object (one of the node types) is an abstract representation in the W3C DOM of an element that contains instructions for an application, but whose content is not treated as part of the document's content tree. Such elements in XML documents are tagged with the format <?*ProcessTarget InstructionText*?>. In the W3C DOM, the two main components are exposed as the target and data string properties, respectively.

q

IE 4 NN *n/a* Moz *all* Saf *all* Op 7 DOM 1

The q object reflects the q element for inline quotations. Although IE for Windows includes (probably erroneously) the cite property for all elements (and causes that property to be listed among the shared properties earlier in this chapter), this object employs the true meaning of the cite property only for IE for Macintosh and W3C DOM browsers.

HTML Equivalent   <q>

Object Model Reference
[window.]document.getElementById("*elementID*")

Object-Specific Properties
None.

Object-Specific Methods
None.

Object-Specific Events

None.

radio

See input.

Range

The W3C DOM Range object—similar in concept to the IE TextRange object—represents a sequence of zero or more rendered text characters in a document. When a text range consists of zero characters, it represents an insertion point between two characters (or before the first or after the last character of the document). The Range object automatically keeps track of the node and character offset references for the start and endpoints of the range, so its methods can copy existing content, delete the range's contents, or insert new contents (in node form) into the existing range while maintaining the integrity of the document tree at every step. Nodeness is important to the Range object, but most of those concerns are handled for you.

A Range object is created via the document.createTextRange( ) method or by turning a user selection into a range via window.getSelection( ).getRangeAt(0). Once a text range is created, use its methods to adjust its start and endpoint to encompass a desired segment of the text. Then choose from a set of additional methods to act on the range. See Online Section V for details and examples of using the Range object and how its syntax varies from that of the IE TextRange object.

Object Model Reference

document.createRange( )

Object-Specific Properties

collapsed	commonAncestorContainer	endContainer
endOffset	startContainer	startOffset

Object-Specific Methods

cloneContents( )	cloneRange( )	collapse( )
compareBoundaryPoints( )	compareNode( )	comparePoint( )
createContextualFragment( )	deleteContents( )	detach( )
extractContents( )	insertNode( )	intersectsNode( )
isPointInRange( )	selectNode( )	selectNodeContents( )
setEnd( )	setEndAfter( )	setEndBefore( )
setStart( )	setStartAfter( )	setStartBefore( )
surroundContents( )	toString( )	

Object-Specific Events
None.

collapsed

IE *n/a* NN *n/a* Moz *all* Saf *all* Op *8* DOM *2*
Read-only

Returns Boolean true if the range's start and endpoints are at the same location, encompassing zero characters. A collapsed range can be located anywhere within the document.

Example
```
if (rng.collapsed) {
    // act on collapsed text range
}
```

Value	Boolean value: true | false.
Default	None.

commonAncestorContainer

IE *n/a* NN *n/a* Moz *all* Saf *all* Op *8* DOM *2*
Read-only

Returns a reference to a document tree node that is the next outermost container that encompasses the current range's start and endpoints. If the start and endpoints are, themselves, in the same node (for example, the same text node), the commonAncestorContainer property returns a reference to that node's parent node. IE TextRange equivalent is parentElement( ).

Example	var containingElem = rng.commonAncestorContainer;
Value	Reference to a node object (commonly an element node type).
Default	None.

endContainer

IE *n/a* NN *n/a* Moz *all* Saf *all* Op *8* DOM *2*
Read-only

Returns a reference to a document tree node that contains the current range's endpoint.

Example	var containingElemRight = rng.endContainer;
Value	Reference to a node object.
Default	None.

endOffset

IE *n/a* NN *n/a* Moz *all* Saf *all* Op *8* DOM *2*
Read-only

Returns an integer count of characters or nodes for the endpoint's location within the node reported by the endContainer property. If the endContainer is a text node, the endOffset property counts the number of characters to the right of the first character of that text node. If the endContainer is an element node, the endOffset property counts the number of nodes between the start of the containing node's content and the endpoint.

As an example, consider the following document segment that shows a text range in bold-face characters, with the start and endpoints signified by pipe characters:

```
<p>One paragraph with |a <span>nested</span>| element inside.</p>
```

Note that the start point is within a text node, while the endpoint sits just outside the span element end tag. The Range object's properties report values as shown in the following table.

Property	Value	Description
commonAncestorContainer	[object HTMLParagraphElement]	The p element embraces both the start and endpoints.
startContainer	[object Text]	Start point is within a text node.
startOffset	19	Start point is at the 20th (zero-based index of 19) character from the start of its container, the text node.
endContainer	[object HTMLParagraphElement]	Endpoint is designated as the end of the span element, which makes the next outer p element the endpoint's container.
endOffset	2	Endpoint is at the 3rd (zero-based index of 2) node in the context of its endContainer p element (first node is a text node; second node is the span element; endpoint is at the start of the third node of the p element).

Example	var rngEndOff = rng.endOffset;
Value	Integer.
Default	None.

startContainer

IE *n/a* NN *n/a* Moz *all* Saf *all* Op *8* DOM *2*

Read-only

Returns a reference to a document tree node that contains the current range's start point.

Example	var containingElemLeft = rng.startContainer;
Value	Reference to a node object.
Default	None.

startOffset

IE *n/a* NN *n/a* Moz *all* Saf *all* Op *8* DOM *2*

Read-only

Returns an integer count of characters or nodes for the start point's location within the node reported by the startContainer property. If the startContainer is a text node, the startOffset property counts the number of characters to the right of the first character of that text node. If the startContainer is an element node, the startOffset property counts the number of nodes between the start of the containing node's content and the start point. See endOffset for more details.

Example	var rngStartOff = rng.startOffset;
Value	Integer.
Default	None.

cloneContents( )

IE *n/a* NN *n/a* Moz *all* Saf *all* Op *8* DOM *2*

Returns a DocumentFragment node containing a copy of the contents from the current range. Any dangling nodes are resolved as part of the cloning process.

Returned Value	Reference to a node of a document fragment type.
Parameters	None.

cloneRange( )

IE *n/a* NN *n/a* Moz *all* Saf *all* Op *8* DOM *2*

Returns a Range object that is a carbon copy of the current range, including references to associated containers. This method lets you preserve a copy of a Range object's specifications while creating a new Range object. Similar to the IE TextRange object's duplicate( ) method.

Returned Value	Reference to a Range object.
Parameters	None.

collapse( )

IE *n/a* NN *n/a* Moz *all* Saf *all* Op *8* DOM *2*

collapse(*toStartFlag*)

Shrinks the current range to an insertion point (start and endpoints are in the same node at the same offset). The Boolean parameter controls whether the range collapses to the start point (true) or endpoint (false) of the current range. A script working its way through a document (e.g., using the String.indexOf( ) method to search for the next instance of a string) usually collapses to the endpoint before shifting the endpoint to the end of the body to perform the next String.indexOf( ) search.

Returned Value	None.

Parameters

toStartFlag

> Boolean value that controls whether collapse occurs at the start point (true) or endpoint (false) of the current range.

compareBoundaryPoints( )

compareBoundaryPoints(*compareType, sourceRangeRef*)

Returns an integer code indicating the relative positioning of one boundary point of the current range's against a boundary point of a different text range. In the simplest case, the two endpoints (one from each range) share the same ancestor container. In such a case, the first parameter determines which endpoints from the two ranges get compared. Use the constants supplied with every Range object, as shown in the following table.

Comparison type	Description
rng.START_TO_START	Comparing the start position of the current range against the start position of the source range
rng.START_TO_END	Comparing the start position of the current range against the endposition of the source range
rng.END_TO_END	Comparing the endposition of the current range against the endposition of the source range
rng.END_TO_START	Comparing the endpoisition of the current range against the start position of the source range

If the first boundary in the comparison occurs earlier in the document than the second boundary, the returned value is -1; if the first boundary comes after the second boundary, the returned value is 1; if the two boundaries are in the identical position, the returned value is 0. Similar to the IE TextRange object's compareEndPoints( ) method.

But the situation can be more complex if the boundary points being compared have different ancestor container nodes. The offset values with respect to container nodes influence the comparison results. Due to the variety of results that can occur with numerous relationships between the compared endpoints, your scripts will need to perform an intricate analysis of boundaries to assure comparisons report the desired sequence. On the other hand, simply looking for unanimity of boundary points is a much simpler prospect. You may prefer to limit your comparisons to looking only for return values of zero (or any other value) for a more binary determination of boundary comparisons.

Returned Value   Integer values -1, 0, or 1.

Parameters

compareType

> Integer values from 0 to 3 corresponding to comparison types. Integer values are not aligned with the W3C DOM standard in Mozilla before version 1.4, but the plain-language constants (such as *rng*.START_TO_START, shown in the table above) produce the correct comparisons.

sourceRangeRef

> Reference to a second, previously defined Range object, perhaps preserved through the cloneRange( ) method.

compareNode( )

compareNode(*nodeReference*)

A Mozilla-only method that returns an integer code indicating the relative position of some other node with respect to the current range. Four plain-language constants are members of every Mozilla Range object, and can be used for comparisons of values returned by the compareNode( ) method. Note that the returned values are from the point of view of the node passed as a parameter, rather than from that of the current range.

Returned values and constants are as follows.

Constant	Value	Description
rng.NODE_BEFORE	0	Entire node comes before the range.
rng.NODE_AFTER	1	Entire node comes after the range.
rng.NODE_BEFORE_AND_AFTER	2	Node starts before the current range and ends after it.
rng.NODE_INSIDE	3	Node is contained in its entirety within the scope of the range.

By way of example:

```
if (rng.compareNode(document.getElementById("myElem")) == rng.NODE_INSIDE) {
    // process for myElem node being contained by the range
}
```

Returned Value   Integer values 0, 1, 2, or 3.

Parameters

nodeReference
Reference to any node in the document tree.

comparePoint( )

compareNode(*nodeReference, offset*)

A Mozilla-only method that returns an integer code indicating the relative position of some other node and offset within that node with respect to the current range. Note that the returned values are from the point of view of the node (more specifically, the point signified by the offset within the node) passed as parameters, rather than from that of the current range.

Returned values are as follows.

Value	Description
-1	Point comes before the start of the range.
0	Point is located within the range.
1	Point comes after the end of the range.

By way of example:

```
if (rng.comparePoint(document.getElementById("myElem"), 2) == 0) {
    // process for offset of 2 within myElem node being contained by the range
}
```

Returned Value   Integer values -1, 0, 1.

Parameters

nodeReference
> Reference to any node in the document tree.

offset
> Integer offset, counting either nested nodes within an element or characters within a text node.

createContextualFragment( )   IE *n/a* NN *n/a* Moz *all* Saf *all* Op *8* DOM *2*

createContextualFragment(*contentString*)

The createContextualFragment( ) method was initially designed as an alternative to the innerHTML convenience property (because the W3C DOM provides little in the way of support for content strings consisting of tags). This method accepts any string—including tagged content—as a parameter, and returns a DocumentFragment type of node, ready for appending or inserting into the document tree. Subsequent adoption of the innerHTML property by the Mozilla browser makes this method redundant, except that it is more consistent with the overall nodeness of the W3C DOM.

Returned Value   Reference to a document fragment type of node outside of the document tree. This node can then be applied to the document tree.

Parameters

contentString
> Document content in string form, including tags and attributes.

deleteContents( )   IE *n/a* NN *n/a* Moz *all* Saf *all* Op *8* DOM *2*

Removes the contents of the current text range from the document tree. If the range is an element node (e.g., with boundaries established via the selectNode( ) method), invoking deleteContents( ) on the range removes the node from the document tree and collapses the range. The Range object remains in memory, but without any content. If you want to capture the content prior to its deletion, do so with other Range object methods (such as cloneRange( ) and, when it works correctly, cloneContents( )).

Returned Value   None.

Parameters   None.

detach( )   IE *n/a* NN *n/a* Moz *all* Saf *all* Op *8* DOM *2*

Destroys the current Range object to the extent that invoking most methods on the object or accessing its properties throw a RangeException of type INVALID_STATE_ERR.

Returned Value   None.

Parameters   None.

extractContents( )

IE *n/a* NN *n/a* Moz *all* Saf *all* Op *8* DOM *2*

Returns a DocumentFragment node containing the contents of the current range, after removing the contents from the document tree. If you experience problems with this method, try setting the range boundaries first set via the selectNodeContents( ) method.

Returned Value   Reference to a node of a document fragment type.

Parameters   None.

insertNode( )

IE *n/a* NN *n/a* Moz *all* Saf *all* Op *8* DOM *2*

insertNode(*nodeReference*)

Inserts a node at the start of the current text range. Most useful when the range is already collapsed as a text insertion pointer. The node being inserted can be created fresh (via document.createElement( )) or fetched from elsewhere in the document tree, in which case it is removed from its old position and inserted into the current range. If you insert a text node adjacent to a spot that also happens to be an existing text node, you can wind up with two adjacent text nodes. Invoke the normalize( ) method on the parent to consolidate the text nodes.

Returned Value   Nothing

Parameters

nodeReference

Reference to any text, element, or document fragment node to be inserted into the range.

intersectsNode( )

IE *n/a* NN *n/a* Moz *all* Saf *all* Op *8* DOM *2*

intersectsNode(*nodeReference*)

Returns Boolean true if any part of the current range overlaps with the text or element node that is passed as a parameter. If your script detects an intersection, it can use the compareNode( ) method to obtain more detail about the intersection.

Returned Value   Boolean value: true | false.

Parameters

nodeReference

Reference to any text or element in the document tree.

isPointInRange( )

IE *n/a* NN *n/a* Moz *all* Saf *all* Op *8* DOM *2*

isPointInRange(*nodeReference, offset*)

Returns Boolean true if the location denoted by the parameter values (a node in the document tree and an offset location within that node) is within the current range.

Returned Value   Boolean value: true | false.

Parameters

nodeReference

Reference to any text or element in the document tree.

offset

Integer offset, counting either nested nodes within an element or characters within a text node.

selectNode( ), selectNodeContents( )   IE *n/a* NN *n/a* Moz *all* Saf *all* Op *8* DOM *2*

selectNode(*nodeReference*) selectNodeContents(*nodeReference*)

Sets the range's boundary points to encompass a node or just the node's contents. Despite the methods' names, no body text in the rendered document is highlighted.

Your choice of method impacts the way the range's startContainer and endContainer properties are filled. In the following sequence, you see what happens to the range and its properties when an element node and a text node are parameters to these methods. The initial HTML segment is:

```
<p>One paragraph with a <span id="myspan">nested</span> element inside.</p>
```

Selecting the span element (with the rng.selectNode(document.getElementById("myspan")) method) sets the range to:

```
<p>One paragraph with a |<span id="myspan">nested</span>| element inside.</p>
```

The Range object's properties report values as follows.

Property	Value	Description
startContainer	[object HTMLParagraphElement]	Start point is right before the span element.
startOffset	1	Start point is at the 2nd (zero-based index of 1) node inside the p element.
endContainer	[object HTMLParagraphElement]	Endpoint is immediately after the span element.
endOffset	2	Endpoint is at the 3rd (zero-based index of 2) node in the context of its endContainer p element.

Using the rng.selectNodeContents(document.getElementById("myspan")) method to select the span element's contents sets the range to:

```
<p>One paragraph with a <span id="myspan">|nested|</span> element inside.</p>
```

The Range object's properties report values as follows.

Property	Value	Description
startContainer	[object HTMLSpanElement]	Start point is just inside the span element.
startOffset	0	Start point is at the 1st (zero-based index of 0) node inside the span element.
endContainer	[object HTMLSpanElement]	Endpoint is immediately after the span element's content.
endOffset	1	Endpoint is at a position where the 2nd (zero-based index of 1) node, if present, would be in the context of its endContainer span element.

Using the `rng.selectNode(document.getElementById("myspan").firstChild)` method to select the text node inside the span element sets the range to:

```
<p>One paragraph with a <span id="myspan">|nested|</span> element inside.</p>
```

Even though the node passed as a parameter is different (and a different node type), the new range selection looks the same as the previous one. In fact, due to the way the node tree is structured, the Range object's properties report identical values as follows.

Property	Value	Description
startContainer	[object HTMLSpanElement]	Start point is just inside the span element.
startOffset	0	Start point is at the 1st (zero-based index of 0) node inside the span element.
endContainer	[object HTMLSpanElement]	Endpoint is immediately after the span element's content.
endOffset	1	Endpoint is at a position where the 2nd (zero-based index of 1) node, if present, would be in the context of its endContainer span element.

Using the `rng.selectNodeContents(document.getElementById("myspan"))` method to select the contents of the text node inside the span element sets the range to:

```
<p>One paragraph with a <span id="myspan">||nested</span> element inside.</p>
```

In other words, the range collapses to an insertion point at the start of the text node (this may be a bug), and the text node becomes the container, as shown in the following property enumeration.

Property	Value	Description
startContainer	[object Text]	Start point is at the beginning of the text node.
startOffset	0	Start point is at the 1st (zero-based index of 0) position of the text node.
endContainer	[object Text]	Endpoint is collapsed.
endOffset	0	Endpoint is collapsed.

Element nodes tend to be the most practical parameter values to pass to either method.

Returned Value   None.

Parameters

nodeReference
    Reference to any text or element in the document tree.

setEnd( ), setStart( )   IE *n/a* NN *n/a* Moz *all* Saf *all* Op *8* DOM *2*

`setEnd(`*nodeReference*, *offset*`)` `setStart(`*nodeReference*, *offset*`)`

Establish the document tree locations for the individual boundary points of an existing Range object. Similar to the IE TextRange object's setEndPoint( ) method. The mapping of a location relies upon a node reference and an offset value relative to that node's starting point and type. Offset values count child nodes when the *nodeReference* is an element node; they count characters when the *nodeReference* is a text node. To set a boundary at a node edge, the associated methods (setEndAfter( ) and three others) are more convenient.

Returned Value   None.

Parameters

nodeReference
> Reference to any element or text node in the document tree.

offset
> Integer offset, counting either nested nodes within an element or characters within a text node.

setEndAfter( ), setEndBefore( ), setStartAfter( ), setStartBefore( )   IE *n/a* NN *n/a* Moz *all* Saf *all* Op *8* DOM *2*

setEndAfter(*nodeReference*) setEndBefore(*nodeReference*) setStartAfter(*nodeReference*) setStartBefore(*nodeReference*)

Establish the document tree locations for the individual boundary points of an existing Range object with respect to a node's edges. These methods assume that you are interested in setting a range's boundaries to places immediately before or after an existing node, and not concerned with other kinds of offsets. Range boundaries do not have to be symmetrical, allowing you to specify the start boundary relative to one node and the end boundary relative to a completely different node later in the document.

Returned Value   None.

Parameters

nodeReference
> Reference to any element or text node in the document tree.

surroundContents( )   IE *n/a* NN *n/a* Moz *all* Saf *all* Op *8* DOM *2*

surroundContents(*parentNodeReference*)

Encapsulates the current range with a new container, usually a new element node created via the document.createElement( ) method. Endpoints of the current range should have the same parent container prior to applying this method.

Returned Value   None.

Parameters

parentNodeReference
> Reference to a node that becomes the new containing parent for the range.

toString( )   IE *n/a* NN *n/a* Moz *all* Saf *all* Op *8* DOM *2*

Returns a string of the body content contained by the range. No tags or attributes accompany the returned value.

Returned Value   String.

Parameters   None.

RangeException   IE *n/a* NN *n/a* Moz *1.0.1* Saf *all* Op *8* DOM *2*

Some operations on W3C DOM Range objects can trigger errors, or, in the vernacular of JavaScript 1.5, throw exceptions if something goes wrong. The W3C DOM defines an object that conveys a code number corresponding to a well-defined, if somewhat limited, list of exceptions specifically related to Range objects. For example, if you attempt to set range boundaries to encompass non-content-related nodes (such as an Attr node), the selectNode( ) method with such a node as a parameter throws an exception whose code number is 2. This number corresponds to the exception that signals an attempt to perform an illegal or logically impossible action on a text range.

Object Model Reference
errorObjectReference

Object-Specific Properties
code

Object-Specific Methods
None.

Object-Specific Events
None.

code   IE *n/a* NN *n/a* Moz *1.0.1* Saf *all* Op *8* DOM *2*

Read-only

Provides the integer corresponding to one of the defined Range object error types, as shown in the following table.

Code	Constant	Most Likely Cause
1	BAD_BOUNDARYPOINTS_ERR	The surroundContents( ) method was applied to a range with a nonapplicable endpoint
2	INVALID_NODE_TYPE_ERR	The method tried to work in a nonapplicable type of node

Value   Integer

Default   Determined by error.

RepetitionElement   IE *n/a* NN *n/a* Moz *n/a* Saf *n/a* Op *9* DOM *n/a*

Any HTML element that is set up in a Web Forms 2.0 environment is an instance of the RepetitionElement, sometimes as a repeated block, other times as a template (depending on attribute settings). This object has a number of properties and methods (listed below) that become members of any HTML element in a supporting browser (such as Opera 9). See the descriptions of these properties and methods among the shared items at the beginning of this chapter.

Object-Specific Properties

repeatMax	repeatMin	repeatStart
repetitionBlocks	repetitionIndex	repetitionTemplate
repetitionType		

Object-Specific Methods

addRepetitionBlock( )	addRepetitionBlockByIndex( )
moveRepetitionBlock( )	removeRepetitionBlock( )

Object-Specific Events
None.

reset

See input.

rows

IE 4   NN n/a   Moz all   Saf all   Op 7   DOM 1

Provides a collection of all tr element objects contained in a single table, tbody, tfoot, or thead element object. The rows collection of a table element includes all rows of the table, regardless of row groups. Collection members are sorted in source code order. Internet Explorer lets you use array notation or parentheses to access a single row in the collection (e.g., document.getElementById("myTable").rows[0], document.all.myTable.rows (0)).

Object Model Reference
document.getElementById("*tableOrSectionID*").rows

Object-Specific Properties

length

Object-Specific Methods

item( )	namedItem( )	tags( )	urns( )

Object-Specific Events
None.

length

IE 4 NN *n/a* Moz *all* Saf *all* Op 7 DOM 1

Read-only

Returns the number of elements in the collection.

Example

```
var howMany = document.getElementById("myTable").rows.length;
```

Value   Integer.

item( )

IE 4 NN *n/a* Moz *all* Saf *all* Op 7 DOM 1

```
item(index[, subindex]) item(index)
```

Returns a single tr object or collection of tr objects corresponding to the element matching the index value (or, optionally in IE, the index and subindex values).

Returned Value   One tr object or collection (array) of tr objects. If there are no matches to the parameters, the returned value is null.

Parameters

index

When the parameter is a zero-based integer, the returned value is a single element corresponding to the specified item in source code order (nested within the current element); when the parameter is a string (IE only), the returned value is a collection of elements with id properties that match that string.

subindex

In IE only, if you specify a string value for the first parameter, you can use the second parameter to specify a zero-based index that retrieves the specified element from the collection with id properties that match the first parameter's string value.

namedItem( )

IE 6 NN *n/a* Moz *all* Saf *all* Op 7 DOM 1

```
namedItem("ID")
```

Returns a single tr object or collection of tr objects corresponding to the element matching the parameter string value.

Returned Value   One tr object or collection (array) of tr objects. If there are no matches to the parameters, the returned value is null.

Parameters

ID

The string that contains the same value as the desired element's id attribute.

tags( )

tags(*tagName*)

Returns a collection of objects (among all objects within the current collection) with tags that match the *tagName* parameter. Redundant here, because all elements have the same tr tag.

Returned Value A collection (array) of objects. If there are no matches to the parameters, the returned value is an array of zero length.

Parameters

tagName

This involves a string of the all-uppercase version of the element tag, for example, document.getElementById("myTable").rows.tags("tr").

urns( )

urns(*URN*)

See the all.urns( ) method.

rb, ruby, rt

Of these three ruby text-related elements, only ruby and rt are officially supported as objects in the IE DOM. But an rb element (even though it has no structural or rendering powers as of IE 7) is also regarded as an element object. Mozilla and Opera treat these as valid HTML element objects of unknown type. See the ruby element in Chapter 1 for details on the usage of these elements. As scriptable objects, they have no properties or methods beyond a generic HTML element object.

Object Model Reference

document.getElementById("*elementID*")

Object-Specific Properties

None.

Object-Specific Methods

None.

Object-Specific Events

None.

rule

See CSSRule.

rules

See CSSRules.

runtimeStyle

IE 5(Win) NN n/a Moz n/a Saf n/a Op n/a DOM n/a

The runtimeStyle object (a property of all HTML element objects in IE 5 and later for Windows) acts like a super-powerful style object: setting any of its properties overrides that property's settings that may exist in explicitly coded style definitions. Thus, it over-powers global, imported, linked, and inline style definitions. This object shares nearly the same long list of properties and methods with the style object.

Object Model Reference
[window.]document.getElementById("*elementID*").runtimeStyle

Object-Specific Properties
See the style object.

Object-Specific Methods
See the style object.

Object-Specific Events
None.

s

See b.

samp

See abbr.

screen

IE 4 NN n/a Moz all Saf all Op 7 DOM n/a

The screen object refers to the video display on which the browser is being viewed. Many video control panel settings influence the property values, but only a handful of properties are shared among browser brands.

Object Model Reference
NN

    screen

IE

    [window.]screen

Object-Specific Properties

availHeight	availLeft	availTop	availWidth
bufferDepth	colorDepth	deviceXDPI	deviceYDPI
fontSmoothingEnabled	height	logicalXDPI	logicalYDPI
pixelDepth	updateInterval	width	

Object-Specific Methods
None.

Object-Specific Events
None.

availHeight, availWidth
IE *4* NN *4* Moz *all* Saf *all* Op *7* DOM *n/a*

Read-only

Provide the height and width of the content region of the user's video monitor in pixels. This measure does not include the 24-pixel task bar (Windows) or 20-pixel system menubar (Macintosh). IE/Macintosh miscalculates the height of the menu bar as 24 pixels. To use these values in creating a pseudo-maximized window, you also have to adjust the top-left position of the window.

Example
```
var newWind = window.open("","","height=" + screen.availHeight +
",width=" + screen.availWidth);
```

Value   Integer of available pixels in vertical and horizontal dimensions.

Default   Depends on the user's monitor size.

availLeft, availTop
IE *n/a* NN *4* Moz *all* Saf *all* Op *n/a* DOM *n/a*

Read-only

Provide the pixel coordinates of the left and top edges of the screen that is available for content. With the standard Windows Taskbar arrangement, both values are zero. But drag the Taskbar to the left or top of the screen, and the corresponding value increases to accommodate the bar's space. Navigator 4 for the Macintosh doesn't start its screen counting until just below the fixed menu bar, but for Mozilla and Safari in Mac OS X, the availTop property returns 22 for the menu bar height.

Example   `window.moveTo(screen.availLeft, screen.availTop);`

Value   Integer.

Default   0 (Windows); 20 (Macintosh)

bufferDepth

IE 4   NN *n/a*   Moz *n/a*   Saf *n/a*   Op *n/a*   DOM *n/a*

Read/Write

Specifies the setting of the offscreen bitmap buffer. Path animation smoothness may improve on some clients if you match the bufferDepth to the colorDepth values. Setting the bufferDepth to -1 forces IE to buffer at the screen's pixel depth (as set in the control panel), and colorDepth is automatically set to that value, as well (plus if a user changes the bits per pixel, the buffer is adjusted accordingly). A setting to any of the other permitted values (1, 4, 8, 15, 16, 24, or 32) buffers at that pixel depth and sets the colorDepth to that value. The client's display must be set to the higher bits-per-pixel values to take advantage of the higher settings in scripts.

Example   screen.bufferDepth = 4;

Value   Any of the following allowed integers: -1 | 0 | 4 | 8 | 15 | 16 | 24 | 32.

Default   0

colorDepth

IE 4   NN 4   Moz *all*   Saf *all*   Op 7   DOM *n/a*

Read-only

Returns the number of bits per pixel used to display color in the video monitor or image buffer. Although this property is read-only, its value can be influenced by settings of the bufferDepth property (IE only). You can determine the color depth of the current video screen and select colors accordingly.

Example
```
if (screen.colorDepth > 8) {
    document.getElementById("pretty").color = "cornflowerblue";
} else {
    document.getElementById("pretty").color = "blue";
}
```

Value   Integer.

Default   Current video control panel setting.

deviceXDPI, deviceYDPI, logicalXDPI, logicalYDPI

IE 6   NN *n/a*   Moz *n/a*   Saf *n/a*   Op *n/a*   DOM *n/a*

Read-only

All four properties concern themselves with the dots-per-inch resolution of display screens along the horizontal (x) and vertical (y) axes. A device density property returns the actual pixel density of the current display screen, as detected by the operating system. The logical density is the "normal" pixel density that most users and page authors work with (typically 96 dots per inch horizontally and vertically). These two sets of properties let scripts examine whether the user has a higher-than-usual pixel density display, which could make fixed-size items, such as images and pixel-sized fonts, appear uncomfortably small on the screen. In such cases, scripts can determine a scaling factor between the device and logical densities, and apply that factor to the style.zoom property of critical elements (or the entire document.body, for that matter). Users of high-density display systems may already have their IE application preferences set to automatic scaling, so these calculations aren't necessary.

Example

```
var normDPI = 96;
if ((screen.deviceXDPI == screen.logicalXDPI) && (screen.deviceXDPI > normDPI)) {
    document.body.style.zoom = normDPI / screen.logicalXDPI;
}
```

Value	Integer.
Default	96

fontSmoothingEnabled

IE 4(Win) NN n/a Moz n/a Saf n/a Op n/a DOM n/a

Read-only

Returns Boolean true if the user has enabled Smooth Edges for fonts in the Windows Display control panel. The setting may influence the font-related style sheet you link into a document.

Example

```
var styleFile = "css/corpStyle.css";
if (screen.fontSmoothingEnabled) {
    styleFile = "css/corpStyleFancy.css";
}
document.write("<link type='text/css' rel='stylesheet' href='"  +
    styleFile + "'>");
```

Value	Boolean value: true	false.
Default	false

height, width

IE 4 NN 4 Moz all Saf all Op 7 DOM n/a

Read-only

Return the number of pixels available vertically and horizontally in the client video monitor. This is the raw dimension. For the amount of screen space not covered by system bars, see availHeight and availWidth.

Example

```
if (screen.height > 480 && screen.width > 640) {
    ...
}
```

Value	Integer of pixel counts.
Default	Depends on video monitor.

logicalXDPI, logicalYDPI

See deviceXDPI.

pixelDepth

IE n/a NN 4 Moz all Saf all Op 7 DOM n/a

Read/Write

Returns the number of bits per pixel used to display color in the video monitor. This value is similar to the colorDepth property, but it is not influenced by a potential custom color palette, as colorDepth is.

Example

```
if (screen.pixelDepth > 8) {
    document.getElementById("pretty").color = "cornflowerblue";
} else {
    document.getElementById("pretty").color = "blue";
}
```

Value   Integer.

Default   Current video control panel setting.

updateInterval

IE 4 NN n/a Moz n/a Saf n/a Op n/a DOM n/a

Provides the time interval (in milliseconds) between screen updates. A value of zero lets the browser select an average that usually works best. The longer the interval, the more animation steps may be buffered and then ignored as the update fires to display the current state.

Example   `screen.updateInterval = 0;`

Value   Positive integer or zero.

Default   0

width

See height.

script

IE 4 NN n/a Moz all Saf all Op 7 DOM 1

The script object reflects the script element. Internet Explorer 4 for Windows chokes on accessing or setting the innerHTML or innerText properties, but the equivalent text property is safe. IE 5 for the Macintosh implements the readyState property (shared among all elements in IE for Windows) for this object. IE has known problems loading external *.js* files vis the setAttribute( ) method on the src attribute; assigning a new URL to the src property is more reliable.

HTML Equivalent   `<script>`

Object Model Reference

[window.]document.getElementById("*elementID*")

Object-Specific Properties

charset	defer	event	htmlFor	src	text	type

Object-Specific Methods
None.

Object-Specific Events

Event	IE	Others	DOM	
error	•	—	—	
load	•	—	—	

charset

IE *6* NN *n/a* Moz *all* Saf *all* Op *7* DOM *1*

Read/Write

Indicates the character encoding of the script content.

Example

```
if (document.getElementById("myScript").charset == "csISO5427Cyrillic") {
    // process for Cyrillic charset
}
```

Value   Case-insensitive alias from the character set registry (*ftp://ftp.isi.edu/in-notes/iana/assignments/character-sets*).

Default   Determined by browser.

defer

IE *4* NN *n/a* Moz *all* Saf *all* Op *7* DOM *1*

Read/Write

Specifies whether the browser should proceed with rendering regular HTML content without looking for the script to generate content as the page loads. This value needs to be set in the script element's tag at runtime. When this property is set to true by the addition of the DEFER attribute to the tag, the browser does not have to hold up rendering further HTML content to parse the content of the script element in search of document.write( ) statements. Changing this property's value after the document loads does not affect the performance of the script or browser. Although all mainstream browsers implement the property, only IE does anything with it.

Example

```
if (document.getElementById("myScript").defer = = "true") {
    ...
}
```

| **Value** | Boolean value: true \| false. |
| **Default** | false |

event

IE *4* NN *n/a* Moz *all* Saf *all* Op *n/a* DOM *1*

Read-only

Internet Explorer's event model allows binding of object events to script elements with the help of the event and for attributes (see Online Section VI). The event property returns the setting for the event attribute. Not functional in other browsers, even though the property is implemented in some.

Example

```
if (document.getElementById("gizmoScript").event == "onresize") {
   ...
}
```

| **Value** | Case-sensitive event name string. |
| **Default** | None. |

htmlFor

IE *4* NN *n/a* Moz *all* Saf *all* Op *n/a* DOM *1*

Read-only

Returns the value (element ID) assigned to the for attribute of a script element. This attribute points to the ID of the element to which the script is bound when a specific event (set by the event attribute) fires for the element. Not functional in browsers other than IE.

Example

```
if (document.getElementById("helpScript").htmlFor == "helpButton") {
   ...
}
```

| **Value** | String. |
| **Default** | None. |

src

IE *4* NN *n/a* Moz *all* Saf *all* Op *7* DOM *1*

Read/Write

Provides the URL of the *.js* script file imported into the current script element. If you assign a new *.js* file to an existing script element in IE, the previous *.js* file's scripts do not disappear. But any duplications of variable or functions names are overwritten by the definitions from the new file.

Example

```
if (document.getElementsByTagName("script")[1].src == "scripts/textlib.js") {
   ...
}
```

| Value | Complete or relative URL as a string. |
| Default | None. |

text

Read/Write

Indicates the text content of the element. Assigning script statements to this object has different results in various browsers. In late versions of IE for Windows, the new value is added to the existing script, even though the property no longer reports the previous script text; in Mozilla, the assigned values are ignored; in IE 5 for Macintosh, the property is treated as read-only; Safari returns only an empty string.

Example	`var scriptText = document.getElementById("script3").text;`
Value	String.
Default	None.

type

Read-only

Provides an advisory about the content type of the script statements. The content type should tell the browser which scripting engine to use to interpret the script statements, such as `text/javascript`. The `type` attribute may eventually replace the `language` attribute as the one defining the scripting language in which the element's statements are written.

Example	`var scriptMIMEtype = document.getElementById("script3").type;`
Value	String.
Default	None.

scripts

A collection of all scripts defined or imported in a document, including those defined in the head or body portion. Collection members are sorted in source code order.

Object Model Reference

`document.scripts`

Object-Specific Properties

`length`

Object-Specific Methods

| `item( )` | `namedItem( )` | `tags( )` | `urns( )` |

Object-Specific Events

None.

length

IE 4 NN *n/a* Moz *all* Saf *all* Op 7 DOM *n/a*

Read-only

Returns the number of elements in the collection.

Example   var howMany = document.scripts.length;

Value   Integer.

item( )

IE 4 NN *n/a* Moz *all* Saf *all* Op 7 DOM *n/a*

item(*index*[, *subindex*])

Returns a single object or collection of objects corresponding to the element matching the index value (or, optionally, the index and subindex values).

Returned Value   One object or collection (array) of objects. If there are no matches to the parameters, the returned value is null.

Parameters

index

When the parameter is a zero-based integer, the returned value is a single element corresponding to the said numbered item in source code order (nested within the current element). When the parameter is a string, the returned value is a collection of elements with id properties that match that string.

subindex

If you specify a string value for the first parameter, you may use the second parameter to specify a zero-based integer to retrieve a specific element from the collection with id properties that match the first parameter's string value.

namedItem( )

IE 4 NN *n/a* Moz *all* Saf *all* Op 7 DOM *n/a*

namedItem("*ID*")

Returns a single script object or collection of script objects corresponding to the element matching the parameter string value.

Returned Value   One script object or collection (array) of script objects. If there are no matches to the parameters, the returned value is null.

Parameters

ID

The string that contains the same value as the desired element's id attribute.

tags( )

tags(*tagName*)

Returns a collection of objects (among all objects within the current collection) with tags that match the *tagName* parameter. Redundant here, because all elements have the same script tag.

Returned Value   A collection (array) of objects. If there are no matches to the parameters, the returned value is an array of zero length.

Parameters

tagName
    A string of the all-uppercase version of the element tag, as in `document.scripts.tags("script")`.

urns( )

urns(*URN*)

See the `all.urns( )` method.

scrollbars

See directories.

select

The select object reflects the select element. This element is a form control that contains option elements. The shared `disabled` property is no available for pre-Mozilla Netscape Navigator.

HTML Equivalent   `<select>`

Object Model Reference
```
[window.]document.formName.selectName
[window.]document.forms[i].elements[i]
[window.]document.getElementById("elementID")
```

Object-Specific Properties

autofocus	data	dataFld	dataSrc	form
forms	labels	length	multiple	name
options[]	selectedIndex	selectedOptions	size	type
validationMessage	validity	value	willValidate	

Object-Specific Methods

add( )	checkValidity( )	dispatchChange( )
dispatchFormChange( )	item( )	namedItem( )
remove( )	setCustomValidity( )	

Object-Specific Events

Event	IE	NN	Opera 9	Others	DOM
afterupdate	•	—	—	—	—
beforeupdate	•	—	—	—	—
change	•	•	•	•	•
formchange	—	—	•	—	—
forminput	—	—	•	—	—
invalid	—	—	•	—	—

autofocus

IE *n/a* NN *n/a* Moz *n/a* Saf *n/a* Op 9 DOM *n/a*

Read/Write

Web Forms 2.0 extension that brings focus to the element after the page loads. Should be assigned to only one form control element per page.

Example   document.getElementById("myselect").autofocus = true;

Value   Boolean: true | false.

Default   false

data

IE *n/a* NN *n/a* Moz *n/a* Saf *n/a* Op *n/a* DOM *n/a*

Read/Write

Web Forms 2.0 extension that allows a form to retrieve initial values for controls from an external XML file. The specification provides some details of the structure and namespaces to be used for the file. Visit *http://www.whatwg.org/* for further information.

Value   URL string.

Default   Empty string.

dataFld

IE *4* NN *n/a* Moz *n/a* Saf *n/a* Op *n/a* DOM *n/a*

Read/Write

Used with IE data binding to associate a remote data source column name with the selectedIndex property of the select object. A datasrc attribute must also be set for the element. Setting both the dataFld and dataSrc properties to empty strings breaks the binding between element and data source. Works only with text file data sources in IE 5/Mac.

Example	`document.forms[0].mySelect.dataFld = "choice";`
Value	Case-sensitive identifier of the data source column.
Default	None.

dataSrc

Used with IE data binding to specify the ID of the page's object element that loads the data source object for remote data access. Setting both the dataFld and dataSrc properties to empty strings breaks the binding between element and data source. Works only with text file data sources in IE 5/Mac.

Example	`document.forms[0].mySelect.dataSrc = "DBSRC3";`
Value	Case-sensitive identifier of the data source.
Default	None.

form

Returns a reference to the form element that contains the current element. When processing an event from this element, the event handler function automatically has access to the select element (as the event object's target or srcElement property). By reading the form property, the script can easily access other controls within the same form.

Example	`var theForm = evt.srcElement.form;`
Value	form element object reference.
Default	None.

forms

Web Forms 2.0 extension that returns an array (NodeList) of references to form objects with which the current select element is associated.

Example	`var formList = document.getElementById("mySelect").forms;`
Value	Array.
Default	One-item array with a reference to any enclosing form element.

labels

Web Forms 2.0 extension that returns an array (HTMLCollection) of references to label element objects associated with the current select element.

Example	var allLabels = document.getElementById("mySelect").labels;
Value	Array of label element object references.
Default	Empty array.

length

Read/Write

The number of option objects nested inside the select object. The value returned is the same as the select object options.length property, and can be safely used as a for loop maximum counter value to iterate through the nested option objects. The W3C DOM specifies that this property is read-only, but because the property has been read/write for some time in mainstream browsers, you can continue to adjust this value. By and large, the only modification made to this property, if at all, should be setting its value to zero to empty all options from the select object. Better still, if you are authoring for IE 5 and later or W3C DOM browsers, use the select.remove( ) and select.add( ) methods to modify the contingent of option elements nested inside the select element.

Example	document.forms[0].mySelect.length = 0;
Value	Integer.
Default	None.

multiple

Read/Write

Specifies whether the browser should render the select element as a list box and allow users to make multiple selections from the list of options. By default, the size property is set to the number of nested option elements, but the value may be overridden with the size property setting. To change a scrolling pick list to a popup menu, set the multiple property to false and the size property to 1. Users can select contiguous items by **Shift**-clicking on the first and last items of the group. To make discontiguous selections, Windows users must **Ctrl**-click on each item; Mac users must **Command**-click on each item. The multiple property has no effect when size is set to 1 to display a popup menu.

Example

```
if (document.entryForm.list3.multiple) {
    ...
}
```

| **Value** | Boolean value: true | false. |
| **Default** | false |

name

This is the identifier associated with the form control. The value of this property is submitted as one-half of the name/value pair when the form is submitted to the server. Names are hidden from user view, since control labels are assigned via other means, depending on the control type. Form control names may also be used by script references to the objects. Despite the modern standards' preference for the id attribute, many browsers still require that a control be assigned a name attribute to allow the control's value to be submitted.

Example   document.orderForm.payment.name = "credcard";

Value   Case-sensitive string identifier that follows the rules of identifier naming: it may contain no whitespace, cannot begin with a numeral, and should avoid punctuation except for the underscore character.

Default   None.

options[ ]

Returns an array of all option objects contained by the current element (in the W3C DOM Level 2, this array is an HTMLOptionsCollection object). Items in this array are indexed (zero-based) in source code order. For details on using this collection in a backward-compatible way for adding and removing option elements from a select element, see the options object. Loop through this collection in select elements set for multiple selections.

Example
```
var selVals = new Array( );
for (var i = 0; i < document.forms[0].mySelect.length; i++) {
    if (document.forms[0].mySelect.options[i].selected) {
        selVals[selVals.length] = document.forms[0].mySelect.options[i].value;
    }
}
```

Value   Array of option objects.

Default   None.

selectedIndex

This is the zero-based integer of the option selected by the user. If the select element is set to allow multiple selections, the selectedIndex property returns the index of the first selected item (see the selected property). You can use this property to gain access to the value or text of the selected item, as shown in the example.

In recent browsers, if no option is selected, the selectedIndex property returns 0 (the first option). Setting the value to -1 deselects all items and empties the display (except in Safari).

Example

```
var list = document.forms[0].selectList;
var listText = list.options[list.selectedIndex].text;
```

Value   Integer.

Default   0

size   IE 4 NN n/a Moz all Saf all Op 7 DOM 1
Read/Write

Controls the number of rows displayed in a scrolling pick list, reflecting the size attribute of the select element. When set to true, the multiple property overrides a size value set to fewer than the number of options. To change a scrolling pick list to a popup menu, set the multiple property to false and the size property to 1.

Example   `document.forms[0].choices.size = 6;`

Value   Integer.

Default   None.

type   IE 4 NN 3 Moz all Saf all Op 7 DOM 1
Read-only

Returns the type of form control element. A select object has two possible values, depending on whether the element is set to be a multiple-choice list. The value is returned in all lowercase letters. It may be necessary to cycle through all form elements in search of specific types to do some processing on (e.g., emptying all form controls of type "text" while leaving other controls untouched).

Note that Navigator 4 incorrectly reports a select object's type as select-multiple if the element's size attribute is set to any value larger than 1, even if the multiple attribute is not set.

Example

```
if (document.forms[0].elements[3].type == "select-multiple") {
    ...
}
```

Value   Any of the following constants (as a string): button | checkbox | file | hidden | image | password | radio | reset | select-multiple | select-one | submit | text | textarea.

Default   Depends on value of multiple.

validationMessage

Read-only

Web Forms 2.0 extension that returns a browser-generated message if the form control fails to validate according to its specifications. This property is meant more for text-oriented form controls, where an empty string means that the entry validates properly.

Value   Empty string.

Default   Empty string.

validity

Read-only

Web Forms 2.0 extension that returns a ValidityState object. See the ValidityState object.

Value   ValidityState object.

Default   ValidityState object.

value

Read/Write

This is the current value associated with the form control that is submitted with the name/value pair for the element. All values are strings, but they may represent other kinds of data, including Boolean and numeric values. Early browsers (pre-Mozilla Netscape and pre-IE 4), scripts had to retrieve the selected option's value by using the select object's selectedIndex property as an index into the options array, then inspect each option object's selected property to find the true one(s).

Example

```
if (document.forms[0].medium.value == "CD-ROM") {
    ...
}
```

Value   String.

Default   None.

add( )

add(*newOptionElement*[, *positionIndex*])
add(*newOptionElement*, *optionElementReference*)

Adds a new option element to the current select element. Unfortunately, IE and W3C DOMs don't agree on the parameter values for this method. While all browsers require a reference to a newly created option element (the value returned from a document. createElement("option") method is appropriate for that), the second parameter varies with browser. In IE, the second parameter is optional and supplies a numeric index to the existing option element; the new option is inserted in front of that element. With no second

Alphabetical DOM Reference

parameter, the new option is appended to the existing option elements. In W3C DOM browsers, the second parameter is required. The parameter is either a reference to an existing option element (the new option is inserted before that referenced option) or null (the new option is appended to the existing options).

Returned Value   None.

Parameters

newOptionElement

Reference to an option element created by script, usually with the document. createElement( ) method.

positionIndex

Optional IE integer parameter signifying the existing nested option element in front of which the new option is to be inserted. Omitting this parameter or assigning a value of -1 causes the new option to be appended to the end of the options list.

optionElementReference

Reference to an option element in front of which the new option is to be inserted. You may also use null to append the new option to the end of the option list.

checkValidity( )   IE *n/a* NN *n/a* Moz *n/a* Saf *n/a* Op *9* DOM *n/a*

Web Forms 2.0 method that returns a Boolean value representing whether the form control element meets its validity criteria—ultimately, whether the validity.valid property is true.

Returned Value   Boolean value: true | false.

Parameters   None.

dispatchChange( ),
dispatchFormChange( )   IE *n/a* NN *n/a* Moz *n/a* Saf *n/a* Op *9* DOM *n/a*

Web Forms 2.0 methods that fire the change and formchange events on the current element. You could, for example "convert" a mouseup event to a change or formchange event by having the onmouseup event handler invoke either method.

Returned Value   None.

Parameters   None.

item( )   IE *5* NN *n/a* Moz *all* Saf *n/a* Op *7* DOM *1*

item(*index*[, *subindex*])
item(*index*)

Returns a single nested option object or collection of nested option objects corresponding to the element matching the index value (or, optionally, the index and subindex values).

Returned Value   One object or collection (array) of objects. If there are no matches to the parameters, the returned value is null.

Parameters

index

When the parameter is a zero-based integer, the returned value is a single element corresponding to the said numbered item in source code order (nested within the current element). When the parameter is a string, the returned value is a collection of elements with id properties that match that string.

subindex

If you specify a string value for the first parameter, you may use the second parameter to specify a zero-based integer to retrieve a specific element from the collection with id properties that match the first parameter's string value.

namedItem( )   IE 6 NN *n/a* Moz *all* Saf *n/a* Op 7 DOM 1

namedItem("*ID*")

Returns a single nested option object or collection of nested option objects corresponding to the element matching the parameter string value.

Returned Value   One option object or collection (array) of option objects. If there are no matches to the parameters, the returned value is null.

Parameters

ID

The string that contains the same value as the desired element's id attribute.

remove( )   IE 5 NN *n/a* Moz *all* Saf *all* Op 7 DOM 1

remove(*positionIndex*)

Deletes an option element from the current select element at the zero-based index position signified by the parameter value. In lieu of setting the select object's length property to zero, you can remove all existing options with a simple loop construction:

```
while (selectElemRef.length > 0) {
    selectElemRef.remove(0);
}
```

At this point, you can populate the list with new options via the various approaches described in the add( ) method discussion and the options object discussion.

Returned Value   None.

Parameters

positionIndex

Zero-based integer signifying the item from the nested options collection to be deleted.

setCustomValidity( )   IE *n/a* NN *n/a* Moz *n/a* Saf *n/a* Op *9* DOM *n/a*

setCustomValidity([*errorString*])

Web Forms 2.0 method that sets the customError Boolean value of the validity property (itself a ValidityState object). This method has no effect on button elements and throws a NOT_SUPPORTED_ERR error.

Returned Value   None.

Parameters

errorString

> If null or an empty string, the parameter resets the validity object's customError property, signifying the form control is not valid. An error string is to be remembered by the browser (during the current session) so that it displays the string upon subsequent validation failures.

selection   IE *4* NN *n/a* Moz *all* Saf *all* Op *7* DOM *1*

The selection object represents zero or more characters that have been explicitly selected in a document by the user or selected under script control. The objects are very different entities across browsers (observe compatibility ratings for properties and methods, below), and there are two incompatible approaches to providing script access to the selection.

In IE for Windows, you create a selection object via the document.selection property, which returns a selection object. To perform substantive actions on the content of the selection object, you then generate a TextRange object from the selection object (via the selection object's createRange( ) method). Use TextRange properties and methods to interact with the content. To convert a TextRange object to a visibly selected stretch of text on the page, use the TextRange object's select( ) method. This close linkage with the TextRange object means that the IE selection object is limited to Win32 versions. The IE selection object can include selected text inside an input (of type text) and textarea element.

In IE for the Macintosh, you don't have a selection object per se. Instead, it implements the Navigator 4 document.getSelection( ) method, which returns only the string contents of the selected text. Speaking of that Navigator 4 method, Mozilla does support it, but the method is deprecated and displays a warning (less harmful than an error) in the JavaScript Console if you use the method.

In Mozilla, create a selection object with the window.getSelection( ) method. Many properties and methods of the Mozilla selection object have analogs with the W3C DOM Range object specification. In fact, it is through the Range object that scripts can highlight even discontiguous text spans on the page: create and size a Range object; then add that Range to the highlighted text via the selection object's addRange( ) method. Mozilla selections (as with the Range object) operate only on body content, and not on text inside editable text boxes.

Safari's support for the selection object is quite limited, returning little more than the selected text. Opera 8 or later tracks the IE object to the extent that you can create an IE TextRange object from the selection; Opera 9 also implements the Mozilla selection object.

It's not uncommon among browsers that a user clicking on a button or link deselects the current text selection. Therefore, all scripted action involving selections in these browsers must be triggered by onselect or onmouseup events, or functions invoked by a timer (see the window.setTimeout( ) method description in Chapter 5).

Object Model Reference

IE (Win), Opera
    document.selection
Mozilla, Safari, Opera 9
    window.getSelection( )

Object-Specific Properties

anchorNode	anchorOffset	focusNode	focusOffset
isCollapsed	rangeCount	type	typeDetail

Object-Specific Methods

addRange( )	clear( )	collapse( )
collapseToEnd( )	collapseToStart( )	containsNode( )
createRange( )	createRangeCollection( )	deleteFromDocument( )
empty( )	extend( )	getRangeAt( )
removeAllRanges( )	removeRange( )	selectAllChildren( )
selectionLanguageChange( )	toString( )	

Object-Specific Events
None.

anchorNode, focusNode

IE *n/a*   NN *n/a*   Moz *all*   Saf *n/a*   Op *9*   DOM *n/a*

Read-only

Return a reference to the node where the user started (anchor) and ended (focus) the selection. Most typically, these are text node types. If the selection is set or extended via the addRange( ) method, these properties point to the node boundaries of the most recently added range.

Example
```
var anchor = selectionRef.anchorNode;
if (anchor.nodeType == 3 && anchor.parentNode.tagName == "td") {
    // process selection start inside a table cell
}
```

Value　　　　Reference to a document tree node, or null if no selection.

Default　　　　null

Alphabetical DOM
Reference

anchorOffset, focusOffset

IE n/a NN n/a Moz all Saf n/a Op 9 DOM n/a
Read-only

Return an integer count of characters or nodes from the beginning of the anchor or focus nodes of the selection (see anchorNode and focusNode properties). If the node is a text node, the offset unit is the character; if the node is an element node, the offset unit is the node. This behavior is similar to the offset properties of a Range object. Most typically, these values count characters within text node types. If the selection is set or extended via the addRange( ) method, these properties point to the node boundary offsets of the most recently added range.

Example   var selStartOffset = selectionRef.anchorOffset;

Value   Integer.

Default   0

isCollapsed

IE n/a NN n/a Moz all Saf n/a Op 9 DOM n/a
Read-only

Returns Boolean true if the anchor and focus boundaries of a selection are identical.

Example
```
if (selectionRef.isCollapsed) {
    // selection is an insertion point
}
```

Value   Boolean value: true | false.

Default   true

rangeCount

IE n/a NN n/a Moz all Saf n/a Op 9 DOM n/a
Read-only

Returns an integer count of Range objects (which may be discontiguous in Mozilla) within the span of the selection. A manual selection by the user always contains one Range, but the addRange( ) method can tack on multiple, discontiguous ranges to the selection. To inspect each highlighted section's properties, use the getRangeAt( ) method.

Example   var howMany = selectionRef.rangeCount;

Value   Integer.

Default   0

type

IE 4(Win) NN n/a Moz n/a Saf all Op n/a DOM n/a
Read-only

Specifies whether the current selection object has one or more characters selected or is merely an insertion point.

Example
```
if (document.selection.type == "Text") {
    ...
}
```

Value　　　　In IE, one of three constant values (as a string): None | Text | Control. The last one is possible only when HTML editing is engaged and control selections are possible. In Safari, one of three constant values (as a string): None | Caret | Range.

Default　　　　None

typeDetail　　　　　IE *5.5*　NN *n/a*　Moz *n/a*　Saf *n/a*　Op *n/a*　DOM *n/a*
Read-only

This property is supplied as a placeholder for other applications that may use the IE browser component. Such an application can provide additional selection type information as needed.

addRange( )　　　　　IE *n/a*　NN *n/a*　Moz *all*　Saf *n/a*　Op *9*　DOM *n/a*
addRange(*RangeReference*)

Turns a Range into a highlighted selection on the page. You can add as many discontiguous ranges to the selection as your application requires. Each addition increments the selection object's rangeCount property. Ranges may also overlap in a selection.

```
var selRef = window.getSelection( );
var rng = document.createRange( );
rng.selectNodeContents(document.getElementById("myP"));
selRef.addRange(rng);
```

Returned Value　　　None.

Parameters
RangeReference
　　Reference to a Range object with boundaries that have been established by Range object methods.

clear( )　　　　　IE *4(Win)*　NN *n/a*　Moz *n/a*　Saf *n/a*　Op *n/a*　DOM *n/a*

Deletes the content of the current selection in a document. For example, the event handler in the following tag deletes any selected text of the p element two seconds after the user starts making the selection:

```
<p onselectstart="setTimeout('document.selection.clear( )',2000);">
```

Returned Value　　　None.

Parameters　　　None.

collapse( )

collapse(*nodeReference, offset*)

Collapses the current selection to a location specified by the two parameters. Any previously highlighted selection returns to normal display.

Returned Value   None.

Parameters

nodeReference
> Reference to a text or element node in the document tree in which the collapsed selection should move.

offset
> Integer count of characters or nodes within the *nodeReference* node where the collapsed selection should move. The count is relative to the start of the node. Units are character for text nodes, nodes for elements.

collapseToEnd( ), collapseToStart( )

Collapses the current selection to a location at the start (collapseToStart( )) or end (collapseToEnd( )) of the selection object. Any previously highlighted selection returns to normal display. If the selection consists of multiple ranges, the start or end boundary used for these collapse methods are at the outermost edges of the combined selection. After the collapse, the selection contains only one range.

Returned Value   None.

Parameters   None.

containsNode( )

containsNode(*nodeReference, entirelyFlag*)

Returns Boolean true if the current selection object contains a node passed as a parameter. The second parameter is supposed to let you loosen or tighten the definition of contains, but the behavior of the method seems backward to the intended purpose of the flag. You can assure accuracy if you pass null as the second parameter, which forces the method to define containment as containing the node in its entirety.

Returned Value   Boolean value: true | false.

Parameters

nodeReference
> Reference to any addressable text or element node in the document tree.

entirelyFlag
> Boolean value or null. Observed behavior is that a value of true means the selection can contain only a part of the node for the method to return true.

createRange( )   IE *4(Win)*   NN *n/a*   Moz *n/a*   Saf *n/a*   Op *8*   DOM *n/a*

Creates a TextRange object from the current selection object. After a statement like the following:

```
var myRange = document.selection.createRange( );
```

scripts can act on the content of the selected text.

Returned Value   TextRange object.

Parameters   None.

createRangeCollection( )   IE *5.5*   NN *n/a*   Moz *n/a*   Saf *n/a*   Op *n/a*   DOM *n/a*

Creates a TextRange collection object. This must be in anticipation of IE supporting multiple, discontiguous selections in the future.

Returned Value   TextRange collection object.

Parameters   None.

deleteFromDocument( )   IE *n/a*   NN *n/a*   Moz *all*   Saf *n/a*   Op *9*   DOM *n/a*

Removes the current selection from the document tree. The node hierarchy adjusts itself by obeying the same rules as Range.deleteContents( ).

Returned Value   None.

Parameters   None.

empty( )   IE *4(Win)*   NN *n/a*   Moz *n/a*   Saf *n/a*   Op *n/a*   DOM *n/a*

Deselects the current selection and sets the selection object's type property to None. There is no change to the content that had been selected.

Returned Value   None.

Parameters   None.

extend( )   IE *n/a*   NN *n/a*   Moz *all*   Saf *n/a*   Op *9*   DOM *n/a*

extend(*nodeReference, offset*)

Moves the end (focus) boundary of the selection to the designated document tree node and offset within that node. The start (anchor) point does not move with this method.

Returned Value   None.

Parameters

nodeReference
> Reference to a text or element node in the document tree in which the selection's focus (endpoint) should move.

offset
> Integer count of characters or nodes within the *nodeReference* node where the collapsed selection should move. The count is relative to the start of the node. Units are character for text nodes, nodes for elements.

getRangeAt( )

IE *n/a* NN *n/a* Moz *all* Saf *n/a* Op *9* DOM *n/a*

getRangeAt(*rangeIndex*)

Returns a reference to the range within a selection object whose zero-based numeric index matches the passed parameter. For contiguous selections, the parameter should be zero. But for discontiguous selections, the getRangeAt( ) method lets you retrieve each range that had been added to the selection for individual manipulation as a Range object. Use the selection.rangeCount property to derive the number of Range objects contained by the selection object. Invoking the method does not disturb the sequence of ranges within the selection.

Returned Value   Range object reference.

Parameters

rangeIndex
> Zero-based integer index value.

removeAllRanges( )

IE *n/a* NN *n/a* Moz *all* Saf *n/a* Op *9* DOM *n/a*

Removes all Range objects from the current selection (not from the document tree). The selection collapses, and the rangeCount property value changes to zero.

Returned Value   None.

Parameters   None.

removeRange( )

IE *n/a* NN *n/a* Moz *all* Saf *n/a* Op *9* DOM *n/a*

removeRange(*rangeReference*)

Removes a single Range object from the current selection (not from the document tree). If you have a multiple-range selection, you can iterate through all Range objects, inspect each for some criterion, and delete the one(s) you want with the following sequence:

```
var oneRange;
var sel = window.getSelection( );
for (var i = 0; i < sel.rangeCount; i++) {
    oneRange = sel.getRangeAt(i);
    if (oneRange.someProperty == someDiscerningValue) {
        sel.removeRange(oneRange);
    }
}
```

Returned Value   None.

Parameters

rangeReference
    Reference to one of the Range objects previously added to the current selection.

selectAllChildren( )   IE *n/a*   NN *n/a*   Moz *all*   Saf *n/a*   Op *9*   DOM *n/a*

`selectAllChildren(`*elementNodeReference*`)`

Forces the `selection` object to encompass the element node passed as a parameter and all of its child nodes. This method is also a shortcut to using a script to select an element node. Using this method on an element node causes the anchor and focus nodes to be that element node. Should you pass a reference to a text node, the resulting selection is collapsed in front of the first character of the text node. Invoking this method on an existing selection replaces all ranges with the new range encompassing the element.

Returned Value   None.

Parameters

elementNodeReference
    Reference to an element node in the document tree that becomes the selection.

selectionLanguageChange( )   IE *n/a*   NN *n/a*   Moz *all*   Saf *n/a*   Op *9*   DOM *n/a*

`selectionLanguageChange(`*RTLFlag*`)`

Controls the cursor Bidi (bi-directional) level.

Returned Value   None.

Parameters

RTLFlag
    Boolean value: `true` for right-to-left; `false` for left-to-right.

toString( )   IE *n/a*   NN *n/a*   Moz *all*   Saf *all*   Op *8*   DOM *n/a*

Returns a string containing only body content from the selection. Tags and attributes are ignored.

Returned Value   String value.

Parameters   None.

small

See b.

span

IE 4   NN *n/a*   Moz *all*   Saf *all*   Op 7   DOM 1

The span object reflects the span element. This element is used primarily as an arbitrary container for assigning styles to inline content elements. You might say that it is the quintessential generic inline element object. In Navigator 4, a span element that is given a position style is treated very much like a layer object for scripting purposes.

HTML Equivalent   <span>

Object Model Reference
[window.]document.getElementById("*elementID*")

Object-Specific Properties
None.

Object-Specific Methods
None.

Object-Specific Events
None.

statusbar

See directories.

strike

See b.

strong

See abbr.

style (element)

IE 4   NN *n/a*   Moz *all*   Saf *all*   Op 7   DOM 1

The style element object reflects the style HTML element. This object is separate from the style object that is accessed as a property of virtually every element in a document. The style element object is generated in a document via the <style> tag, which can have a unique ID value assigned to it; the style (property) object contains all the style properties and their current values as set for a particular element.

HTML Equivalent   <style>

Object Model Reference
[window.]document.getElementById("*elementID*")

Object-Specific Properties

disabled	media	sheet	styleSheet	type

Object-Specific Methods
None.

Object-Specific Events

Event	IE	Others	DOM	
error	•	—	—	
load	•	—	—	

disabled

IE 4 NN n/a Moz all Saf all Op 7 DOM 1
Read/Write

Specifies whether rules in the style sheet should be applied to their selected elements. During page authoring, you can create a button that toggles style sheets on and off to see how the page looks in all types of browsers.

Example	document.getElementById("mainStyle").disabled = true;
Value	Boolean value: true | false.
Default	false

media

IE 4 NN n/a Moz all Saf all Op 7 DOM 1
Read/Write

Indicates the intended output device for the rules of the style element. The media property looks forward to the day when browsers are able to tailor content to specific kinds of devices such as pocket computers, text-to-speech digitizers, or fuzzy television sets.

Example	document.getElementById("myStyle").media = "print";
Value	Any one of the following constant values as a comma-delimited string: all | print | screen.
Default	all

sheet

IE n/a NN n/a Moz all Saf all Op 9 DOM n/a
Read-only

Returns a styleSheet object (W3C DOM type CSSStyleSheet) representing the style sheet defined by the style element. This is an alternate (and nonstandard) way to reference a styleSheet object. The document.styleSheets collection is a better approach.

Example	var oneSheet = document.getElementById("myStyle").sheet;
Value	Reference to a styleSheet object (W3C DOM type CSSStyleSheet).

Alphabetical DOM Reference

Default   None.

styleSheet   IE 6   NN *n/a*   Moz *n/a*   Saf *n/a*   Op *n/a*   DOM *n/a*

Read-only

Returns a styleSheet object representing the style sheet defined by the style element. This is property is present, but doesn't seem to be officially supported. The document. styleSheets collection is a better approach.

Example   `var oneSheet = document.getElementById("myStyle").styleSheet;`

Value   Reference to a styleSheet object.

Default   None.

type   IE 4   NN *n/a*   Moz *all*   Saf *all*   Op 7   DOM 1

Read/Write

This is the style sheet MIME type specified by the type attribute of the style element.

Example
```
if (document.getElementById("myStyle").type == "text/css") {
    // unlikely to be anything else
}
```

Value   MIME type string.

Default   `text/css`

style, CSSStyleDeclaration   IE 4   NN *n/a*   Moz *all*   Saf *all*   Op 7   DOM 2

In its most generic sense, a style object is the access point for scripts to read and write individual CSS properties for a given element. This style object exposes (or has the potential to expose) every style sheet property supported by the browser (the kinds of CSS properties described in Chapter 4).

In practice, however, a style object that you access through an HTML element object's style property (one of the shared properties described early in this chapter) is limited in scope: It reflects only the CSS settings explicitly defined in the element's tag via the style attribute or settings assigned to the element's style property via script (all the properties are there, but their values are empty, false, or zero). But other style sheets associated with the browser (internal style sheets) and the document (explicit style sheet rules defined in the <style> element and rules imported through either a link element or an @import rule) also affect the rendered characteristics of the element. A union of all CSS properties affecting an element—the effective style definition—may be read, but only through browser-dependent syntax. IE (also supported by Opera) uses the currentStyle property of an element, whereas W3C DOM browsers use the document.defaultView. getComputedStyle( ) method. Both syntaxes return an object that lets scripts inspect the value of each effective CSS property value.

While the three IE style-related objects (style, currentStyle, and runtimeStyle) return a style object with properties that expose CSS style properties, the situation is a little more complex on the W3C DOM side. On the one hand, Mozilla, Safari, and Opera implement a version of the W3C DOM CSSStyleDeclaration object that exposes all the CSS properties as scriptable properties. This is the version accessed through an element object's style property (just like IE, thus making an element object's style property work cross-browser). But when you read the effective style sheet (via document.defaultView.getComputedStyle( )), the object that comes back does not expose the CSS properties directly as scriptable properties in Mozilla before 1.4 or Safari. Instead, you must use the CSSStyleDeclaration methods (listed below) to inspect a specific attribute value by name. It's a longer way to reach a particular effective style property value, but very much in keeping with other attribute-reading syntax deployed throughout the W3C DOM. Fortunately, beginning with Mozilla 1.4 and Opera 8, the CSSStyleDeclaration object returned from getComputedStyle( ) exposes all CSS properties as scriptable properties. The property values are read-only (as they are in IE's currentStyle and runtimeStyle objects), but you can use a read-only value in your scripting for if-then decisions and as the basis for arithmetic for numerically oriented values. Once you set a CSS property value via the element object's style property, however, you can read it from the style property cross-browser, and thus avoid the browser compatibility hassle.

This section lists the available style object properties plus the W3C DOM formal methods for accessing those attributes where needed. The W3C DOM lists a large percentage of the style object properties under an object umbrella called CSS2Properties. The specification offers the CSS2Properties object as an optional convenience for browsers (as current Mozilla and Opera apparently use internally to expose computed style properties).

The scriptable properties of the style object listed below correspond to the CSS properties. For more information on a particular property, see the corresponding listing in Chapter 4.

Object Model Reference

All

    [window.]document.getElementById("*elementID*").style

IE

    [window.]document.styleSheets[i].rules[j].style

    [window.]document.styleSheets[i].rules[j].currentStyle

    [window.]document.styleSheets[i].rules[j].runtimeStyle

W3C DOM

    [window.]document.styleSheets[i].cssRules[j].style

Object-Specific Properties

accelerator	azimuth	background
backgroundAttachment	backgroundColor	backgroundImage
backgroundPosition	backgroundPositionX	backgroundPositionY
backgroundRepeat	behavior	blockDirection
border	borderBottom	borderBottomColor

borderBottomStyle	borderBottomWidth	borderCollapse
borderColor	borderLeft	borderLeftColor
borderLeftStyle	borderLeftWidth	borderRight
borderRightColor	borderRightStyle	borderRightWidth
borderSpacing	borderStyle	borderTop
borderTopColor	borderTopStyle	borderTopWidth
borderWidth	bottom	captionSide
clear	clip	clipBottom
clipLeft	clipRight	clipTop
color	content	counterIncrement
counterReset	cssFloat	cssText
cue	cueAfter	cueBefore
cursor	direction	display
elevation	emptyCells	filter
font	fontFamily	fontSize
fontSizeAdjust	fontStretch	fontStyle
fontVariant	fontWeight	height
imeMode	layoutFlow	layoutGrid
layoutGridChar	layoutGridLine	layoutGridMode
layoutGridType	left	length
letterSpacing	lineBreak	lineHeight
listStyle	listStyleImage	listStylePosition
listStyleType	margin	marginBottom
marginLeft	marginRight	marginTop
markerOffset	marks	maxHeight
maxWidth	minHeight	minWidth
MozBorderRadius	MozBorderRadiusBottomleft	MozBorderRadiusBottomright
MozBorderRadiusTopleft	MozBorderRadiusTopright	MozOpacity
opacity	orphans	outline
outlineColor	outlineOffset	outlineStyle
outlineWidth	overflow	overflowX
overflowY	padding	paddingBottom
paddingLeft	paddingRight	paddingTop
page	pageBreakAfter	pageBreakBefore
pageBreakInside	parentRule	pause
pauseAfter	pauseBefore	pitch
pitchRange	pixelBottom	pixelHeight
pixelLeft	pixelRight	pixelTop
pixelWidth	playDuring	posBottom
posHeight	position	posLeft
posRight	posTop	posWidth

quotes	richness	right
rubyAlign	rubyOverhang	rubyPosition
scrollbar3dLightColor	scrollbarArrowColor	scrollbarBaseColor
scrollbarDarkShadowColor	scrollbarFaceColor	scrollbarHighlightColor
scrollbarShadowColor	scrollbarTrackColor	size
speak	speakHeader	speakNumeral
speakPunctuation	speechRate	stress
styleFloat	tableLayout	textAlign
textAlignLast	textAutospace	textDecoration
textDecorationBlink	textDecorationLineThrough	textDecorationNone
textDecorationOverline	textDecorationUnderline	textIndent
textJustify	textKashidaSpace	textOverflow
textShadow	textTransform	textUnderlinePosition
top	unicodeBidi	verticalAlign
visibility	voiceFamily	volume
whiteSpace	widows	width
wordBreak	wordSpacing	wordWrap
writingMode	zIndex	zoom

Object-Specific Methods

getPropertyCSSValue( )	getPropertyPriority( )	getPropertyValue( )
item( )	removeProperty( )	setProperty( )

Object-Specific Events
None.

accelerator

IE 5(Win)   NN n/a   Moz n/a   Saf n/a   Op n/a   DOM n/a

See text

For IE 5 and later running under Windows 2000 or newer version of Windows, users can set a preference to highlight an accelerator key for commands (or web page accessKey letters) when the user presses the **Alt** key. The accelerator key property controls whether the element is treated as a highlightable accelerator key string. Available as a property of the IE currentStyle (read-only) and runtimeStyle (read/write) objects only.

Example   document.getElementById("controlH").style.accelerator = true;

Value   Boolean value: true | false.

Default   false

Alphabetical DOM Reference

azimuth, cue, cueAfter, cueBefore, elevation, pause, pauseAfter, pauseBefore, pitch, pitchRange, playDuring, richness, speak, speakHeader, speakNumeral, speakPunctuation, speechRate, stress, voiceFamily, volume

IE *n/a* NN *n/a* Moz *all* Saf *n/a* Op *(see text)* DOM *2*

Read/Write

This large group of properties comes from CSS attributes intended for browsers that use speech synthesis techniques to vocalize document content. You don't have to be vision-impaired to benefit from this possibility, but Mozilla does not include this feature by default. You can read about these CSS attributes in Chapter 4.

Opera 9 implements its own version of several of these properties (opPhonemes, opVoicePitch, opVoicePitchRange, opVoiceRate, opVoiceStress, opVoiceVolume). The browser maker offers a separate voice plug-in.

Value   All values for these properties are strings.

Default   None.

background

IE *4* NN *n/a* Moz *all* Saf *all* Op *7* DOM *2*

Read/Write

Provides the element's style sheet background attribute. This is a shorthand attribute, so the scripted property consists of a string of space-delimited values for the backgroundAttachment, backgroundColor, backgroundImage, backgroundPosition, and backgroundRepeat property values. One or more values may be in the background value, and the individual values may be in any order. Available in IE as a property of the style and runtimeStyle objects only.

Example

```
document.getElementById("myDiv").style.background = "url(logo.gif) repeat-y";
```

Value   String of space-delimited values corresponding to one or more individual background style properties.

Default   None.

backgroundAttachment

IE *4* NN *n/a* Moz *all* Saf *1.2* Op *7* DOM *2*

Read/Write

Sets how the image is "attached" to the element. The image can either remain fixed within the viewable area of the element (the viewport) or it may scroll with the element as the document is scrolled. During scrolling, the fixed attachment looks like a stationary backdrop to rolling credits of a movie.

Example
document.getElementById("myDiv").style.backgroundAttachment = "fixed";

Value   String of either allowable value: fixed | scroll.

Default   scroll

backgroundColor

IE 4 NN *n/a* Moz *all* Saf *all* Op 7 DOM 2
Read/Write

Provides the background color of the element. If you also set a backgroundImage, the image overlays the color. Transparent pixels of the image allow the color to show through.

Example
document.getElementById("highlighted").style.backgroundColor = "yellow";

Value   Any valid color specification (see description at beginning of the chapter) or transparent.

Default   transparent

backgroundImage

IE 4 NN *n/a* Moz *all* Saf *all* Op 7 DOM 2
Read/Write

URL of the background image of the element. If you also set a backgroundColor, the image overlays the color. Transparent pixels of the image allow the color to show through.

Example
document.getElementById("navbar").style.backgroundImage =
"url(images/navVisited.jpg)";

Value   Any complete or relative URL to an image file in CSS URL format: url(*filePath*).

Default   None.

backgroundPosition

IE 4 NN *n/a* Moz *all* Saf *all* Op 7 DOM 2
Read/Write

Indicates the top and left location of a background image relative to the element's content region (plus padding). Positions may be specified as length values (with numbers and units or percentages) or according to a combination of constants top, right, bottom, left, and center. The property has no effect on a background images set to repeat along both axes. Available as a property of the IE style and runtimeStyle objects only.

Example
document.getElementById("div3").style.backgroundPosition = "20% 50%";

Value

A string containing one value (to be applied to both horizontal and vertical axes) or a space-delimited pair of values. Values may be explicit length values (with units, as in 30px 5px), percentages (e.g., 50% 50%) or position constants that have explicit meanings for their combinations.

Constant value pair	Percentage equivalents	Constant value pair	Percentage equivalents
top left	0% 0%	center center	50% 50%
left top	0% 0%	right	100% 50%
top	50% 0%	right center	100% 50%
top center	50% 0%	center right	100% 50%
center top	50% 0%	bottom left	0% 100%
right top	100% 0%	left bottom	0% 100%
top right	100% 0%	bottom	50% 100%
left	0% 50%	bottom center	50% 100%
left center	0% 50%	center bottom	50% 100%
center left	0% 50%	bottom right	100% 100%
center	50% 50%	right bottom	100% 100%

Percentage values are interpolated logically. For example, a value of 0% means that the image abuts the left or top edge of the element block; a value of 50% centers the image vertically or horizontally; a value of 100% places the image flush right or bottom..

Default   0% 0%

backgroundPositionX, backgroundPositionY

IE 4 NN n/a Moz n/a Saf 1.3/2 Op n/a DOM n/a

Read/Write

Indicate the top and left locations of the background image relative to the element's content region (plus padding). Useful if you wish to adjust the background image along only one axis while not disturbing the other.

Example

```
document.getElementById("div3").style.backgroundPositionX = "20px";
document.getElementById("table2").style.backgroundPositionY = "10px;"
```

Value

You should be able to specify percentage values, which are the percentage of the block-level element's box width and height (respectively) at which point the image (or repeated images) begins. You are safest with pixel values. None of the allowed constants except top and left are recognized.

Default   0

backgroundRepeat

IE 4   NN *n/a*   Moz *all*   Saf *all*   Op 7   DOM 2

Read/Write

Specifies whether a background image (specified with the backgroundImage property) should repeat and, if so, along which axes. You can use repeating background images to create horizontal and vertical bands with some settings.

Example
```
document.getElementById("div3").style.backgroundRepeat = "repeat-y";
```

Value
With a string setting of no-repeat, one instance of the image appears in the location within the element established by the backgroundPosition property (default is top-left corner). Normal repeats are performed along both axes, but you can have the image repeat down a single column (repeat-y) or across a single row (repeat-x). To reestablish the default, assign the value repeat.

Default   repeat

behavior

IE 5(Win)   NN *n/a*   Moz *n/a*   Saf *n/a*   Op *n/a*   DOM *n/a*

Read/Write

Controls whether an IE Windows external behavior is assigned to the element.

Example
```
document.getElementById("div3").style.behavior = "url(#default#userData)";
```

Value   CSS-formatted URL value, with the actual URL pointing to an external . htc file, ID of an object element that loads a behavior ActiveX control into the page, or one of the built-in default behaviors (in the format url(#default#*behaviorName*)).

Default   None.

blockDirection

IE 5(Win)   NN *n/a*   Moz *n/a*   Saf *n/a*   Op *n/a*   DOM *n/a*

Read-only

Returns the writing script direction of the current element. Available as a property of the IE currentStyle object only.

Example
```
if (document.getElementById("myDIV").style.blockDirection = "rtl") {
    // process right-to-left text
}
```

Value   String constant values: ltr | rtl.

Default   ltr

border

Read/Write

Provides a shorthand property for getting or setting the borderColor, borderStyle, and/or borderWidth properties of all four borders around an element in one statement. You must specify a border style (see borderStyle) for changes of this property to affect the display of the element's border (a missing style is interpreted as no style, ergo no border). Numerous other properties allow you to set the width, style, and color of individual edges or groups of edges if you don't want all four edges to be the same. Only those component settings explicitly made in the element's tag attributes are reflected in the property, but you may assign components not part of the original tag. Available in IE as a property of the style and runtimeStyle objects only.

Example document.getElementById("announce").style.border = "inset red 4px";

Value Space-delimited string. For the borderStyle and borderWidth component values, see the respective properties in this chapter. For details on the borderColor value, see the section about CSS colors at the beginning of Chapter 4.

Default None.

borderBottom, borderLeft, borderRight, borderTop

Read/Write

These are shorthand properties for getting or setting the borderColor, borderStyle, and/or borderWidth properties for a single edge of an element in one statement. You must specify a border style (see borderStyle) for changes of these properties to affect the display of the element's border (a missing style is interpreted as no style, ergo no border along the specified edge). If you want all four edges to be the same, see the border attribute. Only those component settings explicitly made in the element's tag attributes are reflected in the property, but you may assign components not part of the original tag. Available in IE as properties of the style and runtimeStyle objects only.

Example
```
document.getElementById("announce").style.borderBottom = "inset red 4px";
document.getElementById("announce").style.borderLeft = "solid #20ff00 2px";
document.getElementById("announce").style.borderRight = "double 3px";
document.getElementById("announce").style.borderTop = "outset red 8px";
```

Value
Space-delimited string. For the border*Side*Style and border*Side*Width component values, see the respective properties in this chapter. For details on the border*Side*Color value formats, see the section about colors at the beginning of Chapter 4.

Default None.

borderBottomColor, borderLeftColor, borderRightColor, borderTopColor

IE 4   NN n/a   Moz all   Saf all   Op 7   DOM 2

Read/Write

Provide the color of a single border edge of an element. It is easy to abuse these properties by mixing colors that don't belong together. See also the borderColor attribute for setting the color for groups of edges in one statement.

Example

```
document.getElementById("announce").style.borderBottomColor = "red";
document.getElementById("announce").style.borderLeftColor = "#20ff00";
document.getElementById("announce").style.borderRightColor = "rgb(100, 75, 0)";
document.getElementById("announce").style.borderTopColor = "rgb(90%, 0%, 25%)";
```

Value   For details on CSS color values, see the section about colors at the beginning of Chapter 4.

Default   None.

borderBottomStyle, borderLeftStyle, borderRightStyle, borderTopStyle

IE 4   NN n/a   Moz all   Saf all   Op 7   DOM 2

Read/Write

Provide the line style of a single border edge of an element. The edge-specific attributes let you override a style that has been applied to all four edges with the border or borderStyle properties. See also the borderStyle property for setting the style for groups of edges in one statement.

Example

```
document.getElementById("announce").style.borderBottomStyle = "groove";
document.getElementById("announce").style.borderLeftStyle = "double";
document.getElementById("announce").style.borderRightStyle = "solid";
document.getElementById("announce").style.borderTopStyle = "inset";
```

Value

Style values are case-insensitive constants that are associated with specific ways of rendering border lines. The CSS style constants are: dashed, dotted, double, groove, hidden, inset, none, outset, ridge, and solid. Not all browsers recognize all the values in the CSS recommendation. See the border-style attribute listing in Chapter 4 for complete details on the available border styles.

Default   None.

Alphabetical DOM Reference

borderBottomWidth, borderLeftWidth, borderRightWidth, borderTopWidth
IE 4 NN n/a Moz all Saf all Op 7 DOM 2
Read/Write

Provide the width of a single border edge of an element. See also the borderWidth property for setting the width for groups of edges in one statement.

Example
```
document.getElementById("announce").style.borderBottomWidth= "thin";
document.getElementById("announce").style.borderLeftWidth = "thick";
document.getElementById("announce").style.borderRightWidth = "2px";
document.getElementById("announce").style.borderTopWidth = "0.5em";
```

Value   Three case-insensitive constants—thin | medium | thick—allow the browser to define how many pixels are used to show the border. For more precision, you can also assign a length value (see the discussion of CSS length values at the beginning of Chapter 4).

Default   medium

borderCollapse
IE 4 NN n/a Moz all Saf 1.3/2 Op 7 DOM 2
Read/Write

Controls which table border model the table element should observe.

Example
```
document.getElementById("myTable").style.borderCollapse = "separate";
```

Value   Two case-insensitive string constants: collapse | separate.

Default   separate

borderColor
IE 4 NN n/a Moz all Saf all Op 7 DOM 2
Read/Write

A shortcut attribute that lets you set multiple border edges to the same or different colors. You may supply one to four space-delimited color values. The number of values determines which sides receive the assigned colors.

Example
```
document.getElementById("announce").style.borderColor = "red";
document.getElementById("announce").style.borderColor = "red green";
document.getElementById("announce").style.borderColor =
"black rgb(100, 75, 0) #c0c0c0";
document.getElementById("announce").style.borderColor = "yellow green blue red";
```

Value
This property accepts one, two, three, or four color values as a string (including transparent as a color), depending on how many and which borders you want to set with

specific colors. See the `border-color` attribute listing in Chapter 4 for complete details on how the number of values affects this property.

Default   The object's color property (if it is set).

borderSpacing

IE 5   NN n/a   Moz all   Saf all   Op 7   DOM 2

Read/Write

Controls the spacing between table cells when the table is in (the default) separate borders mode, similar to a `table` object's `cellSpacing` property. IE 5 for the Macintosh doesn't respond to changes of this property's value. Available in IE as a property of the `style` object only.

Example   `document.getElementById("myTable").style.borderSpacing= "12px";`

Value   CSS length value as a string (see the discussion of CSS length values at the beginning of Chapter 4).

Default   None.

borderStyle

IE 4   NN n/a   Moz all   Saf all   Op 7   DOM 2

Read/Write

This is a shortcut property that lets you set multiple border edges to the same or different style. You may supply one to four space-delimited style values. The number of values determines which sides receive the assigned colors.

Example

```
document.getElementById("announce").style.borderStyle = "solid";
document.getElementById("announce").style.borderStyle = "solid double";
document.getElementById("announce").style.borderStyle =
"double groove groove double";
```

Value

Style values are case-insensitive constants that are associated with specific ways of rendering border lines. The CSS style constants are: `dashed`, `dotted`, `double`, `groove`, `hidden`, `inset`, `none`, `outset`, `ridge`, and `solid`. Not all browsers recognize all the values in the CSS recommendation. See the `border-style` attribute listing in Chapter 4 for complete details on the available border styles.

This property accepts one, two, three, or four style values as a string, depending on how many and which borders you want to set with specific styles. See the `border-style` attribute listing in Chapter 4 for complete details on how the number of values affects this property.

Default   none

borderWidth

Read/Write

This is a shortcut property that lets you set multiple border edges to the same or different width. You may supply one to four space-delimited width length values. The number of values determines which sides receive the assigned widths.

Example

```
document.getElementById("founderQuote").style.borderWidth = "3px 5px";
```

Value

Three case-insensitive constants—thin | medium | thick—allow the browser to define exactly how many pixels are used to show the border. For more precision, you can also assign a length value (see the discussion of length values at the beginning of Chapter 4).

This property accepts one, two, three, or four values, depending on how many and which borders you want to set with specific widths. See the border-width attribute listing in Chapter 4 for complete details on how the number of values affects this property.

Default   medium

bottom

Read/Write

For an absolute-positioned element, defines the position of the bottom edge of an element's box (content plus bottom padding, border, and/or margin) relative to the bottom edge of the next outermost block content container. IE for Windows and Netscape 6 do something unexpected when the positioned element uses the root positioning context. Instead of using the bottom of the document as the comparative edge, these browsers use the bottom of the browser window space (the viewport in CSS terminology). This means that the precise bottom position of the element varies with the user's browser window size. IE 5 for the Macintosh uses the document's bottom as the comparative edge. This discrepancy makes it more practical to use the bottom property for a positioned element nested inside another positioned element. When the element is relative-positioned, the offset is based on the bottom edge of the inline location where the element would normally appear in the content.

For numeric calculations on this value in IE, retrieve the pixelBottom or posBottom style properties, which return genuine numeric values.

Example   `document.getElementById("blockD2").style.bottom = "35px";`

Value   String consisting of a numeric value and length unit measure, a percentage, or auto.

Default   auto

captionSide

Controls the location of a caption element (nested inside a table element) relative to the table's box.

Example   `document.getElementById("myTable").style.captionSide = "bottom";`

Value   Case-insensitive string of any of the following constants: bottom | left | right | top. Some browsers may be limited to only the bottom and top values.

Default   top

clear

Defines whether the element allows itself to be displayed in the same horizontal band as a floating element. Typically, another element in the vicinity has its float style attribute set to left or right. To prevent the current element from being in the same band as the floating block, set the clear property to the same side (left or right). If you aren't sure where the potential overlap might occur, set the clear property to both. An element that has its clear property set to a value other than none is rendered at the beginning of the next available line below the floating element.

Example   `document.getElementById("myDiv").style.clear = "both";`

Value   Case-insensitive string of any of the following constants: both | left | none | right.

Default   none

clip

Defines a clipping region of a positionable element. The clipping region is the area of the element layer in which content is visible. Clipping may not work properly in Internet Explorer 4 for the Macintosh. Available in IE as a property of the style and runtimeStyle objects only.

Example

`document.getElementById("art2").style.clip = "rect(5px 100px 40px 0)";`

Value   Case-insensitive string of either the auto constant or the CSS clip attribute setting that specifies the shape (rect only for now) and the position of the four clip edges relative to the original element's top-left corner. When specifying lengths for each side of the clipping rectangle, observe the clockwise order of values: top, right, bottom, left. See the discussion about CSS length values at the beginning of Chapter 4. A value of auto sets the clipping region to the block that contains the content. In Internet Explorer, the width may extend to the width of the next outermost container (such as the body element).

Default   None.

clipBottom, clipLeft, clipRight, clipTop

IE *5(Win)* NN *n/a* Moz *n/a* Saf *n/a* Op *n/a* DOM *n/a*

Read-only

Return a clipping edge of a positionable element. Available in IE as a property of the currentStyle object only.

Example   var cl = document.getElementById("art2").style.clipLeft;

Value   Case-insensitive length string or auto constant. See the discussion about CSS length values at the beginning of Chapter 4.

Default   None.

color

IE *4* NN *n/a* Moz *all* Saf *all* Op *7* DOM *2*

Read/Write

Sets the foreground (text) color style sheet attribute of the element. For some graphically oriented elements, such as form controls, the color attribute may also be applied to element edges or other features. Such extracurricular behavior is browser specific and may not be the same across browsers.

Example   document.getElementById("specialDiv").style.color = "green";

Value   Case-insensitive CSS color specification (see the discussion at beginning of Chapter 4).

Default   black

content

IE *5(Mac)* NN *n/a* Moz *all* Saf *1.3/2* Op *7* DOM *2*

Read/Write

Defines extra content that is to be displayed before or after and element (in concert with the :before and :after pseudo-classes. Although the property is available for IE 5 Macintosh and Netscape 6, the values are empty strings and the rendered content (which appears in Netscape 6 only) does not change if you assign it a new value.

Value   See the discussion of the content CSS attribute in Chapter 4.

Default   None.

counterIncrement, counterReset

IE *5(Mac)* NN *n/a* Moz *1.8* Saf *n/a* Op *7* DOM *2*

Read/Write

These properties are placeholders for future implementations of automatic counter mechanisms specified in the CSS specification.

Value	See the discussion of the counterIncrement and counterReset CSS attributes in Chapter 4.
Default	None.

cssFloat

Controls the CSS float attribute for an element, allowing adjacent text content to wrap around block elements, such as images. Changing the value in IE 5 for Macintosh has no effect. The "css" prefix for this property name deflects potential conflicts with the float reserved JavaScript keyword.

Example	document.getElementById("myDiv").style.cssFloat = "right";
Value	String of an allowable constant value: left | right | none.
Default	none

cssText

Returns a string of the entire CSS style sheet rule applied to the element. If the rule included shorthand style attribute settings (such as border), browsers return modified versions according to their ideas of what the value means. If you set the style attribute of an element to style="border: groove red 3px", IE for Windows reports the cssText property for that element as:

```
BORDER-RIGHT: red 3px groove; BORDER-TOP: red 3px groove;
BORDER-LEFT: red 3px groove; BORDER-BOTTOM: red 3px groove
```

IE for Macintosh reports:

```
{BORDER-TOP: 3px groove red; BORDER-RIGHT: 3px groove red;
BORDER-BOTTOM: 3px groove red; BORDER-LEFT: 3px groove red}
```

And Mozilla reports:

```
border: 3px groove red;
```

Note how each browser manipulates the sequence of individual values. Even so, you can assign a shorthand value to the property and in any order you like. Available in IE as a property of the style and runtimeStyle objects only.

Example

```
document.getElementById("block3").style.cssText = "margin: 2px; font-size: 14pt";
```

Value	String value of semicolon-delimited style attributes.
Default	None.

cue, cueAfter, cueBefore

See azimuth.

cursor

Read/Write

Specifies the shape of the cursor when the screen pointer is atop the element. The precise look of cursors depends on the operating system. Before deploying a modified cursor, be sure you understand the standard ways that the various types of cursors are used within the browser and operating system. Users expect a cursor design to mean the same thing across all applications. Figure 4-3 in Chapter 4 offers a gallery of cursors for each of the cursor constant settings provided by Internet Explorer.

Setting this property affects the cursor only when it is atop the current element and does not set the cursor immediately on a global basis.

Example　　　`document.getElementById("hotStuff").style.cursor = "pointer";`

Value

Any one cursor constant as a string, as supported by various browsers and versions.

Cursor name	IE/Windows	IE/Mac	Mozilla	Safari	Opera
alias	n/a	n/a	n/a	n/a	n/a
all-scroll	6	n/a	1.8	n/a	n/a
auto	4	4	all	all	7
cell	n/a	n/a	1.8	n/a	n/a
col-resize	6	n/a	1.8	n/a	n/a
context-menu	n/a	n/a	1.8	n/a	n/a
copy	n/a	n/a	1.8	n/a	n/a
count-down	n/a	n/a	n/a	n/a	n/a
count-up	n/a	n/a	n/a	n/a	n/a
count-up-down	n/a	n/a	n/a	n/a	n/a
crosshair	4	4	all	all	7
default	4	4	all	all	7
e-resize	4	4	all	all	7
grab	n/a	n/a	<1	n/a	n/a
grabbing	n/a	n/a	<1	n/a	n/a
hand	4	4	n/a	all	7
help	4	4	all	all	7
move	4	4	all	all	7
n-resize	4	4	all	all	7
ne-resize	4	4	all	all	7
nesw-resize	n/a	n/a	1.8	n/a	n/a
no-drop	6	n/a	1.8	n/a	n/a
none	n/a	n/a	n/a	n/a	n/a
not-allowed	n/a	n/a	n/a	n/a	n/a

Cursor name	IE/Windows	IE/Mac	Mozilla	Safari	Opera
nw-resize	4	4	all	all	7
nwse-resize	n/a	n/a	1.8	n/a	n/a
pointer	4	4	all	all	7
progress	6	n/a	<1	n/a	9
row-resize	6	n/a	1.8	n/a	n/a
s-resize	4	4	all	all	7
se-resize	4	4	all	all	7
spinning	n/a	n/a	all	n/a	n/a
sw-resize	4	4	all	all	7
text	4	4	n/a	n/a	n/a
url(uri)	6	n/a	n/a	n/a	n/a
vertical-text	6	n/a	1.8	n/a	n/a
w-resize	4	4	all	all	7
wait	4	4	all	all	7

The IE 6 setting of an external URL requires an address of a cursor file of extension *.cur* or *.ani*.

Default   auto

direction

Read/Write

Returns the writing script direction of the current element. Intended primarily for elements inside documents with mixed writing script directions (e.g., French text intermingled among Arabic).

Example   `document.getElementById("term3").style.direction = "ltr";`

Value   String constant values: ltr | rtl.

Default   ltr

display

Read/Write

Controls the CSS box type used to render the element. The most common settings for body content dictate whether an element is rendered as a block or inline element. When set to none, the element is hidden, and surrounding content cinches up to fill the space. Some box types are specific to tables and lists.

Example

`document.getElementById("instructionDiv").style.display = "none";`

Value

Any one display type constant as a string, as supported by various browsers and versions.

Display type	IE/Win	IE/Mac	NN	Mozilla	Safari	Opera	CSS
block	5	4	4	all	all	7	2
compact	n/a	n/a	n/a	n/a	n/a	n/a	<2.1
inline	5	4	4	all	all	7	2
inline-block	5.5	n/a	n/a	n/a	n/a	n/a	<2.1
inline-table	n/a	5	n/a	n/a	all	7	2
list-item	5	5	n/a	all	all	7	2
marker	n/a	n/a	n/a	n/a	n/a	n/a	<2.1
none	4	4	4	all	all	7	2
run-in	n/a	5	n/a	n/a	n/a	7	2
table	n/a	5	n/a	all	all	7	2
table-caption	n/a	5	n/a	all	all	7	2
table-cell	n/a	5	n/a	all	all	7	2
table-column-group	n/a	5	n/a	n/a	n/a	n/a	2
table-footer-group	5.5	5	n/a	all	all	7	2
table-header-group	5	5	n/a	all	all	7	2
table-row	n/a	5	n/a	all	all	7	2
table-row-group	n/a	5	n/a	n/a	n/a	n/a	2

Default   Element-dependent.

elevation

See azimuth.

emptyCells   IE 5(Mac) NN n/a Moz all Saf 1.3/2 Op 8 DOM 2

Read/Write

When a table is set to render the separate cell box format (the default), and a border is established for td elements in that table, the emptyCells style property controls whether the table renders borders around cells that have no content.

Example   document.getElementById("myTable").style.emptyCells = "hide";

Value   String of allowable constant values: hide | show.

Default   show

filter

Sets the visual, reveal, or blend filter used to display or change content of an element. A visual filter can be applied to an element to produce effects such as content flipping, glow, drop shadow, and many others. A reveal filter is applied to an element when its visibility changes. The value of the reveal filter determines what visual effect is to be applied to the transition from hidden to shown (or vice versa). This includes effects such as wipes, blinds, and barn doors. A blend filter sets the speed at which a transition between states occurs. Although the `filter` property is present in Internet Explorer for Macintosh, it does not operate there.

Example   `document.getElementById("fancy").style.filter= "dropshadow( )";`

Value

Each filter property may have more than one space-delimited filter type associated with it. Each filter type is followed by a pair of parentheses, which may convey parameters about the behavior of the filter for the current element. A parameter generally consists of a name/value pair, with assignment performed by the equals symbol. Note that Microsoft instituted an entirely new filter syntax starting with IE 5.5 for Windows. The new syntax runs in parallel with the old (for now). See the `filter` style sheet attribute listing in Chapter 4 for details on filter settings and parameters.

Default   None.

font

This is a shorthand property that lets you set one or more font-related properties—`fontFamily`, `fontSize`, `lineHeight` (which must be preceded by a / symbol in this property), `fontStyle`, `fontVariant`, and `fontWeight`—with one assignment statement. A space-delimited list of values (in any sequence) is applied to the specific font properties for which the value is a valid type. Or, you can short-circuit these individual settings by choosing one of the default (operating-system-dependent) system fonts: `caption` | `icon` | `menu` | `message-box` | `small-caption` | `status-bar`.

Example

`document.getElementById("subhead").style.font = "bolder small-caps 16pt";`

Value   For syntax and examples of value types for font-related properties, see the respective property listing.

Default   None.

fontFamily

Provides a prioritized list of font families to be used to render the object's content. One or more font family names may be included in a comma-delimited list of property values. If a font family name consists of multiple words, the family name must be inside a set of inner quotes. Available in IE as a property of the style and runtimeStyle objects only, but the individual font properties are available in currentStyle, as well.

Example

```
document.getElementById("subhead").style.fontFamily =
    "'Century Schoolbook', Times, serif";
```

Value	Any number of font family names, comma delimited. Multiword family names must be quoted. Recognized generic family names are: serif | sans-serif | cursive | fantasy | monospace.
Default	Browser default.

fontSize

Indicates the font size of the element. The font size can be set in several ways. A collection of constants (xx-small, x-small, small, medium, large, x-large, xx-large) defines what are known as *absolute* sizes. In truth, these are absolute only in a single browser in a single operating system, since the reference point for these sizes varies with browser and operating system (analogous to the old HTML font sizes of 1 through 7). But they do let the author have confidence that one element set to large is rendered larger than medium.

Another collection of constants (larger, smaller) is known as relative sizes. Because the font-size style attribute is inherited from the parent element, these relative sizes are applied to the parent element to determine the font size of the current element. It is up to the browser to determine exactly how much larger or smaller the font size is, and a lot depends on how the parent element's font size is set. If it is set with one of the absolute sizes (large, for example), a child's font size of larger means the font is rendered in the browser's x-large size. The increments are not as clear-cut when the parent font size is set with a length or percentage.

If you elect to use a length value for the fontSize property, you will achieve greater consistency across operating systems if units such as pixels (px) or ems (em), instead of points (pt). Em units are calculated with respect to the size of the parent element's font size. Finally, you can set fontSize to a percentage, which is calculated based on the size of the parent element's font size.

Example   `document.getElementById("teeny").style.fontSize = "x-small";`

Value

Case-insensitive string values from any of the following categories. For an absolute size, one of the following constants: xx-small \| x-small \| small \| medium \| large \| x-large \| xx-large. For a relative size, one of the following constants: larger \| smaller. For a length, see the discussion about CSS length values at the beginning of Chapter 4. For a percentage, the percentage value and the % symbol.

Default   Parent element's font size.

fontSizeAdjust

Provides the font aspect value, usually of the first font family in a font-family attribute sequence, forcing alternative font families to calculate their rendered font size to closely match that of the primary font family. Although this property is a member of the style object in IE 5/Mac and Mozilla, neither the style attribute nor scripted changes to it affect the font display.

Example	`document.getElementById("myDIV").style.fontSizeAdjust = "0.56";`
Value	Numeric aspect value as a quoted string, or none.
Default	none

fontStretch

Provides the character spacing for the element, based on available spacing widths available for the current font family. Although this property is a member of the style object in IE 5/Mac and Mozilla, neither the style attribute nor scripted changes to it affect the font display.

Example

`document.getElementById("myDIV").style.fontStretch= "ultra-condensed";`

Value	String of allowable constant values: normal | wider | narrower | ultra-condensed | extra-condensed | condensed | semi-condensed | semi-expanded | expanded | extra-expanded | ultra-expanded, or none.
Default	none

fontStyle

Specifies whether the element is rendered in a normal (roman), italic, or oblique font style. If the fontFamily includes font faces labeled Italic and/or Oblique, the setting of the fontStyle attribute summons those particular font faces from the browser's system. But if the specialized font faces are not available in the system, the normal font face is usually algorithmically slanted to look italic. Output sent to a printer with such font settings relies on the quality of arbitration between the client computer and printer to render an electronically generated italic font style. Personal computer software typically includes other kinds of font rendering under the heading of "Style." See fontVariant and fontWeight for other kinds of font "styles."

Example	`document.getElementById("emphasis").style.fontStyle = "italic";`
Value	One the following string constant values: normal | italic | oblique.
Default	normal

fontVariant

IE 4   NN n/a   Moz all   Saf 1.3/2   Op 7   DOM 2
Read/Write

Specifies whether the element should be rendered in all uppercase letters in such a way that lowercase letters of the source code are rendered in smaller uppercase letters. If a font family contains a small caps variant, the browser should use it automatically. More likely, however, the browser calculates a smaller size for the uppercase letters that take the place of source code lowercase letters. In practice, Internet Explorer 4 renders the entire source code content as uppercase letters of the same size as the parent element's font, regardless of the case of the source code. Later IE versions, Mozilla, Safari, and Opera use two different uppercase sizes.

Example

```
document.getElementById("emphasis").style.fontVariant = "small-caps";
```

Value	Any of the following constant values as strings: normal | small-caps.
Default	normal

fontWeight

IE 4   NN n/a   Moz all   Saf all   Op 7   DOM 2
Read/Write

Sets the weight (boldness) of the element's font. CSS provides a weight rating scheme that is more granular than most browsers render on the screen, but the finely tuned weights may come into play when the content is sent to a printer. The scale is a numeric rating from 100 to 900 at 100-unit increments. Therefore, a fontWeight of 100 would be the least bold that would be displayed, while 900 would be the boldest. A setting of normal (the default weight for any font) is equivalent to a fontWeight value of 400; the standard bold setting is equivalent to 700. Other settings (bolder and lighter) let you specify a weight relative to the parent element's weight.

Example	document.getElementById("hotStuff").style.fontWeight = "bold";
Value	Any of the following constant values: bold | bolder | lighter | normal | 100 | 200 | 300 | 400 | 500 | 600 | 700 | 800 | 900.
Default	normal

height, width

IE 4   NN n/a   Moz all   Saf all   Op 7   DOM 2
Read/Write

Indicate the height and width (and their units) of the element. Because the values are strings containing the assigned units, you cannot use these properties for calculation. Grab copies of the numbers by using parseFloat( ) on the values; or for IE, use pixelHeight, pixelWidth, posHeight, and posWidth properties. Changes to these properties may not be visible unless the element has its position style attribute set.

In IE 6 and 7 standards compatibility mode (where document.compatType == "CSS1Compat"), these dimensions apply to only the content portion of an element, irrespective of borders, padding, or margins. For example, if a positioned element that is equipped with padding and borders must be sized to a precise rectangular size, you must subtract the thicknesses of the padding and borders from the height and width values so that the overall element is the desired size.

Example	`document.getElementById("viewArea").style.height = "450px";`
Value	String consisting of a numeric value and length measure or percentage.
Default	None.

imeMode

IE *5(Win)* NN *n/a* Moz *n/a* Saf *n/a* Op *n/a* DOM *n/a*

Read/Write

Controls the presence of the Input Method Editor in IE for Windows for browser and system versions that support languages such as Chinese, Japanese, and Korean.

Example	`document.getElementById("nameEntry").style.imeMode = "active";`
Value	String of allowable constant values: `active` | `auto` | `disabled` | `inactive`.
Default	`auto`

layoutFlow

IE *5(Win)* NN *n/a* Moz *n/a* Saf *n/a* Op *n/a* DOM *n/a*

Read/Write

Intended primarily for languages that display characters in vertical sentences, controls the progression of content. Replaced starting with IE 5.5 for Windows by the `writingMode` property.

| **Value** | One of the constant values (as a string): `horizontal` \| `vertical-ideographic`. |
| **Default** | `horizontal` |

layoutGrid

IE *5(Win)* NN *n/a* Moz *n/a* Saf *n/a* Op *n/a* DOM *n/a*

Read/Write

This is a shorthand property that lets you set one or more layout grid properties (`layoutGridChar`, `layoutGridLine`, `layoutGridMode`, and `layoutGridType`) with one assignment statement. These attributes are used primarily with Asian language content.

Example

`document.getElementById("subhead").style.layoutGrid = "2em strict";`

| **Value** | For syntax and examples of value types for layoutGrid-related properties, see the respective property listing. |
| **Default** | None. |

Alphabetical DOM Reference

layoutGridChar

IE 5(Win)   NN n/a   Moz n/a   Saf n/a   Op n/a   DOM n/a

Read/Write

Dictates the size of Asian language character grid for block-level elements.

Example   `document.getElementById("subhead").style.layoutGrid Char= "auto";`

Value   String consisting of an explicit CSS length value or auto or none.

Default   `none`

layoutGridLine

IE 5(Win)   NN n/a   Moz n/a   Saf n/a   Op n/a   DOM n/a

Read/Write

Dictates the line height of Asian language character grid for block-level elements.

Example

`document.getElementById("subhead").style.layoutGrid Line= "120%";`

Value   String consisting of an explicit CSS length value or auto or none.

Default   `none`

layoutGridMode

IE 5(Win)   NN n/a   Moz n/a   Saf n/a   Op n/a   DOM n/a

Read/Write

Specifies whether the Asian language character grid should be one- or two-dimensional.

Example

`document.getElementById("subhead").style.layoutGrid Mode= "both";`

Value   String constant values: both | char (for inline elements) | line (for block-level elements) | none.

Default   `both`

layoutGridType

IE 5(Win)   NN n/a   Moz n/a   Saf n/a   Op n/a   DOM n/a

Read/Write

Controls how the layout grid responds to characters of varying width.

Example

`document.getElementById("subhead").style.layoutGrid Type = "strict";`

Value   String constant values: fixed | loose | strict.

Default   `loose`

left

For positionable elements, defines the position of the left edge of an element's box (content plus left padding, border, and/or margin) relative to the left edge of the next outermost block content container. When the element is relative-positioned, the offset is based on the left edge of the inline location of where the element would normally appear in the content.

For calculations on this value, use parseFloat( ) on the returned value; or, in IE, retrieve the pixelLeft or posLeft properties, which return genuine numeric values.

Example   document.getElementById("blockD2").style.left = "45px";

Value   String consisting of a numeric value and length unit measure, a percentage, or auto.

Default   auto

length

Officially a property of the W3C DOM CSSStyleDeclaration object, this property returns the number of individual CSS properties contained by the object.

Value   Integer.

Default   Varies with browser implementation.

letterSpacing

Specifies the spacing between characters within an element. Browsers normally define the character spacing based on font definitions and operating system font rendering. Assigning a negative value tightens the spacing, but be sure to test the effect on the selected font for readability on different operating systems.

Example   document.body.style.letterSpacing = "1.1em";

Value   A string of a length value (with unit of measure) or normal. The best results are achieved by using units that are based on the rendered font size (em and ex). A setting of normal is how the browser sets the letters without any intervention.

Default   normal

lineBreak

Controls line breaking rules for Japanese text.

Example   document.body.style.lineBreak = "strict";

Alphabetical DOM Reference

Value	String constant values: normal	strict.
Default	normal

lineHeight

Indicates the height of the inline box (the box holding one physical line of content). See the line-height style attribute in Chapter 4 for details on browser quirks and inheritance traits of different types of values.

Example	document.getElementById("tight").style.lineHeight = "1.1em";
Value	A string of a length value (with unit of measure) or normal.
Default	normal

listStyle

This is a shorthand property for setting up to three list-style properties in one assignment statement. Whichever attributes you don't explicitly set with this attribute assume their default values. These properties define display characteristics for the markers automatically rendered for list items inside ol and ul elements. This is available in IE as a property of the style and runtimeStyle objects only, but individual properties are properties of currentStyle, as well.

Example

```
document.getElementById("itemList").style.listStyle = "square outside none";
```

Value	See the individual attribute entries for listStyleType, listStylePosition, and listStyleImage for details on acceptable values for each. You may include one, two, or all three values in the list-style attribute setting in any order you wish.
Default	None.

listStyleImage

Provides the URL for an image that is to be used as the marker for a list item. Because this attribute can be inherited, a setting (including none) for an individual list item can override the same attribute or property setting in its parent.

Example

```
document.getElementById("itemList").style.listStyleImage =
"url(images/3DBullet.gif)";
```

Value

Use none (as a string) to override an image assigned to a parent element. Otherwise, supply any valid full or relative URL (in the CSS URL format) to an image file with a MIME type that is readable by the browser.

Default   none

listStylePosition
IE 4   NN n/a   Moz all   Saf all   Op 7   DOM 2

Read/Write

Specifies whether the marker is inside or outside (outdented) the box containing the list item's content. When listStylePosition is set to inside and the content is text, the marker appears to be part of the text block. In this case, the alignment (indent) of the list item is the same as normal, but without the outdented marker.

Example
```
document.getElementById("itemList").style.listStylePosition = "inside";
```

Value   Either constant value as a string: inside | outside.

Default   outside

listStyleType
IE 4   NN n/a   Moz all   Saf all   Op 7   DOM 2

Read/Write

Specifies the kind of item marker to be displayed with each item. This attribute is applied only if listStyleImage is none (or not specified). The constant values available for this attribute are divided into two categories. One set is used with ul elements to present a filled disc, an empty circle, or a filled square. The other set is for ol elements, which has list items that can be marked in sequences of arabic numerals, roman numerals (uppercase or lowercase), letters of the alphabet (uppercase or lowercase), and some other character sequences of other languages if the browser and operating system supports those languages.

Example   `document.getElementById("itemList").style.listStyleType = "circle";`

Value

One constant value as a string that is relevant to the type of list container. For ul: circle | disc | square. For ol: decimal | decimal-leading-zero | lower-roman | upper-roman | lower-greek | lower-alpha | lower-latin | upper-alpha | upper-latin | hebrew | armenian | georgian | cjk-ideographic | hiragana | katakana | hiragana-iroha | katakana-iroha. Commonly supported ol element sequences are treated as shown in the following table.

Type	Example
decimal	1, 2, 3, …
decimal-leading-zero	01, 02, 03, …
lower-alpha	a, b, c, …

Type	Example
lower-greek	α, β, γ, ...
lower-roman	i, ii, iii, ...
upper-alpha	A, B, C, ...
upper-roman	I, II, III, ...

Default disc (for ul); decimal (for ol).

margin

IE 4 NN *n/a* Moz *all* Saf *all* Op 7 DOM 2

Read/Write

This is a shortcut property that can set the margin widths of up to four edges of an element with one statement. A margin is space that extends beyond the border of an element to provide extra empty space between adjacent or nested elements, especially those that have border attributes set. You may supply one to four space-delimited margin values. The number of space-delimited values determines which sides receive the assigned margins.

Example

```
document.getElementById("logoWrapper").style.margin = "5px 8px";
```

Value

This property accepts one, two, three, or four space-delimited values inside one string, depending on how many and which margins you want to set. See the margin attribute listing in Chapter 4 for complete details on how the number of values affects this property. Values for the margins can be lengths, percentages of the next outermost element size, or the auto constant.

Default 0

marginBottom, marginLeft, marginRight, marginTop

IE 4 NN *n/a* Moz *all* Saf *all* Op 7 DOM 2

Read/Write

All four properties set the width of a single margin edge of an element. A margin is space that extends beyond the element's border and is not calculated as part of the element's width or height.

Example

```
document.getElementById("logoWrapper").style.marginTop = "5px";
document.getElementById("navPanel").style.marginLeft = "10%";
```

Value Values for margin widths can be length values, percentages of the next outermost element size, or the auto constant.

Default 0

markerOffset

Read/Write

Controls the space between list item markers (which occupy their own box in the CSS box model) and the box that contains the list item text. Although the property is available for Mozilla and Opera, the value is an empty string and the rendered content does not change if you assign it a new value. Additionally, the corresponding CSS property has been deleted from CSS 2.1.

Value   A string of a length value (with unit of measure) or auto.

Default   None.

marks

Read/Write

Sets crop mark type for an @page rule. Although the property is available for IE 5 Macintosh, Mozilla, and Opera, the values are empty strings and the rendered content does not change if you assign it a new value.

Value

Case-insensitive string of any of the following constants: crop | cross | none.

Default   none

maxHeight, maxWidth, minHeight, minWidth

Read/Write

Define loose heights and widths for an element so that, for "max" properties, an element is allowed to grow no bigger in the designated dimension, or, for "min" properties, an element can expand in the designated dimension to accommodate more than expected content or rendering situations. IE 6 supports only the minHeight property, and it can be used only for tr, th, and td elements. IE 7, however, implements all properties correctly when running in CSS compatibility mode (i.e., with a modern DOCTYPE declaration).

Value   CSS length value (see Chapter 4) as a string.

Default   None.

MozBorderRadius

Read/Write

A shortcut property that lets you set the radius of one or more border corners.

Value   One to four length values as a string. See -moz-border-radius in Chapter 4 for value details.

Default   0

MozBorderRadiusBottomleft, MozBorderRadiusBottomright, MozBorderRadiusTopleft, MozBorderRadiusTopright

IE *n/a*   NN *n/a*   Moz *all*   Saf *n/a*   Op *n/a*   DOM *n/a*

Read/Write

Each property controls the radius of one border corner.

Value   Length value as a string. See -moz-border-radius in Chapter 4 for value details.

Default   0

MozOpacity

IE *n/a*   NN *n/a*   Moz *all*   Saf *n/a*   Op *n/a*   DOM *n/a*

Read/Write

Defines the level of opacity of the element. The lower the value, the more transparent the element becomes. This is the proprietary Mozilla version of the proprietary Microsoft opaque filter, and has been superceded in more recent versions by the genuine opacity property.

Example   document.getElementById("menuWrapper").style.MozOpacity = "40%";

Value   Numeric string value between 0 and 1.

Default   1 (completely opaque)

opacity

IE *n/a*   NN *n/a*   Moz *1.7.2*   Saf *1.2*   Op *9*   DOM *n/a*

Read/Write

Defines the level of opacity of the element. The lower the value, the more transparent the element becomes.

Example   document.getElementById("menuWrapper").style.MozOpacity = "40%";

Value   Numeric string value between 0 and 1.

Default   1 (completely opaque)

orphans, widows

IE *5(Mac)*   NN *n/a*   Moz *all*   Saf *n/a*   Op *7*   DOM *2*

Read/Write

For a block-level element's content that spreads across page boxes, specify the minimum number of lines of the element that must appear at the bottom of the page (orphans) or at the top of the next page (widows). Although these properties are members of the style object in IE 5/Mac, Mozilla, and Opera, neither the style attribute nor scripted changes to it affect the printed output.

Example   document.getElementById("sec23").style.orphans = "3";

| **Value** | Integer as a string. |
| **Default** | None. |

outline

This is a shorthand property for getting or setting the outlineColor, outlineStyle, and/or outlineWidth properties of an outline around an element in one statement. You must specify an outline style (see outlineStyle) for changes of this property to affect the display. An outline is like a border, but overlays the element without occupying any content space or affecting the element's dimensions.

Example	document.getElementById("announce").style.outline = "solid blue 4px";
Value	Space-delimited string. For the outlineStyle and outlineWidth component values, see the respective properties in this chapter. For details on the outlineColor value, see the section about CSS colors at the beginning of Chapter 4.
Default	None.

outlineColor

Controls the color of an outline.

Example
document.getElementById("announce").style.outlineColor = "rgb(100, 75, 0)";

| **Value** | CSS color value or constant invert. For details on CSS color values, see the section about colors at the beginning of Chapter 4. |
| **Default** | invert |

outlineOffset

Controls the distance beyond the element's border (equally in each direction) where the outline is drawn..

Example	document.getElementById("announce").style.outlineOffset = "5px";
Value	A CSS length value. One value controls all sides of the outline.
Default	0

Alphabetical DOM
Reference

outlineStyle

Read/Write

Controls the line type of an outline.

Example	`document.getElementById("announce").style.outlineStyle = "solid";`
Value	Style values are case-insensitive constants that are associated with specific ways of rendering outline (and border) lines. The CSS style constants are: dashed, dotted, double, groove, hidden, inset, none, outset, ridge, and solid.
Default	none

outlineWidth

Read/Write

Controls the thickness of the outline lines.

Example	`document.getElementById("announce").style.outlineWidth = "2px";`
Value	Three case-insensitive constants—thin | medium | thick—allow the browser to define exactly how many pixels are used to show the border. For more precision, you can also assign a length value (see the discussion of CSS length values at the beginning of Chapter 4).
Default	medium

overflow

Read/Write

Specifies how a positioned element should treat content that extends beyond the boundaries established in the style sheet rule. See the discussion of the overflow style sheet attribute in Chapter 4 for details.

Example	`document.getElementById("myDiv").style.overflow = "scroll";`
Value	Any of the following constants as a string: auto | hidden | scroll | visible.
Default	visible

overflowX, overflowY

Read/Write

Specify how a positioned element should treat content that extends beyond the horizontal (overflowX) or vertical (overflowY) boundaries established in the style sheet rule.

Example	`document.getElementById("myDiv").style.overflow X= "scroll";`
Value	Any of the following constants as a string: auto | hidden | scroll | visible.

Default   visible

padding

IE *4* NN *n/a* Moz *all* Saf *all* Op *7* DOM *2*

Read/Write

This is a shortcut property that can set the padding widths of up to four edges of an element with one statement. Padding is space that extends around the content box of an element up to but not including any border that may be specified for the element. Padding picks up the background image or color of its element. As you add padding to an element, you increase the size of the visible rectangle of the element without affecting the content block size. You may supply one to four space-delimited padding values. The number of values determines which sides receive the assigned padding.

Example   `document.getElementById("logoWrapper").style.padding = "3px 5px";`

Value

This property accepts one, two, three, or four space-delimited values inside one string, depending on how many and which edges you want to pad. See the `padding` attribute listing in Chapter 4 for complete details on how the number of values affects this property. Values for padding widths can be lengths, percentages of the next outermost element size, or the auto constant.

Default   0

paddingBottom, paddingLeft, paddingRight, paddingTop

IE *4* NN *n/a* Moz *all* Saf *all* Op *7* DOM *2*

Read/Write

All four properties set the width of a single padding edge of an element. Padding is space that extends between the element's border and content box. Padding is not calculated as part of the element's width or height.

Example

```
document.getElementById("logoWrapper").style.paddingTop = "3px";
document.getElementById("navPanel").style.paddingLeft = "10%";
```

Value   Values for padding widths can be length values, percentages of the next outermost element size, or the auto constant.

Default   0

page

IE *5(Mac)* NN *n/a* Moz *all* Saf *n/a* Op *7* DOM *2*

Read/Write

Points to the name of an existing @page rule (when the rule contains an identifier, such as @page figures {size: landscape}) in order to apply that rule to the current block-level element. Although this property is a member of the style object in IE 5/Mac, Mozilla, and Opera, neither the style attribute nor scripted changes to it affect the printed output.

Alphabetical DOM
Reference

Value   String identifier.

Default   None.

pageBreakAfter, pageBreakBefore   IE 4 NN n/a Moz 1.0.1 Saf 1.3/2 Op 7 DOM 2

Read/Write

Define how content should treat a page break around an element when the document is sent to a printer. Page breaks are not rendered in the visual browser as they may be in word processing programs; on screen, long content flows in one continuous scroll on the screen. Also see the extensive discussion of page breaks in the listing for the page-break-after and page-break-before style attributes in Chapter 4.

Example
```
document.getElementById("hardBR").style.pageBreakAfter = "always";
document.getElementById("navPanel").style.paddingLeft = "10%";
```

Value   All supporting browsers recognize four constant values (as strings): always | auto | left | right. Additionally, IE for Windows supports an empty string, which has the same effect as the W3C CSS avoid constant.

Default   auto

pageBreakInside   IE 5(Mac) NN n/a Moz all Saf n/a Op 7 DOM 2

Read/Write

Defines whether the element allows itself to be split across printed pages. Although this property is a member of the style object in IE 5/Mac, Mozilla, and Opera, neither the style attribute nor scripted changes to it affect the printed output.

Value   A constant value (as a string): auto | avoid.

Default   auto

parentRule   IE n/a NN n/a Moz all Saf 1.2 Op 7 DOM 2

Read-only

Officially a property of the W3C DOM CSSStyleDeclaration object, this property returns a reference to the styleSheet object that is the parent of the current style sheet. This occurs only in nested situation, such as when a style rule is contained in a construction such as an @media block.

Value   Reference to a styleSheet object.

Default   None.

pause, pauseAfter, pauseBefore, pitch, pitchRange

See azimuth.

pixelBottom, pixelLeft, pixelRight, pixelTop

For positionable elements, these properties define the pixel position of the edges of an element's box (content plus padding, border, and/or margin) relative to the corresponding edges of the next outermost block content container. When the element is relative-positioned, the measure is based on the edges of the inline location of where the element would normally appear in the content. Use these properties for calculation (including path animation) instead of the bottom, left, right, and top properties, which store their values as strings with the unit names. Available as a property of the IE style and runtimeStyle objects only.

Example   `document.getElementById("myDIV").style.pixelLeft++;`

Value   Integer.

Default   None.

pixelHeight, pixelWidth

Specify the height and width of the element in pixels. Use these properties for calculation instead of properties such as height and width, which return strings including units. Changes to these properties may not be visible unless the element has its position style attribute set. Available as a property of the IE style and runtimeStyle objects only.

Example
`var midWidth = document.getElementById("myDIV").style.pixelWidth/2;`

Value   Integer

Default   None.

playDuring

See azimuth.

posBottom, posLeft, posRight, posTop

For positionable elements, these properties define the position of the edges of an element's box (content plus padding, border, and/or margin) relative to the corresponding edges of the next outermost block content container. When the element is relative-positioned, the measure is based on the edges of the inline location where the element would normally appear in the content. Most importantly, these properties' values are numeric and in the unit of measure set in the CSS bottom, left, right, or top attribute. Use these properties for calculation (including path animation) instead of the bottom, left, right, and top properties, which store their values as strings with the unit names. All math is in the specified units. Also contrast these properties with the pixelBottom, pixelLeft, pixelRight, and pixelTop properties, which are integer values for pixel measures only. Available as a property of the IE style and runtimeStyle objects only.

Example
```
document.getElementById("myDIV").style.posLeft =
  document.getElementById("myDIV").style.posLeft + 1.5;
```

Value   Floating-point number.

Default   None.

posHeight, posWidth
IE 4 NN *n/a* Moz *n/a* Saf *n/a* Op 7 DOM *n/a*

Read/Write

Specify the numeric height and width of the element in the units set by the CSS positioning-related attributes. Use these properties for calculation instead of properties such as height and width, which return strings including units. All math is in the specified units. Also contrast these properties with the pixelHeight and pixelWidth properties, which are integer values for pixel measures only. Available as a property of the IE style and runtimeStyle objects only.

Example   document.getElementById("myDIV").style.posWidth = 10.5;

Value   Floating-point number.

Default   None.

position
IE 4 NN *n/a* Moz *all* Saf *all* Op 7 DOM 2

Read-only

For positionable elements, returns the value assigned to the style sheet position attribute. This property is actually read/write, but you cannot change a positioned element into a static one or vice-versa.

Example   var posType = document.getElementById("myDIV").style.position;

Value   String constant: absolute | fixed | relative | static. The fixed value is
                     not supported in IE for Windows through Version 6.

Default   None.

quotes
IE 5(Mac) NN *n/a* Moz *all* Saf *n/a* Op 7 DOM 2

Read/Write

Assigns pairs of characters to be used as quote marks (especially for the q element). See the quotes CSS property in Chapter 4 for implementation notes. Don't be surprised if attempts to write new values to this property are unsuccessful.

Value   A string consisting of two or four quoted strings (nested quotes). The
                     first pair provides characters for first-level quotes; the second pair
                     supplies characters to nested quotes.

Default   None.

richness

See azimuth.

right   IE 5   NN *n/a*   Moz *all*   Saf *all*   Op 7   DOM 2

For an absolute-positioned element, defines the position of the right edge of an element's box (content plus right padding, border, and/or margin) relative to the right edge of the next outermost block content container.

For numeric calculations on this value in IE, retrieve the `pixelRight` or `posRight` style properties, which return genuine numeric values.

Example   `document.getElementById("blockD2").style.right = "25px";`

Value   String consisting of a numeric value and length unit measure, a percentage, or auto.

Default   auto

rubyAlign   IE 5   NN *n/a*   Moz *n/a*   Saf *n/a*   Op *n/a*   DOM *n/a*

Controls alignment of content in a ruby element. Changes to this property affect IE for Windows only. Ruby-related styles are defined in CSS3.

Example   `document.getElementById("myRuby").style.rubyAlign = "center";`

Value   Case-insensitive string of any of the following constants: `auto` | `center` | `distribute-letter` | `distribute-space` | `left` | `line-edge` | `right`.

Default   auto

rubyOverhang   IE 5   NN *n/a*   Moz *n/a*   Saf *n/a*   Op *n/a*   DOM *n/a*

Controls text overhang characteristics of content in a ruby element. Changes to this property affect IE for Windows only. Ruby-related styles are defined in CSS3.

Example
`document.getElementById("myRuby").style.rubyOverhang="whitespace";`

Value   Case-insensitive string of any of the following constants: `auto` | `none` | `whitespace`.

Default   auto

rubyPosition

IE 5 NN *n/a* Moz *n/a* Saf *n/a* Op *n/a* DOM *n/a*

Read/Write

Controls whether ruby (rt element) text renders on the same line or above its related ruby base (rb element) text. Changes to this property affect IE for Windows only. Ruby-related styles are defined in CSS3.

Example   document.getElementById("myRuby").style.rubyPosition = "inline";

Value   Case-insensitive string of any of the following constants: above | inline.

Default   above

scrollbar3dLightColor, scrollbarArrowColor, scrollbarBaseColor, scrollbarDarkShadowColor, scrollbarFaceColor, scrollbarHighlightColor, scrollbarShadowColor, scrollbarTrackColor

IE 5.5 NN *n/a* Moz *n/a* Saf *n/a* Op *n/a* DOM *n/a*

Read/Write

Controls the colors for specific components of a scrollbar user interface element associated with an applet, body, div, embed, object, or textarea element. See the description of these CSS attributes in Chapter 4 for details about which component each property governs.

Example
document.getElementById("comments").style.scrollbarArrowColor = "rgb(100, 75, 0)";

Value   Case-insensitive CSS color specification (see discussion at beginning of Chapter 4).

Default   None.

size

IE *n/a* NN *n/a* Moz *all* Saf *n/a* Op 7 DOM 2

Read/Write

For a page context defined by an @page rule, this property controls the page size or orientation. Although the property is available for Mozilla and Opera, the value is an empty strings and the property has no influence over the page context.

Value   CSS length values (as a string) or case-insensitive string of any of the following constants: auto | landscape | portrait. For length values, a single value is applied to height and width; two space-delimited length values are applied to width and height, respectively.

Default   auto

speak, speakHeader, speakNumeral, speakPunctuation, speechRate, stress

See azimuth.

styleFloat

Specifies on which side of the containing box the element aligns so that other content wraps around the element. When the property is set to none, the element appears in its source code sequence, and at most one line of surrounding text content appears in the same horizontal band as the element. See the float style attribute in Chapter 4 for more details. IE 5 for Macintosh duplicates this property as cssFloat, the DOM 2 version.

Example	document.getElementById("myDIV").style.styleFloat = "right";
Value	One of the following constants (as a string): none | left | right.
Default	None.

tableLayout

Acts as a switch at load time to direct the browser to start rendering the table based on column widths set by the first row, or wait until the table data is loaded so that the browser can calculate optimum column widths based on cell contents. Changes to this property have no effect on a rendered table.

Example	document.getElementById("myTable").style.tableLayout = "fixed";
Value	One of the following constants (as a string): auto | fixed.
Default	auto

textAlign

Determines the horizontal alignment of text within an element's box.

Example	document.getElementById("myDIV").style.textAlign = "right";
Value	One of the four constants (as a string): center | justify | left | right.
Default	Depends on default language of the browser.

textAlignLast

Determines the horizontal alignment of the last line of text within an element's box. This style attribute may be helpful to obtain the desired look if you use some of the other proprietary text alignment style properties in IE 5.5.

Example

document.getElementById("myDIV").style.textAlignLast = "justify";

Value   One of the following constants (as a string): auto | center | justify | left | right.

Default   auto

textAutospace   IE 5(Win) NN n/a Moz n/a Saf n/a Op n/a DOM n/a
Read/Write

Controls the spacing between ideographic (typically Asian languages) and nonideographic characters.

Example
```
document.getElementById("myDIV").style.textAutospace = "ideograph-numeric";
```

Value   One of the following constants (as a string): ideograph-alpha | ideograph-numeric | ideograph-parenthesis | ideograph-space | none.

Default   none

textDecoration   IE 4 NN n/a Moz all Saf all Op 7 DOM 2
Read/Write

Specifies additions to the text content of the element in the form of underlines, strikethroughs, overlines, and (in Navigator and CSS) blinking. Browsers use this style attribute internally to assign by default underlines to a elements and strikethroughs to strike elements, so the default value varies with element type. You may specify more than one decoration style by supplying values in a space-delimited list. While browsers accept the (CSS optional) blink value, they (thankfully) do not cause the text to blink. Text decoration has an unusual parent-child relationship. Values are not inherited, but the effect of a decoration carries over to nested items in most cases. Therefore, unless otherwise overridden, an underlined p element underlines a nested b element within. Internet Explorer also includes Boolean properties for each decoration type.

Example
```
document.getElementById("emphasis").style.textDecoration = "underline";
```

Value   In addition to none, any of the following four constants (as a string): blink | line-through | overline | underline. Multiple values may be included in the string as a space-delimited list.

Default   Element and internal style sheet dependent.

textDecorationBlink, textDecorationLineThrough, textDecorationNone, textDecorationOverline, textDecorationUnderline
IE *4* NN *n/a* Moz *n/a* Saf *n/a* Op *n/a* DOM *n/a*

Read/Write

Specifies whether the specified text decoration feature is enabled for the element. Each of these properties corresponds to a value that can be assigned to the text-decoration style attribute in CSS (see Chapter 4). Internet Explorer does not blink text, so the textDecorationBlink property is ignored. Setting textDecorationNone to true sets all other related properties to false. Setting these properties on the Macintosh version of IE 4 does not alter the content. Use the textDecoration property instead—good practice all around.

Example
```
document.getElementById("emphasis").style.textDecorationLineThrough = "true";
```

Value   Boolean value: true | false.

Default   false

textIndent
IE *4* NN *n/a* Moz *all* Saf *all* Op *7* DOM *2*

Read/Write

Specifies the size of the indent at the first line of a block of inline text (such as a p element). Only the first line is affected by this setting. A negative value can be used to outdent the first line, but be sure the text does not run beyond the left edge of the browser window or frame.

Example
```
document.getElementById("firstGraph").style.textIndent = "0.5em";
```

Value   Positive or negative CSS length value (see Chapter 4) as a string.

Default   0px

textJustify
IE *5* NN *n/a* Moz *n/a* Saf *n/a* Op *n/a* DOM *n/a*

Read/Write

Specifies detailed character distribution techniques for any block-level element that has a text-align CSS attribute or a textAlign style property set to justify.

Example
```
document.getElementById("inset").style.textJustify = "distribute-center-last";
```

Value   One of the following constants (as a string): auto | distribute | distribute-all-lines | distribute-center-last | inter-cluster | inter-ideograph | inter-word | kashdia | newspaper. See the text-justify attribute in Chapter 4 for details on the meanings of these values.

Default   auto

textKashidaSpace

For Arabic text in a block-level element with a text alignment style that is set to justify, controls the ratio of kashida expansion to white space expansion.

Example
```
document.getElementById("inset").style.textKashidaSpace = "15%";
```

Value   Percentage value as a string.

Default   0%

textOverflow

Controls whether text content that overflows a fixed box should display an ellipsis (…) at the end of the line to indicate more text is available. The element should also have its overflow style attribute or property set to hidden.

Example
```
document.getElementById("textBox").style.textOverflow = "ellipsis";
```

Value   One of the allowable constant string value: clip | ellipsis.

Default   clip

textShadow

Controls the specifications for shadow effects on the element's text. Although this property is a member of the style object in IE 5/Mac, Mozilla, and Opera, neither the style attribute nor scripted changes to it affect the element's text display.

Value
A string consisting of one or more shadow specifications. Each shadow specification consists of space-delimited values for a color, a length for the offset to the right of the text, a length for the offset below the text, and an optional blur radius value. Multiple shadow specifications are comma-delimited or a value of none to turn off the shadow.

Default   none

textTransform

Controls the capitalization of the element's text. When a value other than none is assigned to this attribute, the cases of all letters in the source text are arranged by the style sheet, overriding the case of the source text characters.

Example
```
document.getElementById("heading").style.textTransform = "capitalize";
```

Value

A value of none allows the case of the source text to be rendered as is. Other available constant values (as strings) are: capitalize | lowercase | uppercase. A value of capitalize sets the first character of every word to uppercase. Values lowercase and uppercase render all characters of the element text in their respective cases.

Default   none

textUnderlinePosition
IE 5.5 NN n/a Moz n/a Saf n/a Op n/a DOM n/a
Read/Write

Controls whether an underline (i.e., an element with a text-decoration style set to underline) is rendered above or below the text.

Example
```
document.getElementById("heading").style.textUnderlinePosition = "above";
```

Value

IE 5.5 recognizes two constant values: above | below. IE 6 adds the values auto and auto-pos (which appear to do the same thing). The default value also changed between versions, from below to auto. In IE 6, the auto value underlines vertical Japanese text "above" (to the right) of the characters.

Default   none (IE 5.5); auto (IE 6).

top
IE 4 NN n/a Moz all Saf all Op 7 DOM 2
Read/Write

For positionable elements, defines the position of the top edge of an element's box (content plus top padding, border, and/or margin) relative to the top edge of the next outermost block content container. When the element is relative-positioned, the offset is based on the top edge of the inline location of where the element would normally appear in the content.

For calculations on this value, use parseFloat( ) on the returned value; or, in IE, retrieve the pixelTop or posTop properties, which return genuine numeric values.

Example   `document.getElementById("blockD2").style.top = "40px";`

Value   String consisting of a numeric value and length unit measure, a percentage, or auto.

Default   auto

Alphabetical DOM Reference

unicodeBidi

IE 5   NN n/a   Moz all   Saf all   Op 8   DOM 2
Read/Write

Controls the embedding of bidirectional text (such as a mixture of French and Arabic) in concert with the direction style attribute.

Example

document.getElementById("blockD2").style.unicodeBidi = "bidi-override";

Value   String constant values: bidi-override | embed | normal.

Default   normal

verticalAlign

IE 4   NN n/a   Moz all   Saf 1.2   Op 7   DOM 2
Read/Write

Specifies the vertical alignment characteristic of the element. This property operates in two spheres, depending on the selection of values you use. See the in-depth discussion of the vertical-align style sheet property in Chapter 4 for details.

Example

document.getElementById("myDIV").style.verticalAlign = "text-top";

Value   String value of an absolute measure (with units), a percentage (relative to the next outer box element), or one of the many constant values: bottom | top | baseline | middle | sub | super | text-bottom | text-top.

Default   baseline

visibility

IE 4   NN n/a   Moz all   Saf all   Op 7   DOM 2
Read/Write

Specifies the state of the positioned element's visibility. Surrounding content does not close up the space left by an element that has its visibility property set to hidden.

Example   document.getElementById("myDIV").style.visibility = "hidden";

Value   One of the constant values (as a string): collapse | hidden | inherit | visible.

Default   visible

voiceFamily, volume

See azimuth.

whiteSpace

Controls intepretation of whitespace (such as leading spaces and line breaks) from the source code.

Example document.getElementById("myDIV").style.whiteSpace = "pre";

Value One of the constant values (as a string): normal | nowrap | pre. Value of normal allows browsers to word-wrap lines in block elements and ignore leading spaces. Value of nowrap causes source code not to word-wrap, but still ignores leading spaces. Value of pre preserves leading spaces, extra spaces, and carriage returns in the source code. Note that IE 6 for Windows does not respond to the pre value unless the DOCTYPE element values place the browser into standards compatibility mode.

Default normal

widows

See orphans.

width

See height.

wordBreak

Specifies the word-break style for ideographic languages or content that mixes Latin and ideographic languages.

Example document.getElementById("myDIV").style.wordBreak = "keep-all";

Value One of the constant values (as a string): break-all | keep-all | normal.

Default normal

wordSpacing

Governs the length of space between words. IE 5 for Macintosh may exhibit overlap problems with the word-spacing of elements nested inside the one being controlled.

Example document.getElementById("myDIV").style.wordSpacing = "1.0em";

Value CSS length value (as a string) or the constant normal.

Default normal

Alphabetical DOM Reference

wordWrap

IE 5.5 NN n/a Moz n/a Saf 1.3/2 Op n/a DOM n/a

Read/Write

Specifies the word-wrapping style for block-level, specifically sized inline, or positioned elements. If a single word (i.e., without any whitespace) extends beyond the width of the element containing box, the normal behavior is to extend the content beyond the normal box width, without breaking. But you can force the long word to break at whatever character position occurs at the edge of the box.

Example	`document.getElementById("myDIV").style.wordWrap = "break-word";`
Value	One of the constant values (as a string): break-word | normal.
Default	`normal`

writingMode

IE 5.5 NN n/a Moz n/a Saf n/a Op n/a DOM n/a

Read/Write

Intended primarily for languages that display characters in vertical sentences, this controls the progression of content, left-to-right, or right-to-left.

Example	`document.getElementById("myDIV").style.writingMode = "lr-tb";`
Value	One of the constant values (as a string): lr-tb | tb-rl. Value of tb-rl can rotate text of some languages by 90 degrees.
Default	`lr-tb`

zIndex

IE 4 NN n/a Moz all Saf all Op 7 DOM 2

Read/Write

For a positioned element, this specifies the stacking order relative to other elements within the same parent container. See Online Section VI for details on relationships of element layering amid multiple containers.

Example	`document.getElementById("myDIV").style.zIndex = "3";`
Value	Integer. Mozilla prefers that this value be in string form (that's how the property returns its value), while IE returns a number.
Default	0

zoom

IE 5.5 NN n/a Moz n/a Saf n/a Op n/a DOM n/a

Read/Write

Governs the magnification of rendered content. Particularly useful for output that might be displayed on monitors with very high pixel density. See `screen.logicalXDPI` property.

Example	`document.body.style.zoom = "200%";`
Value	Percentage value (where 100% is normal), floating-point multiplier (where 1.0 is normal), or constant normal.

Default   `normal`

getPropertyCSSValue( )   IE *n/a* NN *n/a* Moz *1.7* Saf *n/a* Op *n/a* DOM *2*

`getPropertyCSSValue("CSSAttributeName")`

Returns an object that represents a CSS value. In the W3C DOM, the `CSSValue` object returned from this method has properties that reveal the text of the attribute/value pair and a numeric value corresponding to a long list of primitive value types (indicating types such as percentage, pixel lengths, and RGB color).

Returned Value   Reference to a `CSSValue` object.

Parameters

CSSAttributeName
> The CSS attribute name from an inline style declaration (not the DOM version of the property name).

getPropertyPriority( )   IE *n/a* NN *n/a* Moz *all* Saf *all* Op *9* DOM *2*

`getPropertyPriority("CSSAttributeName")`

Returns the string value of any priority (such as `!important`) associated with the inline CSS attribute.

Returned Value   String.

Parameters

CSSAttributeName
> The CSS attribute name from an inline style declaration (not the DOM version of the property name).

getPropertyValue( )   IE *5(Mac)* NN *n/a* Moz *all* Saf *all* Op *7* DOM *2*

`getPropertyValue("CSSAttributeName")`

Returns the string value of the inline CSS attribute/value pair.

Returned Value   String.

Parameters

CSSAttributeName
> The CSS attribute name from an inline style declaration (not the DOM version of the property name).

item( )   IE *5(Mac)* NN *n/a* Moz *all* Saf *all* Op *n/a* DOM *1*

`item(index)`

Returns the attribute name of the inline CSS attribute/value pair corresponding to the integer index value in source code order. Safari incorrectly returns the CSS value, not the name.

Returned Value   String. IE for Macintosh returns name in all-uppercase characters, while Mozilla returns all-lowercase characters.

Parameters

index
  Zero-based integer corresponding to the specified inline CSS attribute/value pair in source code order.

removeProperty( )   IE *n/a* NN *n/a* Moz *all* Saf *all* Op 7 DOM 2

removeProperty("*CSSAttributeName*")

Deletes the inline CSS attribute/value pair and returns a string with the previous value.

Returned Value   String.

Parameters

CSSAttributeName
  The CSS attribute name from an inline style declaration (not the DOM version of the property name).

setProperty( )   IE 5(Mac) NN *n/a* Moz *all* Saf *all* Op 7 DOM 2

setProperty("*CSSAttributeName*", "*value*", "*priority*")

Sets an inline style attribute/value pair. If the attribute already exists, the new value is applied to the existing attribute; otherwise, the attribute and value are added to the element.

Returned Value   None.

Parameters

CSSAttributeName
  The CSS attribute name from an inline style declaration (not the DOM version of the property name).

value
  String of the value in the format applicable to the attribute.

priority
  String of the priority assignment (such as !important) or empty string.

styleSheet, CSSStyleSheet   IE 4 NN *n/a* Moz *all* Saf *all* Op 7 DOM 1

The styleSheet object (CSSStyleSheet object in the W3C DOM abstract model, which inherits the DOM StyleSheet object) represents a style sheet that may have been created as a style element or imported with a link element or @import statement inside a style element. This object is different from the style element object, which strictly reflects the style HTML element and its attributes. The document.styleSheets[] collection contains zero or more styleSheet objects. The shared disabled property is available in all supporting browsers, facilitating the enabling and disabling of entire style sheets with simple Boolean assignments.

Object Model Reference
```
[window.]document.styleSheets[i]
```

Object-Specific Properties

cssRules[]	cssText	href	imports[]	media
ownerNode	ownerRule	owningElement	pages[]	parentStyleSheet
readOnly	rules[]	title	type	

Object-Specific Methods

addImport( )	addRule( )	deleteRule( )	insertRule( )	removeRule( )

Object-Specific Events
None.

---

cssRules[ ]
IE 5(Mac) NN n/a Moz all Saf all Op 7 DOM 2
Read-only

Returns a collection of cssRule objects nested within the current styleSheet object. The IE equivalent is the rules property. See the cssRules object earlier in this chapter for a description of this collection object's property and methods; see the cssRule object earlier in this chapter for a description of the individual members of this collection.

Example   `var allCSSRules = document.styleSheets[0].cssRules;`

Value   Reference to a CSSRules collection object.

Default   Array of zero length.

---

cssText
IE 5 NN n/a Moz n/a Saf n/a Op n/a DOM n/a
Read/Write

Contains the entire text (as a string) of all rules defined in the style sheet. This is useful primarily if you wish to replace the entire set of rules with a new set. To act on the text of an individual rule in IE, access the cssText property of a single rule object (obtained by the styleSheet object's rules[i].cssText property); or, in W3C DOM browsers, you can use the cssRules[i].cssText property.

Example   `var allCSSText = document.styleSheets[0].cssText;`

Value   String.

Default   Empty string.

href

This is the URL specified by a link element's href attribute (when the link is used to import a style sheet). This value is read/write in IE for Windows, but read-only in W3C DOM browsers.

Example	document.styleSheets[1].href = "css/altStyles.css";
Value	String of complete or relative URL.
Default	None.

imports[ ]

Returns a collection (array) of styleSheet objects imported into an explicit styleSheet object via the @import rule. See the imports collection object earlier in this chapter for further discussion. For W3C DOM browsers, you must loop through all cssRule objects of a styleSheet object in search of those with type property values equal to 3 (the same as the cssRule object's IMPORT_RULE constant).

Example	var allImportRules = document.styleSheets[0].imports;
Value	Reference to an imports collection object.
Default	Array of zero length.

media

Specifies the intended output device for the content governed by the style sheet (reflecting the media attribute of the link and style elements). IE uses a string for this value, while W3C DOM browsers use a read-only MediaList object (which has properties and methods of its own).

Example

```
var theMedia = document.styleSheets[2].media;
theMedia = (typeof theMedia.mediaText != "undefined") ? theMedia.mediaText :
theMedia;
if (theMedia.match(/print/) {
    // process for print output
}
```

Value	For IE, any one of the following constant values as a string: all | print | screen; for W3C DOM browsers a MediaList object.
Default	all

---

ownerNode

Read-only

Returns a reference to the document tree node that contains the styleSheet object. This node is either a style or link element, depending on the way the style sheet is defined in the document. The IE (Windows and Mac) equivalent property is owningElement.

Example	var mama = document.styleSheets[2].ownerNode;
Value	Object reference.
Default	None.

ownerRule

Read-only

For a styleSheet object brought into the document via an @import rule, returns a reference to that @import rule object (a W3C DOM CSSImportRule object). The cssRule object earlier in this chapter provides the properties and methods that apply to a CSSImportRule object. For other style sheet types, the property returns null.

Example	var hostRule = document.styleSheets[2].ownerRule;
Value	Object reference or null.
Default	null

owningElement

Read-only

Returns a reference to the style or link element object that defines the current styleSheet object. Each document maintains a collection of style sheets created with both the style and link elements. The comparable W3C DOM property is ownerNode.

Example	var firstStyleID = document.styleSheets[0].owningElement.id;
Value	Element object reference.
Default	None.

pages[ ]

Read-only

Returns a collection (array) of page objects (@page rules) nested within a styleSheet object. For W3C DOM browsers, you must loop through all cssRule objects of a styleSheet object in search of those with type property values equal to 6 (the same as the cssRule object's PAGE_RULE constant). See the page object.

Example	var allPageRules = document.styleSheets[0].pages;
Value	Reference to a pages collection object.
Default	Array of zero length.

parentStyleSheet

IE 4 NN n/a Moz all Saf all Op 7 DOM 2

Read-only

For a styleSheet object generated by virtue of inclusion with an @page rule, the parentStyleSheet property returns a reference to the styleSheet (created as a link or style element) object that imported the current style sheet. For a nonimported style sheet, the property returns null.

Example   var myMaker = document.styleSheets[0].parentStyleSheet;

Value   Reference to a styleSheet object.

Default   null

readOnly

IE 4 NN n/a Moz n/a Saf n/a Op n/a DOM n/a

Read-only

Specifies whether the style sheet can be modified under script control. Style sheets imported through a link element or an @import rule cannot be modified, so they return a value of true.

Value   Boolean value: true | false.

Default   false

rules[ ]

IE 4 NN n/a Moz n/a Saf all Op n/a DOM n/a

Read-only

Returns a collection of rule objects nested within the current styleSheet object. The W3C DOM equivalent is the cssRules property (Safari supports both properties). See the cssRules object earlier in this chapter for a description of this collection object's property and methods; see the cssRule object earlier in this chapter for a description of the individual members of this collection.

Example   var allrules = document.styleSheets[0].rules;

Value   Reference to a rules collection object.

Default   Array of zero length.

title

IE 4 NN n/a Moz all Saf all Op 7 DOM 2

Read/Write

Exposes the title attribute of the style or link element that owns the current styleSheet object. Since the attribute does not affect user interface elements (the elements are unrendered, and thus don't show tool tips), it is available to convey other string information to the styleSheet object under script control.

Example

```
if (document.styleSheets[2].title == "corpStyleWindows") {
    // process for the designated style
}
```

Value	String value.
Default	Empty string.

type
IE 4 NN n/a Moz all Saf all Op 7 DOM 2

Read-only

Returns the style sheet MIME type specified by the type attribute of the style or link element.

Example

```
if (document.styleSheets[0].type == "text/css") {
    ...
}
```

Value	String (text/css for typical CSS style sheets).
Default	None.

addImport( )
IE 4 NN n/a Moz n/a Saf n/a Op n/a DOM n/a

`addImport(url, [index])`

Adds an external style sheet specification to a styleSheet object.

Returned Value Integer of the index position within the styleSheets[] collection where the style sheet was added (in case you omit the second parameter and let the browser find the endposition).

Parameters

url
> A complete or relative URL to the style sheet (*.css*) file.

index
> An optional integer indicating where in the collection the new element should be placed.

addRule( )
IE 4 NN n/a Moz n/a Saf n/a Op n/a DOM n/a

`addRule("selector", "style"[, index])`

Adds a new rule for a style sheet. This method offers a scripted way of adding a rule to an existing styleSheet object:

```
document.styleSheets[1].addRule("p b","color:red");
```

You may duplicate a selector that already exists in the styleSheet and, therefore, override an existing rule for the same element selector. The only prohibition is that you may not override a rule to convert a plain style rule into one that creates a positionable element (or

Alphabetical DOM Reference

vice versa). The new rule is governed by the same cascading rules as all style sheet rules (that includes the rule's source code position among other rules with the same selector). Therefore, a new rule in a styleSheet object does not supersede a style set in an element's style property.

Returned Value   Early versions of IE returned no value. More recently, IE for Windows returns -1, while IE for Macintosh returns null. In the future, the returned value may become the integer of the index location of the new rule.

Parameters

selector
>   The style rule selector as a string.

style
>   One or more style *attribute:value* pairs. Multiple pairs are semicolon delimited, just as they are in the regular style sheet definition.

index
>   An optional integer indicating where in the collection the new element should be placed.

deleteRule( )   IE 5(Mac) NN n/a Moz all Saf all Op 7 DOM 2

deleteRule(*index*)

Removes a rule from the styleSheet object. The integer index parameter value points to the zero-based item in the cssRules array to delete. Note that IE 5 for Macintosh implements both the Microsoft removeRule( ) and W3C DOM deleteRule( ) method for the same operation.

Returned Value   None.

Parameters

index
>   A zero-based integer indicating which rule in the cssRules collection is to be deleted.

insertRule( )   IE 5(Mac) NN n/a Moz all Saf all Op 7 DOM 2

insertRule("*ruleText*", *index*)

Adds a new rule for a style sheet. This method offers a scripted way of adding a rule to an existing W3C DOM styleSheet object:

```
document.styleSheets[1].insertRule("p b {color:red}", 0);
```

You may duplicate a selector that already exists in the styleSheet and, therefore, override an existing rule for the same element selector. The only prohibition is that you may not override a rule to convert a plain style rule into one that creates a positionable element (or vice versa). The new rule is governed by the same cascading rules as all style sheet rules (that includes the rule's source code position among other rules with the same selector). Therefore, a new rule in a styleSheet object does not supersede a style set in an element's style property. Note that IE 5 for the Macintosh implements both the W3C DOM insertRule( ) and Microsoft addRule( ) methods to accomplish the same result.

Returned Value Integer of the index location of the new rule.

Parameters

ruleText
> The entire style rule selector as a string in exactly the same format as assigned in a style element: *selector {attribute:value; attribute:value;...}*.

index
> Zero-based integer indicating where in the cssRules collection the new rule should be placed.

removeRule( ) IE 4 NN *n/a* Moz *n/a* Saf *n/a* Op *n/a* DOM *n/a*

removeRule(*index*)

Removes a rule from the styleSheet object. The integer index parameter value points to the zero-based item in the rules array to delete.

Returned Value None.

Parameters

index
> A zero-based integer indicating which rule in the rules collection is to be deleted.

styleSheets, StyleSheetList IE 4 NN *n/a* Moz *all* Saf *all* Op 7 DOM 2

A collection of styleSheet objects that are members of a document object. The W3C DOM abstract representation of this collection is called a StyleSheetList object. Members of this collection are accessed via their integer index number, but you may iterate through the collection and examine properties of each style sheet object (such as the selectorText property) to distinguish one rule from another.

Object Model Reference
document.styleSheets

Object-Specific Properties
length

Object-Specific Methods
item( )

Object-Specific Events
None.

length

Read-only

Returns the number of elements in the collection.

Example

var howMany = document.styleSheets.length;

Value   Integer.

item( )

item(*index*)

Returns a styleSheet object corresponding to the object matching the index value in source code order.

Returned Value   Reference to a styleSheet object. If there are no matches to the parameters, the returned value is null.

Parameters

index

A zero-based integer corresponding to the specified item in source code order (nested within the current document object).

sub, sup

The sub object reflects the sub element; the sup object reflects the sup element. Browsers tend to render these objects' content in a smaller size than surrounding content. IE 5 for Macintosh provides object-specific, read-only height and width properties for these elements, but no other object model does.

HTML Equivalent

<sub>
<sup>

Object Model Reference

[window.]document.getElementById("*elementID*")

Object-Specific Properties

None.

Object-Specific Methods

None.

Object-Specific Events

None.

submit

See input.

sup

See sub.

table

IE 4 NN *n/a* Moz *all* Saf *all* Op 7 DOM 1

The table object reflects the table element. Other objects related to the table object are: caption, col, colgroup, tbody, td, tfoot, thead, and tr.

HTML Equivalent   `<table>`

Object Model Reference

`[window.]document.getElementById("elementID")`

Object-Specific Properties

align	background	bgColor	border
borderColor	borderColorDark	borderColorLight	caption
cellPadding	cells[]	cellSpacing	cols
dataPageSize	frame	height	rows[]
rules	summary	tbodies[]	tFoot
tHead	width		

Object-Specific Methods

createCaption( )	createTFoot( )	createTHead( )	deleteCaption( )
deleteRow( )	deleteTFoot( )	deleteTHead( )	insertRow( )
lastPage( )	moveRow( )	nextPage( )	previousPage( )
refresh( )			

Object-Specific Events

None.

align

IE 4 NN *n/a* Moz *all* Saf *all* Op 7 DOM 1

Read/Write

Defines the horizontal alignment of the element within its surrounding container.

Example   `document.getElementById("myTable").align = "center";`

Value   Any of the three horizontal alignment constants: center | left | right.

Default   left

background

Provides the URL of the background image for the table. If you set a backgroundColor to the element as well, the color appears if the image fails to load; otherwise, the image overlays the color.

Example
```
document.getElementById("myTable").background = "images/watermark.jpg";
```

Value   Complete or relative URL to the background image file.

Default   None.

bgColor

Specifies the background color of the element. This color setting is not reflected in the style sheet backgroundColor property. Even if the bgcolor attribute or bgColor property is set with a plain-language color name, the returned value is always a hexadecimal triplet.

Example   `document.getElementById("myTable").bgColor = "yellow";`

Value   A hexadecimal triplet or plain-language color name. See Appendix A for acceptable plain-language color names.

Default   Varies with browser and operating system.

border

Specifies the thickness of the border around the table (in pixels). This is the default 3D-look border and should not be confused with borders created with style sheets.

Example   `document.getElementById("myTable").border = 4;`

Value   An integer value. A setting of zero removes the border entirely.

Default   0

borderColor

Specifies the color of the table's border. Internet Explorer applies the color to all four lines that make up the interior border of a cell. Therefore, colors of adjacent cells do not collide.

Example   `document.getElementById("myTable").borderColor = "salmon";`

Value   A hexadecimal triplet or plain-language color name. A setting of empty is interpreted as "#000000" (black). See Appendix A for acceptable plain-language color names.

Default Varies with operating system.

borderColorDark, borderColorLight

The 3D effect of table borders in Internet Explorer is created by careful positioning of light and dark lines around the page's background or default color. You can independently control the colors used for the dark and light lines by assigning values to the borderColorDark (left and top edges of the cell) and borderColorLight (right and bottom edges) properties.

Typically, you should assign complementary colors to the pair of properties. There is also no rule that says you must assign a dark color to borderColorDark. The attributes merely control a well-defined set of lines so you can predict which lines of the border change with each attribute.

Example
```
document.getElementById("myTable").borderColorDark = "blue";
document.getElementById("myTable").borderColorLight = "cornflowerblue";
```

Value A hexadecimal triplet or plain-language color name. A setting of empty is interpreted as "#000000" (black). See Appendix A for acceptable plain-language color names.

Default Varies with operating system.

caption

Returns a reference to a caption element nested inside the table. From this reference you can access properties and methods of the caption object. In W3C DOM browsers, you can create a new caption element, and assign that new element's reference to the caption property of a table, making the property read/write in that browser (although you really should be using the createCaption( ) method). For all browsers, however, you can modify properties of the caption object returned by the caption property.

Example `var capText = document.getElementById("myTable").caption.innerHTML;`

Value Object reference.

Default None.

cellPadding

Specifies the amount of empty space between the (visible or invisible) border of a table cell and the content of the cell. Note that this property applies to space *inside* a cell. Minor adjustments to this property are not as noticeable when the table does not also display borders (in which case the cellSpacing property can assist in adjusting the space between cells).

Example   document.getElementById("myTable").cellPadding = "15";

Value   A string value for a length in pixels or percentage.

Default   0

cells
IE *5(Win)* NN *n/a* Moz *n/a* Saf *all* Op *9* DOM *n/a*

Read-only

Returns a collection of all td elements inside the table. Entries in the array are in source code order of td elements. This property is more widely available for a tr element (one row at a time).

Example   var totCells = document.getElementById("myTable").cells.length;

Value   Reference to a cells collection object.

Default   Array of zero length.

cellSpacing
IE *4* NN *n/a* Moz *all* Saf *all* Op *7* DOM *1*

Read/Write

Specifies the amount of empty space between the outer edges of each table cell. If the table has a border, the effect of setting cellSpacing is to define the thickness of borders rendered between cells. Even without a visible border, the readability of a table often benefits from cell spacing, or a combination of cell spacing and cell padding.

Example   document.getElementById("myTable").cellSpacing = "5";

Value   A string value for a length in pixels or percentage.

Default   0 (with no table border); 2 (with table border).

cols
IE *4* NN *n/a* Moz *n/a* Saf *n/a* Op *n/a* DOM *n/a*

Read/Write

Specifies the number of columns of the table. The corresponding IE-specific cols attribute assists the browser in preparation for rendering the table. Without this attribute, the browser relies on its interpretation of all downloaded tr and td elements to determine how the table is to be divided. You cannot change the column makeup of a table from this property, despite its read/write status. See also the col object earlier in this chapter.

Example   document.getElementById("myTable").cols = 5;

Value   Integer.

Default   None.

dataPageSize

Used with IE data binding, this property advises the browser how many instances of a table row must be rendered to accommodate the number of data source records set by this attribute. See lastPage( ), nextPage( ), and previousPage( ) methods for navigating through groups of records.

Example   document.getElementById("inventoryTable").dataPageSize = 10;

Value   Integer.

Default   None.

frame

Indicates which (if any) sides of a table's outer border (set with the border attribute or border property) are rendered. This property does not affect the interior borders between cells.

Example   document.getElementById("orderForm").frame = "hsides";

Value

Any one case-insensitive frame constant (as a string):

above
    Renders border along top edge of table only
below
    Renders border along bottom edge of table only
border
    Renders all four sides of the border (same as box)
box
    Renders all four sides of the border (same as border)
hsides
    Renders borders on top and bottom edges of table only (a nice look)
lhs
    Renders border on left edge of table only
rhs
    Renders border on right edge of table only
void
    Hides all borders (default in HTML 4)
vsides
    Renders borders on left and right edges of table only

Default   void (when border=0); border (when border is any other value)

Alphabetical DOM
Reference

height, width

Read/Write

Specify the height and width in pixels of the element. Changes to these values are immediately reflected in reflowed content on the page. Only the width property is available in W3C DOM browsers, as the table's height is considered to be the sum of the highest cell in each row.

Example   `document.getElementById("myTable").height = 250;`

Value   Integer.

Default   None.

rows

Read-only

Returns a collection of tr elements inside the entire table. You can also get a group of rows for each table section (tbody, tfoot, and thead element objects).

Example   `var allTableRows = document.getElementById("myTable").rows;`

Value   Reference to a rows collection object.

Default   Array of zero length.

rules

Read/Write

Indicates where (if at all) interior borders between cells are rendered by the browser. In addition to setting the table to draw borders to turn the cells into a matrix, you can set borders to be drawn only to separate borders, columns, or any sanctioned cell grouping (thead, tbody, tfoot, colgroup, or col). The border attribute must be present—either as a Boolean or set to a specific border size—for any cell borders to be drawn. Do not confuse this property with the rules[] collection of styleSheet objects. Scripted changes to this property do not always yield the desired results, especially in early versions of Netscape 6.

Example   `document.getElementById("myTable").rules = "groups";`

Value

Any one case-insensitive rule constants (as a string):

all
    Renders borders around each cell

cols
    Renders borders between columns only

groups
    Renders borders between cell groups as defined by thead, tfoot, tbody, colgroup, or
    col elements

>Hides all interior borders

rows
>Renders borders between rows only

Default none (when border=0); all (when border is any other value).

summary

IE 6 NN n/a Moz all Saf all Op 7 DOM 1
Read-only

Reflects the HTML 4 summary attribute, which provides no particular functionality in mainstream browsers. But you can assign a value to it in the source code to convey data to a script that reads the property.

Example `var data = document.getElementById("myTable").summary;`

Value String.

Default Empty string.

tBodies[ ]

IE 4(Win)/5(Mac) NN n/a Moz all Saf all Op 7 DOM 1
Read-only

Returns a collection of tBody element objects in the current table. Every table element has at least one (explicit or implied) tBody element object nested inside.

Example `var bodSections = document.getElementById("myTable").tBodies;`

Value Reference to a collection of tBody objects.

Default Array of length one.

tFoot

IE 4(Win)/5(Mac) NN n/a Moz all Saf all Op 7 DOM 1
Read-only

Returns a reference to the tfoot element object if one has been defined for the table. If no tfoot element exists, the value is null. You can access tfoot element object properties and methods through this reference if you like.

Example
`var tableFootTxt = document.getElementById("myTable").tFoot.firstChild.nodeValue;`

Value tfoot element object reference.

Default null

tHead　　　　　　　　　　　　IE *4(Win)/5(Mac)*　NN *n/a*　Moz *all*　Saf *all*　Op *7*　DOM *1*

Read-only

Returns a reference to the thead element object if one has been defined for the table. If no thead element exists, the value is null. You can access thead element object properties and methods through this reference if you like.

Example
```
var tableHeadTxt = document.getElementById("myTable").tHead.firstChild.nodevalue;
```

Value　　　　　　thead element object reference.

Default　　　　　null

width

See height.

createCaption( ), deleteCaption( )　　　　IE *4*　NN *n/a*　Moz *all*　Saf *all*　Op *7*　DOM *1*

Add or remove a caption element nested within the current table element. If no caption exists, the creation method produces an empty element, which your scripts must then populate with caption text (through common element content modification techniques). If a caption exists, the method is essentially ignored, and returns a reference to the existing caption element.

Returned Value　　Reference to new caption element (for createCaption( )); nothing for deleteCaption( ).

Parameters　　　None.

createTFoot( ), createTHead( ), deleteTFoot( ), deleteTHead( )　　　IE *4*　NN *n/a*　Moz *all*　Saf *all*　Op *7*　DOM *1*

Add or remove a thead or tfoot element nested within the current table element. If no head or foot table section exists, the creation method produces an empty element, which your scripts must then populate with rows (through thead.insertRow( ) and tfoot. insertRow( ) methods). If the desired table section exists, the method is essentially ignored, and returns a reference to the existing thead or tfoot element.

Returned Value　　Reference to newly created element (for createTFoot( ) and createTHead( )); nothing for deleteTHead( ) and deleteTFoot( ).

Parameters　　　None.

deleteRow( )

deleteRow(*index*)

Removes a tr element nested within the current table element. The integer parameter points to the zero-based item in the rows collection. To repopulate a table with new or sorted content, empty the table (or just a table section) with iterative calls to the deleteRow( ) method:

```
while (tableReference.rows.length > 0) {
    tableReference.deleteRow(0);
}
```

Returned Value   None.

Parameters

index

Zero-based integer corresponding to the said numbered tr element in source code order (nested within the current element).

insertRow( )

insertRow(*index*)

Inserts a tr element nested within the current table element. The integer parameter points to the zero-based index in the rows collection where the new row should go, but in IE you can also use the shortcut value of -1 to append the row to the end of the collection. Adding the row inserts an empty element, to which you add cells via the insertCell( ) method. Unfortunately, scripting the addition of table rows and cells in IE for the Macintosh (including Version 5.1) is very broken, yielding elephantine row and cell dimensions. For nonnested tables, you might be able to get away with regular document tree node creation and insertion instead of the table (and related) object convenience methods.

Returned Value   Reference to the newly inserted row.

Parameters

index

Zero-based integer corresponding to a row of the rows collection before which the new row is to be inserted.

lastPage( ), nextPage( ), previousPage( )

Advises the data binding facilities to load the last, next, or previous group of records from the data source to fill the number of records established with the dataPageSize property. The lastPage( ) method is available in IE 5 or later.

Returned Value   None.

Parameters   None.

moveRow( )

IE 5(Win)   NN n/a   Moz n/a   Saf n/a   Op n/a   DOM n/a

moveRow(*indexToMove, destinationIndex*)

Moves a row in the table from its original location to a different row position. The first parameter is a zero-based index of the row (within the rows collection) you wish to move. The second parameter is the index of the row before which you want to move the row. As a method of the table object, moveRow( )'s index parameters include the first row, which may contain th elements you don't want to move. Invoke the method on the tbody object if you want counting to be just within a table section.

Returned Value   Reference to the moved row.

Parameters

indexToMove
> A zero-based integer pointing to the row to move.

destinationIndex
> A zero-based integer pointing to the row above which the row is to be moved.

refresh( )

IE 4   NN n/a   Moz n/a   Saf n/a   Op n/a   DOM n/a

Advises the data binding facilities to reload the current page of data from the data source. If your table is retrieving frequently changing data from a database, you can create a setTimeout( ) loop to invoke document.getElementById("myTable").refresh( ) as often as users would want updated information from the database.

Returned Value   None.

Parameters   None.

tags

IE n/a   NN |4| Moz n/a   Saf n/a   Op n/a   DOM n/a

The tags object is used by JavaScript syntax for style sheets in Navigator 4 only. As a property of the document object, this tags object is used in building references to particular HTML elements to get or set their style-related properties. The direct properties of the tags object are all HTML element types. For example:

```
[document.]tags.p
[document.]tags.h1
```

There is no need to repeat a list of all HTML elements as properties for this object. These references are usable inside style elements with a type set to text/javascript. That's where you assign values to style sheet properties with JavaScript syntax, as in the following examples:

```
tags.p.color = "green";
tags.h1.fontSize = "14pt";
```

The properties in the following list are not properties of the tags object per se, but rather of the style sheet associated with an element, class, or ID singled out by a JavaScript syntax assignment statement. The properties are listed here for convenience (and historical completeness). Properties dedicated to element positioning are listed separately from regular style properties. For information about these property values, consult the CSS reference chapter, where you can find details of all style sheet properties listed by CSS syntax.

Style Object-Specific Properties

backgroundColor	backgroundImage	borderBottomWidth	borderColor
borderLeftWidth	borderRightWidth	borderStyle	borderTopWidth
borderWidths( )	color	display	fontFamily
fontSize	fontStyle	fontWeight	listStyleType
marginBottom	marginLeft	marginRight	margins( )
marginTop	paddingBottom	paddingLeft	paddingRight
paddings	paddingTop	textAlign	textDecoration
textTransform	verticalAlign	whiteSpace	

Position Object-Specific Properties

background	bgColor	clip	left
top	visibility	zIndex	

tBodies

IE 4 NN n/a Moz all Saf all Op 7 DOM 1

This is a collection of all tbody elements contained within a single table element. Collection members are sorted in source code order.

Object Model Reference
document.getElementById("*tableID*").tBodies

Object-Specific Properties

length

Object-Specific Methods

item( )	namedItem( )	tags( )	urns( )

Object-Specific Events
None.

length

IE 4 NN n/a Moz all Saf all Op 7 DOM 1

Read-only

Returns the number of elements in the collection.

Example   var howMany = document.getElementById("myTable").tBodies.length;

Value   Integer.

item( )   IE 4 NN *n/a* Moz *all* Saf *all* Op 7 DOM 1

item(*index*[, *subindex*]) item(*index*)

Returns a single tBody object or collection of tBody objects corresponding to the element matching the index value (or, optionally in IE, the index and subindex values).

Returned Value   One tBody object or collection (array) of tBody objects. If there are no matches to the parameters, the returned value is null.

Parameters

index

> When the parameter is a zero-based integer, the returned value is a single element corresponding to the specified item in source code order (nested within the current element); when the parameter is a string (IE only), the returned value is a collection of elements with id properties that match that string.

subindex

> In IE only, if you specify a string value for the first parameter, you can use the second parameter to specify a zero-based index that retrieves the specified element from the collection with id properties that match the first parameter's string value.

namedItem( )   IE 6 NN *n/a* Moz *all* Saf *all* Op 7 DOM 1

namedItem("*ID*")

Returns a single tBody object or collection of tBody objects corresponding to the element matching the parameter string value.

Returned Value   One tBody object or collection (array) of tBody objects. If there are no matches to the parameters, the returned value is null.

Parameters

ID

> The string that contains the same value as the desired element's id attribute.

tags( )   IE 4 NN *n/a* Moz *n/a* Saf *n/a* Op *n/a* DOM *n/a*

tags("*tagName*")

Returns a collection of objects (among all objects nested within the current collection) whose tags match the *tagName* parameter.

urns( )   IE 5(Win) NN *n/a* Moz *n/a* Saf *n/a* Op *n/a* DOM *n/a*

urns(*URN*)

See the all.urns( ) method.

tbody, tfoot, thead

IE *4* NN *n/a* Moz *all* Saf *all* Op *7* DOM *1*

The tbody, tfoot, and thead objects reflect the tbody, tfoot, and thead elements, respectively. For scripting purposes, you can treat each of these as a container of row groups inside a table. They all share the same properties and methods, so you need to keep their HTML functionality straight as you script these elements. A table can have only one tfoot and one thead element, but multiple tbody elements. Also, by default, Internet Explorer 4 or later and W3C DOM browsers create a tbody object for every table even if you don't include one in your table's source code. This default tbody element encompasses all rows of the table (except those you have wrapped inside thead or tfoot elements, if any).

HTML Equivalent

```
<tbody>
<tfoot>
<thead>
```

Object Model Reference

```
[window.]document.getElementById("elementID")
[window.]document.getElementById("tableID").tBodies[i]
[window.]document.getElementById("tableID").tfoot
[window.]document.getElementById("tableID").thead
```

Object-Specific Properties

align	bgColor	ch	chOff	rows	vAlign

Object-Specific Methods

deleteRow( )	insertRow( )	moveRow( )

Object-Specific Events

None.

align

IE *4* NN *n/a* Moz *all* Saf *all* Op *7* DOM *1*

Read/Write

Defines the horizontal alignment of content within all cells contained by the tbody element.

Example	document.getElementById("myTbody").align = "center";
Value	One of the three horizontal alignment string constants: center | left | right.
Default	left

bgColor

Read/Write

Specifies the background color of the cells contained by the tbody, tfoot, or thead element. This color setting is not reflected in the style sheet backgroundColor property. Even if the bgcolor attribute or bgColor property is set with a plain-language color name, the returned value is always a hexadecimal triplet.

Example	document.getElementById("myTable").tHead.bgColor = "yellow";
Value	A hexadecimal triplet or plain-language color name. See Appendix A for acceptable plain-language color names.
Default	Varies with browser and operating system.

ch

Read/Write

Defines the text character used as an alignment point for text within a column or column group (reflecting the char attribute). This property is normally of value only for the align attribute set to "char". In practice, even though the table section element object has this property, the browser does not respond to values assigned to it.

Example	document.getElementById("myTBody").ch = ".";
Value	Single character string.
Default	None.

chOff

Read/Write

Defines the offset point at which the character specified by the char attribute is to appear within a cell. In practice, even though the table section element object has this property, the browser does not respond to values assigned to it.

Example	document.getElementById("myTBody").chOff = "80%";
Value	String value of the number of pixels or percentage (within the cell).
Default	None.

rows

Read-only

Returns a collection of tr elements inside the table section. You can also get a group of rows for an entire table in IE for Windows.

Example	var allTableRows = document.getElementById("myTFoot").rows;
Value	Reference to a rows collection object.
Default	Array of zero length.

vAlign

Read/Write

Specifies the manner of vertical alignment of text within the cells contained by the tbody, tfoot, or thead element.

Example   document.getElementById("myTbody").vAlign = "baseline";

Value   Case-insensitive constant (as a string): baseline | bottom | middle | top.

Default   middle

deleteRow( )

deleteRow(*index*)

Removes a tr element nested within the current tbody, tfoot, or thead element. The integer parameter points to the zero-based item in the section's rows collection. To repopulate a table section with new or sorted content, empty the section with iterative calls to the deleteRow( ) method:

```
while (tBodyReference.rows.length > 0) {
    tBodyReference.deleteRow(0);
}
```

Returned Value   None.

Parameters

index

> Zero-based integer corresponding to the said numbered tr element in source code order (nested within the current element).

insertRow( )

insertRow(*index*)

Inserts a tr element nested within the current tbody, tfoot, or thead element. The integer parameter points to the zero-based index in the rows collection where the new row should go, but in IE you can also use the shortcut value of -1 to append the row to the end of the collection. Adding the row inserts an empty element, to which you add cells via the insertCell( ) method. Unfortunately, scripting the addition of table rows and cells in IE for the Macintosh (including Version 5.1) is very broken, yielding elephantine row and cell dimensions. For nonnested tables, you might be able to get away with regular document tree node creation and insertion instead of the table section object convenience methods.

Returned Value   Reference to the newly inserted row.

Parameters

index

> Zero-based integer corresponding to a row of the rows collection before which the new row is to be inserted.

moveRow( )

moveRow(*indexToMove, destinationIndex*)

Moves a row in the tbody, tfoot, or thead element from its original location to a different row position within the same section. The first parameter is a zero-based index of the row (within the rows collection) you wish to move. The second parameter is the index of the row before which you want to move the row.

Returned Value   Reference to the moved row.

Parameters

indexToMove
    A zero-based integer pointing to the row to move.

destinationIndex
    A zero-based integer pointing to the row above which the row is to be moved.

td, th

The td and th objects reflect the td and th elements. From an HTML structure viewpoint, the two elements have different purposes within a table; but from a scripting perspective, the elements share the same properties and methods. A cell is a cell.

While a table cell element may inherit a number of visual properties from containers (e.g., a td element appearing to pick up the bgColor of a tbody or tr element), those inherited property values are not automatically assigned to the td object. Therefore, just because a cell may have a yellow background color doesn't mean its bgColor property is set at all.

HTML Equivalent
```
<td>
<th>
```

Object Model Reference
```
[window.]document.getElementById("elementID")
[window.]document.getElementById("tableRowID").cells[i]
```

Object-Specific Properties

abbr	align	axis	background
bgColor	borderColor	borderColorDark	borderColorLight
cellIndex	ch	chOff	colSpan
headers	height	noWrap	rowSpan
scope	vAlign	width	

Object-Specific Methods
None.

Object-Specific Events
None.

abbr

IE *5(Mac)/6(Win)* NN *n/a* Moz *all* Saf *all* Op *7* DOM *1*

Read/Write

Reflects the `abbr` attribute (cell description for speech), for which mainstream browsers have no functionality at this time.

Value   String.

Default   Empty string.

align

IE *4* NN *n/a* Moz *all* Saf *all* Op *7* DOM *1*

Read/Write

Defines the horizontal alignment of content within the cell.

Example   `document.getElementById("myTD").align = "center";`

Value   Any of the three horizontal alignment constants: `center` | `left` | `right`.

Default   `left`

axis

IE *5(Mac)/6(Win)* NN *n/a* Moz *all* Saf *all* Op *7* DOM *1*

Read/Write

Reflects the `axis` attribute (cell category description for speech), for which mainstream browsers have no functionality at this time.

Value   String.

Default   Empty string.

background

IE *4* NN *n/a* Moz *n/a* Saf *n/a* Op *n/a* DOM *n/a*

Read/Write

Specifies the URL of the background image for the cell. If you set a `bgColor` to the element as well, the color appears if the image fails to load; otherwise, the image overlays the color.

Example

`document.getElementById("myTD").background = "images/watermark.jpg";`

Value   Complete or relative URL to the background image file.

Default   None.

bgColor

IE *4* NN *n/a* Moz *all* Saf *all* Op *7* DOM *1*

Read/Write

Provides the background color of the table cell. This color setting is not reflected in the style sheet `backgroundColor` property. Even if the `bgcolor` attribute or `bgColor` property is set with a plain-language color name, the returned value is always a hexadecimal triplet.

| **Example** | `document.getElementById("myTD").bgColor = "yellow";` |

Value A hexadecimal triplet or plain-language color name. See Appendix A for acceptable plain-language color names.

Default Varies with browser and operating system.

borderColor

Provides the color of the element's border. Internet Explorer applies the color to all four lines that make up the interior border of a cell. Therefore, colors of adjacent cells do not collide.

Example `document.getElementById("myTD").borderColor = "salmon";`

Value A hexadecimal triplet or plain-language color name. A setting of empty is interpreted as "#000000" (black). See Appendix A for acceptable plain-language color names.

Default Varies with operating system.

borderColorDark, borderColorLight

The 3D effect of table borders in Internet Explorer is created by careful positioning of light and dark lines around the page's background or default color. You can independently control the colors used for the dark and light lines by assigning values to the borderColorDark (left and top edges of the cell) and borderColorLight (right and bottom edges) properties.

Typically, you should assign complementary colors to the pair of properties. There is also no rule that says you must assign a dark color to borderColorDark. The attributes merely control a well-defined set of lines so you can predict which lines of the border change with each attribute.

Example
```
document.getElementById("myTD").borderColorDark = "blue";
document.getElementById("myTD").borderColorLight = "cornflowerblue";
```

Value A hexadecimal triplet or plain-language color name. A setting of empty is interpreted as "#000000" (black). See Appendix A for acceptable plain-language color names.

Default Varies with operating system.

cellIndex

Read-only

Returns a zero-based integer representing the position of the current cell among all other td elements in the same row. The count is based on the source code order of the td elements within a tr element.

Example	var whichCell = document.getElementById("myTD").cellIndex;
Value	Integer.
Default	None.

ch

Read/Write

Defines the text character used as an alignment point for text within a cell. This property is normally of value only for the align attribute set to "char". In practice, even though the table section element object has this property, the browser does not respond to values assigned to it.

Example	document.getElementById("myTD").ch = ".";
Value	Single character string.
Default	None.

chOff

Read/Write

Defines the offset point at which the character specified by the char attribute is to appear within a cell. In practice, even though the table section element object has this property, the browser does not respond to values assigned to it.

Example	document.getElementById("myTD").chOff = "80%";
Value	String value of the number of pixels or percentage (within the cell).
Default	None.

colSpan

Read/Write

Specifies the number of columns across which the current table cell should extend itself. For each additional column included in the colSpan count, one less td element is required for the table row. If you set the align property to center or right, the alignment is calculated on the full width of the td element across the specified number of columns. Unless the current cell also specifies a rowspan attribute, the next table row returns to the original column count.

Example	document.getElementById("myTD").colSpan = 2;

| **Value** | Integer, usually 2 or larger. |
| **Default** | 1 |

headers

Read/Write

Points to the ID of a table cell element designated as a column header for the current cell. In practice, no mainstream browsers provide functionality for this property.

| **Value** | String ID value. |
| **Default** | None. |

height, width

Read/Write

Specify the height and width of the element. Changes to these values are immediately reflected in reflowed content on the page.

Example	`document.getElementById("myTD").height = "250";`
Value	Pixel integer count (as a string) or a percentage.
Default	None.

noWrap

Read/Write

Indicates whether the browser should render the cell as wide as is necessary to display a line of nonbreaking text on one line. Abuse of this attribute can force the user into a great deal of inconvenient horizontal scrolling of the page to view all of the content.

Example	`document.getElementById("myTD").noWrap = "true";`
Value	Boolean value: `true` | `false`.
Default	`false`

rowSpan

Read/Write

Specifies the number of rows through which the current table cell should extend itself downward. For each additional row included in the `rowSpan` count, one less `td` element is required for the next table row. If you set the `vAlign` property to `middle`, the alignment is calculated on the full height of the `td` element across the specified number of rows.

Example	`document.getElementById("myTD").rowSpan = 12;`
Value	Integer, usually 2 or larger.
Default	1

scope

Reflects the scope attribute of table cell elements. In practice, no mainstream browsers provide functionality for this property.

| **Value** | One of the recognized string constants: cols | colgroup | rows | rowgroup. |
| **Default** | None. |

vAlign

Specifies the manner of vertical alignment of text within the element's content box.

Example	document.getElementById("myTD").vAlign = "baseline";
Value	Case-insensitive constant (as a string): baseline	bottom	middle	top.
Default	middle

width

See height.

text

See input.

Text, TextNode

A Text object is what this book calls in many places a "text node." Microsoft refers to this object as a TextNode object. This object represents the child object containing the characters that go between start and end tags of an element. The Text object exists in the abstract W3C DOM model by virtue of an inheritance chain between it and the fundamental Node object (Node to CharacterData to Text). The Node object ancestry automatically equips the Text object with a long list of properties and methods described among the shared items at the start of this chapter (and itemized in the Node object section in this chapter). Along this inheritance chain, the Text object gains some additional properties and methods (described below) that let us manipulate the node's content within the constructs dictated by the formal W3C DOM model. Because the DOM is scripting language-independent, you find properties and methods that may be more easily or more powerfully manipulated through JavaScript string handling (see Chapter 5). Feel free to use those techniques in a client-side JavaScript environment of the browser.

Scripts refer to the Text node (or IE TextNode object) only through references that locate the node in the document tree (such as the first child of a particular element node) or as returned by the document.createTextNode( ) method.

Object Model Reference

elementReference.childReference
textNodeReference.siblingReference

Object-Specific Properties

data   length

Object-Specific Methods

appendData( )   deleteData( )   insertData( )   replaceData( )
splitText( )   substringData( )

Object-Specific Events

None.

---

data   IE 5   NN *n/a*   Moz *all*   Saf *all*   Op *7*   DOM *1*
Read/Write

Contains the string of characters in the text node. The value is the same as the nodeValue property value, and there is no reason to favor one property over the other, except perhaps for plain-language syntactic preferences for reading the code.

Example
document.getElementById("myP").firstSibling.data = "Some new text.";

Value   String.

Default   Empty string.

---

length   IE 5   NN *n/a*   Moz *all*   Saf *all*   Op *7*   DOM *1*
Read-only

Provides a count of characters in the text node.

Example   var howMany = document.getElementById("myP").firstSibling.length;

Value   Integer.

Default   0

---

appendData( )   IE *5(Mac)/6(Win)*   NN *n/a*   Moz *all*   Saf *all*   Op *7*   DOM *1*
appendData("*newText*")

Adds characters (passed as a string parameter) to the end of the current text node. The content consists of raw characters, so if you intend to add a sentence to a text node, your scripts are responsible for sentence spacing.

Returned Value   None.

Parameters

newText

String value of text to be appended. A reference that evaluates to a string (such as the data property of another text node in the document) copies the referenced value to the append location.

deleteData( ) IE 5(Mac)/6(Win) NN n/a Moz all Saf all Op 7 DOM 1

deleteData(*startOffset*, *count*)

Removes characters from the current text node starting with the character in (zero-based) position signified by *startOffset*, and for a length of *count* characters in the normal text direction of the current language. If the length specified for deletion goes beyond the length of the data, all characters to the end of the text node are deleted without throwing an exception. Early Mozilla versions include source code whitespace in its counts for both parameters.

Returned Value None.

Parameters

startOffset

Positive integer specifying the zero-based starting character point for the deletion.

count

Positive integer specifying the number of characters to be deleted.

insertData( ) IE 5(Mac)/6(Win) NN n/a Moz all Saf all Op 7 DOM 1

insertData(*startOffset*, "*newText*")

Inserts text into a zero-based character position in the text node.

Returned Value None.

Parameters

startOffset

Positive integer specifying the zero-based character before which the new text is to be inserted.

newText

String value of text to be inserted. A reference that evaluates to a string (such as the data property of another text node in the document) copies the referenced value to the append location.

replaceData( ) IE 5(Mac)/6(Win) NN n/a Moz all Saf all Op 7 DOM 1

replaceData(*startOffset*, *count*, "*newText*")

Replaces text in the current text node with new text. The original content to be removed is signified by the zero-based start position and the number of characters. The string passed as a third parameter goes into the space vacated by the removed text. A bug in IE 5 for Macintosh crops the new text to the length of the removed text.

Returned Value   None.

Parameters

startOffset
>   Positive integer specifying the zero-based starting character point for the deletion.

count
>   Positive integer specifying the number of characters to be deleted.

newText
>   String value of text to be inserted where the remaining text collapses. A reference that evaluates to a string (such as the data property of another text node in the document) copies the referenced value to the append location.

splitText( )   IE *5(Mac)/6(Win)* NN *n/a* Moz *all* Saf *all* Op *7* DOM *1*

splitText(*offset*)

Divides the current text node into two sibling text nodes; otherwise, doesn't disturb the text.

Returned Value   Reference to the second text node.

Parameters

offset
>   Positive integer specifying the zero-based character point before which the split occurs.

substringData( )   IE *5(Mac)/6(Win)* NN *n/a* Moz *all* Saf *all* Op *7* DOM *1*

substringData(*startOffset, count*)

Returns a copy of the designated segment of the text node content. The section to be copied is signified by the zero-based start position and the number of characters

Returned Value   String.

Parameters

startOffset
>   Positive integer specifying the zero-based starting character point for the copy action.

count
>   Positive integer specifying the number of characters to be copied.

textarea   IE *4* NN *n/a* Moz *all* Saf *all* Op *7* DOM *1*

The textarea object reflects the textarea element and is used as a form control. This object is the primary way of getting a user to enter multiple lines of text for submission to the server. Note that the innerHTML property is not available on the Macintosh version of Internet Explorer 4. Only a limited number of properties and methods shown below are available in early browsers that do not support addressing all HTML elements (prior to IE 4 and Netscape 6). IE 5 and later support the shared doScroll( ) method for this object.

HTML Equivalent   `<textarea>`

Object Model Reference

```
[window.]document.formName.elementName
[window.]document.forms[i].elements[j]
[window.]document.getElementById("elementID")
```

Object-Specific Properties

accept	autofocus	cols	dataFld	dataSrc
defaultValue	form	forms[]	inputmode	labels[]
maxlength	name	pattern	readOnly	required
rows	selectionEnd	selectionStart	status	textLength
type	validationMessage	validity	value	willValidate
wrap				

Object-Specific Methods

checkValidity( )	createTextRange( )	dispatchChange( )
dispatchFormChange( )	handleEvent( )	select( )
setCustomValidity( )		

Object-Specific Events

Event	IE	Mozilla	Safari	Opera	W3C DOM
change	•	•	—	•	•
scroll	•	—	—	—	—
select	•	•	—	•	•

accept

IE *n/a*   NN *n/a*   Moz *n/a*   Saf *n/a*   Op *9*   DOM *n/a*

Read/Write

A Web Forms 2.0 extension, the accept attribute specifies one or more MIME types for allowable content to be entered into the element. If the browser provides alternate input editors for content other than straight text, this attribute prepares the element for the content and encodes it correctly for submission with the form.

Example   `document.forms[0].comments.accept = "message/news";`

Value   MIME type string.

Default   Varies with browser and operating system.

autofocus

IE *n/a* NN *n/a* Moz *n/a* Saf *n/a* Op *9* DOM *n/a*

Read/Write

Web Forms 2.0 extension that brings focus to the element after the page loads. Should be assigned to only one form control element per page.

Value	Boolean value: true | false.
Default	false

cols

IE *4* NN *n/a* Moz *all* Saf *all* Op *7* DOM *1*

Read/Write

Specifies the width of the editable space of the textarea element. The value represents the number of monofont characters that are to be displayed within the width. When the font size can be influenced by style sheets, the actual width changes accordingly.

Example	document.forms[0].comments.cols = 60;
Value	Integer.
Default	20 (IE/Windows); -1 (Mozilla, meaning that the attribute or property hasn't been set); 0 (Safari, Windows).

dataFld

IE *4* NN *n/a* Moz *n/a* Saf *n/a* Op *n/a* DOM *n/a*

Read/Write

Used with IE data binding to associate a remote data source column name to a textarea object's value property. A datasrc attribute must also be set for the element. Setting both the dataFld and dataSrc properties to empty strings breaks the binding between element and data source. Works only with text file data sources in IE 5/Mac.

Example	document.myForm.myTextArea.dataFld = "description";
Value	Case-sensitive identifier of the data source column.
Default	None.

dataSrc

IE *4* NN *n/a* Moz *n/a* Saf *n/a* Op *n/a* DOM *n/a*

Read/Write

Used with IE data binding to specify the ID of the page's object element that loads the data source object for remote data access. Content from the data source is specified via the datafld attribute. Setting both the dataFld and dataSrc properties to empty strings breaks the binding between element and data source. Works only with text file data sources in IE 5/Mac.

Example	document.myForm.myTextArea.dataSrc = "DBSRC3";
Value	Case-sensitive identifier of the data source.
Default	None.

defaultValue

Specifies the default text for the textarea element, as established by the text between the start and end tags in the page's source code.

Example
```
var txtAObj = document.forms[0].myTextArea;
if (txtAObj.value != txtAObj.defaultValue ) {
    ...
}
```

Value   Any string value.

Default   None.

form

Returns a reference to the form element that contains the current element. When processing an event from this element, the event handler function automatically has access to the select element (as the event object's target or srcElement property). By reading the form property, the script can easily access other controls within the same form.

Example   var theForm = evt.srcElement.form;

Value   form element object reference.

Default   None.

forms

Web Forms 2.0 extension that returns an array (NodeList) of references to form objects with which the current textarea element is associated.

Example   var formList = document.getElementById("myTextarea").forms;

Value   Array.

Default   One-item array with a reference to any enclosing form element.

inputmode

Web Forms 2.0 extension (adopted whole from the W3C XForms 1.0 specification at *http://www.w3.org/TR/xforms/sliceE.html*) that directs the browser to display the appropriate text input user interface for a written language. Consult the W3C XForms 1.0 documents for details.

Example   document.orderForm.searchText.inputmode = "hiragana";

Value   Written language script token with an optional modifier token (space-delimited). Tokens generally correspond to Unicode scripts (*http://www.unicode.org/unicode/reports/tr24/*).

Default   None.

labels

IE *n/a* NN *n/a* Moz *n/a* Saf *n/a* Op *9* DOM *n/a*

Read-only

Web Forms 2.0 extension that returns an array (HTMLCollection) of references to `label` element objects associated with the current form control element.

Example

```
var textboxLabels = document.getElementById("myTextarea").labels;
```

Value   Array of `label` element object references.

Default   Empty array.

maxlength

IE *n/a* NN *n/a* Moz *n/a* Saf *n/a* Op *9* DOM *n/a*

Read/Write

Web Forms 2.0 extension that defines the maximum number of characters that may be typed into a `textarea` element. In practice, browsers beep or otherwise alert users when a typed character would exceed the `maxlength` value. There is no innate correlation between the `maxlength` and `size` attributes. If the `maxlength` allows for more characters than fit within the specified width of the element, the browser provides horizontal scrolling (albeit awkward for many users) to allow entry and editing of the field.

Example   `document.getElementById("query").maxlength=10;`

Value   Positive integer.

Default   Unlimited.

name

IE *3* NN *2* Moz *all* Saf *all* Op *7* DOM *1*

Read/Write

This is the identifier associated with the form control. The value of this property is submitted as one-half of the name/value pair when the form is submitted to the server. Names are hidden from user view, since control labels are assigned via other means, depending on the control type. Form control names may also be used by script references to the objects. Despite the modern standards' preference for the `id` attribute, many browsers still require that a control be assigned a `name` attribute to allow the control's value to be submitted.

Example   `document.orderForm.myTextArea.name = "customerComment";`

Value   Case-sensitive identifier that follows the rules of identifier naming: it may contain no whitespace, cannot begin with a numeral, and should avoid punctuation except for the underscore character.

Default   None.

pattern

IE *n/a* NN *n/a* Moz *n/a* Saf *n/a* Op *9* DOM *n/a*

Read/Write

Web Forms 2.0 extension that lets you specify a regular expression pattern that the user's input must match to pass validation.

Example   `document.getElementById("partNum").pattern = "[A-Z][0-9]{7}"`

Value   A regular expression (but not surrounded by the slash symbols, as used in JavaScript regular expressions).

Default   None.

readOnly

IE *4* NN *n/a* Moz *all* Saf *all* Op *7* DOM *1*

Read/Write

Indicates whether the form element can be edited on the page by the user. A form control that has its `readOnly` property set to `true` may still be modified by scripts, even though the user may not alter the content.

Example   `document.forms[0].myTextArea.readOnly = "true";`

Value   Boolean value: `true` | `false`.

Default   `false`

required

IE *n/a* NN *n/a* Moz *n/a* Saf *n/a* Op *9* DOM *n/a*

Read/Write

Web Forms 2.0 extension that signifies whether the `textarea` element's value is required for submission. Sets the `missingValue` property of the `ValidityState` object to `true` if the element receives no value.

Value   Boolean value: `true` | `false`.

Default   `false`

rows

IE *4* NN *n/a* Moz *all* Saf *all* Op *7* DOM *1*

Read/Write

Specifies the height of the `textarea` element based on the number of lines of text that are to be displayed without scrolling. The value represents the number of monofont character lines that are to be displayed within the height before the scrollbar becomes active. When the font size can be influenced by style sheets, the actual height changes accordingly.

Example   document.forms[0].comments.rows = 6;

Value   Integer.

Default   2 (IE/Windows); -1 (Mozilla, meaning that the attribute or property hasn't been set); 0 (Safari, Windows).

selectionEnd, selectionStart   IE *n/a* NN *n/a* Moz *all* Saf *1.3/2* Op *8* DOM *n/a*
Read/Write

The selectionEnd and selectionStart properties are convenience properties that allow scripts to get and set the endpositions of a text selection within a text-oriented input element. Values are zero-based integer counters of positions between characters in the text entered into the field. When both properties have the same value, the visual result is the same as a text insertion pointer. For example, to place the cursor at the end of a text box, set the two values to the element's text length (see the textLength property). The equivalent IE functionality requires creating an IE text range in the element, adjusting the range's endpoints, and selecting the range (see the TextRange object).

Example
```
var elem = document.forms[0].myTextarea;
elem.selectionEnd = elem.textLength;
elem.selectionStart = elem.textLength;
```

Value   Positive integer.

Default   None.

status   IE *4* NN *n/a* Moz *n/a* Saf *n/a* Op *n/a* DOM *n/a*
Read/Write

This is implemented in IE, but has no function for the textarea object.

Value   Boolean value: true | false; or null.

Default   null

textLength   IE *n/a* NN *n/a* Moz *1.4* Saf *n/a* Op *8* DOM *n/a*
Read-only

Returns the number of characters in the textarea element.

Value   Integer.

Default   0

type

Returns the type of form control element. The value is returned in all lowercase letters. It may be necessary to cycle through all form elements in search of specific types to do some processing on (e.g., emptying all form controls of type "textarea" while leaving other controls untouched).

Example

```
if (document.forms[0].elements[3].type == "textarea") {
    ...
}
```

Value Any of the following constants (as a string): button | checkbox | file | hidden | image | password | radio | reset | select-multiple | select-one | submit | text | textarea.

Default textarea

validationMessage

Web Forms 2.0 extension that returns a browser-generated message if the form control fails to validate according to its specifications. An empty string means that the entry validates properly.

Value String.

Default Empty string.

validity

Web Forms 2.0 extension that returns a ValidityState object. See the ValidityState object.

Value ValidityState object.

Default ValidityState object.

value

Specifies the current value associated with the form control that is submitted with the name/value pair for the element. All values are strings.

Example var comment = document.forms[0].myTextArea.value;

Value String.

Default None.

willValidate

Read-only

Web Forms 2.0 extension that returns a Boolean value indicating whether the form control element meets criteria for validating under the Web Forms 2.0 mechanism.

Value   Boolean value: true | false.

Default   false

wrap

IE 4 NN *n/a* Moz *n/a* Saf *n/a* Op 9 DOM *n/a*

Read/Write

Indicates whether the browser should wrap text in a textarea element and whether wrapped text should be submitted to the server with soft returns converted to hard carriage returns. A value of hard engages word-wrapping and converts soft returns to CR-LF characters in the value submitted to the server. A value of soft turns on word-wrapping, but does not include the CR-LF characters in the text submitted with the form. A value of off turns word-wrapping off.

Example   document.forms[0].comments.wrap = "soft";

Value   One of the constant values (as a string): hard | off | soft.

Default   soft

checkValidity( )

IE *n/a* NN *n/a* Moz *n/a* Saf *n/a* Op 9 DOM *n/a*

Web Forms 2.0 method that returns a Boolean value representing whether the form control element meets its validity criteria—ultimately, whether the validity.valid property is true.

Returned Value   Boolean value: true | false.

Parameters   None.

createTextRange( )

IE 4(Win) NN *n/a* Moz *n/a* Saf *n/a* Op *n/a* DOM *n/a*

Creates a TextRange object from the content of the textarea object. See the TextRange object for details.

Returned Value   TextRange object.

dispatchChange( ),
dispatchFormChange( )

IE *n/a* NN *n/a* Moz *n/a* Saf *n/a* Op 9 DOM *n/a*

Web Forms 2.0 methods that fire the change and formchange events on the current element. You could, for example "convert" a click event to a change or formchange event by having the onclick event handler invoke either method.

Returned Value   None.

Parameters   None.

handleEvent( )

IE *n/a* NN |4| Moz *n/a* Saf *n/a* Op *n/a* DOM *n/a*

`handleEvent(event)`

Instructs the object to accept and process the event whose specifications are passed as the parameter to the method. The object must have an event handler for the event type to process the event. Navigator 4 only.

Returned Value   None.

Parameters

event

A Navigator 4 event object.

select( )

IE *3* NN *2* Moz *all* Saf *all* Op *7* DOM *1*

Selects all the text displayed in the form element. To position the insertion pointer in a specific location inside a `textarea` element in IE, see the `TextRange` object.

Returned Value   None.

Parameters   None.

setCustomValidity( )

IE *n/a* NN *n/a* Moz *n/a* Saf *n/a* Op *9* DOM *n/a*

`setCustomValidity([errorString])`

Web Forms 2.0 method that sets the `customError` Boolean value of the `validity` property (itself a `ValidityState` object). If the method does not impact an element type, it throws a NOT_SUPPORTED_ERR error.

Returned Value   None.

Parameters

errorString

If null or an empty string, the parameter resets the validity object's `customError` property, signifying the form control is not valid. An error string is to be remembered by the browser (during the current session) so that it displays the string upon subsequent validation failures.

TextNode

See Text.

TextRange

IE *4(Win)* NN *n/a* Moz *n/a* Saf *n/a* Op *n/a* DOM *n/a*

The `TextRange` object--similar in concept to the W3C DOM `Range` object—represents the text of zero or more characters in a document. When a text range consists of zero characters, it represents an insertion point between two characters (or before the first or after the last character).

A TextRange object is created via the createTextRange( ) method associated with the body, button, text, or textarea objects. You can also turn a user selection into a range via the selection object's createRange( ) (note the slight difference in the method name). Once you have created a text range, use its methods to adjust its start and endpoints to encompass a desired segment of the text (such as text that matches a search string). Once the range has been narrowed to the target text, assign values to its text property to change, remove, or insert text (or use pasteHTML( ) to insert HTML into the range). A library of direct commands that perform specific textual modifications can also be invoked to act on the text range. See Online Section V for details and examples of using the TextRange object.

Shared properties and methods from the list at the start of this chapter are: offsetLeft, offsetTop, getBoundingClientRect( ), getClientRects( ), and scrollIntoView( ). Note that the TextRange object and all associated facilities are available only in the Windows version of Internet Explorer.

Object Model Reference

objectRef.createTextRange( )
selectionObjectRef.createRange( )

Object-Specific Properties

boundingHeight	boundingLeft	boundingTop	boundingWidth
htmlText	text		

Object-Specific Methods

collapse( )	compareEndPoints( )	duplicate( )
execCommand( )	expand( )	findText( )
getBookmark( )	inRange( )	isEqual( )
move( )	moveEnd( )	moveStart( )
moveToBookmark( )	moveToElementText( )	moveToPoint( )
parentElement( )	pasteHTML( )	queryCommandEnabled( )
queryCommandIndeterm( )	queryCommandState( )	queryCommandSupported( )
queryCommandText( )	queryCommandValue( )	select( )
setEndPoint( )		

boundingHeight, boundingWidth

IE 4(Win)   NN *n/a*   Moz *n/a*   Saf *n/a*   Op *n/a*   DOM *n/a*

Read-only

Return the pixel measure of the imaginary space occupied by the TextRange object. Although you do not see a TextRange object in the document (unless a script selects it), the area of a TextRange object is identical to the area that a selection highlight would occupy. These values cinch up to measure only as wide or tall as the widest and tallest part of the range. You would arrive at these same values by performing arithmetic on values returned from the getBoundingClientRect( ) method.

Example

```
var rangeWidth = document.forms[0].myTextArea.createTextRange( ).boundingWidth;
```

Value   Integer.

Default   None.

boundingLeft, boundingTop   IE *4(Win)* NN *n/a* Moz *n/a* Saf *n/a* Op *n/a* DOM *n/a*

Read-only

Return the pixel distance between the top or left of the browser window or frame and the top or left edges of the imaginary space occupied by the TextRange object. Although you do not see a TextRange object in the document (unless a script selects it), the area of a TextRange object is identical to the area that a selection highlight would occupy. Values for these properties are measured from the fixed window or frame edges and not the top and left of the document, which may scroll out of view. Therefore, as a document scrolls, these values change.

Example

```
var rangeOffH = document.forms[0].myTextArea.createTextRange( ).boundingLeft;
```

Value   Integer.

Default   None.

htmlText   IE *4(Win)* NN *n/a* Moz *n/a* Saf *n/a* Op *n/a* DOM *n/a*

Read-only

Specifies all HTML of the document for a given element when that element is used as the basis for a TextRange object. For example, if you create a TextRange for the body element (document.body.createTextRange( )), the htmlText property contains all HTML content between (but not including) the body element tags.

Example   `var rangeHTML = document.body.createTextRange( ).htmlText;`

Value   String.

Default   None.

text   IE *4(Win)* NN *n/a* Moz *n/a* Saf *n/a* Op *n/a* DOM *n/a*

Read/Write

Indicates the text contained by the text range. In the case of a TextRange object of a body element, this consists of only the text that is rendered, but none of the HTML tags behind the scenes.

Example   `var rangeText = document.body.createTextRange( ).text;`

Value   String.

Default   None.

collapse( )   IE 4(Win) NN n/a Moz n/a Saf n/a Op n/a DOM n/a

collapse([start])

Reduces the TextRange object to a length of zero (creating an insertion point) at the beginning or end of the text range before it collapsed.

Returned Value   None.

Parameters

start

     Optional Boolean value that controls whether the insertion point goes to the beginning (true) of the original range or the end (false). The default value is true.

compareEndPoints( )   IE 4(Win) NN n/a Moz n/a Saf n/a Op n/a DOM n/a

compareEndPoints("type", comparisonRange)

Compares the relative position of the boundary (start and end) points of two ranges (the current range and one that had been previously saved to a variable). The first parameter defines which boundary points in each range you wish to compare. If the result of the comparison is that the first point is earlier in the range than the other point, the returned value is -1. If the result shows both points to be in the same location, the returned value is 0. If the result shows the first point to be later in the range than the other point, the returned value is 1. For example, if you have saved the first range to a variable r1 and created a new range as r2, you can see the physical relationship between the end of r2 and the start of r1:

```
r1.compareEndPoints("EndToStart", r2)
```

If r1 ends where r2 starts (the insertion point between two characters), the returned value is 0.

Returned Value   -1, 0, or 1.

Parameters

type

     One of the following constants (as a string): StartToEnd | StartToStart | EndToStart | EndToEnd.

comparisonRange

     A TextRange object created earlier and saved to a variable.

duplicate( )   IE 4(Win) NN n/a Moz n/a Saf n/a Op n/a DOM n/a

Creates a new TextRange object with the same values as the current range. The new object is an independent object (the old and new do not equal each other), but their values are initially identical (until you start modifying one range or the other).

Returned Value   TextRange object.

Parameters   None.

execCommand( )   IE 4(Win) NN n/a Moz n/a Saf n/a Op n/a DOM n/a

execCommand("*commandName*"[, *UIFlag*[, *value*]])

Executes the named command on the current TextRange object. Many commands work best when the TextRange object is an insertion point. See Appendix D for a list of commands.

Returned Value   Boolean value: true if command is successful; false if unsuccessful.

Parameters

commandName
> A case-insensitive string value of the command name. See Appendix D.

UIFlag
> Optional Boolean value: true to display any user interface triggered by the command (if any); false to prevent such display.

value
> A parameter value for the command.

expand( )   IE 4(Win) NN n/a Moz n/a Saf n/a Op n/a DOM n/a

expand("*unit*")

Expands the current text range (including a collapsed range) to encompass the textual unit passed as a parameter. For example, if someone selects some characters from a document, you can create the range and expand it to encompass the entire sentence in which the selection takes place:

```
var rng = document.selection.createRange( );
rng.expand("sentence");
```

If the starting range extends across multiple units, the expand( ) method expands the range outward to the next nearest unit.

Returned Value   Boolean value: true if method is successful; false if unsuccessful.

Parameters

unit
> A case-insensitive string value of the desired unit: character | word | sentence | textedit. The textedit value expands the range to the entire original range.

findText( )   IE 4(Win) NN n/a Moz n/a Saf n/a Op n/a DOM n/a

findText("*string*"[, *searchScope*][, *flags*])

Searches the current TextRange object for a match of a string passed as the required first parameter. By default, matching is done on a case-insensitive basis. If there is a match, the TextRange object repositions its start and endpoints to surround the found text. To continue searching in the document, you must reposition the start point of the text range to the end of the found string (with collapse( )).

Optional parameters let you limit the scope of the search within the range to a desired number of characters after the range's start point, or dictate additional matching requirements, such as partial or whole words.

Returned Value   Boolean value: true if a match is found; false if unsuccessful.

Parameters

string

A case-insensitive string to be searched.

searchScope

Integer for the number of characters to search relative to the range's start point. A positive number searches forward; a negative number searches backward, to text earlier in the document than the start point of the text range.

flags

Integer for search detail codes: 0 (match partial words); 1 (match backwards); 2 (match whole words only); 4 (match case).

getBookmark( ), moveToBookmark( )   IE 4(Win) NN n/a Moz n/a Saf n/a Op n/a DOM n/a

getBookmark( ) moveToBookmark(*bookmarkString*)

These two methods work together as a way to temporarily save a text range specification and restore it when needed. The getBookmark( ) method returns an opaque string (containing binary data that is of no value to human users). Once that value is stored in a variable, the range can be modified as needed for the script. Some time later, the book-marked text range can be restored with the moveToBookmark( ) method:

```
var rangeMark = myRange.getBookmark();
...
myRange.moveToBookmark(rangeMark);
```

Returned Value   Boolean value: true if the operation is successful; false if unsuccessful.

Parameters

bookmarkString

An opaque string returned by the getBookmark( ) method.

inRange( )   IE 4(Win) NN n/a Moz n/a Saf n/a Op n/a DOM n/a

inRange(*comparisonRange*)

Determines whether the comparison range is within or equal to the physical range of the current text range.

Returned Value   Boolean value: true if the comparison range is in or equal to the current range; false if not.

Parameters

comparisonRange

TextRange object created earlier and saved to a variable.

isEqual( )   IE 4(Win)   NN n/a   Moz n/a   Saf n/a   Op n/a   DOM n/a

isEqual(*comparisonRange*)

Determines whether the comparison range is identical to the current text range.

Returned Value   Boolean value: true if the comparison range is equal to the current range; false if not.

Parameters

comparisonRange

A TextRange object created earlier and saved to a variable.

move( )   IE 4(Win)   NN n/a   Moz n/a   Saf n/a   Op n/a   DOM n/a

move("*unit*"[, *count*])

Collapses the current text range to an insertion point at the end of the current range and moves it forward or backward from the current position by one or more units.

Returned Value   Integer of the number of units moved.

Parameters

unit

A case-insensitive string value of the desired unit: character | word | sentence | textedit. The textedit value moves the insertion pointer to the start or end of the entire original range.

count

An optional integer of the number of units to move the insertion pointer. Positive values move the pointer forward; negative values move the pointer backward. Default value is 1.

moveEnd( ), moveStart( )   IE 4(Win)   NN n/a   Moz n/a   Saf n/a   Op n/a   DOM n/a

moveEnd("*unit*"[, *count*]) moveStart("*unit*"[, *count*])

Moves only the end or start point (respectively) of the current text range by one or more units. An optional parameter lets you specify both the number of units and direction. To shift the start point of a text range toward the beginning of the original range, be sure to specify a negative value. When moving the endpoint forward by word units, be aware that a word ends with a whitespace character (including a period). Therefore, if a findText( ) method sets the range to a found string that does not end in a space, the first moveEnd("word") method moves the ending point to the spot past the space after the found string rather than to the following word.

Returned Value   Integer of the number of units moved.

Parameters

unit

A case-insensitive string value of the desired unit: character | word | sentence | textedit. The textedit value moves the insertion pointer to the start or end of the entire original range.

count

> An optional integer of the number of units to move the insertion pointer. Positive values move the pointer forward; negative values move the pointer backward. Default value is 1.

moveToBookmark( )

See getBookmark().

moveToElementText( )   IE 4(Win) NN *n/a* Moz *n/a* Saf *n/a* Op *n/a* DOM *n/a*
moveToElementText(*elementObject*)

Moves the current TextRange object's start and endpoints to encase the specified HTML element object. The resulting text range includes the HTML for the element, as well.

Returned Value   None.

Parameters

elementObject

> A scripted reference to the object. This can be in the form of a direct reference (document.getElementById("*elementID*")) or a variable containing the same kind of value.

moveToPoint( )   IE 4(Win) NN *n/a* Moz *n/a* Saf *n/a* Op *n/a* DOM *n/a*
moveToPoint(*x, y*)

Collapses the text range to an insertion pointer and sets its location to the spot indicated by the horizontal and vertical coordinates in the browser window or frame. This is as if the user had clicked on a spot in the window to define an insertion point. Use methods such as expand( ) to enlarge the text range to include a character, word, sentence, or entire text range.

Returned Value   None.

Parameters

x

> Horizontal coordinate of the insertion point in pixels relative to the left edge of the window or frame.

y

> Vertical coordinate of the insertion point in pixels relative to the top edge of the window or frame.

parentElement( )   IE 4(Win) NN *n/a* Moz *n/a* Saf *n/a* Op *n/a* DOM *n/a*

Returns an object reference to the next outermost element that fully contains the TextRange object.

Returned Value   Element object reference.

Parameters   None.

pasteHTML( )   IE *4(Win)* NN *n/a* Moz *n/a* Saf *n/a* Op *n/a* DOM *n/a*
pasteHTML("*HTMLText*")

Replaces the current text range with the HTML content supplied as a parameter string. Typically, this method is used on a zero-length text range object acting as an insertion pointer. All tags are rendered as if they were part of the original source code.

Returned Value   None.

Parameters
HTMLText
    Document source code to be inserted into the document.

queryCommandEnabled( )   IE *4(Win)* NN *n/a* Moz *n/a* Saf *n/a* Op *n/a* DOM *n/a*
queryCommandEnabled("*commandName*")

Indicates whether the command can be invoked in light of the current state of the document or selection.

Returned Value   Boolean value: true if enabled; false if not.

Parameters
commandName
    A case-insensitive string value of the command name. See Appendix D.

queryCommandIndeterm( )   IE *4(Win)* NN *n/a* Moz *n/a* Saf *n/a* Op *n/a* DOM *n/a*
queryCommandIndeterm("*commandName*")

Indicates whether the command is in an indeterminate state.

Returned Value   Boolean value: true | false.

Parameters
commandName
    A case-insensitive string value of the command name. See Appendix D.

queryCommandState( )   IE *4(Win)* NN *n/a* Moz *n/a* Saf *n/a* Op *n/a* DOM *n/a*
queryCommandState("*commandName*")

Determines the current state of the named command.

Returned Value   true if the command has been completed; false if the command has not completed; null if the state cannot be accurately determined.

Parameters
commandName
    A case-insensitive string value of the command name. See Appendix D.

queryCommandSupported( )   IE 4(Win) NN n/a Moz n/a Saf n/a Op n/a DOM n/a

queryCommandSupported("*commandName*")

Determines whether the named command is supported by the document object.

Returned Value   Boolean value: true | false.

Parameters

commandName
> A case-insensitive string value of the command name. See Appendix D.

queryCommandText( )   IE 4(Win) NN n/a Moz n/a Saf n/a Op n/a DOM n/a

queryCommandText("*commandName*")

Returns text associated with the command.

Returned Value   String.

Parameters

commandName
> A case-insensitive string value of the command name. See Appendix D.

queryCommandValue( )   IE 4(Win) NN n/a Moz n/a Saf n/a Op n/a DOM n/a

queryCommandValue("*commandName*")

Returns the value associated with the command, such as the name font of the selection.

Returned Value   Depends on the command.

Parameters

commandName
> A case-insensitive string value of the command name. See Appendix D.

select( )   IE 4(Win) NN n/a Moz n/a Saf n/a Op n/a DOM n/a

Selects all the text that is included in the current TextRange object. This method brings some visual confirmation to users that a script knows about a particular block of text. For example, if you were scripting a search with the findText( ) method, you would then use the scrollIntoView( ) and select( ) methods on that range to show the user where the matching text is.

Returned Value   None.

Parameters   None.

setEndPoint( )   IE 4(Win) NN n/a Moz n/a Saf n/a Op n/a DOM n/a

setEndPoint("*type*", *comparisonRange*)

Sets the endpoint of the current TextRange object to the endpoint of another range that had previously been preserved as a variable reference.

Returned Value   None.

Parameters

type

One of the following constants (as a string): StartToEnd | StartToStart | EndToStart | EndToEnd.

comparisonRange

A TextRange object created earlier and saved to a variable.

TextRectangle   IE *5(Win)* NN *n/a* Moz *n/a* Saf *n/a* Op *n/a* DOM *n/a*

A TextRectangle object contains the coordinates of the four edges of an invisible box that surrounds a string of body text. Two methods of all element objects and the TextRange object produce information about two different kinds of text rectangles. The getClientRects() method returns a collection of line-by-line text rectangles; the getBoundingClientRect() method returns a single TextRectangle object that has coordinates that encompass all line-by-line rectangles.

Invoking either of these methods gets the rectangles' values instantaneously. Resizing the window or altering the content of the target object may change the actual rectangles, but the TextRangle objects obtained earlier do not keep pace with the changes (since the content of each line's rectangle is likely to change). Therefore, obtain TextRectangle values immediately before you need to process them in other script statements.

Object Model Reference

elementOrTextRangeReference.getBoundingClientRect()
elementOrTextRangeReference.getClientRects()[i]

Object-Specific Properties

bottom	left	top	right

Object-Specific Methods
None.

Object-Specific Events
None.

bottom, left, right, top   IE *5(Win)* NN *n/a* Moz *n/a* Saf *n/a* Op *n/a* DOM *n/a*

Read-only

Return integer pixel values for the browser window coordinates of the rectangle edges. Note that these values are not relative to the page. Therefore, values change as the text holder scrolls.

Example

```
var rightMostEdge = document.getElementById("myP").getBoundingClientRect().right;
```

Value	Integer pixel measures
Default	None.

tfoot

See tbody.

th

See td.

thead

See tbody.

title

The title object reflects the title element. If you encounter problems referencing the element object by its id attribute, use the tag access methods, such as document. getElementsByTagName("title")[0].

HTML Equivalent <title>

Object Model Reference
[window.]document.getElementById("*elementID*")

Object-Specific Properties
text

Object-Specific Methods
None.

Object-Specific Events
None.

text

Read/Write

Specifies the text content of the element. For the title element, this is the text between the start and end tags that also appears in the browser window's title bar (usually along with some identification of the browser brand) or tab (when in tabbed browsing). Changes you make to this property do not appear in the source code you view from the browser. Nor does the change appear in the title bar of IE for Windows.

Example   document.getElementsByTagName("title")[0].text = "Welcome, Dave!";

Value	String.
Default	None.

toolbar

See directories.

tr

The tr object reflects the tr element.

HTML Equivalent   <tr>

Object Model Reference

[window.]document.getElementById("*elementID*")
[window.]document.getElementById("*tableID*").rows[i]

Object-Specific Properties

align	bgColor	borderColor	borderColorDark
borderColorLight	cells[]	ch	chOff
height	rowIndex	sectionRowIndex	vAlign

Object-Specific Methods

deleteCell( )	insertCell( )

Object-Specific Events

None.

align

Read/Write

Defines the horizontal alignment of content within all cells of the row.

Example	document.getElementById("myTR").align = "center";
Value	Any of the three horizontal alignment constants: center | left | right.
Default	left

bgColor

Read/Write

Specifies the background color of the table cells in the current row. This color setting is not reflected in the style sheet backgroundColor property. Even if the bgcolor attribute or bgColor property is set with a plain-language color name, the returned value is always a hexadecimal triplet.

Example   document.getElementById("myTR").bgColor = "yellow";

Value   A hexadecimal triplet or plain-language color name. See Appendix A for acceptable plain-language color names.

Default   Varies with browser and operating system.

borderColor   IE 4 NN *n/a* Moz *n/a* Saf *n/a* Op *n/a* DOM *n/a*
Read/Write

Specifies the color of the element's border. Internet Explorer applies the color to all four lines that make up the interior border of a cell. Therefore, colors of adjacent cells do not collide.

Example   document.getElementById("myTR").borderColor = "salmon";

Value   A hexadecimal triplet or plain-language color name. A setting of empty is interpreted as "#000000" (black). See Appendix A for acceptable plain-language color names.

Default   Varies with operating system.

borderColorDark,
borderColorLight   IE 4 NN *n/a* Moz *n/a* Saf *n/a* Op *n/a* DOM *n/a*
Read/Write

The 3D effect of table borders in Internet Explorer is created by careful positioning of light and dark lines around the page's background or default color. You can independently control the colors used for the dark and light lines by assigning values to the borderColorDark (left and top edges of the cell) and borderColorLight (right and bottom edges) properties.

Typically, you should assign complementary colors to the pair of properties. There is also no rule that says you must assign a dark color to borderColorDark. The attributes merely control a well-defined set of lines so you can predict which lines of the border change with each attribute.

Example
document.getElementById("myTR").borderColorDark = "blue";
document.getElementById("myTR").borderColorLight = "cornflowerblue";

Value   A hexadecimal triplet or plain-language color name. A setting of empty is interpreted as "#000000" (black). See Appendix A for acceptable plain-language color names.

Default   Varies with operating system.

cells

Returns a collection of td or th elements nested inside the table row. Items in the collection are in source code order.

Example	`var allRowCells = document.getElementById("myTR").cells;`
Value	Reference to a cells collection object.
Default	Array of zero length.

ch

Defines the text character used as an alignment point for text cells of the row. This property is normally of value only for the align attribute set to "char". In practice, even though the table section element object has this property, the browser does not respond to values assigned to it.

Example	`document.getElementById("myTR").ch = ".";`
Value	Single character string.
Default	None.

chOff

Defines the offset point at which the character specified by the char attribute is to appear within a cell. In practice, even though the table section element object has this property, the browser does not respond to values assigned to it.

Example	`document.getElementById("myTR").chOff = "80%";`
Value	String value of the number of pixels or percentage (within the cell).
Default	None.

height

Specifies the pixel or percentage height of the row. To change the height of a row dynamically, adjust the element's style.height value rather than the height property.

Value	String value of the number of pixels or percentage (within the row).
Default	None.

rowIndex

Returns a zero-based integer representing the position of the current row among all other tr elements in the entire table. The count is based on the source code order of the tr elements.

Example   var whichRow = document.getElementById("myTR").rowIndex;

Value   Integer.

Default   None.

sectionRowIndex

Returns a zero-based integer representing the position of the current row among all other tr elements in the row grouping. A row grouping can be one of the following elements: thead, tbody, tfoot. The count is based on the source code order of the tr elements.

Example   var whichRow = document.getElementById("myTR").sectionRowIndex;

Value   Integer.

Default   None.

vAlign

Indicates the manner of vertical alignment of text within the cells of the current row.

Example   document.getElementById("myTR").vAlign = "baseline";

Value   Case-insensitive constant (as a string): baseline | bottom | middle | top.

Default   middle

deleteCell( )

deleteCell(*index*)

Removes a td or th element nested within the current tr element. The integer parameter points to the zero-based item in the row's cells collection.

Returned Value   None.

Parameters

index

Zero-based integer corresponding to the numbered td element in source code order (nested within the current element).

insertCell( ) IE 4(Win) NN n/a Moz all Saf all Op 7 DOM 1

insertCell(*index*)

Inserts a `td` element nested within the current `tr` element. The integer parameter points to the zero-based index in the `cells` collection where the new cell should go, but in IE you can also use the shortcut value of -1 to append the cell to the end of the collection. Adding the cell inserts an empty element, to which you add content via the various document tree modification techniques. Unfortunately, scripting the addition of table rows and cells in IE for the Macintosh (including Version 5.1) is very broken, yielding elephantine row and cell dimensions. For nonnested tables, you might be able to get away with regular document tree node creation and insertion instead of the table section object convenience methods.

Returned Value   Reference to the newly inserted cell.

Parameters

index

> Zero-based integer corresponding to a row of the `cells` collection before which the new cell is to be inserted.

TreeWalker IE n/a NN n/a Moz 1.0.1 Saf 1.3/2 Op 8 DOM 2

The `TreeWalker` object is a live, hierarchical list of nodes that meet criteria defined by the `document.createTreeWalker( )` method. The list assumes the same parent-descendant hierarchy for its items as the nodes to which its items point. The `createTreeWalker( )` method describes the node where the list begins and which nodes (or classes of nodes) are exempt from the list by way of filtering.

The `TreeWalker` object maintains a kind of pointer inside the list (so that your scripts don't have to). Methods of this object let scripts access the next or previous node (or sibling, child, or parent node) in the list, while moving the pointer in the direction indicated by the method you chose. If scripts modify the document tree after the `TreeWalker` is created, changes to the document tree are automatically reflected in the sequence of nodes in the `TreeWalker`.

While fully usable in an HTML document, the `TreeWalker` can be even more valuable in an XML data document. For example, the W3C DOM does not provide a quick way to access all elements that have a particular attribute name (something that the XPATH standard can do easily on the server). But you can define a `TreeWalker` to point only to nodes that have the desired attribute, and quickly access those nodes sequentially (i.e., without having to script more laborious looping through all nodes in search of the desired elements). As an example, the following filter function allows only those nodes that contain the `author` attribute to be a member of a `TreeWalker` object:

```
function authorAttrFilter(node) {
    if (node.hasAttribute("author")) {
        return NodeFilter.FILTER_ACCEPT;
    }
    return NodeFilter.FILTER_SKIP;
}
```

A reference to this function becomes one of the parameters to a createTreeWalker() method that also limits the list to element nodes:

```
var authorsOnly = document.createTreeWalker(document,
NodeFilter.SHOW_ELEMENT, authorAttrFilter, false);
```

You can then invoke TreeWalker object methods to obtain a reference to one of the nodes in the list. When you invoke the method, the TreeWalker object applies the filter to candidates relative to the current position of the internal pointer in the direction indicated by the method. The next document tree node to meet the method and filter criteria is returned. Once you have that node reference, you can access any DOM node property or method to work with the node, independent of the items in the TreeWalker list.

Object Model Reference
TreeWalkerReference

Object-Specific Properties

currentNode	expandEntityReference	filter	root	whatToShow

Object-Specific Methods

firstChild( )	lastChild( )	nextNode( )	nextSibling( )
parentNode( )	previousNode( )	previousSibling( )	

Object-Specific Events
None.

currentNode
IE *n/a* NN *n/a* Moz *1.0.1* Saf *1.3/2* Op *8* DOM *2*

Read/Write

Returns a reference to the node where the TreeWalker's pointer is positioned. But more importantly, you can also assign a document tree node reference to this property to manually set a new position for the pointer. If the assigned node would normally be filtered out of the list, the next method invocation is performed from the position as if the assigned node were not filtered out of the list.

Example   myTreeWalker.currentNode = document.getElementById("main");

Value   Reference to a document tree node.

Default   First node of the document.

expandEntityReference, filter, root, whatToShow
IE *n/a* NN *n/a* Moz *1.0.1* Saf *1.3/2* Op *8* DOM *2*

Read-only

These four properties reflect the parameter values passed to the document. createTreeWalker() method when the object was created.

firstChild( ), lastChild( ), nextSibling( ), parentNode( ), previousSibling( )
IE *n/a* NN *n/a* Moz *1.0.1* Saf *1.3/2* Op *8* DOM *2*

These methods return references to nodes within the hierarchy of items in the `TreeWalker` object. The parent-descendant relationships between nodes are identical to those of the nodes within the document tree. As you invoke any one of these methods, the `TreeWalker`'s internal pointer moves to a position adjacent to the node's spot within the `TreeWalker` list. If there is no node meeting the desired reference, the method returns `null`. This means that you need to verify the existence of the node before reading any property of the node:

```
if (myTreeWalker.nextSibling( )) {
    var theTag = myTreeWalker.currentNode.tagName;
}
```

If you reference a property of a null reference directly (`myTreeWalker.nextSibling( ). tagName`, for example), a reference error results.

Returned Value Reference to a document tree node.

Parameters None.

nextNode( ), previousNode( )
IE *n/a* NN *n/a* Moz *1.0.1* Saf *1.3/2* Op *8* DOM *2*

Move the internal `NodeIterator` pointer one position forward (`nextNode( )`) or backward (`previousNode( )`), while returning a reference to the node through which the pointer passed en route. These two methods operate as if the hierarchy were flattened (in the manner of a `NodeIterator` object).

Returned Value Reference to a node in the document tree.

Parameters None.

tt

See b.

u

See b.

UIEvent
IE *n/a* NN *n/a* Moz *all* Saf *all* Op *7* DOM *2*

The W3C DOM `UIEvent` object is an abstract object that contains the properties and methods shared by every instance of a W3C DOM focus-related event. This object inherits characteristics from the W3C DOM `Event` object. The properties and method of this object are blended into the directly scripted event object. See the discussion of the event object earlier in this chapter for specific property and method support for this object and how these items are inherited by more specific event types.

Alphabetical DOM Reference

ul

IE 4 NN n/a Moz all Saf all Op 7 DOM 1

The ul object reflects the ul element.

HTML Equivalent `<ul>`

Object Model Reference
`[window.]document.getElementById("elementID")`

Object-Specific Properties

compact   type

Object-Specific Methods
None.

Object-Specific Events
None.

compact

IE 4 NN n/a Moz all Saf all Op 7 DOM 1

Read/Write

When set to true, the compact property should instruct the browser to render items in the list in a more compact format. This property has no effect in mainstream browsers.

Example   `document.getElementById("myUL").compact = true;`

Value   Boolean value: true | false.

Default   `false`

type

IE 4 NN n/a Moz all Saf all Op 7 DOM 1

Read/Write

Specifies the manner in which the leading item markers in the list are displayed.

Example   `document.getElementById("myUL").type = "square";`

Value   Any one of the constant values (as a string): circle | disc | square. Additional choices available through style sheets

Default   `disc`

userProfile

IE 4-6(Win) NN n/a Moz n/a Saf n/a Op n/a DOM n/a

The userProfile object reflects numerous pieces of information stored in the browser's user profile for the current user. This object has four methods that:

- Let you queue requests for individual fields of the profile (items such as name, mailing address, phone numbers, and so on)

- Display the request dialog that lets users see what you're asking for and disallow specific items or the whole thing
- Grab the information
- Clear the request queue

Once the information is retrieved (with the user's permission), it can be slipped into form elements (visible or hidden) for submission to the server. Compatibility listings here indicate support in IE 4 through 6 for Windows only. While IE for Macintosh accepts the method calls without error, there is no functionality attached to those methods. Further details on the user profile are available from Microsoft at *http://msdn.microsoft.com/ workshop/management/profile/profile_assistant.asp*.

Example

```
navigator.userProfile.addReadRequest("vcard.displayname");
navigator.userProfile.doReadRequest("3", "MegaCorp Customer Service");
var custName = navigator.userProfile.getAttribute("vcard.displayname");
navigator.userProfile.clearRequest();
if (custName) {
    ...
}
```

Object Model Reference
```
navigator.userProfile
```

Object-Specific Properties
None.

Object-Specific Methods

addReadRequest( )	clearRequest( )	doReadRequest( )	getAttribute( )

Object-Specific Events
None.

addReadRequest( )　　　　IE 4-6(Win)　NN n/a　Moz n/a　Saf n/a　Op n/a　DOM n/a
```
addReadRequest("attributeName")
```
Adds a request to inspect a particular user profile attribute to a queue that must be executed separately (via the doReadRequest( ) and getAttribute( ) methods). Items added to the queue are displayed to the user to select which item(s) can be submitted to a server. For multiple attributes, use multiple invocations of the addReadRequest( ) method.

Returned Value　　Boolean value: true (if successful) | false (if unsuccessful).

Parameters
attributeName
　　One of the following case-insensitive attribute names as a string:

vCard.Business.City	vCard.Business.Country
vCard.Business.Fax	vCard.Business.Phone

vCard.Business.State	vCard.Business.StreetAddress
vCard.Business.URL	vCard.Business.Zipcode
vCard.Cellular	vCard.Company
vCard.Department	vCard.DisplayName
vCard.Email	vCard.FirstName
vCard.Gender	vCard.Home.City
vCard.Home.Country	vCard.Home.Fax
vCard.Home.Phone	vCard.Home.State
vCard.Home.StreetAddress	vCard.Home.Zipcode
vCard.Homepage	vCard.JobTitle
vCard.LastName	vCard.MiddleName
vCard.Notes	vCard.Office
vCard.Pager	

clearRequest( )   IE 4-6(Win) NN n/a Moz n/a Saf n/a Op n/a DOM n/a

Empties the queue of attribute names to be retrieved. Use this after your script has success-fully retrieved the required information. This prepares the queue for the next list.

Returned Value   None.

Parameters   None.

doReadRequest( )   IE 4-6(Win) NN n/a Moz n/a Saf n/a Op n/a DOM n/a

doReadRequest(*usageCode*[, "*friendlyName*"[, "*domain*"[, "*path*"[, "*expiration*"]]]])

Based on the items in the queue, this method inspects the browser to see whether the user has given permission to inspect these attributes in the past. If not (for some or all), the method displays a dialog box (the Profile Assistant window) that lets users turn off the items that should not be exposed to the server. Parameters provide information for the dialog and for maintenance of the permission (similar to the ways that cookies are managed). Only one doReadRequest( ) method is required, regardless of the number of attributes in the queue.

Returned Value   In Windows, the method returns no value, regardless of how the user responds to the Profile Assistant dialog box. On the Macintosh (which does not support this object fully), the method does not display the Profile Assistant dialog box and returns false.

Parameters

usageCode

One of the following code integers that display human-readable messages defined by the Internet Privacy Working Group, as shown in the following table.

Code	Meaning
0	Used for system administration.
1	Used for research and/or product development.
2	Used for completion and support of current transaction.
3	Used to customize the content and design of a site.
4	Used to improve the content of the site, including advertisements.
5	Used for notifying visitors about updates to the site.
6	Used for contacting visitors for marketing of services or products.
7	Used for linking other collected information.
8	Used by site for other purposes.
9	Disclosed to others for customization or improvement of the content and design of the site.
10	Disclosed to others who may contact you for marketing of services and/or products.
11	Disclosed to others who may contact you for marketing of services and/or products, but you have the opportunity to ask a site not to do this.
12	Disclosed to others for any other purpose.

friendlyName

An optional string containing an identifiable name (and URL) that the user recognizes as the source of the request. This may be a corporate identity.

domain

An optional string containing the domain of the server making the request. If an expiration date is set, this information is stored with the requested attributes to prevent future requests from this domain from interrupting the user with the Profile Assistant dialog box.

path

An optional string containing the path of the server document making the request. If an expiration date is set, this information is stored with the requested attributes to prevent future requests from this domain from interrupting the user with the Profile Assistant dialog box.

expiration

An optional string containing the date on which the user's permissions settings expire. Not recognized in Internet Explorer 4.

getAttribute( ) IE *4-6(Win)* NN *n/a* Moz *n/a* Saf *n/a* Op *n/a* DOM *n/a*

getAttribute("*attributeName*")

Returns the value of the attribute, provided the user has given permission to do so. If that permission was denied, the method returns null. Use one getAttribute( ) method for each attribute value being retrieved.

Returned Value   String value or null.

Alphabetical DOM Reference

Parameters

attributeName
> One of the *v*Card attribute names listed in the addReadRequest( ) method description.

ValidityState

IE n/a NN n/a Moz n/a Saf n/a Op 9 DOM n/a

In Web Forms 2.0, each form control capable of receiving user entry has a validity property whose value is an instance of the ValidityState object. This object contains nine Boolean properties, eight of which may be set to true if the corresponding validity test fails. An input, textarea, and select element (again only the Web Forms 2.0 environment) offers enough supplemental attributes to let a page author preset value types, upper and lower limits, text patterns, and even if user entry is required before the form may be submitted. For example, if a text input element is set up to receive a number within a particular range, the validity.typeMismatch property will be set to true if the user enters a letter; if the user enters a number but it is higher than the expected range, the validity.rangeOverflow property is set to true.

All of this comes into play when the instance of the ValidityState object goes to set the valid property—the gatekeeper to whether the element passes validation. If any of the specific validation error properties is false, then the valid property is also false. In other words, the validation tests must have all "green lights" (i.e., the individual test properties are false) before the valid property is set to true.

The following example demonstrates one way to bring validity tests together with an output element object affiliated with a time-oriented input element, which displays a plain-language error message to the user:

```
<script type="text/javascript"> // <![CDATA[
function validateField(evt) {
   var form = evt.target.form;
   var errField = form.elements[evt.target.name + "Error"];
   if (evt.target.validity.typeMismatch) {
      errField.value = 'You must enter a time (hh:mm).';
   } else if (evt.target.validity.stepMismatch) {
      errField.value = 'Appointments must begin at 0, 15, 30, or 45 past the hour.';
   } else if (evt.target.validity.rangeUnderflow) {
      errField.value = 'The earliest appointment is 9:00 am.';
   } else if (evt.target.validity.rangeOverflow) {
      errField.value = 'The last appointment is 5:00 pm.';
   } else if (evt.target.validity.valueMissing) {
      errField.value = 'You must enter a time.';
   } else {
      errField.value = '';
   }
   evt.preventDefault();
// ]]>
}
</script>
...
<form action="..." method="get" >
<p><label>Desired appointment time:
```

```
        <input type="time" name="apptTime" min="09:00" max="17:00" value="09:00"
step="900"
            required="required" onforminput="validateField(event)" />
    </label>
    <output name="apptTimeError" />
    </p>
    <p>
    <input type="submit" />
    </p>
    </form>
```

Object Model Reference

[window.]document.getElementById("*elementID*")

Object-Specific Properties

customError	patternMismatch	rangeOverflow	rangeUnderflow
stepMismatch	tooLong	typeMismatch	valid
valueMissing			

Object-Specific Methods

None.

customError

Read-only

If true, the control was marked invalid by script intervention.

Value   Boolean value: true | false.

Default   false

patternMismatch

Read-only

If true, the input value does not match the regular expression pattern assigned to it. An empty field results in this property being false.

Value   Boolean value: true | false.

Default   false

rangeOverflow, rangeUnderflow

Read-only

If true, the input value (number, time, date, or file) exceeds the limits set by the max and min attributes, respectively.

Value   Boolean value: true | false.

Default   false

stepMismatch

IE *n/a* NN *n/a* Moz *n/a* Saf *n/a* Op *9* DOM *n/a*

Read-only

If true, the input value does not meet the value increment parameters established by the control's step attribute.

Value   Boolean value: true | false.

Default   false

tooLong

IE *n/a* NN *n/a* Moz *n/a* Saf *n/a* Op *9* DOM *n/a*

Read-only

If true, the input value exceeds the character length established by the control's maxlength attribute.

Value   Boolean value: true | false.

Default   false

typeMismatch

IE *n/a* NN *n/a* Moz *n/a* Saf *n/a* Op *9* DOM *n/a*

Read-only

If true, the input value is not of the value type expected by the control (based on the control's type attribute, or a file input element's accept attribute).

Value   Boolean value: true | false.

Default   false

valid

IE *n/a* NN *n/a* Moz *n/a* Saf *n/a* Op *9* DOM *n/a*

Read-only

If true, all other properties of the object are false, indicating that all controls have passed validation.

Value   Boolean value: true | false.

Default   false

valueMissing

IE *n/a* NN *n/a* Moz *n/a* Saf *n/a* Op *9* DOM *n/a*

Read-only

If true, the input value is empty, and the element's required attribute has been set.

Value   Boolean value: true | false.

Default   false

var

See abbr.

ViewCSS

The W3C DOM ViewCSS object is an abstract object that feeds its getComputedStyle( ) method to the document.defaultView object. This provides the actual rendered style sheet properties for a given element node.

Object Model Reference

[window.]document.defaultView

Object-Specific Properties

None.

Object-Specific Methods

getComputedStyle( )

Object-Specific Events

None.

getComputedStyle( )

getComputedStyle(*elementNodeReference*, "*pseudoElementName*")

Returns a style object (specifically, a CSSStyleDeclaration object in the W3C DOM terminology) showing the net cascade of style settings that affect the element passed as the first parameter. To retrieve a particular style attribute value (including a value inherited from the default browser style sheet), use the getPropertyValue( ) method of the style object returned from this method:

```
var compStyle = getComputedStyle(document.getElementById("myP"), "");
var pBGColor = compStyle.getPropertyValue("background-color");
```

See the style object for additional details.

Returned Value   style (CSSStyleDeclaration) object reference.

Parameters

elementNodeReference

Reference to an element node in the document tree that becomes the selection.

pseudoElementName

String name of a pseudo-element (e.g., :first-line) or an empty string.

wbr

The wbr object reflects the wbr element.

HTML Equivalent   <wbr>

Object Model Reference

[window.]document.getElementById("*elementID*")

Object-Specific Properties
None.

Object-Specific Methods
None.

Object-Specific Events
None.

window
IE *4* NN *n/a* Moz *all* Saf *all* Op *7* DOM *1*

The window object represents the browser window or frame in which document content is displayed. The window object plays a vital role in scripting when scripts must communicate with document objects located in other frames or subwindows. Managing multiple windows can be tricky business because of the transient nature of cross-window references. Strict interpretation of HTML and XHTML standards frowns upon multiple windows, and many confused users may agree.

Although the W3C DOM Level 2 does not provide in-depth specifications for the window object (a window, after all, is outside the scope of document markup), it nevertheless indicates possible future hooks through what it calls "view" objects. Thus, the Netscape 6 document.defaultView property returns the document's window; the Netscape 6 window object also takes on the method of the ViewCSS object to gain the DOM's getComputedStyle( ) method.

The window object has been scriptable since the beginning and bears a considerable legacy of properties and methods. Many of these features are browser-specific, so observe compatibility ratings carefully before adopting a particular object feature.

Object Model Reference
window
self
top
parent

Object Properties

clientInformation	clipboardData	closed	Components
content	controllers	crypto	defaultStatus
dialogArguments	dialogHeight	dialogLeft	dialogTop
dialogWidth	directories	document	event
external	frameElement	frames[]	fullScreen
history	innerHeight	innerWidth	length
location	locationbar	menubar	name
navigator	netscape	offscreenBuffering	opener

outerHeight	outerWidth	pageXOffset	pageYOffset
parent	personalbar	pkcs11	prompter
returnValue	screen	screenLeft	screenTop
screenX	screenY	scrollbars	scrollMaxX
scrollMaxY	scrollX	scrollY	self
sidebar	status	statusbar	toolbar
top	window		

Object Methods

addEventListener( )	alert( )	attachEvent( )
back( )	blur( )	captureEvents( )
clearInterval( )	clearTimeout( )	close( )
confirm( )	createPopup( )	detachEvent( )
disableExternalCapture( )	dispatchEvent( )	dump( )
enableExternalCapture( )	execScript( )	find( )
focus( )	forward( )	GeckoActiveXObject( )
getComputedStyle( )	getSelection( )	home( )
moveBy( )	moveTo( )	navigate( )
open( )	openDialog( )	print( )
prompt( )	releaseEvents( )	removeEventListener( )
resizeBy( )	resizeTo( )	routeEvent( )
scroll( )	scrollBy( )	scrollByLines( )
scrollByPages( )	scrollTo( )	setInterval( )
setTimeout( )	showHelp( )	showModalDialog( )
showModelessDialog( )	sizeToContent( )	stop( )

Object-Specific Events

Event	IE/Windows	Mozilla	Safari	Opera	DOM
afterprint	•	—	—	—	—
beforeprint	•	—	—	—	—
beforeunload	•	—	•	—	—
blur	•	•	•	•	—
dragdrop	—	•	—	—	—
error	•	•	•	•	—
focus	•	•	•	•	—
help	•	—	—	—	—
load	•	•	•	•	—
move	•	—	—	—	—
resize	•	•	•	•	—

Event	IE/Windows	Mozilla	Safari	Opera	DOM
scroll	•	•	•	•	—
unload	•	•	•	•	—

clientInformation

IE *4* NN *n/a* Moz *n/a* Saf *1.2* Op *n/a* DOM *n/a*

Read-only

Returns the navigator object. The navigator object is named after a specific browser brand; the clientInformation property is a nondenominational way of accessing important environment variables that have historically been available through properties and methods of the navigator object (discussed separately earlier in this chapter as its own object).

Example

```
if (parseInt(window.clientInformation.appVersion) >= 4) {
    // process code for IE 4 or later
}
```

Value   The navigator object.

Default   The navigator object.

clipboardData

IE *5(Win)* NN *n/a* Moz *n/a* Saf *n/a* Op *n/a* DOM *n/a*

Read-only

Returns the clipboardData object, discussed separately earlier in this chapter as its own object. The object (accessible as a property of a window or frame object) is a temporary container that scripts in IE 5 and later for Windows can use to transfer text data, particularly during script-controlled operations that simulate cutting, copying, and pasting, or that control dragging.

Example

```
var rng = document.selection.createRange( );
clipboardData.setData("Text",rng.text);
```

Value   The clipboardData object.

Default   The clipboardData object.

closed

IE *4* NN *3* Moz *all* Saf *all* Op *7* DOM *n/a*

Read-only

This is the Boolean value that says whether the referenced window is closed. A value of true means the window is no longer available for referencing its objects or script components. This is used most often to check whether a user has closed a subwindow generated by the window.open( ) method.

Example
```
if (!newWindow.closed) {
    newWindow.document.close( );
}
```

Value   Boolean value: true | false.

Default   None.

Components, content, controllers, prompter, sidebar

IE *n/a* NN *n/a* Moz *all* Saf *n/a* Op *n/a* DOM *n/a*
Read-only

These properties are associated with the proprietary Mozilla xpconnect ("cross-platform" connect) services. These services allow scripts that have the correct security clearance to work with XPCOM (decidedly not MS COM) objects to extend the functionality of the application that uses the Mozilla engine (such as the Netscape 6 browser). Access to these services requires enabling security privileges (typically via signed scripts), as follows:

```
netscape.security.PrivilegeManager.enablePrivilege("UniversalXPConnect");
// your xpconnect access code here
netscape.security.PrivilegeManager.revertPrivilege("UniversalXPConnect");
```

For more details on this mechanism, visit *http://www.mozilla.org/scriptable/*.

crypto, pkcs11

IE *n/a* NN *n/a* Moz *all* Saf *n/a* Op *n/a* DOM *n/a*
Read-only

Return references to objects associated with Mozilla public-key cryptography internals. For more details on this subject, visit *http://www.mozilla.org/projects/security/*.

defaultStatus

IE *3* NN *2* Moz *all* Saf *all* Op *7* DOM *n/a*
Read/Write

Specifies the default message displayed in the browser window's status bar when no browser loading activity is occurring. To temporarily change the message (during mouse rollovers, for example), set the window's status property. Most scriptable browsers and versions have difficulty managing the setting of the defaultStatus property. Expect odd behavior.

Example   `window.defaultStatus = "Make it a great day!";`

Value   Any string value.

Default   None.

dialogArguments

This is the string or other data type passed as extra arguments to a modal dialog window created with the window.showModalDialog( ) or (in IE 5 and later for Windows only) window. showModelessDialog( ) methods. This property is best accessed by a script in the document displayed in the dialog window in order to retrieve whatever data is passed to the new window as arguments. It is up to your script to parse the data if you include more than one argument nugget separated by whatever argument delimiter you choose.

Example

```
// in dialog window
var allArgs = window.dialogArguments;
var firstArg = allArgs.substring(0, allArgs.indexOf(";"));
```

Value   String, number, array, or object.

Default   None.

dialogHeight, dialogWidth

Specify the height and width values of a modal dialog window created with the showModalDialog( ) and showModelessDialog( ) methods. Although Internet Explorer does not balk at modifying these properties (in a script running in the modal dialog window), the changed values are generally not reflected in a resized dialog window. Initial values are set as parameters to the dialog-opening methods.

Example   `var outerWidth = window.dialogWidth;`

Value   String, including the unit value (e.g., 520px).

Default   None.

dialogLeft, dialogTop

Indicate the offset distance of the left and top edges of a modal dialog window (created with the showModalDialog( ) and showModelessDialog( ) methods) relative to the top-left corner of the video screen. Although Internet Explorer does not balk at modifying these properties (in a script running in the modal dialog window), the changed values are generally not reflected in a repositioned dialog window. Initial values are set as parameters to the dialog methods.

Example   `var outerLeft = window.dialogLeft;`

Value   String, including the unit value (e.g., 80px).

Default   None.

directories, locationbar, menubar, personalbar, scrollbars, statusbar, toolbar

Return references to the Navigator browser window feature (the directories property is new for Mozilla). See the discussion of the directories (et al.) objects earlier in this chapter for how to control the visibility of these window features with signed scripts.

Example

```
netscape.security.PrivilegeManager.enablePrivilege("UniversalBrowserWrite")
window.statusbar.visible = "false";
netscape.security.PrivilegeManager.revertPrivilege("UniversalBrowserWrite")
```

Value   Respective object references.

Default   None.

document

Returns a reference to the document object contained by the window. In browsers that offer W3C DOM document tree support, this property points more specifically to the root HTMLDocument node for the document tree loaded in the window. The W3C DOM even describes this property as a member of one of its View objects (analogous to a browser window). This is the property that lets scripts references to document methods and content begin with the word document.

Example   var oneElem = document.getElementById("myP");

Value   Reference to the root document object.

Default   Reference to the root document object.

event

Internet Explorer's event model generates an event object for each user or system event. This event object is a property of the window object. Opera implements a hybrid event mechanism (IE and W3C DOM). The window.event property returns an event object that has both IE and W3C DOM characteristics (e.g., sourceElement and target properties). For details about the IE event object, see Online Section VI and the listing of the event object in this chapter.

Example

```
if (event.altKey) {
    // handle case of Alt key down
}
```

Alphabetical DOM Reference

Value   event object reference.

Default   None.

external

IE 4(Win) NN n/a Moz n/a Saf n/a Op n/a DOM n/a
Read-only

Returns a reference to the external object, which provides access to lower-level functionality of the browser engine (security permissions willing). See the discussion of the external object earlier in this chapter.

Example   external.AddFavorite("http://www.dannyg.com", "Danny Home Page");

Value   external object reference.

Default   external object reference.

frameElement

IE 5.5 NN n/a Moz 1.0.1 Saf 1.2 Op 7 DOM n/a
Read-only

If the current window is a member of a frameset or is an iframe, the frameElement property returns a reference to the frame or iframe element object (distinct from the frame-as-window object). Security restrictions, however, can impede script access to this property.

Example   var frameID = window.frameElement.id;

Value   frame or iframe object reference; or null.

Default   null.

frames[ ]

IE 3 NN 2 Moz all Saf all Op 7 DOM n/a
Read-only

Returns a collection (array) of window objects that are implemented as frames or iframes in the current window. For a frameset's parent or top window, the array contains references to first-generation frame windows. Index values can be zero-based integers (in source code order) or the identifier assigned to the name attribute of the frame element.

Example   parent.frames[1].myFunc( );

Value   Array of frame (window) object references.

Default   Array of length zero.

fullScreen

IE n/a NN n/a Moz 1.4 Saf n/a Op n/a DOM n/a
Read-only

Always returns Boolean false, even if the browser is set to Full Screen mode via the View menu in Windows.

Value	Boolean value: true | false.
Default	false

history

IE *3* NN *2* Moz *all* Saf *all* Op *7* DOM *n/a*
Read-only

Contains the history object for the current window or frame. For details, see the discussion of the history object.

Example

```
if (self.history.length > 4) {
    ...
}
```

Value	history object reference.
Default	Current history object.

innerHeight, innerWidth

IE *n/a* NN *4* Moz *all* Saf *all* Op *7* DOM *n/a*
Read/Write

Specify the pixel measure of the height and width of the content region of a browser window or frame. This area is where the document content appears, exclusive of all window "chrome." For comparable values in IE, see the body element object.

Example

```
window.innerWidth = 600;
window.innerHeight = 400;
```

Value	Integer.
Default	None.

length

IE *4* NN *n/a* Moz *all* Saf *all* Op *7* DOM *n/a*
Read-only

Specifies the number of frames (if any) nested within the current window. This value is the same as that returned by window.frames.length. When no frames are defined for the window, the value is zero.

Example

```
if (window.length > 0) {
    ...
}
```

Value	Integer.
Default	0

location

IE 3   NN 2   Moz *all*   Saf *all*   Op 7   DOM *n/a*

Read/Write

Returns a location object containing URL details of the document currently loaded in the window or frame. To navigate to another page, you assign a URL to the location.href property (or see the navigate( ) method for an IE-only alternative). See the location object.

Example	top.location.href = "index.html";
Value	A full or relative URL as a string.
Default	Current location object.

locationbar

See directories.

menubar

See directories.

name

IE 3   NN 2   Moz *all*   Saf *all*   Op 7   DOM *n/a*

Read/Write

This is the identifier associated with a frame or subwindow for use as the value assigned to target attributes or as script references to the frame/subwindow. For a frame, the value is usually assigned via the name attribute of the frame tag, but it can be modified by a script if necessary. The name of a subwindow is assigned as a parameter to the window.open( ) method. The primary browser window does not have a name by default, but you can assign one via script if you need a subwindow to target a link or form back to the main window.

Example

```
if (parent.frames[1].name == "main") {
    ...
}
```

Value	Case-sensitive identifier that follows the rules of identifier naming: it may contain no whitespace, cannot begin with a numeral, and should avoid punctuation except for the underscore character.
Default	None.

navigator

IE 4   NN *n/a*   Moz *all*   Saf *all*   Op 7   DOM *n/a*

Read-only

Returns a reference to the navigator object. Since the window reference is optional, syntax without the window reference works on all scriptable versions of Internet Explorer and Navigator. See the navigator object.

Example	var theBrowser = navigator.appName;
Value	navigator object reference.
Default	navigator object.

netscape

Returns a reference to the netscape object, which offers limited script access to the inner workings of the application through signed scripts and the user's explicit permission. For example, it is through the netscape object that JavaScript can access the PrivilegeManager.

Example

netscape.security.PrivilegeManager.enablePrivilege("UniversalBrowserWrite");

Value	netscape object reference.
Default	netscape object.

offscreenBuffering

Indicates whether the browser should use offscreen buffering to improve path animation performance. Although the property is implemented in IE 5 for Macintosh, it is unclear that it offers any functionality. Recent versions of IE for Windows connect this property to the DirectX ActiveX control. When the document loads, the property is set to auto. After that, a script may turn buffering on and off by assigning a Boolean value to this property.

Example	window.offscreenBuffering = "true";
Value	Boolean value: true | false.
Default	auto

opener

This is an object reference to the window (or frame) that used a window.open( ) method to generate the current window. This property allows subwindows to assemble references to objects, variables, and functions in the originating window. To access document objects in the creating window, a reference can begin with opener and work its way through the regular document object hierarchy from there, as shown in the left side of the following example statement. The relationship between the opening window and the opened window is not strictly parent-child. The term "parent" has other connotations in scripted window and frame references. IE's dialog windows (the showModalDialog( ) and showModelessDialog( ) windows) do not support this property. Values between the main and dialog windows must be passed at creation time and via the dialog window's returnValue property upon closing.

Example

```
opener.document.forms[0].importedData.value = document.forms[0].entry.value;
```

Value   window object reference.

Default   None.

outerHeight, outerWidth   IE *n/a*   NN *4*   Moz *all*   Saf *all*   Op *7*   DOM *n/a*

Read/Write

Specify the pixel measure of the height and width of the browser window or frame, including (for the top window) all tool bars, scoll bars, and other visible window "chrome. " IE offers no equivalent properties.

Example

```
window.outerWidth = 80;
window.outerHeight = 600;
```

Value   Integer.

Default   None.

pageXOffset, pageYOffset   IE *n/a*   NN *4*   Moz *all*   Saf *all*   Op *7*   DOM *n/a*

Read-only

Specify the pixel measure of the amount of the page's content that has been scrolled upward and/or to the left. For example, if a document has been scrolled so that the topmost 100 pixels of the document (the "page") are not visible because the window is scrolled, the pageYOffset value for the window is 100. When a document is not scrolled, both values are zero.

Example   `var vertScroll = self.pageYOffset;`

Value   Integer.

Default   0

parent   IE *3*   NN *2*   Moz *all*   Saf *all*   Op *7*   DOM *n/a*

Read-only

Returns a reference to the parent window object whose document defined the frameset in which the current frame is specified. Use parent in building a reference from one child frame to variables or methods in the parent document or to variables, methods, and objects in another child frame. For example, if a script in one child frame must reference the content of a text input form element in the other child frame (named "content"), the reference would be:

```
parent.content.document.forms[0].entryField.value
```

For more deeply nested frames, you can access the parent of a parent with syntax such as: `parent.parent.frameName`.

Example	`parent.frames[1].document.forms[0].companyName.value = "MegaCorp";`
Value	window object reference.
Default	Current window object reference.

personalbar

See directories.

pkcs11

See crypto.

prompter

See Components.

returnValue

IE *4(Win)/5(Mac)* NN *n/a* Moz *n/a* Saf *n/a* Op *n/a* DOM *n/a*

Read/Write

A value to be returned to the main window when an IE dialog window (generated by showModalDialog( ) method only) closes. The value assigned to this property in a script running in the dialog window becomes the value returned by the showModalDialog( ) method in the main window. For example, the document in the modal dialog window may have a statement that sets the returnValue property with information from the dialog:

```
window.returnValue = window.document.forms[0].userName.value;
```

The dialog is created in the main document with a statement like the following:

```
var userName = showModalDialog("userNamePrompt.html");
```

Whatever value is assigned to returnValue in the dialog is then assigned to the userName variable when the dialog box closes and script execution continues.

Value	Any scriptable data type.
Default	None.

screen

IE *4* NN *n/a* Moz *all* Saf *all* Op *7* DOM *n/a*

Read-only

Returns a reference to the screen object. Since the window reference is optional, syntax without the window reference works on all scriptable browsers.

Example	`var howHigh = screen.availHeight;`
Value	screen object reference.
Default	screen object.

screenLeft, screenTop

IE *5(Win)*   NN *n/a*   Moz *n/a*   Saf *1.2*   Op *7*   DOM *n/a*

Read-only

Return pixel coordinates of the top-left corner of the browser content area relative to the top-left corner of the screen. A maximized IE browser window returns a screenLeft value of 0, but the screenTop value varies with the complement of toolbars the user chooses to display. Use window.moveTo( ) to change the window position.

Example   var fromTheTop = window.screenTop;

Value   Integer.

Default   User-dependent

screenX, screenY

IE *n/a*   NN *n/a*   Moz *all*   Saf *1.2*   Op *7*   DOM *n/a*

Read/Write

Return pixel coordinates of the top-left corner of the entire browser window (including "chrome") relative to the top-left corner of the screen. A browser window maximized under Windows returns screenX and screenY values of -4 because the chrome extends slightly beyond the screen display. You can adjust the window location through these properties or the window.moveTo( ) method.

Example   var fromTheTop = window.screenY;

Value   Integer.

Default   User-dependent.

scrollbars

See directories.

scrollMaxX, scrollMaxY

IE *n/a*   NN *n/a*   Moz *1.4*   Saf *n/a*   Op *n/a*   DOM *n/a*

Read-only

Return the number of pixels along the horizontal (scrollMaxX) and vertical (scrollMaxY) axes that the current window's content can be scrolled. If there is no scrollbar along an axis, its corresponding value is zero because the window cannot be scrolled in that direction. You can use these properties to determine the total rendered height and width of a scrolled document by adding the window's innerWidth and innerHeight values to the corresponding maximum scroll properties.

Example   var docHeight = window.scrollMaxY + window.innerHeight;

Value   Integer.

Default   0

scrollX, scrollY

Return the pixel distance the window is scrolled along the horizontal (scrollX) and vertical (scrollY) axes. To determine these values in IE, you must take into account compatibility mode settings in IE 6 (see the DOCTYPE element in Chapter 1). In quirks mode and in IE for Macintosh, use the document.body.scrollLeft and document.body.scrollTop properties. In IE 6 standards compatibility mode (where document.compatMode == "CSS1Compat"), use document.body.parentNode.scrollLeft and document.body.parentNode.scrollTop to get the scroll values of the html element.

Example   var scrolledDown = window.scrollY;

Value   Integer.

Default   0

self

This is a reference to the current window or frame. This property is synonymous with window, but is sometimes used to improve clarity in a complex script that refers to many windows or frames. Never use the reference window.self to refer to the current window or frame because some browser versions get confused with the reference.

Example   self.focus( );

Value   window object reference.

Default   Current window.

sidebar

See Components.

status

Specifies the text of the status bar of the browser window. Setting the status bar to some message is recommended only for temporary messages, such as for mouse rollovers atop images. To prevent link spoofing (where the visible text of a link indicates a trustworthy site, but the href of the link points to a Bad Guy's site), the trend in modern browsers is to not allow modifying the status bar when rolling the mouse atop links.

Double or single quotes in the message must be escaped (\'). Many users don't notice incidental text in the status bar, so avoid putting mission-critical information there. Temporary messages conflict with browser-driven use of the status bar for loading progress and other purposes. To set the default status bar message (when all is at rest), see the defaultStatus property.

Example

```
<...onmouseover="window.status='Table of Contents';return true"
onmouseout = "window.status = '';return true">
```

Value   String.

Default   Empty string.

statusbar

See directories.

toolbar

See directories.

top

IE 3   NN 2   Moz *all*   Saf *all*   Op 7   DOM *n/a*

Read-only

This is an object reference to the browser window. Script statements from inside nested frames can refer to the browser window properties and methods or to variables or functions stored in the document loaded in the topmost position. Do not begin a reference with window.top, just top. To replace a frameset with a new document that occupies the entire browser window, assign a URL to the top.location.href property.

Example   top.location.href = "tableOfContents.html";

Value   window object reference.

Default   Browser window.

window

IE 3   NN 2   Moz *all*   Saf *all*   Op 7   DOM *n/a*

Read-only

This is an object reference to the browser window.

Example

```
if (window == top) {
    // load a frameset
    location.href = "mainFrameset.html";
}
```

Value   window object reference.

Default   Browser window.

addEventListener( )   IE *n/a* NN *n/a* Moz *all* Saf *all* Op *7* DOM *n/a*

addEventListener("*eventType*", *listenerFunction, useCapture*)

Although the window object as we know it is not officially part of the W3C DOM, mainstream W3C DOM browsers implement this W3C DOM event model method for the window object. See the addEventListener( ) method discussion among the shared methods described earlier in this chapter.

alert( )   IE *3* NN *2* Moz *all* Saf *all* Op *7* DOM *n/a*

alert("*message*")

Displays an alert dialog box with a message of your choice. Script execution halts while the dialog box appears. A single button lets the user close the dialog. The title bar of the window (and the "JavaScript Alert" legend in earlier browser versions) cannot be altered by script.

Returned Value   None.

Parameters

message
> Any string.

attachEvent( )   IE *5(Win)* NN *n/a* Moz *n/a* Saf *n/a* Op *7* DOM *n/a*

attachEvent("*eventName*", *functionReference*)

This IE event model method, shared among all element objects, is also a member of the window object. See the attachEvent( ) method discussion among the shared methods described earlier in this chapter.

back( )   IE *n/a* NN *4* Moz *all* Saf *n/a* Op *7* DOM *n/a*

Navigates one step backward through the history list of the window or frame. You may prefer the cross-browser history.back( ) method.

Returned Value   None.

Parameters   None.

blur( )   IE *4* NN *3* Moz *all* Saf *all* Op *7* DOM *n/a*

Removes focus from the window and fires a blur event (in IE). No other element necessarily receives focus as a result, but if another browser window is open at the time, the current window moves to the rear of the stack (except in Opera, whose display does not change).

Returned Value   None.

Parameters   None.

Alphabetical DOM Reference

captureEvents( )

IE *n/a* NN *4* Moz *all* Saf *1.2* Op *7* DOM *n/a*

captureEvents(*eventTypeList*)

Instructs the browser to grab events of a specific type before they reach their intended target objects. The object invoking this method must then have event handlers defined for the given event types to process the event. Although this method is part of the Navigator 4 event model, it is supported in Mozilla, Safari, and Opera, creating the equivalent of a W3C DOM capture-mode event listener for the document object. Continue to use this method if you must support Navigator 4, but migrate new code to the W3C DOM event listener syntax as described in Online Section VI. Mozilla's documentation now calls this method obsolete.

Returned Value   None.

Parameters

eventTypeList

A comma-separated list of case-sensitive event types as derived from the available Event object constants, such as Event.CLICK or Event.MOUSEMOVE.

clearInterval( )

IE *4* NN *4* Moz *all* Saf *all* Op *7* DOM *n/a*

clearInterval(*intervalID*)

Turns off the interval looping action referenced by the *intervalID* parameter. See window. setInterval( ) for how to initiate such a loop.

Returned Value   None.

Parameters

intervalID

An integer created as the return value of a setInterval( ) method.

clearTimeout( )

IE *2* NN *2* Moz *all* Saf *all* Op *7* DOM *n/a*

clearTimeout(*timeoutID*)

Turns off the timeout delay counter referenced by the *timeoutID* parameter. See window. setTimeout( ) for how to initiate such a delay.

Returned Value   None.

Parameters

timeoutID

An integer created as the return value of a setTimeout( ) method.

close( )

IE *3* NN *2* Moz *all* Saf *all* Op *7* DOM *n/a*

Closes the current window. A script in a subwindow cannot close the main window without receiving the user's explicit permission from a security dialog box. Mozilla and Safari prevent a window from closing itself, but, like all browsers, a main window can close a subwindow when a script in the main window previously opened the subwindow via the window.open( ) method.

Returned Value   None.

Parameters   None.

confirm( )   IE 3 NN 2 Moz *all* Saf *all* Op 7 DOM *n/a*
confirm("*message*")

Displays a dialog box with a message and two clickable buttons. Script execution halts while the dialog box appears. One button indicates a **Cancel** operation; the other button indicates the user's approval (**OK** or **Yes**). The text of the buttons is not scriptable. The message should ask a question to which either button would be a logical reply. A click of the **Cancel** button returns a value of false; a click of the **OK** button returns a value of true.

Because this method returns a Boolean value, you can use this method inside a condition expression:

```
if (confirm("Reset the entire form?")) {
    document.forms[0].reset( );
}
```

Returned Value   Boolean value: true | false.

Parameters

message
    Any string, usually in the form of a question.

createPopup( )   IE 5.5 NN *n/a* Moz *n/a* Saf *n/a* Op *n/a* DOM *n/a*

Opens a blank popup rectangular space that can be populated with HTML content, yet the space can extend across frame boundaries and even window borders. Scripts must assign content (not an external URL) to the popup object returned by the method. See the popup object for more details and an example of usage.

Returned Value   popup object reference.

Parameters   None.

detachEvent( )   IE 5(Win) NN *n/a* Moz *n/a* Saf *n/a* Op 7 DOM *n/a*
detachEvent("*eventName*", *functionReference*)

This IE event model method, shared among all element objects, is also a member of the window object. See the detachEvent( ) method discussion among the shared methods described earlier in this chapter.

disableExternalCapture( ),
enableExternalCapture( )   IE *n/a* NN |4| Moz *n/a* Saf *n/a* Op *n/a* DOM *n/a*

With signed scripts and the user's permission, a script can capture events in other windows or frames that come from domains other than the one that served the document with event-capturing scripts. Navigator 4 only.

Returned Value   None.

Parameters   None.

dispatchEvent( )   IE *n/a* NN *n/a* Moz *all* Saf *n/a* Op 7 DOM *n/a*

dispatchEvent(*eventObjectReference*)

Although the window object is not officially part of the W3C DOM, Mozilla and Opera implement this W3C DOM event model method for the window object. See the dispatchEvent( ) method discussion among the shared methods described earlier in this chapter.

dump( )   IE *n/a* NN *n/a* Moz *1.4* Saf *n/a* Op *n/a* DOM *n/a*

dump(*message*)

Write's the string passed as a parameter to the console or other device configured to be STDOUT. When this method was first implemented, scripters had to enable the method from the browser's configuration preferences. In more recent versions, however, the preference key is no longer among preferences accessible via the about:config URI.

Returned Value   None.

Parameters

message
   String of a message to be sent to STDOUT.

execScript( )   IE 4 NN *n/a* Moz *n/a* Saf *n/a* Op *n/a* DOM *n/a*

execScript(*expressionList* [, *language*])

Evaluates one or more script expressions in any scripting language embedded in the browser. Expressions must be contained within a single string; multiple expressions are delimited with semicolons:

```
window.execScript("var x = 3; alert(x * 3)")
```

The default script language is JavaScript. If you need to see results of the script execution, provide for the display of resulting data in the script expressions, as shown in the example. The execScript( ) method itself returns no value.

Returned Value   None.

Parameters

expressionList
> String value of one or more semicolon-delimited script expressions.

language
> String value for a scripting language: JavaScript | JScript | VBS | VBScript.

find( )

IE *n/a* NN *4* Moz *1.0.1* Saf *n/a* Op *n/a* DOM *n/a*

find("*searchString*"[, *matchCase*[, *searchUpward*]])

Searches the document body text for a string and selects the first matching string. Optionally, you can specify whether the search should be case-sensitive or should search upward in the document. With the found text selected in Navigator 4, you can then use the document.getSelection( ) method to grab a copy of the found text. You don't, however, have nearly the dynamic content abilities afforded by Internet Explorer 4's TextRange object (for Win32).

Returned Value   Boolean value: true if a match was found; false if not.

Parameters

searchString
> String for which to search the document.

matchCase
> Boolean value: true to allow only exact, case-sensitive matches; false (default) to use case-insensitive search.

searchUpward
> Boolean value: true to search from the current selection position upward through the document; false (default) to search forward from the current selection position.

focus( )

IE *4* NN *3* Moz *all* Saf *all* Op *7* DOM *n/a*

Brings the window to the front of all regular browser windows and fires the onFocus event (in IE). If another window had focus at the time, that other window receives an onBlur event.

Returned Value   None.

Parameters   None.

forward( )

IE *n/a* NN *4* Moz *all* Saf *n/a* Op *7* DOM *n/a*

Navigates one step forward through the history list of the window or frame. If the forward history has no entries, no action takes place.

Returned Value   None.

Parameters   None.

GeckoActiveXObject( )

IE *n/a* NN *n/a* Moz *1.4* Saf *n/a* Op *n/a* DOM *n/a*

`new GeckoActiveXObject("`*`programID`*`")`

A Mozilla constructor function specifically designed to allow the browser to open the Windows Media Player ActiveX control (and no other ActiveX controls). For implementation details, visit: *http://developer.mozilla.org/en/docs/Windows_Media_in_Netscape*.

Returned Value   Reference to the player for further script control.

Parameters

programID
>   Identifier of the desired Windows Media Player control.

getComputedStyle( )

IE *n/a* NN *n/a* Moz *all* Saf *n/a* Op *8* DOM *2*

`getComputedStyle(`*`elementNodeReference`*`, "`*`pseudoElementName`*`")`

Returns a style object (specifically, a `CSSStyleDeclaration` object in the W3C DOM terminology) showing the net cascade of style settings that affect the element passed as the first parameter. To retrieve a particular style attribute value (including a value inherited from the default browser style sheet), use the `getPropertyValue( )` method of the style object returned from this method:

```
var compStyle = getComputedStyle(document.getElementById("myP"), "");
var pBGColor = compStyle.getPropertyValue("background-color");
```

See the style object for additional details. Although Mozilla and Opera allow access to this method via the `window` object, the W3C DOM prefers access through `document. defaultView.getComputedStyle( )`.

Returned Value   style (`CSSStyleDeclaration`) object reference.

Parameters

elementNodeReference
>   Reference to an element node in the document tree that becomes the selection.

pseudoElementName
>   String name of a pseudo-element (e.g., `:first-line`) or an empty string.

getSelection( )

IE *n/a* NN *n/a* Moz *all* Saf *all* Op *9* DOM *n/a*

Returns a selection object in Mozilla and Opera, which can then be turned into a W3C DOM Range object. This method takes the place of the old `document.getSelection( )` method, which is deprecated in Mozilla. Safari returns only the selected text. The corresponding IE operation is the `document.selection` property. See the selection object for details on working with a selection.

Returned Value   selection object reference.

Parameters   None.

home( )

Navigates to the URL designated as the home page for the browser. This is the same as the user clicking on the **Home** button.

Returned Value   None.

Parameters   None.

moveBy( )

moveBy(*deltaX*, *deltaY*)

This is a convenience method that shifts the location of the window by specified pixel amounts along both axes. To shift along only one axis, set the other value to zero. Positive values for *deltaX* shift the window to the right; negative values to the left. Positive values for *deltaY* shift the window downward; negative values upward.

Returned Value   None.

Parameters

deltaX
> Positive or negative pixel count of the change in horizontal direction of the window.

deltaY
> Positive or negative pixel count of the change in vertical direction of the window.

moveTo( )

moveTo(*x*, *y*)

This is a convenience method that shifts the location of the current window to a specific coordinate point. The moveTo( ) method uses the screen coordinate system.

Returned Value   None.

Parameters

x
> Positive or negative pixel count relative to the top of the screen.

y
> Positive or negative pixel count relative to the left edge of the screen.

navigate( )

navigate(*URL*)

Loads a new document into the window or frame. This is the IE-specific way of assigning a value to the window.location.href property.

Returned Value   None.

Parameters

URL
> A complete or relative URL as a string.

Alphabetical DOM Reference

open( ) IE 3 NN 2 Moz *all* Saf *all* Op 7 DOM *n/a*

```
open("URL", "windowName"[, "windowFeatures"])
open("URL", "windowName"[, "windowFeatures"][, replaceFlag])
```

Opens a new window (without closing the original one). You can specify a URL to load into the new window or set that parameter to an empty string to allow scripts to document. write( ) into that new window. The *windowName* parameter lets you assign a name that can be used by target attributes of link and form elements. This name is not to be used in script references as frame names are. Instead, a script reference to a subwindow must be to the window object returned by the window.open( ) method. Therefore, if your scripts must communicate with a window opened in this manner, it is best to save the returned value as a global variable so that future statements can use it.

A potential problem with subwindows is that they can be buried under the main window if the user clicks on the main window (or a script gives it focus). Any script that opens a subwindow should also include a focus( ) method for the subwindow to make sure it comes to the front in case it is already open. Subsequent invocations of the window.open( ) method in which the *windowName* parameter is the same as an earlier call automatically address the previously opened window, even if it is underneath the main window (and thus without bringing the window to the front).

The optional third parameter gives you control over various physical attributes of the subwindow. The *windowFeatures* parameter is a single string consisting of a comma-delimited list (without spaces between items) of attribute/value pairs:

```
newWindow = window.open("someDoc.html","subWind",
"status,menubar,height=400,width=300");
newWindow.focus( );
```

By default, all window attributes are turned on and the subwindow opens to the same size that the browser would use to open a new window from the **File** menu. But if your script specifies even one attribute, all settings are turned off. Therefore, use the *windowFeatures* parameter to specify those features that you want turned on.

If you encounter problems referencing a subwindow immediately after it is created, the problem is most likely a timing issue (affecting IE for Windows more than others). Script statements seem to want to reference the window before it exists completely. To work around the problem, place the code that works with the subwindow in a separate function, and invoke that function via the setTimeout( ) method, usually with no more than 50 milliseconds needed.

Managing multiple windows through scripts can be difficult. Security restrictions across domains frequently foil the best intentions. Most browsers have pop-up window blocking engaged, which may thwart your effort to open a separate window triggered by the load and unload events. In Opera, the new window is restricted to live within the main application window, behaving very differently from other browsers. Users aren't always fond of windows appearing and hiding on their own. If your audience uses newer browsers, consider simulating windows with positioned elements.

Returned Value   Window object reference.

Parameters

URL

> A complete or relative URL as a string. If an empty string, no document loads into the window.

windowName

> An identifier for the window to be used by `target` attributes. This is different from the `title` attribute of the document that loads into the window.

windowFeatures

> A string of comma-delimited features to be turned on in the new window. Do not put spaces after the comma delimiters. The list of possible features is long, but a number of them are specific to Navigator 4 or later and require signed scripts because they are potentially a privacy and security concern to unsuspecting users. The features are listed as follows. To turn on a window feature, simply include its case-insensitive name in the comma-separated list. Only attributes specifying dimensions require values be assigned.

Attribute	IE	Mozilla	Safari	Opera	Description
alwaysLowered	n/a	<1.7	n/a	n/a	Always behind all other browser windows. Signed script required.
alwaysRaised	n/a	<1.7	n/a	n/a	Always in front of all other browser windows. Signed script required.
channelMode	4	n/a	n/a	n/a	Show in theater mode with channel band.
chrome	n/a	1.7	n/a	n/a	Displays content with no chrome, user interface features or keyboard commands. Signed script required.
close	n/a	all	n/a	n/a	For dialog type, set to no to remove close box. Signed script required.
copyhistory	3	all	n/a	n/a	Copy history listing from opening window to new window.
dependent	n/a	all	n/a	n/a	Subwindow closes if the window that opened it closes.
dialog	n/a	1.2	n/a	n/a	Window controls for minimize and maximize hidden.
directories	3	all	n/a	n/a	Display directory buttons.
fullscreen	4	n/a	n/a	n/a	Display no titlebar or menus
height	3	all	all	7	Window height in pixels.
hotkeys	n/a	all	n/a	n/a	Disables menu keyboard shortcuts (except Quit and Security Info).
innerHeight	n/a	all	n/a	n/a	Content region height. Signed script required for very small measures.
innerWidth	n/a	all	n/a	n/a	Content region width. Signed script required for very small measures.
left	4	all	all	n/a	Offset of window's left edge from left edge of screen.

Attribute	IE	Mozilla	Safari	Opera	Description
location	3	all	all	n/a	Display Location (or Address) text field.
menubar	3	all	n/a	n/a	Display menubar (a menubar is always visible on Mac).
minimizable	n/a	1.2	n/a	n/a	For dialog type, includes minimize control.
modal	n/a	1.2	n/a	n/a	Open window as a modal. Signed script required.
outerHeight	n/a	all	n/a	n/a	Total window height. Signed script required for very small measures.
outerWidth	n/a	all	n/a	n/a	Total window width. Signed script required for very small measures.
personalbar	n/a	all	n/a	n/a	Mozilla-specific alternate to the directories attribute.
resizable	3	all	all	n/a	Allow window resizing (always allowed on Mac).
screenX	n/a	all	n/a	n/a	Offset of window's left edge from left edge of screen. Signed script required to move window offscreen.
screenY	n/a	all	n/a	n/a	Offset of window's top edge from top edge of screen. Signed script required to move window offscreen.
scrollbars	3	all	all	n/a	Display scrollbars if document is too large for window.
status	3	all	n/a	n/a	Display status bar.
titlebar	n/a	all	n/a	n/a	Displays titlebar. Set this value to no to hide the titlebar. Signed script required.
toolbar	3	all	n/a	n/a	Display toolbar (with **Back**, **Forward**, and other buttons).
top	4	all	all	7	Offset of window's top edge from top edge of screen.
width	3	all	all	n/a	Window width in pixels.
z-lock	n/a	all	n/a	n/a	New window is fixed below browser windows. Signed script required.

replaceFlag

Boolean value (for IE only) that controls the effect of the new window's URL on the global history of the browser. Set to true to replace the current page with the new window's URL (so that the current page won't be accessed through the **Back** button); set to false to add the new window's URL to the history, as normal.

openDialog( )   IE *n/a*   NN *n/a*   Moz *1.0.1*   Saf *n/a*   Op *n/a*   DOM *n/a*

openDialog("*URL*", "*windowName*"[, "*windowFeatures*"][, *arg1*[, *arg2*[, ...]]])

For use in XUL extensions only (due to security reasons), this method is a variation on the window.open( ) method, offering slightly different ways of handling window features as well as allowing the passage of one or more arguments to the new window (similar to the IE showModalDialog( ) method). Arguments are accessible in the document loaded into the subwindow via the window.arguments property.

Returned Value   Window object reference.

Parameters

URL
> A complete or relative URL as a string. If an empty string, no document loads into the window.

windowName
> An identifier for the window to be used by target attributes. This is different from the title attribute of the document that loads into the window.

windowFeatures
> A string of comma-delimited features to be turned on in the new window. See window. open( ) for details. An additional feature, all, displays (all=yes) or hides (all=no) window features except chrome, dialog, and modal (although each of these may be controlled independently).

arg1, arg2
> JavaScript values of any type. Scripts in the subwindow access the values as items in the window.arguments array.

print( )   IE 5   NN 4   Moz *all*   Saf *all*   Op 7   DOM *n/a*

Starts the printing process for the window or frame. A user must still confirm the print dialog box to send the document to the printer. This method is the same as clicking the browser's **Print** button or selecting **Print** from the **File** menu.

Returned Value   None.

Parameters   None.

prompt( )   IE 3   NN 2   Moz *all*   Saf *all*   Op 7   DOM *n/a*
prompt("*message*", "*defaultReply*")

Displays a dialog box with a message, a one-line text entry field, and two clickable buttons. Script execution halts while the dialog box appears. The message should urge the user to enter a specific kind of answer. One button indicates a **Cancel** operation; the other button indicates the user's approval of the text entered into the field (**OK** or **Yes**). The text of the buttons is not scriptable. A click of the **Cancel** button returns a value of null; a click of the **OK** button returns a string of whatever is in the text entry field at the time (including the possibility of an empty string). It is up to your scripts to test for the type of response (if any) supplied by the user.

Returned Value   When clicking the **OK** button, a string of the text entry field; when clicking **Cancel**, null.

Alphabetical DOM Reference

Parameters

message
> Any string.

defaultReply
> Any string that suggests an answer. Always supply a value, even if an empty string.

releaseEvents( )   IE *n/a* NN 4 Moz *all* Saf *1.2* Op 7 DOM *n/a*

`releaseEvents(eventTypeList)`

The opposite of `window.captureEvents( )`, this method turns off event capture at the window level for one or more specific events named in the parameter list. Although this method is part of the Navigator 4 event model, it is supported in Mozilla, Safari, and Opera, creating the equivalent of a W3C DOM capture-mode event listener for the document object. Continue to use this method if you must support Navigator 4, but migrate new code to the W3C DOM event listener syntax as described in Online Section VI. Mozilla's documentation now calls this method obsolete.

Returned Value   None.

Parameters

eventTypeList
> A comma-separated list of case-sensitive event types as derived from the available Event object constants, such as `Event.CLICK` or `Event.MOUSEMOVE`.

removeEventListener( )   IE *n/a* NN *n/a* Moz *all* Saf *all* Op 7 DOM *n/a*

`removeEventListener("eventType", listenerFunction, useCapture)`

Although the `window` object as we know it is not officially part of the W3C DOM, mainstream W3C DOM browsers implement this W3C DOM event model method for the `window` object. See the `removeEventListener( )` method discussion among the shared methods described earlier in this chapter.

resizeBy( )   IE 4 NN 4 Moz *all* Saf *all* Op *all* DOM *n/a*

`resizeBy(deltaX, deltaY)`

This is a convenience method that shifts the width and height of the window by specified pixel amounts. To adjust along only one axis, set the other value to zero. Positive values for *deltaX* make the window wider; negative values make the window narrower. Positive values for *deltaY* make the window taller; negative values make the window shorter. The top and left edges remain fixed; only the right and bottom edges are moved.

Returned Value   None.

Parameters

deltaX
> Positive or negative pixel count of the change in horizontal dimension of the window.

deltaY

Positive or negative pixel count of the change in vertical dimension of the window.

resizeTo( )   IE *4* NN *4* Moz *all* Saf *all* Op *all* DOM *n/a*

```
resizeTo(x, y)
```

This is a convenience method that adjusts the height and width of the window to specific pixel sizes. The top and left edges of the window remain fixed, while the bottom and right edges move in response to this method.

Returned Value   None.

Parameters

x

Width in pixels of the window.

y

Height in pixels of the window.

routeEvent( )   IE *n/a* NN |*4*| Moz *n/a* Saf *n/a* Op *n/a* DOM *n/a*

```
routeEvent(event)
```

Used inside an event handler function, this method directs Navigator 4 (only) to let the event pass to its intended target object.

Returned Value   None.

Parameters

event

A Navigator 4 event object.

scroll( )   IE *4* NN *3* Moz *all* Saf *all* Op *7* DOM *n/a*

```
scroll(x, y)
```

Sets the scrolled position of the document inside the current window or frame. To return the document to its unscrolled position, set both parameters to zero.

Returned Value   None.

Parameters

x

Horizontal measure of scrolling within the window.

y

Vertical measure of scrolling within the window.

Alphabetical DOM
Reference

scrollBy( )　　　　　　　　　　　IE 4　NN 4　Moz all　Saf all　Op 7　DOM n/a

scrollBy(*deltaX*, *deltaY*)

Scrolls the document in the window by specified pixel amounts along both axes. To adjust along only one axis, set the other value to zero. Positive values for *deltaX* scroll the document to the left (so the user sees content to the right in the document); negative values scroll the document to the right. Positive values for *deltaY* scroll the document upward (so the user sees content lower in the document); negative values scroll the document downward. Scrolling does not continue past the zero coordinate points.

Returned Value　　　None.

Parameters

deltaX

    Positive or negative pixel count of the change in horizontal scroll position.

deltaY

    Positive or negative pixel count of the change in vertical scroll position.

scrollByLines( ), scrollByPages( )　　　IE n/a　NN n/a　Moz all　Saf n/a　Op n/a　DOM n/a

scrollByLines(*intervalCount*) scrollByPages(*intervalCount*)

Scroll the document in the window downward (positive value) or upward (negative value) by the increment of lines or pages. The methods perform the same actions as the user clicking on the arrow and "page" regions of the vertical scrollbar, respectively.

Returned Value　　　None.

Parameters

intervalCount

    Positive or negative count of the change in vertical scroll position. Units are governed by the method choice (lines or pages).

scrollTo( )　　　　　　　　　　　IE 4　NN 4　Moz all　Saf all　Op 7　DOM n/a

scrollTo(*x*, *y*)

Scrolls the document in the window to a specific scrolled pixel position.

Returned Value　　　None.

Parameters

x

    Horizontal position in pixels of the window.

y

    Vertical position in pixels of the window.

setInterval( )   IE *4* NN *4* Moz *all* Saf *all* Op *7* DOM *n/a*

```
setInterval("scriptExpression", msecs[, language])
setInterval(functionReference, msecs[, arg1, ..., argN])
```

Starts a timer that continually invokes the *expression* every *msecs*. Other scripts can run in the time between calls to *expression*. This method is useful for starting animation sequences that must reposition an element along a path at a fixed rate of speed. A repetitive call to an animation function would look like the following:

```
intervalID = setInterval("advanceAnimation( )", 500);
```

The parameter situation can be confusing. The simplest, most cross-browser approach is to invoke a script function (as a string), with the interval time (in milliseconds) as the second parameter. Any script expression will execute, but the expression is evaluated at the time the setInterval( ) method is invoked. Therefore, if you concatenate variables into this expression, their values must be ready when the setInterval( ) method runs, even though the variables won't be used until some milliseconds later.

IE permits a third parameter to specify a different scripting language in which the expression is to run. Unless it is a VBScript expression, you can omit this parameter. You may also substitute a function reference (not a string) as the first parameter, and pass a comma-delimited list of parameters that go to the function call. These parameters go after the *msecs* time, and they can be any data types.

This method returns an ID that should be saved as a global variable and be available as the parameter for the clearInterval( ) method to stop the looping timer. Unless you explicitly clear the interval process, it will continue to execute until the page unloads.

Returned Value   Integer acting as an identifier for this repetitive process.

Parameters

scriptExpression
> Any script expression as a string, but most commonly a function. The function name with parentheses is placed inside the parameter's quoted string.

functionReference
> Nonstring function reference (function name without the parentheses) or anonymous function.

msecs
> The time in milliseconds between invocations of the *expression* or *functionReference*.

args
> An optional comma-delimited list of parameters to be passed to a function used as the *functionReference* parameter. Navigator only.

language
> An optional scripting language specification of the *expression* parameter (default is JavaScript). IE for Windows only.

setTimeout( )   IE 3 NN 2 Moz *all* Saf *all* Op 7 DOM *n/a*

setTimeout("*scriptExpression*", *msecs*[, *language*])
setTimeout(*functionReference*, *msecs*[, *arg1*, ..., *argN*])

Starts a one-time timer that invokes the *scriptExpression* or *functionReference* after a delay of *msecs*. Other scripts can run while the browser waits to invoke the *expression*. A statement that sets the timer would look like the following:

```
timeoutID = setTimeout("finishWindow( )", 50);
```

The parameter situation can be confusing. The simplest, most cross-browser approach is to invoke a script function (as a string), with the interval time (in milliseconds) as the second parameter. Any script expression will execute, but the expression is evaluated at the time the setTimeout( ) method is invoked. Therefore, if you concatenate variables into this expression, their values must be ready when the setTimeout( ) method runs, even though the variables won't be used until some milliseconds later.

IE permits a third parameter to specify a different scripting language in which the expression is to run. Unless it is a VBScript expression, you can omit this parameter. You may also substitute a function reference (not a string) as the first parameter, and pass a comma-delimited list of parameters that go to the function call. These parameters go after the *msecs* time, and they can be any data types.

This method returns an ID that should be saved as a global variable and be available as the parameter for the clearTimeout( ) method to stop the timer before it expires and invokes the delayed action.

The setTimeout( ) method can be made to behave like the setInterval( ) method in some constructions. If you place a setTimeout( ) method as the last statement of a function and direct the method to invoke the very same function, you can create looping execution with a timed delay between executions. This is how earlier browsers (before the setInterval( ) method was available) scripted repetitive tasks, such as displaying updated digital clock displays in form fields or the status bar.

Returned Value   Integer acting as an identifier.

Parameters

scriptExpression
> Any script expression as a string, but most commonly a function. The function name with parentheses is placed inside the parameter's quoted string.

functionReference
> Nonstring function reference (function name without the parentheses) or anonymous function.

msecs
> The time in milliseconds that the browser waits before invoking the *expression*.

args
> An optional comma-delimited list of parameters to be passed to a function used as the *functionReference* parameter. Navigator only.

language
> An optional scripting language specification of the *expression* parameter (default is JavaScript). IE for Windows only.

showHelp( )

showHelp("*URL*")

Displays a **WinHelp** window with the *.hlp* document specified with the *URL* parameter.

Returned Value   None.

Parameters

URL

A complete or relative URL to a WinHelp formatted file as a string.

showModalDialog( )

showModalDialog("*URL*"[, *arguments*[, "*features*"]])

Displays a special window that remains atop all browser windows until the user explicitly closes the dialog window. This kind of window is different from the browser windows generated with the window.open( ) method. A modal dialog has no scriptable relationship with its opening window once the dialog window is opened. All values necessary for displaying content must be in the HTML document that loads into the window or be passed as parameters. The modal dialog may then have a script set its returnValue property, which becomes the value returned to the original script statement that opened the modal dialog box as the returned value of the showModalDialog( ) method.

You can pass arguments to the modal dialog by creating a data structure that best suits the data. For a single value, a string will do. For multiple values, you can create a string with a unique delimiter between values, or create an array and specify the array as the second parameter for the showModalDialog( ) method. A script in the document loaded into the modal dialog can then examine the window.dialogArguments property and parse the arguments as needed for its scripting purposes. See the dialogArguments property for an example.

The third optional parameter lets you set physical characteristics of the dialog window. These characteristics are specified in a CSS-style syntax. Dimensions for dialogWidth, dialogHeight, dialogLeft, and dialogTop should be specified in pixels. An example of a call to a modal dialog is as follows:

```
var answer = window.showModalDialog("subDoc.html",argsVariable,
    "dialogWidth:300px; dialogHeight:200px; center:yes");
```

IE/Macintosh requires that dialog dimensions be at least 201 pixels along both axes.

Modal dialogs can present problems for scripts if the window loads a frameset. A script in one of the frames will likely not be able to reference the parent or top window to gain access to either the window's close( ) method or content in another frame.

Returned Value   The value (if any) assigned to the window.returnValue property in the document loaded into the modal dialog window.

Parameters

URL

A complete or relative URL as a string.

arguments

Data as a number, string, or array to be passed to the scripts in the document loaded into the modal dialog.

features

A string of semicolon-delimited style attributes and values to set the physical characteristics of the modal dialog. Available attributes are as shown in the following table.

Feature	Value	Description
center	yes|no|1|0|on|off	Center the dialog
dialogHeight	Length/units	Outer height of dialog
dialogLeft	Integer	Left pixel offset (overrides center)
dialogTop	Integer	Top pixel offset (overrides center)
dialogWidth	Length/units	Outer width of dialog
edge	raised|sunken	Transition style between border and content area
help	yes|no|1|0|on|off	Display help icon in titlebar
resizable	yes|no|1|0|on|off	Dialog is resizable
status	yes|no|1|0|on|off	Display status bar

showModelessDialog( )   IE *5(Win)* NN *n/a* Moz *n/a* Saf *n/a* Op *n/a* DOM *n/a*

showModelessDialog("*URL*"[, *arguments*[, "*features*"]])

Displays a special window that remains atop all browser windows, yet allows the user to interact with other open windows and their content. Other than browser versions that support it, this method has the same parameters and characteristics as the showModalDialog( ) method. See that method for details.

sizeToContent( )   IE *n/a* NN *n/a* Moz *all* Saf *n/a* Op *n/a* DOM *n/a*

Lets the browser determine the optimum window size to display the window's content. Suitable for subwindows that display a limited amount of information.

Returned Value   None.

Parameters   None.

stop( )   IE *n/a* NN *n/a* Moz *all* Saf *n/a* Op *7* DOM *n/a*

Halts the download of external data of any kind. This method is the same as clicking the browser's **Stop** button.

Returned Value   None.

Parameters   None.

xml

The xml object reflects the Microsoft proprietary xml element, creating a so-called XML data island inside an HTML document. This functionality has largely been replaced by the XMLHttpRequest object.

HTML Equivalent   <xml>

Object Model Reference
[window.]document.getElementById("*elementID*")

Object-Specific Properties

src	XMLDocument

Object-Specific Methods
None.

Object-Specific Events
None.

src

Read/Write

Contains the URL of the external XML document loaded into the data island. To load a new document after the fact, assign a new URL to this property.

Example
document.getElementById("xmlData").src = "xml/latestResults.xml";

Value   Relative or complete URL string.

Default   None.

XMLDocument

Read-only

This is a reference to the Microsoft XML document object. This object resembles the W3C DOM core document object in many ways, but Microsoft provides a different syntax to read and write data from the object. See *http://msdn.microsoft.com/xml/reference/xmldom/ start.asp* for details.

Example   var xmlDoc = document.getElementById("XMLData").XMLDocument;

Value   Reference to an MS XML document object.

Default   None.

Alphabetical DOM Reference

XMLHttpRequest

IE *5(Win)*   NN *n/a*   Moz *all*   Saf *1.2*   Op *8*   DOM *n/a*

The XMLHttpRequest object allows background communication between the currently loaded Web page and a server, without disturbing the current page. In typical usage, the server responds to a request or post of data from the browser and returns an XML document, which the instance of this object stores as one of its properties. Upon successful receipt of the XML document (as revealed by other properties), the browser's scripts can parse the XML data (using W3C DOM document tree properties and methods), usually to extract data for revising part of the current Web page. See Online Section VII for implementation details.

All browsers other than IE implement the XMLHttpRequest exclusively as a native scriptable object. IE 5 through 6 implemented the object as an ActiveX control, but IE 7 includes a native XMLHttpRequest object so that the same syntax instance creation syntax for other browsers (invoking the XMLHttpRequest( ) constructor function) now works for IE.

Beginning with version 1.8, Mozilla browsers added some properties, methods, and events that may find their way into other browsers in the future.

Object Model Reference

new XMLHttpRequest( )

Object Properties

channel	multipart	readyState	responseBody
responseText	responseXML	status	statusText

Object Methods

abort( )	addEventListener( )	dispatchEvent( )
getAllResponseHeaders( )	getResponseHeader( )	open( )
overrideMimeType( )	removeEventListener( )	send( )
setRequestHeader( )		

Object Events

Event	IE/Windows	Mozilla	Safari	Opera	DOM
error	—	•	—	—	—
load	—	•	—	—	—
progress	—	•	—	—	—
readystatechange	•	•	•	•	—

channel

IE *n/a*   NN *n/a*   Moz *1.8*   Saf *n/a*   Op *n/a*   DOM *n/a*

Read-only

Intended for XUL add-ons (and therefore requiring elevated access privileges), the channel property returns a reference to the communications channel that the XMLHttpRequest object will use for its communication with a server. You can view an example of this property in use at: *http://developer.mozilla.org/en/docs/Changing_the_Priority_of_HTTP_Requests.*

Value   Reference to an internal communications channel.

Default   Channel of the current XMLHttpRequest object.

multipart

Mozilla 1.8 and later allows multiple XML documents to be retrieved with a single request. To prepare the XMLHttpRequest object for this kind of transaction, set the multipart property to true. The server's first response must have a MIME type of multipart/x-mixed-replace. The XMLHttpRequest object will fire a load event after each part is received. Subsequent documents within the multipart stream are placed into the response variables one at a time.

Value   Boolean value: true | false.

Default   false

readyState

Returns an integer code corresponding to the current state of the object.

Value

Integer value with the following meanings:

Value	Meaning
0	Uninitialized (the open( ) method has not yet been invoked)
1	Loading (the send( ) method has not yet been invoked)
2	Loaded (the send( ) method has been invoked, and header and status properties are ready for reading)
3	Interactive (the transfer is in progress, partial data available)
4	Complete (all transfer operations are finished)

Default   0

responseBody

Returns the body of the response in a form Microsoft calls "an array of unsigned bytes." The data is not a JavaScript value type, and therefore of little or no value to web page authors.

Value   Byte array.

Default   None.

responseText

IE 5(Win)   NN *n/a*   Moz *all*   Saf *1.2*   Op *8*   DOM *n/a*

Read-only

Returns the received data in string form.

Value   String.

Default   None.

responseXML

IE 5(Win)   NN *n/a*   Moz *all*   Saf *1.2*   Op *8*   DOM *n/a*

Read-only

Returns the received data in the form of an XML document object. You can use DOM node tree parsing techniques (including E4X capabilities in Mozilla, as described in Chapter 5) to extract data as needed for display in the web page or further calculations.

Value   Document object.

Default   None.

status

IE 5(Win)   NN *n/a*   Moz *all*   Saf *1.2*   Op *8*   DOM *n/a*

Read-only

Returns an integer that is the response code received from the server. Typical response codes are 200 (for "OK") and 404 (for "Not Found"). A value of 200 means that the server has sent the content from the URL passed as a parameter to the get( ) method. This property is one way to test for successful completion of a transaction.

Value   Integer.

Default   0

statusText

IE 5(Win)   NN *n/a*   Moz *all*   Saf *1.2*   Op *8*   DOM *n/a*

Read-only

Returns the text portion of the status code returned from the server, such as OK and Not Found. If you use the status property in your code, and you receive a number you don't understand, read the statusText property to get a more plain-language description of the problem.

Value   String.

Default   Empty string.

abort( )

IE 5(Win)   NN *n/a*   Moz *all*   Saf *1.2*   Op *8*   DOM *n/a*

Invoked after the send( ) method, the abort( ) method cancels the current request. The status property is set to zero.

Returned Value   None.

Parameters   None.

addEventListener( ), dispatchEvent( ), removeEventListener( )

Mozilla offers the DOM-standard way of managing events bound to the XMLHttpRequest object, partly because there are more possible events to bind (load, error, and (starting in 1.8) progress) than only the readystatechange implemented in all supporting browsers. Of special interest to this object, you must invoke addEventListener( ) only after the get( ) method because the latter method removes all pending event listeners. See the descriptions of these three methods among the shared items at the beginning of this chapter.

getAllResponseHeaders( )

Returns the complete set of headers received from the server. A header consists of several name/value pairs (in the form name: value), each of which is delimited by carriage return and linefeed characters. Here is an example:

```
ETag: "633bfe1-439-3d7a7301"
Content-Length: 1081
Keep-Alive: timeout=15, max=98
Content-Type: application/xml
Last-Modified: Sat, 07 Sep 2002 21:43:29 GMT
```

Note that there is a CR/LF sequence after the final name/value pair.

Returned Value   String.

Parameters   Empty string.

getResponseHeader( )

getResponseHeader("*headerName*")

Returns only the value of a specific header field whose name matches the value passed as a parameter to the method.

Returned Value   String.

Parameters

headerName
> String consisting of the name of a particular header name/value pair. Do not include the colon delimiter of the name/value pair.

open( )

open("*method*", "*URI*"[, *asyncFlag*[, "*username*"[, "*password*"]]])

Sets key parameters of the request in preparation of the actual request (which occurs via the send( ) method).

Returned Value   None.

Parameters

method
> The HTTP method to be used as a string. Use GET for a typical data request; or POST for submitting lengthy data and SOAP commands.

URI
> The Uniform Resource Identifier of the remote data or service, as a string.

asyncFlag
> Boolean value that directs the request to be made synchronously (false) or asynchronously (true). A synchronous request puts your scripts in peril of locking up if there is a server or network malfunction. Use an asynchronous, and let the readystatechange or load events trigger scripts that act on the received content. The default is true.

username
> A string containing a user name, if required for authentication. But be careful when including sensitive information in a script that could be viewed by others.

password
> A string containing a password, if required for authentication. But be careful when including sensitive information in a script that could be viewed by others.

overrideMimeType( )   IE 5(Win) NN n/a Moz all Saf 1.2 Op 8 DOM n/a
overrideMimeType("*MIMEType*")

Invoke between the get( ) and send( ) methods to force the object to apply the specified MIME type to the data received from the server. This may be necessary when the server is not configured to identify its output as an XML content type (e.g., text/xml).

Returned Value   None.

Parameters

MIMEType
> The desired content type, as a string. For the XMLHttpRequest object to load data into the responseXML property, the data must be received as a valid XML content type, such as text/xml, or overridden with this method to reach the same end.

send( )   IE 5(Win) NN n/a Moz all Saf 1.2 Op 8 DOM n/a
send(*data*)

Transmits data to the server through specifications established in the previous open( ) method.

Returned Value   None.

Parameters

data
> Data sent with the request can be in one of two forms for all supporting browsers and one extra form for IE. The two forms accepted by both are either a string or a DOM

document object (e.g., a document generated via the document.implementation.
createDocument( ) method). The latter is internally serialized (made into a string)
before transmission. IE also allows byte arrays to be specified as the data. Data does
not contain header information, which is set via the setRequestHeader( ) method.

setRequestHeader( )   IE 5(Win) NN n/a Moz all Saf 1.2 Op 8 DOM n/a

```
setRequestHeader("headerLabel", "value")
```

Invoked between the open( ) and send( ) methods, this method lets your script assign one
or more header name/value pairs to the data that is about to be sent.

Returned Value   None.

Parameters

headerLabel
> Name portion of the name/value pair for the header, as a string.

value
> Value portion of the name/value pair for the header, as a string.

XMLSerializer   IE n/a NN n/a Moz 1.0.1 Saf 1.2 Op 8 DOM n/a

The XMLSerializer object transforms an XML document or node object into a string value
consisting of all the markup. Browsers use this object internally for tasks such as converting
XML content into a string that is sent as data via the XMLHttpRequest.send( ) method. But
the object is available to your scripts, if needed for other tasks. Mozilla exposes the
serializeToStream( ) method of the object, but one of the method's parameters is a data
type (output stream) not available to client-side scripts associated with web pages.

Object Model Reference
```
new XMLSerializer( )
```

Object Properties
None.

Object Methods
```
serializeToString( )
```

Object-Specific Events
None.

serializeToString( )   IE n/a NN n/a Moz 1.0.1 Saf 1.2 Op 8 DOM n/a

```
serializeToString(DOMNode)
```

Returns a string consisting of the markup comprising the DOM node passed as a parameter. This node can be either an entire document (nodeType of 9) or other node type,

including a document fragment. The exception is Safari prior to 2.0.2, which worked only on complete document nodes.

Returned Value   String.

Parameters

DOMNode

An XML node object of any type (see above for Safari exception).

xmp

See pre.

Event Reference

The purpose of this chapter is to provide a list of every event type implemented in current mainstream browsers, as well as those specified in the W3C recommendation for the Events module of DOM Level 2. Events are listed alphabetically by their type names—the same format used by the W3C DOM Events modules. Event bindings using an element object property or the IE attachEvent( ) method require the "on" prefix to the event type name. So that you can readily see whether a particular entry applies to the browser(s) you must support, a version table accompanies each term listed in the following pages. This table tells you at a glance the version of Internet Explorer (IE), pre-Mozilla Netscape Navigator (NN), Mozilla (Moz), Apple Safari (Saf), Opera (starting from version 7), and W3C DOM specification in which the term was first introduced.

If a listing for IE signifies Win or Mac, it means that the event is supported only for the Windows or Macintosh operating system version. IE 5.5 or later is for Windows only. Note that a large number of event types are supported only in IE for Windows, and many of those apply only to data binding applications. If you are concerned with cross-browser deployment, pay very close attention to the browser compatibility charts to find the events that work on a broad array of browser brands and versions. Online Section VI contains many guidelines and examples for blending otherwise incompatible event mechanisms into routines that work on many browser types.

In the following listings below, the "Bubbles" category indicates whether the event follows event bubbling propagation (in browsers that support event bubbling, described in Online Section VI), while the "Cancelable" category means that the default action usually associated with the event (such as navigating to a new URL when clicking on an a element) can be canceled by script statements, thus averting the normal operation. The category named "Typical Targets" usually points to broad types of elements to which the event type may be applied. For more specific element support for each event type, consult Chapter 9.

Alphabetical Event Reference

abort

IE 3 NN 4 Moz *all* Saf *all* Op *all* DOM 2
Bubbles: No; Cancelable: No

Fires if an img element's content fails to complete loading due to user interruption (e.g., clicking **Stop** or rapidly navigating to another page) or other failure (e.g., timeout due to network traffic). The W3C DOM applies this event only to the object element, which, in the W3C standards view (but not yet widely supported in browsers), is the desired way to embed an image into a page.

Typical Targets   The img element.

activate

IE 5.5 NN *n/a* Moz *n/a* Saf *n/a* Op *n/a* DOM *n/a*
Bubbles: Yes; Cancelable: No

Fires when an object becomes the active object. Giving an object focus makes it active, but a rendered element can be the active element without having focus. Only one element at a time may be active. See the setActive( ) method of shared objects in Chapter 2. If an element has received focus, the activate event fires before the focusin and then the focus events.

Typical Targets   All rendered elements, plus the document and window objects.

afterprint, beforeprint

IE 5(Win) NN *n/a* Moz *n/a* Saf *n/a* Op *n/a* DOM *n/a*
Bubbles: No; Cancelable: No

Fires after the user clicks the **Print** button in the Print dialog box before content is assembled for the printer (beforeprint) and after the data has been sent to the printer (afterprint). You can use these events to trigger functions that modify a style sheet or other content rendering of a page (so that a potentially different-looking page reaches the printer) and then restore the page for viewing on the screen. This technique can work in lieu of style sheet media settings.

Typical Targets   The body and frameset elements, plus the window object.

afterupdate

IE 4(Win) NN *n/a* Moz *n/a* Saf *n/a* Op *n/a* DOM *n/a*
Bubbles: Yes; Cancelable: No

Fires after data being sent to a writable data source object (through the IE data binding mechanism) has successfully updated the database.

Typical Targets   Elements that accept data input and support data binding.

beforeactivate

IE 6   NN *n/a*   Moz *n/a*   Saf *n/a*   Op *n/a*   DOM *n/a*

Bubbles: Yes; Cancelable: Sometimes

Fires just before an object is to become the active object. Giving an object focus makes it active, but a rendered element can be the active element without having focus. Only one element at a time may be active. See the setActive( ) method of shared objects in Chapter 2. If an element received focus, related events fire in the following sequence: beforeactivate, activate, focusin, and focus.

If you cancel the beforeactivate event, the element does not become active, nor does it receive focus, but only if the intended focus action occurs from explicit user action (clicking and tabbing). An element blocked from receiving focus causes the focus to go to another element: to the next focusable element in tabbing order (when the user tabs to the blocked element) or to the next outermost focusable parent element in the document tree (when a user clicks on the blocked element). Activating or giving focus to an element via the setActive( ) or focus( ) method cannot be blocked by canceling this event.

Typical Targets   All rendered elements, plus the document and window objects.

beforecopy

IE 5(Win)   NN *n/a*   Moz *n/a*   Saf 1.3/2   Op *n/a*   DOM *n/a*

Bubbles: Yes; Cancelable: Yes

Fires just before a user-initiated **Copy** command (via the **Edit** menu, a keyboard shortcut, or a context menu) completes the task of moving the selected content to the system clipboard. At this point in the copy sequence, a function invoked by this event handler can perform additional or substitute processing for the normal system copy action. For example, additional information from the element, such as effective style information of the element containing selected text, can be preserved in the IE clipboardData object (see Chapter 2) for later processing with the help of the beforepaste event handler. Canceling the beforecopy event does not prevent user copying of a selection.

In Internet Explorer, the "before" events fire when the user displays the context menu (i.e., before any menu item is chosen). The events fire in the sequence beforecut, beforecopy, and beforepaste. Moreover, with the context menu approach, the three-event sequence fires twice.

Note that in Safari 1.3/2, you must pass onbeforecopy (rather than beforecopy) to addEventListener( ) to bind the event.

Typical Targets   Rendered elements except form controls.

beforecut

IE 5(Win)   NN *n/a*   Moz *n/a*   Saf 1.3/2   Op *n/a*   DOM *n/a*

Bubbles: Yes; Cancelable: Yes

Fires just before a user-initiated **Cut** command (via the **Edit** menu, a keyboard shortcut, or a context menu) completes the task of removing the content from its current location and moving the selected content to the system clipboard (assuming the browser is in edit mode for body content). At this point in the cut sequence, a function invoked by this event handler can perform additional or substitute processing for the normal system cut action. For example, additional information from the element, such as effective style information of the element containing selected text, can be preserved in the IE `clipboardData` object (see Chapter 2) for later processing with the help of the `beforepaste` event handler. Canceling the `beforecut` event does not prevent user cutting of a selection.

See beforecopy for additional browser-specific notes.

Typical Targets   All rendered elements.

beforedeactivate

IE 5.5   NN *n/a*   Moz *n/a*   Saf *n/a*   Op *n/a*   DOM *n/a*
Bubbles: Yes; Cancelable: Yes

Fires just before an object is about to yield activation to another object because the user clicked on another element, tabbed to another element, or because a script invoked the `setActive( )` or `focus( )` method of another element. If an element has focus and is the active element, the following event sequence fires en route to losing focus: `beforedeactivate`, `deactivate`, and `blur`. Because `beforedeactivate` is cancelable (but `deactivate` is not), cancel this event to prevent an element from deactivating or losing focus—provided you have a good reason to do this other than annoying your visitors.

Typical Targets   All rendered elements, plus the `document` and `window` objects.

beforeeditfocus

IE 5(Win)   NN *n/a*   Moz *n/a*   Saf *n/a*   Op *n/a*   DOM *n/a*
Bubbles: Yes; Cancelable: Yes

Fires just before an editable element receives official focus by a user clicking or tabbing to the element. Editable elements include text-oriented form controls and body elements set to be editable (see the IE 5.5 `contentEditable` property of all elements in Chapter 2). A function invoked from this event handler can perform additional scripted actions, such as setting the color of the element text, before the user begins editing the content.

Typical Targets   Text form controls; rendered elements in edit mode (IE 5.5 or later); content governed by the DHTML Editing ActiveX control (see *http:// msdn.microsoft.com/workshop/browser/mshtml/*).

beforepaste

IE 5(Win)   NN *n/a*   Moz *n/a*   Saf 1.3/2   Op *n/a*   DOM *n/a*
Bubbles: Yes; Cancelable: Yes

Fires just before a user-initiated **Paste** command (via the **Edit** menu, a keyboard shortcut, or a context menu) completes the task of pasting the content from the system clipboard to the current selection. If you are trying to paste custom information from the `clipboardData` object (saved there in an `beforecopy`, `copy`, `beforecut`, or `cut` event handler), you need to have the `beforepaste` and `paste` event handler functions working together. Set `event.returnValue` to false in the beforepaste event handler so that the **Paste** item in the **Edit** (and context) menu is activated, even for a noneditable paste target. When the user selects the **Paste** menu choice, your paste event handler retrieves information from the clipboardData object and perhaps modifies the selected element's HTML content:

```
function handleBeforePaste( ) {
    event.returnValue = false;
}
function handlePaste( ) {
    if (event.srcElement.className == "OK2Paste") {
        event.srcElement.innerText = clipboardData.getData("Text");
    }
}
```

In the above paste operation, the system clipboard never plays a role because your scripts handle the entire data transfer—all without having to go into edit mode.

See beforecopy for additional browser-specific notes.

Typical Targets   All rendered elements and the document object.

beforeprint

See afterprint.

beforeunload   IE 4(Win)/5(Mac) NN n/a Moz 1.7 Saf 1.3/2 Op n/a DOM n/a

Bubbles: No; Cancelable: Yes

Fires just before the current document begins to unload due to impending navigation to a new page, form submission, or window closure. This event fires before the unload event, and gives your scripts and users a chance to cancel the unload action. Some of this activity is automatic to prevent nefarious scripts from trapping users on a page.

In the beforeunload event handler, assign a string to the event.returnValue property to force IE and Mozilla 1.8 or later to display a dialog box that lets the user choose whether the page should stay where it is, or whether the navigation or window closure action that the user requested continues as expected. The string assigned to the event property becomes part of the dialog box message (other text in the message is hard-wired by the browser and may not be removed or modified). The resulting action is controlled by the user's button choice in the dialog box.

Typical Targets   The body and frameset elements, plus the window object.

beforeupdate   IE 4(Win) NN n/a Moz n/a Saf n/a Op n/a DOM n/a

Bubbles: Yes; Cancelable: Yes

Fires just prior to sending data to a writable data source object (through the IE data binding mechanism). You can perform data validation and cancel the update.

Typical Targets   Elements that accept data input and support data binding.

blur
IE 3   NN 2   Moz *all*   Saf *all*   Op *all*   DOM 2
Bubbles: No; Cancelable: No

Fires after the current element loses focus (due to some other element receiving focus) or invoking the blur( ) method of the current element. The blur event fires before the focus event in the other element.

Avoid using the blur event in text input fields to trigger form validation, especially if the validation routine displays an alert dialog box upon discovering an error. Interaction among the blur and focus events, along with the display and hiding of an alert dialog box can put you into an infinite loop. Use change instead.

Although the blur event has been supported for form controls and window objects since the early days of scriptable browsers, modern browsers can fire the event on virtually any other rendered element, provided the tabindex attribute is set for the element. Note that IE for Windows is known to omit firing the blur event on window objects.

Typical Targets   For all browsers, input (of type text and password), textarea, select, and window objects; for IE 5 or later and W3C DOM browsers, add any rendered element for which the tabindex attribute is assigned a value.

bounce
IE 4   NN *n/a*   Moz *n/a*   Saf *n/a*   Op *n/a*   DOM *n/a*
Bubbles: No; Cancelable: Yes

Fires each time the text in a marquee element, whose behavior is set to alternate, touches a boundary and changes direction.

Typical Targets   The marquee element.

cellchange
IE 5(Win)   NN *n/a*   Moz *n/a*   Saf *n/a*   Op *n/a*   DOM *n/a*
Bubbles: Yes; Cancelable: No

Fires on the element hosting a data binding data source object (usually the object element) each time data in the remote database changes its value.

Typical Targets   The object and applet elements.

change
IE 3   NN 2   Moz *all*   Saf *all*   Op *all*   DOM 2
Bubbles: No (IE); Yes (Others); Cancelable: Yes (IE); No (Others)

Fires when a text-oriented form control or select element loses focus *and* its content or chosen item is different from what it was when the element most recently gained focus. Use this event in text-type input and textarea elements to validate an entry for that one field.

But also include form-wide validation with the form element's submit event handler. This event fires before the blur event.

Typical Targets   Text-type input, textarea, and select elements.

click

IE *3* NN *2* Moz *all* Saf *all* Op *all* DOM *2*
Bubbles: Yes; Cancelable: Yes

Fires after the user effects a mouse click or equivalent action. Click equivalents occur naturally on focusable elements (buttons and links for most browsers) by pressing the **Enter** key (and frequently the spacebar) when the item has focus. In modern browsers that support the accesskey attribute, typing the access key combination also triggers a click equivalent.

For mouse click actions, the click event fires only if the mouse button is pressed and released with the pointer atop the same element. In that case, the primary mouse events fire in this order: mousedown, mouseup, and click.

An event object created from a mouse event has numerous properties filled with details such as coordinates of the click and whether any modifier keys were held down during the event. Information about the button used is more reliably accessed through the mousedown or mouseup event. The event handler function can inspect these properties as needed.

Although the click event has been supported for button-oriented form controls and link objects since the early days of scriptable browsers, modern browsers can fire the event on virtually any other rendered element. Note that in Mozilla versions prior to 1.4 and Safari prior to 1.3, mouse events can fire on child text nodes of container-type elements, meaning that the event object's target property references the node, rather than the element. See Online Section VI for details about the impact of this behavior and cross-browser solutions.

Typical Targets   For all browsers, input (of type button, radio, checkbox, reset, and submit), a, and area objects; Version 4 and later support the event for the document and window objects; for IE 4 or later and most W3C DOM browsers (not Opera 9), add any rendered element, as well as text nodes for Mozilla prior to version 1.4.

contextmenu

IE *5(Win)* NN *n/a* Moz *all* Saf *all* Op *n/a* DOM *n/a*
Bubbles: Yes; Cancelable: Yes

Fires after the user clicks the right mouse button (or the button designated the secondary mouse button in the mouse control panel). This mouse button displays the context menu for the item beneath the pointer. For Mozilla prior to 1.4 and Safari prior to 1.3, the event target could be a text node. For all other supporting browsers and versions, the target (or IE event.sourceElement) is the containing element. To block the display of the context menu (and perhaps display a custom one of your own design via DHTML), set event. returnValue to false in the contextmenu event handler. While hiding the context menu may make it more difficult for users to view the source of a page or save an image (assuming you have already opened a document in a window bereft of the menubar), it is not a foolproof way to guard against determined users capturing your page's content. Any scripted solution fails the instant the user disables scripting.

Typical Targets   All rendered elements and the document object.

controlselect
IE *5.5* NN *n/a* Moz *n/a* Saf *n/a* Op *n/a* DOM *n/a*
Bubbles: Yes; Cancelable: Yes

Fires when the user selects an editable element (not its content) while the page is in edit mode. See move for a demonstration of this event.

Typical Targets   All rendered elements and the document object.

copy
IE *5(Win)* NN *n/a* Moz *n/a* Saf *1.3/2* Op *n/a* DOM *n/a*
Bubbles: Yes; Cancelable: Yes

Fires after the user initiates the **Copy** command (via the **Edit** menu, a keyboard shortcut, or a context menu) to place a copy of the selected content into the system clipboard. An event handler function for this event can supplement the copy action by placing additional data of your choice into the clipboardData object (which the paste event handler can read and handle as needed).

To give users access to a **Copy** menu command for an otherwise uneditable element, set event.returnValue to false in the beforecopy event handler for the same object as the copy event handler. On the other hand, to prevent user copying of body content, set event.returnValue to false for the copy event handler. Just don't regard this tactic as a foolproof way to prevent users from copying your prized content.

Note that in Safari 1.3/2, you must pass oncopy (rather than copy) to addEventListener( ) to bind the event.

Typical Targets   Rendered elements except form controls.

cut
IE *5(Win)* NN *n/a* Moz *n/a* Saf *1.3/2* Op *n/a* DOM *n/a*
Bubbles: Yes; Cancelable: Yes

Fires after the user initiates the **Cut** command (via the **Edit** menu, a keyboard shortcut, or a context menu) to place a copy of the selected content into the system clipboard. To cut body content, the containing element must be in edit mode (see the shared contendEditable property in Chapter 2). An event handler function for this event can supplement the cut action by placing additional data of your choice into the clipboardData object (which the paste event handler can read and handle as needed).

To give users access to a **Cut** menu command for an otherwise uneditable element, set event.returnValue to false in the beforecut event handler for the same object as the cut event handler. On the other hand, to prevent user cutting of body or form control content, set event.returnValue to false for the cut event handler.

Note that in Safari 1.3/2, you must pass oncut (rather than cut) to addEventListener( ) to bind the event.

Typical Targets   All rendered elements.

dataavailable, datasetchanged, datasetcomplete

IE 4(Win)   NN n/a   Moz n/a   Saf n/a   Op n/a   DOM n/a

Bubbles: Yes; Cancelable: No

Fire on the element hosting a data binding data source object (usually the object element) each time the remote data source signals it has new data ready for retrieval (dataavailable), a data set has been modified (datasetchanged), or a data set has received all data form the query (datasetcomplete). These events are available only for data source object types capable of asynchronous connections with their remote sources.

Typical Targets   The object and applet elements; the xml element in IE 5 and later.

dblclick

IE 4   NN 4   Moz all   Saf n/a   Op all   DOM n/a

Bubbles: Yes; Cancelable: Yes

Fires after the user effects a second successive mouse click or equivalent action (see click for click equivalents). A double-click requires a specific sequence of mouse events leading up to it. The sequence is mousedown, mouseup, click, mouseup, and dblclick. The amount of time that can elapse between the two clicks is determined by the client computer's mouse control panel settings.

Because the click event fires ahead of dblclick, the associated click event handler (if any) should perform only innocuous actions, such as highlighting an element, much like the way operating system desktop icons operate. If an item requires a double-click, that is the only event that should do something significant. For Mozilla prior to 1.4 and Safari prior to 1.3, the event target could be a text node. For all other supporting browsers and versions, the target (or IE event.sourceElement) is the containing element.

Typical Targets   Support for this event in Navigator 4 is limited to the a element (but not on the Macintosh); IE 4 or later and W3C DOM browsers (except Safari through version 2) support the event on renderable elements and the document object.

deactivate

IE 5.5   NN n/a   Moz n/a   Saf n/a   Op n/a   DOM n/a

Bubbles: Yes; Cancelable: No

Fires after an object has yielded activation to another object because the user clicked on another element or tabbed to another element, or because a script invoked the setActive( ) or focus( ) method of another element. If an element has focus and is the active element, the following event sequence fires en route to losing focus: beforedeactivate, deactivate, and blur. To prevent an element from deactivating or losing focus, cancel the companion beforedeactivate event.

Typical Targets   All rendered elements, plus the document and window objects.

DOMActivate
IE *n/a* NN *n/a* Moz *n/a* Saf *1.3/2* Op *n/a* DOM *2*
Bubbles: Yes; Cancelable: Yes

Fires when a user begins interacting with an element, such as clicking a button or typing a character into a text box. The event object's detail property passes an integer that contains more information about the event: 1 for unmodified single clicks; 2 for actions with modifier keys or double-clicks (what the DOM specification calls *hyperactivation*).

Typical Targets   All rendered elements that are capable of receiving focus normally (such as form controls and links), plus any other rendered element for which the tabindex attribute is assigned a value.

DOMAttrModified
IE *n/a* NN *n/a* Moz *all* Saf *n/a* Op *7* DOM *2*
Bubbles: Yes; Cancelable: No

Fires after a script adds, removes, or changes the value of an element's attribute. Adding or removing an attribute must be done by the setAttribute( ) and removeAttribute( ) methods, but changing an existing attribute may be accomplished either by the setAttribute( ) method or assigning a new value to an element object's property that corresponds to an attribute. Numerous event object properties convey details about the event. See the following properties of the event object in Chapter 2: attrName, attrChange, prevValue, newValue, and relatedNode.

Typical Targets   All elements.

DOMCharacterDataModified
IE *n/a* NN *n/a* Moz *n/a* Saf *n/a* Op *n/a* DOM *2*
Bubbles: Yes; Cancelable: No

Fires after a script changes the value of a CharacterData type of node. See the following properties of the event object in Chapter 2: prevValue and newValue.

Typical Targets   CharacterData nodes.

DOMContentLoaded
IE *n/a* NN *n/a* Moz *1.0.1* Saf *n/a* Op *9* DOM *n/a*
Bubbles: Yes; Cancelable: Yes

Fires immediately after all HTML source code has been interpreted by the browser such that all elements are represented in the DOM. This occurs ahead of further loading of external content (e.g., images, sounds, etc.) that may require more time to complete—after which the load event fires. Using this event instead of load allows DHTML scripts to begin modification of the document tree even while other external content is en route. The event does not fire if the user navigates to the page via the browser history (e.g., **Back** or **Forward** buttons).

Typical Targets   body, document, window DOM objects.

DOMControlValueChanged

IE *n/a*   NN *n/a*   Moz *n/a*   Saf *n/a*   Op *9*   DOM *2*

Bubbles: Yes; Cancelable: No

Fires on a Web Forms 2.0 form control each time its value changes. Binding this event to a form element lets a script execute when any single control's value changes.

Typical Targets   Web Forms 2.0 form control elements and the form element.

DOMFocusIn, DOMFocusOut

IE *n/a*   NN *n/a*   Moz *n/a*   Saf *1.3/2*   Op *9*   DOM *2*

Bubbles: Yes; Cancelable: No

Fires when the current element receives focus (DOMFocusIn) or loses focus (DOMFocusOut). These events fire prior to the focus and blur events, respectively. Similar to the IE focusin and focusout events.

Typical Targets   All rendered elements that are capable of receiving focus normally (such as form controls and links), plus any other rendered element for which the tabindex attribute is assigned a value.

DOMFrameContentLoaded

IE *n/a*   NN *n/a*   Moz *1.0.1*   Saf *n/a*   Op *9*   DOM *n/a*

Bubbles: Yes; Cancelable: Yes

Fires immediately after all HTML source code loading into a frame element has been interpreted by the browser such that all elements are represented in the DOM. This occurs ahead of further loading of external content (e.g., images, sounds, etc.) that may require more time to complete—after which the load event fires. Using this event instead of load allows DHTML scripts to begin modification of the document tree even while other external content is en route. The event does not fire if the user navigates to the page via the browser history (e.g., **Back** or **Forward** buttons). This event is typically bound to frame elements inside the framesetting document.

Typical Target   frame element.

DOMMenuItemActive

IE *n/a* NN *n/a* Moz *1.0.1* Saf *n/a* Op *n/a* DOM *n/a*

Bubbles: Yes; Cancelable: No

Fires on an option element when an option is selected via a keyboard **Up** or **Down** arrow key. For example, if you assign an accesskey to a select element and invoke that key combination, the select element forces a focus event. A press of the **Up** or **Down** arrow key to choose an option fires the DOMMenuItemActive event.

Typical Target   option element.

DOMNodeInserted

IE *n/a* NN *n/a* Moz *all* Saf *1.3/2* Op *9* DOM *2*

Bubbles: Yes; Cancelable: No

Fires on a node when that node is explicitly inserted into an existing node container. If you assign an event listener for this event to an element that is the recipient of an inserted (including appended) node, the DOMNodeInserted event fires on the node being inserted (the srcElement of the event object). If the event bubbles further (i.e., away from the point of insertion), the event listener function can still find out about the new container by reading the relatedNode event property. Note that if the incoming node comes from another location in the same document, the removal of the node from its original container fires the DOMNodeRemoved event on the removed node before it leaves its original container (so that the event can bubble up to its original container).

Typical Targets   All nodes.

DOMNodeInsertedIntoDocument

IE *n/a* NN *n/a* Moz *n/a* Saf *n/a* Op *n/a* DOM *2*

Bubbles: No; Cancelable: No

Fires on a node when that node is inserted into an existing node container, but the origin of the node is from another document. If you assign an event listener for this event and the DOMNodeInserted event, the DOMNodeInsertedIntoDocument event fires first. Note that if the incoming node comes from another location in another document, the removal of the node from its original document fires the DOMNodeRemovedFromDocument and DOMNodeRemoved events on the removed node before it leaves its original container (so that the event can bubble up to its original container).

Typical Targets   All nodes.

DOMNodeRemoved

IE *n/a* NN *n/a* Moz *all* Saf *1.3/2* Op *n/a* DOM *2*

Bubbles: Yes; Cancelable: No

Fires on a node when that node is explicitly removed from a node container. If you assign an event listener for this event to an element that is the container of a removed node, the

DOMNodeRemoved event fires on the node being removed (the srcElement of the event object). If the event bubbles further (i.e., away from the original node location), the event listener function can still find out about the old container by reading the relatedNode event property.

Typical Targets   All nodes.

DOMNodeRemovedFromDocument

IE *n/a* NN *n/a* Moz *n/a* Saf *n/a* Op *n/a* DOM *2*

Bubbles: No; Cancelable: No

Fires on a node when the node is removed because it is being inserted into another document, meaning the node is exiting its original document entirely. If you assign an event listener for this event and the DOMNodeRemoved event, the DOMNodeRemovedFromDocument event fires last.

Typical Targets   All nodes.

DOMSubtreeModified

IE *n/a* NN *n/a* Moz *n/a* Saf *1.3/2* Op *n/a* DOM *2*

Bubbles: No; Cancelable: No

Fires on a node that is inside the document tree and that changes its nested node structure. This event acts like a generic event for the more specific node mutation events, and fires last.

Typical Targets   All nodes.

DOMTitleModified

IE *n/a* NN *n/a* Moz *1.0.1* Saf *n/a* Op *n/a* DOM *2*

Bubbles: No; Cancelable: Yes

Fires when a script modifies the value of the document.title property.

Typical Targets   document node.

drag, dragend, dragstart

IE *5(Win)* NN *n/a* Moz *n/a* Saf *1.3/2* Op *n/a* DOM *n/a*

Bubbles: Yes; Cancelable: Yes

When the user starts dragging a previously created selection, the browser fires one dragstart event on the selection's parent element, followed by a series of drag events, and then one dragend event when the user releases the mouse button. All three event types fire on the same element during the drag.

During the drag operation, the user sees the cursor in one of its various forms, rather than seeing the actual element float around the page. As long as the user keeps the mouse

Event Reference

button down following an initial drag action, the drag event keeps firing. Other drag-related events fire on other elements along the way (events such as dragenter for an element that finds the dragged cursor in its airspace), but the drag event also fires at various instances.

An element with content that is dragged receives events in the following sequence: dragstart, drag (perhaps many times), and dragend. Elements in the path of the drag action receive dragenter, dragover, and dragleave events, while the element at the end of the drag receives the drop event (which fires before the dragend event of the dragged element). The speed of the drag action and client system speed impacts the number of event firings of all drag types. A fast drag on a slow machine may result in some events not firing.

Typical Targets   All rendered elements and document objects. Safari fires the events on text nodes.

dragdrop

IE *n/a* NN |4| Moz *n/a* Saf *n/a* Op *n/a* DOM *n/a*

Bubbles: No; Cancelable: No

Fires (in Navigator 4 only) if the user drags a desktop file to the document. With signed scripts, the browser can read the filename of the dragged item.

Typical Targets   The window object.

dragend

See drag.

dragenter, dragleave, dragover

IE *5(Win)* NN *n/a* Moz *n/a* Saf *1.3/2* Op *n/a* DOM *n/a*

Bubbles: Yes; Cancelable: Yes

Elements in the path of a drag action usually receive dragenter, dragover, and dragleave events in that order. The speed of the drag action and client systems impact the number of event firings of all drag types. A fast drag on a slow machine may result in some events not firing.

If your scripts will be performing customized actions upon the user dropping the dragged item onto a target in the document, you should prevent default actions of the dragenter and dragover events so that the target's drop event can do its job without interference from the normal system response to dragging. See the dataTransfer object in Chapter 2 for an example of drag-related event interaction.

Typical Targets   All rendered elements and document objects.

dragstart

See drag.

drop

IE *5(Win)* NN *n/a* Moz *n/a* Saf *1.3/2* Op *n/a* DOM *n/a*

Bubbles: Yes; Cancelable: Yes

Fires on the drop target element when the user releases the mouse button after a drag action. Fires just before the dragend event of the owner of the dragged content. Prevent default actions of the drop target's dragenter and dragover events (by setting event.returnValue to false in their respective event handler functions) so that the target's drop event can do its job without interference from the normal system response to dragging. See the dataTransfer object in Chapter 2 for an example of drag-related event interaction, including the effectAllowed property, which controls the cursor shape at the drop target.

Typical Targets   All rendered elements and document objects.

error

IE *4* NN *3* Moz *all* Saf *all* Op *all* DOM *2*

Bubbles: No; Cancelable: Yes

Fires after one of a variety of errors occurs, depending on the element or object to which the event handler is assigned. For elements that load external content, such as the img element, errors during loading (such as an invalid URL) fire the error event on the img element. When assigned to the window object (including direct assignment in the <body> tag), overall runtime script errors (not compile-time syntax errors) also fire the error event. A technique that some scripters used in earlier browsers that plastered script error messages inside intrusive alert dialog boxes was to trap all runtime errors in the following manner:

```
function doNothing( ) {return true;}
window.onerror = doNothing;
```

This isn't good for debugging because you need to find errors during development. See the Error object in Chapter 2 for more details on processing errors from this event handler. Eventually, there will enough browsers deployed that use more modern exception handling (see try/catch in Chapter 5).

Typical Targets   Elements that load external content, plus the window object and (in Mozilla) XMLHttpRequest.

errorupdate

IE *4(Win)* NN *n/a* Moz *n/a* Saf *n/a* Op *n/a* DOM *n/a*

Bubbles: Yes; Cancelable: No

Fires if an error occurs while sending data to a writable data source object (through the data binding mechanism).

Typical Targets   Elements that accept data input and support data binding.

filterchange

Fires when an element's filter changes its state and when a transition or blend filter completes its action. You can use the event to cascade a sequence of transitions.

Typical Targets   Most rendered elements.

finish

Fires after the scrolling text in a looping `marquee` element comes to rest after its final motion.

Typical Targets   The `marquee` element.

focus

Fires when the current element receives focus due to user action (clicking or tabbing) or invoking of the `focus( )` method. The blur event of the next previously focused element fires before the focus event in the current element.

Although the focus event has been supported for form controls and window objects since the early days of scriptable browsers, modern browsers can fire the event on virtually any other rendered element, provided the `tabindex` attribute is set for the element. Note that IE for Windows is known to omit firing the focus event on window objects.

Typical Targets   For all browsers, `input` (of type text and password), `textarea`, `select`, and `window` objects; for IE 5 or later and W3C DOM browsers, add any rendered element for which the `tabindex` attribute is assigned a value.

focusin, focusout

Fire when the current element receives focus (`focusin`) or loses focus (`focusout`). These events fire prior to the focus and blur events, respectively. Microsoft suggests that you can use these event handlers to perform style changes (anywhere in the document) in anticipation of an element receiving or losing focus, without disturbing the normal focus and blur actions.

Typical Targets   All rendered elements that are capable of receiving focus normally (such as form controls and links), plus any other rendered element for which the `tabindex` attribute is assigned a value.

formchange

IE *n/a* NN *n/a* Moz *n/a* Saf *n/a* Op *9* DOM *n/a*
Bubbles: No; Cancelable: No

Web Forms 2.0 event that fires after a form control's change event. But unlike the change event, formchange fires on all other controls in the form (except an output element) in source code order, and then the enclosing form element. Therefore, a form control can "know" when any other control in the form has changed.

Typical Targets   Web Forms 2.0 form control elements.

forminput

IE *n/a* NN *n/a* Moz *n/a* Saf *n/a* Op *9* DOM *n/a*
Bubbles: No; Cancelable: No

Web Forms 2.0 event that fires after a form control's input event. But unlike the input event, forminput fires on all other controls in the form (except an output element) in source code order, and then the enclosing form element. Therefore, a form control can "know" when any other control in the form is being changed.

Typical Targets   Web Forms 2.0 form control elements.

help

IE *4* NN *n/a* Moz *n/a* Saf *n/a* Op *n/a* DOM *n/a*
Bubbles: Yes; Cancelable: Yes

Fires when the user presses the **F1** function key. If an element has focus at the time, that is the element that receives the event. You can prevent the default action (displaying the IE **Help** window) and generate your own DHTML-based help system if you like.

Typical Targets   All rendered elements, plus document and window objects, except in IE for Macintosh, which limits this event to the window object.

input

IE *n/a* NN *n/a* Moz *n/a* Saf *n/a* Op *9* DOM *n/a*
Bubbles: Yes; Cancelable: No

Web Forms 2.0 event that fires as a user performs any input action on a form control. For example, each keystroke in a text field fires an input event. Thus, scripts can perform more immediate input validation, rather than waiting for an change event to fire upon the element losing focus.

Typical Targets   Web Forms 2.0 form control elements.

Event Reference

invalid

IE *n/a* NN *n/a* Moz *n/a* Saf *n/a* Op *9* DOM *n/a*

Bubbles: Yes; Cancelable: Yes

Web Forms 2.0 event that fires on a form control just prior to the form's submission and the value does not meet the criteria established via other element attributes. See the output element in Chapter 1 for an example.

Typical Targets   Web Forms 2.0 form control elements.

keydown, keyup

IE *4* NN *4* Moz *all* Saf *all* Op *all* DOM *3*

Bubbles: Yes; Cancelable: Yes

Fire when the user presses (keydown) and releases (keyup) a keyboard key. These two events fire on a focusable element or object for almost every key of the keyboard, including function and navigation keys. The instance of the event object for these events contains information about the key (not the character) pressed. See Online Section VI for details on cross-browser handling of keyboard events. You cannot reliably inhibit critical **Ctrl** character sequences, but if you prevent the default action of the keypress event for a text form control, the character does not arrive at the text field.

Typical Targets   All focusable rendered elements, plus document and window objects.

keypress

IE *4* NN *4* Moz *all* Saf *all* Op *all* DOM *n/a*

Bubbles: Yes; Cancelable: Yes

Fires when the user presses a keyboard character key or holds it down until the computer's auto-repeat mechanism takes hold. During auto-repeat, a new event fires prior to each character registering with the system (e.g., for display in a text box). The event sequence is keydown, keypress, and keyup. For text fields, the keypress event fires before the typed character appears in the text box. Therefore, the value of the event target/srcElement has the text prior to the addition of the typed character. See Online Section VI for details on cross-browser handling of keyboard events.

Typical Targets   All focusable rendered elements, plus the document object.

layoutcomplete

IE *5.5* NN *n/a* Moz *n/a* Saf *n/a* Op *n/a* DOM *n/a*

Bubbles: Yes; Cancelable: Yes

Fires when a print preview LayoutRect object finishes rendering its content. For details on this XML enhancement for IE 5.5 and later, visit *http://msdn.microsoft.com/workshop/browser/hosting/printpreview/reference/reference.asp*.

Typical Targets   An XML LayoutRect object.

load

IE *3* NN *2* Moz *all* Saf *all* Op *all* DOM *2*

Bubbles: No; Cancelable: No

Fires when external content belonging to the current element or object finishes loading and initializing. This event handler for the window object is perhaps the most important because it signals that all content of the document and its elements (including external content) has loaded before the event fires. When that event fires, your scripts can reference any document tree object without error. See also the DOMContentLoaded event.

The event fires for a frameset element only after the load events for all frames have fired (but the event is not bubbling from frame to frameset). Note that if the user or a script loads a new page into a frame after the frameset's initial load, the load event does not fire again for the frameset (but it does for the frame).

Although the load event has been supported for window objects since the early days of scriptable browsers, modern browsers fire the event on virtually any other rendered element that loads external content.

Typical Targets   For all browsers, window objects; for Version 4 browsers or later the img element; for IE 4 or later and current mainstream browsers, add any rendered element capable of loading external content; for Mozilla 1.8 and Safari 1.2, XMLHttpRequest.

losecapture

IE *5(Win)* NN *n/a* Moz *n/a* Saf *n/a* Op *n/a* DOM *n/a*

Bubbles: No; Cancelable: No

Fires when event capture mode for the element becomes disengaged. See the shared setCapture( ) method in Chapter 2.

Typical Targets   All rendered elements.

message

IE *n/a* NN *n/a* Moz *n/a* Saf *n/a* Op *8* DOM *n/a*

Bubbles: Yes; Cancelable: Yes

Fires when one document invokes the postMessage( ) method on another document (e.g., the second document being in an iframe). The event handler to receive and process the event is bound to the destination document object, and the event object's properties convey information such as domain (to help the destination document verify that the event is coming from a desired sender) and data. Data can be only a string value, but the two documents may be served from different domains, bypassing the cross-domain security restrictions of normal JavaScript processing.

Typical Targets   document

Event Reference

mousedown, mouseup

IE *4* NN *4* Moz *all* Saf *all* Op *all* DOM *2*

Bubbles: Yes; Cancelable: Yes

Fires when the user presses down (mousedown) or releases (mouseup) a mouse button. Events related to mouse click actions fire in this order: mousedown, mouseup, and click.

An event object created from a mouse event has numerous properties filled with details such as coordinates of the click, the mouse button used, and whether any modifier keys were held down during the event. The event handler function can inspect these properties as needed.

Note that in Mozilla prior to version 1.4 and Safari prior to version 1.3, mouse events can fire on child text nodes of container-type elements, meaning that the event object's target property references the node, rather than the element. See Online Section VI for details about the impact of this behavior and cross-browser solutions.

Typical Targets   All rendered elements, except in Navigator 4, where the events are limited to button-style input elements, plus a and area elements.

mouseenter, mouseleave

IE *5.5* NN *n/a* Moz *n/a* Saf *n/a* Op *n/a* DOM *n/a*

Bubbles: No; Cancelable: No

Fire when the user rolls the mouse pointer into (mouseenter) or out of (mouseleave) an element's space (including border or padding, but not margin). Each event fires just once per entry and exit. These variations on the mouseover and mouseout events do not bubble.

Typical Targets   All rendered elements.

mousemove

IE *4* NN *4* Moz *all* Saf *all* Op *all* DOM *2*

Bubbles: Yes; Cancelable: No

Fires while the user rolls the mouse pointer atop an element's space, with the mouse button up or down. Note that the event fires repeatedly, although the frequency of firing depends on the speed of the mouse motion and system resources.

An event object created from a mouse event has numerous properties filled with details such as coordinates of the pointer and whether any modifier keys were held down during the event. The event handler function can inspect these properties as needed.

In Navigator 4, this event type can be assigned to the window, document, and layer object, but only in the explicitly defined event capture mode. Note that in Mozilla prior to version 1.4 and Safari prior to version 1.3, mouse events can fire on child text nodes of container-type elements, meaning that the event object's target property references the node, rather than the element. See Online Section VI for details about the impact of this behavior and cross-browser solutions.

Typical Targets   All rendered elements, except as noted earlier for Navigator 4.

mouseout, mouseover

IE *3* NN *2* Moz *all* Saf *all* Op *all* DOM *2*

Bubbles: Yes; Cancelable: Yes

Fire when the user rolls the mouse pointer into (mouseover) or out of (mouseout) an element's space (including border or padding, but not margin). Each event fires just once per entry and exit (except in Navigator 4 for Windows, in which the event fires repeatedly, similar to mousemove).

Because the mouseout event doesn't officially fire until another element in the window fires its mouseover event (whether you have a handler for it or not), the mouseout event may not fire if the target element is at the edge of a window or frame, and the user whisks the pointer outside of the current frame without the first frame's body element ever receiving the mouseover event. If you use mouseout events to restore image swaps, the user could see a stuck image. Leave sufficient space around your swappable images to account for this behavior.

An event object created from a mouse event has numerous properties filled with details such as coordinates of the click, the mouse button used, whether any modifier keys were held down during the event, and where the incoming pointer came from or outgoing pointer has gone. The event handler function can inspect these properties as needed.

Note that in Mozilla prior to version 1.4 and Safari prior to version 1.3, mouse events can fire on child text nodes of container-type elements, meaning that the event object's target property references the node, rather than the element. See Online Section VI for details about the impact of this behavior and cross-browser solutions.

Although these events have been supported in one form or another since the early days of scriptable browsers, only modern browsers can fire the event on virtually any rendered element. For older browsers, the events were limited to a and area elements (where a elements surrounded images to be swapped).

Typical Targets   All rendered elements, except as noted earlier.

mousewheel

IE *6* NN *n/a* Moz *n/a* Saf *n/a* Op *n/a* DOM *n/a*

Bubbles: No; Cancelable: No

Fires as the user spins the mouse wheel (on a mouse equipped with a wheel). The event object's wheelDelta property reveals details about the direction and amount of rotation.

Typical Targets   All rendered elements and the document object.

move

IE *n/a* NN |4| Moz *n/a* Saf *n/a* Op *n/a* DOM *n/a*

Bubbles: No; Cancelable: No

Fires (in Navigator 4 only) if the user or script moves the browser window.

Typical Targets   The window object.

Event Reference

move, moveend, movestart

IE 5.5 NN *n/a* Moz *n/a* Saf *n/a* Op *n/a* DOM *n/a*

Bubbles: Yes; Cancelable: No

When in edit mode, a positionable element set up for dragging receives these events in the following sequence: movestart (upon starting the drag), move (repeatedly during the drag), and moveend (upon release of the mouse button). The following example uses several events to demonstrate IE edit mode scripting (note that the native element dragging mechanism doesn't work well in IE 6 if the <!DOCTYPE> element points to a standards-compatible mode DTD):

```
<html>
<head>
<title>IE 5.5 (Windows) Edit Mode</title>
<style type="text/css">
    body {font-family:Arial, sans-serif}
    #myDIV  {position:absolute; height:100px; width:300px;}
    .regular {border:5px black solid; padding:5px; background-color:lightgreen}
    .moving {border:5px maroon dashed; padding:5px; background-color:lightyellow}
    .chosen {border:5px maroon solid; padding:5px; background-color:lightyellow}
</style>
<script type="text/javascript">
// built-in dragging support
document.execCommand("2D-position",false,true);
// preserve content between modes
var oldHTML = "";

// engage static edit environment
function editOn() {
    var elem = event.srcElement;
    elem.className = "chosen";
}

// engage special edit-move environment
function moveOn() {
    var elem = event.srcElement;
    oldHTML = elem.innerHTML;
    elem.className = "moving";
}

// display coordinates during drag
function trackMove() {
    var elem = event.srcElement;
    elem.innerHTML = "Element is now at: " + elem.offsetLeft + ", " +
                    elem.offsetTop;
}

// turn off special edit-move environment
function moveOff() {
    var elem = event.srcElement;
    elem.innerHTML = oldHTML;
    elem.className = "chosen";
}
```

```
    // restore original environment (wrapper gets onfocusout)
    function editOff( ) {
        var elem = event.srcElement;
        if (elem.id == "wrapper") {
            elem.firstChild.className = "regular";
        }
    }

    // initialize event handlers
    function init( ) {
        document.body.oncontrolselect = editOn;
        document.body.onmovestart = moveOn;
        document.body.onmove = trackMove;
        document.body.onmoveend = moveOff;
        document.body.onfocusout = editOff;
    }

    window.onload = init;
    </script>
    </head>
    <body>
    <div id="wrapper" contenteditable="true">
        <div id="myDIV" class="regular">
            This is a positioned element with some text in it.
        </div>
    </div>
    </body>
    </html>
```

Typical Targets   All rendered elements.

paste

IE *5(Win)* NN *n/a* Moz *n/a* Saf *1.3/2* Op *n/a* DOM *n/a*

Bubbles: Yes; Cancelable: Yes

Fires after the user initiates the **Paste** command (via the **Edit** menu, a keyboard shortcut, or a context menu) to place a copy of the system clipboard into the selected content. An event handler function for this event can supplement the paste action by retrieving additional data from the clipboardData object (information placed there by one of the copy- or cut-related event handler functions).

To give users access to a **Paste** menu command for an otherwise uneditable element, set event.returnValue to false in the beforepaste event handler for the same object as the paste event handler. On the other hand, to prevent user pasting system clipboard content, set event.returnValue to false for the paste event handler.

Typical Targets   All rendered elements.

progress

IE *n/a* NN *n/a* Moz *1.8* Saf *n/a* Op *n/a* DOM *n/a*

Bubbles: No; Cancelable: No

Fires periodically during the receipt of data from the server through the XMLHttpRequest object.

Typical Targets   XMLHttpRequest object.

propertychange

IE *5(Win)* NN *n/a* Moz *n/a* Saf *n/a* Op *n/a* DOM *n/a*

Bubbles: No; Cancelable: No

Fires after the property of an element changes under script control. Property changes occur through direct property assignment and methods, such as setAttribute( ). Changes to an element's property (e.g., a property of an element's style object) also trigger this event. The event object's propertyName property contains the name of the property influenced by the event.

Typical Targets   All rendered elements, plus the document object.

readystatechange

IE *4* NN *n/a* Moz *1.0.1* Saf *1.2* Op *8* DOM *n/a*

Bubbles: No; Cancelable: No

Fires if the readyState property changes for an element. See the shared readyState property in Chapter 2 for details on what affects the property. Most browsers support this event only for the XMLHttpRequest object (see Online Section VII).

Typical Targets   Elements that load external content, including XMLHttpRequest.

reset

IE *4* NN *3* Moz *all* Saf *all* Op *all* DOM *2*

Bubbles: No; Cancelable: Yes

Fires when a form element receives a request to reset the form from a reset-type input element or a scripted reset( ) method. By canceling the event, a script in the reset event handler aborts the normal form reset.

Typical Targets   The form element.

resize

IE *4* NN *4* Moz *all* Saf *all* Op *all* DOM *2*

Bubbles: Yes; Cancelable: No

Fires after an element or object is resized by the user or script control. Note that resizing a window may force other elements in the page to resize themselves. In IE, resize events from those elements bubble to the body and window objects, where a lone resize event handler may be bombarded by events. Safari fires this event on the window object, and not a node in the DOM tree.

Typical Targets   For IE, elements that have dimensions associated with them, plus the window and document objects; for Mozilla and Opera, the window and document objects; for Safari, the window object only.

resizeend, resizestart   IE *5.5* NN *n/a* Moz *n/a* Saf *n/a* Op *n/a* DOM *n/a*

Bubbles: Yes; Cancelable: No

Fire (in edit mode only) when a user resizes an element by dragging its resize handles. See move for a related example.

Typical Targets   All rendered elements.

rowenter, rowexit, rowsdelete, rowsinserted   IE *4(Win)* NN *n/a* Moz *n/a* Saf *n/a* Op *n/a* DOM *n/a*

Bubbles: Yes; Cancelable: No

Fire on the element hosting a data binding data source object (usually the object element) when a row in the remote database table is modified either through database or data source activity.

Typical Targets   The object and applet elements; the xml element in IE 5 and later.

scroll   IE *4* NN *n/a* Moz *n/a* Saf *n/a* Op *n/a* DOM *2*

Bubbles: No; Cancelable: No

Fires each time an element displaying scroll bars or the browser window executes a scroll, either by user action or script control. If a user drags the scroll bar thumb, the event fires repeatedly during the dragging motion, but the frequency of event firings depends on system speeds.

Typical Targets   All rendered elements that can have scrollbars by default (such as textarea and window objects), plus any element that has its overflow style sheet attribute set to scroll; in Mozilla and Safari, the html element; in Opera, the body element and document node.

select

IE 3 NN 2 Moz *all* Saf *all* Op *all* DOM 2

Bubbles: No (IE and Safari); Yes (Others); Cancelable: Yes

Fires when a user drags a selection in a text box (input or textarea elements). Broken in Navigator 4 for Windows. In IE 4 or later for Windows, the event also applies to body text selections.

Typical Targets   Text-type input and textarea elements for all browsers; body element for IE 4 or later for Windows.

selectionchange

IE 5.5 NN *n/a* Moz *n/a* Saf *n/a* Op *n/a* DOM *n/a*

Bubbles: No; Cancelable: No

Fires when the selection type (in IE edit mode) changes.

Typical Targets   The document object.

selectstart

IE 4 NN *n/a* Moz *n/a* Saf *1.3/2* Op *n/a* DOM *n/a*

Bubbles: Yes; Cancelable: Yes

Fires immediately after the user begins dragging a selection on a body element or form control text. If the selection extends across multiple elements, only one event fires, and its target remains the element where the selection began. Canceling this event in the <body> tag (onselectstart="return false") can prevent undesirable and inadvertent user selection and scrolling interaction.

Typical Targets   All rendered elements.

start

IE 4 NN *n/a* Moz *n/a* Saf *n/a* Op *n/a* DOM *n/a*

Bubbles: No; Cancelable: No

Fires when the scrolling text in a looping marquee element begins its motion after a page loads.

Typical Targets   The marquee element.

stop

IE 5(Win) NN *n/a* Moz *n/a* Saf *n/a* Op *n/a* DOM *n/a*

Bubbles: No; Cancelable: No

Fires when the user clicks the browser's **Stop** button, even if the document and its content have successfully loaded.

Typical Targets   The document object.

submit

IE *3* NN *2* Moz *all* Saf *all* Op *all* DOM *2*

Bubbles: No (IE); Yes (Others); Cancelable: Yes

Fires when a `form` element receives a request to submit the form from a submit-type `input` element but *not* from a scripted `submit()` method. This is the event to trigger one final client-side form validation prior to sending a form to the server. By canceling the event, a script in the `submit` event handler aborts the submission.

Typical Targets   The `form` element.

unload

IE *3* NN *2* Moz *all* Saf *all* Op *all* DOM *2*

Bubbles: No; Cancelable: No

Fires just before the current document begins to unload due to impending navigation to a new page, form submission, or window closure. This event fires after the `beforeunload` event in browsers that support that event. In most browsers, the actual document unloading does not wait for the `unload` event handler function to complete. Therefore, if the function performs too many actions, especially those that rely on script variables and elements in the current page, those references may become invalid while the function runs, creating script errors (of the "undefined" or "object not found" variety). Therefore, keep unload processing to a minimum.

Typical Targets   The `body` and `frameset` elements, plus the `window` object.

Style Sheet Property Reference

The purpose of this chapter is to provide a list of every web page style sheet property that is implemented in mainstream browsers, as well as those specified in the W3C recommendations for Cascading Style Sheets. So that you can readily see whether a particular entry applies to the browser(s) you must support, a version table accompanies each term listed in the following pages. This table tells you at a glance the version of Internet Explorer (IE), pre-Mozilla Netscape Navigator (NN), Mozilla (Moz), Apple Safari (Saf), Opera (starting from version 7), and W3C CSS specification in which the term was first introduced. Several properties removed from the specification with the publication of CSS Level 2.1 are marked with CSS version <2.1 (less than 2.1) and should not be used.

This chapter is organized alphabetically by CSS property name. For each property, you can see quickly what the value types are, an example of real-life source code, and how to address the property from the JavaScript language (if the property is scriptable). A few items implemented in available browsers are proposed for CSS Level 3, but only those that are nearing final approval are marked accordingly. Some additional items for the Mozilla, Safari, and Opera browsers are preliminary versions of forthcoming CSS3 properties. To deploy these features ahead of the formal specification, while preventing possible naming collisions with final CSS3 specifications, each browser gives these properties a prefix that identifies the source: -moz- (Mozilla), -khtml- (Safari), and -o- (Opera). Note that none of these prefixes validate under CSS Level 2 due to the leading hyphen. This is intentional. Mozilla and Safari rendering engines also support a number of additional proprietary properties (with -moz- and -khtml- prefixes, respectively) that are not intended for web pages, but for internal use (e.g., Mozilla XUL user interface elements) or applications (e.g., Apple Dashboard widgets or Macintosh applications employing WebKit). These properties are outside the realm of DHTML document creation and are therefore not described in this chapter.

Property Value Types

Many style sheet properties share similar data requirements. For the sake of brevity in the reference listings, this section describes a few common property value types in more detail than is possible within each listing. When you see one of these property value types associated with a property, consult this section for a description of the type.

Length

A length value defines a linear measure of document real estate—usually a horizontal or vertical measurement of distance, height, width, thickness, or size. Length units may be relative or absolute. A relative unit depends upon variables such as the dot pitch or pixel density of the video display that shows a document. Relative units in CSS are pixels (px), ems (em), and exes (ex). An em is the actual height of the element's font (or inherited font) as rendered on a given display device; an ex is the height of a lowercase "x" under the same conditions. The exception to this rule is when em and ex units are used to define the font-size property, in which case the units are relative to the font size of the parent element.

Pay special attention when a relative value is to be inherited by a child element. In those circumstances, the CSS recommendation says that the child element inherits the *computed* value of the property (computed at the time of the property definition in the parent element's assignment), rather than an adjusted value. For example, if the body element specifies a font-size of 20pt and a text-indent of 2em (equaling 40pt), the text-indent value inherited by p or other elements within the body element is equal to 40pt, regardless of what the current font-size of the other elements may be. To override the inherited computed value, the p or other element needs to reassign a text-indent property for that element (or other outer container that intervenes from the body). Mozilla, Safari, Opera, and IE for the Macintosh behave according to the recommendation. But IE for Windows, even in IE 7's standards-compatible mode, ignores this convention. Instead, this browser family recomputes the inherited relative style assignment. Thus, in the example we just discussed, a p element with a font-size set to 10pt does not inherit the 40pt computed text-indent value from the body. Rather, the unstated text-indent value for the p element is recomputed for its 10pt font-size—an effective text-indent value of 20pt. (This type of inconsistency is indicative of occasional cross-browser difficulties with CSS in implementing pixel-perfect identical representations on all platforms.)

Pixel values, while frequently used for font sizes, present their own potential problems. A pixel, as noted earlier, varies in size with the pixel density of the output device. The higher the density, the smaller each pixel is. For printing output on 300- to 600-dpi printers, browsers perform internal scaling calculations to assign more dots per pixel so that a text character sent to the printer approximates the size as viewed on the screen. But don't expect absolutely perfect sizes on all monitors or printers. Allow for scaling approximations for all length value assignments.

Absolute length units are intended for output media with constant physical properties (such as a PostScript printer). Although there is nothing preventing you from using absolute or relative units interchangeably, you need to be aware of the consequences given your audience. Absolute length units in CSS are inches (in), centimeters (cm), millimeters (mm), picas (pi), and points (pt).

URI and URL (and IRI)

Universal Resource Identifier (URI) is a broad term for an address of content on the Web (while an Internationalized Resource Identifier—IRI—is an address that can include Unicode characters to accommodate non-ASCII characters). A Universal Resource Locator (URL) is a type of URI. For most web authoring, you can think of them as one and the same, because most web browsers restrict their focus to URLs. A URL may be complete (including the protocol, host, domain, and the rest) or may be relative to the URL of the current document, with one exception: if the style rule is imported from a *.css* file (perhaps from a different directory), a relative URL uses the path to the *.css* file as the base. The CSS property syntax prescribes a special format for specifying a URI property value, as follows:

```
propertyName: url("actualURL")
```

Quotes surrounding the *actualURL* are optional, but recommended.

Colors

A color value can be assigned either via an RGB (red-green-blue) value or a plain-language equivalent (see Appendix A). For style sheet RGB values, you have a choice of three formats: hexadecimal triplet, decimal values, or percentage values. A hexadecimal triplet consists of three pairs of hexadecimal (base 16) numbers that range between values of 00 and ff, corresponding to the red, green, and blue components of the color. The three pairs of numbers are bunched together and preceded by a pound sign (#). Therefore, the reddest of reds has all red (ff) and none (00) of the other two colors: #ff0000; pure blue is #0000ff. Letters a through f can also be uppercase letters. (An approved notational shortcut allows you to specify one hexadecimal character when the value is intended to be a matching pair of characters. For example, #f0a is interpreted as #ff00aa.)

The other types of RGB values require a prefix of rgb( ) with a comma-delimited list of red, green, and blue values in the parentheses. As decimal values, each color can range from 0 through 255, with zero meaning the complete absence of a particular color. You can also specify each value by a percentage. The following examples show four different ways of specifying pure green:

```
color: green
color: #00ff00
color: rgb(0, 255, 0)
color: rgb(0%, 100%, 0%)
```

If you exceed the maximum allowable values in the last two examples, the browser trims the values back to the maximums.

These numbering schemes obviously lead to a potentially huge number of combinations (over 16 million). In the early days of the web, typical PC display settings (throttled by limitations in processing power and memory) limited output to 256 colors, meaning that subtle differences among the 16 million potential colors were lost on visitors who had those settings. As a result, web content authors commonly used what became known as a *web-safe palette* consisting of 216 distinguishable colors. Although today's computers have sufficient processing power and memory to accommodate millions of colors with ease, some page designers continue to adhere to the more limited palette. A fine online reference of colors that work well on all browsers and PC color display settings can be found at *http://www.lynda.com/hex.asp*.

The CSS2 specification adds another dimension to color naming: you can specify colors that the user has assigned to specific user interface items in the operating system's control panel. Such colors are typically adjustable for items like button label text, scrollbars, 3D shadows, and so on. A color-blind user, for example, may have a carefully crafted set of colors that provide necessary contrast to see screen elements. Use these choices with caution, however, because even the default rendered color can vary widely between browser brands and operating systems. To link those colors to a style, use any of the following keywords in place of the color property value:

activeborder	activecaption	appworkspace
background	buttonface	buttonhighlight
buttontext	captiontext	graytext
highlight	highlighttext	inactiveborder
inactivecaption	inactivecaptiontext	infobackground
infotext	menu	menutext
scrollbar	threeddarkshadow	threedface
threedhighlight	threedlightshadow	threedshadow
window	windowframe	windowtext

Selectors

Most style sheet rules are associated with distinct HTML elements or groups of elements identified via style sheet selectors, such as classes, IDs, and contextual selectors (see Chapter 3). Table 4-1 lists these selectors as defined in W3C recommendations through CSS3, along with mainstream browser version support. In the Format column, *E* and *F* stand for element (i.e., tag) names of two different elements. As shown in Appendix F, the "m18" designation in the Mozilla column indicates an early milestone release number.

Table 4-1. Primary CSS selectors

Name	Format	IE	Mozilla	Safari	Opera	CSS
Adjacent sibling	E + F	7	m18	all	7	2
Attribute (name)	E[attr]	7	m18	all	7	2
Attribute (name and value)	E[attr="val"]	7	m18	all	7	2
Attribute (name and any value)	E[attr~="val"]	7	m18	all	7	2
Attribute (name and any value up to hyphen)	E[attr|="val"]	7	m18	all	7	2
Attribute (name and value start)	E[attr^="val"]	7	1.0.1	all	9	3
Attribute (name and value end)	E[attr$="val"]	7	1.0.1	all	9	3
Attribute (name and value contains)	E[attr*="val"]	7	1.0.1	all	9	3
Child	E > F	7	m18	all	7	2
Class	E.classname	4	m18	all	7	1
Descendant	E F	4	m18	all	7	1
General sibling	E ~ F	7	1.7.2	n/a	9	3
ID	E#id	4	m18	all	7	1
Type	E	4	m18	all	7	1
Universal	*	4	m18	all	7	2

Pseudo-Element and Pseudo-Class Selectors

In rare instances, you might want to assign a style to a well-defined component of an element (pseudo-element) or to all elements that exhibit a particular state (pseudo-class).

Pseudo-Elements

A pseudo-element gets its name because the CSS declaration of this type causes the browser to act as if it has inserted an artificial element into an existing element. For example, CSS defines pseudo-elements for the first letter and first line of a block-level element. The HTML source code for the real element might be something simple:

```
<p>A mere paragraph.</p>
```

But a browser that implements the :first-letter and :first-line pseudo-elements would treat the p element as if it were structured as follows:

```
<p><p:first-line><p:first-letter>A</p:first-letter> mere
paragraph.</p:first-line></p>
```

The location of the </p:first-line> end tag, of course, depends on the rendered version of the p element. If the paragraph were sized to fit a narrow column, and the first line word-wrapped after the word "mere," the :first-line pseudo-element's invisible end tag would follow the space after "mere." The point of all of this is that you can assign numerous style properties to these very specific portions of a block-level element, such as a drop capital letter:

```
p:first-letter {font-size: 36pt; font-weight: 600;
                font-family: Rune, serif; float: left}
```

or an all-uppercase first line:

```
p:first-line{text-transform: uppercase}
```

Regardless of the pseudo-element structure or style assignments, the document tree is unaffected. In the simple p element example, the element contains one text child node.

To help differentiate pseudo-elements from pseudo-classes in CSS markup, CSS3 introduces a new notation using a double colon, as in the following:

```
p::first-line{text-transform: uppercase}
```

Browsers that implement the new notation (all mainstream browsers except IE through version 7) also support the old notation to accommodate legacy code.

As of CSS2, four pseudo-elements have been defined, as shown in Table 4-2. Note that the :first-letter pseudo-element acknowledges style properties only of the following types: background, border, clear, color, float, font, letter-spacing, line-height, margin, padding, text-decoration, text-shadow, text-transform, vertical-align (when float is none), and word-spacing. The :first-line pseudo-element acknowledges style properties only of the following types: background, clear, color, font, letter-spacing, line-height, text-decoration, text-shadow, text-transform, vertical-align, and word-spacing. CSS3 introduces the optional ::selection pseudo-element, whose style properties are to be applied to a user selection (e.g., as a way to style selected text in a printer-friendly manner).

Table 4-2. CSS2 pseudo-elements

Name	IE/Windows	IE/Mac	Moz/Saf/Op	CSS	Description
:after	n/a	n/a	all	2	The space immediately after an element (see content property)
:before	n/a	n/a	all	2	The space immediately before an element (see content property)
:first-letter	5.5	5	all	1	The first letter of a block-level element
:first-line	5.5	5	all	1	The first line of a block-level element

Pseudo-Classes

The a element has readily distinguishable states: a link that has not been visited, a link being clicked on, a link that has been visited in recent history. These states are called *pseudo-classes*; they work like class selector definitions but don't have to be labeled as such in their element tags. A pseudo-class always operates as a kind of modifier to another selector. In the following example, notice how the :hover pseudo-class operates on all a elements in one rule, and applies an extra color property to an a element singled out by its ID:

```
a {text-decoration: none}
a:hover {text-decoration: underline}
#specialA:hover {color: red}
```

The classness of a pseudo-class is not always based on an element's state. Document tree context, page position (right or left), and even language are examples of the possibilities that pseudo-classes afford. For example, the :first-child pseudo-class turns its associated element into a special class (i.e., a class capable of defining its own style propertys) whenever the element is a first child element in a document tree. Thus, the following style rule applies a different font size for every p element that is the first child of any container with the class name section:

```
.section > p:first-child {font-size: 110%}
```

The use here of the > child selector limits the scope of the p:first-child pseudo-class to first children of specific containers. Removing the child selector would cause the rule to apply to any p element that is the first child of any other container.

Table 4-3 provides a summary of pseudo-classes supported by CSS2. Implementation in mainstream browsers is sporadic.

Table 4-3. CSS2 Pseudo-classes

Name	IE/Windows	IE/Mac	Moz/Saf/Op	CSS	Description
:active	4	4	all	1	An a element being clicked on by the user
:first	n/a	n/a	n/a	2	First page of a document (with @page declaration)
:first-child	n/a	5	all	2	Any element that is the first child of another element
:focus	n/a	5	all	2	Any element that has focus
:hover	4	4	all	2	An element that has a cursor on top of it (only a elements in IE 4-6 and in IE 7 quirks mode)
:lang(code)	n/a	5	n/a	2	An element with the same language code
:left	n/a	n/a	n/a	2	A left-facing page (with @page declaration)
:link	4	4	all	1	An a element that has not yet been visited
:right	n/a	n/a	n/a	2	A right-facing page (with @page declaration)
:visited	4	4	all	1	An a element that has been visited within the browser's history

CSS3 introduces a large collection of new pseudo-classes, some of which are already implemented in the latest mainstream browsers. The largest group of new selectors allow you to assign style properties to elements that meet very specific contextual criteria, such as every other row of a table, without burdening the HTML markup with lots of class attributes. Some selectors allow style sheets to complement or replace the browser's default rendering for states, such as a disabled element or a "checked" button. Table 4-4 lists CSS3 selectors as of the latest W3C Working Draft available before going to press.

Table 4-4. CSS3 Pseudo-classes

Name	IE	Mozilla	Safari	Opera	CSS	Description
`:checked`	n/a	n/a	n/a	9	3	A radio or checkbox button is checked
`:disabled`	n/a	n/a	n/a	9	3	A focusable element is disabled
`:empty`	n/a	1.0.1	all	n/a	3	An element containing no child nodes
`:enabled`	n/a	n/a	n/a	9	3	A focusable element is enabled
`:first-of-type`	n/a	n/a	n/a	n/a	3	Any element that matches the tag name and is the first child of a parent element
`:invalid`	n/a	n/a	n/a	9	n/a	A Web Forms 2.0 control element whose value is invalid
`:last-child`	n/a	1.0.1	n/a	n/a	3	Any element that is the last child of a parent element
`:last-of-type`	n/a	n/a	n/a	n/a	3	Any element that matches the tag name and is the last child of a parent element
`:not(`*selector*`)`	n/a	n/a	n/a	n/a	3	Elements not matching *selector*
`:nth-child(`*an+b*`)`	n/a	n/a	n/a	n/a	3	Every *b*th child element in groups of *a*
`:nth-last-child(`*an+b*`)`	n/a	n/a	n/a	n/a	3	Every *b*th child element counting backwards from the last sibling, in groups of *a*
`:nth-last-of-type(`*an+b*`)`	n/a	n/a	n/a	n/a	3	Every *b*th child element with the same tag name counting backwards from the last sibling, in groups of *a*

Table 4-4. CSS3 Pseudo-classes (continued)

Name	IE	Mozilla	Safari	Opera	CSS	Description
`:nth-of-type(`*an+b*`)`	n/a	n/a	n/a	n/a	3	Every *b*th child element with the same tag name in groups of *a*
`:only-child`	n/a	n/a	n/a	n/a	3	An element that has no siblings
`:only-of-type`	n/a	n/a	n/a	n/a	3	An element that has no siblings with the same tag name
`:root`	n/a	n/a	n/a	n/a	3	The HTML element
`:target`	n/a	n/a	n/a	n/a	3	An element contained by an anchor

At-Rules

CSS2 defines an extensible structure for declarations or directives (commands, if you will) that are part of style sheet definitions. They are called *at-rules* because the rule starts with the "at" symbol (@) followed by an identifier for the declaration. Each at-rule may then include one or more descriptors that define the characteristics of the rule.

Although at-rules typically appear as the first declarations in a style sheet, in practice some (@media in particular) work best when only one occupies each style sheet. The following sequence provides different style characteristics for a document when viewed on screen and printed on paper (relative font size on the screen, absolute on paper):

```
<style type="text/css">
@media screen {
    body {font-size: 14px}
}
</style>
<style type="text/css">
@media print {
    body {font-size: 12pt}
}
</style>
```

The @font-face rule can be used to download font definition files to the IE browser, and associate each font definition with a font family name to be assigned by succeeding style assignments. Here is an example that downloads one of the Internet Explorer accepted font file formats, assigning the definition to a font family name called Stylish:

```
<style type="text/css">
@font-face {
    font-family: Stylish;
    font-weight: normal;
```

```
        font-style: normal;
        src: url(fonts/stylish.eot);
    }
</style>
```

IE allows you to define multiple @font-face rules in the same style sheet. Visit *http://msdn.microsoft.com/workshop/author/fontembed/font_embed.asp* for details on how to create font definition files that work with IE for Windows and Macintosh.

Already supported by a few mainstream browsers, CSS3 namespaces are initially declared via the @namepace rule. Any subsequent selectors that wish to reference an element name defined in the namespace must cite the namespace name, followed by a pipe character (|), and then the element name. For example, the following rules would apply the blue color only to td elements defined in the products namespace:

```
@namespace products url(http://www.example.com/DTD/productDB);
products|td {color: blue}
```

Table 4-5 provides a summary of the at-rules supported by CSS and mainstream browsers.

Table 4-5. CSS at-rules

Name	IE/Windows	Mozilla	Safari	Opera	CSS	Description
@namespace	n/a	1.0.1	1.3/2	9	2	Character set used for external style sheet file.
@charset	5	m18	n/a	7	2	Character set used for external style sheet file.
@font-face	4	n/a	n/a	n/a	n/a	Font description to assist in font-matching between an embedded font and the client system font (or downloaded font).
@import	4	m18	all	7	1	Imports an external style sheet. See Chapter 3 for the impact on the cascade.
@media	5	m18	all	7	2	Defines an output media type for one or more style sheet rules. Rules assigned to the same selectors but inside different @media rules (e.g., @media print or @media screen) adhere to media-specific rules when the document is rendered in the specified medium.
@page	n/a	n/a	n/a	7	2	Defines the page box's size, margins, orientation, crop marks, and other page-related properties governing the printing of the document.

Conventions

The CSS syntax descriptions shown throughout this chapter adhere to the following guidelines:

- Words in the `Constant Width` font are keywords or constant values to be used as-is.
- Words in the `Constant Width Italic` font are placeholders for values.
- A value contained by square brackets ([ ]) is optional.
- A series of two or more values separated by a pipe symbol (|) represent items in a list of acceptable values to be used in the position shown.
- A few listings show numbers in brackets ({1,2}) after a value. The numbers indicate the minimum and maximum numbers of space-delimited values you can specify.
- A double-pipe symbol (||) separating multiple values indicates that one or more of the values must be present, but the order is not significant.

The "Applies To" category advises which HTML elements can be influenced by the style property. Some style properties can be applied only to block-level, inline, or replaced elements. A block-level element is one that always starts on a new line and forces a new line after the end of the element (h1 and p elements, for example). An inline element is one that you can place in the middle of a text line without disturbing the content flow (em elements, for example). A replaced element is a block-level or inline element that has content that may be changed dynamically without requiring any reflow of surrounding content. The img element falls into this category because you can swap image source files within an img element's rectangular space.

A listing category called "Initial Value" serves the same purpose as the "Default" category in other reference chapters. The terminology used in this chapter conforms with the terminology of the CSS specification.

Many items contain a category called "Object Model Reference" to show the way scripts can reference the property as properties in a browser's document object model—specifically, as properties of the style object. Consult Chapter 2 for compatibility ratings for the scripted equivalents of style properties, as they frequently differ from the style sheet property implementations shown in this chapter.

Alphabetical Property Reference

azimuth

Inherited: Yes

Given a listener at the center of a circular sound space (like in a surround-sound-equipped theater), azimuth sets the horizontal angle of the source of the sound (for example, in a text-to-speech browser). See also the elevation property.

CSS Syntax

azimuth: *angle* | *angleConstant* || *direction*

Value

Up to two values (other than inherit). One represents the angle, clockwise from straight ahead; the second is a 20-degree incremental movement to the left or right. An *angle* value is any value in the range of −360 to +360 (inclusive) plus the letters "deg", as in 90deg. The value 0deg is directly in front of the listener. To set the angle to the left of the listener, the value can be either -90deg or 270deg. Optionally, you can choose an *angleConstant* value from a large library of descriptions that correspond to fixed points around the circle. If you add the behind modifier, the values shift from in front of the listener to behind the listener.

Value	Equals	Value	Equals
center	0deg	center behind	180deg
center-right	20deg	center-right behind	160deg
right	40deg	right behind	140deg
far-right	60deg	far-right behind	120deg
right-side	90deg	right-side behind	90deg
left-side	270deg	left-side behind	270deg
far-left	300deg	far-left behind	240deg
left	320deg	left behind	220deg
center-left	340deg	center-left behind	200deg

For the *direction* value, you can choose from two constants: leftwards | rightwards. These settings shift the sound 20 degrees in the named direction.

Initial Value   center

Example

h1 {azimuth: 45deg}
p.aside {azimuth: center-right behind}

Applies To   All elements.

background

IE 4 NN n/a Moz all Saf all Op all CSS 1

Inherited: No

This is a shortcut property that lets you set up to five separate (but related) background-style properties in one property statement. Values can be in any order, each one delimited by a space. Although the property is not officially available in Navigator 4, some combinations of values may work with it.

CSS Syntax

background: *background-attachment* || *background-color* || *background-image* || *background-position* || *background-repeat*

Value

Any combination of the five background-style property values, in any order. Any property not specified is assigned its initial value. See each property for details about the expected values.

Initial Value	None.
Example	body {background: url(watermark.jpg) repeat fixed}
Applies To	All elements.

Object Model Reference

[window.]document.getElementById("*elementID*").style.background

background-attachment

IE 4 NN n/a Moz all Saf 1.2 Op all CSS 1

Inherited: No

When an image is applied to the element background (with the background-image property), the background-attachment property sets whether the image scrolls with the document. The image can remain fixed within the viewable area of the element (the viewport), or it may scroll with the element as content scrolls. During scrolling, a fixed attachment looks like a stationary backdrop to rolling credits of a movie.

CSS Syntax

background-attachment: fixed | scroll

Value

The fixed value keeps the image stationary in the element viewport; the scroll value lets the image scroll with the document content.

Initial Value	scroll
Example	body {background-attachment: fixed}
Applies To	All elements.

Object Model Reference

[window.]document.getElementById("*elementID*").style.backgroundAttachment

background-color

IE *4* NN *4* Moz *all* Saf *all* Op *all* CSS *1*

Inherited: No

Sets the background color for the element. Although it may appear as though a nested element's background-color property is inherited, in truth the initial value is transparent, which lets the next-outermost colored element show through whitespace of the current element.

CSS Syntax

background-color: *color* | transparent

Value

Any valid color specification (see description at beginning of the chapter) or transparent.

Initial Value	transparent
Example	.highlighter {background-color: yellow}
Applies To	All elements.

Object Model Reference

[window.]document.getElementById("*elementID*").style.backgroundColor

background-image

IE *4* NN *4* Moz *all* Saf *all* Op *all* CSS *1*

Inherited: No

Sets the background image (if any) for the element. If you set a background-color for the element as well, the color appears if the image fails to load; otherwise, the image overlays the color. Transparent pixels of the image allow a background color to show through. See also the background-attachment property.

CSS Syntax

background-image: *uri* | none

Value

To specify a URL, use the url( ) wrapper for the property value. You can omit the property or specify none to prevent an image from loading into the element's background.

Initial Value	none
Example	h1 {background-image: url(watermark.jpg)}
Applies To	All elements.

Object Model Reference

[window.]document.getElementById("*elementID*").style.backgroundImage

background-position

IE 4 *NN n/a* *Moz all* *Saf all* *Op all* *CSS 1*

Inherited: No

Establishes the location of the left and top edges of the background image specified with the background-image property.

CSS Syntax

background-position: [*percentage* | *length*] {1,2} |
  [top | center | bottom] || [left | center | right]

Value

You can specify one or two percentages, which are the percentages of the block-level element's box width and height (respectively) at which the image (or repeated images) begins. If you supply only one percentage value, it applies to the horizontal measure, and the vertical measure is automatically set to 50%. Instead of percentages, you can specify length values (in the unit of measure that best suits the medium). You can also mix a percentage with a length. In lieu of the numerical values, you can create combinations of values with the two sets of constant values. Select one from each collection, as in top left, top right, or bottom center. Whenever you specify two values, they must be separated by a space.

Initial Value   0% 0%

Example

div.marked {background-image: url(watermark.jpg);
   background-position: center top}

Applies To   Block-level and replaced elements.

Object Model Reference

[window.]document.getElementById("*elementID*").style.backgroundPosition

background-position-x,
background-position-y

IE 4 *NN n/a* *Moz n/a* *Saf 1.3/2* *Op n/a* *CSS n/a*

Inherited: No

Establish the location of the left (x) or top (y) edges of the background image specified with the background-image property.

CSS Syntax

background-position-x: [*percentage* | *length*] | [left | center | right]
background-position-y: [*percentage* | *length*] | [top | center | bottom]

Value

You can specify the percentage of the block-level element's box width or height (respectively) at which the image (or repeated images) begins. Instead of percentages, you can specify length values (in the unit of measure that best suits the medium). In lieu of the numerical values, you may use one axis-specific constant value per property.

Initial Value   0%

Example
```
div.marked {background-image: url(watermark.jpg);
    background-position-x: center}
```

Applies To   Block-level and replaced elements.

Object Model Reference
```
[window.]document.getElementById("elementID").style.backgroundPositionX
[window.]document.getElementById("elementID").style.backgroundPositionY
```

background-repeat

IE *4*   NN *n/a*   Moz *all*   Saf *all*   Op *all*   CSS *1*

Inherited: No

Sets whether a background image (specified with the background-image property) should repeat and, if so, along which axis. You can use repeating background images to create horizontal and vertical bands.

CSS Syntax
```
background-repeat: no-repeat | repeat | repeat-x | repeat-y
```

Value
With a setting of no-repeat, one instance of the image appears in the location within the element established by the background-position property (default is the top-left corner). Normal repeats are performed along both axes, but you can have the image repeat down a single column (repeat-y) or across a single row (repeat-x).

Initial Value   repeat

Example
```
body {background-image: url(icon.gif); background-repeat: repeat-y}
```

Applies To   All elements.

Object Model Reference
```
[window.]document.getElementById("elementID").style.backgroundRepeat
```

behavior

IE *5(Win)*   NN *n/a*   Moz *n/a*   Saf *n/a*   Op *n/a*   CSS *n/a*

Inherited: No

Associates an external behavior definition to the element.

CSS Syntax
```
behavior: uri[, uri[, ...]]
```

Value

CSS-formatted URL value, with the actual URL pointing to an external *.htc* file, ID of an object element that loads a behavior ActiveX control into the page, or one of the built-in default behaviors (in the format url(#default#*behaviorName*)). Default behavior names are:

anchorClick	anim	clientCaps	download
homePage	httpFolder	mediaBar	saveFavorite
saveHistory	saveSnapshot	userData	

For details on what these default behaviors do and under what security conditions you can use them, visit *http://msdn.microsoft.com/workshop/author/behaviors/reference/reference.asp*.

Initial Value   None.

Example   input.numOnly {behavior: url(numInput.htc)}

Applies To   All elements.

Object Model Reference

```
[window.]document.getElementById("elementID").style.behavior
[window.]document.getElementById("elementID").behaviorUrns[i]
```

border

IE 4 NN *n/a* Moz *all* Saf *all* Op *all* CSS 1

Inherited: No

This is a shorthand property for setting the width, style, and/or color of all four borders around an element in one assignment statement. Whichever properties you don't explicitly set with this property assume their initial values. Numerous other properties allow you to set the width, style, and color of individual edges or groups of edges, if you don't want all four edges to be the same.

Due to differences in the way browsers define their default behavior with regard to borders, every style sheet border rule should include the width and style settings. Failure to specify both properties may result in the border not being seen in one browser or the other.

CSS Syntax

```
border: border-width || border-style || color | transparent
```

Value

For the *border-width* and *border-style* property values, see the respective properties in this chapter. For details on the *color* value, see the section about colors at the beginning of this chapter.

Initial Value   None.

Example   p {border: 3px groove darkred}

Applies To

All elements, but only block and replaced elements in IE 4 and 5 for Windows.

Object Model Reference

[window.]document.getElementById("*elementID*").style.border

border-bottom, border-left, border-right, border-top

IE 4 NN *n/a* Moz *all* Saf *all* Op *all* CSS 1

Inherited: No

All four properties are shorthand properties for setting the width, style, and/or color of a single border edge of an element in one assignment statement. Whichever properties you don't explicitly set with this property assume their initial values.

CSS Syntax

```
border-bottom: border-bottom-width || border-bottom-style || color | transparent
border-left: border-left-width || border-left-style || color | transparent
border-right: border-right-width || border-right-style || color | transparent
border-top: border-top-width || border-top-style || color | transparent
```

Value

For the width and style property values, see the border-bottom-width and border-bottom-style properties in this chapter. For details on the *color* value, see the section about colors at the beginning of this chapter.

Initial Value None.

Example

```
p {border-bottom: 3px solid lightgreen}
p {border-left: 6px solid lightgreen}
p {border-right: 3px solid lightgreen}
p {border-top: 6px solid lightgreen}
```

Applies To

All elements, but only block and replaced elements in IE 4 and 5 for Windows.

Object Model Reference

[window.]document.getElementById("*elementID*").style.borderBottom
[window.]document.getElementById("*elementID*").style.borderLeft
[window.]document.getElementById("*elementID*").style.borderRight
[window.]document.getElementById("*elementID*").style.borderTop

border-bottom-color, border-left-color, border-right-color, border-top-color

IE 4 NN *n/a* Moz *all* Saf *all* Op *all* CSS 2

Inherited: No

Each property sets the color of a single border edge of an element. This power is easy to abuse by mixing colors that don't belong together. See also the border-color property for setting the color of multiple edges in one statement.

CSS Syntax

```
border-bottom-color: color | transparent
border-left-color: color | transparent
border-right-color: color | transparent
border-top-color: color | transparent
```

Value

For details on the *color* value, see the section about colors at the beginning of this chapter. Also transparent.

Initial Value   None.

Example

```
p {border-bottom-color: gray}
div {border-left-color: #33c088}
p.special {border-right-color: rgb(150, 75, 0)}
h3 {border-top-color: rgb(100%, 50%, 21%)}
```

Applies To

All elements, but only block and replaced elements in IE 4 and 5 for Windows.

Object Model Reference

```
[window.]document.getElementById("elementID").style.borderBottomColor
[window.]document.getElementById("elementID").style.borderLeftColor
[window.]document.getElementById("elementID").style.borderRightColor
[window.]document.getElementById("elementID").style.borderTopColor
```

border-bottom-style, border-left-style, border-right-style, border-top-style

IE 4   NN *n/a*   Moz *all*   Saf *all*   Op *all*   CSS 2

Inherited: No

Each property sets the line style of a single border edge of an element. The edge-specific properties let you override a style that has been applied to all four edges with the border or border-style properties, but the edge-specific setting must come after the other one (in source code order) in the style sheet rule. See also the border-style property for setting the style of multiple edges in one statement.

CSS Syntax

```
border-bottom-style: style
border-left-style: style
border-right-style: style
border-top-style: style
```

Value

Style values are constants that are associated with specific ways of rendering border lines. Not all browser versions recognize all of the values in the CSS recommendation. Style support is shown in the following table.

Value	IE/Windows	NN	Others	CSS
dashed	5.5	6	all	1
dotted	5.5	6	all	1
double	4	4	all	1
groove	4	4	all	1
hidden	n/a	6	all	2
inset	4	4	all	1
none	4	4	all	1
outset	4	4	all	1
ridge	4	4	all	1
solid	4	4	all	1

The manner in which browsers interpret the definitions of the style values is not universal. Figure 4-1 shows a gallery of all styles as rendered by Internet Explorer, Firefox, Safari, and Opera 9. Don't expect the same look in all browsers.

Initial Value   none

Example

```
p {border-style: solid; border-bottom-style: none}
div {border-left-style: ridge}
```

Applies To   All elements.

Object Model Reference

```
[window.]document.getElementById("elementID").style.borderBottomStyle
[window.]document.getElementById("elementID").style.borderLeftStyle
[window.]document.getElementById("elementID").style.borderRightStyle
[window.]document.getElementById("elementID").style.borderTopStyle
```

border-bottom-width, border-left-width, border-right-width, border-top-width

IE 4   NN 4   Moz *all*   Saf *all*   Op *all*   CSS 1

Inherited: No

Each property sets the width of a single border edge of an element. See also the border-width property for setting the width of multiple edges in one statement.

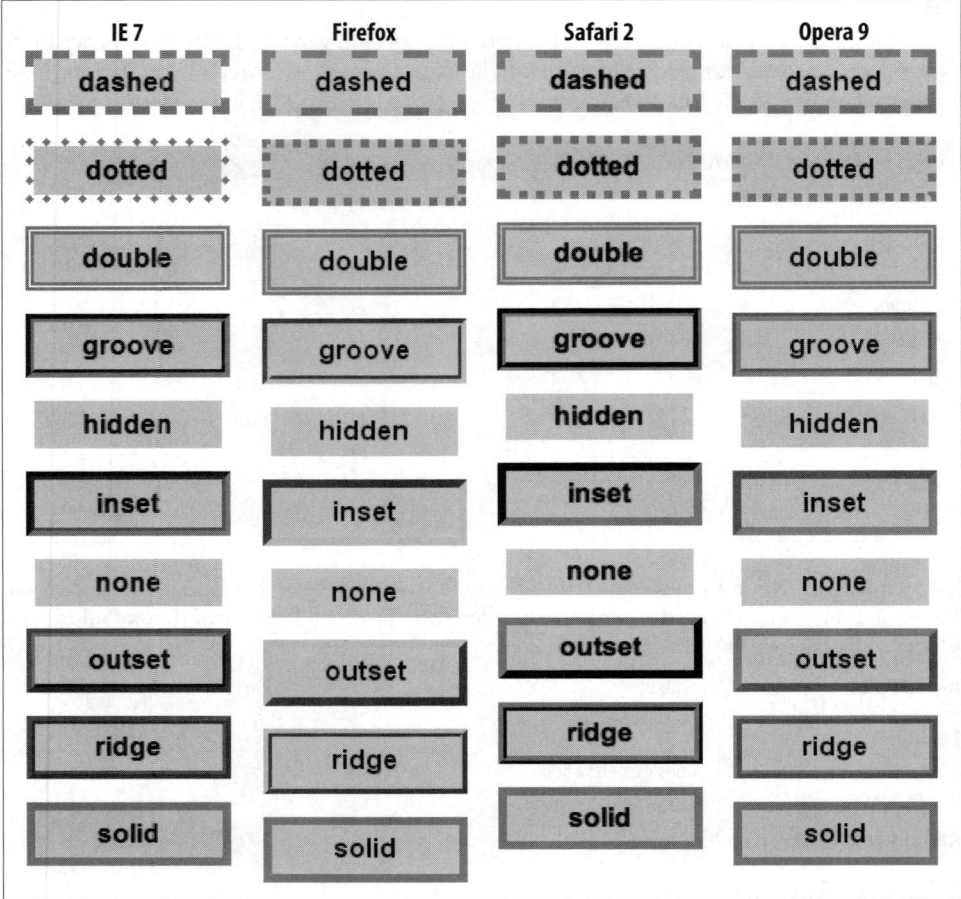

Figure 4-1. Border-style gallery

CSS Syntax

```
border-bottom-width: thin | medium | thick | length
border-left-width: thin | medium | thick | length
border-right-width: thin | medium | thick | length
border-top-width: thin | medium | thick | length
```

Value

Three constants—thin | medium | thick—allow the browser to define how many pixels are used to show the border. For more precision, you can also assign a length value (see the discussion of length values at the beginning of this chapter).

Initial Value   medium

Example

```
h2 {border-bottom-width: 2px}
```

```
div {border-left-width: thin}
p.special {border-right-width: 0.5em}
```

Applies To

All elements, but only block and replaced elements in IE 4 and 5 for Windows.

Object Model Reference

```
[window.]document.getElementById("elementID").style.borderBottomWidth
[window.]document.getElementById("elementID").style.borderLeftWidth
[window.]document.getElementById("elementID").style.borderRightWidth
[window.]document.getElementById("elementID").style.borderTopWidth
```

border-collapse
IE *5(Win)* NN *n/a* Moz *all* Saf *all* Op *all* CSS *2*

Inherited: Yes

Sets whether borders of adjacent table elements (cells, row groups, column groups) are rendered separately or collapsed (merged) to ignore any padding or margins between adjacent borders. A table set to the separate border model may also have its border-spacing and empty-cells style properties set (if supported by the target browsers).

CSS Syntax

```
border-collapse: collapse | separate
```

Value	Constant values: collapse | separate.
Initial Value	separate
Applies To	The table element.

border-color
IE *4* NN *4* Moz *all* Saf *all* Op *all* CSS *1*

Inherited: No

This is a shortcut property that lets you set multiple border edges to the same or different colors. Navigator 4 allows only a single value, which applies to all four edges. For other supporting browsers, you may supply one to four space-delimited color values. The number of values determines which sides receive the assigned colors.

CSS Syntax

```
border-color: color {1,4}
```

Value

For modern browsers, this property accepts one, two, three, or four *color* values, depending on how many and which borders you want to set with specific colors. Value quantities and positions are interpreted as shown in the following table.

Number of values	Effect
1	All four borders set to value
2	Top and bottom borders set to the first value, right and left borders set to the second value
3	Top border set to first value, right and left borders set to second value, bottom border set to third value
4	Top, right, bottom, and left borders set, respectively

Initial Value

The element's color style property (which is inherited if not specifically assigned for the element).

Example

```
h2 {border-color: red blue red}
div {border-color: red rgb(0,0,255) red}
```

Applies To

All elements, but only block and replaced elements in IE 4 and 5 for Windows.

Object Model Reference

`[window.]document.getElementById("elementID").style.borderColor`

border-spacing

IE *n/a* NN *n/a* Moz *all* Saf *all* Op *all* CSS *2*

Inherited: No

Determines the size of the space (if any) between all cell borders in a table. This property requires that the border-collapse property be set to separate (which is typically the default value). If you include only one length value, it applies to both the horizontal and vertical cell spacing; for two values, the first applies to the horizontal and the second to the vertical. See Figure 4-2 for a synopsis of a table's numerous dimension definitions.

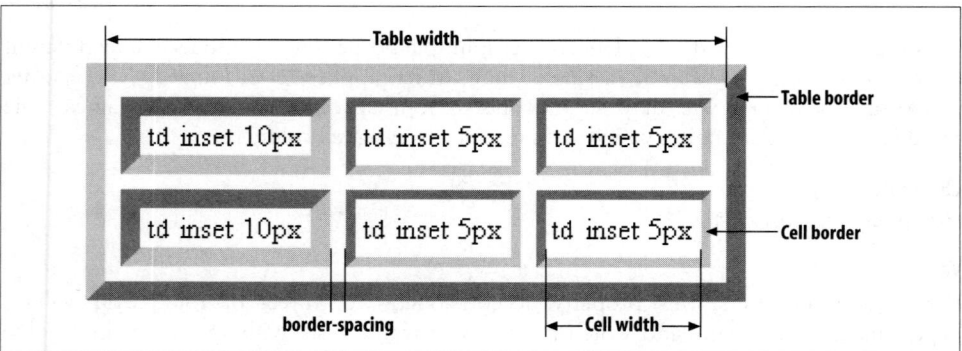

Figure 4-2. The geometry of a table element

CSS Syntax

`border-spacing: length[length]`

Value

See the discussion of length values at the beginning of this chapter. If you want no spacing along one axis, set its value to zero.

Initial Value   0

Applies To   The table element.

border-style

IE 4   NN 4   Moz *all*   Saf *all*   Op *all*   CSS 1

Inherited: No

This is a shortcut property that lets you set multiple border edges to the same or different style. For mainstream browsers, you may supply one to four space-delimited border style values. The number of values determines which sides receive the assigned style.

CSS Syntax

border-style: *borderStyle* {1,4}

Value

Style values are constants that are associated with specific ways of rendering border lines. See border-bottom-style for a list of available values.

The precise manner in which browsers interpret the definitions of the style values is far from universal. Figure 4-1 shows a gallery of all styles as rendered by Internet Explorer 7, Firefox, Safari, and Opera 9. Do not expect the exact same look in all browsers.

This property accepts one, two, three, or four space-delimited *borderStyle* values, depending on how many and which borders you want to set with specific styles. Value quantities and positions are interpreted as shown in the following table.

Number of values	Effect
1	All four borders set to value
2	Top and bottom borders set to the first value, right and left borders set to the second value
3	Top border set to first value, right and left borders set to second value, bottom border set to third value
4	Top, right, bottom, and left borders set, respectively

Initial Value   none

Example

```
h1 {border-style: ridge; border-width: 3px}
div {border-style: solid double; border-width: 4px}
```

Applies To

All elements, but only block and replaced elements in IE 4 and 5 for Windows.

Object Model Reference

[window.]document.getElementById("*elementID*").style.borderStyle

border-width

IE 4   NN 4   Moz *all*   Saf *all*   Op *all*   CSS 1

Inherited: No

This is a shortcut property that lets you set multiple border edges to the same or different widths. You may supply one to four space-delimited width length values. The number of values determines which sides receive the assigned widths.

CSS Syntax

border-width: thin | medium | thick | *length* {1,4}

Value

Three constants—thin | medium | thick—allow the browser to define how many pixels are used to show the border. For more precision, you can also assign a length value (see the discussion of length values at the beginning of this chapter).

This property accepts one, two, three, or four space-delimited *borderWidth* values, depending on how many and which borders you want to set with specific styles. Value quantities and positions are interpreted as follows.

Number of values	Effect
1	All four borders set to value
2	Top and bottom borders set to the first value, right and left borders set to the second value
3	Top border set to first value, right and left borders set to second value, bottom border set to third value
4	Top, right, bottom, and left borders set, respectively

Initial Value   medium

Example

h1 {border-style: ridge; border-width: 3px 5px 3px}
div {border-style: solid double; border-width: 4px}

Applies To

All elements, but only block and replaced elements in IE 4 and 5 for Windows.

Object Model Reference

[window.]document.getElementById("*elementID*").style.borderWidth

bottom

IE 5   NN *n/a*   Moz *all*   Saf *all*   Op *all*   CSS 2

Inherited: No

The CSS specification calls for this property to define the position of the bottom edge of a positioned element's margin edge relative to the bottom edge of the next outermost block content container; in the case of positioned elements using the root document as the positioning context, dimensions of the containing block are determined by the browser window of an unscrolled document. In other words, for a top-level positioned element, instead of using the bottom of the document as the comparative edge, these browsers use the bottom of the browser window space (the viewport in CSS terminology). As a result, the precise bottom position of the element varies with the user's browser window size.

When the element is relative-positioned, the offset is based on the bottom edge of the inline location of where the element would normally appear in the content.

CSS Syntax

bottom: *length* | *percentage* | auto

Value

See the discussion about length values at the beginning of this chapter. Negative lengths may be allowed in some contexts, but be sure to test the results on all browsers. You may also specify a percentage value, which is calculated based on the height of the next outermost container. The setting of auto lets the browser determine the bottom offset of the element box on its naturally flowing offset within the containing box.

Initial Value   auto

Applies To   All positioned elements.

Object Model Reference

[window.]document.getElementById("*elementID*").style.bottom

caption-side   IE 5(Mac) NN n/a Moz all Saf all Op all CSS 2

Inherited: Yes

Positions the caption element above or below the tabular content of the enclosing table element. This property supplants some deprecated align property settings of the caption element.

CSS Syntax

caption-side: top | bottom | left | right

Value

One of the four constant values: top | bottom | left | right. The values left and right were removed from CSS2.1.

Initial Value   top

Applies To   caption elements.

Object Model Reference

[window.]document.getElementById("*elementID*").style.captionSide

clear   IE 4 NN 4 Moz all Saf all Op all CSS 1

Inherited: No

Defines whether a block-level element allows itself to be displayed in the same horizontal band as a nearby floating element, such as an image. Typically, another element in the vicinity has its float style property set to left or right. To prevent the current element from being in the same band as the floating block, set the clear property to the same side (left or right). If you aren't sure where the potential overlap might occur, set the clear property to both. An element with a clear property that is set to a value other than none is rendered at the beginning of the next available line below the floating element.

CSS Syntax

clear: both | left | none | right

Value   Any of the following constants: both | left | none | right.

Initial Value   none

Example

```
<img src="logo.gif" height="40" width="60" style="float: right">
<h1 style="clear: right">Giantco Corporation</h1>
```

Applies To   Block-level elements.

Object Model Reference

[window.]document.getElementById("*elementID*").style.clear

clip

IE 4 NN 4 Moz *all* Saf *all* Op *all* CSS 2

Inherited: No

Defines a clipping region of a positionable element. The clipping region is the area of the element layer in which content is visible. If you encounter problems clipping an element, wrap the content-holding element inside a block-level element whose clip property is set to the desired region.

CSS Syntax

clip: rect(*lengthTop lengthRight lengthBottom lengthLeft*) | auto

Value

Extending to CSS2.1, the only shape recognized for the clip property is rect. Other shapes may be admitted in the future.

When specifying lengths for each side of the clipping rectangle, observe the clockwise order of values: top, right, bottom, left. See the discussion about length values at the beginning of this chapter. A value of auto sets the clipping region to the block that contains the content.

Initial Value   auto

Example

```
<span style="position: absolute; clip: rect(10px 110px 80px 10px)">
<img src="desk1.gif" height="90" width="120">
</span>
```

Applies To   Block-level, replaced, and positioned elements.

Object Model Reference

[window.]document.getElementById("*elementID*").style.clip

color

IE 4   NN 4   Moz all   Saf all   Op all   CSS 1

Inherited: Yes

Defines the foreground text color of the element. For some graphically oriented elements, such as form controls, the color property may also be applied to element edges, checkmarks, or other features. Such extracurricular behavior is browser-specific and may not be the same across browsers.

CSS Syntax
color: *color*

Value
See the discussion of color property values at the beginning of this chapter.

Initial Value   black

Example   th {color: darkred}

Applies To   All elements.

Object Model Reference
[window.]document.getElementById("*elementID*").style.color

content

IE *n/a*   NN *n/a*   Moz all   Saf all   Op all   CSS 2

Inherited: No

Defines the actual content or source of content to be displayed before and/or after the current element. In CSS jargon, this kind of content is called *generated content*. This property may be set only with the :before and :after pseudo-elements associated with a real element. For example, as a result of the following style sheet rule:

blockquote:after {content:"(Reprinted by permission.)"}

a permissions phrase is appended to the end of every blockquote element, although the content does not become a member of the document tree. HTML tags in the content text are not interpreted, but if the situation warrants it, an external document can be assigned to the content property.

CSS Syntax
content: *string* | *uri* | *counter* | attr(*attrName*) | open-quote | close-quote | no-open-quote | no-close-quote | none | normal

Value
The purpose of the "no" quote types is to let you specify the effect of a quote (as far as quote nesting goes) without displaying a quote symbol. Multiple space-delimited strings may follow the content: property name.

Another value (*counter*) is not yet supported by all browsers (see counter-increment), but its potential is significant for documents that would benefit from client-side section number generation. A CSS counter offers a way for a style sheet to control numbering schemes for sequences of elements (such as sections, illustrations, and the like). The assumption is that the numbering is not part of the actual content, but is determined solely by the rendered context of the element within the document. Therefore, if you remove a numbered paragraph from a document in the edit phase, the paragraph numbering of the document adjusts itself automatically when the page is rendered.

The basic operation of a counter entails assigning an identifier to it (thus allowing multiple counters to exist in the same document, such as one for sections, another for subsections). Other CSS properties (counter-increment and counter-reset) require values that point to an identified counter to control the numbering sequence. The following style sheet rule inserts a section label and number in front of every h1 element, and increments the counter number each time the style is applied to an h1 element while the document renders:

```
h1:before {counter-increment: secNum;
          content: "Section " counter(secNum) ". "}
```

When counters are implemented in mainstream browsers, they will provide substantial power to highly structured, long documents.

Initial Value	"" (empty string)
Example	p.note:before {content: "==>"}
Applies To	All elements plus a :before and/or :after pseudo-element.

counter-increment, counter-reset

IE *n/a* NN *n/a* Moz *1.8* Saf *n/a* Op *7* CSS *2*

Inherited: No

These properties control the numbering sequence of a CSS counter used for generated content (see the content property). The counter-increment property sets the amount (and direction) of change each time the counter is accessed during rendering. The counter-reset property lets you set the counter to a specific number (default of zero).

CSS Syntax

```
counter-increment: counterID [ posOrNegInteger ] | none
counter-reset: counterID [ posOrNegInteger ] | none
```

Value

A *counterID* is an identifier assigned to a content: counter(*counterID*) style property. The optional integer value is space-delimited after the *counterID*. You can combine multiple counter IDs in the same style property by stringing together space-delimited pairs of ID and integer values.

Initial Value	none
Example	h1 {counter-reset: subSection}
Applies To	All elements.

cue

Inherited: No

For aural style sheets only, this property provides a shorthand for setting cue-before and cue-after property settings. A cue is a sound (also known as an auditory icon) that can be used to aurally delimit the reading of document content. Cue properties are URIs to sound resources.

CSS Syntax

```
cue: cue-before || cue-after
```

Value

If there are two values, the first is applied to the cue-before property and the second to the cue-after property. If there is only one value, the same auditory icon is applied to both cue-before and cue-after.

Initial Value   none

Applies To   All elements.

cue-after, cue-before

Inherited: No

For aural style sheets only, a cue is a sound (also known as an auditory icon) that can be used to aurally delimit the reading of document content. The cue-before and cue-after properties are URIs to sound files that are to be played before and after the content is rendered via text-to-speech or another aural medium.

CSS Syntax

```
cue-after: uri | none
cue-before: uri | none
```

Value

Any valid complete or relative URL (in CSS format) to a sound file in a MIME type supported by the browser. You may apply the same values to both properties for the same style selector if it makes aural sense for the listener.

Initial Value   none

Example   li {cue-before: url(ding.wav); cue-after: url(dong.wav)}

Applies To   All elements.

cursor

Inherited: Yes

Sets the shape of the cursor when the screen pointer is atop the element. The precise look of cursors depends on the operating system. Before deploying a modified cursor, be sure you understand the standard ways that the various types of cursors are used within the browser and operating system. Users expect a cursor design to mean the same thing across all applications. Figure 4-3 offers a gallery of cursors for each of the cursor constant settings provided by Internet Explorer for Windows.

all-scroll	col-resize	crosshair	e-resize
hand	help	move	n-resize
ne-resize	no-drop	not-allowed	nw-resize
pointer	progress	row-resize	s-resize
se-resize	sw-resize	text	vertical-text
w-resize	wait		

Figure 4-3. Internet Explorer cursor gallery

CSS Syntax

cursor: *cursorType* || *uri*

Value

A cursor type is one of the implemented cursor names. The following table shows which cursor types are supported by various browsers and the CSS standard (3* indicates a proposed value for CSS3).

Cursor name	IE/Windows	IE/Mac	Mozilla	Safari	Opera	CSS
alias	n/a	n/a	n/a	n/a	n/a	3*
all-scroll	6	n/a	1.8	n/a	n/a	3*
auto	4	4	all	all	7	2
cell	n/a	n/a	1.8	n/a	n/a	3*
col-resize	6	n/a	1.8	n/a	n/a	3*
context-menu	n/a	n/a	1.8	n/a	n/a	3*
copy	n/a	n/a	1.8	n/a	n/a	3*
count-down	n/a	n/a	n/a	n/a	n/a	n/a
count-up	n/a	n/a	n/a	n/a	n/a	n/a
count-up-down	n/a	n/a	n/a	n/a	n/a	n/a
crosshair	4	4	all	all	7	2
default	4	4	all	all	7	2
e-resize	4	4	all	all	7	2
grab	n/a	n/a	<1	n/a	n/a	n/a

Cursor name	IE/Windows	IE/Mac	Mozilla	Safari	Opera	CSS
grabbing	n/a	n/a	<1	n/a	n/a	n/a
hand	4	4	n/a	all	7	n/a
help	4	4	all	all	7	2
move	4	4	all	all	7	2
n-resize	4	4	all	all	7	2
ne-resize	4	4	all	all	7	2
nesw-resize	n/a	n/a	1.8	n/a	n/a	3*
no-drop	6	n/a	1.8	n/a	n/a	3*
none	n/a	n/a	n/a	n/a	n/a	3*
not-allowed	n/a	n/a	n/a	n/a	n/a	3*
nw-resize	4	4	all	all	7	2
nwse-resize	n/a	n/a	1.8	n/a	n/a	3*
pointer	4	4	all	all	7	2
progress	6	n/a	<1	n/a	9	2.1
row-resize	6	n/a	1.8	n/a	n/a	3*
s-resize	4	4	all	all	7	2
se-resize	4	4	all	all	7	2
spinning	n/a	n/a	all	n/a	n/a	n/a
sw-resize	4	4	all	all	7	2
text	4	4	n/a	n/a	n/a	2
url(uri)	6	n/a	n/a	n/a	n/a	2
vertical-text	6	n/a	1.8	n/a	n/a	3*
w-resize	4	4	all	all	7	2
wait	4	4	all	all	7	2

Notice that IE 6 or later implements downloadable cursors. The IE setting for an external URL requires an address of a cursor file of extension *.cur* or *.ani* (which you create with a graphics utility that creates Windows cursors).

Initial Value   auto

Example   a.helpLink {cursor: help}

Applies To   All elements.

direction

IE 5 NN *n/a* Moz *all* Saf *all* Op *all* CSS 2

Inherited: Yes

Sets the direction of the flow of inline portions of content (such as text) and the order in which table cells are filled along a row. Analogous to the dir property of most elements, the direction style property lets you override the browser's default rendering direction for other languages or special content.

CSS Syntax

direction: ltr | rtl

Value

Either of two directional constants. The value ltr stands for left-to-right; rtl stands for right-to-left.

Initial Value	ltr
Applies To	All elements.

display

IE *4* NN *4* Moz *all* Saf *all* Op *all* CSS *1*

Inherited: No

This is a multipurpose property that determines how a browser treats invisible boxes that surround every element and text node. For example, a block-level item exhibits specific characteristics that are quite distinct from an inline item (at least with respect to how the element renders in relation to surrounding content). The CSS specification provides numerous types of such boxes, because the space they occupy can be influenced differently by such things as borders or even outright rendering rules (e.g., the way a compact style controls definition list items). In practice, you may not see much, if any, difference between some display types because the browser's built-in style sheet doesn't specify anything different for the variations (e.g., a table element may render the same way if its display style property is set to block or table). At the same time, the display style lets you override the default rendering behavior of elements, such as making a block table render as an inline table.

Additionally, display settings can be applied to arbitrary elements (e.g., divs and spans) to give them the rendering powers of the full-fledged elements in the value names. For example, a collection of hierarchical elements (such as the result of an XML query) can be displayed as a table by applying table-related display values to elements corresponding to groups, rows, and cells.

Perhaps the most frequently used aspect of the display style property in DHTML is setting the scripts to toggle between showing and completely hiding the element and its space. When the property is set to none, the element is hidden from view, and all surrounding content cinches up to occupy whatever space the element would normally occupy. This is different from the visibility property, which reserves space for the element while hiding it from view. But to redisplay the item to its default display mode, you can assign one of the common display types (block and inline) or the more specific type associated with the element (such as list-item for an li element), if supported by your target browsers.

CSS Syntax

display: *displayType*

Value

The CSS specification identifies many display types, but browser support is more limited. The following table shows the supported types. Support for the list-item and all table-related values means that the values can be applied successfully to arbitrary containers.

Display type	IE/ Windows	IE/Mac	NN	Mozilla	Safari	Opera	CSS
block	5	4	4	all	all	7	2
compact	n/a	n/a	n/a	n/a	n/a	n/a	<2.1
inline	5	4	4	all	all	7	2
inline-block	5.5	n/a	n/a	n/a	n/a	n/a	<2.1
inline-table	n/a	5	n/a	n/a	all	7	2
list-item	5	5	n/a	all	all	7	2
marker	n/a	n/a	n/a	n/a	n/a	n/a	<2.1
none	4	4	4	all	all	7	2
run-in	n/a	5	n/a	n/a	n/a	7	2
table	n/a	5	n/a	all	all	7	2
table-caption	n/a	5	n/a	all	all	7	2
table-cell	n/a	5	n/a	all	all	7	2
table-column-group	n/a	5	n/a	n/a	n/a	n/a	2
table-footer-group	5.5	5	n/a	all	all	7	2
table-header-group	5	5	n/a	all	all	7	2
table-row	n/a	5	n/a	all	all	7	2
table-row-group	n/a	5	n/a	n/a	n/a	n/a	2

Initial Value   Element-dependent.

Example   .hidden {display: none}

Applies To   All elements (but some display types are applicable to specific elements).

Object Model Reference
[window.]document.getElementById("*elementID*").style.display

elevation

IE *n/a*   NN *n/a*   Moz *n/a*   Saf *n/a*   Op *n/a*   CSS 2

Inherited: No

Given a listener at the center of a three-dimensional sound space (like in a surround-sound-equipped theater), elevation sets the vertical angle of the source of the sound (for example, in a text-to-speech browser). See also the azimuth property.

CSS Syntax
elevation: *angle* | *angleConstant*

Value

Your choice of a specific angle (in degrees) or one of the five constant values. An angle value is any value in the range of –90 to +90 (inclusive) plus the letters "deg", as in 90deg. The value 0deg is at the same vertical level as the listener's ear. To set the angle above level, the value must be a positive value (45deg); below level requires a negative value (-45deg). Optionally, you can choose an *angleConstant* value from a library of descriptions that correspond to fixed points above and below level.

Value	Equals
above	90deg (directly overhead)
below	-90deg (directly beneath)
higher	+10 degrees from current
level	0deg (at listener's ear level)
lower	−10 degrees from current

In combination with the azimuth property, you can place a sound at any point around a spherical surround-sound stage.

Initial Value   level

Example
```
h1 {elevation: -45deg}
p.heavenly {elevation: above}
```

Applies To   All elements.

empty-cells

Controls whether an empty td element shows its borders and background in a table. Surrounding cells don't change position when an empty cell is hidden. Instead, the cell is essentially transparent, allowing the table's background to show through in the space.

CSS Syntax
```
empty-cells: show | hide
```

Value   One of two constants: show | hide .

Initial Value   show

Example   td {border: salmon inset 3px; empty-cells: hide}

Applies To   td elements.

filter (old style)

Sets the visual, reveal, or blend filter used to display or change content of an element. A visual filter can be applied to an element to produce effects such as content flipping, glow, drop shadow, and many others. A reveal filter is applied to an element when its visibility or appearance changes. The value of the reveal filter determines what visual effect is to be applied to the transition from hidden to shown (or vice versa). This includes effects such as wipes, blinds, and barn doors. A blend filter sets the speed at which a transition between visibility states occurs.

CSS Syntax

```
filter: filterType1(paramName1=value1, paramName2=value2,...)
        filterType2(paramName1=value1,...) ...
```

Value

Each filter property may have more than one space-delimited filter type associated with it. Each filter type is followed by a pair of parentheses, which may convey parameters about the behavior of the filter for the current element. A parameter generally consists of a name/value pair, with assignment performed by the equals symbol. See the "Notes" section below for details on *filterType* values and parameters.

Initial Value   None.

Example   .fastStuff {filter: blur(add=true, direction=225)}

Applies To

body, button, img, input, marquee, table, td, textarea, tfoot, th, thead, tr, and absolute-positioned div and span elements.

Object Model Reference

[window.]document.getElementById("*elementID*").filters["*filterName*"]

Notes

First-generation filters (which continue to be supported at least through IE 7) are divided into three broad categories: visual, reveal, and blend. Each category has its own parameter names. You can mix categories within a single filter property assignment and have quite a bit of fun experimenting with the combinations. Observe carefully the limitations about the elements to which you may assign filters.

The visual filters and their parameters are as follows:

alpha( )

>   Controls transparency level. The opacity and finishopacity parameters can be set from transparent (0) to opaque (100). The style parameter sets the opacity gradient shape: uniform (0), linear (1), radial (2), or rectangular (3). startX and startY set the horizontal and vertical coordinates for opacity gradient start, whereas finishX and finishY set the horizontal and vertical coordinates for opacity gradient end.

blur( )
> Gives the element the appearance of motion. The add parameter specifies whether to add the original image to the blurred image (1) or to omit it (0). direction sets the angle of the blurred image relative to the original image location: above (0); above-right (45); right (90); below-right (135); below (180); below-left (225); left (270); above-left (315). strength indicates the number of pixels for the blurred image to extend.

chroma( )
> Sets a color transparent. The color parameter specifies the hexadecimal triplet value of the color to be made transparent.

dropShadow( )
> Creates an offset shadow for apparent depth. The color parameter sets the hexadecimal triplet value of color for drop shadow. offx and offy specify the number of pixels between the element and the drop shadow along the x and y axes (positive values to the right/down; negative to the left/up). The positive parameter specifies whether only positive pixels generate drop shadows (1) or transparent pixels as well (0).

flipH( )
> Creates a horizontally mirrored image of the element.

flipV( )
> Creates a vertically mirrored image of the element.

glow( )
> Adds radiance to outer edges. The color parameter sets the hexadecimal triplet value of the color for the radiance effect and strength sets the radiance intensity (1-255).

gray( )
> Removes colors but retains luminance.

invert( )
> Reverses the hue, saturation, and brightness (HSV) levels.

light( )
> Shines a light source on the element (numerous filter method calls are available to set specific types of light sources, locations, intensities, and colors).

mask( )
> Creates a transparent mask. The color parameter sets the hexadecimal triplet value of the color applied to transparent regions.

shadow( )
> Displays the element as a solid silhouette. The color parameter sets the hexadecimal triplet value of the color used for shadows and direction sets the angle of the shadow relative to the original image location: above (0); above-right (45); right (90); below-right (135); below (180); below-left (225); left (270); above-left (315).

wave( )
> Renders the element with a sine wave distortion along the x-axis. The add parameter specifies whether to add the original image to waved image (1) or not (0). freq sets the number of waves to be applied to visual distortion, light sets the light strength (0-100), phase sets the percentage offset for the sine wave (0-100 corresponding to to 360 degrees), and strength sets the wave effect intensity (0-255).

xRay( )
> Renders only the edges.

The blend and reveal transition filters and parameters are as follows:

blendTrans( )

Fades the element in or out. The duration parameter sets the floating-point value (*seconds.milliseconds*) of how long the transition effect should take.

revealTrans( )

Sets a transition effect between appearance states of an element. The duration parameter sets the floating-point value (*seconds.milliseconds*) of how long the transition effect should take. transition is a key integer that corresponds to one of the following transition types.

Value	Transition type	Value	Transition type
0	Box in	12	Random dissolve
1	Box out	13	Split vertical in
2	Circle in	14	Split vertical out
3	Circle out	15	Split horizontal in
4	Wipe up	16	Split horizontal out
5	Wipe down	17	Strips left down
6	Wipe right	18	Strips left up
7	Wipe left	19	Strips right down
8	Vertical blinds	20	Strips right up
9	Horizontal blinds	21	Random bars horizontal
10	Checkerboard across	22	Random bars vertical
11	Checkerboard down	23	Random

Both transition filters have a set of three methods: apply( ), play( ), and stop( ). Use apply( ) to freeze the element's display while you change the element's visibility or other visual property; then invoke the play( ) method on the filter to let the transition be seen by the user:

```
document.getElementById("myImg").filters["revealTrans"].apply( );
document.getElementById("myImg").src = "newPix.jpg";
document.getElementById("myImg").filters["revealTrans"].play( );
```

A style sheet rule for the element may have been set to the following:

```
img {filter: revealTrans(transition=2, duration=3)}
```

When the script statements execute, the change from one image to another occurs through a "circle in" reveal transition.

filter (new style)

IE 5.5   NN *n/a*   Moz *n/a*   Saf *n/a*   Op *n/a*   CSS *n/a*

Inherited: No

Sets the static or transition filter used to display or change content of an element with the help of the DXImageTransform ActiveX control, delivered with IE 5.5 or later for Windows. The purpose of the new filter mechanism is the same as the old style one, but the syntax for invoking the ActiveX control is new, as are many of the filter names.

CSS Syntax

```
filter: progid:DXImageTransform.Microsoft.filterType1(paramName1=value1,
paramName2=value2,...)
progid:DXImageTransform.Microsoft.filterType2(paramName1=value1,...) ...
```

Value

Each filter type must be preceded by the reference to the ActiveX control (progid: DXImageTransform.Microsoft.), and multiple filter types for a single filter style property are space delimited. Each filter type is followed by a pair of parentheses, which may convey parameters about the behavior of the filter for the current element. A parameter generally consists of a name/value pair, with assignment performed by the equals symbol. Filter types that control transitions also have methods that scripts invoke to freeze the display while some visible property of the element changes (also under script control) and then play the transition. (See the "Notes" section below for information about *filterType* values and parameters.

Initial Value   None.

Example

```
.fastStuff {filter: progid:DXImageTransform.Microsoft.MotionBlur(add=1,
direction=225)}
```

Applies To   All elements.

Object Model Reference

```
[window.]document.getElementById("elementID").filters[
  "DXImageTransform.Microsoft.filterName"]
```

Notes

Documenting in detail ActiveX controls that work only on Windows versions of Internet Explorer exceeds the scope of this book. But by way of introduction to what the new filter scheme offers in IE 5.5 and later, the following table lists the static and trasition filters available in the DXImageTransform ActiveX control, along with descriptions of what they do. For specific details of properties that go into style sheet rules, as well as the scriptable properties and methods available to each filter, visit *http://msdn.microsoft.com/workshop/ author/filter/filters.asp*.

Filter name	Type	Description
Alpha()	static	Controls transparency level (opacity)
Barn()	transition	A barn-door transition effect, with properties for speed, motion, and orientation
BasicImage()	static	Sets a variety of filter styles (mirror, opacity, grayscale, etc.) for all kinds of elements, but under script control can also rotate the element and alter its color mask
Blinds()	transition	A Venetian-blind transition effect, with properties for direction and thickness of the slats
Blur()	static	Controls the fuzziness of the element

Filter name	Type	Description
Checkerboard( )	transition	A checkboard transition effect with properties for direction, speed, and square sizes
Chroma( )	static	Controls the transparency of a specific color
Compositor( )	static	Combines color filter effects
DropShadow( )	static	Creates an offset shadow for apparent depth, with properties for color, and depth of shadow
Emboss( )	static	Controls an embossed texture effect
Engrave( )	static	Controls an engraved texture effect
Fade( )	transition	A blended transition between views, with properties for speed and the degree of overlap of both views
Glow( )	static	Controls radiance of outer edges
Gradiant( )	statics	Applies a colored gradient texture on the element's background
GradientWipe( )	transition	A wipe transition using a gradient blend at the wipe line, with properties for speed, thickness of the gradient, and direction
ICMFilter( )	static	Applies an external Image Color Management profile to the element
Inset( )	transition	A wipe transition that works along horizontal and vertical axes, but diagonally from one corner to its opposite
Iris( )	transition	A zoom-style transition with properties for speed, direction (in or out), and iris shape (e.g., circle, cross, diamond, plus, square, star)
Light( )	static	Controlled exclusively through scripts, adds effect of light source directed at the element
MaskFilter( )	static	Overlays a transparent mask for a color
Matrix( )	static	Controls rotation, flipping, and scaling of element
MotionBlur( )	static	Simulates motion via artificial blurring
Pixelate( )	transition	Blends between views via an expansion/contraction and blurring/focusing of the content
RadialWipe( )	transition	Blends between views via your choice of styles (clock, wedge, radial)
RandomBars( )	transition	Blends between views via expanding/contracting bars, with properties for orientation and speed
RandomDissolve( )	transition	Blends between views through random pixel changes
Shadow( )	static	Displays element content as a silhouette
Slide( )	transition	Blends between views through banded sliding of various types
Spiral( )	transition	Blends between views through spiral reveals
Stretch( )	transition	Blends between views through various stretch-style reveals
Strips( )	transition	Blends between views with striped effect
Wave( )	static	Adds sine-wave distortion to the element
Wheel( )	transition	Blends between views via wheel spokes emanating from the element center
ZigZag( )	transition	Blends between views via removal of rows of bricks

Successful deployment of these filters, especially on complex content, requires extensive experimentation and testing to make sure that your combination doesn't crash the browser.

float

Inherited: No

Determines on which side of the containing box the element aligns so that other content wraps around the element. When the property is set to none, the element appears in its source code sequence, and at most, one line of surrounding text content appears in the same horizontal band as the element.

Due to the prior reservation of float as a keyword in JavaScript, the property name is not available as a style object property name in object models that use JavaScript. Internet Explorer adopted the styleFloat property name; the W3C DOM uses cssFloat.

CSS Syntax
float: *alignmentSide* | none

Value	An *alignmentSide* is one of the following constants: left	right.
Initial Value	none
Example	img.navButton {float: right}
Applies To	All elements except positioned elements (or generated content).

Object Model Reference
[window.]document.getElementById("*elementID*").style.styleFloat
[window.]document.getElementById("*elementID*").style.cssFloat

font

Inherited: Yes

This is a shorthand property that lets you set multiple font-related properties with one assignment statement. Some browsers are more forgiving than others about required and optional values, but this property should at least specify the *font-size* and font face (either by *font-family* or *CSS2FontConstant* values) in that order. The order of other space-delimited value types is not critical. In CSS2, some additional short-circuit constants apply named system fonts that have fixed values for each of the font-related properties.

CSS Syntax
font: *font-style* || *font-variant* || *font-weight* || *font-size[/line-height]* ||*font-family* | *CSS2FontConstant*

Value
For syntax and examples of value types for font and line properties, see the respective property listing. The construction with the forward slash before the *line-height* value allows the use of a second length value within the potentially long sequence of values for this

property: the *line-height* length value must always accompany the required *font-size* value, separated by a forward slash.

The CSS2 font constants are as follows: caption | icon | menu | message-box | small-caption | status-bar. These constants refer to browser and operating system fonts used by the client. Their precise appearance is therefore different on different operating systems but consistent with the user's expectation for a particular type of font. In other words, these styles should be used when their function mirrors a system or browser function.

Initial Value   None.

Example

```
body {font: 12px serif}
h2 {font: bolder small-caps 16px "Lucida Console", Arial, sans-serif}
.iconCaption {font: 10px/1.1em caption}
```

Applies To   All elements.

Object Model Reference

```
[window.]document.getElementById("elementID").style.font
```

font-family

IE *4* NN *4* Moz *all* Saf *all* Op *all* CSS *1*

Inherited: Yes

Sets a prioritized list of font families to be used to render the content. One or more font family names may be included in a comma-delimited list of property values. If a font family name consists of multiple words, the family name must be inside quotes.

A font family may consist of multiple font definitions. For example, a Helvetica font family may also include a bold version and an italic version—genuinely distinct fonts rather than the approximated versions of bold and italic. When you specify a font family by name, the browser looks into the client's system to see if there is a font available by that name. If not, the browser looks to the next font family name in the list. Therefore, it is wise to include font family names in a sequence that goes from the most esoteric to the most generic. The final font family name should be the generic family (serif, sans-serif, cursive, fantasy, or monospace) that most closely resembles the desired font. Many fonts that are widely installed on one operating system may not be as popular on another operating system.

Browsers following the CSS2 specification should also be smart enough to recognize Unicode character codes and try to match them with named font families that cater to particular languages. Ideally, this will allow a browser to mix fonts from different languages and writing systems in the same element, provided each font-family is listed in the property value.

CSS Syntax

```
font-family: fontFamilyName [, fontFamilyName [, ...]]
```

Value

Any number of font family names, comma delimited. Multiword family names must be quoted. Recognized generic family names are: serif | sans-serif | cursive | fantasy | monospace.

Initial Value	Browser default.
Example	body {font-family: "Century Schoolbook", Times, serif}
Applies To	All elements.

Object Model Reference

[window.]document.getElementById("*elementID*").style.fontFamily

Notes

Internet Explorer provides facilities for downloading font definition files for a browser that doesn't have a special font that the page designer wants for the page. The font definition files must be created by the author using browser-specific font conversion tools. An @font-face style sheet rule downloads the font definition file and associates that font description with an arbitrary font family name:

```
@font-face {font-family: Neato; src: url(http://www.giantco.com/fonts/neato.eot)}
```

See "At-Rules" earlier in this chapter for details on deploying this type of style rule. You then specify the font in regular font-family style properties. If the font has yet to download, the browser displays the page in another font until the downloadable font has arrived. At that point, the page is reflowed with the downloaded font.

font-size

IE 4 NN 4 Moz *all* Saf *all* Op *all* CSS 1

Inherited: Yes

Determines the font size of the element. The font size can be set in several ways. A collection of constants (xx-small, x-small, small, medium, large, x-large, xx-large) defines what are known as absolute sizes. In truth, these are absolute as far as a single browser in a single operating system goes because the reference point for these sizes varies with browser and operating system (analogous to the old HTML font sizes of 1 through 7). See Figure 4-4 for size comparisons viewed on the same video monitors. But they let the author have confidence that one element set to large is rendered larger than another set to medium.

Another collection of constants (larger, smaller) are known as relative sizes. Because the font-size property is inherited from the parent element, these relative sizes are applied to the parent element to determine the font size of the current element. It is up to the browser to determine exactly how much larger or smaller the font size is, and a lot depends on how the parent element's font size is set. If it is set with one of the absolute sizes (large, for example), a child's font size of larger means that the font is rendered in the browser's x-large size. The increments are not as clear cut when the parent font size is set with a length or percentage.

If you elect to use a length value for the font-size property, choose a unit that makes the most sense for fonts rendered on the output medium, such as pixels (px) for screen display and points (pt) or ems (em) for printed output. Em values are calculated relative to the size

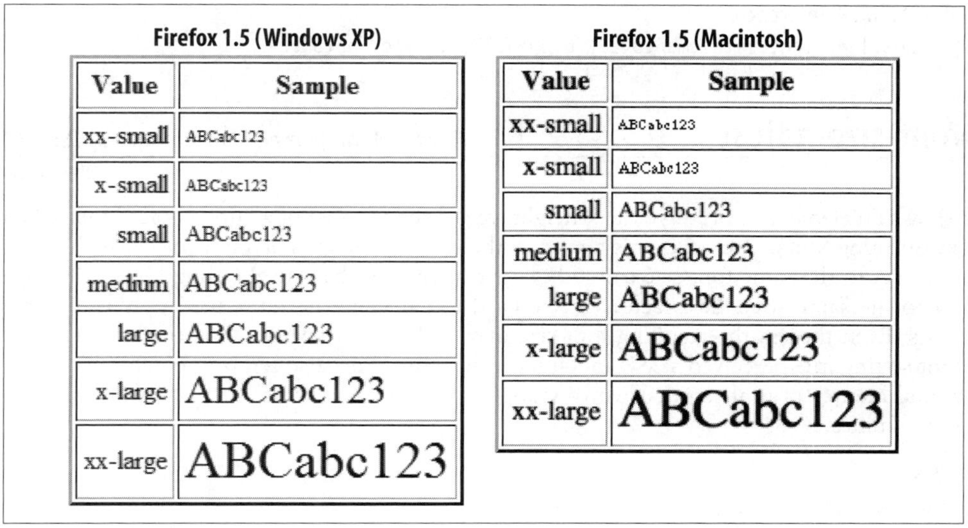

Figure 4-4. Font size constant values in Firefox 1.5 on the Windows and Mac platforms

of the parent element's font size. Finally, you can set the font-size to a percentage, which is calculated based on the size of the parent element's font size.

Some browsers hijack your best efforts at precisely sizing fonts, using their own (or user) settings to establish a "medium" size. That is why many designers prefer to rely on the relative-size constants for their font-size specification schemes. This choice means giving up a level of control over rendering from one browser and operating system to the next, but attempting too strict control on uniform rendering generally leads to utter frustration.

CSS Syntax

font-size: *absoluteSize* | *relativeSize* | *length* | *percentage*

Value

For an absolute size, one of the following constants: xx-small | x-small | small | medium | large | x-large | xx-large. For a relative size, one of the following constants: larger | smaller. For a length, see the discussion about length values at the beginning of this chapter. For a percentage, the percentage value and the % symbol.

Initial Value

medium (for BODY element); the parent element's font-size value (for all others).

Example

```
body {font-size: 14pt}
p.teeny {font-size: x-small}
em {font-size: larger}
span.larger {font-size: 150%}
```

Applies To   All elements.

Object Model Reference

[window.]document.getElementById("*elementID*").style.fontSize

font-size-adjust

IE *n/a* NN *n/a* Moz *n/a* Saf *n/a* Op *n/a* CSS <2.1

Inherited: Yes

Allows an element to preserve the x-height (measured in exes) of a "first choice" font when substituting fonts. The z-factor is a ratio of the em- to x-heights of a font. Because different fonts set to the same font size can look larger or smaller than neighboring fonts on a page set to the same size, the z-factor can be used to calculate the ratio and apply it to other fonts. Even though the resulting font size may be larger or smaller than the "first choice" font setting, the perceived size is much more accurate. This also tends to equalize the horizontal metrics of fonts so that word-wrapped lines break at the same place with different font families.

CSS Syntax

font-size-adjust: 0.47

Value

A number representing the aspect value of the preferred font (perhaps obtainable from the font maker) or none.

Initial Value	none
Applies To	All elements.

Object Model Reference

[window.]document.getElementById("*elementID*").style.fontSizeAdjust

font-stretch

IE *n/a* NN *n/a* Moz *n/a* Saf *n/a* Op *n/a* CSS <2.1

Inherited: Yes

Sets the rendered font to a letter-spacing relative of the specified font family.

CSS Syntax

font-stretch: *stretchType* | normal

Value

For an absolute size, one of the following constants: ultra-condensed | extra-condensed | condensed | semi-condensed | semi-expanded | extra-expanded | ultra-expanded. For a relative size, one of the following constants: narrower | wider.

Initial Value	normal
Applies To	All elements.

Object Model Reference

[window.]document.getElementById("*elementID*").style.fontStretch

font-style

Inherited: Yes

Determines whether the element is rendered in a normal (Roman), italic, or oblique font style. If the font-family includes font faces labeled Italic and/or Oblique, the setting of the font-style property summons those particular font faces from the browser's system. But if the specialized font faces are not available in the system, the normal font face is usually algorithmically slanted to look italic. Output sent to a printer with such font settings relies on the quality of arbitration between the client computer and printer to render an electronically generated italic font style. Although personal computer software typically includes other kinds of font rendering under the heading of "Style," see font-variant and font-weight for other kinds of font "styles."

CSS Syntax
font-style: *fontStyle*

Value
One of the following constants: normal | italic | oblique. Browsers tend to treat italic and oblique settings the same.

Initial Value	normal
Example	h2 em {font-style: italic}
Applies To	All elements.

Object Model Reference
[window.]document.getElementById("*elementID*").style.fontStyle

font-variant

Inherited: Yes

Determines whether the element should be rendered in all uppercase letters in such a way that lowercase letters of the source code are rendered in smaller uppercase letters. If a font family contains a small caps variant, the browser should use it automatically. More likely, however, the browser calculates a smaller size for the uppercase letters that take the place of source code lowercase letters. In practice, Internet Explorer for Windows prior to Version 6 renders the entire source code content as uppercase letters of the same size as the parent element's font, regardless of the case of the source code.

CSS Syntax
font-variant: *fontVariant*

Value	Any of the following constant values: normal	small-caps.
Initial Value	normal
Example	em {font-variant: small-caps}
Applies To	All elements.

Object Model Reference

[window.]document.getElementById("*elementID*").style.fontVariant

font-weight

IE *4* **NN** *n/a* **Moz** *all* **Saf** *all* **Op** *all* **CSS** *1*

Inherited: Yes

Sets the weight (boldness) of the element's font. CSS provides a weight rating scheme that is more granular than most browsers render on the screen, but the finely tuned weights may come into play when the content is sent to a printer. The scale is a numeric rating from 100 to 900 at 100-unit increments. Therefore, a font-weight of 100 is the least bold that can be displayed, whereas 900 is the boldest. A setting of normal (the default weight for any font) is equivalent to a font-weight value of 400; the standard bold setting is equivalent to 700. Other settings (bolder and lighter) let you specify a weight relative to the parent element's weight.

The CSS2 specification offers guidelines about how the weight values should correspond to font family names and internal characteristics of some font definition formats. For example, the OpenType font definition format provides slots for nine font weights. In this case, the numeric font-weight property values map directly to the weight definitions in that font. If the font family contains a face with a name that contains the word Medium and one labeled Book, Regular, Roman, or Normal, the Medium face is equated with a weight value of 500 (whereas the other is at 400). All font face names including the word Bold are equated with a weight of 700. For font families that don't have all nine weights assigned, the browser should do its best to interpolate, but it is very likely that some weight values generate fonts of the same weight as other values.

CSS Syntax

font-weight: *fontWeight*

Value

Any of the following constant values: bold | bolder | lighter | normal | 100 | 200 | 300 | 400 | 500 | 600 | 700 | 800 | 900.

Initial Value	normal
Example	p em {font-weight: bolder}
Applies To	All elements.

Object Model Reference

[window.]document.getElementById("*elementID*").style.fontWeight

height

IE *4* **NN** *4* **Moz** *all* **Saf** *all* **Op** *all* **CSS** *1*

Inherited: No

Sets the height of a block-level, replaced, and positioned element's content height (exclusive of borders, padding, and margins).

IE for Windows counts top and bottom margins, padding, and borders when calculating the height of an element until you reach IE 6 in standards-compatibility mode (see the DOCTYPE element in Chapter 1). When observing the CSS standards, the height applies to only the content portion of an element, irrespective of borders, padding, or margins.

CSS Syntax

height: *length* | *percentage* | auto

Value

See the discussion about length values at the beginning of this chapter. The setting of auto lets the browser determine the height of the element box based on the amount of space required to display the content.

Initial Value

auto

Example

div#announce {height: 240}
textarea {height: 90%}

Applies To

Navigator 4, all absolute-positioned elements; Internet Explorer 4, applet, div, embed, fieldset, hr, iframe, img, input, marquee, object, span, table, and textarea elements; Internet Explorer 5, Mozilla, Safari, and Opera, all elements except nonreplaced inline elements, table column elements, and column group elements.

Object Model Reference

[window.]document.getElementById("*elementID*").style.height

ime-mode

IE 5(Win) NN *n/a* Moz *n/a* Saf *n/a* Op *n/a* CSS *n/a*

Inherited: No

Controls the presence of the Input Method Editor in IE for Windows for browser and system versions that support languages such as Chinese, Japanese, and Korean.

CSS Syntax

ime-mode: active | auto | disabled | inactive

Value One of four constants: active | auto | disabled | inactive.

Initial Value auto

Example input {ime-mode: active}

Applies To input and textarea elements.

Object Model Reference

[window.]document.getElementById("*elementID*").style.imeMode

!important

IE *4* NN *n/a* Moz *all* Saf *all* Op *all* CSS *1*

Inherited: No

Increases the weight (importance) of a property setting with respect to cascading order. This keyword is a declaration rather than a property, but it can be attached to any property setting. The syntax requires an exclamation symbol between the property value and the important keyword. Extra whitespace around the exclamation symbol is acceptable. See Chapter 3.

CSS Syntax
!important

Value	No values assigned to this declaration.
Example	p {font-size: 14pt !important}
Applies To	All elements.

Object Model Reference
[window.]document.getElementById("*elementID*").style.
getPropertyPriority("*styleProperty*")

layer-background-color, layer-background-image

IE *n/a* NN *|4|* Moz *n/a* Saf *n/a* Op *n/a* CSS *n/a*

Inherited: No

These are Navigator 4-only properties that allow a positioned element's background color and image to extend through padding, all the way to the border. Values are the same as for the CSS background-color and background-image properties. See background-color, background-image, and padding.

layout-flow

IE *5.5* NN *n/a* Moz *n/a* Saf *n/a* Op *n/a* CSS *n/a*

Inherited: Yes

Intended primarily for languages that display characters in vertical sentences, this property controls the progression of content, left-to-right, or right-to-left. Microsoft recommends using the writing-mode property instead.

CSS Syntax
layout-flow: horizontal | vertical-ideographic

Value	One of two constants: horizontal	vertical-ideographic.
Initial Value	horizontal
Example	body {layout-flow: vertical-ideographic}
Applies To	All elements.

Object Model Reference

[window.]document.getElementById("*elementID*").style.layoutFlow

layout-grid

IE *5(Win)* NN *n/a* Moz *n/a* Saf *n/a* Op *n/a* CSS *n/a*

Inherited: Yes

This is a shorthand property that lets you set one or more layout grid properties (layoutGridChar, layoutGridLine, layoutGridMode, and layoutGridType) with one assignment statement. These properties are used primarily with Asian language content.

CSS Syntax

layout-grid: *layout-grid-mode* | *layout-grid-type* | *layout-grid-line* | *layout-grid-char*

Value

For syntax and examples of value types for font and line properties, see the respective property listing.

Initial Value   both loose none none

Example   body {layout-grid: both fixed 14px 14px}

Applies To   All elements.

Object Model Reference

[window.]document.getElementById("*elementID*").style.layoutGrid

layout-grid-char

IE *5(Win)* NN *n/a* Moz *n/a* Saf *n/a* Op *n/a* CSS *n/a*

Inherited: Yes

Controls the size of the Asian language character grid for block-level elements.

CSS Syntax

layout-grid-char: *length* | auto | none

Value

Length value as an absolute unit measure, or a percentage. Or one of the following constants: auto | none.

Initial Value   none

Example   body {layout-grid-mode: both; layout-grid-char: 14px}

Applies To   All elements.

Object Model Reference

[window.]document.getElementById("*elementID*").style.layoutGridChar

layout-grid-line

IE *5(Win)* NN *n/a* Moz *n/a* Saf *n/a* Op *n/a* CSS *n/a*

Inherited: Yes

Controls the line height of Asian language character grid for block-level elements.

CSS Syntax

layout-grid-line: *length* | auto | none

Value

Length value as an absolute unit measure, or a percentage. Or one of the following constants: auto | none.

Initial Value	none
Example	body {layout-grid-mode: both; layout-grid-line: 14px}
Applies To	All elements.

Object Model Reference

[window.]document.getElementById("*elementID*").style.layoutGridLine

layout-grid-mode

IE *5(Win)* NN *n/a* Moz *n/a* Saf *n/a* Op *n/a* CSS *n/a*

Inherited: Yes

Controls whether the Asian language character grid should be one- or two-dimensional.

CSS Syntax

layout-grid-mode: *gridMode*

Value

One of the following constants: both | char (for inline elements) | line (for block-level elements) | none.

Initial Value	both
Example	body {layout-grid-mode: both}
Applies To	All elements.

Object Model Reference

[window.]document.getElementById("*elementID*").style.layoutGridMode

layout-grid-type

IE *5(Win)* NN *n/a* Moz *n/a* Saf *n/a* Op *n/a* CSS *n/a*

Inherited: Yes

Controls how the layout grid responds to characters of varying width.

CSS Syntax

layout-grid-type: *gridType*

Value	One of the following constants: fixed	loose	strict.

Initial Value	fixed
Example	div.kor {layout-grid-type: strict}
Applies To	Block-level elements.

Object Model Reference

[window.]document.getElementById("*elementID*").style.layoutGridType

left
IE *4* NN *4* Moz *all* Saf *all* Op *all* CSS *2*

Inherited: No

For positionable elements, defines the offset position of the left margin edge of an element relative to the left edge of the next outermost block content container. When the element is relative-positioned, the offset is based on the left edge of the inline location of where the element would normally appear in the content.

CSS Syntax

left: *length* | *percentage* | auto

Value

See the discussion about length values at the beginning of this chapter. Negative lengths may be allowed in some contexts, but be sure to test the results on all browsers. You may also specify a percentage value, which is calculated based on the width of the next outermost container. The setting of auto lets the browser determine the left offset of the element box within the containing box by virtue of normal element flow.

Initial Value	auto

Example

h1 {position: relative; left: 2em}
#logo {position: absolute; left: 80px; top: 30px}

Applies To	Positioned elements.

Object Model Reference

[window.]document.getElementById("*elementID*").style.left

letter-spacing
IE *4* NN *n/a* Moz *all* Saf *all* Op *all* CSS *1*

Inherited: Yes

Defines the spacing between characters within an element. Browsers normally define the character spacing based on font definitions and operating-system font rendering. To override the settings, assign a length value to the letter-spacing property. A negative value tightens the spacing, but test the effect on the selected font for readability on different operating systems.

CSS Syntax

letter-spacing: *length* | normal

Value

See the discussion at the beginning of this chapter about length values. The best results use units that are based on the rendered font size (em and ex). A setting of normal is how the browser sets the letters without any intervention.

Initial Value   normal

Example

```
.tight {letter-spacing: -0.03em}
blockquote {letter-spacing: 1.1em}
```

Applies To   All elements.

Object Model Reference

[window.]document.getElementById("*elementID*").style.letterSpacing

line-break

IE 5*(Win)* NN *n/a* Moz *n/a* Saf *n/a* Op *n/a* CSS *n/a*

Inherited: Yes

Controls line-breaking rules for Japanese text.

CSS Syntax

```
line-break: normal | strict
```

Value   One of the following constants: normal | strict.

Initial Value   normal

Example   p {letter-break: strict}

Applies To   Block-level elements.

Object Model Reference

[window.]document.getElementById("*elementID*").style.lineBreak

line-height

IE *4* NN *4* Moz *all* Saf *all* Op *all* CSS *1*

Inherited: Yes

Sets the height of the inline box (the box holding one physical line of content). Under normal circumstances, the line-height of the tallest font in a line of text or the tallest object governs the line height for that content line.

CSS Syntax

```
line-height: normal | number | length | percentage
```

Value

A value of normal lets the browser calculate line spacing for the entire element, thus producing a computed value that can be inherited by nested elements. A *number* value (greater than zero) acts as a multiplier for the font-size of the current element. Therefore, if a nested element inherits the line-height multiplier from its parent, that multiplier is applied to the current element's font-size setting (the multiplier, not the computed value of the parent, is inherited). A *length* value assigns an actual value to the inline box height. And a *percentage* value is a multiplier applied to the font size of the current element. In this case, the computer value can be inherited by nested elements.

Initial Value   normal

Example

```
p {line-height: normal}    /* Browser default; actual value is  inheritable */
p {line-height: 1.1}       /* Number value; the number value is inheritable */
p {line-height: 1.1em}     /* Length value; the actual value is inheritable */
p {line-height: 110%}      /* Percentage value; percentage times font size */
                           /* is inheritable /*
```

Applies To   All elements.

Object Model Reference

[window.]document.getElementById("*elementID*").style.lineHeight

list-style   IE 4   NN *n/a*   Moz *all*   Saf *all*   Op *all*   CSS 1

Inherited: Yes

This is a shorthand property for setting up to three list-style properties in one assignment statement. Whichever properties you don't explicitly set with this property assume their initial values. These properties define display characteristics for the markers automatically rendered for list items inside ol and ul elements.

CSS Syntax

list-style: *list-style-type* || *list-style-position* || *list-style-image*

Value

See the individual property entries for list-style-type, list-style-position, and list-style-image for details on acceptable values for each. You may include one, two, or all three values in the list-style property setting in any order you wish.

Initial Value   None.

Example   ul {list-style: square outside none}

Applies To

dd, dt, li, ol, and ul elements and any other element assigned the display: list-item style property.

Object Model Reference

[window.]document.getElementById("*elementID*").style.listStyle

list-style-image

IE *4* NN *n/a* Moz *all* Saf *all* Op *all* CSS *1*

Inherited: Yes

Provides the URL for an image that is to be used as the marker for a list item. Because this property can be inherited, a setting for an individual list item can override the same property setting in its parent.

CSS Syntax

list-style-image: none | *uri*

Value

For *uri*, supply any valid full or relative URL (in the CSS format) to an image file with a MIME type that is readable by the browser.

Initial Value   none

Example

ul {list-style-image: url(images/folder.gif)}
li.file {list-style-image: url(images/doc.gif)}

Applies To

dd, dt, li, ol, and ul elements and any other element assigned the display: list-item style property.

Object Model Reference

[window.]document.getElementById("*elementID*").style.listStyleImage

list-style-position

IE *4* NN *n/a* Moz *all* Saf *all* Op *all* CSS *1*

Inherited: Yes

Determines whether the marker is inside or outside (outdented) from the box containing the list item's content. When the list-style-position is set to inside and the content is text, the marker appears to be part of the text block. In this case, the alignment (indent) of the list item is the same as normal, but without the outdented marker. Figure 4-5 demonstrates the effects of both settings on wrapped list item text.

CSS Syntax

list-style-position: inside | outside

Value   Any of the constant values: inside | outside.

Initial Value   outside

Example   ul {list-style-position: inside}

Applies To

dd, dt, li, ol, and ul elements and any other element assigned the display: list-item style property.

Figure 4-5. Results of list-style-position settings

Object Model Reference

[window.]document.getElementById("*elementID*").style.listStylePosition

list-style-type

IE 4   NN 4   Moz *all*   Saf *all*   Op *all*   CSS 1

Inherited: Yes

Sets the kind of item marker to be displayed with each item. This property applies only if list-style-image is none (or not specified). The constant values available for this property are divided into two categories. One set is used with ul elements to present a filled disc, an empty circle, or a filled square; the other set is for ol elements, which have list items that can be marked in sequences of Arabic numerals, Roman numerals (uppercase or lowercase), or letters of the alphabet (uppercase or lowercase), and some other character sequences of other languages if the browser and operating system supports those languages.

CSS Syntax

list-style-type: *listStyleType*

Value

One constant value that is relevant to the type of list container. For ul: circle | disc | square. For ol: decimal | decimal-leading-zero | lower-roman | upper-roman | lower-greek | lower-alpha | lower-latin | upper-alpha | upper-latin | hebrew | armenian | georgian | cjk-ideographic | hiragana | katakana | hiragana-iroha | katakana-iroha. Commonly supported ol element sequences are treated as shown in the following table.

Type	Example
decimal	1, 2, 3, ...
decimal-leading-zero	01, 02, 03, ...
lower-alpha	a, b, c, ...
lower-greek	α, β, γ, ...
lower-roman	i, ii, iii, ...

Type	Example
upper-alpha	A, B, C, ...
upper-roman	I, II, III, ...

Initial Value   disc (for first level ul); decimal (for ol).

Example
```
ul {list-style-type: circle}
li {list-style-type: upper-roman}
```

Applies To

dd, dt, li, ol, and ul elements and any other element assigned the display: list-item style property.

Object Model Reference
```
[window.]document.getElementById("elementID").style.listStyleType
```

margin

IE 4   NN 4   Moz all   Saf all   Op all   CSS 1

Inherited: No

This is a shortcut property that can set the margin widths of up to four edges of an element with one statement. A margin is space that extends beyond the border of an element to provide extra empty space between adjacent or nested elements, especially those that have border properties set. You may supply one to four space-delimited margin values. The number of values determines which sides receive the assigned margins.

CSS Syntax
```
margin: marginThickness | auto {1,4}
```

Value

This property accepts one, two, three, or four values, depending on how many and which margins you want to set. Values for *marginThickness* can be *lengths*, percentages of the next outermost element size, or the auto constant. Value quantities and positions are interpreted as follows.

Number of values	Effect
1	All four margin edges set to value
2	Top and bottom margins set to the first value, right and left margins set to the second value
3	Top margin set to first value, right and left margins set to second value, bottom margin set to third value
4	Top, right, bottom, and left margin set, respectively

Initial Value   0

Example   `p.highlight {margin: 10px 20px}`

Applies To   All elements.

Object Model Reference

[window.]document.getElementById("*elementID*").style.margin

margin-bottom, margin-left, margin-right, margin-top

IE *4* **NN** *4* **Moz** *all* **Saf** *all* **Op** *all* **CSS** *1*

Inherited: No

All four properties set the width of a single margin edge of an element. A margin is space that extends beyond the element's border and is not calculated as part of the element's width or height.

CSS Syntax

margin-bottom: *marginThickness* | auto
margin-left: *marginThickness* | auto
margin-right: *marginThickness* | auto
margin-top: *marginThickness* | auto

Value

Values for *marginThickness* can be *lengths*, percentages of the next outermost element size, or the auto constant.

Initial Value   0

Example

blockquote {margin-left: 20; margin-top: 10}
#narrowCol {margin-left: 30%; margin-right: 30%}

Applies To   All elements.

Object Model Reference

[window.]document.getElementById("*elementID*").style.marginBottom
[window.]document.getElementById("*elementID*").style.marginLeft
[window.]document.getElementById("*elementID*").style.marginRight
[window.]document.getElementById("*elementID*").style.marginTop

marker-offset

IE *n/a* **NN** *n/a* **Moz** *n/a* **Saf** *n/a* **Op** *n/a* **CSS** *<2.1*

Inherited: No

Controls the space between list item markers (which occupy their own box in the CSS box model) and the box that contains the list item text. Requires that the list item elements be set to a display style marker.

CSS Syntax

marker-offset: *length* | auto

Value

A length value (see the discussion of length values at the beginning of this chapter), or the auto constant.

Initial Value   auto

Example   `li:before {display: marker; marker-offset: 4em}`

Applies To

List elements set to `marker` display mode (generally with a `:before` or `:after` pseudo-class).

marks   IE *n/a* NN *n/a* Moz *n/a* Saf *n/a* Op *n/a* CSS 2

Inherited: n/a

This is a page context property that sets whether the page should be rendered with crop or registration marks outside of the page content area. This property must be set within an @page rule. See "At-Rules," earlier in this chapter for details on deploying this type of style rule.

CSS Syntax

marks: *markType* | none

Value

Available *markType* values are the following constant values: crop | cross. A crop mark shows where pages should be trimmed; a cross mark is used for alignment and registration.

Initial Value   none

Example   `@page {marks: crop}`

Applies To   Page context.

Object Model Reference

`[window.]document.getElementById("elementID").style.marks`

max-height, min-height   IE *(see text)* NN *n/a* Moz *all* Saf *all* Op *all* CSS 2

Inherited: No

These properties let you establish a maximum and/or minimum height for an element's box. You can bracket the permissible height of an element regardless of the height caused by the natural flow of the content.

When you set the max-height property of an element that has content that may extend beyond that maximum, you should also set the overflow style property to hidden so that excess content is cropped. Failure to do so causes the overflowing content to bleed into the succeeding elements' content. Any box enhancements (borders, background color, etc.) shrink or expand to meet the requirements of the content or (if there isn't enough content to fill the box) minimum height.

Internet Explorer 6 supports only the min-height property, and is limited to td, th, and tr elements inside a table with its table-layout style property is set to fixed. This conflicts with the CSS2 specification, which explicitly excludes table-related elements from being influenced by these properties. IE 7, however, implements both properties correctly when running in CSS compatibility mode (i.e., with a modern DOCTYPE declaration). IE 5 for Macintosh supports neither property.

CSS Syntax

```
max-height: length | percentage | none
min-height: length | percentage | none
```

Value

See the discussion of length values at the beginning of the chapter. The value may also be a percentage that is calculated relative to the element's container. A value of none removes all constraints, allowing the content to flow naturally.

Initial Value   none (max-width); none (min-width).

Applies To   See text.

Object Model Reference

```
[window.]document.getElementById("elementID").style.minHeight
[window.]document.getElementById("elementID").style.maxHeight
```

max-width, min-width   IE 7 NN n/a Moz all Saf all Op all CSS 2

Inherited: No

These properties let you establish a minimum and/or maximum width for an element. You can bracket the permissible width of an element regardless of the width caused by the natural flow of the content within a parent container. IE 7 must run in CSS compatibility mode to use these properties

CSS Syntax

```
max-width: length | percentage | none
min-width: length | percentage | none
```

Value

See the discussion of length values at the beginning of the chapter. The value may also be a percentage that is calculated relative to the element's container. A value of none removes all constraints, allowing the content to flow naturally.

Initial Value   none (max-width); none (min-width).

Applies To   All elements.

Object Model Reference

```
[window.]document.getElementById("elementID").style.minWidth
[window.]document.getElementById("elementID").style.maxWidth
```

-moz-border-radius

IE *n/a* NN *n/a* Moz *all* Saf *n/a* Op *n/a* CSS *n/a*

Inherited: No

This is a shortcut property that lets you set the radius of one or more border corners. The number of values determines which sides receive the assigned colors. Note that this value arrangement differs from the preliminary CSS3 border-radius property value setup.

CSS Syntax

-moz-border-radius: *radius* {1,4}

Value

A border corner radius can be defined by a length measure, signifying the length of the radius of the imaginary circle from which the rounded corner comes. The larger the value, the more rounded the corner becomes. For screen display, the pixel length unit is most appropriate. You may also use a percentage value in the range between 0% (no rounding) to 50% (maximum rounding). The rounded border does not crop content of the element.

This property accepts one, two, three, or four *radius* values, depending on how many and which corners you want to make round. Value quantities and positions are interpreted as shown in the following table.

Number of values	Effect
1	All four corners set to same value
2	Top left and bottom right corners set to the first value, top right and bottom left corners set to the second value
3	Top left corner set to first value, top right and bottom left corners set to second value, bottom right corner set to third value
4	Top left, top right, bottom right, and bottom left corners set, respectively

Initial Value   0

Example

div.hotbox {-moz-border-radius: 20px}
div.circle {-moz-border-radius: 50%}

Applies To   All elements.

-moz-border-radius-bottomleft, -moz-border-radius-bottomright, -moz-border-radius-topleft, -moz-border-radius-topright

IE *n/a* NN *n/a* Moz *all* Saf *n/a* Op *n/a* CSS *n/a*

Inherited: No

Controls the radius of one border corner. Note that the value arrangement differs from the preliminary CSS3 corner-specific border-radius property value setup.

CSS Syntax

```
-moz-border-radius-bottomleft: radius
-moz-border-radius-bottomright: radius
-moz-border-radius-topleft: radius
-moz-border-radius-topright: radius
```

Value   See -moz-border-radius.

Initial Value   0

Example

```
div.bizarro {-moz-border-radius-topright:10%; -moz-border-radius-bottomright:10% }
```

Applies To   All elements.

-moz-opacity

IE *n/a*　NN *n/a*　Moz *all*　Saf *n/a*　Op *n/a*　CSS *n/a*

Inherited: No

Controls the level of opacity of the element. The lower the value, the more transparent the element becomes. This is a proprietary Mozilla property that was joined by the CSS3 opacity property in Mozilla 1.7.2.

CSS Syntax

```
-moz-opacity: alphaValue
```

Value

The level of opacity is determined by a floating-point number between 0.0 and 1.0. A completely opaque rendering occurs at a value of 1.0. Percentage values supported in earliest Mozilla versions have been dropped.

Initial Value   1

Example   div#watermark {-moz-opacity: 0.4}

Applies To   All elements.

Object Model Reference

```
[window.]document.getElementById("elementID").style.MozOpacity
```

opacity

IE *n/a*　NN *n/a*　Moz *1.7.2*　Saf *1.2*　Op *9*　CSS *3*

Inherited: No

Controls the level of opacity of the element. The lower the value, the more transparent the element becomes. Although the property is technically not inherited, the opacity of all child elements of a container are governed by the setting of the parent container.

CSS Syntax

```
opacity: alphaValue
```

Value

The level of opacity is determined by a floating-point number between 0.0 and 1.0. A completely opaque rendering occurs at a value of 1.0.

Initial Value	1
Example	div#watermark {opacity: 0.35}
Applies To	All elements.

Object Model Reference

[window.]document.getElementById("*elementID*").style.opacity

orphans
IE 5(Mac) NN n/a Moz n/a Saf n/a Op 7 CSS 2
Inherited: Yes

Sets the minimum number of lines of the start of a paragraph that must be visible at the bottom of a page where a page break occurs. See the widows property for lines to be displayed at the top of a page after a page break.

CSS Syntax

orphans: *lineCount*

Value	An integer of the number of lines.
Initial Value	2
Applies To	Block-level elements.

Object Model Reference

[window.]document.getElementById("*elementID*").style.orphans

outline
IE 5(Mac) NN n/a Moz 1.8.1 Saf 1.2 Op 7 CSS 2
Inherited: No

This is a shorthand property for setting the width, style, and/or color of all four edges of an outline around an element in one assignment statement. Properties that you don't explicitly set with this property assume their initial values.

An outline differs from a border in two primary ways. First, an outline does not occupy space in the CSS box model. Rather, the outline simply hovers atop the element, drawn just beyond the border rectangle. Second, CSS does not restrict an outline to be rectangular, allowing an outline to follow the irregular outline of an unjustified paragraph, for example. IE 5 for the Macintosh draws only rectangular outlines. For earlier versions of Mozilla, a full set of CSS2 outline properties is available with the -moz- prefix (e.g., -moz-outline-color), as well as further proprietary extensions for outline radius corners similar to the -moz-border-radius property.

CSS Syntax

outline: *border-color* || *border-style* || *outline-width*

Value	See the respective properties in the following sections.
Initial Value	None.
Example	`blockquote {outline: darkred ridge 5px}`
Applies To	All elements.

Object Model Reference

`[window.]document.getElementById("elementID").style.outline`

outline-color

IE *5(Mac)* NN *n/a* Moz *1.8.1* Saf *1.2* Op *7* CSS *2*

Inherited: No

Controls the color of an outline around an element.

CSS Syntax

`outline-color: color`

Value

A CSS color value. One value controls all sides of the outline. The CSS specification also calls for a constant called `invert`, which performs an algorithmic inversion of the background color, but this value is not supported in IE 5 Mac.

Initial Value

In IE 5 for Macintosh, `black`. The CSS2 specification suggests invert as a default.

Example

```
h2 {outline-color: salmon}
div {outline-color: rgb(0,0,255)}
```

Applies To	All elements.

Object Model Reference

`[window.]document.getElementById("elementID").style.outlineColor`

outline-offset

IE *n/a* NN *n/a* Moz *1.8.1* Saf *1.2* Op *n/a* CSS *3*

Inherited: No

Controls the distance beyond the element's border (equally in each direction) where the outline is drawn.

CSS Syntax

`outline-offset: length`

Value	A CSS length value. One value controls all sides of the outline.
Initial Value	0
Example	`h2 {outline-offset: 3px}`

Applies To   All elements.

Object Model Reference

[window.]document.getElementById("*elementID*").style.outlineOffset

outline-style   **IE** *5(Mac)* **NN** *n/a* **Moz** *1.8* **Saf** *1.2* **Op** *7* **CSS** *2*

Inherited: No

Controls the style of an outline around an element. These are the same edge designs as border styles.

CSS Syntax

outline-style: *borderStyle*

Value

Style values are constants that are associated with specific ways of rendering border lines. See border-style for a list and illustration. One value controls all sides of the outline.

Initial Value   none

Example

```
h2 {outline-style: solid}
div {outline-style: groove}
```

Applies To   All elements.

Object Model Reference

[window.]document.getElementById("*elementID*").style.outlineStyle

outline-width   **IE** *5(Mac)* **NN** *n/a* **Moz** *1.8.1* **Saf** *1.2* **Op** *7* **CSS** *2*

Inherited: No

Controls the thickness of an outline around an element. To prevent surrounding content from rendering under the outline, you should consider adding a margin around the element.

CSS Syntax

outline-width: thin | medium | thick | *length*

Value

Three constants—thin | medium | thick—allow the browser to define exactly how many pixels are used to show the outline. For more precision, you can also assign a length value (see the discussion of length values at the beginning of this chapter). One value controls all sides of the outline.

Initial Value   medium

Example

```
h1 {outline-style: ridge; outline-width: 5px}
div {outline-style: solid; outline-width: 2px}
```

Applies To   All elements.

Object Model Reference

```
[window.]document.getElementById("elementID").style.outlineWidth
```

overflow   IE 4   NN n/a   Moz all   Saf all   Op all   CSS 2

Inherited: No

Defines how the element treats content with rendered dimensions that exceed the specified height and/or width of the container. Except for some types of content that demand a fixed width (a pre element, for instance), the default behavior of an element is to respect the width property setting and handle the issue of overflow in the height of the element. Assigning the overflow property to the body element in an attempt to control the display of scroll bars is risky business for cross-browser compatibility. Test your overflow code thoroughly on IE for Windows (in quirks and standards-compatible modes).

A setting of visible causes the containing block to expand to allow the full width (if fixed) and height of the content to be displayed. If borders, margins, and padding are set for the element, they are preserved around the expanded content block. If the element has height and width specified, as well as a background image or color, and if the content extends beyond the specified size, the results vary with browser family. IE for Windows in quirks mode expands the height of the background to accommodate the content, pushing succeeding content downward to accommodate the overflowing content. Recent browsers and IE 7 in standards-compatibility mode constrain the background rectangle to the specified size, but the content bleeds beyond the rectangle, and overlaps content that comes after the overflowing element. Because this is the default value for the overflow style property, it is best to specify some other overflow value (or clipping rectangle for a positioned element) whenever you restrict the size of an element.

A setting of hidden forces the block to observe its height and width settings, potentially causing the content to be clipped by the size of the block. Borders and padding are preserved, but margins may be lost along the edges that clip the content. No scrollbars appear with this value.

A setting of scroll usually generates a set of horizontal and vertical scrollbars inside the rectangle of the content block, whether they're needed or not. The bars become active only if the content actually requires scrolling in any direction.

A setting of auto should generate scroll bars only if the content in the block requires it. In practice, browsers tend to add only a vertical scrollbar when the content is text that can adjust to the specified width of its container.

CSS Syntax

```
overflow: overFlowType
```

Value   Any of the following constants: auto | hidden | scroll | visible.

Initial Value   visible

Example

div.aside {position: absolute; top: 200px; left: 10px; height: 100px;
width: 150px; overflow: scroll}

Applies To   Block-level, replaced, and positioned elements.

Object Model Reference

[window.]document.getElementById("*elementID*").style.overflow

overflow-x, overflow-y

IE *5(Win)* NN *n/a* Moz *1.8* Saf *1.2* Op *all* CSS *n/a*

Inherited: No

Defines how the element treats content with rendered dimensions that exceed the specified width (x) or height (y) of the container. The operation of this property is the same as the regular overflow property, but each one operates along a single axis. This is particularly helpful if you want to have only a vertical or only a horizontal scrollbar appear with an element. See the overflow property discussion.

CSS Syntax

overflow-x: *overFlowType*
overflow-y: *overFlowType*

Value

Any of the following constants: auto | hidden | scroll | visible.

Initial Value   visible

Example   body {overflow-x: hidden; overflow-y: scroll}

Applies To   Block-level, replaced, and positioned elements.

Object Model Reference

[window.]document.getElementById("*elementID*").style.overflowX
[window.]document.getElementById("*elementID*").style.overflowY

padding

IE *4* NN *4* Moz *all* Saf *all* Op *all* CSS *1*

Inherited: No

This is a shortcut property that can set the padding widths of up to four edges of an element with one statement. Padding is space that extends around the content box of an element up to but not including any border that may be specified for the element. Padding picks up the background image or color of its element. As you add padding to an element, you increase the size of the visible rectangle of the element without affecting the content block size. You may supply one to four space-delimited padding values. The number of values determines which sides receive the assigned padding.

CSS Syntax

padding: *paddingThickness* {1,4}

Value

This property accepts one, two, three, or four values, depending on how many and which sides you want to assign padding to. Values for *paddingThickness* can be *lengths* or percentages of the next outermost element size. Value quantities and positions are interpreted as follows.

Number of values	Effect
1	All four padding edges set to value
2	Top and bottom padding set to the first value, right and left padding set to the second value
3	Top padding set to first value, right and left padding set to second value, bottom padding set to third value
4	Top, right, bottom, and left padding set, respectively

Initial Value	0; IE for Windows specifies a default value of 1 for td and th elements.
Example	p.highlight {padding: 10px 20px}

Applies To

All elements (IE 5 for Macintosh, IE 5.5 for Windows, and W3C browsers); body, caption, div, iframe, marquee, table, td, textarea, tr, and elements (IE 5 and earlier for Windows). CSS2.1 deletes support for tr, thead, tbody, tfoot, col, and colgroup elements.

Object Model Reference

[window.]document.getElementById("*elementID*").style.padding

padding-bottom, padding-left, padding-right, padding-top

IE 4 NN 4 Moz *all* Saf *all* Op *all* CSS 1

Inherited: No

All four properties set the padding width of a single side of an element. Padding is space that extends around the content box of an element up to but not including any border that may be specified for the element. Padding picks up the background image or color of its element. As you add padding to an element, you increase the size of the visible rectangle of the element without affecting the content block size.

CSS Syntax

padding-bottom: *paddingThickness*
padding-left: *paddingThickness*
padding-right: *paddingThickness*
padding-top: *paddingThickness*

CSS Reference

Value

Values for *paddingThickness* can be *lengths* or percentages of the next outermost container size.

Initial Value   0; IE for Windows specifies a default value of 1 for td and th elements.

Example

```
blockquote {padding-left: 20; padding-top: 10}
#narrowCol {padding-left: 30%; padding-right: 30%}
```

Applies To

All elements (IE 5 for Macintosh, IE 5.5 for Windows, and W3C browsers); body, caption, div, iframe, marquee, table, td, textarea, tr, and elements (IE 5 and earlier for Windows). CSS2.1 deletes support for tr, thead, tbody, tfoot, col, and colgroup elements.

Object Model Reference

```
[window.]document.getElementById("elementID").style.paddingBottom
[window.]document.getElementById("elementID").style.paddingLeft
[window.]document.getElementById("elementID").style.paddingRight
[window.]document.getElementById("elementID").style.paddingTop
```

page   IE 5*(Mac)* NN *n/a* Moz *n/a* Saf *n/a* Op *n/a* CSS 2

Inherited: No

Lets you connect a block-level element to an @page rule through an identifier assigned to the rule.

CSS Syntax

page: *pageRuleIdentifier* | auto

Value

The *pageRuleIdentifier* value is the name given to an @page rule in the same document.

Initial Value   auto

Example   table#results {page: printTable}

Applies To   Block-level elements.

Object Model Reference

```
[window.]document.getElementById("elementID").style.page
```

page-break-after, page-break-before

IE *4*   NN *n/a*   Moz *1.0.1*   Saf *all*   Op *all*   CSS *2*

Inherited: No

Defines how content should treat a page break around an element when the document is sent to a printer. Page breaks are not rendered in the visual browser as they may be in word processing programs; on screen, long content flows in one continuous scroll.

Proper handling of pages for printers relies on the CSS2 concept of the *page box*, which is a rectangular region that ultimately reaches a printed page. Page break style properties help the browser control the precise content of each page box. Without any assistance (or with the auto setting), the browser divides pages for printing much as it has in the past by doing a best-fit for the content to fill up as much of each page as there is space for it.

To force a page break above an element, associate a `page-break-before:` always style setting with the element. Similarly, to force a break after an element, use `page-break-after:` always. For example, if you want a special class of br elements to break after them, you could set up a class selector style rule as follows:

```
<style type="text/css">
br.pageEnd {display: block; page-break-after: always}
</style>
```

Then, whenever you want to force a page break in the document, include the following tag:

```
<br class="pageEnd">
```

Property settings for `left` and `right` assume that the browser is equipped to detect left-facing from right-facing pages for double-sided printing (as specified in CSS2). Because you are likely to set different margins for each side of the gutter, indicating how pages break to start a new section requires forcing sufficient page breaks to plant new sections on the desired page. For example, if you want each h1 element to begin on a right-facing page, you would set a page break style for it as follows:

```
h1 {page-break-before: right}
```

This property forces the browser to at least one and at most two page breaks before the h1 element to make sure it starts on a right-facing page. When the browser generates a second page break for the left or right value, it means that the browser generates a blank page box for the second page break.

Implementation of these properties is somewhat limited. Most modern browsers support `always` and `auto`, while Opera 9 correctly supports `right` and `left`.

CSS Syntax

```
page-break-after: breakType
page-break-before: breakType
```

Value

Four constant values: always | auto | left | right (but treats `left` and `right` the same as always). CSS2 adds avoid, which urges the browser to avoid breaking the page in that element if at all possible.

Initial Value   auto

Example	`div.titlePage {page-break-before: always; page-break-after: always}`
Applies To	Block-level elements.

Object Model Reference

`[window.]document.getElementById("elementID").style.pageBreakAfter`
`[window.]document.getElementById("elementID").style.pageBreakBefore`

page-break-inside
IE *n/a* NN *n/a* Moz *n/a* Saf *n/a* Op 7 CSS 2

Inherited: Yes

Defines whether a printed page break is allowed within an element. Especially useful to define a container of multiple block elements that you want to keep printed on the same page.

CSS Syntax

`page-break-inside: ` *breakType*

Value	One of two constant values: avoid | auto.
Initial Value	auto
Example	`div.together {page-break-inside: avoid}`
Applies To	Block-level elements.

pause
IE *n/a* NN *n/a* Moz *n/a* Saf *n/a* Op *n/a* CSS 2

Inherited: No

For aural style sheets, this is a shorthand property for setting both pause-after and pause-before properties in one statement. You may supply one or two values for this property.

CSS Syntax

`pause: ` *time* `| ` *percentage* ` {1,2}`

Value

This property accepts one or two values, depending on the values you want to assign to the pause-before and pause-after settings. A single value of the pause property is applied to both pause-before and pause-after. When two values are supplied, the first is assigned to pause-before; the second is assigned to pause-after.

Values for *time* are floating-point numbers followed by either the ms (milliseconds) or s (seconds) unit identifier. These settings are therefore absolute durations for pauses. Values for *percentage* are inversely proportional to the words-per-minute values of the speech-rate property setting. Because the speech-rate controls how long it takes for a single word (on average), a pause setting of 100% means that a pause has the same duration as a single word; a setting of 50% would be a pause of one-half the duration of speaking a single word.

Initial Value	Depends on the browser.
Applies To	All elements.

pause-after, pause-before

IE *n/a* NN *n/a* Moz *n/a* Saf *n/a* Op *n/a* CSS 2

Inherited: No

CSS Reference

For aural style sheets, these set the duration of a pause after or before the current element. You can assign both properties to the same element to designate pauses before and after the element is spoken.

CSS Syntax

```
pause-after: time | percentage
pause-before: time | percentage
```

Value

Values for *time* are floating-point numbers followed by either the ms (milliseconds) or s (seconds) unit identifier. These settings are therefore absolute durations for pauses. Values for *percentage* are inversely proportional to the words-per-minute values of the speech-rate property setting. Because the speech-rate controls how long it takes to speak a single word (on average), a pause setting of 100% means that a pause has the same duration as a single word; a setting of 50% would be a pause of one-half the duration of speaking a single word.

Initial Value	Depends on the browser.
Applies To	All elements.

pitch

IE *n/a* NN *n/a* Moz *n/a* Saf *n/a* Op *n/a* CSS 2

Inherited: No

For aural style sheets, this sets the average pitch frequency of the voice used for text-to-speech output.

CSS Syntax

```
pitch: frequency | frequencyConstant
```

Value

A *frequency* value is any positive floating-point number followed by either the Hz (Hertz) or kHz (kiloHertz) units, as in 500Hz or 5.5kHz. Alternatively, you can use any of the following constant values: x-low | low | medium | high | x-high. As of the CSS2 working draft available for this book, no specific frequency values had yet been assigned to these constants.

Initial Value	medium
Applies To	All elements.

pitch-range

IE *n/a* NN *n/a* Moz *n/a* Saf *n/a* Op *n/a* CSS 2

Inherited: No

For aural style sheets, this sets the range over which the average pitch frequency of a text-to-speech voice varies.

CSS Syntax

pitch-range: *number*

Value

Any positive number or zero. A value of 0 is a monotone voice; a value of 50 should offer a normal range; values above 50 might sound animated.

Initial Value   50

Applies To   All elements.

play-during

IE *n/a*   NN *n/a*   Moz *n/a*   Saf *n/a*   Op *n/a*   CSS 2

Inherited: No

For aural style sheets, this sets the sound-mixing properties of a background sound with a text-to-speech rendering of the element's content.

CSS Syntax

play-during: *uri* [mix | repeat] | auto | none

Value

The *uri* value is a link to the sound file to be used as background sound (if desired). Optionally, you can specify that the background sound of the parent element's play-during property is started and mixed with the current element's background sound. If the length of the background sound is shorter than it takes for the element's text to be spoken, the repeat constant tells the browser to repeat the sound until the spoken text has finished. A value of auto means that the parent element's sound continues to play without interruption. And a value of none means that no background sound (from the current or parent element) is heard for this element.

Initial Value   auto

Applies To   All elements.

position

IE *4*   NN *4*   Moz *all*   Saf *all*   Op *all*   CSS 2

Inherited: No

Sets whether the element is positionable, and if so, what type of positionable element it is. The two primary types of positionable elements are set with values relative and absolute, with a third type, fixed, applicable to only some browsers. See Chapter 5 for details and examples.

CSS Syntax

position: *positionConstant*

Value

Browsers and the CSS standard recognize different sets of constant values for this property, as shown in this table.

Value	IE/Windows	IE/Mac	NN	Others
absolute	4	4	4	all
fixed	7	5	6	all
relative	4	4	4	all
static	4	4	6	all

The static value is essentially an unpositioned element, one that flows in the normal rendering sequence of the body content. A fixed-position element is positioned relative to the window (viewport), and remains in its specified location even as the content scrolls underneath it.

Initial Value   static

Applies To   All elements.

Object Model Reference

[window.]document.getElementById("*elementID*").style.position

Notes

Navigator 4 treats elements that set the CSS position property in the following ways: an absolute-positioned element is turned into the same kind of element as that created as a layer element; a relative-positioned element is turned into the same kind of element as that created as an ilayer element. There are some subtle differences between the actual elements and the simulated version, resulting in more reliable behavior in Navigator 4 when the actual layer and ilayer elements were deployed.

quotes   IE *5(Mac)* NN *n/a* Moz *all* Saf *n/a* Op *all* CSS *2*

Inherited: Yes

Controls the characters to be generated for open and close quote symbols in text. The assumption is that the quote symbols are not part of the content, but are generated by the browser because of contextual clues (such as surrounding a quote with a q element). This property must be used with the content property, which, with the help of the :before and :after pseudo-classes, determines where the open-quote and end-quote symbols appear:

```
q {quotes: "«" "»" "'" "'"}
q:before {content: open-quote}
q:after {content: close-quote}
```

CSS Syntax

quotes: *openString closeString* [*nestedOpenString nestedCloseString*] | none

Value

One or two pairs of quoted symbols. The optional second pair defines the symbols used for a nested quote symbol. Entity characters are not permitted.

Initial Value   Depends on browser and system language.

Applies To   All elements.

Object Model Reference
[window.]document.getElementById("*elementID*").style.quotes

Notes
Support in browsers isn't as good as indicated above. IE 5 for the Macintosh doesn't genuinely respond to the quotes property, but does substitute standard two-level quotes for the content property. Mozilla implements only the first level of quotes. Symbol characters outside the ASCII set may not align with the characters you put into the source code with your text editor. Verify the results before deploying this property.

richness
IE n/a NN n/a Moz n/a Saf n/a Op n/a CSS 2

Inherited: Yes

For aural style sheets, this sets the brightness (stridency) of the voice used in text-to-speech rendering of the element.

CSS Syntax
richness: *number*

Value
A positive floating-point number to represent how strident the voice sounds. A value of 50 is normal. Lower values produce a softer, mellower voice; higher values produce a louder, more forceful voice.

| Initial Value | 50 |
| Applies To | All elements. |

right
IE 5 NN n/a Moz all Saf all Op all CSS 2

Inherited: No

For positionable elements, this defines the position of the right margin edge of an element box relative to the right edge of the next outermost block content container. When the element is relative-positioned, the offset is based on the right edge of the inline location of where the element would normally appear in the content.

CSS Syntax
right: *length* | *percentage* | auto

Value
See the discussion about length values at the beginning of this chapter. Negative lengths may be allowed in some contexts, but be sure to test the results on all browsers. You may also specify a percentage value, which is calculated based on the width of the next outermost container. Note, however, that the results you get may seem like the inverse of what you expect: a value of 0% means that the right edge is flush against the right edge of the positioning context, whereas a value of 100% could push the element completely out of view

to the left. The setting of auto lets the browser determine the right offset of the element box on its naturally flowing offset within the containing box.

Initial Value   auto

Applies To   Positioned elements.

Object Model Reference
[window.]document.getElementById("*elementID*").style.right

ruby-align   IE 5   NN *n/a*   Moz *n/a*   Saf *n/a*   Op *n/a*   CSS 3

Inherited: No

Controls alignment of content in a ruby element.

CSS Syntax
ruby-align: *alignType* | auto

Value
One of the following constants: auto | center | distribute-letter | distribute-space | left | line-edge | right. For more details on ruby-related styles, visit *http://www.w3.org/TR/css3-ruby*.

Initial Value   auto

Applies To
IE limits this style to ruby elements only, but the preliminary CSS3 specification suggests it can apply to any element that contains ruby text (and is thus inheritable in that context).

Object Model Reference
[window.]document.getElementById("*elementID*").style.rubyAlign

ruby-overhang   IE 5   NN *n/a*   Moz *n/a*   Saf *n/a*   Op *n/a*   CSS 3

Inherited: Yes

Controls text overhang characteristics of content in a ruby element.

CSS Syntax
ruby-overhang: *alignType* | auto

Value
One of the following constants: auto | none | whitespace. For more details on ruby-related styles, visit *http://www.w3.org/TR/css3-ruby*.

Initial Value   auto

Applies To
ruby elements (or any element that has its display property set to ruby-text).

Object Model Reference

[window.]document.getElementById("*elementID*").style.rubyOverhang

ruby-position

IE *5* NN *n/a* Moz *n/a* Saf *n/a* Op *n/a* CSS *3*

Inherited: Yes

Controls whether nested ruby (rt element) text renders on the same line or above its related ruby base (rb element) text.

CSS Syntax

ruby-position: *positionType*

Value

IE recognizes one of the following constants, above | inline, while the preliminary CSS3 specification prefers these constants: after | before | inline | right. For more details on ruby-related styles, visit *http://www.w3.org/TR/css3-ruby*.

Initial Value   above (IE); before (CSS3).

Applies To

ruby elements (or any element that has its display property set to ruby-text).

Object Model Reference

[window.]document.getElementById("*elementID*").style.rubyPosition

scrollbar-3dlight-color, scrollbar-arrow-color, scrollbar-base-color, scrollbar-darkshadow-color, scrollbar-face-color, scrollbar-highlight-color, scrollbar-shadow-color, scrollbar-track-color

IE *5.5* NN *n/a* Moz *n/a* Saf *n/a* Op *n/a* CSS *n/a*

Inherited: No

Controls the colors for specific components of a scrollbar user interface element associated with scrollable elements. The following table describes which pieces of a scroll bar are controlled by each property.

Property	Description
scrollbar-3dlight-color	Top and left edges of the scroll slider and arrow button boxes
scrollbar-arrow-color	Arrows inside arrow button boxes
scrollbar-base-color	Overall hue of the scroll bar
scrollbar-darkshadow-color	Right and bottom edges of the scroll slider and arrow button boxes
scrollbar-face-color	Forward flat surfaces (e.g., front-facing panel of slider) and alternating pixels of the track
scrollbar-highlight-color	Normally white pixels that create 3D effects, plus alternating pixels of the track

Property	Description
scrollbar-shadow-color	Slighlty thicker edges controlled by scrollbar-darkshadow-color
scrollbar-track-color	Entire track, as solid version of specified color

You can experiment with combinations of multiple scroll bar pieces and colors.

CSS Syntax

```
scrollbar-3dlight-color: color
scrollbar-arrow-color: color
scrollbar-base-color: color
scrollbar-darkshadow-color: color
scrollbar-face-color: color
scrollbar-highlight-color: color
scrollbar-shadow-color: color
scrollbar-track-color: color
```

Value   CSS color values.

Initial Value   Varies with user Display control panel settings.

Example   textarea {scrollbar-face-color: lightyellow}

Applies To   applet, bdo, body, custom, div, embed, object, and textarea elements.

Object Model Reference

```
[window.]document.getElementById("elementID").style.scrollbar3dLightColor
[window.]document.getElementById("elementID").style.scrollbarArrowColor
[window.]document.getElementById("elementID").style.scrollbarBaseColor
[window.]document.getElementById("elementID").style.scrollbarDarkShadowColor
[window.]document.getElementById("elementID").style.scrollbarFaceColor
[window.]document.getElementById("elementID").style.scrollbarHighlightColor
[window.]document.getElementById("elementID").style.scrollbarShadowColor
[window.]document.getElementById("elementID").style.scrollbarTrackColor
```

size

IE *n/a* NN *n/a* Moz *n/a* Saf *n/a* Op *all* CSS *2*

Inherited: n/a

Sets the size and/or orientation of a page box. Intended primarily for printed page formatting, the settings may not affect how content is cropped or oriented on the video screen. This property is set within an @page declaration.

CSS Syntax

```
size: [length {1,2}] auto | portrait | landscape
```

Value

If you specify one or two *length* values, the page box becomes absolute regardless of the paper sheet size; without specific *length* values, the page box is sized relative to the selected paper sheet size. If you supply only one length value, it is applied to both the width and height of the page box; if there are two values, the first controls the page box width and the second controls the page box height. Bear in mind that printers frequently impose a minimum margin around the rendered page box. Even when the size property is set to auto, you can add more breathing space around the page box by adding a margin property to the @page declaration.

Initial Value	auto
Example	@page{size: landscape}
Applies To	Page context.

speak

For aural style sheets, this specifies whether a browser equipped for text-to-speech should speak the element's content, and if so, whether the speech should be as words or spelled out character-by-character.

CSS Syntax

speak: *speechType*

Value

Three possible constant values: none | normal | spell-out. A value of none means that speech is turned off. The browser does not delay over the duration of the speech and any specified pauses (see the volume: silent property value). A value of normal turns on speech and reads the text as words. A value of spell-out turns on speech and reads the content letter-by-letter (certainly applicable to abbr and acronym elements).

Initial Value	normal
Applies To	All elements.

speak-header

For text-to-speech-capable browsers, this specifies whether the browser calls out the name of a table cell's header prior to the cell's value every time that value is read aloud or just one time for all adjacently read cells that share the same header (e.g., navigating downward through a table column).

CSS Syntax

speak-header: *headerFrequency*

Value	Two possible constant values: once	always.
Initial Value	once
Applies To	th elements.

speak-numeral

IE *n/a*   NN *n/a*   Moz *n/a*   Saf *n/a*   Op *n/a*   CSS 2

Inherited: Yes

For aural style sheets, this sets whether numbers are to be read as individual numerals ("one four two") or as full numbers (e.g., "One hundred forty-two"). The language used for the spoken numbers is set with the element's lang property.

CSS Syntax

speak-numeral: *numeralType*

Value	Two possible constant values: digits	continuous.
Initial Value	continuous
Applies To	All elements.

speak-punctuation

IE *n/a*   NN *n/a*   Moz *n/a*   Saf *n/a*   Op *n/a*   CSS 2

Inherited: Yes

For aural style sheets, this sets whether punctuation symbols should be read aloud ("period") or interpreted as the language's natural pauses for the various symbols.

CSS Syntax

speak-punctuation: *punctuationType*

Value

Two possible constant values: code | none. A value of code means that a symbol name is spoken when the symbol is encountered in element text.

Initial Value	none
Applies To	All elements.

speech-rate

IE *n/a*   NN *n/a*   Moz *n/a*   Saf *n/a*   Op *n/a*   CSS 2

Inherited: Yes

For aural style sheets, this sets the number of words per minute of the text-to-speech output.

CSS Syntax

speech-rate: *wordsPerSecond* | *speedConstant*

Value

A *wordsPerSecond* value is any positive floating-point number with no unit appended. Alternatively, you can use any of the following constant values.

Value	Meaning
x-slow	80 words per minute
slow	120 words per minute

Value	Meaning
medium	180-200 words per minute
fast	300 words per minute
x-fast	500 words per minute
slower	Current rate minus 40 words per minute
faster	Current rate plus 40 words per minute

Initial Value   medium

Applies To   All elements.

stress
IE *n/a* NN *n/a* Moz *n/a* Saf *n/a* Op *n/a* CSS 2

Inherited: Yes

For aural style sheets, this sets the amount of stress (inflection) in the spoken voice.

CSS Syntax

stress: *stressLevel*

Value

A *stressLevel* value is any positive floating-point number with no unit appended. A value of 50 is normal.

Initial Value   50

Applies To   All elements.

table-layout
IE *5(Win)* NN *n/a* Moz *1.0.1* Saf *all* Op *7* CSS 2

Inherited: No

Determines whether the browser uses computed heights and widths of the entire table's data to begin rendering the table or relies on the table element's size properties and uses the first row's cell widths to begin rendering table content. When the property is set to auto, the browser must load all of the table cells and their content before the first row of data can be rendered, causing a brief (but perhaps imperceptible) delay in drawing the table. Setting the value to fixed allows table rendering to begin sooner, which is helpful for large tables. If content in succeeding rows is wider than the fixed column size, the content is usually clipped unless you set the overflow style property to visible (but that will likely make a visual jumble in adjacent cells).

CSS Syntax

table-layout: *layoutType*

Value   Two possible constant values: auto | fixed.

Initial Value   auto

Applies To   table elements.

text-align

Determines the horizontal alignment of text within an element. This property is inherited, so it can be set for a container to impact all nested elements, such as a p element within a div element. Values of center, left, and right are supported across the board. The value of justify is not a CSS requirement, but it works in IE 5 or later and other mainstream browsers.

CSS Syntax
text-align: *alignment*

Value One of the four constants: center | justify | left | right.

Initial Value Depends on browser language.

Example
```
p.rightHand {text-align: right}
blockquote {text-align: justify}
```

Applies To
Block-level elements, but right-alignment also works in text-type input and textarea elements in IE 5 and later for Windows, Mozilla, Safari, and Opera.

Object Model Reference
[window.]document.getElementById("*elementID*").style.textAlign

text-align-last

Controls the horizontal alignment of the last line of text within an element's box.

CSS Syntax
text-align-last: *alignment*

Value
One of the following constants: auto | center | justify | left | right. The value of auto picks up the inherited text-align property.

Initial Value auto

Example blockquote {text-align-last: center}

Applies To Block-level elements.

Object Model Reference
[window.]document.getElementById("*elementID*").style.textAlignLast

text-autospace

IE *5(Win)* NN *n/a* Moz *n/a* Saf *n/a* Op *n/a* CSS *n/a*

Inherited: No

Controls the spacing between ideographic (typically Asian languages) and nonideographic characters.

CSS Syntax

text-autospace: *spacingType*

Value

One of the following constants: ideograph-alpha | ideograph-numeric | ideograph-parenthesis | ideograph-space | none.

Initial Value	none
Example	div {text-autospace: ideograph-numeric}
Applies To	All elements.

Object Model Reference

[window.]document.getElementById("*elementID*").style.textAutospace

text-decoration

IE *4* NN *4* Moz *all* Saf *all* Op *all* CSS *1*

Inherited: No

Specifies additions to the text content of the element in the form of underlines, strikethroughs, overlines, and (in Navigator and CSS) blinking. You may specify more than one decoration style by supplying values in a space-delimited list. Thankfully, mainstream browsers ignore the blink setting. Navigator 4 does not recognize the overline decoration.

Text decoration has an unusual parent-child relationship. Values are not inherited, but the effect of a decoration carries over to nested items. Therefore, unless otherwise overridden, an underlined p element underlines a nested span element within, for example.

CSS Syntax

text-decoration: *decorationStyle* | none

Value

In addition to none, any of the following four constants: blink | line-through | overline | underline, but Mozilla ignores blink.

Initial Value	none
Example	div.highlight {text-decoration: underline}
Applies To	All elements.

Object Model Reference

[window.]document.getElementById("*elementID*").style.textDecoration
[window.]document.getElementById("*elementID*").style.textDecorationBlink
[window.]document.getElementById("*elementID*").style.textDecorationLineThrough
[window.]document.getElementById("*elementID*").style.textDecorationNone

```
[window.]document.getElementById("elementID").style.textDecorationOverLine
[window.]document.getElementById("elementID").style.textDecorationUnderline
```

text-indent

IE *4*　**NN** *4*　**Moz** *all*　**Saf** *all*　**Op** *all*　**CSS** *1*

Inherited: Yes

Sets the size of indenting of the first line of a block of inline text (such as a p element). Only the first line is affected by this setting. A negative value can be used to outdent the first line, but be sure the text does not run beyond the left edge of the browser window or frame.

CSS Syntax

text-indent: *length* | *percentage*

Value

See the discussion about length values at the beginning of this chapter. Negative lengths may be allowed in some contexts, but be sure to test the results on all browsers. You may also specify a percentage value, which is calculated based on the width of the next outermost container.

Initial Value　　0

Example

```
body {text-indent: 2em}
p.firstGraphs {text-indent: 0}
```

Applies To　　　Block-level elements.

Object Model Reference

[window.]document.getElementById("*elementID*").style.textIndent

text-justify

IE *5*　**NN** *n/a*　**Moz** *n/a*　**Saf** *n/a*　**Op** *n/a*　**CSS** *n/a*

Inherited: Yes

Controls detailed character distribution techniques for any block-level element that has its text-align CSS property set to justify. This property is designed primarily for Asian or other non-Latin languages.

CSS Syntax

text-justify: *justificationType*

Value

One of the constants shown in the following table.

Value	Meaning
auto	Lets browser choose best type
distribute	Similar to newspaper but optimized for Asian languages
distribute-all-lines	Justifies lines, including the last line, leading to potentially very wide word spacing

Value	Meaning
distribute-center-last	Justifies lines but centers the last line (not implemented)
inter-cluster	Justifies lines lacking word spacing
inter-ideograph	Justifies lines consisting of ideographs
inter-word	Justifies lines by distributing padded space between words (common for Latin languages)
kashida	Justifies Arabic script through elongated strokes (IE 5.5 or later required)
newspaper	Justifies lines by distributing padded space between words and between characters

Initial Value   0

Example   div#col1 {text-align: justify; text-justify: newspaper}

Applies To   Block-level elements.

Object Model Reference
[window.]document.getElementById("*elementID*").style.textJustify

text-kashida-space

IE *5.5* NN *n/a* Moz *n/a* Saf *n/a* Op *n/a* CSS *n/a*

Inherited: Yes

For Arabic text in a block-level element with text alignment style set to justify, controls the ratio of kashida expansion to whitespace expansion.

CSS Syntax
text-kashida-space: *length | percentage*

Value
See the discussion about length values at the beginning of this chapter. You may also specify a percentage value, which is calculated based on the width of the next outermost container.

Initial Value   0%

Example
div#col1 {text-align: justify; text-justify: newspaper; text-kashida-space: 5%}

Applies To   Block-level elements.

Object Model Reference
[window.]document.getElementById("*elementID*").style.textKashidaSpace

text-overflow

IE *6* NN *n/a* Moz *n/a* Saf *1.3/2* Op *(see text)* CSS *n/a*

Inherited: No

Controls whether text content that overflows a fixed box space should display an ellipsis (. . .) at the end of the line to indicate more text is available. The element should also have its overflow style property set to hidden. Opera 9 implements a proprietary version of this property: -o-text-overflow.

CSS Syntax

text-overflow: *overflowType*

Value	One of two constants: clip	ellipsis.
Initial Value	clip
Example	td {overflow: hidden; white-space: nowrap; text-overflow: ellipsis}
Applies To	Block-level elements.

Object Model Reference

[window.]document.getElementById("*elementID*").style.textOverflow

text-shadow

Sets shadow effects for the text of the current element. A text element can have more than one shadow, and each shadow can have its own color, vertical offset, horizontal offset, and blur radius. Each shadow exists in its own minilayer, stacked with the first shadow specification at the bottom of the heap. Values for each shadow are space-delimited, and multiple shadow value sets are comma-delimited.

CSS Syntax

text-shadow: [*color*] *horizLength vertLength blurRadiusLength*,
  [[*color*] *horizLength vertLength blurRadiusLength*] | none

Value

If you omit the *color* property value, the shadow uses the element's color property value (which may, itself, be inherited). The *color* property can be placed before or after whatever length values are set for a shadow. See the discussion of color values at the beginning of this chapter. Values for *horizLength* and *vertLength* are length values (see the beginning of this chapter), and their sign indicates the direction the shadow offset takes from the element text. For the *horizLength* value, a positive value places the shadow to the right of the element; a negative value to the left. For the *vertLength* value, a positive value places the shadow below the text; a negative value places it above. A blur radius is a length value (see the beginning of this chapter) that specifies the extent of the shadow from the edge of the text characters.

Initial Value	none
Applies To	All elements.

text-transform

IE *4* NN *4* Moz *all* Saf *all* Op *all* CSS *1*

Inherited: Yes

Controls the capitalization of the element's text. When a value other than none is assigned to this property, the cases of all letters in the source text are arranged by the style sheet, overriding the case of the source text characters.

CSS Syntax

```
text-transform: caseType | none
```

Value

A value of none allows the case of the source text to be rendered as-is. Other available constant values are capitalize | lowercase | uppercase. A value of capitalize sets the first character of every word to uppercase. The values lowercase and uppercase render all characters of the element text in their respective cases.

Initial Value   none

Example   h2 {text-transform: capitalize}

Applies To   All elements.

Object Model Reference

```
[window.]document.getElementById("elementID").style.textTransform
```

text-underline-position

IE *5.5* NN *n/a* Moz *n/a* Saf *n/a* Op *n/a* CSS *n/a*

Inherited: No

Controls whether an underline (i.e., an element with a text-decoration style set to underline) is rendered above or below the text. Applicable primarily to Asian languages rendered in vertical columns.

CSS Syntax

```
text-underline-position: positionType | none
```

Value

IE 5.5 recognizes two constant values: above | below. IE 6 adds the values auto and auto-pos (which appear to do the same thing). The default value also changed between versions, from below to auto. In IE 6, the auto value underlines vertical Japanese text "above" (to the right) of the characters.

Initial Value   none

Example   h2 {text-underline-position: above}

Applies To   All elements.

Object Model Reference

```
[window.]document.getElementById("elementID").style.textUnderlinePosition
```

top

IE *4* NN *4* Moz *all* Saf *all* Op *all* CSS *2*

Inherited: No

For positioned elements, this defines the position of the top margin edge of an element relative to the top edge of the next outermost block content container.

CSS Syntax

top: *length* | *percentage* | auto

Value

See the discussion about length values at the beginning of this chapter. Negative lengths may be allowed in some contexts, but be sure to test the results on all browsers. You may also specify a percentage value, which is calculated based on the height of the next outermost container. The setting of auto lets the browser determine the top offset of the element box on its naturally flowing offset within the containing box.

Initial Value   auto

Example

```
h1 {position: relative; top:2em}
#logo {position: absolute; left:80px; top:30px}
```

Applies To   Positioned elements.

Object Model Reference

[window.]document.getElementById("*elementID*").style.top

unicode-bidi

IE *5* NN *n/a* Moz *all* Saf *all* Op *8* CSS *2*

Inherited: No

Controls the embedding of bidirectional text (such as a mixture of German and Arabic), in concert with the direction style property.

CSS Syntax

unicode-bidi: *embeddingType*

Value   One of the following constant values: bidi-override | embed | normal.

Initial Value   normal

Example   div.multiLingual {unicode-bidi: embed}

Applies To   All elements.

Object Model Reference

[window.]document.getElementById("*elementID*").style.unicodeBidi

vertical-align

IE *4*   NN *n/a*   Moz *all*   Saf *1.2*   Op *all*   CSS *1*

Inherited: No

There are two sets of values for this property, and they affect different characteristics of the inline element to which they are applied. The major point of reference is that an inline element has its own line box to hold its content. Two values, top and bottom, affect how the text is rendered within the line box. The settings bring the text flush with the top or bottom of the box, respectively.

Application of this property is not limited to inline spans of text. Images and tables can use this style property. All other settings for vertical-align affect how the entire element box is vertically positioned relative to text content of the parent element. The default value, baseline, means that the line box is positioned such that the baselines of both the line box's text (or very bottom of an element such as an img) and the parent text are even. That's how an em element can be its own line box element but still look as though it flows on the same baseline as its containing p element. The rest of the property's constant values (and percentage or length) determine where the element's line box is set with respect to the parent line. A positive percentage or length value positions the element the stated distance above the baseline; a negative value positions the element below the baseline. Percentages are calculated with respect to the line height.

CSS Syntax

vertical-align: *vertAlignType* | *length* | *percentage*

Value

Two constant values apply to alignment of text within the element itself: bottom | top.

Six constant values apply to alignment of the element's line box relative to the surrounding text line (of the parent element): baseline | middle | sub | super | text-bottom | text-top. A value of baseline keeps the baseline of the element and parent element line even. A value of middle aligns the vertical midpoint of the element with the baseline plus one-half the x-height of the parent element's font. Values of sub and super shift the element into position for subscript and superscript but do not by themselves create a true subscript or superscript in that no adjustment to the font size is made with this property. A value of text-bottom aligns the bottom of the element with the bottom of the font line of the parent element text; a value of text-top does the same with the tops of the element and parent.

Initial Value   baseline

Example   span.sup {vertical-align: super; font-size: smaller}

Applies To   Inline elements only.

Object Model Reference

[window.]document.getElementById("*elementID*").style.verticalAlign

visibility

Controls whether the element is rendered on the page. An element hidden via the visibility property preserves space in the document where the element normally appears. If you prefer surrounding content to cinch up the space left by a hidden element, see the display property. The CSS specification suggests that the value of collapse, when applied to table row-related elements, should cinch up the table, but no mainstream browser does that (Mozilla 1.8, Safari 2, and Opera 9 simply hide the row, leaving a blank row space).

The visibility property is inherited when its value is set to inherit. This setting means that if the parent is hidden, the child is also hidden. But, by setting the child's visibility property to visible, you can still keep the parent hidden while showing the child independently.

CSS Syntax

visibility: *visibilityType*

Value

One of the constant values: collapse | hidden | inherit | visible. IE for Windows does not recognize the collapse value. Navigator 4 allows visibility control only of positioned elements.

Initial Value	visible
Example	#congrats {visibility: hidden}
Applies To	All elements.

Object Model Reference

[window.]document.getElementById("*elementID*").style.visibility

voice-family

For aural style sheets, this sets the voice family names the aural browser should try to use for speaking the content. Multiple, comma-delimited values are accepted. This feature is analogous to the font-family setting for visual browsers.

CSS Syntax

voice-family: *voiceFamilyName* [, *voiceFamilyName* [, ...]]

Value

A *voiceFamilyName* may be the identifier for a voice type provided by the aural browser or a generic voice name (yet to be determined by the W3C). As with font-family settings, you should specify multiple voice types, starting with the more specific and ending with the most generic for the type of speech you want for the element's content.

Initial Value	Depends on browser.
Applies To	All elements.

volume

IE *n/a*   NN *n/a*   Moz *n/a*   Saf *n/a*   Op *n/a*   CSS 2

Inherited: No

For aural style sheets, this sets the dynamic range (softness/loudness) of the spoken element. Because normal speech has inflections that prevent an absolute volume to apply at all times, the volume property sets the median volume.

CSS Syntax

volume: *number* | *percentage* | *volumeConstant*

Value

A volume *number* value is any number. A value of zero should represent the minimum audible level for the equipment and ambient noise environment; a value of 100 should represent the maximum comfortable level under the same conditions. A *percentage* value is calculated relative to the parent element's volume property setting. Alternative settings include the following constants (and their representative values): silent (no sound) | x-soft (0) | soft (25) | medium (50) | loud (75) | x-loud (100).

Initial Value   medium

Applies To   All elements.

white-space

IE *5(Mac)/5.5(Win)*   NN *4*   Moz *all*   Saf *all*   Op *all*   CSS 1

Inherited: Yes

Sets how the browser should render whitespace (extra character spaces and carriage returns) that is part of the element's source code. Under normal circumstances, HTML ignores extra whitespace and thus collapses the rendered content around such space. For example, only single spaces are preserved between words, and br elements are required to force a line break within a paragraph. A whitespace property setting of pre treats whitespace as if you had surrounded the element in a pre element. Although browsers have a tradition of rendering pre elements in a monospace font, the look of an ordinary element set to white-space: pre preserves its font characteristics.

CSS Syntax

white-space: *whiteSpaceType*

Value

One of five constants: normal | nowrap | pre | pre-line | pre-wrap (the last two are extensions to the pre value, new to CSS2.1) A value of normal allows regular HTML treatment of whitespace to rule. A value of nowrap (not available in Navigator 4) tells the browser to ignore line breaks in the source text (in case the author breaks up lines for readability in the editor) and break them on the page only where there are explicit HTML line breaks (with a br element, for example). A value of pre has the browser honor all whitespace entered by the author in the source content, without adjusting any font settings of the element.

Initial Value

normal

Example

`div.example {white-space: pre}`

Applies To

All elements.

widows

IE *5(Mac)* NN *6* Moz *n/a* Saf *n/a* Op *7* CSS *2*

Inherited: Yes

Sets the minimum number of lines of a paragraph that must be visible at the top of a page after a page break occurs. See the orphans property for lines to be displayed at the bottom of a page before a page break.

CSS Syntax

widows: *lineCount*

Value	An integer of the number of lines.
Initial Value	2
Applies To	Block-level elements.

width

IE *4* NN *4* Moz *all* Saf *all* Op *all* CSS *1*

Inherited: No

Sets the width of a block-level, replaced, and positioned element's content width (exclusive of borders, padding, and margins).

IE for Windows counts left and right margins, padding, and borders when calculating the width of an element until you reach IE 6 in standards compatibility mode (see the DOCTYPE element in Chapter 1). When observing the CSS standards, the width applies to only the content portion of an element, irrespective of borders, padding, or margins.

CSS Syntax

width: *length* | *percentage* | auto

Value

See the discussion about length values at the beginning of this chapter. The setting of auto lets the browser determine the width of the element box based on the amount of space required to display the content within the current window width.

Initial Value   auto

Example

```
div#announce {position: relative; left: 30; width: 240}
textarea {width: 80%}
```

Applies To

Navigator 4, all absolute-positioned elements; Internet Explorer 4, applet, div, embed, fieldset, hr, iframe, img, input, marquee, object, span, table, and textarea elements; Internet Explorer 5, Mozilla, Safari, and Opera, all elements except nonreplaced inline elements, table column elements, and column group elements.

Object Model Reference

[window.]document.getElementById("elementID").style.width

word-break

IE *5(Win)* NN *n/a* Moz *all* Saf *all* Op *all* CSS *n/a*

Inherited: No

Controls the word-break style for ideographic languages or content that mixes Latin and ideographic languages.

CSS Syntax

word-break: *breakType*

Value	One of the following constant values: break-all | keep-all | normal.
Initial Value	normal
Example	div {word-break: keep-all}
Applies To	Block-level and table-related elements.

Object Model Reference

[window.]document.getElementById("elementID").style.wordBreak

word-spacing

IE *4(Mac)/6(Win)* NN *n/a* Moz *all* Saf *all* Op *all* CSS *1*

Inherited: Yes

Sets the spacing between words when the text is not under external word-spacing constraints (e.g., an align property set to justify). IE 5 for Macintosh may exhibit overlap problems with the word-spacing of elements nested inside the one being controlled.

CSS Syntax

word-spacing: *length* \| normal

Value

A value of normal lets the browser handle word spacing according to its rendering calculations. See the discussion about length values at the beginning of this chapter.

Initial Value	normal
Applies To	All elements.

Object Model Reference

[window.]document.getElementById("elementID").style.wordSpacing

word-wrap

Specifies word-wrapping style for block-level, specifically-sized inline, or positioned elements. If a single word (i.e., without any whitespace) extends beyond the width of the element containing box, the normal behavior is to extend the content beyond the normal box width, without breaking. But with the value of break-word, you can force the long word to break at whatever character position occurs at the edge of the box.

CSS Syntax
word-wrap: *wrapStyle*

Value   One of the constant values: break-word | normal.

Initial Value normal

Applies To   Block-level, sized inline, and positioned elements.

Object Model Reference
[window.]document.getElementById("*elementID*").style.wordWrap

writing-mode

Intended primarily for languages that display characters in vertical sentences, this controls the progression of content, left-to-right, or right-to-left.

CSS Syntax
writing-mode: *direction*

Value
One of the constant values: lr-tb | tb-rl. Value of tb-rl can rotate text of some languages by 90 degrees.

Initial Value lr-tb

Applies To   All elements.

Object Model Reference
[window.]document.getElementById("*elementID*").style.writingMode

z-index

For a positioned element, this sets the stacking order relative to other elements within the same parent container. See Online Section V for details on relationships of element layering amid multiple containers.

CSS Syntax

z-index: *integer* | auto

Value

Any integer value. A value of auto is the same as a value of zero. When all elements in the same parent container have the same z-index value, the stacking order is determined by element source code order.

Initial Value	auto
Example	div#instrux {position: absolute; left: 50; top: 70; z-index: 2}
Applies To	Positioned elements.

Object Model Reference

[window.]document.getElementById("*elementID*").style.zIndex

Notes

Rendering mechanisms in many browsers and versions generate form controls (buttons, text boxes, and especially select elements) in such a way that they always render in front of a positioned element, regardless of z-index property setting. This means that a positioned element may find a form control from the regular content flow sticking out in front of the positioned element, such as a drop-down menu. There is no workaround for this, other than to set the visibility of the form controls (or its form container) to hidden while the positioned element is visible. IE 7 fixes this problem.

zoom

IE *5.5* NN *n/a* Moz *n/a* Saf *n/a* Op *n/a* CSS *n/a*

Inherited: No

Controls the magnification of rendered content. This is particularly useful for output that might be displayed on monitors with very high pixel density. See screen.logicalXDPI property in Chapter 2.

CSS Syntax

zoom: *scale* | *percentage* | normal

Value

Magnification can be denoted as a floating-point number, a scaling factor (1.0 is normal), or a percentage (100% is normal).

Initial Value	normal
Example	body {zoom: 200%}
Applies To	All elements.

Object Model Reference

[window.]document.getElementById("*elementID*").style.zoom

JavaScript Core Language Reference

The previous chapters in the reference part of the book have covered every aspect of Dynamic HTML authoring that affects elements, objects, and styles—the pieces that are often visible on the page. The one part yet to be covered is the scripting glue that makes it possible to access and control the items detailed up to this point—the "D" of DHTML. This chapter covers the core scripting language features that apply to cross-browser application development. This means that VBScript, ActiveX controls, and Java classes accessible through LiveConnect are intentionally omitted here in favor of the core language that is widely deployed in every scriptable browser.

As described in Online Section I, the JavaScript language was a Netscape invention. Microsoft's version of the language is called JScript. But a browser-neutral version of the language has been approved as a common denominator standard for all JavaScript-derived languages: ECMAScript. There is a great deal of agreement in the implementation of the core elements of this scripting language among browser makers and the ECMA standards group. The biggest challenge for writing core language code (i.e., code that is independent of the scriptable document object model) is knowing what version of the language is supported by which versions of the browser. In the entries for this chapter, you can see at a glance which browser version first supported each core language object, property, method, function, operator, and control statement.

With the increased usage of the type attribute of script elements (over the original language attribute), the JavaScript version is of less importance these days than whether a particular browser supports an object, property, or method. Object detection techniques are much preferred over filtering scripts by JavaScript version number (which is possible via the language attribute). Therefore, JavaScript version numbers are not listed in this chapter for individual items.

About Static Objects

Unlike the heavily object-oriented Java language, there is little of the traditional object-oriented vernacular in the object-based JavaScript language. As a result, scripters tend not to think in terms of static objects and object instantiation. But some of that does take place behind the scenes.

Some core language objects act as though they are true static objects. The Math object is a good example; it contains a number of properties and methods that scripts use without ever having to peel off an instance of that object to do some math.

In contrast, the Date object is a static object that generates an instance of itself each time someone creates a new date:

```
var now = new Date( );
```

In this example, the now variable is an instance of the Date object—a snapshot of the object frozen in time. That instance provides access to many methods that let scripts get pieces of date and time, as well as set new values to those pieces. The methods actually live in the static object, but you access them through the instance that holds a value that can be influenced by those methods (yes, these methods are inherited, but JavaScript doesn't use this term much). Only on rare occasions do scripts ever need to look directly at the static Date object for other kinds of assistance (such as the UTC( ) method).

Most objects are either all static (Math) or completely suppress themselves from the scene once you create instances you work with (Object, Array, Number). Only a few objects operate in both modes, depending on whether you need the data of an instance of the object or one of the static properties or methods. You've seen how the Date object performs double duty. The RegExp object also performs this double duty; a regular expression instance object is created for you when you execute a related method. At the same time, you can access static objects (such as String and Array) to modify their basic behavior by assigning new properties and methods to their prototype (via the prototype property). New instances of such modified objects inherit the new properties or methods assigned to the prototype.

Mozilla Get and Set Methods

In anticipation of future ECMA adoption of a new language feature, Mozilla-based browsers provide a mechanism for defining functions that perform the acts of reading (getting) and writing (setting) custom properties of objects, and attaching those functions to objects. To prevent collision with the eventual standardized syntax, the Mozilla version utilizes a special double-double underscore syntax (i.e., two underscore characters on each side of the method name) for two methods of any object's prototype property:

```
objectName.prototype._ _defineGetter_ _("propertyName",
functionReference);objectName.prototype._ _defineSetter_ _("propertyName",
functionReference);
```

The reason this mechanism is different from simply assigning a custom prototype property is that the actions required to get or set a property value may require multiple script statements—handled by the function referenced in the prototype methods.

To demonstrate this facility, the following examples operate on a DOM object (but any object you can reference with JavaScript will do) to provide an innerText property for all HTML element objects. The W3C DOM doesn't offer this property, but you can add it to all elements in the page by having these method statements in the page's scripts. The functions defined here are anonymous functions (for compactness), but any function reference will suffice. In a cross-browser application, these statements would have to be protected so that they run only when the HTMLElement is referenceable and the _ _defineGetter_ _() or _ _defineSetter_ _() method is implemented (all verifiable through object detection):

```
HTMLElement.prototype._ _defineGetter_ _("innerText", function () {
    var rng = document.createRange();
    rng.selectNode(this);
    return rng.toString();
});
HTMLElement.prototype._ _defineSetter_ _("innerText", function(newTxt) {
    var rng = document.createRange();
    rng.selectNodeContents(this);
    rng.deleteContents();
    this.appendChild(document.createTextNode(newTxt));
    return newTxt;
});
```

Whenever a script statement attempts to read the innerText property of an element, the function associated with the _ _defineGetter_ _() method is executed, returning the desired value. Conversely, whenever a value is assigned to the innerText property of an element, the _ _defineSetter_ _() method's function runs.

ECMAScript for XML (E4X)

While the ECMAScript standard (ECMA-262) has been quite stable for some time, it is not standing still. A separate document, ECMA-257, extends the language with new native objects that facilitate creating and manipulating XML data. The shorthand name for this new ECMAScript for XML standard is E4X. In a way, it bridges JavaScript and the W3C DOM because the concepts of elements, attributes, child nodes, and the like are integral parts of the E4X scene. But E4X is also a natural extension to JavaScript in that XML is just another data type (albeit with some powerful methods and constructors).

The obvious outlet for E4X extensions is in AJAX applications, where the new objects facilitate, for example, obtaining an XML document's element data without the otherwise cumbersome DOM node tree parsing. Similarly, when the server side of an AJAX application needs to receive data in XML form from the client (notably in SOAP applications), E4X objects simplify the creation of XML content for transmission as data posted via an XMLHttpRequest object instance.

The E4X standard uses the term "property" to refer to what a DOM scripter considers to be an element or group of elements. That's partly because E4X syntax references elements via ECMAScript property syntax. Discussions in this chapter on the subject, however, tend to stick with calling an element an element to be consistent with the way DOM scripters are accustomed to thinking about those pieces of data.

Much of the development work of the E4X standard was spurred by the Mozilla Foundation. It's not surprising, therefore, that Mozilla-based browsers 1.8 and later would be the first ones to support E4X features. A few E4X constructs will cause script errors in browsers not equipped to handle them. While it is possible to keep most browsers away from E4X code (by specifying the required extension to a script element's type attribute: type="text/javascript; e4x=1"), not all browsers recognize the type extension as being different from the normal text/javascript, and will therefore choke on the E4X notation as the page loads.

ECMAScript Reserved Keywords

The following case-sensitive words may not be used as identifier names:

abstract	boolean	break	byte
case	catch	char	class
const	continue	debugger	default
delete	do	double	else
enum	export	extends	final
finally	float	for	function
goto	if	implements	import
in	instanceof	int	interface
long	native	new	package
private	protected	public	return
short	static	super	switch
synchronized	this	throw	throws
transient	try	typeof	var
void	volatile	while	with

Many of these words are already used in existing JavaScript versions, while the rest are reserved for possible use in future versions.

The following case-sensitive words may not be used as identifier names in E4X scripts:

each   namespace   XML

Core Objects

ActiveXObject   IE 4(Win) NN *n/a* Moz *n/a* Saf *n/a* Op *n/a* ECMA *n/a*

Internet Explorer for Windows provides a direct portal between a web page and an ActiveX control (an *automation object* in Windows jargon) already registered with the Windows system. By creating an instance of the ActiveXObject, you supply your scripts with a reference to that control; use that reference to access the control's properties or invoke its methods. Uncovering the methods and properties of an automation object may require a bit of exploration through the Microsoft Developer Network web site (*http://msdn.microsoft. com*). A Microsoft utility, called OLE/COM Object Viewer, can also open doors for the persistent. A good place to start your exploration is *http://msdn2.microsoft.com/en-us/library/ 7sw4ddf8.aspx*. See also the GetObject( ) global function for a way to obtain a reference to an automation object via its local pathname.

Creating an ActiveXObject
```
var myObj = new ActiveXObject(appName.className[, remoteServerName])
```

Properties   None.

Methods   None.

arguments   IE 4 NN 3 Moz *all* Saf *all* Op 7 ECMA 1

Every function—while it is executing—has an arguments object, which is accessible as a property of the function. The object is created automatically, and cannot be created outside of the function context that owns it. For example, consider a typical function definition:
```
function myFunc( ) {
     // function statements
}
```
A statement inside the function can access the arguments object by the following reference:
```
arguments
```
This object always contains the callee property, which is a reference to the very same function (explained in the callee property discussion). But you can also use the arguments object to access each parameter variable value through array notation. In the above example, a statement inside the myFunc( ) function can access the passed parameter value with the following reference:
```
arguments[0]
```
See the arguments property discussion of the Function object later in this chapter for practical applications.

Properties

callee   length

Methods   None.

callee

Read-only

Provides a reference to the function that created the arguments object. Thus, in an anonymous function, a statement can make a recursive call to the same (unnamed) function via the callee property, as shown in the Example.

Example

```
myObj.doThis = function(input) {
    // function statements that act on parameter value
    if (!someCondition) {
        // make recursive call to this anonymous function
        arguments.callee(input);
    }
}
```

Value   Function object reference.

length

Read-only

Returns the number of arguments passed to the function in its current invocation. The number is not influenced by the number of parameter variables defined for the function.

Example

```
function myFunc() {
    for (var i = 0; i < arguments.length; i++) {
        ...
    }
}
```

Value   Integer.

Array

An array is an ordered collection of one or more pieces of data. JavaScript array entries may be of any data type, and you can mix different data types in the same array. Each entry in an array has an index assigned to it. The default behavior is for the index to be a zero-based integer (the first entry has an index of zero). An index value may also be a string, but the string index acts like a property name of an array object, and does not influence the numeric indices (which is why string-indexed entries cannot be iterated via the array's

---

length property, but can be iterated via a for-in loop). Separate sets of integer- and string-indexed items can coexist within the same array object.

Accessing an entry in an array requires the name of the array and the index in square brackets:

```
cars[0]
cars["Ford"]
```

You may also create an array of arrays to simulate multidimensional arrays. A reference to an item in a two-dimensional array uses syntax as follows:

```
myArray[x][y]
```

The number of entries in a JavaScript array (its length) can vary over time. Therefore, you do not have to initialize an empty array to a specific size (nor is there any particular advantage to doing so). To add a new entry to an array of indeterminant length, assign the value to the next higher array index value:

```
cars[cars.length] = "Bentley";
```

A shortcut array creation technique is available starting in IE 4 and Navigator 4, using square brackets to contain values in literal notation.

Creating an Array

```
var myArray = new Array();
var myArray = new Array(sizeInteger);
var myArray = new Array(element0, element1, ..., elementN);
var myArray = [element0, element1, ..., elementN];
```

Properties

constructor	length	prototype

Methods

concat( )	every( )	filter( )
forEach( )	indexOf( )	join( )
lastIndexOf( )	map( )	pop( )
push( )	reverse( )	shift( )
slice( )	some( )	sort( )
splice( )	toLocaleString( )	toString( )
unshift( )		

constructor

IE 4 NN 4 Moz all Saf all Op 7 ECMA 1

Read/Write

This is a reference to the function that created the instance of an Array object—the native Array( ) constructor function in browsers.

Example

```
if (myVar.constructor == Array) {
    // process native string
}
```

Value   Function object reference.

length   IE 4 NN 3 Moz *all* Saf *all* Op 7 ECMA 1
Read/Write

Provides a count of the number of numerically indexed entries stored in the array. If the constructor function used to create the array specified a preliminary length, the length property reflects that amount, even if data does not occupy every slot.

Example

```
for (var i = C; i < myArray.length; i++) {
    ...
}
```

Value   Integer.

prototype   IE 4 NN 3 Moz *all* Saf *all* Op 7 ECMA 1
Read/Write

This is a property of the static Array object. Use the prototype property to assign new properties and methods to future instances of arrays created in the current document. For example, the following function creates a return-delimited list of elements in an array in reverse order:

```
function formatAsList() {
    var output = "";
    for (var i = this.length - 1; i >= 0; i--) {
        output += this[i] + "\n";
    }
    alert(output);
}
```

To give an array that power, assign this function reference to a prototype property whose name you want to use s the method to invoke this function:

```
Array.prototype.showReverseList = formatAsList;
```

If a script creates an array at this point:

```
var stooges = new Array("Moe", "Larry", "Curly", "Shemp");
```

the new array has the showReverseList( ) method available to it. To invoke the method, the call is:

```
stooges.showReverseList( );
```

You can add properties the same way. These allow you to attach information about the array (its creation time, for example) without disturbing the ordered sequence of array data. When a new document loads into the window or frame, the static Array object starts fresh again.

Example Array.prototype.created = "";

Value Any data, including function references.

concat( )   *IE 4 NN 4 Moz all Saf all Op 7 ECMA 1*

concat(*item1*[, *item2*[, ...*itemN*]])

Returns an array that combines the current array object with one or more array objects (or other values) specified as the method parameter(s):

```
var combinedArray = myArray1.concat(myArray2, someValue);
```

Neither of the original arrays is altered in the process.

Returned Value An Array object.

Parameters

item1...itemN

> Any JavaScript value, including another array.

every( )   *IE n/a NN n/a Moz 1.8 Saf n/a Op n/a ECMA n/a*

every(*functionRef*[, *thisObject*])

Executes a function (callback) on each element of an array. The every( ) function returns true if all function invocations return true; if one function invocation returns false, the every( ) function halts further calls to the external function, and returns false.

Information about the array element is passed to the callback function via three parameters: the value of the element, the index of the element, and a reference to the array, as in the following example:

```
function allNumbers(val, i, array) {
    return (typeof val == "number");
}
var myArray = [10, 100, 1000];
var result = myArray.every(allNumbers);
// result is true for the array
```

The callback function is allowed to modify the original array, which may, at times, impact further callback calls. Only the length of the array is fixed at the time every( ) is invoked, and each element is passed to the callback function with the value in force at the time the callback is made. If an element yet to be reached is deleted, its value is passed to the function as undefined.

If the callback function requires an object for the purposes of scope (i.e., so that a reference to this points to the correct object), you may pass a reference to that object as an optional second parameter (see forEach( ) for an example).

Returned Value Boolean.

Parameters

functionRef

> Reference to a function written to accept three parameters: array value, array index, and array reference. The function should return a Boolean value.

thisObject
> An optional reference to an object whose scope is required by statements (using this) in the callback function.

filter( ) IE *n/a* NN *n/a* Moz *1.8* Saf *n/a* Op *n/a* ECMA *n/a*
`filter(functionRef[, thisObject])`

Executes a function (callback) on each element of an array and returns a new array of values that pass whatever test is performed in the callback function (by the callback function returning true for that value). The original array is not modified unless the callback function makes such changes.

Information about the array element is passed to the callback function via three parameters: the value of the element, the index of the element, and a reference to the array (see every( ) for an example). The function should return a Boolean value indicating whether or not the value is one that should be returned as an element of the new array returned by filter( ). Note that the returned array may be smaller than the original.

The callback function is allowed to modify the original array, which may, at times, impact further callback calls. Only the length of the array is fixed at the time filter( ) is invoked, and each element is passed to the callback function with the value in force at the time the callback is made. If an element yet to be reached is deleted, its value is passed to the function as undefined.

If the callback function requires an object for the purposes of scope (i.e., so that a reference to this points to the correct object), you may pass a reference to that object as an optional second parameter.

Returned Value   Array.

Parameters

functionRef
> Reference to a function written to accept three parameters: array value, array index, and array reference. The function should return a Boolean value.

thisObject
> An optional reference to an object whose scope is required by statements (using this) in the callback function.

forEach( ) IE *n/a* NN *n/a* Moz *1.8* Saf *n/a* Op *n/a* ECMA *n/a*
`forEach(functionRef[, thisObject])`

Executes a function (callback) on each element of an array, without returning any value.

Information about the array element is passed to the callback function via three parameters: the value of one element through each iteration, the index of the element, and a reference to the array.

The callback function is allowed to modify the original array, which may, at times, impact further callback calls. Only the length of the array is fixed at the time forEach( ) is invoked, and each element is passed to the callback function with the value in force at the time the callback is made. If an element yet to be reached is deleted, its value is passed to the function as undefined.

If the callback function requires an object for the purposes of scope (i.e., so that a reference to this points to the correct object), you may pass a reference to that object as an optional second parameter. In the following example, the myObj object is passed as the second parameter to give proper scope for the doNumberTest( ) method to increment a value stored as an object property:

```
var myObj = {
    successCounter: 0,
    doNumberTest: function(val) {
        if (typeof val == "number") {
            this.successCounter++;
        }
    },
    report: function () {
        alert("Successful " + this.successCounter + " times!");
    }
};

var myArray = [10, "100", 1000];
myArray.forEach(myObj.doNumberTest, myObj);
```

You can then invoke the myObj.report( ) method at any time to read the accumulated value of the myObj.successCounter value. In this example the value is incremented twice during each invocation of the forEach( ) method because two of the array's values are numbers.

Returned Value   None.

Parameters

functionRef
> Reference to a function written to accept three parameters: array value, array index, and array reference. The function should not return a value.

thisObject
> An optional reference to an object whose scope is required by statements (using this) in the callback function.

indexOf( )   IE *n/a* NN *n/a* Moz *1.8* Saf *n/a* Op *9* ECMA *n/a*
indexOf(*searchElement*[, *fromIndex*])

Returns an integer indicating the zero-based position within the array where the first instance of a search element is located. If the search element is not found in the array, the return value is -1. The search is always from start of the array to the end and is based on the JavaScript strict equality (===) operator, meaning that the match must consist of the value and data type to be successful. In effect, this method provides a shortcut to find the index within an array of a known value—or just to find out if a value is contained in an array—without having to write looping code that iterates through the array values.

Returned Value

Integer. Zero or greater if the search element is contained in the array; -1 if the search element is not in the array.

Parameters

searchElement
> Any JavaScript value, including another array or DOM object.

fromIndex
> An optional integer indicating the zero-based position within the array elements at which begin the search. A negative value is a count of positions from the end of the array (but the search always works its way toward the end).

join( )   IE 4   NN 3   Moz *all*   Saf *all*   Op 7   ECMA 1

```
join(["delimiterString"])
```

Returns a string consisting of a list of items (as strings) contained by an array. The delimiter character(s) between items is set by the parameter to the method. Note that an array's items are only those items that are accessible via an integer index. Items referenced via string index values are treated as properties of the array object, and are thus independent of integer indexed values (the two sets can coexist in a single array without conflict). The join( ) method works only with the integer-indexed items.

Returned Value   String.

Parameters

delimiterString
> Any string of characters. Nonalphanumeric characters must use URL-encoded equivalents (%0D for carriage return). The default delimiter string is a comma character.

lastIndexOf( )   IE *n/a*   NN *n/a*   Moz *1.8*   Saf *n/a*   Op 9   ECMA *n/a*

```
lastIndexOf(searchElement[, fromIndex])
```

Returns an integer indicating the zero-based position within the array where the first instance of search element is located when searched from the end of the array. If the search element is not found in the array, the return value is -1. The search is always from the end of the array to the beginning and is based on the JavaScript strict equality (===) operator, meaning that the match must consist of the value and data type to be successful. This method is just like indexOf( ) but searches the array in the opposite direction.

Returned Value

Integer. Zero or greater if the search element is contained in the array; -1 if the search element is not in the array.

Parameters

searchElement
> Any JavaScript value, including another array or DOM object.

---

fromIndex

An optional integer indicating the zero-based position within the array elements at which begin the search. A negative value is a count of positions from the end of the array (but the search always works its way toward the beginning).

map( )

`map(functionRef[, thisObject])`

Executes a function (callback) on each element of an array and returns a new array of values that are returned by the callback function. The original array is not modified unless the callback function makes such changes.

Information about the array element is passed to the callback function via three parameters: the value of the element, the index of the element, and a reference to the array. The function should return a value, which then becomes an element of the new array returned by map( ), as in the following example:

```
function makeStringy(val, i, array) {
    return val.toString( );
}
var myArray = [10, 100, 1000];
var newArray = myArray.map(makeStringy);
```

The callback function is allowed to modify the original array, which may, at times, impact further callback calls. Only the length of the array is fixed at the time map( ) is invoked, and each element is passed to the callback function with the value in force at the time the callback is made. If an element yet to be reached is deleted, its value is passed to the function as undefined.

If the callback function requires an object for the purposes of scope (i.e., so that a reference to this points to the correct object), you may pass a reference to that object as an optional second parameter.

Returned Value   Array.

Parameters

functionRef

Reference to a function written to accept three parameters: array value, array index, and array reference. The function should return a value.

thisObject

An optional reference to an object whose scope is required by statements (using this) in the callback function.

pop( )

Returns the value of the last item in an array and removes it from the array. The length of the array decreases by one.

Returned Value   Any JavaScript value.

Parameters   None.

push( )   IE 5.5(Win) NN 4 Moz *all* Saf *all* Op 7 ECMA 2

push(*item1*[, *item2*[, ...*itemN*]])

Appends one or more items to the end of an array. The length of the array increases by one.

Returned Value   The length (integer) of the array after the push operation.

Parameters

item1...itemN
> Comma-delimited list of one or more JavaScript values, including object references.

reverse( )   IE 4 NN 3 Moz *all* Saf *all* Op 7 ECMA 1

Reverses the order of items in the array and returns a copy of the array in the new order. Not only does the reverse( ) method rearrange the values in the array, but it also returns a copy of the reversed array.

Returned Value   An Array object.

Parameters   None.

shift( )   IE 5.5(Win) NN 4 Moz *all* Saf *all* Op 7 ECMA 2

Returns the value of the first item in an array and removes it from the array. The length of the array decreases by one.

Returned Value   Any JavaScript value.

Parameters   None.

slice( )   IE 4 NN 2 Moz *all* Saf *all* Op 7 ECMA 2

slice(*startIndex*[, *endIndex*])

Returns an array that is a subset of contiguous items from the main array. Parameters determine where the selection begins and ends.

Returned Value   An Array object.

Parameters

startIndex
> A zero-based integer of the first item of the subset from the current array.

endIndex
> An optional zero-based integer of the last item of the subset from the current array. If omitted, the selection is made from the *startIndex* position to the end of the array.

some( )

some(*functionRef*[, *thisObject*])

Executes a function (callback) on each element of an array and returns true if the callback function returns true for any one element, or false if no invocations of the callback function return true.

Information about the array element is passed to the callback function via three parameters: the value of the element, the index of the element, and a reference to the array. The function should return a Boolean value.

The callback function is allowed to modify the original array, which may, at times, impact further callback calls. Only the length of the array is fixed at the time some( ) is invoked, and each element is passed to the callback function with the value in force at the time the callback is made. If an element yet to be reached is deleted, its value is passed to the function as undefined.

If the callback function requires an object for the purposes of scope (i.e., so that a reference to this points to the correct object), you may pass a reference to that object as an optional second parameter.

Returned Value   Boolean.

Parameters

functionRef

Reference to a function written to accept three parameters: array value, array index, and array reference. The function should return a Boolean value.

thisObject

An optional reference to an object whose scope is required by statements (using this) in the callback function.

sort( )

sort([*compareFunction*])

Sorts the values of the array either by the ASCII value of string versions of each array entry or according to a comparison function of your own design. The sort( ) method repeatedly invokes the comparison function, passing two values from the array. The comparison function should return an integer value, which is interpreted by the sort( ) function as follows.

Value	Meaning
<0	The second passed value should sort later than the first value.
0	The sort order of the two values should not change.
>0	The first passed value should sort later than the second value.

The following comparison function sorts values of an array in numerical (instead of ASCII) order:

```
function doCompare(a, b) {
    return a - b;
}
```

To sort an array by this function, the statement is:

```
myArray.sort(doCompare);
```

By the time the sort() method has completed its job, it has sent all values to the doCompare() function two values at a time and sorted the values on whether the first value is larger than the second (in the manner of a bubble sort).

If an array's elements consist of objects, you can sort by the property values of those objects. For example, the following sorting function places an array of employee objects in alphabetical order by values of the objects' age properties:

```
function compareByAge(a, b) {
    return a.age - b.age;
}
```

Not only does the sort() method rearrange the values in the array, but it also returns a copy of the sorted array.

Returned Value   An Array object, sorted according to sorting criteria.

Parameters

compareFunction
> A reference to a function that receives two parameters and returns an integer result.

splice( )   IE 5.5 NN 4 Moz *all* Saf *all* Op 7 ECMA 2

splice(*startIndex, deleteCount*[, *item1*[, *item2*[, ...*itemN*]]])

Removes zero or more contiguous items from within an array and, optionally, inserts new items in their places. The length of the array adjusts itself accordingly.

Returned Value   An Array object containing removed items.

Parameters

startIndex
> A zero-based integer of the first item of the subset from the current array.

deleteCount
> An integer denoting how many items from the *startIndex* position are to be removed from the array.

item1...itemN
> Comma-delimited list of JavaScript values to be inserted into the array in place of removed items. The number of items does not have to equal *deleteCount*.

toLocaleString( )   IE 5.5 NN *n/a* Moz *all* Saf *all* Op 7 ECMA 2

Returns a comma-delimited string of values, theoretically in a format tailored to the language and customs of the browser's default language. Implementation details vary with browser and data type. IE 5.5 and later converts numbers of all kinds to strings with two digits to the right of the decimal, but triggers an error for object references. Mozilla leaves integers in their original format and displays object references as [object *objectType*]. The ECMA standard leaves such interpretations up to the browser maker.

Returned Value	Comma-delimited string.
Parameters	None.

toString( )

Returns a comma-delimited string of values, identical to using the `Array.join( )` method with a comma parameter. All values are converted to some string equivalent, including objects (`[object]` in IE/Windows; `[object` *objectType*`]` in IE 5/Macintosh, Mozilla, and Safari).

Returned Value	Comma-delimited string.
Parameters	None.

unshift( )

`unshift(`*item1*`[, `*item2*`[, ...`*itemN*`]])`

Inserts one or more items at the beginning of an array. The length of the array increases by the number of items added, and the method returns the new length of the array.

Returned Value	Integer.

Parameters

item1...itemN
> Comma-delimited list of one or more JavaScript values.

Boolean

A `Boolean` object represents any value that evaluates to `true` or `false`. By and large, you don't have to worry about the `Boolean` object because the browsers automatically create such objects for you when you assign a `true` or `false` value to a variable. Quoted versions of these values are treated only as a string.

Creating a Boolean Object

```
var myValue = new Boolean( );
var myValue = new Boolean(BooleanValue);
var myValue = BooleanValue;
```

Properties

constructor	prototype

Methods

toString( )	valueOf( )

constructor

This is a reference to the function that created the instance of a Boolean object—the native Boolean( ) constructor function in browsers.

Example
```
if (myVar.constructor == Boolean) {
    // process native string
}
```
Value   Function object reference.

prototype

This is a property of the static Boolean object. Use the prototype property to assign new properties and methods to future instances of a Boolean value created in the current document. See the Array.prototype property description for examples. There is little need to create new prototype properties or methods for the Boolean object.

Example   Boolean.prototype.author = "DG";

Value   Any data, including function references.

toString( )

Returns the object's value as a string data type. You don't need this method in practice, because the browsers automatically convert Boolean values to strings when they are needed for display in alert dialogs or in-document rendering.

Returned Value   "true" | "false"

Parameters   None.

valueOf( )

Returns the object's value as a Boolean data type. You don't need this method when you create Boolean objects by simple value assignment.

Returned Value   Boolean value: true | false.

Parameters   None.

Date

The Date object is a static object that generates instances by way of several constructor functions. Each instance of a Date object is a snapshot of the date and time, measured in milliseconds relative to zero hours on January 1, 1970. Negative millisecond values represent time before that date; positive values represent time since that date.

The typical way to work with dates is to generate a new instance of the Date object, either for now or for a specific date and time (past or future, using the client local time). Then use the myriad of available date methods to get or set components of that time (e.g., minutes, hours, date, month). Browsers internally store a date as the millisecond value at Coordinated Universal Time (UTC, which is essentially the same as Greenwich Mean Time, or GMT). When you ask a browser for a component of that time, it automatically converts the value to the local time zone of the browser based on the client computer's control panel setting for the clock and time zone. If the control panel is set incorrectly, time and date calculations may go awry.

Creating a Date Object

```
var now = new Date( );
var myDate = new Date("month dd, yyyy hh:mm:ss");
var myDate = new Date("month dd, yyyy");
var myDate = new Date(yy, mm, dd, hh, mm, ss);
var myDate = new Date(yy, mm, dd);
var myDate = new Date(milliseconds);
```

Properties

constructor	prototype

Methods

getDate( )	getDay( )	getFullYear( )
getHours( )	getMilliseconds( )	getMinutes( )
getMonth( )	getSeconds( )	getTime( )
getTimezoneOffset( )	getUTCDate( )	getUTCDay( )
getUTCFullYear( )	getUTCHours( )	getUTCMilliseconds( )
getUTCMinutes( )	getUTCMonth( )	getUTCSeconds( )
getVarDate( )	getYear( )	parse( )
setDate( )	setFullYear( )	setHours( )
setMilliseconds( )	setMinutes( )	setMonth( )
setSeconds( )	setTime( )	setUTCDate( )
setUTCFullYear( )	setUTCHours( )	setUTCMilliseconds( )
setUTCMinutes( )	setUTCMonth( )	setUTCSeconds( )
setYear( )	toDateString( )	toGMTString( )
toLocaleDateString( )	toLocaleString( )	toLocaleTimeString( )
toString( )	toTimeString( )	toUTCString( )
UTC( )	valueOf( )	

constructor

This is a reference to the function that created the instance of a Date object—the native Date( ) constructor function in browsers.

Example
```
if (myVar.constructor == Date) {
    // process native string
}
```
Value   Function object reference.

prototype

This is a property of the static Date object. Use the prototype property to assign new properties and methods to future instances of a Date value created in the current document. See the Array.prototype property description for examples.

Example   Date.prototype.author = "DG";

Value   Any data, including function references.

getDate( )

Returns the calendar date within the month specified by an instance of the Date object.

Returned Value   Integer between 1 and 31.

Parameters   None.

getDay( )

Returns an integer corresponding to a day of the week for the date specified by an instance of the Date object.

Returned Value   Integer between 0 and 6. Sunday is 0, Monday is 1, and Saturday is 6.

Parameters   None.

getFullYear( )

Returns all digits of the year for the date specified by an instance of the Date object.

Returned Value
Integer. Navigator 4 goes no lower than zero. Internet Explorer and other mainstream browsers return negative year values.

Parameters   None.

getHours( ) IE *3*   NN *2*   Moz *all*   Saf *all*   Op *7*   ECMA *1*

Returns a zero-based integer corresponding to the hours of the day for the date specified by an instance of the Date object. The 24-hour time system is used.

Returned Value   Integer between 0 and 23.

Parameters   None.

getMilliseconds( ) IE *4*   NN *4*   Moz *all*   Saf *all*   Op *7*   ECMA *1*

Returns a zero-based integer corresponding to the number of milliseconds past the seconds value of the date specified by an instance of the Date object.

Returned Value   Integer between 0 and 999.

Parameters   None.

getMinutes( ) IE *3*   NN *2*   Moz *all*   Saf *all*   Op *7*   ECMA *1*

Returns a zero-based integer corresponding to the minute value for the hour and date specified by an instance of the Date object.

Returned Value   Integer between 0 and 59.

Parameters   None.

getMonth( ) IE *3*   NN *2*   Moz *all*   Saf *all*   Op *7*   ECMA *1*

Returns a zero-based integer corresponding to the month value for the date specified by an instance of the Date object. That this method's values are zero-based frequently confuses scripters at first.

Returned Value

Integer between 0 and 11. January is 0, February is 1, and December is 11.

Parameters   None.

getSeconds( ) IE *3*   NN *2*   Moz *all*   Saf *all*   Op *7*   ECMA *1*

Returns a zero-based integer corresponding to the seconds past the nearest full minute for the date specified by an instance of the Date object.

Returned Value   Integer between 0 and 59.

Parameters   None.

getTime( ) IE *3*   NN *2*   Moz *all*   Saf *all*   Op *7*   ECMA *1*

Returns a zero-based integer corresponding to the number of milliseconds since January 1, 1970, to the date specified by an instance of the Date object.

Returned Value   Integer.

Parameters   None.

getTimezoneOffset( )   IE 3 NN 2 Moz *all* Saf *all* Op 7 ECMA 1

Returns a zero-based integer corresponding to the number of minutes difference between GMT and the client computer's clock for an instance of the Date object. Time zones to the west of GMT are positive values; time zones to the east are negative values. Numerous bugs plagued this method in early browsers, especially Macintosh versions.

Returned Value   Integer between -720 and 720.

Parameters   None.

getUTCDate( )   IE 4 NN 4 Moz *all* Saf *all* Op 7 ECMA 1

Returns the calendar date within the month specified by an instance of the Date object but in the UTC time stored internally by the browser.

Returned Value   Integer between 1 and 31.

Parameters   None.

getUTCDay( )   IE 4 NN 4 Moz *all* Saf *all* Op 7 ECMA 1

Returns an integer corresponding to a day of the week for the date specified by an instance of the Date object but in the UTC time stored internally by the browser.

Returned Value   Integer between 0 and 6. Sunday is 0, Monday is 1, and Saturday is 6.

Parameters   None.

getUTCFullYear( )   IE 4 NN 4 Moz *all* Saf *all* Op 7 ECMA 1

Returns all digits of the year for the date specified by an instance of the Date object but in the UTC time stored internally by the browser.

Returned Value

Integer. Navigator 4 goes no lower than zero. Internet Explorer and other mainstream browsers return negative year values.

Parameters   None.

getUTCHours( )   IE 4 NN 4 Moz *all* Saf *all* Op 7 ECMA 1

Returns a zero-based integer corresponding to the hours of the day for the date specified by an instance of the Date object but in the UTC time stored internally by the browser. The 24-hour time system is used.

Returned Value   Integer between 0 and 23.

Parameters   None.

getUTCMilliseconds( )   IE *4* NN *4* Moz *all* Saf *all* Op *7* ECMA *1*

Returns a zero-based integer corresponding to the number of milliseconds past the seconds value of the date specified by an instance of the Date object but in the UTC time stored internally by the browser.

Returned Value   Integer between 0 and 999.

Parameters   None.

getUTCMinutes( )   IE *4* NN *4* Moz *all* Saf *all* Op *7* ECMA *1*

Returns a zero-based integer corresponding to the minute value for the hour and date specified by an instance of the Date object but in the UTC time stored internally by the browser.

Returned Value   Integer between 0 and 59.

Parameters   None.

getUTCMonth( )   IE *4* NN *4* Moz *all* Saf *all* Op *7* ECMA *1*

Returns a zero-based integer corresponding to the month value for the date specified by an instance of the Date object but in the UTC time stored internally by the browser. That this method's values are zero-based frequently confuses scripters at first.

Returned Value

Integer between 0 and 11. January is 0, February is 1, and December is 11.

Parameters   None.

getUTCSeconds( )   IE *4* NN *4* Moz *all* Saf *all* Op *7* ECMA *1*

Returns a zero-based integer corresponding to the seconds value past the nearest full minute of the date specified by an instance of the Date object but in the UTC time stored internally by the browser.

Returned Value   Integer between 0 and 59.

Parameters   None.

getVarDate( )   IE *4* NN *n/a* Moz *n/a* Saf *n/a* Op *n/a* ECMA *n/a*

Returns a date value in a format (called VT_DATE) suitable for a variety of Windows-oriented applications, such as ActiveX controls and VBScript. Not for use with JavaScript date calculations.

Returned Value   VT_DATE format value (not for JavaScript use).

Parameters   None.

getYear( )   IE 3 NN 2 Moz *all* Saf *all* Op 7 ECMA *n/a*

Returns a number corresponding to the year of an instance of the Date object, but exhibits irregular behavior. In theory, the method should return the number of years the date object represents since 1900. This would produce a one- or two-digit value for all years between 1900 and 1999. However, when you reach 2000, the pattern fails. Instead of producing values starting with 100, the getYear( ) method, some browsers return the same four-digit value as getFullYear( ). For this reason, it is best to use getFullYear( ) whenever possible (but observe the browser compatibility for that method). Note that this method is not an ECMA-supported method, whereas getFullYear( ) is.

Returned Value

Integer between 0 and 99 for the years 1900 to 1999; four-digit integer starting with 2000 for some browsers, or a continuation (100+) for others.

Parameters   None.

parse( )   IE 3 NN 2 Moz *all* Saf *all* Op 7 ECMA 1

parse("*dateString*")

Static Date object method that returns the millisecond equivalent of the date specified as a string in the parameter.

Returned Value   Date in milliseconds.

Parameters

dateString
> Any valid string format equivalent to that derived from a Date object. See toString( ), toGMTString( ), and toLocaleString( ) methods for sample formats.

setDate( )   IE 3 NN 2 Moz *all* Saf *all* Op 7 ECMA 1

setDate(*dateInt*)

Sets the date within the month for an instance of the Date object. If you specify a date beyond the end of the object's current month, the object recalculates the date in the succeeding month. For example, if a Date object is set to December 25, 2007, you can find out the calendar date 10 days later with the following construction:

myDate.setDate(myDate.getDate( ) + 10);

After this calculation, the value of myDate is the equivalent of January 4, 2008.

Returned Value   New date in milliseconds.

Parameters

dateInt
> Date integer.

setFullYear( )

setFullYear(*yearInt*)

Assigns the year for an instance of the Date object.

Returned Value

New date in milliseconds.

Parameters

yearInt
> Integer. Navigator 4 allows digits no lower than zero. Internet Explorer and other mainstream browsers allow negative year values.

setHours( )

setHours(*hourInt*)

Sets the hours of the day for an instance of the Date object. The 24-hour time system is used. If you specify an hour beyond the end of the object's current day, the object recalculates the time in the succeeding day(s).

Returned Value

New date in milliseconds.

Parameters

hourInt
> Zero-based integer.

setMilliseconds( )

setMilliseconds(*msInt*)

Sets the number of milliseconds past the seconds value for an instance of the Date object.

Returned Value   New date in milliseconds.

Parameters

msInt
> Zero-based integer of milliseconds.

setMinutes( )

setMinutes(*minuteInt*)

Sets the minute value for the hour and date of an instance of the Date object.

Returned Value   New date in milliseconds.

Parameters

minuteInt
> Zero-based integer.

setMonth( )   IE 3 NN 2 Moz *all* Saf *all* Op 7 ECMA 1

setMonth(*monthInt*)

Sets the month value for the date of an instance of the Date object. That this method's values are zero-based frequently confuses scripters at first.

Returned Value   New date in milliseconds.

Parameters

monthInt

Zero-based integer. January is 0, February is 1, and December is 11. Assigning higher values increases the object to the succeeding year.

setSeconds( )   IE 3 NN 2 Moz *all* Saf *all* Op 7 ECMA 1

setSeconds(*secInt*)

Sets the seconds value past the nearest full minute for an instance of the Date object.

Returned Value   New date in milliseconds.

Parameters

secInt

Zero-based integer.

setTime( )   IE 3 NN 2 Moz *all* Saf *all* Op 7 ECMA 1

setTime(*msInt*)

Sets an instance of the Date object to the number of milliseconds since January 1, 1970.

Returned Value   New date in milliseconds.

Parameters

msInt

Integer of milliseconds.

setUTCDate( )   IE 4 NN 4 Moz *all* Saf *all* Op 7 ECMA 1

setUTCDate(*dateInt*)

Sets the date within the month of an instance of the Date object but in the UTC time stored internally by the browser. If you specify a date beyond the end of the object's current month, the object recalculates the date in the succeeding month. For this and all other setUTC... methods, Safari has Daylight Savings Time problems that were fixed in version 2.02.

Returned Value   New UTC date in milliseconds.

Parameters

dateInt

Integer.

setUTCFullYear( )   IE *4*   NN *4*   Moz *all*   Saf *all*   Op *7*   ECMA *1*

setUTCFullYear(*yearInt*)

Sets all digits of the year for an instance of the Date object but in the UTC time stored internally by the browser.

Returned Value   New UTC date in milliseconds.

Parameters

yearInt

> Integer. Navigator 4 allows values no lower than zero. Internet Explorer and NN 6 allow negative year values.

setUTCHours( )   IE *4*   NN *4*   Moz *all*   Saf *all*   Op *7*   ECMA *1*

setUTCHours(*hourInt*)

Sets the hours of the day for an instance of the Date object but in the UTC time stored internally by the browser. The 24-hour time system is used.

Returned Value   New UTC date in milliseconds.

Parameters

hourInt

> Zero-based integer.

setUTCMilliseconds( )   IE *4*   NN *4*   Moz *all*   Saf *all*   Op *7*   ECMA *1*

setUTCMilliseconds(*msInt*)

Sets the number of milliseconds past the seconds value of an instance of the Date object but in the UTC time stored internally by the browser.

Returned Value   New UTC date in milliseconds.

Parameters

msInt

> Zero-based integer.

setUTCMinutes( )   IE *4*   NN *4*   Moz *all*   Saf *all*   Op *7*   ECMA *1*

setUTCMinutes(*minuteInt*)

Sets the minute value for the hour and date of an instance of the Date object but in the UTC time stored internally by the browser.

Returned Value   New UTC date in milliseconds.

Parameters

minuteInt

> Zero-based integer.

setUTCMonth( )   IE 4   NN 4   Moz all   Saf all   Op 7   ECMA 1

setUTCMonth(monthInt)

Sets the month value for an instance of the Date object but in the UTC time stored internally by the browser. That this method's values are zero-based frequently confuses scripters at first.

Returned Value   New UTC date in milliseconds.

Parameters

monthInt

> Zero-based integer. January is 0, February is 1, and December is 11. Assigning higher values increases the object to the succeeding year.

setUTCSeconds( )   IE 4   NN 4   Moz all   Saf all   Op 7   ECMA 1

setUTCSeconds(secInt)

Sets the seconds value past the nearest full for an instance of the Date object but in the UTC time stored internally by the browser.

Returned Value   New UTC date in milliseconds.

Parameters

secInt

> Zero-based integer.

setYear( )   IE 3   NN 2   Moz all   Saf all   Op 7   ECMA n/a

setYear(yearInt)

Sets the year of an instance of a Date object. Use setFullYear( ) instead. Note that this method is not an ECMA-supported method, whereas setFullYear( ) is.

Returned Value   New date in milliseconds.

Parameters

yearInt

> Four-digit (and sometimes two-digit) integers representing a year.

toDateString( )   IE 5.5   NN n/a   Moz all   Saf all   Op 7   ECMA 3

Returns a string consisting only of the date portion of an instance of a Date object. The precise format is under the control of the browser and language, but U.S. English versions of modern supporting browsers return values in the format *Ddd Mmm dd yyyy*.

Returned Value   String.

Parameters   None.

toGMTString( ) IE *3* NN *2* Moz *all* Saf *all* Op *7* ECMA *1*

Returns a string version of the GMT value of a Date object instance in a standardized format. This method does not alter the original Date object. For use in newer browsers, the toUTCString( ) method is recommended in favor of toGMTString( ).

Returned Value

String in the following format: *dayAbbrev*, *dd mmm yyyy* hh:*mm*:*ss* GMT. For example:

```
Mon 05 Aug 2002 02:33:22 GMT
```

Parameters   None.

toLocaleDateString( ) IE *5.5* NN *n/a* Moz *all* Saf *all* Op *7* ECMA *3*

Returns a string consisting only of the date portion of an instance of a Date object. The precise format is under the control of the browser and language.

Returned Value

String in a variety of possible formats. Examples of U.S. versions of browsers include the following.

Platform	String value
Internet Explorer 7	Sunday, April 01, 2007
Mozilla/Win	Sunday, April 01, 2007
Mozilla/Mac	04/01/2007
Safari	April 1, 2007
Opera	4/1/2007

Parameters   None.

toLocaleString( ) IE *3* NN *2* Moz *all* Saf *all* Op *7* ECMA *1*

Returns a string version of the local time zone value of both the date and time from a Date object instance. The format may be localized for a particular country or an operating system's convention.

Returned Value

String in a variety of possible formats. Examples of U.S. versions of browsers include the following.

Platform	String value
Internet Explorer 7	Sunday, April 01, 2007 10:30:00 AM
Mozilla/Win	Sunday, April 01, 2007 10:30:00 AM
Mozilla/Mac	Sun Apr 1 10:30:00 2007
Safari	April 1, 2007 10:30:00 AM PDT
Opera	4/1/2007 10:30:00 AM

Date

Parameters   None.

toLocaleTimeString( )   IE *5.5*   NN *n/a*   Moz *all*   Saf *all*   Op *7*   ECMA *3*

Returns a string consisting only of the time portion of an instance of a Date object. The precise format is under the control of the browser and language.

Returned Value

String in a variety of possible formats. Examples of U.S. versions of browsers include the following.

Platform	String value
Internet Explorer 7	`10:30:00 AM`
Mozilla/Win	`10:30:00 AM`
Mozilla/Mac	`10:30:00`
Safari	`10:30:00 AM PDT`
Opera	`10:30:00 AM`

Parameters   None.

toString( )   IE *4*   NN *2*   Moz *all*   Saf *all*   Op *7*   ECMA *1*

This is a method used mostly by the browser itself to obtain a string version of an instance of a Date object when needed for display in dialog boxes or on-screen rendering.

Returned Value

String in a variety of possible formats. Here are examples for U.S. versions of browsers.

Platform	String value
Internet Explorer 7	`Sun Apr 1 10:30:00 PDT 2007`
Mozilla/Win	`Sun Apr 01 2007 10:30:00 GMT-0700 (Pacific Daylight Time)`
Mozilla/Mac	`Sun Apr 01 2007 10:30:00 GMT-0700 (PDT)`
Safari	`Sun Apr 01 2007 10:30:00 GMT-0700`
Opera	`Sun, 01 Apr 2007 10:30:00 GMT-0700`

Parameters   None.

toTimeString( )   IE *5.5*   NN *n/a*   Moz *all*   Saf *all*   Op *7*   ECMA *3*

Returns a string consisting only of the time portion of an instance of a Date object. The precise format is under the control of the browser and language.

Returned Value

Platform	String value
Internet Explorer 7	`10:30:00 PDT`
Mozilla/Win	`10:30:00 GMT-0700 (Pacific Daylight Time)`
Mozilla/Mac	`10:30:00 GMT-0700 (PDT)`
Safari	`10:30:00 GMT-0700`
Opera	`10:30:00 GMT-0700`

Parameters   None.

toUTCString( )   IE 4 NN 4 Moz *all* Saf *all* Op 7 ECMA 1

Returns a string version of the UTC value of a `Date` object instance in a standardized format. This method does not alter the original `Date` object. For use in newer browsers, the `toUTCString( )` method is recommended in favor of `toGMTString( )`.

Returned Value

String in the following format: *dayAbbrev dd mmm yyyy hh:mm:ss* GMT. For example:

```
Mon 05 Aug 2002 02:33:22 GMT
```

Parameters   None.

UTC( )   IE 3 NN 2 Moz *all* Saf *all* Op 7 ECMA 1

`Date.UTC(`*yyyy, mm, dd*`[, `*hh*`[, `*mm*`[, `*ss*`[, `*msecs*`]]]])`

This is a static method of the `Date` object that returns a numeric version of the date as stored internally by the browser for a `Date` object. Unlike parameters to the `Date` object constructor, the parameter values for the `UTC( )` method must be in UTC time for the returned value to be accurate. This method does not generate a date object, as the `Date` object constructor does.

Returned Value   Integer of the UTC millisecond value of the date specified as parameters.

Parameters

yyyy
> Four-digit year value.

mm
> Two-digit month number (0-11).

dd
> Two-digit date number (1-31).

hh
> Optional two-digit hour number in 24-hour time (0-23).

mm
> Optional two-digit minute number (0-59).

ss

Optional two-digit second number (0-59).

msec

Optional milliseconds past the last whole second (0-999).

valueOf( )   IE 4   NN 4   Moz *all*   Saf *all*   Op 7   ECMA 1

Returns the object's value.

Returned Value   Integer millisecond count.

Parameters   None.

Enumerator   IE *4(Win)*   NN *n/a*   Moz *n/a*   Saf *n/a*   Op *n/a*   ECMA *n/a*

If an ActiveX control property or method returns a collection of values, the usual Java-Script approach to collections (treating them as arrays) does not work for such values. The Enumerator object gives JavaScript a way to reference items in such collections by control-ling a pointer to the list of items. For additional details, visit *http://msdn.microsoft.com/library/default.asp?url=/library/en-us/script56/html/js56jsobjenumerator.asp*.

Creating an Enumerator`var myEnumObj = new Enumerator(externalCollection);`

Properties   None.

Methods

   atEnd( )   item( )   moveFirst( )   moveNext( )

atEnd( )   IE *4(Win)*   NN *n/a*   Moz *n/a*   Saf *n/a*   Op *n/a*   ECMA *n/a*

Returns Boolean `true` if the Enumerator is pointing at the last item in the collection.

Returned Value   Boolean value: `true | false`.

Parameters   None.

item( )   IE *4(Win)*   NN *n/a*   Moz *n/a*   Saf *n/a*   Op *n/a*   ECMA *n/a*

Returns a value from the collection at the pointer's current position.

Returned Value   Number, string, or other value from the collection.

Parameters   None.

moveFirst( ), moveNext( )   IE *4(Win)*   NN *n/a*   Moz *n/a*   Saf *n/a*   Op *n/a*   ECMA *n/a*

Adjust the location of the pointer within the collection, jumping to the first item in the collection, or ahead by one item.

Returned Value   None.

Parameters   None.

Error

Browsers that implement try-catch exception handling automatically create an instance of the Error object whenever an error occurs during script processing. You can also create an Error object instance that you explicitly throw. The catch portion of the try-catch construction receives the Error object instance as a parameter, which scripts can examine to learn the details of the error, as exposed by the object's properties.

Creating an Error Object

```
var myError = new Error("errorMessage");
```

Properties

constructor	description	fileName	lineNumber
message	name	number	prototype

Methods

toString( )

constructor

Provides a reference to the function that created the instance of an Error object—the native Error( ) constructor function in browsers.

Example

```
if (myVar.constructor == Error) {
    // process native string
}
```

Value   Function object reference.

description

Provides a plain-language description of the error, frequently the same as appears in the IE script error dialog. Use the newer message property if possible.

Example

```
if (myError.description.indexOf("Object expected") != -1) {
    // handle "object expected" error
}
```

Value   String.

fileName

Specifies the URL of the page in which the script error occurred. This information appears in the Mozilla JavaScript/Error Console window for each reported error.

Example   var sourceFile = myError.fileName;

Value   URL string.

lineNumber

Specifies the number of the line in the source code where the current script error occurred. This information appears in the Mozilla JavaScript/Error Console window for each reported error.

Example   var errorLine = myError.lineNumber;

Value   Number in string format.

message

Provides a plain-language description of the error. There is no standard for the format or content of such messages.

Example
```
if (myError.message.indexOf("defined") != -1) {
    // handle error for something being undefined
}
```

Value   String.

name

This is a string that sometimes indicates the type of the current error. The default value of this property is Error. But the browser may also report types EvalError, RangeError, ReferenceError, SyntaxError, TypeError, URIError, and, if supported by the browser, a specific W3C DOM error type.

Example
```
if (myError.name == "SyntaxError") {
    // handle syntax error
}
```

Value   String.

number

Provides a number corresponding to an IE error. You must apply binary arithmetic to the value to derive a meaningful number. Use:

```
var errNum = ErrObj.number & 0xFFFF;
```

Then compare the result against Microsoft's numbered listing at *http://msdn.microsoft.com/ library/default.asp?url=/library/en-us/script56/html/js56jsmscRunTimeErrors.asp.*

Example   `var errNo = myError.number;`

Value   Number.

prototype

This is a property of the static `Error` object. Use the `prototype` property to assign new properties and methods to future instances of a Error object created in the current document. See the `Array.prototype` property description for examples.

Example   `Error.prototype.custom = true;`

Value   Any data, including function references.

stack

Provides a list of functions and possibly an event whose execution led to the error. For each trace back to a function, the stack entry notes the source code line number. This property can be a helpful debugging tool.

Value   Multi-line string.

toString( )

Returns a string representation of the object, but the values differ between browser families. IE returns [object Error], while Mozilla returns a concatenation of the `name` and `message` properties.

Returned Value   String.

Parameters   None.

Function

A function is a group of one or more script statements that can be invoked at any time during or after the loading of a page. Invoking a function requires nothing more than including the function name with a trailing set of parentheses inside another script statement or as a value assigned to an event handler attribute in an HTML tag.

Since the first scriptable browsers, a function is created by the act of defining it with a name inside a script element:

```
function funcName( ) {...}
```

More recent browsers also allow the use of two types of constructors, as shown below in "Creating a Function." These so-called anonymous functions (i.e., they have no names to reference) are especially useful when a property assignment requires a reference to a function, but you don't want to clutter your variable naming space with a function definition's name.

Functions may be built to receive zero or more parameters. Parameters are assigned to comma-delimited parameter variables defined in the parentheses pair following the function name:

```
function doSomething(param1, param2, ... paramN) {...}
```

A parameter value may be any JavaScript data type, including object references and arrays. There is no penalty for not supplying the same number of parameters to the function as are defined for the function. The function object receives all parameters into an array (called arguments), which script statements inside the function may examine to extract parameter data.

A function returns execution to the calling statement when the function's last statement has executed. A value may be returned to the calling statement via the return statement. Also, a return statement anywhere else in the function's statements aborts function statement execution at that point and returns control to the calling statement (optionally with a returned value). If one branch of a conditional construction in a function returns a value, each branch, including the main branch, must also return a value, even if that value is null (IE tends to be more forgiving if you don't balance return statements, but it's good programming practice just the same).

Functions have ready access to all global variables that are defined outside of functions anywhere in the document. But variables defined inside a function (the var keyword is required) are accessible only to statements inside the function.

To reference a function object that is defined elsewhere in the document, use the function name without its parentheses. For example, to assign a function to an event handler property, the syntax is:

```
objReference.eventHandlerProperty = functionName;
```

Starting with Version 4 browsers, you may nest functions inside one another:

```
function myFuncA( ) {
    statements
    function myFuncB( ) {
        statements
    }
}
```

Nested functions (such as myFuncB) can be invoked only by statements in its next outermost function.

All functions belong to the window in which the function is defined. Therefore, if a script must access a function located in a sibling frame (in the global naming space—not nested or anonymous functions), the reference must include the frame and the function name:

```
parent.otherFrame.someFunction( )
```

See also return and yield among the control structures later in this chapter.

Creating a Function
```
function myFunction([param1[, param2[,...paramN]]]) {
    statement(s)
}
var functionRef = function ([param1[, param2[,...paramN]]]) {
    statement(s)
};

var myFunction = new Function([param1[,...paramN], "statement1[; ...
statementN;"])objectRef.methodName = function([param1[, param2[,...paramN]]]) {
    statement(s)
};
```

Properties

arguments	arity	caller	constructor	length	prototype

Methods

apply( )	toString( )	call( )	valueOf( )

arguments

Read-only

Returns an arguments object that contains values passed as arguments to the function. Script statements inside the function can access the values through array syntax, which has numeric index values that correspond to incoming parameter values in the order in which they were passed. The content of the arguments array is independent of the parameter variables defined for the function. Therefore, if the function defines two parameter variables but the calling statement passes 10 parameters, the arguments array captures all 10 values in the order in which they were passed. Statements inside the function may then examine the length of the arguments array and extract values as needed. This allows one function to handle an indeterminate number of parameters if the need arises.

For most browsers, you can simply begin the reference to the object with the name of the property (e.g., arguments[2]). But some older browsers require the name of the enclosing function object, as well. All browsers recognize the longer version.

Example
```
function myFunc( )
    for (var i = 0; i < myFunc.arguments.length; i++) {
        ...
    }
}
```

Value   An arguments object.

arity

Returns an integer representing the number of parameters that are defined for the function. This property may be examined in a statement outside of the function, perhaps in preparation of parameters to be passed to the function. Returns the same value as the length property.

Example   `var paramCount = myFunction.arity;`

Value   Integer.

caller

Returns a reference to a function object that contained the statement invoking the current function. This property is readable only by script statements running in function whose caller you wish to reference. Omitted in some pre-1.0 versions of Mozilla, but back in subsequent versions.

Example
```
function myFunc( )
    if (myFunc.caller == someFuncZ) {
        // process when this function is called by someFuncZ
    }
}
```
Value   Function object.

constructor

This is a reference to the function that created the instance of a Function object—the native Function( ) constructor function in browsers.

Example
```
if (myVar.constructor == Function) {
    // process native function
}
```
Value   Function object reference.

length

Returns an integer representing the number of parameters that are defined for the function. This property may be examined in a statement outside of the function, perhaps in preparation of parameters to be passed to the function.

Example   var paramCount = myFunction.length;

Value   Integer.

prototype   IE 4 NN 3 Moz *all* Saf *all* Op 7 ECMA 1

This is a property of the static Function object. Use the prototype property to assign new properties and methods to future instances of functions created in the current document. See the Array.prototype property description for examples.

Example   Function.prototype.author = "DG";

Value   Any data, including function references.

apply( )   IE 5.5 NN *n/a* Moz *all* Saf *all* Op 7 ECMA 3
apply([*thisObjectRef*[, *argumentsArray*]])

Invokes the current function, optionally specifying an object to be used as the context for which any this references in the function applies. Parameters to the function (if any) are contained in array that is passed as the second parameter of the apply( ) method. The method can be used with anonymous or named functions. Usage of this method is rare, but provides flexibility that is helpful if your script should encounter a reference to a function and needs to invoke that function, particularly within an object's context.

Consider a script function that is assigned as a method of a custom object:

```
// function definition
function myFunc(parm1, parm2, parm3) {
    // statements
}
// custom object constructor
function customObj(arg1, arg2) {
    this.property1 = arg1;
    this.property2 = arg2;
    this.method1 = myFunc;
}
var myObjA = new CustomObj(val1, val2);
var myObjB = new CustomObj(val3, val4);
```

The most common way to execute the myFunc( ) function is as a method of one of the objects:

```
myObjA.method1(parmValue);
```

But you can invoke the function from a reference to the function, and make the function believe it is being invoked through one of the objects:

```
myFunc.apply(myObjB, [parmVal1, parmVal2, parmVal3]);
```

If the function (myFunc in this example) has a statement with the this keyword in it, that term becomes a reference to the object context passed as the first parameter to the apply( ) method (myObjB in this example).

Returned Value   None.

Parameters

thisObjectRef
> Reference to an object that is to act as the context for the function.

argumentsArray
> An array with items that are values to be passed to the function. Array entries are passed to the function in the same order as they are organized in the array.

call( )
IE 5.5 NN *n/a* Moz *all* Saf *all* Op 7 ECMA 3

`call([thisObjectRef[, arg1[, arg2,[...argN]]]])`

Invokes the current function, optionally specifying an object to be used as the context for which any this references in the function applies. Parameters to the function (if any) are contained in a comma-delimited list passed as additional parameters to the call( ) method. Other than the way parameters to the function are assembled, the call( ) and apply( ) methods perform the same tasks. See the apply( ) method for more details.

Returned Value   None.

Parameters

thisObjectRef
> Reference to an object that is to act as the context for the function.

arg1,...argN
> A comma-delimited list of parameters values to be passed to the function.

toString( )
IE 4 NN 4 Moz *all* Saf *all* Op 7 ECMA 1

Returns the object's value (script statement listing and function wrapper) as a string data type. You don't need this method in practice because the browsers automatically convert values to strings when they are needed for display in alert dialogs or in-document rendering.

Returned Value   String.

Parameters   None.

valueOf( )
IE 4 NN 4 Moz *all* Saf *all* Op 7 ECMA 1

Returns the object's value. When displaying the value, such as in an alert dialog box, the browser converts the value to a string, but the true value is an instance of the Function object.

Returned Value   A function object reference.

Parameters   None.

Global

The Global object lives in every window or frame of a JavaScript-enabled browser (it is created for you automatically). You don't ever reference the object explicitly, but you do reference its properties and methods to accomplish tasks such as converting strings to numbers (via the parseInt( ) or parseFloat( ) methods). Properties act as constants, and thus evaluate to themselves. As an object with global scope, it exposes its members to script statements throughout the page.

Properties

Infinity	NaN	undefined

Methods

atob( )	btoa( )	decodeURI( )
decodeURIComponent( )	encodeURI( )	encodeURIComponent( )
escape( )	eval( )	GetObject( )
isFinite( )	isNaN( )	isXMLName( )
parseInt( )	parseFloat( )	ScriptEngine( )
ScriptEngineBuildVersion( )	ScriptEngineMajorVersion( )	ScriptEngineMinorVersion( )
unescape( )	unwatch( )	watch( )

Infinity

Read-only

Provides a numerical positive infinity (or negated with the - operator). We're talking a practical, as opposed to a theoretical, infinity here. Any number smaller than Number.MIN_VALUE or larger than Number.MAX_VALUE is an infinite value in the JavaScript world. How mundane!

Example var authorEgo = Infinity;

Value Infinity

NaN

Read-only

This is a value that is not-a-number. JavaScript returns this value when a numerical operation yields a non-numerical result because of a flaw in one of the operands. If you want to test whether a value is not a number, use the isNaN( ) global function rather than comparing to this property value. This global property is the value that Number.NaN evaluates to.

Value NaN

undefined
IE 5.5 NN *n/a* Moz *all* Saf *all* Op 7 ECMA 2

Read-only

While the undefined data type has been in ECMAScript and browsers since very early times, only recently was it also elevated to a formal property of the Global object. Despite the recent compatibility ratings, you can use its data type (accessed in string form via the typeof operator) comfortably in older browsers.

Value   undefined

atob( ), btoa( )
IE *n/a* NN 4 Moz *all* Saf *n/a* Op *n/a* ECMA *n/a*

atob("*base64EncodedData*") btoa("*stringToBeEncoded*")

These methods let you convert arbitrary strings (including strings conveying characters representing binary data and Unicode values) to a 65-character subset of the U.S.-ASCII character set. Encoding in this so-called base64 scheme allows any data to be conveyed along even the most rudimentary transport mechanism. You can read about the rationale and internal mechanisms of the encoding/decoding conversions in RFC 1521 of the Internet Engineering Task Force (*http://www.ietf.org/rfc/rfc2045.txt*).

Use the btoa( ) method to encode string data into the base64 scheme. The resulting encoded data will consist of ASCII characters a–z, A–Z, 0–9, and three symbols (/, +, =). Use the atob( ) method to decode base64 encoded data back to its original version.

Returned Value   A string.

Parameters

base64EncodedData
> A string containing base64 data either encoded on the client or received as part of a document from a server that performs its own encoding.

stringToBeEncoded
> A string characters to be encoded to base64 for internal or external use. For example, an encoded value could be assigned to the value property of an input element for submission to a server process designed to receive base64 data.

decodeURI( )
IE 5.5 NN *n/a* Moz *all* Saf *all* Op 7 ECMA 3

decodeURI("*ercodedURI*")

Returns a string with most URI-encoded values in the parameter restored to their original symbols. Operates only on escaped (encoded) characters that are encodable via the encodeURI( ) method.

Returned Value   A string.

Parameters

encodedURI
> A string containing a relative or complete encoded URI.

decodeURIComponent( ) IE *5.5* NN *n/a* Moz *all* Saf *all* Op *7* ECMA *3*

decodeURIComponent("*encodedURIComponent*")

Returns a string with all URI-encoded values in the parameter restored to their original symbols. Intended for use on data portions of a URI excluding the protocol. This method replaces the ECMA-deprecated unescape( ) function.

Returned Value   A string.

Parameters

encodedURIComponent

> A string containing a relative or complete encoded URI, or portions thereof.

encodeURI( ) IE *5.5* NN *n/a* Moz *all* Saf *all* Op *7* ECMA *3*

encodeURI("*URIString*")

Returns a string with most URI-encodable values in the parameter converted to their escaped versions (e.g., a space character is converted to %20). This method excludes the following characters from conversion:

>   ; / ? : @ & = + $, #

These characters are valid symbols in URI strings as-is, and should not be converted, and the conversion might invalidate the URI. This method replaces the ECMA-deprecated escape( ) function.

Returned Value   A string.

Parameters

URIString

> A string containing a relative or complete plain-text URI.

encodeURIComponent( ) IE *5.5* NN *n/a* Moz *all* Saf *all* Op *7* ECMA *3*

encodeURIComponent("*URIComponentString*")

Returns a string with all characters except Latin character set letters A through Z (upper and lowercases), digits 0 through 9, and a set of URI-friendly symbols (- _ . ! ~ * ( ) ' *space*) converted to their escaped versions (% symbol followed by the hexadecimal version of their Unicode value). Intended for use on data portions of a URI excluding the protocol.

Returned Value   A string.

Parameters

URIComponentString

> A string containing a relative or complete plain-text URI, or portions thereof.

escape( )

IE 3 NN 2 Moz *all* Saf *all* Op 7 ECMA |1|

escape("*string*"[, 1])

Returns a URL-encoded version of the string passed as a parameter to the function. URL encoding converts most nonalphanumeric characters (except * _ + - . / and, in IE, @) to hexadecimal values (such as %20 for the space character). URL-encoded strings do not normally encode the plus symbol because those symbols are used to separate components of search strings. If you must have the plus symbol encoded as well, Navigator 4 (only) offers a second parameter (a numeral 1) to turn on that switch for the method. Note that this method has been deprecated in favor of the encodeURI( ) and encodeURIComponent( ) methods. This method has been removed from the ECMA 3 specification.

Returned Value   A string.

Parameters

string
    Any string value.

eval( )

IE 3 NN 2 Moz *all* Saf *all* Op 7 ECMA 1

eval("*string*")

Returns an object reference of the object described as a string in the parameter of the function. For example, if a form has a sequence of text fields named entry1, entry2, entry3, and so on, you can still use a for loop to cycle through all items by name if you let the eval( ) function convert the string representation of the names to object references:

```
for (var i = 1; i <=5; i++) {
    oneField = eval("document.forms[0].entry" + i);
    oneValue = oneField.value;
    ...
}
```

Be aware, however, that the eval( ) method is perhaps the most inefficient and performance-draining method of the entire JavaScript language. There are many other, far more efficient, ways to reference a document tree object when you have only the string ID or name, such as the document.getElementById( ) and, for older browsers, named indexes of the document.forms, document.images, and document.formRef.elements arrays.

Returned Value   Object reference.

Parameters

string
    Any string representation of an object reference.

GetObject( )

IE 5(Win) NN *n/a* Moz *n/a* Saf *n/a* Op *n/a* ECMA *n/a*

GetObject("*localPathName*"[, *appName.objectType*])

Returns a reference to an ActiveX object hosted on the client machine whose path name the script is aware of. This is an alternate to creating an instance of an ActiveXObject. In addition to specifying the pathname of the control, you can name a data file to open along with the control's application. Append an exclamation point and the name of the file as part of the *localPathName* parameter. To learn more about invoking ActiveX objects (also called automation objects), visit: *http://msdn2.microsoft.com/en-us/library/7tf9xwsc.aspx*.

Returned Value   Object reference.

Parameters

localPathName
>   A string containing a complete pathname (including volume) to the automation object.

appName.objectType
>   Common syntax to reference a particular application and type of object supported by the automation object whose path is specified in the first parameter.

isFinite( )   IE *4* NN *4* Moz *all* Saf *all* Op *7* ECMA *1*
isFinite(*expression*)

Returns a Boolean value of true if the number passed as a parameter is anything within the range of Number.MIN_VALUE and Number.MAX_VALUE, inclusive. String values passed as parameters cause the function to return false.

Returned Value   Boolean value: true | false.

Parameters

expression
>   Any JavaScript expression.

isNaN( )   IE *3* NN *2* Moz *all* Saf *all* Op *7* ECMA *1*
isNaN(*expression*)

Returns a Boolean value of true if the expression passed as a parameter does not evaluate to a numeric value. Any expression that evaluates to NaN (such as performing parseInt( ) on a string that does not begin with a numeral) causes the isNaN( ) method to return true.

Returned Value   Boolean value: true | false.

Parameters

expression
>   Any JavaScript expression.

isXMLName( )   IE *n/a* NN *n/a* Moz *1.8.1* Saf *n/a* Op *n/a* ECMA *E4X*
isXMLName(*string*)

Returns a Boolean value of true if the string passed as a parameter is a valid local name for XML elements or attributes.

Returned Value   Boolean value: true | false.

Parameters

string

> Any JavaScript string.

parseInt( )   IE 3   NN 2   Moz *all*   Saf *all*   Op 7   ECMA 1

parseInt("*string* "[, *radix*])

Returns an integer value (as a number data type in base-8 or base-10) of the numerals in the string passed as a parameter. The string value must at least begin with a numeral, or the result is NaN. If the string starts with numbers but changes to letters along the way or includes whitespace, only the leading numbers up to the first nonnumeral or whitespace are converted to the integer. Therefore, you can use the expression:

    parseInt(navigator.appVersion)

to extract only the whole number of the version that leads the otherwise long string that is returned from that property.

The optional radix parameter lets you specify the base of the number being passed to the function. A number string that begins with zero is normally treated as an octal number, which gives you the wrong answer. It is a good idea to use the radix value of 10 on all parseInt( ) functions if all of your dealings are in base-10 numbers.

Returned Value   Integer.

Parameters

string

> Any string that begins with one or more numerals, +, or -.

radix

> An integer of the number base of the number passed as the string parameter (e.g., 2, 8, 10, 16).

parseFloat( )   IE 3   NN 2   Moz *all*   Saf *all*   Op 7   ECMA 1

parseFloat(*string*)

Returns a number value (either an integer or floating-point number) of the numerals in the string passed as a parameter. The string value must at least begin with a numeral, or the result is NaN. If the string starts with numbers but changes to letters along the way, only the leading numbers are converted to the integer. Therefore, you can use the expression:

    parseFloat(navigator.appVersion)

to extract the complete version number (e.g., 4.03) that leads the otherwise long string that is returned from that property.

If the converted value doesn't have any nonzero values to the right of the decimal, the returned value is an integer. Floating-point values are returned only when the number calls for it.

Returned Value   Number.

Parameters

string

> Any string that begins with one or more numerals, +, or -.

ScriptEngine( ), ScriptEngineBuildVersion( ), ScriptEngineMajorVersion( ), ScriptEngineMinorVersion( )

IE 4 NN n/a Moz n/a Saf n/a Op n/a ECMA n/a

These Internet Explorer-only functions reveal information about the scripting engine (JScript, VBScript, or VBA) being used to invoke the method and which version of that engine is installed. For JScript, the version refers to the version of the *Jscript.dll* file installed among the browser's support files. The major version is the part of the version number to the left of the version decimal point; the minor version is the part to the right of the decimal point. More granular than that is the internal build number that Microsoft uses to keep track of release generations during development and through release.

Returned Value

ScriptEngine( ) returns a string of one of the following engine names: JScript | VBA | VBScript. All other functions return integer values.

Parameters   None.

unescape( )

IE 3 NN 2 Moz all Saf all Op all ECMA |1|

unescape(*string*)

Returns a decoded version of the URL-encoded string passed as a parameter to the function. URL encoding converts nonalphanumeric characters (except * _ + - . / and, in IE, @) to hexadecimal values (such as %20 for the space character). Note that this method has been deprecated in favor of the decodeURI( ) and decodeURIComponent( ) methods. This method has been removed from the ECMA 3 specification.

Returned Value   String.

Parameters

string

> Any URL-encoded string value.

unwatch( ), watch( )

IE n/a NN 4 Moz all Saf n/a Op n/a ECMA n/a

unwatch(*property*) watch(*property, funcHandler*)

These Navigator- and Mozilla-specific functions are used internally primarily by JavaScript debuggers. When a statement invokes the watch( ) function for an object, the parameters include the property whose value is to be watched and the reference to the function to be invoked whenever the value of the property is changed by an assignment statement. To turn off the watch operation, invoke the unwatch( ) function for the particular property engaged earlier.

Returned Value   Nothing.

Parameters

property
>   The name of the object's property to be watched.

funcHandler
>   The name of the function (no parentheses) to be invoked whenever the watched property's value changes.

Iterator

An iterator can act as a read-only property reader of an object, facilitating single-stepping through all properties of an object in the order in which the properties were originally defined. The JavaScript for-in control structure essentially uses the same technique, but by creating a custom iterator object, you control when the next property in the object is read via the next( ) method. Between invocations of the next( ) method, the iterator object instance remembers which item is next in the queue. When the next( ) method finds no further properties to read, it throws a StopIteration exception.

Create a custom interator object by invoking the Iterator( ) constructor function, passing a reference to the object through which you intend to iterate. An optional Boolean second parameter, when set to true, suppresses the property values being returned by the next( ) method.

Creating an Iterator Object

```
var myIterator = new Iterator(object[, propertyNameOnlyFlag]);
```

Properties

constructor   prototype

Methods

next( )

constructor, prototype

See the corresponding properties in the Array object description.

next( )

next( )

Reads the property of the iterator following the most recent one read. The method returns either an array of the property/value pair or a string of the property name. After the property is read, the iterator keeps the "pointer" in position, awaiting the next invocation of the method. If the method attempts to read a property after the last one, the method throws a

`StopIteration` exception. You can invoke this method in individual steps or within a looping control structure, such as a `while` construction.

Returned Value

Two-element array when the iterator is created with both property name and value (the default), otherwise a string of just the property name. When the method returns an array, the first element is the property name, the second element is the property value, which may be of any type.

Parameters   None.

Math   IE 3   NN 2   Moz *all*   Saf *all*   Op 7   ECMA 1

The `Math` object is used only in its static object form as a library of math constant values and (mostly trigonometric) operations. As a result, there is no constructor function. `Math` object properties are constant values, while methods return a numeric value reflecting some math operation on a value; the original value is not altered when the method is invoked.

Invoking a `Math` object property or method adheres to the following syntax:

```
Math.propertyName
Math.method(param1[, param2])
```

Be sure to observe the uppercase "M" in the `Math` object in script statements. All expressions involving the `Math` object evaluate to or return a value.

Properties

| E | LN10 | LN2 | LOG10E | LOG2E | PI | SQRT1_2 | SQRT2 |

Methods

abs( )	acos( )	asin( )	atan( )	atan2( )	ceil( )
cos( )	exp( )	floor( )	log( )	max( )	min( )
pow( )	random( )	round( )	sin( )	sqrt( )	tan( )

E   IE 3   NN 2   Moz *all*   Saf *all*   Op 7   ECMA 1

Read-only

Returns Euler's constant.

Example   `var num = Math.E;`
Value   2.718281828459045

LN2   IE 3   NN 2   Moz *all*   Saf *all*   Op 7   ECMA 1

Read-only

Returns the natural logarithm of 2.

Example   var num = Math.LN2;

Value   0.6931471805599453

LN10

IE *3*   NN *2*   Moz *all*   Saf *all*   Op *7*   ECMA *1*

Read-only

Returns the natural logarithm of 10.

Example   var num = Math.LN10;

Value   2.302585092994046

LOG2E

IE *3*   NN *2*   Moz *all*   Saf *all*   Op *7*   ECMA *1*

Read-only

Returns the log base-2 of Euler's constant.

Example   var num = Math.LOG2E;

Value   1.4426950408889634

LOG10E

IE *3*   NN *2*   Moz *all*   Saf *all*   Op *7*   ECMA *1*

Read-only

Returns the log base-10 of Euler's constant.

Example   var num = Math.LOG10E;

Value   0.4342944819032518

PI

IE *3*   NN *2*   Moz *all*   Saf *all*   Op *7*   ECMA *1*

Read-only

Returns the value of π.

Example   var num = Math.PI;

Value   3.141592653589793

SQRT1_2

IE *3*   NN *2*   Moz *all*   Saf *all*   Op *7*   ECMA *1*

Read-only

Returns the square root of 0.5.

Example   var num = Math.SQRT1_2;

Value   0.7071067811865476

SQRT2
<specific>IE *3* NN *2* Moz *all* Saf *all* Op *7* ECMA *1*</specific>

Returns the square root of 2.

Example   `var num = Math.SQRT2;`

Value   1.4142135623730951

abs( )
IE *3* NN *2* Moz *all* Saf *all* Op *7* ECMA *1*

`abs(`*number*`)`

Returns the absolute value of the number passed as a parameter.

Returned Value   Positive number or zero.

Parameters

number
    Any number.

acos( )
IE *3* NN *2* Moz *all* Saf *all* Op *7* ECMA *1*

`acos(`*number*`)`

Returns the arc cosine (in radians) of the number passed as a parameter.

Returned Value   Number.

Parameters

number
    Any number from –1 to 1.

asin( )
IE *3* NN *2* Moz *all* Saf *all* Op *7* ECMA *1*

`asin(`*number*`)`

Returns the arc sine (in radians) of the number passed as a parameter.

Returned Value   Number.

Parameters

number
    Any number from –1 to 1.

atan( )
IE *3* NN *2* Moz *all* Saf *all* Op *7* ECMA *1*

`atan(`*number*`)`

Returns the arc tangent (in radians) of the number passed as a parameter.

Returned Value   Number.

Parameters

number

Any number between negative infinity and infinity.

atan2( )
IE *4* NN *2* Moz *all* Saf *all* Op *7* ECMA *1*

`atan2(x, y)`

Returns the angle (in radians) of angle formed by a line to Cartesian point x, y.

Returned Value   Number between $-\pi$ and π.

Parameters

x

Any number.

y

Any number.

ceil( )
IE *3* NN *2* Moz *all* Saf *all* Op *7* ECMA *1*

`ceil(number)`

Returns the next higher integer that is greater than or equal to the number passed as a parameter.

Returned Value   Integer.

Parameters

number

Any number.

cos( )
IE *3* NN *2* Moz *all* Saf *all* Op *7* ECMA *1*

`cos(number)`

Returns the cosine of the number passed as a parameter.

Returned Value   Number.

Parameters

number

Any number.

exp( )
IE *3* NN *2* Moz *all* Saf *all* Op *7* ECMA *1*

`exp(number)`

Returns the value of Euler's constant to the power of the number passed as a parameter.

Returned Value   Number.

Parameters

number
> Any number.

floor( ) IE 3 NN 2 Moz *all* Saf *all* Op 7 ECMA 1

floor(*number*)

Returns the next lower integer that is less than or equal to the number passed as a parameter.

Returned Value   Integer.

Parameters

number
> Any number.

log( ) IE 3 NN 2 Moz *all* Saf *all* Op 7 ECMA 1

log(*number*)

Returns the natural logarithm (base e) of the number passed as a parameter.

Returned Value   Number.

Parameters

number
> Any number.

max( ) IE 3 NN 2 Moz *all* Saf *all* Op 7 ECMA 1

max(*number1*, *number2*)

Returns the greater value of the two parameters.

Returned Value   Number.

Parameters

number1
> Any number.

number2
> Any number.

min( ) IE 3 NN 2 Moz *all* Saf *all* Op 7 ECMA 1

min(*number1*, *number2*)

Returns the lesser value of the two parameters.

Returned Value   Number.

Parameters

number1

> Any number.

number2

> Any number.

pow( ) IE 3 NN 2 Moz *all* Saf *all* Op 7 ECMA 1

pow(*number1, number2*)

Returns the value of the first parameter raised to the power of the second parameter.

Returned Value   Number.

Parameters

number1

> Any number.

number2

> Any number.

random( ) IE 3 NN 2 Moz *all* Saf *all* Op 7 ECMA 1

Returns a pseudo-random number between 0 and 1. To calculate a pseudo-random integer between zero and another maximum value, use the formula:

```
Math.floor(Math.random( ) * (n+1))
```

where *n* is the top integer of the acceptable range. To calculate a pseudo-random integer between a range starting with a number other than zero, use the formula:

```
Math.floor(Math.random( ) * n - m + 1) + m
```

where *m* is the lowest integer of the acceptable range and *n* equals the maximum value of the range. Note that the Math.random( ) method does not work in the Windows and Macintosh versions of Navigator 2.

Returned Value   Number from 0 up to, but not including, 1.

Parameters   None.

round( ) IE 3 NN 2 Moz *all* Saf *all* Op 7 ECMA 1

round(*number*)

Returns an integer that follows rounding rules. If the value of the passed parameter is greater than or equal to $x.5$, the returned value is $x + 1$; otherwise, the returned value is x.

Returned Value   Integer.

Parameters

number

> Any number.

sin( )

IE 3   NN 2   Moz all   Saf all   Op 7   ECMA 1

```
sin(number)
```

Returns the sine (in radians) of the number passed as a parameter.

Returned Value   Number.

Parameters

number

Any number.

sqrt( )

IE 3   NN 2   Moz all   Saf all   Op 7   ECMA 1

```
sqrt(number)
```

Returns the square root of the number passed as a parameter.

Returned Value   Number.

Parameters

number

Any number.

tan( )

IE 3   NN 2   Moz all   Saf all   Op 7   ECMA 1

```
tan(number)
```

Returns the tangent (in radians) of the number passed as a parameter.

Returned Value   Number.

Parameters

number

Any number between negative infinity and infinity.

Namespace

IE n/a   NN n/a   Moz 1.8.1   Saf n/a   Op n/a   ECMA E4X

An instance of the Namespace object (from the E4X standard) is an object that typically associates a URI (whose location contains information about the elements defined for the namespace) with a prefix that is prepended to an element's local name. A namespace object instance has two properties, prefix and uri, both of which are string values. Namespace object instances are used as parameter values for some methods of the XML and XMLList objects.

You can create a namespace object by invoking the Namespace( ) constructor function with zero, one, or two parameters. The most common invocation of the constructor is with two parameter strings, the first being the prefix, and the second being the URI, as follows:

```
var myNamespace = new Namespace("ns", "http://www.example.com/schema");
```

Creating a Namespace Object

```
var myNamespace = new Namespace([prefix],[uri]);
```

Properties

constructor   prefix   prototype
uri

Methods

toString( )

constructor, prototype

IE *n/a* NN *n/a* Moz *1.8.1* Saf *n/a* Op *n/a* ECMA *n/a*

Read/Write

See the corresponding properties in the Array object description.

prefix

IE *n/a* NN *n/a* Moz *1.8.1* Saf *n/a* Op *n/a* ECMA *n/a*

Read-only

A string containing the namespace prefix. An empty string signifies that the namespace is the default namespace for the XML data.

Example   var myPrefix = myNamespace.prefix;

Value   String.

uri

IE *n/a* NN *n/a* Moz *1.8.1* Saf *n/a* Op *n/a* ECMA *n/a*

Read-only

A string containing the namespace URI.

Example   var myNSUri = myNamespace.uri;

Value   String.

toString( )

IE *n/a* NN *n/a* Moz *1.8.1* Saf *n/a* Op *n/a* ECMA *n/a*

Returns the object's value as a string data type. For an instance of a Namespace object, the uri property value is returned.

Returned Value   String.

Parameters   None.

Number

IE *4* NN *3* Moz *all* Saf *all* Op *7* ECMA *1*

A Number object represents any numerical value, whether it is an integer or floating-point number. By and large, you don't have to worry about the Number object because a numerical value automatically becomes a Number object instance whenever you use such a value or assign it to a variable. On the other hand, you might want access to the static properties that only a math major would love.

Creating a Number Object

```
var myValue = number;
var myValue = new Number(number);
```

Properties

constructor	MAX_VALUE	MIN_VALUE	NaN
NEGATIVE_INFINITY	POSITIVE_INFINITY	prototype	

Methods

toExponential( )	toFixed( )	toLocaleString( )	toPrecision( )
toString( )	valueOf( )		

---

constructor

IE 4   NN 4   Moz *all*   Saf *all*   Op 7   ECMA 1

Read/Write

This is a reference to the function that created the instance of a Number object—the native Number( ) constructor function in browsers.

Example

```
if (myVar.constructor == Number) {
    // process native function
}
```

Value   Function object reference.

MAX_VALUE

IE 4   NN 3   Moz *all*   Saf *all*   Op 7   ECMA 1

Read-only

Equal to the highest possible number that JavaScript can handle.

Example   `var tiptop = Number.MAX_VALUE;`

Value   1.7976931348623157e+308

MIN_VALUE

IE 4   NN 3   Moz *all*   Saf *all*   Op 7   ECMA 1

Read-only

Equal to the smallest possible number that JavaScript can handle.

Example   `var itsybitsy = Number.MIN_VALUE;`

Value   5e-324

NaN

IE 4 NN 3 Moz *all* Saf *all* Op 7 ECMA 1
Read-only

Equal to a value that is not-a-number. JavaScript returns this value when a numerical operation yields a non-numerical result because of a flaw in one of the operands. If you want to test whether a value is not a number, use the isNaN( ) global function rather than comparing to this property value.

Value   NaN

NEGATIVE_INFINITY, POSITIVE_INFINITY

IE 4 NN 3 Moz *all* Saf *all* Op 7 ECMA 1
Read-only

Values that are outside of the bounds of Number.MIN_VALUE and Number.MAX_VALUE, respectively.

Example   Number.NEGATIVE_INFINITY

Value   -Infinity; Infinity

prototype

IE 4 NN 3 Moz *all* Saf *all* Op 7 ECMA 1
Read/Write

A property of the static Number object. Use the prototype property to assign new properties and methods to future instances of a Number value created in the current document. See the Array.prototype property description for examples. There is little need to create new prototype properties or methods for the Number object.

Example   Number.prototype.author = "DG";

Value   Any data, including function references.

toExponential( )

IE 5.5 NN *n/a* Moz *all* Saf *all* Op 7 ECMA 3

toExponential(*fractionDigits*)

Returns a string containing the number object's value displayed in JavaScript's exponential notation. The single parameter specifies the number of digits to the right of the decimal to display in the string. For example, if a variable contains the number 9876.54, if you apply the toExponential(10) method, the result is 9.8765400000E+3, with zeroes padding the rightmost digits to reach a total of 10 digits to the right of the decimal. If you specify a parameter that yields a display with fewer digits than in the original number, the returned value is rounded.

Returned Value   String.

Parameters

fractionDigits
    An integer specifying the number of digits to the right of the decimal in the returned string.

---

toFixed( )

`toFixed(fractionDigits)`

Returns a string containing the number object's value displayed with a fixed number of digits to the right of the decimal (useful for currency calculation results). If you specify a parameter that yields a display with fewer significant digits than the original number, the returned value is rounded, but based only on the value of the digit immediately to the right of the last displayed digit (i.e., rounding does not cascade).

Returned Value   String.

Parameters

`fractionDigits`
> An integer specifying the number of digits to the right of the decimal in the returned string.

toLocaleString( )

Returns a string version of the number object's value. The precise format of the returned value is not mandated by the ECMA standard, and may be different from one local currency system to another (as set in the client computer's international preferences). On a U.S. English system, IE 5.5 and later for Windows returns a value with two digits to the right of the decimal (rounding values if necessary), with commas denoting thousands, millions, and so on. IE 5 for Macintosh does the same except for the commas. Mozilla, Safari, and Opera perform no special formatting.

Returned Value   String.

Parameters   None.

toPrecision( )

`toPrecision(precisionDigits)`

Returns a string containing the number object's value displayed with a fixed number of digits, counting digits to the left and right of the decimal. If you specify a parameter that yields a display with fewer digits to the left of the decimal than the original number, the returned value is displayed in exponential notation. Truncated values are rounded, but based only on the value of the digit immediately to the right of the last displayed digit (i.e., rounding does not cascade).

Returned Value   String.

Parameters

`precisionDigits`
> An integer specifying the total number of digits in the returned string.

toString( )   *IE 4 NN 4 Moz all Saf all Op 7 ECMA 1*

Returns the object's value as a string data type. You don't need this method in practice because the browsers automatically convert Number values to strings when they are needed for display in alert dialogs or in-document rendering.

Returned Value   String.

Parameters   None.

valueOf( )   *IE 4 NN 4 Moz all Saf all Op 7 ECMA 1*

Returns the object's value.

Returned Value   A numeric value.

Parameters   None.

Object   *IE 4 NN 3 Moz all Saf all Op 7 ECMA 1*

In addition to serving quietly as the foundation of all native JavaScript objects, the Object object is the pure model of the JavaScript object—including custom script objects you create. Use the Object object to generate things in your scripts with behaviors that are defined by custom properties and/or methods. Most typically, you start by creating a blank object with the constructor function and then assign values to new properties of that object.

Navigator 4, IE 5 or later, and all modern scriptable browsers also let you assign properties and values via a special literal syntax that also creates the Object instance in the process:

```
var myObject = {propName1:propValue1[, propName2:propValue2[,
...propNameN:propValueN]]}
```

You can use objects as data structures for structured custom data in your scripts, much like creating an array with named index values.

Creating an Object Object

```
var myObject = new Object( );
var myObject = {propName1:propVal1[, propName2:propVal2[,...N]]};
var myObject = new constructorFuncName([propVal1[, propVal2[,...N]]]);
```

Properties

constructor   prototype

Methods

hasOwnProperty( )	isPrototypeOf( )	propertyIsEnumerable( )
toLocaleString( )	toString( )	valueOf( )

constructor

Provides a reference to the function that created the instance of an Object object—the native Object( ) constructor function in browsers.

Example

```
if (myVar.constructor == Object) {
    // process native string
}
```

Value   Function object reference.

prototype

This is a property of the static Object. Use the prototype property to assign new properties and methods to future instances of an Object created in the current document. See the Array.prototype property description for examples.

Example   Object.prototype.author = "DG";

Value   Any data, including function references.

hasOwnProperty( )
hasOwnProperty("*propertyName*")

Returns Boolean true if, at the time the current object's instance was created, its constructor (or literal assignment) contained a property with a name that matches the parameter value. A property assigned to an object via its prototype property is not considered one of the object's own properties.

Returned Value   Boolean value: true | false.

Parameters

propertyName
    String containing the name of an object property.

isPrototypeOf( )
isPrototypeOf(*objectReference*)

Returns Boolean true if the current object and the object passed as a parameter coincide at some point along each object's prototype inheritance chain. Note that different browser implementations do not always agree on the results.

Returned Value   Boolean value: true | false.

Parameters

objectReference
Reference to an object that potentially shares prototype inheritance with the current object.

propertyIsEnumerable( )   IE *5.5* NN *n/a* Moz *all* Saf *n/a* Op *7* ECMA *3*

propertyIsEnumerable("*propertyName*")

Returns Boolean true if the property, whose name is passed as a parameter, exposes itself to for-in property inspection through the object.

Returned Value   Boolean value: true | false.

Parameters

propertyName
String containing the name of an object property.

toLocaleString( )   IE *5.5* NN *n/a* Moz *all* Saf *n/a* Op *7* ECMA *3*

Browsers are free to determine how to localize string representations of object instances. For now, they appear to perform the same action as the toString( ) method, returning the value [object Object].

Returned Value   String.

Parameters   None.

toString( )   IE *4* NN *4* Moz *all* Saf *all* Op *7* ECMA *1*

Returns the object's value as a string data type. In recent browsers, this value is [object Object].

Returned Value   String.

Parameters   None.

valueOf( )   IE *4* NN *4* Moz *all* Saf *all* Op *7* ECMA *1*

Returns the object's value.

Returned Value   An object reference.

Parameters   None.

QName   IE *n/a* NN *n/a* Moz *1.8.1* Saf *n/a* Op *n/a* ECMA *E4X*

An instance of the QName object (from the E4X standard) is an object that represents a qualified XML name for an element or attribute. A Qname object instance has two properties, localName and uri, both of which are string values. The name( ) method of an XML object returns a value of this object type.

You can create a Qname object by invoking the QName( ) constructor function with zero, one, or two parameters. The most common invocation of the constructor is with two parameters, the first being an instance of a Namespace object (from which the Qname object derives its uri property value), and the second being a string for the local name, as follows:

```
var myNamespace = new Namespace("ns", "http://www.example.com/schema");
var myQname = new QName(myNamespace, "widgetNumber");
```

Creating a namespace object

```
var myQname = new QName([namespaceObject],["localName"]);
```

Properties

constructor	localName	prototype
uri		

Methods

toString( )

constructor, prototype

IE *n/a* NN *n/a* Moz *1.8.1* Saf *n/a* Op *n/a* ECMA *n/a*
Read/Write

See the corresponding properties in the Array object description.

localName

IE *n/a* NN *n/a* Moz *1.8.1* Saf *n/a* Op *n/a* ECMA *n/a*
Read-only

A string containing the local name portion of a qualified name.

Example   `var myName = myQname.localName;`

Value   String.

uri

IE *n/a* NN *n/a* Moz *1.8.1* Saf *n/a* Op *n/a* ECMA *n/a*
Read-only

A string containing the namespace URI.

Example   `var myNSUri = myQname.uri;`

Value   String.

toString( )

IE *n/a* NN *n/a* Moz *1.8.1* Saf *n/a* Op *n/a* ECMA *n/a*

Returns the object's value as a string data type. For an instance of a QName object, the method returns the uri property value followed by a double colon (the JavaScript/E4X delimiter between a namespace and local name) and the local name.

Returned Value   String in the form: *uri::localName*.

Parameters   None.

RegExp

IE *4* NN *4* Moz *all* Saf *all* Op *all* ECMA *3*

The RegExp object is a static object that both generates instances of a regular expression and monitors all regular expression in the current window or frame. Instances of the RegExp object are covered in the regular expressions object description that follows this section.

Regular expressions assist in locating text that matches patterns of characters or characteristics. For example, a regular expression can be used to find out very quickly if an entry in a text field is a five-digit number. Defining the pattern to match requires knowledge of a separate notation syntax that is beyond the scope of this book (but is covered in *Mastering Regular Expressions*, by Jeffrey E. F. Friedl, published by O'Reilly). A summary of the syntax can be found in the description of the regular expression object.

In some browsers, properties of the RegExp object store information about the last operation of any regular expression in the document. Therefore, it is conceivable that each property could change after each regular expression operation. Such operations include not only the methods of a regular expression object instance (exec( ) and test( )), but also the String object methods that accept regular expressions as parameters (match( ), replace( ), and split( )). Some of these properties are passed to the regular expression object as well, in preparation for the next operation with the regular expression.

Where supported, all properties have verbose names as well as shortcut names that begin with $.

Properties

index	input	lastIndex	lastMatch	lastParen	leftContext
multiline	prototype	rightContext	$1	$2	$3
$4	$5	$6	$7	$8	$9

index

IE *4* NN *n/a* Moz *n/a* Saf *n/a* Op *n/a* ECMA *n/a*

Read-only

This is the zero-based index value of the character position within the string where the most recent search for the pattern began. The lastIndex property provides the end position.

Example   var srchStart = RegExp.index;

Value   Integer.

input

This is the main string against which a regular expression is compared. If the main string is handed to the regular expression operation as a parameter to a method, this value is null. The short version is $_ (dollar sign, underscore). This property is deprecated in JavaScript 1.5.

Example   `RegExp.input = "Four score and seven years ago...";`

Value   String.

lastIndex

This is the zero-based index value of the character within the string where the next search for the pattern begins. In a new search, the value is zero. You can also set the value manually if you wish to start at a different location or skip some characters. This property is echoed in the regular expression object instance, and is supported there in most browsers.

Example   `myRE.lastIndex = 30;`

Value   Integer.

lastMatch

Returns the string that matches the regular expression as a result of the most recent operation. The short version is $&. This property is deprecated in JavaScript 1.5.

Example   `var matched = RegExp.lastMatch;`

Value   String.

lastParen

Returns the string that matches the last parenthesized subcomponent of the regular expression as a result of the most recent operation. The short version is $+. This property is deprecated in JavaScript 1.5.

Example   `var myValue = RegExp.lastParen;`

Value   String.

leftContext, rightContext

The leftContext property returns the string starting with the beginning of the most recent searched text up to, but not including, the matching string. The rightContext property returns the string starting with the main string portion immediately following the matching string and extending to the end of the string. The short versions are $\`$ and $'$, respectively. Because the start of subsequent searches on the same main string move inexorably toward the end of the main string, the starting point of the leftContext value can shift with each operation. These properties are deprecated in JavaScript 1.5.

Example
```
var wholeContext = RegExp.leftContext + RegExp.lastMatch + RegExp.rightContext;
```
Value   String.

multiline   IE *n/a* NN *4* Moz *all* Saf *n/a* Op *n/a* ECMA *n/a*
Read/Write

Although implemented in NN and Mozilla, this property should be read only from an instance of the RegExp object. See the regular expression object.

prototype   IE *4* NN *4* Moz *all* Saf *all* Op *7* ECMA *3*
Read/Write

See this property for the Array object.

$1, ..., $9   IE *4* NN *4* Moz *all* Saf *n/a* Op *n/a* ECMA *n/a*
Read-only

Parenthesized subcomponents of a regular expression return results. These results are stored individually in properties labeled 1 through 9, preceded by the $ shortcut symbol. The order is based on the position of the left parenthesis of a subcomponent: the leftmost subcomponent result is placed into $1. These properties may be used directly within parameters to String methods that use regular expressions (see the String.replace( ) method). These properties are deprecated in JavaScript 1.5.

Example   RegExp.$2

Value   String.

regular expression   IE *4* NN *4* Moz *all* Saf *all* Op *7* ECMA *3*

A regular expression object is an instance of the RegExp object. Each regular expression object consists of a pattern that is used to locate matches within a string. Patterns for a regular expression can be simple strings or significantly more powerful expressions that use a notation that is essentially a language unto itself. The implementation of regular expressions in JavaScript 1.2 is very similar to the way they are implemented in Perl.

To create a regular expression object, surround the pattern with forward slashes, and assign the whole expression to a variable. For example, the following statement creates a regular expression with a pattern that is a simple word:

```
var re = /greet/;
```

The re variable can then be used as a parameter in a variety of methods that search for the pattern within some string (you may also use an expression directly as a method parameter, rather than assigning it to a variable).

Regular expression notation also consists of a number of metacharacters that stand in for sometimes complex ideas, such as the boundary on either side of a word, any numeral, or one or more characters. For example, to search for the pattern of characters shown above but only when the pattern is a word (and not part of a word such as greetings), the regular expression notation uses the metacharacters to indicate that the pattern includes word boundaries on both sides of the pattern:

```
var re = /\bgreet\b/;
```

The following table shows a summary of the regular expression notation used in JavaScript 1.2.

Character	Matches	Example
\b	Word boundary	/\bto/ matches "tomorrow"/to\b/ matches "Soweto"
		/\bto\b/ matches "to"
\B	Word nonboundary	/\Bto/ matches "stool" and "Soweto"/to\B/ matches "stool" and "tomorrow"
		/\Bto\B/ matches "stool"
\d	Numeral 0 through 9	/\d\d/ matches "42"
\D	Nonnumeral	/\D\D/ matches "to"
\s	Single whitespace	/under\sdog/ matches "under dog"
\S	Single nonwhitespace	/under\Sdog/ matches "under-dog"
\w	Letter, numeral, or underscore	/1\w/ matches "1A"
\W	Not a letter, numeral, or underscore	/1\W/ matches "1%"
.	Any character except a newline	/../ matches "Z3"
[...]	Any one of the character set in brackets	/J[aeiou]y/ matches "Joy"
[^...]	Negated character set	/J[^eiou]y/ matches "Jay"
*	Zero or more times	/\d*/ matches "", "5", or "444"
?	Zero or one time	/\d?/ matches "" or "5"
+	One or more times	/\d+/ matches "5" or "444"
{n}	Exactly n times	/\d{2}/ matches "55"
{n,}	n or more times	/\d{2,}/ matches "555"
{n,m}	At least n, at most m times	/\d{2,4}/ matches "5555"
^	At beginning of a string or line	/^Sally/ matches "Sally says..."
$	At end of a string or line	/Sally.$/ matches "Hi, Sally."

When you create a regular expression, you may optionally wire the expression to work globally (as you probably do if the regular expression is doing a search-and-replace operation with a method, and your goal is a "replace all" result) and to ignore case in its matches. The modifiers that turn on these switches are the letters g and i. They may be used by themselves or together as gi. See also the multiline property for the meaning of the m modifier.

Once you have established a pattern with the regular expression notation, all the action takes place in the regular expression object methods and the String object methods that accept regular expression parameters.

Creating a regular expression Object

```
var regExpressionObj = /pattern/ [g | i | m];
var regExpressionObj = new RegExp(["pattern", ["g" | "i" | "m"]]);
```

Properties

constructor	global	ignoreCase	lastIndex	multiline
source				

Methods

compile( )	exec( )	test( )

constructor

IE 4 NN 4 Moz *all* Saf *all* Op 7 ECMA 3

Read/Write

See this property for the Array object.

global, ignoreCase

IE 5(Mac)/5.5(Win) NN 4 Moz *all* Saf *all* Op 7 ECMA 3

Read-only

Returns Boolean true if the regular expression object instance had the g or i modifiers (respectively) set when it was created. If a regular expression object has both modifiers set (gi), you must still test for each property individually.

Example

```
if (myRE.global && myRE.ignoreCase) {
    ...
}
```

Value   Boolean value: true | false.

lastIndex

IE 4 NN 4 Moz *all* Saf *all* Op 7 ECMA 3

Read/Write

This is the zero-based index value of the character within the string where the next search for the pattern begins. In a new search, the value is zero. You can also set the value manually if you wish to start at a different location or skip some characters.

Example   myRE.lastIndex = 30;

Value   Integer.

multiline

The value of the regexp's `multiline` property is determined exclusively by the presence or absence of the "m" flag in the object constructor. In other words, the scripter determines whether the `multiline` property of the regexp object will be `true` by explicitly setting the "m" flag, as in:

    var re = /you/gm;

After the above statement executes, `re.multiline` is true.

Despite its name, the "m" flag has no bearing on the search for text matches extending across multiple lines of text in a string. All searches work across multiple-line strings anyway. The "m" flag does apply, however, when the regular expression includes the ^ or $ symbols. For example, consider the ^ symbol, which indicates that the pattern must start at the beginning of a string. In the following multiline string:

    Are\n
    you\n
    happy?

the regexp /you/ will find a match because the pattern "you" is someplace within the string. The regexp /^you/ will not find a match because the string does not start with the pattern "you". The regexp /^you/m will find a match because the "m" (multiline) flag says it's OK to treat each physical line of a multiline string as a start of a string.

Be careful when you deploy the "m" flag because not all browsers recognize it. Using the "m" flag causes script errors in the older browsers.

Example
```
if (re.multiline) {
    ...
}
```
Value   Boolean.

source

Returns a string version of the characters used to create the regular expression. The value does not include the forward slash delimiters that surround the expression.

Example   `var myREasString = myRE.source;`

Value   String.

compile( )   IE *3*   NN *2*   Moz *all*   Saf *all*   Op *7*   ECMA *n/a*

compile("*pattern*"[, "g" | "i" | "m"])

Compiles a regular expression pattern into a genuine regular expression object. This method is used primarily to recompile a regular expression with a pattern that may change during the execution of a script.

Returned Value   Reference to a regular expression instance.

Parameters

pattern

     Any regular expression pattern as a quoted string. Modifiers for global, ignore case, or both must be supplied as a separate quoted parameter.

exec( )   IE *4*   NN *4*   Moz *all*   Saf *all*   Op *7*   ECMA *3*

exec(*string*)

Performs a search through the string passed as a parameter for the current regular expression pattern. A typical sequence follows the format:

```
var myRE = /somePattern/;
var resultArray = myRE.exec("someString");
```

Properties of both the static RegExp and regular expression instance (myRE in the example) objects are updated with information about the results of the search. In addition, the exec( ) method returns an array of data, much of it similar to RegExp object properties. The returned array includes the following properties:

index

     Zero-based index of starting character in the string that matches the pattern

input

     The original string being searched

[0]

     String of the characters matching the pattern

[1]...[n]

     Strings of the results of the parenthesized component matches

You can stow away the results of the exec( ) method in a variable, whereas the RegExp property values change with the next regular expression operation. If the regular expression is set for global searching, a subsequent call to myRE.exec("*someString*") continues the search from the position of the previous match.

If no match is found for a given call to exec( ), it returns null.

Returned Value   An array of match information if successful; null if there is no match.

Parameters

string

     The string to be searched.

test( )

test(*string*)

Returns Boolean true if there is a match of the regular expression anywhere in the string passed as a parameter, false if not. No additional information is available about the results of the search. This is the fastest way to find out if a string contains a match for a pattern.

Returned Value   Boolean value: true | false.

Parameters

string
    The string to be searched.

String

A String object represents any sequence of zero or more characters that are to be treated strictly as text (that is, no math operations are to be applied). A large library of methods is divided into two categories. One category surrounds a string with a pair of HTML tags for a variety of HTML character formatting. These methods are used primarily to assist statements that use document.write( ) to dynamically create content, but their functionality is now superceded by style sheets. The second, vital method category is the more traditional set of string parsing and manipulation methods that facilitate finding and copying characters and substrings, case changes, and conversion from string lists to JavaScript arrays.

By and large, you don't have to worry about explicitly creating a string beyond a simple assignment of a quoted string value:

    var myString = "howdy";

Occasionally, however, it is helpful to create a string object using the constructor of the static String object. Preparing string values for passage to Java applets often requires this type of string generation:

    var myString = new String("howdy");

Other than the constructor, prototype property, and fromCharCode( ) method, all properties and methods are for use with instances of the String object, rather than the static String object.

Creating a String Object

    var myValue = "*someString*";
    var myValue = new String("*someString*");

Properties

constructor	length	prototype

Methods

anchor( )	big( )	blink( )	bold( )
charAt( )	charCodeAt( )	concat( )	fixed( )
fontcolor( )	fontsize( )	fromCharCode( )	indexOf( )

italics( )	lastIndexOf( )	link( )	localeCompare( )
match( )	replace( )	search( )	slice( )
small( )	split( )	strike( )	sub( )
substr( )	substring( )	sup( )	toLocaleLowerCase( )
toLocaleUpperCase( )	toLowerCase( )	toString( )	toUpperCase( )
valueOf( )			

constructor

IE 4   NN 4   Moz *all*   Saf *all*   Op 7   ECMA 1

Read/Write

This is a reference to the function that created the instance of a String object—the native String( ) constructor function in browsers.

Example
```
if (myVar.constructor == String) {
    // process native string
}
```

Value   Function object reference.

length

IE 3   NN 2   Moz *all*   Saf *all*   Op 7   ECMA 1

Read-only

Provides a count of the number of characters in the string. String values dynamically change their lengths if new values are assigned to them or if other strings are concatenated.

Example
```
for (var i = 0; i < myString.length; i++) {
    ...
}
```

Value   Integer.

prototype

IE 4   NN 3   Moz *all*   Saf *all*   Op 7   ECMA 1

Read/Write

This is a property of the static String object. Use the prototype property to assign new properties and methods to future instances of a String value created in the current document. See the Array.prototype property description for examples.

Example   String.prototype.author = "DG";

Value   Any data, including function references.

anchor( )   IE 3   NN 2   Moz *all*   Saf *all*   Op 7   ECMA *n/a*
anchor("*anchorName*")

Returns a copy of the string embedded within an anchor (<a>) tag set. The value passed as a parameter is assigned to the name attribute of the tag.

Returned Value   A string within an a element.

Parameters
anchorName
    A string to use as the value of the name attribute.

big( )   IE 3   NN 2   Moz *all*   Saf *all*   Op 7   ECMA *n/a*

Returns a copy of the string embedded within a <big> tag set.

Returned Value   A string within a big element.

Parameters   None.

blink( )   IE 3   NN 2   Moz *all*   Saf *all*   Op 7   ECMA *n/a*

Returns a copy of the string embedded within a <blink> tag set.

Returned Value   A string within a blink element.

Parameters   None.

bold( )   IE 3   NN 2   Moz *all*   Saf *all*   Op 7   ECMA *n/a*

Returns a copy of the string embedded within a <b> tag set.

Returned Value   A string within a b element.

Parameters   None.

charAt( )   IE 3   NN 2   Moz *all*   Saf *all*   Op 7   ECMA 1
charAt(*positionIndex*)

Returns a single character string of the character located at the zero-based index position passed as a parameter. Use this method instead of substring( ) when only one character from a known position is needed from a string.

Returned Value

A one-character string. In newer browser versions, an empty string is returned if the parameter value points to a character beyond the length of the string.

Parameters
positionIndex
    Zero-based integer.

charCodeAt( )

charCodeAt(*positionIndex*)

Returns a number of the decimal Unicode value for the character located at the zero-based index position passed as a parameter. For common alphanumeric characters, the Unicode values are the same as ASCII values.

Returned Value

A positive integer. Returns NaN if the parameter value points to a character beyond the length of the string.

Parameters

positionIndex
 Zero-based integer.

concat( )

concat(*string2*)

Returns a string that appends the parameter string to the current string object. The results of this method are the same as concatenating strings with the add (+) or add-by-value (+=) operators. Neither the method nor operators insert spaces between the two string components.

Returned Value   String.

Parameters

string2
 Any string.

fixed( )

Returns a copy of the string embedded within a <tt> tag set.

Returned Value   A string within a tt element.

Parameters   None.

fontcolor( )

fontColor(*color*)

Returns a copy of the string embedded within a font (<font>) tag set. The value passed as a parameter is assigned to the color attribute of the tag.

Returned Value   A string within a font element.

Parameters

color
 A string to use as the value of the color attribute.

fontsize( )

`fontSize(size)`

Returns a copy of the string embedded within a font (`<font>`) tag set. The value passed as a parameter is assigned to the `size` attribute of the tag.

Returned Value   A string within a `font` element.

Parameters

size

An integer to use as the value of the `size` attribute.

fromCharCode( )

`String.fromCharCode(num1, [, num2,[...numN]])`

This is a static method that returns a string of one or more characters with Unicode values that are passed as a comma-delimited list of parameters. For example, the expression:

`String.fromCharCode(120, 121, 122)`

returns "xyz".

Returned Value   A string.

Parameters

num1...numN

One or more integer values in an unquoted, comma-delimited list.

indexOf( )

`indexOf(searchString[, startPositionIndex])`

Returns a zero-based integer of the position within the current string where the *searchString* parameter starts. Normally, the search starts with the first (index of zero) character, but you may have the search begin later in the string by specifying the optional second parameter, which is the index value of where the search should start. If there is no match, the returned value is -1. This is a backward-compatible quick way to find out if one string contains another: if the returned value is -1 then you know the *searchString* is not in the larger string. If the returned value is another number (the precise value doesn't matter), the *searchString* is in the larger string. For browsers that support regular expressions, the String object's search( ) method performs a similar function.

Returned Value   Integer.

Parameters

searchString

A string to look for in the current string object.

startPositionIndex

A zero-based integer indicating the position within the current string object to begin the search of the first parameter.

italics( )
IE 3 NN 2 Moz *all* Saf *all* Op 7 ECMA *n/a*

Returns a copy of the string embedded within an <i> tag set.

Returned Value A string within an i element.

Parameters None.

lastIndexOf( )
IE 3 NN 2 Moz *all* Saf *all* Op 7 ECMA 1

lastIndexOf(*searchString*[, *startPositionIndex*])

Returns a zero-based integer of the position within the current string object where the *searchString* parameter starts. This method works like the indexOf( ) method but begins all searches from the end of the string or some index position. Even though searching starts from the end of the string, the *startPositionIndex* parameter is based on the start of the string, as is the returned value. If there is no match, the returned value is -1.

Returned Value Integer.

Parameters

searchString
A string to look for in the current string object.

startPositionIndex
A zero-based integer indicating the position within the current string object to begin the search of the first parameter. Even though the search starts from the end of the string, this parameter value is relative to the front of the string.

link( )
IE 3 NN 2 Moz *all* Saf *all* Op 7 ECMA *n/a*

link(*URL*)

Returns a copy of the string embedded within an anchor (<a>) tag set. The value passed as a parameter is assigned to the href attribute of the tag.

Returned Value A string within an a element.

Parameters

URL
A string to use as the value of the href attribute.

localeCompare( )
IE 5.5 NN *n/a* Moz *all* Saf *all* Op 7 ECMA 3

localeCompare(*string2*)

Returns a number indicating whether the current string sorts before, the same as, or after the parameter string, based on browser- and system-dependent string localization. If the current string sorts before the parameter string, the return value is a negative number; if they are the same, the return value is 0, if the current string sorts after the parameter string, the return value is a positive number.

Use this method with caution if the strings contain characters outside the Latin character set because each browser can determine what localization equalities are in place. They also calculate the return values differently.

Returned Value   Integer

Parameters

string2

> Any string.

match( )   IE 4 NN 4 Moz *all* Saf *all* Op 7 ECMA 3

match(*regexpression*)

When you create the regular expression with the "g" flag, returns an array of strings within the current string that match the regular expression passed as a parameter. For example, if you pass a regular expression that specifies any five-digit number, the returned value of the match( ) method would be an array of all five-digit numbers (as strings) in the main string. Properties of the RegExp static object are influenced by this method's operation.

When the regular expression is defined without the "g" flag, the method returns an array object whose zero index location is the first matched string, and whose two properties are index (a pointer to the zero-based string character position where the match begins) and input (a copy of the string).

Returned Value   An array of strings.

Parameters

regexpression

> A regular expression object. See the regular expression object for the syntax to create a regular expression object.

replace( )   IE 4 NN 4 Moz *all* Saf *all* Op 7 ECMA 3

replace(*regexpression*, *replaceString*)

Returns the new string that results when matches of the *regexpression* parameter are replaced by the *replaceString* parameter. The original string is unharmed in the process, so you need to capture the returned value in a variable to preserve the changes.

Returned Value   A string.

Parameters

regexpression

> A regular expression object. If you want the replace( ) method to act globally on the string, set the global switch (g) on the regular expression. See the regular expression object for the syntax to create a regular expression object.

replaceString

> A string that is to take the place of all matches of *regexpression* in the current string.

search( ) IE 4 NN 4 Moz *all* Saf *all* Op 7 ECMA 3

search(*regexpression*)

Returns the zero-based indexed value of the first character in the current string that matches the pattern of the *regexpression* parameter. This method is similar to the indexOf( ) method, but the search is performed with a regular expression rather than a straight string.

Returned Value   Integer.

Parameters

regexpression
    A regular expression object. See the regular expression object for the syntax to create a regular expression object.

slice( ) IE 4 NN 4 Moz *all* Saf *all* Op 7 ECMA 3

slice(*startPositionIndex, endPositionIndex*])

Returns a substring of the current string. The substring is copied from the main string starting at the zero-based index count value of the character in the main string. If no second parameter is provided, the substring extends to the end of the main string. The optional second parameter can be another zero-based index value of where the substring should end. This value may also be a negative value, which counts from the end of the string toward the front.

Returned Value   String.

Parameters

startPositionIndex
    A zero-based integer indicating the position within the current string object to start copying characters.

endPositionIndex
    A zero-based integer indicating the position within the current string object to end copying characters. Negative values count inward from the end of the string.

small( ) IE 3 NN 2 Moz *all* Saf *all* Op 7 ECMA *n/a*

Returns a copy of the string embedded within a <small> tag set.

Returned Value   A string within a small element.

Parameters   None.

split( ) IE 4 3 NN 3 Moz *all* Saf *all* Op 7 ECMA 1

split(*delimiter* [, *limitInteger*])

Returns a new array object whose elements are segments of the current string. The current string is divided into array entries at each instance of the delimiter string specified as the first parameter of the method. The delimiter does not become part of the array. You do not have to declare the array prior to stuffing the results of the split( ) method. For example, if a string consists of a comma-delimited list of names, you can convert the list into an array as follows:

```
var listArray = stringList.split(",");
```

You may also use a regular expression as the parameter to divide the string by a pattern rather than a fixed character.

Returned Value   Array.

Parameters

delimiter

A string or regular expression that defines where the main string is divided into elements of the resulting array.

limitInteger

An optional integer that restricts the number of items converted into array elements.

strike( )   IE 3   NN 2   Moz *all*   Saf *all*   Op 7   ECMA *n/a*

Returns a copy of the string embedded within a <strike> tag set.

Returned Value   A string within a strike element.

Parameters   None.

sub( )   IE 3   NN 2   Moz *all*   Saf *all*   Op 7   ECMA *n/a*

Returns a copy of the string embedded within a <sub> tag set.

Returned Value   A string within a sub element.

Parameters   None.

substr( )   IE 4   NN 4   Moz *all*   Saf *all*   Op 7   ECMA *n/a*

substr(*startPositionIndex* [, *length*])

Returns a copy of an extract from the current string. The extract begins at the zero-based index position of the current string as specified by the first parameter of the method. If no other parameter is provided, the extract continues to the end of the main string. The second parameter can specify an integer of the number of characters to be extracted from the main string. In contrast, the substring( ) method's parameters point to the start and end position index values of the main string.

Returned Value   A string.

Parameters

startPositionIndex

A zero-based integer indicating the position within the current string object to start copying characters

length
> An optional integer of the number of characters to extract, starting with the character indicated by the *startPositionIndex* parameter

substring( )   IE 3 NN 2 Moz *all* Saf *all* Op 7 ECMA 1

substring(*startPositionIndex, endPositionIndex*)

Returns a copy of an extract from the current string. The extract begins at the zero-based index position of the current string as specified by the first parameter of the method and ends just before the character whose index is specified by the second parameter. For example, "Frobnitz".substring(0,4) returns the substring from positions 0 through 3: Frob. In contrast, the substr( ) method's parameters point to the start position of the main string and the number of characters (length) to extract.

Returned Value   A string.

Parameters

startPositionIndex
> A zero-based integer indicating the position within the current string object to start copying characters.

endPositionIndex
> A zero-based integer indicating the position within the current string object to end copying characters. In other words, the copy is made from *startPositionIndex* up to, but not including, the character at position *endPositionIndex*.

sup( )   IE 3 NN 2 Moz *all* Saf *all* Op 7 ECMA *n/a*

Returns a copy of the string embedded within a <sup> tag set.

Returned Value   A string within a sup element.

Parameters   None.

toLocaleLowerCase( ), toLocaleUpperCase( )   IE 5.5 NN *n/a* Moz *all* Saf *all* Op 7 ECMA 3

Return a copy of the current string in all lowercase or uppercase letters. Works the same as the regular version, except for some non-Latin alphabets with character mappings that may require special internal handling.

Returned Value   String.

Parameters   None.

toLowerCase( ), toUpperCase( )   IE 3 NN 2 Moz *all* Saf *all* Op 7 ECMA 1

Return a copy of the current string in all lowercase or uppercase letters. If you want to replace the current string with a case-adjusted version, assign the result of the method to the same string:

```
myString = myString.toUpperCase( );
```

It is common to use either one of these methods to create a case-insensitive comparison of two strings. This is especially convenient if one of the strings being compared is entered by a user, who may submit a variety of case situations:

```
if (document.forms[0].entry.value.toLowerCase( ) == compareValue) {
    ...
}
```

Returned Value   String.

Parameters   None.

toString( ), valueOf( )   IE 4 NN 4 Moz *all* Saf *all* Op 7 ECMA 1

Return a string value of the object.

Returned Value   String value.

Parameters   None.

VBArray   IE 4(Win) NN n/a Moz n/a Saf n/a Op n/a ECMA n/a

The VBArray object lets JavaScript communicate with Visual Basic safe arrays. This kind of array is read-only, can be multidimensional, and is sometimes returned as a value from ActiveX controls. Methods of this object give JavaScript access to the VBArray data. For additional details, visit *http://msdn2.microsoft.com/en-us/library/3s0fw3t2.aspx*.

Creating a VBArray var myVBA = new VBArray(*externalArray*);

Properties   None.

Methods

dimensions( )	getItem( )	lbound( )	toArray( )	ubound( )

dimensions( )   IE 4(Win) NN n/a Moz n/a Saf n/a Op n/a ECMA n/a

Returns an integer corresponding to the number of dimensions of the VBArray.

Returned Value   Integer.

Parameters   None.

getItem( )   IE 4(Win) NN n/a Moz n/a Saf n/a Op n/a ECMA n/a

getItem(*dim1*[, *dim2*[,...*dimN*]])

Returns the value of an item from the VBArray. Parameters specify the location in the array.

Returned Value   Number, string, or other value from the VBArray.

Parameters

dimN

Integer for the location within the array. For a multiple-dimension VBArray, use a comma-delimited map to the position.

lbound( ), ubound( )   IE *4(Win)* NN *n/a* Moz *n/a* Saf *n/a* Op *n/a* ECMA *n/a*

lbound(*dim*) ubound(*dim*)

Return an integer of the lowest and highest index values available for a particular dimension of a VBArray.

Returned Value   Integer

Parameters

dim

Integer for the location within the array.

toArray( )   IE *4(Win)* NN *n/a* Moz *n/a* Saf *n/a* Op *n/a* ECMA *n/a*

Returns a JavaScript array version of the VBArray.

Returned Value   Array.

Parameters   None.

XML   IE *n/a* NN *n/a* Moz *1.8.1* Saf *n/a* Op *n/a* ECMA *E4X*

An instance of the XML object (from the E4X standard) is a container of XML data. Such data can range from an empty text node to a complex XML element, such as one representing a SOAP query or a container of multiple "record" elements returned from a database query.

You have two primary ways to create an XML object. The first is via the traditional object constructor function call, as in:

```
var myXml = new XML( );
```

When you don't pass any value as a parameter, the constructor returns an empty text node. But you may also pass a string representing any component of an XML document, from a text node value to nested XML elements, as in:

```
var myXml = new XML("<season><bowl><number>I</number><year>1967</year><winner>
Packers</winner><loser>Chiefs</loser></bowl></season>");
```

Once you have an instance of an XML object, you can then use familiar JavaScript property notation to obtain the value of an element. Given that the instance evaluates to the root node of the data, use "dot" syntax to traverse the hierarchy:

```
var bowlYear = myXml.bowl.year;
```

Even this "extract" from myXml is, itself, an instance of the XML object, and has full use of instance methods, but from the narrower scope of, in this case, the year element only.

When a scripted reference points to an element that is repeated at the same level in the XML data, the expression evaluates to an XMLList object containing all instances of like-named elements at that level as XML objects. For example, if the Super Bowl data had multiple bowl elements for several years (see the XML file described in Online Section IV, as it is used for several examples here), the following expression yields an XML list of all of those bowl elements:

```
var allBowls = myXml.bowl;
```

Therefore, when you drill down one level further, to the following:

```
var allYears = myXml.bowl.year;
```

the expression evaluates to another XMLList object containing all year elements spread across all bowl elements.

E4X provides a notation shortcut when a reference needs to traverse multiple containment levels. The *descendant accessor* (..) searches the XML object on the left side for all instances of elements whose names match the right side, regardless of how deeply they're nested. For example, to obtain references to all of the year elements, the descendant accessor syntax is as follows:

```
var allYears = myXml..year;
```

When you have multiple elements of the same name, you can also target an individual element or like elements if you know one of its subelements and values. For example, consider an XML object containing multiple bowl elements (like the XML data described in Online Section IV). To extract a collection of bowl elements in which the value of the winner element is "Packers," the syntax would be as follows:

```
var thePack = myXml.bowl.(winner=="Packers");
```

The result is a collection of XML objects (XMLList) of zero or more bowl elements meeting the stated criterion.

Use the standard JavaScript assignment operator (=) to plug a new value into the text node of an element:

```
myXml.bowl.number = "II";
myXml.bowl.year = 1968;
```

Similarly, you can add elements, attributes, and values to XML data via assignment operators. For example, to add a winscore element and value to the bowl element of the XML object created above, use the following statement:

```
myXml.bowl.winscore = 35;
```

The resulting XML (pretty printed) is as follows:

```
<season>
  <bowl>
    <number>I</number>
    <year>1967</year>
    <winner>Packers</winner>
    <loser>Chiefs</loser>
    <winscore>35</winscore>
  </bowl>
  ...
</season>
```

To reference an attribute of an element, use the @ prefix. For example, to add an attribute to the number element above, use the following statement:

```
myXml.bowl.number.@type = "Roman Numeral";
```

The resulting element becomes:

```
<number type="Roman Numeral">I</number>
```

Just as arrays and objects have literals to assist in their creation ([ ] and { }, respectively), so, too, do XML objects. The left angle bracket of a tag signals the beginning of an XML object literal, which ends with the corresponding end tag. Note that there are no quotes surrounding the value, but quotes would be embedded within the right side expression to surround attribute values. For example,

```
var myXml = <season>
  <bowl>
    <number type="Roman Numeral">I</number>
    <year>1967</year>
    <winner>Packers</winner>
    <loser>Chiefs</loser>
  </bowl>
</season>;
```

This is the notation that causes the most backward compatibility problems if a browser fails to recognize the text/javascript; e4x=1 type as being different from the regular text/javascript type. Such a browser will interpret the left angle bracket as an operator located in an illegal position.

To place a JavaScript-computed value inside an XML object—perhaps a variable containing an accumulated string or a calculated number result—surround the expression with curly braces, as follows:

```
// a sample global object with some properties/values
var teams = { _1967: {winner:"Packers", loser:"Chiefs"}, _1968: {...}, ...};
// use object properties as element values
var myXml = <season>
  <bowl>
    <number>I</number>
    <year>1967</year>
    <winner>{teams._1967.winner}</winner>
    <loser>{teams._1967.loser}</loser>
  </bowl>
</season>;
```

You can create an empty element and populate it with additional child nodes using Java-Script syntax, as follows:

```
var bowlXML = <bowl/>;
bowlXML.number = "I";
bowlXML.number.@type = "Roman Numeral";
bowlXML.year = 1967;
...
```

While the JavaScript object/property assignment technique works well, you also have a wide range of methods of an XML object that give you more control over the contents of an existing XML object, including inserting and remove elements at specific locations.

To convert an instance of an XML object to a string for posting to a server, use the toString( ) method.

All properties and the defaultSettings( ), setSettings( ), and settings( ) methods described below are members of the static XML object. All other methods are used with instances.

Creating an XML Object

```
var myXml = new XML([XMLString]);
var myXml = XMLMarkup;
```

Properties

constructor	ignoreComments	ignoreProcessingInstructions
ignoreWhitespace	prettyIndent	prettyPrinting
prototype		

Methods

addNamespace( )	appendChild( )	attribute( )
attributes( )	child( )	childIndex( )
children( )	comments( )	contains( )
copy( )	defaultSettings( )	descendants( )
elements( )	hasComplexContent( )	hasOwnProperty( )
hasSimpleContent( )	inScopeNamespaces( )	insertChildAfter( )
insertChildBefore( )	length( )	localName( )
name( )	namespace( )	namespaceDeclarations( )
nodeKind( )	normalize( )	parent( )
prependChild( )	processingInstructions( )	propertyIsEnumerable( )
removeNamespace( )	replace( )	setChildren( )
setLocalName( )	setName( )	setNamespace( )
setSettings( )	settings( )	text( )
toString( )	toXMLString( )	valueOf( )

constructor, prototype   IE *n/a* NN *n/a* Moz *1.8.1* Saf *n/a* Op *n/a* ECMA *n/a*
Read/Write

See the corresponding properties in the Array object description.

ignoreComments   IE *n/a* NN *n/a* Moz *1.8.1* Saf *n/a* Op *n/a* ECMA *E4X*
Read/Write

Instructs the constructor not to create comment nodes, even if comments are included in the source material. The default value is true, so you must explicitly turn on comments if you wish them to be included in the XML code.

| **Example** | XML.ignoreComments = false; |
| **Value** | Boolean. |

ignoreProcessingInstructions   IE *n/a* NN *n/a* Moz *1.8.1* Saf *n/a* Op *n/a* ECMA *E4X*
Read/Write

Instructs the constructor not to create processing instruction nodes, even if they are included in the source material. The default value is true, so you must explicitly turn on processing instructions if you wish them to be included in the XML code.

| **Example** | XML.ignoreProcessingInstructions = false; |
| **Value** | Boolean. |

ignoreWhitespace   IE *n/a* NN *n/a* Moz *1.8.1* Saf *n/a* Op *n/a* ECMA *E4X*
Read/Write

Instructs the constructor to discard insignificant whitespace characters (space, carriage return, line feed, tab), even if they are included in the source material. The default value is true, so you must explicitly turn on whitespace if you wish source code whitespace to be included in the XML code.

| **Example** | XML.ignoreWhitespace = false; |
| **Value** | Boolean. |

prettyIndent   IE *n/a* NN *n/a* Moz *1.8.1* Saf *n/a* Op *n/a* ECMA *E4X*
Read/Write

Controls the number of spaces the browser uses to indent elements when an XML object is converted to a string and the XML.prettyPrinting property is turned on (which it is by default). The default value is 2.

| **Example** | XML.prettyIndent = 3; |
| **Value** | Positive integer or zero. |

prettyPrinting   IE *n/a* NN *n/a* Moz *1.8.1* Saf *n/a* Op *n/a* ECMA *E4X*
Read/Write

Controls whether string conversions of an XML object (via toString( ) or toXMLString( )) formats the output with whitespace (carriage returns, indentation, etc.) or as a contiguous string. The amount of indentation is controlled by the XML.prettyIndent property. The default behavior is for pretty printing to be on (true) and indentation of two spaces per level.

| **Example** | XML.prettyPrinting = false; |
| **Value** | Boolean. |

addNamespace( )

addNamespace(*namespaceObject*)

Inserts a namespace declaration into the root node of an XML object. See the Namespace object for constructor information.

Applies To   XML

Returned Value   Reference to the modified XML object instance.

Example

```
myXml.addNamespace(new Namespace("ex", "http://www.example.com/ns"));
```

Parameters

namespaceObject

> Reference to a namespace object instance.

appendChild( )

appendChild(*childXMLObject*)

Inserts an XML object (typically an element or text node) at the end of all other children (if any) of the root node invoking the method.

Applies To   XML

Returned Value   Reference to the modified XML object instance.

Example

```
myXml.bowl.(year == 1995)[0].appendChild(<stadium>Joe Robbie Stadium</stadium>);
```

Parameters

childXMLObject

> Reference to an XML object instance.

attribute( )

attribute("*attributeName*")

Returns an XMLList object whose items evaluate to values of XML objects that have an attribute matching the value passed as a parameter.

Applies To   XML, XMLList

Returned Value   Xmllist object of zero or more XML objects.

Example   var typeList = myXml.bowl.number.attribute("type");

Parameters

attributeName

> String value of the name of the attribute to look for within the current XML object.

attributes( )
IE *n/a* NN *n/a* Moz *1.8.1* Saf *n/a* Op *n/a* ECMA *E4X*

Returns an XMLList object whose items evaluate to values of all attributes defined for the current XML object.

Applies To   XML, XMLList

Returned Value Xmllist object of zero or more matching XML objects.

Example   `var valueList = myXml.bowl.number.attributes();`

Parameters   None.

child( )
IE *n/a* NN *n/a* Moz *1.8.1* Saf *n/a* Op *n/a* ECMA *E4X*

`child("propertyName")`

Returns an XMLList object whose items evaluate to values of XML objects that are children of the current object(s) and whose element names match the value passed as a parameter. If you were distributing values from XML records down an HTML table column, this method lets you obtain all values for that column via this method.

Applies To   XML, XMLList

Returned Value Xmllist object of zero or more XML objects.

Example   `var yearsList = myXml.bowl.child("year");`

Parameters

propertyName

  String value of the name of the child elements to look for within the current XML object.

childIndex( )
IE *n/a* NN *n/a* Moz *1.8.1* Saf *n/a* Op *n/a* ECMA *E4X*

Returns a zero-based integer indicating the child position of the current XML object within its parent element.

Applies To   XML

Returned Value Positive integer or 0.

Example   `var where = myXml.employee.(id == "2f4");`

Parameters   None.

children( )
IE *n/a* NN *n/a* Moz *1.8.1* Saf *n/a* Op *n/a* ECMA *E4X*

Returns an XMLList object containing references to all child elements of the current XML object. The XMLList object has only as many items as there are immediate children of the current object. But because each item in the list is a reference to an XML object, that object's nested children are also accessible through further inspection.

Applies To   XML, XMLList

Returned Value	Xmllist object.
Example	`var kids = myXml.children( );`
Parameters	None.

comments( )   IE *n/a* NN *n/a* Moz *1.8.1* Saf *n/a* Op *n/a* ECMA *E4X*

Returns an XMLList object containing references to all comment elements among the immediate children of the current object. If scripts are used to create the XML object instance, the `XML.ignoreComments` property must be set to `false` for the comments to become part of the XML object.

Applies To	XML, XMLList
Returned Value	Xmllist object.
Example	`var topLevelComments = myXml.comments( );`
Parameters	None.

contains( )   IE *n/a* NN *n/a* Moz *1.8.1* Saf *n/a* Op *n/a* ECMA *E4X*

`contains("value")`

Returns true if the value of the current XML object (or objects for an XMLList) matches the value passed as a parameter.

Applies To	XML, XMLList
Returned Value	Boolean.
Example	`if (myXml.bowl.winner.contains("Packers")) {...};`

Parameters

value

> String value to compare against the current XML object's value (or values for an XMLList).

copy( )   IE *n/a* NN *n/a* Moz *1.8.1* Saf *n/a* Op *n/a* ECMA *E4X*

Returns a copy of the current XML or XMLList object. All nested elements are included in the copy.

Applies To	XML, XMLList
Returned Value	Xml or XMLList object, depending on type of current object.
Example	`var oneCopy = myXml.copy( );`
Parameters	None.

defaultSettings( )   IE *n/a*   NN *n/a*   Moz *1.8.1*   Saf *n/a*   Op *n/a*   ECMA *E4X*

XML.defaultSettings( )

Returns a JavaScript object whose properties are the entire set of global properties for the static XML object (ignoreComments, ignoreProcessingInstructions, ignoreWhitespace, prettyIndent, and prettyPrinting) and their default values. Use the result of this method as a parameter for setSettings( ) to restore all values to their default settings in one statement.

Returned Value   JavaScript object.

Example   XML.setSettings(XML.defaultSettings( ));

Parameters   None.

descendants( )   IE *n/a*   NN *n/a*   Moz *1.8.1*   Saf *n/a*   Op *n/a*   ECMA *E4X*

descendants(["*elementName*"])

Returns an XMLList object containing XML objects for all descedants of the current object(s) (when no parameter is passed) or only those descendants whose element name matches the passed parameter. The reach of the descendants( ) method includes nested descendants, as well. Each descendant becomes a first-class item in the list, meaning that for a complex set of XML data, the list could be very large.

Applies To   XML, XMLList

Returned Value   Xmllist.

Example   var allDescendants = myXml.descendants( );

Parameters

elementName
> String value to compare against the names of all elements nested in the current object(s).

elements( )   IE *n/a*   NN *n/a*   Moz *1.8.1*   Saf *n/a*   Op *n/a*   ECMA *E4X*

elements("*name*")

Returns an XMLList object whose items evaluate to values of XML objects that are children of the current object(s) (with no parameter) and whose element names match the value passed as a parameter. Only element objects are added to the list, omitting comments and processing instructions (in case they're in the XML data).

Applies To   XML, XMLList

Returned Value   Xmllist object of zero or more XML objects.

Example   var yearsList = myXml.bowl.elements("year");

Parameters

name

String value of the name of the child elements to look for within the current XML object.

hasComplexContent( )   IE *n/a* NN *n/a* Moz *1.8.1* Saf *n/a* Op *n/a* ECMA *E4X*

Returns true if the current XML object contains an element that has child elements, and is thus said to have complex content.

Applies To   XML, XMLList

Returned Value   Boolean.

Example

```
if (myXml.employee[3].hasComplexContent( )) {
    // statements
};
```

Parameters   None.

hasOwnProperty( )   IE *n/a* NN *n/a* Moz *1.8.1* Saf *n/a* Op *n/a* ECMA *E4X*

```
hasOwnProperty("propertyName")
```

Returns true if the current XML object contains an element whose name matches the string passed as a parameter. The method also works on the static XML object, in which case you can test for the presence of properties and methods (e.g., XML.hasOwnProperty("addNamespace")).

Applies To   XML, XMLList

Returned Value   Boolean.

Example

```
if (myXml.hasOwnProperty("age")) {
    // statements
};
```

Parameters

propertyName

String value of the name of elements to look for within the current XML object, or properties/methods of the static XML object.

hasSimpleContent( )   IE *n/a* NN *n/a* Moz *1.8.1* Saf *n/a* Op *n/a* ECMA *E4X*

Returns true if the current XML object contains an element that has no child elements or is a text or attribute node. Note that an element that has a text node for its value and no other child elements is considered simple content.

Applies To   XML, XMLList

Returned Value   Boolean.

Example

```
if (myXml.employee[3].age.hasSimpleContent()) {
    // statements
};
```

Parameters   None.

inScopeNamespaces( )   IE *n/a* NN *n/a* Moz *1.8.1* Saf *n/a* Op *n/a* ECMA *E4X*

Returns an array of Namespace objects within the scope of the current XML object's parent. If no namespaces have been explicitly declared, the result is an empty array.

Applies To   XML

Returned Value   Array.

Example   `var nsList = myXml.inScopeNamespaces();`

Parameters   None.

insertChildAfter( ), insertChildBefore( )   IE *n/a* NN *n/a* Moz *1.8.1* Saf *n/a* Op *n/a* ECMA *E4X*

```
insertChildAfter(referenceChild, newChild)
insertChildBefore(referenceChild, newChild)
```

Inserts a new child element (second parameter) after or before a referenced child (first parameter) of the current XML object, returning a reference to the newly updated XML object. If you pass null as a first parameter, insertChildAfter( ) inserts the new child as the first child (i.e., after none of the child elements), while insertChildBefore( ) inserts the new child as the last child (i.e., before none of the child elements). The current object is modified, as well as returning a reference to the modified object.

Applies To   XML

Returned Value   XML object.

Example

```
myXml.bowl[0].insertChildBefore(myXml.bowl[0].winner[0], <stadium>Lambeau Field</
stadium>);
```

Parameters

referenceChild
> A reference to the child of the current object to be used as a reference point for insertion; also null, which short-circuits the reference point to mean "after" or "before" none of the existing children.

newChild
> An XML object to be inserted.

length( )   IE *n/a*   NN *n/a*   Moz *1.8.1*   Saf *n/a*   Op *n/a*   ECMA *E4X*

Returns an integer count of the number of objects contained by the instance of an XML or XMLList object. The value is always 1 for an XML object, and the actual count for an XMLlist object.

Applies To   XML, XMLList

Returned Value   Integer.

Example   var howMany = myXml.bowl.length( );

Parameters   None.

localName( )   IE *n/a*   NN *n/a*   Moz *1.8.1*   Saf *n/a*   Op *n/a*   ECMA *E4X*

Returns a string of the local name part of an XML object's qualified name. For an element whose names do not have a namespace prefix, the localName( ) and name( ) methods return the same value.

Applies To   XML

Returned Value   String.

Example

```
var myXml = <results xmlns:libBook="http://catalog.example.edu/schema">
    <libBook:title libBook:rarebooks="true">De Principia</libBook:title></results>;
var elemLocName = myX.children( )[0].localName( );
    // result is "title"
```

Parameters   None.

name( )   IE *n/a*   NN *n/a*   Moz *1.8.1*   Saf *n/a*   Op *n/a*   ECMA *E4X*

Returns a string of the fully qualified name part of an XML object. For an element whose names do not have a namespace prefix, the localName( ) and name( ) methods return the same value.

Applies To   XML

Returned Value   String.

Example

```
var myXml = <results xmlns:libBook="http://catalog.example.edu/schema">
    <libBook:title libBook:rarebooks="true">De Principia</libBook:title></results>;
var elemLocName = myX.children( )[0].localName( );
    // result is "title"
```

Parameters   None.

namespace( )   IE *n/a*   NN *n/a*   Moz *1.8.1*   Saf *n/a*   Op *n/a*   ECMA *E4X*

namespace([*"prefix"*])

Returns a namespace object whose properties convey the prefix and URI specified for the namespace for the current XML object. You can optionally specify a prefix as a parameter so that the method returns a value only for a matching prefix. If the prefix does not match, the method returns undefined.

Applies To   XML

Returned Value   Namespace object.

Example

```
var myXml = <results xmlns:libBook="http://catalog.example.edu/schema">
    <libBook:title libBook:rarebooks="true">De Principia</libBook:title></results>;
var elemLocName = myX.children( )[0].namespace("libBook");
    // result is a Namespace object
```

Parameters

prefix
    A string of a qualified name prefix (without a colon).

namespaceDeclarations( )   IE *n/a*   NN *n/a*   Moz *n/a*   Saf *n/a*   Op *n/a*   ECMA *E4X*

Returns an array of namespace objects. Each entry is a namespace that is associated with the current XML object, including those defined in its parent.

Applies To   XML

Returned Value   Array.

Parameters   None.

nodeKind( )   IE *n/a*   NN *n/a*   Moz *1.8.1*   Saf *n/a*   Op *n/a*   ECMA *E4X*

Returns a string that identifies the type of DOM node that the current XML object represents.

Applies To   XML

Returned Value

One of the following string values: element, attribute, comment, processing-instruction, text.

Parameters   None.

normalize( )   IE *n/a*   NN *n/a*   Moz *1.8.1*   Saf *n/a*   Op *n/a*   ECMA *E4X*

Just like the DOM method of the same name, this version unites adjacent text nodes in the current element or XMLList into a single text node. Text nodes inserted into an element (e.

g., via the prependChild( ) method) are maintained as separate nodes (when pretty printed, each text node of an element appears on its own line).

Applies To   XML, XMLList

Returned Value

An XML or XMLList value (depending on the type of object invoking the method) with the normalized content.

Parameters   None.

parent( )   IE *n/a* NN *n/a* Moz *1.8.1* Saf *n/a* Op *n/a* ECMA *E4X*

Returns a reference to the parent element of the current XML or XMLList object.

Applies To   XML, XMLList

Returned Value

An XML or XMLList value (depending on the type of object invoking the method) with the normalized content. If the object has no parent, the method returns an empty object. If the current object is a list of elements that have multiple parents, the method returns undefined.

Example   var parentElem = myXml.bowl.parent( );

Parameters   None.

prependChild( )   IE *n/a* NN *n/a* Moz *1.8.1* Saf *n/a* Op *n/a* ECMA *E4X*
prependChild(*newChild*)

Inserts an XML object as the first child of the current XML object, returning a reference to the current object after the insertion. The original object is also modified.

Applies To   XML

Returned Value   XML object.

Example
```
var txt = new XML("Super Bowl ");
myXml.bowl[20].number[0].prependChild(txt);
```

Parameters
newChild

   An instance of an XML object.

processingInstructions( )   IE *n/a* NN *n/a* Moz *1.8.1* Saf *n/a* Op *n/a* ECMA *E4X*
processingInstructions([*"name"*])

Without a parameter, returns an XMLList of all processing instruction nodes contained by the current XML object. You may optionally pass a name as a parameter, in which case the method returns an XMLList with all processing instruction nodes that have the matching name.

Applies To   XML, XMLList

Returned Value   Xmllist object.

Parameters

name

A string of a processing instruction node's name.

propertyIsEnumerable( )   IE *n/a* NN *n/a* Moz *1.8.1* Saf *n/a* Op *n/a* ECMA *E4X*

Eventually, this method should let a script control whether an element in an XML object is exposed to inspection routines, such as for-in constructions. For the first publication of E4X, however, the method is not connected to a meaningful operation.

Applies To   XML, XMLList

Returned Value   Boolean.

removeNamespace( )   IE *n/a* NN *n/a* Moz *1.8.1* Saf *n/a* Op *n/a* ECMA *E4X*
removeNamespace(*namespaceObject*)

Deletes a namespace declaration from the current XML object. Note, however, that child elements that use the deleted namespace's prefix in element and attribute names continue to have the prefix attached to those items. The method returns a reference to the modified XML object.

Applies To   XML

Returned Value   XML object.

Example
```
var myX = <results xmlns:libBook="http://catalog.example.edu/schema">
    <libBook:title libBook:rarebooks="true">De Principia</libBook:title></results>;
var ns = new Namespace("libBook","http://catalog.example.edu/schema");
myX.removeNamespace(ns);
// returned value (toXMLString( )) is:
//    <results>
//      <libBook:title libBook:rarebooks="true">De Principia</libBook:title>
//    </results>
```

Parameters

namespaceObject

An instance of an Namespace object.

replace( )   IE *n/a* NN *n/a* Moz *1.8.1* Saf *n/a* Op *n/a* ECMA *E4X*

`replace(elementNameStringOrNumber, newValue)`

Replaces one or more child elements of the current object with a different XML object, including an instance of XML (any node type) or XMLList. The first parameter must reference a child element or group of identically named elements by a string or a zero-based integer signifying the index position of the element to be replaced. When the element you intend to replace is, itself, a parent of other elements, all descendants are removed in the operation. When you specify a string element name, if there are multiple elements with the same name, they are all replaced with a single instance of the value of the second parameter. If an element containing a value is replaced by an empty element, the original value is lost in the process (although for a single element, you can construct a script that grabs the value prior to replacement and uses curly braces to script the value of the new element before it is placed in position). The method returns a reference to the modified XML object.

Applies To   XML

Returned Value   XML object.

Example

```
// replace all track elements with one empty track
myXml.mix.replace("track", <track/>);

// replace all year elements with anno elements, preserving values
for each (var elem in myXml.bowl) {
    elem.replace("year", <anno>{elem.year.toString( )}</anno>);
}
```

Parameters

elementNameStringOrNumber

> Either a string of a child element name or a zero-based integer index to the desired child element of the current XML object.

newValue

> An instance of an XML or XMLList object, including a text node.

setChildren( )   IE *n/a* NN *n/a* Moz *1.8.1* Saf *n/a* Op *n/a* ECMA *E4X*

`setChildren(newValue)`

Replaces all child elements of the current object (and their descendants) with a different XML object, including an instance of XML (any node type) or XMLList. The method returns a reference to the modified XML object.

Applies To   XML

Returned Value   XML object.

Example

```
// massive layoff
myXml.employees.setChildren(<vacancy/>);
```

Parameters

newValue

> An instance of an XML or XMLList object, including a text node.

setLocalName( )   IE *n/a* NN *n/a* Moz *1.8.1* Saf *n/a* Op *n/a* ECMA *E4X*

```
setLocalName("newName")
```

Replaces the local name portion of the current XML object with a new value. The prefix is undisturbed.

Applies To   XML

Returned Value   None.

Example

```
var myX = <results xmlns:libBook="http://catalog.example.edu/schema">
    <libBook:title libBook:rarebooks="true">De Principia</libBook:title></results>;
var ns = new Namespace("libBook","http://catalog.example.edu/schema");
myX.ns::title.setLocalName("bookTitle");
// element becomes:
//    <libBook:bookTitle libBook:rarebooks="true">De Principia</libBook:bookTitle>
```

Parameters

newName

> A string value of the new element local name portion.

setName( )   IE *n/a* NN *n/a* Moz *1.8.1* Saf *n/a* Op *n/a* ECMA *E4X*

```
setName("newName")
```

Replaces the name of the current XML object with a new value. If the element's original name has a namespace prefix, the prefix is also removed.

Applies To   XML

Returned Value   None.

Example

```
var myX = <results xmlns:libBook="http://catalog.example.edu/schema">
    <libBook:title libBook:rarebooks="true">De Principia</libBook:title></results>;
var ns = new Namespace("libBook","http://catalog.example.edu/schema");
myX.ns::title.setName("bookTitle");
// element becomes:
//    <bookTitle libBook:rarebooks="true">De Principia</bookTitle>
```

Parameters

newName

> A string value of the new element local name portion.

setNamespace( )   IE *n/a* NN *n/a* Moz *1.8.1* Saf *n/a* Op *n/a* ECMA *E4X*

setNamespace(*namespaceObject*)

Replaces the namespace of the current XML object (element or attribute type) with a new value. To assign a namespace to an element or attribute that doesn't already have a namespace declaration, use addNamespace( ).

Applies To   XML

Returned Value   None.

Example

```
var myX = <results xmlns:libBook="http://catalog.example.edu/schema">
    <libBook:title libBook:rarebooks="true">De Principia</libBook:title></results>;
var ns = new Namespace("libBook","http://catalog.example.edu/schema");
var updatedNS = new Namespace("dg", "http://www.dannyg.com/ns");
myX.ns::title.setNamespace(updatedNS);
// element becomes:
//    <results>
//        <dg:title xmlns:dg="http://www.dannyg.com/ns" libBook:rarebooks="true">De
Principia</libBook:title>
//    </results>
```

Parameters

namespaceObject

> An instance of the Namespace object.

setSettings( )   IE *n/a* NN *n/a* Moz *1.8.1* Saf *n/a* Op *n/a* ECMA *E4X*

XML.setSettings([*settingsObject*])

Controls the global properties of the static XML object in one statement. Passing no parameter, null, or undefined causes all settings to revert to their default values. Otherwise pass an object whose five property names are the names of the five global properties (ignoreComments, ignoreProcessingInstructions, ignoreWhitespace, prettyIndent, and prettyPrinting).

Returned Value   None

Parameters

settingsObject

> An optional JavaScript object whose five properties and values are structured as follows:
>
>> {ignoreComments: Boolean, ignoreProcessingInstructions: Boolean,
>> ignoreWhitespace: Boolean, prettyPrinting: Boolean, prettyIndent: Integer}

settings( )   IE *n/a* NN *n/a* Moz *1.8.1* Saf *n/a* Op *n/a* ECMA *E4X*

XML.settings( )

Returns a JavaScript object whose properties are the entire set of global properties for the static XML object (ignoreComments, ignoreProcessingInstructions, ignoreWhitespace, prettyIndent, and prettyPrinting) and their values. You can use this to preserve a set of custom settings before temporarily changing one or more other properties. Then use the saved value as a parameter to setSettings( ) to restore all values to their previous settings in one statement.

Returned Value   JavaScript object.

Parameters   None.

text( )   IE *n/a* NN *n/a* Moz *1.8.1* Saf *n/a* Op *n/a* ECMA *E4X*

Returns an XMLList of all child text nodes of the current XML object. If the current XML object represents a single element, the returned XMLList has a single item in it, the text node as an XML object. You can obtain the text nodes of all like children by supplying an XMLList of elements that have child text nodes. For example, in the Super Bowl XML data from Online Section IV, there are a series of bowl elements, each of which contains a year element that has a text node. To obtain an XMLList of all of the year element text nodes in the data, the expression would be:

```
myXml.bowl.year.text( )
```

You can usually rely on implicit type conversion on each element of the XMLList to obtain the string value for further script manipulation of those values outside of the XML data. If you encounter difficulty, use the toString( ) method on individual items to obtain string values.

Applies To   XML, XMLList

Returned Value   Xmllist object.

Parameters   None.

toString( )   IE *n/a* NN *n/a* Moz *1.8.1* Saf *n/a* Op *n/a* ECMA *E4X*

Returns a string value type of text node or attribute node portions (simple content) of an element represented as an XML object. For an instance of a single XML object or an XMLList object containing only one item, the returned string is generally usable data. If the current object is a multi-item XMLList, all of the values are scrunched together with no delimiters between element values.

In most cases, you won't need to invoke toString( ) because JavaScript performs implicit type conversion when an expression calls for a string value and you supply an XML object.

Applies To   XML, XMLList

Returned Value   String value.

Parameters   None.

toXMLString( )   IE *n/a* NN *n/a* Moz *1.8.1* Saf *n/a* Op *n/a* ECMA *E4X*

Returns a string value type of the current XML object, complete with tags, attributes, and namespace declarations—a source code view, if you will, of the data. This method applies to both simple XML objects and xmllists. Global values for pretty printing are applied to the output generated by toXMLString( ).

Applies To	XML, XMLList
Returned Value	String value.
Parameters	None.

valueOf( )   IE *n/a* NN *n/a* Moz *1.8.1* Saf *n/a* Op *n/a* ECMA *E4X*

Returns a reference to the current XML object.

Applies To	XML, XMLList
Returned Value	XML object
Parameters	None.

XMLList   IE *n/a* NN *n/a* Moz *1.8.1* Saf *n/a* Op *n/a* ECMA *E4X*

An instance of the XMLList object (from the E4X standard) is a container of zero or more instances of the XML object. For example, consider XML data consisting of one outer element and a repeated series of nested elements (e.g., data representing a customer order with the root element being <order> and a nested <item> element for each product in the order). A reference to the root node (order) returns only one element (along with all of its descendants). A reference to the repeated groups of item elements (order.item) returns an XMLList, with a number of entries identical to the number of item elements in the data. Each one of those items, in turn, may have additional child nodes, and so on.

You can reference an individual item of an XMLList through JavaScript array notation— square brackets and a zero-based integer index, as in:

```
order.item[3]
```

But that's where the similarity between an XMLList and a JavaScript array end. A special E4X control statement, for-each-in, simplifies iteration through the objects in an XMLList object.

The lines between XML and XMLList objects can be fuzzy at times, and that is intentional. The list of methods of an instance of the XMLList object is a subset of methods for an instance of the XML object. See the description of all methods in the XML object listing, and look for the "Applies To" heading to confirm that the method works with XMLList object instances.

Creating an XMLlist Object

```
var myXmlList = new XMLList([XMLList]);
```

Properties	None.

Methods

attribute( )	attributes( )	child( )
children( )	comments( )	contains( )

copy( )	descendants( )	elements( )
hasComplexContent( )	hasOwnProperty( )	hasSimpleContent( )
length( )	normalize( )	parent( )
processingInstructions( )	propertyIsEnumerable( )	text( )
toString( )	toXMLString( )	valueOf( )

Operators

+
IE 3 NN 2 Moz *all* Saf *all* Op 7 ECMA 1

The addition operator works with both numbers and strings, but its results vary with the data types of its operands. When both operands are numbers, the result is the sum of the two numbers; when both operands are strings, the result is a concatenation of the two strings (in the order of the operands); when one operand is a number and the other a string, the number data type is converted to a string, and the two strings are concatenated. To convert a string operand to a number, use the parseInt( ) or parseFloat( ) function.

In an E4X context, the addition operator also works to concatenate XML segments to create XML or XMLList objects.

Example

```
var mySum = number1 + number2;
var newString = "string1" + "string2";
var newXML = <element1>textA</element1> + <element2>textB</element2>; // E4X only
```

+=
IE 3 NN 2 Moz *all* Saf *all* Op 7 ECMA 1

This is the add-by-value operator. This class of operator combines a regular assignment operator (=) with one of the many other operators to carry out the assignment by performing the stated operation on the left operand with the value of the right operand. For example, if a variable named a has a string stored in it, you can append a string to a with the += operator:

```
a += " and some more.";
```

Without the add-by-value operator, the operation has to be structured as follows:

```
a = a + " and some more";
```

The following table shows all the assignment operators that function this way.

Operator	Example	Equivalent
+=	a += b	a = a + b
-=	a -= b	a = a - b
*=	a *= b	a = a * b
/=	a /= b	a = a / b
%=	a %= b	a = a % b
<<=	a <<= b	a = a << b

Operator	Example	Equivalent
>>=	a >>= b	a = a >> b
>>>=	a >>>= b	a = a >>> b
&=	a &= b	a = a & b
|=	a |= b	a = a | b
^=	a ^= b	a = a ^ b

In an E4X context, the add-by-value operator can be used to append XML elements to an existing XML object.

Example
```
output += "<H1>Section 2</H1>";
total *= .95;
```

&&
IE 3   NN 2   Moz all   Saf all   Op 7   ECMA 1

The AND operator compares two Boolean expressions for equality. If both expressions evaluate to true, the result of the && operator also evaluates to true; if either or both expressions are false, the && operator evaluates to false.

A Boolean expression may consist of a comparison expression (using any of the many comparison operators) or a variety of other values. Here are the most common data types, values, and their Boolean value equivalent.

Data type	Boolean equivalent
Number other than zero	true
Zero	false
Any nonempty string	true
Empty string	false
Any object	true
null	false
undefined	false

Using this information, you can create compound conditions with the help of the && operator. For example, if you want to see if someone entered a value into a form field and it is a number greater than 100, the condition would look like the following:

```
var userEntry = document.forms[0].entry.value ;
if (userEntry && parseInt(userEntry) >= 100) {
    ...
}
```

If the user had not entered any value, the string would be an empty string. In the compound condition, when the first operand evaluates to false, the && operator rules mean that the entire expression returns false (because both operands must be true for the operator to return true). Because expressions such as the compound condition are evaluated from left to right, the false value of the first operand short-circuits the condition to return false, meaning that the second operand isn't evaluated.

Example

```
if (a <= b && b >= c) {
    ...
}
```

=	IE 3 NN 2 Moz *all* Saf *all* Op 7 ECMA 1

The assignment operator assigns the evaluated value of the right-hand operand to the variable on the left. After the operation, the variable contains data of the same data type as the original value. Assignment operations can also be chained, with the evaluation of the entire statement starting from the right and working left. Therefore, after the expression:

```
a = b = c = 25;
```

all three variables equal 25.

The right side of the operator can also be JavaScript literals for other value types, such as arrays (surrounded by square brackets), objects (curly braces), and (in E4X) XML data (angle brackets).

Example

```
var myName = "Theodore Roosevelt";
var now = new Date( );
```

&	IE 3 NN 2 Moz *all* Saf *all* Op 7 ECMA 1

The bitwise AND operator performs binary math on two operands (their binary values). Each column of bits is subjected to the Boolean AND operation. If the value of a column in both operands is 1, the result for that column position is 1. All other combinations yield a zero. The resulting value of the operator is the decimal equivalent of the binary result. For example, the binary values of 3 and 6 are 0011 and 0110, respectively. After an AND operation on these two values, the binary result is 0010; the decimal equivalent is 2.

Example   `var n = 3 & 6;`

<<	IE 3 NN 2 Moz *all* Saf *all* Op 7 ECMA 1

The bitwise left-shift operator shifts the bits of the first operand by the number of columns specified by the second operand. For example, if the binary value of 3 (0011) has its bits shifted to the left by 2, the binary result is 1100; the decimal equivalent is 12.

Example   `var shifted = 3 << 2;`

~	IE 3 NN 2 Moz *all* Saf *all* Op 7 ECMA 1

This is the bitwise NOT operator. This unary operator inverts the value of the binary digit in each column of a number. For example, the binary 6 is 0110 (with many more zeros off to the left). After the negation operation on each column's value, the binary result is 1001, plus all zeros to the left inverted to 1s. The decimal equivalent is a negative value (-5).

Example   var n = ~6;

| IE *3* NN *2* Moz *all* Saf *all* Op *7* ECMA *1*

The bitwise OR operator performs binary math on two operands (their binary values). Each column of bits is subjected to the Boolean OR operation. If the value of a column in both operands is 0, the result for that column position is 0. All other combinations yield a 1. The resulting value of the operator is the decimal equivalent of the binary result. For example, the binary values of 3 and 6 are 0011 and 0110, respectively. After an OR operation on these two values, the binary result is 0111; the decimal equivalent is 7.

Example   var n = 3 | 6;

>>   IE *3* NN *2* Moz *all* Saf *all* Op *7* ECMA *1*

The bitwise right-shift operator shifts the bits of the first operand by the number of columns specified by the second operand. For example, if the binary value of 6 (0110) has its bits shifted to the right by 2, the binary result is 0001; the decimal equivalent is 1. Any digits that fall off the right end of the number are discarded.

Example   var shifted = 6 >> 2;

---

^   IE *3* NN *2* Moz *all* Saf *all* Op *7* ECMA *1*

The bitwise exclusive OR (XOR) operator performs binary math on two operands (their binary values). Each column of bits is subjected to the Boolean XOR operation. If the value of a column in either operand (but not both operands) is 1, the result for that column position is 1. All other combinations yield a 0. The resulting value of the operator is the decimal equivalent of the binary result. For example, the binary values of 3 and 6 are 0011 and 0110, respectively. After an XOR operation on these two values, the binary result is 0101; the decimal equivalent is 5.

Example   var n = 3 ^ 6;

>>>   IE *3* NN *2* Moz *all* Saf *all* Op *7* ECMA *1*

This is the bitwise zero-fill right-shift operator. This operator shifts the bits of the first operand (to the right) by the number of columns specified by the second operand. With the bitwise right-shift operator (>>), new digits that fill in from the left end are 1s; with the zero-fill right-shift operator (>>>), the new digits at the left are zeros. Any digits that fall off the right end of the number are discarded. Microsoft also refers to this operator as the unsigned right-shift operator.

Example   var shifted = 6 >>> 2;

The comma operator (with or without optional white space following it) can delimit expressions in the same line of script. It can be used in a number of ways. For example, to declare multiple variables, the syntax would be:

```
var varName1, varName2, ... varNameN;
```

Multiple script statements may also be joined together on the same line. Therefore, the following script line:

```
alert("Howdy"), alert("Doody");
```

presents two alert dialog boxes in sequence (the second one appears after the first is dismissed by the user). Another application is in for loops when you wish to involve two (or more) variables in the loop:

```
for (var i = 0, var j = 2; i < 20; i++, j++) {
    ...
}
```

Example   var isCSS, isIEMac;

?:

The conditional operator provides a shortcut syntax to an if-else control structure. There are three components to the deployment of this operator: a condition and two statements. If the condition evaluates to true, the first of the statements is executed; if the condition evaluates to false, the second statement is evaluated. The syntax is as follows:

```
condition ? statement1 : statement2
```

You can nest these operators as a way of adding more decision paths within a single statement. In the following syntax, if *conditionA* evaluates to false, *conditionB* is evaluated, and the entire expression returns the value of *statement2* or *statement3* depending on the results of *conditionB*:

```
conditionA ? statement1 : (conditionB ? statement2 : statement3)
```

This operator is a shortcut in appearance only. It invokes the same internal processing as an if-else construction.

Example   var newColor = (temp > 100) ? "red" : "blue";

--

The decrement operator (a unary operator) subtracts 1 from the current value of a variable expression. You can place the operator in front of or behind the variable for a different effect. When the operator is in front of the variable, the variable is decremented before it is evaluated in the current statement. For example, in the following sequence:

```
var a, b;
a = 5;
b = --a;
```

one is subtracted from a before being assigned to b. Therefore, both b and a are 4 when these statements finish running. In contrast, in the following sequence:

```
var a, b;
a = 5;
b = a--;
```

the subtraction occurs after a is assigned to b. When the statements complete, b is 5 and a is 4.

This behavior impacts the way for-loop-counting variables are defined and used. Typically, a loop counter that counts backwards from a maximum value decrements the counter after the statements in the loop have run. Thus most loop counters place the operator after the counter variable:

```
for (var i = 10; i >=0; i--) {...}
```

Example

```
--n
n--
```

/   IE 3 NN 2 Moz all Saf all Op 7 ECMA 1

The division operator divides the number to the left of the operator by the number to the right. Both operands must be numbers. An expression with this operator evaluates to a number.

Example   `var myQuotient = number1 / number2;`

==   IE 3 NN 2 Moz all Saf all Op 7 ECMA 1

The equality operator compares two operand values and returns a Boolean result. The behavior of this operator differs with the version of JavaScript specified for the script element. If the language attribute is set to JavaScript or JavaScript1.1, some operands are automatically converted as shown in the following table.

Left operand	Right operand	Description
Object reference	Object reference	Compare evaluation of object references.
Any data type	Boolean	Convert Boolean operand to a number (1 for true; 0 for false) and compare against other operand.
Object reference	String	Convert object to string (via toString( )) and compare strings.
String	Number	Convert string to a number and compare numeric values.

When you explicitly set the script element to language="JavaScript1.2" or later. The browser is more literal about equality, meaning that no automatic data conversions are performed. Therefore, whereas the expression:

```
123 == "123"
```

evaluates to true in most situations due to automatic data type conversion, the expression evaluates to false in statements belonging to JavaScript 1.2 (or later) scripts. Because newer DOM and XHTML standards don't provide a place to specify scripting language versions, you should avoid these special-case situations. If your scripts require tests for absolute equality of operands, use the newer === identity operator instead. For typical value equality testing, the standard equality operators work perfectly well.

Regardless of version, if you wish to compare the values of objects (for example, comparing strings explicitly generated with the new String( ) constructor), you should compare the values derived from methods such as toString( ) or valueOf( ).

Example

```
if (n == m) {
    ...
}
```

>   IE 3 NN 2 Moz *all* Saf *all* Op 7 ECMA 1

The greater-than operator compares the values of operands on either side of the operator. If the numeric value of the left operand is larger than the right operand, the expression evaluates to true. Strings are converted to their Unicode values for comparison of those values.

Example

```
if (a > b) {
    ...
}
```

>=   IE 3 NN 2 Moz *all* Saf *all* Op 7 ECMA 1

The greater-than-or-equal operator compares the values of operands on either side of the operator. If the numeric value of the left operand is larger than or equal to the right operand, the expression evaluates to true. Strings are converted to their Unicode values for comparison of those numeric values.

Example

```
if (a >= b) {
    ...
}
```

===   IE 4 NN 4 Moz *all* Saf *all* Op 7 ECMA 3

The strictly equals (identity) operator compares two operand values and returns a Boolean result. Both the value and data type of the two operands must be identical for this operator to return true (no automatic data type conversions occur). See the equality operator (==) for more liberal equality comparisons.

Example

```
if (n === m) {
    ...
}
```

++ IE *3* NN *2* Moz *all* Saf *all* Op *7* ECMA *1*

The increment operator (a unary operator) adds 1 to the current value of a variable expression. You can place the operator in front of or behind the variable for a different effect. When the operator is in front of the variable, the variable is incremented before it is evaluated in the current statement. For example, in the following sequence:

```
var a, b;
a = 5;
b = ++a;
```

1 is added to a before being assigned to b. Therefore, both b and a are 6 when these statements finish running. In contrast, in the following sequence:

```
var a, b;
a = 5;
b = a++;
```

the addition occurs after a is assigned to b. When these statements complete, b is 5 and a is 6.

This behavior impacts the way for loop-counting variables are defined and used. Typically, a loop counter that counts upward from a minimum value increments the counter after the statements in the loop have run. Thus, most loop counters place the operator after the counter variable:

```
for (var i = 10; i >=0; i++) {...}
```

Example

```
++n
n++
```

!= IE *3* NN *2* Moz *all* Saf *all* Op *7* ECMA *1*

The inequality operator compares two operand values and returns a Boolean result. The behavior of this operator differs with the version of JavaScript specified for the script element. If the language attribute is set to JavaScript or JavaScript1.1, some operands are automatically converted as for the equality (==) operator. The situation is a bit different when the script element is set to language="JavaScript1.2" or later. The browser is more literal about inequality, meaning that no automatic data conversions are performed. Therefore, whereas the expression:

```
123 != "123"
```

evaluates to false in most situations due to automatic data type conversion, the expression evaluates to true in statements belonging to explicitly JavaScript 1.2 (or later) scripts. Because newer DOM and XHTML standards don't provide a place to specify scripting language versions, you should avoid these special-case situations. If your scripts require tests for absolute inequality of operands, use the newer !== identity operator instead. For typical value inequality testing, the standard inequality operators work perfectly well.

Regardless of version, if you wish to compare the values of objects (for example, strings explicitly generated with the new String( ) constructor), you should compare the values derived from methods such as toString( ) or valueOf( ).

Example
```
if (n != m) {
    ...
}
```

| < | IE *3* NN *2* Moz *all* Saf *all* Op *7* ECMA *1* |

The less-than operator compares the values of operands on either side of the operator. If the numeric value of the left operand is smaller than the right operand, the expression evaluates to true. Strings are converted to their Unicode values for comparison of those values.

Example
```
if (a < b) {
    ...
}
```

| <= | IE *3* NN *2* Moz *all* Saf *all* Op *7* ECMA *1* |

The less-than-or-equal operator compares the values of operands on either side of the operator. If the numeric value of the left operand is smaller than or equal to the right operand, the expression evaluates to true. Strings are converted to their Unicode values for comparison of those numeric values.

Example
```
if (a <= b) {
    ...
}
```

| % | IE *3* NN *2* Moz *all* Saf *all* Op *7* ECMA *1* |

The modulus operator divides the number to the left of the operator by the number to the right. If a remainder exists after the division, the expression evaluates to that remainder as an integer. If there is no remainder, the returned value is zero. Both operands must be numbers. An expression with this operator evaluates to a number. Even if you aren't interested in the remainder value, this operator is a quick way to find out if two values are evenly divisible.

Example
```
if ((dayCount % 7) > 0) {
    ...
}
```

| * | IE *3* NN *2* Moz *all* Saf *all* Op *7* ECMA *1* |

The multiplication operator multiplies the number to the left of the operator by the number to the right. Both operands must be numbers. An expression with this operator evaluates to a number.

Example   `var myProduct = `*`number1`*` * `*`number2`*`;`

-   *IE* 3 NN 2 Moz *all* Saf *all* Op 7 ECMA 1

This is the negation operator. This unary operator negates the value of the single operand. For example, in the following statements:

```
a = 5;
b = -a;
```

the value of b becomes -5. A negation operator applied to a negative value returns a positive value.

Example   `var myOpposite = -me;`

!==   *IE* 4 NN 4 Moz *all* Saf *all* Op 7 ECMA 3

The strict-not-equals (nonidentity) operator compares two operand values and returns a Boolean result. Both the value and data type of the two operands must be identical for this operator to return false. For less stringent comparisons, see the inequality operator (!=).

Example
```
if (n !== m) {
    ...
}
```

!   *IE* 3 NN 2 Moz *all* Saf *all* Op 7 ECMA 1

This is the NOT operator. This unary operator evaluates to the negative value of a single Boolean operand. The NOT operator should be used with explicit Boolean values, such as the result of a comparison or a Boolean property setting.

Example
```
if (a == !b) {
    ...
}
```

|| *IE* 3 NN 2 Moz *all* Saf *all* Op 7 ECMA 1

The OR operator compares two Boolean expressions for equality. If either or both expressions evaluate to true, the result of the || operator also evaluates to true; if both expressions are false, the || operator evaluates to false. A Boolean expression may consist of a comparison expression (using any of the many comparison operators) or a variety of other values. See the discussion of the AND operator for a summary of the most common data types, values, and their Boolean value equivalent.

JavaScript Reference

You can create compound conditions with the help of the || operator. For example, if you want to see if either or both of two conditions are true, you would create a condition such as the following:

```
var userEntry1 = document.forms[0].entry1.value;
var userEntry2 = document.forms[0].entry2.value;
if (userEntry1 || userEntry2) {
    ...
}
```

In the compound condition, the || operator wants to know if either or both operands is true before it evaluates to true. If the user entered text into the first field, the condition short-circuits because a true value of either operand yields a true result. If text were entered only in the second field, the second operand is evaluated. Because it evaluates to true (a nonempty string), the condition evaluates to true. Only when both operands evaluate to false does the compound condition evaluate to false.

Example

```
if (a <= b || b >= c) {
    ...
}
```

-   IE 3 NN 2 Moz *all* Saf *all* Op 7 ECMA 1

The subtraction operator subtracts the number to the right of the operator from the number on the left. Both operands must be numbers. An expression with this operator evaluates to a number.

Example   `var myDifference = number1 - number2;`

---

delete   IE 4 NN 4 Moz *all* Saf *all* Op 7 ECMA 1

The delete operator removes a property from an object (e.g., a prototype property from an instance of an object to whose static object your script added the prototype earlier) or an item from a script-generated array. Removing an array entry does not alter the array's length or the numerical indexes of existing items. Instead, the value of the deleted item is simply undefined. The delete operator is not a memory management tool.

In an E4X context, the delete operator can also work on elements and attributes within an XML object. Simply reference the element or attribute to be deleted. If you delete an item in an XMLList object, the numeric index values of items that came after the deleted item are decremented by one, leaving no empty entry (unlike deleting an item of an array).

Example   `delete myString.author;`

---

in   IE 5.5 NN *n/a* Moz *all* Saf *all* Op 7 ECMA *n/a*

The in operator lets scripts quickly uncover whether an object has a particular property or method implemented for it. The left operand is a string containing the name of the property or method (method name without parentheses), while the right operand is a reference to the object. If your exploration requires DOM references entailing "dots," put them in

---

the object reference side of the expression. In other words, instead of trying `"style.filter"` in document.body, use `"filter"` in `document.body.style`. Were it not that so few browsers implement this future ECMA operator, it would be a useful tool in object detection.

Example

```
if ("createDocument" in document.implementation) {
    // go ahead and use document.implementation.createDocument( )
}
```

instanceof
IE 5(Win) NN n/a Moz all Saf all Op 7 ECMA n/a

The instanceof operator lets scripts determine if an object (the left operand) is an instance of a known object (or inherited from the known object). In some ways, this operator is like the typeof operator, but rather than returning a broad object type, an expression with the instanceof operator returns a Boolean value against your test for a more specific object type. In fact, you can query an object against custom objects and, in Mozilla and Opera, W3C DOM tree object prototypes. Whereas the typeof operator on an array returns object, you can find out if an object was instantiated specifically as an array:

```
myVar instanceof Array
```

Note, however, that if the above expression evaluates to true, so does:

```
myVar instanceof Object
```

An array is a descendant of the root Object object, and is thus an instance of that root object, as well.

In Mozilla and Opera, either or both operands can also be references to DOM prototype objects. Therefore, the following expression is legal and operational in both browsers:

```
document.getElementById("widget") instanceof HTMLDivElement
```

Example

```
if (theVal instanceof Array) {
    // go ahead and treat theVal as an array
}
```

new
IE 3 NN 2 Moz all Saf all Op 7 ECMA 1

The new operator creates instances of the following ECMA standard static objects:

```
Array
Boolean
Date
Function
Number
Object
RegExp
String
```

The operator does the same for the following E4X static objects:

```
Namespace
QName
```

JavaScript Reference

> XML
> XMLList

An expression with this operator evaluates to an instance of the object. In other words, invoking this operator makes JavaScript look for a constructor function with the same name. Thus, the new operator also works with custom objects that are formed via custom constructor functions. It also works in IE for Windows for creating instances of proprietary objects, such as ActiveX and VBArray objects.

Syntax rules allow naming the static object, the static object with empty parentheses, and the static object with parameters in parentheses:

```
var myArray = new Array;
var myArray = new Array( );
var myArray = new Array("Larry", "Moe", "Curly");
```

Only the last two examples are guaranteed to work in all scriptable browser versions. With the exception of the Date object, if you omit assigning parameters during the native object creation, the newly minted instance has only the properties that are assigned to the prototype of the static object.

Example   var now = new Date( );

this   IE 3   NN 2   Moz *all*   Saf *all*   Op 7   ECMA 1

Refers to the current object. For example, in a form control object event handler, you can pass the object as a parameter to the function:

```
<input type="text" name="ZIP" onchange="validate(this);">
```

Inside a custom object constructor, the keyword refers to the object itself, allowing you to assign values to its properties (even creating the properties at the same time):

```
function CD(label, num, artist) {
    this.label = label;
    this.num = num;
    this.artist = artist;
}
```

Inside a function, the this keyword refers to the function object. However, if the function is assigned as a method of a custom object constructor, this refers to the instance of the object in whose context the function executes.

Example   `<input type="text" name="phone" onchange="validate(this.value);">`

typeof   IE 3   NN 3   Moz *all*   Saf *all*   Op 7   ECMA 1

The typeof operator returns one of six string descriptions of the data type of a value. Those returned types are:

```
boolean
function
number
object
string
undefined
```

The object type includes arrays, but the operator provides no further information about the type of object or array of the value (see the instanceof operator).

In the E4X context, the typeof operator returns the value of XML for instances of both the XML and XMLList objects.

Example

```
if (typeof someVar == "string") {
    ...
}
```

void

This unary operator evaluates the expression to its right but returns a value of undefined, even if the expression (such as a function call) evaluates to some value. This operator is commonly used with javascript: pseudo-URLs that invoke functions. If the function returns a value, that value is ignored by the calling expression.

Example   `<a href="javascript: void getSound( );" >...</a>`

Control Statements

break

Stops execution of the current loop and returns control to the next script statement following the end of the current loop. Note that without a label parameter, the scope of the break statement is its own loop. To break out of a nested loop, assign labels to each nested layer, and use the desired label as a parameter with the break statement. See the label statement.

Syntax   break [*label*]

Example   See the label statement.

catch

See try.

continue

Stops execution of the current iteration through the loop and returns to the top of the loop for the next pass (executing the update expression if one is specified in a for loop). If you are using nested loop constructions, assign labels to each nested layer, and use the desired label as a parameter with the continue statement. See the label statement.

Syntax   continue [*label*]

Example

```
outerLoop:
for (var i = 0; i <= maxValue1; i++) {
    for (var j = 0; j <= maxValue2; j++) {
        if (j*i == magic2) {
            continue outerLoop;
        }
    }
}
```

do/while

Executes statements in a loop while a condition is true. Because the condition is tested at the end of the loop, the statements inside it are always executed at least one time. It is imperative that the expression that makes up the condition have some aspect of its value potentially altered in the statements. Otherwise, an infinite loop occurs.

Syntax

```
do {
    statements
} while (condition)
```

Example

```
var i = 1;
do {
    window.status = "Loop number " + i++;
} while (i <= 10)
window.status = "";
```

for

This is a construction that allows repeated execution of statements, usually for a controlled number of times.

Syntax

```
for ([initExpression]; [condition]; [updateExpression]) {
    statements
}
```

Example

```
var userEntry = document.forms[0].entry.value;
var oneChar;
for (var i = 0; i < userEntry.length; i++) {
    oneChar = userEntry.charAt(i);
    if (oneChar < "0" || oneChar > "9") {
        alert("The entry must be numerals only.");
    }
}
```

for-in

IE *3* NN *2* Moz *all* Saf *all* Op *7* ECMA *1*

This is a variation of the regular for loop that can extract the property names and values of an object. Only properties (and methods in Mozilla, Safari, and Opera) that are set to be enumerable by the browser internals appear in the output of this construction.

In the E4X context, the object reference is an instance of an XML object, and is automatically treated as an XMLList. As such, the variable acts like an index to the list during the iterations. For example, if myXml is an XMLList with a dozen records, each of which has an element named productID, you could iterate through all of those nested elements as follows:

```
for (var i in myXml..productID) {
    alert("Product ID=" + myXml..productID[i]);
}
```

Syntax

```
for ([var] varName in objectRef) {
    statements
}
```

Example

```
function showProps( ) {
    objName = "image";
    obj = document.images[0];
    var msg = "";
    for (var i in obj) {
        msg += objName + "." + i + "=" + obj[i] + "\n";
    }
    alert(msg);
}
```

for-each-in

IE *n/a* NN *n/a* Moz *1.8.1* Saf *n/a* Op *n/a* ECMA *E4X*

This is a variation of the for-in loop tailored for E4X implementations. Note that in the E4X context, the for-in construction assigns an index to the variable. In contrast, the for-each-in construction assigns an object reference to the variable, facilitating iteration through the objects within an XMLList.

Syntax

```
for each ([var] varName in objectRef) {
    statements
}
```

Example

```
for (var i in myXml..productID) {
    alert("Product ID=" + i);
}
```

if

This is a simple conditional statement that provides one alternate execution path.

Syntax
```
if (condition) {
    statement(s) if true
}
```

Example
```
if (myDateObj.getMonth( ) == 1) {
    calcMonthLength( );
}
```

if-else

This is a conditional statement that provides two execution paths depending on the result of the condition. You can nest another if or if-else statement inside either path of the if-else statement.

Syntax
```
if (condition) {
    statement(s) if true
} else {
    statement(s) if false
}
```

Example
```
var theMonth = myDateObj.getMonth( );
if (theMonth == 1) {
    monLength = calcLeapMonthLength( );
} else {
    monLength = calcMonthLength(theMonth);
}
```

label

You can assign a label identifier to any block of executing statements, including control structures. The purpose of the label is to allow break and continue statements within deeply nested control structures to exit to a nested level that may be at levels beyond the scope of the normal break and continue statements.

Syntax   `labelName:`

Example
```
outerLoop:
for (var i = 0; i <= maxValue1; i++) {
    for (var j = 0; j <= maxValue2; j++) {
        if (i == magic1 && j == magic2) {
            break outerLoop;
```

```
        }
    }
}
```

return

Stops execution of the current function. A return statement can be located anywhere within the function, including inside control structures. You can optionally specify a value to be returned to the calling statement. This return value can be any JavaScript data type. If a return statement that returns a value is in a loop or other control structure, there must be a return statement for each branch of the execution tree, including a default return statement if execution should reach the main execution scope near or at the end of the function.

Syntax   return [*value*]

Example
```
function validateNumber(form) {
    var oneChar;
    for (var i = 0; i < userEntry.length; i++) {
        oneChar = form.entry.value.charAt(i);
        if (oneChar < "0" || oneChar > "9") {
            return false;
        }
    }
    return true;
}
```

switch-case

Provides a shortcut to execution paths for numerous conditions of an expression. The optional break statement at the end of each case block shortcuts execution of the switch statement, and also prevents the inadvertent execution of the default block, if present.

Syntax
```
switch (expression) {
    case label1:
        statements
        [break;]
    case label2:
        statements
        [break;]
    ...
    [default:
        statements]
}
```

Example
```
var productList = document.forms[0].prodList;
var chosenItem = productList.options[productList.selectedIndex].value;
switch(chosenItem) {
```

```
    case "Small Widget":
        document.forms[0].price.value = "44.95";
        break;
    case "Medium Widget":
        document.forms[0].price.value = "54.95";
        break;
    case "Large Widget":
        document.forms[0].price.value = "64.95";
        break;
    default:
        document.forms[0].price.value = "Nothing Selected";
}
```

throw
IE 5 NN n/a Moz all Saf all Op 7 ECMA 3

Triggers an exception condition, passing a value along with the exception. Although the value you pass can be a simple string, ideally you should pass an instance of the JavaScript Error object filled with sufficient information for a catch statement to act intelligently on the error. A throw statement must be enclosed in the try portion of a try-catch construction.

Syntax   throw *value*;

Example

```
function processNumber(inputField) {
    try {
        var inpVal = parseInt(inputField.value, 10);
        if (isNaN(inpVal)) {
            var msg = "Please enter a number only.";
            var err = new Error(msg);
            if (!err.message) {
                err.message = msg;
            }
            throw err;
        }
        // process number
    }
    catch (e) {
        alert(e.message);
        inputField.focus();
        inputField.select();
    }
}
```

try-catch
IE 5 NN n/a Moz all Saf all Op 7 ECMA 3

This construction provides a nondisruptive way to trap for errors (exceptions) and handle them gracefully. Both parts of this exception-handling construction are required. If an error occurs in the try portion, execution immediately branches to the catch portion, where your scripts can display alert dialogs, modify data, or any other task that keeps the JavaScript interpreter from triggering a disruptive error message. Exceptions that occur naturally (i.e., they are not thrown by a throw statement) pass an instance of the Error object as a parameter to the catch section. Statements inside the catch section can examine properties of the error object to determine how to handle exceptions that land there. Thus, one catch portion can handle errors of various types.

You can use try-catch constructions only in browsers that support them. To protect older browsers from seeing this construction, place all affected code inside a <script> tag that explicitly requires JavaScript 1.5 or later (with the language = "JavaScript1.5" or later attribute).

Syntax

```
try {    statement(s) that could cause error
}
catch (errorInfo) {    process error(s) gracefully
}
```

Example

```
function insertOneNode(baseNode, newNode, position) {
    try {
        baseNode.insertBefore(newNode, baseNode.childNodes[position]);
    }
    catch (e) {
        // handle W3C DOM Exception types
        switch (e.name) {
            case "HIERARCHY_REQUEST_ERR" :
                // process bad tree hierarchy reference
                break;
            case "NOT_FOUND_ERR" :
                // process bad refNode reference
                break;
            default :
                // process all other exceptions
        }
    }
    return true;
}
```

while   IE 3   NN 2   Moz *all*   Saf *all*   Op 7   ECMA 1

Executes statements in a loop as long as a condition is true. Because the condition is tested at the beginning of the loop, it is conceivable that under the right conditions, the statements inside the loop do not execute. It is imperative that the expression that makes up the condition have some aspect of its value potentially altered in the statements. Otherwise an infinite loop occurs.

Syntax

```
while (condition) {
    statements
}
```

Example
```
var i = 0;
while (!document.forms[0].radioGroup[i].checked) {
    i++;
}
alert("You selected item number " + (i+1) + ".");
```

with   IE 3   NN 2   Moz *all*   Saf *all*   Op 7   ECMA 1

The with statement adds an object to the scope of every statement nested within. This can shorten the code of some statement groups that rely on a particular object reference. Note that with constructions are generally very inefficient. You can achieve better performance by assigning the object reference to a local variable, and using that variable in your function.

Syntax
```
with (objectRef) {
    statements
}
```

Example
```
with (document.forms[0]) {
    name1 = firstName.value;
    name2 = lastName.value;
    mail = eMail.value;
}
```

yield   IE *n/a*   NN *n/a*   Moz *all*   Saf *1.8.1*   Op *n/a*   ECMA *n/a*

You can turn a function into what is called a generator by inserting the yield keyword into a looping section of the function. Such functions need to be assigned to a variable or as a property value so that the reference can subsequently iterate through the looping section one loop at a time.

When the function is initially invoked, all statements up to the looping section execute as normal. But execution pauses temporarily just before the yield statement. The yield statement can return a value, just like a return statement, but the generator function remains alive, waiting for iterative stepping through the loop section.

To obtain the yielded value, invoke the next( ) method on the function (just like the next( ) method of an iterator object). If there are statements in the function following the yield statement, they execute at this time (perhaps acting on the values of local variables inside the function), but pause in the next time through the loop, just before the yield statement.

Syntax
```
function myFunction( ) {
    statements
    while (true) {
        yield value;
        statements
```

```
    }
}
```

Example

```
function getWords(txt) {
    var words = txt.split(" ");
    for (var i = 0; i < words.length; i++) {
        yield words[i].length;
    }
}

function getAverageWordLength(txt) {
    var lengthCounter = getWords(txt);
    var count = 0;
    var total = 0;
    try {
        while (total += lengthCounter.next()) {
            count++;
        }
    }
    catch(e) {}
    alert("Average word length is: " + (total/count).toFixed(2) + " characters.");
}
```

Miscellaneous Statements

//, /*...*/   IE 3   NN 2   Moz all   Saf all   Op 7   ECMA 1

These are comment statements that let you enter nonexecuting text in a script. Any text following the // symbol anywhere in a statement line is ignored by the language interpreter. The next line of script, unless it begins with another // symbol, is interpreted by the browser.

For multiline comment blocks, you can begin a block with the /* symbol. A comment block may encompass multiple source code lines. The block is closed with the */ symbol, after which the interpreter engages subsequent statements.

Example

```
// convert temp from C to F

/*
many lines
of
comments
*/
```

@cc_on, @if, @end, @set   IE 4(Win) NN n/a Moz n/a Saf n/a Op n/a ECMA n/a

IE for Windows includes a scripting feature called *conditional compilation*. It is a mode that, once turned on via the @cc_on statement, allows JScript statements to run under conditions that are testable within this conditional environment. If you surround conditional compilation statements by JavaScript comments, the conditional statements run only in IE 4 or later for Windows, while not conflicting with other browsers.

The "conditional" part comes from numerous global properties (all preceded with the @ symbol) that reveal environmental properties, such as script engine version, operating system, and CPU type. All of this information is available from the navigator object's properties on a wide range of browsers, so this is not unique information available only to this conditional environment.

To engage conditional compilation, include the following statement in your script:

```
/*@cc_on @*/
```

This is a one-way toggle: once the mode is turned on, it can't be turned off in the current page.

The following fragment shows how the @if and related statements display some environmental information in the window's status bar if the browser is running JScript Version 5.6 or later (IE 6 or later):

```
/*@cc_on @*/
/*@if (@_jscript_version >= 5.6 && @_x86)
    status = "Now running JScript version " + @_jscript_version +
    " with Intel inside.";
  @else @*/
    status = "Have a nice day.";
/*@end @*/
```

The @set statement lets you assign a numeric or Boolean value (no strings) to a variable (a variable with an @ prefix) within a conditional compilation section:

```
@set @isOK = @_win32
```

Once initialized, that variable (including its otherwise unacceptable identifier) can be used in script statements throughout the page. Note that the Visual Basic-inspired syntax of @ statements in conditional compilation statements does not permit semicolons at the end of statements.

On the one hand, conditional compilation could be useful for IE-only deployment to screening older IE versions from new language features that would generate compilation errors (such as try-catch constructions) because such statements compile only under very controllable version situations. In a multibrand browser development shop, however, at most you might find application for IE-only debugging purposes, but probably not for actual application deployment.

Example   See the discussion above.

function   IE 3 NN 2 Moz all Saf all Op 7 ECMA 1

The function keyword begins a named function definition. For anonymous functions, see the Function object.

Example

```
function myFunc(arg1, arg2) {
    // function statements here
}
```

let

The let keyword can be used in a few ways to define variables with a scope separate distinct from other global or local scope within the script. For example, you can limit variable scope to a single expression by first defining the variables inside parentheses, and then using those variables in a single statement, as in the following statements residing inside a function:

```
// local variables
var x = 1;
var y = 10;
alert(let(x = 10, y = y * 5) x*y);
alert(x*y);
```

In the first alert, the computed value is 500, while the second alert displays 10.

If you use a let statement inside a block (e.g., inside braces), the scope of the variable, constant, or function defined via let is within that block, allowing those defined values to be used locally within the block. You can also use the let statement to define for loop counter variables that won't collide with other loops in the same function.

Example

```
for (let i = 0; i < myArray.length; i++) {
    // statements here using i as index variable
}
```

var

A keyword that defines the creation of a new variable. Although the keyword is optional for global variables (those not declared or initialized inside a function), it is good form to use this keyword for each new variable. Using the var keyword inside a function makes the variable local to statements inside the function.

You may simply declare one or more variable names, in which case their initial values are null. Or you can also initialize a new variable with a value.

Example

```
var a, b, c;
var myName = "Susan";
```

Special (Escaped) String Characters

\char   IE *3* NN *2* Moz *all* Saf *all* Op *7* ECMA *1*

JavaScript provides a mechanism for including common whitespace characters (sometimes called control codes) inside strings, as well as symbols that otherwise conflict with string representation. The key is the backslash character (\), followed immediately by a single character with a special meaning. The following table shows the recognized escaped characters and their meanings.

Escape sequence	Description
\b	Backspace
\t	Horizontal tab
\n	Line feed (new line)
\v	Vertical tab
\f	Form feed
\r	Carriage return
\"	Double quote "
\'	Single quote '
\\	Backslash

These characters come in handy for alert, confirm, and prompt dialog box text. For example, if you want to display multiple paragraphs with a blank line between them in an alert box, you would insert line feed characters:

```
alert("First paragraph.\n\nSecond paragraph.")
```

Note that these characters apply to strings, and do not influence HTML content formatting for carriage returns.

Cross References

This part of the book, Chapters 6 through 9, provides a different take on the information of Part I. If you have the name of an HTML attribute or an object property, method, or event handler, you can look it up in one of the indices here to find out which elements and/or objects support it.

HTML/XHTML Attribute Index

Entries in the following index are arranged alphabetically by HTML attribute. Look up an attribute to find out which HTML elements support it. This listing is a union of nonevent attributes defined for elements in Internet Explorer, pre-Mozilla Netscape Navigator, Mozilla, Safari, Opera, Web Forms 2.0, and the latest HTML/XHTML recommendations, including deprecated items. The same attribute name may mean different things for different elements. Be sure to look up the details of the attribute listing in Chapter 1, to find out if the attribute is available for the browser(s) used by your intended audience and whether it does what you want. When you see an attribute with a very long list of elements, the attribute is most likely covered among the shared attributes at the beginning of Chapter 1.

abbr   td, th

above   ilayer, layer

accept   form, input, textarea

accept-charset   form

accesskey   a, abbr, acronym, address, applet, area, b, bdo, big, blockquote, body, button, canvas, caption, center, cite, custom, dd, del, dfn, dir, div, dl, dt, em, embed, fieldset, font, h1, h2, h3, h4, h5, h6, hr, i, img, input, ins, isindex, kbd, label, legend, li, listing, marquee, menu, object, ol, output, p, plaintext, pre, q, rt, ruby, s, samp, select, small, span, strike, strong, sub, sup, table, tbody, td, textarea, tfoot, th, thead, tr, tt, u, ul, var, xmp

action   button, form, input

align   applet, caption, col, colgroup, div, embed, fieldset, h1, h2, h3, h4, h5, h6, hr, iframe, img, input, legend, object, p, select, spacer, table, tbody, td, tfoot, th, thead, tr

alink   body

allowtransparency   iframe

alt   applet, area, embed, img, input, object

archive   applet, object

autocomplete   form, input

autofocus   button, input, select, textarea

axis   td, th

background   body, ilayer, layer, table, td, th, tr

balance   bgsound

behavior   marquee

below   ilayer, layer

bgcolor   body, ilayer, layer, marquee, table, tbody, td, tfoot, th, thead, tr

bgproperties   body

border   frame, frameset, iframe, img, input, object, table

bordercolor   frame, frameset, table, td, th, tr

bordercolordark   table, td, th, tr

bordercolorlight   table, td, th, tr

bottommargin   body

cellpadding   table

cellspacing   table

challenge   keygen

char   col, colgroup, tbody, td, tfoot, th, thead, tr

charoff   col, colgroup, tbody, td, tfoot, th, thead, tr

charset   a, link, script

checked   input

cite   blockquote, del, ins, q

class   a, abbr, acronym, address, applet, area, b, basefont, bdo, bgsound, big, blockquote, body, br, button, caption, canvas, center, cite, code, col, colgroup, datalist, dd, del, dfn, dir, div, dl, dt, em, embed, fieldset, font, form, frame, frameset, h1, h2, h3, h4, h5, h6, head, hr, html, i, iframe, img, input, ins, isindex, kbd, label, legend, li, link, listing, map, marquee, menu, nobr, noframes, noscript, object, ol, optgroup, option, output, p, plaintext, pre, q, rt, ruby, s, samp, script, select, small, span, strike, strong, sub, sup, table, tbody, td, textarea, tfoot, th, thead, tr, tt, u, ul, var, wbr, xmp

classid   object

clear   br

clip   ilayer, layer

code   applet, object

codebase   applet, object

codetype   object

color   basefont, font, hr

cols   frameset, multicol, pre, table, textarea

colspan   td, th

compact   dir, dl, menu, ol, ul

content   meta

contenteditable   a, abbr, acronym, address, b, bdo, big, blockquote, body, button, center, cite, code, custom, dd, del, dfn, dir, div, dl, dt, em, fieldset, font, form, h1, h2, h3, h4, h5, h6, i, input, ins, isindex, kbd, label, legend, li, listing, marquee, menu, nobr, ol, p, plaintext, pre, q, rt, ruby, s,

samp, small, span, strike, strong, sub, sup, textarea, tt, u, ul, var, xmp

coords   a, area

data   form, object, select

datafld   a, applet, button, div, frame, iframe, img, input, label, marquee, param, select, span, td, textarea, th

dataformatas   button, div, label, marquee, param, span

datapagesize   table

datasrc   a, applet, button, div, frame, iframe, img, input, label, marquee, param, select, span, table, textarea

datetime   del, ins

declare   object

defer   script

dir   a, abbr, acronym, address, area, b, basefont, bdo, big, blockquote, body, canvas, caption, center, cite, code, col, colgroup, datalist, dd, del, dfn, dir, div, dl, dt, em, embed, fieldset, font, form, h1, h2, h3, h4, h5, h6, head, html, i, img, input, ins, isindex, kbd, label, legend, li, link, listing, map, marquee, menu, meta, noframes, noscript, object, ol, optgroup, option, output, p, plaintext, pre, q, rt, ruby, s, samp, select, small, span, strike, strong, style, sub, sup, table, tbody, td, textarea, tfoot, th, thead, title, tr, tt, u, ul, var, xmp

direction   marquee,

disabled   a, abbr, acronym, address, b, bdo, big, blockquote, body, button, caption, canvas, center, cite, code, custom, dd, del, dfn, dir, div, dl, dt, em, fieldset, font, form, h1, h2, h3, h4, h5, h6, i, inpu, ins, isindex, kbd, label, legend, li, listing, marquee, menu, nobr, ol, optgroup, option, output, p, plaintext, pre, q, rt, ruby, s, samp, select, small, strike, strong, style, sub, sup, textarea, tt, u, ul, var, xmp

dynsrc   img, input

enctype   button, form, input

event   script

face   basefont, font

for   label, output, script

form   button, fieldset, input, output, select, textarea

frame   table

frameborder   frame, frameset, iframe

framespacing   frameset

galleryimg   img

gutter   multicol

headers   td, th

height   applet, canvas, embed, frame, iframe, ilayer, img, input, layer, marquee, object, spacer, table, td, th

hidden   embed

href   a, area, base, link

hreflang   a, link

hspace   applet, iframe, img, input marquee, object, table

http-equiv   meta

id   a, abbr, acronym, address, applet, area, b, basefont, bdo, bgsound, big, blockquote, body, br, button, caption, canvas, center, cite, code, col, colgroup, datalist, dd, del, dfn, dir, div, dl, dt, em, embed, fieldset, font, form, frame, frameset, h1, h2, h3, h4, h5, h6, head, hr, html, i, iframe, img, input, ins, isindex, kbd, label, legend, li, link, listing, map, marquee, menu, nobr, noframes, noscript, object, ol, optgroup, option, output, p, plaintext, pre, q, rt, ruby, s, samp, script, select, small, span, strike, strong, sub, sup, table, tbody, td, textarea, tfoot, th, thead, tr, tt, u, ul, var, wbr, xmp

inputmode   input, textarea

ismap   img, input

label   optgroup, option

lang   a, abbr, acronym, address, area, b, basefont, bdo, big, blockquote, body, canvas, caption, center, cite, code, col, colgroup, datalist, dd, del, dfn, dir, div, dl, dt, em, embed, fieldset, font, form, h1, h2, h3, h4, h5, h6, head, html, i, img, input, ins, isindex, kbd, label, legend, li, link, listing, map, marquee, menu, meta, noframes, noscript, object, ol, optgroup, option, out-

put, p, plaintext, pre, q, rt, ruby, s, samp, select, small, span, strike, strong, style, sub, sup, table, tbody, td, textarea, tfoot, th, thead, title, tr, tt, u, ul, var, xmp

language   a, abbr, acronym, address, applet, area, b, bdo, big, blockquote, body, button, caption, center, cite, code, custom, dd, del, dfn, dir, div, dl, dt, em, embed, fieldset, font, form, frame, frameset, h1, h2, h3, h4, h5, h6, hr, i, iframe, img, input, ins, isindex, kbd, label, legend, li, listing, map, marquee, nobr, object, ol, option, p, plaintext, pre, q, rt, ruby, s, samp, script, select, small, span, strike, strong, sub, sup, table, tbody, td, textarea, tfoot, th, thead, tr, tt, u, ul, var, xmp

left   ilayer, layer

leftmargin   body

link   body

list   input

longdesc   frame, iframe, img

loop   bgsound, img, input, marquee

lowsrc   img, input

marginheight   body, frame, iframe

marginwidth   body, frame, iframe

max   input

maxlength   input, textarea

mayscript   applet

media   link, style

method   button, form, input

methods   a

min   input

multiple   select

name   a, applet, basefont, button, embed, form, frame, iframe, img, input, keygen, map, meta, object, output, param, rt, ruby, select, textarea

nohref   area

noresize   frame

noshade   hr

nowrap   body, div, td, th

pagex   layer

pagey layer

pattern input

pluginspage embed

pluginurl embed

point-size font

profile head

prompt isindex

rbspan rt

readonly input, textarea

repeat a, abbr, acronym, address, applet, area, b, basefont, bdo, big, blockquote, body, br, button, caption, canvas, center, cite, code, col, colgroup, datalist, dd, del, dfn, dir, div, dl, dt, em, embed, fieldset, font, form, h1, h2, h3, h4, h5, h6, head, hr, i, iframe, img, input, ins, isindex, kbd, label, legend, li, listing, map, marquee, menu, nobr, object, ol, optgroup, option, output, p, plaintext, pre, q, rt, ruby, s, samp, select, small, span, strike, strong, sub, sup, table, tbody, td, textarea, tfoot, th, thead, tr, tt, u, ul, var, wbr, xmp

repeat-max a, abbr, acronym, address, applet, area, b, basefont, bdo, big, blockquote, body, br, button, caption, canvas, center, cite, code, col, colgroup, datalist, dd, del, dfn, dir, div, dl, dt, em, embed, fieldset, font, form, h1, h2, h3, h4, h5, h6, head, hr, i, iframe, img, input, ins, isindex, kbd, label, legend, li, listing, map, marquee, menu, nobr, object, ol, optgroup, option, output, p, plaintext, pre, q, rt, ruby, s, samp, select, small, span, strike, strong, sub, sup, table, tbody, td, textarea, tfoot, th, thead, tr, tt, u, ul, var, wbr, xmp

repeat-min a, abbr, acronym, address, applet, area, b, basefont, bdo, big, blockquote, body, br, button, caption, canvas, center, cite, code, col, colgroup, datalist, dd, del, dfn, dir, div, dl, dt, em, embed, fieldset, font, form, h1, h2, h3, h4, h5, h6, head, hr, i, iframe, img, input, ins, isindex, kbd, label, legend, li, listing, map, marquee, menu, nobr, object, ol, optgroup, option, output, p, plaintext, pre, q, rt, ruby, s, samp, select, small, span, strike, strong,

sub, sup, table, tbody, td, textarea, tfoot, th, thead, tr, tt, u, ul, var, wbr, xmp

repeat-start a, abbr, acronym, address, applet, area, b, basefont, bdo, big, blockquote, body, br, button, caption, canvas, center, cite, code, col, colgroup, datalist, dd, del, dfn, dir, div, dl, dt, em, embed, fieldset, font, form, h1, h2, h3, h4, h5, h6, head, hr, i, iframe, img, input, ins, isindex, kbd, label, legend, li, listing, map, marquee, menu, nobr, object, ol, optgroup, option, output, p, plaintext, pre, q, rt, ruby, s, samp, select, small, span, strike, strong, sub, sup, table, tbody, td, textarea, tfoot, th, thead, tr, tt, u, ul, var, wbr, xmp

repeat-template a, abbr, acronym, address, applet, area, b, basefont, bdo, big, blockquote, body, br, button, caption, canvas, center, cite, code, col, colgroup, datalist, dd, del, dfn, dir, div, dl, dt, em, embed, fieldset, font, form, h1, h2, h3, h4, h5, h6, head, hr, i, iframe, img, input, ins, isindex, kbd, label, legend, li, listing, map, marquee, menu, nobr, object, ol, optgroup, option, output, p, plaintext, pre, q, rt, ruby, s, samp, select, small, span, strike, strong, sub, sup, table, tbody, td, textarea, tfoot, th, thead, tr, tt, u, ul, var, wbr, xmp

rel a, link

replace button, input

required input, textarea

rev a, link

rightmargin body

rows frameset, textarea

rowspan td, th

rules table

scheme meta

scope td, th

scroll body

scrollamount marquee

scrolldelay marquee

scrolling frame, iframe

security frame, iframe

selected option

shape a, area

size basefont, font, hr, input, select, spacer

span col, colgroup

src applet, bgsound, embed, frame, iframe, ilayer, img, input, layer, link, script, xml

standby object

start img, input, ol

step input

style a, abbr, acronym, address, applet, area, b, basefont, bdo, big, blockquote, body, br, button, canvas, caption, center, cite, code, col, colgroup, datalist, dd, del, dfn, dir, div, dl, dt, em, embed, fieldset, font, form, frame, frameset, h1, h2, h3, h4, h5, h6, hr, i, iframe, img, input, ins, isindex, kbd, label, legend, li, link, listing, map, marquee, menu, nobr, noframes, noscript, object, ol, optgroup, option, output, p, plaintext, pre, q, s, samp, select, small, span, strike, strong, sub, sup, table, tbody, td, textarea, tfoot, th, thead, tr, tt, u, ul, var, wbr, xmp

summary table

tabindex a, abbr, acronym, address, applet, area, b, bdo, big, blockquote, body, button, caption, center, cite, custom, dd, del, dfn, dir, div, dl, dt, em, fieldset, font, form, frame, frameset, h1, h2, h3, h4, h5, h6, hr, i, iframe, img, input, ins, isindex, kbd, label, legend, li, listing, marquee, menu, object, ol, p, plaintext, pre, q, rt, ruby, s, samp, select, small, span, strike, strong, sub, sup, table, tbody, td, textarea, tfoot, th, thead, tr, tt, u, ul, var, xmp

target a, area, base, button, form, link

template button, input

text body

title a, abbr, acronym, address, applet, area, b, basefont, bdo, big, blockquote, body, br, button, caption, center, cite, code, col, colgroup, dd, del, dfn, dir, div, dl, dt, em, embed, fieldset, font, form, frame, frameset, h1, h2, h3, h4, h5, h6, hr, i, iframe, img, input, ins, isindex, kbd, label, legend, li, link, listing, map, marquee,

menu, nobr, noframes, noscript, object, ol, optgroup, option, p, plaintext, pre, q, s, samp, select, small, span, strike, strong, sub, sup, table, tbody, td, textarea, tfoot, th, thead, tr, tt, u, ul, var, wbr, xmp

top ilayer, layer

topmargin body

truespeed marquee

type a, button, embed, input, li, link, object, ol, param, script, spacer, style, ul

units embed

unselectable a, abbr, acronym, address, applet, area, b, bdo, big, blockquote, body, button, caption, center, cite, code, custom, dd, del, dfn, dir, div, dl, dt, em, embed, fieldset, font, form, frame, frameset, h1, h2, h3, h4, h5, h6, hr, i, iframe, img, input, ins, isindex, kbd, label, legend, li, listing, marquee, menu, nobr, object, ol, p, plaintext, pre, q, rt, ruby, s, samp, select, small, span, strike, strong, sub, sup, table, tbody, td, textarea, tfoot, thead, tt, u, ul, var, xmp

urn a

usemap img, input, object

valign caption, col, colgroup, tbody, td, tfoot, th, thead, tr

value button, input, li, option, param

valuetype param

vcard_name param

version html, script

visibility ilayer, layer

vlink body

volume bgsound

vspace applet, iframe, img, input, marquee, object, table

weight font

width applet, canvas, col, colgroup, embed, frame, hr, iframe, ilayer, img, input, layer, marquee, multicol, object, pre, spacer, table, td, th

wrap pre, textarea

xmlns html

z-index ilayer, layer

CHAPTER 7
DOM Property Index

Entries in the following index are arranged alphabetically by scriptable object properties. Look up a property to find out which objects support it. You need to be aware, however, of what support means within the context of the way that browser makers and the W3C DOM specify the inner workings of their models using object-oriented approaches. For example, the list of objects that "support" the style property includes several nonrendered HTML element objects, such as head and meta. Inside the browsers, many properties are defined for a generic HTML element, and *all* elements, regardless of their purpose, inherit those properties. Clearly, reading or writing style-related properties of nonrendered elements is a waste of time in actual development; but because these element objects expose the style property, they appear in that property's list. Omitting this information here could cause equally serious problems for scripters who write object- and property-detection scripts. It's better to know that a property is defined (that is, its value type isn't undefined) for a particular object than to be misled into thinking that its omission means that the property is undefined for the object.

The listing below is a union of properties defined for document and browser objects in Internet Explorer, pre-Mozilla Netscape Navigator, Mozilla, Safari, Opera, Web Forms 2.0, and implemented objects from the W3C DOM Levels 2 and 3. (The exception to this rule is that event handler properties are grouped together in Chapter 9 because of the numerous ways events can be bound to objects.) The same property name may mean different things for different objects. Be sure to look up the details of the property listing in Chapter 2, to find if the property is available for the browser(s) used by your intended audience, and whether it does what you want. If an HTML element object and other scriptable object share the same name, the (element) notation follows its name when referring to the element object. When you see a property with a long list of objects, the property is most likely covered among the shared items at the beginning of Chapter 2.

abbr   td, th

ABORT   Event

above   layer

accelerator   currentStyle, runtimeStyle, style

accept   form, input (file), textarea

acceptCharset   form

accessKey   a, abbr, acronym, address, applet, area, b, base, basefont, bdo, bgsound, big, blockquote, body, br, button, caption, center, cite, code, col, colgroup, comment, dd, del, dfn, dir, div, dl, dt, em, embed, fieldset, font, form, frame, frameset, head, hr, html, i, iframe, img, ins, kbd, label, legend, li, link, listing, map, marquee, menu, meta, nobr, noframes, noscript, object, ol, optgroup, option, p, param, plaintext, pre, q, rb, rt, ruby, s, samp, script, select, small, span, strike, strong, style (element), sub, sup, table, tbody, td, textarea, tfoot, th, thead, title, tr, tt, u, var

action   button, form, input

activeElement   document

ADDITION   event

align   applet, caption, col, colgroup, div, embed, fieldset, h1, h2, h3, h4, h5, h6, h2, h3, h4, h5, h6, hr, iframe, img, legend, marquee, object, p, table, tbody, td, tfoot, th, thead, tr

alink   body

alinkColor   document

all   a, abbr, acronym, address, applet, area, b, base, basefont, bdo, bgsound, big, blockquote, body, br, button, canvas, caption, center, cite, code, col, colgroup, comment, datalist, dd, del, dfn, dir, div, dl, document, dt, em, embed, fieldset, font, form, frame, frameset, h1, h2, h3, h4, h5, h6, head, hr, html, i, iframe, img, input, ins, kbd, label, legend, li, link, listing, map, marquee, menu, meta, nobr, noframes, noscript, object, ol, optgroup, option, output, p, param, plaintext, pre, q, rb, rt, ruby, s, samp, script, select, small, span, strike, strong, style (element), sub, sup, table, tbody, td, textarea, tfoot, th, thead, title, tr, tt, u, ul, var, wbr, xmp

allowTransparency   frame, iframe

alt   applet, area, img, input (image), object

altHTML   applet

altHtml   applet, object

altKey   event

altLeft   event

ALT_MASK   Event

anchorNode   selection

anchorOffset   selection

anchors   document

appCodeName   navigator

applets   document

appMinorVersion   navigator

appName   navigator

appVersion   navigator

archive   applet, object

areas   map

async   document

AT_TARGET   event

attrChange   event

ATTRIBUTE_NODE   (constant of all W3C DOM nodes and elements)

attributes   a, abbr, acronym, address, applet, area, Attr, attribute, b, base, basefont, bdo, bgsound, big, blockquote, body, br, button, canvas, caption, center, cite, code, col, colgroup, comment, datalist, dd, del, dfn, dir, div, dl, document, DocumentType, dt, em, embed, fieldset, font, form, frame, frameset, h1, h2, h3, h4, h5, h6, head, hr, html, i, iframe, img, input, ins, kbd, label, legend, li, link, listing, map, marquee, menu, meta, nobr, Node, noframes, noscript, object, ol, optgroup, option, output, p, param, plaintext, pre, q, rb, rt, ruby, s, samp, script, select, small, span, strike, strong, style (element), sub, sup, table, tbody, td, Text, textarea, tfoot, th, thead, title, tr, tt, u, ul, var, wbr, xmp

attrName   event

autocomplete   input

autofocus   button, input, select, textarea

availHeight   screen

availLeft   screen

availTop   screen

availWidth   screen

axis   td, th

azimuth   style

BACK   Event

background   body, currentStyle layer, runtimeStyle, style, table, tags, td, th

backgroundAttachment   currentStyle, runtimeStyle, style

backgroundColor currentStyle, runtimeStyle, style, tags

backgroundImage currentStyle, runtimeStyle, style, tags

backgroundPosition currentStyle, runtimeStyle, style

backgroundPositionX currentStyle, runtimeStyle, style

backgroundPositionY currentStyle, runtimeStyle, style

backgroundRepeat currentStyle, runtimeStyle, style

balance bgsound

BaseHref applet, object

baseURI a, abbr, acronym, address, area, Attr, attribute, b, base, basefont, bdo, big, blockquote, body, br, button, caption, center, cite, code, col, colgroup, comment, dd, del, dfn, dir, div, dl, document, Document-Type, dt, em, embed, fieldset, font, form, frame, frameset, h1, h2, h3, h4, h5, h6, head, hr, html, i, iframe, img, input, ins, kbd, label, legend, li, link, map, marquee, menu, meta, nobr, Node, noframes, noscript, object, ol, optgroup, option, p, param, plaintext, pre, q, rb, rt, ruby, s, samp, script, select, small, span, strike, strong, style (element), sub, sup, table, tbody, td, Text, textarea, tfoot, th, thead, title, tr, tt, u, ul, var, wbr, xmp

behavior currentStyle, marquee, runtimeStyle, style

behaviorCookie event

behaviorPart event

behaviorUrns a, abbr, acronym, address, applet, area, b, base, basefont, bdo, bgsound, big, blockquote, body, br, button, caption, center, cite, code, col, colgroup, comment, dd, del, dfn, dir, div, dl, dt, em, embed, fieldset, font, form, frame, frameset, h1, h2, h3, h4, h5, h6, head, hr, html, i, iframe, img, input, ins, kbd, label, legend, li, link, listing, map, marquee, menu, meta, nobr, noframes, noscript, object, ol, optgroup, option, p, plaintext, pre, q, rt, ruby, s, samp, script, select, small, span, strike,

strong, style (element), sub, sup, table, tbody, td, textarea, tfoot, th, thead, title, tr, tt, u, ul, var, wbr, xml, xmp

below layer

bgColor body, document, layer, marquee, table, tags, tbody, td, tfoot, th, thead, tr

bgProperties body

blockDirection currentStyle

blockFormats Dialog Helper

BLUR Event

body document

bookmarks event

border applet, currentStyle, frame, frameset, iframe, img, object, runtimeStyle, style, table

borderBottom runtimeStyle, style

borderBottomColor currentStyle, runtimeStyle, style

borderBottomStyle currentStyle, runtimeStyle, style

borderBottomWidth currentStyle, runtimeStyle, style, tags

borderCollapse currentStyle, runtimeStyle, style

borderColor currentStyle, frame, frameset,, runtimeStyle, style, table, tags, td, th, tr

borderColorDark table, td, th, tr

borderColorLight table, td, th, tr

borderLeft currentStyle, runtimeStyle, style

borderLeftColor currentStyle, runtimeStyle, style

borderLeftStyle currentStyle, runtimeStyle, style

borderLeftWidth currentStyle, runtimeStyle, style, tags

borderRight currentStyle, runtimeStyle, style

borderRightColor currentStyle, runtimeStyle, style

borderRightStyle currentStyle, runtimeStyle, style

borderRightWidth currentStyle, runtimeStyle, style, tags

borderSpacing currentStyle, style

borderStyle runtimeStyle, style, tags

borderTop currentStyle, runtimeStyle, style

borderTopColor currentStyle, runtimeStyle, style

borderTopStyle currentStyle, runtimeStyle, style

borderTopWidth currentStyle, runtimeStyle, style, tags

borderWidth currentStyle, runtimeStyle, style

borderWidths tags

bottom currentStyle, runtimeStyle, style, TextRectangle

bottomMargin body

boundElements event

boundingHeight TextRange

boundingLeft TextRange

boundingTop TextRange

boundingWidth TextRange

browserLanguage navigator

bubbles event

BUBBLING_PHASE event

bufferDepth screen

button event

cancelable event

cancelBubble event

canHaveChildren a, abbr, acronym, address, applet, area, b, base, basefont, bdo, bgsound, big, blockquote, body, br, button, caption, center, cite, code, col, colgroup, comment, dd, del, dfn, dir, div, dl, dt, em, embed, fieldset, font, form, frame, frameset, h1, h2, h3, h4, h5, h6, head, hr, html, i, iframe, img, input, ins, kbd, label, legend, li, link, listing, map, marquee, menu, meta, nobr, noframes, noscript, object, ol, optgroup, option, p, param, plaintext, pre, q, rb, rt, ruby, s, samp, script, select, small, span, strike, strong, style (element), sub, sup, table, tbody, td, textarea, tfoot, th, thead, title, tr, tt, u, ul, var, wbr, xmp

canHaveHTML a, abbr, acronym, address, applet, area, b, base, basefont, bdo, bgsound, big, blockquote, body, br, button, caption, center, cite, code, col, colgroup, comment, dd, del, dfn, dir, div, dl,

dt, em, embed, fieldset, font, form, frame, frameset, h1, h2, h3, h4, h5, h6, head, hr, html, i, iframe, img, input, ins, kbd, label, legend, li, link, listing, map, marquee, menu, meta, nobr, noframes, noscript, object, ol, optgroup, option, p, param, plaintext, pre, q, rb, rt, ruby, s, samp, script, select, small, span, strike, strong, style (element), sub, sup, table, tbody, td, textarea, tfoot, th, thead, title, tr, tt, u, ul, var, wbr, xml, xmp

canvas CanvasRenderingContext2D

caption table

captionSide currentStyle, style

CAPTURING_PHASE event

CDATA_SECTION_NODE (constant of all W3C DOM nodes and elements)

cellIndex td, th

cellPadding table

cells table, tr

cellSpacing table

ch col, colgroup, tbody, td, tfoot, th, thead, tr

CHANGE event

channel XMLHttpRequest

char col, colgroup

characterSet document

charCode event

charset a, document, link, meta, script

CHARSET_RULE cssRule

checked input (checkbox), input (radio)

childNodes a, abbr, acronym, address, applet, area, Attr, attribute, b, base, basefont, bdo, bgsound, big, blockquote, body, br, button, canvas, caption, center, cite, code, col, colgroup, comment, datalist, dd, del, dfn, dir, div, dl, document, DocumentType, dt, em, embed, fieldset, font, form, frame, frameset, h1, h2, h3, h4, h5, h6, head, hr, html, i, iframe, img, input, ins, kbd, label, legend, li, link, listing, map, marquee, menu, meta, nobr, Node, noframes, noscript, object, ol, optgroup, option, output, p, param, plaintext, pre, q, rb, rt, ruby, s, samp, script, select, small, span, strike, strong, style (element), sub, sup, table, tbody, td, Text, textarea, tfoot, th, thead, title, tr, tt, u, ul, var, wbr, xmp

children a, abbr, acronym, address, applet, area, b, base, basefont, bdo, bgsound, big, blockquote, body, br, button, canvas, caption, center, cite, code, col, colgroup, comment, datalist, dd, del, dfn, dir, div, dl, dt, em, embed, fieldset, font, form, frame, frameset, h1, h2, h3, h4, h5, h6, head, hr, html, i, iframe, img, input, ins, kbd, label, legend, li, link, listing, map, marquee, menu, meta, nobr, noframes, noscript, object, ol, optgroup, option, output, p, param, plaintext, pre, q, rb, rt, ruby, s, samp, script, select, small, span, strike, strong, style (element), sub, sup, table, tbody, td, textarea, tfoot, th, thead, title, tr, tt, u, ul, var, wbr, xmp

chOff col, colgroup, tbody, td, tfoot, th, thead, tr

cite abbr, acronym, address, b, bdo, big, blockquote, caption, center, cite, code, dd, del, dfn, dir, div, dl, dt, em, fieldset, font, h1, h2, h3, h4, h5, h6, html, i, input, ins, ins, kbd, map, menu, meta, nobr, noframes, noscript, ol, optgroup, option, p, param, plaintext, pre, q, rb, rt, ruby, s, samp, script, small, span, strike, strong, sub, sup, title, tt, u, ul, var, wbr, xmp

classid object

className a, abbr, acronym, address, applet, area, b, base, basefont, bdo, bgsound, big, blockquote, body, br, button, canvas, caption, center, cite, code, col, colgroup, comment, datalist, dd, del, dfn, dir, div, dl, dt, em, embed, fieldset, font, form, frame, frameset, h1, h2, h3, h4, h5, h6, head, hr, html, i, iframe, img, input, ins, kbd, label, legend, li, link, listing, map, marquee, menu, meta, nobr, noframes, noscript, object, ol, optgroup, option, output, p, param, plaintext, pre, q, rb, rt, ruby, s, samp, script, select, small, span, strike, strong, style (element), sub, sup, table, tbody, td, textarea, tfoot, th, thead, title, tr, tt, u, ul, var, wbr, xmp

clear br, currentStyle, runtimeStyle, style

CLICK Event

clientHeight a, abbr, acronym, address, applet, area, b, base, basefont, bdo, bgsound, big, blockquote, body, br, button, canvas, caption, center, cite, code, col, colgroup, comment, datalist, dd, del, dfn, dir, div, dl, document, dt, em, embed, fieldset, font, form, frame, frameset, h1, h2, h3, h4, h5, h6, head, hr, html, i, iframe, img, input, ins, kbd, label, legend, li, link, listing, map, marquee, menu, meta, nobr, noframes, noscript, object, ol, optgroup, option, output, p, param, plaintext, pre, q, rb, rt, ruby, s, samp, script, select, small, span, strike, strong, style (element), sub, sup, table, tbody, td, textarea, tfoot, th, thead, title, tr, tt, u, ul, var, wbr, xmp

clientInformation window

clientLeft a, abbr, acronym, address, applet, area, b, base, basefont, bdo, bgsound, big, blockquote, body, br, button, canvas, caption, center, cite, code, col, colgroup, comment, datalist, dd, del, dfn, dir, div, dl, dt, em, embed, fieldset, font, form, frame, frameset, h1, h2, h3, h4, h5, h6, head, hr, html, i, iframe, img, input, ins, kbd, label, legend, li, link, listing, map, marquee, menu, meta, nobr, noframes, noscript, object, ol, optgroup, option, output, p, param, plaintext, pre, q, rb, rt, ruby, s, samp, script, select, small, span, strike, strong, style (element), sub, sup, table, tbody, td, textarea, tfoot, th, thead, title, tr, tt, u, ul, var, wbr, xmp

clientTop a, abbr, acronym, address, applet, area, b, base, basefont, bdo, bgsound, big, blockquote, body, br, button, canvas, caption, center, cite, code, col, colgroup, comment, datalist, dd, del, dfn, dir, div, dl, dt, em, embed, fieldset, font, form, frame, frameset, h1, h2, h3, h4, h5, h6, head, hr, html, i, iframe, img, input, ins, kbd, label, legend, li, link, listing, map, marquee, menu, meta, nobr, noframes, noscript, object, ol, optgroup, option, output, p, param, plaintext, pre, q, rb, rt, ruby, s, samp, script, select, small, span, strike, strong, style (element), sub, sup, table, tbody, td, textarea, tfoot, th, thead, title, tr, tt, u, ul, var, wbr, xmp

clientWidth a, abbr, acronym, address, applet, area, b, base, basefont, bdo, bgsound, big, blockquote, body, br, button, canvas, caption, center, cite, code, col, colgroup, comment, datalist, dd, del, dfn, dir, div, dl, document, dt, em, embed, fieldset, font, form, frame, frameset, h1, h2, h3, h4, h5, h6, head, hr, html, i, iframe, img, input, ins, kbd, label, legend, li, link, listing, map, marquee, menu, meta, nobr, noframes, noscript, object, ol, optgroup, option, output, p, param, plaintext, pre, q, rb, rt, ruby, s, samp, script, select, small, span, strike, strong, style (element), sub, sup, table, tbody, td, textarea, tfoot, th, thead, title, tr, tt, u, ul, var, wbr, xmp

clientX event

clientY event

clip currentStyle, layer, runtimeStyle, style, tags

clipboardData window

clipBottom currentStyle

clipLeft currentStyle

clipRight currentStyle

clipTop currentStyle

closed window

code applet, DOMException, object, RangeException

codeBase applet, object

codeType applet, object

collapsed Range

color basefont, currentStyle, font, hr, runtimeStyle, style, tags

colorDepth screen

cols frameset, table, textarea

colSpan td, th

COMMENT_NODE (constant of all W3C DOM nodes and elements)

commonAncestorContainer Range

compact dir, dl, menu, ol, ul

compatMode document

complete img, input (image)

Components window

content currentStyle, meta, style, window

contentDocument frame, iframe, object

contentEditable a, abbr, acronym, address, applet, area, b, base, basefont, bdo, bgsound, big, blockquote, body, br, button, canvas, caption, center, cite, code, col, colgroup, comment, datalist, dd, del, dfn, dir, div, dl, dt, em, embed, fieldset, font, form, frame, frameset, h1, h2, h3, h4, h5, h6, head, hr, html, i, iframe, img, input, ins, kbd, label, legend, li, link, listing, map, marquee, menu, meta, nobr, noframes, noscript, object, ol, optgroup, option, output, p, param, plaintext, pre, q, rb, rt, ruby, s, samp, script, select, small, span, strike, strong, style (element), sub, sup, table, tbody, td, textarea, tfoot, th, thead, title, tr, tt, u, ul, var, wbr, xmp

contentOverflow event

contentType document

contentWindow frame, iframe, object

CONTROL_MASK Event

controllers textarea, window

cookie document

cookieEnabled navigator

coords a, area

counterIncrement currentStyle, style

counterReset currentStyle, style

cpuClass navigator

crypto window

cssFloat currentStyle, style

cssRules styleSheet

cssText cssRule, currentStyle, runtimeStyle, style, styleSheet

ctrlKey event

ctrlLeft event

cue style

cueAfter style

cueBefore style

current history

currentStyle a, abbr, acronym, address, applet, area, b, base basefont, bdo, bgsound, big, blockquote, body, br, button, canvas, caption, center, cite, code, col, colgroup, comment, datalist, dd, del, dfn, dir, div, dl, dt, em, embed, fieldset, font, form, frame, frameset, h1 h2, h3, h4, h5, h6, head, hr, html, i, iframe, img, input, ins, kbd, label, legend, li, link, listing, map, marquee, menu, meta, nobr, noframes, noscript, object, ol, optgroup, option, output, p, param, plaintext, pre, q, rb, rt, ruby, s, samp, script, select, small, span, strike, strong, style (element), sub, sup, table, tbody, td, textarea, tfoot, th, thead, title, tr, tt, u, ul, var, wbr, xmp

currentTarget event

cursor currentStyle, runtimeStyle, style

customError ValidityState

data comment, datalist, form, object, select, Text

dataFld a, applet, button, div, event, frame, iframe, img, input (button), input (checkbox), input (hidden), input (password), input (radio), input (text), label, marquee, object, select, textarea

dataFormatAs a, button, div, img, label, marquee

dataPageSize table

dataSrc a, applet, button, div, frame, iframe, img, input (button), input (checkbox), input (hidden), input (password), input (radio), input (text), label, marquee, object, select, textarea

dataTransfer event

dateTime abbr. acronym, address, b, bdo, big, blockquote, caption, center, cite, code, dd, del, dfn, dir, div, dl, dt, em, fieldset, font, h1, h2, h3. h4, h5, h6, html, i, input, ins, ins, kbd, map, menu, meta, nobr, noframes, noscript, ol, optgroup, option, p, param, plaintext, pre, rb, rt, ruby, s, samp, script, small, span, strike, strong, sub, sup, title, tt, u, ul, var, wbr, xmp

DBLCLICK Event

declare applet, object

defaultCharset document

defaultChecked input (checkbox), input (radio)

defaultSelected option

defaultStatus window

defaultValue input (file), input (hidden), input (password), input (text), output, textarea

defaultView document

defer script

description mimeType

detail event

deviceXDPI screen

deviceYDPI screen

dialogArguments window

dialogHeight window

dialogLeft window

dialogTop window

dialogWidth window

dir a, abbr, acronym, address, applet, area, b, base, basefont, bdo, bgsound, big, blockquote, body, br, button, canvas, caption, center, cite, code, col, colgroup, comment, datalist, dd, del, dfn, dir, div, dl, document, dt, em, embed, fieldset, font, form, frame, frameset, h1, h2, h3, h4, h5, h6, head, hr, html, i, iframe, img, input, ins, kbd, label, legend, li, link, listing, map, marquee, menu, meta, nobr, noframes, noscript, object, ol, optgroup, option, output, p, param, plaintext, pre, q, rb, rt, ruby, s, samp, script, select, small, span, strike, strong, style (element), sub, sup, table, tbody, td, textarea, tfoot, th, thead, title, tr, tt, u, ul, var, wbr, xmp

direction currentStyle, marquee, runtimeStyle, style

directories window

disabled a, abbr, acronym, address, applet, area, b, base, basefont, bdo, bgsound, big, blockquote, body, br, button, caption, center, cite, code, col, colgroup, comment, dd, del, dfn, dir, div, dl, dt, em, embed, fieldset, font, form, frame, frameset, h1, h2, h3, h4, h5, h6, head, hr, html, i, iframe, img, input, ins, kbd, label, legend, li, link, listing, map, marquee, menu, meta, nobr, noframes, noscript, object, ol, optgroup, option, p, param, plaintext, pre, q, rb, rt, ruby, s, samp, script, select, small, span, strike, strong, style (element), styleSheet, sub, sup, table, tbody, td, textarea, tfoot, th, thead, title, tr, tt, u, ul, var, wbr, xmp

diapatch embed

display currentStyle, runtimeStyle, style, tags

dlgHelper document

doctype document

document a, abbr, acronym, address, applet, area, b, base, basefont, bdo, bgsound, big, blockquote, body, br, button, canvas, caption, center, cite, code, col, colgroup, comment, datalist, dd, del, dfn, dir, div, dl, document, DocumentType, dt, em, embed, fieldset, font, form, frame, frameset, h1, h2, h3, h4, h5, h6, head, hr, html, i, iframe, img, input, ins, kbd, label, legend, li, link, listing, map, marquee, menu, meta, nobr, noframes, noscript, object, ol, optgroup, option, output, p, param, plaintext, popup, pre, q, rb, rt, ruby, s, samp, script, select, small, span, strike, strong, style (element), sub, sup, table, tbody, td, Text, textarea, tfoot, th, thead, title, tr, tt, u, ul, var, wbr, window, xmp

DOCUMENT_FRAGMENT_NODE (constant of all W3C DOM nodes and elements)

DOCUMENT_NODE (constant of all W3C DOM nodes and elements)

DOCUMENT_POSITION_CONTAINED_BY (constant of all W3C DOM nodes and elements)

DOCUMENT_POSITION_CONTAINS (constant of all W3C DOM nodes and elements)

DOCUMENT_POSITION_DISCONNECTED (constant of all W3C DOM nodes and elements)

DOCUMENT_POSITION_FOLLOWING (constant of all W3C DOM nodes and elements)

DOCUMENT_POSITION_IMPLEMENTATION_SPECIFIC (constant of all W3C DOM nodes and elements)

DOCUMENT_POSITION_PRECEDING (constant of all W3C DOM nodes and elements)

DOCUMENT_TYPE_NODE (constant of all W3C DOM nodes and elements)

documentElement document

documentURI document

domain document

domConfig document

DRAGDROP Event

dropEffect clipboardData, dataTransfer

dynsrc img, input (image)

effectAllowed clipboardData, dataTransfer

ELEMENT_NODE (constant of all W3C DOM nodes and elements)

elements form

elevation style

embeds document

emptyCells currentStyle, style

enabledPlugin mimeType

encoding form

enctype button, form, input

endContainer Range

endOffset Range

entities DocumentType

ENTITY_NODE (constant of all W3C DOM nodes and elements)

ENTITY_REFERENCE_NODE (constant of all W3C DOM nodes and elements)

ERROR Event

event script, window

eventPhase event

expandEntityReference NodeIterator, TreeWalker

expando Attr, attribute, document

explicitOriginalTarget event

external window

face basefont, font

fgColor document

fileCreatedDate document, img

fileModifiedDate document, img

fileSize document.img

fileUpdatedDate   document, img

fillStyle   CanvasRenderingContext2D

filter   currentStyle, NodeIterator, runtimeStyle, style, TreeWalker

filters   a, abbr, acronym, address, applet, area, b, base, basefont, bdo, bgsound, big, blockquote, body, br, button, caption, center, cite, code, col, colgroup, comment, dd, del, dfn, dir, div, dl, dt, em, embed, fieldset, font, form, frame, frameset, h1, h2, h3, h4, h5, h6, head, hr, html, i, iframe, img, input, ins, kbd, label, legend, li, link, listing, map, marquee, menu, meta, nobr, noframes, noscript, object, ol, optgroup, option, p, plaintext, pre, q, rt, ruby, s, samp, script, select, small, span, strike, strong, style (element), sub, sup, table, tbody, td, textarea, tfoot, th, thead, title, tr, tt, u, ul, var, wbr, xml, xmp

firstChild   a, abbr, acronym, address, applet, area, Attr, attribute, b, base, basefont, bdo, bgsound, big, blockquote, body, br, button, canvas, caption, center, cite, code, col, colgroup, comment, datalist, dd, del, dfn, dir, div, dl, document, DocumentType, dt, em, embed, fieldset, font, form, frame, frameset, h1, h2, h3, h4, h5, h6, head, hr, html, i, iframe, img, input, ins, kbd, label, legend, li, link, listing, map, marquee, menu, meta, nobr, Node, noframes, noscript, object, ol, optgroup, option, output, p, param, plaintext, pre, q, rb, rt, ruby, s, samp, script, select, small, span, strike, strong, style (element), sub, sup, table, tbody, td, Text, textarea, tfoot, th, thead, title, tr, tt, u, ul, var, wbr, xmp

FOCUS   Event

focusNode   selection

focusOffset   selection

font   currentStyle, runtimeStyle, style

FONT_FACE_RULE   cssRule

fontFamily   currentStyle, runtimeStyle, style, tags

fonts   Dialog Helper

fontSize   currentStyle, runtimeStyle, style, tags

fontSizeAdjust   currentStyle, style

fontSmoothingEnabled   screen

fontStretch   currentStyle, style

fontStyle   currentStyle, runtimeStyle, style, tags

fontVariant   currentStyle, runtimeStyle, style

fontWeight   currentStyle, runtimeStyle, style, tags

form   applet, button, fieldset, input, label, legend, object, option, output, select, textarea

forms   button, document, input, label, legend, output, select, textarea

FORWARD   Event

frame   table

frameBorder   frame, frameset, iframe

frameElement   window

frames   document, window

frameSpacing   frame, frameset, iframe

fromElement   event

fullScreen   window

globalAlpha   CanvasRenderingContext2D

globalCompositeOperation   CanvasRenderingContext2D

hash   a, area, location

hasLayout   currentStyle

headers   td, th

height   applet, canvas, currentStyle, document, embed, frame, iframe, img, input, marquee, object, runtimeStyle, screen, style, table, td, th, tr

HELP   Event

hidden   embed, layer

hideFocus   a, abbr, acronym, address, applet, area, b, base, basefont, bdo, bgsound, big, blockquote, body, br, button, caption, center, cite, code, col, colgroup, comment, dd, del, dfn, dir, div, dl, dt, em, embed, fieldset, font, form, frame, frameset, h1, h2, h3, h4, h5, h6, head, hr, html, i, iframe, img, input, ins, kbd, label, legend, li, link, listing, map, marquee, menu, meta, nobr, noframes, noscript, object, ol, optgroup, option, p, param, plaintext, pre, q, rb, rt, ruby, s, samp, script, select, small, span, strike, strong, style (element), sub, sup, table, tbody, td, textarea, tfoot, th, thead, title, tr, tt, u, ul, var, wbr, xmp

history   window

host   a, area, location

hostname   a, area, location

href   a, area, base, img, link, location, styleSheet

hreflang   a, link

hspace   applet, iframe, img, input (image), marquee, object

htmlFor   label, script

htmlTemplate   button, input

htmlText   TextRange

httpEquiv   meta

id   a, abbr, acronym, address, applet, area, b, base, basefont, bdo, bgsound, big, block-quote, body, br, button, canvas, caption, center, cite, code, col, colgroup, comment, datalist, dd, del, dfn, dir, div, dl, dt, em, embed, fieldset, font, form, frame, frameset, h1, h2, h3, h4, h5, h6, head, hr, html, i, iframe, img, input, ins, kbd, label, legend, li, link, listing, map, marquee, menu, meta, nobr, noframes, noscript, object, ol, optgroup, option, output, p, param, plaintext, pre, q, rb, rt, ruby, s, samp, script, select, small, span, strike, strong, style (element), styleSheet, sub, sup, table, tbody, td, textarea, tfoot, th, thead, title, tr, tt, u, ul, var, wbr, xml, xmp

ids   document

images   document

imeMode   currentStyle, runtimeStyle, style

implementation   document

IMPORT_RULE   cssRule

imports   styleSheet

indeterminate   input (checkbox)

index   option

innerHeight   window

innerHTML   a, abbr, acronym, address, applet, area, b, base, basefont, bdo, bgsound, big, blockquote, body, br, button, canvas, caption, center, cite, code, col, colgroup, comment, datalist, dd, del, dfn, dir, div, dl, dt, em, embed, fieldset, font, form, frame, frameset, h1, h2, h3, h4, h5, h6, head, hr, html, i, iframe, img, input, ins, kbd, label, legend, li, link, listing, map, marquee, menu, meta, nobr, noframes, noscript, object, ol, optgroup, option, output, p, param, plaintext, pre, q, rb, rt, ruby, s, samp, script, select, small, span, strike, strong, style (element), sub, sup, table, tbody, td, textarea, tfoot, th, thead, title, tr, tt, u, ul, var, wbr, xmp

innerText   a, abbr, acronym, address, applet, area, b, base, basefont, bdo, bgsound, big, blockquote, body, br, button, canvas, caption, center, cite, code, col, colgroup, comment, datalist, dd, del, dfn, dir, div, dl, dt, em, embed, fieldset, font, form, frame, frameset, h1, h2, h3, h4, h5, h6, head, hr, html, i, iframe, img, input, ins, kbd, label, legend, li, link, listing, map, marquee, menu, meta, nobr, noframes, noscript, object, ol, optgroup, option, output, p, param, plaintext, pre, q, rb, rt, ruby, s, samp, script, select, small, span, strike, strong, style (element), sub, sup, table, tbody, td, textarea, tfoot, th, thead, title, tr, tt, u, ul, var, wbr, xmp

innerWidth   window

inputEncoding   document

inputmode   input, textarea

internalSubset   DocumentType

isChar   event

isCollapsed   selection

isContentEditable   a, abbr, acronym, address, applet, area, b, base, basefont, bdo, bgsound, big, blockquote, body, br, button, canvas, caption, center, cite, code, col, colgroup, comment, datalist, dd, del, dfn, dir, div, dl, dt, em, embed, fieldset, font, form, frame, frameset, h1, h2, h3, h4, h5, h6, head, hr, html, i, iframe, img, input, ins, kbd, label, legend, li, link, listing, map, marquee, menu, meta, nobr, noframes, noscript, object, ol, optgroup, option, output, p, param, plaintext, pre, q, rb, rt, ruby, s, samp, script, select, small, span, strike, strong, style (element), sub, sup, table, tbody, td, textarea, tfoot, th, thead, title, tr, tt, u, ul, var, wbr, xml, xmp

isDisabled a, abbr, acronym, address, applet, area, b, base, basefont, bdo, bgsound, big, blockquote, body, br, button, caption, center, cite, code, col, colgroup, comment, dd, del, dfn, dir, div, dl, dt, em, embed, fieldset, font, form, frame, frameset, h1, h2, h3, h4, h5, h6, head, hr, html, i, iframe, img, input, ins, kbd, label, legend, li, link, listing, map, marquee, menu, meta, nobr, noframes, noscript, object, ol, optgroup, option, p, param, plaintext, pre, q, rb, rt, ruby, s, samp, script, select, small, span, strike, strong, style (element), sub, sup, table, tbody, td, textarea, tfoot, th, thead, title, tr, tt, u, ul, var, wbr, xml, xmp

isMap img

isMultiLine a, abbr, acronym, address, applet, area, b, base, basefont, bdo, bgsound, big, blockquote, body, br, button, caption, center, cite, code, col, colgroup, comment, dd, del, dfn, dir, div, dl, dt, em, embed, fieldset, font, form, frame, frameset, h1, h2, h3, h4, h5, h6, head, hr, html, i, iframe, img, input, ins, kbd, label, legend, li, link, listing, map, marquee, menu, meta, nobr, noframes, noscript, object, ol, optgroup, option, p, param, plaintext, pre, q, rb, rt, ruby, s, samp, script, select, small, span, strike, strong, style (element), sub, sup, table, tbody, td, textarea, tfoot, th, thead, title, tr, tt, u, ul, var, wbr, xml, xmp

isOpen popup

isTextEdit a, abbr, acronym, address, applet, area, b, base, basefont, bdo, bgsound, big, blockquote, body, br, button, caption, center, cite, code, col, colgroup, comment, dd, del, dfn, dir, div, dl, dt, em, embed, fieldset, font, form, frame, frameset, h1, h2, h3, h4, h5, h6, head, hr, html, i, iframe, img, input, ins, kbd, label, legend, li, link, list-

ing, map, marquee, menu, meta, nobr, noframes, noscript, object, ol, optgroup, option, p, param, plaintext, pre, q, rb, rt, ruby, s, samp, script, select, small, span, strike, strong, style (element), sub, sup, table, tbody, td, textarea, tfoot, th, thead, title, tr, tt, u, ul, var, wbr, xmp

isTrusted event

java window

keyCode event

KEYDOWN Event

KEYPRESS Event

KEYUP Event

label optgroup, option

labels button, input, label, legend, output, select, textarea

lang a, abbr, acronym, address, applet, area, b, base, basefont, bdo, bgsound, big, blockquote, body, br, button, canvas, caption, center, cite, code, col, colgroup, comment, datalist, dd, del, dfn, dir, div, dl, dt, em, embed, fieldset, font, form, frame, frameset, h1, h2, h3, h4, h5, h6, head, hr, html, i, iframe, img, input, ins, kbd, label, legend, li, link, listing, map, marquee, menu, meta, nobr, noframes, noscript, object, ol, optgroup, option, output, p, param, plaintext, pre, q, rb, rt, ruby, s, samp, script, select, small, span, strike, strong, style (element), sub, sup, table, tbody, td, textarea, tfoot, th, thead, title, tr, tt, u, ul, var, wbr, xmp

language a, abbr, acronym, address, applet, area, b, base, basefont, bdo, bgsound, big, blockquote, body, br, button, caption, center, cite, code, col, colgroup, comment, dd, del, dfn, dir, div, dl, dt, em, embed, fieldset, font, form, frame, frameset, h1, h2, h3, h4, h5, h6, head, hr, html, i, iframe, img, input, ins, kbd, label, legend, li, link, listing, map, marquee, menu, meta, navigator, nobr, noframes, noscript, object, ol, optgroup, option, p, param, plaintext, pre, q, rb, rt, ruby, s, samp, script, select, small, span, strike, strong, style (element), sub, sup, table, tbody, td, textarea, tfoot, th, thead, title, tr, tt, u, ul, var, wbr, xmp

lastChild a, abbr, acronym, address, applet, area, Attr, attribute, b, base, basefont, bdo, bgsound, big, blockquote, body, br, button, canvas, caption, center, cite, code, col, colgroup, comment, datalist, dd, del, dfn, dir, div, dl, document, DocumentType, dt, em, embed, fieldset, font, form, frame, frameset, h1, h2, h3, h4, h5, h6, head, hr, html, i, iframe, img, input, ins, kbd, label, legend, li, link, listing, map, marquee, menu, meta, nobr, Node, noframes, noscript, object, ol, optgroup, option, output, p, param, plaintext, pre, q, rb, rt, ruby, s, samp, script, select, small, span, strike, strong, style (element), sub, sup, table, tbody, td, Text, textarea, tfoot, th, thead, title, tr, tt, u, ul, var, wbr, xmp

lastModified document

layers document

layerX event

layerY event

layoutFlow currentStyle, runtimeStyle, style

layoutGrid runtimeStyle, style

layoutGridChar currentStyle, runtimeStyle, style

layoutGridLine currentStyle, runtimeStyle, style

layoutGridMode currentStyle, runtimeStyle, style

layoutGridType currentStyle, runtimeStyle, style

left currentStyle, layer, runtimeStyle, style, tags, TextRectangle

leftMargin body

length all, anchors, applets, areas, attributes, cells, childNodes, children, comment, controlRange, cssRuleList, cssRules, currentStyle, document, elements, embeds, filters, form, forms, frames, history, HTMLCollection, images, imports, links, MediaList, NamedNodeMap, NodeList, options, rows, rules, scripts, select, style, styleSheets, tBodies, Text, window

letterSpacing currentStyle, runtimeStyle, style

lineBreak currentStyle, runtimeStyle, style

lineCap CanvasRenderingContext2D

lineHeight currentStyle, runtimeStyle, style

lineJoin CanvasRenderingContext2D

lineWidth CanvasRenderingContext2D

link body

linkColor document

links document

list input

listStyle currentStyle, runtimeStyle, style

listStyleImage currentStyle, runtimeStyle, style

listStylePosition currentStyle, runtimeStyle, style

listStyleType currentStyle, runtimeStyle, style, tags

LOAD Event

localName a, abbr, acronym, address, applet, area, Attr, attribute, b, base, basefont, bdo, big, blockquote, body, br, button, canvas, caption, center, cite, code, col, colgroup, comment, datalist, dd, del, dfn, dir, div, dl, document, DocumentType, dt, em, embed, fieldset, font, form, frame, frameset, h1, h2, h3, h4, h5, h6, head, hr, html, i, iframe, img, input, ins, kbd, label, legend, li, link, map, marquee, menu, meta, nobr, Node, noframes, noscript, ol, optgroup, option, output, p, param, plaintext, pre, q, rb, rt, ruby, s, samp, script, select, small, span, strike, strong, style (element), sub, sup, table, tbody, td, Text, textarea, tfoot, th, thead, title, tr, tt, u, ul, var, wbr, xmp

LOCATE Event

location document, frame, iframe,window

locationbar window

logicalXDPI screen

logicalYDPI screen

longDesc frame, iframe, img

loop bgsound, img, input (image), marquee

lowsrc img, input (image)

margin currentStyle, runtimeStyle, style

marginBottom currentStyle, runtimeStyle, style, tags

marginHeight frame, iframe

marginLeft currentStyle, runtimeStyle, style, tags

marginRight currentStyle, runtimeStyle, style, tags

margins( ) tags

marginTop currentStyle, runtimeStyle, style, tags

marginWidth frame, iframe

markerOffset currentStyle, style

marks currentStyle, style

maxHeight currentStyle, runtimStyle style

maxLength input (password), input (text)

maxWidth currentStyle, runtimStyle style

media document, link, style (element), styleSheet

MEDIA_RULE cssRule

mediaText MediaList

menubar window

META_MASK Event

metaKey event

method button, form, input

Methods a

mimeType a, document, img

mimeTypes navigator

min input

minHeight currentStyle, runtimeStyle, style

minWidth currentStyle, runtimeStyle, style

miterLimit CanvasRenderingContext2D

MODIFICATION Event

modifiers event

MOUSEDOWN Event

MOUSEDRAG Event

MOUSEMOVE Event

MOUSEOUT Event

MOUSEOVER Event

MOUSEUP Event

MOVE Event

MozBorderRadius style

MozBorderRadiusBottomleft style

MozBorderRadiusBottomright style

MozBorderRadiusTopleft style

MozBorderRadiusTopright style

MozOpacity style

msInterpolationMode currentStyle, runtimeStyle, style

multipart XMLHttpRequest

multiple select

name a, applet, Attr, attribute, button, DocumentType, embed, form, frame, frameset, iframe, img, input, layer, map, meta, object, output, param, select, textarea, window

nameProp a, document, img

namespaces document

namespaceURI a, abbr, acronym, address, applet, area, Attr, attribute, b, base, basefont, bdo, big, blockquote, body, br, button, canvas, caption, center, cite, code, col, colgroup, comment, datalist, dd, del, dfn, dir, div, dl, document, DocumentType, dt, em, embed, fieldset, font, form, frame, frameset, h1, h2, h3, h4, h5, h6, head, hr, html, i, iframe, img, input, ins, kbd, label, legend, li, link, map, marquee, menu, meta, nobr, Node, noframes, noscript, object, ol, optgroup, option, output, p, param, plaintext, pre, q, rb, rt, ruby, s, samp, script, select, small, span, strike, strong, style (element), sub, sup, table, tbody, td, Text, textarea, tfoot, th, thead, title, tr, tt, u, ul, var, wbr, xmp

naturalHeight img

naturalWidth img

navigationMode history

navigator window

newValue event

next history

nextPage event

nextSibling a, abbr, acronym, address, applet, area, Attr, attribute, b, base, basefont, bdo, bgsound, big, blockquote, body, br, button, canvas, caption, center, cite, code, col, colgroup, comment, datalist, dd, del, dfn, dir, div, dl, document, DocumentType, dt, em, embed, fieldset, font, form, frame, frameset, h1, h2, h3, h4, h5, h6, head, hr, html, i, iframe, img, input, ins, kbd, label, legend, li, link, listing, map, marquee, menu, meta, nobr, Node, noframes, noscript, object, ol, optgroup, option, output, p, param, plaintext, pre, q, rb, rt, ruby, s, samp, script, select, small, span, strike, strong, style (element), sub, sup, table, tbody, td, Text, textarea, tfoot, th, thead, title, tr, tt, u, ul, var, wbr, xmp

nodeName   a, abbr, acronym, address, applet, area, Attr, attribute, b, base, basefont, bdo, bgsound, big, blockquote, body, br, button, canvas, caption, center, cite, code, col, colgroup, comment, datalist, dd, del, dfn, dir, div, dl, document, DocumentType, dt, em, embed, fieldset, font, form, frame, frameset, h1, h2, h3, h4, h5, h6, head, hr, html, i, iframe, img, input, ins, kbd, label, legend, li, link, listing, map, marquee, menu, meta, nobr, Node, noframes, noscript, object, ol, optgroup, option, output, p, param, plaintext, pre, q, rb, rt, ruby, s, samp, script, select, small, span, strike, strong, style (element), sub, sup, table, tbody, td, Text, textarea, tfoot, th, thead, title, tr, tt, u, ul, var, wbr, xmp

nodeType   a, abbr, acronym, address, applet, area, Attr, attribute, b, base, basefont, bdo, bgsound, big, blockquote, body, br, button, canvas, caption, center, cite, code, col, colgroup, comment, datalist, dd, del, dfn, dir, div, dl, document, DocumentType, dt, em, embed, fieldset, font, form, frame, frameset, h1, h2, h3, h4, h5, h6, head, hr, html, i, iframe, img, input, ins, kbd, label, legend, li, link, listing, map, marquee, menu, meta, nobr, Node, noframes, noscript, object, ol, optgroup, option, output, p, param, plaintext, pre, q, rb, rt, ruby, s, samp, script, select, small, span, strike, strong, style (element), sub, sup, table, tbody, td, Text, textarea, tfoot, th, thead, title, tr, tt, u, ul, var, wbr, xmp

nodeValue   a, abbr, acronym, address, applet, area, Attr, attribute, b, base, basefont, bdo,

bgsound, big, blockquote, body, br, button, canvas, caption, center, cite, code, col, colgroup, comment, datalist, dd, del, dfn, dir, div, dl, document, DocumentType, dt, em, embed, fieldset, font, form, frame, frameset, h1, h2, h3, h4, h5, h6, head, hr, html, i, iframe, img, input, ins, kbd, label, legend, li, link, listing, map, marquee, menu, meta, nobr, Node, noframes, noscript, object, ol, optgroup, option, output, p, param, plaintext, pre, q, rb, rt, ruby, s, samp, script, select, small, span, strike, strong, style (element), sub, sup, table, tbody, td, Text, textarea, tfoot, th, thead, title, tr, tt, u, ul, var, wbr, xmp

noHref   area

noResize   frame, iframe

noShade   hr

NOTATION_NODE   (constant of all W3C DOM nodes and elements)

notations   DocumentType

noWrap   body, dd, div, dt, td, th

object   applet, object

offscreenBuffering   window

offsetHeight   a, abbr, acronym, address, applet, area, b, base, basefont, bdo, bgsound, big, blockquote, body, br, button, canvas, caption, center, cite, code, col, colgroup, comment, datalist, dd, del, dfn, dir, div, dl, dt, em, embed, fieldset, font, form, frame, frameset, h1, h2, h3, h4, h5, h6, head, hr, html, i, iframe, img, input, ins, kbd, label, legend, li, link, listing, map, marquee, menu, meta, nobr, noframes, noscript, object, ol, optgroup, option, output, p, param, plaintext, pre, q, rb, rt, ruby, s, samp, script, select, small, span, strike, strong, style (element), sub, sup, table, tbody, td, textarea, tfoot, th, thead, title, tr, tt, u, ul, var, wbr, xmp

offsetLeft   a, abbr, acronym, address, applet, area, b, base, basefont, bdo, bgsound, big, blockquote, body, br, button, canvas, caption, center, cite, code, col, colgroup, comment, datalist, dd, del, dfn, dir, div, dl, document, dt, em, embed, fieldset, font,

Cross References

form, frame, frameset, h1, h2, h3, h4, h5, h6, head, hr, html, i, iframe, img, input, ins, kbd, label, legend, li, link, listing, map, marquee, menu, meta, nobr, noframes, noscript, object, ol, optgroup, option, output, p, param, plaintext, pre, q, rb, rt, ruby, s, samp, script, select, small, span, strike, strong, style (element), sub, sup, table, tbody, td, textarea, tfoot, th, thead, title, tr, tt, u, ul, var, wbr, xmp

offsetParent a, abbr, acronym, address, applet, area, b, base, basefont, bdo, bgsound, big, blockquote, body, br, button, canvas, caption, center, cite, code, col, colgroup, comment, datalist, dd, del, dfn, dir, div, dl, document, dt, em, embed, fieldset, font, form, frame, frameset, h1, h2, h3, h4, h5, h6, head, hr, html, i, iframe, img, input, ins, kbd, label, legend, li, link, listing, map, marquee, menu, meta, nobr, noframes, noscript, object, ol, optgroup, option, output, p, param, plaintext, pre, q, rb, rt, ruby, s, samp, script, select, small, span, strike, strong, style (element), sub, sup, table, tbody, td, textarea, tfoot, th, thead, title, tr, tt, u, ul, var, wbr, xmp

offsetTop a, abbr, acronym, address, applet, area, b, base, basefont, bdo, bgsound, big, blockquote, body, br, button, canvas, caption, center, cite, code, col, colgroup, comment, datalist, dd, del, dfn, dir, div, dl, document, dt, em, embed, fieldset, font, form, frame, frameset, h1, h2, h3, h4, h5, h6, head, hr, html, i, iframe, img, input, ins, kbd, label, legend, li, link, listing, map, marquee, menu, meta, nobr, noframes, noscript, object, ol, optgroup, option, output, p, param, plaintext, pre, q, rb, rt, ruby, s, samp, script, select, small, span, strike, strong, style (element), sub, sup, table, tbody, td, textarea, tfoot, th, thead, title, tr, tt, u, ul, var, wbr, xmp

offsetWidth a, abbr, acronym, address, applet, area, b, base, basefont, bdo, bgsound, big, blockquote, body, br, button, canvas, caption, center, cite, code, col, colgroup, comment, datalist, dd, del, dfn, dir, div, dl, dt, em, embed, fieldset, font, form, frame,

frameset, h1, h2, h3, h4, h5, h6, head, hr, html, i, iframe, img, input, ins, kbd, label, legend, li, link, listing, map, marquee, menu, meta, nobr, noframes, noscript, object, ol, optgroup, option, output, p, param, plaintext, pre, q, rb, rt, ruby, s, samp, script, select, small, span, strike, strong, style (element), sub, sup, table, tbody, td, textarea, tfoot, th, thead, title, tr, tt, u, ul, var, wbr, xmp

offsetX event

offsetY event

onLine navigator

opacity currentStyle, style

opener window

opPhonemes currentStyle, style

options datalist, select

opVoicePitch currentStyle, style

opVoicePitchRange currentStyle, style

opVoiceRate currentStyle, style

opVoiceStress currentStyle, style

opVoiceVolume currentStyle, style

originalTarget event

orphans currentStyle, style

oscpu navigator

outerHeight window

outerHTML a, abbr, acronym, address, applet, area, b, base, basefont, bdo, bgsound, big, blockquote, body, br, button, canvas, caption, center, cite, code, col, colgroup, comment, datalist, dd, del, dfn, dir, div, dl, dt, em, embed, fieldset, font, form, frame, frameset, h1, h2, h3, h4, h5, h6, head, hr, html, i, iframe, img, input, ins, kbd, label, legend, li, link, listing, map, marquee, menu, meta, nobr, noframes, noscript, object, ol, optgroup, option, output, p, param, plaintext, pre, q, rb, rt, ruby, s, samp, script, select, small, span, strike, strong, style (element), sub, sup, table, tbody, td, textarea, tfoot, th, thead, title, tr, tt, u, ul, var, wbr, xmp

outerText a, abbr, acronym, address, applet, area, b, base, basefont, bdo, bgsound, big, blockquote, body, br, button, canvas, caption, center, cite, code, col, colgroup, comment, datalist, dd, del, dfn, dir, div, dl, dt, em, embed, fieldset, font, form, frame, frameset, h1, h2, h3, h4, h5, h6, head, hr, html, i, iframe, img, input, ins, kbd, label, legend, li, link, listing, map, marquee, menu, meta, nobr, noframes, noscript, object, ol, optgroup, option, output, p, param, plaintext, pre, q, rb, rt, ruby, s, samp, script, select, small, span, strike, strong, style (element), sub, sup, table, tbody, td, textarea, tfoot, th, thead, title, tr, tt, u, ul, var, wbr, xmp

outerWidth   window

outline   currentStyle, style

outlineColor   currentStyle, style

outlineOffset   style

outlineStyle   currentStyle, style

outlineWidth   currentStyle, style

overflow   currentStyle, runtimeStyle, style

overflowX   currentStyle, runtimeStyle, style

overflowY   currentStyle, runtimeStyle, style

ownerDocument   a, abbr, acronym, address, applet, area, Attr, attribute, b, base, basefont, bdo, bgsound, big, blockquote, body, br, button, canvas, caption, center, cite, code, col, colgroup, comment, datalist, dd, del, dfn, dir, div, dl, document, DocumentType, dt, em, embed, fieldset, font, form, frame, frameset, h1, h2, h3, h4, h5, h6, head, hr, html, i, iframe, img, input, ins, kbd, label, legend, li, link, listing, map, marquee, menu, meta, nobr, Node, noframes, noscript, object, ol, optgroup, option, output, p, param, plaintext, pre, q, rb, rt, ruby, s, samp, script, select, small, span, strike, strong, style (element), sub, sup, table, tbody, td, Text, textarea, tfoot, th, thead, title, tr, tt, u, ul, var, wbr, xmp

ownerElement   attribute

ownerNode   styleSheet

ownerRule   styleSheet

owningElement   styleSheet

padding   currentStyle, runtimeStyle, style

paddingBottom   currentStyle, runtimeStyle, style, tags

paddingLeft   currentStyle, runtimeStyle, style, tags

paddingRight   currentStyle, runtimeStyle, style, tags

paddings   tags

paddingTop   currentStyle, runtimeStyle, style, tags

page   currentStyle, style

PAGE_RULE   cssRule

pageBreakAfter   currentStyle, runtimeStyle, style

pageBreakBefore   currentStyle, runtimeStyle, style

pageBreakInside   style

pages   styleSheet

pageX   event, layer

pageXOffset   window

pageY   event, layer

pageYOffset   window

palette   embed

parent   window

parentElement   a, abbr, acronym, address, applet, area, Attr, attribute, b, base, basefont, bdo, bgsound, big, blockquote, body, br, button, canvas, caption, center, cite, code, col, colgroup, comment, datalist, dd, del, dfn, dir, div, dl, document, dt, em, embed, fieldset, font, form, frame, frameset, h1, h2, h3, h4, h5, h6, head, hr, html, i, iframe, img, input, ins, kbd, label, legend, li, link, listing, map, marquee, menu, meta, nobr, noframes, noscript, object, ol, optgroup, option, output, p, param, plaintext, pre, q, rb, rt, ruby, s, samp, script, select, small, span, strike, strong, style (element), sub, sup, table, tbody, td, textarea, tfoot, th, thead, title, tr, tt, u, ul, var, wbr, xml, xmp

parentLayer   layer

parentNode   a, abbr, acronym, address, applet, area, Attr, attribute, b, base, basefont, bdo, bgsound, big, blockquote, body, br, button, canvas, caption, center, cite, code, col, colgroup, comment, datalist, dd, del, dfn, dir, div, dl, document, DocumentType, dt, em, embed, fieldset, font, form, frame, frameset, h1, h2, h3, h4, h5, h6, head, hr, html, i, iframe, img, input, ins, kbd, label, legend, li, link, listing, map, marquee, menu, meta, nobr, Node, noframes, noscript, object, ol, optgroup, option, output, p, param, plaintext, pre, q, rb, rt, ruby, s, samp, script, select, small, span, strike, strong, style (element), sub, sup, table, tbody, td, Text, textarea, tfoot, th, thead, title, tr, tt, u, ul, var, wbr, xmp

parentRule   cssRule, style

parentStyleSheet   cssRule, styleSheet

parentTextEdit   a, abbr, acronym, address, applet, area, b, base, basefont, bdo, bgsound, big, blockquote, body, br, button, caption, center, cite, code, col, colgroup, comment, dd, del, dfn, dir, div, dl, dt, em, embed, fieldset, font, form, frame, frameset, h1, h2, h3, h4, h5, h6, head, hr, html, i, iframe, img, input, ins, kbd, label, legend, li, link, listing, map, marquee, menu, meta, nobr, noframes, noscript, object, ol, optgroup, option, p, param, plaintext, pre, q, rb, rt, ruby, s, samp, script, select, small, span, strike, strong, style (element), sub, sup, table, tbody, td, textarea, tfoot, th, thead, title, tr, tt, u, ul, var, wbr, xmp

parentWindow   document

pathname   a, area, location

pattern   input, textarea

patternMismatch   ValidityState

pause   currentStyle, style

pauseAfter   currentStyle, style

pauseBefore   currentStyle, style

personalbar   window

pitch   currentStyle, style

pitchRange   currentStyle, style

pixelBottom   currentStyle, style

pixelDepth   screen

pixelHeight   currentStyle, style

pixelLeft   currentStyle, style

pixelRight   currentStyle, style

pixelTop   currentStyle, style

pixelWidth   currentStyle, style

pkcs11   window

platform   navigator

plugins   document, navigator

pluginspage   embed

port   a, area, location

posBottom   currentStyle, runtimeStyle, style

posHeight   currentStyle, runtimeStyle, style

position   currentStyle, runtimeStyle, style

posLeft   currentStyle, runtimeStyle, style

posRight   currentStyle, runtimeStyle, style

posTop   currentStyle, runtimeStyle, style

posWidth   currentStyle, runtimeStyle, style

preferredStylesheetSet   document

prefix   a, abbr, acronym, address, applet, area, Attr, attribute, b, base, basefont, bdo, big, blockquote, body, br, button, canvas, caption, center, cite, code, col, colgroup, datalist, dd, del, dfn, dir, div, dl, document, DocumentType, dt, em, embed, fieldset, font, form, frame, frameset, h1, h2, h3, h4, h5, h6, head, hr, html, i, iframe, img, input, ins, kbd, label, legend, li, link, map, marquee, menu, meta, nobr, Node, noframes, noscript, object, ol, optgroup, option, output, p, param, plaintext, pre, q, rb, rt, ruby, s, samp, script, select, small, span, strike, strong, style (element), sub, sup, table, tbody, td, Text, textarea, tfoot, th, thead, title, tr, tt, u, ul, var, wbr, xmp

previous   history

previousSibling   a, abbr, acronym, address, applet, area, Attr, attribute, b, base, basefont, bdo, bgsound, big, blockquote, body, br, button, canvas, caption, center, cite, code, col, colgroup, comment, datalist, dd, del, dfn, dir, div, dl, document, DocumentType, dt, em, embed, fieldset, font, form, frame, frameset, h1, h2, h3, h4, h5, h6, head, hr, html, i, iframe, img, input, ins, kbd, label, legend, li, link, listing, map, marquee, menu, meta, nobr, Node, noframes, noscript, object, ol, optgroup, option, output, p, param, plaintext, pre, q, rb, rt, ruby, s, samp, script, select, small, span, strike, strong, style (element), sub, sup, table, tbody, td, Text, textarea, tfoot, th, thead, title, tr, tt, u, ul, var, wbr, xmp

prevValue   event

PROCESSING_INSTRUCTION_NODE   (constant of all W3C DOM nodes and elements)

product   navigator

productSub   navigator

profile   head

prompt   isindex

prompter   window

propertyName   event

protocol   a, area, document, img, location

protocolLong   a

publicId   DocumentType

qualifier   event

quotes   currentStyle, style

rangeCount   selection

rangeOffset   event

rangeParent   event

readOnly   input, stylesheet, textarea

readyState   a, abbr, acronym, address, applet, area, b, base, basefont, bdo, bgsound, big, blockquote, body, br, button, caption, center, cite, code, col, colgroup, comment, dd, del, dfn, dir, div, dl, document, dt, em, embed, fieldset, font, form, frame, frameset, h1, h2, h3, h4, h5, h6, head, hr, html, i, iframe, img, input, ins, kbd, label, legend, li, link, listing, map, marquee, menu, meta, nobr, noframes, noscript, object, ol, optgroup, option, p, param, plaintext, pre, q, rb, rt, ruby, s, samp, script, select, small, span, strike, strong, style (element), sub, sup, table, tbody, td, textarea, tfoot, th, thead, title, tr, tt, u, ul, var, wbr, xml, XMLHttpRequest, xmp

reason   event

recordNumber   a, abbr, acronym, address, applet, area, b, base, basefont, bdo, bgsound, big, blockquote, body, br, button, caption, center, cite, code, col, colgroup, comment, dd, del, dfn, dir, div, dl, dt, em, embed, fieldset, font, form, frame, frameset, h1, h2, h3, h4, h5, h6, head, hr, html, i, iframe, img, input, ins, kbd, label, legend, li, link, listing, map, menu, meta, nobr, noframes, noscript, object, ol, optgroup, option, p, param, plaintext, pre, q, rb, rt, ruby, s, samp, script, select, small, span, strike, strong, style (element), sub, sup, table, tbody, td, textarea, tfoot, th, thead, title, tr, tt, u, ul, var, wbr, xmp

recordset   event

referrer   document

rel   a, link

relatedNode   event

relatedTarget   event

REMOVAL   event

repeat   event

repeatMax   a, abbr, acronym, address, applet, area, b, base, basefont, bdo, big, blockquote, body, br, button, canvas, caption, center, cite, code, col, colgroup, datalist, dd, del, dfn, dir, div, dl, dt, em, embed, fieldset, font, form, frame, frameset, h1, h2, h3, h4, h5, h6, head, hr, html, i, iframe, img, input, ins, kbd, label, legend, li, link, map, menu, meta, nobr, noframes, noscript, object, ol, optgroup, option, output, p, param, plaintext, pre, q, rb, RepetitionElement, rt, ruby, s, samp, script, select, small, span, strike, strong, style (element), sub, sup, table, tbody, td, textarea, tfoot, th, thead, title, tr, tt, u, ul, var, wbr, xmp

repeatMin   a, abbr, acronym, address, applet, area, b, base, basefont, bdo, big, blockquote, body, br, button, canvas, caption, center, cite, code, col, colgroup, datalist, dd, del, dfn, dir, div, dl, dt, em, embed, fieldset, font, form, frame, frameset, h1, h2, h3, h4, h5, h6, head, hr, html, i, iframe, img, input, ins, kbd, label, legend, li, link, map, menu, meta, nobr, noframes, noscript, object, ol, optgroup, option, output, p, param, plaintext, pre, q, rb, RepetitionElement, rt, ruby, s, samp, script, select, small, span, strike, strong, style (element), sub, sup, table, tbody, td, textarea, tfoot, th, thead, title, tr, tt, u, ul, var, wbr, xmp

repeatStart a, abbr, acronym, address, applet, area, b, base, basefont, bdo, big, blockquote, body, br, button, canvas, caption, center, cite, code, col, colgroup, datalist, dd, del, dfn, dir, div, dl, dt, em, embed, fieldset, font, form, frame, frameset, h1, h2, h3, h4, h5, h6, head, hr, html, i, iframe, img, input, ins, kbd, label, legend, li, link, map, menu, meta, nobr, noframes, noscript, object, ol, optgroup, option, output, p, param, plaintext, pre, q, rb, RepetitionElement, rt, ruby, s, samp, script, select, small, span, strike, strong, style (element), sub, sup, table, tbody, td, textarea, tfoot, th, thead, title, tr, tt, u, ul, var, wbr, xmp

repetitionBlocks a, abbr, acronym, address, applet, area, b, base, basefont, bdo, big, blockquote, body, br, button, canvas, caption, center, cite, code, col, colgroup, datalist, dd, del, dfn, dir, div, dl, dt, em, embed, fieldset, font, form, frame, frameset, h1, h2, h3, h4, h5, h6, head, hr, html, i, iframe, img, input, ins, kbd, label, legend, li, link, map, menu, meta, nobr, noframes, noscript, object, ol, optgroup, option, output, p, param, plaintext, pre, q, rb, RepetitionElement, rt, ruby, s, samp, script, select, small, span, strike, strong, style (element), sub, sup, table, tbody, td, textarea, tfoot, th, thead, title, tr, tt, u, ul, var, wbr, xmp

repetitionIndex a, abbr, acronym, address, applet, area, b, base, basefont, bdo, big, blockquote, body, br, button, canvas, caption, center, cite, code, col, colgroup, datalist, dd, del, dfn, dir, div, dl, dt, em, embed, fieldset, font, form, frame, frameset, h1, h2, h3, h4, h5, h6, head, hr, html, i, iframe, img, input, ins, kbd, label, legend, li, link,

repetitionTemplate a, abbr, acronym, address, applet, area, b, base, basefont, bdo, big, blockquote, body, br, button, canvas, caption, center, cite, code, col, colgroup, datalist, dd, del, dfn, dir, div, dl, dt, em, embed, fieldset, font, form, frame, frameset, h1, h2, h3, h4, h5, h6, head, hr, html, i, iframe, img, input, ins, kbd, label, legend, li, link, map, menu, meta, nobr, noframes, noscript, object, ol, optgroup, option, output, p, param, plaintext, pre, q, rb, RepetitionElement, rt, ruby, s, samp, script, select, small, span, strike, strong, style (element), sub, sup, table, tbody, td, textarea, tfoot, th, thead, title, tr, tt, u, ul, var, wbr, xmp

repetitionType a, abbr, acronym, address, applet, area, b, base, basefont, bdo, big, blockquote, body, br, button, canvas, caption, center, cite, code, col, colgroup, datalist, dd, del, dfn, dir, div, dl, dt, em, embed, fieldset, font, form, frame, frameset, h1, h2, h3, h4, h5, h6, head, hr, html, i, iframe, img, input, ins, kbd, label, legend, li, link, map, menu, meta, nobr, noframes, noscript, object, ol, optgroup, option, output, p, param, plaintext, pre, q, rb, RepetitionElement, rt, ruby, s, samp, script, select, small, span, strike, strong, style (element), sub, sup, table, tbody, td, textarea, tfoot, th, thead, title, tr, tt, u, ul, var, wbr, xmp

replace button, form, input

required input, textarea

RESET Event

RESIZE Event

responseBody XMLHttpRequest

responseText XMLHttpRequest

responseXML XMLHttpRequest

returnValue event

rev a, link

richness style

right currentStyle,   runtimeStyle,   style,
TextRectangle

rightMargin body

root NodeIterator, TreeWalker

rowIndex tr

rows frameset, table, tbody, textarea, tfoot,
thead

rowSpan td, th

rubyAlign currentStyle, runtimeStyle, style

rubyOverhang currentStyle, runtimeStyle, style

rubyPosition currentStyle, runtimeStyle, style

rules styleSheet, table

runtimeStyle a, abbr, acronym, address, applet,
area, b, base, basefont, bdo, bgsound, big,
blockquote, body, br, button, caption, center, cite, code, col, colgroup, comment, dd,
del, dfn, dir, div, dl, dt, em, embed, fieldset, font, form, frame, frameset, h1, h2, h3,
h4, h5, h6, head, hr, html, i, iframe, img,
input, ins, kbd, label, legend, li, link, listing, map, marquee, menu, meta, nobr, noframes, noscript, object, ol, optgroup,
option, p, param, plaintext, pre, q, rb, rt,
ruby, s, samp, script, select, small, span,
strike, strong, style (element), sub, sup,
table, tbody, td, textarea, tfoot, th, thead,
title, tr, tt, u, ul, var, wbr, xmp

scheme meta

scope td, th

scopeName a, abbr, acronym, address, applet,
area, b, base, basefont, bdo, bgsound, big,
blockquote, body, br, button, caption, center, cite, code, col, colgroup, comment, dd,
del, dfn, dir, div, dl, dt, em, embed, fieldset, font, form, frame, frameset, h1, h2, h3,
h4, h5, h6, head, hr, html, i, iframe, img,
input, ins, kbd, label, legend, li, link, listing, map, marquee, menu, meta, nobr,
noframes, noscript, object, ol, optgroup,
option, p, param, plaintext, pre, q, rb, rt,

ruby, s, samp, script, select, small, span,
strike, strong, style (element), sub, sup,
table, tbody, td, textarea, tfoot, th, thead,
title, tr, tt, u, ul, var, wbr, xml, xmp

screen window

screenLeft window

screenTop window

screenX event, window

screenY event, window

scripts document

scroll body

SCROLL Event

SCROLL_PAGE_DOWN event

SCROLL_PAGE_UP event

scrollAmount marquee

scrollbar3dLightColor currentStyle, runtimeStyle,
style

scrollbarArrowColor currentStyle,   runtimeStyle,
style

scrollbarBaseColor currentStyle,   runtimeStyle,
style

scrollbarDarkShadowColor currentStyle,   runtime-
Style, style

scrollbarFaceColor currentStyle,   runtimeStyle,
style

scrollbarHighlightColor currentStyle,   runtime-
Style, style

scrollbars window

scrollbarShadowColor currentStyle, runtimeStyle,
style

scrollbarTrackColor currentStyle,   runtimeStyle,
style

scrollDelay marquee

scrollHeight a, abbr, acronym, address, applet,
area, b, base, basefont, bdo, bgsound, big,
blockquote, body, br, button, canvas, caption, center, cite, code, col, colgroup, comment, datalist, dd, del, dfn, dir, div, dl,
document, dt, em, embed, fieldset, font,
form, frame, frameset, h1, h2, h3, h4, h5,
h6, head, hr, html, i, iframe, img, input,
ins, kbd, label, legend, li, link, listing, map,
marquee, menu, meta, nobr, noframes,

noscript, object, ol, optgroup, option, output, p, param, plaintext, pre, q, rb, rt, ruby, s, samp, script, select, small, span, strike, strong, style (element), sub, sup, table, tbody, td, textarea, tfoot, th, thead, title, tr, tt, u, ul, var, wbr, xmp

scrolling   frame, iframe

scrollLeft   a, abbr, acronym, address, applet, area, b, base, basefont, bdo, bgsound, big, blockquote, body, br, button, canvas, caption, center, cite, code, col, colgroup, comment, datalist, dd, del, dfn, dir, div, dl, document, dt, em, embed, fieldset, font, form, frame, frameset, h1, h2, h3, h4, h5, h6, head, hr, html, i, iframe, img, input, ins, kbd, label, legend, li, link, listing, map, marquee, menu, meta, nobr, noframes, noscript, object, ol, optgroup, option, output, p, param, plaintext, pre, q, rb, rt, ruby, s, samp, script, select, small, span, strike, strong, style (element), sub, sup, table, tbody, td, textarea, tfoot, th, thead, title, tr, tt, u, ul, var, wbr, xmp

scrollMaxX   window

scrollMaxY   window

scrollTop   a, abbr, acronym, address, applet, area, b, base, basefont, bdo, bgsound, big, blockquote, body, br, button, canvas, caption, center, cite, code, col, colgroup, comment, datalist, dd, del, dfn, dir, div, dl, document, dt, em, embed, fieldset, font, form, frame, frameset, h1, h2, h3, h4, h5, h6, head, hr, html, i, iframe, img, input, ins, kbd, label, legend, li, link, listing, map, marquee, menu, meta, nobr, noframes, noscript, object, ol, optgroup, option, output, p, param, plaintext, pre, q, rb, rt, ruby, s, samp, script, select, small, span, strike, strong, style (element), sub, sup, table, tbody, td, textarea, tfoot, th, thead, title, tr, tt, u, ul, var, wbr, xmp

scrollWidth   a, abbr, acronym, address, applet, area, b, base, basefont, bdo, bgsound, big, blockquote, body, br, button, canvas, caption, center, cite, code, col, colgroup, comment, datalist, dd, del, dfn, dir, div, dl, document, dt, em, embed, fieldset, font,

form, frame, frameset, h1, h2, h3, h4, h5, h6, head, hr, html, i, iframe, img, input, ins, kbd, label, legend, li, link, listing, map, marquee, menu, meta, nobr, noframes, noscript, object, ol, optgroup, option, output, p, param, plaintext, pre, q, rb, rt, ruby, s, samp, script, select, small, span, strike, strong, style (element), sub, sup, table, tbody, td, textarea, tfoot, th, thead, title, tr, tt, u, ul, var, wbr, xmp

scrollX   window

scrollY   window

search   a, area, location

sectionRowIndex   tr

security   document

securityPolicy   navigator

SELECT   Event

selected   option

selectedIndex   options, select

selectedOption   input

selectedOptions   select

selectedStylesheetSet   document

selection   document

selectionEnd   button, input, output, textarea

selectionStart   button, input, output, textarea

selectorText   cssRule

self   window

shadowBlur   CanvasRenderingContext2D

shadowColor   CanvasRenderingContext2D

shadowOffsetX   CanvasRenderingContext2D

shadowOffsetY   CanvasRenderingContext2D

shape   a, area

sheet   link, style (element)

SHIFT_MASK   Event

shiftKey   event

shiftLeft   event

siblingAbove   layer

siblingBelow   layer

sidebar   window

size   basefont, currentStyle, font, hr, input, select, style

sourceIndex   a, abbr, acronym, address, applet, area, b, base, basefont, bdo, bgsound, big, blockquote, body, br, button, canvas, caption, center, cite, code, col, colgroup, comment, datalist, dd, del, dfn, dir, div, dl, dt, em, embed, fieldset, font, form, frame, frameset, h1, h2, h3, h4, h5, h6, head, hr, html, i, iframe, img, input, ins, kbd, label, legend, li, link, listing, map, marquee, menu, meta, nobr, noframes, noscript, object, ol, optgroup, option, output, p, param, plaintext, pre, q, rb, rt, ruby, s, samp, script, select, small, span, strike, strong, style (element), sub, sup, table, tbody, td, textarea, tfoot, th, thead, title, tr, tt, u, ul, var, wbr, xmp

span   col, colgroup, marquee

speak   currentStyle, style

speakHeader   style

speakNumeral   style

speakPunctuation   style

specified   Attr, attribute

speechRate   currentStyle style

src   bgsound, embed, frame, iframe, img, input (image), layer, script, xml

srcElement   event

srcFilter   event

srcUrn   event

standby   applet, object

start   img, input (image), ol

startContainer   Range

startOffset   Range

status   button, input, textarea, window, XMLHttpRequest

statusbar   window

statusText   XMLHttpRequest

stress   style

strictErrorChecking   document

style   a, abbr, acronym, address, area, b, base, basefont, bdo, bgsound, big, blockquote, body, br, button, canvas, caption, center, cite, code, col, colgroup, comment, cssRule, datalist, dd, del, dfn, dir, div, dl, dt,

em, embed, fieldset, font, form, frame, frameset, h1, h2, h3, h4, h5, h6, head, hr, html, i, iframe, img, input, ins, kbd, label, legend, li, link, listing, map, marquee, menu, meta, nobr, noframes, noscript, object, ol, optgroup, option, output, p, param, plaintext, pre, q, rb, rt, ruby, s, samp, script, select, small, span, strike, strong, style (element), sub, sup, table, tbody, td, textarea, tfoot, th, thead, title, tr, tt, u, ul, var, wbr, xmp

STYLE_RULE   cssRule

styleFloat   currentStyle, runtimeStyle, style

styleSheet   link, style (element)

styleSheets   document

SUBMIT   Event

suffixes   mimeType

summary   table

systemId   DocumentType

systemLanguage   navigator

tabIndex   a, abbr, acronym, address, applet, area, b, base, basefont, bdo, bgsound, big, blockquote, body, br, button, caption, center, cite, code, col, colgroup, comment, dd, del, dfn, dir, div, dl, dt, em, embed, fieldset, font, form, frame, frameset, h1, h2, h3, h4, h5, h6, head, hr, html, i, iframe, img, input, ins, kbd, label, legend, li, link, listing, map, marquee, menu, meta, nobr, noframes, noscript, object, ol, optgroup, option, p, param, plaintext, pre, q, rb, rt, ruby, s, samp, script, select, small, span, strike, strong, style (element), sub, sup, table, tbody, td, textarea, tfoot, th, thead, title, tr, tt, u, ul, var, wbr, xmp

tableLayout   currentStyle, runtimeStyle, style

tagName   a, abbr, acronym, address, applet, area, b, base, basefont, bdo, bgsound, big, blockquote, body, br, button, canvas, caption, center, cite, code, col, colgroup, comment, datalist, dd, del, dfn, dir, div, dl, dt, Element, em, embed, fieldset, font, form, frame, frameset, h1, h2, h3, h4, h5, h6, head, hr, html, i, iframe, img, input, ins, kbd, label, legend, li, link, listing, map, marquee, menu, meta, nobr, noframes, noscript, object, ol, optgroup, option, output, p, param, plaintext, pre, q, rb, rt, ruby, s, samp, script, select, small, span, strike, strong, style (element), sub, sup, table, tbody, td, textarea, tfoot, th, thead, title, tr, tt, u, ul, var, wbr, xmp

tags   document

tagUrn   a, abbr, acronym, address, applet, area, b, base, basefont, bdo, bgsound, big, blockquote, body, br, caption, center, cite, code, col, colgroup, comment, dd, del, dfn, dir, div, dl, dt, em, embed, fieldset, font, form, frame, frameset, h1, h2, h3, h4, h5, h6, head, hr, html, i, iframe, img, input, ins, kbd, label, legend, li, link, listing, map, marquee, menu, meta, nobr, noframes, noscript, object, ol, optgroup, option, p, param, plaintext, pre, q, rb, rt, ruby, s, samp, script, select, small, span, strike, strong, style (element), sub, sup, table, tbody, td, tfoot, th, thead, title, tr, tt, u, ul, var, wbr, xml, xmp

target   a, area, base, basefont, button, event, event, form, input, link

tBodies   table

template   button, label, legend, output, textarea

templateElements   form

text   a, abbr, acronym, address, applet, area, b, base, basefont, bdo, big, blockquote, body, br, button, canvas, caption, center, cite, code, comment, datalist, dd, del, dfn, dir, div, dl, document, DocumentType, dt, em, embed, fieldset, font, form, frame, frameset, h1, h2, h3, h4, h5, h6, head, html, i, iframe, img, input, ins, kbd, legend, li, link, map, menu, meta, nobr, noframes, noscript, object, ol, optgroup, option, option, output, p, param, plaintext, pre, q, rb, rt, ruby, s, samp, script, script, small, span, strike, strong, style (element), sub, sup, table, tbody, td, Text, textarea, TextRange, tfoot, th, thead, title, title, tr, tt, u, ul, var, wbr, xmp

TEXT   event

TEXT_NODE   (constant of all W3C DOM nodes and elements)

textAlign   currentStyle, runtimeStyle, style, tags

textAlignLast   currentStyle, runtimeStyle, style

textAutospace   currentStyle, runtimeStyle, style

textContent   a, abbr, acronym, address, applet, area, Attr, attribute, b, base, basefont, bdo, big, blockquote, body, br, button, canvas, caption, center, cite, code, col, colgroup, comment, datalist, dd, del, dfn, dir, div, dl, document, DocumentType, dt, em, embed, fieldset, font, form, frame, frameset, h1, h2, h3, h4, h5, h6, head, hr, html, i, iframe, img, input, ins, kbd, label, legend, li, link, map, marquee, menu, meta, nobr, Node, noframes, noscript, object, ol, optgroup, option, output, p, param, plaintext, pre, q, rb, rt, ruby, s, samp, script, select, small, span, strike, strong, style (element), sub, sup, table, tbody, td, Text, textarea, tfoot, th, thead, title, tr, tt, u, ul, var, wbr, xmp

textDecoration   currentStyle, runtimeStyle, style, tags

textDecorationBlink   runtimeStyle, style

textDecorationLineThrough   runtimeStyle, style

textDecorationNone   runtimeStyle, style

textDecorationOverline   runtimeStyle, style

textDecorationUnderline   runtimeStyle, style

textIndent   currentStyle, runtimeStyle, style

textJustify   currentStyle, runtimeStyle, style

textJustifyTrim   currentStyle, runtimeStyle

textKashida   currentStyle, runtimeStyle

textKashidaSpace   currentStyle, runtimeStyle, style

textLength   output, textarea

textOverflow   currentStyle, runtimeStyle, style

textShadow   currentStyle, style

textTransform   currentStyle, runtimeStyle, style, tags

textUnderlinePosition   currentStyle, runtimeStyle, style

tFoot   table

tHead   table

timeStamp event

title a, abbr, acronym, address, applet, area, b, base, basefont, bdo, bgsound, big, blockquote, body, br, button, canvas, caption, center, cite, code, col, colgroup, comment, datalist, dd, del, dfn, dir, div, dl, document, dt, em, embed, fieldset, font, form, frame, frameset, h1, h2, h3, h4, h5, h6, head, hr, hr, html, i, iframe, img, input, ins, kbd, label, legend, li, link, listing, map, marquee, menu, meta, nobr, noframes, noscript, object, ol, optgroup, option, output, p, param, plaintext, pre, q, rb, rt, ruby, s, samp, script, select, small, span, strike, strong, style (element), styleSheet, sub, sup, table, tbody, td, textarea, tfoot, th, thead, title, tr, tt, u, ul, var, wbr, xmp

toElement event

toolbar window

tooLong ValidityState

top currentStyle, layer, runtimeStyle, style, tags, TextRectangle, window

topMargin body

trueSpeed marquee

type a, applet, button, cssRule, embed, event, event, input, li, link, menu, mimeType, object, ol, param, script, select, selection, style (element), styleSheet, textarea, ul

typeDetail selection

typeMismatch ValidityState

unicodeBidi currentStyle, runtimeStyle, style

uniqueID a, abbr, acronym, address, applet, area, b, base, basefont, bdo, bgsound, big, blockquote, body, br, button, caption, center, cite, code, col, colgroup, comment, dd, del, dfn, dir, div, dl, dt, em, embed, fieldset, font, form, frame, frameset, h1, h2, h3, h4, h5, h6, head, hr, html, i, iframe, img, input, ins, kbd, label, legend, li, link, listing, map, marquee, menu, meta, nobr, noframes, noscript, object, ol, optgroup, option, p, plaintext, pre, q, rt, ruby, s, samp, script, select, small, span, strike, strong, style (element), sub, sup, table, tbody, td, textarea, tfoot, th, thead, title, tr, tt, u, ul, var, wbr, xml, xmp

units embed

UNKNOWN_RULE cssRule

UNLOAD Event

unselectable a, abbr, acronym, address, area, b, base, basefont, bdo, big, blockquote, body, br, canvas, caption, center, cite, code, col, colgroup, datalist, dd, del, dfn, dir, div, dl, dt, em, embed, fieldset, font, form, frame, frameset, h1, h2, h3, h4, h5, h6, head, hr, html, i, iframe, img, input, ins, kbd, label, legend, li, link, map, menu, meta, nobr, noframes, noscript, object, ol, optgroup, option, output, p, param, plaintext, pre, q, rb, rt, ruby, s, samp, script, select, small, strike, strong, style (element), sub, sup, table, tbody, td, textarea, tfoot, th, thead, title, tr, tt, u, ul, var, wbr, xmp

updateInterval screen

URL document

url meta

URLUnencoded document

urn a

useMap applet, img, input (image), object

userAgent navigator

userLanguage navigator

userProfile navigator

valid ValidityState

validationMessage button, input, output, select, textarea

validity button, input, output, select, textarea

vAlign caption, col, colgroup, listing, marquee, tbody, td, tfoot, th, thead, tr

value Attr, attribute, button, button, input, li, option, output, param, select, textarea

valueAsDate input

valueAsNumber input

valueMissing ValidityState

valueType param

vendor navigator

vendorSub navigator

version html

verticalAlign currentStyle, runtimeStyle, style, tags

view event

visibility currentStyle, layer, runtimeStyle, style, tags

visible directories, locationbar, menubar, personalbar, scrollbars, statusbar, toolbar

vLink body

vlinkColor document

voiceFamily currentStyle, style

volume bgsound, currentStyle, style

vrml img

vspace applet, iframe, img, marquee, object

whatToShow NodeIterator, TreeWalker

wheelData event

which event

whiteSpace currentStyle, runtimeStyle, style, tags

widows currentStyle, style

width canvas, col, colgroup, currentStyle, document, embed, frame, hr, iframe, img, input, listing, marquee, object, pre, runtimeStyle, screen, style, table, td, th, tr

willValidate button, input, output, select, textarea

window window

wordBreak currentStyle, runtimeStyle, style

wordSpacing currentStyle, runtimeStyle, style

wordWrap currentStyle, runtimeStyle, style

wrap textarea

writingMode currentStyle, runtimeStyle, style

x event, img

XFER_DONE Event

XMLDocument xml

XMLEncoding document

XMLStandalone document

XMLVersion document

y event, img

zIndex currentStyle, layer, runtimeStyle, style, tags

zoom currentStyle, runtimeStyle, style

DOM Method Index

Entries in the following index are arranged alphabetically by scriptable object methods. Look up a method to find out which document objects support it. You need to be aware, however, of what support means within the context of the way that browser makers and the W3C DOM specify the inner workings of their models using object-oriented approaches. For example, the list of objects that "support" the user-interface-oriented focus( ) method includes several nonrendered HTML element objects, such as head and meta. Inside the browsers, many methods are defined for a generic HTML element, and *all* elements, regardless of their purpose, inherit those methods. Clearly, attempting to set focus to nonrendered elements is a waste of time in actual development; but because these element objects expose the focus( ) method, they appear in that method's list.

Omitting this information here could cause equally serious problems for scripters who write object- and method-detection scripts. It's better to know that a method is defined (that is, its value type is not undefined) for a particular object than to be misled into thinking that its omission means that the method is undefined for the object.

This listing is a union of methods defined for objects in Internet Explorer, pre-Mozilla Netscape Navigator, Mozilla, Safari, Opera, and implemented objects from Web Forms 2.0 and the W3C DOM Levels 2 and 3. The same method name may mean different things for different objects. Be sure to look up the details of the method listing in Chapter 2, to find if the method is available for the browser(s) used by your intended audience and whether it does what you want. If an HTML element object and other scriptable object share the same name, the (element) notation follows its name when referring to the element object. When you see a method with a long list of objects, the method is most likely covered among the shared items at the beginning of Chapter 2.

abort( ) XMLHttpRequest

accept( ) NodeFilter

add( ) controlRange, options,select

addBehavior( ) a, abbr, acronym, address, applet, area, b, base, basefont, bdo, bgsound, big, blockquote, body, br, button, caption, center, cite, code, col, colgroup, comment, dd, del, dfn, dir, div, dl, dt, em, embed, fieldset, font, form, frame, frameset, h1, h2, h3, h4, h5, h6, head, hr, html, i, iframe, img, input, ins, kbd, label, legend, li, link, listing, map, marquee, menu, meta, nobr, noframes, noscript, object, ol, optgroup, option, p, plaintext, pre, q, rt, ruby, s, samp, script, select, small, span, strike, strong, style (element), sub, sup, table, tbody, td, textarea, tfoot, th, thead, title, tr, tt, u, ul, var, wbr, xml, xmp

addBinding( ) document

addEventListener( ) a, abbr, acronym, address, applet, area, attribute, b, base, basefont, big, blockquote, body, br, button, canvas, caption, center, cite, code, col, colgroup, comment, datalist, dd, del, dfn, dir, div, dl, document, DocumentType, dt, em, fieldset, font, form, frame, frameset, h1, h2, h3, h4, h5, h6, head, hr, html, i, iframe, img, input, ins, kbd, label, legend, li, link, map, menu, meta, nobr, noframes, noscript, object, ol, optgroup, option, output, p, param, plaintext, pre, q, rb, ruby, rt, s, samp, script, select, small, span, strike, strong, style (element), sub, sup, table, tbody, td, Text, textarea, tfoot, th, thead, title, tr, tt, u, ul, var, wbr, window, XMLHttpRequest, xmp

addImport( ) styleSheet

addRange( ) selection

addReadRequest( ) userProfile

addRepetitionBlock( ) a, abbr, acronym, address, applet, area, b, base, basefont, big, blockquote, body, br, button, canvas, caption, center, cite, code, col, colgroup, datalist, dd, del, dfn, dir, div, dl, dt, em, embed, fieldset, font, form, frame, frameset, h1, h2, h3, h4, h5, h6, head, hr, html, i, iframe, img, input, ins, kbd, label, legend, li, link, map, menu, meta, nobr, noframes, noscript, object, ol, optgroup, option, output, p, param, plaintext, pre, q, rb, ruby, rt, RepetitionElement, s, samp, script, select, small, span, strike, strong, style (element), sub, sup, table, tbody, td, textarea, tfoot, th, thead, title, tr, tt, u, ul, var, wbr, xmp

addRepetitionBlockByIndex( ) a, abbr, acronym, address, applet, area, b, base, basefont, big, blockquote, body, br, button, canvas, caption, center, cite, code, col, colgroup, datalist, dd, del, dfn, dir, div, dl, dt, em, embed,

fieldset, font, form, frame, frameset, h1, h2, h3, h4, h5, h6, head, hr, html, i, iframe, img, input, ins, kbd, label, legend, li, link, map, menu, meta, nobr, noframes, noscript, object, ol, optgroup, option, output, p, param, plaintext, pre, q, rb, ruby, rt, RepetitionElement, s, samp, script, select, small, span, strike, strong, style (element), sub, sup, table, tbody, td, textarea, tfoot, th, thead, title, tr, tt, u, ul, var, wbr, xmp

addRule( ) styleSheet

adoptNode( ) document

alert( ) window

appendChild( ) a, abbr, acronym, address, applet, area, attribute, b, base, basefont, big, blockquote, body, br, button, canvas, caption, center, cite, code, col, colgroup, comment, datalist, dd, del, dfn, dir, div, dl, document, DocumentType, dt, em, embed, fieldset, font, form, frame, frameset, h1, h2, h3, h4, h5, h6, head, hr, html, i, iframe, img, input, ins, kbd, label, legend, li, link, listing, map, marquee, menu, meta, nobr, Node, noframes, noscript, object, ol, optgroup, option, output, p, param, plaintext, pre, q, rb, ruby, rt, s, samp, script, select, small, span, strike, strong, style (element), sub, sup, table, tbody, td, Text, textarea, tfoot, th, thead, title, tr, tt, u, ul, var, wbr, xmp

appendData( ) comment, Text

appendMedium( ) MediaList

applyElement( ) a, abbr, acronym, address, applet, area, b, base, basefont, bdo, bgsound, big, blockquote, body, br, button, caption, center, cite, code, col, colgroup, comment, dd, del, dfn, dir, div, dl, dt, em, embed, fieldset, font, form, frame, frameset, h1, h2, h3, h4, h5, h6, head, hr, html, i, iframe, img, input, ins, kbd, label, legend, li, link, listing, map, marquee, menu, meta, nobr, noframes, noscript, object, ol, optgroup, option, p, plaintext, pre, q, rt, ruby, s, samp, script, select, small, span, strike, strong, style (element), sub, sup, table, tbody, td, textarea, tfoot, th, thead, title, tr, tt, u, ul, var, wbr, xml, xmp

arc( )   CanvasRenderingContext2D

arcTo( )   CanvasRenderingContext2D

assign( )   location

attachEvent( )   a, abbr, acronym, address, applet, area, b, base, basefont, bgsound, big, blockquote, body, br, button, canvas, caption, center, cite, code, col, colgroup, comment, datalist, dd, del, dfn, dir, div, dl, document, DocumentType, dt, em, embed, fieldset, font, form, frame, frameset, h1, h2, h3, h4, h5, h6, head, hr, html, i, iframe, img, input, ins, kbd, label, legend, li, link, listing, map, menu, meta, nobr, noframes, noscript, object, ol, optgroup, option, output, p, param, plaintext, pre, q, rb, ruby, rt, s, samp, script, select, small, span, strike, strong, style (element), sub, sup, table, tbody, td, Text, textarea, tfoot, th, thead, title, tr, tt, u, ul, var, wbr, window, xmp

back( )   history, window

beginPath( )   CanvasRenderingContext2D

bezierCurveTo( )   CanvasRenderingContext2D

blur( )   a, abbr, acronym, address, applet, area, b, base, basefont, big, blockquote, body, br, button, canvas, caption, center, cite, code, col, colgroup, datalist, dd, del, dfn, dir, div, dl, dt, em, embed, fieldset, font, form, frame, frameset, h1, h2, h3, h4, h5, h6, head, hr, html, i, iframe, img, input, ins, kbd, label, legend, li, link, listing, map, marquee, menu, meta, nobr, noframes, noscript, object, ol, optgroup, option, output, p, param, plaintext, pre, q, rb, ruby, rt, s, samp, script, select, small, span, strike, strong, style (element), sub, sup, table, tbody, td, textarea, tfoot, th, thead, title, tr, tt, u, ul, var, wbr, window, xmp

captureEvents( )   document, layer, window

checkValidity( )   button, form, input, output, select, textarea

ChooseColorDlg( )   Dialog Helper

clear( )   document, selection

clearAttributes( )   a, abbr, acronym, address, applet, area, b, base, basefont, bdo, bgsound, big, blockquote, body, br, button, caption, center, cite, code, col, colgroup, comment, dd, del, dfn, dir, div, dl, dt, em, embed, fieldset, font, form, frame, frameset, h1, h2, h3, h4, h5, h6, head, hr, html, i, iframe, img, input, ins, kbd, label, legend, li, link, listing, map, marquee, menu, meta, nobr, noframes, noscript, object, ol, optgroup, option, p, plaintext, pre, q, rt, ruby, s, samp, script, select, small, span, strike, strong, style (element), sub, sup, table, tbody, td, textarea, tfoot, th, thead, title, tr, tt, u, ul, var, wbr, xml, xmp

clearData( )   clipboardData, dataTransfer

clearInterval( )   window

clearRect( )   CanvasRenderingContext2D

clearRequest( )   userProfile

clearTimeout( )   window

click( )   a, abbr, acronym, address, applet, area, b, base, basefont, bdo, bgsound, big, blockquote, body, br, button, caption, center, cite, code, col, colgroup, comment, dd, del, dfn, dir, div, dl, dt, em, embed, fieldset, font, form, frame, frameset, h1, h2, h3, h4, h5, h6, head, hr, html, i, iframe, img, input, ins, kbd, label, legend, li, link, listing, map, marquee, menu, meta, nobr, noframes, noscript, object, ol, optgroup, option, p, plaintext, pre, q, rt, ruby, s, samp, script, select, small, span, strike, strong, style (element), sub, sup, table, tbody, td, textarea, tfoot, th, thead, title, tr, tt, u, ul, var, wbr, xml, xmp

clip( )   CanvasRenderingContext2D

cloneContents( )   Range

cloneNode( )   a, abbr, acronym, address, applet, area, attribute, b, base, basefont, bgsound, big, blockquote, body, br, button, canvas, caption, center, cite, code, col, colgroup, comment, datalist, dd, del, dfn, dir, div, dl, document, DocumentType, dt, em, embed, fieldset, font, form, frame, frameset, h1, h2, h3, h4, h5, h6, head, hr, html, i, iframe, img, input, ins, kbd, label, legend, li, link, listing, map, marquee, menu, meta, nobr, Node, noframes, noscript, object, ol, optgroup, option, output, p, param, plaintext, pre, q, rb, ruby, rt, s, samp, script, select, small, span, strike, strong, style (element), sub, sup, table, tbody, td, Text, textarea, tfoot, th, thead, title, tr, tt, u, ul, var, wbr, xmp

cloneRange( )   Range

close( )   document, window

closePath( )   CanvasRenderingContext2D

collapse( )   Range, selection, TextRange

collapseToEnd( )   selection

collapseToStart( )   selection

compareBoundaryPoints( )   Range

compareDocumentPosition( )   a, abbr, acronym, address, applet, area, attribute, b, base, basefont, big, blockquote, body, br, button, caption, center, cite, code, col, colgroup, comment, dd, del, dfn, dir, div, dl, document, DocumentType, dt, em, embed, fieldset, font, form, frame, frameset, h1, h2, h3, h4, h5, h6, head, hr, html, i, iframe, img, input, ins, kbd, label, legend, li, link, map, marquee, menu, meta, nobr, Node, noframes, noscript, object, ol, optgroup, option, p, param, plaintext, pre, q, rb, ruby, rt, s, samp, script, select, small, span, strike, strong, style (element), sub, sup, table, tbody, td, Text, textarea, tfoot, th, thead, title, tr, tt, u, ul, var, wbr, xmp

compareEndPoints( )   TextRange

compareNode( )   Range

comparePoint( )   Range

componentFromPoint( )   a, abbr, acronym, address, applet, area, b, base, basefont, bdo, bgsound, big, blockquote, body, br, button, caption, center, cite, code, col, colgroup, comment, dd, del, dfn, dir, div, dl, dt, em, embed, fieldset, font, form, frame, frameset, h1, h2, h3, h4, h5, h6, head, hr, html, i, iframe, img, input, ins, kbd, label, legend, li, link, listing, map, marquee, menu, meta, nobr, noframes, noscript, object, ol, optgroup, option, p, plaintext,

pre, q, rt, ruby, s, samp, script, select, small, span, strike, strong, style (element), sub, sup, table, tbody, td, textarea, tfoot, th, thead, title, tr, tt, u, ul, var, wbr, xml, xmp

confirm( )   window

contains( )   a, abbr, acronym, address, applet, area, attribute, b, base, basefont, big, blockquote, body, br, button, canvas, caption, center, cite, code, col, colgroup, datalist, dd, del, dfn, dir, div, dl, dt, em, embed, fieldset, font, form, frame, h1, h2, h3, h4, h5, h6, head, hr, html, i, iframe, img, input, ins, kbd, label, legend, li, link, listing, map, menu, meta, nobr, noframes, noscript, object, ol, optgroup, option, output, p, param, plaintext, pre, q, rb, ruby, rt, s, samp, script, select, small, span, strike, strong, style (element), sub, sup, table, tbody, td, textarea, tfoot, th, thead, title, tr, tt, u, ul, var, wbr, xmp

containsNode( )   selection

createAttribute( )   document

createAttributeNS( )   document

createCaption( )   table

createCDATASection( )   document

createComment( )   document

createContextualFragment( )   Range

createControlRange( )   a, abbr, acronym, address, applet, area, b, base, basefont, bdo, bgsound, big, blockquote, body, br, button, caption, center, cite, code, col, colgroup, comment, dd, del, dfn, dir, div, dl, dt, em, embed, fieldset, font, form, frame, frameset, h1, h2, h3, h4, h5, h6, head, hr, html, i, iframe, img, input, ins, kbd, label, legend, li, link, listing, map, marquee, menu, meta, nobr, noframes, noscript, object, ol, optgroup, option, p, plaintext, pre, q, rt, ruby, s, samp, script, select, selection, small, span, strike, strong, style (element), sub, sup, table, tbody, td, textarea, tfoot, th, thead, title, tr, tt, u, ul, var, wbr, xml, xmp

createCSSStyleSheet( )   implementation

createDocument( )   implementation

createDocumentFragment( )   document

createDocumentType( )   implementation

createElement( )   document

createElementNS( )   document

createEntityReference( )   document

createEvent( )   document

createEventObject( )   document

createExpression( )   document

createHTMLDocument( )   implementation

createLinearGradient( )
    CanvasRenderingContext2D

createLSInput( )   implementation

createLSOutput( )   implementation

createLSParser( )   implementation

createLSSerializer( )   implementation

createNodeIterator( )   document

createNSResolver( )   document

createPattern( )   CanvasRenderingContext2D

createPopup( )   window

createProcessingInstruction( )   document

createRadialGradient( )
    CanvasRenderingContext2D

createRange( )   document, selection

createRangeCollection( )   selection

createStyleSheet( )   document

createTextNode( )   document

createTextRange( )   body, button, input (button),
    input (hidden), input (password), input
    (reset), input (submit), input (text), text-
    area

createTFoot( )   table

createTHead( )   table

createTreeWalker( )   document

deleteCaption( )   table

deleteCell( )   tr

deleteContents( )   Range

deleteData( )   comment, Text

deleteFromDocument( )   selection

deleteMedium( )   MediaList

deleteRow( )   table, tbody, tfoot, thead

deleteRule( )   styleSheet

deleteTFoot( )   table

deleteTHead( )   table

detach( )   NodeIterator, Range

detachEvent( )   a, abbr, acronym, address,
    applet, area, attribute, b, base, basefont,
    bgsound, big, blockquote, body, br, but-
    ton, canvas, caption, center, cite, code, col,
    colgroup, comment, datalist, dd, del, dfn,
    dir, div, dl, document, DocumentType, dt,
    em, embed, fieldset, font, form, frame,
    frameset, h1, h2, h3, h4, h5, h6, head, hr,
    html, i, iframe, img, input, ins, kbd, label,
    legend, li, link, listing, map, menu, meta,
    nobr, noframes, noscript, object, ol, opt-
    group, option, output, p, param, plaintext,
    pre, q, rb, ruby, rt, s, samp, script, select,
    small, span, strike, strong, style (element),
    sub, sup, table, tbody, td, Text, textarea,
    tfoot, th, thead, title, tr, tt, u, ul, var, wbr,
    window, xmp

disableExternalCapture( )   window

dispatchChange( )   button, input, select, textarea

dispatchEvent( )   a, abbr, acronym, address,
    applet, area, attribute, b, base, basefont,
    big, blockquote, body, br, button, canvas,
    caption, center, cite, code, col, colgroup,
    comment, datalist, dd, del, dfn, dir, div, dl,
    document, DocumentType, dt, em, embed,
    fieldset, font, form, frame, frameset, h1, h2,
    h3, h4, h5, h6, head, hr, html, i, iframe,
    img, input, ins, kbd, label, legend, li, link,
    map, marquee, menu, meta, nobr,
    noframes, noscript, object, ol, optgroup,
    option, output, p, param, plaintext, pre, q,
    rb, ruby, rt, s, samp, script, select, small,
    span, strike, strong, style (element), sub,
    sup, table, tbody, td, Text, textarea, tfoot,
    th, thead, title, tr, tt, u, ul, var, wbr, win-
    dow, XMLHttpRequest, xmp

dispatchFormChange( )   button, form, input,
    select, textarea

dispatchFormInput( )   form

doReadRequest( )   userProfile

doScroll( )   a, abbr, acronym, address, applet,
    area, b, base, basefont, bdo, bgsound, big,

blockquote, body, br, button, caption, center, cite, code, col, colgroup, comment, dd, del, dfn, dir, div, dl, dt, em, embed, fieldset, font, form, frame, frameset, h1, h2, h3, h4, h5, h6, head, hr, html, i, iframe, img, input, ins, kbd, label, legend, li, link, listing, map, marquee, menu, meta, nobr, noframes, noscript, object, ol, optgroup, option, p, plaintext, pre, q, rt, ruby, s, samp, script, select, small, span, strike, strong, style (element), sub, sup, table, tbody, td, textarea, tfoot, th, thead, title, tr, tt, u, ul, var, wbr, xml, xmp

dragDrop( )   a, abbr, acronym, address, applet, area, b, base, basefont, bdo, bgsound, big, blockquote, body, br, button, caption, center, cite, code, col, colgroup, comment, dd, del, dfn, dir, div, dl, dt, em, embed, fieldset, font, form, frame, frameset, h1, h2, h3, h4, h5, h6, head, hr, html, i, iframe, img, input, ins, kbd, label, legend, li, link, listing, map, marquee, menu, meta, nobr, noframes, noscript, object, ol, optgroup, option, p, plaintext, pre, q, rt, ruby, s, samp, script, select, small, span, strike, strong, style (element), sub, sup, table, tbody, td, textarea, tfoot, th, thead, title, tr, tt, u, ul, var, wbr, xml, xmp

drawImage( )   CanvasRenderingContext2D

drawWindow( )   CanvasRenderingContext2D

dump( )   window

duplicate( )   TextRange

elementFromPoint( )   document

empty( )   selection

enableExternalCapture( )   window

evaluate( )   document

execCommand( )   controlRange,   document, TextRange

execScript( )   window

expand( )   TextRange

extend( )   selection

extractContents( )   Range

fill( )   CanvasRenderingContext2D

fillRect( )   CanvasRenderingContext2D

find( )   window

findText( )   TextRange

fireEvent( )   a, abbr, acronym, address, applet, area, b, base, basefont, bdo, bgsound, big, blockquote, body, br, button, caption, center, cite, code, col, colgroup, comment, dd, del, dfn, dir, div, dl, dt, em, embed, fieldset, font, form, frame, frameset, h1, h2, h3, h4, h5, h6, head, hr, html, i, iframe, img, input, ins, kbd, label, legend, li, link, listing, map, marquee, menu, meta, nobr, noframes, noscript, object, ol, optgroup, option, p, plaintext, pre, q, rt, ruby, s, samp, script, select, small, span, strike, strong, style (element), sub, sup, table, tbody, td, textarea, tfoot, th, thead, title, tr, tt, u, ul, var, wbr, xml, xmp

firstChild( )   TreeWalker

focus( )   a, abbr, acronym, address, applet, area, b, base, basefont, big, blockquote, body, br, button, canvas, caption, center, cite, code, col, colgroup, datalist, dd, del, dfn, dir, div, dl, dt, em, embed, fieldset, font, form, frame, frameset, h1, h2, h3, h4, h5, h6, head, hr, html, i, iframe, img, input, ins, kbd, label, legend, li, link, listing, map, marquee, menu, meta, nobr, noframes, noscript, object, ol, optgroup, option, output, p, param, plaintext, pre, q, rb, ruby, rt, s, samp, script, select, small, span, strike, strong, style (element), sub, sup, table, tbody, td, textarea, tfoot, th, thead, title, tr, tt, u, ul, var, wbr, window, xmp

forward( )   history, window

GeckoActiveXObject( )   window

getAdjacentText( )   a, abbr, acronym, address, applet, area, b, base, basefont, bdo, bgsound, big, blockquote, body, br, button, caption, center, cite, code, col, colgroup, comment, dd, del, dfn, dir, div, dl, dt, em, embed, fieldset, font, form, frame, frameset, h1, h2, h3, h4, h5, h6, head, hr, html, i, iframe, img, input, ins, kbd, label, legend, li, link, listing, map, marquee, menu, meta, nobr, noframes, noscript, object, ol, optgroup, option, p, plaintext, pre, q, rt, ruby, s, samp, script, select, small, span, strike, strong, style (element), sub, sup, table, tbody, td, textarea, tfoot, th, thead, title, tr, tt, u, ul, var, wbr, xml, xmp

getAllResponseHeaders( ) XMLHttpRequest

getAnonymousElementByAttribute( ) document

getAnonymousNodes( ) document

getAttribute( ) a, abbr, acronym, address, applet, area, b, base, basefont, bgsound, big, blockquote, body, br, button, canvas, caption, center, cite, code, col, colgroup, datalist, dd, del, dfn, dir, div, dl, dt, Element, em, embed, fieldset, font, form, frame, frameset, h1, h2, h3, h4, h5, h6, head, hr, html, i, iframe, img, input, ins, kbd, label, legend, li, link, listing, map, marquee, menu, meta, nobr, noframes, noscript, object, ol, optgroup, option, output, p, param, plaintext, pre, q, rb, ruby, rt, s, samp, script, select, small, span, strike, strong, style (element), sub, sup, table, tbody, td, textarea, tfoot, th, thead, title, tr, tt, u, ul, var, wbr, xmp

getAttributeNode( ) a, abbr, acronym, address, applet, area, b, base, basefont, bgsound, big, blockquote, body, br, button, canvas, caption, center, cite, code, col, colgroup, datalist, dd, del, dfn, dir, div, dl, dt, Element, em, embed, fieldset, font, form, frame, frameset, h1, h2, h3, h4, h5, h6, head, hr, html, i, iframe, img, input, ins, kbd, label, legend, li, link, listing, map, marquee, menu, meta, nobr, noframes, noscript, object, ol, optgroup, option, output, p, param, plaintext, pre, q, rb, ruby, rt, s, samp, script, select, small, span, strike, strong, style (element), sub, sup, table, tbody, td, textarea, tfoot, th, thead, title, tr, tt, u, ul, var, wbr, xml, xmp

getAttributeNodeNS( ) a, abbr, acronym, address, applet, area, b, base, basefont, big, blockquote, body, br, button, canvas, caption, center, cite, code, col, colgroup, datalist, dd, del, dfn, dir, div, dl, dt, Element, em, embed, fieldset, font, form, frame, frameset, h1, h2, h3, h4, h5, h6, head, hr, html, i, iframe, img, input, ins, kbd, label,

legend, li, link, map, marquee, menu, meta, nobr, noframes, noscript, object, ol, optgroup, option, output, p, param, plaintext, pre, q, rb, ruby, rt, s, samp, script, select, small, span, strike, strong, style (element), sub, sup, table, tbody, td, textarea, tfoot, th, thead, title, tr, tt, u, ul, var, wbr, xmp

getAttributeNS( ) a, abbr, acronym, address, applet, area, b, base, basefont, big, blockquote, body, br, button, canvas, caption, center, cite, code, col, colgroup, datalist, dd, del, dfn, dir, div, dl, dt, Element, em, embed, fieldset, font, form, frame, frameset, h1, h2, h3, h4, h5, h6, head, hr, html, i, iframe, img, input, ins, kbd, label, legend, li, link, map, marquee, menu, meta, nobr, noframes, noscript, object, ol, optgroup, option, output, p, param, plaintext, pre, q, rb, ruby, rt, s, samp, script, select, small, span, strike, strong, style (element), sub, sup, table, tbody, td, textarea, tfoot, th, thead, title, tr, tt, u, ul, var, wbr, xmp

getBindingParent( ) document

getBookmark( ) TextRange

getBoundingClientRect( ) a, abbr, acronym, address, applet, area, b, base, basefont, bdo, bgsound, big, blockquote, body, br, button, caption, center, cite, code, col, colgroup, comment, dd, del, dfn, dir, div, dl, dt, em, embed, fieldset, font, form, frame, frameset, h1, h2, h3, h4, h5, h6, head, hr, html, i, iframe, img, input, ins, kbd, label, legend, li, link, listing, map, marquee, menu, meta, nobr, noframes, noscript, object, ol, optgroup, option, p, plaintext, pre, q, rt, ruby, s, samp, script, select, small, span, strike, strong, style (element), sub, sup, table, tbody, td, textarea, tfoot, th, thead, title, tr, tt, u, ul, var, wbr, xml, xmp

getCharset( ) Dialog Helper

getClientRects( ) a, abbr, acronym, address, applet, area, b, base, basefont, bdo, bgsound, big, blockquote, body, br, button, caption, center, cite, code, col, colgroup, comment, dd, del, dfn, dir, div, dl, dt, em, embed, fieldset, font, form, frame, frameset, h1, h2, h3, h4, h5, h6, head, hr, html, i, iframe, img, input, ins, kbd, label, legend, li, link, listing, map, marquee, menu, meta, nobr, noframes, noscript, object, ol, optgroup, option, p, plaintext, pre, q, rt, ruby, s, samp, script, select, small, span, strike, strong, style (element), sub, sup, table, tbody, td, textarea, tfoot, th, thead, title, tr, tt, u, ul, var, wbr, xml, xmp

getComputedStyle( )   ViewCSS, window

getData( )   clipboardData, dataTransfer

getElementById( )   document

getElementsByName( )   document

getElementsByTagName( )   a, abbr, acronym, address, applet, area, b, base, basefont, bgsound, big, blockquote, body, br, button, canvas, caption, center, cite, code, col, colgroup, datalist, dd, del, dfn, dir, div, dl, document, dt, Element, em, embed, fieldset, font, form, frame, frameset, h1, h2, h3, h4, h5, h6, head, hr, html, i, iframe, img, input, ins, kbd, label, legend, li, link, listing, map, marquee, menu, meta, nobr, noframes, noscript, object, ol, optgroup, option, output, p, param, plaintext, pre, q, rb, ruby, rt, s, samp, script, select, small, span, strike, strong, style (element), sub, sup, table, tbody, td, textarea, tfoot, th, thead, title, tr, tt, u, ul, var, wbr, xmp

getElementsByTagNameNS( )   a, abbr, acronym, address, applet, area, b, base, basefont, big, blockquote, body, br, button, canvas, caption, center, cite, code, col, colgroup, datalist, dd, del, dfn, dir, div, dl, document, dt, Element, em, embed, fieldset, font, form, frame, frameset, h1, h2, h3, h4, h5, h6, head, hr, html, i, iframe, img, input, ins, kbd, label, legend, li, link, map, marquee, menu, meta, nobr, noframes, noscript, object, ol, optgroup, option, output, p, param, plaintext, pre, q, rb, ruby, rt, s, samp, script, select, small, span, strike, strong, style (element), sub, sup, table, tbody, td, textarea, tfoot, th, thead, title, tr, tt, u, ul, var, wbr, xmp

getExpression( )   a, abbr, acronym, address, applet, area, b, base, basefont, bdo, bgsound, big, blockquote, body, br, button, caption, center, cite, code, col, colgroup, comment, dd, del, dfn, dir, div, dl, dt, em, embed, fieldset, font, form, frame, frameset, h1, h2, h3, h4, h5, h6, head, hr, html, i, iframe, img, input, ins, kbd, label, legend, li, link, listing, map, marquee, menu, meta, nobr, noframes, noscript, object, ol, optgroup, option, p, plaintext, pre, q, rt, ruby, s, samp, script, select, small, span, strike, strong, style (element), sub, sup, table, tbody, td, textarea, tfoot, th, thead, title, tr, tt, u, ul, var, wbr, xml, xmp

getFeature( )   a, abbr, acronym, address, applet, area, attribute, b, base, basefont, big, blockquote, body, br, button, canvas, caption, center, cite, code, col, colgroup, comment, datalist, dd, del, dfn, dir, div, dl, document, DocumentType, dt, em, embed, fieldset, font, form, frame, frameset, h1, h2, h3, h4, h5, h6, head, hr, html, i, iframe, img, implementation, input, ins, kbd, label, legend, li, link, map, marquee, menu, meta, nobr, Node, noframes, noscript, object, ol, optgroup, option, output, p, param, plaintext, pre, q, rb, ruby, rt, s, samp, script, select, small, span, strike, strong, style (element), sub, sup, table, tbody, td, Text, textarea, tfoot, th, thead, title, tr, tt, u, ul, var, wbr, xmp

getNamedItem( )   attributes

getNamedItemNS( )   attributes

getOverrideStyle( )   document

getPreventDefault( )   event

getPropertyCSSValue( )   currentStyle, style

getPropertyPriority( )   currentStyle, style

getPropertyValue( )   currentStyle, style

getRangeAt( )   selection

getResponseHeader( )   XMLHttpRequest

getSelection( )   document, window

getSVGDocument( )   embed

go( )   history

handleEvent( ) document, form, input, layer, textarea, window

hasAttribute( ) a, abbr, acronym, address, applet, area, b, base, basefont, big, block-quote, body, br, button, canvas, caption, center, cite, code, col, colgroup, datalist, dd, del, dfn, dir, div, dl, dt, Element, em, embed, fieldset, font, form, frame, frameset, h1, h2, h3, h4, h5, h6, head, hr, html, i, iframe, img, input, ins, kbd, label, legend, li, link, listing, map, marquee, menu, meta, nobr, noframes, noscript, object, ol, optgroup, option, output, p, param, plaintext, pre, q, rb, ruby, rt, s, samp, script, select, small, span, strike, strong, style (element), sub, sup, table, tbody, td, textarea, tfoot, th, thead, title, tr, tt, u, ul, var, wbr, xmp

hasAttributeNS( ) a, abbr, acronym, address, applet, area, b, base, basefont, big, block-quote, body, br, button, canvas, caption, center, cite, code, col, colgroup, datalist, dd, del, dfn, dir, div, dl, dt, Element, em, embed, fieldset, font, form, frame, frameset, h1, h2, h3, h4, h5, h6, head, hr, html, i, iframe, img, input, ins, kbd, label, legend, li, link, map, marquee, menu, meta, nobr, noframes, noscript, object, ol, opt-group, option, output, p, param, plaintext, pre, q, rb, ruby, rt, s, samp, script, select, small, span, strike, strong, style (element), sub, sup, table, tbody, td, textarea, tfoot, th, thead, title, tr, tt, u, ul, var, wbr, xmp

hasAttributes( ) a, abbr, acronym, address, applet, area, attribute, b, base, basefont, big, blockquote, body, br, button, canvas, caption, center, cite, code, col, colgroup, comment, datalist, dd, del, dfn, dir, div, dl, document, DocumentType, dt, em, embed, fieldset, font, form, frame, frameset, h1, h2, h3, h4, h5, h6, head, hr, html, i, iframe, img, input, ins, kbd, label, legend, li, link, listing, map, marquee, menu, meta, nobr, Node, noframes, noscript, object, ol, opt-group, option, output, p, param, plaintext, pre, q, rb, ruby, rt, s, samp, script, select, small, span, strike, strong, style (element), sub, sup, table, tbody, td, Text, textarea,

tfoot, th, thead, title, tr, tt, u, ul, var, wbr, xmp

hasChildNodes( ) a, abbr, acronym, address, applet, area, attribute, b, base, basefont, big, blockquote, body, br, button, canvas, caption, center, cite, code, col, colgroup, comment, datalist, dd, del, dfn, dir, div, dl, document, DocumentType, dt, em, embed, fieldset, font, form, frame, frameset, h1, h2, h3, h4, h5, h6, head, hr, html, i, iframe, img, input, ins, kbd, label, legend, li, link, listing, map, marquee, menu, meta, nobr, Node, noframes, noscript, object, object, ol, optgroup, option, output, p, param, plaintext, pre, q, rb, ruby, rt, s, samp, script, select, small, span, strike, strong, style (element), sub, sup, table, tbody, td, Text, textarea, tfoot, th, thead, title, tr, tt, u, ul, var, wbr, xmp

hasFeature( ) implementation

hasFocus( ) document

hide( ) popup

home( ) window

importNode( ) document

initEvent( ) event

initKeyEvent( ) event

initMouseEvent( ) event

initMutationEvent( ) event

initUIEvent( ) event

inRange( ) TextRange

insertAdjacentElement( ) a, abbr, acronym, address, applet, area, b, base, basefont, bgsound, big, blockquote, body, br, button, canvas, caption, center, cite, code, col, colgroup, datalist, dd, del, dfn, dir, div, dl, dt, em, embed, fieldset, font, form, frame, frameset, h1, h2, h3, h4, h5, h6, head, hr, html, i, iframe, img, input, ins, kbd, label, legend, li, link, listing, map, menu, meta, nobr, noframes, noscript, object, ol, opt-group, option, output, p, param, plaintext, pre, q, rb, ruby, rt, s, samp, script, select, small, span, strike, strong, style (element), sub, sup, table, tbody, td, textarea, tfoot, th, thead, title, tr, tt, u, ul, var, wbr, xmp insertAdjacentHTML( )   a, abbr, acronym, address, applet, area, b, base, basefont, bdo, bgsound, big, blockquote, body, br, button, caption, canvas, center, cite, code, col, colgroup, comment, datalist, dd, del, dfn, dir, div, dl, dt, em, embed, fieldset, font, form, frame, frameset, h1, h2, h3, h4, h5, h6, head, hr, html, i, iframe, img, input, ins, kbd, label, legend, li, link, listing, map, marquee, menu, meta, nobr, noframes, noscript, object, ol, optgroup, option, output, p, plaintext, pre, q, rt, ruby, s, samp, script, select, small, span, strike, strong, style (element), sub, sup, table, tbody, td, textarea, tfoot, th, thead, title, tr, tt, u, ul, var, wbr, xml, xmp

insertAdjacentText( )   a, abbr, acronym, address, applet, area, b, base, basefont, big, blockquote, body, br, button, canvas, caption, center, cite, code, col, colgroup, datalist, dd, del, dfn, dir, div, dl, dt, em, embed, fieldset, font, form, frame, frameset, h1, h2, h3, h4, h5, h6, head, hr, html, i, iframe, img, input, ins, kbd, label, legend, li, link, listing, map, menu, meta, nobr, noframes, noscript, object, ol, optgroup, option, output, p, param, plaintext, pre, q, rb, ruby, rt, s, samp, script, select, small, span, strike, strong, style (element), sub, sup, table, tbody, td, textarea, tfoot, th, thead, title, tr, tt, u, ul, var, wbr, xmp

insertBefore( )   a, abbr, acronym, address, applet, area, attribute, b, base, basefont, big, blockquote, body, br, button, canvas, caption, center, cite, code, col, colgroup, comment, datalist, dd, del, dfn, dir, div, dl, document, DocumentType, dt, em, embed, fieldset, font, form, frame, frameset, h1, h2, h3, h4, h5, h6, head, hr, html, i, iframe, img, input, ins, kbd, label, legend, li, link, listing, map, marquee, menu, meta, nobr, Node, noframes, noscript, object, ol, optgroup, option, output, p, param, plaintext, pre, q, rb, ruby, rt, s, samp, script, select, small, span, strike, strong, style (element), sub, sup, table, tbody, td, Text, textarea, tfoot, th, thead, title, tr, tt, u, ul, var, wbr, xmp

insertCell( )   tr

insertData( )   comment, Text

insertNode( )   Range

insertRow( )   table, tbody, tfoot, thead

insertRule( )   styleSheet

intersectsNode( )   Range

isDefaultNamespace( )   a, abbr, acronym, address, applet, area, attribute, b, base, basefont, big, blockquote, body, br, button, canvas, caption, center, cite, code, col, colgroup, comment, datalist, dd, del, dfn, dir, div, dl, document, DocumentType, dt, em, embed, fieldset, font, form, frame, frameset, h1, h2, h3, h4, h5, h6, head, hr, html, i, iframe, img, input, ins, kbd, label, legend, li, link, map, marquee, menu, meta, nobr, Node, noframes, noscript, object, ol, optgroup, option, output, p, param, plaintext, pre, q, rb, ruby, rt, s, samp, script, select, small, span, strike, strong, style (element), sub, sup, table, tbody, td, Text, textarea, tfoot, th, thead, title, tr, tt, u, ul, var, wbr, xmp

isEqual( )   TextRange

isEqualNode( )   a, abbr, acronym, address, applet, area, attribute, b, base, basefont, big, blockquote, body, br, button, caption, center, cite, code, col, colgroup, comment, dd, del, dfn, dir, div, dl, document, DocumentType, dt, em, embed, fieldset, font, form, frame, frameset, h1, h2, h3, h4, h5, h6, head, hr, html, i, iframe, img, input, ins, kbd, label, legend, li, link, map, marquee, menu, meta, nobr, Node, noframes, noscript, object, ol, optgroup, option, p, param, plaintext, pre, q, rb, ruby, rt, s, samp, script, select, small, span, strike, strong, style (element), sub, sup, table, tbody, td, Text, textarea, tfoot, th, thead, title, tr, tt, u, ul, var, wbr, xmp

isPointInRange( )   Range

isSameNode( )   a, abbr, acronym, address, applet, area, attribute, b, base, basefont, big, blockquote, body, br, button, caption, center, cite, code, col, colgroup, comment, dd, del, dfn, dir, div, dl, document, DocumentType, dt, em, embed, fieldset, font, form, frame, frameset, h1, h2, h3, h4, h5, h6, head, hr, html, i, iframe, img, input, ins, kbd, label, legend, li, link, map, marquee, menu, meta, nobr, Node, noframes, noscript, object, ol, optgroup, option, p, param, plaintext, pre, q, rb, ruby, rt, s, samp, script, select, small, span, strike, strong, style (element), sub, sup, table, tbody, td, Text, textarea, tfoot, th, thead, title, tr, tt, u, ul, var, wbr, xmp

isSupported( ) a, abbr, acronym, address, applet, area, attribute, b, base, basefont, big, blockquote, body, br, button, canvas, caption, center, cite, code, col, colgroup, comment, datalist, dd, del, dfn, dir, div, dl, document, DocumentType, dt, em, embed, fieldset, font, form, frame, frameset, h1, h2, h3, h4, h5, h6, head, hr, html, i, iframe, img, input, ins, kbd, label, legend, li, link, map, marquee, menu, meta, nobr, Node, noframes, noscript, object, ol, optgroup, option, output, p, param, plaintext, pre, q, rb, ruby, rt, s, samp, script, select, small, span, strike, strong, style (element), sub, sup, table, tbody, td, Text, textarea, tfoot, th, thead, title, tr, tt, u, ul, var, wbr, xmp

item( ) all, anchors, applets, areas, attributes, cells, childNodes, children, controlRange, cssRuleList, cssRules, currentStyle, elements, embeds, filters, form, forms, frames, history, HTMLCollection, images, imports, links, MediaList, NodeList, options, rows, rules, scripts, select, style, styleSheets, tBodies

javaEnabled( ) navigator

lastChild( ) TreeWalker

lastPage( ) table

lineTo( ) CanvasRenderingContext2D

load( ) Document, layer

loadBindingDocument( ) document

lookupNamespaceURI( ) a, abbr, acronym, address, applet, area, attribute, b, base, basefont, big, blockquote, body, br, button, canvas, caption, center, cite, code, col, colgroup, comment, datalist, dd, del, dfn, dir, div, dl, document, DocumentType, dt,

em, embed, fieldset, font, form, frame, frameset, h1, h2, h3, h4, h5, h6, head, hr, html, i, iframe, img, input, ins, kbd, label, legend, li, link, map, marquee, menu, meta, nobr, Node, noframes, noscript, object, ol, optgroup, option, output, p, param, plaintext, pre, q, rb, ruby, rt, s, samp, script, select, small, span, strike, strong, style (element), sub, sup, table, tbody, td, Text, textarea, tfoot, th, thead, title, tr, tt, u, ul, var, wbr, xmp

lookupPrefix( ) a, abbr, acronym, address, applet, area, attribute, b, base, basefont, big, blockquote, body, br, button, canvas, caption, center, cite, code, col, colgroup, comment, datalist, dd, del, dfn, dir, div, dl, document, DocumentType, dt, em, embed, fieldset, font, form, frame, frameset, h1, h2, h3, h4, h5, h6, head, hr, html, i, iframe, img, input, ins, kbd, label, legend, li, link, map, marquee, menu, meta, nobr, Node, noframes, noscript, object, ol, optgroup, option, output, p, param, plaintext, pre, q, rb, ruby, rt, s, samp, script, select, small, span, strike, strong, style (element), sub, sup, table, tbody, td, Text, textarea, tfoot, th, thead, title, tr, tt, u, ul, var, wbr, xmp

loop( ) Audio

mergeAttributes( ) a, abbr, acronym, address, applet, area, b, base, basefont, bdo, bgsound, big, blockquote, body, br, button, caption, center, cite, code, col, colgroup, comment, dd, del, dfn, dir, div, dl, dt, em, embed, fieldset, font, form, frame, frameset, h1, h2, h3, h4, h5, h6, head, hr, html, i, iframe, img, input, ins, kbd, label, legend, li, link, listing, map, marquee, menu, meta, nobr, noframes, noscript, object, ol, optgroup, option, p, plaintext, pre, q, rt, ruby, s, samp, script, select, small, span, strike, strong, style (element), sub, sup, table, tbody, td, textarea, tfoot, th, thead, title, tr, tt, u, ul, var, wbr, xml, xmp

move( ) TextRange

moveAbove( ) layer

moveBelow( ) layer

moveBy( )   layer, window

moveEnd( )   TextRange

moveRepetitionBlock( )   a, abbr, acronym, address, applet, area, b, base, basefont, big, block-quote, body, br, button, canvas, caption, center, cite, code, col, colgroup, datalist, dd, del, dfn, dir, div, dl, dt, em, embed, fieldset, font, form, frame, frameset, h1, h2, h3, h4, h5, h6, head, hr, html, i, iframe, img, input, ins, kbd, label, legend, li, link, map, menu, meta, nobr, noframes, noscript, object, ol, optgroup, option, output, p, param, plaintext, pre, q, rb, ruby, rt, RepetitionElement, s, samp, script, select, small, span, strike, strong, style (element), sub, sup, table, tbody, td, textarea, tfoot, th, thead, title, tr, tt, u, ul, var, wbr, xmp

moveRow( )   table, tbody, tfoot, thead

moveStart( )   TextRange

moveTo( )   CanvasRenderingContext2D, layer, window

moveToAbsolute( )   layer

moveToBookmark( )   TextRange

moveToElementText( )   TextRange

moveToPoint( )   TextRange

namedItem( )   all, anchors, applets, areas, cells, children, elements, embeds, filters, form, forms, frames, HTMLCollection, images, links, options, rows, scripts, select, tBodies

navigate( )   window

nextNode( )   NodeIterator, TreeWalker

nextPage( )   table

nextSibling( )   TreeWalker

normalize( )   a, abbr, acronym, address, applet, area, attribute, b, base, basefont, bgsound, big, blockquote, body, br, button, canvas, caption, center, cite, code, col, colgroup, comment, datalist, dd, del, dfn, dir, div, dl, document, DocumentType, dt, em, embed, fieldset, font, form, frame, frameset, h1, h2, h3, h4, h5, h6, head, hr, html, i, iframe, img, input, ins, kbd, label, legend, li, link, listing, map, marquee, menu, meta, nobr, Node, noframes, noscript, object, ol, optgroup, option, output, p, param, plaintext,

pre, q, rb, ruby, rt, s, samp, script, select, small, span, strike, strong, style (element), sub, sup, table, tbody, td, Text, textarea, tfoot, th, thead, title, tr, tt, u, ul, var, wbr, xml, xmp

normalizeDocument( )   document

open( )   document, window, XMLHttpRequest

openDialog( )   window

overrideMimeType( )   XMLHttpRequest

parentElement( )   TextRange

parentNode( )   TreeWalker

parseFromString( )   DOMParser

pasteHTML( )   TextRange

play( )   Audio

postMessage( )   document

preference( )   navigator

preventBubble( )   event

preventCapture( )   event

preventDefault( )   event

previousPage( )   table

previousNode( )   NodeIterator, TreeWalker

previousSibling( )   TreeWalker

print( )   window

prompt( )   window

quadraticCurveTo( )   CanvasRenderingContext2D

queryCommandEnabled( )   controlRange, document, TextRange

queryCommandIndeterm( )   controlRange, document, TextRange

queryCommandState( )   controlRange, document, TextRange

queryCommandSupported( )   controlRange, document, TextRange

queryCommandText( )   TextRange

queryCommandValue( )   controlRange, document, TextRange

recalc( )   document

rect( )   CanvasRenderingContext2D

refresh( )   plugin, table

releaseCapture( )   a, abbr, acronym, address, applet, area, b, base, basefont, bdo, bgsound, big, blockquote, body, br, button, caption, center, cite, code, col, colgroup, comment, dd, del, dfn, dir, div, dl, dt, em, embed, fieldset, font, form, frame, frameset, h1, h2, h3, h4, h5, h6, head, hr, html, i, iframe, img, input, ins, kbd, label, legend, li, link, listing, map, marquee, menu, meta, nobr, noframes, noscript, object, ol, optgroup, option, p, plaintext, pre, q, rt, ruby, s, samp, script, select, small, span, strike, strong, style (element), sub, sup, table, tbody, td, textarea, tfoot, th, thead, title, tr, tt, u, ul, var, wbr, xml, xmp

releaseEvents( )   document, layer, window

reload( )   location

remove( )   controlRange, options, selection

removeAllRanges( )   selection

removeAttribute( )   a, abbr, acronym, address, applet, area, b, base, basefont, bgsound, big, blockquote, body, br, button, canvas, caption, center, cite, code, col, colgroup, datalist, dd, del, dfn, dir, div, dl, dt, Element, em, embed, fieldset, font, form, frame, frameset, h1, h2, h3, h4, h5, h6, head, hr, html, i, iframe, img, input, ins, kbd, label, legend, li, link, listing, map, marquee, menu, meta, nobr, noframes, noscript, object, ol, optgroup, option, output, p, param, plaintext, pre, q, rb, ruby, rt, s, samp, script, select, small, span, strike, strong, style (element), sub, sup, table, tbody, td, textarea, tfoot, th, thead, title, tr, tt, u, ul, var, wbr, xmp

removeAttributeNode( )   a, abbr, acronym, address, applet, area, b, base, basefont, bgsound, big, blockquote, body, br, button, canvas, caption, center, cite, code, col, colgroup, datalist, dd, del, dfn, dir, div, dl, dt, Element, em, embed, fieldset, font, form, frame, frameset, h1, h2, h3, h4, h5, h6, head, hr, html, i, iframe, img, input, ins, kbd, label, legend, li, link, listing, map, marquee, menu, meta, nobr, noframes, noscript, object, ol, optgroup, option, output, p, param, plaintext, pre, q, rb, ruby, rt, s, samp, script, select, small, span, strike,

strong, style (element), sub, sup, table, tbody, td, textarea, tfoot, th, thead, title, tr, tt, u, ul, var, wbr, xml, xmp

removeAttributeNS( )   a, abbr, acronym, address, applet, area, b, base, basefont, big, blockquote, body, br, button, canvas, caption, center, cite, code, col, colgroup, datalist, dd, del, dfn, dir, div, dl, dt, Element, em, embed, fieldset, font, form, frame, frameset, h1, h2, h3, h4, h5, h6, head, hr, html, i, iframe, img, input, ins, kbd, label, legend, li, link, map, marquee, menu, meta, nobr, noframes, noscript, object, ol, optgroup, option, output, p, param, plaintext, pre, q, rb, ruby, rt, s, samp, script, select, small, span, strike, strong, style (element), sub, sup, table, tbody, td, textarea, tfoot, th, thead, title, tr, tt, u, ul, var, wbr, xmp

removeBehavior( )   a, abbr, acronym, address, applet, area, b, base, basefont, bdo, bgsound, big, blockquote, body, br, button, caption, center, cite, code, col, colgroup, comment, dd, del, dfn, dir, div, dl, dt, em, embed, fieldset, font, form, frame, frameset, h1, h2, h3, h4, h5, h6, head, hr, html, i, iframe, img, input, ins, kbd, label, legend, li, link, listing, map, marquee, menu, meta, nobr, noframes, noscript, object, ol, optgroup, option, p, plaintext, pre, q, rt, ruby, s, samp, script, select, small, span, strike, strong, style (element), sub, sup, table, tbody, td, textarea, tfoot, th, thead, title, tr, tt, u, ul, var, wbr, xml, xmp

removeBinding( )   document

removeChild( )   a, abbr, acronym, address, applet, area, attribute, b, base, basefont, big, blockquote, body, br, button, canvas, caption, center, cite, code, col, colgroup, comment, datalist, dd, del, dfn, dir, div, dl, document, DocumentType, dt, em, embed, fieldset, font, form, frame, frameset, h1, h2, h3, h4, h5, h6, head, hr, html, i, iframe, img, input, ins, kbd, label, legend, li, link, listing, map, marquee, menu, meta, nobr, Node, noframes, noscript, object, ol, optgroup, option, output, p, param, plaintext, pre, q, rb, ruby, rt, s, samp, script, select, small, span, strike, strong, style (element), sub, sup, table, tbody, td, Text, textarea, tfoot, th, thead, title, tr, tt, u, ul, var, wbr, xmp

removeEventListener( )   a, abbr, acronym, address, applet, area, attribute, b, base, basefont, big, blockquote, body, br, button, canvas, caption, center, cite, code, col, colgroup, comment, datalist, dd, del, dfn, dir, div, dl, document, DocumentType, dt, em, embed, fieldset, font, form, frame, frameset, h1, h2, h3, h4, h5, h6, head, hr, html, i, iframe, img, input, ins, kbd, label, legend, li, link, map, marquee, menu, meta, nobr, noframes, noscript, object, ol, optgroup, option, output, p, param, plaintext, pre, q, rb, ruby, rt, s, samp, script, select, small, span, strike, strong, style (element), sub, sup, table, tbody, td, Text, textarea, tfoot, th, thead, title, tr, tt, u, ul, var, wbr, window, XMLHttpRequest, xmp

removeExpression( )   a, abbr, acronym, address, applet, area, b, base, basefont, bdo, bgsound, big, blockquote, body, br, button, caption, center, cite, code, col, colgroup, comment, dd, del, dfn, dir, div, dl, dt, em, embed, fieldset, font, form, frame, frameset, h1, h2, h3, h4, h5, h6, head, hr, html, i, iframe, img, input, ins, kbd, label, legend, li, link, listing, map, marquee, menu, meta, nobr, noframes, noscript, object, ol, optgroup, option, p, plaintext, pre, q, rt, ruby, s, samp, script, select, small, span, strike, strong, style (element), sub, sup, table, tbody, td, textarea, tfoot, th, thead, title, tr, tt, u, ul, var, wbr, xml, xmp

removeNamedItem( )   attributes

removeNamedItemNS( )   attributes

removeNode( )   a, abbr, acronym, address, applet, area, b, base, basefont, bdo, bgsound, big, blockquote, body, br, button, canvas, caption, center, cite, code, col, colgroup, comment, datalist, dd, del, dfn, dir, div, dl, dt, em, embed, fieldset, font, form, frame, frameset, h1, h2, h3, h4, h5, h6, head, hr, html, i, iframe, img, input,

ins, kbd, label, legend, li, link, listing, map, marquee, menu, meta, nobr, noframes, noscript, object, ol, optgroup, option, output, p, plaintext, pre, q, rt, ruby, s, samp, script, select, small, span, strike, strong, style (element), sub, sup, table, tbody, td, textarea, tfoot, th, thead, title, tr, tt, u, ul, var, wbr, xml, xmp

removeProperty( )   currentStyle, style

removeRange( )   selection

removeRepetitionBlock( )   a, abbr, acronym, address, applet, area, b, base, basefont, big, blockquote, body, br, button, canvas, caption, center, cite, code, col, colgroup, datalist, dd, del, dfn, dir, div, dl, dt, em, embed, fieldset, font, form, frame, frameset, h1, h2, h3, h4, h5, h6, head, hr, html, i, iframe, img, input, ins, kbd, label, legend, li, link, map, menu, meta, nobr, noframes, noscript, object, ol, optgroup, option, output, p, param, plaintext, pre, q, rb, ruby, rt, RepetitionElement, s, samp, script, select, small, span, strike, strong, style (element), sub, sup, table, tbody, td, textarea, tfoot, th, thead, title, tr, tt, u, ul, var, wbr, xmp

removeRule( )   styleSheet

renameNode( )   document

replace( )   location

replaceAdjacentText( )   a, abbr, acronym, address, applet, area, b, base, basefont, bdo, bgsound, big, blockquote, body, br, button, caption, center, cite, code, col, colgroup, comment, dd, del, dfn, dir, div, dl, dt, em, embed, fieldset, font, form, frame, frameset, h1, h2, h3, h4, h5, h6, head, hr, html, i, iframe, img, input, ins, kbd, label, legend, li, link, listing, map, marquee, menu, meta, nobr, noframes, noscript, object, ol, optgroup, option, p, plaintext, pre, q, rt, ruby, s, samp, script, select, small, span, strike, strong, style (element), sub, sup, table, tbody, td, textarea, tfoot, th, thead, title, tr, tt, u, ul, var, wbr, xml, xmp

replaceChild( )   a, abbr, acronym, address, applet, area, attribute, b, base, basefont, big, blockquote, body, br, button, canvas, caption, center, cite, code, col, colgroup, comment, datalist, dd, del, dfn, dir, div, dl, document, DocumentType, dt, em, embed, fieldset, font, form, frame, frameset, h1, h2, h3, h4, h5, h6, head, hr, html, i, iframe, img, input, ins, kbd, label, legend, li, link, listing, map, marquee, menu, meta, nobr, Node, noframes, noscript, object, ol, optgroup, option, output, p, param, plaintext, pre, q, rb, ruby, rt, s, samp, script, select, small, span, strike, strong, style (element), sub, sup, table, tbody, td, Text, textarea, tfoot, th, thead, title, tr, tt, u, ul, var, wbr, xmp

replaceData( )   comment, Text

replaceNode( )   a, abbr, acronym, address, applet, area, b, base, basefont, bdo, bgsound, big, blockquote, body, br, button, caption, center, cite, code, col, colgroup, comment, dd, del, dfn, dir, div, dl, dt, em, embed, fieldset, font, form, frame, frameset, h1, h2, h3, h4, h5, h6, head, hr, html, i, iframe, img, input, ins, kbd, label, legend, li, link, listing, map, marquee, menu, meta, nobr, noframes, noscript, object, ol, optgroup, option, p, plaintext, pre, q, rt, ruby, s, samp, script, select, small, span, strike, strong, style (element), sub, sup, table, tbody, td, textarea, tfoot, th, thead, title, tr, tt, u, ul, var, wbr, xml, xmp

reset( )   form

resetFromData( )   form

resizeBy( )   layer, window

resizeTo( )   layer, window

restore( )   CanvasRenderingContext2D

rotate( )   CanvasRenderingContext2D

routeEvent( )   document, layer, window

save( )   CanvasRenderingContext2D

scale( )   CanvasRenderingContext2D

scroll( )   window

scrollBy( )   window

scrollByLines( )   window

scrollByPages( )   window

scrollIntoView( )   a, abbr, acronym, address, applet, area, b, base, basefont, big, blockquote, body, br, button, canvas, caption, center, cite, code, col, colgroup, controlRange, datalist, dd, del, dfn, dir, div, dl, dt, em, embed, fieldset, font, form, frame, frameset, h1, h2, h3, h4, h5, h6, head, hr, html, i, iframe, img, input, ins, kbd, label, legend, li, link, listing, map, menu, meta, nobr, noframes, noscript, object, ol, optgroup, option, output, p, param, plaintext, pre, q, rb, ruby, rt, s, samp, script, select, small, span, strike, strong, style (element), sub, sup, table, tbody, td, textarea, tfoot, th, thead, title, tr, tt, u, ul, var, wbr, xmp

scrollTo( )   window

select( )   controlRange, input, textarea, TextRange

selectAllChildren( )   selection

selectionLanguageChange( )   selection

selectNode( )   Range

selectNodeContents( )   Range

send( )   XMLHttpRequest

serializeToString( )   XMLSerializer

setActive( )   a, abbr, acronym, address, applet, area, b, base, basefont, bdo, bgsound, big, blockquote, body, br, button, caption, center, cite, code, col, colgroup, comment, dd, del, dfn, dir, div, dl, dt, em, embed, fieldset, font, form, frame, frameset, h1, h2, h3, h4, h5, h6, head, hr, html, i, iframe, img, input, ins, kbd, label, legend, li, link, listing, map, marquee, menu, meta, nobr, noframes, noscript, object, ol, optgroup, option, p, plaintext, pre, q, rt, ruby, s, samp, script, select, small, span, strike, strong, style (element), sub, sup, table, tbody, td, textarea, tfoot, th, thead, title, tr, tt, u, ul, var, wbr, xml, xmp

setAttribute( )   a, abbr, acronym, address, applet, area, b, base, basefont, bgsound, big, blockquote, body, br, button, canvas, caption, center, cite, code, col, colgroup, datalist, dd, del, dfn, dir, div, dl, dt, Element, em, embed, fieldset, font, form, frame, frameset, h1, h2, h3, h4, h5, h6, head, hr, html, i, iframe, img, input, ins, kbd, label, legend, li, link, listing, map, marquee, menu, meta, nobr, noframes, noscript, object, ol, optgroup, option, output, p, param, plaintext, pre, q, rb, ruby, rt, s, samp, script, select, small, span, strike, strong, style (element), sub, sup, table, tbody, td, textarea, tfoot, th, thead, title, tr, tt, u, ul, var, wbr, xmp

setAttributeNode( ) a, abbr, acronym, address, applet, area, b, base, basefont, bgsound, big, blockquote, body, br, button, canvas, caption, center, cite, code, col, colgroup, datalist, dd, del, dfn, dir, div, dl, dt, Element, em, embed, fieldset, font, form, frame, frameset, h1, h2, h3, h4, h5, h6, head, hr, html, i, iframe, img, input, ins, kbd, label, legend, li, link, listing, map, marquee, menu, meta, nobr, noframes, noscript, object, ol, optgroup, option, output, p, param, plaintext, pre, q, rb, ruby, rt, s, samp, script, select, small, span, strike, strong, style (element), sub, sup, table, tbody, td, textarea, tfoot, th, thead, title, tr, tt, u, ul, var, wbr, xml, xmp

setAttributeNodeNS( ) a, abbr, acronym, address, applet, area, b, base, basefont, big, blockquote, body, br, button, canvas, caption, center, cite, code, col, colgroup, datalist, dd, del, dfn, dir, div, dl, dt, Element, em, embed, fieldset, font, form, frame, frameset, h1, h2, h3, h4, h5, h6, head, hr, html, i, iframe, img, input, ins, kbd, label, legend, li, link, map, marquee, menu, meta, nobr, noframes, noscript, object, ol, optgroup, option, output, p, param, plaintext, pre, q, rb, ruby, rt, s, samp, script, select, small, span, strike, strong, style (element), sub, sup, table, tbody, td, textarea, tfoot, th, thead, title, tr, tt, u, ul, var, wbr, xmp

setAttributeNS( ) a, abbr, acronym, address, applet, area, b, base, basefont, big, blockquote, body, br, button, canvas, caption, center, cite, code, col, colgroup, datalist, dd, del, dfn, dir, div, dl, dt, Element, em, embed, fieldset, font, form, frame, frameset, h1, h2, h3, h4, h5, h6, head, hr, html, i, iframe, img, input, ins, kbd, label,

legend, li, link, map, marquee, menu, meta, nobr, noframes, noscript, object, ol, optgroup, option, output, p, param, plaintext, pre, q, rb, ruby, rt, s, samp, script, select, small, span, strike, strong, style (element), sub, sup, table, tbody, td, textarea, tfoot, th, thead, title, tr, tt, u, ul, var, wbr, xmp

setCapture( ) a, abbr, acronym, address, applet, area, b, base, basefont, bdo, bgsound, big, blockquote, body, br, button, caption, center, cite, code, col, colgroup, comment, dd, del, dfn, dir, div, dl, dt, em, embed, fieldset, font, form, frame, frameset, h1, h2, h3, h4, h5, h6, head, hr, html, i, iframe, img, input, ins, kbd, label, legend, li, link, listing, map, marquee, menu, meta, nobr, noframes, noscript, object, ol, optgroup, option, p, plaintext, pre, q, rt, ruby, s, samp, script, select, small, span, strike, strong, style (element), sub, sup, table, tbody, td, textarea, tfoot, th, thead, title, tr, tt, u, ul, var, wbr, xml, xmp

setCursor( ) window

setCustomValidity( ) button, input, output, select

setData( ) clipboardData, dataTransfer

setEnd( ) Range

setEndAfter( ) Range

setEndBefore( ) Range

setEndPoint( ) TextRange

setExpression( ) a, abbr, acronym, address, applet, area, b, base, basefont, bdo, bgsound, big, blockquote, body, br, button, caption, center, cite, code, col, colgroup, comment, dd, del, dfn, dir, div, dl, dt, em, embed, fieldset, font, form, frame, frameset, h1, h2, h3, h4, h5, h6, head, hr, html, i, iframe, img, input, ins, kbd, label, legend, li, link, listing, map, marquee, menu, meta, nobr, noframes, noscript, object, ol, optgroup, option, p, plaintext, pre, q, rt, ruby, s, samp, script, select, small, span, strike, strong, style (element), sub, sup, table, tbody, td, textarea, tfoot, th, thead, title, tr, tt, u, ul, var, wbr, xml, xmp

setInterval( ) window

setNamedItem( ) attributes

setNamedItemNS( ) attributes

setProperty( ) currentStyle, style

setRequestHeader( ) XMLHttpRequest

setResizable( ) window

setSelectionRange( ) textarea

setStart( ) Range

setStartAfter( ) Range

setStartBefore( ) Range

setTimeout( ) window

show( ) popup

showHelp( ) window

showModalDialog( ) window

showModelessDialog( ) window

sizeToContent( ) window

splitText( ) Text

start( ) marquee

stop( ) Audio, marquee, window

stopPropagation( ) event

submit( ) form

substringData( ) comment, Text

surroundContents( ) Range

swapNode( ) a, abbr, acronym, address, applet, area, b, base, basefont, bdo, bgsound, big, blockquote, body, br, button, caption, center, cite, code, col, colgroup, comment, dd, del, dfn, dir, div, dl, dt, em, embed, fieldset, font, form, frame, frameset, h1, h2, h3, h4, h5, h6, head, hr, html, i, iframe, img, input, ins, kbd, label, legend, li, link, listing, map, marquee, menu, meta, nobr,
noframes, noscript, object, ol, optgroup, option, p, plaintext, pre, q, rt, ruby, s, samp, script, select, small, span, strike, strong, style (element), sub, sup, table, tbody, td, textarea, tfoot, th, thead, title, tr, tt, u, ul, var, wbr, xml, xmp

tags( ) all, anchors, applets, areas, cells, children, elements, embeds, forms, images, links, options, rows, scripts, tBodies

taintEnabled( ) navigator

toDataURL( ) canvas

toString( ) abbr, acronym, address, applet, area, b, base, basefont, big, blockquote, body, br, button, canvas, caption, center, cite, code, col, colgroup, datalist, dd, del, dfn, dir, div, dl, dt, em, embed, fieldset, font, form, frame, frameset, h1, h2, h3, h4, h5, h6, head, hr, html, i, iframe, img, input, ins, kbd, label, legend, li, link, map, menu, meta, nobr, noframes, noscript, object, ol, optgroup, option, output, p, param, plaintext, pre, q, Range, rb, ruby, rt, s, samp, script, select, selection, small, span, strike, strong, style (element), sub, sup, table, tbody, td, textarea, tfoot, th, thead, title, tr, tt, u, ul, var, wbr, xmp

translate( ) CanvasRenderingContext2D

updateCommands( ) window

urns( ) all, anchors, areas, cells, childNodes, children, forms, images, links, options, rows, scripts, tBodies

write( ) document

writeln( ) document

CHAPTER 9
DOM Events Index

Entries in the following index are arranged alphabetically by scriptable object event type. Look up an event type to find out which objects support it. This listing is a union of events defined for objects in Internet Explorer, pre-Mozilla Netscape Navigator, Mozilla, Safari, Opera, and the W3C DOM Levels 2 and 3. When an event type in its latest incarnation applies to all HTML element objects, the listing indicates that fact without repeating the list of all object names.

The same event handler name may mean different things for different objects. Be sure to look up the details of the event listings in Chapter 2, to find if the event handler is available for the browser(s) used by your intended audience and whether it does what you want. Details of the events themselves are in Chapter 3. All event types are listed here in all lowercase and without the "on" prefix that need to be added when used as object properties or attaching events in Internet Explorer.

abort   img, object

activate   All rendered element objects, document, window

afterprint   body, frameset, window

afterupdate   a, bdo, button, div, frame, iframe, img, input (checkbox), input (hidden), input (password), input (radio), input (text), label, legend, marquee, rt, ruby, select, span, textarea

beforeactivate   All rendered element objects, document, window

beforecopy   a, abbr, acronym, address, area, b, bdo, big, blockquote, caption, center, cite, code, dd, dfn, dir, div, dl, dt, em, fieldset, form, h1, h2, h3, h4, h5, h6, i, img, label, legend, li, listing, menu, nobr, ol, p, plaintext, pre, s, samp, small, span, strike, strong, sub, sup, td, textarea, th, tr, tt, u, ul

beforecut   All rendered element objects, document

beforedeactivate   All rendered element objects, document, window

beforeeditfocus   a, abbr, acronym, address, applet, area, b, bdo, big, blockquote, body, button, caption, center, cite, code, dd, del, dfn, dir, div, dl, document, dt, em, fieldset, font, form, h1, h2, h3, h4, h5, h6, i, input (except hidden), ins, isindex, kbd, label, legend, li, listing, marquee, menu, nobr, object, ol, p, plaintext, pre, q, rt, ruby, s, samp, select, small, span, strike, strong, sub, sup, table, td, textarea, tr, tt, u, ul, var, xmp

beforepaste   All rendered element objects, document

beforeprint   body, frameset, window

beforeunload   body, frameset, window

beforeupdate   a, button, div, frame, iframe, img, input (checkbox), input (hidden), input (password), input (radio), input (text), textarea, label, legend, marquee, select, span, bdo, rt, ruby

blur   All rendered element objects, document, window

bounce   marquee

cellchange   applet, object

change   input (text), select, textarea

click   All rendered element objects, document, window

contextmenu   All rendered element objects, document

controlselect   All rendered element objects, document

copy   a, abbr, acronym, address, area, b, bdo, big, blockquote, caption, center, cite, code, dd, dfn, dir, div, dl, dt, em, fieldset, form, h1, h2, h3, h4, h5, h6, hr, i, img, legend, li, listing, menu, nobr, ol, p, plaintext, pre, s, samp, small, span, strike, strong, sub, sup, td, th, tr, tt, u, ul

cut   All rendered element objects, document

dataavailable   applet, object, xml

datasetchanged   applet, object, xml

datasetcomplete   applet, object, xml

dblclick   All rendered element objects, document

deactivate   All rendered element objects, document, window

DOMActivate   All rendered element objects

DOMAttrModified   All element objects

DOMCharacterDataModified   characterDataNode

DOMControlValueChanged   button, form, input, output, select, textarea

DOMFocusIn   All rendered element objects

DOMFocusOut   All rendered element objects

DOMFrameContentLoaded   frame

DOMMenuItemActive   option

DOMNodeInserted   All nodes in document tree

DOMNodeInsertedIntoDocument   All nodes in document tree

DOMNodeRemoved   All nodes in document tree

DOMNodeRemovedFromDocument   All nodes in document tree

DOMSubtreeModified   All nodes in document tree

DOMTitleModified   document

drag   All rendered element objects, document

dragdrop   window

dragend   All rendered element objects, document

dragenter   All rendered element objects, document

dragleave   All rendered element objects, document

dragover   All rendered element objects, document

dragstart   All rendered element objects, document

drop   All rendered element objects, document

error   body, frameset, img, link, object, script, style, window, XMLHttpRequest

errorupdate   a, button, div, frame, iframe, img, input, textarea, label, legend, marquee, select, span, bdo, rt, ruby

filterchange   bdo, body, button, div, fieldset, img, input (except hidden), marquee, rt, ruby, span, table, td, textarea, th, tb

finish   marquee

focus   All rendered element objects, document, window

focusin   All rendered element objects, document, window

focusout   All rendered element objects, document, window

formchange   button, form, input, output, select, textarea

forminput   button, form, input, output, select, textarea

help   All rendered element objects, document, window

invalid   form, input, output, select, textarea

keydown   All rendered element objects, document, window

keypress   All rendered element objects, document

keyup   All rendered element objects, document, window

layoutcomplete   LayoutRect

load   applet, body, embed, frame, frameset,
   iframe, img, layer, link, object, script,
   style, window, XMLHttpRequest

losecapture   All rendered element objects

message   document

mousedown   All rendered element objects

mouseenter   All rendered element objects

mouseleave   All rendered element objects

mousemove   All rendered element objects

mouseout   All rendered element objects

mouseover   All rendered element objects

mouseup   All rendered element objects

mousewheel   All rendered element objects,
   document

move   All rendered element objects, window

moveend   All rendered element objects

movestart   All rendered element objects

paste   All rendered element objects

progress   XMLHttpRequest

propertychange   All rendered element objects,
   document

readystatechange   applet, body, embed, frame,
   frameset, iframe, img, link, object, script,
   style, window, XMLHttpRequest

reset   form

resize   All rendered element objects, document, frameset, window

resizeend   All rendered element objects

resizestart   All rendered element objects

rowenter   applet, object, xml

rowexit   applet, object, xml

rowsdelete   applet, object, xml

rowsinserted   applet, object, xml

scroll   applet, bdo, body, div, document,
   embed, html, map, marquee, object, table,
   textarea, window

select   body, input (text), textarea

selectionchange   document

selectstart   All rendered element objects

start   marquee

start   document

submit   form

unload   body, frameset, window

Appendixes

This part provides quick access to useful HTML authoring and scripting information. The glossary offers quick explanations of some of the new and potentially confusing terminology of DHTML.

Appendix A, *Color Names and RGB Values*

Appendix B, *HTML Character Entities*

Appendix C, *Keyboard Event Character Values*

Appendix D, *Editable Content Commands*

Appendix E, *HTML/XHTML DTD Support*

Appendix F, *The Mozilla Browser Version Trail*

Glossary

Color Names and RGB Values

Netscape was the first to deploy a library of color names (originally adopted from the X Window System palette known as X11 color names) that could be used as attribute and scripted object property color values in place of hexadecimal triplet values. Virtually all modern browsers support the use of these values, and CSS Level 3 puts the list into a published standard. Color names in both tag attributes, scripts, and CSS properties are case-insensitive. Typically, if you set a color attribute or property to one of the named colors, the object property is reflected in scripts as the hexadecimal triplet value for that color. For additional convenience, the following table also shows the decimal equivalents of the RGB value in case you use these color values in style sheet rules. Be aware that some colors in this collection require 16- or 24-bit color to achieve the proper hue.

A small subset of these colors—16 to be exact—appear within the HTML 4 specification. Those colors are shown in the table followed by an asterisk (*).

Color name	Red	Green	Blue	Red	Green	Blue
aliceblue	F0	F8	FF	240	248	255
antiquewhite	FA	EB	D7	250	235	215
aqua*	00	FF	FF	0	255	255
aquamarine	7F	FF	D4	127	255	212
azure	F0	FF	FF	240	255	255
beige	F5	F5	DC	245	245	220
bisque	FF	E4	C4	255	228	196
black*	00	00	00	0	0	0
blanchedalmond	FF	EB	CD	255	235	205
blue*	00	00	FF	0	0	255
blueviolet	8A	2B	E2	138	43	226
brown	A5	2A	2A	165	42	42
burlywood	DE	B8	87	222	184	135
cadetblue	5F	9E	A0	95	158	160

Color name	Red	Green	Blue	Red	Green	Blue
chartreuse	7F	FF	00	127	255	0
chocolate	D2	69	1E	210	105	30
coral	FF	7F	50	255	127	80
cornflowerblue	64	95	ED	100	149	237
cornsilk	FF	F8	DC	255	248	220
crimson	DC	14	3C	220	20	60
cyan	00	FF	FF	0	255	255
darkblue	00	00	8B	0	0	139
darkcyan	00	8B	8B	0	139	139
darkgoldenrod	B8	86	0B	184	134	11
darkgray	A9	A9	A9	169	169	169
darkgreen	00	64	00	0	100	0
darkgrey	A9	A9	A9	169	169	169
darkkhaki	BD	B7	6B	189	183	107
darkmagenta	8B	00	8B	139	0	139
darkolivegreen	55	6B	2F	85	107	47
darkorange	FF	8C	00	255	140	0
darkorchid	99	32	CC	153	50	204
darkred	8B	00	00	139	0	0
darksalmon	E9	96	7A	233	150	122
darkseagreen	8F	BC	8F	143	188	143
darkslateblue	48	3D	8B	72	61	139
darkslategray	2F	4F	4F	47	79	79
darkslategrey	2F	4F	4F	47	79	79
darkturquoise	00	CE	D1	0	206	209
darkviolet	94	00	D3	148	0	211
deeppink	FF	14	93	255	20	147
deepskyblue	00	BF	FF	0	191	255
dimgray	69	69	69	105	105	105
dimgrey	69	69	69	105	105	105
dodgerblue	1E	90	FF	30	144	255
firebrick	B2	22	22	178	34	34
floralwhite	FF	FA	F0	255	250	240
forestgreen	22	8B	22	34	139	34
fuchsia*	FF	00	FF	255	0	255
gainsboro	DC	DC	DC	220	220	220
ghostwhite	F8	F8	FF	248	248	255
gold	FF	D7	00	255	215	0
goldenrod	DA	A5	20	218	165	32
gray*	80	80	80	128	128	128

Color name	Red	Green	Blue	Red	Green	Blue
grey	80	80	80	128	128	128
green*	00	80	00	0	128	0
greenyellow	AD	FF	2F	173	255	47
honeydew	F0	FF	F0	240	255	240
hotpink	FF	69	B4	255	105	180
indianred	CD	5C	5C	205	92	92
indigo	4B	00	82	75	0	130
ivory	FF	FF	F0	255	255	240
khaki	F0	E6	8C	240	230	140
lavender	E6	E6	FA	230	230	250
lavenderblush	FF	F0	F5	255	240	245
lawngreen	7C	FC	00	124	252	0
lemonchiffon	FF	FA	CD	255	250	205
lightblue	AD	D8	E6	173	216	230
lightcoral	F0	80	80	240	128	128
lightcyan	E0	FF	FF	224	255	255
lightgoldenrodyellow	FA	FA	D2	250	250	210
lightgray	D3	D3	D3	211	211	211
lightgreen	90	EE	90	144	238	144
lightgrey	D3	D3	D3	211	211	211
lightpink	FF	B6	C1	255	182	193
lightsalmon	FF	A0	7A	255	160	122
lightseagreen	20	B2	AA	32	178	170
lightskyblue	87	CE	FA	135	206	250
lightslategray	77	88	99	119	136	153
lightslategrey	77	88	99	119	136	153
lightsteelblue	B0	C4	DE	176	196	222
lightyellow	FF	FF	E0	255	255	224
lime*	00	FF	00	0	255	0
limegreen	32	CD	32	50	205	50
linen	FA	F0	E6	250	240	230
magenta	FF	00	FF	255	0	255
maroon*	80	00	00	128	0	0
mediumaquamarine	66	CD	AA	102	205	170
mediumblue	00	00	CD	0	0	205
mediumorchid	BA	55	D3	186	85	211
mediumpurple	93	70	DB	147	112	219
mediumseagreen	3C	B3	71	60	179	113
mediumslateblue	7B	68	EE	123	104	238
mediumspringgreen	00	FA	9A	0	250	154

Color name	Red	Green	Blue	Red	Green	Blue
mediumturquoise	48	D1	CC	72	209	204
mediumvioletred	C7	15	85	199	21	133
midnightblue	19	19	70	25	25	112
mintcream	F5	FF	FA	245	255	250
mistyrose	FF	E4	E1	255	228	225
moccasin	FF	E4	B5	255	228	181
navajowhite	FF	DE	AD	255	222	173
navy*	00	00	80	0	0	128
oldlace	FD	F5	E6	253	245	230
olive*	80	80	00	128	128	0
olivedrab	6B	8E	23	107	142	35
orange	FF	A5	00	255	165	0
orangered	FF	45	00	255	69	0
orchid	DA	70	D6	218	112	214
palegoldenrod	EE	E8	AA	238	232	170
palegreen	98	FB	98	152	251	152
paleturquoise	AF	EE	EE	175	238	238
palevioletred	DB	70	93	219	112	147
papayawhip	FF	EF	D5	255	239	213
peachpuff	FF	DA	B9	255	218	185
peru	CD	85	3F	205	133	63
pink	FF	C0	CB	255	192	203
plum	DD	A0	DD	221	160	221
powderblue	B0	E0	E6	176	224	230
purple*	80	00	80	128	0	128
red*	FF	00	00	255	0	0
rosybrown	BC	8F	8F	188	143	143
royalblue	41	69	E1	65	105	225
saddlebrown	8B	45	13	139	69	19
salmon	FA	80	72	250	128	114
sandybrown	F4	A4	60	244	164	96
seagreen	2E	8B	57	46	139	87
seashell	FF	F5	EE	255	245	238
sienna	A0	52	2D	160	82	45
silver*	C0	C0	C0	192	192	192
skyblue	87	CE	EB	135	206	235
slateblue	6A	5A	CD	106	90	205
slategray	70	80	90	112	128	144
slategrey	70	80	90	112	128	144
snow	FF	FA	FA	255	250	250

Color name	Red	Green	Blue	Red	Green	Blue
springgreen	00	FF	7F	0	255	127
steelblue	46	82	B4	70	130	180
tan	D2	B4	8C	210	180	140
teal*	00	80	80	0	128	128
thistle	D8	BF	D8	216	191	216
tomato	FF	63	47	255	99	71
turquoise	40	E0	D0	64	224	208
violet	EE	82	EE	238	130	238
wheat	F5	DE	B3	245	222	179
white*	FF	FF	FF	255	255	255
whitesmoke	F5	F5	F5	245	245	245
yellow*	FF	FF	00	255	255	0
yellowgreen	9A	CD	32	154	205	50

HTML Character Entities

To display symbols and characters beyond the collection of common ASCII alphanumeric values (0-127), browsers recognize a special coding that lets you insert such characters into HTML document content. These *entity* characters start with an ampersand symbol (&) and end with a semicolon (;). Between those symbols goes a representation of the desired character in your choice of letters or numbers. For example, the numeric entity value for a copyright symbol is 169. An HTML statement using that symbol looks as follows:

```
<p style="text-align: center">&#169;2002 MegaCorp, Inc. All Rights Reserved.</p>
```

Because the numbering system is not easy to remember, entities also have case-sensitive word or abbreviation equivalents for their values. For the copyright symbol, for example, the entity is ©. This makes the code more readable, as in the following:

```
<p style="text-align: center">&copy;2002 MegaCorp, Inc. All Rights Reserved.</p>
```

This table lists every entity defined in the HTML 4 specification in alphabetical order. Recent browsers support the vast majority of these characters, but the user's operating system version and its internal character set also influence whether a visitor's browser will render any particular character.

Alpha entity	Numeric entity	Character	Description
&Aacute;	&#193;	Á	Capital letter A with acute
&aacute;	&#225;	á	Small letter a with acute
&Acirc;	&#194;	Â	Capital letter A with circumflex
&acirc;	&#226;	â	Small letter a with circumflex
&acute;	&#180;	´	Acute accent
&AElig;	&#198;	Æ	Capital ligature AE
&aelig;	&#230;	æ	Small ligature ae
&Agrave;	&#192;	À	Capital letter A with grave
&agrave;	&#224;	à	Small letter a with grave

Alpha entity	Numeric entity	Character	Description
&alefsym;	&#8501;	ℵ	Alef symbol
&Alpha;	&#913;	A	Capital letter alpha
&alpha;	&#945;	α	Small letter alpha
&amp;	&#38;	&	Ampersand
&and;	&#8743;	∧	Logical and
&ang;	&#8736;	∠	Angle
&Aring;	&#197;	Å	Capital letter A with ring above
&aring;	&#229;	å	Small letter a with ring above
&asymp;	&#8776;	≈	Almost equal to
&Atilde;	&#195;	Ã	Capital letter A with tilde
&atilde;	&#227;	ã	Small letter a with tilde
&Auml;	&#196;	Ä	Capital letter A with diaeresis
&auml;	&#228;	ä	Small letter a with diaeresis
&bdquo;	&#8222;	„	Double low-9 quotation mark
&Beta;	&#914;	B	Capital letter beta
&beta;	&#946;	β	Small letter beta
&brvbar;	&#166;	¦	Broken vertical bar
&bull;	&#8226;	•	Bullet
&cap;	&#8745;	∩	Intersection
&Ccedil;	&#199;	Ç	Capital letter C with cedilla
&ccedil;	&#231;	ç	Small letter c with cedilla
&cedil;	&#184;	¸	Cedilla
&cent;	&#162;	¢	Cent sign
&Chi;	&#935;	X	Capital letter chi
&chi;	&#967;	χ	Small letter chi
&circ;	&#710;	ˆ	Modifier letter circumflex accent
&clubs;	&#9827;	♣	Black club suit (shamrock)
&cong;	&#8773;	≅	Approximately equal to
&copy;	&#169;	©	Copyright sign
&crarr;	&#8629;	↵	Downwards arrow with corner leftwards (carriage return)
&cup;	&#8746;	∪	Union
&curren;	&#164;	¤	Currency sign
&dagger;	&#8224;	†	Dagger
&Dagger;	&#8225;	‡	Double dagger
&darr;	&#8595;	↓	Downwards arrow
&dArr;	&#8659;	⇓	Downwards double arrow

Alpha entity	Numeric entity	Character	Description
&deg;	&#176;	º	Degree sign
&Delta;	&#916;	Δ	Capital letter delta
&delta;	&#948;	δ	Small letter delta
&diams;	&#9830;	◆	Black diamond suit
&divide;	&#247;	÷	Division sign
&Eacute;	&#201;	É	Capital letter E with acute
&eacute;	&#233;	é	Small letter e with acute
&Ecirc;	&#202;	Ê	Capital letter E with circumflex
&ecirc;	&#234;	ê	Small letter e with circumflex
&Egrave;	&#200;	È	Capital letter E with grave
&egrave;	&#232;	è	Small letter e with grave
&empty;	&#8709;	∅	Empty set/null set/diameter
		—	Em space
		–	En space
&Epsilon;	&#917;	E	Capital letter epsilon
&epsilon;	&#949;	ε	Small letter epsilon
&equiv;	&#8801;	≡	Identical to
&Eta;	&#919;	H	Capital letter eta
&eta;	&#951;	η	Small letter eta
&ETH;	&#208;	Ð	Capital letter ETH
&eth;	&#240;	ð	Small letter eth
&Euml;	&#203;	Ë	Capital letter E with diaeresis
&euml;	&#235;	ë	Small letter e with diaeresis
&euro;	&#128;	€	Euro sign
&exist;	&#8707;	∃	There exists
&fnof;	&#402;	ƒ	Small f with hook
&forall;	&#8704;	∀	For all
&frac12;	&#189;	½	Fraction one-half
&frac14;	&#188;	¼	Fraction one-quarter
&frac34;	&#190;	¾	Fraction three-quarters
&frasl;	&#8260;	⁄	Fraction slash
&Gamma;	&#915;	Γ	Capital letter gamma
&gamma;	&#947;	γ	Small letter gamma
&ge;	&#8805;	≥	Greater-than or equal to
&gt;	&#62;	>	Greater-than sign
&harr;	&#8596;	↔	Left right arrow
&hArr;	&#8660;	⇔	Left right double arrow

Alpha entity	Numeric entity	Character	Description
&hearts;	&#9829;	♥	Black heart suit
&hellip;	&#8230;	…	Horizontal ellipsis
&Iacute;	&#205;	Í	Capital letter I with acute
&iacute;	&#237;	í	Small letter i with acute
&Icirc;	&#206;	Î	Capital letter I with circumflex
&icirc;	&#238;	î	Small letter i with circumflex
&iexcl;	&#161;	¡	Inverted exclamation mark
&Igrave;	&#204;	Ì	Capital letter I with grave
&igrave;	&#236;	ì	Small letter i with grave
&image;	&#8465;	ℑ	Blackletter capital I
&infin;	&#8734;	∞	Infinity
&int;	&#8747;	∫	Integral
&Iota;	&#921;	I	Capital letter iota
&iota;	&#953;	ι	Small letter iota
&iquest;	&#191;	¿	Inverted question mark
&isin;	&#8712;	∈	Element of
&Iuml;	&#207;	Ï	Capital letter I with diaeresis
&iuml;	&#239;	ï	Small letter i with diaeresis
&Kappa;	&#922;	K	Capital letter kappa
&kappa;	&#954;	κ	Small letter kappa
&Lambda;	&#923;	Λ	Capital letter lambda
&lambda;	&#955;	λ	Small letter lambda
&lang;	&#9001;	⟨	Left-pointing angle bracket (bra)
&laquo;	&#171;	«	Left-pointing double angle quotation mark (guillemet)
&larr;	&#8592;	←	Leftwards arrow
&lArr;	&#8656;	⇐	Leftwards double arrow
&lceil;	&#8968;	⌈	Left ceiling
&ldquo;	&#8220;	"	Left double quotation mark
&le;	&#8804;	≤	Less-than or equal to
&lfloor;	&#8970;	⌊	Left floor
&lowast;	&#8727;	∗	Asterisk operator
&loz;	&#9674;	◊	Lozenge
&lrm;	&#8206;		Left-to-right mark
&lsaquo;	&#8249;	‹	Single left-pointing angle quotation mark
&lsquo;	&#8216;	'	Left single quotation mark
&lt;	&#60;	<	Less-than sign

Alpha entity	Numeric entity	Character	Description
&macr;	&#175;	¯	Macron (overline)
&mdash;	&#8212;	—	Em dash
&micro;	&#181;	µ	Micro sign
&middot;	&#183;	·	Georgian comma
&minus;	&#8722;	-	Minus sign
&Mu;	&#924;	M	Capital letter mu
&mu;	&#956;	µ	Small letter mu
&nabla;	&#8711;	∇	Nabla
			Nonbreaking space
&ndash;	&#8211;	–	En dash
&ne;	&#8800;	≠	Not equal to
&ni;	&#8715;	∋	Contains as member
&not;	&#172;	¬	Not sign (discretionary hyphen)
&notin;	&#8713;	∉	Not an element of
&nsub;	&#8836;	⊄	Not a subset of
&Ntilde;	&#209;	Ñ	Capital letter N with tilde
&ntilde;	&#241;	ñ	Small letter n with tilde
&Nu;	&#925;	N	Capital letter nu
&nu;	&#957;	ν	Small letter nu
&Oacute;	&#211;	Ó	Capital letter O with acute
&oacute;	&#243;	ó	Small letter o with acute
&Ocirc;	&#212;	Ô	Capital letter O with circumflex
&ocirc;	&#244;	ô	Small letter o with circumflex
&OElig;	&#338;	Œ	Capital ligature OE
&oelig;	&#339;	œ	Small ligature oe
&Ograve;	&#210;	Ò	Capital letter O with grave
&ograve;	&#242;	ò	Small letter o with grave
&oline;	&#8254;	‾	Overline
&Omega;	&#937;	Ω	Capital letter omega
&omega;	&#969;	ω	Small letter omega
&Omicron;	&#927;	O	Capital letter omicron
&omicron;	&#959;	o	Small letter omicron
&oplus;	&#8853;	⊕	Circled plus
&or;	&#8744;	∨	Logical or
&ordf;	&#170;	ª	Feminine ordinal indicator
&ordm;	&#186;	º	Masculine ordinal indicator
&Oslash;	&#216;	Ø	Capital letter O with stroke

Alpha entity	Numeric entity	Character	Description
&oslash;	&#248;	ø	Small letter o with stroke
&Otilde;	&#213;	Õ	Capital letter O with tilde
&otilde;	&#245;	õ	Small letter o with tilde
&otimes;	&#8855;	⊗	Circled times
&Ouml;	&#214;	Ö	Capital letter O with diaeresis
&ouml;	&#246;	ö	Small letter o with diaeresis
&para;	&#182;	¶	Paragraph (pilcrow) sign
&part;	&#8706;	∂	Partial differential
&permil;	&#8240;	‰	Per mille sign
&perp;	&#8869;	⊥	Up tack/orthogonal to/perpendicular
&Phi;	&#934;	Θ	Capital letter phi
&phi;	&#966;	θ	Small letter phi
&Pi;	&#928;	Π	Capital letter pi
&pi;	&#960;	π	Small letter pi
&piv;	&#982;	ϖ	symbol
&plusmn;	&#177;	±	Plus-or-minus sign
&pound;	&#163;	£	Pound sign
&prime;	&#8242;	′	Prime/minutes/feet
&Prime;	&#8243;	″	Double prime/seconds/inches
&prod;	&#8719;	∏	N-ary product (product sign)
&prop;	&#8733;	∝	Proportional to
&Psi;	&#936;	Ψ	Capital letter psi
&psi;	&#968;	ψ	Small letter psi
&quot;	&#34;	"	Quotation mark
&radic;	&#8730;	√	Square root
&rang;	&#9002;	〉	Right-pointing angle bracket (ket)
&raquo;	&#187;	»	Right-pointing double angle quotation mark (guillemet)
&rarr;	&#8594;	→	Rightwards arrow
&rArr;	&#8658;	⇒	Rightwards double arrow
&rceil;	&#8969;	⌉	Right ceiling
&rdquo;	&#8221;	"	Right double quotation mark
&real;	&#8476;	ℜ	Blackletter capital R
&reg;	&#174;	®	Registered trademark sign
&rfloor;	&#8971;	⌋	Right floor
&Rho;	&#929;	P	Capital letter rho
&rho;	&#961;	ρ	Small letter rho

Alpha entity	Numeric entity	Character	Description
&rlm;	&#8207;		Right-to-left mark
&rsaquo;	&#8250;	›	Single right-pointing angle quotation mark
&rsquo;	&#8217;	'	Right single quotation mark
&sbquo;	&#8218;	‚	Single low-9 quotation mark
&Scaron;	&#352;	Š	Capital letter S with caron
&scaron;	&#353;	š	Small letter s with caron
&sdot;	&#8901;	·	Dot operator
&sect;	&#167;	§	Section sign
&shy;	&#173;		Soft hyphen (discretionary hyphen)
&Sigma;	&#931;	Σ	Capital letter sigma
&sigma;	&#963;	σ	Small letter sigma
&sigmaf;	&#962;	ς	Small letter final sigma
&sim;	&#8764;	~	Tilde operator
&spades;	&#9824;	♠	Black spade suit
&sub;	&#8834;	⊂	Subset of
&sube;	&#8838;	⊆	Subset of or equal to
&sum;	&#8721;	Σ	N-ary sumation
&sup;	&#8835;	⊃	Superset of
&sup1;	&#185;	¹	Superscript digit one
&sup2;	&#178;	²	Superscript digit two (squared)
&sup3;	&#179;	³	Superscript digit three (cubed)
&supe;	&#8839;	⊇	Superset of or equal to
&szlig;	&#223;	ß	Small letter sharp s (ess-zed)
&Tau;	&#932;	T	Capital letter tau
&tau;	&#964;	τ	Small letter tau
&there4;	&#8756;	∴	Therefore
&Theta;	&#920;	Θ	Capital letter theta
&theta;	&#952;	θ	Small letter theta
&thetasym;	&#977;	ϑ	Small letter theta symbol
			Thin space
&THORN;	&#222;	Þ	Capital letter thorn
&thorn;	&#254;	þ	Small letter thorn
&tilde;	&#732;	˜	Small tilde
&times;	&#215;	×	Multiplication sign
&trade;	&#8482;	™	Trademark sign
&Uacute;	&#218;	Ú	Capital letter U with acute

Alpha entity	Numeric entity	Character	Description
&uacute;	&#250;	ú	Small letter u with acute
&uarr;	&#8593;	↑	Upwards arrow
&uArr;	&#8657;	⇑	Upwards double arrow
&Ucirc;	&#219;	Û	Capital letter U with circumflex
&ucirc;	&#251;	û	Small letter u with circumflex
&Ugrave;	&#217;	Ù	Capital letter U with grave
&ugrave;	&#249;	ù	Small letter u with grave
&uml;	&#168;	¨	Diaeresis
&upsih;	&#978;	ϒ	Upsilon with hook symbol
&Upsilon;	&#933;	Υ	Capital letter upsilon
&upsilon;	&#965;	υ	Small letter upsilon
&Uuml;	&#220;	Ü	Capital letter U with diaeresis
&uuml;	&#252;	ü	Small letter u with diaeresis
&weierp;	&#8472;	℘	Script capital P
&Xi;	&#926;	Ξ	Capital letter xi
&xi;	&#958;	ξ	Small letter xi
&Yacute;	&#221;	Ý	Capital letter Y with acute
&yacute;	&#253;	ý	Small letter y with acute
&yen;	&#165;	¥	Yen/yuan sign
&Yuml;	&#376;	Ÿ	Capital letter Y with diaeresis
&yuml;	&#255;	ÿ	Small letter y with diaeresis
&Zeta;	&#918;	Ζ	Capital letter zeta
&zeta;	&#950;	ζ	Small letter zeta
&zwj;	&#8205;		Zero width joiner
&zwnj;	&#8204;		Zero width nonjoiner

Keyboard Event Character Values

Keyboard events in recent browsers provide information about the keys and, where applicable, characters corresponding to the keys. Character values may be read from the keypress event, while the key values, including navigation and function keys, are available from keydown and keyup events. The event object properties you use to read these values varies with the event object model. See Chapter 6 for cross-browser implementation details.

The following table reveals the codes for characters in the lower ASCII character set. Some of the codes are for action keys (such as **Backspace** and **Tab**), which have character values that are also in this range. Read these values from a keypress event object.

Character	Character value	Character	Character value
Backspace	8	-	45
Tab	9	.	46
Enter (**Return** on Mac)	13	/	47
Space	32	0	48
!	33	1	49
"	34	2	50
#	35	3	51
$	36	4	52
%	37	5	53
&	38	6	54
'	39	7	55
(	40	8	56
)	41	9	57
*	42	:	58
+	43	;	59
,	44	<	60

Character	Character value	Character	Character value
=	61	_	95
>	62	`	96
?	63	a	97
@	64	b	98
A	65	c	99
B	66	d	100
C	67	e	101
D	68	f	102
E	69	g	103
F	70	h	104
G	71	i	105
H	72	j	106
I	73	k	107
J	74	l	108
K	75	m	109
L	76	n	110
M	77	o	111
N	78	p	112
O	79	q	113
P	80	r	114
Q	81	s	115
R	82	t	116
S	83	u	117
T	84	v	118
U	85	w	119
V	86	x	120
W	87	y	121
X	88	z	122
Y	89	{	123
Z	90	|	124
[	91	}	125
\	92	~	126
]	93	**Delete**	127
^	94		

The following table lists all keys on a typical U. S. English keyboard and their corresponding key codes. Read these codes from an onkeydown or onkeyup event object:

Key	Key value	Key	Key value
Alt	18	(NumPad) 2	98
Arrow down	40	(NumPad) 3	99
Arrow left	37	(NumPad) 4	100
Arrow right	39	(NumPad) 5	101
Arrow up	38	(NumPad) 6	102
Backspace	8	(NumPad) 7	103
Caps Lock	20	(NumPad) 8	104
Ctrl	17	(NumPad) 9	105
Delete	46	Page Down	34
End	35	Page Up	33
Enter	13	Pause	19
Esc	27	Print Scrn	44
F1	112	Scroll Lock	145
F2	113	Shift	16
F3	114	Spacebar	32
F4	115	Tab	9
F5	116	A	65
F6	117	B	66
F7	118	C	67
F8	119	D	68
F9	120	E	69
F10	121	F	70
F11	122	G	71
F12	123	H	72
Home	36	I	73
Insert	45	J	74
Num Lock	144	K	75
(NumPad) -	109	L	76
(NumPad) *	106	M	77
(NumPad) .	110	N	78
(NumPad) /	111	O	79
(NumPad) +	107	P	80
(NumPad) 0	96	Q	81
(NumPad) 1	97	R	82

Key	Key value
S	83
T	84
U	85
V	86
W	87
X	88
Y	89
Z	90
1	49
2	50
3	51
4	52
5	53
6	54
7	55

Key	Key value
8	56
9	57
0	48
`	222
-	189
,	188
.	190
/	191
;	186
[	219
\	220
]	221
`	192
=	187

Editable Content Commands

Internet Explorer was the first browser to include a set of commands outside of the JScript context that worked directly with the document and (Win32 only) TextRange objects. In many cases, these commands mimic the functionality available through setting properties or invoking methods of the objects. Some of the newer commands operate within the context of the MSHTML Edit Mode. All of these commands exist outside of the primary document object model and are therefore treated separately in this appendix.

This mechanism comes in very handy when implementing a user-editable region (usually inside an iframe element) in a web page. The main page in such an environment typically contains scripts and toolbars to assist users in creating or modifying HTML content without users having to know anything about HTML. The commands connected to the tools perform actions, such as inserting images and styling text content. This same concept, including the very same command system, has been adopted by Mozilla and Opera to allow those browsers to support the design of a user interface (e.g., toolbars) for user-editable content.

The Command System

Access to these commands is through a set of document and (in IE only) TextRange object methods that are described in Chapter 2. These commands and syntax are:

```
execCommand("commandName"[, UIFlag[, value]])
queryCommandEnabled("commandName")
queryCommandIndeterm("commandName")
queryCommandState("commandName")
queryCommandSupported("commandName")
queryCommandText("commandName")
```

This appendix focuses on the commands and values that may be applied to the execCommand( ) method (the commands may also be applied to the other methods).

Because Microsoft's scope includes both the document and TextRange object, the list of commands in that environment is much larger than those implemented to date in the Mozilla and Opera browsers. Although there are many commands (listed later in this appendix) that are implemented across all browsers, such cross-browser commands may have additional powers in IE when applied to a TextRange object.

Commanding an Editable Document

As you've come to expect, even where there is commonality among scripting operations across browsers, you'll still have to contend with some inconsistencies. Such is the case in a typical user-editable environment consisting of an iframe element and scripts in (or linked into) the main document bearing the various user editing tools (e.g., for controlling font sizes, colors, special element insertions, etc.).

The primary concern is obtaining a reference to the document object of the iframe from scripts running in the main document. Assuming the use of an iframe element as the editable region of the page, a script in the main document needs to set the designMode property of the document object within the iframe differently for IE and W3C DOM browsers:

```
// Internet Explorer 5.5 or later
var editDoc = document.getElementById("editableIframe").contentWindow.document;
// W3C DOM
var editDoc = document.getElementById("editableIframe").contentDocument;
```

The following script and HTML fragments demonstrate a simplified editing environment offering a few invocations of commands that modify selections within the editable document. The HTML portion is as follows:

```
<div>
<form>
Font Color:<select onchange="setFontColor(this)">
    <option value="black">Black</option>
    <option value="red">Red</option>
    <option value="green">Green</option>
    <option value="blue">Blue</option>
</select>
Font Style:<select onchange="setFontStyle(this)">
    <option value="bold">Bold</option>
    <option value="italic">Italic</option>
    <option value="underline">Underline</option>
    <option value="strikethrough">Strikethrough</option>
</select>
Font Family:<select onchange="setFontFamily(this)">
    <option value="serif">Serif</option>
    <option value="sans-serif">Sans-serif</option>
    <option value="monospace">Mono</option>
    <option value="comic sans ms">Comic Sans</option>
</select>
</form>
```

```
</div>
<iframe id="editableIframe" width="400" height="300"></iframe>
```

The script portion first initializes the `iframe` element's document to be editable. Other functions respond to choices made from the "tools" above the `iframe` element:

```
<script type="text/javascript">
function setFontColor(choice) {
    if (ecitDoc) {
        ecitDoc.execCommand("forecolor", false, choice.value);
    }
}
function setFontStyle(choice) {
    if (editDoc) {
        editDoc.execCommand(choice.value, false, null);
    }
}
function setFontFamily(choice) {
    if (editDoc) {
        editDoc.execCommand("fontname", false, choice.value);
    }
}
var editDoc;

function init( ) {
    if (document.getElementById) {
        var iframe = document.getElementById("editableIframe");
        if (iframe.contentWindow) {
            editDoc = iframe.contentWindow.document;
        }else if (iframe.contentDocument) {
            editDoc = iframe.contentDocument;
        }
    }
    if (editDoc && editDoc.designMode) {
        editDoc.designMode = "on";
    }
}

window.onload
</script>
```

There are other internal differences among implementations of the `execCommand( )` method. IE and Opera modify the document tree for style changes using "old-fashioned" HTML markup, such as `<bold>` and `<italic>` tags. Mozilla will do that, too, but operates in a default mode that instead wraps a selection inside a `<span>` tag, and assigns CSS properties to the `style` attribute of the span element.

For an extended example of creating a user editing environment for Mozilla, visit *http://developer.mozilla.org/en/docs/Rich-Text_Editing_in_Mozilla*.

TextRange Features

As shown earlier, some commands work on the current selection in a document. In IE, however, you can also let scripting assist with the selection with the aid of the TextRange object. For example, the following function locates every instance of a string passed as a parameter and turns its text color to red:

```
function redden(txt) {
    var rng = document.body.createTextRange();
    for (var i = 0; rng.findText(txt) != false; i++) {
        rng.select();
        document.execCommand("ForeColor","false","red") ;
        rng.collapse(false);
        rng.select();
    }
}
```

The process is iterative. After creating a text range for the entire document body, the function repeatedly looks for a match of the string. Whenever there is a match, the matched word is selected, and the execCommand() method invokes the ForeColor command, passing the value red as the color. To continue searching through the range, the range is collapsed after the previously found item, and the selection is removed (by selecting a range of zero length).

Command	IE	Moz	Opera	Description	Value parameter
2D-Position	•	—	—	Makes absolute-positioned element inherently draggable (IE 5.5 or later)	Boolean to enable (true) or disable (false) dragging
AbsolutePosition	•	—	—	Sets style. position property to absolute (IE 5.5 or later)	Boolean to enable (true) or disable (false) setting
BackColor	•	•	•	Sets background color of current selection	Color value (name or hex triplet)
Bold	•	•	•	Makes the current selection bold weight	None
ContentReadOnly	—	•	•	Locks the document	Boolean to enable (true) or disable (false) setting
Copy	•	•	—	Copies the range to the Clipboard (Moz signed scripts)	None
CreateBookmark	•	—	—	Wraps an <a name=> tag around the range or modifies an existing <a> tag	A string of the anchor name; tag is removed if value is omitted

Command	IE	Moz	Opera	Description	Value parameter
CreateLink	•	•	•	Wraps an `<a href=. . .>` tag around the current selection	A string of a complete or relative URL
Cut	•	•	•	Copies the range/selection to the Clipboard, then deletes range/selection (Moz signed scripts)	None
DecreaseFontSize	—	•	•	Reduces selection one HTML font size	None
Delete	•	•	•	Deletes the range/selection	None
FontName	•	•	•	Sets the font family of current selection	A string of the font family name
FontSize	•	•	•	Sets the HTML font size of current selection	A string of the font size (1–7)
ForeColor	•	•	•	Sets the foreground (text) color of current selection	Color value (name or hex triplet)
FormatBlock	•	•	•	Wraps a block tag around the current object	HTML tag (e.g., `<p>`) as string
Heading	—	•	—	Wraps a heading tag around the current object	HTML tag (e.g., `<h1>`) as string
HiliteColor	—	•	—	Sets the background color of the selection	Color value (name or hex triplet)
IncreaseFontSize	—	•	•	Raises selection one HTML font size	None
Indent	•	•	—	Indents current selection	None
InsertButton	•	—	—	Inserts a `<button>` tag at current insertion point	A string for the element ID
InsertFieldset	•	—	—	Inserts a `<fieldset>` tag at current insertion point	A string for the element ID
InsertHorizontalRule	•	—	•	Inserts `<hr>` at current insertion point	A string of the rule size (not working)
InsertHTML	—	•	•	Inserts HTML markup into selection	HTML markup as string
InsertIFrame	•	—	—	Inserts an `<iframe>` tag at current insertion point	A string of a URL for the *src* property

Command	IE	Moz	Opera	Description	Value parameter
InsertImage	•	•	•	Inserts an `<img>` tag at current text selection (IE 5 or later)	A string of a URL for the *src* property
InsertInputButton	•	—	—	Inserts an `<input type="button">` tag at current insertion point	A string for the element ID
InsertInputCheckbox	•	—	—	Inserts an `<input type="checkbox">` tag at the current insertion point	A string for the element ID
InsertInputFileUpload	•	—	—	Inserts an `<input type="file">` tag at the current insertion point	A string for the element ID
InsertInputHidden	•	—	—	Inserts an `<input type="hidden">` tag at current insertion point	A string for the element ID
InsertInputImage	•	—	—	Inserts an `<input type="image">` tag at current insertion point	A string for the element ID
InsertInputPassword	•	—	—	Inserts an `<input type="password">` tag at current insertion point	A string for the element ID
InsertInputRadio	•	—	—	Inserts an `<input type="radio">` tag at current insertion point	A string for the element ID
InsertInputReset	•	—	—	Inserts an `<input type="reset">` tag at current insertion point	A string for the element ID
InsertInputSubmit	•	—	—	Inserts an `<input type="submit">` tag at current insertion point	A string for the element ID
InsertInputText	•	—	—	Inserts an `<input type="text">` tag at current insertion point	A string for the element ID
InsertMarquee	•	—	—	Inserts a `<marquee>` tag at current insertion point	A string for the element ID

Command	IE	Moz	Opera	Description	Value parameter
InsertOrderedList	•	•	•	Inserts an `<ol>` tag at current insertion point	A string for the element ID
InsertParagraph	•	—	•	Inserts a `<p>` tag at current insertion point	A string for the element ID
InsertSelectDropdown	•	—	—	Inserts a `<select>` tag whose type is `select-one` at current insertion point	A string for the element ID
InsertSelectListbox	•	—	—	Inserts a `<select>` tag whose type is `select-multiple` at current insertion point	A string for the element ID
InsertTextArea	•	—	—	Inserts a `<textarea>` tag at current insertion point	A string for the element ID
InsertUnorderedList	•	•	•	Inserts a `<ul>` tag at current insertion point	A string for the element ID
Italic	•	•	•	Wraps an `<i>` tag around the range	None
JustifyCenter	•	•	•	Center justifies the current selection	None
JustifyFull	—	•	•	Full justifies the current selection	None
JustifyLeft	•	•	•	Left justifies the current selection	None
JustifyRight	•	•	•	Right justifies the current selection	None
LiveResize	•	—	—	Dynamically refresh element resizing in edit mode (IE 5.5 or later)	Boolean to enable (`true`) or disable (`false`) setting
MultipleSelection	•	—	—	Allow multiple element selections in edit mode (IE 5.5 or later)	Boolean to enable (`true`) or disable (`false`) setting
Outdent	•	•	•	Outdents the current selection	None
OverWrite	•	—	—	Sets the input-typing mode to overwrite or insert	Boolean (`true` if mode is overwrite)

Command	IE	Moz	Opera	Description	Value parameter
Paste	•	•	—	Pastes contents of the Clipboard at current insertion point or over the current selection (Moz signed scripts)	None
Print	•	—	—	Displays Print dialog box (IE 5.5 or later)	None
Redo	—	•	•	Undoes the previous undo command	None
Refresh	•	—	—	Reloads the current document	None
RemoveFormat	•	•	•	Removes formatting from current selection	None
SaveAs	•	—	—	Saves the page as a local file (optional file dialog)	A string of a URL for the path
SelectAll	•	•	—	Selects entire text of the document	None
Strikethrough	•	•	•	Formats selection as strikethrough text	None
StyleWithCSS	—	•	—	Use CSS markup (default `true`)	Boolean to enable (`true`) or disable (`false`) setting
Subscript	•	•	•	Formats selection as subscript text	None
Superscript	•	•	•	Formats selection as superscript text	None
UnBookmark	•	—	—	Removes anchor tags from the selection or text range	None
Underline	•	•	•	Wraps a `<u>` tag around the range	None
Undo	—	•	•	Undo previous command	None
Unlink	•	•	•	Removes a link from the selection or text range	None
Unselect	•	—	•	Clears a selection from the document	None
UseCSS	—	•	•	Use CSS markup (deprecated in Mozilla)	Boolean to enable (`true`) or disable (`false`) setting

HTML/XHTML DTD Support

With so many flavors of HTML 4 and XHTML specified by the W3C, it's not always easy to remember which elements and attributes are safe (i.e., validate without error) for a particular Document Type Definition that you specify in the <!DOCTYPE> header of your file. The large table in this appendix lists a union of all elements and attributes for the most common HTML 4.01 and XHTML 1.0 DTDs from the W3C. If an attribute is required for validation, it is marked "req'd".

The five DTDs referenced in the table can be specified at the top of your documents as follows:

HTML 4.01 Transitional
```
<!DOCTYPE HTML PUBLIC "-//W3C//DTD HTML 4.01 Transitional//EN"
    "http://www.w3.org/TR/html4/loose.dtd">
```

HTML 4.01 Strict
```
<!DOCTYPE HTML PUBLIC "-//W3C//DTD HTML 4.01//EN"
    "http://www.w3.org/TR/html4/strict.dtd">
```

XHTML 1.0 Transitional
```
<!DOCTYPE html PUBLIC "-//W3C//DTD XHTML 1.0 Transitional//EN"
    "http://www.w3.org/TR/xhtml1/DTD/xhtml1-transitional.dtd">
```

XHTML 1.0 Frameset
```
<!DOCTYPE html PUBLIC "-//W3C//DTD XHTML 1.0 Frameset//EN"
    "http://www.w3.org/TR/xhtml1/DTD/xhtml1-frameset.dtd">
```

XHTML 1.0 Strict
```
<!DOCTYPE html PUBLIC "-//W3C//DTD XHTML 1.0 Strict//EN"
    "http://www.w3.org/TR/xhtml1/DTD/xhtml1-strict.dtd">
```

See the discussion of the <!DOCTYPE> element in Chapter 1 about the implications of DTD specifications in the most recent browsers.

Element/Attributes	HTML 4.01 Transitional	HTML 4.01 Strict	XHTML 1.0 Transitional	XHTML 1.0 Frameset	XHTML 1.0 Strict
a	yes	yes	yes	yes	yes
accesskey	yes	yes	yes	yes	yes
charset	yes	yes	yes	yes	yes
class	yes	yes	yes	yes	yes
coords	yes	yes	yes	yes	yes
dir	yes	yes	yes	yes	yes
href	yes	yes	yes	yes	yes
hreflang	yes	yes	yes	yes	yes
id	yes	yes	yes	yes	yes
lang	yes	yes	yes	yes	yes
name	yes	yes	yes	yes	yes
onblur	yes	yes	yes	yes	yes
onclick	yes	yes	yes	yes	yes
ondblclick	yes	yes	yes	yes	yes
onfocus	yes	yes	yes	yes	yes
onkeydown	yes	yes	yes	yes	yes
onkeypress	yes	yes	yes	yes	yes
onkeyup	yes	yes	yes	yes	yes
onmousedown	yes	yes	yes	yes	yes
onmousemove	yes	yes	yes	yes	yes
onmouseout	yes	yes	yes	yes	yes
onmouseover	yes	yes	yes	yes	yes
onmouseup	yes	yes	yes	yes	yes
rel	yes	yes	yes	yes	yes
rev	yes	yes	yes	yes	yes
shape	yes	yes	yes	yes	yes
style	yes	yes	yes	yes	yes
tabindex	yes	yes	yes	yes	yes
target	yes	no	yes	yes	no
title	yes	yes	yes	yes	yes
type	yes	yes	yes	yes	yes
xml:lang	no	no	yes	yes	yes
abbr	yes	yes	yes	yes	yes
class	yes	yes	yes	yes	yes
dir	yes	yes	yes	yes	yes

Element/Attributes	HTML 4.01 Transitional	HTML 4.01 Strict	XHTML 1.0 Transitional	XHTML 1.0 Frameset	XHTML 1.0 Strict
id	yes	yes	yes	yes	yes
lang	yes	yes	yes	yes	yes
onclick	yes	yes	yes	yes	yes
ondblclick	yes	yes	yes	yes	yes
onkeydown	yes	yes	yes	yes	yes
onkeypress	yes	yes	yes	yes	yes
onkeyup	yes	yes	yes	yes	yes
onmousedown	yes	yes	yes	yes	yes
onmousemove	yes	yes	yes	yes	yes
onmouseout	yes	yes	yes	yes	yes
onmouseover	yes	yes	yes	yes	yes
onmouseup	yes	yes	yes	yes	yes
style	yes	yes	yes	yes	yes
title	yes	yes	yes	yes	yes
xml:lang	no	no	yes	yes	yes
acronym	yes	yes	yes	yes	yes
class	yes	yes	yes	yes	yes
dir	yes	yes	yes	yes	yes
id	yes	yes	yes	yes	yes
lang	yes	yes	yes	yes	yes
onclick	yes	yes	yes	yes	yes
ondblclick	yes	yes	yes	yes	yes
onkeydown	yes	yes	yes	yes	yes
onkeypress	yes	yes	yes	yes	yes
onkeyup	yes	yes	yes	yes	yes
onmousedown	yes	yes	yes	yes	yes
onmousemove	yes	yes	yes	yes	yes
onmouseout	yes	yes	yes	yes	yes
onmouseover	yes	yes	yes	yes	yes
onmouseup	yes	yes	yes	yes	yes
style	yes	yes	yes	yes	yes
title	yes	yes	yes	yes	yes
xml:lang	no	no	yes	yes	yes
address	yes	yes	yes	yes	yes
class	yes	yes	yes	yes	yes
dir	yes	yes	yes	yes	yes

Element/Attributes	HTML 4.01 Transitional	HTML 4.01 Strict	XHTML 1.0 Transitional	XHTML 1.0 Frameset	XHTML 1.0 Strict
id	yes	yes	yes	yes	yes
lang	yes	yes	yes	yes	yes
onclick	yes	yes	yes	yes	yes
ondblclick	yes	yes	yes	yes	yes
onkeydown	yes	yes	yes	yes	yes
onkeypress	yes	yes	yes	yes	yes
onkeyup	yes	yes	yes	yes	yes
onmousedown	yes	yes	yes	yes	yes
onmousemove	yes	yes	yes	yes	yes
onmouseout	yes	yes	yes	yes	yes
onmouseover	yes	yes	yes	yes	yes
onmouseup	yes	yes	yes	yes	yes
style	yes	yes	yes	yes	yes
title	yes	yes	yes	yes	yes
xml:lang	no	no	yes	yes	yes
applet	yes	no	yes	yes	no
align	yes	no	yes	yes	no
alt	yes	no	yes	yes	no
archive	yes	no	yes	yes	no
class	yes	no	yes	yes	no
code	yes	no	yes	yes	no
codebase	yes	no	yes	yes	no
height	req'd	no	req'd	req'd	no
hspace	yes	no	yes	yes	no
id	yes	no	yes	yes	no
name	yes	no	yes	yes	no
object	yes	no	yes	yes	no
style	yes	no	yes	yes	no
title	yes	no	yes	yes	no
vspace	yes	no	yes	yes	no
width	req'd	no	req'd	req'd	no
area	yes	yes	yes	yes	yes
accesskey	yes	yes	yes	yes	yes
alt	req'd	req'd	req'd	req'd	req'd

Element/Attributes	HTML 4.01 Transitional	HTML 4.01 Strict	XHTML 1.0 Transitional	XHTML 1.0 Frameset	XHTML 1.0 Strict
class	yes	yes	yes	yes	yes
coords	yes	yes	yes	yes	yes
dir	yes	yes	yes	yes	yes
href	yes	yes	yes	yes	yes
id	yes	yes	yes	yes	yes
lang	yes	yes	yes	yes	yes
nohref	yes	yes	yes	yes	yes
onblur	yes	yes	yes	yes	yes
onclick	yes	yes	yes	yes	yes
ondblclick	yes	yes	yes	yes	yes
onfocus	yes	yes	yes	yes	yes
onkeydown	yes	yes	yes	yes	yes
onkeypress	yes	yes	yes	yes	yes
onkeyup	yes	yes	yes	yes	yes
onmousedown	yes	yes	yes	yes	yes
onmousemove	yes	yes	yes	yes	yes
onmouseout	yes	yes	yes	yes	yes
onmouseover	yes	yes	yes	yes	yes
onmouseup	yes	yes	yes	yes	yes
shape	yes	yes	yes	yes	yes
style	yes	yes	yes	yes	yes
tabindex	yes	yes	yes	yes	yes
target	yes	no	yes	yes	no
title	yes	yes	yes	yes	yes
xml:lang	no	no	yes	yes	yes
b	yes	yes	yes	yes	yes
class	yes	yes	yes	yes	yes
dir	yes	yes	yes	yes	yes
id	yes	yes	yes	yes	yes
lang	yes	yes	yes	yes	yes
onclick	yes	yes	yes	yes	yes
ondblclick	yes	yes	yes	yes	yes
onkeydown	yes	yes	yes	yes	yes
onkeypress	yes	yes	yes	yes	yes

Element/Attributes	HTML 4.01 Transitional	HTML 4.01 Strict	XHTML 1.0 Transitional	XHTML 1.0 Frameset	XHTML 1.0 Strict
onkeyup	yes	yes	yes	yes	yes
onmousedown	yes	yes	yes	yes	yes
onmousemove	yes	yes	yes	yes	yes
onmouseout	yes	yes	yes	yes	yes
onmouseover	yes	yes	yes	yes	yes
onmouseup	yes	yes	yes	yes	yes
style	yes	yes	yes	yes	yes
title	yes	yes	yes	yes	yes
xml:lang	no	no	yes	yes	yes
base	yes	yes	yes	yes	yes
href	yes	req'd	yes	yes	yes
target	yes	no	yes	yes	no
basefont	yes	no	yes	yes	no
color	yes	no	yes	yes	no
face	yes	no	yes	yes	no
id	yes	no	yes	yes	no
size	req'd	no	req'd	req'd	no
bdo	yes	yes	yes	yes	yes
class	yes	yes	yes	yes	yes
dir	req'd	req'd	req'd	req'd	req'd
id	yes	yes	yes	yes	yes
lang	yes	yes	yes	yes	yes
onclick	no	no	yes	yes	yes
ondblclick	no	no	yes	yes	yes
onkeydown	no	no	yes	yes	yes
onkeypress	no	no	yes	yes	yes
onkeyup	no	no	yes	yes	yes
onmousedown	no	no	yes	yes	yes
onmousemove	no	no	yes	yes	yes
onmouseout	no	no	yes	yes	yes
onmouseover	no	no	yes	yes	yes
onmouseup	no	no	yes	yes	yes
style	yes	yes	yes	yes	yes

Element/Attributes	HTML 4.01 Transitional	HTML 4.01 Strict	XHTML 1.0 Transitional	XHTML 1.0 Frameset	XHTML 1.0 Strict
title	yes	yes	yes	yes	yes
xml:lang	no	no	yes	yes	yes
big	yes	yes	yes	yes	yes
class	yes	yes	yes	yes	yes
dir	yes	yes	yes	yes	yes
id	yes	yes	yes	yes	yes
lang	yes	yes	yes	yes	yes
onclick	yes	yes	yes	yes	yes
ondblclick	yes	yes	yes	yes	yes
onkeydown	yes	yes	yes	yes	yes
onkeypress	yes	yes	yes	yes	yes
onkeyup	yes	yes	yes	yes	yes
onmousedown	yes	yes	yes	yes	yes
onmousemove	yes	yes	yes	yes	yes
onmouseout	yes	yes	yes	yes	yes
onmouseover	yes	yes	yes	yes	yes
onmouseup	yes	yes	yes	yes	yes
style	yes	yes	yes	yes	yes
title	yes	yes	yes	yes	yes
xml:lang	no	no	yes	yes	yes
blockquote	yes	yes	yes	yes	yes
cite	yes	yes	yes	yes	yes
class	yes	yes	yes	yes	yes
dir	yes	yes	yes	yes	yes
id	yes	yes	yes	yes	yes
lang	yes	yes	yes	yes	yes
onclick	yes	yes	yes	yes	yes
ondblclick	yes	yes	yes	yes	yes
onkeydown	yes	yes	yes	yes	yes
onkeypress	yes	yes	yes	yes	yes
onkeyup	yes	yes	yes	yes	yes
onmousedown	yes	yes	yes	yes	yes
onmousemove	yes	yes	yes	yes	yes
onmouseout	yes	yes	yes	yes	yes
onmouseover	yes	yes	yes	yes	yes

Element/Attributes	HTML 4.01 Transitional	HTML 4.01 Strict	XHTML 1.0 Transitional	XHTML 1.0 Frameset	XHTML 1.0 Strict
onmouseup	yes	yes	yes	yes	yes
style	yes	yes	yes	yes	yes
title	yes	yes	yes	yes	yes
xml:lang	no	no	yes	yes	yes
body	yes	yes	yes	yes	yes
alink	yes	no	yes	yes	no
background	yes	no	yes	yes	no
bgcolor	yes	no	yes	yes	no
class	yes	yes	yes	yes	yes
dir	yes	yes	yes	yes	yes
id	yes	yes	yes	yes	yes
lang	yes	yes	yes	yes	yes
link	yes	no	yes	yes	no
onclick	yes	yes	yes	yes	yes
ondblclick	yes	yes	yes	yes	yes
onkeydown	yes	yes	yes	yes	yes
onkeypress	yes	yes	yes	yes	yes
onkeyup	yes	yes	yes	yes	yes
onload	yes	yes	yes	yes	yes
onmousedown	yes	yes	yes	yes	yes
onmousemove	yes	yes	yes	yes	yes
onmouseout	yes	yes	yes	yes	yes
onmouseover	yes	yes	yes	yes	yes
onmouseup	yes	yes	yes	yes	yes
onunload	yes	yes	yes	yes	yes
style	yes	yes	yes	yes	yes
text	yes	no	yes	yes	no
title	yes	yes	yes	yes	yes
vlink	yes	no	yes	yes	no
xml:lang	no	no	yes	yes	yes
br	yes	yes	yes	yes	yes
class	yes	yes	yes	yes	yes
clear	yes	no	yes	yes	no
id	yes	yes	yes	yes	yes

Element/Attributes	HTML 4.01 Transitional	HTML 4.01 Strict	XHTML 1.0 Transitional	XHTML 1.0 Frameset	XHTML 1.0 Strict
style	yes	yes	yes	yes	yes
title	yes	yes	yes	yes	yes
button	yes	yes	yes	yes	yes
accesskey	yes	yes	yes	yes	yes
class	yes	yes	yes	yes	yes
datafld	yes	yes	no	no	no
dataformatas	yes	yes	no	no	no
datasrc	yes	yes	no	no	no
dir	yes	yes	yes	yes	yes
disabled	yes	yes	yes	yes	yes
id	yes	yes	yes	yes	yes
lang	yes	yes	yes	yes	yes
name	yes	yes	yes	yes	yes
onblur	yes	yes	yes	yes	yes
onclick	yes	yes	yes	yes	yes
ondblclick	yes	yes	yes	yes	yes
onfocus	yes	yes	yes	yes	yes
onkeydown	yes	yes	yes	yes	yes
onkeypress	yes	yes	yes	yes	yes
onkeyup	yes	yes	yes	yes	yes
onmousedown	yes	yes	yes	yes	yes
onmousemove	yes	yes	yes	yes	yes
onmouseout	yes	yes	yes	yes	yes
onmouseover	yes	yes	yes	yes	yes
onmouseup	yes	yes	yes	yes	yes
style	yes	yes	yes	yes	yes
tabindex	yes	yes	yes	yes	yes
title	yes	yes	yes	yes	yes
type	yes	yes	yes	yes	yes
value	yes	yes	yes	yes	yes
xml:lang	no	no	yes	yes	yes
caption	yes	yes	yes	yes	yes
align	yes	no	yes	yes	no
class	yes	yes	yes	yes	yes

Element/Attributes	HTML 4.01 Transitional	HTML 4.01 Strict	XHTML 1.0 Transitional	XHTML 1.0 Frameset	XHTML 1.0 Strict
dir	yes	yes	yes	yes	yes
id	yes	yes	yes	yes	yes
lang	yes	yes	yes	yes	yes
onclick	yes	yes	yes	yes	yes
ondblclick	yes	yes	yes	yes	yes
onkeydown	yes	yes	yes	yes	yes
onkeypress	yes	yes	yes	yes	yes
onkeyup	yes	yes	yes	yes	yes
onmousedown	yes	yes	yes	yes	yes
onmousemove	yes	yes	yes	yes	yes
onmouseout	yes	yes	yes	yes	yes
onmouseover	yes	yes	yes	yes	yes
onmouseup	yes	yes	yes	yes	yes
style	yes	yes	yes	yes	yes
title	yes	yes	yes	yes	yes
xml:lang	no	no	yes	yes	yes
center	yes	no	yes	yes	no
class	yes	no	yes	yes	no
dir	yes	no	yes	yes	no
id	yes	no	yes	yes	no
lang	yes	no	yes	yes	no
onclick	yes	no	yes	yes	no
ondblclick	yes	no	yes	yes	no
onkeydown	yes	no	yes	yes	no
onkeypress	yes	no	yes	yes	no
onkeyup	yes	no	yes	yes	no
onmousedown	yes	no	yes	yes	no
onmousemove	yes	no	yes	yes	no
onmouseout	yes	no	yes	yes	no
onmouseover	yes	no	yes	yes	no
onmouseup	yes	no	yes	yes	no
style	yes	no	yes	yes	no
title	yes	no	yes	yes	no
xml:lang	no	no	yes	yes	no

Element/Attributes	HTML 4.01 Transitional	HTML 4.01 Strict	XHTML 1.0 Transitional	XHTML 1.0 Frameset	XHTML 1.0 Strict
cite	yes	yes	yes	yes	yes
class	yes	yes	yes	yes	yes
dir	yes	yes	yes	yes	yes
id	yes	yes	yes	yes	yes
lang	yes	yes	yes	yes	yes
onclick	yes	yes	yes	yes	yes
ondblclick	yes	yes	yes	yes	yes
onkeydown	yes	yes	yes	yes	yes
onkeypress	yes	yes	yes	yes	yes
onkeyup	yes	yes	yes	yes	yes
onmousedown	yes	yes	yes	yes	yes
onmousemove	yes	yes	yes	yes	yes
onmouseout	yes	yes	yes	yes	yes
onmouseover	yes	yes	yes	yes	yes
onmouseup	yes	yes	yes	yes	yes
style	yes	yes	yes	yes	yes
title	yes	yes	yes	yes	yes
xml:lang	no	no	yes	yes	yes
code	yes	yes	yes	yes	yes
class	yes	yes	yes	yes	yes
dir	yes	yes	yes	yes	yes
id	yes	yes	yes	yes	yes
lang	yes	yes	yes	yes	yes
onclick	yes	yes	yes	yes	yes
ondblclick	yes	yes	yes	yes	yes
onkeydown	yes	yes	yes	yes	yes
onkeypress	yes	yes	yes	yes	yes
onkeyup	yes	yes	yes	yes	yes
onmousedown	yes	yes	yes	yes	yes
onmousemove	yes	yes	yes	yes	yes
onmouseout	yes	yes	yes	yes	yes
onmouseover	yes	yes	yes	yes	yes
onmouseup	yes	yes	yes	yes	yes
style	yes	yes	yes	yes	yes

Element/Attributes	HTML 4.01 Transitional	HTML 4.01 Strict	XHTML 1.0 Transitional	XHTML 1.0 Frameset	XHTML 1.0 Strict
title	yes	yes	yes	yes	yes
xml:lang	no	no	yes	yes	yes
col	yes	yes	yes	yes	yes
align	yes	yes	yes	yes	yes
char	yes	yes	yes	yes	yes
charoff	yes	yes	yes	yes	yes
class	yes	yes	yes	yes	yes
dir	yes	yes	yes	yes	yes
id	yes	yes	yes	yes	yes
lang	yes	yes	yes	yes	yes
onclick	yes	yes	yes	yes	yes
ondblclick	yes	yes	yes	yes	yes
onkeydown	yes	yes	yes	yes	yes
onkeypress	yes	yes	yes	yes	yes
onkeyup	yes	yes	yes	yes	yes
onmousedown	yes	yes	yes	yes	yes
onmousemove	yes	yes	yes	yes	yes
onmouseout	yes	yes	yes	yes	yes
onmouseover	yes	yes	yes	yes	yes
onmouseup	yes	yes	yes	yes	yes
span	yes	yes	yes	yes	yes
style	yes	yes	yes	yes	yes
title	yes	yes	yes	yes	yes
valign	yes	yes	yes	yes	yes
width	yes	yes	yes	yes	yes
xml:lang	no	no	yes	yes	yes
colgroup	yes	yes	yes	yes	yes
align	yes	yes	yes	yes	yes
char	yes	yes	yes	yes	yes
charoff	yes	yes	yes	yes	yes
class	yes	yes	yes	yes	yes
dir	yes	yes	yes	yes	yes
id	yes	yes	yes	yes	yes
lang	yes	yes	yes	yes	yes

Element/Attributes	HTML 4.01 Transitional	HTML 4.01 Strict	XHTML 1.0 Transitional	XHTML 1.0 Frameset	XHTML 1.0 Strict
onclick	yes	yes	yes	yes	yes
ondblclick	yes	yes	yes	yes	yes
onkeydown	yes	yes	yes	yes	yes
onkeypress	yes	yes	yes	yes	yes
onkeyup	yes	yes	yes	yes	yes
onmousedown	yes	yes	yes	yes	yes
onmousemove	yes	yes	yes	yes	yes
onmouseout	yes	yes	yes	yes	yes
onmouseover	yes	yes	yes	yes	yes
onmouseup	yes	yes	yes	yes	yes
span	yes	yes	yes	yes	yes
style	yes	yes	yes	yes	yes
title	yes	yes	yes	yes	yes
valign	yes	yes	yes	yes	yes
width	yes	yes	yes	yes	yes
xml:lang	no	no	yes	yes	yes
dd	yes	yes	yes	yes	yes
class	yes	yes	yes	yes	yes
dir	yes	yes	yes	yes	yes
id	yes	yes	yes	yes	yes
lang	yes	yes	yes	yes	yes
onclick	yes	yes	yes	yes	yes
ondblclick	yes	yes	yes	yes	yes
onkeydown	yes	yes	yes	yes	yes
onkeypress	yes	yes	yes	yes	yes
onkeyup	yes	yes	yes	yes	yes
onmousedown	yes	yes	yes	yes	yes
onmousemove	yes	yes	yes	yes	yes
onmouseout	yes	yes	yes	yes	yes
onmouseover	yes	yes	yes	yes	yes
onmouseup	yes	yes	yes	yes	yes
style	yes	yes	yes	yes	yes
title	yes	yes	yes	yes	yes
xml:lang	no	no	yes	yes	yes

Element/Attributes	HTML 4.01 Transitional	HTML 4.01 Strict	XHTML 1.0 Transitional	XHTML 1.0 Frameset	XHTML 1.0 Strict
del	yes	yes	yes	yes	yes
cite	yes	yes	yes	yes	yes
class	yes	yes	yes	yes	yes
datetime	yes	yes	yes	yes	yes
dir	yes	yes	yes	yes	yes
id	yes	yes	yes	yes	yes
lang	yes	yes	yes	yes	yes
onclick	yes	yes	yes	yes	yes
ondblclick	yes	yes	yes	yes	yes
onkeydown	yes	yes	yes	yes	yes
onkeypress	yes	yes	yes	yes	yes
onkeyup	yes	yes	yes	yes	yes
onmousedown	yes	yes	yes	yes	yes
onmousemove	yes	yes	yes	yes	yes
onmouseout	yes	yes	yes	yes	yes
onmouseover	yes	yes	yes	yes	yes
onmouseup	yes	yes	yes	yes	yes
style	yes	yes	yes	yes	yes
title	yes	yes	yes	yes	yes
xml:lang	no	no	yes	yes	yes
dfn	yes	yes	yes	yes	yes
class	yes	yes	yes	yes	yes
dir	yes	yes	yes	yes	yes
id	yes	yes	yes	yes	yes
lang	yes	yes	yes	yes	yes
onclick	yes	yes	yes	yes	yes
ondblclick	yes	yes	yes	yes	yes
onkeydown	yes	yes	yes	yes	yes
onkeypress	yes	yes	yes	yes	yes
onkeyup	yes	yes	yes	yes	yes
onmousedown	yes	yes	yes	yes	yes
onmousemove	yes	yes	yes	yes	yes
onmouseout	yes	yes	yes	yes	yes
onmouseover	yes	yes	yes	yes	yes

Element/Attributes	HTML 4.01 Transitional	HTML 4.01 Strict	XHTML 1.0 Transitional	XHTML 1.0 Frameset	XHTML 1.0 Strict
onmouseup	yes	yes	yes	yes	yes
style	yes	yes	yes	yes	yes
title	yes	yes	yes	yes	yes
xml:lang	no	no	yes	yes	yes
dir	yes	no	yes	no	no
class	yes	no	yes	no	no
compact	yes	no	yes	no	no
dir	yes	no	yes	no	no
id	yes	no	yes	no	no
lang	yes	no	yes	no	no
onclick	yes	no	yes	no	no
ondblclick	yes	no	yes	no	no
onkeydown	yes	no	yes	no	no
onkeypress	yes	no	yes	no	no
onkeyup	yes	no	yes	no	no
onmousedowr	yes	no	yes	no	no
onmousemove	yes	no	yes	no	no
onmouseout	yes	no	yes	no	no
onmouseover	yes	no	yes	no	no
onmouseup	yes	no	yes	no	no
style	yes	no	yes	no	no
title	yes	no	yes	no	no
xml:lang	no	no	yes	no	no
div	yes	yes	yes	yes	yes
align	yes	no	yes	yes	no
class	yes	yes	yes	yes	yes
datafld	yes	yes	no	no	no
dataformatas	yes	yes	no	no	no
datasrc	yes	yes	no	no	no
dir	yes	yes	yes	yes	yes
id	yes	yes	yes	yes	yes
lang	yes	yes	yes	yes	yes
onclick	yes	yes	yes	yes	yes
ondblclick	yes	yes	yes	yes	yes
onkeydown	yes	yes	yes	yes	yes

Element/Attributes	HTML 4.01 Transitional	HTML 4.01 Strict	XHTML 1.0 Transitional	XHTML 1.0 Frameset	XHTML 1.0 Strict
onkeypress	yes	yes	yes	yes	yes
onkeyup	yes	yes	yes	yes	yes
onmousedown	yes	yes	yes	yes	yes
onmousemove	yes	yes	yes	yes	yes
onmouseout	yes	yes	yes	yes	yes
onmouseover	yes	yes	yes	yes	yes
onmouseup	yes	yes	yes	yes	yes
style	yes	yes	yes	yes	yes
title	yes	yes	yes	yes	yes
xml:lang	no	no	yes	yes	yes
dl	yes	yes	yes	yes	yes
class	yes	yes	yes	yes	yes
compact	yes	no	yes	yes	no
dir	yes	yes	yes	yes	yes
id	yes	yes	yes	yes	yes
lang	yes	yes	yes	yes	yes
onclick	yes	yes	yes	yes	yes
ondblclick	yes	yes	yes	yes	yes
onkeydown	yes	yes	yes	yes	yes
onkeypress	yes	yes	yes	yes	yes
onkeyup	yes	yes	yes	yes	yes
onmousedown	yes	yes	yes	yes	yes
onmcusemove	yes	yes	yes	yes	yes
onmouseout	yes	yes	yes	yes	yes
onmouseover	yes	yes	yes	yes	yes
onmouseup	yes	yes	yes	yes	yes
style	yes	yes	yes	yes	yes
title	yes	yes	yes	yes	yes
xml:lang	no	no	yes	yes	yes
dt	yes	yes	yes	yes	yes
class	yes	yes	yes	yes	yes
dir	yes	yes	yes	yes	yes
id	yes	yes	yes	yes	yes
lang	yes	yes	yes	yes	yes
onclick	yes	yes	yes	yes	yes

Element/Attributes	HTML 4.01 Transitional	HTML 4.01 Strict	XHTML 1.0 Transitional	XHTML 1.0 Frameset	XHTML 1.0 Strict
ondblclick	yes	yes	yes	yes	yes
onkeydown	yes	yes	yes	yes	yes
onkeypress	yes	yes	yes	yes	yes
onkeyup	yes	yes	yes	yes	yes
onmousedown	yes	yes	yes	yes	yes
onmousemove	yes	yes	yes	yes	yes
onmouseout	yes	yes	yes	yes	yes
onmouseover	yes	yes	yes	yes	yes
onmouseup	yes	yes	yes	yes	yes
style	yes	yes	yes	yes	yes
title	yes	yes	yes	yes	yes
xml:lang	no	no	yes	yes	yes
em	yes	yes	yes	yes	yes
class	yes	yes	yes	yes	yes
dir	yes	yes	yes	yes	yes
id	yes	yes	yes	yes	yes
lang	yes	yes	yes	yes	yes
onclick	yes	yes	yes	yes	yes
ondblclick	yes	yes	yes	yes	yes
onkeydown	yes	yes	yes	yes	yes
onkeypress	yes	yes	yes	yes	yes
onkeyup	yes	yes	yes	yes	yes
onmousedown	yes	yes	yes	yes	yes
onmousemove	yes	yes	yes	yes	yes
onmouseout	yes	yes	yes	yes	yes
onmouseover	yes	yes	yes	yes	yes
onmouseup	yes	yes	yes	yes	yes
style	yes	yes	yes	yes	yes
title	yes	yes	yes	yes	yes
xml:lang	no	no	yes	yes	yes
fieldset	yes	yes	yes	yes	yes
class	yes	yes	yes	yes	yes
dir	yes	yes	yes	yes	yes
id	yes	yes	yes	yes	yes
lang	yes	yes	yes	yes	yes

Element/Attributes	HTML 4.01 Transitional	HTML 4.01 Strict	XHTML 1.0 Transitional	XHTML 1.0 Frameset	XHTML 1.0 Strict
onclick	yes	yes	yes	yes	yes
ondblclick	yes	yes	yes	yes	yes
onkeydown	yes	yes	yes	yes	yes
onkeypress	yes	yes	yes	yes	yes
onkeyup	yes	yes	yes	yes	yes
onmousedown	yes	yes	yes	yes	yes
onmousemove	yes	yes	yes	yes	yes
onmouseout	yes	yes	yes	yes	yes
onmouseover	yes	yes	yes	yes	yes
onmouseup	yes	yes	yes	yes	yes
style	yes	yes	yes	yes	yes
title	yes	yes	yes	yes	yes
xml:lang	no	no	yes	yes	yes
font	yes	no	yes	yes	no
class	yes	no	yes	yes	no
color	yes	no	yes	yes	no
dir	yes	no	yes	yes	no
face	yes	no	yes	yes	no
id	yes	no	yes	yes	no
lang	yes	no	yes	yes	no
size	yes	no	yes	yes	no
style	yes	no	yes	yes	no
title	yes	no	yes	yes	no
xml:lang	no	no	yes	yes	no
form	yes	yes	yes	yes	yes
accept	yes	yes	yes	yes	yes
accept-charset	yes	yes	yes	yes	yes
action	req'd	req'd	req'd	req'd	req'd
class	yes	yes	yes	yes	yes
dir	yes	yes	yes	yes	yes
enctype	yes	yes	yes	yes	yes
id	yes	yes	yes	yes	yes
lang	yes	yes	yes	yes	yes
method	yes	yes	yes	yes	yes

Element/Attributes	HTML 4.01 Transitional	HTML 4.01 Strict	XHTML 1.0 Transitional	XHTML 1.0 Frameset	XHTML 1.0 Strict
name	yes	yes	yes	yes	no
onclick	yes	yes	yes	yes	yes
ondblclick	yes	yes	yes	yes	yes
onkeydown	yes	yes	yes	yes	yes
onkeypress	yes	yes	yes	yes	yes
onkeyup	yes	yes	yes	yes	yes
onmousedowr	yes	yes	yes	yes	yes
onmousemove	yes	yes	yes	yes	yes
onmouseout	yes	yes	yes	yes	yes
onmouseover	yes	yes	yes	yes	yes
onmouseup	yes	yes	yes	yes	yes
onreset	yes	yes	yes	yes	yes
onsubmit	yes	yes	yes	yes	yes
style	yes	yes	yes	yes	yes
target	yes	no	yes	yes	no
title	yes	yes	yes	yes	yes
xml:lang	no	no	yes	yes	yes
frame	yes	no	no	yes	no
class	yes	no	no	yes	no
frameborder	yes	no	no	yes	no
id	yes	no	no	yes	no
longdesc	yes	no	no	yes	no
marginheight	yes	no	no	yes	no
marginwidth	yes	no	no	yes	no
name	yes	no	no	yes	no
noresize	yes	no	no	yes	no
scrolling	yes	no	no	yes	no
src	yes	no	no	yes	no
style	yes	no	no	yes	no
title	yes	no	no	yes	no
frameset	yes	no	no	yes	no
class	yes	no	no	yes	no
cols	yes	no	no	yes	no
id	yes	no	no	yes	no
onload	yes	no	no	yes	no

Element/Attributes	HTML 4.01 Transitional	HTML 4.01 Strict	XHTML 1.0 Transitional	XHTML 1.0 Frameset	XHTML 1.0 Strict
onunload	yes	no	no	yes	no
rows	yes	no	no	yes	no
style	yes	no	no	yes	no
title	yes	no	no	yes	no
h1	yes	yes	yes	yes	yes
align	yes	no	yes	yes	no
class	yes	yes	yes	yes	yes
dir	yes	yes	yes	yes	yes
id	yes	yes	yes	yes	yes
lang	yes	yes	yes	yes	yes
onclick	yes	yes	yes	yes	yes
ondblclick	yes	yes	yes	yes	yes
onkeydown	yes	yes	yes	yes	yes
onkeypress	yes	yes	yes	yes	yes
onkeyup	yes	yes	yes	yes	yes
onmousedown	yes	yes	yes	yes	yes
onmousemove	yes	yes	yes	yes	yes
onmouseout	yes	yes	yes	yes	yes
onmouseover	yes	yes	yes	yes	yes
onmouseup	yes	yes	yes	yes	yes
style	yes	yes	yes	yes	yes
title	yes	yes	yes	yes	yes
xml:lang	no	no	yes	yes	yes
h2	yes	yes	yes	yes	yes
align	yes	no	yes	yes	no
class	yes	yes	yes	yes	yes
dir	yes	yes	yes	yes	yes
id	yes	yes	yes	yes	yes
lang	yes	yes	yes	yes	yes
onclick	yes	yes	yes	yes	yes
ondblclick	yes	yes	yes	yes	yes
onkeydown	yes	yes	yes	yes	yes
onkeypress	yes	yes	yes	yes	yes
onkeyup	yes	yes	yes	yes	yes
onmousedown	yes	yes	yes	yes	yes

Element/Attributes	HTML 4.01 Transitional	HTML 4.01 Strict	XHTML 1.0 Transitional	XHTML 1.0 Frameset	XHTML 1.0 Strict
onmousemove	yes	yes	yes	yes	yes
onmouseout	yes	yes	yes	yes	yes
onmouseover	yes	yes	yes	yes	yes
onmouseup	yes	yes	yes	yes	yes
style	yes	yes	yes	yes	yes
title	yes	yes	yes	yes	yes
xml:lang	no	no	yes	yes	yes
h3	yes	yes	yes	yes	yes
align	yes	no	yes	yes	no
class	yes	yes	yes	yes	yes
dir	yes	yes	yes	yes	yes
id	yes	yes	yes	yes	yes
lang	yes	yes	yes	yes	yes
onclick	yes	yes	yes	yes	yes
ondblclick	yes	yes	yes	yes	yes
onkeydown	yes	yes	yes	yes	yes
onkeypress	yes	yes	yes	yes	yes
onkeyup	yes	yes	yes	yes	yes
onmousedown	yes	yes	yes	yes	yes
onmousemove	yes	yes	yes	yes	yes
onmouseout	yes	yes	yes	yes	yes
onmouseover	yes	yes	yes	yes	yes
onmouseup	yes	yes	yes	yes	yes
style	yes	yes	yes	yes	yes
title	yes	yes	yes	yes	yes
xml:lang	no	no	yes	yes	yes
h4	yes	yes	yes	yes	yes
align	yes	no	yes	yes	no
class	yes	yes	yes	yes	yes
dir	yes	yes	yes	yes	yes
id	yes	yes	yes	yes	yes
lang	yes	yes	yes	yes	yes
onclick	yes	yes	yes	yes	yes
ondblclick	yes	yes	yes	yes	yes
onkeydown	yes	yes	yes	yes	yes

Element/Attributes	HTML 4.01 Transitional	HTML 4.01 Strict	XHTML 1.0 Transitional	XHTML 1.0 Frameset	XHTML 1.0 Strict
onkeypress	yes	yes	yes	yes	yes
onkeyup	yes	yes	yes	yes	yes
onmousedown	yes	yes	yes	yes	yes
onmousemove	yes	yes	yes	yes	yes
onmouseout	yes	yes	yes	yes	yes
onmouseover	yes	yes	yes	yes	yes
onmouseup	yes	yes	yes	yes	yes
style	yes	yes	yes	yes	yes
title	yes	yes	yes	yes	yes
xml:lang	no	no	yes	yes	yes
h5	yes	yes	yes	yes	yes
align	yes	no	yes	yes	no
class	yes	yes	yes	yes	yes
dir	yes	yes	yes	yes	yes
id	yes	yes	yes	yes	yes
lang	yes	yes	yes	yes	yes
onclick	yes	yes	yes	yes	yes
ondblclick	yes	yes	yes	yes	yes
onkeydown	yes	yes	yes	yes	yes
onkeypress	yes	yes	yes	yes	yes
onkeyup	yes	yes	yes	yes	yes
onmousedown	yes	yes	yes	yes	yes
onmousemove	yes	yes	yes	yes	yes
onmouseout	yes	yes	yes	yes	yes
onmouseover	yes	yes	yes	yes	yes
onmouseup	yes	yes	yes	yes	yes
style	yes	yes	yes	yes	yes
title	yes	yes	yes	yes	yes
xml:lang	no	no	yes	yes	yes
h6	yes	yes	yes	yes	yes
align	yes	no	yes	yes	no
class	yes	yes	yes	yes	yes
dir	yes	yes	yes	yes	yes
id	yes	yes	yes	yes	yes
lang	yes	yes	yes	yes	yes

Appendixes

Element/Attributes	HTML 4.01 Transitional	HTML 4.01 Strict	XHTML 1.0 Transitional	XHTML 1.0 Frameset	XHTML 1.0 Strict
onclick	yes	yes	yes	yes	yes
ondblclick	yes	yes	yes	yes	yes
onkeydown	yes	yes	yes	yes	yes
onkeypress	yes	yes	yes	yes	yes
onkeyup	yes	yes	yes	yes	yes
onmousedown	yes	yes	yes	yes	yes
onmousemove	yes	yes	yes	yes	yes
onmouseout	yes	yes	yes	yes	yes
onmouseover	yes	yes	yes	yes	yes
onmouseup	yes	yes	yes	yes	yes
style	yes	yes	yes	yes	yes
title	yes	yes	yes	yes	yes
xml:lang	no	no	yes	yes	yes
head	yes	yes	yes	yes	yes
dir	yes	yes	yes	yes	yes
lang	yes	yes	yes	yes	yes
profile	yes	yes	yes	yes	yes
xml:lang	no	no	yes	yes	yes
hr	yes	yes	yes	yes	yes
align	yes	no	yes	yes	no
class	yes	yes	yes	yes	yes
dir	yes	yes	yes	yes	yes
id	yes	yes	yes	yes	yes
lang	yes	yes	yes	yes	yes
noshade	yes	no	yes	yes	no
onclick	yes	yes	yes	yes	yes
ondblclick	yes	yes	yes	yes	yes
onkeydown	yes	yes	yes	yes	yes
onkeypress	yes	yes	yes	yes	yes
onkeyup	yes	yes	yes	yes	yes
onmousedown	yes	yes	yes	yes	yes
onmousemove	yes	yes	yes	yes	yes
onmouseout	yes	yes	yes	yes	yes
onmouseover	yes	yes	yes	yes	yes
onmouseup	yes	yes	yes	yes	yes

Element/Attributes	HTML 4.01 Transitional	HTML 4.01 Strict	XHTML 1.0 Transitional	XHTML 1.0 Frameset	XHTML 1.0 Strict
size	yes	no	yes	yes	no
style	yes	yes	yes	yes	yes
title	yes	yes	yes	yes	yes
width	yes	no	yes	yes	no
xml:lang	no	no	yes	yes	yes
html	yes	yes	yes	yes	yes
dir	yes	yes	yes	yes	yes
lang	yes	yes	yes	yes	yes
version	yes	no	no	no	no
xml:lang	no	no	yes	yes	yes
xmlns	no	no	yes	yes	yes
i	yes	yes	yes	yes	yes
class	yes	yes	yes	yes	yes
dir	yes	yes	yes	yes	yes
id	yes	yes	yes	yes	yes
lang	yes	yes	yes	yes	yes
onclick	yes	yes	yes	yes	yes
ondblclick	yes	yes	yes	yes	yes
onkeydown	yes	yes	yes	yes	yes
onkeypress	yes	yes	yes	yes	yes
onkeyup	yes	yes	yes	yes	yes
onmousedown	yes	yes	yes	yes	yes
onmousemove	yes	yes	yes	yes	yes
onmouseout	yes	yes	yes	yes	yes
onmouseover	yes	yes	yes	yes	yes
onmouseup	yes	yes	yes	yes	yes
style	yes	yes	yes	yes	yes
title	yes	yes	yes	yes	yes
xml:lang	no	no	yes	yes	yes
iframe	yes	no	yes	yes	no
align	yes	no	yes	yes	no
class	yes	no	yes	yes	no
frameborder	yes	no	yes	yes	no
height	yes	no	yes	yes	no
id	yes	no	yes	yes	no

Element/Attributes	HTML 4.01 Transitional	HTML 4.01 Strict	XHTML 1.0 Transitional	XHTML 1.0 Frameset	XHTML 1.0 Strict
longdesc	yes	no	yes	yes	no
marginheight	yes	no	yes	yes	no
marginwidth	yes	no	yes	yes	no
name	yes	no	yes	yes	no
scrolling	yes	no	yes	yes	no
src	yes	no	yes	yes	no
style	yes	no	yes	yes	no
title	yes	no	yes	yes	no
width	yes	no	yes	yes	no
img	yes	yes	yes	yes	yes
align	yes	yes	yes	yes	yes
alt	req'd	req'd	req'd	req'd	req'd
border	yes	no	yes	yes	no
class	yes	yes	yes	yes	yes
dir	yes	yes	yes	yes	yes
height	yes	yes	yes	yes	yes
hspace	yes	no	yes	yes	no
id	yes	yes	yes	yes	yes
ismap	yes	yes	yes	yes	yes
lang	yes	yes	yes	yes	yes
longdesc	yes	yes	yes	yes	yes
name	yes	yes	yes	yes	no
onclick	yes	yes	yes	yes	yes
ondblclick	yes	yes	yes	yes	yes
onkeydown	yes	yes	yes	yes	yes
onkeypress	yes	yes	yes	yes	yes
onkeyup	yes	yes	yes	yes	yes
onmousedown	yes	yes	yes	yes	yes
onmousemove	yes	yes	yes	yes	yes
onmouseout	yes	yes	yes	yes	yes
onmouseover	yes	yes	yes	yes	yes
onmouseup	yes	yes	yes	yes	yes
src	req'd	req'd	req'd	req'd	req'd
style	yes	yes	yes	yes	yes
title	yes	yes	yes	yes	yes
usemap	yes	yes	yes	yes	yes

Element/Attributes	HTML 4.01 Transitional	HTML 4.01 Strict	XHTML 1.0 Transitional	XHTML 1.0 Frameset	XHTML 1.0 Strict
vspace	yes	no	yes	yes	no
width	yes	yes	yes	yes	yes
xml:lang	no	no	yes	yes	yes
input	yes	yes	yes	yes	yes
accept	yes	yes	yes	yes	yes
accesskey	yes	yes	yes	yes	yes
align	yes	yes	yes	yes	yes
alt	yes	yes	yes	yes	yes
checked	yes	yes	yes	yes	yes
class	yes	yes	yes	yes	yes
datafld	yes	yes	no	no	no
dataformatas	yes	yes	no	no	no
datasrc	yes	yes	no	no	no
dir	yes	yes	yes	yes	yes
disabled	yes	yes	yes	yes	yes
id	yes	yes	yes	yes	yes
ismap	yes	yes	yes	yes	yes
lang	yes	yes	yes	yes	yes
maxlength	yes	yes	yes	yes	yes
name	yes	yes	yes	yes	yes
onblur	yes	yes	yes	yes	yes
onchange	yes	yes	yes	yes	yes
onclick	yes	yes	yes	yes	yes
ondblclick	yes	yes	yes	yes	yes
onfocus	yes	yes	yes	yes	yes
onkeydown	yes	yes	yes	yes	yes
onkeypress	yes	yes	yes	yes	yes
onkeyup	yes	yes	yes	yes	yes
onmousedown	yes	yes	yes	yes	yes
onmousemove	yes	yes	yes	yes	yes
onmouseout	yes	yes	yes	yes	yes
onmouseover	yes	yes	yes	yes	yes
onmouseup	yes	yes	yes	yes	yes
onselect	yes	yes	yes	yes	yes
readonly	yes	yes	yes	yes	yes
size	yes	yes	yes	yes	yes

Element/Attributes	HTML 4.01 Transitional	HTML 4.01 Strict	XHTML 1.0 Transitional	XHTML 1.0 Frameset	XHTML 1.0 Strict
src	yes	yes	yes	yes	yes
style	yes	yes	yes	yes	yes
tabindex	yes	yes	yes	yes	yes
title	yes	yes	yes	yes	yes
type	yes	yes	yes	yes	yes
usemap	yes	yes	yes	yes	yes
value	yes	yes	yes	yes	yes
xml:lang	no	no	yes	yes	yes
ins	yes	yes	yes	yes	yes
cite	yes	yes	yes	yes	yes
class	yes	yes	yes	yes	yes
datetime	yes	yes	yes	yes	yes
dir	yes	yes	yes	yes	yes
id	yes	yes	yes	yes	yes
lang	yes	yes	yes	yes	yes
onclick	yes	yes	yes	yes	yes
ondblclick	yes	yes	yes	yes	yes
onkeydown	yes	yes	yes	yes	yes
onkeypress	yes	yes	yes	yes	yes
onkeyup	yes	yes	yes	yes	yes
onmousedowr	yes	yes	yes	yes	yes
onmousemove	yes	yes	yes	yes	yes
onmouseout	yes	yes	yes	yes	yes
onmouseover	yes	yes	yes	yes	yes
onmouseup	yes	yes	yes	yes	yes
style	yes	yes	yes	yes	yes
title	yes	yes	yes	yes	yes
xml:lang	no	no	yes	yes	yes
isindex	yes	no	yes	yes	no
class	yes	no	yes	yes	no
dir	yes	no	yes	yes	no
id	yes	no	yes	yes	no
lang	yes	no	yes	yes	no
prompt	yes	no	yes	yes	no
style	yes	no	yes	yes	no
title	yes	no	yes	yes	no
xml:lang	no	no	yes	yes	no

Element/Attributes	HTML 4.01 Transitional	HTML 4.01 Strict	XHTML 1.0 Transitional	XHTML 1.0 Frameset	XHTML 1.0 Strict
kbd	yes	yes	yes	yes	yes
class	yes	yes	yes	yes	yes
dir	yes	yes	yes	yes	yes
id	yes	yes	yes	yes	yes
lang	yes	yes	yes	yes	yes
onclick	yes	yes	yes	yes	yes
ondblclick	yes	yes	yes	yes	yes
onkeydown	yes	yes	yes	yes	yes
onkeypress	yes	yes	yes	yes	yes
onkeyup	yes	yes	yes	yes	yes
onmousedown	yes	yes	yes	yes	yes
onmousemove	yes	yes	yes	yes	yes
onmouseout	yes	yes	yes	yes	yes
onmouseover	yes	yes	yes	yes	yes
onmouseup	yes	yes	yes	yes	yes
style	yes	yes	yes	yes	yes
title	yes	yes	yes	yes	yes
xml:lang	no	no	yes	yes	yes
label	yes	yes	yes	yes	yes
accesskey	yes	yes	yes	yes	yes
class	yes	yes	yes	yes	yes
dir	yes	yes	yes	yes	yes
for	yes	yes	yes	yes	yes
id	yes	yes	yes	yes	yes
lang	yes	yes	yes	yes	yes
onblur	yes	yes	yes	yes	yes
onclick	yes	yes	yes	yes	yes
ondblclick	yes	yes	yes	yes	yes
onfocus	yes	yes	yes	yes	yes
onkeydown	yes	yes	yes	yes	yes
onkeypress	yes	yes	yes	yes	yes
onkeyup	yes	yes	yes	yes	yes
onmousedown	yes	yes	yes	yes	yes
onmousemove	yes	yes	yes	yes	yes
onmouseout	yes	yes	yes	yes	yes
onmouseover	yes	yes	yes	yes	yes

Element/Attributes	HTML 4.01 Transitional	HTML 4.01 Strict	XHTML 1.0 Transitional	XHTML 1.0 Frameset	XHTML 1.0 Strict
onmouseup	yes	yes	yes	yes	yes
style	yes	yes	yes	yes	yes
title	yes	yes	yes	yes	yes
xml:lang	no	no	yes	yes	yes
legend	yes	yes	yes	yes	yes
accesskey	yes	yes	yes	yes	yes
align	yes	no	yes	yes	no
class	yes	yes	yes	yes	yes
dir	yes	yes	yes	yes	yes
id	yes	yes	yes	yes	yes
lang	yes	yes	yes	yes	yes
onclick	yes	yes	yes	yes	yes
ondblclick	yes	yes	yes	yes	yes
onkeydown	yes	yes	yes	yes	yes
onkeypress	yes	yes	yes	yes	yes
onkeyup	yes	yes	yes	yes	yes
onmousedown	yes	yes	yes	yes	yes
onmousemove	yes	yes	yes	yes	yes
onmouseout	yes	yes	yes	yes	yes
onmouseover	yes	yes	yes	yes	yes
onmouseup	yes	yes	yes	yes	yes
style	yes	yes	yes	yes	yes
title	yes	yes	yes	yes	yes
xml:lang	no	no	yes	yes	yes
li	yes	yes	yes	yes	yes
class	yes	yes	yes	yes	yes
dir	yes	yes	yes	yes	yes
id	yes	yes	yes	yes	yes
lang	yes	yes	yes	yes	yes
onclick	yes	yes	yes	yes	yes
ondblclick	yes	yes	yes	yes	yes
onkeydown	yes	yes	yes	yes	yes
onkeypress	yes	yes	yes	yes	yes
onkeyup	yes	yes	yes	yes	yes
onmousedown	yes	yes	yes	yes	yes
onmousemove	yes	yes	yes	yes	yes

Element/Attributes	HTML 4.01 Transitional	HTML 4.01 Strict	XHTML 1.0 Transitional	XHTML 1.0 Frameset	XHTML 1.0 Strict
onmouseout	yes	yes	yes	yes	yes
onmouseover	yes	yes	yes	yes	yes
onmouseup	yes	yes	yes	yes	yes
style	yes	yes	yes	yes	yes
title	yes	yes	yes	yes	yes
type	yes	no	yes	yes	no
value	yes	no	yes	yes	no
xml:lang	no	no	yes	yes	yes
link	yes	yes	yes	yes	yes
charset	yes	yes	yes	yes	yes
class	yes	yes	yes	yes	yes
dir	yes	yes	yes	yes	yes
href	yes	yes	yes	yes	yes
hreflang	yes	yes	yes	yes	yes
id	yes	yes	yes	yes	yes
lang	yes	yes	yes	yes	yes
media	yes	yes	yes	yes	yes
onclick	yes	yes	yes	yes	yes
ondblclick	yes	yes	yes	yes	yes
onkeydown	yes	yes	yes	yes	yes
onkeypress	yes	yes	yes	yes	yes
onkeyup	yes	yes	yes	yes	yes
onmousedown	yes	yes	yes	yes	yes
onmousemove	yes	yes	yes	yes	yes
onmouseout	yes	yes	yes	yes	yes
onmouseover	yes	yes	yes	yes	yes
onmouseup	yes	yes	yes	yes	yes
rel	yes	yes	yes	yes	yes
rev	yes	yes	yes	yes	yes
style	yes	yes	yes	yes	yes
target	yes	no	yes	yes	no
title	yes	yes	yes	yes	yes
type	yes	yes	yes	yes	yes
xml:lang	no	no	yes	yes	yes
map	yes	yes	yes	yes	yes
class	yes	yes	yes	yes	yes
dir	yes	yes	yes	yes	yes

Element/Attributes	HTML 4.01 Transitional	HTML 4.01 Strict	XHTML 1.0 Transitional	XHTML 1.0 Frameset	XHTML 1.0 Strict
id	yes	yes	req'd	req'd	req'd
lang	yes	yes	yes	yes	yes
name	req'd	req'd	yes	yes	yes
onclick	yes	yes	yes	yes	yes
ondblclick	yes	yes	yes	yes	yes
onkeydown	yes	yes	yes	yes	yes
onkeypress	yes	yes	yes	yes	yes
onkeyup	yes	yes	yes	yes	yes
onmousedown	yes	yes	yes	yes	yes
onmousemove	yes	yes	yes	yes	yes
onmouseout	yes	yes	yes	yes	yes
onmouseover	yes	yes	yes	yes	yes
onmouseup	yes	yes	yes	yes	yes
style	yes	yes	yes	yes	yes
title	yes	yes	yes	yes	yes
xml:lang	no	no	yes	yes	yes
menu	yes	no	yes	no	no
class	yes	no	yes	no	no
compact	yes	no	yes	no	no
dir	yes	no	yes	no	no
id	yes	no	yes	no	no
lang	yes	no	yes	no	no
onclick	yes	no	yes	no	no
ondblclick	yes	no	yes	no	no
onkeydown	yes	no	yes	no	no
onkeypress	yes	no	yes	no	no
onkeyup	yes	no	yes	no	no
onmousedown	yes	no	yes	no	no
onmousemove	yes	no	yes	no	no
onmouseout	yes	no	yes	no	no
onmouseover	yes	no	yes	no	no
onmouseup	yes	no	yes	no	no
style	yes	no	yes	no	no
title	yes	no	yes	no	no
xml:lang	no	no	yes	no	no

Element/Attributes	HTML 4.01 Transitional	HTML 4.01 Strict	XHTML 1.0 Transitional	XHTML 1.0 Frameset	XHTML 1.0 Strict
meta	yes	yes	yes	yes	yes
content	req'd	req'd	req'd	req'd	req'd
dir	yes	yes	yes	yes	yes
http-equiv	yes	yes	yes	yes	yes
lang	yes	yes	yes	yes	yes
name	yes	yes	yes	yes	yes
scheme	yes	yes	yes	yes	yes
xml:lang	no	no	yes	yes	yes
noframes	yes	no	yes	yes	no
class	yes	no	yes	yes	no
dir	yes	no	yes	yes	no
id	yes	no	yes	yes	no
lang	yes	no	yes	yes	no
onclick	yes	no	yes	yes	no
ondblclick	yes	no	yes	yes	no
onkeydown	yes	no	yes	yes	no
onkeypress	yes	no	yes	yes	no
onkeyup	yes	no	yes	yes	no
onmousedown	yes	no	yes	yes	no
onmousemove	yes	no	yes	yes	no
onmouseout	yes	no	yes	yes	no
onmouseover	yes	no	yes	yes	no
onmouseup	yes	no	yes	yes	no
style	yes	no	yes	yes	no
title	yes	no	yes	yes	no
xml:lang	no	no	yes	yes	no
noscript	yes	yes	yes	yes	yes
class	yes	yes	yes	yes	yes
dir	yes	yes	yes	yes	yes
id	yes	yes	yes	yes	yes
lang	yes	yes	yes	yes	yes
onclick	yes	yes	yes	yes	yes
ondblclick	yes	yes	yes	yes	yes
onkeydown	yes	yes	yes	yes	yes
onkeypress	yes	yes	yes	yes	yes
onkeyup	yes	yes	yes	yes	yes

Element/Attributes	HTML 4.01 Transitional	HTML 4.01 Strict	XHTML 1.0 Transitional	XHTML 1.0 Frameset	XHTML 1.0 Strict
onmousedown	yes	yes	yes	yes	yes
onmousemove	yes	yes	yes	yes	yes
onmouseout	yes	yes	yes	yes	yes
onmouseover	yes	yes	yes	yes	yes
onmouseup	yes	yes	yes	yes	yes
style	yes	yes	yes	yes	yes
title	yes	yes	yes	yes	yes
xml:lang	no	no	yes	yes	yes
object	yes	yes	yes	yes	yes
align	yes	no	yes	yes	no
archive	yes	yes	yes	yes	yes
border	yes	no	yes	yes	no
class	yes	yes	yes	yes	yes
classid	yes	yes	yes	yes	yes
codebase	yes	yes	yes	yes	yes
codetype	yes	yes	yes	yes	yes
data	yes	yes	yes	yes	yes
datafld	yes	yes	no	no	no
dataformatas	yes	yes	no	no	no
datasrc	yes	yes	no	no	no
declare	yes	yes	yes	yes	yes
dir	yes	yes	yes	yes	yes
height	yes	yes	yes	yes	yes
hspace	yes	no	yes	yes	no
id	yes	yes	yes	yes	yes
lang	yes	yes	yes	yes	yes
name	yes	yes	yes	yes	yes
onclick	yes	yes	yes	yes	yes
ondblclick	yes	yes	yes	yes	yes
onkeydown	yes	yes	yes	yes	yes
onkeypress	yes	yes	yes	yes	yes
onkeyup	yes	yes	yes	yes	yes
onmousedown	yes	yes	yes	yes	yes
onmousemove	yes	yes	yes	yes	yes
onmouseout	yes	yes	yes	yes	yes
onmouseover	yes	yes	yes	yes	yes

Element/Attributes	HTML 4.01 Transitional	HTML 4.01 Strict	XHTML 1.0 Transitional	XHTML 1.0 Frameset	XHTML 1.0 Strict
onmouseup	yes	yes	yes	yes	yes
standby	yes	yes	yes	yes	yes
style	yes	yes	yes	yes	yes
tabindex	yes	yes	yes	yes	yes
title	yes	yes	yes	yes	yes
type	yes	yes	yes	yes	yes
usemap	yes	yes	yes	yes	yes
vspace	yes	no	yes	yes	no
width	yes	yes	yes	yes	yes
xml:lang	no	no	yes	yes	yes
ol	yes	yes	yes	yes	yes
class	yes	yes	yes	yes	yes
compact	yes	no	yes	yes	no
dir	yes	yes	yes	yes	yes
id	yes	yes	yes	yes	yes
lang	yes	yes	yes	yes	yes
onclick	yes	yes	yes	yes	yes
ondblclick	yes	yes	yes	yes	yes
onkeydown	yes	yes	yes	yes	yes
onkeypress	yes	yes	yes	yes	yes
onkeyup	yes	yes	yes	yes	yes
onmousedown	yes	yes	yes	yes	yes
onmousemove	yes	yes	yes	yes	yes
onmouseout	yes	yes	yes	yes	yes
onmouseover	yes	yes	yes	yes	yes
onmouseup	yes	yes	yes	yes	yes
start	yes	no	yes	yes	no
style	yes	yes	yes	yes	yes
title	yes	yes	yes	yes	yes
type	yes	no	yes	yes	no
xml:lang	no	no	yes	yes	yes
optgroup	yes	yes	yes	yes	yes
class	yes	yes	yes	yes	yes
dir	yes	yes	yes	yes	yes
disabled	yes	yes	yes	yes	yes

Element/Attributes	HTML 4.01 Transitional	HTML 4.01 Strict	XHTML 1.0 Transitional	XHTML 1.0 Frameset	XHTML 1.0 Strict
id	yes	yes	yes	yes	yes
label	req'd	req'd	req'd	req'd	req'd
lang	yes	yes	yes	yes	yes
onclick	yes	yes	yes	yes	yes
ondblclick	yes	yes	yes	yes	yes
onkeydown	yes	yes	yes	yes	yes
onkeypress	yes	yes	yes	yes	yes
onkeyup	yes	yes	yes	yes	yes
onmousedown	yes	yes	yes	yes	yes
onmousemove	yes	yes	yes	yes	yes
onmouseout	yes	yes	yes	yes	yes
onmouseover	yes	yes	yes	yes	yes
onmouseup	yes	yes	yes	yes	yes
style	yes	yes	yes	yes	yes
title	yes	yes	yes	yes	yes
xml:lang	no	no	yes	yes	yes
option	yes	yes	yes	yes	yes
class	yes	yes	yes	yes	yes
dir	yes	yes	yes	yes	yes
disabled	yes	yes	yes	yes	yes
id	yes	yes	yes	yes	yes
label	yes	yes	yes	yes	yes
lang	yes	yes	yes	yes	yes
onclick	yes	yes	yes	yes	yes
ondblclick	yes	yes	yes	yes	yes
onkeydown	yes	yes	yes	yes	yes
onkeypress	yes	yes	yes	yes	yes
onkeyup	yes	yes	yes	yes	yes
onmousedown	yes	yes	yes	yes	yes
onmousemove	yes	yes	yes	yes	yes
onmouseout	yes	yes	yes	yes	yes
onmouseover	yes	yes	yes	yes	yes
onmouseup	yes	yes	yes	yes	yes
selected	yes	yes	yes	yes	yes
style	yes	yes	yes	yes	yes
title	yes	yes	yes	yes	yes

Element/Attributes	HTML 4.01 Transitional	HTML 4.01 Strict	XHTML 1.0 Transitional	XHTML 1.0 Frameset	XHTML 1.0 Strict
value	yes	yes	yes	yes	yes
xml:lang	no	no	yes	yes	yes
p	yes	yes	yes	yes	yes
align	yes	no	yes	yes	no
class	yes	yes	yes	yes	yes
dir	yes	yes	yes	yes	yes
id	yes	yes	yes	yes	yes
lang	yes	yes	yes	yes	yes
onclick	yes	yes	yes	yes	yes
ondblclick	yes	yes	yes	yes	yes
onkeydown	yes	yes	yes	yes	yes
onkeypress	yes	yes	yes	yes	yes
onkeyup	yes	yes	yes	yes	yes
onmousedown	yes	yes	yes	yes	yes
onmousemove	yes	yes	yes	yes	yes
onmouseout	yes	yes	yes	yes	yes
onmouseover	yes	yes	yes	yes	yes
onmouseup	yes	yes	yes	yes	yes
style	yes	yes	yes	yes	yes
title	yes	yes	yes	yes	yes
xml:lang	no	no	yes	yes	yes
param	yes	yes	yes	yes	yes
id	yes	yes	yes	yes	yes
name	req'd	req'd	req'd	req'd	yes
type	yes	yes	yes	yes	yes
value	yes	yes	yes	yes	yes
valuetype	yes	yes	yes	yes	yes
pre	yes	yes	yes	yes	yes
class	yes	yes	yes	yes	yes
dir	yes	yes	yes	yes	yes
id	yes	yes	yes	yes	yes
lang	yes	yes	yes	yes	yes
onclick	yes	yes	yes	yes	yes
ondblclick	yes	yes	yes	yes	yes
onkeydown	yes	yes	yes	yes	yes
onkeypress	yes	yes	yes	yes	yes

Element/Attributes	HTML 4.01 Transitional	HTML 4.01 Strict	XHTML 1.0 Transitional	XHTML 1.0 Frameset	XHTML 1.0 Strict
onkeyup	yes	yes	yes	yes	yes
onmousedown	yes	yes	yes	yes	yes
onmousemove	yes	yes	yes	yes	yes
onmouseout	yes	yes	yes	yes	yes
onmouseover	yes	yes	yes	yes	yes
onmouseup	yes	yes	yes	yes	yes
style	yes	yes	yes	yes	yes
title	yes	yes	yes	yes	yes
width	yes	no	yes	yes	no
xml:lang	no	no	yes	yes	yes
xml:space	no	no	yes	yes	yes
q	yes	yes	yes	yes	yes
cite	yes	yes	yes	yes	yes
class	yes	yes	yes	yes	yes
dir	yes	yes	yes	yes	yes
id	yes	yes	yes	yes	yes
lang	yes	yes	yes	yes	yes
onclick	yes	yes	yes	yes	yes
ondblclick	yes	yes	yes	yes	yes
onkeydown	yes	yes	yes	yes	yes
onkeypress	yes	yes	yes	yes	yes
onkeyup	yes	yes	yes	yes	yes
onmousedown	yes	yes	yes	yes	yes
onmousemove	yes	yes	yes	yes	yes
onmouseout	yes	yes	yes	yes	yes
onmouseover	yes	yes	yes	yes	yes
onmouseup	yes	yes	yes	yes	yes
style	yes	yes	yes	yes	yes
title	yes	yes	yes	yes	yes
xml:lang	no	no	yes	yes	yes
s	yes	no	yes	yes	no
class	yes	no	yes	yes	no
dir	yes	no	yes	yes	no
id	yes	no	yes	yes	no
lang	yes	no	yes	yes	no
onclick	yes	no	yes	yes	no

Element/Attributes	HTML 4.01 Transitional	HTML 4.01 Strict	XHTML 1.0 Transitional	XHTML 1.0 Frameset	XHTML 1.0 Strict
ondblclick	yes	no	yes	yes	no
onkeydown	yes	no	yes	yes	no
onkeypress	yes	no	yes	yes	no
onkeyup	yes	no	yes	yes	no
onmousedown	yes	no	yes	yes	no
onmousemove	yes	no	yes	yes	no
onmouseout	yes	no	yes	yes	no
onmouseover	yes	no	yes	yes	no
onmouseup	yes	no	yes	yes	no
style	yes	no	yes	yes	no
title	yes	no	yes	yes	no
xml:lang	no	no	yes	yes	no
samp	yes	yes	yes	yes	yes
class	yes	yes	yes	yes	yes
dir	yes	yes	yes	yes	yes
id	yes	yes	yes	yes	yes
lang	yes	yes	yes	yes	yes
onclick	yes	yes	yes	yes	yes
ondblclick	yes	yes	yes	yes	yes
onkeydown	yes	yes	yes	yes	yes
onkeypress	yes	yes	yes	yes	yes
onkeyup	yes	yes	yes	yes	yes
onmousedown	yes	yes	yes	yes	yes
onmousemove	yes	yes	yes	yes	yes
onmouseout	yes	yes	yes	yes	yes
onmouseover	yes	yes	yes	yes	yes
onmouseup	yes	yes	yes	yes	yes
style	yes	yes	yes	yes	yes
title	yes	yes	yes	yes	yes
xml:lang	no	no	yes	yes	yes
script	yes	yes	yes	yes	yes
charset	yes	yes	yes	yes	yes
defer	yes	yes	no	no	no
event	yes	yes	no	no	no
for	yes	yes	no	no	no
language	yes	no	yes	yes	no

Element/Attributes	HTML 4.01 Transitional	HTML 4.01 Strict	XHTML 1.0 Transitional	XHTML 1.0 Frameset	XHTML 1.0 Strict
src	yes	yes	yes	yes	yes
type	req'd	req'd	req'd	req'd	req'd
xml:space	no	no	yes	yes	yes
select	yes	yes	yes	yes	yes
class	yes	yes	yes	yes	yes
datafld	yes	yes	yes	yes	yes
dataformatas	yes	yes	yes	yes	yes
datasrc	yes	yes	yes	yes	yes
dir	yes	yes	yes	yes	yes
disabled	yes	yes	yes	yes	yes
id	yes	yes	yes	yes	yes
lang	yes	yes	yes	yes	yes
multiple	yes	yes	yes	yes	yes
name	yes	yes	yes	yes	yes
onblur	yes	yes	yes	yes	yes
onchange	yes	yes	yes	yes	yes
onclick	yes	yes	yes	yes	yes
ondblclick	yes	yes	yes	yes	yes
onfocus	yes	yes	yes	yes	yes
onkeydown	yes	yes	yes	yes	yes
onkeypress	yes	yes	yes	yes	yes
onkeyup	yes	yes	yes	yes	yes
onmousedown	yes	yes	yes	yes	yes
onmousemove	yes	yes	yes	yes	yes
onmouseout	yes	yes	yes	yes	yes
onmouseover	yes	yes	yes	yes	yes
onmouseup	yes	yes	yes	yes	yes
size	yes	yes	yes	yes	yes
style	yes	yes	yes	yes	yes
tabindex	yes	yes	yes	yes	yes
title	yes	yes	yes	yes	yes
xml:lang	no	no	yes	yes	yes
small	yes	yes	yes	yes	yes
class	yes	yes	yes	yes	yes
dir	yes	yes	yes	yes	yes

Element/Attributes	HTML 4.01 Transitional	HTML 4.01 Strict	XHTML 1.0 Transitional	XHTML 1.0 Frameset	XHTML 1.0 Strict
id	yes	yes	yes	yes	yes
lang	yes	yes	yes	yes	yes
onclick	yes	yes	yes	yes	yes
ondblclick	yes	yes	yes	yes	yes
onkeydown	yes	yes	yes	yes	yes
onkeypress	yes	yes	yes	yes	yes
onkeyup	yes	yes	yes	yes	yes
onmousedown	yes	yes	yes	yes	yes
onmousemove	yes	yes	yes	yes	yes
onmouseout	yes	yes	yes	yes	yes
onmouseover	yes	yes	yes	yes	yes
onmouseup	yes	yes	yes	yes	yes
style	yes	yes	yes	yes	yes
title	yes	yes	yes	yes	yes
xml:lang	no	no	yes	yes	yes
span	yes	yes	yes	yes	yes
class	yes	yes	yes	yes	yes
datafld	yes	yes	no	no	no
dataformatas	yes	yes	no	no	no
datasrc	yes	yes	no	no	no
dir	yes	yes	yes	yes	yes
id	yes	yes	yes	yes	yes
lang	yes	yes	yes	yes	yes
onclick	yes	yes	yes	yes	yes
ondblclick	yes	yes	yes	yes	yes
onkeydown	yes	yes	yes	yes	yes
onkeypress	yes	yes	yes	yes	yes
onkeyup	yes	yes	yes	yes	yes
onmousedown	yes	yes	yes	yes	yes
onmousemove	yes	yes	yes	yes	yes
onmouseout	yes	yes	yes	yes	yes
onmouseover	yes	yes	yes	yes	yes
onmouseup	yes	yes	yes	yes	yes
style	yes	yes	yes	yes	yes
title	yes	yes	yes	yes	yes
xml:lang	no	no	yes	yes	yes

Element/Attributes	HTML 4.01 Transitional	HTML 4.01 Strict	XHTML 1.0 Transitional	XHTML 1.0 Frameset	XHTML 1.0 Strict
strike	yes	no	yes	yes	no
class	yes	no	yes	yes	no
dir	yes	no	yes	yes	no
id	yes	no	yes	yes	no
lang	yes	no	yes	yes	no
onclick	yes	no	yes	yes	no
ondblclick	yes	no	yes	yes	no
onkeydown	yes	no	yes	yes	no
onkeypress	yes	no	yes	yes	no
onkeyup	yes	no	yes	yes	no
onmousedown	yes	no	yes	yes	no
onmousemove	yes	no	yes	yes	no
onmouseout	yes	no	yes	yes	no
onmouseover	yes	no	yes	yes	no
onmouseup	yes	no	yes	yes	no
style	yes	no	yes	yes	no
title	yes	no	yes	yes	no
xml:lang	no	no	yes	yes	no
strong	yes	yes	yes	yes	yes
class	yes	yes	yes	yes	yes
dir	yes	yes	yes	yes	yes
id	yes	yes	yes	yes	yes
lang	yes	yes	yes	yes	yes
onclick	yes	yes	yes	yes	yes
ondblclick	yes	yes	yes	yes	yes
onkeydown	yes	yes	yes	yes	yes
onkeypress	yes	yes	yes	yes	yes
onkeyup	yes	yes	yes	yes	yes
onmousedown	yes	yes	yes	yes	yes
onmousemove	yes	yes	yes	yes	yes
onmouseout	yes	yes	yes	yes	yes
onmouseover	yes	yes	yes	yes	yes
onmouseup	yes	yes	yes	yes	yes
style	yes	yes	yes	yes	yes
title	yes	yes	yes	yes	yes
xml:lang	no	no	yes	yes	yes

Element/Attributes	HTML 4.01 Transitional	HTML 4.01 Strict	XHTML 1.0 Transitional	XHTML 1.0 Frameset	XHTML 1.0 Strict
style	yes	yes	yes	yes	yes
dir	yes	yes	yes	yes	yes
lang	yes	yes	yes	yes	yes
media	yes	yes	yes	yes	yes
title	yes	yes	yes	yes	yes
type	req'd	req'd	req'd	req'd	req'd
xml:lang	no	no	yes	yes	yes
xml:space	no	no	yes	yes	yes
sub	yes	yes	yes	yes	yes
class	yes	yes	yes	yes	yes
dir	yes	yes	yes	yes	yes
id	yes	yes	yes	yes	yes
lang	yes	yes	yes	yes	yes
onclick	yes	yes	yes	yes	yes
ondblclick	yes	yes	yes	yes	yes
onkeydown	yes	yes	yes	yes	yes
onkeypress	yes	yes	yes	yes	yes
onkeyup	yes	yes	yes	yes	yes
onmousedown	yes	yes	yes	yes	yes
onmousemove	yes	yes	yes	yes	yes
onmouseout	yes	yes	yes	yes	yes
onmouseover	yes	yes	yes	yes	yes
onmouseup	yes	yes	yes	yes	yes
style	yes	yes	yes	yes	yes
title	yes	yes	yes	yes	yes
xml:lang	no	no	yes	yes	yes
sup	yes	yes	yes	yes	yes
class	yes	yes	yes	yes	yes
dir	yes	yes	yes	yes	yes
id	yes	yes	yes	yes	yes
lang	yes	yes	yes	yes	yes
onclick	yes	yes	yes	yes	yes
ondblclick	yes	yes	yes	yes	yes
onkeydown	yes	yes	yes	yes	yes
onkeypress	yes	yes	yes	yes	yes
onkeyup	yes	yes	yes	yes	yes

Element/Attributes	HTML 4.01 Transitional	HTML 4.01 Strict	XHTML 1.0 Transitional	XHTML 1.0 Frameset	XHTML 1.0 Strict
onmousedown	yes	yes	yes	yes	yes
onmousemove	yes	yes	yes	yes	yes
onmouseout	yes	yes	yes	yes	yes
onmouseover	yes	yes	yes	yes	yes
onmouseup	yes	yes	yes	yes	yes
style	yes	yes	yes	yes	yes
title	yes	yes	yes	yes	yes
xml:lang	no	no	yes	yes	yes
table	yes	yes	yes	yes	yes
align	yes	yes	yes	yes	no
bgcolor	yes	yes	yes	yes	no
border	yes	yes	yes	yes	yes
cellpadding	yes	yes	yes	yes	yes
cellspacing	yes	yes	yes	yes	yes
class	yes	yes	yes	yes	yes
datafld	yes	yes	no	no	no
dataformatas	yes	yes	no	no	no
datapagesize	yes	yes	no	no	no
datasrc	yes	yes	no	no	no
dir	yes	yes	yes	yes	yes
frame	yes	yes	yes	yes	yes
id	yes	yes	yes	yes	yes
lang	yes	yes	yes	yes	yes
onclick	yes	yes	yes	yes	yes
ondblclick	yes	yes	yes	yes	yes
onkeydown	yes	yes	yes	yes	yes
onkeypress	yes	yes	yes	yes	yes
onkeyup	yes	yes	yes	yes	yes
onmousedown	yes	yes	yes	yes	yes
onmousemove	yes	yes	yes	yes	yes
onmouseout	yes	yes	yes	yes	yes
onmouseover	yes	yes	yes	yes	yes
onmouseup	yes	yes	yes	yes	yes
rules	yes	yes	yes	yes	yes
style	yes	yes	yes	yes	yes
summary	yes	yes	yes	yes	yes

Element/Attributes	HTML 4.01 Transitional	HTML 4.01 Strict	XHTML 1.0 Transitional	XHTML 1.0 Frameset	XHTML 1.0 Strict
title	yes	yes	yes	yes	yes
width	yes	yes	yes	yes	yes
xml:lang	no	no	yes	yes	yes
tbody	yes	yes	yes	yes	yes
align	yes	yes	yes	yes	yes
char	yes	yes	yes	yes	yes
charoff	yes	yes	yes	yes	yes
class	yes	yes	yes	yes	yes
dir	yes	yes	yes	yes	yes
id	yes	yes	yes	yes	yes
lang	yes	yes	yes	yes	yes
onclick	yes	yes	yes	yes	yes
ondblclick	yes	yes	yes	yes	yes
onkeydown	yes	yes	yes	yes	yes
onkeypress	yes	yes	yes	yes	yes
onkeyup	yes	yes	yes	yes	yes
onmousedown	yes	yes	yes	yes	yes
onmousemove	yes	yes	yes	yes	yes
onmouseout	yes	yes	yes	yes	yes
onmouseover	yes	yes	yes	yes	yes
onmouseup	yes	yes	yes	yes	yes
style	yes	yes	yes	yes	yes
title	yes	yes	yes	yes	yes
valign	yes	yes	yes	yes	yes
xml:lang	no	no	yes	yes	yes
td	yes	yes	yes	yes	yes
abbr	yes	yes	yes	yes	yes
align	yes	yes	yes	yes	yes
axis	yes	yes	yes	yes	yes
bgcolor	yes	no	yes	yes	no
char	yes	yes	yes	yes	yes
charoff	yes	yes	yes	yes	yes
class	yes	yes	yes	yes	yes
colspan	yes	yes	yes	yes	yes
dir	yes	yes	yes	yes	yes
headers	yes	yes	yes	yes	yes

Element/Attributes	HTML 4.01 Transitional	HTML 4.01 Strict	XHTML 1.0 Transitional	XHTML 1.0 Frameset	XHTML 1.0 Strict
height	yes	no	yes	yes	no
id	yes	yes	yes	yes	yes
lang	yes	yes	yes	yes	yes
nowrap	yes	no	yes	yes	no
onclick	yes	yes	yes	yes	yes
ondblclick	yes	yes	yes	yes	yes
onkeydown	yes	yes	yes	yes	yes
onkeypress	yes	yes	yes	yes	yes
onkeyup	yes	yes	yes	yes	yes
onmousedown	yes	yes	yes	yes	yes
onmousemove	yes	yes	yes	yes	yes
onmouseout	yes	yes	yes	yes	yes
onmouseover	yes	yes	yes	yes	yes
onmouseup	yes	yes	yes	yes	yes
rowspan	yes	yes	yes	yes	yes
scope	yes	yes	yes	yes	yes
style	yes	yes	yes	yes	yes
title	yes	yes	yes	yes	yes
valign	yes	yes	yes	yes	yes
width	yes	no	yes	yes	no
xml:lang	no	no	yes	yes	yes
textarea	yes	yes	yes	yes	yes
accesskey	yes	yes	yes	yes	yes
class	yes	yes	yes	yes	yes
cols	req'd	req'd	req'd	req'd	req'd
datafld	yes	yes	no	no	no
dataformatas	yes	yes	no	no	no
datasrc	yes	yes	no	no	no
dir	yes	yes	yes	yes	yes
disabled	yes	yes	yes	yes	yes
id	yes	yes	yes	yes	yes
lang	yes	yes	yes	yes	yes
name	yes	yes	yes	yes	yes
onblur	yes	yes	yes	yes	yes
onchange	yes	yes	yes	yes	yes
onclick	yes	yes	yes	yes	yes

Element/Attributes	HTML 4.01 Transitional	HTML 4.01 Strict	XHTML 1.0 Transitional	XHTML 1.0 Frameset	XHTML 1.0 Strict
ondblclick	yes	yes	yes	yes	yes
onfocus	yes	yes	yes	yes	yes
onkeydown	yes	yes	yes	yes	yes
onkeypress	yes	yes	yes	yes	yes
onkeyup	yes	yes	yes	yes	yes
onmousedown	yes	yes	yes	yes	yes
onmousemove	yes	yes	yes	yes	yes
onmouseout	yes	yes	yes	yes	yes
onmouseover	yes	yes	yes	yes	yes
onmouseup	yes	yes	yes	yes	yes
onselect	yes	yes	yes	yes	yes
readonly	yes	yes	yes	yes	yes
rows	req'd	req'd	req'd	req'd	req'd
style	yes	yes	yes	yes	yes
tabindex	yes	yes	yes	yes	yes
title	yes	yes	yes	yes	yes
xml:lang	no	no	yes	yes	yes
tfoot	yes	yes	yes	yes	yes
align	yes	yes	yes	yes	yes
char	yes	yes	yes	yes	yes
charoff	yes	yes	yes	yes	yes
class	yes	yes	yes	yes	yes
dir	yes	yes	yes	yes	yes
id	yes	yes	yes	yes	yes
lang	yes	yes	yes	yes	yes
onclick	yes	yes	yes	yes	yes
ondblclick	yes	yes	yes	yes	yes
onkeydown	yes	yes	yes	yes	yes
onkeypress	yes	yes	yes	yes	yes
onkeyup	yes	yes	yes	yes	yes
onmousedown	yes	yes	yes	yes	yes
onmousemove	yes	yes	yes	yes	yes
onmouseout	yes	yes	yes	yes	yes
onmouseover	yes	yes	yes	yes	yes
onmouseup	yes	yes	yes	yes	yes

Element/Attributes	HTML 4.01 Transitional	HTML 4.01 Strict	XHTML 1.0 Transitional	XHTML 1.0 Frameset	XHTML 1.0 Strict
style	yes	yes	yes	yes	yes
title	yes	yes	yes	yes	yes
valign	yes	yes	yes	yes	yes
xml:lang	no	no	yes	yes	yes
th	yes	yes	yes	yes	yes
abbr	yes	yes	yes	yes	yes
align	yes	yes	yes	yes	yes
axis	yes	yes	yes	yes	yes
bgcolor	yes	no	yes	yes	no
char	yes	yes	yes	yes	yes
charoff	yes	yes	yes	yes	yes
class	yes	yes	yes	yes	yes
colspan	yes	yes	yes	yes	yes
dir	yes	yes	yes	yes	yes
headers	yes	yes	yes	yes	yes
height	yes	no	yes	yes	no
id	yes	yes	yes	yes	yes
lang	yes	yes	yes	yes	yes
nowrap	yes	no	yes	yes	no
onclick	yes	yes	yes	yes	yes
ondblclick	yes	yes	yes	yes	yes
onkeydown	yes	yes	yes	yes	yes
onkeypress	yes	yes	yes	yes	yes
onkeyup	yes	yes	yes	yes	yes
onmousedown	yes	yes	yes	yes	yes
onmousemove	yes	yes	yes	yes	yes
onmouseout	yes	yes	yes	yes	yes
onmouseover	yes	yes	yes	yes	yes
onmouseup	yes	yes	yes	yes	yes
rowspan	yes	yes	yes	yes	yes
scope	yes	yes	yes	yes	yes
style	yes	yes	yes	yes	yes
title	yes	yes	yes	yes	yes
valign	yes	yes	yes	yes	yes
width	yes	no	yes	yes	no
xml:lang	no	no	yes	yes	yes

Element/Attributes	HTML 4.01 Transitional	HTML 4.01 Strict	XHTML 1.0 Transitional	XHTML 1.0 Frameset	XHTML 1.0 Strict
thead	yes	yes	yes	yes	yes
align	yes	yes	yes	yes	yes
char	yes	yes	yes	yes	yes
charoff	yes	yes	yes	yes	yes
class	yes	yes	yes	yes	yes
dir	yes	yes	yes	yes	yes
id	yes	yes	yes	yes	yes
lang	yes	yes	yes	yes	yes
onclick	yes	yes	yes	yes	yes
ondblclick	yes	yes	yes	yes	yes
onkeydown	yes	yes	yes	yes	yes
onkeypress	yes	yes	yes	yes	yes
onkeyup	yes	yes	yes	yes	yes
onmousedown	yes	yes	yes	yes	yes
onmousemove	yes	yes	yes	yes	yes
onmouseout	yes	yes	yes	yes	yes
onmouseover	yes	yes	yes	yes	yes
onmouseup	yes	yes	yes	yes	yes
style	yes	yes	yes	yes	yes
title	yes	yes	yes	yes	yes
valign	yes	yes	yes	yes	yes
xml:lang	no	no	yes	yes	yes
title	yes	yes	yes	yes	yes
dir	yes	yes	yes	yes	yes
lang	yes	yes	yes	yes	yes
xml:lang	no	no	yes	yes	yes
tr	yes	yes	yes	yes	yes
align	yes	yes	yes	yes	yes
bgcolor	yes	no	yes	yes	no
char	yes	yes	yes	yes	yes
charoff	yes	yes	yes	yes	yes
class	yes	yes	yes	yes	yes
dir	yes	yes	yes	yes	yes
id	yes	yes	yes	yes	yes
lang	yes	yes	yes	yes	yes
onclick	yes	yes	yes	yes	yes

Element/Attributes	HTML 4.01 Transitional	HTML 4.01 Strict	XHTML 1.0 Transitional	XHTML 1.0 Frameset	XHTML 1.0 Strict
ondblclick	yes	yes	yes	yes	yes
onkeydown	yes	yes	yes	yes	yes
onkeypress	yes	yes	yes	yes	yes
onkeyup	yes	yes	yes	yes	yes
onmousedown	yes	yes	yes	yes	yes
onmousemove	yes	yes	yes	yes	yes
onmouseout	yes	yes	yes	yes	yes
onmouseover	yes	yes	yes	yes	yes
onmouseup	yes	yes	yes	yes	yes
style	yes	yes	yes	yes	yes
title	yes	yes	yes	yes	yes
valign	yes	yes	yes	yes	yes
xml:lang	no	no	yes	yes	yes
tt	yes	yes	yes	yes	yes
class	yes	yes	yes	yes	yes
dir	yes	yes	yes	yes	yes
id	yes	yes	yes	yes	yes
lang	yes	yes	yes	yes	yes
onclick	yes	yes	yes	yes	yes
ondblclick	yes	yes	yes	yes	yes
onkeydown	yes	yes	yes	yes	yes
onkeypress	yes	yes	yes	yes	yes
onkeyup	yes	yes	yes	yes	yes
onmousedown	yes	yes	yes	yes	yes
onmousemove	yes	yes	yes	yes	yes
onmouseout	yes	yes	yes	yes	yes
onmouseover	yes	yes	yes	yes	yes
onmouseup	yes	yes	yes	yes	yes
style	yes	yes	yes	yes	yes
title	yes	yes	yes	yes	yes
xml:lang	no	no	yes	yes	yes
u	yes	no	yes	yes	no
class	yes	no	yes	yes	no
dir	yes	no	yes	yes	no
id	yes	no	yes	yes	no

Element/Attributes	HTML 4.01 Transitional	HTML 4.01 Strict	XHTML 1.0 Transitional	XHTML 1.0 Frameset	XHTML 1.0 Strict
lang	yes	no	yes	yes	no
onclick	yes	no	yes	yes	no
ondblclick	yes	no	yes	yes	no
onkeydown	yes	no	yes	yes	no
onkeypress	yes	no	yes	yes	no
onkeyup	yes	no	yes	yes	no
onmousedown	yes	no	yes	yes	no
onmousemove	yes	no	yes	yes	no
onmouseout	yes	no	yes	yes	no
onmouseover	yes	no	yes	yes	no
onmouseup	yes	no	yes	yes	no
style	yes	no	yes	yes	no
title	yes	no	yes	yes	no
xml:lang	no	no	yes	yes	no
ul	yes	yes	yes	yes	yes
class	yes	yes	yes	yes	yes
compact	yes	no	yes	yes	no
dir	yes	yes	yes	yes	yes
id	yes	yes	yes	yes	yes
lang	yes	yes	yes	yes	yes
onclick	yes	yes	yes	yes	yes
ondblclick	yes	yes	yes	yes	yes
onkeydown	yes	yes	yes	yes	yes
onkeypress	yes	yes	yes	yes	yes
onkeyup	yes	yes	yes	yes	yes
onmousedown	yes	yes	yes	yes	yes
onmousemove	yes	yes	yes	yes	yes
onmouseout	yes	yes	yes	yes	yes
onmouseover	yes	yes	yes	yes	yes
onmouseup	yes	yes	yes	yes	yes
style	yes	yes	yes	yes	yes
title	yes	yes	yes	yes	yes
type	yes	no	yes	yes	no
xml:lang	no	no	yes	yes	yes

Element/Attributes	HTML 4.01 Transitional	HTML 4.01 Strict	XHTML 1.0 Transitional	XHTML 1.0 Frameset	XHTML 1.0 Strict
var	yes	yes	yes	yes	yes
class	yes	yes	yes	yes	yes
dir	yes	yes	yes	yes	yes
id	yes	yes	yes	yes	yes
lang	yes	yes	yes	yes	yes
onclick	yes	yes	yes	yes	yes
ondblclick	yes	yes	yes	yes	yes
onkeydown	yes	yes	yes	yes	yes
onkeypress	yes	yes	yes	yes	yes
onkeyup	yes	yes	yes	yes	yes
onmousedown	yes	yes	yes	yes	yes
onmousemove	yes	yes	yes	yes	yes
onmouseout	yes	yes	yes	yes	yes
onmouseover	yes	yes	yes	yes	yes
onmouseup	yes	yes	yes	yes	yes
style	yes	yes	yes	yes	yes
title	yes	yes	yes	yes	yes
xml:lang	no	no	yes	yes	yes

The Mozilla Browser Version Trail

Keeping track of browser versions gets complicated when discussing browsers built using the open source browser engine produced by what is known today as The Mozilla Foundation. At least three well-known browsers—Firefox, Netscape 6 or later, and Camino (for the Macintosh)—are built upon Mozilla. Unfortunately, each browser (including Mozilla, itself) has its own version numbering system. Detailing the version number of each browser to signify compatibility with or support for a particular language feature gets tedious and confusing very quickly. Instead, this book relies on the underlying Mozilla version number to reference all browsers spawned therefrom. The following conversion table will help you identify corresponding versions of major releases of the different trade-named browsers. For example, if an item is designated as implemented in Mozilla 1.4, then it is also supported in Netscape 7.1 or later, Firefox 1.0 or later, and Camino 1.0 or later. Pre-1.0 versions of Firefox (including those under abandoned names) and Camino are intentionally omitted from the table on the assumption that users of pre-release versions of these browsers have very likely upgraded to 1.0 or greater versions. The m18 desgination stands for milestone build number 18, a convention later dropped in favor of traditional numbering.

Mozilla	Netscape	Firefox	Camino
m18	6.0		
0.9.4	6.2		
1.0.1	7.0		
1.4	7.1		
1.7.2	7.2		
1.7.5	8.0-8.1	1.0	
1.8		1.5	1.0
1.8.1		2.0	

Glossary

absolute positioning

Setting the precise location of an element within the coordinate system of the next outermost container. An absolute-positioned element exists in its own transparent layer; it is removed from the flow of content that surrounds it in the HTML source code.

abstract object

A specification for the characteristics of other, real objects with which scripts come into contact. Modern document object model designers frequently blend the characteristics of multiple abstract objects into a single scriptable object. For example, the properties, methods, and event handlers for a specific HTML p element object in a document loaded into Mozilla are derived from many W3C DOM specification abstract objects: the `Node`, `Element`, `HTMLElement`, `HTMLParagraphElement`, `ElementCSSInlineStyle`, and `EventTarget` objects.

accessibility

The design concern for allowing users with physical disabilities to make as full a use of web content as possible. For example, aural style sheets provide increased web accessibility to users who have vision impairments. See also *WAI* and *unobtrusive JavaScript*.

AJAX

Asynchronous JavaScript and XML, a term coined by Jesse James Garret to embrace the combination of technologies of a scriptable Document Object Model and asynchronous background communication between a Web page and server through the `XMLHttpRequest` object.

API

Application Programming Interface, which is usually a collection of methods and properties that operate as a convenient layer between programmers and more complex internal computer activity. In Dynamic HTML, it is common to use or create a custom API to act as a buffer between the browser-specific implementations of element positioning and the programmer's desire to use a single coding scheme regardless of browser.

anonymous function

A way of defining a function without explicitly giving the function a name. Common usage is to assign a function to an object property to create a method of the object.

at-rule

A type of CSS command used inside a style sheet definition. Typical at-rule commands import external style sheets or download font specifications. An at-rule statement begins with the @ symbol.

attribute

A property of an HTML (and XHTML) element. Attributes are usually assigned values by way of operators (the = symbol for HTML). In HTML, sometimes the presence of the attribute name is enough to turn on a feature associated with that attribute (regardless of the value assigned), but XHTML requires that all attributes have values assigned to them. HTML attribute names are case-insensitive; XHTML attribute names are case-sensitive.

block-level element

An HTML element that automatically forces a new line before and after the element, assuring that no other element appears in the same horizontal band of the page (unless another element is absolute-positioned on top of it). An example of a block-level element is the h1 element.

border

In CSS, a region that exists outside of the content and padding area of a block-level element. The border is always present, even if its thickness is zero, and it can't be seen. A border is sandwiched between the *margin* and *padding*.

browser sniffing

A scripting technique (usually involving properties of the navigator object) that sets global variables signifying the current browser's brand, version, operating system, and other environment capabilities. Scripts use the variables to branch code execution to accommodate browser-specific syntax for operations to work across multiple, incompatible browsers. The technique is gradually being displaced by *object detection*.

cascading rule

One of the sequence of decisions that a CSS-equipped browser uses to determine which one of several possible overlapping style sheet rules applies to a given element. Each cascading rule assigns a value to a specificity rating that helps determine which style sheet rule (and attributes within that rule) applies to the element.

class

In CSS, a collection of one or more elements (of the same or different tag type) that are grouped together for the purpose of assigning the same style sheet rule

throughout the document. Assigning a class identifier to elements via the class attribute (and using that class selector in a style sheet rule) lets authors create element groupings that cannot be created only out of tag names or IDs.

collection

A group of scriptable objects of the same type. Scripts may reference individual members of the collection via standard numeric array index syntax (*collectionName*[*index*]), aided by the collection's length property for iterative access inside for loops, if desired. In recent browsers, methods allow access via numeric index (*collectionName*.item (*index*)) or, if the objects have names associated with them, their names (*collectionName*.namedItem("*name*")). Internet Explorer also allows references through its own collection notation (*collectionName* (*index*)). Many DOM properties and methods return values in the form of a collection.

container

Any element that holds other elements of any type. Tags for contained elements appear between the container's start and end tags.

contextual selector

In CSS, a way of specifying under what containment circumstances a particular type of element should have a style sheet rule applied to it. The containment hierarchy is denoted in the selector by a space-delimited list. Thus, the rule p em {color: red} applies the red text color to all em elements that are contained by p elements; an em element inside an li element is unaffected by this style sheet rule.

CSS

Acronym for Cascading Style Sheets, a recommended standard created under the auspices of the World Wide Web Consortium (W3C). The acronym is commonly followed by a number designating the version number of the standard. Level 2 of CSS is known as CSS2. Beginning with Level 2, the CSS specification is divided into separate modules, such as Core, HTML, Events, and so on.

CSS-P

Acronym for Cascading Style Sheets-Positioning. Initially undertaken as an effort separate from the CSS work, the two standards come together in CSS2, and the CSS-P terminology is no longer needed.

data binding

A facility in Microsoft Internet Explorer that allows web page content to be dynamically linked to a data source, such as a server database. For example, a marquee element can grab the latest headlines from a database field as the page loads into the client and display those headlines as a scrolling tickertape. Windows versions have two-way access to many data source types, but IE for Macintosh's data binding works only with static tab- or comma-delimited text file sources.

declaration

In CSS, the combination of a property name, colon operator, and value assigned to the property. Multiple declarations in a single style sheet rule are separated by semicolons.

deprecated

A web standard or language feature (commonly an HTML element or attribute and corresponding DOM equivalent) that is still supported in a standards release version, the use of which is discouraged in documents that support the version. A term that is deprecated in one version release is usually removed in the following release. Browser support for deprecated items usually continues for many generations for backward compatibility with existing documents that use the element or attribute.

DHTML

Acronym for Dynamic Hypertext Markup Language. DHTML is an amalgam of several standards, including HTML (and XHTML), CSS, DOM, and ECMAScript. In practice, scripts modify element styles or the makeup of the document tree without requiring refreshing of the page from the server.

DOM

Acronym for the Document Object Model standards effort headed by the W3C. The term in all uppercase letters is commonly, but perhaps inappropriately, applied to a specific implementation of a document object model in a particular browser.

DTD

Acronym for the Document Type Definition, a document that defines in excruciating detail the types of elements, attributes, and attribute values that are permissible in an SGML (and thus HTML or XML) document. Users never see DTD documents, but they are commonly referenced within the <!DOCTYPE> element at the top of a document to define the markup rules followed by the document's content. Anyone may create a custom DTD for their documents, but most HTML documents adhere to one of the W3C-published DTDs.

dynamic content

Any HTML content that changes after the document has loaded. Content that does not require a reflow of the page can be accommodated in Navigator 3 and onward and Internet Explorer 4 and onward. The replaced img element is an example. IE 4 or later and W3C DOM browsers also allow body content to be changed after the document loads by automatically reflowing the page after the content changes.

E4X

ECMAScript For XML, an extension of the ECMAScript standard designed to simplify scripted access to components of an XML document. First implemented among mainstream browsers in Mozilla 1.8.

ECMA

A Switzerland-based standards body formerly known as the European Computer Manufacturers Association.

ECMAScript

The common name for the Java-Script-based scripting language standard ECMA-262. The standard defines a core scripting language, without any specific references to web-based content. The functionality of the first edition of ECMA-262 is roughly equivalent to Java-Script 1.1 as deployed in Navigator 3. The second edition corrected errors of the first, while the third edition adds new features common to JavaScript 1.5.

element

Refers to a portion of a document that has a specific context within the document defined by an angle-bracketed tag or tag pair (start and end tag set). For example, the <body> tag creates a body element in the document.

event binding

A technique of instructing an object to process a particular event type when the event fires on that object.

event bubbling

The Internet Explorer 4 or later and W3C DOM event model mechanism that propagates events from the target element upward through the HTML element hierarchy. After the event is processed (at the scripter's option) by the target element, event handlers higher up the hierarchy may perform further processing on the event. Event propagation can be halted at any point via the cancelBubble property or, in W3C DOM browsers, the stopPropagation( ) method.

event handler

A script-oriented keyword that intercepts an event action (such as a mouse click) and initiates the execution of one or more script statements. An event handler can be specified as an attribute of an HTML element, assigned as a property of the scriptable object version of the element, or associated with the object through event model-specific methods (attachEvent( ) or addEventListener( )). Each element responds to a specific set of events.

event propagation

The process of event information coursing its way through the element or object hierarchy of a document. In recent browsers, an event propagates from the window, document, or body element (depending on the event type) inward toward the target element. At that point the event propagation performs a U-turn, and bubbles upward through the same container path. For an object to process an event as it passes toward the target element, the object must be set up to capture the event. Event bubbling is automatic for most event types.

filter

A rendering feature of Internet Explorer 4 or later (for the Windows platform) that adds typographic effects to text content and animated transitions between views. A filter is assigned to an element by way of CSS syntax.

HTML

Acronym for Hypertext Markup Language, a simplified version of SGML tailored for content that is published across a network via the Hypertext Transfer Protocol (HTTP). Version 4 of the HTML standard (under the auspices of the W3C) extends the notion of separating content from form by letting HTML elements define the context of content, rather than its specific look. HTML 4.01 is the foundation of initial specifications for *XHTML*.

ID

An identifier for an element that should be unique among all elements within a single document. The ID of an element is assigned by the id attribute supported by every HTML 4 tag. An ID is used for many purposes, including associating a CSS style sheet rule with a single element among all elements of a document and simplifying script references to a specific element.

identifier

A name assigned to an id, class, or name attribute of an element, as well as names for objects and variables in a scripting language. The names can begin with any uppercase or lowercase letter of the English alphabet, but subsequent characters may include letters, numerals, or the underscore character.

inline element

An HTML element that is rendered as part of the same text line as its surrounding HTML content. An em element that signifies an emphasized portion of a paragraph is an inline element because its content does not disturb the regular linear flow of the content. The opposite of an inline element is a *block-level element*.

intrinsic events

Events defined by the HTML 4 standard as belonging to virtually every element that is rendered on the page. These events are primarily the common mouse and keyboard events.

JavaScript

A programming language devised by Brendan Eich at Netscape for simplified server and client programming. Originally developed under the name LiveScript, the name changed (under license from Sun Microsystems) before the first commercial release of a scriptable browser, Navigator 2. JavaScript became the basis for ECMAScript. Microsoft's name for its implementation of JavaScript is JScript.

JavaScript Style Sheets

A Navigator 4-only syntax for defining style sheet rules.

JScript

Microsoft's formal name for the JavaScript-based scripting language built into Internet Explorer 3 and later. Compatible with ECMAScript and JavaScript.

JSON

JavaScript Object Notation, a way of conveying JavaScript data types such as arrays and custom objects via string values. The notation uses the square brackets (arrays) and curly braces (objects), but within strings that can be reconverted to their native objects via the eval( ) function.

layer

Derived from Navigator 4's now-abandoned model for a positionable element, the term is currently a generic reference to any element with a CSS position property assigned a value such as absolute, relative, or fixed. Each positioned element exists in its own transparent layer above the main document body.

margin

In CSS, a region that extends outside of an element's *border*. Every element has a margin, even if its thickness is zero.

media

In CSS, a reference to the type of output for which the rule is to be applied. Mainstream browsers commonly support the screen and print media, but the other possible media include projection, audio, and small screen displays of portable devices.

method

A scriptable object's action that can be initiated by any script statement. A reference to a JavaScript-syntax method is easily recognizable by the set of parentheses that follows the method name. Zero or more parameters may be included inside the parentheses. A method may return a value depending on what it has been programmed to do, but it isn't a requirement.

modifier key

A keyboard key that is usually pressed in concert with a character key or mouse action to initiate a special action. Modifier keys common to all operating system platforms include the Shift, Control, and Alt keys. Modern Microsoft keyboards also have the Windows key; Macintosh keyboards have the Command key. Keyboard and mouse events can be examined for which (if any) modifier keys were being held down at the time of the character key's event.

modularization

A tendency in recent W3C standards tracks to divide large standards into multiple modules, each of which has a specific focus, such as the Events module of the W3C DOM recommendation.

Mozilla-based browser

A Web browser built with the Gecko engine, whose development is managed by The Mozilla Foundation. Popular Mozilla-based browsers include Netscape 6 or later, Firefox, and Camino.

node

In a document object model, an object that can be referenced within the document's hierarchical structure. Some node types act as containers of additional, nested nodes, while other types contain nothing but document text content.

object

A representation of an HTML element or other programmable item in a scripting language, such as JavaScript. An object may have properties and methods that define the behavior and/or appearance of the object. Scripts typically read or modify object properties or invoke object methods to affect some change of value or appearance of the object. Objects in a browser's document object model reflect HTML elements defined by the document source code. For example, in recent browser versions, if a script assigns a new URL to the value of the src property of an img object, the new graphic replaces the old within the rectangular space occupied by the img element on the page. Other types of objects, such as dates and strings, do not appear on the screen directly but are used in script execution.

object detection

A scripting technique that verifies whether a browser supports a particular object, property, or method before attempting to execute a statement with that term in it. This technique is gaining favor over *browser sniffing*.

padding

In CSS, a region that extends between the element's content and the border. Padding provides some breathing space between the content and a border (if one is specified). Every element has padding, even if its thickness is zero.

parent

For HTML elements, the next outermost element in source code order (the tr element that surrounds a td element, for example). For positioned elements, the parent element determines the coordinate plane for an element's positioning. For scriptable window objects, a frame's parent is the frameset document that defines the frame holding the current document.

platform

A software or hardware system that forms the basis for further product development. For web browsers, the term may apply to a browser brand or the operating system on which a browser brand operates (Windows XP, Mac OS X, Solaris, etc.). In this book, *platform* usually applies to the browser brand.

positioning

Specifying the precise location of an element on the page. An element may be absolute-, relative-, or (in some browsers) fixed-positioned.

property

A single characteristic of an object, such as its ID or value, which can be retrieved (and sometimes set) with the help of scripting. Style sheet attributes are also sometimes referred to as properties because they can be scripted as properties of the style object. In CSS a property is a style characteristic (e.g., color or background-image) whose value is assigned within a style sheet rule

pseudo-class

A style sheet selector that points to a particular state or behavior of an HTML element, such as an a element set up as a link that has been visited recently by the user (a:visited).

pseudo-element

A style sheet selector that points to a very specific piece of an element, such as the first letter of a paragraph (p:first-letter).

quirks (mode)

Reference to a mode whereby modern browsers emulate the nonstandard behaviors of their earlier versions for the sake of backward compatibility with existing HTML and CSS code. The operational mode (quirks versus standards-compatible modes) is controlled by settings in the `<!DOCTYPE>` tag for browsers such as IE 6 or 7 and Mozilla-based browsers.

relative positioning

Setting the precise location of an element within the coordinate system established by the location where the element would normally appear if it were not positioned. Documents preserve the blank space originally designated for a relative-positioned element so that surrounding content does not cinch up around the place left vacant by a positioned element.

replaced element

An inline or block-level element that can have its content replaced without requiring any adjustment of the document. An `img` element, for example, can have its content replaced by a script after the page has loaded.

RGB

An acronym for red-green-blue, the three base colors (in that order) for a popular color specification system, including those used for HTML and CSS color-related attributes. Values for each color are in the range between 0-255 (none to maximum saturation), in decimal or hexadecimal notation.

rule

In CSS, a set of style declarations that are associated with one selector. A rule can also be embedded within an element as the value assigned to the `style` attribute of the element's tag.

selector

In CSS, the name of the element(s), ID(s), class(es), or other permissible element groupings to which a style declaration is bound. The combination of a selector and declaration creates a style sheet rule.

standards-compatible mode

Reference to a mode whereby browsers attempt to more strictly observe CSS specifications for items such as the box model.

Internet Explorer 6 and 7 use this mode to cancel legacy effects, known as quirks mode. The operational mode (quirks versus standards-compatible modes) is controlled by settings in the `<!DOCTYPE>` tag for browsers such as IE 6 or 7 and Mozilla-based browsers.

style sheet

In CSS, one or more rules that define how a particular segment of document content should be rendered by the browser. A style sheet may be defined in an external document, in the style element, or assigned to an element via its `style` attribute.

transition

In Internet Explorer for Windows, a visual effect for hiding and showing elements. Transitions are controlled via filters.

unobtrusive JavaScript

A way of designing scripts for Web pages that allows mission-critical information and navigation to operate without scripting being enabled. At load time, a script-aware browser can modify the document (without the visitor being explicitly aware of the modifications) to add enhancements that offer additional features for visitors with scriptable browsers. This design methodology means that visitors using browsers for accessibility are not deprived of the primary content of the Web site or application.

validation

Passing source code through a program that compares the code against a standards-based measuring stick for syntactic accuracy, structural integrity, and adherence to standards requirements.

VBScript

A scripting language alternate to JScript in Internet Explorer for Windows. You can combine script blocks in VBScript and JScript in the same document, and statements in each block may reference variables and objects in the other.

W3C

An acronym for the World Wide Web Consortium (*http://www.w3.org*).

Appendixes

WAI

An acronym for the Web Accessibility Initiative activity of the W3C; their goal is to promote web resources for users with disabilities (*http://www.w3.org/WAI*).

Web 2.0

Primarily a marketing term signifying Web sites and applications that emphasize heavy interaction with site visitors in the way of rich user interfaces, visitor-created content, or AJAX technology.

Web Forms 2.0

One section of the Web Applications 1.0 specification created by WHATWG. Web Forms 2.0 is designed to build in form control validation without scripting.

WHATWG

Web Hypertext Application Technology Working Group (*http://whatwg.org*), an organization operating outside of the W3C to establish updated standards for deploying applications over the World Wide Web. Their primary specification, called Web Applications 1.0 (also known as HTML5), includes standards for self-validating forms (Web Forms 2.0) and other features. Opera 9 is the first browser to implement Web Forms 2.0 and the Audio object.

XHTML

An acronym for the Extensible Hypertext Markup Language recommendation of the W3C. This branch of the HTML activity is a version of HTML implemented as an XML application (*http://www.w3.org/MarkUp*).

XML

An acronym for the Extensible Markup Language recommendation of the W3C, which provides the basis for structuring data in a way that facilitates its storage and transfer around the Web (*http://www.w3.org/XML*).

XMLHttpRequest

Name of the scriptable object through which Web page scripts can communicate with a server asynchronously to retrieve and/or post XML data without disturbing the layout of the current page. Originally implemented as an ActiveX control in Internet Explorer 5, the object is now a native object in Mozilla, Safari, Opera, and Internet Explorer 7.

Index

We'd like to hear your suggestions for improving our indexes. Send email to *index@oreilly.com*.

dir, 325
dir attribute, 11
dir object, 471
<dir> tag, 78
direction style sheet property, 961
directories object, 472
disabled, 325
disabled attribute, 11
dispatchEvent( ), 352
div object, 473
<div> tag, 78–81
division (/) operator, 1131
dl object, 475
<dl> tag, 81
do/while statement, 1140
document, 325
document object, 475–512
   HTMLDocument node, 513
DocumentFragment object, 514
DocumentType object, 515–517
DOM (Document Object Model)
   events, 1200–1202
   methods, 1183–1199
   properties, 1158–1182
DOM objects, static, 311
DOMActivate event, 912
DOMAttrModified event, 912
DOMCharacterDataModified event, 912
DOMContentLoaded event, 912
DOMControlValueChanged event, 913
DOMException object, 517–519
DOMFocusIn event, 913
DOMFocusOut event, 913
DOMFrameContentLoader event, 913
DOMMenuItemActive event, 914
DOMNodeInserted event, 914
DOMNodeInsertedIntoDocument
   event, 914
DOMNodeRemoved event, 914
DOMNodeRemovedFromDocument
   event, 915
DOMParser object, 519
DOMSubtreeModified event, 915
DOMTitleModified event, 915
doScroll( ), 352
drag event, 915
dragdrop event, 916
dragDrop( ), 353
dragend event, 915
dragenter event, 916
dragleave event, 916
dragover event, 916

dragstart event, 915
drop event, 917
dt object, 520
<dt> tag, 85

E

editable content commands, 1222–1229
editable documents
   commands, 1223
   TextRange object, 1225
Element object, 521
ElementCSSInlineStyle object, 521
elements object, 522
elevation style sheet property, 963
em object, 386
<em> tag, 86
embed object, 523
<embed> tag, 86–92
embeds object, 527
empty-cells style sheet property, 964
Enumerator object, 1056
equal (===) operator, 1132
equality (==) operator, 1131
error event, 917
Error object, 1057–1059
errorupdate event, 917
event handlers, DOM, 1200–1202
Event object, 556–557
event object, 528–556
events, 310, 904
   abort, 904
   activate, 904
   afterupdate, 904
   beforeactivate, 905
   beforecopy, 905
   beforecut, 905
   beforedeactivate, 906
   beforeeditfocus, 906
   beforepaste, 906
   beforeprint, 904
   beforeunload, 907
   beforeupdate, 907
   blur, 908
   bounce, 908
   cellchange, 908
   change, 908
   click, 909
   context menu, 909
   controlselect, 910
   copy, 910
   cut, 910
   dataavailable, 911

T

word-spacing style sheet property, 1022
word-wrap style sheet property, 1023
writing-mode style sheet property, 1023

X

XHTML, DTD support, 1230
XML object, 1106–1125
xml object, 895
<xml> tag, 300
xml:lang attribute, 16
XMLHttpRequest object, 896–901
XMLList object, 1125
XMLSerializer object, 901
<xmp> tag, 301

Y

yield statement, 1146

Z

z-index style sheet property, 1023
zoom style sheet property, 1024

About the Author

Danny Goodman has been writing about personal computers and consumer electronics since the late 1970s. In 2006, he celebrated 25 years as a freelance writer and programmer, having published hundreds of magazine articles, several commercial software products, and three dozen computer books. Through the years, his most popular book titles—on HyperCard, AppleScript, JavaScript, and Dynamic HTML—have covered programming environments that are accessible to nonprofessionals yet powerful enough to engage experts. He is the author of O'Reilly's popular *JavaScript and DHTML Cookbook*.

To keep up to date on the needs of web developers for his recent books, Danny is also a programming consultant to some of the industry's top intranet development groups and corporations. His expertise in implementing sensible cross-browser client-side scripting solutions is in high demand and allows him to, in his words, "get code under my fingernails while solving real-world problems."

Danny was born in Chicago, Illinois during the Truman Administration. He earned a B.A. and M.A. in Classical Antiquity from the University of Wisconsin, Madison. He moved to California in 1983 and lives in a small San Francisco–area coastal community, where he alternates views between computer screens and the Pacific Ocean.

Colophon

The animal on the cover of *Dynamic HTML: The Definitive Reference*, Third Edition, is a flamingo. Flamingos are easily identifiable by their long legs and neck, turned-down bill, and bright color, which ranges from white to pink to bright red. There are five living species of flamingo, encompassing the family *Phoenicopteridae*. Flamingos are found in Asia, Africa, Europe, South American, and the Caribbean islands. Although wild flamingos are sometimes seen in Florida, they do not naturally nest in the United States.

Flamingos feed on small crustaceans, algae, and other unicellular organisms. Their unusually shaped bills provide flamingos with a unique food-filtering system. A flamingo eats by placing its head upside down below the water surface and sucking in water and small food particles through the serrated edges of its bill. The flamingo then pushes its thick, fleshy tongue forward, forcing the water out but trapping the food particles on lamellae inside the beak.

In the wild, flamingos tend to live in remote, difficult-to-reach areas. In the suburbs, however, they stand guard over many a front lawn.

The cover image is from Dover Pictorial Archive. The cover font is Adobe ITC Garamond. The text font is Linotype Birka; the heading font is Adobe Myriad Condensed; and the code font is LucasFont's TheSans Mono Condensed.

Better than e-books

Buy *Dynamic HTML: The Definitive Reference*, 2nd Edition, and access the digital edition FREE on Safari for 45 days.

Go to www.oreilly.com/go/safarienabled
and type in coupon code SNMEBWH

Search
thousands of
top tech books

Download
whole chapters

Cut and Paste
code examples

Find
answers fast

Search Safari! The premier electronic reference
library for programmers and IT professionals.

Related Titles from O'Reilly

Web Programming

ActionScript 3 Cookbook

ActionScript for Flash MX: The
Definitive Guide, *2nd Edition*

Ajax Design Patterns

Ajax Hacks

Building Scalable Web Sites

Dynamic HTML: The Definitive
Reference, *2nd Edition*

Flash Hacks

Essential PHP Security

Google Advertising Tools

Google Hacks, *2nd Edition*

Google Map Hacks

Google Pocket Guide

Google: The Missing Manual,
2nd Edition

Head First HTML
with CSS & XHTML

Head Rush Ajax

HTTP: The Definitive Guide

JavaScript & DHTML
Cookbook

JavaScript Pocket Reference,
2nd Edition

JavaScript: The Definitive Guide,
4th Edition

Learning PHP 5

Learning PHP and MySQL

PHP Cookbook

PHP Hacks

PHP in a Nutshell

PHP Pocket Reference,
2nd Edition

PHPUnit Pocket Guide

Programming ColdFusion MX,
2nd Edition

Programming PHP, *2nd Edition*

Upgrading to PHP 5

Web Database Applications
with PHP and MySQL,
2nd Edition

Web Site Cookbook

Webmaster in a Nutshell,
3rd Edition

Web Administration

Apache Cookbook

Apache Pocket Reference

Apache: The Definitive Guide,
3rd Edition

Perl for Web Site Management

Squid: The Definitive Guide

Web Performance Tuning,
2nd Edition